DICTIONARY OF
THE HISTORY OF IDEAS

DICTIONARY
OF THE HISTORY
OF IDEAS

Studies of Selected Pivotal Ideas

PHILIP P. WIENER

EDITOR IN CHIEF

VOLUME I

Abstraction in the Formation of Concepts

TO

Design Argument

CHARLES SCRIBNER'S SONS · NEW YORK

The Publishers are grateful for permission to quote from
previously published works in the following articles:

"Agnosticism"

　from *Language, Truth and Logic*, by A. J. Ayer, copyright 1935,
　by permission of Victor Gollancz Ltd.

"Ambiguity as Aesthetic Principle"

　from Virgil, *Aeneid*, trans. H. R. Fairclough, Loeb Classical
　Library, by permission of Harvard University Press

　from *Camoens: The Lusiads*, trans. W. C. Atkinson, copyright
　1952, by permission of Penguin Books, Ltd.

　from *The Odes of Pindar*, trans. Richmond Lattimore, copyright
　1947 by The University of Chicago. All rights reserved.

　from *Richard of Saint Victor*, ed. Clare Kirchberger, © 1957,
　by permission of Harper & Row, Publishers

"Catharsis"

　from *The Oxford Translation of Aristotle*, trans. W. D. Ross,
　copyright 1925, by permission of The Clarendon Press, Oxford

"Cosmology"

　from *Early Science in Oxford*, by R. T. Gunther, copyright
　1931, by permission of The Clarendon Press, Oxford

PRINTED IN THE UNITED STATES OF AMERICA

Library of Congress Catalog Card Number 72-7943

SBN 684-16422-1 (pbk.)　Volume I
SBN 684-16423-X (pbk.)　Volume II
SBN 684-16424-8 (pbk.)　Volume III
SBN 684-16425-6 (pbk.)　Volume IV
SBN 684-16426-4 (pbk.)　Index
SBN 684-16418-3 (pbk.)　Set

PREFACE

Artists, writers, and scientists do not hesitate in their creative efforts and researches to borrow ideas outside their own special fields whenever their themes reach beyond established forms, styles, or traditional methods. The languages of the arts will often show the impact of literary themes, scientific discoveries, economic conditions, and political change. The physical, biological, psychological, and social sciences have branched out from ancient mythical and metaphysical ideas of nature and man, and in their historical development have utilized the results of analyses and experimental methods that have emerged from the cross-fertilization of tested ideas and methods. This outward reaching of the mind motivates the historian of ideas to explore the pivotal clues to man's artistic and scientific achievements in diverse fields. While respecting the integrity and need for specialized departments of learning, the historian of ideas makes his particular contribution to knowledge by tracing the cultural roots and historical ramifications of the major and minor specialized concerns of the mind.

The editors have invited contributions from scholars of many countries, especially those scholars who have shown a particular awareness of the cultural and historical affiliations of their respective disciplines with other allied fields. Departmental and national boundaries have thus been crossed in the cooperative exchange of ideas and cultural perspectives among editors and contributors.

We cannot emphasize too strongly the point expressed in the subtitle of our work, that we are presenting a varied array of *selected* pivotal topics in intellectual history and of methods of writing about such topics. Although the number of topics discussed is large, we do not pretend that these volumes represent the entire range of intellectual history. To attempt a complete history of ideas would be to attempt (of course, in vain) to exhaust the history of the human mind; hence, the limited number of topics dealt with, and even these contain lacunae which we hope will encourage further studies. Students of the history of ideas should profit from the substance and methods of interpretation contained in the scholarship of our contributors, and in future research the cross-references, bibliographies, and index should be valuable aids.

The topics chosen are intended to exhibit the intriguing variety of ways in which ideas in one domain tend to migrate into other domains. The diffusion of these ideas may be traced in three directions: horizontally across disciplines in a given cultural period, vertically or chronologically through the ages, and "in depth" by analysis of the internal structure of pervasive and pivotal ideas. Internal analysis is needed if one is to discover the component ideas that have become elements of newer and larger thoughts or movements. A now classic model is Arthur O. Lovejoy's historical study and internal analysis of the Great Chain of Being into its component "unit-ideas" of continuity, gradation, and plenitude. These unit-ideas are not descriptions of the whole organic cultural and historical setting of thought, but products of analysis, which Lovejoy proposed as aids to the unravelling of complex ideas and of their roles in different contexts. However, no single method or model has been prescribed or adopted as exclusive by either editors or contributors. We have, therefore, studies of three different sorts: cross-cultural studies limited to a given century or period, studies that trace an idea from antiquity to later periods, and studies that explicate the meaning of a pervasive idea and its development in the minds of its leading proponents. Minor figures cannot be neglected since they often reflect the prevailing climate of opinion of their times.

The cross-references appended to each article have been carefully prepared to direct the reader to related articles in which the same or similar idea occurs within a different domain, often modified and even transformed by the different context. But despite our interdisciplinary aim, we do not ignore the fact that departments of study are established in academic and other specialized institutions. The *Dictionary* will facilitate the reader's transition from the ideas familiar to him in his special area of study to those very ideas operative in, and transformed by, related ideas in other fields with which he is less familiar.

In some cases the same word will have entirely distinct meanings in different disciplines, so that it is important not to confound words with ideas; for example, it is a sophistic confusion to draw inferences from the theory of relativity in physics to relativism in morals, or to impose seventeenth-century mechanical models on organic or social phenomena. But it is germane to the history of thought and culture to record the historical role of such pervasive models in diverse fields. Consequently, we did not seek to collect topics for articles at random, but organized an analytical table of contents into a seven-fold grouping of topics, thus discovering important relationships which might otherwise have been overlooked. The following domains and disciplines, of course, involve unavoidable overlapping, but form the basic framework of the selected topics contributed.

I. The history of ideas about the external order of nature studied by the physical and biological sciences, ideas also present in common usage, imaginative literature, myths about nature, metaphysical speculation.

II. The history of ideas about human nature in anthropology, psychology, religion, and philosophy as well as in literature and common sense.

III. The history of ideas in literature and the arts in aesthetic theory and literary criticism.

IV. The history of ideas about or attitudes to history, historiography, and historical criticism.

V. The historical development of economic, legal, and political ideas and institutions, ideologies, and movements.

VI. The history of religious and philosophical ideas.

VII. The history of formal mathematical, logical, linguistic, and methodological ideas.

Few of the pivotal ideas presented fall squarely and only within any one group. Even the ancillary topics will lead outward to still other clusters of ideas. The "Faust Theme," for example, is an illustration of the more general idea of "Motif" in the history of literature, but the Faust theme is itself pregnant with symbolic references to the problem of evil, to the ideas of tragedy, of macrocosm and microcosm.

Although the intensive synchronic study of any "period" of cultural or intellectual history may reveal the predominance of certain artistic, scientific, industrial, political, religious, or philosophical ideas, there is no *a priori* ranking of these groups of ideas. Nor can it be presumed that they are all of equal importance through all periods of cultural development viewed diachronically. The *Dictionary*'s emphasis on interdisciplinary, cross-cultural relations is not intended as a substitute for the specialized histories of the various disciplines, but rather serves to indicate actual and possible interrelations.

The purpose of these studies of the historical interrelationships of ideas is to help establish some sense of the unity of human thought and its cultural manifestations in a world of ever-increasing specialization and alienation. These cumulative acquisitions of centuries of work in the arts and sciences constitute our best insurance against intellectual and cultural bankruptcy. Taking stock of the ideas that have created our cultural heritage is a prerequisite of the future growth and flourishing of the human spirit.

The editors are indeed grateful for the cooperation of so many scholars, including advisers and readers as well as contributors and the staff of the publisher. Without the unstinting aid and constant encouragement of Mr. Charles Scribner, who initiated the idea of this *Dictionary*, the project would not have come to fruition.

PHILIP P. WIENER

ANALYTICAL TABLE OF CONTENTS

I. The history of ideas about the external order of nature studied by the physical and biological sciences, ideas also present in common usage, imaginative literature, myths about nature, metaphysical speculation.

Alchemy

Astrology

Atomism: Antiquity to the Seventeenth Century

Atomism in the Seventeenth Century

Biological Conceptions in Antiquity

Biological Homologies and Analogies

Biological Models

Conservation of Natural Resources

Cosmic Images

Cosmic Voyages

Cosmology from Antiquity to 1850

Cosmology since 1850

Entropy

Environment

Environment and Culture

Evolutionism

Experimental Science and Mechanics in the Middle Ages

Genetic Continuity

Health and Disease

Indeterminacy in Physics

Inheritance of Acquired Characteristics (Lamarckian)

Inheritance through Pangenesis

Longevity

Changing Concepts of Matter from Antiquity to Newton

Nature

Newton and the Method of Analysis

Optics and Vision

Organicism

Recapitulation

Relativity

Space

Spontaneous Generation

Technology

Time and Measurement

Uniformitarianism and Catastrophism

ix

ANALYTICAL TABLE OF CONTENTS

II. The history of ideas about human nature in anthropology, psychology, religion, and philosophy as well as in literature and common sense.

Association of Ideas	Psychological Ideas in Antiquity
Behaviorism	Psychological Schools in European Thought
Empathy	Psychological Theories in American Thought
Imprinting and Learning Early in Life	Renaissance Idea of the Dignity of Man
Types of Individualism	Theriophily
Love	Universal Man
Man-Machine from the Greeks to the Computer	*Virtù* in and since the Renaissance
Pre-Platonic Conceptions of Human Nature	Virtuoso
Primitivism	Wisdom of the Fool
Primitivism in the Eighteenth Century	Witchcraft

III. The history of ideas in literature and the arts in aesthetic theory and literary criticism.

Allegory in Literary History	Demonology
Ambiguity as Aesthetic Principle	Evolution of Literature
Ancients and Moderns in the Eighteenth Century	Expressionism in Literature
Art and Play	Form in the History of Aesthetics
Art for Art's Sake	Genius from the Renaissance to 1770
Baroque in Literature	Genius: Individualism in Art and Artists
Theories of Beauty to the Mid-Nineteenth Century	Musical Genius
Theories of Beauty since the Mid-Nineteenth Century	Concept of Gothic
Catharsis	Harmony or Rapture in Music
Chance Images	Iconography
Classicism in Literature	Impressionism in Art
Classification of the Arts	Irony
Sense of the Comic	Literature and Its Cognates
Creativity in Art	Literary Paradox
Literary Criticism	Millenarianism

Mimesis

Motif

Motif in Literature: The Faust Theme

Literary Attitudes Toward Mountains

Music and Science

Music as a Demonic Art

Music as a Divine Art

Myth in Antiquity

Myth in Biblical Times

Myth in the Middle Ages and the Renaissance

Myth in English Literature: Seventeenth and Eighteenth Centuries

Myth in the Eighteenth and Early Nineteenth Centuries

Myth in the Nineteenth and Twentieth Centuries

Naturalism in Art

Neo-Classicism in Art

Newton's *Opticks* and Eighteenth-Century Imagination

Periodization in Literary History

Rhetoric and Literary Theory in Platonism

Poetry and Poetics from Antiquity to the Mid-Eighteenth Century

Realism in Literature

Rhetoric after Plato

Romanticism in Literature

Romanticism (ca. 1780-ca. 1830)

Satire

Victorian Sensibility and Sentiment

Style in Literature

Sublime in External Nature

Symbol and Symbolism in Literature

Taste in the History of Aesthetics from the Renaissance to 1770

Temperance (*Sōphrosynē*) and the Canon of the Cardinal Virtues

Sense of the Tragic

Ut pictura poesis

IV. The history of ideas about or attitudes to history, historiography, and historical criticism.

China in Western Thought and Culture

Crisis in History

Cultural Development in Antiquity

Culture and Civilization in Modern Times

Cycles

Determinism in History

Enlightenment

The Counter-Enlightenment

Fortune, Fate, and Chance

Freedom of Speech in Antiquity

Historicism

Historiography

The Influence of Ideas on Ancient Greek Historiography

Humanism in Italy

Oriental Ideas in American Thought

Periodization in History

Progress in Classical Antiquity

ANALYTICAL TABLE OF CONTENTS

Progress in the Modern Era

Idea of Renaissance

Renaissance Humanism

Renaissance Literature and Historiography

Volksgeist

Zeitgeist

V. *The historical development of economic, legal, and political ideas and institutions, ideologies, and movements.*

Academic Freedom

Alienation in Hegel and Marx

Analogy of the Body Politic

Anarchism

Authority

Balance of Power

Causation in Law

The City

Civil Disobedience

Class

Conservatism

Constitutionalism

Democracy

Despotism

Economic History

Economic Theory of Natural Liberty

Education

Equality

Equity in Law and Ethics

Legal Concept of Freedom

General Will

Historical and Dialectical Materialism

Ideology

Ideology of Soviet Communism

Justice

Ancient Greek Ideas of Law

Ancient Roman Ideas of Law

Common Law

Concept of Law

Due Process in Law

Equal Protection in Law

Natural Law and Natural Rights

Legal Precedent

Legal Responsibility

Liberalism

Loyalty

Machiavellism

Marxism

Marxist Revisionism: From Bernstein to Modern Forms

Medieval and Renaissance Ideas of Nation

Nationalism

International Peace

Philanthropy

Property

Protest Movements

Revolution

Romanticism in Political Thought

Social Contract

Social Democracy in Germany and Revisionism

Socialism from Antiquity to Marx

State

Totalitarianism

Utility and Value in Economic Thought

Utopia

Vox populi

War and Militarism

Welfare State

Social Attitudes Towards Women

Work

VI. *The history of religious and philosophical ideas.*

Abstraction in the Formation of Concepts

Agnosticism

Alienation in Christian Theology

Analogy in Early Greek Thought

Analogy in Patristic and Medieval Thought

Antinomy of Pure Reason

Appearance and Reality

Baconianism

Buddhism

Causation in the Seventeenth Century

Causation in the Seventeenth Century, Final Causes

Certainty in Seventeenth-Century Thought

Certainty since the Seventeenth Century

Chain of Being

Christianity in History

Church as an Institution

Modernism in the Christian Church

Cosmic Fall

Creation in Religion

Cynicism

Death and Immortality

Deism

Design Argument

Determinism in Theology: Predestination

Double Truth

Dualism in Philosophy and Religion

Epicureanism and Free Will

Eschatology

Problem of Evil

Existentialism

Faith, Hope, and Charity

Free Will and Determinism

Free Will in Theology

Gnosticism

Idea of God from Prehistory to the Middle Ages

Idea of God, 1400–1800

Idea of God since 1800

Happiness and Pleasure

ANALYTICAL TABLE OF CONTENTS

Hegelian Political and Religious Ideas

Heresy in the Middle Ages

Heresy, Renaissance and Later

Hermeticism

Hierarchy and Order

Holy (The Sacred)

Idea

Ideal in Philosophy from the Renaissance to 1780

Impiety in the Classical World

Irrationalism in the History of Philosophy

Islamic Conception of Intellectual Life

Macrocosm and Microcosm

Metaphor in Philosophy

Metaphor in Religious Discourse

Metaphysical Imagination

Moral Sense

Necessity

Neo-Platonism

Ethics of Peace

Perennial Philosophy

Perfectibility of Man

Pietism

Platonism in Philosophy and Poetry

Platonism in the Renaissance

Platonism since the Enlightenment

Positivism in Europe to 1900

Positivism in Latin America

Positivism in the Twentieth Century (Logical Empiricism)

Pragmatism

Prophecy in Hebrew Scripture

Prophecy in the Middle Ages

Pythagorean Doctrines to 300 B.C.

Pythagorean Harmony of the Universe

Ramism

Rationality among the Greeks and Romans

Reformation

Relativism in Ethics

Origins of Religion

Ritual in Religion

Religion and Science in the Nineteenth Century

Religious Enlightenment in American Thought

Religious Toleration

Right and Good

Romanticism in Post-Kantian Philosophy

Sin and Salvation

Skepticism in Antiquity

Skepticism in Modern Thought

Ethics of Stoicism

Theodicy

Time

Utilitarianism

VII. The history of formal mathematical, logical, linguistic, and methodological ideas.

Anthropomorphism in Science

Axiomatization

Casuistry

Causation

Causation in History

Causation in Islamic Thought

Chance

Classification of the Sciences

Continuity and Discontinuity in Nature and Knowledge

Game Theory

Infinity

Study of Language

Linguistics

Linguistic Theories in British Seventeenth-Century Philosophy

Relativity of Standards of Mathematical Rigor

Mathematics in Cultural History

Number

Probability: Objective Theory

Formal Theories of Social Welfare

Structuralism

Symmetry and Asymmetry

Uniformitarianism in Linguistics

Unity of Science from Plato to Kant

LIST OF ARTICLES

Abstraction in the Formation of Concepts I 1

Academic Freedom I 9

Agnosticism I 17

Alchemy I 27

Alienation in Christian Theology I 34

Alienation in Hegel and Marx I 37

Allegory in Literary History I 41

Ambiguity as Aesthetic Principle I 48

Analogy in Early Greek Thought I 60

Analogy in Patristic and Medieval Thought I 64

Analogy of the Body Politic I 67

Anarchism I 70

Ancients and Moderns in the Eighteenth Century I 76

Anthropomorphism in Science I 87

Antinomy of Pure Reason I 91

Appearance and Reality I 94

Art and Play I 99

Art for Art's Sake I 108

Association of Ideas I 111

Astrology I 118

Atomism: Antiquity to the Seventeenth Century I 126

Atomism in the Seventeenth Century I 132

Authority I 141

Axiomatization I 162

Baconianism I 172

Balance of Power I 179

Baroque in Literature I 188

Theories of Beauty to the Mid-Nineteenth Century I 195

Theories of Beauty since the Mid-Nineteenth Century I 207

Behaviorism I 214

Biological Conceptions in Antiquity I 229

Biological Homologies and Analogies I 236

Biological Models I 242

Buddhism I 247

Casuistry I 257

Catharsis I 264

Causation I 270

Causation in History I 279

Causation in Islamic Thought I 286

Causation in Law I 289

Causation in the Seventeenth Century I 294

xvii

LIST OF ARTICLES

Causation in the Seventeenth Century,
Final Causes — I 300

Certainty in Seventeenth-Century Thought — I 304

Certainty since the Seventeenth Century — I 312

Chain of Being — I 325

Chance — I 335

Chance Images — I 340

China in Western Thought and Culture — I 353

Christianity in History — I 373

Church as an Institution — I 412

Modernism in the Christian Church — I 418

The City — I 427

Civil Disobedience — I 434

Class — I 441

Classicism in Literature — I 449

Classification of the Arts — I 456

Classification of the Sciences — I 462

Sense of the Comic — I 467

Conservation of Natural Resources — I 470

Conservatism — I 477

Constitutionalism — I 485

Continuity and Discontinuity in Nature
and Knowledge — I 492

Cosmic Fall — I 504

Cosmic Images — I 513

Cosmic Voyages — I 524

Cosmology from Antiquity to 1850 — I 535

Cosmology since 1850 — I 554

Creation in Religion — I 571

Creativity in Art — I 577

Crisis in History — I 589

Literary Criticism — I 596

Cultural Development in Antiquity — I 607

Culture and Civilization in Modern Times — I 613

Cycles — I 621

Cynicism — I 627

Death and Immortality — I 634

Deism — I 646

Democracy — I 652

Demonology — I 667

Design Argument — I 670

Despotism — II 1

Determinism in History — II 18

Determinism in Theology: Predestination — II 25

Double Truth — II 31

Dualism in Philosophy and Religion — II 38

Economic History — II 44

Economic Theory of Natural Liberty — II 61

Education — II 71

Empathy — II 85

Enlightenment — II 89

The Counter-Enlightenment — II 100

Entropy — II 112

Environment — II 120

Environment and Culture — II 127

Epicureanism and Free Will — II 134

Equality — II 138

Equity in Law and Ethics	II 148
Eschatology	II 154
Problem of Evil	II 161
Evolution of Literature	II 169
Evolutionism	II 174
Existentialism	II 189
Experimental Science and Mechanics in the Middle Ages	II 196
Expressionism in Literature	II 206
Faith, Hope, and Charity	II 209
Form in the History of Aesthetics	II 216
Fortune, Fate, and Chance	II 225
Free Will and Determinism	II 236
Free Will in Theology	II 242
Legal Concept of Freedom	II 248
Freedom of Speech in Antiquity	II 252
Game Theory	II 263
General Will	II 275
Genetic Continuity	II 281
Genius from the Renaissance to 1770	II 293
Genius: Individualism in Art and Artists	II 297
Musical Genius	II 312
Gnosticism	II 326
Idea of God from Prehistory to the Middle Ages	II 331
Idea of God, 1400–1800	II 346
Idea of God since 1800	II 354
Concept of Gothic	II 366
Happiness and Pleasure	II 374
Harmony or Rapture in Music	II 388
Health and Disease	II 395
Hegelian Political and Religious Ideas	II 407
Heresy in the Middle Ages	II 416
Heresy, Renaissance and Later	II 424
Hermeticism	II 431
Hierarchy and Order	II 434
Historical and Dialectical Materialism	II 450
Historicism	II 456
Historiography	II 464
The Influence of Ideas on Ancient Greek Historiography	II 499
Holy (The Sacred)	II 511
Humanism in Italy	II 515
Iconography	II 524
Idea	II 542
Ideal in Philosophy from the Renaissance to 1780	II 549
Ideology	II 552
Ideology of Soviet Communism	II 559
Impiety in the Classical World	II 564
Impressionism in Art	II 567
Imprinting and Learning Early in Life	II 583
Indeterminacy in Physics	II 586
Types of Individualism	II 594
Infinity	II 604
Inheritance of Acquired Characteristics (Lamarckian)	II 617
Inheritance through Pangenesis	II 622

LIST OF ARTICLES

Irony   II 626

Irrationalism in the History of Philosophy   II 634

Islamic Conception of Intellectual Life   II 638

Justice   II 652

Study of Language   II 659

Ancient Greek Ideas of Law   II 673

Ancient Roman Ideas of Law   II 685

Common Law   II 691

Concept of Law   III 1

Due Process in Law   III 6

Equal Protection in Law   III 10

Natural Law and Natural Rights   III 13

Legal Precedent   III 27

Legal Responsibility   III 33

Liberalism   III 36

Linguistics   III 61

Linguistic Theories in British Seventeenth-Century Philosophy   III 73

Literary Paradox   III 76

Literature and Its Cognates   III 81

Longevity   III 89

Love   III 94

Loyalty   III 108

Machiavellism   III 116

Macrocosm and Microcosm   III 126

Man-Machine from the Greeks to the Computer   III 131

Marxism   III 146

Marxist Revisionism: From Bernstein to Modern Forms   III 161

Relativity of Standards of Mathematical Rigor   III 170

Mathematics in Cultural History   III 177

Changing Concepts of Matter from Antiquity to Newton   III 185

Metaphor in Philosophy   III 196

Metaphor in Religious Discourse   III 201

Metaphysical Imagination   III 208

Millenarianism   III 223

Mimesis   III 225

Moral Sense   III 230

Motif   III 235

Motif in Literature: The Faust Theme   III 244

Literary Attitudes Toward Mountains   III 253

Music and Science   III 260

Music as a Demonic Art   III 264

Music as a Divine Art   III 267

Myth in Antiquity   III 272

Myth in Biblical Times   III 275

Myth in the Middle Ages and the Renaissance   III 286

Myth in English Literature: Seventeenth and Eighteenth Centuries   III 294

Myth in the Eighteenth and Early Nineteenth Centuries   III 300

Myth in the Nineteenth and Twentieth Centuries   III 307

Medieval and Renaissance Ideas of Nation   III 318

Nationalism   III 324

XX

Naturalism in Art	**III**	339
Nature	**III**	346
Necessity	**III**	351
Neo-Classicism in Art	**III**	362
Neo-Platonism	**III**	371
Newton and the Method of Analysis	**III**	378
Newton's *Opticks* and Eighteenth-Century Imagination	**III**	391
Number	**III**	399
Optics and Vision	**III**	407
Organicism	**III**	421
Oriental Ideas in American Thought	**III**	427
Ethics of Peace	**III**	440
International Peace	**III**	448
Perennial Philosophy	**III**	457
Perfectibility of Man	**III**	463
Periodization in History	**III**	476
Periodization in Literary History	**III**	481
Philanthropy	**III**	486
Pietism	**III**	493
Rhetoric and Literary Theory in Platonism	**III**	495
Platonism in Philosophy and Poetry	**III**	502
Platonism in the Renaissance	**III**	508
Platonism since the Enlightenment	**III**	515
Poetry and Poetics from Antiquity to the Mid-Eighteenth Century	**III**	525
Positivism in Europe to 1900	**III**	532
Positivism in Latin America	**III**	539

Positivism in the Twentieth Century (Logical Empiricism)	**III**	545
Pragmatism	**III**	551
Pre-Platonic Conceptions of Human Nature	**III**	570
Primitivism	**III**	577
Primitivism in the Eighteenth Century	**III**	598
Probability: Objective Theory	**III**	605
Progress in Classical Antiquity	**III**	623
Progress in the Modern Era	**III**	633
Property	**III**	650
Prophecy in Hebrew Scripture	**III**	657
Prophecy in the Middle Ages	**III**	664
Protest Movements	**III**	670
Psychological Ideas in Antiquity	**IV**	1
Psychological Schools in European Thought	**IV**	10
Psychological Theories in American Thought	**IV**	16
Pythagorean Doctrines to 300 B.C.	**IV**	30
Pythagorean Harmony of the Universe	**IV**	38
Ramism	**IV**	42
Rationality among the Greeks and Romans	**IV**	46
Realism in Literature	**IV**	51
Recapitulation	**IV**	56
Reformation	**IV**	60
Relativism in Ethics	**IV**	70
Relativity	**IV**	74
Origins of Religion	**IV**	92
Ritual in Religion	**IV**	99

LIST OF ARTICLES

Religion and Science in the Nineteenth Century   IV 106

Religious Enlightenment in American Thought   IV 109

Religious Toleration   IV 112

Idea of Renaissance   IV 121

Renaissance Humanism   IV 129

Renaissance Idea of the Dignity of Man   IV 136

Renaissance Literature and Historiography   IV 147

Revolution   IV 152

Rhetoric after Plato   IV 167

Right and Good   IV 173

Romanticism in Literature   IV 187

Romanticism (ca. 1780-ca. 1830)   IV 198

Romanticism in Political Thought   IV 205

Romanticism in Post-Kantian Philosophy   IV 208

Satire   IV 211

Victorian Sensibility and Sentiment   IV 217

Sin and Salvation   IV 224

Skepticism in Antiquity   IV 234

Skepticism in Modern Thought   IV 240

Social Contract   IV 251

Social Democracy in Germany and Revisionism   IV 263

Formal Theories of Social Welfare   IV 276

Socialism from Antiquity to Marx   IV 284

Space   IV 295

Spontaneous Generation   IV 307

The State   IV 312

Ethics of Stoicism   IV 319

Structuralism   IV 322

Style in Literature   IV 330

Sublime in External Nature   IV 333

Symbol and Symbolism in Literature   IV 337

Symmetry and Asymmetry   IV 345

Taste in the History of Aesthetics from the Renaissance to 1770   IV 353

Technology   IV 357

Temperance (Sōphrosynē) and the Canon of the Cardinal Virtues   IV 365

Theodicy   IV 378

Theriophily   IV 384

Time   IV 389

Time and Measurement   IV 398

Totalitarianism   IV 406

Sense of the Tragic   IV 411

Uniformitarianism and Catastrophism   IV 417

Uniformitarianism in Linguistics   IV 423

Unity of Science from Plato to Kant   IV 431

Universal Man   IV 437

Utilitarianism   IV 444

Utility and Value in Economic Thought   IV 450

Utopia   IV 458

Ut pictura poesis   IV 465

Virtù in and since the Renaissance   IV 476

Virtuoso   IV 486

Volksgeist   IV 490

Vox populi   IV 496   Witchcraft   IV 521

War and Militarism   IV 500   Social Attitudes Towards Women   IV 523

Welfare State   IV 509   Work   IV 530

Wisdom of the Fool   IV 515   *Zeitgeist*   IV 535

LIST OF CONTRIBUTORS

Listed below are the contributors to the *Dictionary of the History of Ideas*. Each author's name is followed by his institutional affiliation at the time of publication and the titles of articles written. The symbol † indicates that an author is deceased.

NICOLA ABBAGNANO. Professor of the History of Philosophy, University of Turin. *Renaissance Humanism.*

H. B. ACTON. Professor, University of Edinburgh. *Hegelian Political and Religious Ideas.*

JOSEPH AGASSI. Professor of Philosophy and History of Science, Boston University and Tel Aviv University. *Anthropomorphism in Science.*

A. OWEN ALDRIDGE. Editor, *Comparative Literature Studies,* University of Illinois. *Ancients and Moderns in the Eighteenth Century; Primitivism in the Eighteenth Century.*

A. HILARY ARMSTRONG. Gladstone Professor of Greek, University of Liverpool. *Neo-Platonism.*

KENNETH J. ARROW. Professor of Economics, Harvard University. *Formal Theories of Social Welfare.*

STUART ATKINS. Professor of German, University of California at Santa Barbara. *Motif in Literature: The Faust Theme.*

EDWARD G. BALLARD. Professor of Philosophy, Tulane University. *Sense of the Comic; Sense of the Tragic.*

D. M. BALME. Professor, University of London. *Biological Conceptions in Antiquity.*

MOSHE BARASCH. Hebrew University. *The City.*

FREDERICK M. BARNARD. Professor, University of Western Ontario. *Culture and Civilization in Modern Times.*

FELICE BATTAGLIA. Professor, University of Bologna. *Work.*

FRANKLIN L. BAUMER. Randolph W. Townsend Jr. Professor of History, Yale University. *Romanticism (ca. 1780 to ca. 1830).*

MONROE C. BEARDSLEY. Professor, Temple University. *Theories of Beauty since the Mid-Nineteenth Century.*

LEWIS WHITE BECK. Burbank Professor of Intellectual and Moral Philosophy, University of Rochester. *Antinomy of Pure Reason.*

ISAIAH BERLIN. President of Wolfson College, University of Oxford. *The Counter-Enlightenment.*

BERNARD BEROFSKY. Associate Professor of Philosophy, Columbia University. *Free Will and Determinism.*

PETER A. BERTOCCI. Borden Parker Bowne Professor of Philosophy, Boston University. *Creation in Religion.*

JAN BIALOSTOCKI. Professor of Art History, University of Warsaw; Curator, National Museum in Warsaw. *Iconography.*

ROBERT BLANCHÉ. Honorary Professor, University of Toulouse. *Axiomatization.*

GEORGE BOAS. Professor Emeritus of the History of Philosophy, The Johns Hopkins University. *Cycles; Idea; Macrocosm and Microcosm; Nature; Primitivism; Theriophily;* Vox populi.

SALOMON BOCHNER. Professor Emeritus of Mathematics, Princeton University; Professor of Mathematics and Chairman of the Department, Rice University. *Continuity and Discontinuity in Nature and Knowledge; Infinity; Mathematics in Cultural History; Space; Symmetry and Asymmetry.*

KENNETH E. BOULDING. Professor of Economics, University of Colorado. *Economic Theory of Natural Liberty.*

KARL DIETRICH BRACHER. Professor of Political Science and Contemporary History, University of Bonn. *Totalitarianism.*

S. G. F. BRANDON.† *Church as an Institution; Idea of God from Prehistory to the Middle Ages; Origins of Religion; Ritual in Religion; Sin and Salvation.*

ASA BRIGGS. Professor of History and Vice-Chancellor, University of Sussex. *Welfare State.*

TEDDY BRUNIUS. Professor, Institute of Aesthetics, University of Uppsala. *Catharsis.*

HERBERT BUTTERFIELD. Hon. Fellow of Peterhouse and Emeritus Regius Professor of Modern History, University of Cambridge. *Balance of Power; Christianity in History; Historiography.*

MILIČ ČAPEK. Professor of Philosophy, Graduate School, Boston University. *Time.*

D. S. L. CARDWELL. University of Manchester. *Technology.*

PETER CAWS. Professor of Philosophy, Hunter College and Graduate Center, City University of New York. *Structuralism.*

W. OWEN CHADWICK. Regius Professor of Modern History, University of Cambridge. *Religion and Science in the Nineteenth Century.*

JACQUES CHORON.† *Death and Immortality.*

VINCENZO CIOFFARI. Visiting Professor and Scholar-in-Residence, Boston University. *Fortune, Fate, and Chance.*

THOMAS COLE. Professor of Greek and Latin, Yale University. *Cultural Development in Antiquity.*

ROSALIE L. COLIE. Nancy Duke Lewis Professor of Comparative Literature, Brown University. *Literary Paradox.*

JAMES COLLINS. Professor of Philosophy, Saint Louis University. *Idea of God, 1400–1800.*

LEWIS A. COSER. Distinguished Professor of Sociology, State University of New York at Stony Brook. *Class.*

THOMAS A. COWAN. Professor of Law, Rutgers, The State University, Newark. *Causation in Law.*

MERLE CURTI. Professor Emeritus of History, University of Wisconsin, Madison. *Philanthropy; Psychological Theories in American Thought.*

MARY DALY. Associate Professor of Theology, Boston College. *Faith, Hope, and Charity; Social Attitudes Towards Women.*

RAYMOND F. DASMANN. Senior Ecologist, International Union for the Conservation of Nature. *Conservation of Natural Resources.*

ENRICO DE ANGELIS. University of Pisa. *Causation in the Seventeenth Century, Final Causes.*

ALLEN G. DEBUS. Professor of the History of Science, University of Chicago (The Morris Fishbein Center for the Study of the History of Science and Medicine, Department of History). *Alchemy.*

PHILLIP DE LACY. Professor of Classical Studies, University of Pennsylvania. *Skepticism in Antiquity.*

ALEXANDER PASSERIN D'ENTRÈVES. Professor of Political Theory, University of Turin. *The State.*

DENIS DE ROUGEMONT. Director, Graduate Institute for European Studies, Geneva. *Love.*

R. W. M. DIAS. Magdalene College, University of Cambridge. *Legal Concept of Freedom.*

HERBERT DIECKMANN. Avalon Foundation Professor in the Humanities, Cornell University. *Theories of Beauty to the Mid-Nineteenth Century.*

E. R. DODDS. Professor, University of Oxford. *Progress in Classical Antiquity.*

ALAN DONAGAN. Professor of Philosophy, University of Chicago. *Determinism in History.*

WILLIS DONEY. Professor of Philosophy, Dartmouth College. *Causation in the Seventeenth Century.*

JACQUES DROZ. Professor, Sorbonne. *Romanticism in Political Thought.*

RENÉ DUBOS. Professor, Rockefeller University. *Environment.*

WAYNE DYNES. Assistant Professor, Columbia University. *Concept of Gothic.*

ABRAHAM EDEL. Distinguished Professor of Philosophy, Graduate Center, City University of New York. *Happiness and Pleasure; Right and Good.*

MIRCEA ELIADE. University of Chicago. *Myth in the Nineteenth and Twentieth Centuries.*

JULIUS A. ELIAS. Associate Professor of Philosophy, City College, City University of New York. *Art and Play.*

ALVAR ELLEGÅRD. Gothenburg University. *Study of Language.*

ROGER L. EMERSON. The Institute for Advanced Study in the Humanities, University of Edinburgh. *Deism; Utopia.*

AUSTIN FARRER.† *Free Will in Theology.*

HERBERT FEIGL. Regents' Professor of Philosophy Emeritus, University of Minnesota; Director, Minnesota Center for the Philosophy of Science (1953–71). *Positivism in the Twentieth Century (Logical Empiricism).*

BLOSSOM FEINSTEIN. Assistant Professor of English, C. W. Post College, Long Island University. *Hermeticism.*

BURTON FELDMAN. Professor, University of Denver. *Myth in the Eighteenth and Early Nineteenth Centuries.*

DAVID FELLMAN. Vilas Professor of Political Science, University of Wisconsin, Madison. *Academic Freedom; Constitutionalism.*

FREDERICK FERRÉ. Charles A. Dana Professor of Philosophy, Dickinson College. *Design Argument; Metaphor in Religious Discourse.*

GRETCHEN LUDKE FINNEY. *Harmony or Rapture in Music.*

JOHN FISHER. Professor of Philosophy, Temple University. *Platonism in Philosophy and Poetry.*

ANGUS FLETCHER. Professor of English, State University of New York at Buffalo. *Allegory in Literary History.*

ELIZABETH FLOWER. University of Pennsylvania. *Ethics of Peace.*

PAUL FORIERS. Professor, and Dean of the Law School, University of Brussels. *Natural Law and Natural Rights.*

MORRIS D. FORKOSCH. Professor, University of San Diego Law School. *Justice; Due Process in Law; Equal Protection in Law.*

LIA FORMIGARI. Professor, Philosophy of Language, University of Messina. *Chain of Being; Linguistic Theories in British Seventeenth-Century Philosophy.*

WILLIAM K. FRANKENA. Professor of Philosophy, University of Michigan. *Education.*

WOLFGANG G. FRIEDMANN.† *Property.*

DAVID FURLEY. Princeton University. *Rationality among the Greeks and Romans.*

JOAN KELLY GADOL. City College, City University of New York. *Universal Man.*

PATRICK GARDINER. Fellow and Tutor of Philosophy, Magdalen College, University of Oxford. *Causation in History.*

CHARLES EDWARD GAUSS. Formerly Elton Professor of Philosophy, George Washington University. *Empathy.*

HILDA GEIRINGER. Professor Emeritus of Mathematics, Harvard University. *Probability: Objective Theory.*

NICHOLAS GEORGESCU-ROEGEN. Distinguished Professor of Economics, Vanderbilt University. *Utility and Value in Economic Thought.*

DIETRICH GERHARD. Professor Emeritus, Washington University and University of Cologne. *Periodization in History.*

FELIX GILBERT. Professor, School of Historical Studies, Institute for Advanced Study. *Machiavellism; Revolution.*

LANGDON GILKEY. Professor of Theology, Divinity School, University of Chicago. *Idea of God since 1800.*

MORRIS GINSBERG.† *Progress in the Modern Era.*

CLARENCE J. GLACKEN. Professor of Geography, University of California at Berkeley. *Environment and Culture.*

BENTLEY GLASS. Distinguished Professor of Biology, State University of New York at Stony Brook. *Genetic Continuity.*

THOMAS A. GOUDGE. Professor of Philosophy, University of Toronto. *Evolutionism.*

JOHN GRAHAM. Associate Professor, University of Virginia. *Ut pictura poesis.*

ROBERT M. GRANT. Professor of New Testament and Early Christianity, Divinity School, University of Chicago. *Gnosticism.*

STEPHEN R. GRAUBARD. Professor of History, Brown University. *Democracy.*

MOSHE GREENBERG. Professor of Bible, Hebrew University. *Prophecy in Hebrew Scripture.*

G. M. A. GRUBE. University of Toronto. *Rhetoric and Literary Theory in Platonism.*

GERALD J. GRUMAN, M.D. Special Research Fellow, Wayne State University; Center for Studies of Suicide Prevention; National Institute of Mental Health. *Longevity.*

HENRY GUERLAC. Goldwin Smith Professor of the History of Science, Cornell University. *Newton and the Method of Analysis.*

JAMES GUTMANN. Professor Emeritus of Philosophy, Columbia University. *Romanticism in Post-Kantian Philosophy.*

JAMES HAAR. Professor of Music, New York University. *Pythagorean Harmony of the Universe.*

DAVID G. HALE. Associate Professor of English, State University of New York at Brockport. *Analogy of the Body Politic.*

REINHOLD HAMMERSTEIN. Professor, Director of the Music Seminar, University of Heidelberg. *Music as a Demonic Art; Music as a Divine Art.*

FREDERICK HARD. Professor of English Literature, University of California at Santa Cruz. *Myth in English Literature: Seventeenth and Eighteenth Centuries.*

DENYS HAY. Professor of Medieval History, University of Edinburgh. *Idea of Renaissance.*

R. W. HEPBURN. Professor of Philosophy, University of Edinburgh. *Cosmic Fall.*

PETER HERDE. Professor of History and Director of the Historical Seminar, University of Frankfurt. *Humanism in Italy.*

RONALD HILTON. Professor, Stanford University; Executive Director, California Institute of International Studies. *Positivism in Latin America.*

HENRY M. HOENIGSWALD. Professor of Linguistics, University of Pennsylvania. *Linguistics.*

BANESH HOFFMANN. Professor of Mathematics, Queens College, City University of New York. *Relativity.*

RAGNAR HÖISTAD. Assistant Professor, University of Uppsala. *Cynicism.*

DAVID LARRIMORE HOLLAND. Professor of Church History, McCormick Theological Seminary. *Heresy, Renaissance and Later.*

SIDNEY HOOK. Professor Emeritus, New York University. *Marxism.*

PAMELA M. HUBY. Senior Lecturer in Philosophy, University of Liverpool. *Epicureanism and Free Will.*

GRAHAM HUGHES. Professor of Law, New York University. *Concept of Law.*

GEORG G. IGGERS. Professor of History, State University of New York at Buffalo. *Historicism.*

DAVID IRWIN. Head of Department of History of Art, University of Aberdeen. *Neo-Classicism in Art.*

CARL T. JACKSON. Associate Professor of History, University of Texas, El Paso. *Oriental Ideas in American Thought.*

MAX JAMMER. Professor of Physics, Bar-Ilan University. *Entropy; Indeterminacy in Physics.*

H. W. JANSON. Professor of Fine Arts, New York University. *Chance Images.*

IREDELL JENKINS. University of Alabama. *Art for Art's Sake.*

HAROLD J. JOHNSON. Professor of Philosophy, University of Western Ontario. *Changing Concepts of Matter from Antiquity to Newton.*

DAVID JORAVSKY. Professor of History, Northwestern University. *Inheritance of Acquired Characteristics (Lamarckian).*

CHARLES H. KAHN. Professor of Philosophy, University of Pennsylvania. *Pre-Platonic Conceptions of Human Nature.*

WALTER KAISER. Professor of English and Comparative Literature, Harvard University. *Wisdom of the Fool.*

ROBERT H. KARGON. Associate Professor of the History of Science, The Johns Hopkins University. *Atomism in the Seventeenth Century.*

STUART A. KAUFFMAN, M.D. Assistant Professor, Department of Theoretical Biology and Department of Medicine, University of Chicago. *Biological Homologies and Analogies.*

MAURICE KENDALL. Chairman, Scientific Control Systems, London. *Chance.*

ALVIN B. KERNAN. Professor of English, Yale University. *Satire.*

R. K. KINDERSLEY. St. Anthony's College, University of Oxford. *Marxist Revisionism from Bernstein to Modern Forms.*

ROBERT M. KINGDON. Professor of History, University of Wisconsin, Madison. *Determinism in Theology: Predestination.*

FRANK H. KNIGHT.† *Economic History.*

NORMAN D. KNOX.† *Irony.*

HANS KOHN.† *Nationalism.*

MILTON R. KONVITZ. Professor of Law and Professor of Industrial and Labor Relations, Cornell University. *Equity in Law and Ethics; Loyalty.*

STEPHAN KÖRNER. Professor of Philosophy, University of Bristol and Yale University. *Necessity.*

LEONARD KRIEGER. University Professor, University of Chicago. *Authority.*

WARREN F. KUEHL. Professor of History, University of Akron. *International Peace.*

ELISABETH LABROUSSE. Maître de Recherche, Centre de la Recherche Scientifique. *Religious Toleration.*

DONALD F. LACH. B. E. Schmitt Professor of Modern History, University of Chicago. *China in Western Thought and Culture.*

SANFORD A. LAKOFF. Professor of Political Science, University of Toronto. *Socialism from Antiquity to Marx.*

GORDON LEFF. Professor of History, University of York. *Heresy in the Middle Ages; Prophecy in the Middle Ages.*

ARTHUR LEHNING. International Institute of Social History, Amsterdam. *Anarchism.*

SHIRLEY ROBIN LETWIN. Department of Philosophy, London School of Economics. *Certainty since the Seventeeth Century.*

HARRY LEVIN. Irving Babbitt Professor of Comparative Literature, Harvard University. *Motif.*

MICHAEL LEVIN. Lecturer, Department of Political Science, University College of Wales. *Social Contract.*

R. C. LEWONTIN. Louis Block Professor of Biological Sciences, University of Chicago. *Biological Models.*

GEORGE LICHTHEIM. *Historical and Dialectical Materialism.*

G. E. R. LLOYD. University Lecturer, University of Cambridge. *Analogy in Early Greek Thought.*

LEROY E. LOEMKER. Professor Emeritus of Philosophy, Emory University. *Perennial Philosophy; Theodicy.*

ANTHONY A. LONG. Reader in Greek and Latin, University College, London. *Psychological Ideas in Antiquity; Ethics of Stoicism.*

EDWARD E. LOWINSKY. Ferdinand Schevill Distinguished Service Professor, University of Chicago. *Musical Genius.*

STEVEN LUKES. Fellow and Tutor in Politics, Balliol College, University of Oxford. *Types of Individualism.*

DAVID McLELLAN. Senior Lecturer in Politics, University of Kent. *Alienation in Hegel and Marx.*

ROBERT McRAE. Professor, Department of Philosophy, University of Toronto. *Unity of Science from Plato to Kant.*

EDWARD H. MADDEN. Professor of Philosophy, State University of New York at Buffalo. *Civil Disobedience.*

WILLIAM A. MADDEN. Professor of English, University of Minnesota. *Victorian Sensibility and Sentiment.*

ERNST MORITZ MANASSE. Chairman, Department of Latin and Philosophy, North Carolina Central University. *Platonism since the Enlightenment.*

ANTHONY MANSER. Professor of Philosophy, University of Southampton. *Existentialism.*

MICHAEL E. MARMURA. Professor, Department of Islamic Studies, University of Toronto. *Causation in Islamic Thought.*

GERHARD MASUR. Professor Emeritus of History, Sweet Briar College and University of Berlin. *Crisis in History.*

ARMAND MAURER. Professor of Philosophy, Pontifical Institute of Mediaeval Studies and University of Toronto. *Analogy in Patristic and Medieval Thought.*

ARNALDO MOMIGLIANO. University College, London. *Freedom of Speech in Antiquity; Impiety in the Classical World.*

D. H. MONRO. Professor of Philosophy, Monash University. *Relativism in Ethics; Utilitarianism.*

MICHAEL MORAN. Lecturer in Philosophy, Chairman of Intellectual History, School of European Studies, University of Sussex. *Metaphysical Imagination.*

OSKAR MORGENSTERN. Professor of Economics, New York University. *Game Theory.*

HERBERT MORRIS. Professor of Law and Philosophy, University of California at Los Angeles. *Legal Responsibility.*

LLOYD MOTZ. Professor, Columbia University. *Cosmology since 1850.*

FERNAND-LUCIEN MUELLER. Professor, University of Geneva; Secrétaire général des Rencontres Internationales de Genève; Member of Executive Council, Société Européenne de Culture. *Psychological Schools in European Thought.*

THOMAS MUNRO. Professor Emeritus of Art, Case Western Reserve University; formerly Curator of Education, Cleveland Museum of Art. *Impressionism in Art.*

MILTON C. NAHM. Professor of Philosophy, Leslie Clark Professor of the Humanities, Bryn Mawr College. *Creativity in Art.*

HAJIME NAKAMURA. University of Tokyo. *Buddhism.*

SEYYED HOSSEIN NASR. Professor of Philosophy and Dean, Faculty of Letters and Humanities, Tehran University. *Islamic Conception of Intellectual Life.*

JOHN CHARLES NELSON. Professor, Columbia University. *Platonism in the Renaissance.*

J. P. NETTL.† *Social Democracy in Germany and Revisionism.*

MARJORIE HOPE NICOLSON. William Peterfield Trent Professor Emeritus, Department of English and Comparative Literature, Columbia University. *Cosmic Voyages; Literary Attitudes Toward Mountains; Newton's* Opticks *and Eighteenth-Century Imagination; Sublime in External Nature; Virtuoso.*

KAI NIELSEN. Professor of Philosophy, University of Calgary. *Agnosticism.*

HELEN F. NORTH. Professor of Classics, Swarthmore College. *Temperance (Sōphrosynē) and the Canon of the Cardinal Virtues.*

FRITZ NOVOTNY. Professor, formerly Director of Österreichische Galerie, Vienna. *Naturalism in Art.*

WALTER JACKSON ONG, S.J. Professor of English and Professor of Humanities in Psychiatry, Saint Louis University. *Ramism.*

JANE OPPENHEIMER. Class of 1897 Professor of Biology, Bryn Mawr College. *Recapitulation.*

GIAN NAPOLEONE GIORDANO ORSINI. Professor of Comparative Literature, University of Wisconsin, Madison. *Organicism.*

MARTIN OSTWALD. Professor of Classics, Swarthmore College and University of Pennsylvania. *Ancient Greek Ideas of Law.*

WILLARD GURDON OXTOBY. Professor of Religious Studies and Near Eastern Studies, University of Toronto. *Holy (The Sacred).*

CLAUDE V. PALISCA. Professor of the History of Music, Yale University. *Music and Science.*

R. R. PALMER. Professor of History, Yale University. *Equality.*

HELLMUT O. PAPPE. Professor Emeritus of Law, Reader in the History of Social Thought, University of Sussex. *Enlightenment.*

JOHN PASSMORE. Professor of Philosophy, Research School of Social Sciences, Australian National University. *Perfectibility of Man.*

C. A. PATRIDES. Reader in English Literature, University of York. *Hierarchy and Order.*

JAROSLAV PELIKAN. Professor of Religious Studies, Yale University. *Pietism.*

STEPHEN C. PEPPER.† *Metaphor in Philosophy.*

CHAIM PERELMAN. Professor, University of Brussels; formerly Dean of the School of Philosophy and Letters. *Natural Law and Natural Rights.*

R. S. PETERS. Professor of Philosophy of Education, University of London Institute of Education. *Behaviorism.*

SIMONE PÉTREMENT. Agrégée de Philosophie, Docteur ès Lettres, Conservateur à la Bibliothèque Nationale, Paris. *Dualism in Philosophy and Religion.*

JAMES PHILIP. Dean of Arts and Science, Bishop's University. *Pythagorean Doctrines to 300 B.C.*

MARTIN PINE. Assistant Professor of History, Queens College, City University of New York. *Double Truth.*

DAVID PINGREE. Professor, Brown University. *Astrology.*

JOHN PLAMENATZ. *Liberalism.*

RICHARD H. POPKIN. Professor of Philosophy, Lehman College, City University of New York. *Skepticism in Modern Thought.*

GAINES POST. Professor Emeritus of History, Princeton University. *Ancient Roman Ideas of Law; Medieval and Renaissance Ideas of Nation.*

D. D. RAPHAEL. Professor of Philosophy, University of Reading. *Moral Sense.*

JOHN RATTÉ. Associate Professor of History, Amherst College. *Modernism in the Christian Church.*

MOSTAFA REJAI. Professor of Political Science, Miami University. *Ideology.*

MELVIN RICHTER. Professor of Political Science, Hunter College and Graduate Center, City University of New York. *Despotism.*

VASCO RONCHI. Professor, President of National Institute of Optics, Arcetri. *Optics and Vision.*

THEODORE ROPP. Professor of History, Duke University. *War and Militarism.*

EDWARD ROSEN. City College, City University of New York. *Cosmology from Antiquity to 1850.*

PAOLO ROSSI. Professor, Università degli Studi di Firenze. *Baconianism.*

NATHAN ROTENSTREICH. Ahad Haam Professor of Philosophy, Hebrew University. *Volksgeist; Zeitgeist.*

R. A. SAYCE. Reader in French Literature, Worcester College, University of Oxford. *Style in Literature.*

WALTER SCHMITHALS. *Eschatology.*

HERBERT W. SCHNEIDER. Professor Emeritus of Philosophy, Columbia University and Claremont Graduate School. *Religious Enlightenment in American Thought.*

PIERRE-MAXIME SCHUHL. Professor, Sorbonne; Membre de L'Institut de France. *Myth in Antiquity.*

CHRISTOPH J. SCRIBA. Professor, Lehrstuhl für Geschichte der exakten Wissenschaften und der Technik an der Technischen, University of Berlin. *Number.*

JERROLD E. SEIGEL. Associate Professor of History, Princeton University. *Virtù in and since the Renaissance.*

JEAN SEZNEC. Marshal Foch Professor of French Literature, University of Oxford. *Myth in the Middle Ages and the Renaissance.*

JUDITH N. SHKLAR. Harvard University. *General Will.*

WALTER SIMON.† *Positivism in Europe to 1900.*

W. SLUCKIN. Professor of Psychology, University of Leicester. *Imprinting and Learning Early in Life.*

T. B. SMITH. Professor, University of Edinburgh. *Legal Precedent.*

BORIS SOUVARINE. Institut d'Histoire Sociale. *Ideology of Soviet Communism.*

PIERRE SPEZIALI. Professor of Mathematics, Collège Voltaire de Genève; also associated with University of Geneva. *Classification of the Sciences.*

LEWIS W. SPITZ. Professor of History, Stanford University. *Reformation.*

WERNER STARK. Professor of Sociology, Fordham University. *Casuistry.*

PETER N. STEARNS. Professor, Rutgers, The State University, New Brunswick. *Protest Movements.*

PETER STEIN. Regius Professor of Civil Law, University of Cambridge. *Common Law.*

TOM TASHIRO. City College, City University of New York. *Ambiguity as Aesthetic Principle.*

W. TATARKIEWICZ. Professor, University of Warsaw; Member of Polish Academy of Sciences and Letters; Visiting Mills Professor, University of California at Berkeley (1967–68). *Classification of the Arts; Form in the History of Aesthetics; Mimesis.*

OWSEI TEMKIN. Professor Emeritus of the History of Medicine, The Johns Hopkins University. *Health and Disease.*

E. N. TIGERSTEDT. Professor of Comparative Literature, University of Stockholm. *Poetry and Poetics from Antiquity to the Mid-Eighteenth Century.*

GIORGIO TONELLI. Professor of Philosophy, State University of New York at Binghamton. *Genius from the Renaissance to 1770; Ideal in Philosophy from the Renaissance to 1780; Taste in the History of Aesthetics from the Renaissance to 1770.*

HELEN P. TRIMPI. Lecturer in English, Stanford University. *Demonology; Witchcraft.*

CHARLES TRINKAUS. University of Michigan. *Renaissance Idea of the Dignity of Man.*

RADOSLAV A. TSANOFF. McManis Professor of Philosophy, Rice University. *Problem of Evil.*

ERNEST TUVESON. Professor of English, University of California at Berkeley. *Alienation in Christian Theology; Millenarianism.*

HÉLÈNE L. TUZET. Doctor in Comparative Literature, University of Poitiers. *Cosmic Images.*

FRANCIS LEE UTLEY. Professor of English, Ohio State University. *Myth in Biblical Times.*

HENRY G. VAN LEEUWEN. Professor of Philosophy, Hanover College. *Certainty in Seventeenth-Century Thought.*

A. G. M. VAN MELSEN. Professor of Philosophy, President of the University, University of Nijmegen. *Atomism: Antiquity to the Seventeenth Century.*

ARAM VARTANIAN. Professor of French, New York University. *Man-Machine from the Greeks to the Computer; Spontaneous Generation.*

RUDOLF VIERHAUS. Professor, Director of Max-Planck-Institut für Geschichte, Göttingen. *Conservatism.*

KURT VON FRITZ. Professor Emeritus, University of Munich. *The Influence of Ideas on Ancient Greek Historiography.*

PETER VORZIMMER. Professor of History, Temple University. *Inheritance through Pangenesis.*

JEAN WAHL. Professor, Sorbonne. *Irrationalism in the History of Philosophy.*

WILLIAM A. WALLACE. Professor of History and Philosophy of Science. The Catholic University of America. *Experimental Science and Mechanics in the Middle Ages.*

BERNARD WEINBERG. Robert Maynard Hutchins Distinguished Service Professor, Department of Romance Languages, University of Chicago. *Rhetoric after Plato.*

JULIUS WEINBERG.† *Abstraction in the Formation of Concepts; Causation.*

HERBERT WEISINGER. Professor of English, Dean of the Graduate School, State University of New York at Stony Brook. *Renaissance Literature and Historiography.*

ULRICH WEISSTEIN. Professor of German and of Comparative Literature, Indiana University. *Expressionism in Literature.*

RENÉ WELLEK. Sterling Professor of Comparative Literature, Yale University. *Baroque in Literature; Classicism in Literature; Literary Criticism; Evolution of Literature; Literature and Its Cognates; Periodization in Literary History; Realism in Literature; Romanticism in Literature; Symbol and Symbolism in Literature.*

RULON WELLS. Yale University. *Uniformitarianism in Linguistics.*

G. J. WHITROW. University of London. *Time and Measurement.*

PHILIP P. WIENER. Editor, *Journal of the History of Ideas*, Temple University. *Pragmatism.*

RAYMOND L. WILDER. Professor Emeritus, University of Michigan. *Relativity of Standards of Mathematical Rigor.*

LEONARD G. WILSON. Professor of the History of Medicine, University of Minnesota. *Uniformitarianism and Catastrophism.*

RUDOLF WITTKOWER.† *Genius: Individualism in Art and Artists.*

JOHN W. YOLTON. Professor and Chairman, Department of Philosophy, York University, Toronto. *Appearance and Reality.*

ROBERT M. YOUNG. Director, Wellcome Unit for the History of Medicine, Fellow of King's College, University of Cambridge. *Association of Ideas.*

NOTE TO THE READER

Each article is followed by a list of cross-references to other articles in the *Dictionary*. Cross-references appearing in bold-face type indicate articles which contain particularly significant treatment of a related topic. When appearing as cross-references, titles of articles are often given in abbreviated form. When referring to a group of articles on the same subject, a simple reference is used instead of a listing of all articles in that category. Thus, a cross-reference to "Platonism" is meant to indicate all four articles dealing with Platonism.

DICTIONARY OF
THE HISTORY OF IDEAS

ABSTRACTION IN THE FORMATION OF CONCEPTS

THE TERM "abstraction" is the usual expression in medieval philosophical terminology for several processes distinguished in Aristotle's writings by different terms, viz., *aphairesis* (ἀφαίρεσις) and *korismos* (χωρισμός) described in different ways. In all probability, it was Boethius who introduced the Latin *abstractio* and *abstrahere* to translate these Greek nouns and the related verbs.

The main theories of concept formation in Greek antiquity were those of Democritus, Plato, and Aristotle (Beare, 1906). According to all these theories, sense perception and intellectual cognition have to be distinguished both by their objects and by their nature. For Democritus and the Atomists, knowledge as well as sense perception arises from effluvia of atoms which are continually thrown off from the surfaces of physical objects, and eventually enter the percipient through the various sense organs. Intellectual cognition depends on finer and subtler effluvia. This theory was further developed by the Epicureans.

The difference between sense objects and the objects of intellectual cognition were also recognized by Plato but accounted for in a very different way. It is generally assumed that Plato adopted the Heraclitean view that the physical world is in continuous flux so that it never exhibits stable objects for sensory cognition. Because we know, for example, the objects of moral ideals and of mathematics, it was necessary to assume a nonsensory origin of this knowledge. Objects of knowledge really are; objects of sense are perpetually becoming. The objects of intellectual cognition, accordingly, must have been stored up in us from a previous existence. Knowledge, properly so-called, is reminiscence.

As the Platonic Forms are separate from the physical world of flux, the knowledge of Forms can only be suggested by the approximations to them that the physical world is able temporarily to manifest. The theory, which Plato expressly defended in the *Meno* (81C), *Phaedo* (73A), and *Phaedrus* (247C) and nowhere expressly abandoned, is that we possess knowledge of the Forms from a previous existence, and that so-called learning is really reminiscence. Accordingly, we should not expect to find anything like a doctrine of abstraction in Plato's writings. The need for such a doctrine as we find in Aristotle is occasioned by Aristotle's insistence that the Forms of material things are not separate realities, yet we seem to be able to consider them without considering the matter or without considering other concrete features of material things. Separate Forms provide us with difficulties but not with this particular one. Plato's insistence that we are acquainted with objects that are nowhere completely realized in the physical world requires a different account of our knowledge of such objects, and Plato found the theory of reminiscence the only suitable explanation.

But if there is no doctrine of abstraction in Plato's works, there are passages which might have suggested the doctrine to his successor, Aristotle. It is sufficient to mention here only the passage in the *Phaedrus* (249B–C) where it is written that "man must needs understand the language of Forms, passing from a plurality of perceptions to a unity gathered together by reasoning" (Hackforth, 1952). Since, in the very next sentence, we are informed that "this understanding is the recollection of those things which our souls beheld aforetime . . . ," the intention of the passage is clear enough. But the notion that this unity (ἕν) is somehow connected with a multitude of perceptions might have been one of the suggestions which led Aristotle to his doctrine of abstraction.

It was Aristotle's view that form and matter are joined in physical objects that made a theory of abstraction both possible and necessary: possible because forms otherwise could not be known by way of perception and necessary because now perception is the only immediate source of cognition. Aristotle uses the term "abstraction" (ἀφαίρεσις) in connection with the objects of mathematics, which "Platonists" had held were separate from the material world (Ross, p. 566). Aristotle maintained that these mathematical features were, in fact, inseparable from material things but could be thought of separately. In the *Metaphysics* (1060a 28–1061b 31) the process is described as follows: in the mathematician's investigations, he takes away everything that is sensible, e.g., weight and lightness, hardness and softness, heat and cold, and all other sensible contrarieties, and leaves only quantity and continuity in one, two, or three dimensions, as well as the affections (πάθη) of these quantities. Elsewhere (*Post. Anal.* 81b 3; *De anima* 431b 12ff.; *Nic. Eth.* 1142a; *De caelo* III, 1, 299a 15) we are repeatedly informed that the objects of mathematics are treated as separate but cannot exist separately. It is this formulation which is repeated throughout the subsequent history of abstraction both by those who follow Aristotle and by those who reject his views.

A point here is worthy of remark. The authors from Boethius to modern times speak of abstracting forms (both accidental and mathematical) from matter, whereas Aristotle (as Owens has pointed out) in describing mathematical abstraction speaks of taking away the sensible qualities, and leaving only the quantitative features of physical objects.

Although the process of coming to know the universal from repeated perceptions of particulars is not *called* abstraction—Aristotle here uses "separation" (χωρίζειν)—there is at least one passage which, indirectly, connects these two activities (*Post. Anal.* 81b 3). In both these cases, induction (ἐπαγωγή) is associated with the process of coming to know the universal, whether mathematical or physical. In the case of mathematical abstraction, it is sometimes indicated that the observed object suggests something which is not actually presented, but the prevailing impression is that the mathematical features are literally in the object, and are discovered by removing from consideration all other sensible qualities.

The description of cognition given in *De anima* and in the *Parva naturalia* is important for the later development of the doctrine of abstraction as we find it in medieval writers. The forms of sensible objects without their matter enter the soul, so that we know objects by the presence of their forms in consciousness. The form as it exists in the soul is, presumably, numerically different though specifically the same as the form in the object of perception (*De anima* III; VIII, 431b 26ff.). The forms of objects existing in the soul are, Aristotle assumes, the fundamental elements of thought which are the referents of the verbal symbols of spoken discourse (*De interpretatione* I, 16a 3ff; cf. *De anima* III, 6, 430a 26–430b 33). So, in many cases at any rate, the general terms of discourse stand for isolable objects of intellectual consideration. There are, however, exceptions to this, the most important of which are the analogical or systematically ambiguous terms of metaphysics. Still, the assumption that verbal terms usually stand for affections of the soul is one of the important ingredients of the doctrine of abstraction which was later developed by the medieval philosophers.

There are two doctrines of Aristotle which throw some light on his views about abstraction. One is the contention that human cognition first comprehends the generic features of physical things and only later comes to the specific differentiae (*Physica* I, 1). The other is the view that the essence of an organism is discovered regressively by first knowing the activities, then the powers, and by subsequently discovering the essence on which such powers depend (*De anima* II). The former doctrine indicates that there are generic concepts. The latter suggests that the concepts of essences, in the case of those of organisms, are really no more than conjunctions of powers. But the view that an essence is an essential unity obviously conflicts with this, because the coexistence of powers expressed by a conjunction of formulae could not constitute the sort of unity of essence that Aristotle seemed to have had

in mind. It is, therefore, difficult to understand exactly how the form of anything comes to exist in the soul as an essential unity.

Two main features, then, characterize Aristotle's view of abstraction: formal aspects of physical reality exist in the soul as separate from matter even though such a separation is impossible in the physical world itself. This is true of generic concepts, of mathematical aspects of things, and, of course, the specific concepts of things. Cognition occurs when a form exists in the soul.

That abstraction need not involve any falsification is insisted upon by the medievals, and the first statement of this is to be found in Aristotle. The mathematician is concerned with the shape and size of objects such as the sun or the moon, for example; but he does not consider them as limits of natural bodies, or with any properties of shape or size insofar as they are aspects of physical objects. On the other hand, he separates shape, etc., though without any falsity resulting from such conceptual separation (*Physica* II, 2, 193b 33ff.).

The accounts which have come down concerning the theories of concept-formation of Stoics and Epicureans contain nothing that can properly be described as a theory of abstraction. Neither of these schools accepted the form-matter distinction; they both maintained a materialistic view of nature, and the Stoics, at least, were nominalists in some sense.

For the Stoics, the main function of reason was the grasp of the conclusion of demonstrations such as the existence of gods and their providential activity. General notions (νουμένα), they maintained, are gained by contact or by resemblance; some come from analogy, still others by composition or contrariety. In another testimony, general notions are said to arise by way of enlargement or diminution of what is perceived, or by privation (Diog. Laërt. VII, 52–53).

Epicurus and his school, in addition to their atomistic materialism, held that we see, for example, shapes, and think of shapes by virtue of the entrance into the body of something coming from external objects. The effluence of atoms coming from the surfaces of physical objects enters the sense organs and produces images. Universal ideas are stored in the mind so that when, for instance, the word "man" is heard, it calls up the shape stored in the mind. As all this must reduce to a physical pattern, it is clear that all notions are ultimately derived from perception by contact, analogy, resemblance, or conjunction. None of this can be called abstraction.

Since Plotinus rejected the Aristotelian theory of sensory cognition, there is no place for a doctrine of abstraction in his account of our conceptual knowledge

(*Enneads* IV, 6, 1–3). The same remark holds for Augustine. In his account of sensory cognition, the soul suffers no changes from the sense organs, but is essentially active, taking note of changes in the body by a kind of vital attention. Hence there can be no taking of a form into the soul from physical nature. An abstraction, therefore, is out of the question in his view of perception. The doctrine that the laws of numbers and of wisdom are somehow given to human consciousness by interior illumination from a divine source takes the place of abstraction. As Augustine's views on these and other questions were derived from Plotinus and, indirectly, from Plato, this is to be expected.

The commentator, Alexander of Aphrodisias, uses the phrase ἐξ ἀφαιρέσεως in describing the process of obtaining any form in consciousness as separated from the material which it determines in the external world, and it is from this source (Alexander, *De anima*, pp. 107, 34) that Boethius derived his account of abstraction (*In Isagogen Porphyrii commenta* I, 11).

According to Boethius, there are many things which cannot actually be separated but which are separated by the soul and by thought—e.g., no one can actually separate a triangle from its material substratum, but a person can mentally separate the triangle and its properties from matter, and contemplate it. This separation does not involve any falsification because falsification can only occur when something is asserted to exist separately which does not or cannot exist separately. Thus the separation achieved by abstraction is not only not false, but is indispensable to the discovery of truth. This means, we propose, that abstraction provides the concepts which are to be united in affirmative propositions which truly state what characteristics things possess.

This account of abstraction follows along lines already laid down by Aristotle and is repeated, with elaborations, by the logicians of the twelfth century. Thus Abelard tells us that, although matter and form are always together, the mind can consider each separately. Thus abstraction does not falsify because there is no assertion that anything has just the abstracted property and no others. The mind considers only one feature but does not assert its separation in fact from other features. "For the thing does not have only it, but the thing is considered only as having it" (*Logica ingredientibus*). John of Salisbury provides a similar account. In abstracting a line or surface, the abstracting intellect does not conceive it as existing apart from matter. Abstraction is simply a contemplation of form without considering its matter even though the form cannot exist without the matter (*Metalogicon* II, Ch. 20). Again, some things resemble others and the mind abstracts from these particular individuals and considers only the resemblance. In this way, the concept of "man" is abstracted from the perceptions of individuals, and the concept of "animal" from man, horse, etc. (ibid.).

Similar views about abstraction are developed by the anonymous author of *De intellectibus* (cf. V. Cousin, 1859) and it is clear that this general agreement can be accounted for by the fact that all the schoolmen of this period read Boethius, and, perhaps, also by the influence of Abelard.

The Arabic translations of Aristotle and some of his earlier Greek commentators made the doctrine of abstraction available to the Islamic and Jewish philosophers. But there were also translations or epitomes of the writings of Plotinus and Proclus and, even when there was no confusion between Neo-Platonic and Aristotelian views, attempts were made to harmonize Aristotelian and Neo-Platonic doctrine. In particular, the Neo-Platonic system of emanations was grafted onto that doctrine of Aristotle which concerned the connection of the Agent Intellect to individual human cognitive activities. The Active Intellect in Aristotle's psychology was identified with the last Intelligence. In some of these systems, the illuminative activity of the active intellect consists in the radiation of forms into the material world and into the human mind. Attempts to combine this doctrine with the doctrine of abstraction produced strange consequences. In Avicenna's (Ibn Sina, 980–1037) treatises on psychology, for example, there are various degrees of abstraction of forms which correspond to the ascending sequence of cognitive powers, the sensitive, the imaginative, the estimative, and finally the intellective. His account of abstraction of sensible forms seems to conform to the Aristotelian psychology of taking the form of a material object apart from the matter (Avicenna, *Psychology*, p. 40). But forms which have no embodiment or which are embodied accidentally must be received from the Agent Intellect when the individual human souls have been prepared by the appropriate sense experience to receive these emanations (Avicenna, *De anima* 5; cf. Al-Ghazali, *Metaphysics*, pp. 174ff.). This explanation of how we know the nature of qualities and of things thus combines a theory of abstraction properly so-called with a doctrine which accounts for conceptual knowledge by emanations of forms from a suprahuman source. This made it congenial to many of the earlier scholastics of the thirteenth century.

Another feature of Avicenna's views must be mentioned: the doctrine of distinctions. This became important for the scholastics of the thirteenth and fourteenth centuries, and figures in the discussions of the seventeenth century. One of the important sources is

Aristotle's statement in the *Topics* that "if one thing is capable of existing without the other, the former will not be the same as the latter" (*Topics* Book VII, Ch. 2; Becker, p. 152 b34). This was taken to be the test of a real distinction of two things. According to Avicenna, that which is asserted is other than that which is not asserted, and what is conceded is different from what is not conceded (*De anima* I, 1). So, if someone can assert or concede that he exists even though he does not assert or admit that his body exists, this is sufficient ground for holding a real distinction between the mind and the body. A similar idea underlies Descartes' mind-body distinction as a consequence of *cogito, ergo sum.*

Yet another aspect of Avicenna's thought, important to the history of abstraction, is his doctrine of the common nature. Although Avicenna vehemently denies that universals have any extra-mental existence and although he asseverates that individuals alone exist, he maintains that a nature can be contemplated which, in itself, is neither one nor many (numerically) but is simply the nature that it intrinsically is: horseness is simply horseness. This theory of natures was to be used by the thirteenth-century scholastics in diverse ways. Aquinas draws upon it to avoid the Platonic paradox about the one and the many in his *De ente et essentia,* and it is essential to the views of Duns Scotus. According to the latter, the common nature has a unity less than numerical unity so that the paradox of one nature or form in many individuals is again avoided. And it continues to receive support in the fourteenth century in the critique of Ockham by Richard of Campsall: *Illa natura . . . non est pleures nec una (Logica,* Ch. 15).

This theory that a nature as such is neither one nor many is essential to Scotus' doctrine of abstraction. For although such a nature cannot be separated, even by divine power, from the individual differences by which each thing is individuated, it can nonetheless be considered apart from such individuating features by abstraction.

Al-Ghazali (1058–1111) criticized Avicenna's view of abstraction along lines which immediately call to mind similar criticisms made later by some fourteenth-century nominalists (especially Ockham) and by some of the nominalists of the seventeenth and eighteenth centuries (especially Hobbes and Berkeley). Against the view that the intelligible universal in the intellect is divested of all specifying or individuating determinations, Al-Ghazali urges that everything in the intellect is derived from the senses and retains all the concrete determinateness of sense experience. True, the intellect can separate parts of a composite, but each part thus separated is just as individual as was the aggregate from which it was separated. Each wholly determinate part of an aggregate thus separated functions as a universal insofar as it is conceived as standing in a relation to all similar individuals, and serves as an image for all other things similar to it (*Tahafut . . . ,* 1958; cf. Averroës, *Tahafut,* 1954). Al-Ghazali may, therefore, be regarded as a precursor of the sort of criticism of abstraction which later nominalists in Christendom were to exploit. There is, of course, no likelihood of any literary influence because this part of Al-Ghazali was not accessible in Latin until the sixteenth century (Zedler, 1961). Moreover, Averroës opposed Al-Ghazali on this point and continued to uphold the Aristotelian doctrine. We find that Maimonides (1135–1204) also adheres to a doctrine of abstraction derived mostly from Avicenna's *Guide of the Perplexed.*

In the philosophical writings of the early thirteenth century in Christendom attempts were made to accommodate the views of Aristotle to those of Saint Augustine. Avicenna's writings on psychology made this accommodation feasible especially to the Franciscans. But we should glance at one of the first attempts in this vein by Robert Grosseteste.

In his commentary on the *Posterior Analytics,* Grosseteste taught that the mind is capable of knowledge without the aid of the senses. Due to its incarceration in the body, however, the mind is darkened and requires the aid of sensation. Accordingly, abstraction of forms from the data of sensation is normally required. So the intellect separates out for special consideration the features of things which are confused in sensation. Abstraction of forms usually is derived from many individual objects presented to the senses. But the knowledge thus attained is not of the highest grade.

A representative view of the Franciscans can be found in Matthew of Aquasparta. Because the human soul is a sort of mean between God and creatures, it has two aspects, one of which, the superior part, is turned toward God; the other, the inferior part, is turned toward creatures. According to the doctrine of "the two faces of the soul," the correct explanation of human knowledge is a medium between the position of Augustine and Aristotle.

Knowledge of the world is generated in man by sensation, memory, and experience from which the universal concepts of art and science are derived. But in order fully to understand the natures of things thus abstracted from sensation we require an illumination from the Divine Light. Although we do not see Divine Light in our earthly existence, we see the natures of things by its means. The existence of this illumination is explained as follows: we know eternal truths with certainty. These truths are immutable yet everything in the world about us and our very minds are mutable. So, the immutable and necessary features of our knowledge require the illumination of the Divine Light.

Matthew adopts the Augustinian theory that the corporeal world cannot produce changes in the soul (the inferior cannot affect the superior). Rather the soul is actively aware of changes occurring anywhere in the body. The data which the soul makes from its notice of corporeal changes are rendered intelligible by the Agent Intellect which, Matthew says, is what Aristotle calls *abstractions*. But these abstractions are understood in the light of the immutable rules provided by divine illumination. This combination of "abstraction" and illumination is to be found in a number of Franciscan thinkers of the thirteenth century.

Saint Thomas Aquinas. Aquinas expounds a theory of abstraction according to which things (in the sense of objects of apprehension) can be considered, one aspect apart from another, in cases in which the two things cannot exist separated from one another. In cases in which one thing can exist apart from another we should speak of "separation" rather than abstraction (*Commentary on Boethius' De Trinitate*, Q5, a.3). Since substance, which is the intelligible matter of quantity, can exist without quantity, it is possible to consider substance without quantity. Again, to consider "animal" without considering "stone" is not to abstract *animal* from *stone*. Thus it is only in cases where things cannot exist separately but can be *considered* separately that we can properly speak of abstraction.

Abstraction is of two kinds: the one, mathematical abstraction, involves a consideration of form from sensible matter. The other is the abstraction of the universal from the particular. The possibility of abstraction depends on the fact that things (features of things) exist in one way in the realm of matter, but in another in an intellect which apprehends them. Thus, because the mind is immaterial, the natures of material things exist in the mind in a way suitable to the mind, i.e., they have an immaterial existence in the mind. But the simple apprehension of the mind does not involve any assertion that the features of things exist thus in reality, because simple apprehension is not an act which asserts or denies anything at all. The mathematical abstraction which considers only the quantitative features of physical things does not assert that lines, planes, etc., exist independently of such objects. It merely considers these features without attending to other aspects of physical objects, although the mathematical or quantitative features cannot exist isolated from physical objects.

In the case of the abstraction of the universal from particulars, the mind considers the specific nature of, say, man or dog, apart from the individuating aspects of individual men or dogs. Again, *abstrahentium non est mendacium* ("abstraction is not falsification") because the mind does not assert that the specific nature of man can exist apart from particular men.

The generic nature common to several species can be abstracted so that the mind thinks only of the generic aspect of these several species and ignores the specific differences. "What is joined in reality, the intellect can at times receive separately, when one of the elements is not included in the notion of the other" (*Summa contra gentiles* I, c. 54, para. 3). So, because the concept of the genus "animal" does not explicitly contain the concept of, say, "rational," the mind can consider "animal" without considering any particular kind of animal. But this "animal" is not something existing apart from particular kinds of animal any more than these particular kinds can exist apart from individual animals. Only in the mind that apprehends the form of animal stripped of its individuating and specifying characteristics does animal as such exist (ibid., I, c. 26, para. 5).

Nothing exists in a genus which does not exist in some species of that genus (ibid., I, c. 25, para. 2). *Animal* cannot exist *in re* without the differentia "rational" or the differentia "irrational." Still animal can be considered without these differentiae (ibid., I, c. 26, para. 11). There is, however, no purely generic exemplar in the divine mind (*Summa theol.* I, 15a. 3 ad 4).

Duns Scotus adopted from Avicenna the doctrine of a common nature which is in itself neither one nor many but simply what is indicated in the definition or description of such a nature. This nature can be individuated in the individuals of a species by the further determination of an individual difference or "haecceity" (i.e., "thisness" in contrast to "quiddity" or "whatness"), or it can be rendered a universal concept by the action of the active intellect; but in itself it is neither one nor many.

The process of abstracting a universal concept from the common nature so conceived is not a "real action" because the common nature is already present in the individuals and formally distinguished from the individual differences prior to and independent of any action of the intellect (Duns Scotus, *Quaestiones in metaphyisicorum libros*, VII, q. 18; *Opus oxoniense* II d. 1, q. 5 [q. 6], n. 5). This formal distinction of the specific nature from the individual differences which contract it to a numerical unity in the various individuals of the species applies just as well to the distinction between the specific and the generic features of a common nature, for these also are formally distinct in such a way that the mind can think of the generic nature as such. There is, therefore, no distortion or falsification in the result of abstraction, because abstrac-

5

tion amounts to considering one aspect of a nature without considering the others (*Opus oxon.* III, d. 14, q. 2, n. 12).

Thus, the distinctive feature of Scotus' contribution to the doctrine of abstraction depends upon his doctrine of the formal distinction between the individuating and the common nature which exists prior to any action of mind on the data of observation.

William of Ockham. Ockham uses the term "abstraction" and provides a number of meanings for it, but he departs from his predecessors on one very important point: he denies that we can think as separate what is incapable of existing separately in reality. However, he allows that we can understand one thing without understanding another at the same time even though the two things do, in fact, coexist. Thus he states "To abstract is to understand one thing without understanding another at the same time even though in reality the one is not separated from the other, e.g., sometimes the intellect understands the whiteness which is in milk and does not understand the sweetness of milk. Abstraction in this sense can belong even to a sense, for a sense can apprehend one sensible without apprehending another" (*Expositio physicorum,* fol. 111c).

In his commentary on the *Sentences* (II, qq. 14, 15 xx) Ockham tells us that the abstraction of the agent intellect is twofold. On the one hand, it produces a thought (an intellection) which is either intuitive or abstractive, is wholly abstracted from matter because it is immaterial in itself, and has its existence in something immaterial (i.e., in the soul). On the other hand, the abstraction produces a universal, i.e., a universal concept of a thing in representative existence.

In still another sense, abstraction occurs when one predicable is predicated of a subject and another predicable is not predicable of that subject even though the latter predicable applies to the subject. This takes place in mathematics. For the mathematician considers only such statements as "Every body is divisible, is so long and so deep," and ignores statements about bodies which pertain to motion, to the composition of matter and form in physical things, etc.

Accordingly, Ockham allows that many things are really distinct which constitute a unity, as in the case of matter and form, or substance and accident. Now it is true that, in such cases, the mind can separate or divide these from one another so as to understand one and not understand the other. But if *a* and *b* are one thing and *a* may not be really distinguished from *b*, it is impossible that the mind may divide *a* from *b* so as to understand either without understanding the other (*Sent.* I, d. 2, q. 3, H).

Hence, Ockham rejects any abstraction of a common nature or form from its instances in such a way that the mind can contemplate the common nature as such. The only distinction Ockham will allow is the real distinction of one thing from another thing. A distinction between the common nature and an individual difference which Scotus had defended is, for Ockham, entirely out of the question (*Sent.* I d, qq. 1–4).

The reason why Ockham can allow the abstraction of matter and form in an individual physical object is because, for him, this matter and this form could exist apart from one another, at least by divine power. The same is true of accident and substance. An accident can be thought without its substratum because an accident and its substratum are two really distinct things, and one can exist without the other (*Sent.* II, q. 5, M; cf. I, d. 30, q. 1, P).

Thus Ockham, as Vignaux observed, adopted the principle, much later exploited by Hume, that whatever is distinguishable is separable. And like Hume, he practically rejected the distinction of reason. The result was a rejection of the central tenet of the classical doctrine of abstraction, set forth by Aristotle and defended, in one form or another, by many of the scholastics of the twelfth and later centuries.

Descartes. There were many elaborations of the Thomistic doctrine among the later scholastics of the fifteenth and sixteenth centuries by Cajetan, Suarez, John of St. Thomas and others. Suarez in particular, was responsible for sharpening the differences between abstraction and distinction (or "separation" as Saint Thomas had called it). And this, in turn, was almost certainly the immediate source of Descartes' views.

While Descartes allows that abstraction takes place in the mind, he is always at pains to notice that abstraction renders our concepts inadequate in such a way that we cannot discover the important distinction of things. Thus, the distinction of reason by which a substance is distinguished from its principal attribute (of thought or extension as the case may be) is effected by abstracting one from the other. This is accomplished only with some difficulty and the result does not correspond with anything in the way of a real separation of a substance from its nature or attribute (*Principles of Philosophy*, I, 63). Thus the valuable operation of the mind is that which provides us with a real distinction. This Descartes sometimes calls "exclusion." The principal difference which Descartes makes between abstraction and exclusion is that, in the case of abstraction we consider one thing without considering that from which abstraction has been made and so may not be aware that abstraction has rendered a concept inadequate, whereas in *distinguishing* one thing from another, we must keep both clearly before us. Considering an abstraction by itself prevents us from knowing well what it has been abstracted from (Letter to Clerselier, 12 Jan. 1646).

The influence of Descartes on the so-called Port-Royal Logic of Antoine Arnauld (1612–94) is obvious. But this famous treatise presents an account of abstraction which agrees in essential features with the standard medieval view. Arnauld had argued, in his critique of Descartes, that the genus can be conceived without conceiving its species so that, for example, one can conceive figure without conceiving any of the characteristics proper to such a particular figure as a circle ("Fourth Objections"). Again, length can be conceived without breadth or depth. But such abstraction, properly so-called, is only between aspects of things which are only distinct by a distinction of reason. Where things really distinct are distinguished, abstraction does not occur (*La Logique ou l'art de penser* [1662], Part I, Ch. 5).

John Locke. The discussion of abstraction which is perhaps most familiar to modern readers is to be found in Locke's *Essay Concerning Human Understanding.*

Words become general by being made the signs of general ideas; and ideas become general by separating from them the circumstances of time and place, and any other ideas that may determine them to this or that particular existence. By this way of abstraction they are made capable of representing more individuals than one; each of which having in it a conformity to that abstract idea, is (as we call it) of that sort (Book III, Ch. 3, para. 6).

He goes on to suggest immediately that nothing new is introduced in this process but that it is rather a process of omitting all individuating features, and retaining only what is common to all of a set of resembling particulars. This omission, he explains elsewhere (Book II, Ch. 13, para. 13), is a kind of partial consideration which does not imply a separation. But Locke applies the notion of abstraction to cases which go beyond the mere omission of particular spatiotemporal determinations. In the famous example of forming the general idea of a triangle, Locke says that this idea of triangle in general is "something imperfect that cannot exist, an idea wherein some parts of several different and inconsistent ideas are put together" (Book IV, Ch. 7, para. 9). Whatever Locke may have thought this "putting together" amounted to, it is certainly not achieved simply by omitting particularizing features of several particular triangles. The fact is that no single doctrine of abstraction can be found in Locke, as I. A. Aaron has shown (Aaron, 1937).

Berkeley and Hume. Berkeley's critique of abstraction proceeds along lines which were relatively new to his readers but which had already been worked out by Al-Ghazali in the eleventh century and even by Ockham in the fourteenth century. If two things (in Berkeley's philosophy, of course, two ideas) can exist separately, the mind can abstract one from the other. But if it is granted that two things cannot exist one apart from the other, i.e., that there would be a contradiction if *a* were supposed to exist without *b* (or conversely), the mind cannot think of *a* without *b* or of *b* without *a*. To argue otherwise would be to attribute to the human mind a power which not even God can be supposed to have or to exercise.

Hume adopted Berkeley's critique and elaborated a positive theory of the function of general terms which goes beyond Berkeley. Although every idea is particular, some ideas can function as general ones by being associated with a name of a number of particulars which resemble one another exactly or only approximately. In the latter case, the name is associated with a number of qualitatively different but resembling images. One of these associated images will be dominant, the others relatively recessive but, as Hume puts it, "present in power to be recalled by design or necessity." Thus, although a red image may be recalled when the word "color" is pronounced, heard, read, or recalled, other color-images less strongly associated with the word "color" tend to appear in consciousness, are "present in power," and will be recalled if there is danger of a mistakenly narrow use of "color" presenting itself. This then, is Hume's alternative to the doctrine that there are either genuine images or abstract general ideas. The traditional explanation of the origin of abstract concepts persisted, with some modifications, among the philosophers of the eighteenth century.

A considerable advance in the understanding of the nature and function of concepts seems to have been made by Immanuel Kant. The verb, adjective, and noun frequently occur in Kant's *Critique of Pure Reason* (*Werke*, A54, A70 [B95], A76, A96) without any special explanation. But Kant's doctrine of pure as well as *a posteriori* concepts leaves no doubt that abstraction alone cannot account for the existence or employment of concepts (*Werke*, VII, 400–01). "The form of a concept, as a discursive representation is always constructed." As Kant puts it in the *Prolegomena to any Future Metaphysics* (para. 20), empirical concepts would not be possible unless a pure concept were added to the particular concept which has been abstracted from intuition. And, finally, in the *Critique of Pure Reason*, the concept is presented as a *rule* by means of which the imagination can outline, for example, the figure of a certain quadruped (say, a *dog*) without limiting it to such a determinate figure as one's experience or concrete images might present. Kant calls this a schema. Without such a schema (which is an application of the pure concepts of the under-

7

standing) neither images nor a conceptualization of images would be possible.

Kant's doctrine that pure concepts, i.e., the categories of the understanding, be at the basis of all conceptual thinking thus makes the process of abstraction subsidiary to and dependent upon faculties which are logically prior to any process of abstraction from empirical data. As more than one writer has recently pointed out, empirical concepts are more like dispositions than like static constituents of consciousness. There is, however, no suggestion in Kant that abstraction does not occur. That this new view of the activities of the mind would require an entirely different account of abstraction is not made very plain in Kant's writings.

In the development of metaphysical Idealism in the post-Kantian philosophers, the notion of abstraction becomes very general, so general in fact that the original meanings of the term seem almost lost. What makes the matter even more difficult to discuss is the fact that, among these Idealists, any separation or isolation of one content or feature of experience or thought from another is condemned as falsification, so that "to abstract," "abstract," "abstraction," all acquire a pejorative sense. To separate the cognizing subject from its object, to attend to one discriminable element apart from its surrounding, and the like, are all condemned as falsifications of reality. This condemnation rests on the Hegelian doctrine that "the Truth is the Whole," i.e., that all aspects of thought and reality are dialectically interconnected.

Other more significant attacks on the doctrine that general concepts result from abstraction come from Husserl's thorough critique of Locke and his eighteenth-century critics. While insisting on the absurdity of Locke's doctrine, Husserl attacked with equal vehemence the theories of Berkeley, Hume, and Mill. He insisted that the general attributes are given to consciousness initially, and thus repudiated the traditional doctrine of abstraction. There are similar views to be found in some of the writings of Whitehead and Santayana. The "eternal objects" of Whitehead and the "essences" of Santayana are supposed to be discoveries rather than constructions; they are not the results of creations of mental activities, and thus are not the result of abstraction as it was traditionally expounded, although the accounts of abstraction in terms of attention and comparisons would be consistent with such views.

One of the most significant critiques of abstraction comes from Gottlob Frege, in his *Grundlagen der Arithmetik* (1884). While Frege appears to allow that "color, weight, and hardness" are abstracted from objects, he holds that *number* is not so abstracted. His theory of the concept of cardinal number makes it

impossible to obtain the number concept by simply omitting features of empirically accessible objects. Because a number is a "property" of properties, it is not available from empirical inspection of individuals. And if we examine Frege's definitions of particular finite cardinals we see at once why the notion of cardinal numbers can hardly be extracted as traditional abstraction doctrines suggest. The number one, for example, is a characteristic of any "property F" which satisfies the following condition: there is that which is F and which is the same as anything which is F, more exactly: $(\exists x) (Fx. (y) (Fy. \supset . y = x)$. It is readily seen, if we remove the expression "F" from the above formula thus obtaining $(\exists x). (-x. (y) - y. \supset . y = x)$, that the property of F is expressible solely in terms of logical constants. Now because these constants function in discourse in a manner that is not comparable with the way indicative or descriptive expressions function, it is hardly surprising that there is nothing available empirically from which they can be abstracted or upon which attention may be concentrated. A psychological account of the origin of the notion of number will doubtless be a very complicated affair but it will necessarily be radically different from *abstraction*.

The technique employed by Frege, Georg Cantor, and some others to elucidate the mathematical notions of cardinal number was recognized by Bertrand Russell as an application of a general principle which Russell called "the principle of abstraction." But he added that it would have been better called the principle "for the avoidance of abstraction." The principle is this: for any relation S which is transitive and symmetrical there is a relation R which is a many-one relation such that whenever xSy, there is a unique term z such that xRz and yRz; conversely, if there is a many-one relation R such that there is a unique term z so that xRz and yRz, there is a relation S which is transitive and symmetrical (*Principia Mathematica*, Vol. 1, °72).

The essential principle to notice here is that, instead of attempting to account for the concept by a psychological theory by which the concept is derived somehow from the data of the senses or from some innate or at least internal feature of human consciousness, the concept is constructed by logical means from fairly simple relational concepts. Thus, a cardinal number is defined as either a class of those classes whose numbers can be bi-uniquely correlated (in a one to one correspondence) with one another, or, as a property P of those properties q^1, q^2, . . . , q^n such that those things having any one of these properties can be correlated bi-uniquely with the things having any other of these properties.

The formal definition of cardinal number brings into

prominence the fact that it is constructed by means of variables ranging over individuals and properties, and by logical connectives and quantifiers. There is nothing about such a construction which even suggests that it could have been "abstracted" (in the traditional sense) from sense given materials or that there is some "inner" source of the notion. It can be objected to all this that this logical construction of concepts of cardinal and ordinal numbers does not explain their psychological origin. Doubtless this is correct. Frege and Russell probably both supposed that they were elucidating the nature of mathematical objects which are somehow given (in some very different way from abstraction), whereas they were actually recommending the replacement of obscure notions by clear ones. But whatever the psychological origin of mathematical concepts may be, the Frege-Russell construction shows that it must be far more complex than anything proposed by the traditional abstraction theories. So, while the psychological question remains a highly interesting one, the focus of interest has shifted to the logical content of formal concepts.

BIBLIOGRAPHY

For main developments in Greek thought, see J. I. Beare, *Greek Theories of Elementary Cognition* (Oxford, 1906). See also Diogenes Laertius, *Lives of the Philosophers*, Loeb Classical Library (London and New York, 1925), esp. VII, 52–53; R. Hackforth, *Plato's Phaedrus* (Cambridge, 1952), p. 86; Joseph Owens, *The Doctrine of Being in the Aristotelian Metaphysics*, 2nd ed. (Toronto, 1963); W. D. Ross, *Aristotle's Prior and Posterior Analytics* (Oxford, 1949), p. 566.

For Alexander of Aphrodisias, see his *De anima* (Berlin, 1887), pp 107, 34. Boethius is found in *In Isagogen Porphyrii Commenta, Corpus Scriptorem Ecclesiasticorum Latinorum*, Vol. XLVIII (Vienna, 1906), 135–69; also *Quomodo substantiae in eo quod sint bonae sint cum non sint substantialia bona* (London, 1928), pp. 44–45; and in *De Trinitate* (London, 1928), Q5, a. 3.

The sources for medieval figures include: Abelard, *Logica ingredientibus*, ed. B. Geyer, *Beiträge zur Geschichte der Philosophie des Mittelalters*, Band XXI (Münster in W., 1921), Heft L, 25; and *P. Abelardi opera hactenus inedita*, ed. V. Cousin (Paris, 1849; Vol. II, 1859), II, 733–45; Al-Ghazali, *Algazal's Metaphysics*, ed. J. T. Muckle (Toronto, 1933), Part II (IV, 5), pp. 174ff.; and *Tahafut Al-Falasifah* (*Destruction of the Philosophers*), trans. S. A. Kameli (Lahore, 1958), pp. 218–20; Averroës, *Tahafut*, trans. S. van der Bergh (London, 1954), pp. 345–55; Avicenna, *Psychology*, trans. F. Rahman (Oxford, 1952), p. 40, also *De anima* (Venice, 1508), I, 1 and V, 5; Duns Scotus, *Quaestiones in metaphysicorum libros* (Lyon, 1639), VII, q. 18, also *Opus oxoniense* (Lyon, 1639), and *Sentences* (Lyon, 1639); John of Salisbury, *Metalogicon* (Berkeley, 1955), II, Ch. 20; Maimonides, *The Guide of the Perplexed*, trans. Shlomo Pines (Chicago, 1963), Part I, Ch. 68, pp. 163–64; J. R. O'Donnell, ed., *Nine Medieval Thinkers* (Toronto, 1955), p. 191, is the source for Richard of Campsall. For Saint Thomas Aquinas, *Summa contra gentiles*, the standard Latin text is edited by Leonina Manvalis (Rome, 1946), and an English translation is that by Anton Pegis et al. (Garden City, N.Y., 1955–56); for *Summa theologica*, the standard Latin text is edited by M. E. Marietti (Turin, 1952), and an English version is *Basic Writings of Saint Thomas Aquinas*, ed. Anton Pegis (New York, 1945). See also Beatrice H. Zedler, ed., *Averroës Destructio destructionum* (Milwaukee, 1961), pp. 18–31.

Since the Renaissance, principal sources include I. A. Aaron, *John Locke* (Oxford, 1937), pp. 194–200; A. Arnauld, *La Logique, ou l'art de penser*, 5th ed. (Paris, 1683), Part I, Ch. 5; René Descartes, Letter to P. Mesland, 2 May 1644, *Principles of Philosophy*, ed. Charles Adam and Paul Tannery, 12 vols. (Paris, 1897–1913; 1964), I, 63 and VIII, 31. See also *Replies to First Objections*, ed. Charles Adam and Paul Tannery (Paris, 1964), VII, 120, and *Quartae objectiones*, in the Haldane and Ross translation (Cambridge, 1912), II, 82; John Locke, *Essay Concerning Human Understanding* (London, 1690), Book III, Ch. 3, para. 6. I. A; Immanuel Kant, *Werke*, ed. E. Cassirer, 11 vols. (Berlin, 1912–22), VII, 400–01; idem, *Kritik der reinen Vernunft* (Leipzig, 1924), A, 1781, B, 1787; H. Scholz and H. Schweitzer, *Die sogenannte Definitionen durch Abstraktion* (Leipzig, 1935).

JULIUS WEINBERG

[See also Analogy; **Axiomatization;** Experimental Science; **Islamic Conception;** Number; Optics and Vision; Organicism; **Platonism; Rationality.**]

ACADEMIC FREEDOM

I

ACADEMIC freedom is the liberty of thought which is claimed by teachers and other elements of the educational community. While the claim to freedom of the mind has a very long history—it was asserted in ancient Athens, for example, by Socrates—academic freedom, as the more specialized concern of the schools, is a rather modern phenomenon, having been first recognized in some of the universities of Western Europe in the sixteenth and seventeenth centuries. Emerging in the twelfth and thirteenth centuries, the university in the medieval age was to a considerable extent an autonomous corporate institution, but the master or teacher was subject to powerful restraints, both internal and external, and to the inhibiting force of authoritative tradition. Beginning with the founding of the university at Leiden in 1575, academic freedom began to take root in the Western world, albeit very slowly, as a consequence of the gradual development of an atmosphere of tolerance nurtured by the rise of religious, political, and economic liberalism, and the growth of the so-called new sciences. Francis Bacon's *Advancement of Learning* (1605) proclaimed the philosophical underpinning of the case for freedom of experimental inquiry with respect to the new sciences. The fierce, destructive, sectarian religious and political conflicts which characterized the struggle between the Reformation and the Counter-Reformation led a decimated and exhausted Western Europe to comprehend the values of toleration. The steady growth of commerce, which, among other things, drew attention to the desirable consequences of competitive enterprise, together with the rise of the liberal state, led to the emergence of a philosophy of knowledge which stressed the basic contingency of ideas, and the utility of testing the value of ideas, not in terms of the power of those who espoused them, but rather in terms of their capacity to stand up under the competition of other ideas. There was a logical transition from the competition of the marketplace to the competition of ideas.

While academic freedom has by no means achieved universal acceptance in the contemporary world, it is accepted as the normal expectation in most countries of Western Europe, with the exception of the dictatorships on the Iberian peninsula. It is not accepted by the communist or communist-dominated countries in Central and Eastern Europe and in Asia. It is significant that academic freedom is regarded, at least in principle, as a necessary and desirable aspect of higher education in many of the developing countries of Africa, the Middle East, and the Far East. In the many countries where academic freedom is understood and respected, however, there are two uses of the term which, if not fundamentally different, seem to differ in their points of emphasis. Thus, in Great Britain the term generally refers to the freedom of the educational institution as a whole from outside influences, political or otherwise.

While this usage of the term is by no means unknown in the United States, in America it almost invariably refers to the freedom of the individual professor. Of course, outside influences are often brought to bear upon American colleges and universities, and the concept of academic freedom requires the institution to resist any attacks upon its freedom to act as a corporate body. Nevertheless, in accordance with the individualistic tendency of the concept of rights in American constitutional law, the claim to academic freedom is generally stated and tested in terms of individual teachers. Whatever may be the force of outside influ-

ences, the concept holds that the institution has an obligation to protect the rights of academic freedom for all of its faculty members. Since the ultimate power of control over an American college or university is vested in its governing board, a dismissal in violation of a professor's academic freedom simply cannot happen unless the board decrees it. It follows that in the American system of higher education, responsibility for protecting the academic freedom of teachers rests with those who are legally in control of the institution, and who have the power not only to condone violations of that freedom, for example, by making improper dismissals, but also the power to protect the faculty against outside pressures and to defend their freedom. American experience indicates that even though a university may enjoy complete institutional autonomy, so far as external pressures are concerned, it is still possible for the university's administration to act in a manner which is injurious to the faculty's claim to academic freedom.

II

Academic freedom is usually described as the right of each individual member of the faculty of an institution to enjoy the freedom to study, to inquire, to speak his mind, to communicate his ideas, and to assert the truth as he sees it. In the United States, the professor's academic freedom is often defined in terms of full freedom in research and in the publication of the results, in classroom discussion of his subject, and in the exercise extra-murally of his basic rights as a citizen. But in America, and increasingly in other parts of the world, the concept of academic freedom has been broadened to include students as well as teachers. The freedom of the professor to teach is merely one side of the coin of academic freedom, the other side being the freedom of the student to learn.

In the historical sense this concept is neither very novel nor particularly American. It was a familiar point in the great days of German higher education, during the half century preceding World War I, that a close affinity between *Lehrfreiheit* and *Lernfreiheit* was recognized, though for the student the freedom to learn assumed characteristics not generally to be found in other countries. Once he had received the *abitur* (an examination taken at age 19 or 20, at the end of the *gymnasium* period), he was free to wander from school to school, to attend classes as he chose, and to take examinations whenever he felt prepared, and to try again if he failed. Otherwise he was never given grades and the flunk-out for unsatisfactory scholarship was unknown. This sort of student freedom was not widely practiced or recognized in other countries.

By the third quarter of the twentieth century, university students in the United States, and indeed all other elements of the university community, became more and more interested in those aspects of academic freedom which are of immediate concern to students. Various student associations began to draft statements of specific rights which they thought they were entitled to claim as against interference by college and university authorities. Civil liberties organizations and professorial groups also became active in this effort to spell out the academic freedom rights of the students. This activity produced, in 1967, a *Joint Statement on Rights and Freedoms of Students*, drafted by a joint committee made up of representatives of the American Association of University Professors, the U. S. National Student Association, the Association of American Colleges, the National Association of Student Personnel Administrators, and the National Association of Women Deans and Counselors. Other educational associations have endorsed the *Statement* since its formulation, and thus it is rapidly acquiring standing as an authoritative statement of desirable normative principles.

The *Statement* points out that "freedom to teach and freedom to learn are inseparable facets of academic freedom." It is noted that since "free inquiry and free expression are indispensable to the attainment" of the goals of academic institutions—which are: "the transmission of knowledge, the pursuit of truth, the development of students, and the general well-being of society"—"students should be encouraged to develop the capacity for critical judgment and to engage in a sustained and independent search for truth." To this end, the *Statement* spells out the rights of students as regards institutional admission policies, in the classroom, in respect to student records, student affairs, and off-campus activities. In the area of student affairs, various standards are stated with respect to freedom of association, freedom of inquiry and expression, participation in institutional government, and student publications. A detailed final section seeks to delineate, with considerable particularity, procedural standards in disciplinary proceedings, to the end that students may enjoy a full measure of due process.

III

The fundamental case for academic freedom has always been that while it confers desired benefits upon the professors who enjoy it, it is defensible mainly on the ground that the unhampered search for the truth is for the benefit of society as a whole. A basic premiss is that final truth in all branches of human knowledge has not yet been achieved, and that new truths will emerge only as ideas clash with ideas in an unrestricted marketplace of ideas. In the words of Cardinal Newman (1872), a true university or college is a place "in which the intellect may safely range and speculate, sure to find its equal in some antagonistic activity, and its judge in the tribunal of truth. It is a place where inquiry is pushed forward, and discoveries verified and perfected, and rashness rendered innocuous, and error exposed, by the collision of mind with mind, and knowledge with knowledge" ("What is a University?," *Historical Sketches* [1872], I, 16). Thus it has been asserted that academic freedom exists "in order that society may have the benefit of honest judgment and independent criticism which otherwise might be withheld because of fear of offending a dominant group or transient social attitude" (Clark Byse and Louis Joughin, *Tenure in American Higher Education* [1959], p. 4).

The eminent scholars (including the distinguished historian of ideas, Arthur O. Lovejoy) who founded the American Association of University Professors in 1915 published a *Declaration of Principles* which stated the rationale for academic freedom that has been generally accepted by the American academic community. They pointed out that while professors are the appointees of the university's trustees, they are not in any proper sense the trustees' employees, just as federal judges are appointed by the President without becoming, as a consequence, the Chief Executive's employees. "For, once appointed," they declared, "the scholar has professional functions to perform in which the appointing authorities have neither competency nor moral right to intervene." And they added: "A university is a great and indispensable organ of the higher life of a civilized community, in the work of which the trustees hold an essential and highly honorable place, but in which the faculties hold an independent place, with quite equal responsibilities—and in relation to purely scientific and educational questions, the primary responsibility." Stressing the nature of the academic calling, they wrote that "if education is the cornerstone of the structure of society, and if progress in scientific knowledge is essential to civilization, few things can be more important than to enhance the dignity of the scholar's profession, with a view to attracting to its ranks men of the highest ability, of sound learning, and of strong and independent character."

A similar conception of the nature of academic freedom has, in recent years, been adopted by the United States Supreme Court. Speaking for the Court in 1957, Chief Justice Warren declared:

The essentiality of freedom in the community of American universities is almost self-evident. No one should underestimate the vital role in a democracy that is played by those who guide and train our youth. To impose any strait jacket upon the intellectual leaders in our colleges and universities would imperil the future of our Nation. No field of education

11

is so thoroughly comprehended by man that new discoveries cannot yet be made. Particularly is that true in the social sciences, where few, if any, principles are accepted as absolutes. Scholarship cannot flourish in an atmosphere of suspicion and distrust. Teachers and students must always remain free to inquire, to study and to evaluate, to gain new maturity and understanding; otherwise our civilization will stagnate and die (*Sweezy* v. *New Hampshire*, 354 U.S. 234, 250).

Similarly, in a concurring opinion filed in this case, Justice Frankfurter wrote:

These pages need not be burdened with proof, based on the testimony of a cloud of impressive witnesses, of the dependence of a free society on free universities. This means the exclusion of governmental intervention in the intellectual life of a university. It matters little whether such intervention occurs avowedly or through action that inevitably tends to check the ardor and fearlessness of scholars, qualities at once so fragile and so indispensable for fruitful academic labor (ibid., 354 U.S. 262).

More recently, again speaking for the Supreme Court, Justice Brennan observed:

Our Nation is deeply committed to safeguarding academic freedom, which is of transcendent value to all of us and not merely to the teachers concerned. That freedom is therefore a special concern of the First Amendment, which does not tolerate laws that cast a pall of orthodoxy over the classroom. "The vigilant protection of constitutional freedom is nowhere more vital than in the community of American schools." . . . The classroom is peculiarly the "marketplace of ideas." The Nation's future depends upon leaders trained through wide exposure to that robust exchange of ideas which discovers truth "out of a multitude of tongues, [rather] than through any kind of authoritative selection" (*Keyishian* v. *Board of Regents of New York*, 385 U.S. 589, 603 [1967]).

Thus, by the late 1960's, the concept of academic freedom had been accepted by the United States Supreme Court as an integral part of the civil liberties law of the country. This concept was by then also regarded by the academic community as an essential element of the American system of intellectual freedom. It was widely believed that the schools play an indispensable role in the progress of civilization, that the colleges and universities were the country's most important instruments for the generation and testing of new ideas and the advancement of scientific knowledge, and for the training of new leadership in government, in the professions, and in the economy. Since leaders in a rapidly changing world should not be slaves to routine, but must, on the contrary, be able to take the initiative, handle new ideas, solve new problems, evaluate evidence, think rationally, and act purposefully, it was felt that only a free educational system

can produce such leadership. In a broader sense, it was widely understood that in a fluid, open, democratic society, in which the legally protected right to dissent inevitably creates an atmosphere of controversy, the schools cannot insulate their students from controversy, since this would leave them unprepared to take their rightful places in a society in which controversy is a daily and indispensable condition. Furthermore, a democratic, self-governing society cannot afford the risk of having an ignorant and unenlightened citizenry. Self-government means that the citizen must be able to govern himself, that is to say, to control his emotions, to use his reason, and to be concerned with the public interest. To this end the schools, functioning in an atmosphere of academic freedom, make a weighty contribution. It follows that the freedom of teachers to teach and of students to learn is essential to democracy, to progress, to the security of a way of life committed to the maximizing of human freedom.

IV

The world over, wherever the principle of academic freedom has been understood and respected, it has been closely tied to the concept of tenure, since security of employment is an essential precondition for the unhampered exercise of academic freedom. While there are variations on the general theme, the concept of tenure which has taken root in the United States comes to this: after a teacher has served on a faculty for a limited, prescribed number of years in probationary status, he acquires a permanent position.

The American Association of University Professors has sought, during the past half century, to standardize the maximum duration of the probationary period. The influential 1940 *Statement of Principles*, which it negotiated with the Association of American Colleges, and which has been endorsed by over sixty learned societies since its adoption, prescribed that the maximum duration of the probationary period should be seven years. That is to say, after a teacher has served on a faculty for seven years in probationary status, the institution has an obligation to make up its mind whether to let him go or keep him permanently by granting him tenure. Tenure means that the teacher, having been found adequate by the institution during the probationary period, is now entitled to hold his position until retirement. It is recognized, however, that the concept does not mean that a tenured professor can never be dismissed under any conceivable circumstances. On the contrary, it is agreed that the institution has a right to dismiss a tenured professor, but only if there is adequate cause for the dismissal, and only if adequate cause is established by procedures which satisfy the rigorous demands of due process. In addition, it is recognized that an institution may find it necessary to terminate a continuous appointment because of financial exigency—though it is insisted, in the 1940 *Statement*, that such financial exigency "should be demonstrably bona fide."

The essence of the tenure concept, then, is the recognition of the right to serve until retirement, unless there is an earlier dismissal for an adequate reason established through procedures which measure up to the requirements of justice by assuring the individual concerned the protection of due process. This means that before the administration of an institution makes an unfavorable recommendation to the governing board, the faculty member must be given a statement of specific charges, served upon him long enough in advance so that he has adequate time to prepare his defense. Following the service of charges, he is entitled to be heard, in the first instance, by a faculty committee, preferably an elected committee not directly controlled by the administration. Due process also assures the individual all of the elements of a fair hearing, such as the right to be heard in his own defense, the right to counsel, the right to offer witnesses and to confront and cross-examine witnesses who appear against him, and a right to a stenographic record of all hearings. Due process also demands that findings of fact and the ultimate decision should be based on the hearing record.

In addition, the burden of proof to establish the existence of adequate cause for a dismissal is on those who brought the charges, since the grant of tenure establishes a presumption of competence comparable to the presumption of innocence which defendants enjoy in criminal cases. If the faculty hearing committee decides in favor of the involved faculty member, the normal expectation is that the charges will be dropped. If the administration persists in bringing the charges to the governing body for final action, then that body is expected to give the individual a hearing embracing all of the basic elements of due process. When a faculty committee has made a decision favorable to the individual, then an especially heavy burden of proof rests upon those who persist in pressing the charges.

Thus, the real protection for the tenured professor, so far as dismissal is concerned, depends far more upon the procedures available to him, than upon any substantive definition of the term academic freedom. Furthermore, while the rules of academic due process seek to protect the professor against injustice, they also protect the institution and its administration from acting unjustly and making mistakes. Speaking in the wider context of governmental action, Justice Jackson urged that it should not be overlooked that "due proc-

ess of law is not for the sole benefit of an accused. It is the best insurance for the Government itself against those blunders which leave lasting stains on a system of justice but which are bound to occur on ex parte consideration" (*Shaughnessy* v. *United States ex rel. Mezei*, 345 U.S. 206, 224–25 [1953], dissenting opinion). When a professor is dismissed arbitrarily, without charges and a chance to be heard in a fair proceeding, not only is the professor treated wrongly, but the institution deprives itself of the benefits and guidance which would be secured by following proper procedures. An arbitrary dismissal also prevents the academic community from having confidence in the institution's course of action, since there are bound to be doubts about the acceptability of administrative decisions which were taken with faulty procedure. Due process is regarded as vital for the academic community, as it is in the general community, because it is society's best assurance that the action was taken justly.

V

In the United States there are a number of associations concerned with defining and defending the professor's claim to academic freedom, such as the American Civil Liberties Union, various teachers' unions, the American Association for Higher Education (an affiliate of the National Educational Association), and many other groups. Since its establishment in 1915, however, the chief spokesman for the academic freedom rights of teachers in the world of higher education has been the American Association of University Professors. Over the years the Association has spelled out the content of academic freedom, both substantive and procedural, in numerous statements of principles and has dealt with specific complaints submitted to it by aggrieved professors. Complaints alleging improper dismissals are referred to the Association's oldest and most influential committee, Committee A, on Academic Freedom and Tenure. During the past half century the Committee, with the assistance of professional staff in the central office in Washington, has dealt with hundreds of cases, and has developed a large and sophisticated body of interpretations and common law principles which relate to various aspects of academic freedom.

Once the General Secretary of the Association has concluded that there is a *prima facie* case for believing that a serious violation of an important principle of academic freedom and tenure has occurred, he appoints an investigating committee of disinterested scholars. Following its investigation, the ad hoc committee reports to Committee A, which then decides whether to accept the report, and whether it should be published in the quarterly journal of the Association.

13

Once a year, at the annual delegate meeting of the Association, Committee A decides whether to recommend for or against censure of the administration concerned. The ultimate weapon of the Association is a public censure, which is no more, and no less, than an expression of moral disapproval. Through the instrumentality of censure the Association pronounces its special form of anathema upon the administration of an institution, declaring that in its informed and solemn judgment, proper conditions of academic freedom do not exist there. This is communicated to the academic world through the Association's publications, through the mass media, and through the efforts of other learned societies.

There is every reason to believe that this weapon of the Association is very effective, even though it does not go beyond the expression of moral disapproval. Administrations on censure are removed from the list by vote of the annual delegate meeting of the Association on the recommendation of Committee A. This occurs when it has been decided that the dereliction which led to the censure action has been corrected. Generally this takes the form of changes in the institution's rules and procedures, and the award to the injured party of some sort of redress.

There are active associations of university teachers in the other English-speaking countries, notably Great Britain, Canada, Australia, in the Scandinavian countries, and rather less effective associations in most of the other countries of Western Europe. In addition there is an International Association of University Professors and Lecturers, with a part-time Secretary-General, but this is essentially an association of autonomous national bodies, and is limited in activity to the holding of periodical conferences and seminars.

VI

The concept of academic freedom embraces more than mere protection against arbitrary dismissals, though the central purpose of tenure is to protect the teacher against such dismissals. In fact, professors often have occasion to complain about many other forms of mistreatment. The American Association, for example, has received frequent complaints about denial of salary increases, or the receipt of increases below the average, or the assignment of inconvenient hours or unwelcome courses, and other forms of unwanted action taking the form and having the purpose of harassment. If professors are to be free from external restraints in their pursuit of the truth, they must be as free from harassment as they are from the crippling pressure of the possibility of summary dismissal. The American Association of University Professors has always taken the position that the best security against most forms of

harassment is to be found within the machinery of the institution itself. Thus, an essential element of the prevailing American conception of academic freedom is the principle of maximum faculty participation in the decision-making processes of the institution. Through faculty meetings, faculty committees, and other devices of communication, the faculty, it is believed, can achieve a responsible place in the making of institutional decisions. For example, institutions are encouraged to have faculty grievance committees, built into the official organizational system of the institution, for the adjustment of complaints.

The whole concept of faculty involvement in institutional government took a giant step forward in 1966, when three major groups in American higher education, the American Council on Education, the American Association of University Professors, and the Association of Governing Boards of Universities and Colleges, reached agreement on a joint *Statement on Government of Colleges and Universities*. This *Statement* recognizes that college or university government is the joint responsibility of the various major elements of the academic community, faculties, administrators, governing boards, and students, since, it is noted, "the variety and complexity of the tasks performed by institutions of higher education produce an inescapable interdependence" among them. Joint efforts by all components of the institution are needed for effective planning and communication, for budgeting, for the selection of the chief academic officials, and for the optimum use of facilities. More particularly, the tripartite *Statement* recognizes that the faculty has "primary responsibility" with respect to curriculum, subject matter and methods of instruction, research, and those elements of student life which relate to the educational process. The faculty determines the requirements for the degrees offered in courses, and decides when and how degree requirements have been met. It is also recognized that the faculty has primary responsibility with respect to academic appointments, reappointments, decisions not to reappoint, promotions, the granting of tenure, and dismissals. This responsibility rests upon the fact that scholars in a particular field have the chief competence for making judgments on all these matters of faculty status.

Of course, administrative review and board approval are part of the complicated procedures which are involved in making decisions on questions of faculty status, but faculty judgment on these matters should normally be decisive, and should not be overruled except for very compelling reasons, and in accordance with procedures spelled out in advance with explicit detail. In addition, it is agreed that the faculty should be consulted in the selection of department chairmen, deans and presidents, and in the making of budget policy. Finally, it is recognized that if faculty participation is to be meaningful, the institution must have suitable agencies for participation through regularly scheduled faculty meetings, representative assemblies, and faculty committees, of which at least the most important should be elected directly by the faculty.

The tripartite *Statement* reflects a dramatic change in the structure of American colleges and universities, for in the early days of higher education in America the faculty was weak and the president of the institution was in a very commanding position. The historic position of the American university president was a powerful one from the very beginning, but changes have occurred in the course of history, and this has resulted in significant changes in the distribution of power within the institution. The basic historic fact is that in the United States there were college presidents long before there were professionally-trained, full-time, competent faculties completely committed to the teaching profession. The earliest teachers in the American colleges were mainly preachers who taught part-time, or who taught occasionally as an alternative to other activities. In contrast, from the very start the president was a full-time, fully-committed chief officer of the institution. The colleges were weak, professional faculties were unknown, and the only person who could speak for the college, defend it against its enemies in the community, and secure the necessary support, was the president. Thus, the president was strong because the faculty was weak.

The conditions which created the powerful president, however, disappeared with the rise of strong, professionally-competent, full-time faculties, made up of scholars and teachers, able to insist upon sharing with the institution's administration the responsibility for making basic policy decisions. The growing involvement of American professors in the governance of their institution is a consequence of their professional competence. This is not to suggest that presidents are unimportant or without power, but in the modern age the professors have assumed the responsibility of exercising a large portion of the innovative function in higher education, for the president has become an extremely busy academic entrepreneur who lacks the time and energy to be concerned very much or very often with educational innovation.

The concept of a partnership between administration, teaching faculty, and students now dominates the American education scene. Professors do not regard themselves as mere employees who can be hired and fired at will, and the theory and practice of academic freedom, suitably buttressed by faculty participation in the governance of the institution, has rendered wholly untenable the conception of the professor as a hired hand.

Finally, the modern concept of academic freedom insists that the professor has a right to exercise all of the rights of citizenship, including freedom of speech and freedom of association, and that in exercising these rights he should be subjected to no institutional interference or academic penalties. The 1940 *Statement* declares that the faculty member, as a citizen, has the right to speak or write free from institutional censorship or discipline, though attention is called to the professor's special obligation to be accurate, to exercise appropriate restraint, to show respect for the opinion of others, and to make every effort to indicate that he is not an institutional spokesman. It is widely recognized in the American academic community that a faculty member, like other citizens, should be free to engage in political activities so far as he can do so consistently with his professional obligations as a teacher and scholar.

VII

The main elements of academic freedom are securely established in those countries which recognize and respect the principles of intellectual and political freedom. Academic freedom does not exist in dictatorship countries, or in countries which practice thought-control. This suggests that while academic freedom has its own special characteristics, it is invariably part of a larger pattern of human freedom. Furthermore, just as the other rights which modern man claims are subject to the manifold pressures of a complex, problem-ridden, changing world, so does the right to academic freedom encounter powerful pressures which weaken or challenge the concept, and indeed, on some occasions and in some places, threaten its very existence.

Some difficulties result, in the United States, from the very structure of the system of higher education which is, in reality, no system at all. There is no national ministry of education, and the role of the national government in education at all levels is largely limited to making and administering financial grants. For the public institutions the power of control rests in the fifty state governments, and in the governing boards created by these governments. For the private institutions the power of control rests in the boards of trustees. Some measure of conformity with minimum general standards is achieved through the several regional accrediting associations, and through the efforts of national professional associations in specialized schools and colleges, such as those of law, medicine, pharmacy, architecture, and journalism. But on the whole, variety and local control are the central features of the American system of higher education. While the 15 spirit of localism may serve to insulate problems, including violations of academic freedom, it also encourages a chaotic tendency for the locally autonomous institution to proceed on an *ad hoc* basis free from the restraining influence of centralized standards of performance. The still very considerable administrative power of the typical American college or university president, exercised locally in a self-defining situation, gives a willful or determined man great scope in which to operate with respect to his institution's personnel.

In varying degrees throughout the world, the professor's academic freedom is often under pressure from all sorts of external forces—political parties and factions, politicians, economic interests, religious groups, patriotic organizations, racial and national origins groups, and many others. In most institutions the influence of alumni and private donors is persistent and may be very weighty. In many countries, and especially in the United States, there is a wide-spread, latent anti-intellectualism in large segments of the population which, under certain conditions, may contribute to the outside pressures which challenge or weaken the academic freedom of the teachers. In a broader sense it may be noted that, in the nature of their calling, professors deal with new ideas, and it is often painful to work with new ideas in areas where popular values are deeply entrenched. Furthermore, the remarkable expansion of the social sciences in recent years has had the result of involving professors more and more with public issues on which large segments of the population are deeply divided. Such issues as those involving war and peace, labor relations, regulation of the economy, public ownership, and basic political change are likely to be highly combustible.

During the period following World War II the outstanding political fact on a global scale was the protracted Cold War between the communist and democratic communities of nations, particularly between the United States and the Soviet Union. The severe pressures generated by the Cold War exerted a profoundly disturbing impact upon educational institutions. In the United States the Cold War led to the imposition of various forms of loyalty oaths, which many professors regarded as invidiously insulting to them, to legislative investigations, and sundry purges. In addition, and again particularly in the United States, the post-World War II period witnessed an agonizing conflict over race relations, and the colleges and universities were deeply involved in situations growing out of this conflict. In many institutions the freedom of professors to take sides in this struggle was sharply challenged, and administrative reprisals were by no means unknown. Many censure actions of the American Association of

University Professors, for example, were by-products of tensions generated by the race issue.

Finally, all over the world, the decade of the 1960's was a time of serious student dissatisfaction and unrest. In many places student dissent ripened into disruption and violence, and led to stern measures on the part of institutional administrations and governments. There were large-scale police actions at such distinguished institutions as the University of California in Berkeley and Columbia University in New York, and massive military intervention against students in such cities as Paris, Mexico City, and Tokyo. The academic freedom of the institution as a whole was inevitably drawn into the maelstrom of issues which large-scale student violence created.

Like so many other freedoms, academic freedom is experienced unevenly in the contemporary world. It is securely established in some countries, and scarcely exists in others, and in between the extremes it exists in varying degrees of amplitude and security. Where academic freedom is well-defined and respected, the teaching profession understands that the principle protects the professor against the devastating consequences of arbitrary dismissal. It is recognized that the teacher can be dismissed only for adequate cause, as established in a proceeding which measures up to the requirements of due process, including a hearing before a tribunal consisting of his academic peers. It is well understood that the security of the professor depends not so much upon the substantive definition of what constitutes adequate cause, as upon the procedures which are followed. That proper procedure is an indispensable element of justice in the life of the state is a commonplace observation. Proper procedure is equally essential if academic freedom is to remain a viable concept.

BIBLIOGRAPHY

The leading history of academic freedom, with special reference to the United States, is Richard Hofstadter and Walter P. Metzger, *The Development of Academic Freedom in the United States* (New York, 1955). The principal study of the tenure concept in American higher education is by Clark Byse and Louis Joughin, *Tenure in American Higher Education* (Ithaca, N.Y., 1959). Louis Joughin, ed., *Academic Freedom and Tenure* (Madison, 1967), contains most of the basic statements of principles adopted by the American Association of University Professors, as well as six important journal articles on the subject of academic freedom and tenure. Policy statements of the American Civil Liberties Union on academic freedom and due process are reprinted in the American Association of University Professors, *Bulletin*, **42** (1956), 517–29, 655–61, and **48** (1962), 111–15. The place of academic freedom in American public law is reviewed in a symposium in *Law and Contemporary Problems*,

28 (1963), 429–671, and in William P. Murphy, "Educational Freedom in the Courts," American Association of University Professors, *Bulletin*, **49** (1963), 309–27. The philosophy of academic freedom is reviewed and evaluated in Russell Kirk, *Academic Freedom; An Essay in Definition* (Chicago, 1955), and in Robert M. MacIver, *Academic Freedom in Our Time* (New York, 1955). Specific academic freedom cases are reported on in almost every issue of the *Bulletin* of the American Association of University Professors.

DAVID FELLMAN

[See also **Democracy**; Economic Theory of Natural Liberty; Education; **Freedom**; Law, Due Process in; Loyalty; **Protest Movements**; Religious Toleration.]

AGNOSTICISM

I

AGNOSTICISM is a philosophical and theological concept which has been understood in various ways by different philosophers and theologians. T. H. Huxley coined the term in 1869, and its first home was in the disputes about science and religion, naturalism and supernaturalism, that reached a climax during the nineteenth century. To be an agnostic is to hold that nothing can be known or at least that it is very unlikely that anything will be known or soundly believed concerning whether God or any transcendent reality or state exists.

It is very natural for certain people conditioned in certain ways to believe that there must be some power "behind," "beyond," or "underlying" the universe which is responsible for its order and all the incredible features that are observed and studied by the sciences even though these same people will readily grant that we do not know that there is such a power or have good grounds for believing that there is such a power. While the admission of ignorance concerning things divine is usually made by someone outside the circle of faith, it can and indeed has been made by fideistic Jews and Christians as well.

Some writers, e.g., Robert Flint and James Ward, so construed "agnosticism" that (1) it was identified with "philosophical skepticism" and (2) it allowed for there being "theistic agnostics" and "Christian agnostics." However, the more typical employment of "agnosticism" is such that it would not be correct to count as agnostics either fideistic believers or Jews and Christians who claim that we can only gain knowledge of God through some mystical awareness or "ineffable knowledge." It surely was this standard but more circumscribed sense of "agnosticism" that William James

had in mind when he made his famous remark in his essay "The Will to Believe" that agnosticism was the worst thing that "ever came out of the philosopher's workshop." Without implying or suggesting any support at all for James's value judgment, we shall construe agnosticism in this rather more typical manner. Given this construal (1) "theistic agnosticism" is a contradiction and thus one cannot be a Jew or a Christian and be an agnostic and (2) also agnosticism is *neutral* vis-à-vis the claim that there can be no philosophical knowledge or even scientific or common-sense knowledge. We shall then take agnosticism to be the more limited claim that we either do not or cannot know that God or any other transcendent reality or state exists and thus we should suspend judgment concerning the assertion that God exists. That is to say, the agnostic neither affirms nor denies it. This, as should be evident from the above characterization, can take further specification and indeed later such specifications will be supplied. But such a construal captures in its characterization both what was essentially at issue in the great agnostic debates in the nineteenth century and the issue as it has come down to us.

II

T. H. Huxley was by training a biologist, but he had strong philosophical interests and as a champion of Darwinism he became a major intellectual figure in the nineteenth century. In his "Science and Christian Tradition" (in *Collected Essays*), Huxley remarks that agnosticism is a method, a stance taken toward putative religious truth-claims, the core of which is to refuse to assent to religious doctrines for which there is no adequate evidence, but to retain an open-mindedness about the possibility of sometime attaining adequate evidence. We ought never to assert that we know a proposition to be true or indeed even to assent to that proposition unless we have adequate evidence to support it.

After his youthful reading of the Scottish metaphysician William Hamilton's *Philosophy of the Unconditioned* (1829), Huxley repeatedly returned to questions about the limits of our possible knowledge and came, as did Leslie Stephen, to the empiricist conclusion that we cannot know anything about God or any alleged states or realities "beyond phenomena." Whether there is a God, a world of demons, an immortal soul, whether indeed "the spiritual world" is other than human fantasy or projection, were all taken by Huxley to be *factual questions* open to careful and systematic empirical investigation. In short, however humanly important such questions were, they were also "matters of the intellect" and in such contexts the central maxim of the method of agnosticism is to "follow your reason as far as it will take you, without regard to any other consideration. And negatively: In matters of the intellect do not pretend that conclusions are certain which are not demonstrated or demonstrable" (Huxley, pp. 245–46). Operating in accordance with such a method does not justify "the denial of the existence of any Supernature; but simply the denial of the validity of the evidence adduced in favour of this, or that, extant form of Supernaturalism" (p. 126). Huxley found that he could no more endorse materialism, idealism, atheism, or pantheism than he could theism; they all claimed too much about essentially contested matters. Huxley felt that people espousing such world views were too ready to claim a solution to the "problem of existence," while he remained painfully aware that he had not succeeded in coming by such a solution and in addition retained "a pretty strong conviction that the problem was insoluble" (pp. 237–38).

This conviction is at the heart of his agnosticism. Huxley was convinced that Kant and Hamilton had established that reason fails us—and indeed *must* fail us—when we try to establish that the world is finite in space or time or indefinite in space or time, rational or irrational, an ordered whole or simply manifesting certain ordered features but not something properly to be called an ordered whole. Answers to such questions reveal something about our attitudes but can never provide us with propositions we can justifiably claim to be true or even know to be false. Agnosticism is a confession of honesty here. It is "the only position for people who object to say that they know what they are quite aware they do not know" (p. 210).

Such skepticism concerning the truth-claims of religion and metaphysics, including, of course, metaphysical religiosity, should not be taken as a denial that there can be reliable knowledge. Rather Huxley argued, as John Dewey did far more systematically later, that we can and do gain experimental and experiential knowledge of nature, including human nature, and that this, by contrast with so-called "supernatural knowledge," becomes increasingly more extensive and reliable. And while remaining an agnostic, Huxley saw in science—basically the scientific way of fixing belief—a fundamental and well grounded challenge to the authority of the theory of the "spiritual world."

Whatever may have been the case in the seventeenth century, there was in Huxley's time a state of war between science and religion. Huxley took science to be a challenge to claims of biblical infallibility and revelation. The whole supernatural world view built on the authority of the Bible and revelation must come under scientific scrutiny and when this is done it becomes gradually apparent that the use of the scientific method and appeals to scientific canons of criticism give us a far more reliable method of settling belief than do the scriptures and revelation.

To commit ourselves to the Bible as an infallible authority is to commit ourselves to a world view in which we must believe that devils were cast out of a man and went into a herd of swine, that the deluge was universal, that the world was made in six days, and the like. Yet such claims are plainly and massively contravened by our actual empirical knowledge such that they are quite beyond the boundaries of responsible belief. About such matters, Huxley argues, we ought not to be at all agnostic. Moreover, we cannot take them simply as myths, important for the biblical and Christian understanding of the world, if we are to take seriously biblical infallibility and the authority of revelation. For the Jewish-Christian world view to establish its validity, it must provide us with adequate grounds for believing that there are demons. But there is no good evidence for such alleged realities and to believe in them is the grossest form of superstition (Huxley, p. 215).

Even if we fall back on a severe Christology, we are still in difficulties, for it is evident enough that Jesus believed in demons and if we are to adopt a radical Christology and take Jesus as our infallible guide to the divine, we are going to have to accept such superstitious beliefs. Such beliefs affront not only our intellect—our credibility concerning what it is reasonable to believe—they also affront our moral sense as well (p. 226). Yet once we give up the Gospel claim that there are "demons who can be transferred from a man to a pig," the other stories of "demonic possession fall under suspicion." Once we start on this slide, once we challenge the ultimate authority of the Bible, and follow experimental and scientific procedures, the ground for the whole Judeo-Christian world view is undermined.

Huxley obviously thinks its credibility and probability is of a very low order; an order which would make Christian or Jewish belief quite impossible for a reasonable and tolerably well informed man. Those who claim to know that there are such unseen and indeed utterly unseeable realities, are very likely people who have taken "cunning phrases for answers," where real answers are "not merely actually impossible, but theoretically inconceivable." Yet as an agnostic one must always—even for such problematical transcendental claims—remain open to conviction where evidence can be brought to establish the truth of such transcendent religious claims.

Leslie Stephen in his neglected *An Agnostic's*

Apology (1893) remarks that he uses "agnostic" in a sense close to that of T. H. Huxley. To be an agnostic, according to Stephen, is to reject what he calls "Dogmatic Atheism," i.e., "the doctrine that there is no God, whatever is meant by God. . ."; it is, instead, (1) to affirm "what no one denies," namely "that there are limits to the sphere of human intelligence" and (2) also to affirm the controversial empiricist thesis "that those limits are such as to exclude at least what Lewes called 'Metempirical knowledge'" (p. 1). ("Metempirical knowledge" is meant to designate all forms of knowledge of a transcendent, numinal, nonempirical sort.)

Stephen makes apparent the empiricist commitments of his conception of agnosticism in characterizing gnosticism, the view agnosticism is deliberately set against. To be a gnostic is to believe that "we can attain truths not capable of verification and not needing verification by actual experiment or observation" (ibid., pp. 1–2). In gaining such a knowledge gnostics in opposition to both Hume and Kant claim that by the use of our reason we can attain a knowledge that transcends "the narrow limits of experience" (p. 1). But the agnostic, firmly in the empiricist tradition, denies that there can be any knowledge of the world, including anything about its origin and destiny, which transcends experience and comprehends "the sorry scheme of things entire." Such putative knowledge, Stephen maintains, is illusory and not something "essential to the highest interests of mankind," providing us, as speculative metaphysicians believe, with the solution to "the dark riddle of the universe" (p. 2).

In a manner that anticipates the challenge to the claims of religion and metaphysics made by the logical empiricists, Stephen says that in addition to the problem of whether they can establish the truth or probable truth of "religious truth-claims" there is the further consideration—actually a logically prior question—of whether such putative claims "have any meaning" (p. 3).

It should be noted that Stephen does not begin "An Agnostic's Apology" by discussing semantical difficulties in putative religious truth-claims but starts with problems connected with what W. K. Clifford was later to call "the ethics of belief." We indeed would all want—if we could do it honestly—to accept the claim that "evil is transitory . . . good eternal" and that the "world is really an embodiment of love and wisdom, however dark it may appear to us" (p. 2). But the rub is that many of us cannot believe that and in a question of such inestimable human value, we have "the most sacred obligations to recognize the facts" and make our judgments in accordance with the facts. But the facts do not give us grounds for confidence in the viability of Judeo-Christian beliefs. Rather we are strongly inclined when we inspect these beliefs to believe they are wish fulfillments. And while it may indeed be true that for the moment dreams may be pleasanter than realities, it is also true that if we are bent on attaining a more permanent measure of happiness, it "must be won by adapting our lives to the realities," for we know from experience that illusory consolations "are the bitterest of mockeries" (ibid.). The religious platitudes "Pain is not an evil," "Death is not a separation," and "Sickness is but a blessing in disguise" have tortured sufferers far more than "the gloomiest speculations of avowed pessimists" (ibid.).

However, the problem of *meaning* cuts to a deeper conceptual level than do such arguments about the ethics of belief. Where Judeo-Christianity does not have a fideistic basis, it is committed to what Stephen calls gnosticism. But does not such a doctrine fail "to recognize the limits of possible knowledge" and in trying to transcend these limits does it not in effect commit the gnostic to pseudo-propositions which are devoid of literal meaning? Logical empiricists later answered this question in the affirmative and while it is not crystal clear that Stephen's answer is quite that definite, it would appear that this is what he wants to maintain. And if that is what Stephen is maintaining, there can, of course, be no knowledge of the divine.

Stephen raises this key question concerning the intelligibility of such gnostic God-talk, but he does little with it. Instead he focuses on some key questions concerning attempts by theologians to undermine agnosticism. He first points out that an appeal to revelation is no answer to the agnostic's denial that we have knowledge of transcendent realities or states, for in claiming to rely exclusively on revelation these theologians acknowledge that "natural man can know nothing of the Divine nature." But this Stephen replies, is not only to grant but in effect to assert the agnostic's fundamental principle (p. 5). He points out that H. L. Mansel in effect and in substance affirms agnosticism and that Cardinal Newman with his appeal to the testimony of conscience does not provide a reliable argument on which to base a belief in God nor does he undermine the agnostic's position, for "the voice of conscience has been very differently interpreted." Some of these interpretations, secular though they be, have all the appearances of being at least as valid as Newman's, for all that Newman or anyone else has shown. Moreover, on any reasonable reading of a principle of parsimony, they are far simpler than Newman's interpretation. Thus Newman's arguments in reality prove, as do Mansel's, that a man ought to be an agnostic concerning such ultimate questions where reason remains his guide and where he does not make an appeal to the *authority* of the Church. They, of   19 course, would have us accept the authority of the Church, but how can we reasonably do so when there are so many Churches, so many conflicting authorities, and so many putative revelations? Where reason can only lead us to agnosticism concerning religious matters, we can have no ground for accepting one Church, one religious authority, or one putative revelation rather than another. We simply have no way of knowing which course is the better course. Agnosticism, Stephen concludes, is the only reasonable and viable alternative.

Like Huxley, and like Hume before him, Stephen is skeptical of the *a priori* arguments of metaphysics and natural theology. "There is not a single proof of natural theology," he asserts, "of which the negative has not been maintained as vigorously as the affirmative" (p. 9). In such a context, where there is no substantial agreement, but just endless and irresolvable philosophical controversy, it is the duty of a reasonable man to profess ignorance (p. 9). In trying to escape the bounds of sense—in trying to gain some metempirical knowledge—philosophers continue to contradict flatly the first principles of their predecessors and no vantage point is attained where we can objectively assess these endemic metaphysical conflicts that divide philosophers. To escape utter skepticism, we must be agnostics and argue that such metaphysical and theological controversies lead to "transcending the limits of reason" (p. 10). But the only widely accepted characterization of these limits "comes in substance to an exclusion of ontology" and an adherence to empirically based truth-claims as the only legitimate truth-claims.

It will not help, Stephen argues, to maintain that the Numinous, i.e., the divine, is essentially mysterious and that religious understanding—a seeing through a glass darkly—is a knowledge of something which is irreducibly and inescapably mysterious. In such talk in such contexts, there is linguistic legerdemain: we call our doubts mysteries and what is now being appealed to as "the mystery of faith" is but the theological phrase for agnosticism (p. 22).

Stephen argues that one could believe knowledge of the standard types was quite possible and indeed actual and remain skeptical about metaphysics. It is just such a position that many (perhaps most) contemporary philosophers would take. In taking this position himself, Stephen came to believe that metaphysical claims are "nothing but the bare husks of meaningless words." To gain genuine knowledge, we must firmly put aside such meaningless metaphysical claims and recognize the more limited extent of our knowledge claims. A firm recognition here will enable us to avoid utter skepticism because we come to see that within

the limits of the experiential "we have been able to discover certain reliable truths" and with them "we shall find sufficient guidance for the needs of life" (p. 26). So while we remain religious skeptics and skeptical of the claims of transcendental metaphysics, we are not generally skeptical about man's capacity to attain reliable knowledge. Yet it remains the case that nothing is known or can be known, of the alleged "ultimate reality"—the Infinite and Absolute—of traditional metaphysics and natural theology (p. 26). And thus nothing can be known of God.

III

Before moving on to a consideration of some twentieth-century formulations of agnosticism and to a critical examination of all forms of agnosticism, let us consider briefly a question that the above characterization of Huxley and Stephen certainly should give rise to. Given the correctness of the above criticisms of Judaism and Christianity, do we not have good grounds for rejecting these religions and is not this in effect an espousal of atheism rather than agnosticism?

We should answer differently for Huxley than we do for Stephen. Huxley's arguments, if correct, would give us good grounds for rejecting Christianity and Judaism; but they are not sufficient by themselves for jettisoning a belief in God, though they would require us to suspend judgment about the putative knowledge-claim that God exists and created the world. But it must be remembered that agnosticism is the general claim that we do not know and (more typically) cannot know or have good grounds for believing that there is a God. But to accept this is not to accept the claim that there is no God, unless we accept the premiss that what cannot even in principle be known cannot exist. This was not a premiss to which Huxley and Stephen were committed. Rather they accepted the standard agnostic view that since we cannot know or have good reasons for believing that God exists we should suspend judgment concerning his existence or nonexistence. Moreover, as we shall see, forms of Jewish and Christian fideism when linked with modern biblical scholarship could accept at least most of Huxley's arguments and still defend an acceptance of the Jewish or Christian faith.

Stephen's key arguments are more epistemologically oriented and are more definitely committed to an empiricist account of meaning and the limits of conceivability. As we shall see in examining the contentions of some contemporary critics of religion, it is more difficult to see what, given the correctness of Stephen's own account, it could *mean* to affirm, deny, or even doubt the existence of God. The very concept of God on such an account becomes problematical. And this makes what it would be to be an agnostic, an atheist, or a theist problematical.

The cultural context in which we speak of religion is very different in the twentieth century than it was in the nineteenth (cf. MacIntyre, Ricoeur). For most twentieth-century people with even a minimal amount of education, the authority of science has cut much deeper than it did in previous centuries. The cosmological claims in the biblical stories are no longer taken at face value by the overwhelming majority of educated people both religious and non-religious. Theologians working from within the circle of faith have carried out an extensive program of de-mythologizing such biblical claims. Thus it is evident that in one quite obvious respect the nineteenth-century agnostics have clearly been victorious. There is no longer any serious attempt to defend the truth of the cosmological claims in the type of biblical stories that Huxley discusses.

However, what has not received such wide acceptance is the claim that the acceptance of such a de-mythologizing undermines Judaism and Christianity and drives an honest man in the direction of agnosticism or atheism. Many would claim that such de-mythologizing only purifies Judaism and Christianity of extraneous cultural material. The first thing to ask is whether or not a steady recognition of the fact that these biblical stories are false supports agnosticism as strongly as Huxley thinks it does.

Here the new historical perspective on the Bible is a crucial factor. The very concept of the authority of the Bible undergoes a sea change with the new look in historical scholarship. It is and has been widely acknowledged both now and in the nineteenth century that Judaism and Christianity are both integrally linked with certain historical claims. They are not sufficient to establish the truth of either of these religions, but they are necessary. Yet modern historical research—to put it minimally—places many of these historical claims in an equivocal light and makes it quite impossible to accept claims about the literal infallibility of the Bible. Conservative evangelicalists (fundamentalists) try to resist this tide and in reality still battle with Huxley. They reject the basic findings of modern biblical scholarship and in contrast to modernists treat the Bible not as a fallible and myth-laden account of God's self-revelation in history but as a fully inspired and infallible historical record. Conservative evangelicalists agree with modernists that revelation consists in God's self-disclosure to man, but they further believe that the Bible is an infallible testimony of God's self-unveiling. Modernists by contrast believe that we must discover what the crucial historical but yet divine events and realities are like by a painstaking historical investigation of the biblical material. This involves all

the techniques of modern historical research. The various accounts in the Bible must be sifted by methodical inquiry and independently acquired knowledge of the culture and the times must be used whenever possible.

Conservative evangelicalism is still strong as a cultural phenomenon in North America, though it is steadily losing strength. However it is not a serious influence in the major seminaries and modernism has thoroughly won the day in the intellectually respectable centers of Jewish and Christian learning. Huxley's arguments do come into conflict with conservative evangelicalism and his arguments about the plain falsity, utter incoherence, and sometimes questionable morality of the miracle stories and stories of Jesus' actions would have to be met by such conservative evangelicalists. But the modernists would be on Huxley's side here. So, for a large and respectable element of the Jewish and Christian community, Huxley's arguments, which lead him to reject Christianity and accept agnosticism, are accepted but not taken as at all undermining the foundations of Judaism or Christianity.

Huxley's sort of endeavor, like the more systematic endeavors of David Strauss, simply helps Christians rid the world of the historically contingent cultural trappings of the biblical writers. Once this has been cut away, modernists argue, the true import of the biblical message can be seen as something of decisive relevance that transcends the vicissitudes of time.

However, this is not all that should be said vis-à-vis the conflict between science and religion and agnosticism. It is often said that the conflict between science and religion came to a head in the nineteenth century and now has been transcended. Science, it is averred, is now seen to be neutral concerning materialism or any other metaphysical thesis and theology—the enterprise of attempting to provide ever deeper, clearer, and more reasonable statements and explications of the truths of religion—is more sophisticated and less vulnerable to attacks by science or scientifically oriented thinkers. Still it may be the case that there remain some conflicts between science and religion which have not been overcome even with a sophisticated analysis of religion, where that analysis takes the religions of the world and Christianity and Judaism in particular to be making truth-claims.

Let us consider how such difficulties might arise. Most Christians, for example, would want to claim as something central to their religion that Christ rose from the dead and that there is a life after the death of our earthly bodies. These claims seem at least to run athwart our scientific understanding of the world so that it is difficult to know how we could both accept scientific method as the most reliable method of settling

21

disputes about the facts and accept these central Christian claims. Moreover, given what science teaches us about the world, these things could not happen or have happened. Yet it is also true that the by now widely accepted new historical perspective on the Bible recognizes and indeed stresses mythical and poetical strands in the biblical stories. And surely it is in this non-literal way that the stories about demons, Jonah in the whale's belly, and Noah and his ark are to be taken, but how far is this to be carried with the other biblical claims? Are we to extend it to such central Christian claims as "Christ rose from the Dead," "Man shall survive the death of his earthly body," "God is in Christ"? If we do, it becomes completely unclear as to what it could mean to speak of either the truth or falsity of the Christian religion. If we do not, then it would seem that some central Christian truth-claims do clash with scientific claims and orientations so that there is after all a conflict between science and religion.

Given such a dilemma, the agnostic or atheist could then go on to claim that either these key religious utterances do not function propositionally as truth-claims at all or there is indeed such a clash. But if there is such a clash, the scientific claims are clearly the claims to be preferred, for of all the rival ways of fixing belief, the scientific way of fixing belief is clearly the most reliable. Thus if there are good empirical, scientific reasons (as there are) for thinking that people who die are not resurrected, that when our earthly bodies die we die, and that there is no evidence at all, and indeed not even any clear meaning to the claim that there are "resurrection bodies" and a "resurrection world" utterly distinct from the cosmos, we have the strongest of reasons for not accepting the Christian claim that "Christ rose from the Dead." The scientific beliefs in conflict with that belief are ones that it would be foolish to jettison. But it is only by a sacrifice of our scientific way of conceiving of things that we could assent to such a central religious claim. Thus it is fair to say that our scientific understanding drives us in the direction of either atheism or agnosticism.

Some contemporary theologians have responded to such contentions by arguing that there are good conceptual reasons why there could not be, appearances to the contrary notwithstanding, such a conflict. "Christ" is not equivalent to "Jesus" but to "the son of God" and God is not a physical reality. Christianity centers on a belief in a deity who is beyond the world, who is creator of the world. But such a reality is in principle, since it is transcendent to the cosmos, not capable of being investigated scientifically but must

be understood in some other way. God in his proper non-anthropomorphic forms is beyond the reach of evidence. Only crude anthropomorphic forms of Christian belief could be disproved by modern scientific investigations.

To believe that Christ rose from the dead is to be committed to a belief in miracles. But, it has been forcefully argued by Ninian Smart, this does not commit us to something which is anti-scientific or that can be ruled out *a priori* (Smart [1964], Ch. II; [1966], pp. 44–45). A miracle is an event of divine significance which is an exception to at least one law of nature. Scientific laws are not, it is important to remember, falsified by single exceptions but only by a class of experimentally repeatable events. Thus we can believe in the miracle of Christ's resurrection without clashing with anything sanctioned by science. It is a dogma, the critic of agnosticism could continue, to think that everything that can be known can be known by the method of science or by simple observation. A thoroughly scientific mind quite devoid of credulity could remain committed to Judaism or Christianity, believe in God, and accept such crucial miracle stories without abandoning a scientific attitude, i.e., he could accept all the findings of science and accept its authority as the most efficient method for ascertaining what is the case when ascertaining what is the case comes to predicting and retrodicting classes of experimentally repeatable events or processes.

Christians as well as agnostics can and do recognize the obscurity and mysteriousness of religious claims. The Christian should go on to say that a nonmysterious God, a God whose reality is evident, would not be the God of Judeo-Christianity—the God to be accepted on faith with fear and trembling. It is only for a God who moves in mysterious ways, that the characteristic Jewish and Christian attitudes of discipleship, adoration, and faith are appropriate. If the existence of God and what it was to act in accordance with His will were perfectly evident or clearly establishable by hard intellectual work, faith would lose its force and rationale. Faith involves risk, trust, and commitment. Judaism or Christianity is not something one simply must believe in if one will only think the matter through as clearly and honestly as possible.

What is evident is that the agnosticism of a Huxley and a Stephen at least—and a Bertrand Russell as well—rests on a philosophical view not dictated by science. James Ward saw this around the turn of the century and argued in his *Naturalism and Agnosticism* that agnosticism "is an inherently unstable position" unless it is supplemented by some general philosophical view such as materialism or idealism (p. 21). Yet it is just such overall views that Huxley and Stephen were anxious to avoid and along Humean lines viewed with a thoroughgoing skepticism.

In sum, the claim is that only if such an overall philosophical view is justified is it the case that there may be good grounds for being an agnostic rather than a Christian or a Jew. The overall position necessary for such a justification is either a position of empiricism or materialism and if it is the former it must be a form of empiricism which in Karl Popper's terms is also a scientism. By this we mean the claim that there are no facts which science cannot explore: that what cannot at least in principle be known by the method of science cannot be known. Where alternatively scientism is part of a reductive materialist metaphysics, there is a commitment to what has been called an "existence-monism," namely, the view that there is only one sort of level or order of existence and that is spatiotemporal existence. That is to say, such an existence-monist believes that to exist is to have a place in space-time. In support of this, he may point out that we can always ask about a thing that is supposed to exist *where* it exists. This, it is claimed, indicates how we in reality operate on materialist assumptions. And note that if that question is not apposite, "exists" and its equivalents are *not* being employed in their standard senses, but are being used in a secondary sense as in "Ghosts and gremlins exist merely in one's mind." Besides existence-monism there is the even more pervasive and distinctively empiricist position—a position shared by the logical empiricists, by Bertrand Russell, and by John Dewey—referred to as "methodological-monism": to wit "that all statements of fact are such that they can be investigated scientifically, i.e., that they can in principle be falsified by observation" (Smart [1966], p. 8).

However, critics of agnosticism have responded, as has Ninian Smart, by pointing out that these philosophical positions are vulnerable to a variety of fairly obvious and long-standing criticisms. Perhaps these criticisms can be and have been met, but these positions are highly controversial. If agnosticism is tied to them, do we not have as good grounds for being skeptical of agnosticism as the agnostics have for being skeptical of the claims of religion?

Some samplings of the grounds for being skeptical about the philosophical underpinnings for agnosticism are these. When I suddenly remember that I left my key in my car, it makes sense to speak of the space-time location of my car but, it is at least plausibly argued, not of the space-time location of my sudden thought. Moreover numbers exist but it hardly makes sense to ask *where* they exist. It is not the case that for all

standard uses of "exist" that to exist is to have a place in space-time. Methodological-monism is also beset with difficulties. There are in science theoretically unobservable entities and "from quite early times, the central concepts of religion, such as God and nirvana already include the notion that what they stand for cannot literally be observed" (Smart [1962], p. 8). Moreover it is not evident that we could falsify statements such as "There are some graylings in Michigan" or "Every human being has some neurotic traits" or "Photons really exist, they are not simply scientific fictions." Yet we do recognize them (or so at least it would seem) as intelligible statements of fact. Such considerations lead Ninian Smart to claim confidently in his *The Teacher and Christian Belief* (London, 1966) that "it remains merely a dogma to claim that all facts are facts about moons and flowers and humans and other denizens of the cosmos. There need be no general embargo upon belief in a transcendent reality, provided such belief is not merely based on uncontrolled speculation" (p. 51). Smart goes on to conclude that "the exclusion of transcendent fact rests on a mere decision" (p. 52). So it would appear, from what has been said above, that agnosticism has no solid rational foundation.

The dialectic of the argument over agnosticism is not nearly at an end and it shall be the burden of the argument here to establish that agnosticism still has much to be said for it. First of all, even granting, for the reasons outlined above, that neither the development of science nor an appeal to scientism or empiricism establishes agnosticism, there are other considerations which give it strong support. David Hume's *Dialogues on Natural Religion* (1779) and Immanuel Kant's *Critique of Pure Reason* (1781) make it quite evident that none of the proofs for the existence of God work, i.e., they are not sound or reliable arguments. Furthermore it should be noted that their arguments do not for the most part depend for their force on empiricist assumptions and they most certainly do not depend on the development of science.

The most rigorous contemporary work in the philosophy of religion has not always supported the detailed arguments of Hume and Kant but it has for the most part supported their overall conclusions on this issue. Alvin Plantinga, for example, in his *God and Other Minds* (1967) rejects rather thoroughly the principles and assumptions of both existence-monism and methodological-monism and he subjects the particulars of Hume's and Kant's views to careful criticism, yet in the very course of giving a defense of what he takes to be the rationality of Christian belief, he argues that none of the attempts at a demonstration of the existence of God have succeeded. He is echoed in this claim by such important contemporary analytical theologians as John Hick and Diogenes Allen. This lack of validated knowledge of the divine or lack of such warranted belief strengthens the hand of the agnostics, though it is also compatible with fideism or a revelationist view such as Barth's, which holds that man on his own can know nothing of God but must rely utterly on God's self-disclosure.

IV

In the twentieth century a distinct element comes to the fore which counts in favor of agnosticism but also gives it a particular twist. This new turn leads to a reformulation of agnosticism. It states agnosticism in such a manner that it becomes evident how it is a relevant response to one of the major elements in contemporary philosophical perplexities over religion.

We have hitherto been talking as if God-talk is used in certain central contexts to make statements of whose truth-value we are in doubt. That is, there is no doubt that they have a truth-value but there is a doubt which truth-value they actually have. Theists think that at least some of the key Jewish or Christian claims are true, atheists think they are false, and traditional agnostics, as H. H. Price puts it in his *Belief* (London, 1969), suspend "judgement on the ground that we do not have sufficient evidence to decide the question and so far as he [the agnostic] can tell there is no likelihood that we ever shall have" (p. 455). But in the twentieth century with certain analytic philosophers the question has come to the fore about whether these key religious utterances have any truth-value at all.

A. J. Ayer defending the modern variety of empiricism called "logical empiricism" argued in his *Language, Truth and Logic* (London, 1935) that such key religious utterances are devoid of cognitive meaning. Such considerations lead Ayer to deny that he or anyone taking such a position could be either a theist, an atheist, or even an agnostic. In a well known passage Ayer comments that it is very important not to confuse his view with agnosticism or atheism, for, as he puts it,

It is a characteristic of an agnostic to hold that the existence of a god is a possibility in which there is no good reason either to believe or disbelieve; and it is characteristic of an atheist to hold that it is at least probable that no god exists. And our view that all utterances about the nature of God are nonsensical, so far from being identical with, or even lending any support to, either of these familiar contentions, is actually incompatible with them. For if the assertion that there is a god is nonsensical, then the atheist's assertion that there is no god is equally nonsensical, since it is only a significant proposition that can be significantly

contradicted. As for the agnostic, although he refrains from saying either that there is or that there is not a god, he does not deny that the question whether a transcendent god exists is a genuine question. He does not deny that the two sentences "There is a transcendent god" and "There is no transcendent god" express propositions one of which is actually true and the other false. All he says is that we have no means of telling which of them is true, and therefore ought not to commit ourselves to either. But we have seen that the sentences in question do not express propositions at all. And this means that agnosticism also is ruled out (p. 219).

Ayer goes on to remark that the theist's putative claims are neither valid nor invalid; they say nothing at all and thus the theist cannot rightly be "accused of saying anything false, or anything for which he has insufficient grounds" (ibid., p. 219). It is only when the Christian, so to speak, turns meta-theologian and claims that in asserting the existence of a Transcendent God he is expressing a genuine proposition "that we are entitled to disagree with him" (ibid.).

The central point Ayer is making is that such religious utterances do not assert anything and thus they can be neither doubted, believed, nor even asserted to be false. With such considerations pushed to the front, the key question becomes whether such religious utterances have any informative content at all.

There is something very strange here. Ayer, as we have seen, does not regard his position as atheistical or agnostic, for since such key religious utterances could not even be false, they could not be intelligibly denied and since they make no claim to be intelligibly questioned, they could not be sensibly doubted. But, as Susan Stebbing rightly observed, "the plain man would not find it easy to see the difference between Mr. Ayer's non-atheism and the fool's atheism" (Stebbing, p. 264). But before we say "so much the worse for the plain man," we should remember that to believe that such key religious utterances are unbelievable because nonsensical is even a more basic rejection of religious belief than simply asserting the falsity of the putative truth-claims of Christianity, but allowing for the *possibility* that they might be true.

Because of this altered conceptualization of the situation, Price, Edwards, and Nielsen have characterized both agnosticism and atheism in a broader and more adequate way which takes into account these problems about meaning. A contemporary agnostic who is alert to such questions about meaning would maintain that judgments concerning putatively assertive God-talk should be suspended for either of two reasons, depending on the exact nature of the God-talk in question: (1) the claims, though genuine truth-claims, are without sufficient evidence to warrant either their belief or categorical rejection, or (2) their meaning is so problematical that it is doubtful whether there is something there which is sufficiently intelligible or coherent to be believed. Where God is conceived somewhat anthropomorphically the first condition obtains and where God is conceived non-anthropomorphically the second condition obtains. The contemporary agnostic believes that "God" in the most typical religious employments is so indeterminate in meaning that he must simply suspend judgment about whether there is anything that it stands for which can intelligibly be believed. His position, as Price points out, is like the traditional agnostic's in being neutral between theism and atheism (p. 454). He believes that neither such positive judgment is justified, but unlike a contemporary atheist, on the one hand, he is not so confident of the unintelligibility or incoherence of religious utterances that he feels that religious belief is irrational and is to be rejected, but, on the other hand, he does not believe one is justified in taking these problematic utterances as being obscurely revelatory of Divine Truth. Neither atheism nor any of the several forms of fideism is acceptable to him.

The contemporary agnostic sensitive to problems about the logical status of religious utterances simply stresses that the reasonable and on the whole justified course of action here is simply to suspend judgment. His doubts are primarily *doubts about the possibility of there being anything to doubt,* but, second-order as they are, they have an effect similar to the effect of classical agnosticism and they lead to a similar attitude toward religion. There is neither the classical atheistic denial that there is anything to the claims of religion nor is there the fideistic avowal that in spite of all their obscurity and *seeming* unintelligibility that there still is something there *worthy* of belief. Instead there is a genuine suspension of judgment.

The thing to ask is whether the doubts leading to a suspension of judgment are actually sufficient to *justify* such a suspension or, everything considered, (1) would a leap of faith be more justified or (2) would the overcoming of doubt in the direction of atheism be more reasonable? Or is it the case that there is no way of making a rational decision here or of reasonably deciding what one ought to do or believe?

It may indeed be true, as many a sophisticated theologian has argued, that religious commitment is perfectly compatible with a high degree of ignorance about God and the nature—whatever that may mean—of "ultimate reality." But, if this is the case and if our ignorance here is as invincible as much contemporary philosophical argumentation would have us believe, *natural theology* seems at least to be thoroughly undermined. In trying to establish whether the world is contingent or non-contingent, whether there is or can be something "beyond the world" upon which the world in some sense depends, or whether there is or could be an unlimited reality which is still in some sense personal, theological reasonings have been notoriously unsuccessful. About the best that has been done is to establish that it is not entirely evident that these questions are meaningless or utterly unanswerable.

Here a Barthian turn away from natural theology is equally fruitless. To say that man can by his own endeavors know nothing of God but simply must await an unpredictable and rationally inexplicable self-disclosure of God—the core notion of God revealing himself to man—is of no help, for when we look at religions in an honest anthropological light, we will see, when all the world is our stage, that we have multitudes of conflicting alleged revelations with no means at all of deciding, without the aid of natural theology or philosophical analysis, which, if any, of these putative revelations are genuine revelations. It is true enough that if something is actually a divine revelation, it cannot be assessed by man, but must simply be accepted. But the agnostic reminds the revelationist that we have a multitude of conflicting candidate revelations with no means of reasonably deciding which one to accept. In such a context a reasonable man will remain agnostic concerning such matters. To simply accept the authorative claims of a Church in such a circumstance is to fly in the face of reason.

The most crucial problem raised by the so-called truth-claims of Judaism and Christianity is that of conceivability—to borrow a term that Herbert Spencer used in the nineteenth century and thereby suggesting that there are more lines of continuity between the old agnosticism and the new than this essay has indicated. The *incredibility*—to use Spencer's contrasting term—of these central religious claims is tied, at least in part, to their *inconceivability.* "God" is not supposed to refer to a being among beings; by definition God is no finite object or process in the world. But then how is the referring to be done? What are we really talking about when we speak of God? How do we or can we fix the reference range of "God"? God surely cannot be identified in the same manner we identify the sole realities compatible with existence-monism. There can be no picking God out as we would a discrete entity in space-time. Alternatively there are theologians who will say that when we come to recognize that it is just a brute fact that there is that indefinitely immense collection of finite and contingent masses or conglomerations of things, we use the phrase "the world" to refer to, and when we recognize it could have been the case—eternally the case—that there was no world at all, we can come quite naturally to feel puzzled about why there is a world at all.

Is there anything that would account for the existence of all finite reality and not itself be a reality that needed to be similarly explained? In speaking of God we are speaking of such a reality, if indeed there is such a reality. We are concerned with a reality not simply—as the world might be—infinite in space and time, but a reality such that it would not make sense to ask *why* it exists. Such a reality could not be a physical reality.

In sum, we have, if we reflect at all, a developing sense of the contingency of the world. The word "God" in part means, in Jewish and Christian discourses, whatever it is that is non-contingent upon which all these contingent realities continuously depend. God is the completeness that would fill in the essential incompleteness of the world. We have feelings of dependency, creatureliness, finitude and in having those feelings, it is argued, we have some sense of that which is without limit. "God" refers to such alleged ultimate realities and to something richer as well. But surely this, the critic of agnosticism will reply, sufficiently fixes the reference range of "God," such that it would be a mistake to assert that "God" is a term supposedly used to refer to a referent but nothing coherently specifiable counts as a possible referent for "God," where "God" has a non-anthropomorphic employment.

Surely such a referent is not something which can be clearly conceived, but, as we have seen, a nonmysterious God would not be the God of Judeo-Christianity. But has language gone on a holiday? We certainly, given our religious conditioning, have a *feeling* that we understand what we are saying here. But do we? Perhaps, as Axel Hägerström thought, "contingent thing," "finite thing," and "finite reality" are pleonastic. For anything at all that exists, we seem to be able to ask, without being linguistically or conceptually deviant, why it exists. "The world" or "the cosmos" does not stand for an entity or a *class* of things, but is an umbrella term for all those things and their structural relations that religious people call "finite things" and many others just call "things." What are we talking about when we say there is something infinite and utterly different from these "finite realities" and that this "utterly other reality" is neither physical nor temporal nor purely conceptual nor simply imaginary, but, while being unique and radically distinct from all these things, continuously sustains all these "finite things" and is a mysterious something upon which they are utterly dependent? Surely this is very odd talk and "sustains" and "dependent" have no unproblematical use in this context.

These difficulties and a host of difficultie

make it doubtful whether the discourse used to spell out the reference range of "God" is sufficiently intelligible to make such God-talk coherent. An agnostic of the contemporary sort is a man who suspends judgment, oscillating between rejecting God-talk as an irrational form of discourse containing at crucial junctures incoherent or rationally unjustifiable putative truth-claims and accepting this discourse as something which, obscure as it is, makes a sufficiently intelligible and humanly important reference to be worthy of belief.

One reading of the situation is that the network of fundamental concepts constitutive of nonanthropomorphic God-talk in Judeo-Christianity is so problematical that the most reasonable thing to do is to opt for atheism, particularly when we realize that we do not need these religions or any religion to make sense of our lives or to buttress morality. But agnosticism, particularly of the contemporary kind specified here, need not be an evasion and perhaps is the most reasonable alternative for the individual who wishes, concerning an appraisal of competing world views and ways of life, to operate on a principle of maximum caution.

BIBLIOGRAPHY

Two extensive discussions are in Robert Flint, *Agnosticism* (London, 1903); and in R. A. Armstrong, *Agnosticism and Theism in the Nineteenth Century* (London, 1905). See also James Ward, *Naturalism and Agnosticism* (London, 1899). The central works from Hume and Kant relevant here are David Hume, *Enquiry concerning Human Understanding* (1748), and *Dialogues concerning Natural Religion* (London, 1779); Immanuel Kant, *Kritik der reinen Vernunft* (1781), and *Die Religion innerhalb der Grenzen der blossen Vernunft* (1793). For the paradigmatic nineteenth-century statements of agnosticism see T. H. Huxley, *Collected Essays,* 9 vols. (London, 1894), Vol. V; and Leslie Stephen, *An Agnostic's Apology and Other Essays* (London, 1893), and *English Thought in the Eighteenth Century* (London, 1876).

The following works are central to the nineteenth-century debate over agnosticism: Sir William Hamilton, "Philosophy of the Unconditioned," *The Edinburgh Review* (1829); H. L. Mansel, *The Limits of Religious Thought* (London, 1858); J. S. Mill, *Three Essays on Religion* (London, 1874); and Herbert Spencer, *First Principles* (London, 1862). Noel Annan, *Leslie Stephen* (London, 1952); William Irvine, *Thomas Henry Huxley* (London, 1960); John Holloway, *The Victorian Sage* (New York, 1953); Basil Willey, *Nineteenth Century Studies* (London, 1950); and J. A. Passmore, *A Hundred Years of Philosophy* (London, 1957), provide basic secondary sources. For material carrying over to the twentieth-century debate see R. Garrigou-Lagrange, *Dieu, son existence et sa nature; solution thomiste des antinomies agnostiques* (Paris, 1915); and J. M. Cameron, *The Night Battle* (London, 1962). For some contemporary defenses of agnosticism see Ronald W. Hepbu *dox* (New York, 1966); Bertrand Russell, *Why I am Not a Christian* (London, 1957); H. J. Blackman, ed., *Objections To Humanism* (London, 1963); *Religion and Humanism*, no editor, various authors—Ronald Hepburn, David Jenkins, Howard Root, Renford Bambrough, Ninian Smart (London, 1964); William James, *The Will to Believe and Other Essays* . . . (New York, 1897), attacked agnosticism.

The following books by contemporary philosophers or analytically oriented philosophical theologians make arguments relevant to our discussion. A. J. Ayer, *Language, Truth and Logic* (London, 1935); Axel Hägerström, *Philosophy and Religion*, trans. Robert T. Sandin (London, 1964); John Hick, *Faith and Knowledge*, 2nd ed. (Ithaca, 1966); R. B. Braithwaite, *An Empiricist's View of the Nature of Religious Belief* (Cambridge, 1955); Diogenes Allen, *The Reasonableness of Faith* (Washington and Cleveland, 1968); Ninian Smart, *The Teacher and Christian Belief* (London, 1966); idem, *Philosophers and Religious Truth* (London, 1964); idem, *Theology, Philosophy and Natural Sciences* (Birmingham, England, 1962). Alasdair MacIntyre, *Secularization and Moral Change* (London, 1967); idem and Paul Ricoeur, *The Religious Significance of Atheism* (New York, 1969); H. H. Price, *Belief* (London, 1969); L. Susan Stebbing, "Critical Notice, *Language, Truth and Logic*," *Mind*, new series, **45** (1936); Kai Nielsen, "In Defense of Atheism," in *Perspectives in Education, Religion and the Arts*, eds. Howard Kiefer and Milton Munitz (New York, 1970); Paul Holmer, "Atheism and Theism," *Lutheran World*, **13** (1966); Alvin Plantinga, *God and Other Minds* (Ithaca, 1967); George Mavrodes, *Belief in God* (New York, 1970).

Some good critical and historical commentary on Hume occurs in Bernard Williams, "Hume on Religion," in *David Hume: A Symposium*, ed. D. F. Pears (London, 1963); in the essays by James Noxon, William H. Capitan, and George J. Nathan, reprinted in V. C. Chapell, ed., *Hume: A Collection of Critical Essays* (New York, 1966); and in Norman Kemp Smith's masterful and indispensable introduction to Hume's Dialogues. See David Hume, *Dialogues Concerning Natural Religion*, ed. and introduction by Norman Kemp Smith (Edinburgh, 1947). For Kant see W. H. Walsh, "Kant's Moral Theology," *Proceedings of the British Academy*, **49** (1963).

KAI NIELSEN

[See also **Gnosticism**; God; Positivism; **Skepticism**.]

ALCHEMY

THE ALCHEMY of the sixteenth and the seventeenth centuries represents a fusion of many seemingly disparate themes derived from ancient and medieval Near and Far Eastern sources. A simple definition is difficult if not impossible. The alchemists always maintained a special interest in the changes of matter and surely most of them accepted the concept of transmutation, but there were other significant strains evident in alchemical thought as well. Important among these was the early and persistent belief that the study of alchemy had a special role in medicine through the preparation of remedies and the search for the prolongation of life. In addition to this was the belief that alchemy was the fundamental science for the investigation of nature. And yet, if the alchemists spoke repeatedly of experience and observation as the true keys to nature, they also maintained a fervent belief in a universe unified through the relationship of the macrocosm and the microcosm—a relationship that of necessity tied this science to astrology. The alchemists were convinced further that their search for the truths of nature might be conceived in terms of a religious quest which would result in a greater knowledge of the Creator. It is not surprising then to find a late sixteenth-century author defining medicine as "the searching out of the secretes of nature," a goal that was to be accomplished by resort to "mathematicall and supernaturall precepts, the exercise whereof is Mechanicall, and to be accomplished with labor." Having thus defined medicine, he went on to state that the real name of this art was simply chemistry or alchemy (Bostocke, 1585).

In short, while few would deny that there were elements of modern science in alchemy, it is also true that this was a study permeated with a mysticism foreign to the post-Newtonian world.

ALCHEMY IN ANTIQUITY

The difficulty in dating alchemical texts has resulted in a long-standing controversy over its origins. Yet, if the priority of Near Eastern, Indian, and Chinese alchemists remains in dispute, there is general agreement among scholars that the student in search of the roots of alchemy must be concerned not only with early concepts of nature, but also with the practical craft traditions of antiquity. The oldest surviving works of metal craftsmen combine an emphasis on the change in the appearance of metals with the acceptance of a vitalistic view of nature—a view that included the belief that metals live and grow within the earth in a fashion analogous to the growth of a human fetus. It was to become fundamental to alchemical thought that the operator might hasten the natural process of metallic growth in his laboratory and thus bring about perfection in a period of time far less than that required by nature.

Several texts point to the existence of a practical proto-alchemical literature in the ancient Near East. The recent study of two Babylonian tablets (Oppenheim, 1966) dating from the thirteenth century B.C.

but copied from still earlier originals describes the production of "silver" from a copper/bronze mixture. These early recipes already contain elements of ritual and the processes themselves call for secrecy. Both were to become common themes in later alchemical literature. The Leiden and Stockholm papyri (ca. third century A.D.) would appear to be part of the same practical tradition. Here, among some three hundred recipes, will be found directions for the imitation of the noble metals. A method for the doubling of *asem* (the gold-silver alloy, electrum) indicates the future direction of alchemical literature. The similarity between the directions given in these papyri and passages in the *Physica et Mystica* of Bolos Democritos of Mendes (perhaps as early as 200 B.C.) indicates that the latter work also profited from an acquaintance with the metal craft tradition. However, mystical passages in his work were to become the subject of exegesis for Hellenistic alchemists of late antiquity. The pseudo-Democritos was revered by them as a sage of great authority and his work thus forms a connecting link between the practical metal craft tradition and the true Alexandrian alchemy of late antiquity.

Alexandrian alchemy was based on Greek philosophy as well as on the practical tradition of the craftsmen. The early comparisons of man and nature found in the pre-Socratics and in Plato's *Timaeus* fostered an interest in the relationship of the macrocosm and the microcosm, a doctrine which played a major role in alchemical thought well into the seventeenth century. Systems of intermediary beings and the *pneuma* were employed by the Stoics, the Neo-Platonists, and other philosophical sects in antiquity to provide connecting links between the two worlds.

Also important for the development of alchemical thought was the long tradition of speculation on the Creation. The philosopher interested in both the Creation and Nature was inevitably drawn to the question of the origin of the elements and the possibility of a *prima materia*. The views of the pre-Socratics on the prime matter formed a springboard from which later authors launched their own concepts. Thus Aristotle conveniently summarized the views of his predecessors prior to refuting them in his *Metaphysics*. However, the subject was one of no less importance to him than it had been to them. Aristotle accepted the four Empedoclean elements (earth, air, water, and fire) with their attendant qualities and he believed that they were mutually transmutable.

The genesis of the elements also forms an important section of Plato's *Timaeus* where the subject is developed mathematically, but to alchemical authors of late antiquity who were influenced by Neo-Platonic, Gnostic, and Christian sources, the accounts found in Gene-

sis and the *Pymander* attributed to Hermes Trismegistus were no less significant. Surely the alchemical literature was stamped with a Creation-element theme throughout its existence. In the sixteenth and the seventeenth centuries chemical authors still focused on the elements in their defense or attack of any given system. An important example may be found in Gerhard Dorn's defense of the Paracelsians which he based on an analysis of the "Physics of Genesis" and the "Physics of Hermes." Similarly Robert Boyle placed special emphasis on the problem of the elements in his criticism of the Aristotelians and the Paracelsian chemists in the *Sceptical Chymist* (1661).

The earliest true alchemical texts in Greek date from the end of the third century A.D. These are clearly connected with the earlier practical tradition as well as with current philosophical and religious thought. Two of the more important authors are Zosimos, author of the encyclopedic *Cheirokmeta*, whose work links these alchemical texts with the book of Bolos Democritos, and Maria the Jewess, whose text is significant for its detailed description of the laboratory equipment of the Alexandrian alchemist. The latter work indicates that the emphasis on distillation and sublimation processes—still so pronounced in the Renaissance—was already characteristic of alchemical recipes in late antiquity. These Alexandrian texts are openly concerned with transmutation. The processes given stress color change as a guide to progress—from black to white to yellow to violet. The sequence was clearly associated with the change from a chaotic and undefined primal matter to metallic perfection. And although the final stage was eventually to be changed from violet to red, the emphasis on color was to remain a basic theme in descriptions of the Great Work.

Although practical recipes form part of these third- and fourth-century texts there is also present in them a pronounced interest in secrecy and mysticism. Allegorical dream sequences form part of this literature, and the role of spirits is considered important in the transformation of matter. And while one may extract some scientific information from the Greek alchemical codices, he will find it difficult to separate this material from the ever-present religious aura that pervades these works. An example may be seen in the analogous treatment of metals and mankind. Because of the truth of this it was felt that the operator might follow the death and resurrection theme as he pursued his work. It was this aspect of alchemical thought that dominates the later Greek texts. The work of Stephanos (ca. 610–41) is replete with prayers, invocations, and allegorical descriptions. There is little indication here that the alchemist still had close personal contact with the laboratory. The text of Stephanos was highly influential and it was used by later alchemists both as a model and as a subject for commentaries. Alexandrian alchemy did not continue much longer as a living tradition. Before the tenth century the basic texts had been codified and few new texts were composed in Greek after that time.

Although Pliny and Dioscorides refer to mineral substances of medical value, Hellenistic alchemical texts do not indicate any real concern with pharmaceutical chemistry. This is in marked contrast with the development of alchemy in China and India. As early as the eighth century B.C. there was a belief in physical immortality in China, and this was later to become closely associated with Taoist thought. A text from the second century B.C. refers to the transmutation of cinnabar to gold and within a few hundred years the concept of longevity was to be clearly connected with chemically prepared drugs and elixirs. This is evident in the *Nei P'ien* of Ko Hung (ca. A.D. 320) which was to become a standard Chinese text on this subject. In it will be found sections on the transmutation of metals and on elixirs of life—and all this mixed with rules for the attainment of long life and immortality. Chinese alchemy paralleled Alexandrian alchemy in its frequent reference to the macrocosm-microcosm analogy as well as in the development of both esoteric and exoteric approaches to this subject. Thus, while the Chinese alchemist sought a potable gold and various chemically prepared drugs in his quest for longevity and immortality, the texts also indicate a real interest in alchemy as the search for the inner perfection of the soul.

From India the Sanskrit *Atharva Veda* (perhaps as early as the eighth century B.C.) refers to the use of gold as a means of preserving life, and there are other early texts relating gold to immortality. Buddhist texts of the second to the fifth centuries A.D. discuss the transmutation of base metals to gold by means of a juice concocted from vegetable and mineral sources. The still later tantric-Hatha yoga texts (post-eighth century) show the same trend toward increased mysticism already noted in the Greek and the Chinese sources. Here the operator undergoes the experience of an initiatory death and this is followed by a resurrection. In metals the result may be seen in the perfection of gold—in man, the alchemist induces in his own person a similar separation of spirit from gross matter. In this case the result is a perfected person with an infinitely prolonged youth.

ISLAMIC ALCHEMY

Similarities between Chinese and Indian alchemy have long led to speculations regarding the possible transmission of common concepts. To date, however, few facts have come to light to substantiate these speculations. The origins of Islamic alchemy are somewhat easier to discern. Here there is little question about the importance of Greek sources. Traditionally Prince Khalid ibn Yazid (d. 704) was the first Muslim convert to alchemy and it is significant that his teacher was said to be one Morienos, a pupil of the legendary Stephanos of Alexandria. Although there is little likelihood of truth in this story, the strong Greek influence on Islamic alchemy may be further confirmed by frequent references to Alexandrian authors and the general use of Greek philosophical concepts. Translations were made into Arabic at learned centers throughout the Near East not only of the works of such major figures as Aristotle, Galen, and Ptolemy, but also of Zosimos, Bolos Democritos, and Stephanos. Among these centers the old Sassanian academy at Jundi-Shapur played a role. Similarly a group of Sabians at Harran were influential in transmitting Indian alchemical and astrological thought into the Islamic tradition.

The ascription of alchemical works to earlier authors was as common to Islamic authors as it had been to their Greek predecessors. The short alchemical classic, the "Emerald Table," was said to have been written by Hermes Trismegistus, but the earliest surviving version is in an early ninth-century Arabic text ascribed to the first-century (A.D.) magician, Apollonios of Tyana. A similar problem exists in regard to the *Turba philosophorum*. This exists only in Latin, but it has been shown by E. J. Holmyard and J. Ruska to have been composed originally in Arabic early in the tenth century. The dialogue form is used in the *Turba* and the speakers are supposedly the Greek philosophers of antiquity. Islamic alchemy did not confine itself to Greek sages and gods alone in this regard. The eighth-century scholar, Jabir-ibn-Hayyan, probably authored only a few works on alchemy. However, some two thousand titles are ascribed to him. The great bulk of these seem to derive from members of the Isma'ilya sect, the Brotherhood of Purity, and they date from the ninth and the tenth centuries.

Islamic alchemy is characterized by both the practical and the mystical elements seen in the earlier Greek texts. There are frequent warnings that the information being revealed is for the initiated alone and there is a continued use of the allegorical approach which had become common in late Greek works. The religious nature of the art is emphasized and the predominant vitalism favored by alchemical authors may be seen in discussions of the generation of metals, and in the sexual interpretation of fundamental stages of the great work. As in the Alexandrian texts the progress of the operator may be followed through the now standard sequence of color changes. The concept of the philosopher's stone is also well developed in the Arabic literature. This stone allegedly provided a substance which brought about the rapid transmutation of base metals to gold. It derived from the earlier concept of special elixirs which might cure illnesses in man and which in an analogous fashion might perfect—or cure—imperfect metals in inanimate nature.

Aristotelian element theory is commonly employed in the Arabic texts, but in addition the Jabirian works employed the Sulphur-Mercury theory of the metals. This concept suggests that all metals are composed of different proportions of a sophic sulphur and a sophic mercury. While there was general agreement that these two substances have a resemblance to common sulphur and mercury, it was asserted that they were much purer than anything that could be produced in the laboratory. A quantitative relationship between the two was implied, but the mathematical relationship expressed in these texts may be most easily related to the number mysticism favored by the Neo-Pythagoreans and Eastern mystics. Although the Sulphur-Mercury theory appears first in this literature, it seems to be a modification of the concept of the two exhalations within the earth that lead to the formation of minerals and metals. This concept is discussed in the fourth book of Aristotle's *Meteorologica*.

In the Arabic literature the reader finds an emphasis on medical chemistry for the first time outside of the Far East and India. The work of the physician al-Razi (Rhazes, 860–925) is decidedly practical in nature. Although he accepted the truth of transmutation and discussed elixirs of varying powers, in the *Book of the Secret of Secrets* Razi spoke at length of chemical equipment and he described in detail the laboratory operations requisite for the chemist. In addition he described a large number of laboratory reagents and classified them into the categories of "animal," "mineral," "vegetable," and "derivative." Chemical texts continued to employ the first three of these as a basic scheme for arrangement until well into the eighteenth century. Razi's interest in medicine and practical chemistry influenced later Islamic work in medical chemistry. The work of ibn-Sina (Avicenna, 980–1037) and Abu Mansur Muwaffak (late tenth century) indicates a special interest in chemically prepared substances of pharmaceutical value.

THE EARLY LATIN ALCHEMY OF THE WEST

Western alchemy developed from Arabic sources. As Islamic scholars had sought alchemical texts in the eighth century, so their Latin counterparts sought similar works four centuries later. The earliest dated Latin translation of this genre is the story of Prince Khalid and Morienos. This was completed by Robert of Chester on the eleventh of February, 1144, a year after he had translated the Koran and a year prior to the completion of his translation of the *Algebra* of al-Khwarizmi. The *De compositione alchemiae* of Morienos proved to be only the first of many such translations made during the following century.

There are frequent references to alchemy in the work of Thomas Aquinas and from the commentaries on Aristotle written by Albertus Magnus it is clear that the subject was of great interest to thirteenth-century scholars. Albertus knew the work of Avicenna and he commented on the fact that this Islamic scholar had both accepted and denied the possibility of transmutation in different works ascribed to him. Although Albertus believed in the truth of transmutation himself, he remained skeptical of the "transmuted" metals he had seen, since the artificial product had not been able to withstand the heat of the fire. With Albertus we also have early evidence of the application of the sulphur-mercury theory in the West. In his *De mineralibus* he referred to the ancient concept of the exhalations, but he went on to discuss a new theory that attributed the origin of metals to sulphur and mercury.

Some of the most interesting medieval alchemical treatises date from the late thirteenth and the early fourteenth centuries. The *Pretiosa Margarita Novella* of Petrus Bonus of Ferrara (ca. 1330) reflects the influence of scholasticism in its tripartite structure. Arguments in favor of transmutation follow the initial refutations, and these in turn are followed by positive answers to the objections. Peter accepted transmutation himself, and he further stated that the true process might easily be learned in an hour. At the same time he was honest enough to admit that he did not know how to produce gold himself. No less influential was the *Summa perfectionis* which was ascribed to Jabir (Latinized as Geber, late thirteenth century). As in the *Precious Pearl* the sulphur-mercury theory forms the theoretical basis for an understanding of the metals, and the alchemist is informed that he must arrange these substances (understood as ideal substances resembling most in nature common sulphur and mercury) in perfect proportions for the consummation of the Great Work. Geber described in considerable detail the laboratory processes and equipment of the alchemist. This text reflects an important change in distillation techniques that seems to have originated among twelfth- and thirteenth-century chemists. The introduction of condensation at this time made possible the collection of low boiling fractions for the first time. As a result we find in the literature of the mid-twelfth century the first reference to alcohol. Geber confirms this change in equipment and procedure. He described condensation apparatus in detail, and in addition he was the first to give a method for the preparation of a mineral acid—our nitric acid. These substances plus the mixtures of other mineral acids placed powerful new reagents in the hands of alchemists who were to use them regularly after this period.

The alchemy of the late fourteenth and the fifteenth centuries indicates an increasing interest in allegorical and mystical themes. Thomas Norton's *Ordinall of Alchimy* (1477) is little concerned with clear-cut descriptions of chemical processes or laboratory equipment. Rather, we meet here with a lengthy poetical account of the difficult nature of the work, the need of virtue for its successful conclusion, and veiled descriptions of the true process. These and similar texts were accompanied by a widespread reaction against alchemy. The unsavory characterization of the alchemist in medieval literature knows no better example than Chaucer's "Canon's Yeoman's Tale" (ca. 1390) while on an official level there were the decrees and statutes of Pope John XXII (1317) and Henry IV of England (1404) directed against those who attempted to multiply gold.

Closely connected with the widespread medieval interest in transmutation was a parallel trend toward medical chemistry. By the fourteenth century distillation and other chemical processes were in use among Italian physicians as a means of identifying the dissolved substances in the much frequented mineral water spas. A century later Michael Savonarola ordered these tests into a procedural form that became the basis of the later methods of aqueous analyses composed by Gabriel Fallopius and Robert Boyle in the sixteenth and seventeenth centuries.

No less important was the medieval physicians' dependence on alchemy as a source for new medicines. The Eastern interest in the prolongation of life is evident here. This may be seen as early as the mid-thirteenth century in the work of Roger Bacon. Bacon fully accepted the truth of metallic transmutation and he suggested that this might be utilized to alleviate the poverty of mankind. For Bacon alchemy was a major field of experimental science and he explicitly stated that one of its goals was the search for a lengthened life span. In the *Opus tertium* (1267) he commented that although many physicians used chemical processes to prepare their medicines, very few of them knew how to make metals and fewer still knew how to perform those works which led to the prolongation of life.

The same theme occurs in the work of Bacon's younger contemporary, Arnold of Villanova, who argued that alchemy must play an important role in the much needed reform of medicine. In this way new remedies and the elixir of life might be found. The alchemist John of Rupescissa (mid-fourteenth century) insisted that the only real purpose of alchemy was to benefit mankind. His works abound with medicinal preparations derived from metals and minerals and he

emphasized distillation processes which seemingly separated pure quintessences from the gross matter of the natural substances. It was this medieval tradition of medical chemistry that bore fruit in the Renaissance "distillation books" of Hieronymus Brunschwig, Conrad Gesner, and others who looked on alchemy and chemical operations as a basic tool for the preparation of medicines rather than the search for gold.

RENAISSANCE ALCHEMY AND THE "NEW SCIENCE"

The work of Marsilio Ficino and his followers associated with the Platonic Academy in Florence resulted in a heightened interest in the mystical texts of late antiquity. Ficino himself translated the Hermetic corpus (1463) and this text was of great influence in the revival of Natural Magic, Astrology, and Alchemy. Interest in these subjects is closely intertwined with the course of the Scientific Revolution. Indeed, the sixteenth and the early seventeenth centuries witnessed an ever-quickening concern with alchemy. This new interest reached a peak in the middle years of the latter century before declining. It was just at this time that the major collected editions of alchemical classics were being prepared by Zetzner (1602, 1622, 1659–61), Ashmole (1652), and Manget (1702).

The fresh flavor of Renaissance alchemy is perhaps best seen in the work of Paracelsus (1493–1541) and his followers. The iatrochemists of the sixteenth and the seventeenth centuries follow directly in the steps of their medieval predecessors. Like them, they expressed an interest in transmutation, but they were primarily concerned with the medical applications of alchemy. For some this meant the preparation of chemical drugs, but for others it meant a mystical alchemical approach to medicine that might apply to macrocosmic as well as to microcosmic phenomena.

Paracelsus may be characterized as one of the many nature philosophers of his time, but he differs from others in his emphasis on the importance of medicine and alchemy as bases for a new understanding of the universe. Characteristic of the Paracelsians was their firm opposition to the dominant Aristotelian-Galenic tradition of the universities. They were unyielding in their opposition to Scholasticism which they sought to replace with a philosophy influenced by the recently translated Neo-Platonic and Hermetic texts. The religious nature of their quest is ever present. Man was to seek an understanding of his Creator through the two books of divine revelation; the Holy Scriptures and the Book of Creation—Nature. The Paracelsians constantly called for a new observational approach to nature, and for them chemistry or alchemy seemed to be the best example of what this new science should be. The Paracelsians were quick to offer an alchemical interpretation of Genesis. Here they pictured the Creation as the work of a divine alchemist separating the beings and objects of the earth and the heavens from the unformed *prima materia* much as the alchemist may distill pure quintessence from a grosser form of matter.

The search for physical truth in the biblical account of the Creation focused special attention on the formation of the elements. Paracelsus regularly used the Aristotelian elements, but he also introduced the *tria prima*—the principles of Salt, Sulphur, and Mercury. The latter were a modification of the old sulphur-mercury theory of the metals, but they differed from the older concept in that they were to apply to all things rather than being limited to the metals alone. The introduction of these principles had the effect of calling into question the whole framework of ancient medicine and natural philosophy since these had been grounded upon the Aristotelian elements. Furthermore, the fact that Paracelsus had not clearly defined his principles tended to make the whole question of elementary substances an ill-defined one.

The Paracelsians sought to interpret their world in terms of alchemy or chemistry. On the macrocosmic level they spoke of meteorological events in terms of chemical analogies. On the geocosmic level they argued over differing chemical interpretations of the growth of minerals and the origin of mountain springs. And in their search for agricultural improvements they postulated the importance of dissolved salts as the reason for the beneficial result of fertilizing with manure. For them this was the familiar universal salt of the alchemists.

The Paracelsians approached medicine in a similar fashion. They felt assured that their knowledge of the macrocosm might be properly applied to the microcosm. Thus, if an aerial sulphur and niter were the cause of thunder and lightning in the heavens, the same aerial effluvia might be inhaled and generate burning diseases in the body. Similarly, chemical deposits were formed when the internal archei governing the various organs failed to properly eliminate impurities from the system.

The Renaissance was a period of new and violent diseases and the chemical physicians stated that their new stronger remedies were essential for the proper cures. The work of Paracelsus is reminiscent of medieval distillation chemistry, but by the end of the century iatrochemists were turning less to distilled quintessences and more to precipitates and residues in their search for new remedies. In all cases it was argued that alchemical procedures resulted in the separation of pure substances from inactive impurities.

In the century between 1550 and 1650 conflicts between Paracelsian iatrochemists and more traditional

Galenists were common. The detailed critique of the Paracelsian position by Thomas Erastus became a fundamental text for those who opposed the chemical medicine, and a sharp confrontation between chemists and Galenists followed in Paris in the first decade of the seventeenth century. Here the debate centered largely around the possible dangers of the new medicines. Both Andreas Libavius and Daniel Sennert reviewed this controversy and concluded that the best course for physicians would be to accept the useful remedies of both the old and the new systems. This was the compromise position taken by the compilers of the *Pharmacopoeia* of the Royal College of Physicians of London (1618) and after this time there were few who denied the value of chemistry for medicine.

Yet, if the chemists debated with more traditional philosophers and physicians, they disagreed no less among themselves. At the opening of the seventeenth century Robert Fludd defended the chemically oriented views of the Rosicrucians and he described his mystical alchemical interpretation of nature and supernature in a series of folio volumes on the macrocosm and the microcosm. Here he placed considerable emphasis on an alchemical interpretation of the Creation and he utilized mechanical examples to support his views. His work gave support to the alchemical plea for a new science and it was viewed with alarm by Johannes Kepler, Marin Mersenne, and Pierre Gassendi.

Jean Baptiste van Helmont was no less a chemical philosopher than Fludd, and he described in detail his transmutation of mercury to gold by means of a small sample of the philosopher's stone. Van Helmont sought a chemical understanding of man through medicine, but, in contrast to Fludd and most Paracelsians, he rejected the macrocosm-microcosm analogy. Van Helmont thus was less interested in macrocosmic and geocosmic phenomena than Fludd and he concentrated more on practical and theoretical medical questions. The influence of both authors was considerable in an age when great uncertainty existed about the future course of the new science. As late as 1650 John French could still suggest that only chemistry should properly be considered the basis for a reform of the universities. Similarly John Webster (1654) stated that the new learning must be grounded principally upon the works of Francis Bacon and Robert Fludd.

EPILOGUE

If the chemical philosophy seemed a plausible alternative to the work of the mechanical philosophers in the middle decades of the seventeenth century, this alternative did not remain a viable one for long. The impressive results of the mechanists—culminating in the *Principia mathematica* of Isaac Newton (1687)—stamped on "respectable" natural philosophy the mathematical abstraction of the new physics. And yet, this is not to say that alchemical thought died after a final flowering in the sixteenth and the seventeenth centuries. The collection of manuscripts at King's College, Cambridge leaves little doubt that Isaac Newton was passionately concerned with the traditional problems of transmutation. Furthermore, recent research indicates that Newton's alchemical speculations may have been instrumental in the crystallization of some of his more acceptable concepts of physics. Similarly, Robert Boyle was influenced by alchemical thought. He published on the degradation of silver and his theoretical views were strongly influenced by his early reading of van Helmont. However, it is possible to go beyond these examples. Alchemical works were written by the important practical chemist, Johann Rudolf Glauber and the medical chemistry of the Renaissance alchemists found a new proponent in the revision of Franciscus Sylvius de la Böe whose work went through numerous seventeenth- and eighteenth-century editions. In like manner many elements of Paracelsian chemistry were retained in somewhat altered form in the texts of the eighteenth-century phlogiston chemists. At the same time the German revival of alchemy and Rosicrucianism stimulated a new interest in earlier interpretations of a vitalistic and mystically oriented universe. The impact of this on the growth of the nineteenth-century *Naturphilosophie* has yet to be assessed.

Many characteristic themes of alchemical thought and style are present in the earliest texts that have survived. Both the secrecy and the practical recipes of the metallic craft tradition are evident in the works of the late Hellenistic authors dating from the late third and the fourth centuries A.D. The allegorical and symbolical style of later alchemical works is also present here, and this is a reflection of the mystical tenor of the current philosophies and religions of the late Empire. The medical theme is absent in the Greek tradition and this seems to have been derived from Eastern sources. First found in Chinese alchemical works emphasizing the lengthening of life and the search for immortality, medical alchemy was integrated first into Islamic and then into Western alchemy and medicine.

There is little doubt that alchemy, understood in its broadest sense as a chemical key to nature, played a significant role in the development of the Scientific Revolution. The claim that this mystical science should replace the Aristotelianism and Galenism of the schools was looked on with dismay by early seventeenth-century mechanists who were forced to clarify their own views in their attacks on authors such as Paracelsus and Robert Fludd. At the same time, however, the chemical and alchemical call for a new science based on new observations in nature was important in a period that witnessed an ever-lessening adherence to scholastic authority. Finally, the Paracelsian and iatrochemical adoption of the primary goal of the medical alchemy of the Middle Ages resulted in the permanent acceptance of chemistry as a legitimate tool of the physician and the pharmacist.

BIBLIOGRAPHY

The standard source for Greek alchemy is the *Catalogue des manuscrits alchimiques Grecs* edited by J. Bidez, F. Cumont, J. L. Heiberg, O. Lagercrantz, et al., 8 vols. (Brussels, 1924–32). Earlier, but still useful is the *Collection des anciens alchimistes Grecs* by M. P. Berthelot and C. E. Rouelle, 3 vols. (Paris, 1887–88). Recent editions of Chinese alchemical texts include *Alchemy, Medicine and Religion in the China of* A.D. *320. The Nei P'ien of Ko Hung*, trans. and edited by James R. Ware (Cambridge, Mass., 1966), and Nathan Sivin, *Chinese Alchemy: Preliminary Studies* (Cambridge, Mass., 1968). A collection of Arabic and Syriac texts will be found in M. P. Berthelot, *La chimie au moyen âge*, 3 vols. (Paris, 1893). The latter work should be supplemented with the numerous studies of Julius Ruska on all aspects of Islamic alchemy and the intensive study of Paul Kraus, *Jābir ibn Hayyān*, 2 vols. (Cairo, 1942–43). Basic collected editions of the Latin alchemical texts include the six-volume *Theatrum chemicum* published by Lazarus Zetzner (Strassburg 1659–61) and the two-volume *Bibliotheca chemica curiosa* edited by Jean Jacques Manget (Geneva, 1702). The most extensive German collection is the *Deutsches Theatrum Chemicum* prepared by Friedrich Roth-Scholtz, 3 vols. (Nuremberg, 1728–32). The standard French collection is the *Bibliothèque des philosophes chimiques* prepared by Jean Maugin de Richebourg, 4 vols. (Paris, 1741–54). The most extensive collection of alchemical poetry in English is that of Elias Ashmole, *Theatrum Chemicum Britannicum* (London, 1652), reprinted with an intro. by A. G. Debus (New York, 1967). The standard edition of the works of Paracelsus is that of Karl Sudhoff and Wilhelm Matthiessen, *Sämtliche Werke*, 15 vols. (Munich and Berlin, 1922–33), and the collected works of van Helmont went through numerous editions in several languages from 1648 to 1707.

Bibliographies of alchemical texts date from an early period, but the two standard lists are J. Ferguson, *Bibliotheca Chemica*, 2 vols. (Glasgow, 1906), and Denis I. Duveen, *Bibliotheca Alchemica et Chemica* (London, 1949). A survey of recent scholarship in the field will be found in Allen G. Debus, "The Significance of the History of Early Chemistry," *Cahiers d'Histoire Mondiale*, **9** (1965), 39–58, and extensive bibliographies including recent research will be found in R. P. Multhauf's *The Origins of Chemistry* (London, 1966), pp. 355–89, and Mircea Eliade's *The Forge and the Crucible* (New York, 1962), pp. 186–204. Eliade updated the latter bibliography in his "The Forge and the Crucible: A Postscript," *History of Religions*, **8** (1968), 74–88. For a bibliography of Paracelsus and the later Paracelsians see Karl Sudhoff, *Bibliographia Paracelsica* (Berlin, 1894; reprint Graz, 1958), and "Ein Beitrag zur Bibliographie der Paracelsisten im 16. Jahrhundert," *Centralblatt für Bibliothekswesen*, **10** (1893), 316–26, 385–407. Recent research in this field is covered by the *Paracelsus-Bibliographie 1932–1960 mit einem Verzeichnis neu entdeckter Paracelsus-Handschriften* (*1900–1960*), compiled by Karl-Heinz Weimann (Wiesbaden, 1963). In these bibliographies the reader is directed particularly to the works of Ernst Darmstaedter, Allen G. Debus, Mircea Eliade, Wilhelm Ganzenmuller, Gerald J. Gruman, E. J. Holmyard, C. G. Jung, Hermann Kopp, Edmund O. von Lippmann, R. P. Multhauf, A. Leo Oppenheim, Walter Pagel, J. R. Partington, P. Ray, John Read, Julius Ruska, H. J. Sheppard, John Maxson Stillman, Frank Sherwood Taylor, and R. Campbell Thompson.

ALLEN G. DEBUS

[See also Allegory; Creation in Religion; **Experimental Science in the Middle Ages; Hermeticism;** Islamic Conception; Macrocosm; Neo-Platonism.]

ALIENATION IN CHRISTIAN THEOLOGY

ALIENATION, in theology, refers to the idea that the relation of the worshippers to God may be analogous to the alienation, or estrangement, between human beings. The word implies that a close relationship of affection, family, friendship, or another close tie has been broken, often with detrimental effects on the psyche. The disorganization of the self, worries about guilt, and loss of identity which the breaking of a long and very close bond between people may bring are all familiar. The idea that man, by his sin and indifference, may similarly alienate himself from a loving Father is a distinguishing feature of the Judaic and Christian religious traditions.

The Judaic conception of God and his people came increasingly to be of a familial situation. The story of the creation and fall of man stresses the point that Adam and Eve were both disobedient and potentially dangerous to the high God, since they were ambitious of raising themselves to divine status and might find the means of doing so (Genesis 1:22). Jehovah appears as a jealous ruler. But there is a critical change when the Lord adopts Abram as a son, as a child is adopted, giving him the new name Abraham (Genesis 17), just as later, Jacob is renamed Israel. God is thought of

not merely as the familiar protector of a nation, but, uniquely among ancient cults, as the Father of a human family—the tribes of Israel. The paradigm of the family, with its tensions of affection, hate, loyalties, and fears, permeates the Old Testament. Again and again the children are disobedient and become estranged from their Father: again and again, there is reconciliation between a sorrowing, merciful but divine parent and his loved, but wayward, family. As in a human family, there is a separation between faithful, appreciative siblings and willful, rebellious ones. Sometimes the children wander off to other gods in place of their own Father.

The prophets are the agents through whom God communicates his love for his children, his repeated disappointment and anger over their behavior, and his plans for effecting a final reconciliation. The prophets do not merely warn of terrible punishments if the chosen people continue to disobey the Lord: they constantly use figures from the patriarchal family to embody their message. In one of the most poignant passages of the Old Testament, Hosea represents the Lord yearning over his people Israel just as a patriarch might speak of his sons:

When Israel was a child, I loved him, and out of Egypt I called my son. The more I called them, the more they went from me; they kept sacrificing to the Baals, and burning incense to idols. Yet it was I who taught Ephraim to walk, I took them up in my arms; but they did not know that I healed them. I led them with cords of compassion, with the bands of love; . . . and I bent down to them and fed them. . . . How can I give you up, O Ephraim! . . . My heart recoils within me, my compassion grows warm and tender (Hosea 11:1-8, Revised Standard Version).

Elsewhere, the relationship is that of husband and wife: "And in that day, says the Lord, you will call me, 'My husband,' and no longer will you call me, 'My baal'" (Hosea 2:16).

It is hard to find anything in other world-religions to compare with this moving, divine domestic drama. Even in Islam, Allah appears as judge and sustainer of order only; man is created to fulfill the *amr*, the divine commandment. In Neo-Platonism, it has been asserted, there is a form of alienation, for man is seen as separated from his true divine source and home. The soul has been corrupted by matter, the lowest stage of the emanations from the One, and so has turned away from its higher origin, the Intellect. The very metaphysical structure and impersonality of this system, however, precludes anything like the relationships and dynamic tensions among different psyches which are implied in alienation as we have defined it. The process of return to the Intellect, which certainly never yearns over a lost soul, in fact implies something like de-personalization. Love, for example, must be universalized and purified from being directed to any one person or object. Similarly, in Manicheism, two powers, neither of which is a true personality, fight for domination. Mankind, like the hero of a fairy tale, is held by enchantment in a dark prison—this world. He can be rescued only by being taught the secret of his true nature as a child of light, and through learning thaumaturgic formulas which will enable him to escape to his heavenly home.

Alienation-reconciliation is the central pattern of Saint Paul's interpretation of salvation. In adjusting the Hebraic tradition of a chosen people to a universal religion, however, he necessarily had to make some extremely important changes. The later prophets had begun to think of ultimate redemption in terms of all mankind, not just Israel. Paul completed the transformation: all of the human race are members of God's family, and so all human beings necessarily have become alienated from their Father. Obviously, there must have sprung up serious faults in basic human nature which have estranged all men, not merely some, from God. There is a generalized malaise in the human experience, alienated as all men are from the source of all truth and values. Paul implies that for the Jewish people the alienation was at least partially cured; addressing the Gentiles, he recalls their desperate situation before Christ:

. . . remember that you were at that time separated from Christ, alienated from the commonwealth of Israel, and strangers to the covenants of promise having no hope and without God in the world (Ephesians 2:12).

He describes the plight of fallen man in terms of what the psychiatrist would immediately recognize as "alienation":

And you, who once were estranged and hostile in mind, doing evil deeds, he has now reconciled in his body of flesh by his death, . . . (Colossians 1:21).

This statement demonstrates that alienation and reconciliation are always combined in Paul's teaching, for salvation is reconciliation with God. The Father has reunited and gathered his estranged human family, not by revealing the law through prophets, not by sending a teacher to reveal the secret way out of this evil world, but by curing human nature through joining the divine with the human. In the union of the two in Christ's unified personality, alienation has ended. The Christian message, Paul stresses again and again, is that "God through Christ reconciled us to himself and gave us the ministry of reconciliation" (II Corinthians 5:18). The Christian is "reconciled to God." Thus it would be illuminating to speak of the "alienating sin" instead of "original sin" and of redemption as "reconciliation."

Whether this emphasis would survive in Christianity became the great issue of the first and second centuries.

Opposed to such a view of salvation was the movement known as "Gnosticism." Although it took a vast number of forms, this sect essentially continued Manicheism with Christian coloration. The good God, it taught, is not the creator and ruler of the irredeemably evil world in which man lives and suffers. Men, however, have a spark of "light" which can enable them to escape. Christ was a heavenly spirit, child of a heavenly spirit; both he and his mother were human only in appearance, having no real bodies. Christ's mission was to reveal the *gnosis*, the secret wisdom. The whole thrust is that Christ did *not* join divine and human personalities. There is no reconciliation, here, nor any analogy with human experience. Man is saved by totally rejecting material nature, by heroic denial of one side of his being. It is interesting to speculate as to what kind of world we should have if, say, the Albigensians of the Middle Ages, who apparently carried on this kind of belief, had triumphed.

In the late second century, Saint Irenaeus, in a classical attack on Gnosticism, stated the essence of the great division in Christianity:

. . . if we devise another substance of our Lord's Flesh, then will his statement about Reconciliation no longer hang together. For that only is reconciled, which at one time was in enmity. But if our Lord brought with Him flesh of another substance, then no longer was the same thing reconciled to God, which by transgression has become hostile. But now by Man's participation of Himself our Lord hath reconciled him to God the Father (*Against the Heresies*, trans. John Keble, V:14:3).

Irenaeus adds an important idea: that under the Mosaic law, Israel was never truly reconciled with God, but was only in a "servile" state; now God has truly adopted all mankind, without favoritism, and men once more are his "sons." Hence they should have both more fear and love of God; "for sons ought to fear more than slaves, and to have greater love towards their Father" (ibid., IV:16:5). This paradoxical combination underlies the conception of Christian liberty, and it could exist only in a relationship of alienation-reconciliation.

Saint Augustine in the course of his spiritual wanderings became a Manichean, and he left that sect precisely because it offered no hope of real reconciliation with the Father. He says, in a sermon for Christmas, that God, ". . . remaining God, was made man, so that even as the Son of man he is rightly called *God with us*, not 'God in the one case, man in the other.'" How could Christ, if we believe, with the Gnostics, in the "crucifixion of a phantasm," abolish the "enmity" which man's sins have created between him and God? (*Confessions* 5:19).

Augustine's spiritual quest was for a faith that would combine a return to a reconciliation with God, and to a strong sense that the Deity is truly transcendent and omnipotent; hence his struggles to formulate free will in accordance with divine power. So he vehemently opposed the Pelagians, who denied that man's nature is intrinsically alienated by sin, and that anyone may, like the prodigal son, decide on his own volition to arise and return to his Father. Augustine—and the mainstream of Christianity after his time—emphasized the one-sidedness of the reconciliation. Only as omnipotent God reaches out to the individual soul can reconciliation begin. Augustine's *Confessions* eloquently expresses the idea that natural man suffers from naturally incurable psychical unrest and distress, and therefore yearns for something to save him; and it expresses the joy, the sense of repose and contentment when his estrangement from his Father is ended.

Augustine, following a concept implied in the prophets, describes another kind of alienation. The human family itself, which should live in harmony under the Fatherhood of its God, continues in an incurable state of estrangement within itself. Believers (the adopted people) and unbelievers, even though living and working side by side, are really in deep enmity. This alienation, moreover, is deceptive. The eye of worldly wisdom regards the City of God as composed simply of malcontents, since it is out of sympathy with the ideals and convictions of the "world," which often professes good ideals and intentions. But, of course, it really is the "world" that is alienated from the source of all goodness. Thus there has been a continuing impression that alienation within society is inevitable, and that the righteous are permanently estranged from the "establishment," the dominant powers of the world.

Medieval scholasticism attempted to bring into a syncretic harmony the many strains of thought that had gone into Christianity. The pattern of alienation-reconciliation was not dropped, but the desire to find precise metaphysical formulation for the experience of salvation greatly reduced it in importance. Saint Thomas Aquinas, for example, defining the end in life as—in Aristotelian terms—pure contemplation, envisioned something quite different from the reconciliation of personalities Paul described. The metaphysical definitions inevitably reduced the impression of immediate relationships between God and man. On the other side, the medieval mystical tradition, with its goal of absorption of the individual soul into the divine, worked against the conception of reconciliation, which implies the continuation of the individual self in all its integrity. Augustine certainly would have wished for a mind at one with God's, but not to cease to be Augustine. Finally, the obsession in popular religion with a crudely thaumaturgic salvation—sin being purged by rituals, relics, pardons, etc.—reduced the sense of alienation and reconciliation.

Essential to Martin Luther's reform was a return to Irenaeus' point: that man is redeemed when he returns to become again, literally, a child of God. Luther puts the point in homely, deliberately nontheological terms, like speeches in a domestic drama:

Christ says: formerly you were my enemies; but now you are friends because I regard you as friends, not because you do many good things to Me. . . . I die for the sort of friends who have done Me no good. I have just loved them and made them my friends . . . (*Commentary on John 15*).

God, like a (medieval) father, plays and sports with his children, pretending to be enraged with them to test their loyalty. Christ, unlike angels, lived with us, "ate, drank, became angry, prayed, became sad, cried." And in Luther, as commonly in Christianity, there is an implication, very strong if seldom clearly defined, that it is better for the human soul to have undergone alienation with subsequent reconciliation than it would have been never to have been estranged from God. The joy over the return of the prodigal son was greater than that over the continued faithfulness of his brother. In any event, the relation of a husband and wife, or of friends who have been seriously estranged and then reconciled, is very different from what it was at first. The fall of man was a *felix culpa*, then, in the sense that a new and perhaps deeper relation of God to man has been established, symbolized by the cross. A mystique of alienation has been evident throughout the history of Christianity.

Thus in Western civilization the condition of alienation has, so to speak, been institutionalized in religion. The expectation that alienation is part of the human condition has endured even when specific Christian belief has gone. Romanticism viewed man as "alienated" from nature. Wordsworth's *The Prelude*, for example, tells the story of a boy, nurtured by the divine Spirit of nature, subsequently alienated from it by the temptations and corruptions of civilization, and finally reconciled. In one very important respect, however, the tradition has changed it. The Judeo-Christian religions, as we have seen, closely connected alienation and reconciliation. The gloom of the Christian doctrine of "original sin" is greatly lightened by the idea that this condition is a kind of nightmare from which those who receive grace have awakened. It is the dark before the light. Modern views of man as alienated, however, have no such solution of the dilemma. Man appears to be afflicted by this state, but its cause and cure are uncertain. Hence we have lost the paradoxical sense of optimism that accompanied the idea of alienation in Christianity.

BIBLIOGRAPHY

The main bibliographical items for this subject are mentioned in the text. In addition, the following may be cited: J. M. Ward, *Hosea: A Theological Commentary* (New York, 1966); Saint Augustine, *Sermons for Christmas and Epiphany*, trans. T. C. Lawler (Westminster, Md., 1952); Martin Luther, *Lectures on Romans*, trans. W. Pauck (Philadelphia, 1961); G. B. Hammond, *Man in Estrangement* (Nashville, 1965); and G. Sykes, *Alienation: The Cultural Climate of Our Times* (New York, 1964).

ERNEST TUVESON

[See also **Alienation;** Christianity; Dualism; Free Will; Gnosticism; **God;** Heresy; Romanticism; **Sin and Salvation.**]

ALIENATION IN HEGEL AND MARX

ALTHOUGH its roots lie far back in the Judeo-Christian tradition, the concept of alienation first gained prominence in the philosophy of Hegel, and particularly in his mature writings. There are signs of the idea in his earlier works, but it is not until the *Phenomenology* (1808), thought by many to be Hegel's most important work, that alienation occupies a central place in his writings.

In the opening sections of the *Phenomenology* Hegel attacked the views of common sense and simplified natural science that the world consisted of discrete objects independent of man's consciousness. Truth, for Hegel, was not to be found in knowledge that was purified of any influence from man's own desires and feelings. Ultimately Hegel considered that there could be no truth that was not intimately linked with the ongoing process of human beings as thinking subjects; truth was *their* truth. The supposed objectivity of the world of nature was in fact an alienation, for man's task was to discover, behind these appearances, his own essential life and finally to view everything as a facet of his own self-consciousness. The same principle applied to the world of culture in which such spheres as art and religion, if viewed as independent of man, constituted so many alienations to be overcome by integration into the final understanding and recapitulation which was Absolute Knowledge.

The central actor in this process for Hegel was Spirit. Hegel thought that reality was Spirit developing itself. In this process Spirit produced a world that it thought at first was external; only later did it realize that this world was its own production. Spirit was not something separated from this productive activity; it only existed in and through this activity. At the beginning of this process Spirit was not aware that it was externalizing or alienating itself. Only gradually did Spirit realize that the world was not external to it. It was the failure to realize this that constituted, for Hegel, alienation. This alienation would cease when men became fully self-conscious and understood their environment and their culture to be emanations of Spirit. Freedom consisted in this understanding, and freedom was the aim of history.

Hegel had created a system; and all his disciples agreed that it was the final one. However, when it came to applying the system to particular problems, they conceived their Master's system to be ambivalent. The fact that alienation seemed to them to be a challenge, something to be overcome, led them to put the emphasis on the concepts of dialectic and negativity in Hegel's system; and thus they challenged, first in religion and then in politics, the Master's view that the problem of alienation had, at least in principle, been solved. The foremost among these radical disciples of Hegel, Bruno Bauer, applied the concept of alienation to the religious field. Bauer, who lectured in theology and made his name as a Gospel critic, considered that religious beliefs, and in particular Christianity, caused a division in man's consciousness by becoming opposed to this consciousness as a separate power. Thus religion was an attitude towards the essence of self-consciousness that had become estranged from itself. In this context, Bauer promoted the use of the expression "self-alienation" that soon became current among the Young Hegelians.

Like Bruno Bauer, Ludwig Feuerbach was also fascinated by the problem of religious alienation, but his concept of it was much simpler. Whereas Bauer considered that men's religious creations eventually adopted an inhuman form, Feuerbach saw in religion simply the projection of man's essential desires and capacities. Since what was ascribed to God were really attributes of man, man was separated from himself, and thus alienated. This idea was elaborated in Feuerbach's best known book *The Essence of Christianity*, published in 1841. Feuerbach described the "fundamental idea" of his book thus: "The objective essence of religion, particularly the Christian religion, is nothing but the essence of human, and particularly Christian, feeling. The secret of theology is therefore anthropology. . . . The foundation of a new science is laid here in that the philosophy of religion is conceived of and presented as esoteric or secret anthropology or psychology" (McLellan [1969], p. 88).

Feuerbach made an even greater impact through his *Preliminary Theses for the Reform of Philosophy* and his *Foundations of the Philosophy of the Future*, both published in 1843. Their major purpose was to point out that Hegel's philosophy was just as alienating a force as religion and needed to be reabsorbed in the same manner. Feuerbach began his *Theses* with the statement "the secret of theology is anthropology, but the secret of speculative philosophy is theology" (ibid., p. 98). In Feuerbach's view, the great deficiency in Hegel's philosophy was its negation of theology "from the standpoint of theology." Thus Hegel—the German Proclus—never managed to break out of the circle of ideas and could not realize the true relationship of thought to being: "being is the subject, thought the predicate." As a philosopher in his own right, Feuerbach was only of the second rank: basically he had one idea that he expounded in many different ways. As Marx said later: "Compared with Hegel, Feuerbach is very poor. Nevertheless, after Hegel he was epoch-making because he put the emphasis on certain points, uncomfortable for the Christian consciousness and important for the progress of criticism, which Hegel had left in a sort of mystical twilight between clarity and obscurity" (ibid., p. 113).

It was in this atmosphere of rapid secularization that Marx evolved his own concept of alienation. Bruno Bauer had talked of alienation in religion; Feuerbach had carried this further by pointing out that Hegel's philosophy was itself the last bastion of theology; finally Moses Hess—nicknamed "the communist rabbi"—had transferred Feuerbach's ideas to the realm of economics, by analyzing, in his essay *On the Essence of Money* (1844), money as the alienated essence of man. Marx accepted all these accounts of alienation, considering economics to be fundamental inasmuch as work was man's basic activity. In all these fields Marx's common idea was that man had alienated to someone or something what was essential to his nature—principally, to be in control of his own activities, to be the subject and initiator of the historical process. In the different forms of alienation some other entity had obtained what was proper to man: in religion it was God, in politics the State, in economics the market process and cash nexus. (A note is necessary on the German originals of the term "alienation." Marx uses two words to express the concept of alienation: *Entfremdung* and *Entäusserung*. His distinction between these two words is by no means as precise as that of Hegel. Often they appear to be synonymous and are used together for rhetorical effect. If anything, *Entfremdung* conveys the sense of alienation in which

two people are said to be alienated from each other; while *Entäusserung* has more the sense of "making external to oneself" with legal and commercial overtones. Neither of these words is to be confused with *Vergegenständlichung*, that is, "objectification," which, in Marx as opposed to Hegel, is a neutral process that can be either good or bad according to the particular circumstances.)

Marx first worked out his ideas in detail with regard to political alienation in his *Critique of Hegel's Philosophy of Right*. Here Marx examined paragraph by paragraph Hegel's *Philosophy of Right* and claimed that the state, described by Hegel as productive of, and superior to, its own elements, constituted an alienation of man's essence. Applying to Hegel Feuerbach's reversal of subject and predicate, Marx wrote: "The Idea is made subjective and the true relationship of the family and civil society to the state is conceived of as their imaginary activity. The family and civil society are the presuppositions of the state; they are its properly active elements. But in speculation the relationship is inverted. When the Idea is made a subject, the civil society, the family, 'circumstances, caprice' etc. become unreal objective phrases of the Idea and have a completely different significance" (*Early Texts*, p. 62).

The place where Marx wrote at greatest length on his concept of alienation and his debt to Hegel are two passages in the *Paris Manuscripts*. In the passage on "alienated labour" (ibid., pp. 133ff.), Marx deals with the relationship of the worker to his product. The fact that the worker is related to the product of his labor as to an alien object means that the more the worker produces the more he approaches loss of work and starvation. Marx goes on to detail four types of alienated labor: the alienation of the product from the producer; the alienation of the act of production; the alienation of nature from men; and finally of man from his species-being (a term borrowed from Feuerbach meaning the common factors making up man's nature). This negative picture is complemented by the description that Marx gives of unalienated man in the notes that he made on James Mill at the same time as the writing of the *Manuscripts*. Put rather roughly, what Marx means when he talks of alienation is this: it is man's nature to be his own creator; he forms and develops himself by working on and transforming the world outside him in cooperation with his fellow men. In this progressive interchange between man and the world, it is man's nature to be in control of this process, to be the initiator, the subject in which the process originates. However, this nature has become alien to man; that is, it is no longer his and belongs to another person or thing. In religion, for example, it is God who is the subject of the historical process and man is in a state of dependence on His grace. In economics, according to Marx, it is money and the processes of the market that maneuver men around instead of being controlled by them. The central point is that man has lost control of his own evolution and has seen this control invested in other entities. What is proper to man has become the attribute of something else, and thus alien to him.

The second passage of importance in the *Paris Manuscripts* is the final section entitled *Critique of Hegel's Dialectic* (ibid., pp. 157ff.). Here Marx began by describing Feuerbach's "great achievement" which was to have demonstrated that Hegel's philosophy was merely a different form of the alienation of man's nature; Feuerbach had reestablished the primacy of man's social relationship to man. Marx readily acknowledged his own debt to Hegel. "Therefore the greatness of Hegel's *Phenomenology*," he wrote, "and its final product, the dialectic of negativity as the moving and creating principle, is that Hegel conceived of the self-creation of man as a process, objectification as loss of the object, as externalisation and the transcendence of this externalisation. This means, therefore, that he grasps the nature of labour and understands objective man, true, because real man, as the result of his own labour" (ibid., p. 164). Nevertheless, Hegel's conception of labor was of abstract, mental labor and he only succeeded in overcoming alienation in the realm of consciousness.

Although Hegel said that man suffered from economic and political alienation, it was only the thought of economics and politics in which Hegel was interested. The whole process ended in Absolute Knowledge, with the result that it was the philosopher who judged the world. In other words, Hegel had confused alienation and objectivity. Thus, according to Hegel, "What is supposed to be the essence of alienation that needs to be transcended is not that man's being objectifies itself in an inhuman way in opposition to itself, but that it objectifies itself in distinction from and in opposition to, abstract thought. The appropriation of man's objectified and alienated faculties is thus firstly only an appropriation that occurs in the mind, in pure thought, i.e. in abstraction" (ibid., pp. 162f.). Marx's central criticism of Hegel, therefore, was that alienation would not cease with the supposed abolition of the external world. The external world, according to Marx, was part of man's nature and the point was to establish the right relationship between man and his environment. Marx therefore rejected Hegel's notion of Spirit and replaced its supposed antithesis to the external world by the antithesis between man and his social being.

In his early writings, therefore, Marx sketched a notion of alienation which, taking the analyses in religion and politics of his contemporary Young Hegelians as models, had its roots in the socioeconomic situation of the worker in capitalist society. Yet in the 1930's and '40's, alienation did not play any part in the many discussions of Marx's thought. In the 1960's, however, it was accepted that it is *the* major theme running through the whole of his writings. Those who wish to maintain that there is a break between the "young" and the "old" Marx usually maintain that alienation is a concept that was entirely restricted to Marx's early thought and later abandoned. However, these statements can be shown to be incorrect.

The term itself occurs much more frequently, even in *Capital,* than is commonly realized. In *Capital* Marx writes, for example: "The character of independence and estrangement which the capitalist modes of production as a whole give to the instruments of labour and the product, as against the workman, is developed by means of machinery into a thorough antagonism" (I, 432). Yet it is not only a question of terminology: the content, too, of *Capital* is a continuation of Marx's early thoughts. The main discussion of Volume One of *Capital* rests on the equation of work and value that goes back to the conception of man as a being who creates himself and the conditions of his life—a conception outlined in the *Paris Manuscripts.* It is man's nature, according to the Marx of the *Paris Manuscripts,* to be constantly developing, in cooperation with other men, himself and the world about him. What Marx in *Capital* is describing is how this fundamental role of man, to be the initiator and controller of the historical process, has been transferred, or alienated, and how it belongs to the inhuman power of Capital.

The counterpart of alienated man, the unalienated or "total" man of the *Manuscripts,* also appears in *Capital.* In the chapter of Volume One on "Machinery and Modern Industry" Marx makes the same contrast between the effects of alienated and unalienated modes of production on the development of human potentiality. He writes: "Modern industry, indeed, compels society, under penalty of death, to replace the detailworker of today, crippled by the life-long repetition of one and the same trivial operation, and thus reduced to the mere fragment of a man, by the fully developed individual, fit for a variety of labours, ready to face any change of production, and to whom the different social functions he performs, are but so many modes of giving free scope to his own natural and acquired powers." The fact that, in *Capital,* the conclusion is supported by a detailed analysis of the effects of advanced technology, should not obscure the continuity.

The section of *Capital* that most recalls the early writings, is the final section of Chapter One, entitled "Fetishism of Commodities." The whole section is reminiscent of the passage on alienated labor in the

Paris Manuscripts and of the notes on James Mill that Marx composed in 1844. Marx writes:

A commodity is therefore a mysterious thing, simply because in it the social character of man's labour appears to them as an objective character stamped upon that labour; because the relation of the producers to the sum total of their labour, is presented to them as a social relation, existing not between themselves, but between the products of their labour (I, 488).

However, the writing that best shows the centrality of the concept of alienation to Marx's thought is the *Grundrisse*. This manuscript is the thousand-page draft that served Marx as a basis for *Capital* but remained unpublished until 1941. The *Grundrisse*, of which the *Critique of Political Economy* and *Capital* are only partial elaborations, is the centerpiece of Marx's work. It is the basic work which permitted the generalizations in the famous *Preface* to the *Critique of Political Economy*. For *Capital* is only the first of the six volumes in which Marx wished to develop his *Economics*, the title by which he referred to his *magnum opus* on the alienation of man through Capital and the State.

The scope of the *Grundrisse* being wider than that of *Capital*, Marx's thought is best viewed as a continuing meditation on themes begun in 1844, the high point in which meditation occurred in 1857–58. The continuity between the *Manuscripts* and the *Grundrisse* is evident. Marx himself talked of the *Grundrisse* as "the result of fifteen years of research, thus the best period of my life." This letter was written in November 1858, exactly fifteen years after Marx's arrival in Paris in November 1843. He also says, in the *Preface* of 1859: "the total material lies before me in the form of monographs, which were written at widely separated periods, for self-clarification, not for publication, and whose coherent elaboration according to the plan indicated will depend on external circumstances." This can only refer to the *Paris Manuscripts* of 1844 and the London notebooks of 1850–52. Marx constantly used, and at the same time revised, material from an earlier date: for instance, he used his notebooks of 1843–45 while writing *Capital*.

The content of the *Grundrisse* only serves to confirm what is plain from the external evidence: the beginning of the chapter on *Capital* reproduces almost word for word the passages in the *Manuscripts* on human need, man as a species-being, the individual as a social being, the idea of nature as, in a sense, man's body, the parallels between religious and economic alienation, the utopian and almost millennial elements, etc. One point in particular emphasizes this continuity: the *Grundrisse* are as Hegelian as the *Paris Manuscripts* and the central concept of both of them is alienation.

Aided by the publication of Marx's early writings,

the increasing complexity and anonymity of capitalist society, and the gap between ideology and reality in many socialist ones, the concept of alienation has become very topical. Its very topicality, however, is in danger of rendering the concept of alienation vacuous; for often it seems merely to be used to designate any state of affairs that is considered unsatisfactory. However, Marx's description of alienation, particularly as contained in the *Paris Manuscripts*, is by no means as vacuous as many of its contemporary interpretations. For it contains both an account of the relationship between socioeconomic conditions and psychological states that is, to some extent at least, testable, and also a far from vague view of human nature. Because it contains both of these it is also a concept in which facts and values are inextricably bound together, and so one which runs counter to the prevailing demand for a sharp distinction between evaluative and descriptive statements. Thus, although Marx was always writing with certain initial value judgments presupposed, empirical criteria are, up to a point, applicable to his hypotheses. Marx's concept can be further clarified by asking what he would consider as nonalienation. This positive side of Marx's critique is less well-known. But the passage on "alienated labour" in the *Paris Manuscripts* should be read in close conjunction with his description of "production in a human manner" contained in his notes on James Mill, and with the conception of the future communist society outlined in the *Grundrisse*. The metaphysical and ethical elements of the concept of alienation that originated with Hegel and Feuerbach still persist to some extent in Marx, but they are given a socioeconomic context that makes them all the more interesting to the modern mind.

BIBLIOGRAPHY

H. Arvon, *Ludwig Feuerbach, ou la tranformation du Sacré* (Paris, 1957). S. Avineri, *The Social and Political Thought of Karl Marx* (Cambridge, 1968). H. Barth, *Wahrheit und Ideologie* (Zurich, 1945). J.-Y. Calvez, *La Pensée de Karl Marx* (Paris, 1956). L. Dupré, *The Philosophical Foundations of Marxism* (New York, 1966). L. Feuerbach, *The Essence of Christianity* (London, 1853). J. Findlay, *Hegel: A Re-examination* (London, 1958). E. Fromm, *Marx's Concept of Man* (New York, 1961). G. Hegel, *Phenomenology of Mind* (London and New York, 1910). J. Hyppolite, *Genèse et Structure da la phénoménologie de l'esprit de Hegel* (Paris, 1947). E. Kamenka, *The Ethical Foundations of Marxism* (London, 1962). W. Kaufmann, *Hegel* (New York, 1965). A. Kojève, *Introduction à la lecture de Hegel* (Paris, 1947). J. Loewenberg, *Hegel's Phenomenology* (La Salle, 1965). H. Marcuse, *Reason and Revolution* (London, 1941). K. Marx, *Capital*, 3 vols. (Moscow, 1961–62); idem, *Selected Writings in Sociology and Social Philosophy*, ed. T. Bottomore and M. Rubel (London, 1956); idem, *The Early Texts*, ed. D.

McLellan (Oxford, 1971); idem, *Writings of the Young Marx on Philosophy and Society*, ed. L. Easton and K. Guddat (New York, 1967). D. McLellan, *Marx before Marxism* (New York, 1970), with extensive bibliography on the early Marx; idem, *Marx's Grundrisse* (New York, 1971); idem, *The Thought of Karl Marx* (New York, 1971), with extensive bibliography on Marxist thought as a whole; idem, *The Young Hegelians and Karl Marx* (London, 1969). B. Ollman, *Alienation: Marx's Concept of Man in Capitalist Society* (Cambridge, 1971). J. Plamenatz, *Man and Society*, Vol. 2 (London, 1963). S. Rawidowicz, *Ludwig Feuerbachs Philosophie* (Berlin, 1931). R. Tucker, *Philosophy and Myth in Karl Marx* (Cambridge, 1961).

DAVID McLELLAN

[See also Alienation in Western Theology; Economic History; Economic Theory of Natural Liberty; **Hegelian Political and Religious Ideas; Historical and Dialectical Materialism; Marxism;** Socialism.]

ALLEGORY IN LITERARY HISTORY

IN THE EXPANSION of Western thought allegory has played a major part from the earliest times to the present. Allegories have taken many forms, from mere emblems like the eagle and the dove, to the simple fables of Aesop and parables of Christ, to vast poetic structures like *The Divine Comedy* and equally large forms like the patristic glosses and commentaries on the Bible. Essentially a means of structuring language so as to produce continuously linked series of double or multiple meanings, this symbolic mode depends largely upon syncretic mixtures of symbols from which it builds up "levels of meaning," sometimes as few as two, or as many as seven. Minimally it holds that no single literal meaning can stand alone, but that a valid utterance must possess a transcendent meaning as well, a symbolic surplus beyond the literal level. Most allegories are images of cosmic order, and their fixed, hierarchical, and timeless character becomes problematic whenever such cosmic orders are subjected to temporal analysis. The key to the permanence of allegory throughout history appears to be its ornamental surface, which allies it with changes in cosmology and decorum and gives it an exploratory as well as a traditional and conservationist function.

Terminology. Following classical tradition, the seventh-century scholar Isidore of Seville called allegory an inversion of speech, *alieni loquium, aliud enim sonat, aliud intelligitur,* whereby, in saying one thing a person conveys or understands something else (*Etymologiae* I, 47.22). Such deceptively simple formulas, which abound in the history of allegory, suggest, if nothing else, the fundamentally oblique character of this symbolic mode. When Saint Augustine speaks of "a mode of speech in which one thing is understood by another," his very open definition is based on the assumption that some primary or literal ($\dot{\rho}\eta\tau\dot{\eta}$) level of sense may include another secondary or even more remote sense, which the trained interpreter will seek out through a process of reflection. Such secondary meanings may be imposed upon a text, or an author may clearly build them into a text, but no clear distinction separates the interpretive and creative aspects of allegory, since the two are poles in a single communicative method. The allegorical poet encodes an oblique, multiple (Dante called it a "polysemous") meaning in his fiction, using emblems and iconographic devices, for example, the scythe of time, or the apple of discord, and the stories that go with them.

The allegorical interpreter decodes this same complex message, which assumes that allegory is a structural reality within the text. Nevertheless, though allegory may exist in a text as a structure, the key to this structure is usually found in some system of values or ideas that lies outside the immediate context. "The allegorical method means the interpretation of a text in terms of something else, irrespective of what that something else is. That something else may be book learning, it may be practical wisdom, or it may be one's inner consciousness. All these are matters which depend upon external circumstances" (Wolfson, *Philo*, I, 134). Allegory thus not only assumes a certain stability of literal meaning, but also the legitimacy of a movement back and forth between that literal meaning and some external frame of reference. In the history of the mode both creators and interpreters have enjoyed wide freedom in the ways they have understood the internal and external dimensions of their texts, and the historian is faced with a bewildering variety of allegorical procedures. Theologians, however, have often sought to systematize the allegorical method.

A plethora of traditional technical terms conveys the encyclopedic spirit of this procedure. Hardly an idea in the history of Western thought has failed to find allegorical expression, at some period or other. Major allegorists like Dante and Spenser have often summed up the world views of their time. The term "allegory" itself comes from the teachings of Greco-Roman rhetoricians, Demetrius, Cicero, Quintilian, and others, who take it to mean a series of linked metaphors, as exemplified in Horace's *Ode* (I, 14), in which the poet elaborates on the "ship of state," subdividing the single main figure of speech into a series of nautical/political

41

parallels. Unlike the single metaphor, however, allegory tends to depart from the world of sense-experience, moving toward rumination. Metaphor sees, but allegory thinks, and thus often creates an effect of geometric abstraction. Allegory is furthermore highly ornamental, using elaborate symbolism and personification.

Deriving from Greek *allos* + *agoreuein* ("other + speak out"), allegory implies only the most general kind of semantic doubling, and classical rhetoric draws rather uncertain lines between allegory and other figures of speech, metaphor, synecdoche, metonymy, and the like. It associates allegory with notions of design, with terms like *paradeigma* and *schema,* and later critics link allegory with *figura, impresa,* and *emblema,* which point to vision, structure, and external form.

By contrast the older Greek term for allegorical meaning refers us to a veiling function of language. *Hyponoia* (ὑπόνοια) was the term which, Plutarch tells us (*De audiendis poetis* 4.19), the "ancients" had used, and it implies a hidden meaning, a conjectural or suppositious sense, buried *under* the literal surface. Plato (*Republic* II. 378d), Euripides (*Phoenicians* 1131–33), Aristophanes (*Frogs* 1425–31), Xenophon (*Symposium* III, 6), all use *hyponoia* to mean what is later subsumed under allegory (Pépin, pp. 85–86). *Hyponoia* furthermore has a noetic character; the reader or listener will have to think his way through a semantic barrier, beyond which lies a realm of mystic knowledge. Thus Philo Judaeus may equate the *hyponoia* of a text with its latent theme, its mystery, its secret, its unexpressed, unseen, nonliteral, or simply intelligible meaning. While theological and other exegetes stress the mysteries of allegory, and classical rhetoric stresses its semantic form, analyzing the shift from hidden to open meaning as a semantic inversion, both exegetes and rhetoricians alike possess a large store of technical synonyms, among them *parabole, typos, fabula, symbolon, ennoia, fictio, figmentum, insinuatio, significatio, similitudo, figura, imago, interpretatio, involucrum, integumentum.* Some of these terms define the "external circumstances" of allegory as a theological framework, others as philosophy, still others as rhetoric or poetics. In most of the terms obliquity and mystery are the chief emphasis. Augustine observes in his *De doctrina* (2.7–8) that "when something is searched for with difficulty it is, as a result, more delightfully discovered."

If an ascetic interpretive rigor is one main source of pleasure in allegory, exegetical intricacy is the vice of the mode. From a certain angle allegory is merely a mode of systematic commentary upon a text, as opposed to an unmediated, direct, or literal reading of the text, and thus exegesis must depart from its source in the text. This departure may become obsessive. Dante labels his *Commedia* "digressive," while typically the medieval commentator ringed his text with marginalia. The medieval distinction between a gloss and a commentary allowed the latter to stray further from the literal sense. The interpreter often thought of himself as boring his way through a "rind" or "bark," so as to allow the hidden symbolic truth to flow outward from the textual center. In the Middle Ages at least a text would be valued in the measure to which its lode of inner meaning appeared to defy exhaustion.

Continuities in the History of Allegory. A literary method which encourages the search for multiplicity of sense is bound to provoke attack from rationalist quarters, a situation we observe with Plato, whose rejection of the poets from his ideal republic includes a rejection of the allegorical defense of Homeric myth. Early Greek philosophers, among them Heraclitus and Pythagoras, had found a piety toward god, nature, and man in apparently scandalous passages concerning the gods. Philosophy inverted myth, so that, for example, the jealousy of a god would "truly" represent the physical activity of a natural force. Such a means of saving Homer for morality proved both superficial and irrational in the light of Plato's dialectical analysis. For Plato this allegorical transformation of evil-minded myths did more harm than good, for it permitted the continuance of poetry in preference to the higher pursuit of philosophy. The wisdom saved thereby was, in principle, sophistry. Ironically, Plato himself provided the most substantial mechanism and authority for the persistence of Western allegory.

The Platonic theory of ideas has two aspects which lead to allegorical interpretations of both signs and things, provided the overarching authority of dialectic is allowed to fade from sight. In the first place the ideas may be taken to constitute the formulas, if not exactly the forms, by which the allegorist's "something" is interpreted *as* "something else." If the snake is an emblem of jealousy, then it is the idea *jealousy* that organizes the "coaptation" of the snake for this symbolic purpose. To speak of "the idea of a thing" is almost to invoke the allegorical process, for the idea transcends the thing, much as the allegorist's fiction departs from the literal sense of an utterance. Yet this is not the strongest Platonic support for allegory, powerful though it is.

More important is the Platonic arrangement of the theory of ideas as a vast hierarchical construct, from lower to higher forms. By adopting the "principle of plenitude," the notion that an intelligible world would possess all possible forms of all possible things—as the effluence of the One—Plato answered the allegorist's encyclopedic demand for a plenitude of "somethings" by which to symbolize his "anythings." Plenitude also implied an infinitely subdivided universe, while it led to an otherworldly tendency within the whole approach to life, such that a Platonizing allegorist would always be happy to think of X in terms of Y, since this would achieve transcendency beyond the bonds of mere material reference. By questioning the essential value of material nature, the Platonic dialectic opens the way to a spiritualizing of nature, and in the case of Plato himself this leads to the use of allegory precisely at the moment in his dialogues when the analysis of nature has reached the highest point of transcendence describable in natural, human terms. At that point a leap of iconographic faith takes place, as in the vision of love Diotima gives Socrates, when the realistic and human drama of the *Symposium* gives way to a "conceptual myth," a spiritual diagram of a love which cannot be represented "in terms of" ordinary human experience. The Platonic use of allegory, itself allegorized in the Myth of the Cave, reaches a climax in the *Timaeus*. There, since the universe is not explicable in purely natural terms, its ideal character is permitted to surge up in a fanciful, visionary theory of cosmic order.

The Platonic example may be archetypal for the history of allegory, in that his attack upon Homeric allegorizing is not as general or consistent as at first it seems. He is perhaps open to the charge that he is attacking any allegory which differs in its frame of reference from his own. Throughout the complex development of Hebraic-Christian exegesis such private invectives are common. The Christian exegetes attack their pagan counterparts, and then proceed to employ the rejected hermeneutic method.

At the same time, while rejection and resistance to allegory occur periodically within and between contending schools of thought, the method can survive attack largely because its principle of semantic inversion enables the allegorist to shift his ground freely whenever an opponent questions him. Since in the theological context of most serious ancient allegory there is scarcely room for a scientific theory of language, since, in short, language is here a means of revelation, there seems to have been no way for the allegorist to gain perspective on his own activity. By the second century A.D., as a treatise like Plutarch's *Of Isis and Osiris* will show, a multiplicity of Mediterranean religions had grown up, yielding an unrestrained exchange of figures between variant faiths, each one providing the materials for iconography within the framework of some other faith.

In spite of the intricacy of much exegesis the mode generally depends for its force upon the belief that words have magical power, a belief that is evident in the influential treatises of Pseudo-Dionysius, *On the Celestial Hierarchy* and *On the Divine Names*. Plotinus had already systematized the hierarchical aspect of the Platonic ideas, giving to each hypostasis of the One a particular magical quantum of effluence and influence. Within such frameworks allegory can play a double role. In its Neo-Platonic aspect it looks "upward" to a transcendental plane of purer Being, but at the same time it retains the primitivist drive of a language system in which every term has its own share of magical force. By the same token most allegorical fictions are romantic myths, in which the characters make full use of magical weapons, vehicles, settings, and quests. The history of allegory is, strictly speaking, not the history of rival theologies and philosophies. The logic of allegory is only remotely rationalistic. Instead, we observe a struggle of magic-thinking to survive within a climate of ever-increasing intellectual and semantic sophistication. This is the more curious in the light of the allegorist's frequent pretense of being logical and rational. The pretense covers the true situation, which is that allegories are strict in the manner of magic rituals, substituting mechanical for rational rigor.

Allegorical Syncretism. The creation and interpretation of allegorical texts seems to depend on an acceptance of syncretism, the kind of colloidal mixture of religious, philosophical, and cultural beliefs which particularly marks the Hellenistic Age, the second century A.D., and the High Renaissance, although in the Renaissance syncretism is strongly aesthetic in its combination of elements. Syncretism may be iconographically distinguished from synthesis, insofar as the former preserves the individual traits of the combining beliefs, whereas the latter would achieve a radical transformation of disparate cultural forces, until a single set among them came to dominate and control the assimilation of other sets as minor premises in the logic of the culture as a whole. Syncretism is the cult of diversity within a culture yearning for unified order. It is often to be associated with gnostic spirituality, since the experience of *gnosis* includes a transcendence of the multiplicity of faiths by entertaining all their claims on an equal footing. Thus Gnosticism finds its sources in Greek Orphism, Pythagoreanism, Mazdean dualism, Jewish apocalyptic, Egyptian mystery-religions, Hellenistic astrological cult, and various kinds of numerology, "along with the crass 'spirituality' of mediums, quacks, and religious adventurers" (Grant, *Roman Hellenism*, p. 74).

The early centuries of Christian expansion spanned a period of syncretism in the Mediterranean world, a fact not without its bearing on the development of

Christian exegesis. The Alexandrian School, most notably Clement and Origen, who anticipated the visions of the fourth-century fathers, Basil of Caesarea, Gregory Nazianzen, and Gregory of Nyssa, introduced key notions from Greek philosophy, which was given authority for them by the syncretism of Philo, who, although a Jew, stands at the head of this tradition. The broadly allegorical structure of Augustine's two cities, of God and Man, may owe something to his own syncretic background. In such a climate the religious convert may bring remnants of his former faith with him into the new faith. Syncretism has this great advantage for the allegorist: it gathers in, rather than expels; but at the same time it preserves the sense of diverse origins and intellectual styles.

A similar, if theologically less complicated syncretism surrounds the artist, poet, and scientist during the Renaissance. The "survival of the pagan gods" can occur then, as during the Middle Ages, because while their pagan attributes are assimilated by allegory to moral and mystical frameworks, all of which are guided by Christian principle, their identities as pagan gods are still preserved in ornamental forms within the work of art. This "neo-paganism," as we may call it, had arisen early in the West and its legacy remains alive even during the Middle Ages, although only when the Renaissance saw a fresh sense of freedom within the domain of vision and imagination could the cult of diversity be permitted to express itself in designs of universal harmony. There is thus no conflict in the fact that Spenser, in *The Faerie Queene*, bases an important episode and much of the detail of his Fifth Book on "Egyptian" lore, coming from Plutarch, *Of Isis and Osiris*, and Lucian, *De Syria dea*, while allegorically the poet ties these materials to the legend of Saint George of England, the Arthurian Legend, fairy lore, and so on, weaving the whole structure with fine traces of Hermetic philosophy, number symbolism, and the cosmology of Giordano Bruno. Such combinations *suspend* their elements in a sort of mosaic. On the surface such iconographies are richly textured and decorated.

Piety may be the chief source of syncretic abundance. The allegorist does not wish to lose any of the materials present to his mind. This is clear in the case of both Homeric and biblical allegory. A range of motives may contribute to such systematic "accommodation." Piety begins with the mystery of the word itself, spoken in fine verses or written down in magical alphabetic characters. Ancient allegory also displays a reverence for age, naturally enough, since men obeyed inherited social, political, and religious forms of authority. Finally, piety includes the widely held belief that poets, prophets, lawmakers, priests, and philosophers—wise men, in short—enjoyed their wisdom because they were divinely inspired. Inspiration in particular could account for the jumble of disparate pieces that, over time, found its way into a sacred canon. The inspired and mystical meaning was proved rather than disproved by the appearance of arbitrary inclusion. The more erotic the Song of Songs, the better its candidacy for allegorical interpretation as a myth of hierogamy between divine and human partners. Once the alien document is compressed into the overall vision, its message, assumed to be an inspired revelation, takes on a transcendental character, and allegory must follow.

To piety as the conservative force of syncretism may be added its debased form, superstition. A higher motive, which is harder to define, is the conciliatory and accommodating desire to permit a diverse world of many faces and characters. This motive comes into play when rival world views meet in conflict at their borders, when the opposite impulse would, as with iconoclasm, seek to destroy the rival iconography. Allegory here becomes a diplomatic medium of thought. Pseudo-Heraclitus, for example, tries to balance different interests in his *Homeric Problems* (first century A.D.). He claims that Homer's Apollo represents the sun, in a physical allegory of the origins of the plague in the *Iliad*, while his concern is with cosmogony in reading *Iliad* XVIII, where the Shield of Achilles becomes for him a vast cosmological symbol. Yet with these materialist readings he aligns others of a different sort, as when he moralizes Athena to mean wisdom, or Hermes to mean eloquence and reason. Finally, his overall syncretism stretches to include a quasi-historical allegory, by which the adultery of Ares and Aphrodite represents the mythic origin of metalworking, while the ejection of Hephaistos from heaven stands for the physical discovery that heat can be focussed by mirrors, to create fire. The immediate aim of these varied interpretations is the defense of Homer against his moralizing detractors, but beyond this, and perhaps more deeply felt, is the exegete's desire to use Homer as the encyclopedic container for a wide and disparate variety of intellectual disciplines. Philosophy ceases to be the framework for Homer; Homer becomes the framework for philosophy. Homer has attained the canonical status of a sacred literary body.

The bolder allegorical syncretisms arise when the elements to be contained by the allegory are historically accidental inclusions within an inherited literary corpus. The problem is clearest with the Old Testament. Origen, who believes in the mysterious revelations of Scripture, is aware how absurd it is to believe, literally, that God planted a garden like a farmer, or that He walked about in the garden. With the New Testament Origen recognized the patently implausible character of the story that the Devil could show the kingdoms of the earth from a single mountain top. "And the careful reader will detect thousands of other passages in the gospels like this, which will convince him that events which did not take place at all are woven into the records of what literally did happen" (*De principiis* IV.3.1). The allegorist therefore proposes to supplant the literal inconsistency by a spiritual equivalent possessed of inner truth, precisely, in short, what had been veiled by the inconsistent literal surface. Believing that "the skillful plan of [God] the providential ruler is not so clear in things on earth as it is in regard to the sun and moon and stars," Origen asserts the revelatory function of language when dealing with sacred literature.

Origen is influenced by Philo Judaeus, through the intermediary Clement of Alexandria, and this Alexandrian tradition, which would show parallels in the development of Hellenistic allegory, suggests that major allegory requires a belief in miracles and epiphenomena, at least on a verbal level. Origen notes that it is "the most wonderful thing" that spiritual truths could be veiled under "stories of wars and conquerors and the conquered," and he notes that "the Word of God has arranged for certain stumbling-blocks, as it were, and hindrances and impossibilities to be inserted in the midst of the law and the history." Such barriers are providential—the more strange they seem, the more they goad the reader to "learn from the Scriptures." Like many allegorists, Origen can suddenly undercut his own appearance of caprice. He holds that the historically true passages are "far more numerous than those which are composed with purely spiritual meanings." Yet whenever a historical scandal appears, he can, if he chooses, fall back on a spiritual interpretation. For this reason his method has appeared to one of his close students "unchartably subjective. . . . Whatever Origen's theory of allegory may have been, it is quite inaccurate to call his application of its systematic" (Hanson, p. 245). Now, if allegory is expected to have what Hanson calls "rules," it seems clear that Origen and all other major allegorists are "unchartably subjective." But then, so is syncretism in general, and for that reason, in describing his own work, Dante used his term "polysemous," or ambiguous.

Yet another approach will demand both more and less from allegorical syncretism and will perhaps justify its endless prolixity. This approach is to be found in the Origenist and Philonic belief in the mystery of the Word. Prophecy assumes that the prophet not only sees the vision of the truth, but can "speak out" for this vision, sharing in the divine Logos. Philo may allegorize any portion of the Old Testament, any single image or word, any story, any disparity or contra-

dictory episode. But he does not do this in a spirit of negative or defensive reaction, but rather as the expression of an intellectual or speculative freedom. This mode employs philosophic methods, but Philo is perhaps less a philosopher than a prophet of philosophy. Thus he may go beyond the Platonic use of the Ideas as the forms, or paradigms, of things in the universe, and can hold that the Logos is everywhere immanent in the cosmos—"the totality of the powers of God existing within the cosmos itself" (Wolfson, *Philo*, p. 327). This Logos, unlike the Stoics' material logos, is immaterial, and on that basis can lead to allegories judged "unchartably subjective" from the perspective of natural and human history. Phrased differently, the Philonic use of an immanent logos directs hermeneutic towards mystery, which is buried within the Word, whereas the Stoic logos directs it away from mystery towards reason. Yet Philo and the allegorical tradition stemming from him may not be identified with the *via negativa* of the mystics, since rather than draw his cosmological interpretations into such a spiritualism of the Logos that they reach evanescence, in a cloud of unknowing, he draws them toward an infinitely ramified, but consistently word-centered universe of discourse. What saves his allegory from irrationality is its recognition that "rationality, when conceived as complete, as excluding all arbitrariness, becomes itself a kind of irrationality" (Lovejoy, *Great Chain of Being*, p. 331). Philo is continuously interested in the verbal, linguistic aspect of the Word. He shares the almost immemorial use of exegetical etymologizing, which is finally canonized in the encyclopedic *Etymologiae* of Saint Isidore. If we broaden the Philonic approach to include images and figures of speech as well as the literal or referential materials of language, we may speak of the "logology" of poets and artists as well as of theologians and philosophers (Burke, *Rhetoric of Religion*).

The underlying wisdom of the Philonic strain of allegory is its stress on the freedom of the interpreting mind, on what a seventeenth-century divine called "the liberty of prophesying." Its vice is ingenuity, but its virtue is the corresponding one of a compulsion to investigate and comment upon the Word and its progeny, words. The noblest document composed with such allegory in mind is the Fourth Gospel. Common to all such Logos-centered allegories is the belief that words contain wisdom, and the form in which we inherit words from the past is itself not without reason, if we can only discover the inner web of motives that led to the slow formation of that legacy. It is often said that allegory, outside the specifically historical mode known as typology, is antihistorical. When morality and ethics are the reference-point, this is true enough.

But because words are an essential mechanism of human thought, their recorded forms of combination and formation are primary resources of the historian, and the allegorist's accommodative impulse includes a desire to preserve these resources, rather than see them destroyed by advances or regressions of a cultural set. When the ancient gloss identifies Zeus as "life," because his name coincides with the Greek word for life, an element of history enters the interpretation through what may be a false etymology. Such equations hold that the universe is coherent when read as a logos.

Allegory and the Cosmos. The history of allegory is tuned to the history of cosmological speculation, so much so that allegory might be defined as figurative cosmology. Each such fiction presents the image of a universe (and this is true even of short works), or implies that its details fit into a cosmic picture. Yet this imagery is not identical with the scientist's use of theoretical models. The allegorist does not prove and disprove hypotheses which are then dropped if they fail to hold up as fact. Allegory does not move toward the certainty of fact; it moves toward tenacity of belief. Analogy serves the allegorist, as it serves the cosmologist, but here the test of the figurative *schema* is not its yield of experiment or observation, but its fertility in leading to still further figuration. The allegorist treats his universe as if its being were literal, as if it were a book. Thus there arises the tradition of "book as symbol," in which Homer and the Bible hold the first place. Such works are simply large enough to contain a world of words. In them the cult of the One gives way to a cult of the Universe.

As distinct from the Hellenic, a somewhat less physical notion of cosmos governs the Hebraic-Christian tradition. Here, from the encyclopedic resources of the Old Testament come theories of the Law as the form of the universe. Philo found the Law "complete and true and good," and in this *total* system "anything that seemed to be lacking in it was really hidden behind the literalness of the words and it was the task of the student to search it out" (Wolfson, *Church Fathers*, p. 25). Not necessarily the truth or the goodness of the Torah led to its exegetical treatment, but rather its assumed completeness. For Christians this unity carried over into the fulfillment of Old Testament prophecy by events recounted in the New. The structure of the Bible as it finally evolved into the canonical Books, bounded by Genesis and the Apocalypse, implies the cosmic analogy on which its Logos is ordered.

Syncretism in ancient Mediterranean religious life raised the question of universal order, while the influence of Alexander also led in this direction. The monolithic pretensions of Augustan Rome may likewise have influenced the strongly allegorical cast of Vergi-

lian and Ovidian poetry, so different from Homer. But it was not until the Middle Ages that the drive toward universal containment and encirclement led to the complete dominance of allegorical methods. From the eleventh century onwards influences from Pseudo-Dionysius, Plato, and Plotinus give exegetes a secure sense of philosophic direction. The *Timaeus* and the *Celestial Hierarchy* provide terms and images. But in all areas of life this period shows universalist pretensions, which Maurice de Wulf characterized simply as "a tendency toward unity." Political dreams of a universal brotherhood, intellectual dreams of a totally organized body of knowledge, theological dreams of a total theological *summa*—these were the natural background for allegorical literature. Bernard of Clairvaux finds infinite detail in a closed world, by imagining four infinitely reflexive "mirrors" of knowledge—the natural, intellectual, moral, and historical. Dante's *Commedia*, whose form and setting rival the universe, finds a parallel in his *De monarchia*, a theory of political unification. By symmetry the actual physical universe is converted into a symbol, and we can speak of a "symbolic mentality" which denied the more immediate puzzles presented by the senses. The flight from the limited toward the infinity of the Divine Being kept its balance only, if at all, by asserting that man's world was closed and finite. Ockham's principle of parsimony was invented, it seems, to stem this iconographic tide, since scholastic thought, at first rationalizing, ends by absorbing the medieval compulsion to turn relations into icons.

In a sense allegory thrives even more abundantly during the Renaissance, because the new cosmology does not at once drive out the old, so that visionary and scientific cosmologies coexist, their very difference enriching the imagery of poets and theologians. The main development of the mode is the gradual rejection of the theory of "levels" of meaning. Most allegorists have in fact used two levels, whatever they may have claimed to do. They take a sentence and give it a double meaning. At its simplest this process will be seen in the parables of Christ. Clement of Alexandria, however, distinguished four levels on which he could read a sacred text, a literal level and three subsidiary symbolic stages, the moral, physical, and theological. Origen held that as man is made of body, soul, and spirit, so interpretation must yield three levels of meaning, the literal, moral, and spiritual. Jerome invoked the literal, tropological, and mystical. Augustine held that all readings of Scripture, however structured, should express charity, yet he too could speak of a hierarchy of levels, for instance, historical, aetiological, analogical, and allegorical (*De utilitate credendi*, 3.5). What became the classical formulation of Christian method, the fourfold theory, appeared in Saint John Cassian, who set forth a system of historical (literal), tropological (moral), allegorical, and anagogical. This theory is encapsulated in the mnemonic distich, first cited in 1330, by Augustin de Dacie:

> *Littera gesta docet, quid credas allegoria,*
> *Moralia quid agas, quo tendas anagogica.*

The effect of such planar theories of reading is that allegory becomes more mechanical in theory than it can or need ever be in practice.

What was once available only to the instructed interpreter is now the common property of the experiencing subject. It is an error, however, to believe that romantic "symbolism" destroys allegory, although it loosens and reorders the "levels" on which texts are made and read. Shelley's *Prometheus Unbound* is as much an allegory as the *Psychomachia* of Prudentius (348–?410). Where the mode radically declines in force is not as a creative method, but in the interpretive divisions of theology, where the new criticism of the Bible, with its scientific research into textual evolution, raises questions about the literary level which are so searching that the dependent symbolic levels pale in theological importance.

Allegory and Time. "Rationality has nothing to do with dates." Thus Lovejoy epitomized the static and "absolutely rigid" form of the Great Chain of Being as it had set up the framework of traditional allegory. The stasis of hierarchy is mirrored in the markedly static character of most allegorical fictions, be they stories, dramas, lyrics, or whatever. Allegorical narrative yields a fixated image of change, in which time is synchronic, never diachronic. Augustine imagines human destiny in the shape of a city, following the Book of Revelation. Joachim of Floris diagrams history as an allegorical tree with stems and branches. Time becomes a hypostatized form of becoming.

Two aspects of the mode are thus historically problematic. (1) The Hebraic-Christian belief in prophecy asserts that historical figures may prefigure other historical figures, Joshua becoming the "type" of Jesus. Scholars have held that the historicity of the *figurae* radically differentiates them from allegorical emblems, such as the anchor of faith. Yet the typological figure is under constant pressure to revert to a timeless symbol, since typology in fact is collapsing the diachronic time-span and stopping the fluent openness of time by envisioning miraculous *kairoi*, or prophetic moments when time "stands still." (2) Modern science attacks the fixation of allegory in yet another quarter, and here perhaps there exists a possibility of a radical change in the allegorical method. During and after the Renaissance new methods arise for the analysis and exploration of the *origins* of things, along with their progressive development away from those origins. The text of the Bible is one such object of study, but the physical universe and the historical world of men are more crucial. In the Monads of Bruno and Leibniz the Great Chain of Being is "temporalized," as the closed world of Ptolemy, so useful to the poet's need for a cosmos, gives way to an infinite universe.

Even more upsetting is the discovery of anthropological development. With the Renaissance a somewhat aesthetic cult of Euhemerus arises, finding human origins for the gods, who are regarded as divinized heroes. Such beliefs lead, along with new historical and archeological knowledge, to new theories of human evolution, beginning with primitive forms and advancing to more complex societies. After Vico it is no longer possible for mythology or iconography to divorce itself from temporal change. First the *philosophes* of the Enlightenment debunk the allegorizing of the gods and daemons, then the ground shifts under all forms of imagination, so that developmental myths take over from the former static world view. The "new allegorism" tends to be more monolithic than the old, permitting a single theory of change, whatever it may be, to explain various possible modes of change.

Allegory and Decorum. While a large view may portend the general undermining of allegory in the modern period, the close-up analysis of allegory makes this appear an unlikely development. Allegories are, as a symbolic mode, composed of ornaments—not, strictly speaking, metaphors. Thus, the Greek term for the larger outlines of a major allegory would be *kosmos*, while in classical Greek the same term does double duty for the rhetorician's "ornament." The same double usage appears in Latin *decus*, which grows into the English terms "decoration" and "decorum." Allegory expresses the interplay of little and great worlds, which are ornamentally reflecting surfaces of microcosm and macrocosm.

There is no reason to suppose that men will cease to decorate themselves or fail to recognize decorum. But modes of ornament continuously change. Conceivably the present world, with its increased standardization of artifacts and its diminishing barriers to travel, will see the speeding-up of allegorical processes. Whether revolutions undermine or reorder cosmologies has become the allegorist's chief problem. Allegory can no longer be what for centuries it had tried to be, the image of permanence in a world of flux. Franz Kafka is perhaps the greatest allegorical writer of modern times, and his work revels in cloudy interactions between wierdly undefined characters. Yet Kafka looks at this obscure scene with microscopic delicacy. He bases his fictions largely upon "the Law," on which, **47** following the ancient Jewish tradition, he meditates and builds a vision of man's destiny as a creature caught up in a closed, imprisoning world.

Generally speaking, modern allegory shows signs of breaking down many of the normal divisions between things, either by use of dream-mechanisms or by other surrealistic devices. The mode is creatively perhaps most alive in science-fiction, but it permeates the art of advertising, wherever decoration and decorum are the primary commercial interests. Philosophically and theologically there is less place for allegory than in earlier centuries, but one can discern traces of it in the subjectivism of the phenomenologist's concept of transcendence, and in the actual use of fiction by existentialist authors (for example, the novels of Camus, or earlier, the quasi-fictional treatises of Kierkegaard). As in previous times, the allegorist can today use many different media, including music (with "programs" and leitmotifs) and the visual arts (with emblems and icons).

BIBLIOGRAPHY

General discussions: Kenneth Burke, *The Rhetoric of Religion* (Boston, 1961); Jean Daniélou, *Sacramentum futuri: études sur les origines de la typologie biblique* (Paris, 1950); Angus Fletcher, *Allegory: The Theory of a Symbolic Mode* (Ithaca, 1964); Northrop Frye, "Allegory," *Dictionary of Poetry and Poetics* (Princeton, 1967); R. P. C. Hanson, *Allegory and Event: A Study of the Sources and Significance of Origen's Interpretation of Scripture* (London, 1959); Roger Hinks, *Myth and Allegory in Ancient Art* (London, 1939); Henri de Lubac, *Exégèse médiévale: les quatre sens de l'écriture*, Parts I and II (Paris, 1959–64); Erwin Panofsky, *Studies in Iconology: Humanistic Themes in the Art of the Renaissance* (New York, 1939); Jean Pépin, *Mythe et allégorie: les origines grecques et les contestations judéo-chrétiennes* (Paris, 1958); Rosemond Tuve, *Allegorical Imagery* (Princeton, 1968); H. A. Wolfson, *The Philosophy of the Church Fathers*, Vol. I: *Faith, Trinity, Incarnation* (Cambridge, Mass., 1956); idem, *Philo: Foundations of Religious Philosophy in Judaism, Christianity, and Islam*, 2 vols. (Cambridge, Mass., 1947).

More specialized treatments: Erich Auerbach, "Figura," *Scenes from the Drama of European Literature: Six Essays* (New York, 1959); Edgar de Bruyne, *Études d'esthétique médiévale* (Bruges, 1946); Rudolf Bultmann et al., *Kerygma and Myth: A Theological Debate* (New York, 1961), translated from the German, *Kerygma und Mythos*, Vol. I; Manfred Bukofzer, "Allegory in Baroque Music," *Journal of the Warburg and Courtauld Institutes*, 3 (1939–40); M. L. Colish, *The Mirror of Language: A Study in the Medieval Theory of Knowledge* (New Haven, 1968); C. H. Dodd, *The Interpretation of the Fourth Gospel* (Cambridge, 1953); E. R. Dodds, *Pagan and Christian in an Age of Anxiety: Some Aspects of Religious Experience from Marcus Aurelius to Constantine* (Cambridge, 1968); Austin Farrer, *A Rebirth of Images: the Making of St. John's Apocalypse* (London,

1949); Rosemary Freeman, *English Emblem Books* (London, 1948); F. C. Grant, *Roman Hellenism and the New Testament* (New York, 1962); Adolf Katzellenbogen, *Allegories of the Virtues and Vices in Mediaeval Art* (London, 1939); G. B. Ladner, *The Idea of Reform: Its Impact on Christian Thought and Action in the Age of the Fathers* (Cambridge, Mass., 1959); A. O. Lovejoy, *The Great Chain of Being: a Study of the History of an Idea* (Cambridge, Mass., 1936); Frank Manuel, *The Eighteenth Century Confronts the Gods* (Cambridge, Mass., 1959); René Roques, *L'Univers dionysien: Structure hiérarchique du monde selon le Pseudo-Denys* (Paris, 1954); Jean Seznec, *The Survival of the Pagan Gods: the Mythological Tradition and its Place in Renaissance Humanism and Art* (New York, 1953); C. S. Singleton, "Allegory," *Essays on Dante*, ed. Mark Musa (Bloomington, 1964); Leo Spitzer, *Classical and Christian Ideas of World Harmony* (Baltimore, 1963); Maurice de Wulf, *Philosophy and Civilization in the Middle Ages* (Princeton, 1913); Edgar Wind, *Pagan Mysteries in the Renaissance* (London, 1958).

On literary conventions: Harry Berger, Jr., *The Allegorical Temper* (New York, 1957); Ernst Curtius, *European Literature in the Latin Middle Ages*, trans. W. Trask (New York, 1953); Edmond Faral, *Les Arts poétiques du XII et du XIII siècle* (Paris, 1924); Edwin Honig, *Dark Conceit: the Making of Allegory* (Evanston, 1959); C. S. Lewis, *The Allegory of Love* (Oxford, 1936); E. D. Leyburn, *Satiric Allegory: the Mirror of Man* (New Haven, 1956); Michael Murrin, *The Veil of Allegory* (Chicago, 1969).

A crucial, but very recent, publication is D. C. Allen, *Mysteriously Meant: The Rediscovery of Pagan Symbolism and Allegorical Interpretation in the Renaissance* (Baltimore, 1970).

ANGUS FLETCHER

[See also Ambiguity; **Analogy;** Chain of Being; Hermeticism; **Iconography; Prophecy;** Symbol.]

AMBIGUITY AS AESTHETIC PRINCIPLE

IN WESTERN cultural history *ambiguity* has been a pejorative term until the twentieth century. This bias against the presence of two or more meanings in any statement reflects the general bias of the civilization which traditionally from Classical Greek times has placed its faith in reason and an orderly universe—a civilization which, by extension, has operated on a tacit belief in the reliability of the reasoning process and its correspondence with external reality. Consequently men for centuries did not question the relationship between words and things, and were able to assume that no responsible statement could contradict any other, that if apparent contradictions emerged in speaking, clarity and coherence, hence truth, could be achieved by amplification. Thus the Greek word for universe (κόσμος) carried both a scientific and an aesthetic meaning. Ambiguity in this cultural context represented therefore a failure at truth, a failure in communication attributable either to excessive brevity, deliberate obscurity of phrasing, or to ineptitude.

Nevertheless, in spite of this general prejudice against confusing or misleading statements, certain kinds of ambiguous utterances were acceptable to the ancient Greeks. The earliest examples of these ambiguities are sub-literary and are cast in forms that still reflect the primitive faith in a world that contains precise answers to all questions. Oracular utterances emanating from holy places presupposed the accuracy of the priestess's veiled message, since it was the voice of God that spoke through her. Because the passive role of medium did not include comprehension, elucidation for the priestess as well as the petitioner came with the passage of time. With arcane formulae and recipes the speaker assumed an active role—curses, spells, charms, and ritual signs and dances being early examples of human attempts to control external events through empirical means. The body of knowledge behind these practical skills was invariably recorded in symbolic language, but the obscurity of this form of technical jargon could have been ambiguous only to the non-initiates of occult fraternities.

Closer to art in our sense of the word are riddles which are self-annihilating word games, a form of social entertainment that also presupposes the existence of precise answers to questions, but which require the agency of interlocutor and respondee to complete the process: riddles cease to exist when the meaning is discovered. The contrivance of an endpoint of only one possible answer or meaning differentiates riddles from enigmas, myths, and genuine works of art for which there are no determinable endpoints of contemplation. Ambiguity as an aesthetic principle emerged therefore when artists deliberately contrived complex structures that generated a plurality of meanings.

In Greek literature it was the mantic Pindar who modified the oracular tradition for artistic purposes. In the *Hymn to Zeus* (only fragments of which have survived) God announces that no beauty is complete without praise. By inference, therefore, the poet's status was holy and his function was to celebrate. But what Pindar was celebrating in his hymns of victory for athletes, and why the odes are apparently lacking in unity constitute an enigma. While there is no mystery as to to whom the ἐπινίκια were addressed, there is ambiguity as to the true subject of the poems. Moreover the praises characteristically open brilliantly, as all readers have remarked, but trail off and merely stop, a criticism that may not be relevant to works meant to be orchestrated and choreographed. Nevertheless the structural peculiarities may point to another level of meaning if the poems are accepted as Pindar's records of theophanies that occurred at religious games, an institution that was more ancient than Homer and the Trojan War. Traditionally, the arena in which the contest took place was sacred ground, the athletic event an *agon*, and the victory a *kairos* that transformed the contestant into a hero, a term originally applied only to the dead, but progressively applied to the living.

This cultural change created a third, ambiguous middle zone between the natural and supernatural worlds, in metaphysical terms a new ontological category to which the living aspired. Through excellence which led to transcendence, the presence of the gods could be summoned to this juncture between two worlds. Victory conferred therefore a multivalent status upon the hero, the attainment of a more complete state of being poised between time and eternity. But the duration of this achievement was also ambiguous, since on the level of actuality the victory won by the individual could be lost at the next festival. It is likely, therefore, that the poet's solution to this cultural paradox was the juxtaposition of his favorite images in the context of an amorphous structure: gold representing the permanence of the state of pure being; light representing the incandescent moment of victory when the hero became a presence, its occurrence a metaphor for the process of heroization, and its visible behavior mysterious and of short duration. The waning structure of the Pindarics may allude therefore to metaphysical problems that had no solutions, problems that in a prelogical age could be expressed only in mythopoeic terms.

The traditional practice of classifying according to the place of the festival might have been consonant with Pindar's intention, for if the poems were records of theophanies, where they occurred was more important than other considerations. The *Olympia I*, in Richmond Lattimore's translation, begins:

Best of all things is water; but gold, like a gleaming fire
by night, outshines all pride of wealth beside.
But, my heart, would you chant the glory of games,
look never beyond the sun
by day for any star shining brighter through the deserted
   air,
nor any contest than Olympia greater to sing.
It is thence that the song winds strands
in the hearts of the skilled to celebrate
the son of Kronos. They come their ways
to the magnificent board of Hieron. . . .

A prose reading structured according to hierarchy might be as follows:

Water is the best of all things if usefulness is the criterion, but it is too humble and ordinary to attract attention. Gold, on the other hand, not only has the appearance of excellence but is in fact more valuable than other metals. But better than either of these is my ode composed at Olympia, sacred to Zeus, and occasioned by the victory of Syracusan Hieron. . . .

That this univocal lucidity was achieved by limiting meanings either by amplification or its opposites, compression or suppression, reveals something of the aims and techniques of Pindar. A multivalenced reading might superimpose upon the prose version the following:

Water is the best of all things because it supports life which is the best of all things. But what is best in the world of nature is not best in the metaphysical realm, since the gold of pure being outshines the earthly fame that adheres to the possessors of great wealth. But I am a poet, and poetry is of this world. Therefore in the search for subjects I look no further than the visible world, but choose excellence. The sun has no rivals for brilliance by day, Olympia—sacred to the son of Kronos—none for antiquity and dignity. . . .

Pindar has contrived different levels of reality with different criteria of excellence through the use of gnomic opening, riddle, paradox, symbol, myth, and a multiplicity of meanings through overlapping categories. Moreover, suppressed information that must be inferred is not only technique but meaning in poems that both celebrate and are theophanies. Olympia is compared to the sun that makes invisible lesser stars. That Pythia, Isthmia, and Nemea are not mentioned may be more than tact. Also, the term "Son of Kronos" is not only traditional formula, but a way of evoking both gods for the purpose of opposing Time with Permanence if the self-manifestation of Zeus is the true subject of the poem. Standing, as it were, historically between Mycenae and Athens, and artistically between temple and hippodrome, the Theban Pindar in life was awarded the right to an equal share of first-fruit offerings by the Pythian priestess of Delphi, and after death, heroization, his ghost being invited annually to dine with Apollo (Gilbert Norwood, *Pindar* [1945]). But religious games, Thebes, and Pindar were all anachronisms in the light of world history, for the political reality of the expansion of the Persian Empire and the need for a Greek response gave the leadership of that civilization to Athens.

The rapidity of change that accounts for the ultimate displacement of the arts in Athens also explains the ascendance of drama over lyric in the early stages of this process. For, according to John H. Finley, Jr., Aeschylus was "the inventor of the idea of meaningful

time" (*Pindar and Aeschylus* [1955]). But the optimistic view of history presented in Aeschylus' *Oresteia* gave way to the inconclusive debate in Sophocles' *Antigone,* and to the doubts raised as to the ambiguous benefits of language in Euripides' *Hippolytus,* for the cultural relativity introduced by the Sophists had challenged not only the traditional content of the arts, but the connection between words and things, as well. Thus on the one hand Aristophanes complained that "They have dethroned Zeus, and Vortex is King" (Georgio di Santillana, *The Origins of Scientific Thought* [1961]). On the other hand, the new status of language as reasoning instrument made words the domain of creators of systems: the scientists, philosophers, and historians in whom the tacit faith of the dramatists was continued. Their assertion of the inevitability of consequences from acts knowingly or unwittingly committed was abstracted as the uniformity of nature's laws which could be discovered by following the laws of logic. For the rationalists, therefore, ambiguity was neither thing nor principle, but a phase in the reasoning process between perception and knowledge. But the history of this movement was also one of degeneration, since "Men seemed to be capable of sacrificing the Law of Contradiction for the sake of comfort" (George Boas, *Rationalism in Greek Philosophy* [1961]).

The history of rationalism parallels the story of introspection and the discovery of the self. The reduction of the wealth of Homeric terms for what subsequently were the simplified categories of "body" and "soul" reveals the metamorphosis of the conception of man from aggregate to unit, a change confirmed in art by the abandonment of the geometric style of the late archaic period (Bruno Snell, *The Discovery of the Mind: The Greek Origins of European Thought* [1953]). This unification through simplification produced at the same time a common denominator that could be projected either as causal nexus or as focus of interest for artistic purposes. The failure of Greek politics thus gave a new direction to the arts in the Greco-Roman period (Moses Hadas, *Hellenistic Culture: Fusion and Diffusion* [1959]). The emergence of the spiritual landscape of the pastoral lyric asserted the validity of the private and subjective world; the improbable world of the romances proclaimed at the same time the unpredictability of Fortune and a faith in an incomprehensible but benign Providence; and the composition of spiritual biographies called aretologies that transformed moral teachers into cult figures—all point to the kind of consolation men sought.

Nevertheless, after Aristotle, literary works addressed to the reason as well as to the sentiments were subject to more stringent standards of consistency, hence the criticism of Vergil's *Aeneid* that persists to this day. Apparently in the cultural climate of his time, even the political success of Augustan Rome did not prevent the poet from longing for the other world, and this moral ambivalence produced an artistic duplicity in an epic that attempted to satisfy by simple juxtaposition the rival claims of both worlds. The two halves of the epic are thus disjunctive, the first modeled upon the horizontal plan of the *Odyssey*, the second upon the vertical transcendence of the *Iliad*, with no attempt to relate them. At mid-point between the two halves Vergil placed the gates from the underworld (VI, 888–98; *Loeb Library*, I, 571):

And when Anchises had led his son over every scene, and fired his soul with love of fame that was to be, he tells him then of the wars he must thereafter wage, and instructs him of the Laurentine peoples and the city of Latinus and how he is to flee or face each toil.

Two gates of Sleep there are, whereof the one is said to be of horn, and thereby an easy outlet is given to true shades; the other gleaming with the sheen of polished ivory, but false are the dreams sent by the spirits to the world above. There then with these words Anchises attends both his son and the Sibyl, and dismisses them by the ivory gate.

Because this episode is pivotal, its interpretation will determine the meaning of the whole work. The easiest solution is to conjecture a mistake on the part of the author. The principle of *durior lectio*, on the other hand, requires a reading of the text as it stands. Clearly Aeneas and the Sibyl have made their exit from the wrong gate if the world of political Rome is not to be dismissed as a vain dream; alternatively if the reality of Rome is asserted, Aeneas himself is a false dream. Thus the Law of Contradiction is evoked, and as the two halves of the epic seem mutually exclusive, centuries of readers have in effect discarded the last six books. It is likely, however, that the poet was in fact asserting both worlds but could find no satisfactory solution to his problem. The characterization of his eponymous hero as "pious" was Vergil's way of making him both historical founder and presiding genius of city and empire. Whereas the fusion of two roles in one character succeeded, the work as a whole did not, and the poet's instruction in his will that the epic be destroyed may be interpreted as the recognition of his failure to reconcile the ideas of history and eternity, a conjecture made more probable by the fact that Vergil died in Greece while revising the *Aeneid*. The precise destination of Vergil's cultural pilgrimage is unknown, but it was at Alexandria, through Philo's multileveled but unified interpretation of sacred history, that a solution was found. Philo's elaborate ramifications of the allegorical method are, therefore, the first critical treatises on one, perhaps the most rational, type of ambiguity.

Among the backgrounds to the solution of this twofold problem was typology, a chronological projection of allegory that was one of the several innovations of the Old Testament Prophets. Responding to the immediate political needs of a threatened Judea, their messianic message fused policy with prophecy by historical analogy. The recurrent cycle of slavery and deliverance encouraged faith in a redeemer; therefore some of these leaders saw their lives as both fact and symbol: they were "types" of Moses and Messiah, intermediary figures that recapitulated past events while prophetically living the future. And by generalizing and extending in both directions it was possible to join together the end of history with its beginning, erasing the distinction between prophecy and apocalypse; thus for Isaiah, the Messiah that he prophesied was to be another Adam in another Paradise:

And there shall come forth a rod out of the stem of Jesse. . . . And righteousness shall be the girdle of his loins, and faithfulness the girdle of his reins. The wolf also shall dwell with the lamb, and the leopard shall lie down with the kid. . . . And the lion shall eat straw like the ox (Isaiah 11:1, 5–7).

Isaiah's inclusion of a genealogy was an expression of faith in the continuity of history, even as his projection of a Messiah documented the need for a cult figure (as alternative to relapse into idolatry) to focus the aspirations of a people in troubled times. Centuries later the selection of Jesus as the announced Second Adam gave to his followers a fixed point for their interpretation of history, and Moses was then reduced to a "type" who prefigured the Christ in whom the Law and the Prophetic promises were fulfilled. Allegory became therefore an indispensable tool for this new religion with evangelical and universalist aims.

The Prophetic interpretation of political events constituted in effect the invention of world history. And because history was the revealed will of God, approved records of the past were subsequently organized into a canon and elevated to the status of Scripture. The transcendence implied by this new category of writing produced therefore works in Greco-Roman times that took on the character of vulgate romances with apocryphal additions. The linear projection of history was now abandoned in favor of a single character who anachronistically embodied the past and future experience of the people. But world history could also be projected in this fashion, as in the case of the gigantic statue of Nebuchadnezzar's dream, the different materials of which the figure was made representing the chronology of kingdoms, the last or fifth monarchy being the millenium. The author of the Book of Daniel (a figure unrecorded elsewhere before the second century) retold therefore the history of the Jews, composing a "myth" of the Old Testament as nucleus to a story intended to encourage the people persecuted under the Seleucid King, Antiochus Epiphanes. Although he set his story in Babylonia and Persia, in the stratified characterization of Daniel the reader recognizes Joseph and Solomon, and in the apocryphal additions the ritualistic bias of the Haggidic tradition. In short, the character of Daniel is an "historical exemplum," and the technique of deliberate anachronism allowed the author to shift from Hebrew to late Aramaic in mid-sentence, a fact that could not be passed unobserved by his first readers. Seen in this light, the Book of Daniel served the same aretalogical purpose as the Gospels, the author's open-ended scheme consistent with a religion historically predicated on the metaphysical principle of becoming. But unlike the Gospels, Daniel records the Jewish retreat from universalism, a fact that also explains their rejection of Philo as biblical exegete. Contrary to his intentions, therefore, Philo became the ancestor to the medieval Christian philosophers (Harry Austryn Wolfson, *Philo*, 2 vols. [1962]).

The allegorization that unified the Old and New Testaments for the Christians also transformed their Bible into a universal history; therefore the word allegory acquired a new meaning. For the Greek rationalists, allegory referred merely to a figurative use of language—in short, a fiction. But for the Christians symbols were nothing less than visible signs of the Truth they were instructed to propagate universally. In the resulting conflicts the production of apologies in response to attacks progressively clarified doctrine and assumptions (Claude Tresmontant, *La Métaphysique du christianisme et la naissance de la philosophie chrétienne* [1961]) that later received systematic treatment (Étienne Gilson, *La Philosophie au Moyen Age* [1952]).

But it was on the level of sentiment that the appeal of Christianity lay, since the pessimism inherent in the Greek cyclical notion of history, and its counterpart for the individual, endless reincarnation in an unchanging world governed by eternal laws—could not compete against a religion that recognized the individual soul and offered a personal redeemer, a compassionate God, and a progressive, meaningful world history. The conversion of Constantine that automatically made Christianity the official religion of the empire, and the expansion of the Church's boundaries as other forms of rule failed marked the extent and degree of this cultural revolution. According to Erwin Panofsky, (*Gothic Architecture and Scholasticism* [1951], pp. 3, 4):

To the Carolingian revival of the arts there corresponds, in philosophy, the phenomenon of John the Scot, equally magnificent, equally unexpected. . . . About a hundred years of fermentation in both fields were followed, in art,

by a variety and contrariety of Romanesque . . . and, in theology and philosophy, by a similar multiplicity of divergent currents, from uncompromising fideism and ruthless rationalism to the proto-humanism of . . . the school of Chartres.

The allegory, analogy, and symbolism that characterized medieval thought was the very foundation of the Gothic church, beginning with the cruciform groundplan and the general orientation of the structure. The common supposition that everything visible was a symbol led William Durandus, the thirteenth-century Bishop of Mende, to compile and invent in his *Rationale divinorum officiorum* layer upon layer of meaning to every detail of church, ornaments, rites, and ceremonies. Thus the foundation of the church represented Faith; the roof Charity, because it covered a multitude of sins; the door, Obedience—"If thou wilt enter into life, keep the Commandments" (Matthew 19:17). Moreover, the sacristy symbolized the womb of the Virgin Mary where Christ put on his humanity, since that was where the priests, his representatives on earth, put on their robes.

Because the main entrance to the church, the west door, faced the material world from which the laity came to worship, church facades became visual synopses of theology, and in some instances the anonymous artists found ways to represent doctrinal ambiguities. Among the statues and the high relief carvings that make up the facade of the Cathedral of Notre Dame in Paris is a standing niche figure of the Virgin Mary, heavy with Child. What distinguishes this work from others that serve a similar architectural function (Adolf Katzenellenbogen, *The Sculptural Programs of Chartres Cathedral: Christ-Mary-Ecclesia* [1959]) is the series of choices the artist made. Like his contemporaries, in his wish to recall an event in Time and to evoke its Eternal meaning he engaged in deliberate anachronism, for his Virgin is not yet the Mother of Jesus; nevertheless she is already crowned the Queen of Heaven. But beyond these conventional details is the more significant combination of the Virgin's enigmatic smile and the gesture of her hands, arrested in mid-motion. The viewer is uncertain whether she (*Figlia del tuo Figlio*) is blessing the Fruit of her Womb or whether she is praying to the Eternal God. The ambiguity in the intent of her gesture reflected that of her status, for on the one hand the doctrine of Christ's humanity allowed one to believe that a dutiful Son would be obedient to the wishes of his Mother. On the other, it was also held that the Incarnation was the greatest indignity suffered by God—in which case the status of the Virgin was merely that of the Chosen Vessel which gave her a place of honor but not necessarily any authority in heaven. Consequently both rank and function of Queen of Heaven and Mediatrix of Grace, titles for which no authority existed, were doubtful.

On the practical level the wish of the Church on Earth to be in accord with the one in Heaven raised questions touching upon the validity of unauthorized modes of worship. It is probable that the influence of Saint Bernard of Clairvaux, the Marian Doctor, encouraged the church's toleration of this form of idolatry as counter-measure against the growing popularity of the secular cult of the Lady, no longer obscurely deified in *trobar clus*, but openly in the vernacular romances (Maurice Valency, *In Praise of Love* [1958]). The ambiguities that surround the statue in question stem from the authoritative statement of doctrine, the Creed, which remains officially a Mystery even today. The implications of a triune God, his dual nature, and the manner of his birth challenged the artist to present a mind in tacit play with unanswerable questions of faith inherent in the figures, both depicted and concealed.

The economic recovery of Europe that permitted the building of cathedrals also formalized education institutionally (Charles Homer Haskins, *The Renaissance of the 12th Century* [1927]) a fact that may explain the shift from positive to systematic theology. But the pedagogue's shift of focus from a theory of knowledge to a theory of learning led not only to a reclassification of things according to theoretical, practical, mechanical, and logical categories, but to empiricism, as well. Consequently in their theological-aesthetic *didascalica* they were natural theologians who believed that the Creator could best be understood by his Creation, and thereby gave an impetus to the study of the world of things.

They were also mystical theologians who thought in terms of a sequence of experience out of which knowledge was to be derived for the unification of man's mind with that of God. Hence the structural metaphor of the voyage for Saint Bonaventure's *Itinerarium*, the nuptial metaphor in Hugh of Saint Victor's *De arraha animae*, and the figure of Jacob in the *Benjamin Minor* of the later Victorine, Richard. For Richard, man's ascent from earth to heaven by means of the mystical ladder was premiss and conclusion. What he analyzed was each episode of Jacob's life as aspects—ways of seeing and interpreting—of the ultimate unity of things that was implied by the oneness of God. The two wives of Jacob served therefore two functions of as many views of the subject "Man" as the author cared to contemplate. The fertility of Leah and the sterility of Rachel, on one level, were interpreted as the appetites of the mind (*Richard of Saint Victor*, ed. and trans. Clare Kirchberger [1957], p. 91):

For as it is Leah's part to love since she is the affection of the soul, so it is Rachel's part to know, for she is reason. The former gives birth to ordered affection; the latter to the reason or the pure intelligence. Judah represents to us . . . love of the highest good. And when Judah is born . . . then Rachel begins to desire children passionately, for she wants to know. Where love is there is vision . . . and certainly he who can love invisible things will immediately desire to know them and to see them by the intelligence.

The canon regulars of Saint Victor (in whose writings are preserved the earliest systematic treatment of the four-fold interpretation of Scripture: literal, allegorical, moral, and anagogical) were the ancestors of the author of the *Epistle to Can Grande*. But in adapting this type of multivalenced textual criticism to the *Divine Comedy* the author of the letter (if it was Dante) stipulated only two, the literal and the unspecified symbolic, ambiguously stating that the work was *"polysemos, hoc est plurium sensuum,"* thus leaving open the question of how many levels of meaning apply.

From a structural point of view the *Commedia* might have included a fourth part, since the Christian heaven was located outside the closed Ptolemaic cosmos. But while staying within this universe, Dante chose to open up his world conditionally. Consequently the problem that confronts the reader at the end of *Purgatorio* is similar to the pivotal episode in the *Aeneid*. But unlike Vergil's disjunctive ambiguity, Dante's Garden of Eden is a conjunctive symbol, the most complex and open of nexuses in Western letters. In Eden the pilgrim Dante sees in a vision a giant temporalized emblem (more complex than Dürer's for the Emperor Maximilian I) that is a pageant of the Church. This allegory has been glossed alternatively as the Church Militant on earth or the Church Triumphant in Heaven, but the probability that Dante intended both is made more likely by the location of this episode in the work. For the purposes of his narrative, from Eden the pilgrim Dante continued his voyage to God in the *Paradiso*, but in terms of the meaning of the work, the untold story of the future of mankind also begins at this point. Thus, on earth, the closed world of moral categories is obliterated by the recovery of innocence, and even the memory of past history is washed away by the waters of Lethe or Divine forgiveness, since Scripture assures us that "When He forgives He forgets." This uncanonical second baptism constitutes therefore a new opportunity for man under the new dispensation of Christian hedonism. Thus Vergil's valedictory benediction to Dante (*Purgatorio*, XXVII, 131, 142): . . . *lo tuo piacere omai prendi per duce . . . per ch'io te sovra te corono e mitrio* ("Now take pleasure as your guide . . . [because you are now master of yourself, body and soul,] I therefore crown and mitre you"). 53

The withdrawal of Vergil as Dante's guide was the poet's way of announcing the obsolescence of reason as governing principle for human action or principle of political organization, since the second baptism made instinctive man's knowledge of natural order, the poet's definition of Good. His projection of Evil in the *Inferno* recalls therefore the statue in the *Book of Daniel*, a human anatomy analyzed both tropologically and chronologically but inverted, its posture representing the stance of sin in relation to the natural order created by God. Conversely, the figure of redemption in the *Purgatorio* is represented upright, the attainment of the *recta ratio* by man paradoxically obliterating his need for it. Consequently the problem that is raised is the connection in Dante's mind between the ideas of the possible intellect and plenitude, and what these terms meant to him. In his political theory, stated in metaphysical terms, Dante was explicit on the first topic, but not the second (*De Monarchia*, trans. H. W. Schneider [1957], p. 6):

. . . since this power can not be completely actualized in a single man or in any of the particular communities . . . there must be a multitude in mankind through whom this whole power can be actualized; just as there must be a multitude of created beings to manifest adequately the whole power of prime matter. . . . With this judgment Averroes agrees in his commentary on *De anima*.

The cultural rebirth of man announced by Dante was projected two centuries later as a revolution in education by Rabelais, for whom the exploration of human possibilities through actualization automatically meant the rejection of allegory and multiple levels of reality. He therefore blasted, in the Prologue to the First Book of *Gargantua*, the tradition that had extended from Philo to his day (trans. J. M. Cohen, Penguin Classics [1955], p. 38):

But do you faithfully believe that Homer, in writing his *Iliad* and *Odyssey*, ever had in mind the allegories squeezed out of him by Plutarch, Heraclides Ponticus, Eustathius, and Phornutus, and which Politian afterwards stole from them in his turn? If you do, you are not within a hand's or a foot's length of my opinion. For I believe them to have been as little dreamed of by Homer as the Gospel mysteries were by Ovid in his *Metamorphoses;* a case which a certain Friar Lubin, a true bacon-picker, has actually tried to prove, in the hope that 'he may meet others as crazy as himself and—as the proverb says—a lid to fit his kettle.

It was not, however, the force of Rabelais' language, but the Scientific Revolution that destroyed the allegorical method. According to Herbert Butterfield in *The Origins of Modern Science* (1957), pp. 7, 8:

. . . it outshines everything since the rise of Christianity and reduces the Renaissance and Reformation to the rank of mere episodes, mere internal displacements, within the system of medieval Christendom. . . . it changed the character of men's habitual mental operations . . . [and] looms so large as the real origin both of the modern world and of the modern mentality that our customary periodisation of European history has become an anachronism and an encumbrance.

Accordingly, we will approach the centuries extending from the Florentine Renaissance to the First World War as a single epoch, tracing the principle of ambiguity under three headings, all ultimately derived from geographical and cosmological exploration.

1. Accidentalism in Open Systems. The seeming haphazardness of horizontal and open-ended works in the Renaissance was implicitly a new projection of ambiguity, for the sole rule of the Abbey of Thélème—*Fay ce que vouldras*—when translated to aesthetic principle produced compositions as savory and variegated (but unpredictable) as the *Adventures of Pantagruel*. Adventures, which for other men had led to the accidental discovery of new continents while merely searching for new ways of traveling to places long known, thus unwittingly shifted the center of the world from the Mediterranean to the Atlantic, and added impetus to the nationalism that challenged with a rival theory of sovereignty the first modern state, the Church. Similarly the faith in the goodness of instinct that dignified the study of man's actual behavior led to the discovery of the ego. But because the ambiguities of accidentalism at this time had to be conceptualized by alternative characterizations of God as either the rational or the capricious Uncreated Being, the result for men was fideistic optimism or nescience. Thus Rabelais' optimism shaded into skepticism for Montaigne, since the purposeless exploration of the inner world of man raised more questions than he could answer, or that he answered with another question: *"Que sçay-je?"* This impatient shrug of Montaigne reflects the quickened time-sense of the age that now found essays and short novellas more congenial fare than long accretions. But it was in the developed drama with its possibilities for the simultaneous presentation of multiple relationships and causal connections that the eclecticism and the ambiguities of an open world were best expressed.

No treatment of ambiguity can avoid the problem of *Hamlet*, since for so many both character and play have become synonymous with the term. But some of the problems are the invention of modern critics, dating no earlier than the advent of the proscenium stage which introduced not only a different theater but also a different technique of interpreting drama. The multiple playing areas of the Elizabethan stage, simultaneous action, multiple motives, and the several levels of reality that are the bases of Shakespearean dramaturgy were flattened out by the box-stage, realistic decor, and notions of verisimilitude and linear progression of action that characterize the novels of Zola. Therefore the delight of the critic in the multivalence of Hamlet's madness, or speculation on the motives for the delay in revenge are false problems; Hamlet is under palace arrest, and only by his assumed antic disposition (plan known to Horatio) does he have license to prowl and to spy.

The genuine ambiguities have to do with the ideas explored by Shakespeare, and with the structure and scope of the play. First, revenge is throughout Shakespeare a negative term, at best what Francis Bacon calls "a kind of wild justice, which the more man's nature runs to, the more ought law to weed it out." Whether Shakespeare meant to say that revenge is acceptable when purged of passion and executed more in sorrow than in anger, or whether revenge is all that remains of justice when the times are out of joint must remain a moot point. Secondly, two notions of kingship are present in the play: on the political level, Denmark's kings are elected; on the theological level succession of reigns and of dynasties are foreordained by God. Thus, upon his providential return to Denmark, after Hamlet has proof of Claudius' guilt and the assurance that he is God's chosen instrument, he announces his royal pretension with "I, Hamlet the Dane." Later, in reviewing with Horatio the evidence against Claudius, he declares that "the interim is mine," suggesting that the eldest crime has made invalid the present reign. Hamlet, therefore, is his father's successor, the purpose of his uncrowned rule to bring to an end a dynasty and his own life which are parts of the general rottenness of Denmark. Hamlet thus is both scourge of God and victim whose double role in life requires premeditation of all action to prevent the tainting of his mind, that purity rewarded in death by an apotheosis hymned by flights of angels.

But death for the other characters is also a consummation, the manner of their dying indicating, but not revealing entirely, the ambiguous connection between the actualization of God's will that is providence, and justice on earth. Among the problems that Hamlet ponders therefore are the purposes of knowledge, the limits of reason, and God's will. But ultimately all attempts at the capturing of God's mind are not only vain but blasphemous; therefore augury must be defied, and like the fallen sparrow man is God's captive, nescience reason's response to omniscience, and readiness the proper state of the will in relation to providence.

The historical setting and the scope of the play are impossible to determine, since on the one hand the ostensible reason for dispatching Hamlet to England is for the collection of the Danegeld (ca. ninth century); on the other hand, he is a student at Wittenberg which was founded in 1502, but which did not enjoy a foreign reputation until Shakespeare's day. Obviously anachronism is present, but the usual function of collapsing time does not seem to apply. In *Hamlet* the author's motive appears to be the opposite: the extension of Danish and English history centuries beyond the two months required by the action. Similarly, the dramatic structure, "all beginning," becomes appropriate when it is perceived that Shakespeare was experimenting with the hero *in posse*, a risky artistic challenge that requires the identification of an adolescent protagonist with his potentialities rather than with his achievements, with *becoming* rather than with *being*: "For he was likely, had he been put on, to have prov'd most royal."

Technically, Shakespeare had to negotiate the constant shift in focus from the drama on the stage to the drama within Hamlet's inexperienced but learning mind by regularly suspending the action with an abnormal number of internalizing soliloquies. That Shakespeare thought he succeeded in his attempts may be seen in Fortinbras' epilogue, for when the poet feels secure in his accomplishment he characteristically violates the illusion he has created in order to reveal his hand as creator. As for the meaning of so protean a play, the history of *Hamlet* criticism parodies Polonius' response to cloud formations, the various interpretations placed upon Hamlet's antic disposition by the other characters, and their various reactions to the play within the play—all these examples anticipating the Rorschach Test (1923) which is based upon the interpretation of an articulate but amorphous shape that elicits self-revealing commentary. The work is therefore informed with its own literary criticism, including the tacit assertion that works of art may be exercises in criticism as well as creation, endeavors always subject to the fashions of the day. The explicitness of this awareness Shakespeare reserved for his Cleopatra (*Antony and Cleopatra*, V, ii):

> The quick comedians
> Extemporally will stage us and present
> Our Alexandrian revels. Antony
> Shall be brought drunken forth, and I shall see
> Some squeaking Cleopatra boy my greatness
> I'th' posture of a whore.

But the poet's desire to free his work from himself and from Time is also present in *Hamlet,* for the play concludes with an infinite regress. Horatio offers to follow his prince in death, but his duties are not yet over. He is not only to report Hamlet's cause aright to the unsatisfied, but also, in this harsh world, to draw his breath in pain "to tell my story." Because Shakespeare's Hamlet is not the Hamlet of saga, chronicle, romance, or other dramatic presentations, telling the story aright requires returning to the beginning, *da capo,* and re-experiencing the play, a simple form of regress that was a familiar device in music.

2. *The Autonomy of Art and Self-Reference.* The multivocality of Shakespearean drama that conceals the author's point of view finds its counterpart in painting with Leonardo's invention of *sfumato.* This shading and blurring of outline in combination with the disjunctive background explains the enigmatic quality of the Mona Lisa (E. H. Gombrich, *The Story of Art,* 9th ed. [1958]). A comparison of her smile with that of the Virgin of Notre Dame described above reveals the historic changes in artistic aims, since repeated viewings of the medieval statue will add nothing to the doctrinal ambiguities once they are perceived, for the work, like the church's sacraments, was no more than a visible sign for a reality that existed elsewhere. But in the case of Leonardo it is precisely the repeated viewings that convince the beholder that her expressions change. Because the moods of the beholder that are read into the picture are *ipso facto*

FIGURE 1. J. Vermeer van Delft, *An Artist in his Studio.* ca. 1670.

valid, viewing the Mona Lisa becomes a continuous process of collaborative recreation. Thus the roles of artist and audience are temporally reversed, and the question of who is who and what is what remains an open one. This problem was made the subject of a painting by Vermeer (Figure 1).

The original title of "An Artist in His Studio" was "The Painter's Art" (Lawrence Gowing, *Vermeer* [1952]) which tells us a great deal more about the meaning of the work. Vermeer has depicted an artist painting from a human model costumed and furnished with the trumpet of fame, the book of history, and the crown of immortality. But a number of questions are raised in the viewer's mind. First, the impersonation of Immortality, whether it can be done, and what reality there is in the artist's portrait of her. It has therefore been conjectured that the artist was painting Hope although his model represented another figure. Secondly, the causal connection between fame and the artist's work have been reversed, for fame is a by-product of, not the subject of a painting.

But more importantly, who is the artist? The identity of the painter depicted by Vermeer is concealed from the viewer since he is seen only from the back. And when one steps outside the frame of the canvas, the same question is posed in a different context, for the beholder is standing where Vermeer must have stood as he painted the picture. While this last point may be made of all easel paintings, it has special relevance to this particular work because of the subject and its treatment. On the left side of the canvas is part of a tapestry painted to look as though it might have been hanging over the canvas itself. But an equally possible interpretation is that it hangs in the doorway that separates two rooms. In either case it is pulled back to reveal an artist in his studio—or, "An Artist in His Studio." Whosoever the hand that pulls back the tapestry to reveal the painter painting, the viewer is permitted an insight into the creative process itself, the most secret of mysteries. Yet at the same time it is also public and cosmic, for fame is the judgment of the world, but the governance of the world may be providential or entirely fortuitous, an historical accident.

What then is the "subject" of this painting whose surface lucidity, explicitness of detail, and quietness of statement conceal as many ambiguities as the beholder can think up? It is astonishing that something originating in so small and contained an area as a narrow Dutch room can have such wide application. But to say that an event "originates" in a specific place is to make an arbitrary decision, for within the context of the assumptions implicit in the painting, this need not be the case. If no limits of inference are set and if the categories of causal relations are placed in doubt, each detail in the painting may at the same time be both cause and effect. Moreover, the abstraction that is Fame and the anonymity of the artist depicted place them in the category of common, not proper nouns. Consequently it may be surmised that Vermeer was handling abstractions that touch upon communication and the human understanding, both within the self and the public at large; that Vermeer was analyzing the interpenetration of working, thinking, and creating, as well as the possibility of an almost infinite succession of appreciation. That Vermeer's legal executor was the pioneer microbiologist Leeuwenhoek, famous for his microscopes, is perhaps not without significance.

The self-reference in a painting about painting was an acknowledgment of the disappearance of traditional content from art. When secularization also came to music, it had certain natural advantages that perhaps explains its ascendancy in the eighteenth century. Divorced from reference to the outside world, it became not only the most abstract and formal of the arts, but also a language without a subject. Or, stated in another way, it became the subject of its own discourse. Thus when the composers turned their attention to the exploration of formal patterns their realization that reiteration was the only referential mode available to this kind of music prompted them to explore the ambiguities intrinsic to any melody. The pleasure they derived in contriving these excursions is recorded by the number and extent of variations upon themes, whether their own or those of others, for such exercises could be cast as independent works, as are the *Goldberg Variations* of Bach, or as part of a larger work. Because the point about themes and variations can most conveniently be made by the simplest of examples, we choose the second movement of Haydn's G Major *Symphony No. 94*, the "Surprise," one of the twelve he composed for the London season of 1792. In it Haydn projected a series of physical postures, psychological states, and courtly ceremonies that concluded in the genial nescience of a quiddity: What is a tune? For the oddity of reiterative utterances is that through repetition the original statement is both strengthened and undermined, and credence in its validity is progressively obliterated into nonexistence or modified to the status of an enigma, as the title of a work of Elgar's declares.

The surprise commemorated in the informal title of Haydn's symphony refers to the fortissimo crash in the 16th measure of the second movement, a social joke that records Haydn's disapproval of the conventions of the time that permitted dozing at concerts. But since jokes do not bear repeating, *Variationen* was a useful solution to an artistic problem. Thus the technically simple, superficially naive work begins with the most innocent of melodies, the first half of which the modern listener associates with "Twinkle, Twinkle, Little Star." This toy of a tune is introduced by the first and second violins, then as if to put finger to lip and walk tiptoe, the first violins play it again very softly, while the second violins disappear pizzicato into the accompaniment. The listener is now ready for something to happen—but not the loud crash he just heard. While he is recovering from his surprise, Haydn with mock innocence gives the second half of the melody.

The variations begin in the 33rd measure when the melody is abandoned to the second strings and the first warbles momentarily with the flutes. The second variation, beginning with the 49th measure, introduces a series of questions. Is it possible to make this music-box tune heroic? Haydn shifts to the minor and increases volume. The result is as ludicrous as the listener expected. But surprisingly, when it is repeated exactly, something ominous creeps into the music. Bemused, the listener now expects to hear the second half of the melody repeated; instead Haydn shifts to the relative key and engages in private mutterings. The listener feels excluded from what seemed to have been a conversation. All patterns of expectancy are undermined by this digression, and the listener gradually realizes the destructive function of irrelevance (measures 57 to 74). Haydn then pretends to apologize for his inhospitality by returning to the tune with the notes playfully doubled as though in compensation for his lapse of attention. The listener is safely back in the world of the miniature. But is he? As it turns out, he has been led back only to hear loudly proclaimed the martial and genuine heroic possibilities of the melody. The conclusion of the second movement however is not coterminal with its performance, for the question of what a melody is remains. Haydn's selection of a well-known theme that had been used as popular French folk song and German religious chorale might have been his way of alluding to other possibilities, possibilities that are now being gathered in the La Rue Union Thematic Catalogue of 18th-Century Symphonies. The two versions familiar to Haydn's audience were:

HAYDN:

FRENCH FOLK SONG:

Ah vous dirai–je maman ce qui cause mon tourment

BACH:

O Lamm Gottes unschuldig

In addition to the demonstration of the ambiguity of melody, Haydn has also suggested in the *da capo* portions that repetition does not exist. But there are other paths open to musicians if they are preoccupied with the irretrievability of experience. Guarantees that preclude the possibility of recurrence can be built into compositions, and some of the works of the twentieth-century John Cage, along with other moderns who are attempting to rejuvenate music, are so conceived. The problem of modernity is important to ambiguity as aesthetic principle, for it traces at the same time the decline of multivalence and opens up the question of what the word "Art" means.

3. *Modernity and the Rejuvenation of the Arts.* The idea of modernity clearly present from the early Renaissance was not formulated as aesthetic principle until the nineteenth century. The oddity of this fact is perhaps best explained by the artists' unwillingness to abandon notions of hierarchy; consequently the story of the Scientific Revolution from their point of view is largely that of resistance. The New Science had its distinctly negative aspect, since the collapse of the old cosmology (Alexandre Koyré, *From the Closed World to the Infinite Universe* [1957]) had taken with it those older sciences that had been assimilated to it. The decline of symbolism (Johann Huizinga, *The Waning of the Middle Ages* [1924]) was hastened therefore, and the astrology, the faculty psychology, and the humoral medicine that relied upon the stars were automatically discredited. Thus the complex, multivalenced resonances that the artists had been able to achieve through correspondence and cross-reference were now lost. The coincidental revival of magic indicated therefore not only a new phase of empiricism necessary for the reconstruction of the sciences, but also a longing for secret, ancient wisdom, the possession of which gave one the power and status of an adept. Hence the flourishing of witchcraft with its arcane formulae and recipes, the *Hieroglyphics* of Horapollo, the Cabbalah, the further additions to the Hermetic corpus, and the emblem books that had as their last readers women and children in seventeenth-century Holland.

For the artists not committed to such exotica the problem was acute, since it was not only the traditional sciences, but also one of the major props of their activity, the siderealized classical myths, that had been undermined (Jean Seznec, *The Survival of the Pagan Gods* [1953]). As for the poets, the limits of language became painfully apparent, and this dilemma was expressed both in their works and in the collections of paradoxes that attempted to join together different worlds by verbal statements while acknowledging at the same time the impossibility of the undertaking (Rosalie L. Colie, *Paradoxia epidemica* [1966]). The century following Shakespeare's was the last to concern itself with theodicies since the role of God was now passive; He existed, as it were, in the past tense merely as the Creator of the world described by a Descartes, a Newton, or a Darwin (John C. Greene, *The Death of Adam: Evolution and its Impact on Western Thought* [1959]). Poets had learned to perceive the world differently, but their delight was of short duration (Marjorie Hope Nicolson, *Newton Demands the Muse: Newton's 'Opticks' and the Eighteenth Century Poets* [1946]) and as a class they never again recaptured the authority they formerly enjoyed. Their work, along with that of the painters, degenerated into academic exercises stripped, as it were, of content, since they had imposed upon themselves unnecessarily long the task of upholding a no longer viable tradition.

The new direction for the arts—rooted in the commerce and technology that was one facet of the Renaissance—had been stated centuries earlier by the sixteenth-century Portugese, Camoens, born in the same year that Vasco da Gama died. His epic, *Os Lusíadas,* had opened with a declaration for actuality and modernity (trans. William C. Atkinson [1952], p. 39):

This is the story of heroes who . . . opened a way to Ceylon, and further, across seas no man had ever sailed before. . . . Let us hear no more then of Ulysses and Aeneas, no more of Alexander and Trajan. The heroes and poets of old have had their day.

This plea was for the most part ignored by the poets and painters, and not for want of heroes or themes since Spain, England, and France had their Vasco da Gamas also. Moreover, the seventeenth-century battle between the Ancients and the Moderns was primarily the concern of the critics and fought on different grounds well after the war was over. The revolution in modernity that should have re-defined the meaning of the word "Art" was delayed; meanwhile the significant achievements from this period were coming from practical men: the architects who quickly rebuilt the churches and hospitals after the Great Fire of London, the craftsmen who planned the English manor houses and laid out the gardens, the artisans in the ateliers of France who designed furniture, and the Dutch factory workers who turned out porcelain and china. It was only when Baudelaire, the contemporary of Darwin, pronounced modernity as an aesthetic principle that *in extremis* the artists finally responded and the arts were rejuvenated. But one of the consequences of this late re-orientation in critical theory was to make ambiguous what constituted an art, for anything could aspire to that condition or be analyzed in aesthetic terms. Not only a life-style like Baudelaire's Dandy, but cities, factories, and subsequently, plans for regional development and political states—not to mention found objects—have been so appraised. Understandably, modernity could not always be distinguished from mere novelty, since the rapid development of technology along with the sciences made inescapable the awareness of change and the shifting grounds of reality.

For radical changes had been taking place in the sciences, as well, and the complete causality implicit in Newton's reduction of all physical phenomena to matter, motion, time, and space was now challenged. In the Einsteinian world wherein matter had dissolved into energy, time was a geometric projection, and the motion of individual charged particles unpredictable, Niels Bohr and J. Robert Oppenheimer began to ponder the latest physical discoveries in terms of radical problems of the understanding. Because the laws that had governed the familiar world of large objects did not seem to operate on the atomic level on which that world is built, the introduction of the conjunctive principles of correspondence and contrariety became an operational necessity. Since, however, these principles were admitted to be merely "a new mode of description" that conjoined different categories of analysis, the ambiguities of language, mind, reasoning, and levels of reality were now assimilated to physical research and theory. The epistemological quandary that the physicists since Einstein found themselves in gave added impetus to the cultural relativity explored by the psychologists, anthropologists, linguists, and historians whose interest was to analyze structures of thought and patterns of behavior.

The cumulative effect of these various endeavors was the total reappraisal of the meaning of history and of human culture. It was in this context that "ambiguity" as applied to the arts underwent a semantic shift (William Empson, *Seven Types of Ambiguity* [1949]) for in the bewildering diversity of categories of thought one response was to take pleasure in complexity; hence the presence of a multiplicity of meaning in a work, or the possibility of a variety of readings was equated with the positive value of richness. The term became therefore one of approbation, and attention was now directed to the psychology of ambiguity (Ernst Kris, *Psychoanalytic Explorations in Art* [1952]). For the

aestheticians also the isolation of the locus of ambiguity seemed to be a more fruitful line of inquiry than a taxonomy, since artists have not limited themselves to one type, and the combination of types in a single work allowed for different analyses. Both approaches are obviously ahistorical. Ambiguities for us, however, have referred to something and often point to the central concern of the artist, to the ideas and problems in cultural history that ought to be explored for purposes of appreciation.

In the long history of ambiguity as a pejorative term, an important distinction must be made. As stated above, for the critics ambiguity represented an annoyance in the cognitive process that was to be eliminated as quickly as the rules of logic would permit. For artists the embarrassment of dilemmas and the delay in their resolution was the very focus of their interest; hence saying more than one thing at a time to express the complexity of experience has normally been one of their aims. Thus in spite of the ultimate agreement on the uniformity of nature's laws, artists, critics, and scientists have for centuries addressed themselves to different orders of reality.

This condition may be coming to an end, for the current trend away from formal logic in favor of nondiscursive modes may be pointing to a new basis of agreement more intimate than in the past. The merging of function of studio and laboratory which is illustrative of this union might also mean the end of pessimism in the arts, since both are at present being utilized for the exploration of the limits of human perception, of tolerance, attention-span, and how the interpretation of events occurs. Accordingly, the researches of the neuro-psychologists are analogous to the experimentations of Op Artists and Electronic Composers (Fritz Winckel, *Music, Sound, Sensation: A Modern Exposition* [1967]) and the results of these collaborative efforts within the framework of the new biology may signify the emergence of a new image of man. What is certain is that under pressure of historical changes, all disciplines in the post-critical age are forced to revalue their methods of gathering data and drawing inferences, and are consequently preoccupied with the problems of heuristics. Thus the art of interpretation for Michael Polanyi and Elizabeth Sewell is subsumed under their cover-term, *discovery*, a way of approaching problems, whether scientific, philosophical, or artistic, those categories themselves no longer meaningful in the realignment of disciplines that constitutes for them an intellectual revolution.

Seen in this light, the periodic restructuring of human knowledge and the invention of new methods of reasoning have as their purpose the elimination of

59

ambiguities and the preservation of the notions of unity, both in man and in nature. But it may be observed that each new way of reasoning generates new ambiguities which in turn provoke the search for more comprehensive theories of causality. Consequently, if knowledge has no limits, ambiguity must remain a permanent part of the human experience. Under these conditions it is likely that artists will continue to search for significance through the cultural paradoxes exposed by their perceptions of discrepancies. And from the complexity and multivalence of their experiences they will continue to provide others with that special kind of entertainment that we call the arts.

BIBLIOGRAPHY

There exists no single work that traces ambiguity or multivalence through the whole of Western culture; therefore the suggested readings are arranged historically. Jean Daniélou, S. J., *Sacramentum futuri: Études sur les origines de la typologie biblique* (Paris, 1950). Jean Pépin, *Mythe et allégorie: les origines grecques et les contestations judéo-chrétiennes* (Paris, 1958). For Eastern Christianity see R. P. C. Hanson, *Allegory and Event: A Study of the Sources and Significance of Origen's Interpretation of Scripture* (London, 1959). For the history of mystical theology, Pierre Pourrat, *La Spiritualité chrétienne*, 3 vols. (Paris, 1921–27), trans. W. H. Mitchell and S. P. Jacques as *Christian Spirituality*, 3 vols. (London, 1922–27). Henri de Lubac, S. J., *Exégèse médiévale: les quatre sens de l'écriture*, 3 vols. (Paris, 1959–61). For literary tropes, Ernst Robert Curtius, *Europäische Literatur und lateinisches Mittelalter* (Berne, 1948), trans. Willard R. Trask as *European Literature and the Latin Middle Ages* (New York, 1953) and their counterpart in the visual arts, Erwin Panofsky, *Studies in Iconology: Humanistic Themes in the Art of the Renaissance* (New York, and London, 1939). For theological aesthetics see Gerardus van der Leeuw, *Sacred and Profane Beauty: The Holy in Art* (London, 1963); for philosophical criticism and a brief history of aesthetics, the studies of Monroe C. Beardsley; also E. H. Gombrich, *Art and Illusion* (New York, 1960), Northrop Frye *Anatomy of Criticism* (Princeton, 1957), and George Boas, *The Heaven of Invention* (Baltimore, 1961). For more specialized studies, Winifred Nowottny, *The Language Poets Use* (Oxford, 1962), R. P. Blackmur, *Language As Gesture* (New York, 1952), Kenneth Burke, *A Grammar of Motives* (New York, 1954), and W. K. Wimsatt, *The Verbal Icon* (Lexington, Ky., 1954). For the relationship between structural linguistics, mythology, and cultural anthropology, Claude Lévi-Strauss, *Structural Anthropology*, trans. Claire Jacobson and Brooke Grundfest Schoepf (New York, 1963). For a new epistemology grounded in the ambiguities of heuristics, Michael Polanyi, *The Tacit Dimension* (New York, 1966).

TOM TASHIRO

[See also **Analogy;** Chain of Being; Hierarchy; **Metaphor;** Myth; Poetry; **Symbol.**]

ANALOGY IN EARLY GREEK THOUGHT

I

ANALOGY, in its broadest sense, comprehends any mode of reasoning that depends on the suggestion or recognition of a relationship of similarity between two objects or sets of objects. It includes not only four-term proportional relationships of the type A:B::C:D (for which the Greek term is ἀναλογία), but also both explicit and implicit comparisons, for example the use of models (παραδείγματα) and of images (εἰκόνες). In early Greek thought analogies played a fundamental role in the expression of cosmological doctrines, in the development of natural science, and in ethical and political arguments.

The three most important types of images used in cosmological theories are (1) political and social, (2) vitalist, and (3) technological, in which, roughly speaking, the cosmos is conceived as a state, as a living being, and as an artifact respectively.

1. Political and Social Images. The use of political and social concepts is widespread in pre-Socratic cosmology. The idea of cosmic order as a balance of power between equal opposed forces goes back to Anaximander, who describes the relation between certain cosmic factors in legal terms: "They pay the penalty and recompense to one another for their injustice according to the assessment of time." Heraclitus, on the other hand, stresses the constant war and strife between opposites: "One must realize that war is common and justice is strife and everything happens through strife and necessity" (frag. 80). But both Parmenides in the *Way of Seeming* and Empedocles in his poem *On Nature* revert to the idea of a cosmic balance of power. In Empedocles, for example, Love and Strife are equals: they gain the upper hand in the world in turn, and these alternations are governed by a "broad oath," that is, by some sort of contract between them.

Anaxagoras and Diogenes of Apollonia use a third type of political model, ascribing supreme power to a single cosmic principle, and Plato similarly attributes supreme power to Reason which governs and arranges all things for the best. Superficially this last group of images resembles the traditional descriptions of Zeus as supreme god; but there is this fundamental difference, that the philosophers ascribe supreme power not to a capricious deity, but to the principle of order and rationality itself, to Mind or Reason or, in the case of Diogenes, to Air, thought of as the seat of intelligence. These authoritarian images too, like the egalitarian ones of Anaximander and Empedocles, serve to express the idea of cosmic order, although they do so from a different point of view and with different associations.

All these philosophers describe the cosmos in terms of a concrete political or social situation, whether of a balance of power and equality of rights, or of constant war and aggression, or of benevolent, authoritarian rule. Plato's antidemocratic, authoritarian political inclinations are echoed in his descriptions of Reason as a supreme, benevolent cosmic ruler, but the evidence concerning earlier philosophers is too scanty to allow us to determine how closely their cosmological images tallied with their particular political ideologies. However, there are two ways in which their images may be related to their historical and social background.

First, the development of the Greek city-state from about the seventh century B.C. was accompanied by an increasing political awareness and a new conception of political rights. In particular the framing of constitutions and the codification of laws led to a much less arbitrary administration of justice than had been the case in earlier periods. These changes had their counterparts in the political images used by the cosmologists; varied as those images are, they have in common the notion that cosmological changes are governed by rules that are independent of the caprice of individuals. The development in the attitude towards justice in the city-state is reflected in the development of Greek cosmology itself, since it was largely by means of the ideas of law and justice that the pre-Socratic thinkers expressed the notion that the changes affecting the primary substances in the world are orderly and regulated by immutable principles.

Secondly, the very variety of images and of the cosmological doctrines themselves is significant. As in the political sphere the rise of the city-state is accompanied by a proliferation of constitutional forms ranging from extreme democracy to tyranny, the merits of each of which were much debated, so similarly in the field of speculative thought the philosophers felt free to reject earlier ideas and to attempt to resolve each problem for themselves, and each new theory as it was advanced was discussed and criticized openly.

It is difficult to decide how far any of the pre-Socratics recognized an element of transference in applying political and social conceptions to the cosmos. No philosopher before Plato explicitly refers to his cosmological images as images (εἰκόνες), and yet it is unlikely that any of them simply failed to differentiate at all between the realm of society and that of nature, the relations between which had become, by the end of the fifth century at least, the subject of heated controversy. Heraclitus, for instance, tacitly distinguishes between human laws and the divine law, while saying that the former depend on the latter, in frag.

114. Evidently he did not simply confuse human society and cosmic order. Yet law and justice applied to the cosmos were no mere figures of speech, for order in the human sphere was regularly conceived as *part* of the wider cosmic order and as somehow derived from it.

2. Vitalist Images. Most of the earlier pre-Socratic philosophers imagined that the primary stuff out of which things are made or from which they originate is not merely *like* something that is alive, but is *indeed* instinct with life. This is true of all three Milesian philosophers and of Heraclitus; when he describes the world-order as an "ever-living" fire in frag. 30, "ever-living" is not simply a poetical equivalent for "everlasting," for he held that fire is indeed the substance of which our own souls consist. Later the Atomists too seem to have believed that the mass of atoms from which worlds originate is instinct with life in the sense that it is permeated by soul-atoms. Although Aristotle ridiculed the belief that soul is intermingled in the whole universe, he himself held that the heavenly bodies are alive, and indeed some of his general physical theories, for example the doctrine of potentiality and actuality, are much influenced by ideas which apply primarily to the sphere of living things.

These and other vitalist beliefs affected the development of Greek cosmology in three main ways. First, the earliest philosophers were "hylozoists"; they assumed that the primary substance, being alive, is in motion. The question of the origin or cause of movement only came to be recognized as a problem after Parmenides had denied the possibility of change.

Secondly, vitalist notions are naturally very important in accounts of how the world developed from an original, undifferentiated state. Anaximander, for example, pictured the world evolving from a seed that separated off from the Boundless, and some of the Pythagoreans too thought that the One from which the cosmos developed was composed of seed.

Thirdly, the structure of the cosmos was sometimes compared with that of man and vice versa. The idea that the world is a living creature may underlie the comparison that Anaximenes drew between the role of air in the world and that of breath in man. But two of the Hippocratic treatises put forward much more elaborate analogies between the microcosm and the macrocosm. In *De victu* man's body is said to be a copy of the world-whole, the stomach being compared with the sea and so on. And *De hebdomadibus* suggests detailed correspondences both between the substances in the body and those in the universe—where the bones correspond to the stony core of the earth, for example—and between the various parts of the body and different geographical areas—where the Thracian Bosphorus is said to correspond to the feet, the Peloponnese to the head, and so on. While Plato proposed no detailed analogy between the anatomy of man and the structure of the universe, he stated unequivocally his conviction that "this world is in truth a living creature, endowed with soul and reason" (*Timaeus* 30b), and according to the *Philebus* (29b ff.) both our body and our soul are derived from the body and the soul of the world-whole respectively.

3. Technological Images. Several of the pre-Socratics use the metaphor of steering in their cosmologies, but the first to employ a wide range of technological images is Empedocles, and then both Plato and Aristotle use them extensively in two contexts, especially, (1) to describe the role of a moving or efficient cause, and (2) to express the idea of intelligent design in the cosmos.

In Empedocles' system everything is composed of the four "roots," earth, water, air, and fire, together with Love and Strife, and in describing how complex substances and the organs in the body come to be he assigns to Love the role of craftsman, the four elements being the material on which it works. It would be anachronistic to attribute a clear distinction between "material" and "efficient" causes to Empedocles; but it is in the descriptions of the craftsmanlike activity of Love that he comes closest to treating it as a purely efficient cause. Plato's *Timaeus* is the first Greek text to describe the formation of the world as a whole as the work of a Craftsman. In Plato the Demiurge takes over already existing matter and imposes order on its disorderly movements, and his account of the details of creation is full of images drawn from carpentry, weaving, modelling, metallurgy, and agricultural technology. Aristotle's unmoved mover, unlike Plato's Craftsman, is only a final, not an efficient cause; but Aristotle too believes that final causes are at work in natural processes, and he uses comparisons drawn from the arts and crafts extensively to illustrate this. Despite their unconcealed contempt for the life led by merely human artisans, both Plato and Aristotle found technological imagery indispensable for expressing their belief in the rational design of the universe.

II

The history of early Greek cosmology is largely the history of the interpretation of the cosmos in terms of various ideas derived from the three fields of politics, biology, and technology. Aristotle, especially, criticized many such ideas, as for example the belief that such substances as air or fire are alive. Yet these three types of images continued to be influential long after him. The Stoics, in particular, not only represented the cosmos as a living creature and believed in the purposeful, craftsmanlike activity of Nature, but also described the world as a state governed by divine law, and similar ideas had a long history in the Middle Ages and in the Renaissance.

Moreover while Greek cosmology owed many ideas to politics and biology, Greek biological theories and political thought were similarly colored by the use of images drawn from one another. For example, the twin ideas that health depends on the equality of rights (ἰσονομία) of opposed powers in the body, and that disease results from the supreme rule (μοναρχία) of one such power, go back to Alcmaeon and thereafter become commonplaces of Greek pathology and therapeutics. Aristotle, too, compares the living creature with a well-governed city, describing the heart as the central seat of authority in the body (e.g., *De motu animalium* 703a 29ff.).

Conversely Greek political theorists sometimes compare the state with a living organism, and the influence of other biological and technological analogies on Greek ethics is marked. Here Plato provides the best examples. First he constructed an elaborate analogy between the state and the individual in the *Republic*, suggesting, for instance, that both may be divided into three parts, one of which—the Guardians in the state and reason in the soul—should be in overall control. A second important analogy in Plato is that between justice and health. This provides the main grounds for the two theses, (1) that the just man is happier than the unjust, and (2) that once having done wrong, it is better to suffer than to escape punishment—for punishment is the "cure" for injustice. And a third recurrent analogy is that between the politician and the artist or craftsman, where Plato suggests that the statesman must be an expert in politics in a way comparable with that in which a pilot is expert in navigation or a doctor in medicine. We find similar types of analogies in Aristotle, too. In the *Politics* (1295a 40f.) he describes the constitution as the life, as it were, of the state, and in the *Nicomachean Ethics* (1113a 25ff.) he draws a comparison between the good man and the healthy: just as a sick person may be mistaken about what is hot or cold or sweet or bitter, and the judge of these things is the normal, healthy man, so, he argues, the good man (ὁ σπουδαῖος) is the judge of what is right and wrong.

Greek ideas on nature and art, on the state, the living organism, and the world as a whole, are linked by a series of interlocking analogies. Most of the major fifth- and fourth-century philosophers put forward analogies of one or other of the types we have considered. Yet the particular forms that their analogies take are very varied, and no single version of any of them dominates the period. Had any such orthodoxy existed, these analogies might have impeded the development of certain inquiries far more than they did. As it was, although some Hippocratic writers produced elaborate versions of the microcosm-macrocosm analogy, this did not prevent other theorists from making considerable progress in both the study of anatomy and in astronomy, during the fourth century. Again, both Plato and Aristotle held that the stars are alive and divine, although this had been denied by such thinkers as Anaxagoras; yet this belief did not prevent Aristotle from attempting a detailed mechanical account of the movements of the heavenly bodies, based on Eudoxus' theory of concentric spheres.

III

Two other features of the role of analogy in early Greek thought that are especially notable are (1) their use as a method of suggesting or supporting explanations of particular natural phenomena, and (2) the gradual exploration of the logic of analogy. The beginnings of the first use go back to the Milesians, who based many of their accounts of obscure astronomical, meteorological, and geological phenomena on simple analogies with familiar objects. Thus Anaximenes compared lightning with the flash made by an oar in water, believing both phenomena to be the result of a cleaving process. His predecessor Anaximander suggested a more elaborate and artificial analogy in which he pictured the heavenly bodies as wheels of fire enclosed in mist; the stars themselves are seen through openings in the mist, and he described eclipses of the sun and moon as being due to the temporary blocking of their apertures. Primitive though this theory is, it ranks as the first known attempt to construct a mechanical model of the heavenly bodies.

The use of such comparisons grows as the range of problems investigated is extended. Empedocles and some of the Hippocratic writers, especially, propose ingenious analogies to explain processes that take place within the body. Thus Empedocles compares the process of respiration with the action of a clepsydra (water clock). *De natura pueri* compares the formation of a membrane round the seed in the womb with that of a crust on bread as it is baked, and *De morbis* IV compares the formation of stones in the bladder with the smelting of iron ore. The same writer also illustrates how the humors travel between different parts of the body by referring to the way in which a system of three or more intercommunicating vessels may be filled with a liquid or emptied by filling or emptying one of them, and on other occasions, too, Greek scientists refer to simple tests carried out on substances outside the body in their search for analogies for biological processes.

These writers rarely examine explicitly the question of how the analogies they propose apply to the phenomena they were supposed to explain, and many of their ideas seem farfetched. Even so, analogy provided an important, indeed in some cases the only, means of bringing empirical evidence to bear on obscure or intractable problems, especially in such fields as astronomy and meteorology, embryology and pathology, where direct experimentation was generally out of the question.

Various writers, beginning with Anaxagoras at the end of the fifth century, refer to this use of analogy under the general heading of making "phenomena the vision of things that are obscure" (ὄψις τῶν ἀδήλων τὰ φαινόμενα), and awareness of most of the different modes of analogy grows rapidly in the fourth century. Plato, himself one of the chief exponents of reasoning from analogy, was the first to point out how deceptive similarities may be, and to draw attention to the difference between merely probable arguments, including emotive images and myths, and demonstrations. Then Aristotle analyzed analogical argument as such in the form of the paradigm, explaining its relation to induction and showing that it is not formally demonstrative. Nevertheless he granted its usefulness as a persuasive argument in the field of rhetoric, and he even described how a dialectician may exploit similarities in order to deceive an opponent. Plato and Aristotle made decisive advances in exploring the logic of arguments from analogy: yet the effect of their work was not, of course, to preclude the use of such arguments, but rather to show that they are not formally valid. Moreover while Aristotle successfully analyzed analogy as a method of inference, neither he nor any later Greek logician made much progress towards elucidating the other important function of analogy, namely as a method of discovery in natural science.

BIBLIOGRAPHY

The principal texts are discussed in G. E. R. Lloyd, *Polarity and Analogy: two types of argumentation in early Greek thought* (Cambridge, 1966), which includes an extensive bibliography. See also especially H. Diller, "ὄψις τῶν ἀδήλων τὰ φαινόμενα," *Hermes,* **67** (1932), 14–42; H. Gomperz, "Problems and Methods of Early Greek Science," *Journal of the History of Ideas,* 4 (1943), 161–76; W. K. C. Guthrie, "Man's Role in the Cosmos," *The Living Heritage of Greek Antiquity* (The Hague, 1967), pp. 56–73; C. W. Müller, *Gleiches zu Gleichem: ein Prinzip frühgriechischen Denkens* (Wiesbaden, 1965); O. Regenbogen, *Eine Forschungsmethode antiker Naturwissenschaft,* Quell. u. Stud. zur Gesch. der Mathematik, Astronomie u. Physik, B I, 2 (Berlin, 1930); F. Solmsen, "Nature as Craftsman in Greek Thought," *Journal of the History of Ideas,* **24** (1963), 473–96.

G. E. R. LLOYD

[See also **Atomism; **Balance of Power; **Cosmology; **Creation; **Nature; **Pythagorean Doctrines to 300 B.C.; Stoicism.]

ANALOGY IN PATRISTIC AND MEDIEVAL THOUGHT

THE MIDDLE Ages made abundant use of analogy and symbolism in all aspects of its culture. Indeed, its mentality has rightly been described as symbolic. At the end of the Middle Ages Dante's *Divine Comedy* perfectly expresses this mentality; but as early as the first centuries after Christ the bases of medieval symbolism were laid down by the Church Fathers.

1. The Patristic Period. The Fathers of the Church cultivated symbolism both as a means of interpreting Scripture and of understanding the world and God, its transcendent cause. Influenced by Philo, Clement of Alexandria makes frequent use of symbolism. For him, symbolism expresses the basic unity in all things, despite their multiplicity and diversity. Invisible harmonies, likenesses, and proportions bind the universe together, and these can be interpreted by symbols and allegories. Thus symbolism reveals the hidden connection between things and points to their underlying unity. Allegorical interpretation of Scripture is needed because its truth is veiled in symbols. Clement justifies the concealing of truth in symbols as a means of giving truth greater power over minds. Moreover, by their ambiguity symbols contain a richness and complexity of meaning, in contrast to clear statements, that convey but one message to the reader.

Clement's pupil, Origen, distinguishes between the literal or historical meaning of Scripture and its spiritual or allegorical meaning. The spiritual sense, lying beneath the obvious, literal meaning, is the one principally intended by the Holy Spirit, the main author of Scripture, and it can be grasped only by the enlightened and initiated.

For Origen, the allegorical interpretation of Scripture is justified by the fact that the cosmos itself is a vast set of symbols created by God to lead the mind to him. Visible nature is a symbol of the invisible world in which each individual has its ideal model or type. Hence all things, Scripture included, have two facets: one corporeal and sensible, the other spiritual and mystical. Because God is the author of both Scripture and Nature, we should expect similar problems in understanding them (*De principiis* IV, 1, 7). Like Scripture, nature is a sacred mystery that can be best expressed by symbols. Only by deciphering the imprint left by God on the world can we raise ourselves to the transcendent, invisible world; for God has so ordered his creation, has so linked the lower to the higher by subtle signatures and affinities, that the world we see is, as it were, a great staircase by which the mind of man must climb upwards to spiritual intelligence (*In canticum canticorum* 3).

Cosmic symbolism was most clearly expressed for the Middle Ages by Denis, the Pseudo-Areopagite (fifth century A.D.). The word ἀναλογία often appears in his writings, generally with the meaning of relation or proportion. The proportion denoted by the term is not abstract or mathematical but the concrete relation of love between creatures and God. On the one hand, it means the creature's desire for deification, and, on the other, God's appearance (theophany) to creatures. Denis also uses the term to denote the divine ideas, which define the creature's position in the hierarchy of creation and his capacity to receive divine gifts. It also means the creature's capacity for these gifts and his loving response to God.

For Denis a symbol (σύμβολον) is the relating or adapting of visible forms in order to reveal something invisible. Symbols are "unlike likenesses," and hence when applied to God they both conceal and reveal him. No symbol, however, can give us a positive knowledge of the divinity. Following Plotinus and Proclus he conceives God as infinite and one, transcending being or reality and every conceivable positive perfection. As infinite, he is strictly inimitable by anything finite; and yet the finite universe participates in his riches. This justifies our giving positive names to him, such as "goodness" and "being." More suitable are negative names like "one" and "infinite." More appropriate still are superlative names like "super-good" and "super-being." In the end we know God best by realizing our ignorance of him (*Divine Names* 7, 3; PG 3, 872B).

Following Cicero and the Latin grammarians, the Latin Fathers used *proportio* as the equivalent of ἀναλογία. In the broad sense it meant any likeness or comparison; more strictly it denoted a likeness or identity of proportions: as *a* is to *b*, so *c* is to *d*. For Saint Augustine analogy is a method of scriptural interpretation by which the harmony of the Old and New Testaments is established. This differs from allegory, which reveals the figurative, as opposed to the literal, sense of Scripture. In the strict sense, Augustine denies that there is an analogy between the trinity of faculties of the soul (memory, intelligence, and will) and the trinity of divine Persons, because this is not a true comparison between them leading to a knowledge of the Trinity (*Sermo 52*, 10; PL 38, 364).

Augustine prefers the term "sign" to "analogy." A sign is any word or thing that leads to a knowledge of something else. If it points to the divine, it is a *sacramentum*. The universe itself is holy (a sacrament), for it contains signs leading the mind above itself to God. Words have a proper meaning (*signa propria*) but they also have a figurative sense (*signa translata*), expressing the mysteries hidden within things. In the interpretation of Scripture and in the study of nature he has recourse to allegory and symbols drawn from both biblical and classical sources. Numbers, for example, have mysterious and symbolic meanings.

The Dionysian and Augustinian symbolism derive from Neo-Platonism, though the former places more emphasis on cosmic symbolism and the latter on the symbolic value of human signs and history as instruments of spiritual experience. Both tend to devalue the physical contents of reality and the importance of scientific explanation through intrinsic causes, and to place the true significance of reality in its essential reference to the transcendent God.

2. The Early Middle Ages. Like Augustine, Boethius transmitted classical philosophical ideas to the Middle Ages. In his logical works he translates ἀγαλογία as *comparatio* or *proportio*, ἀνάλογον as *proportionale*. *Proportio* he defines as the comparison of similar things. For example, there is a proportion between the relation of 4 to 2 and 40 to 20. Similarly genus is related to specific difference as matter is related to form, e.g., animality to rationality in the definition of man.

When treating of our knowledge of God, Boethius does not appeal to this Aristotelian type of analogy but to the Platonic notions of participation and image. This is because he denies any comparison between the infinite and finite (*De consolatione philosophiae* II, prose 7). Thus God is said to be good by substance, whereas creatures are called good because they come from his goodness and participate in it. This is shown by their tendency to goodness. They are "similar to the primal goodness" and hence are called good in reference to it.

This rests on the Neo-Platonic notion that by participation the intelligible, divine world descends into matter. The former is the archetype, the latter is its image, and as such it is the visible representation of spiritual realities.

In the Byzantine world this same principle was used by Saint John Damascene to defend the cult of sacred images. The prototype really exists in its image, he contended. Hence Christ and the saints are really present in icons; they are there by way of image (εἰκονικός). Thus an icon is a visible means by which God can be sensibly worshiped. An icon contains its subject "sacramentally." It is a part of the heavenly world projected into the earthly. As such, it is the seat of spiritual powers which are communicated to a worshiper suitably disposed to receive them.

The iconoclasts of the East dismissed these ideas as essentially pagan and forbade the making of icons. The Western Church at the time of Charlemagne considered sacred images useful as adornments and as instructive in historical matters. But the *Libri Carolini*

forbade the worship of images as repositories of spiritual powers. At this period the West had no interest in, or understanding of, the Christian Neo-Platonic interpretation of images as projections of spiritual forces into matter. It was scarcely ready to receive the works of John Scotus Erigena, who a century after Charlemagne translated into Latin the *Corpus Dionysiacum* and incorporated Denis' Christian Neo-Platonism into his own writings.

The patristic theme of the symbolic value of visible creation for the revelation of God was familiar to writers of the eleventh and twelfth centuries. Thus Hugh of Saint Victor compares the sensible universe to a book written by the finger of God. Everything in it is a figure, not invented by human ingenuity, but instituted by the divine will, in order to manifest and signify in some way the hidden attributes of God. Alain of Lille puts this notion in poetry: *Omnis mundi creatura/ Quasi liber et pictura/ Nobis est et speculum* (*Rythmus;* PL 210, 579). Aelred of Rievaulx speaks of the visible world as the first garment of God, the second being Scripture.

Cosmological analogies, often borrowed from biblical and classical sources, abound in early medieval writings. Thus Macrobius speaks of the glory of God illuminating the whole world "as one face fills many mirrors placed in due order." Alain of Lille compares the universe to a feudal city, with its periphery inverted. The empyrean is the central castle where the emperor (God) sits enthroned. The lower heaven is occupied by the angelic knighthood; while we on earth are outside the city wall. These are but two aspects of the "discarded image" of the Middle Ages (to use C. S. Lewis' phrase). Both, incidentally, appear in Dante's *Divine Comedy*.

Political and ecclesiastical analogies played significant roles in medieval society. In the twelfth century the term "mystical body of Christ," previously applied to the consecrated host, was gradually transferred to the Christian people, whose head is Christ. By analogy this theological notion was then applied to the body politic, which was called "the mystical body of the commonweal." Secular rulers borrowed the insignia of spiritual dignitaries; kings were thought of as married to their realms as Christ is married to the Church. In the English Tudor period this developed into the notion of "the King's two bodies"—his natural body and his body politic. On the other hand, medieval spiritual leaders borrowed the symbols of the secular powers. The pope, for example, was called "prince" and "true emperor" in the later Middle Ages.

The logical basis of such analogies occupied early medieval logicians such as Abelard. Discussing the transference (*transumptio*) of terms, he points out that **65** a term that principally signifies one thing may be applied to another because of some likeness. Thus we can say "The meadow smiles," transferring "smiles" from its proper usage to a metaphorical one. Rules were laid down for arguments based on such transference of terms. Abelard bases the argument by analogy on the maxim: "What occurs in the case of some proportional things happens in others." Thus one can argue that the ruler of a city should not be chosen by lot but for his knowledge, for this is how the pilot of a ship should be chosen (*Dialectica*, ed. De Rijk, p. 442).

3. The Late Middle Ages. With the discovery of the complete works of Aristotle in the twelfth and thirteenth centuries, medieval theories of analogy came more decisively under his influence. No less than the Church Fathers, the scholastics of the later Middle Ages viewed the universe through religious eyes. For them, too, the universe bears witness to the existence and attributes of its creator. But under the impact of Aristotelianism, a Christian naturalism arose that accorded to the universe a secular dimension unknown to the early Middle Ages. Creatures were not *pure* symbols: transparent films, so to speak, through which God's glory shines. They were created natures with values and ends of their own, though subordinate to their creator. The scholastic doctrines of analogy (especially that of Saint Thomas Aquinas) were designed to express this fact.

No scholastic caught the spirit of the Fathers better than Saint Bonaventure. His *Journey of the Mind to God* traces the stages by which the human mind ascends to its creator. The first stage is the discovery of God's "footprints" (*vestigia*) in the sensible world. Like a mirror this world reflects its creator in a distant way, e.g., through its being or existence. He is seen more closely and intimately through his image implanted in the spiritual soul. The sensible world is an exterior "book," the mind an interior one, in which its creator can be read.

Bonaventure distinguishes between two kinds of analogy. The first is based on the unequal participation of several things in one nature, as both man and dog are called animals, though man possesses animal nature more perfectly. The second is based on the unity not of nature, but of proportional likeness. This is the kind of analogy between God and creatures. They do not participate in one nature but there is a proportional similitude between them. Hence terms such as "goodness" can be predicated by analogy of both of them. Proportional unity is sometimes found among creatures; e.g., "light" is predicated of heavenly and earthly bodies, not because they share in one nature but because of their proportional likeness. Analogy always

implies similarity and dissimilarity; in the case of God and creatures the dissimilarity is greater than the similarity.

For Saint Thomas Aquinas, as for Saint Bonaventure, names apply to God and creatures only by analogy. Names cannot be predicated of them univocally, i.e., in entirely the same sense, for this would imply that they have a nature in common. Aquinas defines a univocal term as one whose meaning is entirely the same when predicated of several things; e.g., "animal" predicated of horse and cow. An equivocal term is attributed to several things with entirely different meanings; e.g., "dog" predicated of the animal and the constellation. Analogous terms are predicated of several subjects with a meaning that is partly the same and partly different. More precisely, their meaning is absolutely (*simpliciter*) different and relatively or proportionately (*secundum quid*) the same. For example, both animals and food are called healthy: animals because they possess health in the proper sense of the term, food because it is a cause of health.

Thus predication by analogy means predication according to a relation or proportion. This may be a relation of one thing to another, as in the above example of health. Or it may be a likeness of proportions, or proportionality; e.g., "sight" is attributed to both the eye and the intellect, because as sight is in the eye, so understanding is in the mind (Saint Thomas Aquinas, *On Truth*, 2, 11). In some proportionalities names are transferred to things to which they do not properly belong, the transference being justified by a similarity of effects. For example, God is called a "sun" because he is the source of spiritual life as the sun is the source of physical life. Such a transference of a name Thomas calls a metaphor. He points out that Scripture contains many metaphors of corporeal properties being transferred to spiritual realities because of a dynamic likeness. Thus grace is said to efface spiritual stains as water washes away bodily stains.

In other proportionalities there is no figurative transference of terms. The term is ascribed to several things in its proper sense, though they possess the property denoted by the term in different modes. Thus "being" is ascribed to man and stone in its proper sense, but their being is only proportionately the same, for each exists or is a being in proportion to its nature. Similarly "goodness" is attributed to God and creatures in its proper sense, though God possesses goodness in a higher mode than creatures.

The Thomistic doctrine of analogy makes it possible to speak meaningfully of God and to establish a theology, i.e., a science of God. But it does not allow us to know what God is in himself. Our knowledge of God is either negative (as when we know that he is not material or not finite), or it is analogical (i.e., he is known insofar as he is represented by creatures by proportional similitude).

Duns Scotus, on the contrary, contended that negative and analogical knowledge of God presupposes more basic univocal concepts of God and creatures. He argued that we cannot know what God is not, unless we first know what he is. Hence we must conceive God through positive concepts, derived from creatures, which apply to them in exactly the same sense. Examples of such univocal concepts are "being" and the transcendental properties of being such as "goodness." Scotus also argued that we cannot know God by analogy with creatures unless we know the two terms of the analogy, and for this we need absolute (i.e., nonrelational) concepts of what God is in himself. Such knowledge is given through univocal concepts, especially that of being. For Scotus, however, being is a univocal concept only when abstracted from all its modalities. When beings are considered as they actually exist, they are either infinite and uncreated being (God), or they are finite and created being (creatures). Thus conceived, they are beings only by analogy.

Toward the close of the Middle Ages theories of analogy came more strongly under the influence of Neo-Platonism. In particular, there was a revival of Boethian and Dionysian perspectives on analogy in the works of Eckhart and Nicholas of Cusa.

For Master Eckhart God is the analogous cause of creatures. Since there is both similarity and dissimilarity between the creator and his creatures, names given to them in common, such as "unity," "being," and "goodness," are neither univocal nor equivocal but analogous. Things participate in the divine perfections but they do not possess them as their own. In themselves they are pure nothingness. They are said to be, to be one or good, only in reference to God, who alone is Being, Unity, and Goodness. These perfections are ascribed to creatures entirely from without and they never positively take root in them.

Nicholas of Cusa resorted to symbolism to arrive at a knowledge of spiritual realities. Convinced that the visible universe is a faithful reflection of the invisible divine world, he thought it legitimate to use images to reach the latter analogically. He praised the Platonists, especially Augustine and Boethius, for realizing that the most perfect images of spiritual realities are drawn from mathematics—the science that gives the greatest certitude. Cusa himself often used mathematical symbols in his mystical ascent to God. Thus for him the coincidence of an infinite straight line with an infinite circle and triangle shows by analogy the coincidence of opposites in the infinite God (*De docta ignorantia* I, 11–16).

BIBLIOGRAPHY

Étienne Gilson, *History of Christian Philosophy in the Middle Ages* (New York, 1955). *The Cambridge History of Later Greek and Early Medieval Philosophy*, ed. A. H. Armstrong (Cambridge, 1967). H. DeLubac, *Exégèse médiévale: les quatre sens de l'écriture*, 4 vols. (Paris, 1959–62). M.-D. Chenu, *Nature, Man, and Society in the Twelfth Century*, trans. J. Taylor, L. K. Little (Chicago, 1968). E. F. Osborn, *The Philosophy of Clement of Alexandria* (Cambridge, 1957). V. Lossky, "La notion des 'analogies' chez Denys le pseudo-Aréopagite," *Archives d'histoire doctrinale et littéraire du Moyen Age*, **5** (1930), 279–309. J. Koch, "Zur analogielehre Meister Eckharts," *Mélanges offerts à Étienne Gilson* (Toronto and Paris, 1959), pp. 327–50. G. P. Klubertanz, *St. Thomas Aquinas on Analogy* (Chicago, 1960). C. S. Lewis, *The Discarded Image* (Cambridge, 1964).

ARMAND MAURER

[See also **Allegory;** Analogy in Early Greek Thought; **Creation in Religion;** God; Hierarchy; Holy; Infinity; Love; Nature; Number; Platonism; Symbol.]

ANALOGY OF THE BODY POLITIC

THE ANALOGY of the body politic is the perception and elaboration of correspondences between society or the state and the individual human body. These correspondences may then be applied in a variety of ways in political analysis or argument. In their simplest form, these arguments assert that given the organic nature of the state, then certain political structures or actions are necessarily appropriate. A "natural" society is one which functions in a manner similar to the human body. In the history of political philosophy and polemic, the analogy has been applied to many different forms of government and in support of a variety of particular opinions. In general, however, these states are hierarchical and authoritarian and the ideas being supported are conservative, stressing social order and obedience. There are a number of important exceptions. As a strategy of argumentation, moreover, the analogy is used in many different genres—philosophical treatise, political exhortation, sermon, poem, or drama. The analogy may appear as an allusive phrase or it may provide the structure for an extended discussion. Historically speaking, the analogy was used extensively from the time of the Greeks to the seventeenth century, when it was effectively challenged by another analogy, that of the social contract; in the nineteenth century developments in the study of biological evolution gave new impetus and application to the analogy.

ANALOGY OF THE BODY POLITIC

The analogy of the body politic rests on two principles which were articulated by the Greeks. First, the doctrine of hylozoism asserts that mind or life permeates the natural world. The individual possesses life or soul or mind which is in some way identical to the *homonoia* which animates, unifies, and directs the state. This mind is the source of the regularity in nature which makes possible science, including political science. This concept permits discussion of the relative health or sickness of the body politic and the suggesting of cures, perhaps by a ruler acting as a physician. The second basic principle asserts that one simple pattern exists at many levels of being; this pattern is most perfectly manifested in the human body (Plato, *Timaeus* 30c). In a variety of accounts, creation consists of the imposition of this pattern on previously chaotic matter. Since the citizen, the microcosm, and the larger world of the state possess an identical life and an identical physical structure, then more specific description and prescription are possible.

The earliest, though fragmentary, examples of the analogy come from India. The *Rig-Veda* (X, 90) contains a hymn describing the creation of four castes—priests, warriors, shepherds, and servants—from the body of Purusa, a sacrificial personification of the world-soul. The *Mahabharata* (XIV, xxii) gives a debate between the mind and the perceiving organs, the point of which is that human arrogance comes from an ignorance of how the members of society must cooperate.

More substantial examples appear in Greek political writers, who specifically apply the analogy to the *polis*. Plato begins the *Republic* by establishing analogy as a mode of inquiry: if justice in a state can be defined, then justice in an individual can also be determined. He then contrasts a simple, "healthy" society and a "feverish" one corrupted by luxury. By an extension of the analogy, the cure for a "festering" society is not the multiplication of petty laws, but a rigorous transformation of the state and the individual so that both will exhibit a centralized, rational control and an appropriate division of labor. In the later *Laws* (628c ff.) Plato characterizes the highest good as a peaceful, friendly state, like a healthy body that does not require medical attention. The organic nature of the state is specifically enunciated by Aristotle: "Thus the state is by nature clearly prior to the family and the individual . . . for example, if the whole body be destroyed, there will be no foot or hand . . ." (*Politics* 1253a). Society, therefore, is a creation of nature, not of man; man's greatest fulfillment comes from being a part of the *polis*.

Other Greek writers also used the analogy. Aristophanes sees one function of the comic poet as the difficult task of curing the diseases of the state (*Wasps*

650–51). Demosthenes regards Philip of Macedon as an attack of fever which Athens must resist. Of particular interest is the Aesopic fable of the belly and the members (*Aesopica*, ed. B. E. Perry, Urbana, Ill. [1952], No. 130). In its simplest form the fable teaches the cooperative structural relationship between the generals and soldiers in an army. The fable is explicitly political in the Roman tradition (Livy, II, 32) in which Menenius Agrippa ends a plebeian secession by explaining the nourishment the belly (Senate) provides for the hands and feet (common people). The analogy was also applied occasionally to smaller groups; in Xenophon's *Memorabilia* (II, iii) Socrates urges reconciliation between quarreling brothers by citing the harmony of pairs of hands, feet, and eyes.

After the conquests of Alexander, the city-state was a much less relevant political unit; by praying for *homonoia* between Macedonians and Persians, Alexander indicated that the analogy of the body politic could be applied to the much larger Hellenistic monarchy or even all mankind. Philo Judaeus urges acceptance of personal disaster by comparing the actions of divine providence to an amputation performed by a surgeon on a partially diseased body. The writings of the Roman Stoics contain many passages which argue analogically for the necessity of subordinating the desires of the individual to the well-being of the state or humanity. Cicero writes that if each part of the body tries to appropriate the health of the others, then the body will die; such behavior in men would be equally destructive (*De officiis* III, 22). Echoing Plato and Aristotle, Seneca says that as it is unnatural for the hands to destroy the feet, so the need for harmony, love, and mutual protection causes mankind to protect individuals (*De ira* II, 31).

Such statements are the source of one of the most influential uses of the analogy, Saint Paul's first epistle to the Corinthians: "For as the body is one, and hath many members . . . so also is Christ. . . . And the eye cannot say unto the hand, I have no need of thee: nor again the head to the feet, I have no need of you. . . . Now ye are the body of Christ and members in particular . . ." (I Corinthians 12:12–27). Love (*agapē*) between the members unifies the body (I Corinthians 6:15–16). Though some of Paul's language is traditional, the application of the analogy to the followers of Christ is a significant departure, which contains the radical implication that faith determines the body of which a man is a part. In the early Church, Paul's words were frequently quoted in admonitions against dissension and factionalism (e.g., Saint Basil's Letters 66, 203, 222). Saint Augustine occasionally describes the Cities of God and Man as bodies, but his emphasis is on the concept of a mystical body of the faithful, united by having sacramentally eaten the body of Christ.

In the Middle Ages the analogy of the body was developed substantially. Most previous applications had been rather brief; medieval authors extend it in elaborate, sometimes fantastic detail. Though its influence on the West is uncertain, the tenth-century *Encyclopedia* of the Arabic Brotherhood of Sincerity uses organic analogies at great length: the human body is compared to a city and a kingdom; the senses are to the soul as counsellors to a king, and so on. Among Christian writers the analogy is used for a variety of purposes. Most simply, it appears in devotional literature to explain charity, grace, or some other aspect of doctrine. It could supplement the concept of the three estates: clergy-eyes-guidance, nobility-hands-defense, peasants-feet-agriculture. John of Salisbury's *Policraticus* (1159) adopts for its structure a substantial comparison of the human body and a kingdom. After identifying the soul and the clergy, John discusses in detail the other members of the body: head-prince, heart-senate, hands-soldiers, stomach-treasury, and feet-farmers. He emphasizes the need for spiritual unity in the state and proposes cures for various political diseases, including tyranny. The fable of the belly explains and defends systems of taxation.

The Church developed Paul's words about the body of Christ to explain the structure and importance of ecclesiastical institutions. The Church becomes *corpus mysticum et politicum* of which the Pope is the head, kings and emperors but members. Organic analogies buttress both sides of the period's most profound political controversies. Saint Thomas Aquinas finds four points of identity which unify both natural and mystical bodies, and asserts that the supremacy of the spiritual authority corresponds to the soul's rule of the body. There are three responses to such claims: to proclaim the importance of some other organ, such as the heart, with which a king may be equated; to define the state as a body distinct from the body of the Church; or to deny the importance of the papacy by claiming that only Christ is the head of the Church. In the late Middle Ages the second alternative, an extension of the idea of a "mystical body," is a convenient illustration of the growing self-consciousness of the national states. Sir John Fortescue's *De laudibus legum Angliae* (ca. 1470) says that a body politic, specifically England, is a *corpus mysticum;* the laws are the nerves which unite the body and public spirit is the life-giving blood. An example of the third alternative is Henry VIII's assumption of the title "Supreme Head of the Church in England."

In the sixteenth and seventeenth centuries the analogy persisted as part of the period's vigorous medieval heritage, but at the same time other ideas developed which effectively challenged the validity of the analogy. The three main questions to which the analogy was applied are the nature of the Church, the nature of the state, and the relationship of the two. Theologians and polemicists had much to say about the effect of the Reformation on the body of the Church. Kings and popes competed for the title "head," and they denied that each other's institutions could be described by organic analogies.

Secular rulers invoked the analogy repeatedly to enforce conformity and at least passive obedience. Even in matters of religion, the word of the prince had to be followed; rebellion in the state was as unnatural as internal conflict in a body. The Elizabethan *Homily Against Disobedience* claims that for a subject to judge a ruler is impiety, "as though the foot must judge of the head. . . ." At a more perceptive level, the analogy became a vehicle for social criticism. Thomas Starkey's *Dialogue between Pole and Lupset,* early in the sixteenth century, catalogues diseases or imbalances in the four humors as a structure for discussing political and economic abuses and proposing remedies. A few more radical applications appeared, as in John Milton's *Of Reformation in England* (1641), which transforms the old fable of the belly to attack the episcopacy as a cancerous wen.

Shakespeare's *Coriolanus* is perhaps the most thoughtful consideration of the applicability of organic analogies in politics. In the first scene, derived from Livy and Plutarch, Menenius recounts the fable of the belly in a partially successful attempt to calm a rioting mob. Organic imagery recurs frequently through the play as the characters attempt to define the suitability of the proud protagonist. The action shows that the Senate is not a generous nourisher of the state, the plebeians are not docile workers; Coriolanus vigorously denies any unity, organic or otherwise, with the lower classes. The distinction of Shakespeare's play is that it dramatizes the gap between the ideal commonwealth suggested by the idea of a body politic, and the political behavior of men. In some instances the familiar analogy appears to be little more than a pious fraud perpetrated by ruthless aristocrats.

The doubts Shakespeare raises about the validity of the analogy are part of a larger process of questioning and substitution. Some writers differentiated the bodies as politic and natural; Fernando Vasquez observes that in a man a limb cannot change its position, no other part can become the head, authority always resides in the head, and the death of the head always causes the death of the body—but none of these is true of the body politic (*Controversarium* III). Hugo Grotius made a similar distinction by pointing out the contractual origin of the state and the right of a part to protect itself by secession or other means (*De jure* II).

To this increasing general skepticism must be added two very significant factors which essentially destroyed the traditional analogy. The first is the new science which undercut the basic premisses. Materialism replaced hylozoism. The pattern which permitted structural correspondences could be dismissed as the vain attempt of men to find order where none in fact existed. The analogy of the body politic exemplifies the Baconian Idols which obstruct scientific inquiry.

Secondly, the concept of a body politic was effectively replaced by the old, but not widely popular, idea of a social contract. For Calvin and his followers the Church as mystical body was supplemented by a great emphasis on a covenant, modeled on the one between God and Abraham. These theories of covenant and contract view church and state as artificial institutions, created by an act of will of their individual members and subject to change by them. The new analogy attempts definition in terms of origin, for which organic analogies seemed deficient. A striking fusion of the two traditions is Hobbes' statement (in *Leviathan*, Part I, Introduction) that the state is an artificial body, a machine assembled by man. More typical of the transition are these words from the Mayflower Compact (1620): "We . . . covenant and combine ourselves together into a Civil Body Politike. . . ." The main point is the combining; "Body Politike" is simply a synonym for "political entity" with no further analogical meanings intended.

For the last three centuries extended organic analogies have been generally absent from discussions of political issues. The phrase "body politic" persists, but as a dead metaphor rather than a meaningful concept for analysis or argument. Two types of exceptions may be cited from the nineteenth century. First, there was a moderate amount of imagery used to characterize the Industrial Revolution and an ideal alternative which might exist in the future or the medieval past. Thomas Carlyle writes in *Sartor Resartus* (1833) that government is the "outward *Skin* of the Body Politic," binding and protecting its constituent parts; the vivifying nervous system is religion. Mechanism, capitalism, and utilitarianism are symptoms of a "universal Social Gangrene"; England is "writhing powerless on its fever-bed. . . ." To recreate something like the organic interdependency of the Middle Ages, Carlyle advocates hero-worship, "a new body . . . with a resuscitated soul" (*Past and Present*, 1843).

A new development was the application of biological evolution to the study of political institutions, e.g., in so-called Social Darwinism. Herbert Spencer's *The Principles of Sociology* (3 vols., 1876–96) contains as

many comparisons between natural and politic bodies as anything from the past. The significant differences are a much greater variety of bodies and a concern for change from one form to another. A primitive society evolves into an industrial nation just as a small, simple form of life becomes a larger, more complex organism. Though the state may partially resemble a living being, few modern thinkers are willing to extend similarity to identity.

BIBLIOGRAPHY

There is no comprehensive discussion of the topic. Various aspects are treated in R. Allers, "Microcosmus from Anaximandros to Paracelsus," *Traditio*, **2** (1944), 319–407; P. Archambault, "The Analogy of the 'Body' in Renaissance Political Literature," *Bibliotèque d'humanisme et renaissance*, **29** (1967), 21–53; N. O. Brown, *Love's Body* (New York, 1966); A.-H. Chroust, "The Corporate Idea and the Body Politic in the Middle Ages," *Review of Politics*, **9** (1947), 423–52; F. W. Coker, *Organismic Theories of the State: Nineteenth-Century Interpretations of the State as Organism or as Person* (New York, 1910); G. P. Conger, *Theories of Macrocosm and Microcosm in the History of Philosophy* (New York, 1922); O. Gierke, *Natural Law and the Theory of Society*, trans. E. Barker, 2 vols. (Cambridge, 1934); idem, *Political Theories of the Middle Ages*, trans. F. Maitland (Cambridge, 1900); D. G. Hale, *The Body Politic: A Political Metaphor in Renaissance English Literature* (The Hague, 1971); E. H. Kantorowicz, *The King's Two Bodies* (Princeton, 1957); E. Lewis, "Organic Tendencies in Medieval Political Thought," *American Political Science Review*, **32** (1938), 849–76; H. de Lubac, *Corpus Mysticum: L'Eucharistie et l'église au moyen âge* (Paris, 1949); W. Nestle, "Die Fabel des Menenius Agrippa," *Klio*, **21** (1927), 350–60; J. E. Phillips, *The State in Shakespeare's Greek and Roman Plays* (New York, 1940); E. M. W. Tillyard, *The Elizabethan World Picture* (London, 1943; New York, 1961).

DAVID G. HALE

[See also Class; Evolutionism; General Will; Health and Disease; **Macrocosm and Microcosm;** Myth; Nature; Organicism.]

ANARCHISM

General Principles. Anarchism is a social philosophy and a political doctrine based on the value of individual freedom. As such it is linked up with liberal and all other kinds of progressive ideas. Essential for anarchist thought, however, is the rejection of all coercive authority exercised by men over men. The Greek word *an-archy* must have meant absence of authority or government. The word "anarchy," describing a stateless society, was for the first time used by Louis Armand de Lahontan in his *Nouveaux voyages dans l'Amérique septentrionale* (1703), describing the Indians living in a society without state, laws, prisons, priests, private property, in short, "in anarchy." Colloquially however, anarchy became identical with confusion and disorder.

A wide diversity of anarchist views can be found in the works of philosophers, religious thinkers, writers, and poets throughout the ages; for example, in Diderot's "I don't wish either to give or to obey laws," we have a short and perfect statement of the anarchist creed. Opposing Plato's "state communism," Zeno, the founder of the Stoa school, advocated a society without government. Laws should be abolished, since virtue and morality could only be achieved in liberty.

As a general principle, anarchism advocates a society from which the coercive elements have been removed. Like anarchism, liberalism stemmed from the concern for freedom, and the wish to keep the activities of the state and the functions of government to a minimum. Anarchism, however, holds that liberal postulates are realizable only on the basis of the abolition of economic monopoly and the coercive institutions of political power because, while equality is quite possible without liberty, there can be no liberty without social and economic equality; "liberty without socialism is privilege, injustice; and socialism without liberty is slavery and brutality" (Bakunin). The liberal view of the "minimization" of the state and its replacement by free federalist groups, was first expounded by Wilhelm von Humboldt in his treatise, *Ideen zu einem Versuch, die Grenzen der Wirksamkeit des Staats zu bestimmen*, written in 1792 and published in 1851 (English trans. *The Sphere and Duties of Government*, 1854). John Stuart Mill was influenced by this work in writing *On Liberty* (1859). Both works exposed the danger in democracy of the "tyranny of the majority," using principles very close to anarchist doctrine.

Anarchism holds that there is no conflict or irreconcilability between the rights of the individual and society. Sociologically anarchism is based on the distinction between state and society. As men continually are bound to work together for almost any purpose, their aims will be achieved more efficiently if the guiding principle is solidarity or "mutual aid." The individual is not only a single entity, but his very existence presupposes also a collective relationship. Anarchism postulates that human potentialities, spontaneity, individuality, and initiative, buried in an authoritarian society and in a network of bureaucratic institutions, can be freed by de-institutionalizing society. Life-enhancing processes of society will be liberated with the passing of the domination of the state,

which is regarded as a tumor on the body politic. The state, the supreme authority, with its machinery (the government) which carries more power than is required for administration—i.e., the "political surplus"—should be abolished.

Education has always played an important part in anarchist doctrines. Modern psychology and education, with its child-centered principle of self-education and self-discipline, has distinctive anarchist implications in this respect. In recent times new schools in criminology (especially in the USA, and partly in England and the Netherlands) have advocated a change of attitude in judging delinquents and in recognizing their right to some forms of deviant behavior, and to being regarded as equals instead of being made by authority to adapt to the actual dominant pattern. The abolition of the punitive element in justice as well as the abolition of prisons as "seminars of vice," "where man comes out worse than he enters" (William Godwin), is gaining ground.

The essence of the artist as a creative individual implies absolute freedom to realize his aesthetic aims, and *suo ipso* anarchistic thought, even if he is not aware of its theoretical basis. In our age, without abandoning its traditional aesthetic norms in art this need for freedom becomes even more evident. Anarchism postulates that without coercion and stringent outside regulations everyone would have greater possibilities to develop his potential creative personality.

Different Trends. Although different trends—anarcho-communism, individualism, collectivism, mutualism, and all the intermediate programs—can be distinguished, all anarchist schools of thought have a fundamental conception in common, viz., freedom of the individual, rejection of government, state, and all coercive institutions. These forms of anarchism are simply the ways considered best for achieving freedom and solidarity in economic life, the ways believed to correspond most closely with justice and freedom for the distribution of the means of production and the products of labor among men. It is the constant searching for a more secure guarantee of freedom which is the common factor amongst anarchists even when divided into different schools. "The achievement of the greatest measures of individualism is in direct ratio to the amount of communism that is possible; that is to say, a maximum of solidarity in order to enjoy a maximum of freedom" (Malatesta [1926], p. 82).

Bakunist anarchism was called in the late 1860's "collectivism." Anarcho-communism, rejecting the extreme of individualist anarchism, as a variation of collectivism laid the emphasis on communist distribution and local and communal association. Developed mainly by Kropotkin since the end of the seventies, this communal form became the dominating trend of anarchism in the following decades. The anarcho-communists who regarded trade unions as instruments in the struggle for the economic and social improvement of the working class within the framework of existing society and as the means to carry out revolution and social reconstruction, called themselves anarcho-syndicalists. The ultimate goal of anarcho-syndicalism, identical with that of collective anarchism, is to raise the masses to independent management of production and distribution by the common action of all manual and intellectual working men of every branch in industry.

Violence is not an essential part of anarchism. Neither is terrorism. Because of the spectacular *attentats* and outrages, connected with the names of Ravachol, Auguste Vaillant, Emil Henry, Santo Caserio, mainly in France (1891–94), and of later syndicalist bombings, anarchism and terrorism became associated in the public mind. Their acts were usually retaliation for the persecution and repression by the government and they did not believe in any social organization by the working class, or in propaganda, and acted in a state of rebellion against society. However, their acts of rebellion were isolated, and the number of anarchists who took part in them was always very small. Most of the terrorists in modern times were not anarchists.

Some anarchist currents, like Christian and Tolstoyan anarchism, reject all violence. Central to Leo Tolstoy's religious anarchism, derived from the Scriptures, is the rejection of the state and of all authority exercised by men over men, the denial of property, and the need for moral revolution by persuasion and example, as well as by experiments of communal living. Men should destroy the state by ceasing to cooperate with it, and by forming new social organizations and patterns of behavior. Refusal to obey, an essential principle of Tolstoy's teaching, influenced Gandhi in his principle of nonviolent noncooperation. Gandhi was inspired also by Henry David Thoreau's treatise *On the Duty of Civil Disobedience* (1849). These ideas of individual resistance can be summarized in the words of Étienne de la Boétie: "Resolve no longer to serve and you will be free." Anselme Bellegarrique would write (1850): "There are no tyrants, there are only slaves." Noncooperation, nonretaliation, nonviolent resistance, war resistance, boycott, and direct action are applications all derived from these principles.

Political Doctrine. Anarchist thought exercised its main influence as a political doctrine. As such it is part of the history of socialist thought, of which it represents the libertarian and anti-Jacobin trend. Like socialism, anarchism is a product of the political and industrial revolutions. As a matter of fact the history of modern

anarchist thought and anarchist movement is bound up since the middle of the nineteenth century with the history of the labor movement. It is strongly influenced by Marxist ideas about the class struggle and the emphasis of the economic side of the emancipation of the laboring classes.

Anarchism—in contrast with Marxian theory—rejects the theory of the political organization of the labor class with a view to the conquest of the state. It rejects pressure through the mechanism of parliamentary parties as well as dictatorship in the period of the revolution as instruments to achieve these ends. It objects to representative government and to parliamentary democracy because it denies that in a political sense one man should represent another, unless he is a delegate to represent a group in relation to a definite issue or form of activity, and is always subject to recall.

Marx, and Engels too, defined anarchy as the final stage of socialism, i.e., a classless and stateless society. Anarchism however regards the Marxian theory of the inevitability of the historical economic process, leading to the conquest of power and subsequently the "withering away of the state" as a fallacy and as utopian dialectics.

Anarchism recognizes only regional differences and demands for every group the right of self-determination in solidarity with all other associations of an economic or territorial order. Federalism is an essential part of its doctrine. In place of the present state organization, anarchism would establish a federation of free communities which would be bound to one another by their common and social interests, and would arrange their affairs by mutual agreement and free contract.

Theorists. The first systematic exposition is the political treatise of William Godwin, *An Enquiry concerning Political Justice and its Influence on General Virtue and Happiness* (1793). The title is a good summary of the content. The main claim of Godwin as founder of modern anarchism is that in Godwin's opinion all moral evils are caused by political institutions. A disciple of eighteenth-century philosophical rationalism and belief in the perfectibility of man, i.e., a continuous advance towards higher rationality, Godwin believed that men behaved irrationally because the conventional institutions of society led them to stray from reason. Man's character depends on external circumstances, and social prejudice and government should be abolished, as government constitutes the frequent source of crime, villainy, and injustice. Godwin questioned the legitimacy of every form of government and coercion, and envisaged a future of free enlightened cooperation of individuals, grouped in small communities.

The importance Godwin attached to education, i.e., to the purpose of developing the child's autonomy, is common to most anarchist schools of thought. The emphasis on the influence of environment in the formation of character and in the shaping of human conduct, was to be taken over by Robert Owen and developed as an integral part of Owenite socialism. Godwin's anarchism rested on an absolute exaltation of the claim of individual conscience enlightened by reason, involving a repudiation of any duty of obedience, save to the demands of reason. Through Shelley, who adopted his philosophy and who wrote to Godwin: "You are the regulator and former of my mind," anarchism became a theme of world literature.

If Godwin tried to persuade, Charles Fourier emphasized the example of small communities (*phalanstères*), free and voluntary associations (*communes sociétaires*), mainly agricultural, without any authority and coercion, and with a variety of types of work suited for every person, corresponding to the natural variety of human desires. He analyzed the psychological conditions of work, and believed he had discovered the law of "attraction," a permanent contribution to the problem of work and of the incentives and their relations to it. Free experiments are an essential part of anti-authoritarian socialism.

William Thompson, influenced by Godwin, Bentham, and Owen, advocated direct action by the producers, using trade unionism as a means for their own emancipation without the help of the government. He devised a constructive plan for the emancipation of labor by establishing cooperative societies of production and thus constructing a new society.

The system of Co-operative Industry accomplishes this, not by the vain search after foreign markets throughout the globe, no sooner found than over-stocked and glutted by the restless competition of the starving producers, but by the voluntary union of the industrious or productive classes, in such numbers as to afford *a market to each other,* by working together *for each other,* for the mutual supply, directly by themselves, of all their most indispensable wants, in the way of food, clothing, dwelling, and furniture (Thompson, p. III).

Nineteenth-century anarchism first received form and content from Pierre-Joseph Proudhon. The use of the words "anarchy" and "anarchist" in the nineteenth century goes back to Proudhon, who used "anarchy" for the first time in the sense of absence of sovereignty (*What is Property?*, 1840). Later Proudhon spoke, in his *Solution du problème social*, of the ideal republic as *a positive anarchy.* "It is neither liberty, subordinated to order, as in a constitutional monarchy, nor liberty in presenting order. It is reciprocal liberty and not limited liberty; liberty is not the daughter but the

mother of order" (Cole, I, 202). Proudhon's influence on subsequent anarchist thought has been threefold: (1) his attack on the Jacobin principle, his denunciation of the State, and his rejection of representative democracy; (2) his proposal to replace the State by groups of individuals, united for productive purposes; (3) his theory of federalism. According to Proudhon, economic and social exploitation was correlated with political oppression. Nothing is feasible by spontaneous initiative, independent actions of individuals and collectivities as long as they are in the presence of this colossal power which is given to the State by centralization. Proudhon rejected a state corporation as advocated by Louis Blanc. Although he thought mainly in terms of small-scale economic activity, he envisaged for the future large industry and agriculture developed from association. Proudhon advocated a great central Credit Bank, an independent institution apart from the State, making through subsidiary branches interest-free advances of capital, to ensure means of labor to each producer, or workers' organizations to ensure to each producer the full product of his labor. Products would be exchanged at cost value by means of labor checks based on the labor-time theory of value associated with Robert Owen and the Ricardian socialists. Proudhon called this system "mutualism."

Two outstanding representatives of anarchist individualism are Max Stirner and Benjamin Tucker. In *Der Einzige und sein Eigenthum* (1844; trans. as *The Ego and his Own*), Stirner, a philosopher and a social and political thinker, developed the view that law and the State deprived the individual of his uniqueness. As all forms of government arise from the principle that all right and all authority belong to the collectivity, it is indifferent who exercises the authority, for the collectivity is always above the individual. The State acts with violence and claims that its laws are sacred. He who affronts them is a criminal. Every man's welfare demands that a social life based solely on the welfare of the individual take the place of the State. The State exists through voluntary servitude. What do laws amount to if no one obeys them? What do orders amount to if nobody lets himself be ordered? The State is not imaginable without rulers and servitude; for the State must will to be the lord of all that it embraces, and this will be called the "will of the State." The workers have the most enormous power in their hands and if they once became thoroughly conscious of it and used it, nothing would withstand them. The State rests on the slavery of labor. If labor becomes free, the State is lost.

Benjamin R. Tucker rejected any communistic solution of the social problem as incompatible with the "sovereignty of the individual," as postulated by the first American exponents of individual anarchism such as Josiah Warren and Stephen Pearl Andrews. Their intellectual development was not influenced by European libertarian or radical ideas, but rooted in the liberal principles of the Declaration of Independence. In the first half of the nineteenth century, American "philosophical anarchism" was a product of the social conditions of the country. There was a belief in the effectiveness of practical experiments, and their social and economic ideas were based on the right to full product of one's labor, an equitable commerce on the basis of cost as the limit of price, i.e., similar to what Proudhon had conceived in his "mutualist" ideas.

Michael Bakunin, a prolific but incoherent writer, developed his anarchist ideas from 1864 on. Starting from Hegel's idealism, Bakunin's philosophical ideas were molded by the humanism of Ludwig Feuerbach. Atheism became an essential part of his doctrine. He regarded the idea of God as fundamentally inconsistent with human freedom. With Bakunin, anarchist thought became linked with anarchist organizations and working-class movements, and became a political movement. His doctrine inspired socialist movements in France, Italy, Switzerland, and in Spain, where its influence lasted longest. Like Proudhon, Bakunin attacked the concept of the centralized state even when it appeared as the democratic representation of the people or as the instrument of a hitherto exploited class. He envisaged a revolution to expropriate capital and land, but not by the state, which to be able to fulfil its political and economic mission (as state-socialists advocate) would necessarily have to be very powerful and strongly concentrated. He foresaw even greater exploitation, and in the development of the modern great powers and in the growing influence of economic monopoly, the greatest danger for the future of Europe.

Bakunin's anarchist ideas are most fully expressed in the programs—mostly drafts—which he wrote for the secret societies he tried to organize. He was convinced that a small number of individuals, acting in common with the masses, could and should essentially influence the course of historic events. Bakunin's social theory is a critical application of anarchism with a view to changing the political and social system. He rejected Proudhon's mutualism as a solution of the social problem, and also the belief in the possibility of eliminating capitalism by peaceful means. However, Proudhon's anti-Jacobin and federalist ideas influenced him, but he rejected every form of state socialism:

I detest communism because it is the negation of liberty and I can conceive nothing human without liberty. I am no communist because communism concentrates and aims at the absorption of all powers of society; the radical extir-

pation of that principle of authority and guardianship of the state which under the pretext of moralizing and civilizing men, has hitherto enslaved, oppressed, exploited and depraved them (Bakunin [1873], p. 28; trans. G. D. H. Cole).

He stood for the organization of society arranged from below upward on the basis of collective and social property, by way of free association.

Bakunin, the great antagonist of Marx in the "First International" (1864), not only objected to the theory of the state and dictatorship but regarded the Marxian interpretation of Hegel's dialectic, that socialism would be the result of an inevitable, historically determined, scientific process, as a fallacy. He was very critical of the prospect that science would regulate human and social affairs, "the reign of scientific intelligence would be a despotism, more demoralizing and worse than any previous despotism, and resulting in a new class, a hierarchy of real and fictitious scientists, and the world would be divided between a minority in the name of science and an immense ignorant majority" (*Archives Bakounine*, II, 204).

Peter Kropotkin, scientist, historian, and social reformer, contributed perhaps more then anyone else to the elaboration and propagation of anarchism. In his classic, anti-Darwinist, sociological work *Mutual Aid: a Factor of Evolution* (1902) he sets out to show that mutual aid is as important an aspect in nature and in society as the struggle for survival. The dominating importance of the principle of mutual aid appears also in the domain of ethics. Konrad Lorenz wrote that mutual aid is the only phylogenetical adapted mechanism of behavior. By combining his scientific and social aspirations, Kropotkin tried to find a scientific basis of anarchism but never found a very convincing one. The very basis of his faith is a belief in cooperativeness as a natural human quality. The process of individualization, or "individuation" as modern psychologists would call it, i.e., self-realization, will not lead to isolation, but to an intense and more universal collective solidarity. He believed in the coordination of industry and agriculture; small communities which would control the means of production and counteract the tendency of centralized mass production. He always stressed the importance of the institutes created by the workers themselves as cooperative societies and trade unions. After the Russian Revolution he stated (1919) that as long as the country was governed by a party dictatorship, the workers' and peasant councils lost their entire significance.

Errico Malatesta, who spent a life of incessant revolutionary activity spreading anarchist propaganda in Europe and in America, was, like Kropotkin, an anarcho-communist. But while Kropotkin stressed the importance of free association, Malatesta emphasized the role of the conscious minority and of revolutionary actions. Malatesta started his anarchist career in the 1870's as a follower of Bakunin, but in later years he thought the economic and historical approach of Bakunin too Marxist. Although no opponent of syndicalism, he did not share with the anarcho-syndicalists their belief that creating a mass movement through the trade unions was an essential, constructive element in the revolution. He accepted the syndicalist theory of the general strike insofar as it was insurrectional and expropriative, in fact, insofar as it was an effective means of social transformation. He did not share Kropotkin's optimism, or his scientific interpretation of anarchism. He was a pragmatic anarchist and held that the mean task of anarchists was to make and to help to make the revolution. He advanced the revolution as much as possible in his constructive as well as destructive roles, always opposing the formation of any government. He also held that abolition of political power without the simultaneous destruction of economic privilege was not possible. He shared these views with Bakunin, including the rejection of terror. In revolution one must attack institutions; then it will not be necessary to destroy people, and to foster the inevitable reaction which is always caused by the massacre of men. "Terror," wrote Malatesta, "has always been the instrument of tyranny."

The Russian Revolution developed initially on Bakuninist lines: the state and its institutions were destroyed and replaced by "soviets," i.e., councils of workers and peasants, who expropriated the factories and the land. These soviets, in which the constructive element of the revolution was embodied, disintegrated after the Bolsheviks had succeeded in founding a "revolutionary state" and a party dictatorship. The liquidation by the Red Army (March 1921) of the Commune of Kronstadt, which stood for "all power to the Soviets and not to the Party," marked the end of the independent soviets.

The most important historical example of an attempt to put anarchist principles into practice was the industrial and agricultural "collectivizations" during the first months of the Spanish Civil War. Within forty-eight hours of the uprising, on July 19, 1936, the whole economic and social life of Catalonia and many other parts of Spain was taken over by the syndicates. Factories, railways, and workshops, as well as all social services, were run by workers' councils. The continuation of the armed struggle, the government control of production and finance, the counterrevolutionary policy of the communists after the Stalin intervention, the compromises made in the name of "victory over Franco," e.g., the participation of the anarchists'

leaders in the government, were all factors tending to undermine this kind of social reconstruction.

In order to define the role played by anarchism in the light of the experience of a rapidly changing society, two different tendencies can be noticed. Since the defeat of the powerful anarchist movement in the Spanish Civil War, anarchist movements everywhere have declined and lost their impetus. But anarchist ideas have outlived their partisans and may still be of value as doctrines of social reconstruction. The state has changed its character. The laissez-faire state of the nineteenth century has developed into an ever increasing bureaucracy. In a growing process powerful political institutions and industrial monopolies are intertwined in an excessively centralized structure not dreamed of by any anarchist thinker.

The anarchist criticism of the state and of authority, far from being invalidated by this modern development, may be more relevant than when the theory was created. This may explain the growing interest in the 1960's in anarchist ideas. Kropotkin's ideal of a regionally decentralized economy could be regarded at the time as rather utopian and irreconcilable with the economic and political trend of society. But the new developments in an age of cybernetic potentially unlimited technology could easily free society of work and want, to live in a world of plenty. The use of new sources of power may reduce the necessity of present-day, gigantic economic units, and may make the widest distribution of industry, agriculture, and culture possible in the political as well as in the social field. This however would not guarantee automatically a decreased authority, as new communications and computer techniques could just as well produce a greater development of authority. In other words, such a trend to decentralization would only be realized if based on an interregional federation, in which the region, as defined by Lewis Mumford, is the basic configuration in human life, a permanent sphere of cultural influence, and a center of economic activity.

BIBLIOGRAPHY

General. The standard work on the history of anarchism is by Max Nettlau, whose works, collections, and manuscripts, acquired by the International Institute of Social History in Amsterdam, are a monumental source for the history of anti-authoritarian thought and libertarian socialism. Max Nettlau, *Der Vorfrühling der Anarchie: Ihre historische Entwicklung von den Anfängen bis zum Jahre 1864* (Berlin, 1925); idem, *Der Anarchismus von Proudhon zu Kropotkin. Seine historische Entwicklung in den Jahren 1859–1880* (Berlin, 1927); idem, *Anarchisten und Sozialrevolutionäre: Die historische Entwicklung des Anarchismus in den Jahren 1880–1886* (Berlin, 1931). Four more volumes dealing with the period 1886–1914 are still unpublished. Spanish summary: *l'Anarquia a través de los tiempos* (Barcelona, 1935); Max Nettlau, *Bibliographie de l'Anarchie* (Brussels, 1897). The most complete bibliography today is the subject catalog on anarchism (about 18,000 titles) of the Library of the International Institute of Social History, Amsterdam.

Other works are: G. D. H. Cole, *History of Socialist Thought*, 2 vols. (London and New York, 1953–60), Vol. I: *The Forerunners, 1789–1850;* Vol. II: *Marxism and Anarchism, 1850–1890* (London, 1953, 1954); Paul Eltzbacher, *Anarchism: Seven Exponents of the Anarchist Philosophy* (1900; rev. ed New York, 1960); Charles Gide and Charles Rist, *A History of Economic Doctrines*, 2nd. ed. (Boston, 1948); Daniel Guérin, *l'Anarchisme. De la doctrine à l'action* (Paris, 1965); idem, *Ni Dieu, ni maître: Anthologie historique du mouvement anarchiste* (Paris, 1966); James Joll, *The Anarchists* (London, 1964); Leonard I. Krimerman and Lewis Perry, *Patterns of Anarchy: A Collection of Writings on the Anarchist Tradition* (New York, 1966); Peter Kropotkin, "Anarchism" in *Encyclopaedia Britannica*, 11th ed. (London and New York, 1910–11); D. Novak, "The Place of Anarchism in the History of Political Thought," *Review of Politics*, **20** (July 1958); George Woodcock, *Anarchism, A History of Libertarian Ideas and Movements* (London, 1962).

Special works, biographies, studies. Michel Bakounine, *Oeuvres*, 6 vols. (Paris, 1895–1913); idem, *Werke*, 3 vols. (Berlin, 1921–24); idem, *The Political Philosophy of Bakunin*, edited and compiled by G. P. Maximoff (Glencoe, Ill., 1953); idem, *Archives Bakounine* (Leyden, 1961–), edition of the complete works in progress; idem, *Mémoire de la Fédération jurassienne*, pièces justificatives (Sonvillier, 1873); also Max Nettlau, *Bakunin. Eine Biographie*, 3 vols. (London, 1896–1900); E. H. Carr, *Michael Bakunin* (London, 1937); A. Comfort, *Authority and Delinquency in the Modern State: A Criminological Approach to the Problem of Power* (London, 1950); Peter Kropotkin, *Memoirs of a Revolutionist* (1900; reprint New York, 1962); *Kropotkin's Revolutionary Pamphlets*, ed. Roger N. Baldwin (New York, 1927); Errico Malatesta. "Comunismo e Individualismo," *Pensiero e Volontà* (1 April, 1926). Max Nettlau, *Errico Malatesta: Das Leben eines Anarchisten* (Berlin, 1922); idem, *Elisée Reclus, Anarchist und Gelehrter, 1830–1905* (Berlin, 1928); Pierre-Joseph Proudhon, *Les confessions d'un révolutionnaire. Pour servir à l'histoire de la Révolution de Février* (Paris, 1849); idem, *Idée générale de la révolution au XIXe siècle* (Paris, 1851); English trans. (London, 1923); idem, *l'Actualité de Proudhon, Colloque de novembre 1965* (Brussels, 1967); Herbert Read, *Education through Art* (New York, 1945); idem, "Pragmatic Anarchism," in *Encounter*, **15** (January 1968); Vernon Richards, ed., *Errico Malatesta: Life and Ideas* (London, 1965); Rudolf Rocker, *Nationalism and Culture* (New York, 1937); idem, *Pioneers of American Freedom* (Los Angeles, 1949); William Thompson, *Practical Directions for the Speedy and Economical Establishment of COMMUNITIES on the principles of Mutual Co-operation, United Possessions and Equality of Exertions and of the means of Enjoyments* (London, 1830); Franco Venturi, *Roots of Revolution: A History of the Populist and Socialist Movements*

in 19th-century Russia (New York, 1960); G. Woodcock and I. Avakumovič, *The Anarchist Prince: A Biographical Study of Peter Kropotkin* (London, 1950).

ARTHUR LEHNING

[See also **Authority;** Education; Equality; **Freedom;** Ideology; **Individualism;** Law, Natural; Perfectibility; Socialism; State; Work.]

ANCIENTS AND MODERNS IN THE EIGHTEENTH CENTURY

THE IDEA of progress, finding expression in many forms and levels, was most vociferously discussed during the eighteenth century in the literary quarrel of the ancients and moderns, which embraced questions of authority, antiquarianism, and the new experimental science. The attack on authority in science and literary criticism first foreshadowed and later paralleled the challenging of authority in religion and politics, which developed during the Enlightenment in systems of deism and political democracy.

Most of the arguments in favor of modern learning as opposed to ancient grew out of the efforts of Descartes and Bacon to persuade their respective countrymen to adopt a new method of judging and seeking truth. Both rejected the authority of the ancients in scientific questions—Bacon as part of his inductive method and Descartes as part of his system of "methodical doubt." Descartes asserted in the first article, *The Passions of the Mind* (1649):

What the ancients have taught is so scanty and for the most part so lacking in credibility that I may not hope for any kind of approach toward truth except by rejecting all the paths which they have followed.

Aristotle, was first attacked and discredited in the realm of science, and then disputed in literature. Homer developed as another natural target. Critics assumed that if they could sufficiently tarnish his image, they would succeed in proving the superiority of the modern age.

Abbé Pons in France, for example, praised Descartes for subjecting the scientific system of Aristotle to rigid scrutiny and exposing the latter's deviations from truth. Then he pointed to the parallel between the long reign of Aristotle in science and that of Homer in literature. He argued in his *Letter on the "Iliad" of La Motte* (*Lettre sur "l'Iliade" de la Motte*, 1714) that the rejection of Aristotle furnished a presentiment of the imminent fall of Homer. Two years later, the English poet

Sir Richard Blackmore drew the same parallel between science and criticism in his *Essay upon Epick Poetry:* "Unless the Admirers of *Homer* will assert and prove their Infallibility," he challenged, "why may they not be deceiv'd as well as the Disciples and Adorers of *Aristotle*?"

Even after Aristotle had been dethroned in the realm of science, it remained difficult to budge Homer from his pedestal. Critical opinion in the late seventeenth century generally agreed with Boileau that since Homer had been constantly admired and followed throughout the ages, he should always continue to be admired and imitated. The abbé Terrasson, however, in his *Critical Dissertation on the "Iliad"* (*Dissertation critique sur "l'Iliade,"* 1715) revolted against this logic. For him, literary work should not be judged according to the reputation it had enjoyed in the past, but according to its conformity to reason and nature. Literary criticism, according to Terrasson, should adopt the philosophic spirit which had been responsible for progress in the natural sciences, acknowledging the superiority of "reason which leads us to attribute each phenomenon to its proper and natural principle," independent of the opinion of other men. Blackmore said essentially the same:

It's clear, that *Aristotle* form'd all his Axioms and Doctrines in Poetry, from the Patterns of Homer and other Greek Writers; and without assigning any Reason of his Positions. . . . But it is not the Authority of the greatest Masters, but solid and convincing Evidence, that must engage our Belief.

The debate concerned not only the two separate issues of which age possessed greater genius or mental powers and which possessed greater knowledge, but also a far more important one; did an increase of knowledge mean progress? This is another way of asking whether people are actually happier in the modern world. The partisans of the ancients were obviously accepting a form of cultural primitivism. Some men who did not profess any form of primitivism, nevertheless considered the new science as nothing more than an interesting development, which did nothing to change man's nature or to make him any happier. Others justified their indifference to the question by appealing to the commonplace observation of the century—that human nature never changes. Lord Chesterfield, for example, prided himself on the discovery "that nature was the same three thousand years ago as it is at present; that men were but men then as well as now." He was willing to grant that modes and customs often vary, but insisted that "human nature is always the same." Taking a commonplace metaphor, originally introduced by Montaigne, he argued in a letter to his son, 7 February 1749, that there is no more reason to assume that men were

better, braver, or wiser in ancient times than "to suppose that the animals or vegetables were better then than they are now." La Bruyère in another famous analogy, from his *Caractères* (1687), compared authors who espoused the side of the moderns to robust infants who suck the nourishing milk of their nurses and then revolt and beat them.

The major disputants in the quarrel between ancients and moderns made use of three primary metaphorical expressions which passed from pen to pen without acknowledgment: (1) the paradox that modern men are the real ancients; (2) the image of the human race as a single man; and (3) the image of a giant with a dwarf on his shoulders.

(1) The paradox concerning the antiquity of modern men derives from Bacon, who expressed it in Latin, *Antiquitas saeculi juventus mundi* ("Ancient times are the youth of the world"). Our times then are the ancient times "when the world is ancient and not those which we account *ordine retrogrado* by a computation backward from ourselves." The same paradox may be found in Descartes, Pascal, and Malebranche. The *Encyclopédie*, in the article, "Anciens," called it an ingenious sophism, equivalent to the pleasantry, *le monde est si vieux qu'il radote* ("the world is so old it drivels"). In the last decade of the eighteenth century, Thomas Paine gave the argument a political twist in *The Rights of Man* (1791) in order to discredit Burke's concept of prescription. The only reason for studying governments in the ancient world, as far as Paine was concerned, was to profit by their errors and to perceive later improvements by contrast. "Those who lived a hundred or a thousand years ago," Paine affirmed, "were then moderns as we are now."

(2) The image of the human race as a single man compared the life span of the entire human race to one man's progress from cradle to grave. It exists in both Roger Bacon and Francis Bacon and in all the major participants in the ancient-moderns dispute. The figure could be used by one side to show that the race was already approaching senility, and by the other side to characterize the ancients as infants.

(3) The giant-dwarf image represents the ancients as giants supporting the moderns as dwarfs on their shoulders so that the latter may have an advantageous view of nature. The metaphor figured prominently during the Renaissance in the writing of the Spaniard, Juan Luis Vives (1492–1540), and in Ben Jonson (1572–1637), and was reintroduced by Fontenelle. This image may also be used to support either side of the controversy: the ancients interpreted the puny figure of the modern dwarf as a sign of decay, but the moderns considered his advantageous position as a symbol of the superior knowledge of modern times.

The debate was introduced into the literary realm by Alessandro Tassoni in the last of his *Ten Books of Miscellaneous Thoughts* (*Dieci libri di pensieri diversi* [1620]). In theory he seemed to favor the ancients by attacking the argument that knowledge is cumulative and that, therefore, it must always be the latest generation which has the greatest amount of it. Such reasoning, he affirmed, would hold only if study and research were continuously carried on by outstanding minds, but in actuality learning has frequently been captured by hostile forces or inferior intellects and thus learning may decline instead of advance. In his pragmatic survey of the concrete achievements of civilization, however, Tassoni acknowledged the superiority of the moderns. It follows from Tassoni's arguments that progress does not need to take place in a straight line, but it may occur in spurts and jumps; some areas may go forward while others go backwards, and there may even be occasional periods of total retrogression.

In France, the preliminary skirmishes began in 1635, when a minor poet, Boisrobert, who had probably read Tassoni in translation, attacked the ancients before the French Academy. He was followed by Desmarets de Saint-Sorlin who argued passionately in his *Discourse to Prove That Only Christian Subjects are Appropriate to Heroic Poetry* (*Discours pour prouver que les sujets chrétiens sont seuls propres à la poésie héroïque* [1673]), that Christian miracles are far superior to pagan mythology as subjects for heroic poetry. Although the dispute over the use of Christian subject matter in the epic tradition developed in England as a separate contest, completely independent of that between the ancients and moderns, the two contests are thematically related. The advocates of Christian poetry took up their position with the moderns, for the substitution of Christian materials for the classical deities represents a triumph of the contemporary world over the past. Desmarets maintained that the epic poet must be not only a story-teller, but also an authority on "history, geography, astronomy, matters of nature, logic, ethics, rhetoric, fables, agriculture, architecture, painting, sculpture, perspective, and music." This requirement of extensive knowledge for the epic poet obviously put the ancients at a great disadvantage. John Dryden similarly required the epic poet to combine the "natural endowments, of a large invention, a ripe judgment, and a strong memory" with "the knowledge of liberal arts and sciences, and particularly moral philosophy, the mathematics, geography, and history."

Carrying the controversy to the completely different area of linguistics, François Charpentier in 1683 published a treatise, *On the Excellence of the French Language* (*De l'Excellence de la langue française*), arguing that modern French rather than the classical languages should be the medium for inscriptions on public monuments. Taking a position which Alexander Pope was to express a generation later in his satires, (*First Epistle of the Second Book of Horace* [1737]), and Marivaux in his *Miroir* (XI [1755]), Charpentier maintained that those who expressed a preference for the ancients did so because they were jealous of contemporary authors.

In 1687 Charles Perrault united literary and scientific considerations in a poem exalting his own times, *The Century of Louis XIV* (*Le Siècle de Louis le Grand*) which he read before the Academy. The ancients were great in their way, he admitted, but still had all the limitations of human beings. Homer had written under the disadvantages of living in a primitive society and, therefore, had fallen into various errors which he could have avoided had he written in the modern world. Without qualification Perrault affirmed that the ancient authorities in science and history, Aristotle and Herodotus, had already been discredited. As symbols of the scientific superiority of the moderns, Perrault featured in his poem a detailed description of the telescope and microscope. We may find close parallels to these passages in many French and English poems as well as in a Russian Georgic poem, *Letter on the Use of Glass* (1752) by M. V. Lomonosov.

Perrault further developed his notions in a prose dialogue, *Parallels between Ancients and Moderns* (1688–96), not actually intended to show parallels, but instead differences and distinctions. For the gathering of ammunition against the ancients, he appealed to the astronomer Huygens, who supplied him with information concerning the advance of science. On the literary side Perrault repeated his charge that Homer and Vergil had been guilty of an infinite number of errors because they lacked knowledge which came to light in later times. As one example of Homer's great deficiencies, his lack of verisimilitude, Perrault pointed to the victory of Ulysses and three of his friends over 108 suitors of Penelope: the four warriors surmounting impossible odds to kill their foes without taking them by surprise, while Ulysses in the midst of the fray delivered a long moral discourse.

Mme Dacier answered the objections to the errors and implausibilities of the ancients by affirming that whatever reproaches are made against Homer may be made equally against the Old Testament. In the preface to her translation of the *Iliad* (1711) she confined the argument to social customs rather than to scientific knowledge. The epic poet must portray customs and behavior exactly as they are in his own times; otherwise his imitation of nature will be false and his heroes no more credible than heroes of romances. "In a word, the poem imitates what exists and not that which has come into being only after it." Since Homer could not conform to the usages of later centuries, it is necessary for later centuries to comprehend the customs of his century.

In 1688 Fontenelle published a volume of pastoral poetry in which he inserted a *Digression sur les anciens et les modernes*. Here he maintained that the question of the preeminence of ancients or moderns may be reduced to a consideration of whether the trees of former times were taller than those growing at present, a problem which had been presented by Montaigne in the *Apologie de Raymond Sebond*. This is a phase of the related theological doctrine of the degeneration of the world. Fontenelle argued that if biological differences exist in man as well as in plants, these differences are caused by geography and climate, not by chronology. And since the climate is essentially the same in Greece, Italy, and France, all human beings, including the ancients and moderns, Greeks, Romans, and French, are biologically equal. A scientist of modern times, he affirmed, because of the accumulation of information knows ten times more than one of the times of Augustus, and he has ten times greater facility in acquiring his knowledge. The great reputation of the ancients is based upon prejudice and tradition. In literature, the names of the ancients sound better to our ears merely because they are Greek and Latin. Before Fontenelle, eloquence and poetry had been the main subjects of contention, but for him they counted less than the sciences. He admitted that the ancients could theoretically have attained perfection in eloquence and poetry, but granted that they had actually attained it only in the former. Critics were accustomed to consider both Greeks and Romans as ancients, but Fontenelle affirmed that in a relative sense the Romans were moderns. In literary merit, he placed Cicero over Demosthenes, Vergil over both Theocritus and Homer, Horace over Pindar, and Livy over the Greek historians. And he asserted for his contemporaries a further claim to superiority—that they had developed new literary forms like the novel, and the *lettres galantes* which had not existed in antiquity.

Fontenelle also touched on the faults of Homer, which the latter's admirers had attempted to exonerate or vindicate under the plea of poetic license. Homer, for example, indiscriminately mingled as many as five dialects in a single line, a process equivalent to a French poet's blending the dialects of Picardy, Gascony, Normandy, and Brittany with ordinary French. Both Perrault and Fontenelle used the single man image, but the latter refused to carry the comparison to its logical end, resolutely affirming that the human race would never degenerate into senility.

Fontenelle, nevertheless, had no illusions concerning the intrinsic merits of mankind, but shared the cautious skepticism of those who rejected the doctrine of progress. In an imaginary dialogue between Montaigne and Socrates (1683), he represents the former as charging, in connection with the doctrine of universal degeneration, that men do not know how to use the knowledge they acquire. They are like birds too ignorant to stay away from a net which has already snared thousands of their kind. Pierre Bayle pessimistically observed in like vein in his *Historical and Critical Dictionary* (1695–97), that "the world is too undisciplined to profit from the maladies of former centuries." "Each century behaves as though it were the first."

During the seventeenth century Nicolas Boileau-Despréaux was considered to be the foremost French theoretician of classicism and defender of the Ancients. In his *Critical Reflections on Longinus* (1694), he emphasized what he considered to be one of the strongest arguments in favor of ancient writers, the constant admiration in which they have continually been held; a sure and infallible proof, he felt, that they should always be admired. Yet he also admitted in a letter to Perrault, published by the latter in 1701, that although no French Cicero or Vergil had yet appeared, the Age of Louis XIV had surpassed any previous age in tragedy, painting, architecture, and especially in philosophy and science. He virtually abandoned the ancients when he admitted, "the Age of Louis XIV is not only comparable but superior to the most famous ages of antiquity, even the Age of Augustus." Had the debate depended on authority alone, Boileau's capitulation would have meant the total victory of the moderns at least in France, but other critics continued to exalt the preeminence of the ancients as still others disparaged them.

Abbé Jean Terrasson in a posthumous work, *Philosophy Applicable to All Subjects* (1754), affirmed that the superiority of the moderns is a necessary and natural effect of the very constitution of the human spirit. Fontenelle was wrong, he believed, in resting the argument on a comparison between trees in various centuries. Since trees in all ages remain the same, the parallel merely places the moderns on an equal plane with the ancients. Men, unlike trees, endow their progeny with their knowledge and advice. The progress of the human spirit Terrasson illustrated with the old allegory of the human race as a single man. Instead of accepting such a system, which provides us infants for teachers and models, Terrasson exhorted us to respect our nephews over our ancestors. Our progeny will inevitably have greater enlightenment than we ourselves.

This is not far from the confident assertion of M. J. de Condorcet in his *Historical Sketch of the Progress of the Human Mind* (1793) that no limit can be prescribed to the improvement of the human species. Observations of various races of lower animals had demonstrated to Condorcet's satisfaction, long before Darwin, that improvement in physical faculties could be transmitted from one generation to the next. Human beings, he reasoned, could also pass on to their progeny that part of their physical organism on which their intelligence, mental energy, and moral sensibility depend, and proper education could bring about modification and unlimited improvement of these qualities.

In England after Bacon's initial attack on authority in science, the debate shifted to literary theory. Most late seventeenth-century literary critics limited themselves to discussing the Aristotelian rules without mentioning the Stagirite's outmoded science. Dryden, for example, constantly vacillated between adhering to the rules and violating them. He admired Shakespeare, but condemned him by the rules; he praised Milton, but placed Homer and Vergil higher. In opening a complimentary address to his "Honour'd Friend Dr. Charleton" (1663), however, he declared,

> The longest Tyranny that ever sway'd
> Was that wherein our Ancestors betray'd
> Their free-born *Reason* to the *Stagirite*.

One of the few Restoration critics unequivocally to repudiate slavish obeisance to the ancients was Charles Gildon, who in *Miscellaneous Letters and Essays* (1694) drew the parallel with scientific knowledge. He considered it beyond doubt that the Greeks were far behind the moderns in physics and other sciences, which for the ancients "chiefly consisted in words." Since authority had been for many years considered as a deterrent to scientific inquiry he could see no reason why his contemporaries not only continued to accept it but blindly followed it in poetry "since 'tis perhaps almost as prejudicial to our imitation of Nature in This, as to our discovery of it in the Other."

The French had debated the relative merits of the French language and the classical ones, the moderns unequivocally affirming the superiority of their own tongue. The English Restoration critics, however, accepted the theory that English had been a barbarous language until their own times, and even the most vigorous moderns in England granted the preference to classical idioms. Addison went so far as to assert in the *Spectator* (No. 417) that if "*Paradise Lost* falls short of the *Aeneid* or *Iliad*, it proceeds from the fault of the language in which it is written. . . . So divine a poem in English is like a stately palace built of brick." Later David Hume suggested that if "Waller had been born in Rome during the reign of Tiberius, his first productions had been despised, when compared to the finished odes of Horace" ("Of the Rise and Progress of the Arts and Sciences" [1742]).

In England, the formal controversy broke out in full force in 1690 when Sir William Temple published *An Essay upon Ancient and Modern Learning*, asserting the superiority of the ancients in every area and denying that the moderns profit from their inheritance. According to his argument, learning which is derived may weaken invention and dilute genius. "So a Man that only Translates, shall never be a Poet, nor a Painter that only copies, nor a Swimmer that swims always with Bladders." A few pages later he inconsistently demolished this argument by attributing the revival of learning in the modern world to the restoration of Greek and pure Latin after the Middle Ages.

Temple adapted the single man metaphor to his purpose by imagining a strong and vigorous man who should at the age of thirty fall ill and decline until sixty when he should recover and then be more vigorous than most men of this age. Although it could be said that he had grown more in strength during the ten years from 60 to 70 than at any other period, he had still not acquired more strength and vigor than he had possessed at the age of thirty. Temple similarly interpreted the giant-dwarf image to the detriment of the moderns. As Temple viewed it, the dwarf, despite his advantageous position, sees less than the giant if he is naturally shorter-sighted, if he is less observant, or if he is dazzled by height.

By speculating on the possibility that our ancients had their own ancients with a period of intellectual stagnation intervening between them and their forerunners, a period comparable to the Middle Ages, Temple introduced a cyclical theory of history refuting the idea of progress. According to his reasoning, the arts and sciences came to the West from India and perhaps ultimately from China. For information to support this theory—although not the theory itself—Temple relied upon two major sources, Thomas Burnet's *Telluris theoria sacra* (*Sacred Theory of the Earth*, 1681–89) and John Nieuhoff's *Voyages and Travels into Brasil* (1682). The cyclical theory itself was current in the Renaissance and had been refuted by Bacon.

William Wotton answered Temple in *Reflections upon Ancient and Modern Learning* (1694), a lengthy treatise, covering all phases of the arts and sciences, which draws heavily upon Perrault for the arts and on the defenders of the Royal Society for the sciences. Quite moderate in his advocacy of the moderns, Wotton refused to follow Fontenelle in claiming superiority for his own times in oratory and the arts. With impressive logic he observed that values in the arts are based upon opinion and are subject to debate;

whereas values in the sciences are objective and may be ascertained by comparison. In the second edition of his *Reflections* (1697), Wotton added an appendix by a noted scholar, Richard Bentley, who shifted the controversy to the area of philological scholarship.

Bentley used his linguistic learning to prove that the Greek works of Phalaris and Aesop, which Temple had extolled as ancients were spurious and really compositions of modern times. Charles Boyle joined the fray against Bentley, and finally Swift, as a partisan of Temple and the ancients, produced a masterful satire on the entire controversy, *The Battle of the Books* (1704). Swift's mock epic in prose casts the books in St. James Library arrayed in two armies, Moderns and Ancients, disputing a plot of ground on Mount Parnassus. The spirit of the work is succinctly conveyed by one of its mock-epic conventions: the episode of the spider and the bee. The two insects, representing Moderns and Ancients respectively, argue over which of the two is regarded by the outside world as the superior creature. The spider affirms that the bee is a plunderer of nature, stealing from every variety of flower; whereas the spider himself is a domestic animal erecting his dwelling entirely through his own efforts and with materials extracted from his own person. The bee admits ranging over field and garden, but asserts that his collecting of nectar does no harm to the flowers he visits; whereas the spider pours out poison from his breast to spin his web, which perpetually gathers dirt and sweepings. Aesop, who is chosen to moderate the dispute, decides in favor of the bee, whom he associates with himself as an Ancient.

Whatever we have got, has been by infinite labour and search, and ranging through every corner of nature; the difference is that, instead of dirt and poison, we have rather chosen to fill our hives with honey and wax, thus furnishing mankind with the two noblest of things, which are sweetness and light.

Bacon had preceded Swift in the image of the spider and Ben Jonson in the image of the bee, and Temple had vastly extended the latter in an essay *Of Poetry* (1690). Matthew Arnold later adopted the metaphor "sweetness and light" as the symbol of classical culture in a famous essay defending it, *Culture and Anarchy* (1869).

Diderot, a moderate in the controversy, allegorized the quarrel of ancients and moderns somewhat in the vein of the episode of the spider and the bee in a digression inserted in a licentious novel written for the amusement of his mistress, *Les Bijoux indiscrets* (1748). One of the characters in a dream finds himself accompanied by the Goddess Minerva in a gallery of statues and books symbolizing the ancients. A crowd of men burn incense and adorn the statues with garlands, at the same time abusing those of their number who fail to bow profoundly enough before the statues. These are succeeded by a horde of pygmies, who hack at the statues and try to tear them apart. Minerva explains that this quarrel has been going on for a long time, and always to the disadvantage of the pygmies. The statues run some risk of being tarnished by the incense of the worshippers, she explains, but the efforts of the pygmies to destroy them only make them more brilliant.

Swift, in a companion piece to his *Battle of the Books*, *A Tale of the Tub* (1704), ironically pointed to Homer's gross ignorance of the laws of England and the doctrines of the Anglican Church as a means of repudiating the moderns' method of judging Homer by the standards of a later and more sophisticated age than his. Similarly he ridiculed the moderns as critics whose art consisted merely in the discovering and collecting of faults. "Their imaginations are so entirely possessed and replete with the defects of other pens," he charged, "that the very quintessence of what is bad does of necessity distil into their own."

The method of subjecting Homer to the test of verisimilitude and good taste was applied in earnest by La Motte and Terrasson. The former condemned such "low" images as Achilles' asking Thetis to remove the flies from the wounds of Patroclus; the latter found fault because the *Iliad* does not conform to rational principles of stylistic organization; because the action does not adhere to the theme of the work; and because Agamemnon commits capital crimes against religion and justice. The strong implication of both La Motte and Terrasson was that Homer was as much a barbarian as a poet. The principle argument of La Motte was that Homer must be subjected to the judgment of reason and not accepted as the voice of authority. In his opinion, the only pleasures which Homer provides are those based on novelty, on antiquarianism, on respect for authority, and on prejudice. None of these have any relation to reason, the single quality on which aesthetic appreciation should be based (*Discours sur Homère*, 1714). La Motte admitted that it was illogical to attack Homer for not conforming to the dignity of later ages. But he insisted that criticism had the right to condemn Homeric times for their barbarousness and to indicate that the description of them in the *Iliad* appeared disagreeable to the more fastidious standards of later ages.

In 1716, Sir Richard Blackmore published "An Account of the present controversy concerning Homer's *Iliad*," in which he also refused to submit to the authority of ancient writers "unless they were supported by Reason." He condemned the ludicrousness of rivers making speeches and horses shedding tears and labelled the manners and behavior of the pagan Gods a reproach to human nature. Yet he suggested that Fénelon's highly praised modern prose epic, *Télémaque*, had many worse faults than the *Iliad*, particularly in the author's introducing heathen machines and having Grecian pagans speak in the manner of Jews, Egyptians, and Chaldeans.

Pope in *An Essay on Criticism* (1711), however, returned to an almost unanswerable defense of the alleged blemishes in Homer—the argument of the French critics that they were intentional—designed to provide variety and to present his most sublime passages in relief.

> Those oft are stratagems which error seem,
> Nor is it Homer nods, but we that dream.
> (I, 179–80)

This is a couplet based on Horace's *The Art of Poetry* (lines 359–60), but Pope's defense is stronger than Horace's. The latter merely suggests that soporific passages may be condoned in a poem which is very long.

The contention in England over the age of the writings of Aesop and Phalaris, which was waged on linguistic grounds, had its counterpart in France in disagreements over the theory of translation. Madame Dacier in the Preface to her translation of the *Iliad* (1711), argued that the more sublime and beautiful a work is in the original, the more it loses in translation. No writer suffers as much as Homer does, for it is impossible in French to communicate the harmony, nobility, and majesty of his expressions. Characterizing the French language as timid and circumspect because of its formality and blind adherence to custom, she condemned it for lacking the boldness and liberty necessary to reveal the beauties of Homer. Although she was a confirmed classicist, Mme Dacier, in defending Homer, anticipated by a century the linguistic arguments of the romanticists which were based on freedom from restraint. Of Lucretius she remarked that his philosophy and principles were absurd and false, but that the verses in which they were expressed would charm every ear by their beauty and harmony.

Abbé La Motte replied in his *Discours sur Homère* (1714) that no one in the modern world could know the dead languages well enough to appreciate their nuances and beauties. Those who prided themselves on understanding the beauties and negligences of Homer, that is, the bold strokes which his admirers praised him for, could have only an approximate knowledge of ancient Greek. These critics vaunted themselves for possessing knowledge of a language which they understood only partially and imperfectly.

La Motte went even further and declared that the French language was the equal of Greek in beauty of expression. He found examples to illustrate its clarity in history, sublimity in panegyric, saltiness in satire, dignity in tragedy, naiveté in fable, and tenderness in opera. Each language, he maintained, has utilitarian communication as its function, and harmony and sonority are only secondary. It is only because French has kept itself within the limits of good sense and clarity that it can be reproached for lacking boldness. Audacious and daring terms exist in French speech, but if they should ever become commonplace, French would become degenerate and corrupt. It is precisely the good sense of the French language, La Motte insisted, which represents its greatest richness.

Because many French men of letters shared La Motte's pride in the French language, it was possible for the great French seventeenth-century authors eventually to displace the ancients as classic models in French culture. In England, the respect for the vernacular did not reach these heights, and as a result, English neo-classicism never attained the authority of the French.

Abbé Dubos took an eclectic position in his *Critical Reflections on Poetry and Painting* (1719), one of the major documents in the controversy, but on the question of translation he stood firmly with the ancients. It is form alone in Homer which gives pleasure, he affirmed, and therefore Homer must be translated exactly. But Dubos also maintained that no translation can do justice to the beauty of a poetic original since the rhythm and harmony of classical verse cannot be rendered in another language. The *Aeneid* in French is not the same poem as the *Aeneid* in Latin. Dubos argued, moreover, that those who cannot read an ancient poem in the original must accept the judgment about it of those who can. One cannot rely on one's own appraisal of a translation no matter how rational the appraisal may be, since the translation and the original are different entities. The beauties of a poem are judged by sentiment, not reason, and "the general agreement of the senses of other men, is next to the agreement of our own, the most certain means we have of judging phenomena which are ranked under sentiment."

With these arguments Dubos was opposing those moderns like La Motte, who considered that the chief value of studying the ancients was to obtain historical and sociological information and that the purpose of criticism was to place an author in his philosophical and historical context. In rejecting sociological criticism, Dubos discounted the need for verisimilitude and historical accuracy in art. We do not read poetry to look for contradictions, he affirmed, but for the pleasure of being moved emotionally. Holding that the only purpose of poetry is to excite sentiments, not to persuade the reason, he considered it a matter of indifference whether a poem be completely contrary to reality. In his emphasis on sentiment, therefore, Dubos entirely abandoned the Cartesian theory of the advance of knowledge through reason. In his opinion, the greatest discoveries in science—the compass, the printing press, the weight of air, the movement of the earth, and the circulation of blood—came by chance, not by following rational procedures. Cartesian reason he affirmed produces nothing but absurd theories such as that of the beast machine. Sentiment and imagination, therefore, are more important for progress, according to Dubos, than reason.

The sociological criticism which Dubos opposed could be used, however, to the advantage of the Ancients. Fénelon in a *Letter on the Activities of the Academy* (1716), suggested that the deformity and crudeness of religion and the lack of true morality in Homeric times served to make Homer's artistic achievement all the more admirable by contrast. The great epic poet had portrayed with superb imagery and verbal power concepts which in themselves are absurd and shocking. Jean Bovin in his *Apology for Homer* (1715), made a comparison with China, which was emerging at that time as a popular theme. What he enjoyed in reading about China, he said, was Chinese customs. "If the heroes of the century of Homer do not resemble ours, this difference should give us pleasure."

Although Giambattista Vico in Italy wrote his *New Science* (*Scienza Nuova* [1725; 1744]), with absolutely no reference to the critical dispute raging in France and England, the fundamental thought of his treatise completely contradicts those who attributed philosophical discrimination to the ancients. Vico believed that it was fear which first led men to create gods in their imaginations and that their first form of expression was poetical. Contrary to all the ancient philosophers, including Plato and Aristotle, Vico believed that "it was the deficiency of human reasoning power that gave rise to poetry," and he concluded that his discovery of "the origins of poetry does away with the opinion of the matchless wisdom of the ancients."

Addison in the *Spectator* (No. 160 [1711]), used Homer as his only example of natural genius in a distinction between the contributions to humanity which depend upon native inspiration alone and those which have depended upon accumulated experience. Those in the first category of genius have ". . . by the mere Strength of natural Parts, and without any Assistance of Art of Learning, . . . produced Works that were the Delight of their own Times and the Wonder of

Posterity." The second category, "formed themselves by Rules, and submitted the Greatness of their natural Talents to the Corrections and Restraints of Art." Homer was Addison's single example of the first class, and Plato, Aristotle, Vergil, Cicero, Milton, and Bacon of the second. Abbé Dubos converted this distinction to one between ancients and moderns. He affirmed that the moderns are undoubtedly more advanced in the sciences, but their superiority depends on the prior accumulation of a mass of knowledge, not on genius. Modern reason, therefore, is not really superior to ancient. In the realm of art, moreover, time and experience are of no value. The high esteem in which Homer is held, Dubos maintained, is not due to the reign of Aristotle and should not be reduced because the latter has fallen from favor; instead Homer's reputation is based entirely on the pleasure which people of all ages have found in his work.

Pope in *An Essay on Criticism* attempted to blur the distinction between genius and acquired experience by affirming that to follow nature and to imitate the ancients is the same thing.

> Learn for ancient rules a just esteem;
> To copy nature is to copy them.

Like most classicists, Pope advocated the imitation of the ancients in order to attain nature. His friend Edward Young, however, in *Conjectures on Original Composition* (1752), prescribed the opposite method. Instead of imitating Homer, the poet should imitate nature: "drink where he drank, at the true Helicon, that is, at the breast of nature." Young recognized that in both science and the arts, the respect for authority inculcated by the ancients leads simply to imitation of their models and to acceptance of their beliefs. His theory is summarized by the paradox: "The less we copy the renowned ancients, we shall resemble them the more." A Spanish critic G. M. Jovellanos in an essay *On the Necessity of Uniting the Study of Literature and the Sciences* (1797), took his inspiration directly from Young in explaining why the moderns with much greater knowledge than the ancients nevertheless displayed less genius: "because the ancients created, and we imitate; because the ancients studied nature, and we study them. Why do we not follow their track? And if we wish to equal them, why do we not study as they did?"

Diderot, however, in a highly-regarded critical essay, *Salon de 1767*, affirmed that precisely because the Greeks had based their artistic creation on nature, their work could never be excelled. "The inviolable laws of Nature must be executed; Nature does nothing by leaps and bounds, and this is no less true in the arts than in the cosmos." Despite the possibility of going directly to nature for models and inspiration, Diderot affirmed that it is impossible for modern artists ever to equal the ancients—they can only be imitators. Goethe in the section of his autobiography *Poetry and Truth* (*Dichtung und Wahrheit*, 1811–33), devoted to the "Antique and the Present," reiterated and supported this view.

Marivaux in *The Mirror* (1755) offered an explanation of the paradox that literary works could be greater in ancient times than in modern despite the accumulation and proliferation of knowledge in the modern world. He maintained that ideas and taste are not parallel and, therefore, do not increase at the same rate. Each generation which comes on the earth adds its own portion to the stock of ideas, and these never entirely disappear: their impression remains indelibly in humanity. But even though modern times may have a greater accumulation of ideas than existed in the past, there is unfortunately less of taste. The augmentation of ideas is an infallible consequence of the duration of the world, Marivaux concluded, but the art of employing those ideas in works of the spirit may decline—in which event belles lettres may sink, criticism and taste disappear. Marivaux concluded, therefore, that there had never been a period to equal that of the ancients.

Vauvenargues in his *Discourse on the Character of Various Centuries* (1745) made a parallel admission that ineffably greater knowledge is available in modern times than in the past, but he questioned whether the average man was capable of assimilating or utilizing this knowledge. As far as Vauvenargues was concerned, that which depends on the spirit receives no increase from the proliferation of the products of the intellect, and since taste depends on the spirit, knowledge is being increased in vain: "our judgment is instructed, but our taste is not improved."

Even Turgot, one of the most ardent exponents of perfectibility, conceded that while the capacity for knowledge of the nature of truth is as infinite as truth itself, the development of the arts is as limited as man himself. Poetry, painting, and music have a fixed point determined by language and by the sensibility of our organs. This fixed point, Turgot believed, had been attained by the men of the Age of Augustus, who, therefore, will remain as models for all subsequent generations (*Second Discourse . . . on the Progress of the Human Mind*, 1750).

Abbé Terrasson refused to accept the separation of arts and sciences as valid in the measurement of human progress, condemning the division as artificial by means of an original variant of the single-man image. In a discourse with the pertinent title, *Philosophy Applicable to all the objects of the Mind and Reason* (1754), he affirmed that such a separation would perhaps be applicable to a creature with two souls, but it does not fit humanity. He maintained, moreover, that inferior as the ancients were in the sciences, they knew more about them, particularly geometry and astronomy, than they knew about the true principles of reason and humanity, "unique source of the true use of belles-lettres in prose and poetry."

The first critic to suggest the possibility that the fine arts may progress, just as the sciences do, was Edward Young. As part of his campaign against the principle of imitation in literature, he urged poets not only to go beyond the ancients in representing nature, but even to go beyond nature itself and to develop a world of pure imagination. "In the fairyland of fancy," he remarked in his *Conjectures*, "genius may wander wild; there it has creative power, and may reign arbitrarily over its own empire of chimeras." This is the essence of the ultra-modern spirit, and Young himself recognized that it was partly rant. But he declared unequivocally, "all arts and sciences are making considerable advance," and he did not hesitate to ask, "why may not poetry go forward with this advancement?"

Condorcet, probably the most ardent "perfectibilian" of the century, vigorously supported the view that progress occurs in the fine arts. In his *Historical Sketch* (1793) he made an original distinction between "that which belongs really to the progress of art and that which is due only to the talent of the artist." In the past, he contended, critics had judged artists rather than works, giving rise to the adulation of the ancient authors and the growth of a cult requiring imitation of the first models. Although not making any aesthetic comparisons between specific ancient and modern authors, Condorcet affirmed that the arts are improved by and draw profit from advances in philosophy and science—either through more precise knowledge of the effects and powers of these arts themselves or through the destruction of prejudices against them. Reasoning such as this may have inspired the poet Shelley to speculate in the Preface to *The Revolt of Islam* (1817), that "there may be such a thing as perfectibility in works of fiction."

This doctrine of perfectibility is related to the sociological criticism of La Motte since both systems assume that literature is as much a product of society as of individuals. The concept of the interaction of literature and society directly opposes all theories of absolute values, including that of the supremacy of the ancients. Mme de Staël fully developed the concept in her pioneer treatise *Literature Considered in Its Relations with Social Institutions* (*De la Littérature considerée dans ses rapports avec les institutions sociales*, 1800).

In Spain, ever since Luis Vives in the sixteenth century had used literary arguments against the doctrine of the degeneration of the world, critics in that country confidently extolled the originality and vigor of Spanish literature. During the middle of the eighteenth century, however, a Dominican priest, Benito Jeronimo Feijoo, considered to be one of the most progressive as well as prolific minds in Spain at the time, published an essay "Resurrection of the Arts and Defense of the Ancients" (1750), taking a moderate position in the controversy, but leaning toward the side of the ancients. On the subject of the arts he asked: "What is there in our century which can compete with the beauties of the poetry and eloquence of the century of Augustus?" And with respect to the sciences he affirmed that if the stories told of the intellectual penetration of some of the ancients are true, "certainly one may infer that their physical knowledge was much superior to all the philosophers of these times." Two of his examples of this penetration are revealing: Democritus was able merely by tasting milk to tell that it came from a black goat which had been pregnant only once. And the same philosopher, saluting a girl whom he had greeted the night before *Salve virgo*, used the words *Salve mulier* in the morning; it was later discovered that she had been violated. Feijoo reflected the point of view of Temple that the ancients really deserve the credit for many of the discoveries ascribed to the moderns, including circulation of the blood, the telescope, printing, and the compass. He insisted moreover that the first discovery of a principle or art is worthy of more praise than its subsequent development by the moderns.

In France the debate continued on scientific as well as aesthetic grounds. Father Noël Regnault, in his *Ancient Origin of New Physics* (*L'Origine ancienne de la physique nouvelle* [1734]), stressed the great debt which modern science owes to the ancients and argued that the improvements of his day would not have been possible without the ancients. A French Protestant clergyman, living in England, Louis Dutens, published in 1766 *An Inquiry into the Origin of the Discoveries attributed to the Moderns: Wherein It is Demonstrated, That our most celebrated Philosophers have, for most part, taken what they advance from the Works of the Ancients, and that many important Truths in Religion were known to the Pagan Sages*. Considering the works of his predecessors, Perrault, Fontenelle, Wotton, and Temple as comprising fine declamation and rhetoric rather than proofs or demonstrations, Dutens attempted to reveal the enormous share the ancients have had in "modern discoveries." He followed Addison and Dubos in distinguishing between those arts and sciences "which require long experience and practice to bring them to perfection, and those which depend solely on talent and genius." He admitted that the moderns have

brought the former to higher stages of development, and that the Christian religion has even extended morality itself. Also in the area of scientific inventions, he distinguished between the products of genius and philosophy and the "mere effects of chance, or the lucky hits of some ignorant artisans." After including printing, gunpowder, and the compass in the category of lucky hits he tried to trace to the ancients the systems of logic and metaphysics of Descartes, Leibniz, Malebranche, and Locke; Buffon's theories of universal matter, generation, and nutrition: Newton's theory of colors; Harvey's theory of the circulation of blood; the plurality of worlds; the motion of the earth around the sun; and the sexual system of plants. On the subjects of architecture, sculpture, poetry, eloquence, and history, Dutens took for granted the preeminence of the ancients, affirming that "The moderns themselves will not contest with them; on the contrary the height of their ambition is, to imitate them." Dutens concluded that the ancients had preceded or prepared the way for the moderns "in almost all truths of the greatest importance." Supporting the theory of Temple that the ancients had their own ancients, as well as commenting on the opinion of Perrault that recent discoveries had been so extensive that there was little left to be learned, he quoted Seneca concerning the future: "Had even everything been found out by the ancients, there would still this remain to be done anew, to put their inventions into *use* and make their knowledge ours" (*Epistle 64*). Though Dutens' work is today virtually unknown, it was widely circulated in its own time. John Wesley, for example, republished it in abridged form in later editions of his *Survey of the Wisdom of God in Creation*—a text-book of popular science originally published in 1763—which went through several editions in England and the United States. Summarizing his own impression, Wesley exclaimed: "Alas! how little new has been discovered, even by Gassendi, Malebranche, Mr. Locke, or Sir Isaac Newton! How plain is it, that in philosophy, as well as the course of human affairs, 'there is nothing new under the sun.'"

A number of replies to this objection of the lack of novelty, which Wesley was quoting from *Ecclesiastes* in the Old Testament (1:9), were already in print. In order to discourage literary imitations, La Motte ridiculed the concept that no new thoughts are possible and that the human mind had already imagined everything that could be said. He compared ideas to the variety in human physiognomies and affirmed that experience shows that no two men will ever be born who are exactly alike. In like manner, even though ideas may always follow certain common paths, there will always be infinite opportunity for original applications (*Discourse on Poetry* [1707]). Marivaux in *The*

Mirror (1755) made exactly the same comparison and added as a further analogy that just as man has not discovered all the forms of which matter is susceptible, he has not exhausted all the ways of thinking and feeling.

Dubos similarly argued that artists of genius do not use the works of their predecessors as models, but go directly to nature. "Nature is more abundant in different or varied subjects than the genius of artisans in ways of imitating them." Dubos made the original observation, moreover, that particular subjects are compatible for the talents of particular artists, and that some subjects remain virtually untouched because no artist has yet discovered them. Thomas Paine characteristically scoffed in an essay in *The Pennsylvania Magazine* (1775) that the notion that "*We have found out everything* has been the motto of every age," and that this species of vanity was stronger among the ancients than the moderns. Combining chronological and cultural primitivism, he diverted himself by looking back and imagining "a circle of original Indians haranguing on the sublime perfection of the age."

Voltaire associated the quarrel of ancients and moderns with one of the most important scientific projects of the century, twin expeditions organized by the French Academy of Science to measure the latitude at the North Pole and at the Equator and thus to test Newton's hypothesis that the earth is flattened at the poles. In a congratulatory poem to the scientists ("A Messieurs de l'Académie des Sciences" [1738]), Voltaire unequivocally espoused the side of the moderns. Addressing the ancient Greeks, Voltaire bid them to be ashamed and embarrassed at their poor performance in contrast to the great exploits of his contemporaries. "Your century" he declared "is vanquished by the century in which we are." According to Voltaire, opinion in the past had universally favored the Greeks, only because it had been in bondage to lies and prejudices. In a note to his poem, Voltaire reaffirmed the parallel between science and literature, but his examples reveal his own prejudices. He declared that two minor French musical tragedies, *Alcine* and *Armide*, were worth more than all Greek poetry put together and that Thales and Pythagoras were not fit to study under Newton. "But the first-comers seized the Temple of Glory, time confirmed their claim, and the late-comers find the area occupied." In one of his tales, "The World as It is" (1746) Voltaire insisted that the first efforts in every art are always crude despite the preference which critics stubbornly accord to the ancients over the moderns. In his seminal history *The Century of Louis XIV* (1752), he unequivocally asserted "the prodigious superiority of our century over the ancients" and added that at least as far as philosophy is concerned the

dispute is definitely decided in favor of the moderns. In a later dialogue bearing the title *Ancients and Moderns* (1765), Voltaire retreated to the more moderate position of Fontenelle that the controversy could best be resolved by granting that the modern world had discovered new laws of physics, but had not improved upon the ancients' rules of eloquence.

Oliver Goldsmith maintained that there exists no real basis of comparison between ancients and moderns, calling in question, in his *An Enquiry into the Present State of Polite Learning* (1759), the commonplace that nature is always the same. According to Goldsmith, both ancients and moderns imitated nature as they found it, but nature was different for each culture. Both ancients and moderns should then be considered excellent in their separate imitations. Homer would have been despised by the Greeks if he had written like Milton, and Milton would have been ridiculous if he had adopted Homer's religion. One should not condemn Plautus for failing to depict characters like Molière's, nor the reverse. To do so would be as absurd as condemning "a geographer for not introducing more rivers, or promontories, into a country, than nature had given it; or the natural historian, for not enlivening his description of a dead landscape with a torrent, cataract, or a volcano."

For Herder in Germany, it was not precisely nature which changes from one chronological period to another, but national cultures which differ one from another. Classical art he described, in an essay *Homer und Ossian* (1795), as an expression of national, cultural and social conditions which no longer exist in the modern world. Imitations of ancient art, therefore, are false and without soul since they do not express the emotions of the artist. According to Herder, a German poet of the eighteenth century cannot create ancient art just as an apple tree cannot bear pears.

Herder argued moreover in his *Philosophy of the History of the Development of Mankind (Philosophie der Geschichte zur Bildung der Menschheit* [1774]) that just as there exists no "absolute" human being, but all members of the human race differ one from another, there can be no one historical form of culture—the ancient or any other—which can be made as an "absolute ideal." The classic norm forced the poet to be an imitator, not a creator. Herder, like Goldsmith, was a moderate. He did not try to elevate either the ancient or the modern world over the other, but he agreed with virtually all of his predecessors on the side of the moderns that the artist should follow his own inspiration or native talent rather than the standards or models of the past.

New impetus for studying and understanding the ancients came during the second half of the eighteenth century in the wake of extensive excavations and archeological investigations, which led to a Greek Revival in art and architecture. The movement was most significant in Germany, giving rise to Winckelmann's esthetic treatise, *Thoughts concerning the Imitation of Greek Works in Painting and Sculpture* (1755), in which he emphasized the artistic importance of simplicity, not merely that of nature, but that of the absolute or ideal. Schiller in the sixth of his *Letters concerning the Esthetic Education of Mankind* (1795) analyzed the civilization of the ancient Greeks and concluded that the form of culture it represented had then attained maximum development. Continued progress in culture, he felt, had to be based upon a split between intellect and feeling. In his most important critical work, *On Naive and Sentimental Poetry* (*Über naive und sentimentalische Dichtung* [1795–96]), he reformulated "the old Ancient-Modern debate by a new dichotomy," in which he endeavored to justify his own art and modern art in general (René Wellek, *History of Modern Criticism*, I, 234). In Schiller's usage, naive refers to the mode of expression of the ancients based upon instantaneous reaction to primitive manners and the simplicity of nature; sentimental refers to the mode of expression of the moderns based upon an emotional attitude toward nature and manners, reconstructed in tranquility. The ancients portray only that which is happening at the moment; the moderns portray strong feelings conditioned by moral concepts and calm reflection. The moderns, ineffably below the ancients in everything related to nature, still have a better understanding of it. The ancients had conformed to nature, but the moderns in sophisticated society, by controlling nature, oppose it. Schiller granted the superiority of the ancients in the plastic arts, where observation is paramount, but found the moderns superior in all areas based upon ideas where reflection is supreme.

BIBLIOGRAPHY

The best general treatment is that of J. B. Bury in *The Idea of Progress* (London 1920; New York, 1932). The Renaissance background is exhaustively presented by José Antonio Maravall in *Antiguos y Modernos. La idea del progresso en el desarrollo inicial de una sociedad* (Madrid, 1966). The French aspect is treated by H. Rigault in *Histoire de la querelle des modernes* (Paris, 1856), which is supplemented by A. Lombard, *La Querelle des anciens et des modernes. l'abbé Dubos* (Neuchâtel, 1908). The German phase is presented by E. M. Butler in *The Tyranny of Greece over Germany* (New York, 1935), and the English by R. F. Jones in *Ancients and Moderns. A Study of the Rise of the Scientific Movement in Seventeenth-Century England*, 2nd ed. (St. Louis, 1961).

The three most valuable scholarly editions of relevant works are J. Swift, *A Tale of a Tub, The Battle of the Books . . .* , ed. A. C. Guthkelch and D. Nichol Smith (Oxford, 1920); Bernard le Bovier de Fontenelle, *Entretiens sur la pluralité des mondes* and *Digression sur les anciens et les modernes*, ed. Robert Shackleton (Oxford, 1955), and F. M. A. de Voltaire, *La Henriade*, ed. Owen R. Taylor (Geneva, 1965).

Most of the above works contain extensive bibliographies. The edition of *La Henriade* is especially valuable for the literary phase of the debate.

A. OWEN ALDRIDGE

[See also **Baconianism**; Criticism, Literary; Cycles; Deism; Literature and its Cognates; Mimesis; Nature; Perfectibility; Poetry and Poetics; **Primitivism**; **Progress**.]

ANTHROPOMORPHISM IN SCIENCE

ANTHROPOMORPHISM is an inveterate tendency to project human qualities into natural phenomena—consciously or not. The standard and most important variant of anthropomorphism is animism which sees a soul in everything in nature. Before entering into the role of anthropomorphism in the history of science, let us consider a few important and usually neglected logical aspects of the idea.

First, when we draw an analogy from humans to nature, we assume that we know humans; that is to say, we make an analogy from known human qualities to unknown natural qualities. However, it is not what we *know* of human beings, but what we *assume* to be human that we read into nature. For all we know, the analogy may go the other way: like sticks and stones, human beings may not have souls. At the very least, we may leave the question, "Do human souls exist?" open, and still speak of animism as based on an analogy—not so much from known human qualities to unknown natural qualities, but from assumed human qualities to nonhuman qualities.

The second characteristic of anthropomorphism in need of critical attention is one related to the "genetic fallacy." When we make an anthropomorphic assumption, the assumption may be true or false; it is not decisive to show that it is anthropomorphic, just as it is no criticism of any idea to point to its origins. Some anthropomorphic assumptions are known to be false, but not simply because they are anthropomorphic, since other assumptions, e.g., that animals behave like humans in certain respects, may indeed be anthropomorphic and yet true. Nevertheless, it is assumed by and large that when we make an anthropomorphic assumption, it is not likely to be true. This, however, may rest on a more general situation, in which any guess—whether based on analogy or not—is not very likely to be true simply as a guess. If we want our guesses to be more likely than wild fancies, we may suggest a theory concerning the increase of the likelihood of *a priori* guesses. But then, this theory may be false as well. And therefore we have, at least for the time being, to leave open the question "Are any anthropomorphic assumptions true?" Nevertheless, on different grounds we may suggest that practically all anthropomorphic assumptions are likely to be false. The reason is very simple. Looking at the history of culture, we can see that the deeper we go into the past, the more likely we are to find anthropomorphisms; and the nearer we come to our era, the less anthropomorphic our theories become. We also know that the deeper we go into the past, the more likely we are to find erroneous views, or at least, views we consider erroneous today. For this historical reason, we may claim that by and large, anthropomorphism is "out." The question which this approach raises, of course, is "Is there some fundamental defect in anthropomorphism?"

This leads us to the third point. We know certainly that some anthropomorphisms are based on false assumptions (or at least on views which are unacceptable to us)—indeed often one false assumption may generate quite a few analogies. We speak pejoratively of anthropomorphic analogies which present no problems to us because they depend on unacceptable assumptions. The most prominent example is anthropocentrism, namely, the idea that the universe is created for the benefit of man and, therefore, may be judged from the viewpoint of its utility to man. For instance, the essence of wood, Aristotle suggests in his *Physics*, is that it is floatable and combustible, for the obvious reason that the most important functions that wood played in the ancient world were in its use as material for ship-building and as fuel. One may wonder, were Aristotle living today, whether he would make the essence of wood reside in its capability of becoming printing paper. A similar criticism of Aristotle is actually to be found in the late Renaissance and the seventeenth century; for instance, in the works of Robert Boyle, who suggested the following observation: for many people the essence of ice is that it is meltable into water, and thus, in essence, is water; whereas, for doctors, who use ice for lowering temperatures, the essence of water may be that it is freezable into ice.

The criticism made thus far of anthropocentrism, is,

of course, not decisive. It is quite possible to claim that though it is an error to judge wood, and ice, on the basis of their use to mankind at present, we should judge the essence of wood or ice from the viewpoint of mankind throughout the whole of human history. Perhaps it is very difficult to find out the total possible uses of wood or ice to mankind from its beginning to its end; but anthropocentrists might claim that this is what science should be about—that science is more difficult than Aristotle thought, precisely because scientific knowledge grows by attempting to find out the uses of different natural things for mankind through all the ages. It looks as if this generalized anthropocentrism is merely an intellectual exercise, but one may interpret instrumentalism in science as just that. Instrumentalists, however, will object. Somehow, the evidence that anthropocentrism happened to be parochial in the past was taken as evidence that anthropocentrism in any form must be parochial; and parochialism, of course, must be rejected.

We come, finally, to the fourth and last point about anthropomorphism. Anthropomorphism may be viewed (rightly or wrongly) as a version of the parochialism that Sir Francis Bacon designated as the Idols of the Tribe and of the Cave. Parochialism is the projection of our present knowledge of our limited environment into the whole universe. Parochialism is also the idea the worm in the apple has, that the whole world is an apple. And, of course, anthropomorphism may be viewed as a version of parochialism in the sense that we are very close to ourselves, and having some notions of our human traits, we generalize and project them into the universe at large.

So we seem to have arrived at the final condemnation of anthropomorphism. Somehow, we all condemn parochialism and we have the feeling that, viewed historically, science on the whole aims to break down parochial barriers, to give us a better view of the universe, rather than to reinforce the views into which we are born or which are due to space-time accidents of birth, and so forth. And in as much as anthropomorphism is historically parochial, or has its roots historically in parochial philosophy, this fact itself leaves no doubt that anthropomorphism runs against the spirit of science, and that as such, it condemns itself.

On the other hand, there is, no doubt, quite a different aspect or positive value of anthropomorphism in the history of science, which cannot be condemned as parochialism, viz., the human uses of science. To take very simple and obvious examples, scientists have devised many sorts of machines that imitate human operations. This, at least in part, is a technological matter of purely practical significance, interest, or value. We all want to jettison as many of our human burdens as possible with impunity; we try to dump them on machines. Thus engineers will apply science to the designing of machines to perform as accurately as possible as many human functions as possible. One might say all this technology is devoid of intellectual value. But this is only partly true. There is much to be gained scientifically in the theories of servo-mechanisms and "thinking machines" as they are half-jokingly called: we do want to embody part of our views of our functions and of our thought-processes in the observable operations of models, and thus form generalizations in a more scientific and interesting manner. What we learn from these mechanical models may then be used in research—say in biology.

Whether we try to apply our knowledge of machines to humans, or our knowledge of humans to machines, there is in each case an intellectual—even philosophic—interest. We can give examples of both cases, and show thereby that there are certain interactions between the human sciences and nonhuman sciences, as well as between sciences and technologies, which are very stimulating, very suggestive, intellectually very fruitful—and thereby justifiable. Take examples of the applications of scientific knowledge of the inanimate world to the animate world, to humans in particular. Not only have scientists claimed in a succession of hypotheses that the eye is the camera obscura, that the eye is a (lensed) camera, but also that the eye is a television camera of some sort. These are various physiological views of the function of the eyes. We also attempt the opposite when we apply the theories that were first created for explaining human phenomena to the explanation of nonhuman phenomena; there is no reason to discard such hypotheses just because of their anthropomorphic origin. To give a simple example, and a very well-known one indeed, Darwin was influenced by Malthus. Malthus wrote on economic competition and struggle for food in limiting population growth, and Darwin wrote on the origin of species and of biological ecology; nobody ever dreamt of censuring Darwin just because he was indebted to Malthus.

To give another simple example, perhaps more intricate but more important in history, there is nothing more evidently anthropomorphic than the ideas of attraction and repulsion, of love and hate. The introduction of the ideas of love and hate into physics by the Stoics, and in modern times by William Gilbert in his *De magnete* (1600) and by Sir Isaac Newton, is certainly not in itself condemnable. There is even something very interesting in the further development of the theory of love and hate, or attraction and repulsion, in the history of physics. When attraction and repulsion appear together in Newton's *Principia* (1687), they are put together as a theory of force, and the idea of force was considered at that time to be highly animistic. Newton was criticized for his animism and for his occult qualities. He insists in his *Opticks* (1704) that his theories are proper rather than *ad hoc* explanations, and true (because they provide precise predictions), so that one ought not complain about them even if they may need further explanation to fit them into Cartesian philosophy.

Newton's theory of force was abstract—at least as compared to ideas of force we employ when we speak of applying force to break through locked doors, etc.—the force of the muscles, the actions of the muscles, the disposition of the muscles to act. James Clerk Maxwell, in his *Treatise on Electricity and Magnetism* (1873), compared Faraday's tubes of force to muscles. The tubes of force by which Faraday operated, however abstract they were, had two qualities. They tend to shorten and to become wider, in a manner very similar to that of a tube of a muscle. So one can condone the criticism, launched against Faraday by the Newtonians of the day, that his theory was very distinctly anthropomorphic and less abstract than the Newtonian theory. Indeed, those in the Newtonian camp (who were indulgent towards Faraday), such as John Tyndall and H. L. F. von Helmholtz, stressed the fact that they had no quarrel with Faraday's use of those concrete images because of his "want of mathematical culture": people who were better versed in mathematics than Faraday, it follows, need not use his anthropomorphic analogy. This is why historically Maxwell's work was so important: he translated Faraday's images into a mathematical language; even Tyndall was very impressed.

There is correspondence between Faraday and Tyndall published in the *Philosophical Magazine* (1856), where Tyndall says to Faraday that he cannot imagine how space, empty space, that is, can have all these strange properties he ascribes to it, as it pulsates with tensions and strains. Faraday answers Tyndall by declaring him to be unimaginative, and in need of a more developed intuition.

In the history of science misplaced concreteness may have all sorts of different manifestations. We may fill space with a material "ether" which will accomodate strains and stresses. We may suggest that the world is simple because we prefer simplicity, or economy of thought. We may suggest that science should be mathematical since reality is mathematical (Galileo: "The Book of Nature is written in geometrical characters."). We may suggest as a speculation that the world is composed of fragmentary units of "atomic facts" because we state our information about the world in fragmentary propositions. The picture theory of language is perhaps one of the most significant manifestations of anthropomorphism insofar as it imputes to reality the limitations of our mode of representing it. It was crystallized in the twentieth century in the early work of Ludwig Wittgenstein (*Tractatus-Philosophicus*, 1922), and, for a while, was also held by Bertrand Russell.

Is anthropomorphism still alive? One aspect of anthropomorphism is parochialism, and it is typical of parochialism that its holders don't consider themselves parochial. That is to say, we never know how parochial we are. We only know how parochial our predecessors were in comparison with us. It is quite possible that we still hold various versions of anthropomorphism that may be rejected by our successors if they are to get rid of our errors and parochial limitations.

In spite of this caution, it is possible to explain a few facts about the historical development of science as it moves away from anthropomorphism. Examples have been given of interaction between ideas in the social sciences and those in biology and physics. What is condemnable about anthropomorphism is mainly its parochialism. Now it is very hard to draw a very clear line between parochial and nonparochial anthropomorphisms, because the main feature of anthropomorphism is its use of analogy from human phenomena to nonhuman phenomena and the idea of analogy is often very vague. Let us go back to the theory of space, pulsating with stresses and strains, which is common to Faraday's view and to Einstein's in his theory of relativity. It is very easy to suggest that however abstract the idea of pulsating space is in comparison with the theory of the pulsating ether in space, there still is an analogy between Einstein's space and any piece of elastic material such as plain rubber. In other words, however abstract our scientific ideas are, we can draw analogies between them and more concrete ideas, and so we can claim that our ideas are always lamentably concrete and parochial, that we are still rooted in our space-time environment, in local contingent conditions, whether physiological, biological, or social.

Although from time to time we may find analogies that are stimulating, exciting, and interesting, the substance of scientific progress cannot be based on analogies to the given, but rather on novel ideas, on ever increasing abstractions. This explains the situation that was alluded to early in this discussion: historically, the more we go into the distant past, the more we see anthropomorphism in more stark-naked versions. The progress of science is a progress from the more immediate, from the more parochial, to the more abstract, to the more general. And this very increase of generality and abstraction moves us away from anthropomorphism.

It is exactly this characteristic that explains why even our views of human nature, whether psychological, anthropological, sociological, economical, or any other, are increasingly less anthropomorphic, increasingly more abstract. There are very well-known, clamorous protests about making the science of men so abstract as to dehumanize it; for example, it is said that economists have defiled economics by the invention of that monster, the economic man. There is, perhaps, some truth in such claims, but there is also a Luddite attitude lurking in them, to destroy what seems to threaten us. Once we realize that anthropomorphism often takes the familiar and the comfortably acceptable to be true, we see that anthropomorphism may be objectionable even in the social sciences. Still, it is hard to speak against anthropomorphism in human sciences; we do better to speak against parochialism.

BIBLIOGRAPHY

For Aristotle's anthropomorphism, see his *Physics*, ed. and trans. W. D. Ross (Oxford, 1930), Book II, Ch. 8. The *locus classicus* of the critique of anthropomorphism is Bacon's doctrine of the Idols, in *Novum Organum*, Book I (Aphorisms XXXVII–LXVIII), and in *Valerius Terminus*, in *Works*, eds. R. L. Ellis, J. Spedding, and D. D. Heath, 14 vols. (London, 1857–74). But *Novum Organum*, Book II is notoriously anthropomorphic with its "thin" and "thick" essences (cf. I. B. Cohen, below). See also B. Spinoza, *Ethics*, IV, and *Treatise on the Correction of the Understanding* (London, 1910); and John Locke, *An Essay Concerning Human Understanding*, 5th ed. (London, 1706). References to animism, the discussion of the nineteenth-century anthropologists' attitude towards it, and the indication as to the Baconian character of this attitude, are in E. E. Evans-Pritchard, *Theories of Primitive Religion* (Oxford, 1965); esp. references in the Index: Art, Animism, Fetishism, and Ghost Theory. The *locus classicus* of the critique of anthropomorphism and parochialism is found in Galileo's *Dialogue on the Great World Systems*, trans. Thomas Salusbury, ed. G. de Santillana (Chicago, 1953), esp. the First Day. See, however, the discussion of the abstract and the concrete in the Second Day and Santillana's reference (p. 221) to *The Assayer*, from which the quotation about "geometrical characters" is taken. Also compare Galileo on abstractness with J. C. Maxwell on the same topic (and on Faraday) in his *Treatise on Electricity and Magnetism*, 3rd ed., 2 vols. (Oxford, 1904; New York, 1954), paragraphs 529, 541, and 546ff. See also Maxwell's comparison of Faraday's fields to muscles in "On Action at a Distance," *Proceedings of the Royal Institution of Great Britain*, **7**, reprinted in *Scientific Papers*, ed. W. O. Niven (Cambridge, 1890; reprint New York, 1965), II, 311–23; the analogy on 320–21. Cf. John Tyndall's *Faraday as a Discoverer* (London, 1870), and Helmholtz' Preface to the German edition of that book, translated in *Nature*, **2**

(1870). Cf. J. Agassi, "Analogies as Generalizations," in *Philosophy of Science*, **31**, 4 (1964). For the Faraday-Tyndall correspondence, see Tyndall, "On the Existence of a Magnetic Medium in Space," *Philosophical Magazine*, **9** (1855), 205–09; and M. Faraday, "Magnetic Remarks," ibid., 253–55. For Newton's discussion of the attack on his theory as postulating occult qualities, see I. B. Cohen, *Franklin and Newton . . .* (Philadelphia, 1956), Ch. IV, and last sections of Ch. VI. Finally, for the role of language as a veil between man and nature, thus making some measure of parochialism inevitable, see Bertrand Russell's essay, "Mysticism and Logic," in his *Mysticism and Logic* (London, 1910); and Karl R. Popper, "Why Are the Calculi of Logic and Arithmetic Applicable to Reality?" especially the last section, and his "Language and the Body-Mind Problem," both in his *Conjectures and Refutations* (London and New York, 1963). See in this connection Bacon's *Novum Organum* (Aphorisms LIX–LX) on the Idols of the Market Place; and Max Black, *Models and Metaphors* (Ithaca, 1962), the essays on "Benjamin Lee Whorf" and on "Models."

JOSEPH AGASSI

[See also Abstraction; **Analogy**; **Baconianism**; Relativity; Stoicism.]

ANTINOMY OF PURE REASON

KANT CALLS the antinomy of pure reason "the most singular phenomenon of human reason" and praises it as "a very powerful agent to arouse philosophy from its dogmatic slumber and to stimulate it to the arduous task of undertaking a critique of reason itself" (*Prolegomena*, §§53, 53a). It has been thought that the discovery of the antinomy must have played a decisive role in the development of Kant's thought from the pre-critical to the critical stage, about 1770; but efforts to fix the date and to determine the occasion of the discovery have led only to disputable and dubious results. Unlike other Kantian themes, this one underwent no gradual development in his published writings, but sprang full-grown in its most elaborate form, all at once, in the second chapter of the Transcendental Dialectic of the *Critique of Pure Reason*.

The word "antinomy," like many of Kant's technical terms, was derived from jurisprudence, where it referred to a conflict between laws; or from biblical exegesis, where it referred to a conflict between passages of scripture. (For a standard scholastic treatment of the term in logic, law, and exegesis, see Rudolf Goclenius, *Lexicon philosophicum* [1613; reprint 1964],

under "Antinomia.") Kant, influenced probably by Bayle's article on Zeno in his *Dictionnaire* (1697), saw Zeno as the inventor of the antinomic mode of argumentation or the "skeptical method" "of watching, or rather provoking, a conflict of assertions, not for the purpose of deciding in favor of one or the other side, but of investigating whether the object of the controversy is not perhaps a deceptive appearance which each vainly tries to grasp, and in regard to which, even if there were no opposition to overcome, neither can arrive at any result" (*Critique of Pure Reason*, 2nd. ed., p. 451; all page references to this edition). The skeptical method is not skepticism but aims, rather, at certainty; it is unresolved conflict of assertions which induces skepticism.

The Transcendental Dialectic seeks to dispel the illusion that pure reason can give knowledge of what lies beyond the limits of sense experience. The categories (pure concepts of the understanding) organize sense experience into knowledge of phenomena. Extended by the demands of reason for total explanations in metaphysics, the categories are thought to be concepts of unconditioned objects of reason (noumena) and are accordingly called, following Plato, ideas of reason. When thus extended either to some supersensible substances (the soul or God) or to the totality of phenomena which is not *itself* given as a totality in perception (the world as a whole), they become involved in various logical fallacies and produce "transcendental illusions" which are natural to the mind and inescapable until exposed by the critical philosophy. The antinomy is the conflict inherent in the "cosmological idea" of the world as a whole; looked at historically, it is the conflict between opposing theories in rational cosmology (one of the four divisions of metaphysics in the Leibniz-Wolffian system then current in Germany).

The opposed propositions are: Thesis 1, The world has, as to time and space, a beginning; Thesis 2, Everything in the world consists of elements which are simple; Thesis 3, There are in the world causes through freedom (spontaneous causes); Thesis 4, In the series of causes in the world, there is some necessary being; Antithesis 1, The world is as to time and space infinite; Antithesis 2, There is nothing simple, but everything is composite; Antithesis 3, There is no freedom, but all is nature (a complex of causes in space and time); and Antithesis 4, There is nothing necessary in the world, but all is contingent.

The theses, Kant holds, constitute the claims of "dogmatic philosophy" about what cannot be experienced; he calls them "rationalistic" and "Platonic," and they are, in fact, the teachings of the Leibniz-Wolffian rational cosmology. The antitheses are described as the teachings of "empiricism," "naturalism," and "Epicureanism," and represent the claims of empirical science when extended into metaphysics. The moral interests of mankind, Kant holds, are invested in the theses while the speculative (i.e., theoretical) interest favors the antitheses, which forbid any "break in the thread of physical inquiries" and urge "moderation in our pretensions, modesty in our assertions, and the greatest possible extension of our understanding . . . through experience" (p. 498).

The antinomy arises, in each of its four phases, by a formally identical argument. The major premiss is a true proposition: "If the conditioned is given, the entire series of all its conditions is likewise given." The minor premiss is also true: "Objects of the senses are given as conditioned." It follows that the entire series of conditions for any object of the senses is given, and is or contains its sufficient condition. The sufficient condition can be either (a) some ultimate condition within the series (e.g., an indivisible element, a beginning in time, a necessary being); or (b) the infinite series of conditions itself, no one of which is sufficient. Conclusion (a) is drawn by proponents of the theses, who deny the validity of an explanation requiring an infinite regress; and conclusion (b) is drawn by proponents of the antitheses, who refuse to recognize any limits which would terminate the temporal, spatial, and causal regress of conditions.

Kant's resolution of the antinomy has two steps. (1) The syllogism underlying both theses and antitheses is fallacious, since it involves an equivocation of the term "conditioned." In the major premiss, it is taken in "the transcendental sense of a pure category," while in the minor it is taken in "the empirical sense of a category applied to mere phenomena" (p. 527). Hence neither (a) nor (b) is proved. (2) But, though the arguments are invalid, it might be said that *either* theses or antitheses must be true since they are contradictories. Kant replies (p. 532) that they are not contradictories ("analytically opposed") but only "dialectically opposed," each asserting more than is required for it to be the analytical contradictory of the other. Hence both thesis and antithesis may be false, and are false if the additional element in them is false. This additional element is the same in every thesis and every antithesis, namely, the assumption that the things in the world are given in experience as they are in themselves. The resolution of the antinomy requires the denial of this assumption common to both sides.

Kant thereby achieves an indirect argument for his doctrine of "the transcendental ideality of appearances" (p. 534), the doctrine that the world we experience is not, and does not contain, a thing in itself but is only phenomenal.

He derives a second indirect argument for the same teaching by the important distinction he draws between the mathematical (first and second) and the dynamical (third and fourth) antinomies (p. 557). The former concern conditions homogeneous with the conditioned, i.e., spatiotemporal conditions which would be finite (if the theses were true) or infinite (if the antitheses were true). The dynamical antinomies concern conditions heterogeneous with the conditioned, i.e., something supersensible (free causes or necessary beings) as the condition for what is perceived— asserting them (in the theses) or denying them (in the antitheses). The first two theses and antitheses are all false, but the theses and antitheses of the dynamical antinomies *may* all be true (p. 560). The theses may be true of the supersensible world of noumena (though we do not *know* that they are true), while the antitheses are known to be true of the phenomenal world (from argument in the Analytic of the *Critique*). He claims to have shown that there is no reason in logic against Theses 3 and 4, and if there is good reason to believe them to be true, no theoretical argument can forbid their being affirmed ("primacy of practical reason"). This resolution of the third and fourth conflicts thus leads to Kant's "denying [theoretical, metaphysical] knowledge in order to make room for [moral or rational] faith" (p. xxx) which requires acceptance, without apodictic proof, of the theses. Kant accordingly refers to the antinomy as "the most fortunate perplexity into which human reason could ever fall," for without it the case for the antitheses, which produce a metaphysical dogmatism "always at war with morality," would be too strong.

While the outcome of the doctrine of the antinomy is the destruction of the dogmatic metaphysics of both the rationalistic and naturalistic schools, in the context of Kant's own philosophy the antinomy also has an important constructive function. The opposing propositions, denied their metaphysical pretensions, become regulative principles or maxims for the conduct of inquiry. The totality of conditions is not given (*gegeben*) but the search for the totality of conditions (the unconditioned) is assigned (*aufgegeben*) us as a task which must be performed without end. Thus, for example, the second antinomy might well be summarized in Whitehead's aphorism, "Seek simplicity, but distrust it"; and the third in the opposing programs of the ethical and the anthropological enterprises, one seeing man as free (thesis) and the other seeing him as product and part of nature under deterministic natural laws (antithesis).

In his *Critique of Practical Reason* and *Critique of Judgment* Kant develops three further antinomies. In the former, an antinomy concerning the relation of happiness to virtue in the *summum bonum* is resolved by the doctrine of the primacy of practical reason and the postulates of pure practical reason. In the latter, there are two antinomies. The antinomy of taste arises in the conflict between the maxim, *De gustibus non est disputandum* and the fact that one does dispute about taste; it is resolved by a clarification of what is meant by an aesthetic concept. The antinomy of teleological judgment, between the theses of teleology and mechanism, is resolved by converting them into regulative maxims and requiring that they complement each other in the explanation of nature. But in neither of the later *Critiques* is the doctrine of the antinomy worked out with the extensive detail and wide ramifications to be found in the first, and the antinomic form of argument is not entirely suitable to Kant's intentions in these works.

Recent criticism of the Kantian theory of antinomy has focussed on testing the validity of arguments for each thesis and antithesis, especially the first and second in the light of modern mathematical analysis of the concept of infinity; and on evaluating Kant's claim that the resolution of the antinomy provides an indirect proof of transcendental idealism or phenomenalism. The third antinomy attracts most attention nowadays from philosophers who defend or attack the theory of the compatibility of freedom and determinism. The fourth antinomy is of little interest, since it concerns a scientific problem no longer pressing, and what is philosophically interesting in it is better dealt with in the following chapter of the *Dialectic*, the critique of theoretical arguments for the existence of God.

Antinomic arguments (though not the name "antinomy") are widely used in philosophy. "An antinomy produces a self-contradiction by accepted ways of reasoning. It establishes that some tacit and trusted pattern of reasoning must be made explicit and henceforward be avoided or revised," writes a modern logician W. V. Quine, in *The Ways of Paradox* (1966), p. 7. It is perhaps the most typical form of argument in the Platonic dialogues. Among Kant's predecessors who employed explicitly antinomic arguments and who may have specifically influenced him were Arthur Collier in his treatment of space (*Clavis universalis*, 1713), and Christian August Crusius in his treatment of causality and freedom (*Entwurf der nothwendigen Vernunftwahrheiten* [1745]). Nor should the rhetorical conclusion of Hume's *Natural History of Religion* (1757) be overlooked as a possible stimulus to Kant.

The antinomic procedure was extravagantly developed by Fichte and Hegel, Hegel complaining that Kant erroneously limited the antinomies to the cosmological ideas and, even worse, limited them to notions and principles when, in fact, the world itself is full of contradictions (*Science of Logic*, first part originally published in 1812; translated by W. H. Johnston and L. C. Struthers [1929], I, 253). At a time of growing irrationalism in philosophy, the antinomies were highly esteemed as striking down the pretensions of reason. Among later philosophers, the influence of Kant's antinomies can be seen in Charles Renouvier's *Les dilemmes de la métaphysique pure* (1901) and other works, and in Nicolai Hartmann's "aporetic method" in all his books.

BIBLIOGRAPHY

Kant gives a simplified account of the antinomy in *Prolegomena* (1783), §§50–54. The most extensive study of the antinomy is Heinz Heimsoeth's *Transzendentale Dialektik*, Part II: *Vierfache Vernunftantinomie* (Berlin, 1967). In English, the authoritative (but very unsympathetic and critical) study is Norman Kemp Smith's *Commentary to Kant's Critique of Practical Reason* (London, 1918; 2nd ed., 1923), pp. 378–521.

Detailed evaluations of the antinomy in the spirit of the antepenultimate paragraph of this article are in P. F. Strawson's *The Bounds of Sense* (London, 1967), pp. 176–206, and (chosen from a very large periodical literature) M. S. Gram's "Kant's First Antinomy," *The Monist*, **51** (1967), 499–518.

On the origin of Kant's theory of antinomy, see: Karl Siegel, "Kant's Antinomienlehre im Lichte der Inauguraldissertation," *Kant-Studien*, **30** (1925), 67–86; L. Robinson, "Contributions à l'histoire de l'évolution philosophique de Kant," *Revue de Métaphysique et de Morale*, **31** (1924), 268–353, especially 308–39; and reply by H. J. de Vleeschauwer, "Les antinomies kantiennes et la *Clavis universalis* d'Arthur Collier," *Mind*, **47** (1933), 303–20; Joong Fang, *Das Antinomienproblem im Entstehungsgang der Transzendentalphilosophie* (Mainz Diss., 1960); and Norbert Hinske, "Kant's Begriff der Antinomie und die Etappen seiner Ausarbeitung," *Kant-Studien*, **56** (1966), 485–96.

On the antinomies in the later *Critiques*, see L. W. Beck, *A Commentary on Kant's Critique of Practical Reason* (Chicago, 1962), Ch. 13, and H. W. Cassirer, *A Commentary on Kant's Critique of Judgment* (London, 1938).

On Crusius as an antinomic thinker with resemblances to and influence upon Kant, see Heimsoeth's *Studien zur Philosophie Immanuel Kants* (Cologne, 1956), Ch. 3, and Beck's *Early German Philosophy* (Cambridge, Mass., 1969), Ch. 16.

On Hegel as an elaborator and critic of Kant's theory of antinomy see M. Gueroult, "Le jugement de Hegel sur l'antithétique de la raison pure," *Revue de Métaphysique et de Morale*, **38** (1931), 413–39.

LEWIS WHITE BECK

[See also Causation, Final Causes; Cosmology; Free Will and Determinism; **God**; Happiness and Pleasure; Hegelian; **Infinity**; Metaphor; Rationality.]

APPEARANCE AND REALITY

THE GENERAL sense of the contrast between appearance and reality would be any difference between what is the case and what appears to be so. Thus, the ordinary appearance of a person frequently conceals his real feelings and thoughts, the appearance of a village may be one of tranquility, but the reality one of turmoil, hatred, etc. The more specific sense of this contrast arose out of philosophical concerns about the nature of the world. The concept of "world" and of "reality" in this philosophical concern is related to but different from the ordinary concept. Early Greek cosmologists interpreted the perceived world in terms of causal and intentional forces of the gods. Pre-Socratic philosophers, searching for secular explanations, came to draw a sharp contrast between the perceived world and the ultimate "real stuff." Water, air, atoms, abstract notions like "unlimited" or "boundless," and "mind" were offered as the stuff of which the world is really made or in terms of which understanding of the world must be made. Greek atomism is a prime example. All observed properties and qualities of objects were explained in terms of the shape and motion of insensible material particles. This account of reality was not only important in itself, it was, at least to Lucretius later, of ethical and emotional value in leading man via understanding to happiness (cf. Spinoza).

The atomistic way of thinking of the cause and ground of the perceived world is easiest for us to accept since it fits in well with the early forms of atomism in modern physics. As recent science has moved to more and more abstractions, e.g., energy, force, fields, etc., the analogy of real world to the perceived world has given way. Those abstract concepts in Greek thought—the boundless, Parmenides' One, Plato's Forms—likewise required a different mode of thought for their understanding. Even though Parmenides may have thought of the One as in some way physical, the geometrical concepts easily emerged from his conceptualization of the One. The contrast between what appears to be the case and what is in fact so is sharp and striking. Parmenides' recommendation, again as much for moral as for intellectual reasons, was to turn our backs on the way of appearance and to contemplate the way of truth and reality. The contrast was so complete that sense experience was contradictory to reality: what the senses report cannot be true since motion is unreal. The paradoxes of Zeno simply played upon this Parmenidean contrast of appearance and reality. The senses are denied, are unreal.

This striking Parmenidean contrast set many problems for Plato and subsequent philosophers. The challenge of the paradoxes had to be met, one cannot carry out Parmenides' radical denial of all that our senses report. The most fundamental difficulty in a concept of reality such as Parmenides advanced is the implied if not explicit denial to the perceived world of *any* status in reality. Bradley was much later to point out that, no matter how different our philosophy may make appearances from reality, there is an important sense in which the appearances must occupy some place in reality. The Bradleyan concept of reality owes much to Hegel, where radical contrasts and differences tend to disappear in a dialectical flow: reality becomes the totality of that which is, Spinoza's *facies totius Universi* ("the whole aspect of the universe"). But quite apart from such an Hegelian transformation of the concept of reality, there is an important truth in the insistence that anything, appearances as well as nonappearances, *are* in some sense. At least the status is that they *exist* as appearances. Plato put the point trenchantly in having Socrates ask (*Republic* V, 476D), "When you know something, do you know something that is or something that is not?" The conclusion from this question has to be (as both Plato and Parmenides agreed) that that which is not can neither be nor be conceived.

To make room for sense perception which reveals a world of change and motion, of diversity and difference, Plato elaborated a conception of different degrees and kinds of realness. The most real—his Forms—fulfill the role of reality in the more simple notions of appearance and reality: the Forms play causal, semantic, and moral roles. The intellectual understanding of the Forms has an alternate, aesthetic mode. Both modes are sought for social, political, and ethical enlightenment and guidance. Plato stresses a pattern frequently repeated in the history of this idea. While it is reasonable to conclude that it was the moral fervor of Socrates seeking definitions of ethical concepts which led Plato to the notions of permanent, unchanging standards, the intellectual puzzles of Parmenides and Zeno influenced the later development of Plato's doctrine. Ideas of Sameness, Difference, and Existence found their elaboration in the later doctrine of Forms, always as a way of explaining and accounting for the appearance of development and change in our sensory experiences. Moral dilemmas in the earlier dialogues gave way in the later ones (*Parmenides, Sophist, Statesman*) to logical puzzles and challenges.

Conceiving of the reality of abstractions like Sameness and Difference, the Large and the Small, Justice and Beauty, is difficult if we use the familiar world of perception as our touchstone for reality. What Plato's notion of degrees of reality can do for us is to lead the way to viewing the world as composed of a wide variety of things. We need not go all the way with the Great Chain of Being, from lowest and earliest cells to Angels and God, but it is important for a proper understanding of our many-faceted world to have a way of fitting everything into a coherent view of reality. The concept of degrees or kinds of reality enables us to do just that, to see that anything experienced or mentioned, observable or conceivable belongs to the world in some way. We may want to make some distinctions, to place some items in our scheme of things in more prominent, more basic places, to order and relate the ingredients of our world in particular ways. What we cannot do is to label some items "appearance," if we intend thereby to exclude them from the real. This is not to say that the pressures leading philosophers to contrast appearance with reality are any the less forceful and demanding. It is only to say that, however we view the contrast between sensing and conceiving, between concrete particulars and abstract concepts, we have to recognize that that contrast is itself made within reality.

The Platonic doctrine of degrees of reality lends itself to religion in two different ways. In the hands of Plotinus it leads to a mystical metaphysic with a divine One as the culmination of the scale of being. All else is conceived as emanations from this One. Spinoza gave voice later to a similar metaphysic of totality—as Parmenides did before—but with more intellectual and less mystical content, though Spinoza's goal was also moral and religious. The doctrine of degrees of reality also lends itself to the intellectual attempts to articulate and justify a belief in God. Both Saint Anselm and Descartes made use of this notion in their proofs for God's existence. This use of the notion is, however, not central to the idea of appearance and reality. What is central and characteristic of much seventeenth-century philosophical use of this idea is Descartes' insistence that physical reality can be *understood*, not sensed or imagined. What the understanding reveals is a world of geometrical properties, extension being the essential category. The famous wax example in his *Meditations* (Part I) echoes the Greek rejection of the sense-world as real; his proof for body concludes that there is body but that it may not be as it seems to our senses.

A strong motive behind the metaphysic of Descartes was the concern to find a conceptual basis for the formulation and understanding of science; he sought to provide the categories and the method for seeing the world in scientific terms. The category of extension, like its corresponding category of thought, was a nonsensory concept. Descartes did not think of sense experience as less real (though he exploited its possibilities for deception), but he insisted that sensation will not yield a knowledge of matter or mind. Importance is clearly given to the nonsensory. The basic principles

of science were to be found in the basic simples (the simple natures) of his metaphysic.

The seventeenth-century philosophers were particularly concerned with science. Leibniz is equally representative with Descartes. The concept of monads—immaterial atoms, each very much like Parmenides' One—was Leibniz' metaphysical way of capturing some of the principles he thought science needed to explain and formulate the nature of body and motion. Activity for him was a basic scientific and metaphysical category. Leibniz' program is especially important in the history of this idea of appearance and reality because of the way in which the philosophical expression of that idea in his metaphysical writings was anticipated by his own attempts to deal mathematically and intellectually with the science of motion. The threefold appeal of this idea in the history of thought—the religious, the scientific, and the metaphysical—is at work in Leibniz. He liked to say that the experienced phenomena (the appearances) were well-founded: just the sort of phenomena we would expect if the world was really composed of the immaterial atoms he said it was. At the metaphysical level, we find in Leibniz a whole series of translations from ordinary language and experience to the language and reality of monads. The world conceived as colonies of different kinds of monads has God as a sort of super-monad. Immateriality and self-contained actions are the basic features of the world at the real (i.e., monadic) level.

Conceptualization of monads is not easy. Acceptance of tiny imperceptible material monads or atoms has always proved far easier. The Corpuscular Hypothesis used by seventeenth-century scientists in England, adopted by Locke in his philosophy, does not make any unnecessary demands on our thought, since it thinks of those corpuscular entities on analogy with gross bodies. Whenever philosophers move into a metaphysic of appearance and reality, where some of the items ascribed to reality put a strain on our easy conceptualization rooted in the perceptual world, special problems arise about explaining what the real status of those items is. In almost all cases, such transcendent items can be seen to work well as *explanatory* concepts. The difficulties appear when those items are given an ontological status as well. Leibniz seems to have recognized something of these difficulties in his *Discourse on Metaphysics* (1686) where, at one point, he suggests that talk of monads may only be a manner of speaking. To conceive of almost any transcendent abstraction as having ontological status, without deifying it, is indeed troublesome.

One interesting way around some of these problems is found in Spinoza's use of the distinction of appearance and reality. What Spinoza did was to eliminate from his metaphysic all transcendent items, including the traditional God of the Judeo-Christian tradition. Instead, the totality of that which is is itself deified. Traditional divine attributes are still ascribed to this totality, but Spinoza is very explicit in warning us not to be misled by these ascriptions. God or Substance is infinite, possessed of infinite attributes, cause of all and cause of itself, but is not different from all that is. What Spinoza's use of this idea requires is a shift in our understanding, not an acceptance of any new or strange metaphysical entities. Everything in the world, the most common and ordinary as well, can be viewed and understood in two different ways. From the point of view of appearance and ordinary perception, this glass of water, this table, this book is finite, in time, caused, subject to change, and possessed of the sensory properties we sense it as having. But these same objects can be placed in a different perspective where their particularity does not disappear, but where it is viewed from the perspective of the totality and that particularity can be seen as modifications of the totality. Viewing the world (better, the totality of everything) as a whole, as a unit, very general categories can be used to encompass everything. Of all that there is that we know (and Spinoza accepted the limitation of human knowledge), it is either extended or immaterial (i.e., thought). These categories *are* properties of the whole, but only insofar as there are particular extended and thinking things. Viewing particular objects in this way takes us outside time and causation, because time and causation are features of particular objects only. The totality is timeless and uncaused.

Parmenides is obviously reincarnated but transformed in this Spinozistic conception. The problem of conceiving of transcendent entities has disappeared, to be replaced by what may be a difference in kind of predication. That is, when Spinoza says God or Substance is cause of itself, is "cause" being used in the same way, with the same meaning, as in more ordinary causal judgments? Clearly not, in part because *causa sui* really means "uncaused," in part because the ascription of extension or thought to the totality which is Spinoza's Substance is a tacit way of ascribing these predicates to particular objects. Only particular members of the totality change and are caused, occupy space and time. But because these individuals taken together constitute the totality, the totality—not as a collection but as a whole—also *has* these properties, but not in the sense that it occupies space and time, changes, and is caused.

One cannot be sure to what extent the borrowed meanings of his concepts from traditional religious doctrine gave a religious flavor to Spinoza's demythologized metaphysic of Substance. Spinoza was an intense, meditative man; his attitude towards life was moralist and humane rather than coolly intellectual. The concepts of his metaphysic were not fashioned to deal with logical puzzles; they were to deliver him and mankind from human bondage: "from his intellect / And from the stillness of abstracted thought / He asked repose" (Wordsworth, "The Wanderer," lines 313–15). Intellectual understanding is in the service of enlightenment and well-being. The *Ethics* of Spinoza offers us a way of life, not one that requires us to forsake practice and action but one which adds understanding and peace of mind to our daily lives. But of course, such a way to happiness and well-being is not practicable or even feasible for many. The mental and emotional state of mind requisite for finding, in this abstract concretizing of appearance and reality, the peace (one could almost say beatitude) that does not pass but comes through understanding is rare in mankind.

While the naturalization of deity, characteristic of seventeenth-century deists, easily lends itself to the kind of romantic religious attitude toward nature found in Wordsworth, it would be difficult to think of Spinoza's deification of nature finding a direct application in literature. One might expect to find something like it in the metaphysical poets, but their conceits were abstract and often contorted though not metaphysical. For artists usually, for Wordsworth in particular, experience of nature, not abstracted thought, provides the mark of reality. Sometimes the artist is content to record the appearance of things, the sensuous content is valuable enough. At other times, as in Wordsworth's case, familiar perceptual objects are seen as having an "inward meaning," they reveal "the one Presence, and the Life / Of the great whole" (*The Prelude*, II, lines 129–31). Unlike the academic studies at Cambridge, which seemed to the poet of *The Prelude* to take him away from the "sentiment of Being," experience of nature—the woods, mountains, lakes of Windermere—enables him to converse "With things that really are" (II, lines 412–13). The boundaries of our perceptual world, the "cabinet of our sensations," can be transcended if we respond to "the latent qualities / And essences of things" (II, lines 223–29, 344–45). "To thee, unblinded by these outward shows, / The unity of all has been reveal'd" (II, lines 225–26).

There is Platonism, of course, in Wordsworth. The eternal Beauty of the Forms reappears, with the famous "Ode—Intimations of Immortality" typifying this feature of his thought. But the important characteristic of Wordsworth's poetry for the history of the idea of appearance and reality is the deistic, natural religion of his longer poems. The intellectual tradition upon which Wordsworth drew in his nature poetry is the same one to which deists and Spinoza belonged. No sharp contrast between appearance and reality is drawn, the totality of appearances and phenomena *is* reality, but the perceptive person will come to view those objects in a way which reveals the meanings latent in them. Deists, Wordsworth, and Spinoza, in their respective ways worked within a unified, non-transcendent notion of reality but drew distinctions of value within the one Being. All three did so for inspirational purposes. Appearances are not rejected or denied a place in reality, they become reality when experienced and understood in the proper way.

William Blake is another interesting though obscure example of a literary application of metaphysical concepts. The interpretation of Blake is difficult. Platonism and Berkeleyan idealism at least seem to have combined to influence his literary and aesthetic convictions. Northrop Frye (*Fearful Symmetry* . . .) cites those passages where Blake clearly echoes Berkeley, e.g., "nothing is real beyond the imaginative patterns men make of reality" (p. 19). Wordsworth's deism is misleading for Blake, since it credits to nature the realities of the imagination. The Platonism of Blake, which G. M. Harper stresses in his study, *The Neoplatonism of William Blake*, finds expression in such passages as "Imagination, the real and eternal World of which this Vegetable Universe is but a faint shadow" ("Jerusalem," in Blake, *The Complete Writings*, ed. G. Keynes [1957], p. 717), and "There Exist in that Eternal World the Permanent Realities of Every Thing which we see reflected in this Vegetable Glass of Nature" ("A Vision of the Last Judgment," ibid., pp. 605–06). Harper cites several passages which seem to show Blake giving independent existence to the Forms discovered (or created) by the imagination. For example, "Whatever can be Created can be Annihilated: Forms cannot: / The Oak is cut down by the Ax, the Lamb falls by the Knife, / But their Forms Eternal Exist For-ever" ("Milton," ibid., p. 522). While Blake also seems to retain something of the doctrine of "degrees or kinds of reality," e.g., in speaking of the worlds of vision, sight, and memory, Frye insists that "These are not three different worlds"; they are rather three different ways of looking at the one world (p. 26).

Whether we view Blake through the metaphysics of Berkeley or of Plato is not all that important, though both ingredients seem to be there. What is important to see—and Blake is an ideal case—is the way in which metaphysical concepts are used but transmuted by the literary mind. Blake was more interested in artistic and aesthetic adaptations of Plato and Berkeley than in their doctrines themselves. The concept of form as a metaphysical entity is replaced by that of archetype. The artist generally is one who, via vision working on particulars, captures universal and archetypal forms. Metaphysical idealism supplies the artist with an intellectual justification of the truths he learns from his own experience about the creative imagination and the activity of the mind. Platonism enables him to give more than a passing reality to the forms of the imagination. The Platonic real world becomes the world of the imagination.

Kant's philosophy provided many of the Romantics, especially Coleridge, with an even stronger and more attractive philosophical understanding for their artistic activities. Schiller's aesthetic interpretations of Kant probably had a strong influence upon the conceptualizations of the romantic imagination. Kant provided a different kind of merging of phenomenal and real from that of Spinoza. Working with the same totality of things, Kant gave to the mind the fundamental formative and shaping powers of the world of experience. The real world just *is* the world we experience, but its structure and order are not contingent and external to mind, for they are necessary products of mental activity. Kant's moral philosophy might seem to retain a separation between phenomenal (appearance) and real, with its appeal to an intelligible world as a way of explaining how human action can break out of the causal uniformities of nature, but the conceptual grounding of the *Metaphysical Foundations of Morals* (1797) should more properly be seen as a recognition of the difference in the causality of events and actions. The causality of agency in action (and by extension, of creative imagination) was an important philosophical prop for artists, especially poets, of the eighteenth century, in freeing them from what was believed (albeit falsely) to be Locke's failure to recognize the activity of mind in his influential account of the human understanding.

Interestingly, the philosophical recognition of mental activity, even to the extent of giving to mind formative and determining functions of reality, emerged out of a metaphysic which rejected the sharp separation of appearance and reality. Where artists interpret their goal as capturing reality, dualisms which place reality in a realm separate from direct experience of phenomena place a barrier in front of artistic activity. Platonic visionaries could claim access into the realm of Forms (experience of beauty was one path to the Forms recognized by Plato), Wordsworthian and Spinozistic deists and pantheists could claim the ability to capture the living forms in nature. But still more attractive is the notion that the creative imagination takes its place alongside the other mental apparatus elaborated by Kant and plays a formative role in determining the real. Since Kant, most literary and artistic support in philosophy has come from the Kantian and Hegelian merging of appearance and reality.

Hegel gave the most grandiose construction to this new metaphysics. The *Phenomenology of Mind* (1807) is a rich and, in its own way, artistic work. The philosophical tradition is that of Spinoza, deists, and pantheists, with many a debt to Kant. No sharp breaks in the scale of being, smooth transitions from one level or kind to the next, until in Absolute Spirit we have Hegel's attempt to formulate in abstract and semireligious concepts the unified totality of all the levels and kinds of reality and appearance. Unlike the aesthetic approach of Wordsworth, which revealed the most abstract truth of reality by sensory exposure, Hegel's conceptual genius enables us to apply the concepts of his metaphysic to sensory, social, political, and religious experiences. We find in Hegel an application of metaphysical concepts to illuminate life, not just art. The social tensions of master and slave, of ruler and ruled, the intellectual tensions of experience and understanding, of change and law are viewed through the dialectic and structure of his metaphysic.

The Hegelian influence was massive, even within the English-speaking world. It also was largely responsible for the decline and rejection of metaphysics in twentieth-century English philosophy: those who were opposed to metaphysics took Hegel as their example, even though few of the positivists and scientific empiricists had any intimate understanding of Hegel. Nevertheless, even within these new forms of empiricism, with their reliance upon logic and science, dualisms of appearance and reality emerged again. Philosophers saw science as the authority on the nature of the world; but, since the scientific account talked of unobservable particles, the world of ordinary human experience had to be given some place in reality. The sense-datum theories of Bertrand Russell, G. E. Moore, C. D. Broad, and H. H. Price tried to relate appearances to reality as effect to cause. Human knowledge was immediately and mainly of sense qualities, indirectly and inferentially of the scientifically designated causes. Knowledge by acquaintance and knowledge by description (a distinction first made by William James in *Principles of Psychology*, New York [1890], I, 221) was Russell's way of formulating the epistemic access we have to appearances and reality. The transitions and developments of dualism and phenomenalism of previous centuries now reappeared (almost as Hegel's dialectic predicted) in the new but transformed garbs of New Realism, Critical Realism, and Common Sense Direct Realism. These have been almost exclusively English

and American formulations, debates still not completed. (See R. J. Hirst's *The Problems of Perception* for a good summary and discussion of many of these issues.)

Continental metaphysical concerns during the twentieth century have stayed strictly within the Kantian and Hegelian tradition. Edmund Husserl's phenomenology became the dominant mode. Two features characterize Husserl's philosophy: a method of analysis and a new ontology of meaning. The metaphysical dictum here is "the world is my world," the world of lived, human experience. The whole realm of experience becomes a field for analysis, everything now becomes phenomena. Perhaps more stress has been placed by Husserl's followers upon the method of analysis—supposedly unbiased and free from all ontological prejudices—than upon the ontology. Questions of reality are supposed to be set aside as useless, attention is then free to look to the descriptions of all and any phenomena. But there is a metaphysic here all the same, a metaphysic of experience which is clearly Kantian and Hegelian. Since the stress is upon experience as lived and interpreted by men, meaning becomes the central concept, meaning for me. The union of reality in and for itself (*en-soi et pour-soi*), upon which the phenomenological metaphysic of experience rests, has been reformulated by Sartre in *Being and Nothingness* (*L'Etre et le néant*, 1943). That union is possible only because man is the center of this world.

Sartre and other existentialist writers, in their literary productions, seized upon the emotions of man as the most significant definers of reality: anguish, dread, loneliness. The reality of a life can be experienced best, they believe, in confrontations with death, fear, and dread—a far cry from the tranquility and peace of Wordsworth's real world. Husserl's phenomenology has had widespread impact upon literature, psychology, psychoanalysis, religion, and philosophy, even upon social science and education. Moreover, that impact has finally been felt in the English-speaking world. But the existentialist writers—and the art of the absurd in general—have narrowed the scope of reality so much that some of them are close to denying all reality. "Authentic" experience is privileged and rare, perhaps impossible; reality as meaning for a person may be slipping from our grasp: such seems to be the message of much of existentialist writing. They are close to presenting us with the negation of the romantic striving for and belief in a new and better reality in or behind appearances. Samuel Beckett's noncharacters find no meaning and very little reality in their experience. It makes little difference whether Godot is given a religious interpretation, or whether it is secularized and taken to signify a meaning for the world. Beckett's early characters are waiting for meaning to appear out of the routine concatenation of ordinary events. His later characters have given up entirely on Godot, and merely live out their meaningless experiences in absurd and unreal environments. Autonomy, creativity, and value have been replaced by one-dimensional man living out his time in a controlled but meaningless world. Parmenides' denial to appearances of any status in reality has found its contemporary formulation within a metaphysic which identifies reality with appearances. The total annihilation threatened by the bomb has found its literary and philosophic counterpart in this denial of reality to the only reality left, the reality of lived human experience.

It is difficult to predict the future of this idea of appearance and reality. Its apotheosis in metaphysics and literature has had a parallel in religion and theology: the transcendence of God has struggled with the meaningful immanence of human life. In many modern theologies, religious meaning seems to have followed the direction of existentialist writers, being located in personal attitudes towards man and the world. The metaphysic of transcendent entities thus seems on all fronts to have given way to the phenomenological categories: reality is as it is interpreted as being in human experience. What there is has become a function of what man finds meaningful and valuable in his experience. Parmenides denied reality to appearances. Our contemporaries are close to denying reality to reality. Such an ultimate denial would be the complete reversal of the appearance-reality distinction.

BIBLIOGRAPHY

F. H. Bradley, *Appearance and Reality, A Metaphysical Essay* (Oxford and New York, 1930). Dorothy M. Emmet, *The Nature of Metaphysical Thinking* (New York, 1945; London, 1949). N. Frye, *Fearful Symmetry, A Study of William Blake* (Princeton, N. J., 1947). G. M. Harper, *The Neoplatonism of William Blake* (Chapel Hill, N. C., 1961). G. W. F. Hegel, *The Phenomenology of Mind*, trans. J. B. Baillie (London, 1931). R. J. Hirst, *The Problems of Perception* (London and New York, 1959). J. H. Muirhead, *The Platonic Tradition in Anglo-Saxon Philosophy* (London, 1931). J.-P. Sartre, *Being and Nothingness*, trans. H. Barnes (London, 1966). G. Vlastos, "Degrees of Reality in Plato," in *New Essays on Plato and Aristotle*, ed. R. Bambrough (London and New York, 1965), pp. 1–19. W. H. Walsh, *Metaphysics* (London and New York, 1964). J. W. Yolton, *Metaphysical Analysis* (Toronto, 1967).

JOHN W. YOLTON

[See also Atomism; Causation; **Cosmic Images;** Creativity in Art; Deism; **Existentialism; Neo-Platonism; Platonism;** Romanticism; Structuralism.]

ART AND PLAY

AN ANALOGY between art and play, ranging from mere metaphor to literal identification, has been asserted, for better or worse, in an extraordinary variety of ways. The most obvious of these contrast art and play with work, with the "serious," with activities carried out under compulsion of some kind, whether moral, political, economic, psychological, or genetic. Such analogies have been as frequently rebutted by those who insist that art is too serious for such an equation as they have been affirmed by those who have seen art as only hedonic or entertaining.

Between these extremes are those who find positive merit in both aspects of art, and we shall concentrate our attention on such affirmative theories. Associated with these ideas about art and its cultural significance are: (1) the surplus energy or leisure theory of culture, seeing art and play as products of superfluity after basic needs have been met; (2) education, imitation, and vicarious experience theories, whereby art and play are valued for the way in which men can encounter harsh realities harmlessly; (3) metaphysical theories equating the two because of an "as if" element in both, ultimately extending to epistemology and science; (4) "the child-in-the-man" theories emphasizing naiveté and unconscious processes as contrasted with sophisticated hyperrationality.

It is exceedingly rare in antiquity for play to be associated with art at all, and where it is, the connection is usually found in a condescending attitude towards both, or at least towards play where the function of art is conceived rather more loftily. For the most part, however, play is thought of as an activity of animals and children, and, given the relatively unsentimental attitude towards both in antiquity, play is reduced to a fairly low status. It is thought of as nonpurposive, noncognitive, frivolous, time-wasting, and hedonic. No doubt there were in antiquity, as at all times, those who found the highest value of art in pleasure, relaxation, entertainment, and the like, and if they equated art with play it was more likely to damn the former than to praise the latter. Despite these unpromising beginnings, however, there is early evidence of some redeeming qualities and among these may be traced the origins of ideas immensely fruitful in the development of later theories of play and art.

The leading notions are found in the connection of play with *imitation* and *education*, and by way of these the affinity with art may be seen ultimately to draw ever closer. Scattered references may be found in Homer (e.g., *Iliad* XV, 363) as well as in other authors of antiquity (cf. Pauly-Wissowa, article "Spiel") in which the propaedeutic value of childhood games is

99

brought out. Many of these references are to games with clay, sand, and stone pre-figuring sculpture and architecture, but their importance should not be exaggerated. It would be necessary at first to cast the net rather widely to find the connections among ideas whose interrelatedness as seen in later perspective was scarcely apparent in earlier times, and so run the risk of appearing to impute to our seminal thinkers a degree of coherence on the present topic of which they were innocent. On the other hand, the problem of play as it is concerned with culture generally, with psychological theories of man and beast, or even with more obviously related topics such as the drama or the *agon* as "play," are all beyond the scope of this article; for many of these broader issues the reader is referred to the works of Groos and Huizinga, among others. Likewise the connection between sympathetic magic or religious ritual (especially in the sublimated forms of symbolic sacrifice) and imitation cannot be explored here even though there are obvious points of contact between these and certain aspects of play.

In all of these something is represented or acted out or made to stand for something else in a manner that deliberately falls short of the literal or actual enactment of the something else. To this extent, at least, direct utilitarian or cognitive purposes are not served (even if they are never far from the surface) and therewith a key aspect of play as such is manifest. Against this view it is frequently argued that the "primitive" mind is incapable of distinguishing symbol from thing symbolized, and so what appears to be indirect, "playful," vicarious, etc., to more sophisticated minds has been misapprehended. The point is valid but complements rather than weakens the argument advanced here. It is rare for the most sophisticated (or even the most prosaic) of minds wholly to lose the ability to be immersed in the world of fantasy and imagination, or to abandon "reality" for the nonce, however easily it might be recovered at need. Even where primitive languages treat "play" as childish, frivolous, and so forth, and do not adequately distinguish what we should think of as play or symbolic activities from "real" ones, people's actual conduct will display their grasp of the distinction.

Methodologically it will always be a problem to isolate play as it is manifested in art from the many other factors with which play is associated, e.g., human nature and psychology, the "leisure theory of culture," childish (or childlike) things, imitation, vicarious experience, education, epistemology, anticipations of knowledge or of "serious things," creativity, metaphysics. For example, the references to play in Plato display many of the entanglements of the related themes considered above. Play is harmless enough in

very young children, but all too soon it takes on the aspect of an irrationality (and therewith unreality) that it becomes the task of education to remedy. Play only becomes tolerable when it is channeled in desirable directions. To take another example, play as vicarious experience is significant both in Plato and Aristotle. The emphasis in Plato lies rather in the joint subordination of art and play to education (itself in the service of ethics and metaphysics); hence, as will become apparent in many other writers, it is very difficult to separate play in art from its manifestations under other aspects. In Aristotle, the emphasis, to be discussed in greater detail below, is on catharsis, in which the emotions aroused and discharged by the action of the drama are serious but harmless—two features that almost universally are included in the concept of play and art. Only in recent years (say, since Karl Groos and, most notably, Huizinga) has a conscious attempt been made to analyze the concept of play so as to elicit its specific features. Until this century the innumerable discussions of the subject, of which only a few important examples can be given here, appear in contexts displaying the leading interests of their authors; art and play have frequently been only incidental to those interests, however.

I. PLATO

Plato's standard position is clear enough: play is intimately connected with imitation: boys play at being soldiers (*Republic* V, 466E ff.), and more generally, children play at being their elders, the bard imitates in his narrative the speech and action of heroes and, much less acceptably, the actor does this directly; the poet imitates the Muse who inspires him. Since the force of imitation is construed in Plato's educational psychology as making the imitator resemble what is imitated, the truth of the model is all-important. At *Republic* 425A ". . . children in their earliest play are [to be] imbued with the spirit of law and order through their music" (*mousike* here refers to the arts generally, and not necessarily only to music); at 536E children are to be introduced to their studies by play and not by compulsion.

From these observations follows much of the criticism of poetry and the arts for which Plato is notorious; but we shall be concerned here only with those aspects of the criticism that bear on play and art. Certainly a man will not want to imitate anything unworthy of him (*Republic* III, 395A ff.), "except for the sake of play (*paidia*)" (396E). This last reservation finds an echo in *Laws* (II, 667DE) where play is associated both with art and pleasure. Play is here defined as harmless pleasure doing neither good nor harm. But doubts are at once raised by the Athenian whether the performance of a work of art, because it is primarily concerned with imitations and representations of real things, could ever harmlessly misrepresent those things (cf. 658E, 659E). Thus the argument returns to the standard position in which Plato's references to art and play are subordinated to education and moral training within the metaphysical framework of his system.

Repeatedly, whenever the question of play, amusement, entertainment, pleasure, etc., is raised, whether in connection with art or not, Plato allows that these involve a certain charm if their pursuit is appropriate to the age and mental development of the players. But judgment is not so easily disarmed and older and wiser heads keep knowledgeable watch, since nothing that is not true can be beautiful, good, or even harmless.

Plato's views on art have been much attacked and, taken superficially, they may appear disappointing. The overtones of censorship, regimentation, and confident self-righteousness have alienated many commentators. But it is always a mistake to read Plato as though he were describing a feasible reconstruction of the world; he repeatedly distinguishes the ideally desirable from the actually attainable, and in so doing is playing a game of his own—a political game realized with consummate art within metaphysical rules asserted to be self-evidently true for the sake of the game. Seen in this light he has been called *ludimagister* (Rahner [1967], p. 12); Plato himself refers (*Letter* VI, 323D), if genuine, to "the jesting that is kin to earnest," and his own use of myth will bear comparison with Socratic irony as a playful device of art. The *Republic*, in particular, is the model of all subsequent positive Utopias— the negative ones are grimmer and lack the imaginative exploitation of possibilities, even the wishful thinking, that characterize the *Republic* and its successors— qualities shared, as we shall see, by play and art.

II. ARISTOTLE

Much that is at most implied in Plato is made explicit by Aristotle. There is a shift in the underlying metaphysical presuppositions and these yield a theory that is at once richer, more accessible and comfortable, and more "realistic."

The main points of departure lie in two developments of Platonic positions by Aristotle: imitation and the ultimate objectives of human existence. Imitation is broadened so that its validity is not constrained within the limits of the "real"; and one key concept introduced by Aristotle to vindicate man's existence is "leisure" (*schole*).

We are told in the *Poetics* that art imitates not only what is (as in Plato), but what "ought to be" and what "might be." The latter two liberate the Platonic theory from its offensive literalness and dogmatism. What

ought to be represents the morally ideal and only incidentally concerns us here; but what might be refers directly to our theme. Imagination is not bound by the actual, but is free to range over the possible and the plausible. The latter is given even more significance than the former, because the mind may grant credence to something factually impossible, but accepted as plausible for the sake of some argument the value of which does not rest on factual truth. Here (*Poetics*, Ch. 26) Aristotle relies, as Plato does (*Theaetetus* 191B, *Republic* IX, 588C ff.) on the ability of the mind to juxtapose images disparately drawn from experience in order to construct monsters and other imaginary beings and situations, sometimes for some immediate further purpose (if only to frighten children), but not necessarily so. Aristotle draws attention to the power of creating metaphors as a sign of genius, "the one thing that cannot be taught."

This position does not differ significantly from the Kantian notion of the free play of the imagination, and it also anticipates a further element of great importance in later thought. This is the balance between factual (or logical) and aesthetic truth. The former is "objective" and serious; the latter "subjective" and playful. Yet if the latter is to be redeemed of frivolity and childishness some connection with factual truth must be maintained. In Aristotle the connection is somewhat stronger than Coleridge's "willing suspension of disbelief." It was Aristotle who first drew attention to the confusion between the two, as illustrated by the yokel in the audience who rushes on stage to prevent one character from killing another. This involves the inability to follow out all the implications of a situation allowed ex hypothesi; or to follow a set of self-imposed rules or conventions not sanctioned by external reality: yet these are features of play at every level.

The interrelation of art and play in drama is illustrated by two senses of vicarious experience: (1) what can I learn from what has happened to another, and (2) what can be learned from the imaginable alternatives to any given situation. Both senses rely on the assumption that art is justified by its indirect service to knowledge and individual resource in facing future situations; and as such may be seen as a development of the propaedeutic justification for children's play and the adult *agon*. The manner of art, i.e., the depiction of universals, further enhances its usefulness for these ends. By stripping away the fortuitous and accidental circumstances in which individual occurrences arise, "poetry is more universal than history" because it can crystallize the essence of a situation. We are thus exposed to all the advantages of the widest conceivable range of experience without exposure to dangers that might rather crush than edify. The notable difference between Greek and Roman sports and plays supports this view: Greek games were never bloody, nor was bloodshed ever directly shown in the Greek theater.

The doctrine of catharsis may be viewed in the same context as applicable to the emotions aroused by ideal situations. Pity edifies though terror crushes, and the two together perform the function of play—serious but harmless. Pity or compassion is the emotion by which we empathize with the tragic hero, seeing ourselves in him. We use him as surrogate for what we dare not do ourselves. He carries out in a postulated reality all our secret desires, our blasphemies, our impossible quests. Our elation is intensified by his temporary successes: almost we could wish to follow him, but our fascination is no less morbid and we as much desire his failure. His daring is a reproach to our mediocrity, and so the inevitability of his doom reflects our consciousness of human limitations as much as the jealousy of the gods.

The play element lies in a series of "as if" propositions pursued with logical rigor to an inevitable conclusion: let there be a hero nobler by birth and breeding than any member of the audience; let him be wiser, stronger, shrewder, prideful as befits these qualities, but still recognizably human; let him challenge the peace of the gods; and let the gods prove the power of their sanctions. We are content with the thought that if the hero, preeminently possessed of all human virtues, cannot succeed, then how much less can we expect of ourselves. We are thus reconciled to the governance of the cosmos and of our lowly role in its economy.

Aristotle seems to be the originator of, or at least the first to write about, leisure as the basis of culture. The discussion in *Politics* II is long, but a few major points should be presented. A truly human nature can be fulfilled only on the assumption that an environment can be created within which the individual can actualize all his potentialities. But an individual who is obliged to satisfy his needs by his own resources alone would be forced to function at a very limited level of activity, living from hand to mouth with no respite from those activities needed merely to sustain life. The division of labor serves the dual function of enabling the individual to confine his activities to what he can do best, and of furnishing leisure for some individuals in a society to think of matters that transcend the exigencies of the moment. There will be many ways in which such thought accrues to the benefit of the society; only some of these, of course, will bear directly on play and art.

There is a typology of human nature in Aristotle, not unlike the class structure of the *Republic:* some people will be content with practical and productive activities, and for these the value of art and play lies largely in recreation and entertainment, the restoration of energies exhausted in labor, or the dissipation of excess energy when no purposive activity is needed, as in the interval between seeding and harvesting crops, or for simple variety or change of pace, or to keep physical and mental capacities sharpened. But other individuals have superior needs: theoretical and mythopoetic; and these point to the stationing of some men in Aristotle's hierarchy of being above common men and below the gods, though following his advice "to be as divine as they can be" (*Nicomachean Ethics* X. vii). For these the object of all lower activities is to provide the leisure needed for contemplation and those modes of creation appropriate to such men: both part of and operating upon nature. The relationship in Aristotle between activities instrumental for some higher ends and those intrinsically good in themselves is not always clear—nor, perhaps, can it be, in view of his well-known antipathy to infinite regress. At the end of the line, as concerns human activity, are found such notions as happiness and leisure. The latter he mostly (e.g., *Ethics* X. vii) speaks of as instrumental, enabling further happiness-inducing activities distinguished by their not being engaged in under the duress of need (and thus sharing a key aspect of play); indeed, leisure comes close to being an end itself and a goal of human existence, which in its moments of leisure enjoys the highest felicity. Aristotle quotes with approval (*Ethics* X. vi) "The maxim of Anacharsis, 'Play so that you may be serious.'"

III. THE THEORY LAPSES

One searches the literature of later antiquity in vain for the development of these ideas. It is not merely that the epigoni of the post-Aristotelian schools lacked originality, rather the topic seems to lapse into neglect. There are, to be sure, scattered references to children's play, to gaiety of spirit and the like, e.g., in Lucian, Horace, Pliny, Plutarch, and even in Cicero; and the history of aesthetics continued to be served, but the connection between them is broken. Play as such is not neglected but passes into the fierce competition of the *agon* to make a Roman holiday. The magic child of many pagan traditions is absorbed, especially by Augustine, into Christianity, and combines great simplicity and wisdom as before (cf. Boas, 1966), but there is no connection with art.

Perhaps too much joy had escaped the life of reason in the sequence of Greek collapse, stern Ciceronian injunctions to duty, Roman decline, and Christian asceticism. Even Roman comedy displays little of the lightness of touch that might suggest that a practical connection continued even though the theory might be lacking. The Church Fathers frowned on anything that might distract the Christian from the grim search for salvation: Chrysostom, for example, in the Sixth Homily of his *Commentary on Matthew*, tells us "It is not God who gives us the chance to play, but the devil" (PG 57, 70D). These strictures of course had a target, for while the dominant theories to govern human nature had changed, that nature no doubt remained the same.

A contribution to our theme is to be found, therefore, only by default, for the same antipathy to play is also directed against art. The latter was only to be redeemed by the subordination of its subject matter to doctrinally sound topics expressed in a rigid formal perfection taken to be the microcosm of the universe. Not until we reach Aquinas do we find a revival of the generous Aristotelian view: in his commentary on the *Nicomachean Ethics* Saint Thomas favorably explicates the concept of *eutrapelia*, a lightness of spirit midway between boorishness and frivolity (cf. Rahner [1967], p. 99). The emphasis here, as in the *Summa theologica* (II-II, q. 168 a. 2), is however on play as relaxation from labor and tension, without reference to art.

For a long time there seems to have been little patience with play as a feature of imagination, creativity, and art, whether we search among British empiricists or continental rationalists, or among thinkers not so easily labeled. For one thing all these shared in common a view that is in essence hostile to the innocence of art (or simply hostile to innocence) and so we find three aspects, variously emphasized, all of which illustrate the decline of interest in play. The first is rarely explicit, since it treats some forms of art as scarcely worthy of notice: the sort of art that might be associated with play is taken as childish, vulgar (popular), primarily time-killing entertainment, and thus not a fit subject for intellectual inquiry (Schleiermacher).

The second and third views involve even loftier pretensions in which art is justified predominantly with reference to cognition and morality. The position of Leibniz usefully exemplifies the second view: such validity as art possesses lies in its anticipation of positive knowledge. Aesthetic vision yields *petites perceptions* as the first of four grades of perceiving reality in the world. As the mind advances toward fully rational knowledge the lower grades are superseded. Moses Mendelssohn pointed out in criticism of this view that art is thus assumed to have no intrinsic value of its own; and that therefore as positive knowledge increases, the significance of art will decline. The third aspect is found more frequently where the concept of taste and its educability comes to the fore, e.g., in

Hume, Burke, Vico, Lessing, and Herder, among others. Here taste becomes a function of sophistication and wide experience, and so cannot be assimilated to the play theory. Where formal perfection is a major objective of art (e.g., in the theory and practice of Dryden or Pope) this further militates against an analogy with play. For that formal perfection is not infrequently seen as the aesthetic counterpart of a wholly rational world (conceived not only scientifically, but as part of a theodicy) such that art is not an exploration beyond what is currently known, so much as a confirmation of the philosophically demonstrable.

Such views may be mathematically static (as in Leibniz) or historically dynamic (as in Vico). One could quote indefinitely, but Vico may speak for all:

The studies of metaphysics and poetry are in natural opposition one to the other; for the former purges the mind of childish prejudice and the latter immerses and drowns it in the same: the former offers resistance to the judgment of the senses, while the latter makes this its chief rule . . . the former strives that the learned may know the truth of things stripped of all passion: the latter that the vulgar may act only by means of intense excitement of the senses, without which stimulant they assuredly would not act at all (*Scienza Nuova* I, iii, 26; in Croce, *Aesthetic*, pp. 221–22).

A whole family of related views subordinates the culture role of play: historically oriented figures like Vico, Herder, Hegel, Croce, to name only a few, all treat art as something to be superseded—a fortiori imagination and play will be left behind for if ontogeny recapitulates phylogeny, they belong to infancy: "Whoever turns to writing poetry in an age of reflection is returning to childhood and putting his mind in fetters" (Vico: letter to De Angelis of Dec. 25, 1725). Perhaps, after all, the theory of an analogy between play and art did not lapse, but was merely pursued to the detriment of both! But, happily, more affirmative positions are near.

IV. KANT

In Kant the term "play" occurs so often in the discussion of art that some commentators have been led to exaggerate the importance in his system of "the free play of imagination" or of ideas. Yet while no well-articulated theory can be attributed directly to Kant, it remains true all the same that the connections among play, art, and freedom to be found explicitly in the *Critique of Judgment* are the primary source of Schiller's position, and therewith of all subsequent views on the question before us—to the possible exclusion of "surplus energy" theories.

The point of departure lies in the significance of "freedom" in Kant's position. Cognitive judgments are bound by the necessity of their conformity to the   103 modalities by which the human mind forms concepts, i.e., by the forms of intuition and the categories. These impose a logical structure on concepts and the relations among them that in turn leads to the uniformity of the knowledge possessed by all minds and thus justifies the claim for the possibility of a science of the phenomenal world. Ethical judgments, while not bound by fact (which would make ethics merely empirical) are bound by the nature of reason such that certain "ideas of pure reason" are binding on all rational minds so that, on Kant's view, a science of ethics is also possible.

But aesthetic judgments are not bound in either of these ways: they are not referable back in any necessary way to concepts depending on experience, nor are they such as to be uniform for all rational minds. They are necessarily subjective (*Critique of Judgment*—hereafter CJ—Bernard trans., §2, p. 39). Satisfaction in the beautiful must not only be distinguished from cognition and morality, but also from sensory pleasure (§3, 40) which exerts its own tyranny. In all these cases we have an interest in the existence of the object that gives rise to these judgments and feelings; but aesthetic judgment is disinterested and contemplative, i.e., it is free of constraint whether coerced by fact or logic or pain and pleasure: "The cognitive powers, which are involved by this representation, are here in free play, because no definite concept limits them to a definite rule of cognition" (§9, 52).

It should be noted that, at the same time that Kant stresses the freedom (and therewith the subjectivity) of aesthetic judgment, he is not prepared to abandon altogether the notion of the uniformity of such judgments (they *ought* to be necessary and universal): "We are conscious that this subjective relation, suitable for cognition in general, must be valid for everyone, and thus must be universally communicable, just as if it were a definite cognition, resting always on that relation as its subjective condition" (ibid.). And this leads him to claim a "universal subjective validity" that restores the possibility of rational discourse on aesthetic judgment.

In the "Analytic of the Sublime" (ibid.) Kant returns to the question of play as it more specifically applies to art. We find him here furnishing support to those who find the notion of art as play profoundly offensive. Indeed, as we noted earlier, art is often viewed as play only when it is intended to disparage both; but where art is assigned a nobler role, there is a tendency to emphasize the rational (cognitive and ethical) aspects at the expense of play. Kant's position reflects the dialectical tension of these extremes. In §43 he draws distinctions between art and nature, science, and

handicraft on the one hand, but warns (p. 147) against "many modern educators" who "believe that the best way to produce a free art is to remove it from all constraint, and thus to change it from work into mere play." What redeems art from this charge, as we see from numerous other passages, is that the ideas with which imagination plays must have appeal to understanding and reason: so much for the content of art; as to its form, "e.g., in poetry there must be an accuracy and wealth of language, and also prosody and measure." Kant's rationalism and formalism are not lightly to be cast aside, and thus we find him balancing the claims of freedom against those of the rule of reason which may be thought by those "modern educators" (to say nothing of even more modern artists) to constrict imagination within the framework either of drab representationism or of decaying forms:

[Poetry] plays with illusion (*Schein*), which it produces at pleasure, but without deceiving by it; for it declares its exercise to be mere play, which however can be purposively used by the understanding (§53, p. 171).

A final observation before we continue to trace the later fate of these influential ideas. In the *Critique of Pure Reason* (A141–42 = B180–81) we read that while

. . . the *image* is a product of the empirical faculty of reproductive imagination, the *schema* of sensible concepts, such as of figures in space, is a product and, as it were, a monogram, of pure a priori imagination, through which, and in accordance with which, images themselves first become possible.

This doctrine of schematism strongly suggests Kant's philosophical motives for retaining a rational foundation for art. It is that the mind can propose forms to itself that in turn make images of particulars possible; but given the structure of the human mind and its uniformity, there are limitations as to the forms that can be entertained, and these have (or ought to have) universal appeal, constituting the basis for communication and meaningfulness. Yet he clearly confused historically and culturally determined forms (e.g., in poetry and painting) for existentially determined ones, and so placed fortuitous restrictions on what might properly constitute art as well as on the power of imagination to propose other forms (whether in art or in science). We may therefore expect to find in his successors an attack on these restrictions, as well as on the necessary uniformity of human rationality. The farthest-reaching attack, however, will derive from implications of his metaphysics that he could hardly have foreseen (e.g., the unknowability of the thing-in-itself and the "as if" aspects of our explanations of reality).

V. SCHILLER

The most important theory in the entire history of this topic is found in the aesthetic writings of Friedrich Schiller. It is odd but worthy of note that the significance of his contribution has been seriously underestimated both by students of Schiller and of play theory. His originality in the matter, despite the obvious debts to Kant and to Rousseau's educational theories, to say nothing of those of Lessing and Herder, lies in the breadth of the metaphysical claims he makes on behalf of the aesthetic, and in his modifications of the Kantian position.

The most important of these are: (1) in the absence of access to the "thing-in-itself," metaphysical presuppositions are in principle unverifiable—hence man is free to construct explanatory schemes of various kinds to render his experience comprehensible to himself; (2) such schemes in the first place reflect typological differences of temperament (*Naive and Sentimental Poetry*—hereafter NS—176) in which particular "modes of perception" (*Empfindungsweisen*) result in diverse accounts of reality, each compatible with facts and logic though incompatible with each other—two such types are the "realist" and the "idealist," each of whom is persuaded by his idiosyncratic perspective that the other is wrong, but in view of (1) above, both are wrong; (3) thus, instead of the uniform human nature presupposed by Kant as the foundation of "objective" knowledge, Schiller's postulation of two human natures accounts for the insolubility of metaphysical, ethical, and political questions and for the dogmatic assertion by each type of the truth of its own position at the expense of the other; (4) a crucial aspect of Schiller's account of human nature follows from the importance of form and content in Kant. These are seen by Schiller as distinctive features of human modes of experience in terms of impulses (*Triebe*). The form impulse is seen as the tendency of the human mind to structure experience in particular ways and is connected with predominantly rationalist explanations of the world (the idealist position), while the material impulse (*Stofftrieb*) supposes its explanations to be given along with concrete facts (the realist position). A third principle, the play impulse (*Spieltrieb*) is advanced as mediating between these two. (Two parenthetical observatic .: (a) these *Triebe* are not to be confused with the impulses or drives of more recent psychologies, though many commentators have mistakenly praised Schiller for anticipating Freud, while others have denounced him for not being enough of a Freudian; the impulses are rather "dispositions," tendencies to think and act in characteristic ways; (b) it is typical of Schiller's dialectical method to find a third principle to mediate between and reconcile the differences between polar opposites); (5) the divergencies of perspective do not arise at the level of fact or logic, but in disputed interpretations of facts themselves not in dispute.

From these divergencies from Kant, Schiller adumbrates, but does not fully develop, a remarkable theory. Schiller has often been called the poet of freedom; in his *Aesthetic Letters* this is manifested by his search for a means to liberate man from the coercion of industrialized society, and in NS from the compulsion of genetic endowment, environment, and temperament. *On the Sublime* seeks to overcome the ultimate compulsion, that of a fixed unalterable reality (whether conceived of as Nature, Fate, or the laws of physics). The concepts of reality produced by the theologian, the historian, the scientist, or the metaphysician are all simply an illusion or appearance (*Schein*); they are inventions, not discoveries about the world. Nonetheless they are all too frequently mistaken for ultimate truths, and this in turn leads to the dogmatism and even fanaticism that appear justified by premature ontological commitment to their truth.

Only the artist is free of illusions about his illusions; in his creations no claim to reality is made. Rather he *plays* with the appearances he constructs; what he proposes is without ontological commitment, it is a game operating within self-imposed rules, as well as within the limiting conditions of fact and logic. It is contemplative and detached as befits aesthetic creation; but it is also carried out for its own sake as befits a game. (Schiller also makes use of the role of play as preparation for "serious" activity, and of re-creation following the tensions of labor, but neither of these is central.) The Kantian notions of heuristic devices are thus brought a stage further. The aesthetic attitude becomes the paradigm of all human perspectives on the world. Schiller sharply attacks the philosopher who dogmatically insists on all the details of an elaborate system erected on metaphysical assumptions whose origin and validity have never been investigated: "The philosopher is a caricature compared with the poet."

Schiller is well aware of the dangers of such a position and is at pains to forestall criticisms of solipsism and aestheticism, to say nothing of self-indulgent daydreaming and triviality. By his insistence on the Kantian foundations of objective knowledge, the facts are, as it were, stipulated by all parties, so that the Kantian notion of "objective," or at least "universally subjective" knowledge is preserved—nothing is the case simply because someone says so. Nor is a retreat into fantasy permissible, for this too belies the facts. Instead, much the way the hero in tragedy preserves his dignity intact amid physical defeat, so the aesthetic attitude permits moral superiority to the facts, not empirical subordination to them. Nor will the charge of triviality stand, for, as Schiller puts it, "Man is never so serious as when he plays." A quite extraordinary demand is being made here: at the metaphysical level it is that we somehow resolve the problem how to maintain our deepest and most serious beliefs strongly enough to be able to act on them, while at the same time recognizing that those beliefs have no final justification. The latter part of this proposition is closest to play, and such a prospect will seem melancholy to some, but Schiller chooses to be exhilarated by it; we are free to build tragedy or comedy indifferently on the same data. There will be poignant exceptions, but under ideal conditions man "is wholly man only when he plays" (15th of the *Aesthetic Letters*). Then man possesses the childlike quality of grace, aesthetic education is complete, and in spontaneity and harmony one plays the game of life.

Of those directly influenced by Schiller the most notable are Schopenhauer and Nietzsche. Schopenhauer, in particular, after condemning metaphysical explanations of the world as illusory, finds almost the only redemption in art, because we are aware that we are playing a game, and also because we are contemplating Platonic ideas, and the illusion is harmless. But perhaps the most consummate realization of Schiller's ideas is found in Hermann Hesse's *Glasperlenspiel* (*Magister Ludi*): the account of the Music Master is closest of all.

VI. RECENT AND CURRENT VIEWS

A shallow reflection of Schiller's views is found in Herbert Spencer, who vaguely remembers reading about the play theory in some German author whose name escaped him. While what he has to say has little bearing on art, it is included in a simple version of the "surplus energy" theory:

We find that time and strength are not wholly absorbed in providing for immediate needs . . . Hence play of all kinds—hence the tendency to superfluous and useless exercise of faculties that have been quiescent (Spencer [1870–72]).

About the turn of this century there was a significant revival of interest in the topic of play, with some bearing on art. Karl Groos' two books chiefly rely on the role of imitation, empathy, and education in the learning and socialization process:

. . . play leads from what is easy to more difficult tasks, since only deliberate conquest can produce the feeling of pleasure in success (1901, p. 8).

Lange, who follows Groos fairly closely, stresses the structure of self-imposed rules which call for the exercise of imagination. He opposes the passivity of the spectator to the activity of the creator, and extends his argument from play to art in pointing to the invention of a context developed in the course of creation of a work of art.

Of the many commentaries on the surplus energy and education theories a few examples may be cited. Dessoir (pp. 318ff.) treats the Kant-Schiller approaches favorably and with great penetration. Croce (p. 83), followed by Collingwood, accepts the "freedom from causality" argument of Schiller as "possible," but finds the surplus energy argument, especially as found in Spencer "outrageous." Guyau, on the other hand (p. 174), accepts the latter argument, but sees "art as too involved with life to be mere play." And Huizinga, whose splendid book goes much beyond our scope here, treats Schiller quite harshly (p. 168), having evidently misunderstood his case.

A lengthy literature from the utopian socialists to the 1960's expands the leisure theory to incorporate art and play into the activities appropriate to an increasingly affluent society. The education theories are currently in the uncertain stewardship of the schools of education and the learning psychologists; a staggering array of studies pursue the related problems of value-free finger-painting and learning by playing in a manner that has gone far to discredit the whole argument.

The metaphysical and psychological theories remain worthy of serious consideration. As to the first there has been a significant tendency to extend creativity, innovation, conventional (self-imposed) rule-making as obvious features of play and art beyond these to scientific and even to cosmological explanations. Charles S. Peirce, who acknowledges his debt to Friedrich Schiller (p. 401), develops (pp. 360f.) a notion of free aesthetic contemplation—"Pure Play"—culminating in "Musement" concerning "some wonder in one of the Universes." Koestler (1964, especially pp. 509ff.) displays the interconnectedness of humor, art, and science with a wealth of illustration. But the most succinct statement in recent literature on the subject is found in Kroeber (1948, p. 357):

Generically, all the discoveries and innovations of pure science and fine art—those intellectual and aesthetic pursuits which are carried on without reference to technology or utility—may be credited to functioning of the human play impulses. . . . They rest on the play impulse, which is connected with growth but is dissociated from preservation, comfort, or utility, and which in science and art is translated into the realm of imagination, abstraction, relations, and sensuous form.

Finally, there is another area, almost too vague to document precisely, but pervasive enough in recent decades, in which certain childlike qualities (including playfulness) are assimilated to some desirable features of art. While its origins may be traced back to Plato at least, the combination is modern, especially in its emphasis on the unconscious nature of creativity. If, as Ellen Key argued in her famous book, this is *The Century of the Child* (1909), much that is relevant to our theme will be displayed in what George Boas has called *The Cult of Childhood* (1966). Emphasis is laid on the child's naiveté, spontaneity, and unconsciousness, and on the self-absorption of the child's activities—these are preferred to the calculation and purposiveness of adult behavior. The child's vision is taken to be innocent, fresh, unencumbered by conceptual fixity or subordination to cognitive or moral criteria. The artist (e.g., Rilke, Klee) is seen as liberated from the exigencies either of representationalism in content or of set formal patterns. It would be a mistake to insist that all aspects of this shift in aesthetic objectives are connected with nostalgia for childlike simplicity and still less with play. In part it must be associated rather with the metaphysical anarchy currently fashionable and that dates from some of the post-Kantian developments we have traced. Among relevant contemporary positions in aesthetics mention must be made at least of Freudian psychology and proponents of "aesthetic surface."

An important paper of Freud's, "Creative Writers and Day-Dreaming," associates imagination, creativity, and play, and draws on a parallelism between the child and the writer, each of whom creates a world of his own. This world is taken seriously, for the opposite of play is not the serious but the real. (Freud makes the further point that this play is not wholly unconnected with the real, otherwise we have fantasy not play.) From this it follows that features of the real world are rearranged by the child in his play and by the artist in his creation. The difference between these and day-dreaming is that the latter entails a degree of wish-fulfilment that moves in the direction of neurosis or psychosis; but the differences appear to be of degree not kind: ". . . a piece of creative writing, like a day-dream, is a continuation of, and a substitute for, what was once the play of childhood." The elaboration of these insights by the various psychoanalytic schools, particularly by Jung and Rank, is immensely detailed. And it is but a step from these to a great variety of perspectives advanced by existentialist and phenomenological writers on aesthetics who make a great deal of the "child's vision."

This brings us close to the notion of "aesthetic surface" (D. W. Prall, *Aesthetic Analysis*, New York,

1929) and "sheer appearance" (S. Langer, *Philosophy in a New Key* . . . , Cambridge, Mass., 1942). Again, the emphasis here is on the avoidance of conceptual rigidity, allowing the object to speak to imagination, a playing with the possible things the aesthetic object might be, as in Dada for example. These illustrate the tendency in art and play for forms and structures to be explored and exploited more than the specific content of the artwork or game; much is made of the paradoxical status of "commitment" in the sense that play and aesthetic experience are contemplative, i.e., they do not require that what is encountered be translated into action, yet they furnish a rich stock of paradigm situations in largely vicarious experience that is in fact deployed where knowledge and action are called for. The "high seriousness" of play and aesthetic immersion is one of the ways in which many thinkers have tried to give expression to this phenomenon; and it derives from the dual capacity of art to be directly an end-in-itself yet indirectly a means to irrelevant or seemingly opposed ends.

BIBLIOGRAPHY

G. Boas, *The Cult of Childhood* (London, 1966). R. Caillois, *Man, Play and Games* (New York, 1961). R. G. Collingwood, *The Principles of Art* (Oxford, 1938). B. Croce, *Aesthetic* (London, 1922). M. Dessoir, *Aesthetik und allgemeine Kunstwissenschaft in den Grundzügen* (Stuttgart, 1906). J. Dewey, *Art as Experience* (New York, 1934). C. J. Ducasse, *The Philosophy of Art* (New York, 1929). S. Freud, "Creative Writers and Day-Dreaming," in *Standard Works*, Vol. IX., trans. James Strachey (London, 1959). K. Groos, *The Play of Man*, trans. E. L. Baldwin (New York, 1901). J. M. Guyau, *The Problems of Contemporary Aesthetics* (Los Angeles, 1947). J. Huizinga, *Homo Ludens, A Study of the Play-Element in Culture* (Boston, 1950). Immanuel Kant, *Critique of Judgment*, trans. J. H. Bernard (London, 1892; New York, 1951). Arthur Koestler, *The Act of Creation* (London and New York, 1964). A. L. Kroeber, *Anthropology* (New York, 1948). K. Lange, *Das Wesen der Kunst* (Berlin, 1901). H. Noack, "Das Spiel: über die Versuche seiner Erklärung und die Aufgaben seiner Sinndeutung," *Zeitschrift für Aesthetik*, **27** (1933), 97–131. Pauly-Wissowa, *Reallexikon des klassischen Altertums*, article "Spiel". C. S. Peirce, *Selected Writings*, ed. P. P. Wiener (New York, 1958). Hugo Rahner, *Man at Play* (New York, 1967). Friedrich Schiller, *Naïve and Sentimental Poetry* and *On the Sublime*, trans. J. A. Elias (New York, 1966). Winfried Sdun, "Zum Begriff des Spiels bei Kant und Schiller," *Kant-Studien*, **57** (1966), 500–18. Herbert Spencer, *Principles of Psychology* (London, 1870–72).

JULIUS A. ELIAS

[See also Comic; Creativity in Art; **Culture;** Education; Empathy; **Happiness and Pleasure; Primitivism;** Utopia; Wisdom of the Fool.]

ART FOR ART'S SAKE

THE PHRASE "art for art's sake" expresses both a battle cry and a creed; it is an appeal to emotion as well as to mind. Time after time, when artists have felt themselves threatened from one direction or another, and have had to justify themselves and their activities, they have done this by insisting that art serves no ulterior purposes but is purely an end in itself. When asked what art is good for, in the sense of what utility it has, they have replied that art is not something to be used as a means to something else, but simply to be accepted and enjoyed on its own terms.

The explicit and purposive assertion of art for art's sake is a strictly modern phenomenon. The phrase itself begins to appear only in the early years of the nineteenth century, and it is some time after that before a recognizable meaning and intention can be said to emerge. This is quite as would be expected. For before there can be any need and reason to assert that artistic activity is self-sufficient and works of art are ends in themselves, a certain intellectual and cultural climate must occur. The essential catalyzing agent in this process can be identified in a few words: it consists in the tendency of the human career toward complexity, specialization, and fragmentation. So long as the structure of life—individual and social, economic and functional, theoretical and practical—is relatively compact and cohesive, there is little occasion for the emergence of private groups with a strong sense of their own interests and tasks as opposed to those of other groups. Men had obviously all along filled different roles requiring different skills and directed toward different purposes; and their respective duties, responsibilities, and powers had varied across a wide spectrum. But both the actual structure of society and the attitude of men towards society, were largely holistic and organismic. Consequently, the pursuits that we now distinguish quite sharply, such as religion, morality, politics, law, science, technology, art, etc., were not formerly regarded or practiced in such a separatist manner. The same individuals were often engaged in several of these activities, which were viewed as aspects of a single undertaking rather than as distinct endeavors. Though men had certainly practiced art, they had not, with certain exceptions, been highly conscious of themselves as artists.

Beginning with the Renaissance, this cohesive cultural and intellectual unity starts to crumble, and the end of the eighteenth century sees it thoroughly disintegrated. By then, divergent and divisive tendencies are at work throughout the social fabric, finding expression in what we call the religious, political, scientific, and industrial revolutions. Men's newly awakened interests contrast with their old habits and commitments. Inspired by an intense dedication to specific values and purposes, they are drawn together into various groups, each with a strong sense of its own identity and mission. As the result of this broad social and cultural movement, men begin to think of themselves as scientists, ministers, politicians, financiers, or artists; and they assert that as such they have a function of particular importance and so require particular privileges.

The more precise intellectual matrix of the doctrine of art for art's sake can most plausibly be located in the philosophical system of Immanuel Kant, though it must at once be added that Kant certainly did not intend this outcome and would have repudiated it vehemently. But he still made it possible and even inevitable. Through the three *Critiques*, of *Pure Reason, Practical Reason,* and *Judgment,* Kant established a triadic division of man's mental capacities and functions. To paraphrase somewhat loosely Kant's formidable terminology, man is endowed with understanding or cognition, with a sense of duty or conscience, and with aesthetic taste or sensibility. Kant's interest was focused on the first two of these; he was anxious to place science and morality on a firm foundation, and so to avoid the drift toward relativism and skepticism that had reached a climax in the work of Hume. The third *Critique,* that of *Judgment,* plays a more ancillary role, with its significance deriving from architectonic considerations rather than from the intrinsic interest of its subject matter.

Even if this was true of Kant, and the question is highly debatable, it was certainly not true of his immediate converts and followers in German Idealism. For what Kant had done was establish the aesthetic as an autonomous domain, coordinate with man's cognitive and moral faculties and playing a distinct role of its own in the life of the mind. The Idealists were quick to see the possibilities that this schema offered them. Revolting more or less consciously against Rationalist tradition, with its emphasis upon balance and proportion, its insistence upon strict adherence to rules of composition, its exaltation of reason and science, and its morality of detachment and calculation, the Romantics were anxious to find a way to escape from the confinement of this creed and to justify those other aspects of human nature and existence that rationalists neglected or denigrated.

Friedrich Schiller was the first to exploit Kant's doctrine of the aesthetic for this purpose. But he was followed in rapid succession by Friedrich Schelling, Hegel, and Schopenhauer; and then, at only a slight remove, by the wave of Romanticism that swept over France and England as well as Germany, propelled on the thought of men of such diverse temperaments and talents as Herder and Goethe, Wordsworth, Coleridge, Shelley, the brothers Schlegel, and Baudelaire, to mention but a random few. Despite its varied manifestations, this movement had a form and unity deriving from two dominant themes.

First, and more generally, there was the common conviction that art played a serious and significant role in life, that it exercised a human faculty that nothing else could touch, and that it made a unique contribution to man's understanding of the world. Before this, the value of works of art had been primarily regarded as either utilitarian or ornamental; art was thought of as a subsidiary and derivative phenomenon. Now the aesthetic life was raised to a position of high dignity and importance. Second, and more specifically, art was now defined by reference to a particular human faculty and need that brought it into being. Interpretations of this aesthetic source varied, but it was always localized in the sensuous, emotional, and perceptual aspect of man's nature. It was held that artists grasped reality in an immediate and intuitive manner, embodied it in a material form, and so made it available to direct apprehension. In short, art yields concrete insight into the reality that reason can present only in the guise of abstract concepts.

The stage was thus set for the appearance of the idea of art for art's sake. But its actual entrance still required two further developments. Artists had to acquire a strong sense of their identity as artists, of the intrinsic significance of the art they created, and of their need to create freely without interference and harassment. And other established social groups and institutions had to become afraid of the threat that such free artistic expression might pose to their conventional values, beliefs, and practices. Once these conditions existed, censorship, though already widely imposed on literature since the Renaissance, was now directed against many forms of art, both by the church and the state, in an effort to control and direct art, or keep it subservient to special uses and standards. Artists replied by asserting that art was an end in itself, to be created and judged in terms of purely aesthetic criteria.

The idea of art for art's sake is thus to be seen as partly a declaration of artistic independence and partly an expression of the alienation of the artist from society. It is at once a claim and a complaint. Insofar as artists are men, their rejection by society causes them to suffer psychically as well as economically; insofar as they are artists, they glory in it as a proof of their uniqueness. So the alienation that the artist expresses when he dedicates himself to art for art's sake is a compound of protest and pride. In this guise, the idea serves chiefly to sustain the artist's ego.

As a declaration of artistic independence, the idea plays a far more significant and constructive role. For here it becomes a device by which artists justify themselves in the paths they follow and protect their work against attack from an outraged society. So the history of art for art's sake is essentially a history of the various attempts that are made to subvert art, as the artists envisage it, by subordinating art to other purposes and demands; the idea takes shape gradually and erratically, as the threat comes now from one quarter now from another. Although there is very little continuity and development to be found in this history, it can be seen as containing four major chapters, each consisting of a counterattack against a different enemy. These enemies can be conveniently labeled as conventional morality and religion, utility and didacticism, science, and subject matter.

Apparently the first to use the phrase *l'art pour l'art* was Benjamin Constant in an entry in his *Journal intime* for February 11, 1804. It is introduced quite casually to refer to the aesthetic doctrines of Kant and Schelling, which Constant finds "very ingenious." The idea then occurs with increasing frequency in the writings of the Romantics and of all those who, like the Romantics, felt the special calling of the artist and the alienation and lack of understanding under which artists suffered: this list would include particularly Baudelaire, Gautier, Hugo, Flaubert, and Mallarmé in France; Whistler, Pater, and Oscar Wilde in England. In the course of time, the phrase accretes around itself a large but miscellaneous body of passions, convictions, commitments, complaints, and especially antipathies.

In accord with the pattern suggested above, these artistic attitudes and purposes can be seen as clustered around four poles. Artists inveigh against conventional bourgeois morality, with its prudery and hypocrisy, and against all of the measures through which the government, the church, and the press seek to impose this morality and suppress any deviations from it. They repudiate with equal vehemence and scorn the spirit of utility, which asks of everything what practical purpose it serves and is incapable of accepting and enjoying anything as simply good in itself. In a similar vein, they reject the claims of didacticism, refusing to acknowledge that their art should proclaim any moral truths or lessons. Artists also express an intense anxiety about the inroads of science and the spread of the scientific mentality, with its emphasis on material things and mechanical processes, and its worship of brute facts. Finally, artists reproach the sentimentality of the public, which looks not at their works of art but merely at the objects, scenes, and events that these depict; that is, they resent the slavery of subject matter.

The tone and content of these complaints can best

be conveyed by a few quotations from the artists themselves. James A. McNeill Whistler, the painter, made a habit of delivering lectures, granting interviews, and writing letters to newspapers, all of which had the dual purpose of ridiculing popular opinions and tastes concerning art and preaching the doctrine of art for art's sake. These have since been collected in a volume under the title of *The Gentle Art of Making Enemies* (1890), and they constitute a rich mine of doctrine and diatribe. Whistler's statement of the case is direct and pungent:

People have acquired the habit of looking, as who should say, not *at* a picture, but *through* it, at some human fact, that shall, or shall not, from a social point of view, better their mental or moral state. . . . Alas! Ladies and gentlemen, Art has been maligned. She has nought in common with such practices. . . . Purposing in no way to better others, . . . having no desire to teach. . . . Nature contains the elements, in colour and form, of all pictures, as the keyboard contains the notes of all music! . . . To say to the painter, that Nature is to be taken as she is, is to say to the player, that he may sit on the piano (pp. 138, 136, 142–43).

Théophile Gautier urges a similar doctrine, insisting particularly upon the necessity for an absolute divorce between man's artistic and practical pursuits. His argument is brief and pointed: "Only those things that are altogether useless can be truly beautiful; anything that is useful is ugly, for it is the expression of some need, and the needs of man are base and disgusting, as his nature is weak and poor" (Gautier [1834], p. 22).

Walter Pater puts the case in a more philosophical way, seeking not only to extol art but also to explain and justify its preeminent importance. His argument rests upon the contrast between the richness and fleetingness of immediate experience and the bare abstract concepts to which analytical thought seeks to reduce it. And he insists that the entire meaning and value of life reside in the wealth and intensity of experiences. The highest wisdom lies in explaining things, much less in using them, but simply in sensing and feeling them. He concludes in these terms: "Of such wisdom, the poetic passion, the desire of beauty, the love of art for its own sake, has most. For art comes to you proposing frankly to give nothing but the highest quality of your moments as they pass, and simply for these moments' sake" (Pater [1873], pp. 238–39).

In the twentieth century the idea of art for art's sake undergoes a rather radical transformation, generating a more serious and systematic doctrine, and exerting a more positive influence upon artistic creation. It now appears in new interpretations of such concepts as "pure poetry," "significant form," "plastic form." The significance of this movement lies in the insistence that

the work of art is an autonomous and self-contained entity; its meaning and value are exhaustively contained in its material and formal being. Works of art do not need to borrow significance from biographical, psychological, historical, or sociological sources; their significance lies in the formal structures that they realize in a material medium. These ideas had already found eloquent expression as early as 1854 in Eduard Hanslick's book, *The Beautiful in Music;* they were forcefully restated for the context of literature by A. C. Bradley in his *Oxford Lectures on Poetry* (1909); they received their most incisive advocacy in Clive Bell's *Art* (1919) and Roger Fry's *Vision and Design* (1920). Since then, this doctrine has become a commonplace of artistic creation and criticism, and has served as the theoretical source and justification of such important—and divergent—contemporary developments as those of abstract, nonobjective, nonrepresentational, and constructivist art, as well as Dada, Surrealism, and Cubism.

So the idea of art for art's sake has now ceased to be an instrument of protest and defense, and has become one of the central tenets of official aesthetic dogma. It is not he who does or praises art for art's sake who must justify himself, but rather he who would assign to art any values, or judge art by any standards, other than those that are intrinsic to it. Yet the adherents of art for art's sake seem to be as uneasy in their new security as they were in their former alienation. At the same time that they proclaim the autonomy of the artist and his art, their freedom from any extrinsic purpose or obligation, they also insist that the artist is a seer and a prophet, and that through his art he makes available both a truth and a mode of existence that are essential to human well-being. The most startling illustration of this ambivalence occurs in Clive Bell's *Art*, where, within the brief span of forty pages, Bell first urges a rigid doctrine of pure art and then proclaims that art makes us aware "of the God in everything, of the universal in the particular, of the all-pervading rhythm" (Bell [1914], p. 54). But similar conflicts of intention crop up on virtually every occasion when contemporary artists write about their art.

The truth of the matter seems to be that the idea of art for art's sake is one of that numerous class of important half-truths whose validity and vitality are dependent upon the effective presence of their complementary half-truths. This idea is necessary to preserve the independence of the artist and the integrity of the artistic enterprise. But its other half, which is the idea of art for life's sake, is equally necessary to guarantee the integration of the artist into his society and hence the meaningfulness of his art.

BIBLIOGRAPHY

Albert C. Barnes, *The Art in Painting*, 2nd ed. (New York, 1928). Monroe C. Beardsley, *Aesthetics from Classical Greece to the Present* (New York, 1966). Clive Bell, *Art* (London, 1914). A. C. Bradley, *Oxford Lectures on Poetry* (Oxford, 1909). Albert Cassagne, *La Théorie de l'art pour l'art en France* (Paris, 1906). Rose Egan, *The Genesis of the Theory of Art for Art's Sake* (Northampton, 1921; 1924). Roger Fry, *Vision and Design* (London, 1920). Théophile Gautier, *Mademoiselle de Maupin* (Paris, 1834). Edmund Gurney, *The Power of Sound* (London, 1880). Eduard Hanslick, *The Beautiful in Music* (London, 1891). Hilaire Hiler, *Why Abstract?* (New York, 1945). José Ortega y Gasset, *The Dehumanization of Art* (Princeton, 1948). Walter Pater, *The Renaissance* (Oxford, 1873). Louise Rosenblatt, *L'Idée de l'art pour l'art dans la littérature anglaise pendant la période victorienne* (Paris, 1931). Irving Singer, "The Aesthetics of 'Art for Art's Sake,'" *JAAC*, **12**, 3 (1954), 343–59. James A. McNeill Whistler, *The Gentle Art of Making Enemies* (London, 1890). John Wilcox, "The Beginnings of L'art pour l'art," *JAAC*, **11** (1953), 860–77.

IREDELL JENKINS

[See also **Romanticism in Literature;** Romanticism in Post-Kantian Philosophy.]

ASSOCIATION OF IDEAS

SINCE the middle of the eighteenth century the concept of the association of ideas has increasingly been seen as the most basic, the most fecund, and the most pervasive explanatory principle in the human and, to a lesser extent, the biological sciences. The tendency to identify the association of ideas with the school of associationist psychology which flourished in the late nineteenth century has helped to obscure the fact that the principle in its most general form has played the central role in attempts to apply the methods and assumptions of science to the study of man. The principle has two aspects: (1) that complex mental phenomena are formed from simple elements derived ultimately from sensations and (2) that the mechanism by which these are formed depends on similarity and/or repeated juxtaposition of the simple elements in space and time. The association of ideas provides a mechanism for *ordered change through experience* which complements (and plays an analogous role to) the concept of attraction (or gravity) in the physico-chemical sciences. Aside from its obvious position in empiricist epistemology and in psychological theories of learning, it has played a fundamental role in the idea of progress; in utilitarian legislative, economic, and moral theory; in theories of organic evolution; in functionalist social theory; in theories of the functions of the nervous system; and in psychoanalysis. Many of these theories are themselves closely interrelated and can be seen as parts of a coherent tradition in the history of ideas.

In the first systematic elaboration of an associationist theory of mind and brain, David Hartley points out the long prehistory of the concept:

The influence of Association over our Ideas, Opinions, and Affections, is so great and obvious, as scarce to have escaped the Notice of any Writer who has treated of these, though the word *Association*, in the particular Sense here affixed to it, was first brought into Use by Mr. *Locke*. But all that has been delivered by the Ancients and Moderns, concerning the Power of Habit, Custom, Example, Education, Authority, Party-prejudice, the Manner of learning the manual and liberal arts, &c. goes upon this Doctrine as its Foundation, and may be considered as the Detail of it, in various Circumstances" (*Observations on Man* [1749], I, 65).

It is true, as so often in the history of ideas, that aspects of the association of ideas were mentioned by numerous writers prior to Locke, e.g., Plato, Aristotle, Vives, Hobbes. The development of the concept as a central principle of explanation depended, however, on a series of related developments in seventeenth-century ontology, epistemology, and scientific methodology, most of which were formulated in opposition to aspects of the Aristotelian tradition. These combined to provide an intellectual context in which the association of ideas became the central explanatory conception in the interpretation of the nonmaterial world.

The twin impacts of Cartesian mind-body dualism and of the increasing acceptance of the mechanical philosophy as the most fruitful interpretation of the material world separated man's mind from his body and from the world of objects outside the mind, and made the epistemological problem of how we acquire veridical knowledge more, not less, acute. If one accepted, as Locke did, the mind-body dualism but did not share Descartes' belief in innate ideas, the explanation of the acquisition of knowledge and the operations of the mind was left (literally) with no materials with which to work.

It is possible to interpret Descartes' views on man and on animal automatism as providing the basis for a theory of conditioning, and this interpretation was made in France and again in nineteenth-century Britain, e.g., by T. H. Huxley, thereby placing his work as a seminal influence on the early development of associationism. In more recent times Descartes has been credited with such a theory, but these last attribu-

111

tions are clearly examples of "Whig" historiography —looking for precursors without considering the contemporary (as opposed to the current) intellectual context. The theory is here being considered as it was understood in the seventeenth century, with particular reference to the reception of Descartes' ideas in Britain. His epistemology and his ontology implied a rigid dualism, and his ideas on acquired, involuntary movements provided no warrant for a learning theory, since learning referred to "experience" in the *mental* realm. In order to attribute to him a theory of conditioning which could be said to be relevant to *human* learning, one would have to commit an anachronism. In establishing the contemporary impact of his views— and especially in considering the reactions of Locke, Gay, and Newton as precursors to Hartley—it is necessary to take care *not* to interpret Descartes' automatism as applying to human learning. It is important to appreciate that the British (unlike the French) did not interpret Descartes as implying a theory of automatic learning, if only because they considered his mechanistic physiology very crude and were not prepared to indulge in the reductionism which is required to derive a theory of *human* learning from his views on animals and on the passions of men. The modern fusion of the Cartesian animal physiology with associationism was a product of the late eighteenth and nineteenth centuries.

Descartes defined the concept of mind negatively as all that does not pertain to the body. The concepts which were proving so fruitful in physics and astronomy were unavailable to epistemology and psychology. The mind was not for Descartes a possible object for scientific knowledge. It was unextended and indivisible, and its essence was thought or free will. The philosophical consequence of this situation was that there was no language for describing mind except by *analogy*.

Locke wished to emphasize the primacy of experience in the acquisition of ideas. He took the units of experience from contemporary, non-Cartesian expressions of the mechanical philosophy. Despite their common medical experience, Locke, like Hartley, drew his analogies for the analysis of experience from physics. His general mechanical point of view was Newtonian, but the physics of his *An Essay Concerning Human Understanding* (1690) was the corpuscular physics of Robert Boyle, while the epistemology owes much to Pierre Gassendi's revived atomistic sensationalism. Thus Locke laid the foundation of one aspect of associationism in accounting for the origin of ideas by means of the juxtaposition in experience of simple ideas to form complex ones. This was a mechanistic, though not a materialistic, epistemology. It is often pointed out that the section called "Of the Association of Ideas" in Locke's *Essay* was an afterthought. It was a brief discussion added to the fourth edition in 1700 (Book II, Sec. xxxiii), to account for aberrant, irrational, and customary connections between ideas. While granting this, one's attention should not be diverted from the fact that although Locke's preoccupation with epistemology led him to give a cursory treatment to the psychological aspects of his views, his discussion of the association of ideas was consistent with and consequent upon the whole complex of ideas which led to the establishment of the empiricist tradition in science and philosophy.

There were two further conceptual prerequisites for the systematic exploitation of Locke's paradigm for interpreting experience. Edmund Law prefaced his translation of Archbishop King's *Essay on the Origin of Evil* (1731) with a "Preliminary Dissertation concerning the Fundamental Principle of Virtue or Morality." The anonymous author, Rev. John Gay, employed Locke's conception in opposition to the innatist theory of the origin of moral sentiments and disinterested affections advocated by Francis Hutcheson. Gay applied the association of ideas to the domains of ethics and psychology and argued that the moral sense and all the passions were acquired in experience. Men seek pleasure and avoid pain, he argued, and the habitual union of these experiences with the principle of association produces our moral and emotional dispositions.

As some men have imagin'd *Innate Ideas*, because forgetting how they came by them; so others have set up almost as many distinct *Instincts* as there are *acquired Principles* of acting (2nd ed. [1732], p. liii).

Gay's dissertation was the first coherent expression of the main tenets of utilitarian ethical theory and the associationist school of psychology.

The second element which contributed to the systematic associationist view appeared in queries which Isaac Newton raised at the end of the *Principia Mathematica* and appended to his *Optics*. These provided a physical *basis* for the association of ideas (which, it should be recalled, was itself based on a physical analogy). He suggested that the vibrations of corpuscles of light might cause vibrations in the retina of the eye and the brain and produce the sensation of sight. He also noticed the persistence of sensations, e.g., of a glowing coal being whirled in a circle, after the object had moved. Locke had explicitly eschewed speculations on the somatic basis of associations. Newton's queries suggested that the vibrations of physical corpuscles might account for the phenomena of sensation, its propagation in the nervous system, and its persistence, i.e., memory.

In his *Observations on Man, His Frame, His Duty, and His Expectations* (1749), David Hartley relates that he had read of Gay's attempts to deduce all our intellectual pleasures and pains from association and that this had led him to consider the power of association. From this he went on to investigate both its consequences with respect to morality and religion and its physical cause. He developed a systematic psychophysiology, explicitly drawn from the ideas of Newton, Locke, and Gay, which was based on the association of ideas in the mind and on corpuscular vibrations in the nervous system.

The Doctrine of *Vibrations* may appear at first Sight to have no Connection with that of *Association;* however, if these Doctrines be found in fact to contain the Laws of the Bodily and Mental Powers respectively, they must be related to each other, since the Body and Mind are. One may expect, that *Vibrations* should infer Association as their Effect, and *Association* point to *Vibrations* as its cause (I, 6).

What follows is a tour de force in which Hartley argues, case by case, that physical vibrations in the brain, spinal cord, and nerves are the basis of all sensations, all ideas, and all motions of men and animals and that all learning is the consequence of repetitive juxtapositions of corpuscular vibrations and mental associations in space and time, producing habits according to the pleasure-pain principle. This principle, like that of association, has a long history, but in the new context of corpuscular physics and empiricist epistemology it took on a new significance. The persistence of the pleasure-pain principle in biology, psychology, and the social sciences has allowed these disciplines to employ the physical analogies of the association of ideas without abandoning qualitative concepts based on the subjective world of experience.

Although Hartley was orthodox in his belief that nature and man were the products of Design and saw the concept of utility in the context of Natural Theology, his highly specific exposition of the principle of association in a general psychophysiological learning theory played an important role in the secularization of the concepts of adaptation and utility by providing a mechanism for them. This was part of a wider movement in philosophy and science whereby final causes were replaced by material and efficient ones. Although Hartley's learning theory was confined to individual experience, and the "expectations" discussed in his second volume were concerned with the afterlife, others extended his theory and used it as a general warrant for explaining changing utilities and adaptations by means of the pleasurable and painful results or *consequences* of actions. The extension of the time scale beyond the life-span of an individual made this general paradigm available as a potential mechanism for ideas of progress and evolution. Similarly, although Hartley denied, in a general scholium, that his theory had reductionist implications, he did accept its determinist consequences:

The Consequence I mean is that of the Mechanism or Necessity of human Actions, in Opposition to what is generally termed Free-will. . . . By the Mechanism of human Actions I mean, that each Action results from the previous Circumstances of Body and Mind, in the same manner, and with the same Certainty, as other Effects do from their mechanical Causes; . . . (ibid., 500).

Thus, by the mid-eighteenth century two of the main tenets of Cartesian dualism had been effectively challenged—the mind's indivisibility and the concept of free will.

In the same period two other writers had independently, but less systematically, developed sensationalist epistemologies and learning theories under the influence of Locke and Newton. E. B. de Condillac's *Traité des sensations* (1754) was as seminal on the Continent as Hartley's work was in Britain in the development of the sensationalist and physiological theories of human nature which achieved prominence in the French Enlightenment and in the speculative and experimental work of the *Idéologues* whose work, in turn, laid the conceptual foundations for the emergence of physiological psychology in France and Germany in the nineteenth century. It was also from this tradition that the Marquis de Condorcet drew the mechanism for his remarkably sanguine *L'esquisse d'un tableau historique des progrès de l'esprit humain* (1795) and from which J. B. Lamarck drew one aspect of his theory of evolution, that is, the inheritance of acquired characteristics.

Similarly, David Hume's *A Treatise of Human Nature* (1738) was concerned primarily with another topic, epistemology, but he based the principle of causality on the association of ideas ("constant conjunction"). He also grasped the generality of the principle of association:

Here is a kind of *attraction*, which in the mental world will be found to have as extraordinary effects as in the natural, and to show itself in as many and as various forms. Its effects are everywhere conspicuous; but, as to its causes, they are mostly unknown, and must be resolved into *original* qualities of human nature, which I pretend not to explain (Book I, Part I, Sec. IV).

Hume undoubtedly played a crucial part in the development of the empiricist tradition and debates on the issues which he raised were continued in nineteenth-century and in later work in the philosophy of science. However, various extensions of Hartley's doctrine provided the most striking applications of the association of ideas in materialism, utilitarianism, the idea of progress, and evolutionary theories.

All of the principal utilitarian theorists (Joseph Priestley, William Paley, Jeremy Bentham, James Mill, and J. S. Mill) united the search for general (Newtonian) laws of human nature with the psychology of Hartley in the development of their psychological, educational, economic, social, and legislative theories. The "consequences" of the hedonist or pleasure-pain theory of human nature were progressively reinterpreted as the *sanctions* of utilitarian reformist theories. In the course of the nineteenth century it became apparent to many that particular policies cannot be deduced from universal principles of human nature, but in the meantime the associationist-utilitarian point of view became the basis of the editorial policies of the journals of the Philosophic Radicals and their partial allies among the Comtists: *The Westminster Review, The Leader, The Fortnightly Review*. This approach also found an extreme form in the "Gradgrind" approach to education in Britain and resulted in the system of "payment by results" to schoolteachers, whose earnings and facilities depended on the number of their pupils who passed exams.

Although most utilitarian followers of Hartley retained some vestige of mind-body dualism, one of them, Joseph Priestley, interpreted Hartley in a way which foreshadowed conclusions which were later drawn on other grounds. Priestley argued in his edition of Hartley (1775), in a way which was consistent with Priestley's Unitarianism, that Hartley's dualism was superfluous. As Dugald Stewart ruefully observed, Hartley and Condillac's speculations "stopped short of what is called Materialism, . . . but touched its threshold. Thither, it must be owned, their philosophy pointed, and thither their followers proceeded" (*Encyclopaedia Britannica*, 8th ed. [1860], I, 379). Just as Condorcet had drawn on Continental associationism for his idea of inevitable social progress, in England William Godwin's *Political Justice* (1793) combined the theories of Hartley's first volume with a secular transposition of the hopes expressed in the second volume to argue for inevitable social progress, transcending the limits of the passions and the body. Adam Smith (*The Wealth of Nations*, 1776) had earlier employed the principles of association and utility to account for the causes of economic equilibrium and wealth. His laissez-faire theory based its claims for a natural identity of interests among men on a mixture of theological and utilitarian assumptions. T. R. Malthus reacted strongly against the optimism of Godwin and Condorcet and drew on Smith's principles in his account of the causes of poverty. Unlike Smith, he could not believe that the principle of utility produced harmonious equilibrium, and unlike Godwin and Condorcet, he could not believe that it produced inevitable progress. Rather, he translated the sanctions of pleasure and pain into social terms, and combined them with the conflict between nature's niggardliness and man's sexual appetites to produce checks on prosperity and on population itself. Society was in equilibrium because of poverty, vice, misery, famine, war, and death. This equilibrium was a painful one, and what progress there was occurred by means of struggle, slightly tempered by "moral restraint" in the avoidance of premature marriage.

The English parallel to Lamarck's theory of evolution by means of the inheritance of acquired characteristics is to be found in the *Zoonomia* (1794–96) of Erasmus Darwin (a close friend of Priestley, who shared with him and with Godwin and Condorcet a profound sympathy for the progressive, egalitarian aims of the French Revolution). Once again, Hartley's ideas, suitably secularized and generalized, provided the basis for a general theory of ordered, progressive change through cumulative experience:

The ingenious Dr. Hartley in his work on man, and some other philosophers, have been of the opinion, that our immortal part acquires during this life certain habits of action or of sentiment, which become for ever indissoluble, continuing after death in a future state of existence; and add, that if these habits are of the malevolent kind, they must render the possessor miserable even in heaven. I would apply this ingenious idea to the generation or production of the embryo, or new animal, which partakes so much of the form and propensities of the parent (*Zoonomia*, Sec. XXXIX).

Darwin argued that animals develop through experience in their lifetimes, and these structural changes are passed on to the next generation, eventually producing the evolution of new species. The second volume of *Zoonomia* was concerned with medicine and contained an elaborate attempt to classify all diseases on the basis of the pleasure-pain principle and the concepts of sensation, irritation, volition, and association.

Within a century the principles underlying the association of ideas had been extended well beyond their original domain as the source of objections to fixed, designed, innate ideas (Locke). They had provided a basis for all learning and, in biology, for replacement of the belief in fixed species of organisms by one of gradual evolution. The origins of ideas, of knowledge, and of biological species were seen as the result of ordered change through experience. By the last decades of the eighteenth century the paradigm of small, cumulative changes occurring over long periods of time was widely represented in Continental and English thought. Theoreticians in many apparently disparate disciplines were beginning to grasp the fact that very large-scale changes could be accounted for by this general mechanism.

In order to connect the foregoing account with related developments in nineteenth-century biology it is necessary to mention the emergence of uniformitarian geology. The interpretation of the history of the earth in terms of the uniform operation of natural causes over vast periods of time was a part of the wider movement based on belief in the uniformity of nature, of which associationism was a parallel manifestation. The time scale and natural mechanisms of uniformitarian geology, when combined with aspects of naturalistic theories of species change, produced theories of organic evolution.

The evolutionary theorist who drew most directly on the association of ideas was Herbert Spencer. His primary interest lay in finding a scientific basis for his belief in inevitable social progress. He felt that utilitarian social theory did not provide this, while psychology and biology might. He was profoundly influenced by Charles Lyell's *Principles of Geology* (1830–33) but exploited it for his own purposes. That is, he was convinced by Lyell's general belief in uniform natural processes as sufficient to account for the history of the earth, but he did not accept Lyell's refutation of Lamarck's evolutionary theory. Instead, he grasped one aspect of that theory and combined it with associationist psychology (under the influence of George Eliot, G. H. Lewes, and J. S. Mill) and argued in a way that is reminiscent of Erasmus Darwin, that the evolution of species, and even the origin of the forms of thought, could be accounted for by an extension of the association of ideas. In 1855 he expressed these views in his *Principles of Psychology*. The theory was simplicity itself:

The familiar doctrine of association here undergoes a great extension; for it is held that not only in the individual do ideas become connected when in experience the things producing them have repeatedly occurred together, but that such results of repeated occurrences accumulate in successions of individuals: the effects of associations are supposed to be transmitted as modifications of the nervous system (*An Autobiography* [1904], I, 470).

Thus, Spencer combined the Lamarckian idea of the inheritance of acquired characteristics with the law of association, and he extended sensationalism from the tabula rasa of the individual to that of the race. Although Spencer's conception of the mechanism of evolution has since been rejected in favor of natural selection, his general impact on social theory has been enormous. His role in propagating the naturalist and evolutionist point of view was greater than that of the other evolutionists, and his influence in changing the context within which mental phenomena are viewed from epistemology to biology was decisive in psychology. By the end of his massive *Synthetic Philosophy* (1862–93) Spencer believed that he had provided the scientific guarantee for progress which classical utilitarianism lacked. It lay in a very generalized version of evolutionary theory which embraced all of nature and entailed psychological, sociological, and ethical theories—all based on a cosmic version of the association of ideas. It was a very romantic philosophy for all its scientific verbiage, and it is ironic that one of its most enduring influences in social theory was in the extreme laissez-faire views of the (misnamed) "Social Darwinists." Beginning with Walter Bagehot's *Physics and Politics* (1869) and taking its most extreme forms in the writings of W. G. Sumner and the behavior of the American "Robber Barons," the idea of progress by means of the survival of the (economically and socially) fittest was used as a justification for some of the grossest excesses of monopolistic capitalism and imperialism, and it is not without its current advocates. Spencer's writings had other influences on social theorists in China, Japan, Britain, France, and America, while more basic themes in his writings, e.g., his conception of the division of labor and his functionalist approach have had a pervasive influence in sociology and social theory.

Charles Darwin had studied Lamarck's theory of evolution when he was a medical student, but neither this nor his grandfather's theory had shaken his belief in the fixity of species by the time he became a professional naturalist in 1830. The evolutionary theory developed by Darwin and by A. R. Wallace drew less explicitly on the associationist tradition, but it should be mentioned that the theory of natural selection which they arrived at independently was profoundly influenced by the writings of Malthus, which in turn, depended in part on the most general versions of the utilitarian paradigm. In Darwin and Wallace's mechanism for evolutionary change, the sanctions of survival and extinction in the struggle for existence were explicit generalizations of the Malthusian theory of population. Similarly, Darwin's peers and supporters found his theory appealing partly because of its conformity with their empiricist, phenomenalist view of nature and human nature.

The union of the theory of evolution with studies in comparative psychology which Darwin and Spencer inspired led, by way of the work of G. J. Romanes (to whom Darwin gave his notes on psychology), C. L. Morgan (Romanes' pupil and editor), E. L. Thorndike, J. Loeb, William McDougall, and others, to the dominant traditions in modern experimental psychology. However, the establishment of these depended on the increasing independence of classical associationism from the epistemological preoccupations of the empiricist tradition and on the integration of associationism with the study of the physiology of the nervous system. Locke, Hume, Priestley, Thomas Brown, and James Mill had chosen not to investigate the physiological basis of associations, but concomitant developments in neurophysiology had involved the interpretation of the functions of progressively higher parts of the central nervous system in terms of reflexes, and this approach had close conceptual affinities with the discovery that the anterior and posterior spinal nerves roots and higher structures were differentiated and served the functions of motion and sensation.

These theories were developed in the physiological and medical literature of France, Britain, and Germany. The parallel between sensory-motor physiology (Bell, Magendie, Mueller, Carpenter) and reflex theory (Prochaska, Whytt, Hall, Laycock) on the one hand and the associationist tradition in psychology on the other had been noticed by many writers since Hartley and E. Darwin, but the systematic integration was not undertaken until the 1850's in the work of Alexander Bain, which was lavishly praised by J. S. Mill as the highest point reached by the empiricist tradition. Bain stressed the role of movement in learning, and his work led to an increasing interest in behavior which complemented the emphasis on sensation in the British and French traditions. His work was the culmination of classical associationism and was very influential in the development of a new sensory-motor psychophysiology which concerned itself with associated sensations and motions in the nervous system paralleled by ideas of sensation and motion in the mind. This approach was soon reinterpreted in the context of the evolutionary theories of Spencer and Darwin and provided a great stimulus to research in comparative psychology, neurology, neurophysiology, and psychiatry. In particular, the theories of Bain, Spencer, Laycock, and Lewes, through their influence on J. H. Jackson and David Ferrier, led to important advances in clinical neurology and in the experimental localization of functions in the brain. Their work provided the basis for the modern interpretation of the functions of the nervous system in learning and in other forms of adaptive behavior.

The most important contributors to this experimental work were C. S. Sherrington in England and I. P. Pavlov in Russia. They were concerned with the nature of fixed and modifiable (i.e., learned or conditioned) reflexes. By the end of the nineteenth century the neurone theory had provided what seemed a perfect parallelism between brain cells and their connections on the one hand and ideas and their associations on the other. The physiology of conditioned reflexes and the psychology of learning were increasingly seen as one topic of research.

In the same period, important aspects of the psychoanalytic theory of Sigmund Freud also developed from a neurological tradition. The language of Freud's metapsychology employed analogies such as mental "energies," "forces," and "structures" which were taken from German physicalist physiology, while he employed the concept of the reflex in his model for the mental apparatus. His associationist theories of mental function and his biological concepts were derived from English and German associationists and from the theories of suggestion of French and German hypnotists which were also associationist in structure. Finally, his postulate of psychophysical parallelism was avowedly drawn from the writings of Spencer and Jackson. Although there were important features of Freud's theories which were not part of the matrix of associationist neuropsychology and although he directed his attention to new topics in psychological and social theory, the basic assumptions of his approach remained constant throughout his writings and were elaborated in his early and rather orthodox associationist works.

Classical associationism was also influential in the development of the experimental introspective studies of H. Ebbinghaus and W. Wundt in Germany and of E. B. Titchener in America, leading to the establishment of a "structural" school in psychology. This approach gained its identity in the course of a debate with a "functionalist" school which was developing in America under the influence of British classical and evolutionary associationists. The main figures in this school were William James, John Dewey, George H. Mead, and James R. Angell and their work gave rise to much of twentieth-century American social theory.

Aspects of American functional psychology were combined with the related theory of conditioned reflexes and research on localization of functions in the brain to produce recent experimental work in brain and behavior and in that of learning theory. Most of these researchers and theorists have retained an implicit or explicit form of mind-body dualism—psychophysical parallelism—but one line of development, behaviorism, has attempted a reductionist analysis. Since Hartley and Priestley, many have seen that the grounds for traditional dualism have been progressively eroded by the acceptance of mental determinism and the use of physical analogies in associationist psychology. Comparative psychology and evolutionism, coupled with the findings of physiological psychology, led J. B. Watson, the American founder of behaviorism, to argue that both the methodology and the ontology of psychology should be concerned with objective phenomena. Thus, he made the step from "We cannot do science about minds" to "There are no minds." Positivist philosophy and operationism in physics made this move very philosophically appealing, and the step from physical and chemical *analogies* to mind-body *identity* theory has become fashionable in recent philosophical psychology.

In the period from 1916 to the present the concepts of sensation, motion, and association have been reinterpreted in allegedly objective language as "stimulus," "response," and "conditioning." Although a great deal of experimental work has been done and a greater amount of ink has been spilled in attempts to spell out the laws of learning in these terms, the point to be made here is that S-R, statistical, operant, cybernetic and related learning theories remain, along with brainwashing and teaching machines, just as much manifestations of the tradition of association of ideas as do the free associations of the psychoanalytic patient. Historians and practitioners of recent psychology have repeatedly observed that in spite of changes in terminology and fashion and the bitter quarrels in experimental psychology, psychiatry, and social theory, associationism is the only general theory of human nature which has been available to the human and related sciences.

Having emphasized the pervasive influence of the association of ideas since the mid-eighteenth century, it is necessary to stress that the strengths of this approach were balanced by disadvantages which were frequently pointed out. The most persistent objection has been a straightforward rejection of the alleged all-sufficiency of the determinism of associationism on the part of those who wish to maintain that man has free will. Others have objected on some combination of aesthetic and moral grounds that life and nature are more than accretions of sensations. For example, S. T. Coleridge and J. S. Mill rejected aspects of Hartley's theory because they felt that his psychology failed to give sufficient scope to the role of imagination in life, while romantic poets extended this criticism to oppose the whole mechanistic view of nature. Similarly, George Eliot's novels can be seen as complementing the psychological and social theories of her utilitarian and positivist circle in a way which allowed for the portrayal of the nuances of human nature.

In its emphasis on the interactions of the simplest elements and processes, the associationist tradition has provided no basis for classification of larger elements analogous to the physicists' table of fundamental particles or the chemists' periodic table of elements. It has therefore failed to show how the phenomena of human experience can be synthesized from simple, psycho-physiological elements. It provides no basis for the unity of psychological and social life. Even its most ardent exponents have found it necessary to supplement the theory with classifications of faculties or functions which are not derived from the theory itself. Recourse has also been made to vague principles which hypostatize the problem and call it a solution, e.g., "integrative functions," "functional unity," "ego," "Gestalt." Theorists of instinct, emotion, and personality in psychology have made repeated appeals to these and other additional explanatory principles, while social theorists find that the analytic bias of associationism provides no basis for evaluating competing social theories and ideologies. The result, when these issues are raised, has tended to be an approach to psychology and psychotherapy, and to social and political philosophy, which elevates "adjustment" or "adaptation" to the status of a relatively unquestioned goal.

It should not be surprising that associationism and its many derivative theories, e.g., utilitarianism, functionalism, and psychoanalysis, are of little help in the interpretation and evaluation (as opposed to the analysis) of the purposive behavior of men and other organisms. One must recall that it is based on an analogy with a physical paradigm which was explicitly elaborated in the seventeenth century in order to banish anthropomorphism, teleology, and purposive explanation from science. For reasons which are intrinsic to the nature of human existence, associationism has not precluded the effort to extrapolate meaning and purpose from the collisions and accretions of atoms in the void. However, it provides no determinate mechanism for performing the operation and thus no stable criteria of propriety or impropriety in the effort: the goals of men differ.

BIBLIOGRAPHY

R. I. Aaron, *John Locke*, 2nd ed. (Oxford, 1955). E. Albee, *A History of English Utilitarianism* (New York, 1901; reprint 1962). J. M. Baldwin, ed., *Dictionary of Philosophy and Psychology*, 2nd ed., 3 vols. (New York, 1925); Vol. 3 is a comprehensive bibliography by B. Rand. G. S. Brett, "Associationism and 'Act' Psychology," in C. Murchison, ed., *Psychologies of 1930* (Worcester, Mass., 1930), pp. 39–55. J. W. Burrow, *Evolution and Society* (Cambridge, 1966). E. A. Burtt, *The Metaphysical Foundations of Modern Physical Science*, 2nd ed. (London, 1932). S. T. Coleridge, *Biographia Literaria* (London, 1817; various reprints). W. Dennis, ed., *Readings in the History of Psychology* (New York, 1948). C. H. Driver, "Walter Bagehot and the Social Psychologists" and "The Development of a Psychological Approach to Politics in English Speculation before 1869," in F. J. C. Hearnshaw, ed., *The Social and Political Ideas of Some Representative Thinkers of the Victorian Age* (London, 1933), pp. 194–221, 251–71. É. Halévy, *The Growth of Philosophic Radicalism*, rev. ed. (London, 1952). R. J. Herrnstein and E. G. Boring, eds., *A Source Book in the History of Psychology* (Cambridge, Mass., 1965). R. Hofstadter, *Social Darwinism in American Thought*, rev. ed. (Boston, 1955). G. H. Lewes, *The Biographical History of Philosophy*, 2nd ed. (London, 1857). Sir J. Mackintosh, "The Progress of Ethical Philosophy," *Encyclopaedia Britannica*, 8th ed. (Edinburgh, 1860), I, 291–446. J. S. Mill, "Bain's Psychology," *Edinburgh Review*, **110** (1859), 287–321. G. Murphy, *Historical Introduction to Modern Psychology*, rev. ed. (New York, 1949). G. L. Nesbitt, *Benthamite Reviewing* (New York, 1934). R. S. Peters, ed., *Brett's History of Psychology* (London, 1953). T. Ribot, *English Psychology* (London, 1873). L. Stephen, *The English Utilitarians*, 3 vols. (London, 1900). D. Stewart, "The Progress of Metaphysical and Ethical Philosophy," *Encyclopaedia Britannica*, 8th ed. (Edinburgh, 1860), I, 1–289. H. C. Warren, *A History of the Association Psychology* (New York, 1921). R. M. Young, "Scholarship and the History of the Behavioural Sciences," *History of Science*, **5** (1966), 1–51. R. M. Young, "Malthus and the Evolutionists: the Common Context of Biological and Social Theory," *Past and Present*, **43** (1969), 109–45. R. M. Young, *Mind, Brain and Adaptation in the Nineteenth Century* (Oxford, 1970).

ROBERT M. YOUNG

[See also Evolutionism; **Psychological Schools, Theories;** Uniformitarianism; **Utilitarianism.**]

ASTROLOGY

ASTROLOGY is the study of the impact of the celestial bodies—Moon, Mercury, Venus, Sun, Mars, Jupiter, Saturn, the fixed stars, and sometimes the lunar nodes—upon the sublunar world. It presupposes a geocentric and finite universe. The influence of the celestial bodies is variously considered to be absolutely determinative of all motions of the four sublunar elements (Aristotelian physics is accepted as the basis for describing this influence, in a form somewhat modified by Neo-Platonic concepts); to be directional (that is, to indicate trends which may be changed by future astral influences or by the intervention of a supernatural being, usually on the pleading or at the behest of an astrologer or of a priest); or to be merely indicative of the divine will. Astrology so defined could not have existed before the Hellenistic period, and is certainly *not* of Babylonian, Egyptian, or Indian origin.

There are four broad categories of astrological practice. Genethlialogy relates the situation of the heavens at the moment of an individual's nativity to all aspects of his life. General astrology relates the situation of the heavens at particularly significant moments—e.g., at the vernal equinox, at an eclipse, or at a conjunction of the planets—to events affecting broad classes of people, nations, or the entire world. Catarchic astrology is the determination, from an examination of the situation of the heavens, of whether or not a particular moment is suitable for the commencement of a particular act. And interrogatory astrology is the answering of specific questions on the basis of the situation of the heavens at the time of the query. Other types of astrology—e.g., medical astrology or military astrology—are merely adaptations of methods used in the four basic types enumerated above.

***Celestial Omens* (Omina).** Though not properly astrological, but rather only that part of the Mesopotamian science of divination which is concerned with super-terrestrial phenomena, celestial *omina* are frequently combined with strictly astrological material in post-Babylonian sources; in the West they are often included under the rubric, "natural astrology." Like other omens, celestial phenomena were regarded by the Mesopotamians as indicators of the will of the gods, not as in themselves influential. And they never became as important to Mesopotamian diviners as were, for example, liver omens, probably because the gods could not be questioned through them and because no manipulation of the procedures of divination by means of them was possible.

Celestial omens first began to be used as portents on a large scale in the period of the first dynasty of Babylon (eighteenth to fifteenth centuries B.C.), though it is probable that lunar eclipses had at an earlier period been regarded as ominous. The collection and codification of the celestial omens into a series, however, is not definitely attested before the beginning of the first millennium B.C., though fragmentary material in Hittite hints at a possibly much earlier date for a primitive version of *Enûma Anu Enlil*. But the available cuneiform tablets indicate that a standard version was never attained; each copy had its own peculiarities.

As is true of most Mesopotamian omen-series, the predictions of *Enûma Anu Enlil* relate exclusively to the royal court and to the nation; the professional reader of omens, the *bāru*, performed his duties solely in order to advise the king of the future course of events. The gods communicate their message to the *bāru* by means of a symbolic language employing the phenomena of nature according to a complex system elaborately set forth on the tablets of his scholastic tradition. The overriding characteristic of this, as of all Babylonian omen-series, is the extreme systematization of the material; even non-occurring phenomena are, for the sake of symmetry, treated as omens.

The common organization of the elements of this symbolic language in *Enûma Anu Enlil* is in four sections. *Sin*, the Moon, contains omens relating to such phenomena as lunar visibility, eclipses, halos, and conjunctions with fixed stars; Šamaš, the Sun, omens relating to solar eclipses, doublings (observations of two suns simultaneously), and perihelia; Adad, the weather-god, omens involving meteorological phenomena and earthquakes; and Ištar, Venus, omens relating to the first and last visibilities, the stations, and the acronychal risings of the planets, and their conjunctions with the fixed stars. These omina, and especially those from Sin, are often referred to in the reports of the diviners sent to the Assyrian kings in the eighth and seventh centuries B.C., but seem to have lost their popularity by the late Persian period, when new attempts were made to discern the meaning of the celestial signs revealed to mankind by the divinities. But, before this replacement of the ancient system of Enûma Anu Enlil, it had spread, under the aegis of the Persian Empire, to Egypt, to Greece, to the Near East, and to India.

A demotic papyrus based on an original of ca. 500 B.C. is our earliest evidence for the spread of Mesopotamian celestial omina (in this case lunar) to Egypt (R. A. Parker, *A Vienna Demotic Papyrus on Eclipse- and Lunar-omina*, Providence, 1959). The influence is more impressively evident in the fragments of the Greek astrological work composed in Egypt in the second century B.C. and cast in the form of the instructions of the priest Petosiris to the king Nechepso; from this source (and perhaps from Eudoxus, who is often said to have written on celestial omens) it penetrates the second book of Ptolemy's Ἀποτελεσματικά or "Astrological Influences" (ca. 150), the first of Hephaestio of Thebes' Ἀποτελεσματικά (ca. 415), and the Περὶ σημείων (On Signs) of John Lydus (560). Furthermore, a poem on divination from earthquakes, the Περὶ σεισμῶν, is attributed either to the Egyptian Hermes or the Greek Orpheus. Many other such treatises could be mentioned.

In Judaic tradition one of the principal diviners had been the prophet and oneirocritic (dream-interpreter) Daniel. An *Apocalypse* of Daniel which circulated in antiquity in the Near East dealt with various topics from Sin, Šamaš, and Adad. It survives today in Greek, Syriac, and Arabic versions. Other old texts of this genre translated from Syriac into Arabic are ascribed to Hermes, and presumably represent the lore of the Harrānians. The Mandaeans of southern Iraq have also preserved old Mesopotamian traditions in their *Book of the Zodiac;* and they are also to be discerned in the Syriac *Book of the Bee.* The Arabic texts, in celestial omina as in the various categories of astrology proper, are extremely difficult to analyze as they represent admixtures of this older Near Eastern element with the derivative traditions of Greece and India.

In India the earliest surviving omen text is the original of the (at least) three versions of the *Gargasaṃhitā*, parts of which can be dated to the beginning of the Christian era; but the sources undoubtedly go back to translations made from Aramaic into Sanskrit during the nearly two centuries that the Achemenids were the dominant power in northwestern India. The *Gargasaṃhitā* embraces not only the material of *Enûma Anu Enlil*, but also that of several other Mesopotamian series. All was modified so as to fit into the Indian conception of a society of four castes in which the primary duty of the twice-born is the performance of the saṃskāras, but the fundamental dependence of the Indian on its Babylonian antecedent is clear from the identity of many entire omen statements—both protasis and apodosis.

A number of Sanskrit collections of omina, or saṃhitās, are preserved, of which the most notable are the *Bṛhatsaṃhitā* of Varāhamihira (ca. 550), the Jaina *Bhadrabāhusaṃhitā* (tenth century?), and the *Pariśiṣṭas* of the *Atharvaveda* (tenth or eleventh century?); in works of the thirteenth century and later, entitled tājika, a massive infusion of the Arabic versions of celestial omina, as transmitted through Persian (Tājik) translations, is evident. But the main impact of Mesopotamian omens on Indian ideas was in the fields of military astrology (yātrā) and the common Indian form of catarchic astrology (muhūrta), which will be discussed in greater detail below.

Genethlialogy. In the Hellenistic world the various philosophical schools developed theories of the places of man and of the planets in the universe that facilitated the growth of astrology. Platonists and Peripatetics both emphasized the superiority of the celestial spheres, the Platonists claiming that the motions of the stars, being subject to mathematical laws, are more perfect reflections of the divine Reason (νοῦς) than are earthly activities, and the Aristotelians asserting that the circular motion of the planets not only is better (since eternal) than the linear motions of the four sublunary elements (and therefore is evidence of a fifth element and of more intellectual beings than man), but also acts to transmit the initial motion of the prime mover into the world of earth, air, fire, and water. It also became a commonplace of the Hellenistic world that the human body is an image of the cosmos, and the human soul of the cosmic soul. These and similar philosophical assumptions facilitated the acceptance of astrology among intellectuals; the Stoics and Neo-Platonists were particularly prone to succumb to its allure.

By some as yet obscure personages in Egypt in the early second century B.C. the microcosm-macrocosm thesis was mathematicized and, in conjunction with the methods of utilizing celestial omens at the moment of an individual's conception and birth to predict certain things about his life, which were developed in Mesopotamia in the fourth and third centuries B.C., converted into genethlialogy.

The astrologer conceives of the ecliptic as divided into twelve equal parts, or signs, each containing thirty degrees. Each sign is the house of a planet; and each is divided into various subdivisions (decans, *fines*, etc.) of which each is also ruled by a planet. Scattered at various points throughout the zodiac are the planets' degrees of exaltation (the opposite are their degrees of dejection). Furthermore, each sign corresponds to a part of the human body, Aries to the head and Pisces to the feet. The four elements find their counterparts in the four triplicities; and numerous Pythagorean pairs of opposites (male—female, diurnal—nocturnal, hot—cold, etc.) are attributed to consecutive pairs of signs. Finally, a wide variety of substances in the sublunar world and attributes of human character are rather arbitrarily associated with each of the signs.

The planets' particular influences are related to those that they exercised in *Enûma Anu Enlil* and to their traits as deities in Greek mythology; but on them is also superimposed the system of four elements, the Pythagorean opposites, and lists of sublunar substances. Furthermore, their motions are carefully taken into account; their strength is largely determined by their phases with respect to the Sun and distance from their degrees of exaltation and their houses and *fines*, and they exert a mutual influence on each other both by occupying each other's houses and *fines* and by means of conjunctions and aspects. Aspects are of four varieties: opposition (to the seventh sign) and quartile (to the fourth) are generally bad, and trine (to the fifth) and sextile (to the third) good.

As the planets revolve through the zodiac by their various motions, direct and retrograde, the zodiac revolves around the earth. From a particular spot on the earth's surface this motion appears as a succession of signs rising one after another above the eastern horizon. The sign that at any moment—say, that of an individual's birth—is just rising, is the horoscope or the first place; this determines the soul of the native for whom a birth-horoscope is cast. The next sign below the horizon, the second place, determines his wealth; the third his brothers; the fourth his home; the fifth his children; and so on through all the aspects of his life.

The astrologer, therefore, when informed of the exact moment and place of a native's birth, casts his horoscope by fixing the boundaries of the twelve places with respect to the moving ecliptic and calculates the momentary longitudes and latitudes of the planets. He then can predict various aspects of the native's life by examining the intricate relations of the zodiacal signs and their parts and the planets to the appropriate places and to each other. Of course any horoscopic diagram will yield an enormous number of predictions which will contradict each other or which will be quite extravagant; the astrologer must use his knowledge of the native's social, ethnic, and economic background and his experience and good judgment to extract from this congeries a satisfactory reading.

This methodology, expounded above in an extremely simplified form, did not prove completely satisfactory; and the history of astrology is a tale of the application of ever increasing complexities to a system whose basic flaw (allowing for the moment that the idea of astral influence is a correct one) lies precisely in the fact that the multiplicity of predictions it generates renders it too imprecise to be useful.

We have little secure information about the genethlialogy of the last two centuries before Christ, but in the work of Dorotheus of Sidon, written in about A.D. 75, we find three of the more important refinements already present.

The first of these is the system of lots (κλῆροι), which are points as distant from some specified points in the horoscopic diagram as two planets are from each other. Greek astrologers generally used only the two principle lots—the Lot of Fortune and its counterpart, the Lot of the Demon; but the list kept growing, until Abū Maʿshar in the ninth century can enumerate well over a hundred.

The prorogator (ἀφέτης) is a point on the ecliptic (discovered by complicated rules) which determines the length of life of the native. It travels, at the rate of one degree of oblique ascension in a year, toward either the ascendent or descendent point; and as it comes into conjunction with a malefic planet, or is aspected by one, the native's life is threatened or perhaps even destroyed; at any rate he dies when the prorogator has reached the point which was on the horizon in the horoscopic diagram. The system is clearly a modification of the older method, ascribed to the Babylonians, of fixing the maximum length of a native's life as the number of degrees of oblique ascension between the ascendent and midheaven. A common variant on or adjunct to the prorogator is the Lord of the Year, which is the strongest planet in the horoscopic diagram; it travels at the same rate as does the prorogator and, as it moves with respect to the other, stable elements of the horoscopic diagram, determines the events of each year.

Finally, Dorotheus is familiar with a form of continuous horoscopy designed to guarantee the astrologer constant patronage. Continuous horoscopy assumes that the basic natal reading is valid in general, but that a new horoscopic diagram (antigennesis) must be cast on every anniversary (or even at the beginning of every month, week, day, or hour) and compared with that of the native's birth. An elaborate system of planetary transits of the places in the base-horoscope, then, will give a specific reading (or set of readings) for the next year (or month, week, day, or hour).

Associated with the Hermetic tradition is yet another method of deciding the course of events at different times during a native's life; this is the system of planetary periods. According to this doctrine each planet depending on its synodic period (but the Metonic cycle for the Sun, the Egyptian lunar period for the Moon), governs a specific fraction of the native's life, or a specific number of months; then each period is divided into subperiods according to the same proportions, and each subperiod may be further subdivided *ad infinitum*. The primary ruler of the period sets the tone of the whole, but the rulers of the subperiods introduce their own modifications. When the system of periods is combined with that of the Lord of the Year and that of continuous horoscopy, the assessment of the relative weights of resulting predictions is a complex matter indeed. No surviving Greek text provides a satisfactory treatment of the problems involved in applying these rules.

This may suffice to give the reader at least a rough idea of the methods of genethlialogy. Though some authorities, like Vettius Valens (ca. A.D. 175) and his favorite source, Critodemus (beginning of the first century A.D.?) describe strange new ways of manipulating the horoscopic diagram, they were not very influential. There are two intellectually respectable traditions of parallel authority (in fact, they agree with each other at many points): the Dorothean, whose principal adherents are Firmicus Maternus (ca. 335) and Hephaestio of Thebes (ca. 415), and the Ptolemaic, which is followed by Porphyrius (ca. 250), Paul of Alexandria (379), Hephaestio, and Rhetorius of Egypt (ca. 520). But the papyri and fragments of lost works indicate that the practices of popular astrologers were much simpler and cruder than those outlined above.

For astrology in the Roman Empire, as well as being regarded as a system of thought worthy of attempts at scientific or philosophical validation or repudiation, was practically applied on a large scale. The emperors beginning with Tiberius found its influence dangerous enough to warrant the banishment of all astrologers from Italy and the forbiddance of the casting of the Imperial horoscope. Yet the histories of the Roman Empire are filled with sad stories of the credulity of the Augusti and of those who aspired to their power. The belief of the common people is attested by the astrological papyri and by numerous inscriptions.

Among the intellectuals the conflict over the validity

of astrology revolved around two main points: free will and the uniqueness and accuracy of any horoscopic diagram. The latter argument was evolved by the members of the Middle Academy, who claimed that no horoscopic diagram applied to one individual only and that the time of birth was not in any case subject to determination with absolute accuracy. The astrologers could and did reply to the first point that the stars are only one factor in determining the life history of any particular individual (cf. especially Bardesanes), and to the second that they could obtain a good enough approximation to the true situation of the heavens at the time of a native's birth to make their predictions useful.

The other argument, that concerning free will, derives from the necessity of ethics. Astrology could not be allowed to relieve man of his responsibility for his own actions. The astrologer could make two replies to such an attack if he did not choose to assert that ethics are superfluous. He could claim that the human soul, insofar as it is divine, is not subject to astral influences and can resist them; or he could claim that astrology is only an attempt to interpret the divine will, which is manifested by God in the heavens. It is man's responsibility then, and not his necessity, to see that his life conforms to the astrologer's predictions. Neither argument sufficed to assuage the Christian polemicists.

In the first half of the second century A.D. there was written in Egypt, and probably at Alexandria, a Greek handbook of astrology on a rather popular level which exercised an enormous influence on vast multitudes of men, though even its title is not now known. For, in A.D. 149–50, it was translated into Sanskrit in Western India by a scholar known to us today only as Yavaneśvara—"the Lord of the Greeks." His work, through the versification made by Sphujidhvaja in 269–70, together with another lost translation utilized by Satya, is the root of Indian astrology.

The basic methods of Indian genethlialogy are not surprisingly, then, similar to those of its Hellenistic counterpart. But the techniques only, not the philosophical underpinnings, were transmitted; and the whole was thoroughly modified so that the predictions, originally meant to apply to Greek and Roman society, would be meaningful in India; in particular, the caste system, the doctrine of metempsychosis, the Indian system of five elements (without Aristotelian physics, of course), and the Indian system of values were introduced. Moreover, the *nakṣatras* or lunar mansions joined the zodiacal signs in having significance, and an elaborate system of three categories of *yogas* or planetary combinations was developed. Soon the Greek methods of continuous horoscopy were developed into new forms—the planetary periods into a dozen different varieties of *daśās*, and the transits into the elaborate theory of the *aṣṭakavarga*.

Indian genethlialogy in the pre-Islamic period evolved increasingly complex forms. The two lunar nodes were soon treated as new planets, making a total of nine; a series of *upagrahas* or imaginary subplanets took over, as it were, the place of the Greek lots, which appear in Sanskrit texts only through translations of Arabic and Persian texts. Fantastically complicated rules were devised for ascertaining the relative strengths and weaknesses of the planets and zodiacal signs; and new subdivisions of the signs—*horās* or halves, *saptāṃśas* or sevenths, and most importantly, *navāṃśas* or ninths—increased the dominions of the planets beyond the decans, the *fines*, and the twelfths.

This Indian system of genethlialogy, as all of Indian astrology, flourished absolutely without opposition, as its tenets in no way contradicted those of Indian philosophy or religion. It could easily be subsumed as an indicator of the chain of causality that links the acts of a former existence with the circumstances of the present, or regarded as yet one further manifestation of the world of *māyā* from which the enlightened must strive, by knowledge or by faith, to be released. Insofar as we know it was never criticized in India for denying free will, perhaps because free will has always of necessity exercised against the individual's fate or *karma*. And astrology, itself so complex, when it impinged on a social structure as intricate as that of India, could effortlessly have evaded the assaults of the critics from the Middle Academy had they come.

The *tājika* texts of the thirteenth and later centuries brought to Indian genethlialogy some elements of Hellenistic and of Sassano-Arab astrology; the lots have already been mentioned, and to them may be added the prorogator, the Lord of the Year, and the triplicities as employed by Dorotheus. Other ideas have more recently been interjected from the West. But still the *joshi's* principal text, which he consults when he casts the horoscopes of perhaps ninety per cent of the population of India, is the *Bṛhajjātaka* written by Varāhamihira, ca. A.D. 550.

Iran, before the rise of the Sassanids, was evidently open to the influence of some Mesopotamian theories of celestial and other *omina*. The Sanskrit translations of the pre-Mauryan period testify to the existence of omen series in Iran in the Achemenid period. Moreover, the Greek fragments of the Magusean works ascribed to Zoroaster, Ostanes, and others, though probably composed outside of Iran in Asia Minor and therefore reflecting a westernized version of Zoroastrianism, demonstrate a knowledge of some of the techniques of late Babylonian genethlialogy. That system

of genethlialogy, of course, continued to be used in Mesopotamia itself down to the first century A.D., though its possible dependence in its latest manifestations on the Hellenistic science developed in Egypt has yet to be investigated.

But certainly not long after Ardashir founded the Sassanian Empire in A.D. 226 a substantial transmission of Greek and Indian astrological works to Persian took place. The works of Dorotheus of Sidon and Vettius Valens and some treatises ascribed to Hermes were translated from Greek into Pahlavī in the third century. Contemporaneously a Sanskrit text was translated, ascribed in the Arab sources (to which we owe our knowledge of Sassanian astrology) to one Farmasb; later translations from both Greek and Sanskrit into Pahlavī continued to be made, at least till the middle of the sixth century.

The Pahlavī originals of all of these texts are unfortunately lost; but much can be reconstructed from Arabic translations of the eighth and ninth centuries. From these it is clear that Sassanian genethlialogy was essentially an imitation of the Hellenistic (without, however, all the philosophical overtones) onto which were grafted some Indian features, such as the use of the ninths (*navāṃśas*) and the Śaivite interpretations of the Greco-Egyptian Decans; it specialized in various forms of continuous astrology. This form of astrology, but even more what we have called general astrology, profoundly influenced society, and especially the upper classes, in Sassanian Iran; we shall say more of this later. Astrological ideas are also commonly met with in Manichaean texts (as is to be expected in Gnostic sources) and in the chiliastic theories of history of the Zoroastrians; but the level of astrology encountered in what survives of Pahlavī literature is abysmally low.

Genethlialogy reached Islam in three more or less simultaneous streams, as did also astronomy. Greek and Syriac texts representing the Hellenistic science, Sanskrit works of the Indian adaptation of that science, and Pahlavī amalgams of the other two were translated into Arabic in vast numbers in the late eighth and early ninth centuries. Islamic astrology, then, combined the Hellenistic basis, further fortified by a strong reliance on a Neo-Platonic definition of the mode of astral influence in terms of Aristotelian physics, transmitted through the self-styled Ṣabians of Harrān, with the Indian innovations and a Sassanian emphasis on continuous astrology. This combination is particularly apparent in the astrological and astronomical theories of Abū Maʿshar (786–886), Islam's most influential astrologer. This material they refined and developed in their own way, multiplying the number of lots, making more complex the complicated rules governing the prorogator and the Lord of the Year, and, in imitation of the

Indians and the Harranians, devising elaborate rituals to avert or alter the influences of the planets. Their innovations began to enter Byzantium in the tenth century, the Latin West in the twelfth, and India in the thirteenth, profoundly affecting the late pre-modern developments of astrology in all three cultural areas.

As in the Christian world, so in Islam genethlialogy met with strong religious opposition, primarily over the questions of free will and of the illimitable nature of Allah's power. Its principal intellectual advocates and defenders were those philosophers who were influenced by Neo-Platonism, and religious leaders of Shiʿite and especially Ismaʿīlī, inclinations. The intellectuals in Islam eventually dropped it under the pressure of the religiously orthodox as did those in the West and in Byzantium; but it continues to survive and flourish at a popular level among both Christians and Muslims. In India it retains (except among the very Westernized) all of its former intellectual respectability, and continues to be seriously studied and developed in institutes of higher learning.

General Astrology. Babylonian celestial *omina*, as we have seen, were designed to provide predictions relating to all of society or to its representatives, the court; these *omina*, as modified by Greek diviners, continued in use in the Hellenistic period and after. But neither the Greeks (the Romans of course banned astrological predictions regarding the Emperors) nor the Indians in general developed techniques of applying horoscopy to general astrology, though there were horoscopes cast at the founding of cities in the Roman Empire. This innovation was left to the Sassanians who accomplished it by combining the Zoroastrian belief in the creation and destruction of the material world at the beginning and end respectively of a 12,000-year period with Hellenistic continuous astrology. The basic concept was chiliastic, the fate of the cosmos being represented by a point moving 30° on the zodiac every millennium; but other points were invented which traveled 30° a century, decade, and year, or 1° a millennium, century, decade, or year. These points, then, are analogous to the Lord of the Year in continuous astrology.

An approximation of the millennium was observed in the fact that the two superior planets, Saturn and Jupiter, conjoin within the same triplicity twelve consecutive times in 240 years or thirteen times in 260 years and travel, then, through the four triplicities in something very close to 1,000 years. In this form of astrology a simple conjunction every 20 years determines the fate of noble families and kings, the transfer of the conjunctions to a new triplicity every 240 or 260 years the change of a dynasty, and the revolution

of the conjunctions through the four triplicities in 1,000 years the rise of a new prophet. The details are determined by the horoscopic diagram of the vernal equinox of the year in which the conjunction takes place. Similarly, horoscopes were cast at every vernal equinox to decide the year's events, a practice popular in Europe until the seventeenth century and still extensively practiced in India. This method of prediction is, of course, based on the antigennesis used in the continuous astrology of genethlialogy.

A third technique is to grant certain lengthy periods of time (*fardārs*) to each of the planets to rule in turn; and each planet in turn shares a subperiod of the *fardār* with its ruler. This system is modeled on that of the seven planetary periods embracing the native's lifespan in genethlialogy.

These and similar practices allowed the Sassanians to make astrology a potent source of political propaganda; and we have many Arabic astrological histories which culminate in a future absolute victory for the author's chosen party. Already in the late eighth century general astrology was used by an unknown Byzantine writer to prove the imminent collapse of Islam, and at the same time Persian partisans were predicting the restoration of the Sassanian empire. In the thirteenth century certain aspects of general astrology were introduced into India, where they continue to exercise a strong influence on people's attitudes toward political, meteorological, economic, and agricultural developments; and in the fourteenth century it became extremely popular in Western Europe. The millennial aspects in particular appealed to Christian and Islamic audiences (the Ismaʿīlīs are particularly fond of them), but are utterly ignored by the Indians who think in terms of tremendous periods of time between Brahma's inbreathings and outbreathings of the material world.

Catarchic Astrology. The idea behind most forms of catarchic astrology is that any act is influenced by the horoscope of its inception as is any individual by the horoscope of his birth; for certain types of activity, however, celestial omens are also significant. Whoever, then, wishes to perform an act should select the time for its beginning at which the planets are most favorably positioned for the successful completion of that act. The astrologer, in conceding that a person has the free will to choose the astrologically propitious moment for commencing his activities, to some extent negates the genethlialogical predictions; he may reply to his critics, however, that both the genethlialogical and the catarchic horoscopes influence the course of any particular enterprise, and it would be folly to attempt to gauge the future without considering both.

Catarchic astrology begins in the second or first **123**

century B.C. with Hermetic texts on iatromathematics (the application of astrology to medicine) and on general catarchic astrology and with the work of Serapion. From its beginning the use of specially devised Lots (κλῆροι) played a prominent role; their number increases in the course of time till they reach their peak in the works of Abū Maʿshar. They still play a relatively modest role in the fifth book of Dorotheus of Sidon, which is the main font of the tradition of catarchic astrology in the West. Dorotheus also emphasizes the cardines and their lords, the decans, the Sun, and especially the Moon. The Dorothean tradition is continued by "Manetho," Firmicus Maternus, Hephaestio of Thebes, Maximus, Rhetorius, Theophilus of Edessa, and pseudo-Palchus; it also influenced strongly the Islamic tradition. It is in the form of catarchic astrology that astrology had its greatest effect upon society as a whole; for before one could enter into a marriage, begin a business venture, or set out on a journey the astrologer had to determine the proper and propitious moment.

In India catarchic astrology has its roots in the necessity to perform certain Vedic rituals when the Moon is in particular nakṣatras. Certainly by the fifth century B.C. a form of muhūrtaśāstra—the science of determining the proper moment—already existed. It was primarily applied to the saṃskāras, or rites (classically sixteen in number), which a dvija underwent during the course of his life; the timing of other agricultural, domestic, and governmental activities could be determined on the same principles, however.

This simple version of muhūrtaśāstra, largely dependent on the position of the Moon, began to be contaminated by Hellenistic catarchic astrology in the first or second century A.D.; one notices this mixture in the earliest form of the Gargasaṃhitā and in the Yavanajātaka of Sphujidhvaja. But we have no works devoted exclusively to muhūrtaśāstra before the eleventh century. Thereafter it assumes increasing importance, and correspondingly becomes increasingly complex. It is now perhaps the most frequently practiced form of astrology in India as the timing of the saṃskāras (including marriage) as well as many commercial, agricultural, and governmental projects is dependent on the decision of the expert on muhūrtas.

In Islamic countries catarchic astrology is, as one would suspect, a combination of the Dorothean and Indian systems with some admixture of material of pre-Islamic Arab origin relating to the manāzil al-qamar ("mansions of the Moon"). Catarchic astrology in Arabic is often called aḥkām al-nujūm—the judgments of the stars, a name from which we derive our term "judicial astrology." As such it was the subject of a number of vast compilations; the most noteworthy

are those of al-Saymarī, al-Qasrānī and ʿAlī ibn abī al-Rijāl.

Interrogations. This final form of astrology that we shall consider is based on the idea that the horoscope of the moment when someone formally presents a question about a specific subject to the astrologer, determines the correct answer. In divination one distinguishes between omens which naturally occur, which are the freely vouchsafed indications of the divine will, and omens requested of the gods, which represent their answers to man's questions. Other forms of astrology are parallel to the first type of divination, interrogations alone to the second.

In Babylonian divination, and in the divination of other cultures, the successful practice of the second type normally depends on the ritual preparation of the diviner (and sometimes of the interrogator as well) before the question is put. In Greece we do not know that any religious rites were performed by the astrologer before he cast the horoscope of an interrogation, though Firmicus Maternus does indicate that the astrologer should possess "religious" qualities of purity. Rather, in the West interrogations seem to have developed naturally from catarchic astrology when the client asked the astrologer not only, "When should I begin an act in the future?" but "What will be the result of the particular course of action I am engaged in now?" Again, the primary text is Dorotheus' fifth book, though interrogations are fairly infrequent before the Byzantine period.

In India, however, where interrogations like genethlialogy were introduced in the second century by the Yavanajātaka, the relationship of the art to the second type of divination (familiar through the versions of Babylonian omen literature in the saṃhitās) was not ignored; from the earliest times the need for ritual purity and preparation is stressed. Interrogations, or praśnajñāna, never achieved the popularity of genethlialogy or catarchic astrology in India; but there do exist some early works on the subject, notably by Pṛthuyaśas, Varāhamihira's son, by Bādarāyaṇa, and by Bhaṭṭotpala. Only insofar as it influenced military astrology was it of any great significance.

In Islam interrogations experienced their greatest development. From the late eighth century on, one of an astrologer's main occupations was the answering of queries, and we have numerous manuals offering them guidance. These apparently are exclusively dependent on the Dorothean tradition mingled with some Sassanian material; there is no trace yet identified either of Indian ideas or of the necessity for ritual purity. The most interesting texts in this field are the collections of examples, of which the foremost is the *Mudhākarāt* of Abū Maʿshar's pupil Shādhān. Historically many of these examples are extremely valuable as they involve interrogations about their chances of success posed by aspirants to political or military power.

Astrology and Religion. In Mesopotamia it was customary to call the planets the stars of certain deities (Šamaš and Sin, the Sun and Moon, were of course always divinities), though cuneiform texts are not always consistent in connecting the same god with the same planet. But there were no religious activities directed to these gods in their character as planetary deities. The planets were divine, but they were not gods to whom prayers, supplications, vows, or offerings would be made. As there was no astrology in Mesopotamia there could be no developed form of cults of the planets.

This was true in pre-Hellenistic Greece also, of course; the planets did not even receive their names until the fourth century B.C. But already in the *Epinomis* (which was probably written by Philip of Opus) honor is to be paid to the planets, though more through the study of astronomy than through priestly ritual. As the concept of the cosmocrator (ruler of the cosmos) developed, however, the position of the planets in a hierarchy of divinities became clear.

Evidently it was first in Hermeticism that the position of the planets as intermediaries between the One and the sublunar world, which man inhabits, was established; they operate in the celestial spheres as manifestations of the divine will, and the demons act on their behalf below the sphere of the Moon. With this conception begins the long tradition of approaching the One through the planets or the demons, a tradition whose most common manifestation is in the talismans of the theurgists. The theological quibbles which arose over the interpretation of the precise nature of planetary or stellar divinity need not detain us here; it will suffice to mention Mithraists, Chaldaeans (that is, followers of the *Chaldaean Oracles*), and Neo-Platonists among the number of those who normally believed that the astrological power of the planets existed as part of the plan of the Cosmocrator, and that the planets were in some sense divine beings worthy of their own cults. A Cosmocrator is also frequently met with in the various city-religions of Syria in the first and following centuries A.D.; and at Heliopolis and Palmyra anyway he is shown as controlling the planets. But a cult of the planets in this region at that time cannot be established. However, the Syrian background of such philosophers as Bardesanes, Porphyrius, and Iamblichus make one suspect that perhaps there was more to these religions than the monuments tell us.

In many Gnostic sects the position of the planets as subordinate to the supreme deity disappears, though their astrological powers remain an integral part of the cosmological system. They become the instruments of the Spirit of Evil's plans, however, a part of the vast machinery of the physical world devised by Satan or his equivalent to serve as the prison of the captivated portion of the Good which is shared by the souls of men. The planets, then, are not gods to be praised and propitiated, but demons to be overcome by the superior power of the soul cleansed of the impurities of the elementary world.

In India the worship of the planets goes back to the time of the introduction of planetary omens into Sanskrit literature on divination; it is, in fact, particularly prevalent in the texts on military astrology. But it flourished in India because Indians did not have the Greek view of the celestial spheres as forming a *cosmos*, as being a perfectly constructed and eternally moving expression of the ideas of the demiurge. The planets, of course, are divine, as are all parts of the world; they particularly ought to be worshiped as they possess the capability of affecting man's life. In this capability they dispense of their own power, not that of a Cosmocrator. They are, then, more easily persuaded to alter the edict of Fate than would be, for example, the Neo-Platonic planets.

In Sassanian Iran doctrines close to those of the Gnostics prevailed; but there was some controversy over whether the planets in their motions acted on behalf of Ohrmazd or Ahriman. In any case, the imperial iconography represented the King of Kings as a Cosmocrator ruling the motions of the heavenly bodies; and the use of talismans to influence the planets, those intermediaries between man and the supernatural powers, was evidently widespread.

The most interesting case of an elaborate cult of the planets, however, was at Harrān in northern Mesopotamia. There the religious tradition—a mixture of Hermetic, Neo-Platonic, Sassanian, and Indian elements known to us mainly through Arab descriptions—centered entirely about the indirect worship of the One through the planets and through certain Ideas. To this end all of the paraphernalia of the rituals, including the material and shapes of the temples, the apparel of the officiating priests, and the objects sacrificed were determined by astrology. In accordance with the precepts of the *Epinomis* the Harrānians manifested their awe of the planets by studying the science of their motions, and are to be numbered among the foremost astronomers of the ninth century; but they also magnified the significance of astrological theories and practices beyond what any previous group had attempted. The Muslims rewarded their faithfulness to the stars with utter destruction.

125

The rise of modern science in the West has just as effectively caused the annihilation of astrology as an intellectually important idea at the present time, though its popularity among the masses in the West is increasing and it still has a significant following among educated people in India. These last believers better than I can foretell its future fate.

BIBLIOGRAPHY

The following bibliography is intended only to acquaint the reader with the most convenient guides to the vast literature on astrology.

Babylonian celestial omens: P. Hilaire de Wynghene, *Les présages astrologiques* (Rome, 1932) and E. Weidner, "Die astrologische Serie Enûma Anu Enlil," *Archiv für Orientforschung*, **14** (1941/44), 172–95 and 308–18, and **17** (1954/56), 71–89. Greek astrology: A. Bouché-Leclercq, *L'astrologie grecque* (Paris, 1899) and W. and H. G. Gundel, *Astrologumena* (Wiesbaden, 1966). Indian astrology: D. Pingree, *Census of the Exact Sciences in Sanskrit* (Philadelphia, 1970, and following). Islamic astrology: C. A. Nallino, "Astrologia e astronomia presso i Musulmani. 1. Astrologia," *Raccolta di scritti editi e inediti* (Rome 1944), 5, 1–41. Astrology and religion: D. Amand, *Fatalisme et liberté dans l'antiquité grecque* (Louvain, 1945); F. Cumont, *Astrology and Religion among the Greeks and Romans* (New York and London, 1912), and idem, *Lux Perpetua* (Paris, 1949); R. P. Festugière, *La révélation d'Hermès Trismégiste*, 4 vols. (Paris, 1944–54); and H. Lewy, *Chaldaean Oracles and Theurgy* (Cairo, 1956).

DAVID PINGREE

[See also **Cosmic Images;** Cosmology; Demonology; Dualism; Free Will and Determinism; Gnosticism; **Hermeticism;** Islamic Conception; **Neo-Platonism;** Prophecy; Pythagorean . . .; Stoicism.]

ATOMISM: ANTIQUITY TO THE SEVENTEENTH CENTURY

THE AIM of this study is to examine in what way the different Greek and medieval conceptions of nature have contributed to paving the way for the scientific theories of modern times. Within this general framework we shall pay special attention to the classical atomic theory in its different variants, because the development of this theory illustrates to what extent modern science, with its underlying conception of nature, can be traced to the speculations of Greek philosophy.

The very fact that the atomic theory has a long history does not make it easy to define its content in such a way as to comprehend its different variations.

In its widest sense it may be defined, however, as the theory that nature is composed of relatively simple and relatively unchangeable minute particles, which are too small to be directly observable. The observable changes in nature can be explained, however, by their reduction to changes in the configuration of the particles. The observable multiplicity of the existing forms in nature must likewise be based upon differences of forms and of configuration of the particles.

Within this general atomistic conception a distinction can be made between atomism in the strict sense, and other forms. Atomism in the strict sense, propounded by Leucippus and Democritus (fifth century B.C.), is the doctrine that the particles, of which the material things are composed, are simple and unchangeable in an absolute sense (hence the name "atoms," which means indivisible). Whatever may be the changes in configuration of these atoms, the atoms themselves remain intrinsically unchanged. The observable differences in nature, however, are not exclusively based upon differences in configuration of the atoms. Another ground of difference is to be found in the atoms themselves. Although the atoms do not differ qualitatively, they are supposed to have different sizes and shapes, even in an infinite multitude. Consequently, the infinite variety of observable things can be explained by these different sizes and shapes and by the different ways in which the atoms can be combined.

As to the question of what causes the atoms to combine and recombine, Democritus points to motion as a primitive property of atoms. This motion itself is not caused by an outside force; it is an inherent property of the atoms. Like the atoms themselves, their motion is eternal and incorruptible.

Other forms of Greek atomism differ from the atomism of Democritus mainly in three points. First, they do not restrict the differences between the atoms to purely quantitative ones, but also accept differences in quality. Anaxagoras (fifth century B.C.) assumed even as many qualitatively different atoms as there are different natural kinds of substances. As a rule, however, the more "liberal" forms of atomism accept only a limited number of types of primitive atoms. Their qualitative differences are usually based upon the widespread doctrine of the four elements: earth, water, air, and fire (Empedocles, fifth century B.C.).

A second point of difference concerns the *indivisibility* of the atoms. Whereas Democritus holds that this indivisibility has to be taken in a strict sense, other forms of "atomism" speak of an indivisibility only in a relative sense. The smallest particles of a certain substance could be divided, but then they change their nature. Here again Anaxagoras has a different opinion. In his conception the particles could infinitely be divided without losing their specific nature. In view of its importance in the Middle Ages the most interesting doctrine is that which found its origin in the circles of Aristotle's commentators. Finally, the most general characteristic which distinguishes Democritus' atomism from other doctrines is probably its conception of nature. Whatever forms may be found in nature, their origin has to be sought exclusively in the inherent properties of the atoms: their number, size, shape, and their motion. Other doctrines assume, in one way or another, some fundamental nonmaterial principle as the source of the order in nature.

The best way to understand the specific features of Democritus' atomism is to examine the problems for which he sought a solution. These were not the kind of problems in which modern scientific atomic theory is engaged. This is not to say that there is no connection at all, for there is an unmistakable historical connection, but the intellectual climate of the fifth century B.C. differed considerably from ours. Not only are modern scientific problems posed within the context of already existing scientific theories and hypotheses, but they also presuppose an intellectual tradition. The first Greek philosophers, however, had to find their way without such a tradition; their task was the very creation of an intellectual climate in which scientific theories could be formulated.

Shortly before Democritus, Parmenides and Heraclitus had already considerably contributed to the creation of such a climate. Parmenides (about 500 B.C.) was greatly impressed by the cognitive power, possessed by the human intellect: only that can exist which can be understood (cf. Diels, frag. B. 3). Guided by this principle, Parmenides, through subtle arguments, came to the conclusion that reality must be one and immutable, despite the apparent testimony of the senses to the contrary. At first sight, Parmenides' thesis does not at all seem favorable for the rise of modern science. This science is based upon the careful observation of facts, and the empirical evidence of plurality and change in nature is indisputable. Nevertheless, a closer consideration of Parmenides' thesis about the unity and immutability of reality reveals its profound meaning for physical science too. Without immutability in nature, there would be no room at all for scientific *laws*. Without unity in nature, there would be no room for *universal* laws.

Nevertheless, the approach of Parmenides to understanding reality was too one-sided. It did not take the testimony of the senses seriously enough. This same testimony led his contemporary Heraclitus to the assertion that everything is mutable (πάντα ρει) and nothing remains. Democritus' atomism has to be understood as an attempt to combine the fundamental thesis of Parmenides, prerequisite for any rational explanation, with the reality of change and multiplicity. For this reason the atoms are unchangeable and qualitatively the same. The observable multiplicity and qualitative change can sufficiently be explained by the quantitative differences between the atoms and by their motion, which opens up the possibility of their combination and recombination. Why did Democritus think his retouching of Parmenides' thesis was justified? Justification lay in the fact that changes in configuration and quantitative difference are mathematically intelligible. Thus he did not come into conflict with Parmenides' first principle: "Only that can exist which can be understood."

Parmenides' great impact of Greek thought is shown by the fact that his considerations form the starting point of practically all later Greek conceptions of nature, including those conceptions which greatly differ from Democritus' atomism.

The main reason why later philosophers, such as Plato and Aristotle, rejected Democritus' solution of the problems of change and multiplicity was not on account of the general idea of atoms, but because of the one-sidedness of the atomic theory, considered as a universal theory. For Democritus the theory was not merely intended as an explanation of natural phenomena, such as evaporation, or the existence of different states of aggregation. Its aim was to give an ultimate explanation of change as change, including also those changes occurring in man's mental activity. For this reason Democritus assumed atoms of a special form and shape for the composition of the soul. Because they are fine and round, the atoms of the soul can penetrate the whole body, move it, and thus cause its vital functions. Whatever may be the fruitfulness of the atomistic approach to the explanation of natural phenomena, the atomic theory of Democritus was not judged on its merits as a merely physical theory, for such a theory did not yet exist. The theory was judged on its merits as a universal explanation of the whole of reality. As such it was rejected. It was too materialistic, in reducing all qualities and feelings to quantities of atoms, and their configuration. Only gradually did man learn to distinguish methodically the different problems which are interwoven in Democritus' system. In Greek thought philosophy and science still formed a unity. This holds true also of other forms of atomism, which can be distinguished from atomism in the strict sense.

Plato, for example, in the *Timaeus* propounded an atomic theory of his own, but only as a minor aspect of a much broader idealistic conception of nature. In order to understand this conception we must return again to the sharply contrasting views of Parmenides and Heraclitus. For Parmenides reality was immutable being; for Heraclitus it was continuous change. Plato accepts both views, but with respect to different realities, the unchangeable world of ideas and the changing world of sense perception, respectively. The latter world is a shadow of the first, or its imperfect embodiment. Consequently, true knowledge is not directed towards the imperfect world of change, but towards the real unchangeable world. On account of the imperfection and continuous change of the natural things natural science could only be an imperfect science. A further consequence of Plato's conception of the two worlds is that the principle of order in nature was not to be found in nature itself, but in the world from which it is derived. This also explains the great value Plato assigned to mathematics. For the object of mathematics is not the observable realization of a circle or a triangle, but their ideas or essences in their unobservable, logical purity.

A few words remain to be said about Plato's atomic theory. He accepts the elements which Empedocles has proposed on empirical grounds: fire, air, water, and earth. In accordance with his views of the importance of mathematics, Plato tries to characterize the atoms of these elements by means of their mathematical form. Fire has the form of a tetrahedron, air of an octahedron, water of an icosahedron, and earth of a cube. The concrete characterization is, of course, arbitrary, but the idea of connecting physical properties with mathematical structures is in itself extremely fruitful. Yet no physical science could arise from this general idea. The distance between the observable phenomena and the hypothetical structure was too great.

Aristotle approached the problems of natural science much more empirically than either Democritus or Plato. He could not accept the viewpoint of Democritus that all observable change is only accidental, and differed with Plato mainly on the theory of knowledge. For Aristotle experience was the sole fount of human knowledge, including the knowledge of abstract pure concepts. As a consequence, he rejected the distinction between the unchangeable world of ideas and the observable world of change. Having safeguarded the reality of the sensible world, Aristotle faced the difficulties of Parmenides. How is real change possible? Atomism certainly opened up the possibility of explaining accidental changes, in which things did not change their nature, but it could not explain changes, in which things lost their nature. Nor did it account for the existing variety of natural things. It could account for the accidental variety, but not for the fact that nature showed a fixed order in the variety of things, an order which remained constant through the transitory existence of phenomena. Thus the first task

imposed upon Aristotle was a critical reexamination of Parmenides' thesis.

In order to be intelligible, the possibility of change presupposes a certain fundamental complexity rather than simplicity in material things. Otherwise it is not possible to account for both aspects that are present in change: the aspect of certain permanence, and the aspect of something that is really new. To a certain extent Democritus followed the same line of thought. Democritus, however, "substantialized" the permanent aspect, for the atoms were *things*, which existed as such. Thus the possibility of change was narrowed down to accidental changes of configuration. In the eyes of Aristotle, the permanent aspect could not be a thing, but only a principle, i.e., something that does not exist in itself, but only as a component of a whole. Aristotle calls it *matter (hylē)*. Matter is not a substance, but only the capacity to receive "forms." Since matter is not itself a substance, even the most radical changes are possible. For existing things are composed of matter and form, i.e., matter that has received a form. Things can change, because one form can supersede another. The most radical changes are those in which things receive a new substantial form. In this case their nature changes.

The way in which Aristotle discusses the possibility of change makes it clear that he has quite another conception of nature than that of Democritus' atomism. With Aristotle nature refers to something fundamental in material things, which is both the source and the end of their growth, their movements, and their changes. "The primary and proper meaning of 'nature' is the essence of things which have in themselves (*qua* themselves) a principle of motion" (*Metaphysics,* Book IV). Because each thing acts according to its nature, i.e., according to its natural form, each thing strives for its proper end, i.e., its place in the whole of the cosmos. Thus there is a kind of "built-in" natural order, based upon a natural series of final causes.

In these conceptions of Aristotle there is, of course, no place for unchangeable atoms. This does not mean, however, that Aristotle had no thought of minute particles. Although he did not propound a corpuscular theory of his own, we find a few remarks that could have been the starting point for such a theory. The remarks form part of Aristotle's criticism of Anaxagoras' theory about the infinite divisibility of material things. Somewhere there must be a limit to divisibility, which limit is determined by the specific nature of the things in question. It was left to Aristotle's Hellenistic, Arabian, and medieval commentators to develop the casual remarks of their master into the *minima naturalia* theory, stating that each kind of substance has its specific *minima naturalia*. These commentators combined the empirical approach of Aristotle with the more rational approach of Democritus. Thus they prepared the way for the scientific atomic theory of modern times.

Before we discuss, however, the gradual shift of emphasis from a philosophic to a scientific atomic theory, we must first turn our attention to an aspect of the Greek ideas of "nature," which played an important role namely, the ethical dimension of their concept of nature. It is interesting to note that the use of the term "natural law" arose first in the ethical realm. The reason may have been that the phenomena of nature at first impressed man as much more unpredictable than human behavior, which was subject to fixed laws. The Greeks themselves did not even use the term "natural law" in the sense it has nowadays in physical science: the latter sense dates from modern times. This does not mean, as we have seen, that the Greeks were not familiar with the idea of a rational order in nature. On the contrary, this idea was central to their thought, but they did not express it in terms of laws. Even with respect to the ethical sense, the coupling of nature and law into a single expression does not seem to have occurred before the last phase of Greek philosophy as represented by Stoicism.

By speaking of "natural law" the Stoics revived to a certain extent the pre-rationalistic conception of mythological thought, in which hardly any distinction was made between the orders of nature, of culture, and of ethics. The difference was, however, that the Stoics were convinced of the rationality of the all-embracing order of nature. Because nature is permeated with rationality, and rationality constitutes the nature of man, the Stoic philosophers could return to the identification of the natural and the ethical order, without losing sight of the special position which man occupies in the natural order. For precisely the reflection on this position has marked the transition from the mythological to the rational phase in Greek thought. By his reason (*ratio*) man could know his own place in the natural order, and by his free will he could live in accordance with the ethical obligations, which followed from his own place in this order. It is, therefore, no coincidence that long ago the term "nature" also acquired the meaning of "essence." The study of the order of natural things and the place of man in it revealed both the essence of natural things and that of man.

It is not easy to summarize in a few words the general characteristics of the Greek conception of nature. The great diversity of opinion among Greek philosophers makes it even impossible to speak of *the* Greek conception. Yet the ethical connotation, which the term "nature" could acquire, indicates a certain common conviction with almost all Greek philosophers, namely, that the order of nature is an order which man cannot change and which he has to accept as it is. Within the order there was a certain room for human intervention, but the possibilities of this intervention did not apply to nature as a whole, but only to those aspects of it which invited man, as it were, to utilize them. The room in nature for human culture confirmed rather than weakened the idea of the order of nature.

Closely connected with the conception of nature as an unchangeable order, which man has to respect both in his technology and in his ethics, was the conviction that the order of nature was something "supernatural." It should be noted, however, that this last conviction was less general than the first.

In the Christian era the Greek conceptions of nature were taken over, albeit with an important correction. The order of nature became a *created* order. Christian thought broke with the identification of the natural and the supernatural, and with the identification of the natural and the ethical order. The transcendent Creator as the origin of nature and of man made it possible to place man apart from nature, even though their common origin was maintained. The ethical concept, "natural law," could be preserved, but it now had a different sense, because man's relationship to the Creator differs fundamentally from his relation to nature. Both nature and man are subjected to the divine law, but not on the same level. Man's freedom with respect to nature was, in principle, safeguarded; nature was at his disposal. To what extent man could "cultivate" nature was, however, not clear. Man had still to find out.

As long as natural science seemed to be no more than a rational affair, the conception of nature as an order which man could understand but not change remained predominant. Even after the Middle Ages when mathematical rationality superseded philosophical rationality, this predominance was not seriously affected. The new rationality of science changed the idea of the order of nature insofar as this order became the order of a mechanism. It became the construction of a chief engineer, but it still remained an order, which could not be altered by man. He simply seemed to lack the necessary power. Only after it became clear that in order to reach its rational end science had to use experimental means, could a new conception of nature appear. The laws of nature (in the scientific sense) were not only the signs of the rationality of nature, but also the means for the manipulation of nature. The actual order of nature lost its supernatural and normative character. Through an apparently fixed order of nature man saw an unlimited field of possibilities, based upon the fundamental forces of nature.

In the process that led to this view of nature, the development of the atomistic conceptions into an experimental scientific theory played an important role. How did this development take place? For the answer to this question let us return to the Greek atomic conceptions and follow their development through the centuries until the seventeenth century. As we have pointed out, there could not have been a straightforward development from the Greek atomic theories to the scientific atomic theories of modern times. The main reason why this was impossible was not that the Greek theories were, first of all, *philosophical* theories, propounded to explain the possibility of change in general. This was, of course, a reason, but there were nevertheless enough physical aspects in the atomistic doctrines which could function as the beginning of a fruitful physical theory. The main difficulty was that there was too great a gap between the observable phenomena and the theories in question, even with respect to their physical aspects. Accordingly, it was not the atomic theory which was destined to be the first fruitful physical theory. This had to be a theory in which the observable phenomena were much more directly suited to be fitted in a mathematical model. It is, therefore, not accidental that the first fruitful general physical theory, namely mechanics, was of astronomical origin. Only after a general theory of mechanics was developed, which could be applied to the hypothetical atoms, was the time ripe for a physical atomic theory.

With respect to a *chemical* atomic theory, the situation was different. Of course, this theory had to wait also until more general theories were developed, but typical corpuscular considerations could play a part in the coming into existence of these theories. It was easier to characterize the hypothetical atoms by their chemical than by their physical properties. It is obvious that of the two important Greek corpuscular schools of thought, the atomism of Democritus and the minima doctrine of the commentators of Aristotle, the latter, with its specific minima for each kind of substance, offered more possibilities for chemical considerations. The interesting point is that one of the main aspects of the development of the minima doctrine lies precisely in a gradual development from a more philosophical to a more chemical theory. Atomism does not show such a development. This is mainly due to the fact that its spiritual father Democritus had already elaborated a more or less complete doctrine, and that

it had only a few adherents between the fifth century B.C. and the seventeenth century; the most important are Epicurus and the Latin poet Lucretius Carus.

Epicurus introduced the idea of a chance swerve (*clinamen*) of the atoms, which he and Lucretius thought would make intelligible new qualities and free will. What atomism needed for its development was, above all, the connection with observable chemical phenomena. And for such a development it was less suited than the minima theory. When atomism came to occupy again a central position in the seventeenth century, it could profit from the development the minima theory meanwhile had made. What were the main stages in this development?

To Aristotle himself the minima did not mean much more than a theoretical limit to divisibility; they were potentialities rather than actualities. Nothing indicates that he attributed to the minima a certain measure of independent existence. As early as the Greek commentators of Aristotle—Alexander of Aphrodisias (second century A.D.), Themistius (fourth century), and John Philoponus (sixth century)—we find an important development. In their thought the smallest particles are more than just potentialities, the commentators speak of the *elachista*, the Greek equivalent of minima, as if they actually existed. Furthermore, in reading these commentators we get the impression that they used the term *elachista* in a special, technical sense. Just as for Democritus the term *atomos* does not mean exclusively *indivisible*, but is also a technical term for smallest particles, so also something similar seems to be the case with the word *elachista*. Each specific substance has its own *elachista*.

Averroës (1126–98), the most important Arabian commentator on Aristotle, followed up this line of thought. With him we find the suggestion that the *elachista* or minima play an important role during chemical reactions. His Latin followers elaborated this point. They do not leave us in doubt that they attributed to the minima not only an independent existence, but also a certain function in several physical and chemical reactions. In their opinion the minima were the actual building stones of reality. Consequently, the increase or decrease in quantity of a substance amounts to the addition or subtraction of a certain number of minima. Agostino Nifo (1473–1538) assures us that a chemical reaction takes place among the minima. When elements react upon each other they are divided into minima.

The next step was now to examine how the properties of the minima, responsible for chemical and physical reactions, could be connected with the specific observable properties of different substances. The first attempt to do so was, of course, not very spectacular, but the attempt in itself was already important for the coming into existence of chemical and physical theories. According to J. C. Scaliger (1484–1558), some properties of matter, such as fineness and coarseness, depend on the properties of the minima themselves, while others depend on the manner in which they are joined. Rain, snow, and hail are all of the same *coarseness*, because they are composed of the same minima, but their density is different, because the minima of these three substances are at a smaller or a greater distance from one another. Scaliger knew not only minima of elements, but also of compounds, although he does not mention the latter as systematically as the former. As to the chemical reaction, Scaliger is not satisfied with the Aristotelian definition: the union of the reagents, because the role of the minima is not mentioned. He is not satisfied with Democritus either, because Democritus' atoms could not really form a new unity. Hence Scaliger's definition: chemical composition is the motion of the minima towards mutual contact so that union is effected. As a follower of Aristotle, Scaliger is convinced that for a true chemical composition a new substantial form is required.

The interesting point with such men as Scaliger and Nifo is that on the one hand they develop their ideas within the conceptual framework of Aristotle's philosophy, whereas on the other hand they transcend it. Unlike certain Aristotelian circles, as those of the Thomists and Scotists, who limited themselves to the discussion of the minima and of chemical composition merely with philosophical concepts such as actual, potential, form, etc., the Averroists make efforts to express in a more scientific way the relation between the forms of the elements and the form of the compound. Without abandoning the Aristotelian unity of form in the compound, they transform this concept in the direction of what we may call the concept of "structure." Thus they paved the way for a new framework of concepts, in which scientific theories could be formulated.

In the seventeenth century the creation of this new conceptual framework made great progress. This can be shown from the fact that the philosophical differences between the corpuscular systems were soon pushed into the background, while the more scientific aspects that were held in common came to the foreground. Daniel Sennert (1572–1657) offers a clear example of this tendency. Basically, his corpuscular theory was derived from the minima doctrine, but it also contained typical ideas of Democritus' atomism, that in Sennert's days came to occupy a central position. Sennert was, however, interested mainly in a chemical theory, not in philosophical disputes. He was of the opinion that, from a chemical point of view, atomism and minima theory amount to the same thing. In order to maintain this opinion, Sennert had to revise the atomistic doctrine. As a chemist, Sennert was convinced that elementary atoms differ qualitatively and that a clear distinction should be made between elementary atoms and atoms of compounds (*prima mista*). Modern chemistry followed Sennert in this respect. It shows how important the minima doctrine has been.

Does this mean that the revival of atomism in the strict sense did not have any real effect? The contrary is true. The real significance of this revival must, however, not be sought in the revival of the general idea of reducing the observable phenomena to changes in the configuration of atoms, but in the inspiring conviction that nature formed a unity, which quantitatively could be analyzed. This fundamental idea remained alive in modern science, even when at first the number of qualitatively different elementary atoms had to be increased from four to more than ninety. Whereas the minima doctrine (and later on the chemical atomic theory) accepted the existence of qualitatively different elementary atoms as an irreducible fact, atomism did not accept such an irreducibility. Whatever may be the differences of the elementary atoms, these have to be reduced to the fundamental properties of all matter. This idea has been proved successful when the structure of the atoms themselves became an object of scientific research. And it is still vivid in our times when the number of sub-atomic elementary particles has increased tremendously. Science is again looking for unity in this diversity.

BIBLIOGRAPHY

R. G. Collingwood, *The Idea of Nature*, 2nd ed. (New York, 1960). E. J. Dijksterhuis, *The Mechanization of the World Picture* (Oxford, 1960). R. W. Hepburn, "Philosophical Ideas of Nature," in *The Encyclopedia of Philosophy* (New York, 1967), V, 454–58. F. A. Lange, *Geschichte des Materialismus und Kritik seiner Bedeutung in der Gegenwart* (Iserlohn and Leipzig, 1866); trans. E. C. Thomas as *History of Materialism* (reprint, New York, 1950). K. Lasswitz, *Geschichte der Atomistik vom Mittelalter bis Newton*, 2 vols., 2nd ed. (Leipzig, 1926). A. G. M. van Melsen, *From Atomos to Atom, the History of the Concept Atom*, 2nd. ed. (New York, 1960); idem, *Physical Science and Ethics, a Reflection on the Relationship between Nature and Morality* (Pittsburgh, 1967). C. J. de Vogel, *Theoria, studies over de griekse wijsbegeerte* ("Studies Concerning Greek Philosophy") (Assen, 1967). L. L. Whyte, *Essay on Atomism: From Democritus to 1960* (London, 1961).

A. G. M. VAN MELSEN

[See also **Atomism in the Seventeenth Century; Causation;** Epicureanism; Law, Natural; Matter; **Nature;** Platonism; Rationality; Stoicism.]

ATOMISM IN THE
SEVENTEENTH CENTURY

DURING the course of the seventeenth century, an increasing number of natural philosophers turned to one or another versions of the atomic doctrine as an explanatory framework for natural phenomena. By the end of the century, an overwhelming majority of natural philosophers no longer held serious doubts about the existence of atoms in nature. The reasons for this turn of events are numerous and complex, and the depths of the problem are only now being explored by historians of the period.

Atomism appealed to many men of the seventeenth century on several levels. First of all, they saw in atomism a systematic mode of explanation, sanctified by time, with which they could confront the alternatives of Aristotelianism and Paracelsianism which many found intellectually stultifying and, because of the adherents of these other paths, often socially unacceptable. Secondly, the relationships posited by atomism—the motions and impacts of material objects—were close to their experience with gross bodies. Furthermore, the intrusion of machines into the daily and economic lives of men of the seventeenth century became increasingly evident. Scientists draw the analogies employed in natural explanation from experience; these machines, which illustrated impact or utilized the presence of a vacuum provided an impetus for the employment of a "mechanical" explanation. After such explanation was decided upon, atomism provided a way of interpreting those other phenomena which were patently nonmechanical on the visible level. In short, atomism was considered by its adherents over-optimistically as more practical and more "realistic" than its alternatives.

Simon Patrick, a member of the Royal Society of London, illustrated this point in his *Brief Account of the New Sect of Latitude Men* (1662). Patrick related the story of a farmer whose clock was in need of repair. He consulted a "Perpatetick artificer" who explained the material, formal, and efficient causes of clocks, the presence of the formal cause and its privation before it was made. He went on to demonstrate that the nature of the clock-work was a principle of motion by an "inward device of its own accord," and lacking that, the broken clock was now indeed no clock at all. The farmer's son, a university man, who had read Magirus (a favorite late sixteenth-century Aristotelian author), happened along and explained the matter and form of the clock; its primary and secondary qualities; the occult quality in the dial; its "sympathy" with bell, etc. However, the clock remained broken. After a while, the landlord came by. He, an ingenious gentle-man, was impatient with all the scholastic jargon and explained to the farmer the true mechanical principles of the clock. He told the son that "he should take no more notice of the substantial forms and qualities of a clock, and told him that he rejected principles, and therefore would not dispute with him" (p. 19).

"How far," Patrick concluded, "the Clock-menders discourse resembles the Scholastick Philosophy or the Gentlemans [sic] the atomicall, let others judge." But, he continued, "how can we satisfy our selves with the four Elements of *Aristotle*, or the three principles of the Chymists, . . . ? Truly to them that have once tasted of the Mechanical Philosophy, formes and qualities are like to give as little satisfaction, as the Clock-mender did to the Intelligent Gentleman in the Story" (pp. 19–22). It should be made clear, however, that the reception and establishment of the atomic doctrine was neither so simple or rapid as Patrick's story may have implied. The road was a somewhat rocky one and the following will attempt to outline some of the major events of that reception.

Atomism in the Renaissance. During the Middle Ages the works of the great atomist and poet-philosopher, Lucretius, were largely known second-hand. Interest in his works, however, took a sharp turn upward in the fifteenth century owing primarily to the Italian humanist, Poggio Bracciolini. An apostolic secretary to the Pope, Poggio explored the monasteries of Europe in search of forgotten Latin manuscripts. In the years around 1415, he apparently found a copy of the original first-century (B.C.) work *De rerum natura* (*On the Nature of Things*), of Lucretius. Gradually, during the fifteenth century, this great work of atomist philosophy became known throughout western Europe. One of the earliest philosophers to study critically the resurrected Lucretius was the Platonist, Marsilio Ficino. In 1473, at Brescia, an edition of *De rerum natura* appeared, and was swiftly followed by at least three more by 1500. For the first time in many centuries, a complete treatise of atomist natural philosophy became available to western scholars.

Another important source of atomist thought in the Renaissance was the *Lives of the Philosophers*, a third-century work of Diogenes Laërtius which was first printed in 1533. Diogenes' *Lives* includes those of Democritus and Leucippus, and the entire tenth book is devoted to the great Hellenistic atomist, Epicurus. Included in the tenth book are letters from Epicurus to Herodotus and Pythocles, the former being one of the clearest and most concise statements of atomist natural philosophy. In sum, ample writings of the ancients became available in the sixteenth century to fill out and encourage the interest in atomism which had been increasing since Poggio's discovery. The interest took several forms. At first, it was primarily literary; the works of Montaigne and Edmund Spenser, for example, demonstrate the influence of Lucretius. It was not as a natural philosopher that European savants accepted Lucretius; for them, Lucretius was a sublime poet. As a philosopher he fell short of meeting the minimum Christian requirements.

It was not until the writings of Giordano Bruno that the atomists' view of the physical world began to hold meaning for Western philosophers. Indeed, in the work of Bruno, atomism became the key to understanding the universe and its Creator. For Bruno, atomism was the metaphysical principle on the basis of which the underlying unity of all nature could be demonstrated. In the minimum spiritual atom or *monad* he saw the germ of all existence. The atom in its metaphysical role is the matrix for all reality and, moreover, is the substance of the soul. Through the agency of the monad, God becomes the source for all change in nature, as well as the source of its existence. If the atom served a metaphysico-theological purpose in the writings of Bruno, it also was utilized as a mathematical and physical standard. In his *De triplici minimo et mensura* (1591), the minimum has three senses: in physics, mathematics, and metaphysics. In short, the monad was the keystone of Bruno's all-embracing universal scheme.

The atom played an entirely different role in the writings of certain other natural philosophers of the late sixteenth and early seventeenth century. These men, perhaps more recognizable in modern parlance as "scientists," utilized the concept of the atom as an explanatory tool, a tool made necessary by what was to them the demise of Aristotelianism. Of these new atomists three stand out: Galileo Galilei, Thomas Hariot, and Isaac Beeckman.

Beeckman and Hariot are two fascinating and unfortunately neglected scientific figures. Isaac was fortunate enough to have received a good education, and later became master of the Latin school at Dordrecht. Like his predecessor, Leonardo da Vinci, and his contemporary, Hariot, Beeckman published nothing of scientific value in his lifetime. It is only with the posthumous publication (in the twentieth century) of his *Journal* that many of his interesting and important researches have come to light. One of his most successful endeavors was to derive the law of falling bodies; E. J. Dijksterhuis has also shown that Beeckman arrived at some form of the inertial principle. But what interests us here is that behind Beeckman's physics was an atomistic view of nature that was essentially mechanical.

According to Beeckman, a vacuum must exist in nature; directly in opposition to Aristotle, Beeckman

looked to the existence of motion to prove it. In this void, matter consists of atomic parts. The qualities of bodies depend on the magnitude, arrangement, and motion of these atoms. For example, cold and heat consist of the motion (or in the case of cold, the lack of motion) of the constituent atoms. Wetness and dryness are merely results of the figure or shape of the atomic particles. Dry bodies are composed of sharpened atoms; wet bodies of rounded ones. In fact, the four so-called elements of the Aristotelians may easily be derived from the differing shapes of atoms. Out of a first kind comes air, fire by a second, earth by a third, and water by a fourth type. Light and sound, moreover, can be seen to have "material" causes. For example, according to Beeckman the reflection and refraction of light are caused by the interaction of light and the atoms of gross matter. Beeckman's atomism, unlike that of Bruno, was a philosophy intended for a specific physical purpose: it was to replace those worn forms and qualities of the scholastics which were unimaginable or unpicturable in any physical way. It was not an original atomic philosophy, nor did Beeckman employ it in any novel manner. His atomism was an ad hoc device, invented to explain certain physical phenomena—Beeckman's primary interest.

Similarly, the atomism of Thomas Hariot served as a useful, physical hypothesis, invented to render understandable mathematical ideas and chemical and physical phenomena. Hariot was born and educated at Oxford, graduating from St. Mary's Hall in 1579. After receiving his degree, he entered the service of Sir Walter Raleigh as mathematical tutor. Raleigh arranged for Hariot to accompany Grenville's voyage to Virginia in 1585; there Hariot collected a great deal of data concerning Virginia and its inhabitants. He returned to England in 1586 and began writing his *Briefe and True Report of the New Found Land of Virginia;* it appeared in 1588, the only published work of Hariot to appear in his lifetime.

Soon after returning to England Hariot entered the service of the "Wizard Earl," Henry Percy, the ninth Earl of Northumberland. The Earl, who himself enjoyed mathematical and chemical studies, established Hariot in Sion House, near Isleworth, outside London. There Hariot began his labors in mathematics, astronomy, navigation, and physics. Behind Hariot's physical researches lay the hypothesis of atomism. As he wrote to his friend, Johannes Kepler, Hariot advocated the atomic doctrine as the key to natural phenomena:

I have now led you to the doors of nature's house, wherein lie its mysteries. If you cannot enter because the doors are too narrow, then abstract and contract yourself into an atom, and you will enter easily. (Letter of 2 December 1606, in J. Kepler, *Werke*, XV, 368.)

Hariot's atomism was simple, and resembled the views of the ancients, Democritus and Hero of Alexandria: the universe is composed of atoms and interposed void space; the physical qualities of gross bodies depend upon the magnitude, shape, and motion of the constituent atoms.

Hariot published nothing concerning his atomist views; he wrote to Kepler that he could not philosophize freely on those subjects. Hariot was reluctant to make his views known because he faced a problem which many atomists in Europe faced during the remainder of the seventeenth century: atomism, with its pagan, atheistic origins, was theologically suspect. Most seventeenth-century thought was profoundly religious; its scientific practitioners were not exempt from the pious demands of the age. In order for atomism to be acceptable as a scientific doctrine, it first had to become acceptable theologically.

A third physicist who utilized the atomic doctrine, though perhaps with more novelty, was Galileo Galilei. Galileo is, of course, famous as the founder of the modern science of mechanics, and as an astronomer. His use of the atomic doctrine is less widely commented upon. Galileo's *Discourses concerning Two New Sciences* is the work in which he gave his most complete rendering of his atomism. Written in the form of a conversation between three interlocutors, the work is divided into "Days." In the very First Day, Galileo was concerned with a discussion of cohesion, and it is in this discussion that his atomism took shape. Through ingenious experiments, Galileo showed that the "force of the large vacuum" is insufficient to explain the cohesion of bodies. According to Galileo, a vacuum in nature exerts its own force (*virtù*); to illustrate this force he described the following experiment. If one takes two polished, smooth plates of marble or glass and places them face to face, they will glide or slide over one another easily, thus showing that there is nothing between them to hold them together. But when one tries to separate them, one finds that the plates require a great effort to bring them apart. Indeed, the lower one will actually be lifted into the air by the upper! This resistance to separation, Galileo concludes, is caused by "the aversion of nature to empty space" (p. 11) and is present also in keeping the parts of a solid together.

Galileo went on to measure cleverly the force of the vacuum (*forza del vacuo*) by determining how much of its own weight a column of a particular substance (e.g., water or copper) will sustain. He concluded that the resistance of the large vacuum is small in comparison to the cohesive force which binds the small parts of a body. Why then do bodies cohere? It is not merely the force of the external vacuum, but rather the pressure of many tiny internal vacua which account for this cohesion. "And who knows," Galileo writes, "but that there may be other extremely small vacua which affect the smallest particles so that that which binds together the contiguous parts is throughout of the same mintage?" (p. 19). Although the force of each minute vacuum is small, there are so many of them, that their total force is significant. Some picture of Galileo's atomism now emerges. Matter is made up of an infinite number of infinitely small particles, interwoven with an infinity of minute vacua. Galileo's atomism is related to the theories of Democritus and Hero of Alexandria, but is far more subtle and far more mathematical.

It is clear that the atomisms of Beeckman, Hariot, and Galileo are all prototypes of the mechanical philosophies which would later emerge in the writings of Hobbes, Gassendi, and Descartes. It is not surprising; Beeckman was the mentor of both Descartes and Gassendi; Hobbes and the others were familiar with Galileo's *Discourses*. But there is a significant gulf between the atomism of the former group and the corpuscular philosophies of the latter. Beeckman, Hariot, and Galileo were primarily concerned with the explanation of specific physical problems. Galileo, for example, was interested in the problem of cohesion; Hariot was often occupied with the phenomenon of refraction; Beeckman looked for the material basis for motion, light, sound, etc. The later mechanical philosophers, however, took a more systematic tack. They were concerned with complete explanations of the natural world, explanations designed to replace those of their grand opponent, Aristotle. Compared to the mechanical philosophies of Descartes or Gassendi, the atomism of the early physicists was fragmentary, and ad hoc.

Yet the similarities among them are important. Beeckman, Hariot, and Galileo all were concerned with the atheistic implications of atomism; Galileo's foil, Simplicio, remarks on the First Day: "It seems to me that you are travelling along toward those vacua advocated by a certain ancient philosopher." Galileo replies through the character Salviati: "But you have failed to add, 'who denied Divine Providence,' an inapt remark" (p. 25). Later on, Descartes and Gassendi (if not Hobbes) were concerned with ridding the mechanical philosophy of charges of atheism. This *theological* problem of atomism was one of the major obstacles to its acceptance as a reputable natural philosophy in the seventeenth century. How could atomism, with its pagan, atheistic origins and implications become acceptable? This was a question which had to be answered by the promoters of atomism in the course of the scientific revolution.

There was another obstacle which became a major difficulty barring the quick and easy establishment of the mechanical philosophy in the seventeenth century. This hurdle was erected by Sir Francis Bacon, and was one primarily of methodology. Whatever twentieth-century philosophers or historians may think of Bacon's view of science and method, seventeenth-century scientists, e.g., Robert Boyle and Hooke, regarded his writings highly and held them in great esteem. An understanding of Bacon's attitude towards atomism is necessary, therefore, for the understanding of his disciples in the Royal Society during the Restoration.

In Bacon's *magnum opus*, the *New Organon* (or "new engine"), he condemned the spinning of theories, *a priori*, by the Greek philosophers and their followers. Bacon's goal in the *New Organon* was a novel union of theory and practice, an examination of nature leading to secure certain axioms concerning what later writers might call "natural laws." His book was conceived as an engine or machine to assist the mind in discovering natural truth; the mind, left to itself, is capable of producing only fantasies. The evil of contemporary philosophy, Bacon wrote in the preface, is that it presents nature as something already known and understood, whereas, in truth, it remains to be uncovered and illuminated. The systematizers, or Rational School, include both the scholastic followers of Aristotle and the followers of the atomists—although the latter were more moderate in their claims. There have been some, Bacon continued, (like William Gilbert and his followers) who form the Empirical School of philosophy. They fly up to rash generalizations merely on the basis of a few experiments. Both the Greek philosophers and the "Empirics" suffer in their natural philosophies from sterility of method; neither provides a reasonable rule of procedure to facilitate true and certain knowledge. This rule of procedure is what Bacon hoped to present to his readers. His method in natural philosophy, was, simply put, the following:

I propose to establish progressive stages of certainty. The evidence of the sense, helped and guarded by a certain process of correction, I retain. But the mental operation which follows the act of sense I for the most part reject; and instead of it I open and lay out a new and certain path for the mind to proceed in, starting directly from the simple sensuous perception (*New Organon*, author's preface).

Bacon was quite clear and concise; no summary would do him justice. His goal was *certainty* in natural philosophy, and his method utilized what he called an "engine" to assist the mind and, indeed, constrain it. Bacon sought, in general, to undermine what he called "the mischievous authorities of systems," and replace them with a science founded upon orderly procedure.

A corollary of Bacon's insistence upon restraint of the mind's fancy in science was his rejection of the systems of the ancients—atomistic mechanism as well as Aristotelian matter and form. The history of the establishment of the mechanical philosophy in the remainder of the seventeenth century can, in part, be viewed as the reconciliation of the mechanical philosophy with the methodological requirements of Baconianism.

The establishment of atomism as a widely employed scientific explanation began with the formulation of coherent, workable *systems* or theories; the protagonists here are the French philosophers René Descartes and Pierre Gassendi, and the Englishman (famous also in another context), Thomas Hobbes. The story of the acceptance and utilization of their mechanical philosophies involves two major themes: the reconciliation with Baconian methodology mentioned above and the theological purification of the mechanical philosophy. Hariot was made to see the dangers which mechanism held for traditional theology; it would be the task of later atomic philosophers to rid atomism and mechanism of its atheistic taint.

It was the 1640's that marked the flowering of atomism and of Cartesianism, its plenist partner in mechanism. Paris in those years was the world center of natural philosophy. Giants such as René Descartes, Pierre Gassendi, and Thomas Hobbes were bolstered by such talented and provocative controversialists as Roberval, Mydorge, Mersenne, and such liberal patrons as William Cavendish (the Earl and, later Duke, of Newcastle) and his brother Sir Charles Cavendish. The Newcastle Circle—including the Earl and Sir Charles, Thomas Hobbes, John Pell, William Petty, Sir Kenelm Digby, Lady Margaret (later the famous Duchess of Newcastle)—was the center of British émigré interest in the new philosophies. The Earl's table, it was reported, provided a forum for discussion unmatched in Europe.

In 1644, Descartes published his *Principles of Philosophy*, which, though certainly not atomist in character, greatly affected the fortunes of the atomic philosophy both in Britain and on the Continent. The Cartesian universe is composed of a prime matter whose essential characteristic is its extension. Space, too, possesses extension and consequently differs from matter only in the imagination. Unlike the atomists, Descartes insisted that matter is infinitely divisible and since space and body are indistinguishable, there exists no "void space" in nature. Strictly speaking, therefore, Descartes was not an atomist but a vorticist and plenist.

The chief reviver of the atomic philosophies of Epicurus and Lucretius was Pierre Gassendi, a French priest, astronomer, and natural philosopher. Gassendi's

135

atomism was virtually an updated, Christianized version of Epicurus. All physical phenomena, Gassendi claimed, resulted from the diverse motions, figures, and weight of indivisible atoms in motion through the void. Gassendi relied heavily upon material *effluvia* to effect the forces of nature in the physical world. For example, electrical and magnetic attraction are caused by exhalations from the attracting bodies of appropriate streams of small corpuscles.

The systems of Epicurus, the pagan, and Gassendi, the Catholic priest, have important differences. The latter wished to exorcise from atomism the taint of atheism. According to Gassendi, the universe requires the existence of God who not only created it but gave its constituent atoms a *vis motrix* or motive force which provides for motion and by which Gassendi's God regulates the world.

Both Cartesian and Gassendist corpuscularianism exerted great influence upon atomist natural philosophers on the continent and in England. The reaction of the Newcastle Circle to these two approaches is interesting and not unimportant. First, the group around Hobbes and Newcastle were in large part responsible for the initial "importation" of atomism from the continent to England in the period after 1650, when many of the émigrés returned. Secondly, the spectrum of atomic philosophies among the members of the group offers an intriguing tableau of English atomism of the Restoration period, an atomism which was highly eclectic. On the one hand, the group included Sir Kenelm Digby, who was one of the last Aristotelian minimalists. He tried to link the corpuscular notions of Descartes, Gassendi, William Gilbert, and others to Aristotelian natural philosophy. Digby's smallest particles were not atoms but rather the *minima divisibilia* of the scholastics; he employed them, like the modern atomists, in a quasi-mechanical way. On the other hand, Thomas Hobbes was in the 1640's a much more orthodox atomist.

In 1644 Hobbes, who was a close personal friend of Gassendi, took the latter's part against Descartes. At this time, Hobbes indicated a belief both in atoms and in void. Had he published his major work, *De corpore*, which he had already begun in 1644, at that time, he would have shown himself on the side of Gassendi and the atomists. However, it appeared in print only in 1655, and by that time Hobbes had abandoned the vacuist position for belief in an all-pervading aether, probably because such a medium greatly facilitated Hobbes' mechanistic explanations of various forces in nature.

A good example of the similarities and differences in the physical theories of Descartes, Gassendi, and Hobbes can be found in their explanations of the phenomenon of solidity or firmness. According to Descartes, the hardness of a body is an effect of the relative state of rest of the component particles. "I do not believe," he wrote, "that one can imagine a cement more suitable to join together the parts of hard bodies than their own repose" (*Oeuvres*, III, 110). Gassendi, on the other hand, relied upon the grossness and complicated shapes of the atoms of hard bodies to account for firmness, the branches and sharp parts becoming interlaced and making movement difficult, if not impossible. Hobbes relied upon *motion* to account for solidity, and explained hardness as a quality which owes its existence to the pressure of confined rapidly moving atoms. This "kinetic theory" illustrates quite clearly Hobbes's reliance upon *motion* as the instrument of scientific explanation.

After the execution of King Charles I, the Royalist cause began to fade, and Hobbes and the other members of the Newcastle Circle, longing to be back in England, returned home and brought with them the atomic philosophy. As soon as she was established, Lady Margaret (the Duchess of Newcastle) began to publish her atomist poetry, and John Evelyn put out his edition of Lucretius. In the circle of Sir Charles Cavendish, William Petty, and the others it became fashionable to talk among their learned friends about the mechanical philosophy and atomism. It was in this manner that Gassendi's atomism began to influence English scientific thought.

Because of its pagan, atheistic origins, atomism had always been viewed with suspicion, but now, its troubles were compounded. Thomas Hobbes was *also* accused of being an atheist. Gassendi and Descartes, although mechanical philosophers, were exempt from this criticism. In their mechanical universe, Gassendi and Descartes had made room for an immaterial, noncorporeal Divine Being. Both of these philosophers, moreover, admitted that man's soul, as well, is immaterial and spiritual. Hobbes, however, was more consistent. He insisted that man's soul, in a material, mechanical universe, must be material. Later, he admitted to Bishop Bramhall that even God is material and corporeal. To all Englishmen, High Church Anglican and Puritan alike, this was heresy; this was atheism.

In addition to its own intrinsic difficulties, therefore, atomism had to bear the burden of having notorious friends. Because of Hobbes, the atomists, most of whom were actually pious Christians, were laid open to charges of impiety and heresy. These more orthodox atomists were greatly disturbed about the situation, and set about to *purify* atomism and to dissociate it from atheism and impiety.

136

Among the early opponents of the revived Epicurean atomism were several of the famous Cambridge Platonists, particularly John Smith and Henry More. "Epicurism," Smith maintained, "is but atheism under a mask" (*Select Discourses* [1660], p. 41). He focused his criticism on three concepts: (1) that motion is inherent in matter, (2) that the soul is material and mortal, and (3) that the world could be formed without a Divine Architect. In 1653 Henry More published his *Antidote Against Atheism* which criticized Epicurean atomism. He objected specifically to material and mechanical causes for motion, and to the notion that the complex universe could be explained without divine intervention.

It was these objections which Walter Charleton, a friend of the Duchess of Newcastle, a pious Christian and a convinced atomist, tried to meet in his long atomic treatise of 1654. This work, entitled *Physiologia Epicuro-Gassendo-Charltoniana*, was designed to answer the attacks on atomism and to purify it in the eyes of believing Christians. In response to the attacks, Charleton set about to defend atomism cleverly and effectively. His approach was threefold. First, he tried to demonstrate that modern Epicurean atomism was purged of the heresies which admittedly contaminated the pagan formulations of Epicurus and Lucretius, specifically that the soul is material and mortal, and that motion is inherent in matter. Charleton denied both. Secondly, he attempted to dissociate the atomic doctrine of Gassendi from classical atomism by *joining* the attack on the *atheistic* aspects of it. He denigrated what he called "this false doctrine of Epicurus" that atoms were eternally existent and that their motion was inherent in them. According to Charleton, atoms were created *ex nihilo* by God and were infused by Him with a motive virtue or "Internal Energy," which is the first cause of all natural phenomena. Finally, Charleton tried to turn the tables on those who were calling atomism atheistic by declaring that, so far from being impious, atomism actually was a *proof* of the existence and power of God. Who could pretend that such a complex atomic system could come together by the actions of millions upon millions of little atoms alone? Some Divine Being, Charleton insisted, was necessary for this magnificent structure.

Charleton's book was, in large measure, successful. Over a period of several decades it was read by many, including Robert Boyle and Isaac Newton. After Charleton's *Physiologia*, almost all English atomist works contained the pious alterations which he had included. Moreover, it made the atomistic physics of Gassendi readily available to those whose Latin was weak (and these were more numerous than they admitted) and to those to whom Gassendi's works were not readily available. The purification was so successful that even the Cambridge Platonists, especially Ralph Cudworth, began to use a "purified" version of atomism in their works.

A second, and doubtless more formidable, obstacle to the establishment of atomism as a viable natural philosophy was a central contradiction within its own structure. Atomism was held to be, by its proponents, a truer, more useful representation of nature than opposing views—the chimerical inheritance of the Paracelsians or the empty shell of Aristotelianism. Yet how was this "progressive" character of atomism to be affirmed? Neither the methodical doubt of the Cartesians nor the empiricism of the Gassendists and Baconians would seem to admit the highly speculative atomic doctrine. All mechanical philosophies, orthodox atomism included, depended ultimately upon unobservable corpuscles acting upon each other in ways which had to remain inaccessible to natural philosophers despite marvelous advances in instrumentation. How was atomism (or Cartesian corpuscularianism) to be fitted into scientific explanation?

The contradiction was recognized by the major mechanical philosophers, and resolved (to their satisfaction) by recourse to a very special mode of scientific explanation, a mode which can be described by the term "hypothetical physics." All the mechanical philosophers—the atomists Hobbes and Gassendi as well as the plenist Descartes—recognized that they possessed no workable method of directly observing nature at the micro-level, and thus were prevented from gaining real knowledge of the atomic clockwork which to them doubtless existed. This fault, they claimed, was fundamental to natural philosophy; "physics" at the ultimate atomic (or corpuscular) level was inherently barred from certitude. The certainty which all desired (of either the Euclidean deductive or Baconian inductive variety) was impossible when dealing with the basic particles of nature and their interactions. The natural philosopher was therefore constrained to invent *hypotheses* of possible pictures of the inner mechanism of the natural world. There were of course limitations on these "fancies": they had to be internally consistent to lead logically to no obvious absurdity and finally to be consistent with external experience. Descartes, for example, wrote to Father Mersenne in 1638:

To require of me geometrical demonstrations in a question which concerns physics is to ask me to do the impossible. . . . In such matters we have to rely upon suppositions which, even if they are not exactly true, are yet not manifestly contrary to experience, and in speaking of which we argue consistently, without falling into paralogisms. . . .

137

Take it therefore, that there are only two ways of refuting what I have written, either that of proving by certain experience or reasons that the things I have supposed are false or else of showing that what I have deduced from them cannot be so deduced (trans. N. Kemp Smith, pp. 96–107).

Descartes (though not an atomist) has here provided a new standard of scientific explanation which the atomists would likewise agree upon. Physics of the microworld is restricted to the invention of plausible hidden mechanisms which must be self-consistent and conformable to experience. Descartes (like Gassendi and Hobbes) accepted as satisfactory scientific explanations all those "Hypotheses" which satisfied the consistency criteria. Naturally, there were very many such hypotheses for any given phenomenon; competition grew intense for the most *ingenious.*

"Hypothetical physics" as a mode of explanation, though apparently forced upon atomists owing to the limitations of their own doctrine, was modified or rejected by the leading natural philosophers of the next generation. Younger men, like Christopher Wren, Robert Boyle, and eventually Isaac Newton, were dissatisfied with what they took to be the *indecisiveness* of the hypothetical physics. All retained the framework of atomism, or a form of it, and sought new criteria for scientific explanations and new methods to obtain certainty in science. Atomism in the seventeenth century could not, of course, attain the status of a certain science; the result of these forays into new patterns of explanation was to define the boundaries of the use of atomism in natural philosophy.

The Reform of Atomism. The renovation of atomism by the modification of the hypothetical physics was a task which was Europe-wide, carried out on the continent by scientists such as Christian Huygens (1629–95) and in England by those natural philosophers congregating at the Royal Society of London. The virtuosi of the Royal Society, purporting to put into practice (but not always with success) their motto *Nullius in verba*, were uncomfortable with atomism and with Cartesianism even after the efforts of Charleton and others to purify the new philosophy. Without question, the intellectual "patron saint" of this new group founded in 1660 was Francis Bacon, and it was from him that many of the members appropriated their vision of science. [See: Baconianism.] Bacon's call for certainty in science through experience was echoed by his disciples in the Royal Society. The revolt against the systematizers Descartes, Gassendi, and Hobbes (who was excluded from the Society on several grounds) took various forms. This spectrum of response is usually obscured by the haste with which most British natural philosophers assumed the too-encompassing rubric "Baconian." First there were the "empirics,"

who deeply suspected atomism. Like Bacon, they were suspicious of the tenuous and hypothetical foundation of the atomic philosophy, and though they preferred it to Aristotelianism, they could not accept it without serious qualifications. A typical member in this regard was Samuel Parker, Bishop of Oxford, who wrote in *Free and Impartial Censure of the Platonick Philosophie:*

I am lately grown such a despairing Sceptick in all Physiologicall i.e., physical *Theories* that I cannot concern my self in the truth or Falshood of any Hypotheses before any other, yet me thinks their contexture is too slight and brittle to have stresse laid on them . . . for their parts which rather lie than hang together being supported only by the thin filme of a brittle conjecture (not annexed by experience and observation) if that fail anywhere, the whole systeme of the Hypothesis unavoidably shatters (p. 46).

Parker has here laid out the major objection of the empirics: existing theories were based loosely on a string of conjectures with no pretense to—and what is worse, no aspirations toward—certainty in science. The time for theory, they claimed, is not yet ripe; what the members of the Royal Society must do is patiently collect data of all kinds in anticipation of the day when theory is possible. The diagnosis of the ills of atomism by the empirics was doubtless correct; their prescription, however, led mainly to the rather uncritical collections for which the early Society is notorious.

A second "Baconian" reaction to the hypothetical physics of the atomists and the Cartesians can be identified with the Society's most illustrious early member, Robert Boyle. Boyle wished to "reform" the hypothetical physics by bringing it within the compass of experimental philosophy. He was not able, of course, to prove experimentally even the existence of atoms, much less the truth of the hypotheses of his mentors Descartes and Gassendi. He aimed instead at *illustrating* the ideas of the mechanical philosophers and thereby demonstrating that, at least, the corpuscular philosophy was conformable to experiment. In practice the experiments which Boyle adduced were employed by him more to discredit the Aristotelian or Spagyrical views than to "prove" in any sense the truth of a particular atomic or corpuscularian position. "I hoped," Boyle wrote, "I might at least do no unseasonable piece of service to the corpuscular philosophies by illustrating some of their notions with sensible experiments" (*Works,* ed. Birch, I, 356). In the course of this illustration, Boyle advocated what he termed "the corpuscular philosophy," i.e., a generalization of atomist and Cartesian hypotheses. Boyle attempted to depict, therefore, that a mechanical view, based upon matter and motion, was consistent with laboratory experience, whereas Aristotelianism and many alchemical notions were not.

A good instance of Boyle's efforts is the *Experiments, Notes, etc. About the Mechanical Origine . . . of . . . Qualities* (1675). In this work Boyle attempted to show, in his own words, "not that mechanical principles are the necessary and only things, whereby qualities may be explained, but that probably they will be found sufficient for their explication." The qualities which Boyle discussed were heat, cold, colors, odors, tastes, etc. He tried to undercut the Aristotelian mode of explanation in the case of odor, for example, in the following fashion: he produced an odor from a non-odorous body merely by adding water; he took two malodorous chemicals and produced a fragrant product; he took two bodies and produced a mixture the smell of which was markedly different in character from the smell of either constituent. Boyle insisted that these changes could not have been produced by the exchange of Aristotelian forms. His readers evidently agreed with him, and the atomistic, mechanical view advanced by default.

The Anti-hypothetical View. The third variety of the "Baconian" reactions to the hypothetical physics was more complex. There were those in the Royal Society, who, accepting Bacon's demand for certainty and not finding it in the hypothetical physics, empha-sized the necessity for a more Archimedean approach: what they called *mathematics* and what today might be termed *mathematical physics.* The aim of this group, which included Christopher Wren, Isaac Barrow, and, ultimately, Isaac Newton, was primarily to forge de-ductive theories from first principles made secure by experiment. Instead of accepting the built-in hypo-thetical character of physical thought about the ulti-mate structure of matter, these men opted for the possibility of a more rigorous approach. It should be stressed that all were in some sense *atomists;* it was their faith, unfulfilled in their lifetimes, that the atomic motions at the root of all phenomena could be mathe-matically described and secured experimentally.

A leader in this Archimedean-Baconian reaction was Christopher Wren. In his 1657 Inaugural Address as Professor of Astronomy at Gresham College, Wren insisted that:

Mathematical Demonstrations being built upon the im-pregnable Foundation of Geometry and Arithmetick are the only Truths that can sink into the mind of Man void of all Uncertainty; and all other Discourses participate more or less of Truth according as their subjects are more or less capable of Mathematical Demonstration (*Parentalia*, p. 200).

What must be done in natural philosophy, Wren claimed, is to wed the force of mathematical demon-stration with the empirical certitude of experiment and observation. Regarding insight into the hidden atomic

motions underlying all gross phenomena, Wren had great hopes for future success using recently developed and improved optical instruments.

Natural Philosophy having of late been ordered into a geometrical way of reasoning from ocular Experiment, that it might prove a real Science of Nature, *not an Hypothesis of what Nature might be,* the Perfection of Telescopes and Microscopes by which our Sense is so infinitely advanc'd seems to be the only Way to penetrate into the most hidden Parts of Nature and to make the most of the Creation (ibid., p. 204; emphasis added).

It is to be stressed that Wren is here directly con-fronting the hypothetical physics, i.e., that view which constrained natural philosophy to hypotheses "of what Nature might be" instead of reaching, through experi-ment and demonstration, towards certitude.

In consequence, Wren saw the aim and function of the Royal Society as none other than "to establish certain and correct uncertain theories in Philosophy" (ibid., p. 197). Before the Society, Wren produced an instrument made to represent the effects of collision between two hard globes. By adjusting the velocity and size of one or both of these atomic models, Wren hoped to arrive at, in Sprat's words, "the *Principles* of all *Demonstrations* in natural Philosophy . . . for all the Vicissitudes of *Nature* are nothing else but the Effects arising from the meeting of Little Bodies of different Figures, Magnitudes and Velocities" (Sprat, p. 311).

That the mechanical laws which Wren hoped would come out of his "instrument" were later to be laws of atomic motion is not insignificant. It was held, im-plicitly at least, by these last critics of the hypothetical physics that providing a science of mechanics was the first step in the long route around the unresolved seventeenth-century contradiction of holding to an atomic view and desiring certainty in science as well.

Similarly, Isaac Barrow mounted an attack on the hypothetical physics in a fashion quite similar to the earlier (1657) one by Wren. In a series of lectures given in 1664–65 (English version, 1734), which Newton attended, Barrow offered a course of action which differed from the prevailing hypotheticalism of the atomists and was quite similar to that of Wren. What, he asked, do the philosophers offer but ad hoc hy-potheses?

And for the Dispatch of every question or the Explication of a Phaenomenon, a new and distinct Hypothesis is in-vented. From Whence it happens that in what is called and accounted the same science are found hypotheses with-out number (Barrow, p. 61).

True science, according to Barrow, must end all causes of disputation. The resolution of present diffi- 139 culties must be, not merely natural philosophy, but *mathematical* philosophy.

Mathematicians [Barrow wrote] only meddle with such things as are certain passing by those that are doubtful and unknown. . . . What they know to be true and can make good by invincible arguments, that they publish (ibid., p. 64).

By the time Isaac Newton was prepared to enter the scientific lists with the publication of his optical papers (1671–72), atomism had already been established as a viable natural philosophy. The theological disputes surrounding its reception in the early years had largely abated; the problem of method, particularly how to justify the use of atomistic hypotheses in an empirical way, had been papered over (not solved) by such leading lights in the Royal Society as Wren, Boyle and Hooke.

What was Newton's "solution"? How could Newton, answering Barrow's call for *certainty* in science, likewise adhere to an admittedly unconfirmable atomistic conception of nature? First of all, Newton did not doubt the existence of atoms, but attempted to mitigate their hypothetical character by reducing *his* atomism to its barest bones and by concentrating instead upon experimental and mathematical natural philosophy.

His famous theory of color, expanded in the 1671–72 papers, did not rest, he insisted, on any hypothesis concerning the nature of light. As he wrote to Pardies, "I would rather have my views rejected as vain and empty speculations than acknowledged even as a hypothesis" (Newton, *Papers*, p. 92), concluding, "If the possibility of hypotheses is to be the test of truth and reality of things, I see not how certainty can be obtained in any science" (ibid., p. 106). Later he retorted that "to examine how colors may be explained hypothetically is besides my purpose" (ibid., p. 144). Newton best explained his position and made explicit his rejection of the hypothetical physics, in a *suppressed* part of the first optical letter. Newton wrote, in the original: "What I shall tell them is not an Hypothesis but most rigid consequence, not conjectured by barely inferring 'tis thus because not otherwise or because it satisfies all phaenomena (the Philosophers universall Topick) but evinced by ye mediation of experiments concluding directly and without any suspicion of doubt" (*Correspondence*, I, 96–97). The discrepancy between the manuscript and printed versions has apparently unfortunately gone largely unnoticed; in it is contained important evidence of Newton's awareness of and reaction to the hypothetical physics.

The *Principia Mathematica* of 1687, though not an atomistic work, per se, was linked to Newton's atomic views. Much of the *Principia* can be, and was viewed

as presenting the mechanics of atomic motion, although the work referred primarily to visible bodies. He believed his efforts to be applicable to atoms as well. Rule III of the famous *Rules of Reasoning* in the second edition of the *Principia* enabled Newton to extrapolate from sensible experiences to understand the workings of submicroscopic bodies. Thus, Newton was able to state:

The extension, hardness, impenetrability, mobility, and inertia of the whole result from the extension, hardness, impenetrability, mobility and inertia of the parts, and hence we conclude the least particles of all bodies to be also extended and hard impenetrable and movable and endowed with their proper inertia. And this is the foundation of all philosophy (*Principia*, Book III, Rule iii).

BIBLIOGRAPHY

Xenia Atanassievitch, *La Doctrine métaphysique et géométrique de Bruno* (Paris, 1923). Francis Bacon, *New Organon*, ed. Fulton Anderson (Indianapolis and New York, 1960). Isaac Barrow, *Mathematical Lectures Read in the Publick Schools*, trans. John Kirkby (London, 1734). Isaac Beeckman, *Journal, tenu par Isaac Beeckman de 1604–1634*, ed. de Waard, 3 vols. (LaHaye, 1939–45). Marie Boas, "The Establishment of the Mechanical Philosophy," *Osiris*, **10** (1952), 412–51. Robert Boyle, *The Works of the Honourable Robert Boyle*, ed. Thomas Birch, 6 vols. (London, 1772). Walter Charleton, *Physiologia Epicuro-Gassendo Charltoniana* (London, 1654). René Descartes, *Oeuvres*, ed. V. Cousin, 11 vols. (Paris, 1824–26). See also *Oeuvres de Descartes*, ed. C. Adam and P. Tannery, 13 vols. (Paris, 1897–1913). Diogenes Laërtius, *Lives of Eminent Philosophers*, trans. R. D. Hicks (London, 1925). Galileo Galilei, *Dialogues concerning Two New Sciences*, trans. H. Crew and A. de Salvio (New York, 1914). Pierre Gassendi, *Animadversiones in decimum librum Diogenis Laertii* (Lyons, 1649). G. D. Hadzsits, *Lucretius and his Influence* (New York, 1935). Thomas Hariot, *Briefe and True Report of the New Found Land of Virginia* (London, 1588). Thomas Hobbes, *English Works*, ed. Sir William Molesworth, 11 vols. (London, 1839–45). R. Hooykaas, "Experimental Origin of Chemical Atomic and Molecular Theory before Boyle," *Chymia*, **2** (1949), 65–80. Robert Kargon, *Atomism in England: from Hariot to Newton* (Oxford, 1966). Kurd Lasswitz, *Geschichte der Atomistik vom Mittalter bis Newton*, 2 vols. (Hamburg, 1892). Lucretius, (*On the Nature of Things*) *On the Nature of the Universe*, trans. Ronald Latham (Baltimore, 1951). Frank Manuel, *A Portrait of Isaac Newton* (Cambridge, Mass., 1968). Henry More, *Collection of Several Philosophical Writings* (London, 1662). Isaac Newton, *Correspondence*, ed. H. W. Turnbull, Vol. I (Cambridge, 1959); idem, *Mathematical Principles of Natural Philosophy*, trans. A. Motte, rev. F. Cajori (Berkeley, 1962). *Isaac Newton's Papers and Letters on Natural Philosophy*, ed. I. B. Cohen (Cambridge, Mass., 1958). Samuel Parker, *Free and Impartial Censure of the Platonick Philosophie*, 2nd ed. (Oxford, 1667). Simon Patrick, *A Brief Ac-*

count of the New Sect of Latitude Men (London, 1662). John Smith, *Select Discourses* (London, 1660). N. Kemp Smith, *New Studies in the Philosophy of Descartes* (London, 1952). Thomas Sprat, *History of the Royal Society of London for the Improving of Natural Knowledge* (London, 1667). Christopher Wren, *Parentalia, or Memoirs of the Family of the Wrens* (London, 1750).

ROBERT H. KARGON

[See also **Atomism: Antiquity to the Seventeenth Century;** Baconianism; **Biological Homologies; Causation;** Nature.]

AUTHORITY

I

THE IDEA of authority has no single historical definition. Originally, its dominant meaning was the capacity to evoke voluntary compliance or assent, on grounds distinct from coercive power or rational conviction. Currently, its dominant meaning is the capacity to evoke compliance or assent, whether voluntary or not, on grounds which confer an official right upon coercive power and a compulsory force upon rational conviction. The substantive grounds of the original capacity, moreover, like the substantive sources of the subsequent titles to power, have varied markedly with time and circumstance. The history of the idea, therefore, is not the simple course of a single category in response to external changes of practical conditions and ideological associations. The history of the idea is composed rather of the changing proportions between its own dominant meanings and of the changing identities assumed by both these dominant forms. It is a history, then, in which the internal relations of the idea reflect and clarify the variety of its external roles.

The chameleonic qualities of authority raise the special problem of locating it within any historical complex of ideas. The obvious key to the recognition of authority in history is the application of an analytical definition in terms of the constant social function of authority. But the general danger run by this conceptual mode of intellectual history—the danger of anachronism in the imputation to the past of concepts relevant to the present—is confirmed in the case of authority by its cumulative shift from one meaning to another in its overall development. An analytical definition of authority in the current terms of such categories as dominion, government, and power must fail to account for the changing relationship of these categories to authority in the past, and it is precisely this relationship which is the primary historical problem of authority.

To avoid this danger without reverting to the outworn philological mode of intellectual history—i.e., the mechanical recognition of the idea by the word—the following method will be used here: since the term "authority" is a Latin derivative, the original ideas of authority will be defined first by induction from the kinds of situations which the Romans devised the term to meet: these semantically defined ideas, in turn, become the marks of recognition for subsequent forms of authority, whatever their nomenclature. This method, it should be noted, entails the exclusion of non-Western and pre-Roman ideas of authority from consideration, since the authority which is the object of these ideas is a different kind of authority from the composite object continuously derivative from initial Roman usage.

Far from the linear development of the voluntary to the coercible grounds of obedience which is the superficial historical scheme of the idea of authority in the West, the actual history which emerges from the blend of philological and categorical methods reveals a spiral process from the ancient Romans to the present. In this process the successive centers of cultural innovation provoked successive recurrences of the original idea of voluntary authority, to be followed at each stage by the equally recurrent attenuation of its voluntary character under the pull of antithetical ideas of liberty and dominion and by the reformulation of the idea of authority into a rationale of power. There have been four such complete stages, each comprising both a distinct period in Western culture and a specific context for the recurrent process of authority. The Romans devised the idea of authority with special reference to law and ended with a legal justification of sovereignty. Medieval men recapitulated the same process for religion, early modern men for politics, and most recently modern man for society. These dovetailed stages, each constituted by the two successive basic forms of authority, make up the general history of the idea.

II

There is common agreement that the idea of authority, in the full range of meanings that have given it an integral intellectual life to the present, had its origins during the Roman Republic with the coinage of the distinctive term, *auctoritas,* to cover several kinds of primarily, albeit not exclusively, legal relationships. The problem with the ancient Roman origins of authority, indeed, is an embarrassment of riches: it is the problem of inferring a characteristic and coherent Roman idea from the welter of literal usages developed for the term. The wealth of scholarly inquiries into the Roman term and concept has resolved part of this problem, in that several ideas of authority have been identified from classifications of the term's myriad functions (Heinze, pp. 349–55; Fürst, *passim;* Lütcke, pp. 13–29). But what the commentators agree on stresses the importance of what remains problematic. They agree that the frequency and variety of the Romans' applications of these ideas to both their private and their public life demonstrate the fundamental importance of authority for the whole of Roman society, and they agree too that this importance implies a cultural coherence among the Roman ideas of authority. But there is no consensus on what this coherence was.

The reason for the disagreement at this level would seem to be the insistence upon a rigorous coherence in the form of a definite hierarchy among the ideas of authority or in the form of one definite, integral idea which logically or semantically comprehends the rest. But the actual contexts of the partial ideas of Roman authority are simply too variegated and irreducible to bear such a stringent unity. What was common to them was not a synthetic idea to which they contributed but a general attitude which underlay them all. The coherent Roman idea of authority is a formulation of this attitude. It can be ascertained through an inquiry into the pattern formed by the various partial ideas that went into it and into the historical development of this pattern.

Three partial ideas of authority can be inferred from the types of application which the Romans made of the term since remote republican times.

First, among the earliest traceable meanings shared by ideas clustered around the distinctive term, *auctoritas* (or the root term, *auctor,* signifying the agent whose identifying capacity was his *auctoritas*), was the extra confirmation or guarantee of a transaction which was added to its normal legal sanctions by a special responsibility of one party in the transaction. In the field of private law, for example, "the authority of the trustee" meant the trustee's confirmation of a ward's action which made the action legally binding and the trustee legally accountable to the ward for all resulting injuries. Again, "the authority of the lord" (*auctoritas domini*) meant an imposition of the lord's will upon the slave in addition to the lord's regular right of coercive command (*iussum*), and where the related but more inclusive "authority of the patron" spelled out the legally incremental quality of authority by specifying it as that which the paterfamilias exercises in addition to his governing power (*imperium*) over his family (including slaves) and without governing power over his clients.

These private-law applications of authority help to identify an analogous meaning of political authority in Roman public life. The most overt link between the two fields for this meaning of authority was provided by the idea of "patriarchal authority" (*auctoritas patrum*), which was permanently associated with "the authority of the Senate" (*auctoritas Senatus*), synonymously during the early Republic and as one of its formal capacities during the later. Denoting the Senate's function, as a council of elders, of approving the resolutions of the popular assemblies before they could become law, the patriarchal authority of the Senate was obviously the public analogy of the private authority inherent in the certificatory function of the trustee. This aspect of senatorial authority was a formal instance of a public authority expressly recognized in all high governmental officials as a consequence but not a derivative of their legal prerogative or power (*imperium* or *potestas*). It was a prime example of what we may call the incremental or tutelary idea of authority—the idea, that is, of a kind of control over men that is additional to regular legal sanctions and is itself grounded in fiduciary legal status.

A second, even more pervasive, meaning of authority, diffused as it was through the literature of Roman private life as well as of law and politics, was the imputation of the personal—especially moral—qualities of agents, counsellors, or officials to their decisions, judgments, and regulations for the purpose of extending the trust in these model persons to their official deeds. This partial idea of authority has been characterized as "personality-power" or "prestige-power" by subsequent commentators. Where the first, or incremental, idea of authority was distinguished from command and power in order to complement them, the second, or personal, idea of authority was distinguished from counsel and opinion in order to complement them.

Scattered profusely through Roman literature in references taking the general form of "doing something by someone's authority" (*ex auctoritate alicuius*), distinctively personal grounds of authority were imputed to propositions, testimony, and arguments. They ranged from the advice of any trustworthy individual in his private capacity to the private and public recommendations of poets, philosophers, and scholars revered as seers or experts—which were mere counsels and opinions in themselves but whose source made them accepted as law and truth, obligating their recipients in fact far beyond their formal capacity to bind. Cicero, whose habit of joining Stoic principles to Roman practice has made him a veritable source-book for the personal and moral genesis of social and political authority, explicitly substantiated this genesis by analyzing it into the qualities of nature—i.e., virtue—and of time—i.e., original talent, wealth, experience, knowledge, and age—which made certain personalities especially imposing and their activities especially influential upon other people.

In political contexts the Romans also attributed authority to such socially oriented personal qualities as "honor" (*dignitas*), or "influence" (*gratia:* literally, the disposition to make connections and dispense favors), or meritorious acts, or old age (*auctoritas maiorum*). The authority attributed to these personal qualities often shaded insensibly into the incremental authority of public office. In its application to such executive officials as consuls and military leaders the preeminence derivative from personal merits and the preeminence derivative from the perquisites and responsibilities of the offices themselves were obviously osmotic, and even in the case of the Senate the moral prestige of ancestral families and of noble lineage merged into the incremental political role of the council of elders.

But the distinctive features of personal authority—its continuity with example and advice and its contrast to official power—nonetheless retained their identities as persistent ingredients of the characteristic Roman approach to political authority. Their most notable political contributions were to the crucial, related, and otherwise undefinable Roman ideas of the authority of the Senate and the authority of the princeps.

"The authority of the Senate" grew, during the later Republic, to be something more than the above-mentioned incremental patriarchal authority with which it had been wholly identified, and the homage paid to the personal qualities associated with Senators participated in this growth. The authority of the Senate came now to mean the specially effective consultative function which was in fact the elusive mode of government of the Republic's sovereign organ—a function which, in the memorable phrase of Mommsen's *Römisches Staatsrecht,* made *auctoritas* "more than a counsel and less than a command; rather a counsel with which one could not properly avoid compliance" (Mommsen, III, 2, p. 1034). This idea of authority covered all the characteristic operations of the Senate, including both its enactment of final decrees (*senatūs consulta*), which had the formal force of law, and its recommendation of imperfect resolutions, which did not have the formal force of law. Both activities were subsumed under counselling, and the Senate's "authority" was attributed to the actual binding force of its counsels, whatever their form.

Thus Cicero acknowledged "authority," in this sense of factually prescriptive consultation, to be the principle of the Senate's political preeminence, and he contrasted it explicitly with "the power" (*potestas*) of the magistrates and "the liberty" (*libertas*) of the people in one context or with the "power" and the "sover-eignty" (*potestas* and *majestas*) of the people in other contexts. For Cicero as for other witnesses, moreover, much of the prescriptive force that was imputed to the "counsels" of the Senate stemmed from the personal attributes of lineage, propertied wealth, and character associated with the Senators.

Related to senatorial authority but even more definitely personal in its origins and extralegal in its operation was the Roman idea of a "principal authority," or *auctoritas principis* (Magdelain, pp. 1–76). Obviously of decisive importance for the transition from republic to empire during the period of the "principate," the concept of the authority of the "princeps" (for lack of a precise equivalent, the Latin term has been carried over into English) developed its characteristic connotations, which the emperors and their legists would later use, during republican times. In its explicit Ciceronian version the princeps is the "ruler of the commonwealth" (*rector rei publicae*) in a purely ideal sense: as princeps, he occupies no official position and possesses no legal power, but he actually guides the balanced constitution of the Roman state from the outside as it were, whatever his formal political function, by dint of the magnetic moral virtues and merits which made "the best citizen" (*optimus civis*) also "the first, or chief, citizen" (*princeps*). Working preferably—albeit not necessarily—upon the Senate, the first citizens's characteristic mode of de facto government is, like the Senate's, from personal preeminence and through "counsel" (*concilium*), a mode of government which is summed up in its entirety as *auctoritas*. But unlike the Senate, which as a council of elders was a regular constitutional organ however irregular its function, the authority of the princeps not only characterized his political activity but constituted his very existence. Hence not only was authority something "of the first citizen's" (*auctoritas principis*) but someone was a first citizen through authority (*princeps auctoritate*), and Cicero's synonymous use of "honor" in this context as the constituent property of the first citizen (*princeps dignitate*) clearly indicate the personal focus of the princeps' authority during the republic. It was confirmed by the extraordinary function, also attributed to the princeps by both Cicero and Augustus, of supplying "private counsel" directly to the body politic (*res publica*) for the purpose of "liberating" it from the degeneration of its public organs.

The third and final partial idea of authority for the Romans was the quality of creation or initiation which we still primarily associate with the terms, "author" and "authorize." In its references to general human relations, this kind of authority denoted the source of a rumor or of a doctrine or of a decision, with the definite implication that the very identification of this

143

sponsor, independently of his legal function or of his moral qualities, carried with it grounds for others to conform voluntarily to what he authorized. And this in either of two ways. His designation as source (*auctor*) implied either his own continuing responsibility for the information, opinions, and actions in question or the rightful origin of information, opinions, and action whose original right had been transferred.

In the first alternative, authority referred to the special respect that was due to the accountable originator (author) of a complete idea or activity by those who simply comply with it; in the second, authority refers to the originator's (authorizer's) rightful transfer of his claim on this special respect to those who comply with his original incomplete idea or activity by completing it. A prominent instance of original authority in the first sense was the inclusion of the proposal of law within the function of an official's "authority," as shown by the synonymous use, in this context, of *auctor legis* and *lator legis* (Berger, pp. 368–69). The most far-reaching applications of original authority in the second sense were obviously to political power. This kind of authority, for example, was central to the princeps' function—over and above his personal or private counselling functions—of public counselling on critical issues. Not only was he himself "the leader" (*dux*) of the state solely by virtue of his "authority" as the initiator (*auctor*) of proposals—a respect for initiative entirely comprehensible in the normal stasis of a balanced republican constitution—but the regular public organs which enacted his counsel into legislation acted as much by the transferred authority which they acquired along with his counsel as by the coercive power of their own offices.

The Romans themselves never either reduced or synthesized their three categorical ideas of authority—the incremental, the personal, and the initiatory—in a single coherent concept, although subsequent commentators have not been wanting who have tried, on etymological or logical grounds, to do it for them. It is generally agreed that the etymological root of Roman "authority" (*auctoritas*) is "augment" (*augere*), and Cicero did occasionally identify *auctoritas* with a function of "increasing" honor or the general welfare. But however close to the incremental idea this verbal root may be, the lack of a direct etymological connection between this root and other, very different meanings of the word—such as authorship, from *auctor*—which are appropriate to the other partial ideas of authority has led to a simple repetition of the intellectual problem on the etymological level. Hence there is general disagreement on the relevance of the etymology to the concept of authority (Heinze, p. 352; Lütcke, p. 23).

Conceptually, moreover, both in their relationships with the idea of "power" and in their relationships with the idea of "reason" the partial ideas of authority showed themselves to be not merely heterogeneous but mutually opposed. In their relationships to "power" the respective ideas of authority were sometimes explicitly defined in contradistinction from it and sometimes explicitly asserted as the basis of it. In their relationships to "reason" the ideas of authority were sometimes implicitly tied to it (as in the authority associated with counselling), sometimes made explicitly compatible with it as a kind of shorthand for an alternate path to the same truth (e.g., Cicero's acceptance of the "authority" of the Greek philosophers when they do not "deliver their reasons" [*rationem redderent*]), sometimes explicitly opposed to it—and when opposed to reason authority was deemed sometimes an option to be preferred and sometimes an option to be rejected. These variations in the external relations of the various partial ideas of authority highlight the difficulty of arriving at a generic Roman idea of authority by either a semantical or logical analysis of its parts.

But it is possible to arrive at such a generic idea by a historical analysis, which aligns variations along a temporal axis and demonstrates them as coherent stages of an idea in the process of change. Roman public law—always, as we have seen, a crossroads for the sundry partial ideas of authority—furnished the context for the historical passage from republic to empire which makes the integration of the various forms of authority a matter not so much of historiographical interpretation as of historical fact. The crucial document in the reconstruction of this history is undoubtedly the famous Chapter 34 of Augustus' *Res gestae*, into whose formulation of authority republican ideas flowed and from whose formulation the pattern of the imperial idea emerged. Describing the position which was his after 27 B.C., when the Senate conferred upon him the title of "Augustus, for my reward," in gratitude for his formal reestablishment of the republic, the consul Octavius delivered the most revealing pronouncement in the whole history of the idea of authority: "After this time," he wrote, "I was superior to all by my authority (*auctoritate omnibus praestiti*), but I had no more power (*potestatis . . . nihilo amplius*) than the others who were also colleagues in the magistracy" (Magdelain, pp. vii, 53). The appeal to the typical republican idea of a personal and unofficial authority, categorically distinct from official power, seems obvious enough, but what is equally significant, albeit more covert, was the new constitutional role which its association here with the title "Augustus" symbolized for this authority.

The implicit link in this association was the function

of the princeps, which was identified both with Octavian's republican reference to his personal moral preeminence and with his definition of his official title in the initiatory sense of the princeps' authority as "the author of the best condition of state," i.e., *auctor optimi status* (ibid., pp. 56–62). Through its connection with the extralegal republican ideas of authority on the one hand and with the legal title of "Augustus" on the other, the Augustan principate initiated, under personal auspices, the process which would be completed, under institutional auspices, in the later Empire: the compression of loose-jointed authority, in response to the needs of official political organs, into a compact legal basis of constitutional power.

In Augustus' hands, indeed, the various strands of the princeps' authority were unified while the discrete powers of his sundry other offices—each was granted in a different senatorial decree, at a different time, and for a different period from the others—were deliberately kept separate, with the result that authority became recognized as the unitary basis of the several formal powers in the Empire. Augustus achieved this status for his authority by explicitly asserting both his princeps' authority and his magisterial power as official capacities and by implicitly blending the various meanings of authority into a single principal idea of it in the service of its political function. He combined in himself and secured legal sanction for both kinds of authority associated with the two traditions of the princeps (the initiatory public counsellor of the Senate and the personally revered private counsellor of the people). He merged these, moreover, in a new third type of princeps' authority—a guardian authority as trustee of the commonwealth (*custos*, or *pater patriae*), officially charged by the Senate with the safekeeping of the whole community (*cura et tutela rei publicae*). Although still without coercive power itself, this authority both partook of and contributed to the legal obligation of the statutes through the continuous personal identity and overall controlling function of Augustus as both the official bearer of the authority which attracted obedience and the official magistrate with the power to compel it.

With the development of the Augustan empire from a covert to an overt absolutism, the uneasy personal balance between authority and power in Augustus was resolved into a definite legal and logical connection in his successors. The legal texts and commentaries from the second century A.D. onward, abound in references to "our authority" and to "the authority of the laws" as the valid source of particular statutes. They are applied, moreover, not only to "our" authority in the traditional sense of "the authority of the princeps" (*principalis auctoritas*) and to the "authority of the resolutions" (*constitutionum auctoritas*) which were his characteristic mode of recommendation, but also to "our" authority in the novel sense of "imperial" and "sovereign authority" (*imperialis auctoritas* and *auctoritas nostrae majestatis*) and to the "authority" of the regular coercive laws of the sovereign power (*auctoritas juris* and *auctoritas legum*).

The official context and the juristic commentaries make it clear that these references to both a principal consultative and a governmental coercive agency of authority were not, as in republican times, references to two different kinds of authority, but rather to one continuous function of authority. This function was part of the legal and political process which merged the offices of princeps and Imperator and gave to the "resolutions" (*constitutiones*) of the princeps the formal coercive "force of the law" (*vigorem legis*) which was the Emperor's by virtue of the people's delegation of their sovereignty to him.

With the juncture of deliberative authority and magisterial power in the legislative sovereignty of the princeps-Emperor, the varied ancestral, moral, and initiatory grounds of traditional Roman authority converged into a single epitomal quality of the laws themselves, conveying the sense of an obligation to obey them beyond the application of either adequate reason or adequate compulsion. Hence the Imperial jurist, Ulpian (third century A.D.), revealed the political function as well as the legal destination of the Roman idea of authority when he declared the decrees, edicts, and judgments of the "emperor" (*imperator*) to be "statutes" (*leges*) which were "popularly" (*vulgo*) called "resolutions" (*constitutiones*) of the princeps.

The historical development of the Roman attitude to authority demonstrates an essential attribute of the general idea which reappears in every stage of its history and runs through its history in the large: the instability—stemming from the elusiveness of its original fragmented meaning—which made its proponents susceptible to the attraction of settled political power. But the Roman development also reveals, within the original fragmented idea of authority, the potential coherence which was actualized by the magnetic requirements of political power and can be traced through its response to them.

Both the terminological persistence of "princeps" as an Imperial title and of "consider," "assess," "resolve" (*arbitror, censeo, placet*) to define the activity of the princeps, and the formal logical priority which "authority" as the source of law and over the "power" which specified and executed it, were traces of the idea's original meanings which lasted through the Empire as compatible supports of the Emperor's sovereignty, and furnish clues to their common meaning. 145

The idea of authority in general arose when men freely chose final human depositories for their trust, and the various principles on which the choice was made became mutually reinforcing when they were aligned in a series directed toward the crucial problem of establishing a basis for government beyond the specific punishments its organs could impose, and the specific benefits they could deliver. In this constitutional context the personal basis of authority was conceived in terms of a civic morality; the creative basis of authority was conceived in terms of a political initiative; and the commitment of both to validating the origins of political power served to reinforce the trust reposed in the legal guardian who added his responsibility for its results. Thus both of the main discrepancies in the various meanings of authority—the discrepancy between the personal grounds and public effects of moral authority and the discrepancy between the initiatory and confirmatory grounds of responsible authority (that is, between the rights of authorship and the duties of augmentation)—were resolved into sequential relations when they were spread out along a legal axis to supply the organs of government with a single principle of origins and of guaranteed results that was more venerable and more unified than the combination of political appointment, physical sanctions, and promised welfare associated with official power.

This political integration of authority made manifest the three common traits which had always underlain the original variety of its overt principles. First, authority was essentially fiduciary: where the correlative of reason was conviction and the correlative of power was obedience, the correlative of authority was trust. Secondly, authority was essentially transitional: its function was to bring principles from a higher realm of being to bear upon the activities in a lower realm of being: ideas of authority modulated the principles so as to make them relevant without divesting them of their superiority. Thirdly, authority was essentially hierarchical: where power and liberty could both be located anywhere and exercised in any direction, men who used the idea of authority distinctively assumed that the superiority of the realm of its origin over the realm of its exercise required a parallel hierarchy within the realm of its exercise; only higher principles which were selective in their application were authoritative principles; those who appropriated them were the superiors, and those who recognized them were the subordinates.

Thus two generic ideas of authority emerged from the Roman experience: an actual idea which was a quality of sovereign power and a potential idea, independent of the idea of power, which persisted under the cover of the legal actuality. With the actualization of the coherent idea of autonomous authority under new auspices at the start of the next era, the overt relations of the two ideas came to constitute the intellectual history of authority.

III

Overlapping the later Roman Empire, absorbing the forms of its culture while assisting at its demise, the Christian Church perpetuated Roman ideas of authority along with the Latin terms for them. But the Churchmen introduced these ideas into new situations and used them in new contexts which both changed the substance and reinforced the pattern of relations already established between the autonomous and the hybrid ideas of authority. Starting from the reformulation of Roman concepts under the theological and ecclesiastical auspices of the Latin Church Fathers and running through the Protestant and Catholic Reformations of the sixteenth century, the idea of authority was revitalized by the special affinity of Christian religiosity for it. Association with an intellectually and institutionally autonomous Christianity restored the independence of the original pure idea of authority and made the Church, both in its internal and external relations, the main arena in the medieval history of the idea.

The new authority in the Christian dispensation was attributed to God's revealed truth. Its pervasive impact stemmed from the combination of its acknowledged supremacy over all other kinds of authority with its continuous relevance to all forms of temporal life in general and to temporal government and power in particular. The initial effect of this new Christian dimension of authority upon the Roman traditions of authority which it absorbed was to loosen the Imperial combination of authority with temporal political power by intruding a source of authority independent of political power. Subsequently, the theologians and the canonists re-knit the bonds between authority and political power to include the originally autonomous authority of religion in a hierarchical system of official Christian authorities.

The three main steps in this medieval process of successive disruption and re-integration which would become paradigmatic for every new stage in the history of the idea of authority were: the development of Revelation into a Christian authority *sui generis;* the primary interaction of Christian religion and ecclesiastical politics in the constitution of the Catholic Church; the conclusive interaction of religion, Church, and temporal government in the organization of the universal Christian community. Each step contributed an analytically distinct source of the idea and, despite the overlap among them, these religious, doctrinal, and institutional ideas of Christian authority also represented successive chronological emphases within the Christian era. The Reformations of the sixteenth century, in this schema, can be viewed as so many attempted restorations of the initial, purely religious idea of authority which developed, under the pervasive late-medieval conditions of religio-secular interpenetration, into conflicting versions of institutional authority.

1. Religious Authority. The idea of a transcendent and ultimate depository of human trust, not dependent in principle on earthly offices, took several compatible forms in early Christian disquisitions.

First, the idea of "divine authority," stipulated by Augustine (in his *De ordine*) as the "supreme" (*summa*) authority, juxtaposed notions of authority grounded on origination (God as author or cause of his creation), on metaphysical hierarchy (God as the worker of miracles for the limited human capacity of comprehension), and on responsible power (God as both infinite power [*potestas*] over men and as infinite mercy [*clementia*] for men). Second, the idea of "Christ's authority" (*auctoritas Christi*) juxtaposed the notion of authorization (delegation of the Creator's authority to the mediator), the anthropological belief in family hierarchy (the derivation of the authority of the Son from the authority of the Father), the appeal of personal influence (the person of Christ as authoritative "example"), and the commitment to an ultimate source (Christ as "author of the Gospel"). Third, the idea of "Scriptural authority" (*auctoritas divinae scripturae*) juxtaposed the notion of authorization (the Bible as the Word of God, embodying "the authority of God") with the incremental respect due the guarantor (the Bible as "apostolic authority"—that is, the testimony of apostolic witnesses who confirmed the truth of the Gospel for future generations of believers). Fourth, the idea of patristic authority (*auctoritas patrum* or *auctoritas sanctorum*) juxtaposed the notion of authorization (the inspiration of the Fathers by Holy Scripture), the notion of persuasion apart from or prior to rational demonstration, the notion of personal expertise in the juristic formulation of a canonical faith, and the anthropological reverence for the elders (*auctoritas maiorum* as the respect due the fathers of a Christian doctrinal tradition). The idea of church authority (*auctoritas ecclesiae*), finally, juxtaposed ideas of authorized power (the delegation of "divine authority" to the Church by Christ), of unbroken binding tradition (the authority of the Church as the transmitter of the authoritative "tradition of the elders"), of universal persuasion (the real meaning of Augustine's famous declaration in his anti-Manichaean *Contra epistolam quam vocant fundamenti* that "I would not believe the Gospel if the authority of the Catholic Church did not impel me to it"), and of confirmation (the role of the Church in reinforcing Scriptural faith).

Despite the linkage of "authority" and "power" which Christianity carried over into theological ideas of the Divinity and which led medieval men to use the terms interchangeably in many contexts, the addition of the specifically Christian dimension to the idea of authority endowed it with a renewed independence · in its relations with the idea of power. The authority in the authority-power syndrome referred always to the higher, otherworldly source of the force being exercised, whereas power referred to the source of the force within the realm of its exercise. If the easy convertibility of authority and power testified to the interpenetration of spiritual and natural realms in the Middle Ages, the spiritual explosions in the name of authority both at the beginning and the end of that period testified to the countervailing effort to keep a realm of superior being at once apart from and influential upon the powers of this world.

This general contribution of Christianity, as a religion, to the idea of authority—its combination of transcendence and immanence to provide a platform outside this world for the agencies which could bind men within this world—had its model in the specific contribution of Augustine. He traced the ultimate source of authority over men to the person of Christ: it was through His "authority" that the power of God was modulated into the power of the Church and it was the relationship of His divine to His human nature, at once distinct and effluent, that epitomized all Christian authority, at once transcendent and effective.

2. Doctrinal Authority. Between the early applications of Roman legal concepts to the Christian State Church in the fourth century A.D. and the church-state polemics of the late thirteenth, Christian ideas of authority developed primarily under the impetus given by the internal organization of the Catholic Church. Of the two organizational levels—the doctrinal and the constitutional—it was the former that proved to be the more provocative of distinctively Christian ideas of authority.

The articulation of a Catholic doctrine shaped ideas of authority by defining them vis-à-vis the ideas of tradition on the one side and of reason on the other. As the set of religious practices and beliefs hallowed by long usage and predicated upon the universal consensus of the faithful over the generations, tradition took its place during the early Middle Ages alongside Scripture, official administrative position, and canon law as separate, frequently competing, subheadings of authority. This position was eroded away by the growth of papal power and the consolidation of a hierarchical official order within the Church, until by

147

the end of the Investiture conflict in the twelfth century the idea of tradition as an explicit kind of authority had all but disappeared. It was subordinated to papal discretion, absorbed into official canonical jurisprudence, or, alternatively, distilled into constitutional doctrines of conciliar authority (Morrison, pp. 33, 345–46, 354–55). Among the sources of doctrinal authority, tradition clearly represented what was most distinctive in the original idea of uncoercive authority. The historical process which made the definition of it a function of the claimants to official authoritative power in the Church reflected the process of unification and subjection undergone by the idea itself.

The shifting theological relationship of authority and reason shows, *mutatis mutandis,* a similar tendency toward the collapsing of authority's distinctive flexibility. The history of this relationship is tortuous, for it assumed a different shape with each medieval theologian of consequence and, indeed, along with the issue of reason and faith, was a prime topic for the articulation of doctrinal conflicts. As in the case of the relations between authority and tradition, the changing course of the relations between authority and reason postulated a change in the predominant idea of authority as such.

In its early medieval phase the emphasis was on its spiritual source, its personal incidence, its originative function, and its practical effectiveness: it was the active counterpart of faith; it was faith translated into a rule for living in this world, compatible with the faculty of reason, to which it furnished first principles. In its middle phase authority became a bridging principle, one of the crucial concepts which lent verisimilitude to the scholastic syntheses of transcendental Christianity and Aristotelian naturalism by representing each overlap of faith and reason as an identifiable principle. The idea of authority could have this function because of its inherited spectrum of meanings, ranging from the claims of spirit to the demands of power. In a figure like Aquinas Scripture and Aristotle were dovetailed as "authorities," and the idea of authority itself could be used both for "the principle of origins . . . in divine matters" and for the agency of "coercive force" in "public" affairs (ed. Deferrari, pp. 96–97). The effect of the idea in its synthetic employment was to provide an ontological backing for the dominion of some men over others: thus Aquinas could assert authority to be the natural relationship of superior to inferior in any society of men, whether prelapsarian or postlapsarian, on the principle that through their guidance and direction the superiors were the causes or authors of the actions of their inferiors. In its late medieval phase the idea of authority, which was disjoined from reason along with the

disjunction of faith and reason, tended itself increasingly to become a quality of will and power. Duns Scotus merged the worship due God for his authority as "author" or "cause" of life with that due God for his "omnipotence" (Scotus, VIII, 816–17). When John of Paris distinguished between direction and dominion as modes of control, he assigned the label "authority" (*modum auctoritatis*) to dominion (ed. Alan Gewirth, pp. xlix–l). Ockham finally epitomized the subjugation of authority as a distinctive concept by denying it any role as intermediary between faith and reason. The disjunction *between* the realms of faith and reason entailed, in this view, the primacy of the power of will and of the principle of individuation *within* each realm. In matters of faith, authority was subordinated to the power of the Holy Spirit over individual conscience. In matters of reason the authority both of logic and the moral law was subordinate to individual existences and prescriptions created directly by divine omnipotence.

3. Institutional Authority. The early institutionally conditioned idea of authority found its archetypal expression in the fifth-century formula of Pope Gelasius I on the twofold government of the world: "the sacred authority of the popes (*auctoritas sacrata pontificum*) and the power of kings (*potestas regalis*), with the former the greater of the two by virtue of the account which the popes must render of the kings themselves to God" (Ullmann, p. 23). Authority in this distinctive phase had four characteristic connotations. First, it was spiritual in the double sense that it was the direction of men toward the salvation of their souls and that its agency was separate from the agency of coercive force. Second, it was unified in the double sense that only a unified guidance could lead to man's single final end—i.e., salvation—and that it was indivisible, in contrast to power, which could be divided. Third, it was superior, in the sense that it prescribed what was executed by the wielders of power. Finally, authority was literally transitional in the sense that it was the transfer into the temporal world of what was power in the spiritual world.

In its internal ecclesiastical applications, consequently, there was from the start the tendency toward a terminological confusion of *auctoritas* and *potestas,* since the inherited distinction between the capacity to evoke assent and the right to command obedience was blurred in its application to the "principate of the Roman Church," conceived to be a realm of spirit innocent of physical coercion but yet ordained with a spiritual "power of the keys." "Plenary authority" and "plenary power," for example, were used interchangeably to characterize the administrative mandate conferred on popes and bishops by election (Tierney, pp. 143–46). By and large it may be said that down to the thirteenth century the ideas of authority and power tended to merge in their application within the Roman Church but, as the persistence of the Gelasian formula indicates, they retained their distinctive meanings in their application to the relations between the organized Church and the Christian society as a whole. The net result was an attitude toward authority which equipped its bearers with the power of ecclesiastical coercion in spiritual matters and with the influence to guide action in temporal matters.

But from the thirteenth century conditions both within the Roman Church (heretical and conciliar movements) and outside it (conflict with the temporal powers) converged with the revival of classical modes of thinking to produce a notable change in the medieval idea of authority. The change tended to blend the meanings of the idea in the spiritual and temporal realms of the Christian society, and to produce a simplified notion of authority as the basis of coercive power. Because spiritual authority within the Church became disunited and disputed during this period, Papalists and Conciliarists alike resolved the ecclesiastical ambiguity of authority and power in favor of the more manageable idea of power, with the idea of authority adduced simply to add the connotation of rightful origin to the rightful title already inherent in the idea of power. This idea of authoritative spiritual power within the Roman Church had its analogue in the relations between the emerging separate institutions of church and state, for whether in the Papalist's form of the Pope's "authority" in temporal affairs or the Conciliarist acknowledgment of the temporal ruler's independent "authority" over the externals of ecclesiastical organization, the idea of authority in church-state relations too became inseparable from coercive dominion.

The Papalist version of the late medieval idea of authority was the more explicit. The Papalist writers came to rely increasingly upon the doctrine of the "plenitude of power," redefined during the thirteenth and fourteenth centuries so that it no longer signified the circumscribed papal and episcopal "plenary authority" within the Church, but now referred to the Pope's exclusive and unlimited sovereignty, derived from Christ through Saint Peter and applicable to spiritual and temporal matters alike. Within the Church this doctrine was accompanied by the emphasis on "the power of jurisdiction"—i.e., the governmental power over the Church transmitted from Christ to the Pope alone—and on the subordination of the "sacramental power" bequeathed by Christ to all priests (Wilks, pp. 375–77). Outside the Church, the Pope's plenitude of jurisdictional power was called "authority" no longer, as in the Gelasian formula, to characterize a mere spiritual superiority over the power of temporal rulers but to denote the "supreme temporal power" itself, as it was possessed in its integrity by the Pope before he delegated it to be exercised by secular rulers under his direction. Papal authority, in short, was the form taken by the Pope's spiritual power in the temporal arena.

Against this papal offensive, the intellectual defenders of the secular rulers sought in the main to make a cogent doctrine out of the traditional pluralism in the medieval attitude toward authority. This they did by streamlining the functional multiplicity of the several ordained authorities into a dual track of ecclesiastical authority in the realm of spirit and an Imperial or royal authority in the temporal realm, with this "regal authority" equivalent in function and superior in power to pontifical authority. Only the Conciliar writers, engaging the Papalists all along the extended and wavering line between the spiritual and temporal realms, developed a mirror image of the Papalist idea of authority and carried even further the idea of authority as the absolute spiritual ground of political power. Where the Papalists used the ambiguous meaning of the "church" (*ecclesia*) to include within its spiritual power a spiritual aspect of the temporal realm, the Conciliarists used the ambiguous meaning of the "state" (*civitas* or *regnum*) to include a temporal aspect of the spiritual realm. Moreover, when the Conciliarists argued Christ's direct authorization of "a general council composed of all Christians or of the weightier part of them" as the "principal authority" in the Church and carried it over by implied analogy to "the whole body of citizens, or the weightier part thereof" as the "primary authority" in the state (Marsilius, pp. 45, 280), they placed a Christian imprimatur on the pyramidal model of political authority, operating through representation, to counter the Papalist legacy of the hieratic model of authority, operating through delegation.

Reformations of the sixteenth century initiated nothing essentially new in the principle of authority, but they did mark the denouement of its medieval stage. The Protestant reformers sealed off further development of the Christian idea of authority by merely recapitulating its medieval development. But while they did not significantly change the idea, they did significantly change the conditions to which the idea applied, and they contributed thereby to the change of the idea under other auspices. Whether Luther's break with the Roman Church is explained in terms of religious individualism, arrogant disobedience, or the revolt of the son against the father, it is clear that what he wanted was the institution of different authorities

149

in religion rather than no authorities in religion, and it is clear too that the main-line Protestant reformers—Zwingli and Calvin—followed him in this. To all three, the Word of God was the supreme objective authority for all individuals; this authority took a form external to individuals, since it was manifest in Scripture, an externality epitomized by radicals' reference to the main-liners' Scripture as the "paper Pope."

For the determination of right doctrine and the correct administration of essential sacraments, Scriptural authority was vested in community churches, and the individual's submission to their transmitted authority thus became necessary to salvation. Submission to the temporal authorities was prescribed, finally, for all occasions save the most flagrant political violation of God's Word, on the grounds of the divine ordination of the temporal hierarchy to make possible the untrammelled spiritual operation of the true Church (Davies, passim). This generic position of the main Protestant church-fathers shows even their original conception of their mission to have been not the overthrow of ecclesiastical authority in the name of religious liberty but the reversion to the early spiritual type of religious authority against the late medieval tendency to make the ideas of authority and power overlap.

And yet the Protestant churches of the Reformation developed precisely in the same direction as the Catholic Church which they attacked. Whether in the form of theocracies or of state churches, ecclesiastical authority and political power tended increasingly to merge in Lutheranism, Zwinglianism, Calvinism. The sectarian movements of the radical Reformation resisted the merger precisely as the heretical movements of the later Middle Ages had resisted the merger of authority and power in the Roman Church, and even more strongly in the Protestant than in the Catholic case, the radical sects carried their despair of official authoritative churches to the point of condemning authority along with power in all matters of religion. They called instead upon the immediacy of the Holy Spirit in individuals to replace the authority of tradition, community, and Scripture itself in the mediation of salvation. And when the Protestant churches—notably the Calvinist—did devise a doctrine of resistance to authority in the name of religious liberty during the latter part of the sixteenth century, it was given the same label (monarchomach) and it took the same form as the concurrent Catholic doctrine of resistance to Protestant authority—a form that meant not a new development away from the idea of ecclesiastical authoritative power but only a denial of it to the wrong Church. The problem of authority versus liberty in the determination of ultimate religious truth would, to be

sure, develop into a perennial and provocative concern of Protestant theology, but it did so only in tandem with the more general confrontation which had its main focus in a secular sphere.

The competition of analogous Protestant and Catholic doctrines of authoritative power marked the outer limit of creative religious authority. The situation of several ecclesiastical authorities striving for the monopolistic direction of coercive power was obviously untenable. Since the idea of authority had come to provide a necessary higher unity for the collective thought and action of human communities, a more unified authority than the competing claims to divine ordination could afford became an urgent intellectual and practical necessity. The resulting shift in the locus of authority, from transcendent religion to natural politics, and the concomitant revival of its autonomous function, was part of the new mentality which introduced the modern period of Western history.

IV

The third period in the history of the idea of authority comprised the era from the late sixteenth to the late nineteenth centuries, the era in which the realm of politics became its central arena and the contiguous realm of nature was consistently invoked as its source. The older hybrid traditions of authority as the titles of one or another power-wielding hierarchy—family, church, aristocracy—persisted in the new era, but political authority now overshadowed them, paradoxically as the one kind of authority that underwent change by being distinguished in principle from the power it exercised. It was also the one idea of authority that was to have a continuous history in the period, hardening gradually into an attitude which subjected political authority once more to the idea of power. But if this rigidification of the idea of political authority in the eighteenth and nineteenth centuries was a familiar process, there was one development of authority in its political period which was entirely unprecedented: a liberal response to politicized authority arose which for the first time accepted the necessity of power to authority, conceived human freedom as the antithesis of rather than an assumption for the exercise of authority, and rejected the very principle of authority as a dominant value of the human community. The categorical character of this break in the development of the idea makes it advisable to distinguish the early-modern from the modern phase of political authority.

1. The Early-Modern Idea of Political Authority. The pioneering political theorists of the sixteenth and seventeenth centuries detached human nature from its upper linkages to the sources of divine, moral, and ancestral authority and retained its lower linkage with men's political communities. The cause of the detachment was the conflict among the religious, ethical, and familial principles of authority which vitiated their crucial function of providing an unquestioned unified basis of social organization, and the result was to connect nature with politics as the rationally necessary source of the social unity that states were achieving in practice. Authority was now conceived to be the voluntary creation of natural individuals for the expressly political function of providing the coercive power of governments with an origin and a purpose which transcended this power but was directly relevant to it.

The idea of authority thus became the characteristic principle connecting natural with political man; the orbit of authority became an outermost ring of politics. The establishment of this uncoercive sphere within an expanded realm of politics meant more than the formal dislocation of authority from the acknowledged superiority of higher over lower realms in the human hierarchy to the acknowledged superiority of the final over the instrumental orbits of the same realm. The shift also brought with it a substantive alteration in the grounds of authority: whereas the older mediation had stressed the origins of the authority as the primary ground of its validity, the newer stressed the inseparability of the origins of the authority and the ends for which it was originated.

One of the consequences of this change, obviously, was to prepare the way theoretically for the modern emphasis on the attainment of ends as the dominant criterion of the validity of authority. But a more immediate consequence was the paradoxical authoritarianism of the early-modern phase whereby the political authority produced by the joint decision of roughly equal individuals was deemed by those individuals to be more irresistible than had been the traditional authorities who were part of the fundamental structure of the universe. The obvious reason for the intensification of a political authority theoretically grounded in the free consent of its constituent subjects was the voluntary factor originally built into it, but more important for the irreversibility of this authority was the stipulation of social unity as a final end for this authority which transcended any particular exercise or abuse of its coercive powers.

Integral as this distinctive idea of political authority proved to be, its formulation was the gradual product of the various emphases brought to bear by different early-modern theorists on the several aspects of the process. Machiavelli, for example, suspect and misunderstood as his apparent focus on naked power may have been, did contribute the detachment of the authority of divine providence, Christian morality, and "ancestral usages" from politics. However ambiguous his position on the ends of politics was, moreover, his distinction between the insecurity of de facto princely power, on the one hand, and the pre-coercive authority of the people who empower their elected officials or the uncoercive authority of the "legislator" who establishes the principles of government and then divests himself of its power, on the other, adumbrated the differential origins of political power and authority as such.

Jean Bodin, in turn, was ambiguous on the origins of political authority, attributing it alternately to the free choice of family-heads and "to all those who have recognized power to command another," but he contributed to the conversion of old antitheses between political and suprapolitical goals into a hierarchy of instrumental and final ends, appropriate to the exercise of political power and authority, respectively. From the point of view of power—i.e., "necessity"—the material activities of the state have priority, followed by its moral activities and its intellectual activities in that order. From the point of view of the state's authority—i.e., "dignity"—the priorities are precisely reversed (Bodin, pp. 5–18).

For the combination of these factors making for an independent idea of political authority—that is, for the combination of natural origins prior to the exercise of power with the final ends exceeding the exercise of power—we must look to Hobbes. Positing a natural equality of human capacities, wants, and necessities which abolished the natural and moral hierarchies behind traditional authority and positing too an idea of power as a natural force which "no man can transfer . . . in a natural manner," Hobbes developed an explicit definition of political authority which was both consistent with the presumption of extra-political equality and indispensable to the establishment of a distinctively political—that is, of transferred—power. Hobbes defined authority literally and exclusively in terms of authorization—that is, as the "right of doing any act" which is commissioned by an "author," who has the original right, to a "representative," whose actions in this commission continue to be "owned" by the original author and are thus "done by Authority" (Hobbes, pp. 83–85). This general definition of authority, moreover, was obviously preliminary to the political definition of the sovereign as the "common representer," "one person, of whose acts a great multitude, by mutual covenants one with another, have made themselves every one the author, to the end he may use the strength and means of them all . . ." (pp. 87, 89). The authorities of individual men are thereby unified into the one authority of the sovereign, since each member of the multitude avows himself in advance to be "the

151

author" of the acts undertaken by the "one will" of the sovereign. It is thus through the medium of authority that "power and strength" are conveyed to and legitimated in the sovereign.

This function of political authority in Hobbes and his followers was obviously an attempt to re-think the *origins* of temporal government so as to root it in the new atomized and unhierarchical conception of reality: political authority in this sense was the concept which represented the conversion of ultimate individual wills into the support of a single collective power. But the function of political authority here was also crucially related to the *ends* of temporal government. Ostensibly, the end of the state in Hobbes is simple: "peace and common defence" (ibid., p. 90). Actually, however, this formula masks an apparent dilemma between the prudential versus the moral character of this end and of the obligations prescribed by it. On the one hand, the sovereign power to achieve the common peace and defence is the product of a positive calculation by which individuals "confer" their natural power, in exchange for the benefit of security; the obverse is the negative calculation whereby each individual limits his natural power over things in consideration of an equally tangible "fear of punishment" by the sovereign power. But, on the other hand, Hobbes also insisted that when individuals "confer" their natural power they do more than merely exchange it for visible benefits or limit it in view of visible punishments. The conferment of individual powers upon a sovereign power creates a moral obligation of obedience over and above any finite calculation of benefits because the subject has "authorized" every action of the sovereign in advance and because the subject is bound by his own "intention" in instituting government. Both grounds refer to a source of obligation which transcends the public power—that is, to political authority.

The expansibility of the state by the dimension of its authority so clearly implied in the curious flexibility of the rigorous Hobbes, was precisely stated by his follower, Samuel Pufendorf, in his correlative concepts of the ruler's "imperfect rights" and the subject's "imperfect obligations" (Pufendorf, II, 289). These rights and obligations referred to rulers' prescriptions and citizens' compliance which were both valid and unenforceable. Here, exactly, was the operational increment added by political authority to political power.

2. The Modern Idea of Political Authority. The early-modern consensus on political authority as the valid authorization of political power developed into two opposing attitudes toward authority. A liberal attitude, by and large predominant henceforward, made authority an aspect of political power and reduced it to the status of a necessary evil, inevitably opposed and normatively inferior to individual freedom. A conservative attitude resurrected the autonomy of extra-political authority—that is, of the old social and ontological hierarchies—and made political power their logical consequence. This conservative version stressed the voluntary and even spontaneous commitment of subordinates to their authorities, and contrasted it to the potential reality of a democratic dictatorship which made the enforcement of equal liberty an aspect of political power.

In each of these versions the inferior principle was acknowledged as valid in its own sphere, however inferior: the liberals reluctantly recognized a delimited sphere of authoritative power, and the conservatives admitted the validity of an individual liberty whose exercise must be regulated. Despite their overt conflict over the value of authority, liberals and conservatives thus shared mirror images of the proportionate relation between authority and liberty. They also shared a susceptibility to the intellectual currents of the modern period. The actual content of modern ideas of political authority came from the succession of empirical, idealist, and scientist intellectual modes which affected liberals and authoritarians alike. The sequence produced, as exemplars, Locke, Rousseau, Marx, and Mill in the liberal school, and Burke, Hegel, and Comte in the conservative school.

The initial assumptions of the liberal position were set by Locke when he used the empirical employment of reason to posit the primacy of intellectual freedom, and the natural-law idea of government to posit the primacy of freedom in politics. For Locke and the empiricists who followed him, intellectual authority was associated both with the repressiveness of sectarian dogma and with the compulsion of deductive reasoning from putatively self-evident axioms on the Cartesian model. What was freely embraced as self-evident by some must be taken on trust by others, and what was necessarily concluded from it must take on the aspect of coercion from the outside. In politics, analogously, the empiricists associated authority with power and, by virtue of this association, remained chronically suspicious of it. Locke persisted in refuting as invalid "paternal power" that which Filmer justified as "fatherly authority," and Locke himself referred to the legislative sovereign, which he so stringently limited, indiscriminately as the "Supream Authority" and the "Supream Power" (Filmer, pp. 58, 62; Locke, pp. 162, 376–78).

But the generally hostile attitude of the empiricists toward authority, based upon their view of it as an aspect of power, was qualified by their acknowledgment of an uncoercive dimension of it, transitional and subordinate in scope but adequate to explain the limited validity which was conceded to authoritative power. Thus Locke implicitly accepted the temporary intellectual authority of men who show the way to truth through their exemplary use of the "natural faculties" common to all over those who first receive such truth as "imperfect and unsteady notions." In politics he explicitly provided for a valid if sporadic autonomous role for authority when he legitimated the exercise of supreme legislative power over society only "by Authority received" from the society itself; and the supreme power, therefore, was a trustee of this authority (Locke, p. 374). Since Locke declared the supreme power to be sacred and inviolable in its execution of the trust, save for egregious violation, the original authority was confined to an emergency role while the transferred authority simply legitimated the daily exercise of political power.

Rousseau pioneered the application of idealism to the liberal idea of authority, laying down the doctrines that would run as assumptions from Kant to Giuseppe Mazzini. The anti-authoritarian cast of liberal idealism was patent in Rousseau's use of equality to provide the uniformity which had been the traditional function of authority. He rejected any "natural authority" of one man over another, and he made no distinction between the invalid claims to such authority and the invalid exercise of power by the claimant. Moreover, his labelling of the general will interchangeably as the "sovereign power" and the "sovereign authority" left little autonomous scope for an idea of authority between the equal rights of the constituent individuals and the collective legislative power into which they were immediately converted. Thus an act of sovereignty on the one hand involves no "superior" and "inferior" or even any conformity of one person's will to another's; but on the other hand it is guaranteed by "the public force" (Rousseau, II, 27–45). The social contract produces, not authority as in seventeenth-century theory, but the transmutation of one kind of liberty (natural) into another (civil and moral).

But Rousseau did provide for one kind of exceptional authority, distinct both from the citizen's rights and the government's powers. In appearance an atavistic classical revival, it foreshadowed the one generally acceptable function of autonomous authority in modern times. Rousseau resorted to the initiative of the unofficial, extralegal "Legislator" who, "capable of using neither force nor reason, must recur to an authority of another order, which can engage men without violence and persuade without convincing them" (Rousseau, II, 51–53). This was an archaic formulation of the inimitable innovative role of authority. In the form of a temporary dictatorship of the virtuous elite who would inaugurate regimes of democratic freedom Robespierre and Mazzini would modernize this role of authority into the one kind of power that was not reducible to men's liberties and yet would be a final resort of liberals in search of a lever for change.

Karl Marx and John Stuart Mill, each in his own way, applied the logic of science to the principles of liberal idealism and thereby developed the liberal attitude toward authority into a definite but compound concept of authority. In this liberal concept authority was indissolubly joined to power, but there was in it a categorical distinction between the conservative function of authority which subordinates it to the needs of any established power and the innovative function of authority which subordinates the executive powers to its own transcendent design. For Marx, authority in the first function was a simple rationalization of oppressive power and material exploitation; as such, it has characterized every stable society. Authority in the second sense would be embodied in the dictatorship of the proletariat, as the transitional agency with the function of directing political power beyond the class purposes which are essential to political power into the classless society which dispenses with political power. "Revolution," admitted Engels in his article "On Authority," "is the most authoritarian thing there is" (F. Engels, "Über das Autoritätsprinzip (Dell' Autorità)," in *Die Neue Zeit*, **32,** 1 [1914]).

Mill articulated his idea of authority as a principle of control even more precisely when he pronounced the most prominent theme in modern history to be the persistent "struggle between Liberty and Authority" in which liberty was the superior principle and authority, in the sense of political power abetted by the social tyranny of the majority, the threat to it (Mill, pp. 121–33). In the main line of Mill's argument, authority, power, and compulsion were equivalent, and they represented the collective antithesis of liberty—conceived as exclusively individual—which must necessarily either limit them or be limited by them. "The authority of society over the individual" was inevitably a coercive authority, using political power and social constraints as equivalent means and validly employed only in the compulsive function of enforcing the protection of its members from injury. In his essay "On Liberty," Mill denied the whole category of uncoercive authority which had traditionally mediated between official power and individual freedom, for he rejected the functions it was designed to perform for individuals in favor of functions to be performed by individuals for themselves. When he addressed himself to the time-honored function of authority in producing social unity, Mill not only denied authority as a means but repudiated the hitherto sacred quest for unity as an end, exalting individuality and diversity in its stead. 153

For men to act "in a way prescribed to them by authority, and, therefore, by the necessary conditions of the case, the same for all," is to follow "a narrow theory of life" (Mill, pp. 177–78).

But like other liberals Mill too resurrected an autonomous authority as a kind of *deus ex machina* to initiate movement between the rigidly balanced spheres of freedom and power. Mill's theoretical stasis resulted from the antinomy in his theory of anti-authoritarian democracy: the majority of the individuals whom he declared liberated from superior authority themselves formed a coercive uniform authority over the rest, imposing thereby not only a new kind of egalitarian tyranny but, by crushing originality, a paralysis of human affairs. "No government by a democracy or a numerous aristocracy, either in its political acts or in the opinions, qualities, and tone of mind which it fosters, ever did or could rise above mediocrity, except insofar as the sovereign Many have let themselves be guided . . . by the counsels and influence of a more highly gifted and instructed One or Few" (ibid., pp. 181–82).

Characteristically, in view of the political orientation of the period, Mill proposed that this innovative authority occupy a higher, uncoercive level within government itself. His formula for government was "the greatest dissemination of power consistent with efficiency, but the greatest possible centralization of information and diffusion of it from the center," and he expected that in contrast to its limited "actual power" the central governmental organ of this function would issue "advice," which "would naturally carry much authority" (ibid., pp. 227–28). Thus in the final analysis, even this remnant of independent innovating authority remained connected with the authority in power, with the effect of merely softening the harsh impact of necessary coercion upon human liberty.

Conservative theorists of authority between the mid-eighteenth and the mid-nineteenth centuries reversed the relationships posited by the liberals and emerged with a different idea of authority itself. Where the liberals aligned authority with power and acknowledged a subordinate place to both vis-à-vis freedom, conservatives aligned freedom with power and acknowledged a subordinate place to both vis-à-vis authority. Since the theory of conservatism (as distinct from men's hoary conservative attitude) arose to counter the offensive of liberal theory the correspondence is hardly surprising. The conservatives, like the liberals, acknowledged the association of authority with political power—in view of the period's actual focus on political and constitutional issues they could hardly do otherwise—but where the liberals acknowledged persistent authority as a function of power the conservatives acknowledged power as an outgrowth of persistent authority. And where liberals tended to conceive the relationship of authority and liberty disjunctively, as an opposition of coercion and freedom, reconcilable only through the intermittent innovative function of authority, the conservatives conceived the relationship conjunctively. For them men's liberty and the authoritative control over its valid extent were complements; men's continuous assent to the permanent ordering function of authority made for a constant harmony between liberty and coercion.

The conservative theory of authority first arose from Edmund Burke's empirical approach to the stratified reality of the eighteenth-century political society in his *Reflections on the Revolution in France* (1790). He made ideas out of the facts of most men's persistent loyalties to their traditional institutions, and deliberately opposed them to the despotic union of freedom and force. Declaring that "liberty, when men act in bodies, is power," Burke invoked an organic compound of accepted institutions, traditions, and beliefs—a compound covered by the idea of autonomous authorities—to restrain the liberty and shape the power. When it acts "as if in the presence of canonized forefathers, the spirit of freedom, leading in itself to misrule and excess, is tempered with an awful gravity." The governing power, similarly, should be viewed as constituted by a whole series of "establishments"—"established church," "established monarchy," "established aristocracy," and "established democracy"—whose function is to build the authority of religious principle, fundamental law, permanent property, and local attachment into the very exercise of political power. Thus is "power" rendered "gentle" by the support of "ancient opinions and rules of life" (Burke, pp. 19, 33, 43, 62, 90–91, 105–08).

The same idealistic impulse which developed the idea of liberty into the doctrine of freedom elaborated the revived appreciation of tradition into a new philosophy of authority. Starting from the insight vouchsafed by the individualistic premises of the liberal spokesmen, conservative idealists approached authority as a fundamental type of interpersonal relations. The most profound of these—indeed, the most penetrating and fruitful analysis of authority ever written—was undoubtedly in Hegel's discussion of "Lordship and Bondage" (*Herrschaft und Knechtschaft*) in his *Phenomenology of Mind* of 1807 (Hegel, *Phenomenology*, pp. 228–40). As in the rest of the *Phenomenology* the reference of the analysis was at once historical and ontological: the master-servant relationship of a past era was the historical form of the universal relationship of independence and dependence among individuals which has been built into every consciousness as a persistent category of human experience. The differentiation of individuals into superiors and subordinates, in this analysis, is a necessary moment in the essential process of the individual's realizing his own identity by becoming conscious of himself as an independent being. This process is a common social enterprise because individuals can become certain of their own identities only when they are confirmed by the recognition of others, and the distinction between superior and subordinate consciousnesses is an essential mode of recognition in this common enterprise. The distinction is essential originally because there is an inevitable superiority of the individual who secures recognition of his independence over the individual who recognizes it by serving him. But if the *ascertainment* of individual identity through recognition thus starts from an initial one-directional hierarchy of independent and dependent individuals, with equal necessity its *realization* requires the development of reciprocity and of mutual recognition. The relationship thus begins to assume the character of a division of function within the common enterprise of achieving the self-identity of all individuals. For the master becomes dependent upon the servant for the recognition of his independence and requires an independence in the servant for this external recognition; the servant, analogously, internalizes the independence he recognizes in the ruler and confirms his own identity in the external form which he gives to his labor for the master.

The crucial features of Hegel's analysis were, first, the demonstration that the recognition of the superior by the subordinate for his function in an enterprise common to both is the fundamental factor in an authoritative relationship and, second, his explicit inference that this relationship must inevitably transcend the power of the master over the servant to entail the mutual dependence of their functions and the reciprocal independence of their identities as superior and subordinate.

Thus unlimited hierarchical power, the original form of authority, was essentially modified in Hegel's scheme by the equalizing exchange of its qualities between the superior who becomes dependent and the subordinate who gets oriented toward independence as each looks to the other in their joint realization of authority. From this scheme two consequences could follow: the master-servant dialectic could proceed to the complete equalization and mutual identification of the parties or the original hierarchy and determinate identities of superior and subordinate could be synthesized in an open-ended process which would preserve the essential elements of both. The Young Hegelians, including Marx, would draw the first conclusion. Hegel himself proceeded to draw the second. He produced the standard conservative philosophy of political authority, in which the publicly recognized political power of the sovereign over his subjects was the mold which gave a hierarchical form to the ultimate values of free individuals. Political authority furnished the only principle of hierarchy whose origin was acceptable to free individuals and whose purpose transcended the range of its original power. For Hegel, this authority of the state, vis-à-vis its constituent individuals and families, was both "their higher power" and "their immanent purpose." The function of the sovereign monarch is precisely to unite authority and power in the state. The princely power, and the other powers of the state *a fortiori*, are valid only as organs in the service of the "unconditioned," "self-starting," and "self-determined" authority of the monarch to realize the moral unity of the state (Hegel, *Philosophie des Rechts*, pp. 209–16, 240–45). For Hegel, and for conservative idealists in general, the coercive powers of these organs are appropriate instruments of this moral authority.

Scientism, in the shape of French positivism, provided still a third dimension to the conservative doctrine of authority. Positivism as such, with its rejection of belief and its insistence upon observation, experience, experiment, and *a posteriori* reasoning, seemed to offer a hostile environment for ideas of authority, as Mill's version of the doctrine attests, and even in its native French form it would sponsor progressive sociology as well as authoritarian politics. But the conservative political line of positivist origin was not therefore merely fortuitous. The commitment to authority which seemed eccentric and ambiguous in Auguste Comte, the founder of positivism, would be regularized into firm political principle in later positivists like Hippolyte Taine, Charles Maurras, and Vilfredo Pareto. For the mechanics of scientific political conservatism it is nonetheless to Comte that we must look. His combination of the modern claims for social science with the equally modern view of political authority as the official exercise of power first revealed the distinctive feature in the modern conservative idea of political authority—the insistence both upon the immunity of social superiors from political power and upon their capacity to employ political power.

Comte explicitly posed the problem by declaring the crucial issue for society to be precisely the relationship between spiritual and temporal authority. Spiritual authorities—i.e., the intellectual elite—direct social belief through "neither force nor reason," but rather through the "confidence spontaneously accorded intellectual and moral superiority." Temporal authorities—i.e., the political governors—control social action through the application of "practical or material power." Comte's overt solution of their relationship was to assign spiritual authority innovative priority in the direction of social progress (in "dynamic sociology") and political authority conservative priority in the maintenance of social order (in "static sociology"), and to insist upon their mutual separation and inviolability. Actually, however, he went beyond this nominal solution, which scarcely differed in principle from the liberal Mill's, to the characteristic conservative device of connecting the uncoercive authority of the innovator or the founder with the coercive authority of the organs which would enforce the innovation. Comte created the conservative model of this device by stipulating the orderly mission of the innovation and the quasi-political structure of the innovating authority. Thus the function of spiritual authority in the static positivist society of the future will be to educate men continuously in the understanding of the social order as a whole. As such, spiritual authority was associated with temporal power in the sense of "attaching morality to politics as the latter's point of departure." By dint of this attachment, in turn, spiritual authority assumed the equivalent of a political structure. This authority is a "moral government"; it "rules ideas and morals"; it must "institute a system of public and private manners (*habitudes*) favoring the growth of the feeling of social solidarity, on the model of [medieval] Catholicism"; it arbitrates social disputes and includes international relations within its competence. In its social monopoly over education, the intellectual authority is "decisive," as is the temporal authority in the sphere of politics (Comte, II, 485–602).

Comte's innovative intellectual authority may be viewed as the limiting case for the modern conservative idea of authority in general. Whenever the function of nonpolitical authority was conceived to be the extension of human community rather than training for the rights of man, this authority was deemed both continuous with and formative of valid political authority. Whether such nonpolitical authority was progressive and intellectual like Comte's or traditional and corporate like Taine's, its political role was made theoretically possible by the osmotic exchange through which conservative theorists modified the principled independence of social from political authority. They admitted a social equivalent of political power in the functioning of social authority and a moral equivalent of social authority in the ultimate ends of political power. They sought thereby to regularize and modernize the principle of hierarchy which was being compressed by the dominant liberal temper of nineteenth-century Europe to the status of a chronic anachronism with at best a transitional validity.

V

In the recent period of its history, the idea of authority has been examined most intensively in its social context and the idea has been developed most revealingly in social science and social theory. As in the other main periods and contexts of its development, two distinct stages must be identified. From the late nineteenth century to the 1920's changes in the approach to authority were embodied especially in the writings of sociologists who took over from the preceding period the integral association of authority and power in politics but who sought to work out autonomous roles for social authority as such, consonant with the autonomy of the social science which they were establishing. In its second stage the ideas of social authority have been reunited with political power both approvingly in the ideology of fascist totalitarianism and reprovingly in the equally total revulsion of the New—i.e., post-communist—Left from it.

1. Sociology of Authority. Because they reflected the new preeminence of industrial society as the primary unit of human association and the main arena of collective activity, the great pioneers of sociology assiduously recast authority into a social relation signifying a voluntary or conventional interaction categorically detached from its political connection with coercive power. But because this early age of the industrial society was also a period of democratization these founders of sociology had also to take into account the interpenetration of society and state. They tended also to be political sociologists who approached politics as a special kind of social relation. Hence they sought to develop the idea of autonomous social authorities which were independent of the modern state in their origins but were integrated into it, as a social dimension of politics, in their contemporary effects. They thus carried one stage further the sociological politics of the conservative positivists and reversed their priorities: where the positivists extended the state into society and applied political criteria of coercion to social relations, the sociologists extended society into the state and sought to develop double-edged concepts appropriate to the intersection.

The only pure—i.e., spontaneous and uncoercive—social authorities in the new sociology tended to be dead authorities. Almost invariably these authorities were identified as prestigious individuals, patriarchal elders, hallowed traditions, or divinely anointed men and offices whose origins in and relevance to an earlier stage of society were emphatically acknowledged by the sociologists. They also acknowledged the persistence of such authorities into modern times, to be sure, but only as atavisms. Thus the early Émile Durkheim

(1893) assigned authority to the declining repressive type of society and equality to the progressing organic type. "The authority of the collective conscience is . . . in large part composed of the authority of tradition," and, in turn, "it is the authority of age [the old people, the unique intermediary between the present and the past] which gives tradition its authority." Both of these associated authorities—of tradition and the elders—"necessarily diminish" along with the archaic, segmental type of society from which they come (Durkheim, *Division of Labor*, pp. 291–93).

The sociologists' atavistic definition of social authority received a precise terminological confirmation from Max Weber, divergent as his sociological assumptions were from Durkheim's in other respects. Weber carefully distinguished from the concept of "power" (*Macht*) the "more precise sociological concept of 'authority'" (*Herrschaft*), defining power as "any probability of imposing one's will within a social relationship even against resistance" and authority as "the probability of securing obedience to definite commands from a relevant group of men" (Weber, *Grundriss*, pp. 28–29). Weber's general definition of authority was obviously designed to include within the sociological concept the social dimension of political "commands" which produced obedience without coercion, but, as the connotation of *Herrschaft*—lordship or dominion—indicates, this general definition enclosed an ambiguity between the more or less compelling motives of obedience. Weber made no explicit distinctions of principle within authority as *Herrschaft*, since he acknowledged "the belief in legitimacy" to be the indispensable basis of all its forms, but in his elaboration of the three main types of authority a verbal distinction appeared which reflected a subtle differentiation within his idea of authority. When analyzing the concept of *Herrschaft* in the context of the "compliance, . . . the will to obey" on the part of its objects, Weber added the imported term *Autorität* in apposition with *Herrschaft*, and in his analysis of the three legitimate bases of *Herrschaft* he applied *Autorität* to the charismatic and traditional types of authority but only *Herrschaft* to the legal, or bureaucratic, type (ibid., p. 122; Weber, *Religionssoziologie*, I, 268–73). Since Weber thought of the three types as successively dominant in the development of society he was implying a distinctive connotation of authority—*Autorität*—for the two types he recognized frankly to be primarily representative of "the past" and to extend only "as survivals" into the present.

The obvious point of this historical approach to social authority was to indicate as sociological fact what had for some three centuries been proposed as anthropological principle: that the religious and natural hierarchies, such as the church and the family, which had traditionally anchored the social roots of authority were now declining institutions, supported rather by the inertia of past social relations than by relevance to contemporary society. But this empirical confirmation was not the main function of the social analysis. Its main function was rather to set in relief the separate identity of the principle of authority which was relevant to the contemporary industrial society. This modern principle of authority had to be defined both in terms of the new dependence upon the rational calculations of coercive power which distinguished it from the outmoded autonomous social authorities of the past, and in terms of its inheritance from these social authorities of the past. Hence the sociologists analyzed the relationship of the old and new authorities as both a difference of type and a succession of stages for the purposes of demonstrating the political categories dominating modern ideas of authority and examining the modern role of the atavistic social authorities. The results of these inquiries indicated, in general, the actual role of modern ideas of authority to be the social buttressing of political hierarchy, but their *normative* role to be the rational organization of the highly integrated modern industrial society. For an example of the first kind of analysis we may refer to Pareto's revealing categories. For an example of the second we may refer to the collaborative sociological study by Max Horkheimer's Institute for Social Research on "authority and family."

Although Pareto, in *The Mind and Society*, distinguished formally between "a governing, political elite" and "a non-governing, non-political elite" within the generic elite class and defined membership in this generic elite by a superior capacity in any social activity whatsoever, he proceeded to work out the authority of this elite in terms of its relations with political power. It became, in the context of its authority over the nonelite, simply "the higher stratum of society, which usually contains the rulers"; their superior capacities were epitomized into what was suitable for "keeping them in power" and "exercising the functions of government" and what kept them "willing enough to use force" (Pareto, #2041–57). The circulation of elites, moreover, is a process which is effected primarily in the lower-class nonelite's moving into the governing elite and in elitists' dropping out of the governing class through a process which demonstrates the inevitable triumph of superior political capacity, wherever it may be found, over social "label." Thus Pareto's theory of the elite served both to blur the lines between social and political dominant classes in favor

157

of the latter and to subordinate authority, as a tool of social persuasion, to the ever-changing possessors of political power.

In their monumental *Studien über Autorität und Familie* (*Studies of Authority and the Family*) of 1936, the team of democratic socialists associated with Horkheimer in the Institute for Social Research (*Institut für Sozialforschung*) faced squarely the decisive problem raised by the sociological approach to authority: that social authority was a characteristic product of the declining, pre-industrial stage of Western civilization and yet that authority in some form remained a prominent feature of the industrial age. Alerted by the recent rise of fascist totalitarianism—in Horkheimer's words, by "the transition to so-called authoritative forms of state in the present period"—the Institute team, which included Erich Fromm and Herbert Marcuse, saw authority, in the general sense of the "affirmed dependence" of "the larger part of men" upc.. "the smaller," as a central category of "all forms of society," both archaic and modern, and they conceived their mission to be the understanding of the changing forms of authority which corresponded to the changing forms of society (*Studien*, pp. 22–25).

The most striking theoretical contribution of the project was embodied in the convergent demonstration (by Horkheimer, Fromm, and Marcuse from their respective sociological, socio-psychological, and socio-philosophical approaches) of the underlying authoritarianism in the apparently anti-authoritarian attitudes of the modern, liberal. "bourgeois" era. Liberals, in this view, created a new form of authority by stressing the voluntary submission of putatively free individuals to natural, metaphysical, or psychic constraints which were actually reified forms of authoritarian control by a dominant social group. The Institute team acknowledged, from this historical analysis, that authority had both progressive (innovative) and reactionary (repressive) functions for society. But they stopped short of applying their models of authority to the mature industrial society of their own day. The signs of dissolution in the characteristically bourgeois forms of authority—the forms of economic exploitation—were both obviously perceptible and theoretically accountable, but contemporary forms of authority to replace them were not. For there was a profound difference between the team's theoretical expectation of a "rational authority," freely accepted by "the executors" from "the directors" of joint social enterprises in the common interest of both, and their actual perception of the "total-authoritarian state" which made impossible "the hierarchy of authorities" in society necessary for any "system of authority" (ibid., pp. 48, 134–35, 219–22).

Nor was the problem posed by the gulf between the normative and actual tendencies of modern authority resolved by the Institute's empirical inquiry into the structure of the contemporary family, which was approached not as an archaic locus of authority but rather as a social microcosm of all authority. The empirical section of the *Studien* was a progress report, stipulating the completeness of the method and the incompleteness of the result. Only the tentative indication of a social split between a peasantry still involved in the patriarchal family, an urban working class inclined toward the matriarchal family, and a lower middle class (*Mittelstand*) caught indecisively between both tendencies, furnished a substantive confirmation of the crisis of divided social authorities which was throwing the social "education for authority" into the hands of the totalitarian state (ibid., pp. 75, 304–18, 905).

2. *Totalitarian Authority.* Even the furthest sociological advance toward the definition of a modern principle of social authority fell short of the reality of contemporary society and remained an essentially historical definition. The further development of the idea of authority lay with the political totalitarians and with the radical antitotalitarians who have reacted constructively against them. Both groups acknowledge that the contemporary vacuum of social authority is being filled with political instruments of social control. Both the totalitarians and the radical antitotalitarians of the twentieth century have thus gone a crucial step beyond the conservatives and liberals of the nineteenth: where nineteenth-century political thinkers had defended the superiority of authority or liberty respectively but admitted the autonomy and subordinate validity of the opposite principle, their twentieth-century socio-political successors asserted the exclusive validity of authority or liberty respectively, and categorically worked out the entire absorption or denial of the opposite principle.

The development of a distinctive totalitarian idea of authority has been largely the work of fascists, for however authoritarian in practice the structure and policies of communist parties and regimes may be, they correspond to no viable idea of authority. Soviet ideology has tended to exacerbate the special ambiguity of authority which arose when Lenin specified Marx's innovative dictatorship of the majority to be in the charge of a centralized and disciplined professional vanguard who would use violence and terror to initiate the regime of freedom—the ambiguity, that is, of stressing power and liberty to the detriment of any intermediary concept of authority. Thus the occasional ideological concessions, during the Stalin period, to the factual conversion of the revolutionary vanguard into a long-term political and bureaucratic elite—concessions manifest in such concepts of authority as "the vocation of leadership" and the "monolithic Party"—remained theoretically isolated, alternating with the more frequent endorsement of democratic controls from below and excluded from the dominant theory which justifies present political power in terms of future freedom from politics (Moore, passim).

Despite the actual penetration of state and party into the society, moreover, communists distinguish in principle between the political power which withers away and the social organization which remains, a distinction which again obscures the idea of authority. For it remains uncertain, in doctrine, whether the replacement of the government of men by the administration of things is making for a rational society with an uncoercive guiding authority or for a free society with a functionally differentiated collaboration among equals.

For the fascists, on the contrary, the idea of authority was so central to both their programs and their policies as to escape the problems of interpretation which the professed instrumentalism of their doctrine and the glaring inconsistencies of their theory and practice raise for so many of their other ideas. Certain of these problems, indeed—like the relations between the conservative and revolutionary facets of fascism—are illuminated by the clarity of their approach to authority. For the fascists, the political model of authority—the recognition of legitimacy in the organs which actually exercise the collective power of the society—was the model of authority as such, and the conservative retention or the revolutionary dismantling of the existing social authorities varied with the requirements of the political model.

The political definition of social authority was explicit in *La dottrina del Fascismo*, published under Mussolini's name but written by Giovanni Gentile, philosopher of Italian Fascism: "The State not only is authority which governs and molds individual wills with laws and values of spiritual life, but it is also power which makes its will prevail abroad. . . . For the Fascist, everything is within the State and . . . neither individuals or groups are outside the State. . . . For Fascism the State is an absolute, before which individuals and groups are only relative" (Mussolini, pp. 12–16, 33). The Fascist model of political authority thus extended through the social structure and the external spheres of private rights to implant the rule of coercive power within the innermost spirit of the individual. "The Fascist State . . . is the form and internal norm of the whole person. . . . Fascism aims at discipline, and at an authority which penetrates the soul and rules there incontestably" (ibid., pp. 17–18). For, as Gentile would explain in his own name, there

is no essential distinction between "the two terms 'State' and 'individual': far from being "a limit to his liberty," the State "is the universal aspect of the individual, . . . the concrete actuality of his will" (Gentile, pp. 124–31).

Like fascists in general, the German National Socialists used the idea of authority in a political context to link the public power with an original principle detached from any roots in and responsibility to social tradition or democratic rights. In *Mein Kampf* Hitler almost invariably referred to authority as "state authority" (*Staatsautorität*) and he repeatedly characterized the Nazi conception of authority as one "which knows only an authority which proceeds downward from the top and a responsibility which proceeds upward from the bottom" (*Speeches*, I, 180, 201, 502). But unlike the Italian Fascists, the Nazis denied the cultural primacy of the State and hence undermined the ultimacy of its authority as the valid source of political power. For Hitler, the belief that the very existence of the State is the ground of its sanctity and requires "the dog-like veneration of the so-called state authority" was a "legitimist" absurdity which distorted a means into an end-in-itself. Actually, the State is "a means to the end of maintaining and promoting the racial nation (*Volkstum*)," and the State authority is "the sovereign incorporation of a racial nation's instinct and common will for self-preservation" (*Mein Kampf*, pp. 426, 433, 440). For the Nazis, then, political authority was explicitly instrumental, and they referred it, for its own legitimacy, to the suprapolitical good of the race whose instrument it was. Here was the basis in Nazi doctrine for the later claim, to be made by Nazis and anti-Nazis alike, that National Socialism neither espoused nor realized the totalitarian state, since political institutions composed but one of its several lines of control. But it was precisely because it was deemed a political instrument that the principle of authority became crucial in the Nazi scheme, for it became the transferable means of applying the political model of power to all the lines of fascist control—Party, corporate, and personal—and made possible a plural totalitarianism transcending the traditional organs of state.

The idea of authority was the point at which the traditional principle of hierarchy and the modern principle of national sovereignty were joined to become compatible means of power for all social organizations whatsoever. Hitler, for example, endorsed two ideas of authority which were reminiscent of its original meanings, but he now linked them closely to the exercise of coercive power: first, "the authority of personality," which cannot brook control by "any majority"; secondly, the authority of leadership in the sense of initiation, which is a power conferred by the community, is "a high responsibility to the community," and makes the fundamental natural relationship between "initiation" (*Führung*) and "execution" (*Ausführung*) the justification of the power relationship between "domination" (*Überordnung*) and "subordination" (*Unterordnung*) (Hitler, *Tischgespräche*, p. 171).

Thus Hitler, and the fascists in general, took the distinctive ideas of authority out of their original personal and social contexts, applied them to the justification of coercive power, and in this politicized form, reapplied them to the organization of man's social and personal activities and to the molding of his ideas about them. Since, indeed, the idea of authority laid particular stress upon the voluntary component in the submission to power, it was particularly appropriate to totalitarian use for thought-control.

3. *Post-totalitarian Ideas of Authority.* The contemporary intellectual opposition to fascism tended to defend familiar liberal ideas, including those of the democratic limits upon and accountability of authority. The intellectually significant response to totalitarianism has been a post-fascist phenomenon. The change from the liberal view of authority to a radical attack on authority was developed after World War II by the movements of the New Left, which sees in fascism not a case of the political abuse of authority but a key to the ubiquity of oppressive authoritative power throughout society.

This conviction of the New Left has taken two forms, depending on whether the oppression in the power-authority syndrome is seen to come primarily from the power or from the authority. The first of these alternatives has been developed by those in the New Left who represent a connection with the old: for them social authority, in the sense of the force for voluntary submission in men's primary relation, is the characteristic means of power produced by advanced industrial society; it is essentially a pre-coercive power which controls men's will by determining their needs and as such it is continuous with the coercive political power which is merely its extension. "Contemporary industrial society," in the formulation of Herbert Marcuse, a prominent spokesman for this group, is "one-dimensional." It "tends to be totalitarian. For 'totalitarian' is not only a terroristic political coordination of society, but also a non-terroristic economic-technical coordination which operates through the manipulation of needs by vested interests. . . . Under the rule of a repressive whole, liberty can be made into a powerful instrument of domination" (Marcuse, *One-Dimensional Man*, pp. 3, 7).

But this strand of the New Left has not gone the whole way to the rejection of authority. It condemns

every real form of authority because of its unvarying association with repressive power rather than the idea of authority as such. Marcuse, for example, asserts the desirability of "the combination of centralized authority and direct democracy" and implies the authority of Reason in the shape of the "dialectical concept" and "the critical theory of society"—forms of authority devoid of social or political power. The categorical rejection of authority is the result rather of other spokesmen of the New Left whose deliberately formless attitudes are most clearly grasped in the glosses they have contributed to anarchism. The most obvious shift of emphasis in the new anarchism has been from the concentration on political authority characteristic of "historical anarchism"—i.e., the anarchism of Godwin, Proudhon, Bakunin, and Kropotkin—to "the rejection of authority as such, whatever its form or field" (Heintz, pp. 9–12).

But this shift has been more than one of scope, for along with the expansion of the anarchist target from all political forms to all social forms of authority has come a shift from the denial of authority as the source of compulsive power to the denial of the very elements which have always distinguished the idea of authority from the idea of power. First, where the historical anarchists denied the validity of any natural hierarchy or scale of moral values or conferral of rights which could serve as the basis of the *legal* authority of some individuals over others, the neo-anarchists insist upon the natural, moral, social, intellectual, and personal equality of all individuals and upon the consequent illegitimacy of any relationship based on the pretended superiority of some individuals over others, whether innate, ethical, conventional, or contracted. Second, neo-anarchism condemns all institutions—that is, enduring arrangements—not only because of their inevitable tendency toward bureaucratization (as in historical anarchism) but more fundamentally because as such they inevitably entail the authority of the past over the present. Finally, the neo-anarchists insist on the spontaneity, the open-endedness, and the planlessness of their enterprises because the definition of universal ends and the elaboration of programmatic designs toward those ends entail the authority of the future over the present.

In this set of rejections the New Left clearly denies the whole set of original, unperverted meanings of authority. It denies the personal authority of natural capacity and acquired merit; it denies the creation of authority by transfer or delegation of rights; it denies the authority of age and experience, whether in families or traditions; and it denies the authority of the author, both in terms of a special regard for founders and their foundations and in terms of the viability of designs which require the execution by some of what is initiated by others. And all these authentic kinds of authority are denied, moreover, not because they have been corrupted by their association with power but because they are in themselves illegitimate exercises of power and because the functions of personal respect, social continuity, and communicated creation which these authorities purport to serve are better served by the untrammeled interaction of absolutely free and equal individuals.

VI

The ideology of totalitarian fascism has been in abeyance for a generation, and the resonance of the total antifascism of the New Left remains uncertain. Still, their extreme formulations of the idea of authority, opposite in their evaluations but coincident in their convictions about its pervasiveness in modern society as the official mark of power, do seem to signify a logical conclusion to the long development of the idea. They represent the categorical extremes of prevalent attitudes toward social authority which elide its original tensions vis-à-vis the governmental powers and view it simply as a stable form of control.

But there are indications that the present generation may be attending at the birth of still a fifth stage in the history of the idea of authority. The arena of this fifth stage would be the individual himself, and authority would be a quality of the internal relations among his psychic elements. Certainly the hierarchical ranking of the individual's faculties and the attribution of authority to the higher over the lower have been prominent features of Western thought at least back to the ancient Greeks. But heretofore the internal polity of the individual has been in concordance with the external and conditioning structure of the outside world, whether of nature, super-nature, politics, or society. The best known of the recent discussions of authority and the individual, indeed, have been those which have internalized the social relations of authoritative power. Some of our most familiar contemporary characters are precisely such internalizations: the submissive refugee from freedom (in Fromm's *Escape from Freedom*, 1941); the "authoritarian personality," "continuously molded from above" to be both "jealous of his independence and inclined to submit blindly to power and authority" (in T. W. Adorno, et al., *The Authoritarian Personality* [1950], pp. ix, 976); the "inner-directed" and "outer-directed" "character types," equally and successively programmed by society toward "conformity" (in Riesman's *Lonely Crowd*, 1950). But if these analyses are in the familiar mold of demonstrating the continuity between the hierarchy of the cosmos and the hierarchy of the psyche—just as the analyses of

Plato, Saint Augustine, and Descartes did in past eras—such exercises in social psychology also contain the possibility of a new departure by looking to a revised psychic hierarchy as a crucial lever for the dismantling or at least the scaling down of social hierarchy.

The implication of such concluding unscientific postscripts for a distinctive psychological idea of authority has been obscured by their persistence in a social context which makes any psychic assertion by individuals against social repression an act of "autonomy." But within the field of individual psychology itself—and especially in the field of psychoanalytic theory—recent doctrines point toward the transcendence of social repression not through the mere permissive freedom of individual desires but rather through the substitution of uncoerced authority for repression in the relationship of the elements within the psyche and through the assertion of this authority, in its original sense of moral direction, against the repressive power of the society.

The incipient articulation of a psychological context for authority is being most prominently undertaken by neo-Freudians who have begun to develop in theory a structure of harmonious authority within the psyche with the mission of eradicating coercion from social authority as the necessary condition of its own realization. Where Freud himself could not get beyond the dualistic and pessimistic mutual convertibility of "ontogenic" and "phylogenic" repression—a limit directly related to the coercive idea of authority through the paradigmatic figure of the "Primal Father" in both the myths of the species and the fantasies of the individual child—radical neo-Freudians like Marcuse and Norman Brown have proposed the reversal of the psychic hierarchy of super-ego, ego, and id to serve as the ground for the reorganization of social relations. The neo-Freudians insist, like the later Freud, on the continuity of individuals and society, but whether in the form of Marcuse's "idea of non-repressive sublimation" (*Eros and Civilization*) or Brown's "construction of a Dionysian ego" (*Life against Death*) the proper ordering of the instincts (pleasure and reality, love and death) and reason becomes a psychic model for the whole society, creating "its own hierarchy" and replacing (in Marcuse's terminology) "irrational authority" by "rational authority"—that is, replacing an authority that is not compatible with freedom by an authority that is (*Eros*, pp. 205–06).

In general, however, both psychoanalytic doctrine and the common language of the age tend to characterize such reversions to voluntary hierarchies, whether of psychic factors or of individualized moral values as conditions of freedom rather than as forms of pure authority. In part this preference testifies to the traditional reference of authority to interpersonal rather than to intrapersonal relations, but in part too it testifies to the cumulative history of the idea of authority which has led to the general acceptance of the meaning which associates it indelibly with the exercise of coercive power. But even if it is not literally identified with the original idea of authority, the current commitment to a normative psychic hierarchy which should serve to direct the reorganization of society is an indication that the recurrent pattern of a pure, uncoercive authority remains viable. With whatever idea it will henceforth be identified, the diffusion of cultural innovation by men who have no access to the means of power persists as a recurrent theme of the idea of authority, balancing its more dubious contribution to extending the range of compulsion in men's lives.

BIBLIOGRAPHY

No comprehensive history or bibliography of authority exists. The following have been used in the preparation of this article.

Sources. T. W. Adorno, et al., *The Authoritarian Personality* (New York, 1950). *The 'Opus Magus' of Roger Bacon*, ed. John Henry Bridges, trans. Robert Belle Burke (New York, 1962). Jean Bodin, *Six Books of the Commonwealth*, trans. M. J. Tooley (Oxford, n.d.). Norman O. Brown, *Life against Death* (New York, 1959). Edmund Burke, *Reflections on the Revolution in France* (1790; New York, 1961). Carolo du Fresne du Cange, *Glossarium mediae et infimae latinitatis* (Paris, 1678; 1840–46). Auguste Comte, *La philosophie positive*, ed. Jules Rig (Paris, 1880). Roy J. Deferrari and M. Inviolata Barry, with Ignatius McGuinness, *A Lexicon of St. Thomas Aquinas* (Baltimore, 1948). Johannes Duns Scotus, *Opera omnia* (Hildesheim, 1968). Émile Durkheim, *The Division of Labor in Society*, trans. George Simpson (New York, 1964); idem, *L'éducation morale* (Paris, 1925). Robert Filmer, *Patriarcha*, ed. Peter Laslett (Oxford, 1949). Erich Fromm, *Escape from Freedom* (New York, 1941). Giovanni Gentile, *Genesis and Structure of Society*, trans. H. S. Harris (Urbana, 1960). G. W. F. Hegel, *Grundlinien der Philosophie des Rechts*, 4th ed. (Hamburg, 1955); idem, *The Phenomenology of Mind*, trans. J. B. Baillie (New York, 1931). Adolf Hitler, *Mein Kampf*, new ed. (Munich, 1943). *The Speeches of Adolf Hitler*, ed. Norman H. Baynes (New York, 1942). *Hitlers Tischgespräche im Führerhauptquartier 1941–1942*, ed. Henry Picker (Stuttgart, 1963). Thomas Hobbes, *Leviathan* (1651; New York, 1914). John Locke, *Two Treatises of Government*, ed. Peter Laslett (Cambridge, 1964). Niccolò Machiavelli, *The Prince and the Discourses* (New York, 1950). Herbert Marcuse, *Eros and Civilization* (New York, 1962); idem, *One-Dimensional Man* (Boston, 1966). Marsilius of Padua, *The Defender of the Peace*, ed. Alan Gewirth (New York, 1967). Robert Michels, *Political Parties: a Sociological Study of the Oligarchical Tendencies of Modern Democracies*, trans. Eden and Cedar Paul (New York, 1959). John Stuart Mill, *On Liberty* (1859), in *Selected Writings*, ed. Maurice Cowling (New York, 1968). *Mittellateinisches Wörterbuch bis zum ausgehenden 13. Jahrhundert* (Munich, 1967). Benito Mussolini, *La dottrina del Fascismo* (Milan, 1935). Vilfredo Pareto, *The Mind and Society*, new ed. (New York, 1963). Samuel Pufendorf, *De jure naturae et gentium* (1672; Oxford, 1934). David Riesman, et al., *The Lonely Crowd* (Garden City, n.d.). Jean Jacques Rousseau, *The Political Writings*, ed. C. E. Vaughan (New York, 1962). Max Weber, *Gesammelte Aufsätze zur Religionssoziologie* (Tübingen, 1922); idem, *Grundriss der Sozialökonomik; III. Abteilung: Wirtschaft und Gesellschaft* (Tübingen, 1932).

Commentaries. *Authority*, ed. Carl J. Friedrich (Cambridge, Mass., 1958). Leon Baudry, *Guillaume d'Occam* (Paris, 1949). Adolf Berger, *Encyclopedic Dictionary of Roman Law* (Philadelphia, 1953). Rupert E. Davies, *The Problem of Authority in the Continental Reformers* (London, 1946). Fritz Fürst, *Die Bedeutung der Auctoritas im privaten und öffentlichen Leben der römischen Republik* (Marburg, 1934). Peter Heintz, *Anarchismus und Gegenwart* (Zurich, 1951). R. Heinze, "Auctoritas," in *Hermes*, **60** (1925). Bertrand de Jouvenel, *Power: the Natural History of its Growth* (London, 1948); idem, *Sovereignty: an Inquiry into the Political Good* (Cambridge, 1957). Harold Laski, *Authority in the Modern State* (New Haven, 1919). Karl-Heinrich Lütcke, *"Auctoritas" bei Augustin, mit einer Einleitung zur römischen Vorgeschichte des Begriffs* (Stuttgart, 1968). A. J. MacDonald, *Authority and Reason in the Early Middle Ages* (London, 1933). André Magdelain, *Auctoritas principis* (Paris, 1947). Theodor Mommsen, *Römisches Staatsrecht* (Leipzig, 1887–88). Barrington Moore, Jr., *Soviet Politics—The Dilemma of Power: The Role of Ideas in Social Change* (Cambridge, Mass., 1959). Karl F. Morrison, *Tradition and Authority in the Western Church, 300–1140* (Princeton, 1969). Anton von Premerstein, *Vom Werden und Wesen des Prinzipats* (Munich, 1937). *Staatslexikon*, 6th ed. (Freiburg, 1957). *Studien über Autorität und Familie* (Paris, 1936). Brian Tierney, *Foundations of the Conciliar Theory* (Cambridge, Mass., 1955). Walter Ullmann, *The Growth of Papal Government in the Middle Ages* (London, 1955); idem; *Principles of Government and Politics in the Middle Ages* (London, 1961). Howard Warrender, *The Political Philosophy of Hobbes* (Oxford, 1957). Michael Wilks, *The Problem of Sovereignty in the Later Middle Ages* (Cambridge, 1963).

LEONARD KRIEGER

[See also Constitutionalism; **Democracy;** Liberalism; **Marxism;** Reformation; **Social Contract;** State; Totalitarianism.]

AXIOMATIZATION

AXIOMATIZATION as the organization of a deductive system in a strictly axiomatic form dates from the last part of the last century. The very use of the term

"Axiomatics" as a noun is even more recent; it is not to be found in recent editions of the *Encyclopedia Britannica* (1962). It is mentioned in the *Enciclopedia Italiana* (1949); there it is defined as the "name adopted recently to signify that branch of mathematical science which deals with the ordering of principles" (F. Enriques). If we adhered rigidly to this narrow definition, the history of "axiomatics" and of axiomatization would be a brief one, and its domain would be confined to mathematics alone. Here we must adopt the broader interpretation in which these terms are often understood and in which the very word "axiom" is included: an axiomatic system is one composed of propositions deducible from a small number of initial propositions posited as axioms. But what then is an "axiom"?

"There is," Leibniz says, "a class of propositions which, under the name of *maxims* or *axioms,* pass as the *principles* of the sciences. . . . The scholastic philosophers said that these propositions were self-evident *ex terminis,* that is, as soon as the terms in them are understood" (*New Essays* IV, vii, 1). And Bossuet declares: "Those propositions which are clear and intelligible by themselves are called axioms or first principles" (*Connaissance de Dieu* I, 13). Thus, in its classical usage—with various modifications which we shall see later—an axiom is characterized as combining two features: as a *principle* it is the beginning or the basis of a group of propositions which it serves to demonstrate; as a *self-evident* truth known immediately as such, it compels conviction without the aid of any proof. It is, therefore, at one and the same time a certainty by itself and the basis of our certainty with respect to the propositions following from it.

Axiomatization will then consist in organizing a body of propositions into a deductive system such that the principles of this system appear indubitable by virtue of their own self-evidence; the result is that the deductive apparatus performs the functions of communicating or transmitting to the group of propositions of the system the evidence and consequently the certainty of the axioms; this produces what has been called a "transfer of evidence." The deduction is in such a case categorical; it is *demonstrative* in the sense in which Aristotle defines demonstration as the "syllogism of the necessary," the necessity residing both in the connection of the propositions and in the very positing of the initial propositions. Such should be the ideal form of scientific exposition, according to Aristotle: "it is necessary that scientific demonstration start from premises which are true, primitive, immediate and more evident than the conclusions, being prior to them as their cause" (*Posterior Analytic* I, 2). This ideal was to be perpetuated, with few exceptions, until the beginning of the modern era.

I

The typical example, which has been invoked for more than twenty centuries as an unsurpassable model, is the method with which Euclid (ca. 300 B.C.) expounded geometry in his *Elements.* Most of the subject matter had already been acquired; Euclid's merit is due to the manner in which he organized it. "Euclid," Proclus says, "assembled the elements, arranged in order many truths discovered by Eudoxus, completed what had been begun by Theaetetus, and proved more rigorously what had also been too loosely shown before him."

It is well known how Euclid's system is presented. At the beginning of Book I appear statements of definitions (ὅροι), postulates (αἰτήματα), and common notions (κοιναὶ ἔννοιαι). Each of the succeeding books opens with additional definitions intended to introduce the geometrical entities belonging to each book. However, the common notions and postulates given in the first book suffice to demonstrate all the propositions and solve all the problems constituting the whole work with the sole exception (in the middle of Book I) of two supplementary postulates about perpendiculars and parallels. The "common notions" correspond to what later generations called "axioms"; for example, things equal to the same thing are equal to each other. Thus Euclid accomplished the transformation of geometry from an empirical science to a rational science after its initiation by Pythagoras. No longer are merely isolated problems treated "abstractly and by pure intelligence" (Eudemus), but the whole of geometry is organized in a close network in which all the propositions are linked to each other by logical relations, so that each proposition is made absolutely clear to the mind, either through its own self-evidence or through its logical dependence on the primary data.

This accomplishment was henceforth looked upon as a model for all the sciences which, beginning with Physics, were going in turn to be expounded in the geometrical manner (*more geometrico*) even if they do not attain the same level of systematic order as Euclid's *Elements.* In antiquity, as a case in point, Euclid's *Optics* was constructed on a few initial principles such as the one which postulates that light rays are transmitted in a straight line; then also Archimedes' *On the equilibrium of planes* (third century B.C.) demonstrated its propositions by starting with a few postulates such as: equal weights suspended from a lever at equal distances from the fulcrum are in equilibrium.

We can therefore understand why Euclid has been regarded as the initiator of axiomatization. Although not inaccurate, this view must be tempered, however, by a few reservations. First, the fact is that Euclid's *Elements* is not as logically perfect a work as had been thought for a long time, and also it falls far short of satisfying all the requirements of modern axiomatics. It is also a fact that Euclid's *Elements* did not emerge suddenly as an absolute novelty. Hippocrates of Chios (fifth century B.C.) had also written an *Elements*, a work unfortunately lost; but we know that he had attempted in this work a systematic organization of mathematics. Between the work of Hippocrates and that of Euclid other efforts had been made by the mathematicians Leo, Eudoxus, and Theudius.

It would be unjust to overlook certain works before Euclid's, including even nonmathematical works in which a very clear approach is made to an axiomatic treatment. First of all, we find it in Aristotle, not in his *Physics*, which, though attempting to be demonstrative, is still far from axiomatic in form or rigor, but in his logic or more precisely in his syllogistic theory as it appears in the *Prior Analytics*. Of course, Aristotle does not proceed explicitly through initial axioms and demonstration of theorems. But from the standpoint of modern formal logic, as has been shown by J. Łukasiewicz (*Aristotle's Syllogistic from the Standpoint of Modern Logic*, Oxford [1951]; 2nd ed. enlarged [1957]), Aristotle's text allows one to read it as an axiomatic work. To do that, it must be remembered that Aristotle formulates his syllogisms not as schema of inference as the later philosophers did, beginning with Alexander of Aphrodisias and Boethius, but as logical theses; for example, for the syllogism, later called *Barbara*: if A is predicated of all B and B of all C, then A is predicated of all C. This point rectified, it appears that the four moods of the first figure—the so-called "perfect" moods being self-evident without demonstration—play exactly the same role as axioms do, on which the moods of the other figures depend as theorems; the "reduction" of these moods to those of the first figure is really the same as demonstrating them from axioms. And then we must regard as primitive terms of the syllogistic theory the four operators which function in the axioms to connect the variables A, B, C, in the elementary propositions: "belongs to all . . . ," "belongs to none . . . ," etc. Aristotle advanced even further his reduction of the implicit axiomatic base of his syllogistic theory when he went on to demonstrate the third and fourth moods (AII and EIO) of the first figure, by means of only the universal moods (AAA and EAE), which may thus be counted as only two axioms.

The Megaric-Stoic logic, contemporary with Aristotle's, also offers an example of progress towards axiomatization. As a point of departure, five undemonstrated (ἀναπόδεικτοι) propositions are postulated, which can easily be translated into the symbolism of modern logistics; for example, the first proposition

would read: $((p \supset q) \cdot p) \supset q$. They obviously involve propositional variables connected by a few logical operators taken as primitive terms. Not only did they draw from these primitive propositions, as Cicero assures us, "innumerable conclusions," but they boasted being able to reduce every logically important type of reasoning to these primitive propositions. This was accomplished by means of four rules of inference explicitly detached and formulated. What marks this Megaric-Stoic logic as an advance over Aristotle's are the following three features: the clear distinction between axioms and explicitly formulated rules of inference; the line drawn expressly between concrete reasoning (λόγος) and its formal schema (τρόπος); and the claim—not challenged by their adversaries so far as we know, but our inadequate information prevents our checking this—to have erected a system which would today be called "complete." This logic is in fact a move in the direction of modern axiomatics, anticipating our modern calculus of propositions (see Benson Mates, *Stoic Logic*, Berkeley and Los Angeles [1953]).

Later, and until we reach the rigorous axiomatic systems of modern symbolic logic, several attempts at a logic demonstrated in geometric fashion were expressly made, from Galen (second century A.D.) with his proposed *Logica ordine geometrica demonstrata* to the *Logica demonstrativa* of Saccheri (1692).

Thus towards the end of Greek antiquity, mathematics, logic, and certain parts of physics had shown in various degrees the beginnings of axiomatization.

II

At the start of the modern period, the instrumental and exemplary nature of mathematics recognized by the new science led to extending the mathematical mode of exposition to various disciplines. This occurred first in the extension of the work begun by the Greeks to the science of nature and, more exactly, to that part which is generally regarded as its foundation, namely, Mechanics. Galileo was inspired by the method of Archimedes, and tried to do for Dynamics what Archimedes had done for Statics. Descartes, in his *Principles of Philosophy* (*Principia philosophiae*, 1644), postulated three "laws of nature" dealing with motion, justifying them *a priori* through God's perfection, and claiming that he could demonstrate all of physics by means of these three laws. Finally, and above all, Newton in his *Mathematical Principles of Natural Philosophy* (*Philosophiae naturalis principia mathematica*, 1687), organized Mechanics in the form of a logical system which has remained classical. It was taught often best, especially in France, as a mathematical discipline. Newton's work opens with the statement of eight definitions and three axioms or laws of motion, starting from which

Books I and II demonstrate a great many theorems.

However, the prestige of the Euclidean axiomatic model was such that after going beyond mathematics, it won over disciplines which are outside of science properly speaking. Descartes, while maintaining his preference for the analytical order of his *Meditations*, had already agreed, to satisfy the authors of the *Second Objections*, to expound in synthetic order the "reasons which prove the existence of God and the distinction between the mind and the human body, the reasons arranged in a geometric manner," demonstrating his propositions through definitions, postulates, and axioms. His example was followed by Spinoza, with a breadth and rigor which fascinated many minds, in his *Ethics, demonstrated in a geometric order* (*Ethica ordine geometrica demonstrata*, 1677); Spinoza's work was expounded by subjecting it, from one end to the other with no exceptions, to the requirements of Euclidean standards with definitions, postulates, and axioms followed by propositions, demonstrations, corollaries, lemmas, and scholia.

Jurisprudence, along with metaphysics and ethics, also entered upon the road of axiomatization. Whenever Leibniz wished to give examples of disciplines containing rigorous reasoning he mentioned the works of the Roman jurisconsults as well as of the Greek mathematicians. He offered an example himself of a juridical exposition by definitions and theorems in his sample of legal persuasion or demonstration (*Specimen certitudinis seu demonstrationum in jure*, 1669) in which he refers to "those ancients who arranged their rebuttals by means of very certain and quasi-mathematical demonstrations." Not long before, Samuel von Pufendorf had published his *Elementa jurisprudentia universalis* (1660), written under the double inspiration of Grotius and his own teacher Weigel who taught both law and mathematics. Pufendorf wished to show that law, rising above historical contingencies, contains a body of propositions which are perfectly certain and universally valid, and capable of being made the conclusions of a demonstrative science. As a matter of fact, here, as in Leibniz, axiomatization was still only making a start. Instead of producing the propositions and their proofs as logical consequences of principles, Pufendorf presented them substantially in extensive commentaries which follow each one of his twenty-one definitions in order to avoid, he said, "a certain aridity which might have run the risk of distorting this discipline if we had presented it by cutting it up into small parts, as is the manner of mathematics." In the wake of Pufendorf the so-called school of "natural law and human right" elaborated for more than a century theories in which "one deduces through a continuous chain leading from the very nature of man to all his obliga-

tions and all his rights," restating the subtitle of one of Christian Wolff's works. Wolff, as a disciple of Leibniz, boasted of accomplishing what others had only proposed to do, namely, to deal with the theory of human actions according to the demonstrative method of the mathematicians (*Philosophia practica universalis, methodo scientifica pertracta*, Frankfurt and Leipzig, 1738–39). Nevertheless, here also, we are quite far from the logical rigor and even the mode of presentation of Euclidean geometry.

III

The systems we have discussed—logical, mathematical, physical, metaphysical, ethical, or legal—all have in common a dogmatic character. Axioms were supposed to compel assent through their inherent self-evidence transmitted to later propositions by means of demonstrations. In the modern period we see this conception gradually disintegrating, until we reach by degrees our present conception of axiomatics. This conception was attained by a progressive dissociation of the two hitherto intimately related components of the idea of axiom (self-evident and primary proposition). The transformation was accomplished in two stages: the first, in the seventeenth century in connection with the advent of experimental physics; the second, the beginning of which can be dated in the early nineteenth century, with the construction of non-Euclidean geometries.

Descartes still required that the principles of philosophy (including natural philosophy or physics) satisfy two conditions at the same time: ". . . one, that they be so clear and so self-evident that the human mind cannot doubt their truth when it concentrates on judging them; second, that the knowledge of other things depends on the principles which can be known without these other things but not conversely" (Letter, preface to the French version of the *Principles of Philosophy*, 1647). Nevertheless, he admitted, and practiced himself, when he needed to, another mode of exposition, although he regarded it as less perfect than the deductive mode. This other mode consisted in regarding basic propositions (general principles) not as principles of demonstration but as requiring, on the contrary, proof by the empirical verification of their consequences. In this he was in agreement, albeit accidentally, with the practice of the new seventeenth-century physicists who, following Galileo and Torricelli, were active around him and Mersenne: Pascal, Roberval, Gassendi. These principles, that is to say, the propositions from which deduction starts, are only "suppositions" or "hypotheses" in two senses of these words: premises and conjectures. For, as Pascal maintained, in physics the experiments furnish the true principles, that is, the foundations of our knowledge. When in the order of exposition, though not in the order of discovery, the order of the propositions is always the same, viz., that of a deductive synthesis, the meaning of the proof is reversed: instead of extending beyond the premisses to the consequences, the truth rebounds from the consequences to support the premisses.

The operational distinction in Physics between the propositions which it states as its principles and those that it invokes to establish them, is nowhere better illustrated than in the Newtonian theory of gravitation, expounded in Book III of the *Principia;* it instigated the battle between Cartesians and Newtonians that lasted for half a century. One of the chief reasons for the antagonism of the Cartesians was the idea of attraction or action at a distance, which, far from being a clear idea demanding assent as self-evident, was on the contrary, unintelligible to them. To which the Newtonians replied: clear or obscure, self-evident or not, the principle of gravitation is still a compelling truth because experience confirms it in very many precise ways.

Thus classical science was faced with the institution of a sharp separation between the experimental method of the physicists and the demonstrative method of the mathematicians. The result was the uncertain status of Mechanics, halfway between geometry and physics. In the middle of the eighteenth century, the Academy of Berlin offered a prize for the best answer to the question whether the laws of nature are necessary or contingent truths, that is to say, whether they are directly or indirectly purely rational statements or, on the contrary, simply experimental findings. D'Alembert, a declared Newtonian, replied in the way a Cartesian would, and presented Dynamics as a demonstrative science. And in the next century, William Whewell still wondered about the "paradox of necessary truths acquired by experience," which suggested to him his theory about the "progress of evidence."

A nondogmatic use of deductive method was, in a manner of speaking, quite ancient. Without discussing the accidental employment of this method by the mathematician in his indirect proofs, or by the dialectician in his refutations through reduction of his adversary's arguments to absurdity, we find in antiquity a systematic use of the hypothetico-deductive method in expounding one of the sciences of nature which had already reached a high level of development. Alongside of physical astronomy there had actually developed, after Plato, a so-called formal or mathematical astronomy which was connected especially with Ptolemy's work, and which continued to thrive in the Middle Ages; it did not require that its principles should be true but only that they allow one to calculate exactly the empirical data ("to save the phenomena," σώζειν

τὰ φαινόμενα). This was the notion to which Osiander also referred when, in his introduction to Copernicus' *De revolutionibus orbium coelestium* (1543), he asked the astronomer "to imagine and invent any hypotheses whatsoever," adding: "it is not necessary for these hypotheses to be true or even probable, the only sufficient condition is that they must lend themselves to a calculation which agrees with the observations." However, the new physics was just as opposed to these hypotheses which are neither true nor false, as it was to dogmatic theses. If it no longer posits its principles as self-evident, it nevertheless proposes them as truths. As Newton expressly says in the first of his *Rules for Philosophy (Regulae philosophandi)* it does not suffice that the causes invoked by the scientist should be fit to explain the phenomena, but they must be true in addition. This new way of employing the hypothetico-deductive method would discredit in time and relegate to oblivion the ancient method of "saving the phenomena."

To summarize, the deductive order, or axiomatic order in the wide sense, may function in three different ways, depending on the identifiable nature of its basic propositions: (1) a categorical deduction which demonstrates the truth of the consequences by the truth of the principles laid down dogmatically; (2) a hypothetical deduction which proves *a posteriori* the truth of its provisional hypotheses by the truth of their consequences; finally, (3) a pure hypothetical deduction whose principles are introduced as fictions removed from the domain of what is true or false, so that truth comes into play only on the level of logical consequences. Whereas Mechanics tried for a while to persevere still in the first conception (categorical deduction), classical physics opted clearly for the second (*a posteriori* hypothetical inference), rejecting the two past legacies of demonstrative physics and fictive physics. Even when Physics seeks to combine a body of experimental laws into a unifying theory and even when it reduces this theory to a certain mathematical structure, as did J. Lagrange in his *Analytical Mechanics (Mécanique analytique,* 1788), Joseph Fourier in his thermodynamics (*Théorie analytique de la chaleur,* 1822), and J. C. Maxwell in his *Treatise on Electricity and Magnetism* (1873), it does not postulate its axioms either as necessary truths or as arbitrary fictions, but as a system of hypotheses; the truth of these hypotheses being tested finally by the precise and unerring agreement of the many consequences of the hypotheses with the experiential data. It was only around 1900 that this radically hypothetical conception of Physics was revived, on the one hand with the critique of scientific dogmatism by H. Poincaré, P. Duhem, and H. Vaihinger's *Philosophy of As If (Philosophie des als ob,* 1911); on the other hand, and above all, the hypothetical conception came to the fore when the logico-mathematical sciences were put into axiomatic form, in the strict and most rigorous sense which the term "axiomatic" has assumed today.

IV

This new transformation of the logico-mathematical sciences started with the working out of the non-Euclidean geometries (N. Lobatchevsky, 1826; 1855; W. F. Bolyai 1828; and B. Riemann, 1854); since they reflected on the Euclidean axiomatization itself it stood in need of logical reinterpretation. It became clear that Euclid's postulates are not necessary truths since it is possible to construct perfectly consistent logical systems on the negation of some of the postulates. As a result, the thought gradually arose that truth in pure mathematics was no longer a property of isolated statements or formulas but must refer solely to the formal consistency of the whole system. Demonstration ceased to be categorical, and no longer aimed to advance evidence but simply to establish a link from principles as premises to consequences as conclusions, i.e., between primitive propositions and theorems. Mathematics has thus become a hypothetico-deductive science, to use M. Pieri's expression. Of the two functions which mathematical principles served conjointly, only one remains, namely, to serve as premises of a deductive system.

By the same token, demonstration also retains only one of its former functions, but finds it necessary to fulfill this function by meeting new formal requirements. So long as the material truth of propositions was the chief concern, demonstration, in trying to establish the latter, only played the role of a means; one might eventually do without it, tolerate its gap and its ambiguities, provided that intuition could fill the gap by playing its persuasive role. Everything changed when the *logical* organization of the system came to the foreground. The aim of demonstration is no longer a pedagogical or didactic one; it aims to establish "objective relations" (B. Bolzano) which hold between propositions. And logical rigor has to be imposed all the more, because in the generalized systems of geometry the new propositions are often resistant to our intuition and can therefore be supported only by a logical apparatus that is faultless. These new requirements reflect naturally on the Euclidean system itself in which some inadequacies become more apparent; namely, the concealment of links in the logical reasoning with appeal to diagrams as substitutes, a confusion between the fruitful principles of theory and the governing rules of reasoning, the inclusion of definitions among the principles, etc.

In 1882 M. Pasch in his lectures on the new geometry (*Vorlesungen über neuere Geometrie*) formulated the following conditions for a rigorous deductive exposition: (1) primitive terms and primitive propositions, through which all other terms are defined and all other propositions are demonstrated, must be stated explicitly with no omissions; (2) the relations among the primitive terms formulated in the primitive propositions must be purely logical relations without the intrusion of geometrical intuitions, and the demonstrations must appeal only to these logical relations.

A theory axiomatized according to these requirements will then no longer contain at its base the three kinds of propositions (definitions, axioms, postulates) in the traditional geometrical demonstrations inspired by Euclid, but will consist of a group of propositions of a single kind; it will make no difference whether they are called postulates or axioms since the axioms, having lost their privileged self-evidence, have henceforth the same function as postulates. These primitive propositions, like all the others belonging to the system, are composed of two sorts of terms: those which belong distinctly to the theory—in this case, the geometrical terms, e.g., in Pasch: *point, segment, plane, superposable on* . . . —and those which serve to state the logical relations among these primitive terms, for example, *all, and, not, if* . . . *, then, is a* . . . , etc., eventually with terms borrowed from presupposed theories, for example, the terms of arithmetic in this case. Just as the primitive propositions are simply postulated without proof or even strictly asserted, so the primitive terms are taken as indefinable for analogous reasons, since definitions cannot be reduced indefinitely to others. But how will their meaning be determined, if there is no question of allowing one to refer to some prior intuitive meaning? It will be determined, and exclusively so, by the relations among them which the primitive propositions state within the relational framework set by the axioms.

This last point is especially important in that its effect is to subordinate terms to relations, that being the direction already of all modern science in opposition to that of the ancients. Without going into its philosophical implications this reversal has had a considerable scientific bearing. It determined a turn in the employment of axiomatization by making of it not only a mode of exposition supremely satisfactory from a logical point of view, but also a new scientific tool whose importance soon became apparent. It has become clear that this sort of "implicit definition" of the primitive terms by the group of axioms, as J. Gergonne already knew, only determines their meaning as a total system in an equivocal manner which makes possible a variety of interpretations, as, for example, in certain systems of equations the values of the unknowns are determinable by the whole group of the terms in their mutual relations, not each one separately, thus allowing very many interpretations. In other words, only the relations are determined exactly and universally by the axioms, but nothing prevents the same system of *relations* from being able to support different systems of specific *interpretations*. The object of an axiomatic system is therefore, properly speaking, a certain abstract structure. Such a structure, which undoubtedly has been suggested by some concrete embodiment, is nevertheless capable of being interpreted by many other "models" which possess a structural identity (isomorphism). However, the structure can also be studied by itself by going past the "threshold of abstraction" (F. Gonseth), without regard for the more concrete interpretations. Far from being indigent or destitute of meaning, this relative indeterminateness accounts, on the contrary, for the chief value of axiomatic systems in that it enables one to disengage what many diverse and apparently heterogeneous theories have in common from a formal viewpoint, and thus to think the many in the one (εἰς ἕν τὰ πολλά).

The truth is that it was not necessary to wait for modern axiomatics or even non-Euclidean geometries to become aware of the fact that the same system of relations might handle different contents. Physicists and mathematicians could not have failed to notice this fact. Thus it was, for example, that the projective geometry of J. V. Poncelet made use of the "principle of duality" which enabled Gergonne to expound its principles (1824) by writing them in two columns, in which the terms *point* and *plane* were interchanged when one passed from right to left, the relations of these two terms to *straight lines*, as fixed by the axioms of the theory, being identical. However, the generalization of this procedure, which seemed so exceptional, did not appear clearly until the systematic development of axiomatics at the beginning of the twentieth century. The idea came to be clearly perceived already in the first axiomatic systems constructed in conformity with the ideal conceived by Pasch. This occurred in the system of arithmetic by G. Peano (*Arithmetices principia nova methodo exposito*, Turin, 1899) which rests on five axioms containing three primitive terms, and in the system of geometry by D. Hilbert who in his *Foundations of Geometry* (*Grundlagen der Geometrie*, Leipzig, 1899) divides its twenty-one axioms into five groups depending on whether they deal with connection, order, congruence, parallelism, and continuity respectively. These axiomatic systems have been followed in this century by many others, and they tend to be concentrated on the theory of sets as the basis of the whole of mathematics (cf., Hao Wang and R. McNaughton, *Les systèmes axiomatiques de la théorie des ensembles*, Paris, 1953).

V

We see then that what had happened in antiquity recurred, on a higher level of development, about 1900: the axiomatization of mathematics duplicated the axiomatization of logic. In 1879, Frege had offered the first truly axiomatic formulation of the calculus of propositions. However, the two disciplines of logic and mathematics are now intimately tied together, as the very titles of fundamental works show: G. Frege's *The Foundations of Arithmetic, a Logico-mathematical Enquiry into the Concept of Number* (New York, 1950, trans. of *Die Grundlagen der Arithmetik, eine logisch-mathematische Untersuchung über den Begriff der Zahl*, Breslau, 1884), and *Fundamental Laws of Arithmetic, derived by symbolic representation of concepts* (*Grundgesetze der Arithmetik begriffsschriftlich abgeleitet*, Jena 1893–1903); A. N. Whitehead and B. Russell, *Principia Mathematica*, 3 vols. (Cambridge, 1910–13, reprinted 1925–27), the classic of the new symbolic logic or "logistics." The nineteenth century had arithmetized mathematics; the proposal of Frege and Russell was to logicize arithmetic, that is, to construct its primitive terms and primitive propositions with the aid of purely logical terms and purely logical propositions. The latter would themselves be reduced to a small number of initial statements; thus the *Principia Mathematica* makes the whole calculus of propositions rest on two undefined terms, negation ($\sim$) and disjunction ($\vee$, the nonexclusive "or") and on five axioms. By thus deducing arithmetic from logic, the relative indeterminateness of the foundations of arithmetic was to be corrected; such an indeterminateness was making of arithmetic, and with it of the whole of mathematics, a purely formal science in which, as Russell said in a well-known sally, "one never knows what one is saying or whether what is said is true." However, such an attempt made sense only on condition that it would not invest the principles of logic with a similar indeterminateness, that is to say, that we accord to the fundamental ideas of logic an exact meaning and to its laws an absolute truth. As completely axiomatic as it might be, logic, in order to offer a solid basis for the whole mathematical structure, should itself rest on evidence and assert its principles categorically as mathematics also used to do until recently.

But this logical dogmatism soon had to yield, as, not long before, it was mathematical dogmatism which had to yield in the wake of physical dogmatism. Just as geometry in the nineteenth century had proliferated into a multitude of non-Euclidean geometries, and had besides, by its axiomatization, eliminated intuitive representations, so, around 1920, logic all at once in its turn went on to diversify itself and empty itself of its substance. On the one hand, J. Łukasiewicz (1920) and

E. L. Post (1921) constructed the first three-valued and *n*-valued logics respectively; these were soon followed by a proliferation of non-Russellian systems. On the other hand, L. Wittgenstein in his *Tractatus logico-philosophicus* (London, 1922) characterized logical laws, axioms, or theorems as simple tautologies, understanding by that term that they are devoid of all content: "all propositions of logic say the same thing, that is, nothing"; they are pure forms which remain valid whatever material contents are poured into them. The primitive terms no longer retain anything of their intuitive and pre-axiomatic meaning, which was properly a logical one; they retain only what the group of axioms as a whole determines in its systematic ambiguity; and although many systems are still concerned with maintaining a very close correspondence between these two meanings, there is no longer any obligation to do so.

The axiomatization of logic is thus allied to that of mathematics: its terms become rid of their semantic burden; its axioms lose their self-evidence and fall into the rank of postulates which are set up in a more or less arbitrary manner, either to recover as consequences a body of formulas previously given or simply to see what set of formulas might be derived from them. Or better it may be necessary to say that because of its complete vacuity a system of logical axioms cannot be distinguished from a system of mathematical axioms or even, more generally, from any system of axioms whatsoever. The distinction would only reappear if, in descending from a pure science to applications, we recognize that some system lends itself better to an interpretation in logical notions and propositions, and some others to interpretation by mathematical ideas and propositions, taking the words "logical" and "mathematical" here in their intuitive and pre-axiomatic meaning. Strictly speaking it is only on this level of concrete or nearly concrete interpretations that we rediscover the idea of truth. In a purely axiomatic system, the axioms are no longer genuine propositions, but simply "propositional functions," i.e., empty formulas which become genuine propositions for every interpretation of the primitive terms, and become true propositions if this interpretation satisfies all of the axioms. In this last case, every theorem of the system, i.e., every propositional formula deducible, directly or indirectly from the interpreted axioms, becomes truly a proposition and also a proposition which is true.

VI

Compared to the axiomatic efforts made at the end of the nineteenth and beginning of the twentieth centuries, which can be regarded retrospectively as naive or semi-concrete, contemporary axiomatization is characterized by three features anticipated, of course, by what preceded it, but now sharply asserted and inseparably united: symbolization, formalization, and appeal to meta-theories.

Symbolization consists in substituting for the spoken natural languages, with their national differences and especially their imperfections in logical respects, a system of written signs, a "characteristic," which is an immediate ideographic representation not exactly of the ideas belonging to the theory axiomatized, if the ideas happen to be already represented by signs, but of the logical articulations of the discourse in which the theory is developed. It is also not yet a question, therefore, of "the *universal* characteristic" dreamed of by Leibniz, but only of a *logical* characteristic which allows one to express in an entirely artificial symbolism the doctrines which, like Arithmetic, already make use of a symbolism which is appropriated for their ideas and operations. Frege in his *Begriffsschrift* (Halle, 1879) and Peano in his *Notations de logique mathématique* (Turin, 1894) proposed such systems of symbolic logic. Frege's symbolism was quite cumbersome and has not survived, whereas Peano's notation, essentially what Russell adopted, has passed into the current usage of symbolic logic.

The chief value of this symbolic notation is to make possible a formal treatment of the sort of reasoning about ideas, which is still tainted more or less with subjectivity or with appeals to intuition in judging the correctness of logical inferences, by replacing such reasoning by a calculus of signs. Here Leibniz' ideal of a calculus of reasoning (*calculus ratiocinator*) comes to the fore again. Now in order to avoid any dispute in the practice of such a calculus, it is first necessary, as in a well-regulated game, that the rules governing the calculus be explicitly formulated, and in such a manner that they admit no ambiguity about their mode of application. That is why formal axiomatic systems state the rules according to which calculation may take place besides stating the axioms serving as a basis for the calculus. In that way the confusion was cleared up which had prevailed for a long time with respect to the distinction, on the level of logical principles, between premises and rules of inference. The rules of inference are now made explicit and are expressly distinguished from the system of premises on which the calculus operates governed by the rules. These rules are generally divided into two groups, depending on whether they govern the formation or the transformation of expressions. Demonstration then amounts to transforming progressively, without omitting any step, one or more formulas correctly formed (the abbreviation "w.f.f." is used for "well formed formulas") and already admitted as axioms or theorems, by indicating at each step the number of the rule authorizing this transformation, until step by step the formula to be demonstrated is finally reached. Such a task has become performable, in theory and in fact for relatively simple cases, by a suitably constructed and programmed machine; the computing machine can with extreme rapidity try the various combinations authorized by the rules of inference and retain only those combinations which yield the result sought.

But how can one be sure, in the unrolling of the theorems derivable from the axioms according to these rules, that one will never run into a contradiction, that is to say, into the possibility of proving both a formula and the same formula preceded by the sign of negation? Such a question was hardly a problem for the first axiomatic systems which started from a system of propositions practically certified, such as the body of Euclidean geometry or that of classical arithmetic, and simply proposed to make the system rest on a minimal basis, entirely explicit. However, the problem of the consistency of a system arises as soon as there is a doubt about it, and furthermore, the problem of consistency arises also in the reverse direction, when a certain number of axioms are arbitrarily posited in order to see what consequences flow from these axioms. In order to be sure that the very axioms of a system are indeed compatible, we must rise to a new level and take this system as itself an object of study. In his *Foundations of Geometry* of 1899, Hilbert had already raised questions about his axioms when he investigated their mutual independence, their subdivision into five groups, and the limitations which each had to impose on its own respective domain. Taking very clearly into consideration the specificity of this class of problems, he proposed in 1917 the institution of a new science, "Metamathematics," which takes as its object of study the language of mathematics already symbolized and formalized, and in abstraction from its meaning proceeds entirely on its own in a mathematical manner to create rigorous proofs. In this new science the problem of the proof of the noncontradictoriness of an axiomatized mathematical system naturally occupied an important place. In truth, however, the difficulty had only been pushed back, for it was then necessary to guarantee the validity of the metamathematical procedures themselves. Whence arose the attempts to find a means of proving the noncontradictoriness of a system by means of the very axioms and rules of inference within the system itself.

The halting of these attempts and their futility were explained and sanctioned by the famous proof by K. Gödel (1931); the proof itself was drawn by the rigorous procedures of metamathematics and established that the proposition which states the noncontradictori-

ness of a system in which arithmetic can be developed is not decidable within this system. In other words, in order to prove that a formal system is not contradictory, it is necessary to appeal to stronger means of demonstration than those used by the system itself, and by means of which the question of noncontradiction is consequently carried over. Hence the theory about a calculus cannot be constructed by means of the resources alone of this calculus, nor can one speak about a language without employing a metalanguage, which would yield the same uncomfortable situation. In short, formalism is not self-sufficient; its closure on itself is impossible. The ideal of the *calculus ratiocinator* and that of the *caracteristica universalis* are in the end incompatible. One can postpone indefinitely but cannot eliminate altogether the appeal to logical intuitions.

This check on one of the objectives of metamathematics is, in other respects, an important result to credit to it. Besides, metamathematical logic poses many other problems concerning completeness, decidability, categoricity, isomorphism, etc.; the very analysis of these ideas leads to their further diversification by greater refinements and nuances. As an example, the idea of noncontradiction appears as a special case of the more general idea of consistency which is itself presented in various forms.

Because of the close relationship between logic and mathematics, which is highlighted by the formalizing of their axiomatic systems, logic itself has experienced analogous developments. By analogy with Hilbert's metamathematics, Tarski constructed metalogic as a distinct discipline. Beside the questions of syntax which had at first been the main concern of metatheories, Tarski emphasized the importance of the semantic point of view. Through this new approach he established limiting conditions under which the semantic notion of truth replaces the syntactical idea of derivability; this he showed in a theorem (1935) which, conjoined to other results, came at the same time in various forms to converge on Gödel's result. But here also, the field of metatheory was extended to many other problems. Metalogic today occupies in the activities of logicians a place equal at least in importance to that of logic properly so-called, since beyond the studies specifically assigned to metalogic there is scarcely any work in logic not accompanied by a critical examination on the metalogical level.

VII

Modern axiomatic theory, in the beginning, did not seem to come into science except as a rigorous procedure of exposition and as a refinement of the deductive presentation of a theory. Axiomatics is now an integral part of science, as a new discipline having its own field of studies. But it becomes at the same time a general scientific tool; used once simply as a means of expression it assumes now the role of a method of research. In this third aspect, axiomatic theory is intimately associated with the modern theory of groups. An axiomatic system may itself be regarded as the representation of a group, namely, the group of operational transformations which it permits its terms to undergo. Both axiomatics and group theory are devoted to disengaging formal structures, and thereby succeed in exposing the unexpected relationships among apparently heterogeneous theories. Since the beginning of this century, therefore, not only have all branches of mathematics, from set theory to the calculus of probabilities, been axiomatized in many ways, but this work of axiomatization has in addition had the effect of reorganizing the division of various mathematical disciplines; and redistribution of such disciplines is no longer based on the nature of the objects studied but on the common or different features of their fundamental structures.

Axiomatization has proceeded from logic and mathematics, from which it arose, to become progressively extended to the whole gamut of the sciences. An idea which is intimately related to it, the idea of a model, explains this extension. This can be seen, for example, by the place occupied by the idea of model (or interpretation of a formal system of axioms) in the *Proceedings of the 1960 International Congress of Logic, Methodology, and Philosophy of Science* (Stanford, 1962) and by the generally acknowledged importance of models in contemporary scientific work. The term "model of a deductive theory" is applied to another deductive theory which has the same logical structure; that is to say, all of the terms and propositions of the model are in a "biunique" relation to the first theory; the first theory can then, of course, be regarded reciprocally as a model of the second. So it is possible for two or more concrete or semi-concrete theories, even when they bear on totally different objects, to be expressed by one and the same abstract calculus, or in other words, they may be derived from the same axiomatic system of which they are simply different interpretations. We can thus understand how axiomatics was able to become a universal scientific tool; the axiomatized systems of logic and mathematics were only particular applications of this intellectual instrument to a privileged but in no sense exclusive domain.

It was natural, nevertheless, for Mechanics and Physics, the most mathematized sciences, to have soonest and best appropriated the axiomatic method. Theoretical physics had for a long time been expounded in deductive form. It had, when occasion called for it, transposed one formal structure to another (e.g., electromagnetic theory to the theory of light waves), and it was from the language of physics that axiomatics borrowed the very term "model" (e.g., Kelvin's mechanical model of electricity). Theoretical physics now gradually lends itself to the growing needs of axiomatization, not only for the presentation of classical theories, but also for introducing new theories: e.g., the special theory of relativity (H. Reichenbach, *Axiomatik der relativistischen Raum-Zeit Lehre*, Vieweg, Braunschweig, 1924) and quantum-theory (H. Weyl, *Gruppentheorie und Quantenmechanik*, Leipzig, 1923). Then, axiomatization has been applied to scientific domains scarcely mathematized; because of the very fact that a formal axiomatic system eliminated the memory of the intuitive ideas which had gone into it and had thus ceased to remain attached to strictly mathematical notions, it became aptly disengaged from them in such domains. Thus, it was possible to extend axiomatization to Biology (J. H. Woodger, *The Axiomatic Method in Biology*, Cambridge, 1937) and to Psychology (C. L. Hull, *Mathematico-Deductive Theory of Rote Learning: a Study in Scientific Methodology*, New Haven and London, 1940). These theories do not then reach the complete formalization which the theories of Logic and Mathematics have attained by being reduced to pure calculi on signs; nevertheless, they are on the road to formalization.

We venture even to say that today axiomatization, if not in all its rigor at least in spirit, inspires the present refurbishing of methods in the human sciences. In the nineteenth century the economists of the so-called "classical" school had frequently proceeded in a deductive manner (D. Ricardo), and certain ones had even introduced the use of algebraic formulas (A. Cournot, L. Walras). But in our own time we witness a wide movement, bearing on the totality of the sciences of man under the impetus and example of linguistics, to modify profoundly their style of inquiry; instead of limiting research by the Baconian precept of mounting gradually by prescribed steps (*per gradus debitos*) from the experienced facts to more and more general laws, some scientists, without giving up such an empirical investigation of new materials, try to go immediately from observation of the facts to the construction of a formal theory conceived as a system of relations and performing the role of an axiomatic system for these facts. Confronted with social, economic, linguistic, ethnological facts, contemporary structuralism tries, as Claude Lévi-Strauss said to an interviewer (*Le Nouvel Observateur*, 25–31 Jan., 1967), "to represent these facts in the form of models taking always into consideration not the terms but the *relations* among the terms. It then treats each system of relations as a particular case of other systems, real or merely possible, and seeks to explain them as a whole on the level of the rules of *transformation* which permit one to go from one system to another." The exemplary status of axiomatic procedures is well shown when, for instance, we see some linguists today aiming at the construction of a "formalized grammar" apt to eliminate intuition in the learning of a foreign language, thus bypassing the traditional inductive procedure by a radical reversal, in the name of a "Cartesian linguistics" (N. Chomsky, *Cartesian Linguistics*, New York, 1967).

Axiomatic formalization is tried also in other domains, which this time transcend the boundaries of science, properly speaking, viz., in cases where the evaluation of a statement is no longer in terms of what is true or false, but according to what is just and unjust. Confined for a long time to deductive statements, logic has for the last few decades been extended to normative, evaluative, and imperative sentences. Many works have been devoted to the constitution of a "deontic logic," following G. H. Wright (*An Essay in Modal Logic*, Amsterdam, 1951). Now such a logic is exactly adapted to the language of the law, and many efforts are being made today to construct a "logic of law" (V. Klug, *Juristische Logik*, Berlin, 1951); or if this expression appears disputable, in order to try to give to the language of the law a logically rigorous form, what today can only mean a formalized axiomatic. It is true that attention has been concentrated on the applications of law, i.e., to the analysis of legal arguments rather than to the axiomatizing of the legal doctrines themselves; but the idea is on the way. One can well judge what the value of the success of such ventures would be not only as a speculative but also as a practical matter. The editors of legal codes, of constitutions, international treaties, and even of contracts only, are haunted by the two preoccupations of avoiding contradictions and loopholes. These are precisely the problems of consistency and completeness in the theory of axiomatic systems. It would be obviously advantageous to be able to solve these problems whenever the system reaches a certain degree of complexity, by substituting a formalized demonstration for an intuition which is always likely to be fallible and incommunicable.

BIBLIOGRAPHY

The works which mark the principal historical stages of axiomatization have been indicated in the course of the article. Among contemporary works which deal with axiomatics, without being themselves axiomatic, are the following: H. Scholz, *Die Axiomatik der Alten* (1930–31), reprinted in *Mathesis universalis* (Basel-Stuttgart, 1961); F. Gonseth, *Les Mathématiques et la réalité, essai sur la méthode axiomatique* (Paris, 1936); J. Cavaillès, *Méthode axiomatique et formalisme* (Paris, 1938); G. G. Granger, *Pensée formelle et sciences de l'homme* (Paris, 1960), esp. Ch. VI; W. and M. Kneale, *The Development of Logic* (Oxford, 1962). For an introductory exposition: R. Blanché, *L'axiomatique* (Paris, 1955), trans. as *Axiomatics* (London, 1962). Also A. Tarski, *Introduction to Logic and to the Methodology of the Deductive Sciences*, 3rd ed. rev. (New York, 1965), pp. 140, 234ff; R. L. Wilder, *Introduction to the Foundations of Mathematics* (New York, 1952); F. Enriques, *Historic Development of Logic*, trans. J. Rosenthal (New York, 1933).

ROBERT BLANCHÉ

[See also **Abstraction in the Formation of Concepts; Mathematical Rigor; Number; Structuralism.**]

BACONIANISM

I

THE FORTUNES of Bacon in modern thought are extraordinarily rich in controversies and questionings. They are closely bound up with a clash, often very harsh in tone, between diverse and opposed conceptions of philosophy and scientific knowledge. Was Bacon the father of modern philosophy or an heir of Renaissance naturalism? Was he the father of modern science or the builder of a huge and useless "logical machine"? Theorist of the new method of investigating nature or thinker bound to the most characteristic themes of the traditional magico-alchemy? Theorist of progress or the thinker at the source of those processes of alienation and estrangement present in modern industrial society?

Confrontation with or discussion of Bacon's ideas is an integral part not only of the philosophies of Boyle, Vico, Leibniz, Newton, Diderot, Comte, and Dewey but of the great currents and movements of modern culture: the Enlightenment, romantic spiritualism, positivism, and pragmatism. Controversy over Baconian ideas seems alive even today: the expounders of the so-called critical theory of society still see in Bacon or in Baconianism the symbol of the impious Promethean and Faustian ideal of a total instrumental mechanization of reality.

II

The impatience of the humanists and English Ramists with the disputative science of Scholasticism, the naturalism of Italian thought in the Renaissance, the practical elements of the magico-alchemical tradition, the revaluation of technical knowledge in the works of the mechanists (*meccanici*) in the sixteenth century, the ethico-political realism of Machiavelli, the treatises on rhetoric and on the arts of discourse—all these had a decisive influence on the cultural development of Francis Bacon. But what makes his thought modern is not so much his adhesion to the most progressive movements of contemporary culture as the transformed *function* which Bacon assigns to learning. He understands knowledge not as contemplation or recognition of a given reality, but as a *venatio*, a hunt, an exploration of unknown lands, a discovery of the unknown. Bacon wished to be the *buccinator* or herald of a new world, and his true greatness consists precisely in this function of his as herald. He formulated no revolutionary scientific hypothesis and contributed to none of the discoveries destined to alter to any large extent the horizon of modern science. But he did inquire into and wrote on the function of science in human life, and worked out an ethics of scientific research flatly opposed to the typically magical mentality dominant in his time. He tried to think up a new technique of approach to nature, and laid the bases of that encyclopedia of the sciences which was destined to become one of the most important enterprises of European culture. With energy and clarity he formulated a number of theses which are now an integral part of our civilization and which warrant our ranking him, with Descartes and Galileo, among the founders of modern thought. These theses are the following: science can and should transform the condition of human life on earth; science, even if it is internally value-free, is not in reality indifferent to the values of ethics and the reaches of political and social life: it is an instrument constructed by man with a view to the realization of the values of fraternity and progress; these values must be strengthened and reinforced by that same science in which collaboration, humility before Nature, and the will to be clear are the rule; the logic of the humanists, constructed with a view to persuasion, is to be replaced by a logic of invention and discovery useful in the construction of works rather than in the disputations of the learned; the extension of man's power over nature is never the work of a single investigator who keeps his results secret, but is the fruit of an organized collectivity of scientists financed by the State or by public bodies; in the historical world, science always has a precise practical function and every reform of learning is always a reform also of cultural institutions and universities.

Many of these ideas seem familiar to us nowadays. Nevertheless they were born of a long historical labor and have had a revolutionary significance. To make this clear it will be useful to consider briefly five salient ideas or viewpoints in the Baconian philosophy to which the later course of thought appealed, positively or negatively, and which exerted a decisive influence on the Enlightenment and on positivism. These conceptions may be listed as follows: (1) the evaluation of tradition; (2) the idea of science; (3) the revaluation of technology; (4) the search for a method; (5) the notion of natural history.

(1) Bacon was convinced that culture had entered a period of radical crisis, had come to a "dead end," and that a new epoch was about to be born. However, the vast change about to happen was not to affect only philosophy or speculative thought, Bacon believed. It was rather bound up with a whole series of material factors which have modified man's way of life and must consequently modify, too, their way of thinking. The great inventions of the compass, the printing press, and gunpowder, the new growth of the mechanical arts, the voyages of exploration and geographical discoveries, and the new political conditions in Europe have modified the conditions of living. It would be shameful for men to be confined within the boundaries of the ancient intellectual world after they have opened out to infinity the boundaries of the *globus mundi*. Since the conditions of the time are ripe, Bacon presents his works as a child of the time (*temporis partus masculus*) rather than of the mind of a genius. The considerations developed in *Temporis partus masculus* (1602–03), *Cogitata et visa* (1607), *Redargutio philosophiarum* (1608), and then restated in different form in the major works are not interpretable as a kind of invective or polemical outburst: they are born of the consciousness that a new age requires a new philosophy and a new vision of the world, that it requires above all an end to that attitude of veneration of the past which hitherto has characterized culture. What Bacon attacks in the ancient philosophers (Plato, Aristotle, Galen, Cicero, Seneca, Plutarch) and in those of the Middle Ages and the Renaissance (Thomas, Duns Scotus, Ramus, Cardan, Paracelsus, Telesio) is not a series of theoretical errors. These philosophies can all be put on the same level because they are all in reality products of ages that had characteristics, purposes, goals different from those of the modern age. It is not a question of attacking or denying the glory of the traditional philosophers. If we followed in their path, Bacon says again and again, we should certainly come to results inferior to those they arrived at. It is a question of rejecting their goals and their methods, showing the historical character—historical, and therefore not eternal or supertemporal—of these philosophies, making clear how the limits of these philosophies are precisely the limits of Greek civilization, close to the time of the fables of the poets and poor in history, and of medieval civilization, built by men of acute mind and too ample

leisure (confined moreover to convent cells), who sought impiously to reduce theology to a science and wrote commentaries far more obscure than the sacred texts they professed to interpret.

(2) Science, as Bacon conceives it, must abandon the terrain of chance, of the arbitrary, of the hasty synthesis, and must proceed on the basis of an experimentalism constructed not *ex analogia hominis* but *ex analogia universi*. John Dewey has very justly written that many misunderstandings of Bacon's thought would have been avoided had proper notice been taken of the emphasis Bacon places on the social factor both in the search for knowledge and in the goal of knowledge. Bacon did not succeed in carrying out any of his numerous projects for a reformation of cultural institutions, but he insisted at length on the public, democratic, and collaborative nature of scientific inquiry. The conception of science as resulting from a series of individual contributions to a communal success, the patrimony of all, put Bacon in a position of radical conflict on the one hand with the debater's science of Scholasticism, on the other with the magical mentality largely dominant in the culture of the Renaissance. Against Cardan, against Agrippa, against many of the Renaissance naturalists Bacon carried on an unrelenting polemic. In the *Redargutio philosophiarum*, and then in the general preface to the *Instauratio magna*, he struck with singular penetration and power at the roots of the characteristic attitudes of magical alchemy. If among innumerable falsities magic and alchemy come to some results, that still happens out of love of novelty and for the sake of exciting wonder, not with a view to the benefit of humankind. Philosophy tends, through demonstrations, to make things seem less wonderful and miraculous than in reality they are; magic and imposture on the contrary make things seem more wonderful than they are in reality. Men must continue the attempt characteristic of magic, to make themselves masters of nature, but must reject the methods and the procedures magic has linked to these attempts. Every attitude which would substitute the wisdom of one man for the organized efforts of humanity is to be rebuffed. Every doctrine that places science in the service of some one man rather than in the service of the whole human race is to be rejected. Bacon accordingly interprets magic as imposture, as a craving for applause, a mania for greatness and fame. For technique and its sweat and laboriousness magic pretends to be able to substitute some easy arrangement of bodies. But the interpretation of the oracles of nature demands an infinite patience, and the pages of the great book of nature are to be read with humility and reverence. To learn to read in this book means renouncing the pretence

of miracle-making to amaze the vulgar; it means to become as little children. Magicians and alchemists repeat the same gestures endlessly, put their trust in an inalterable ritual. Magic and alchemy are by nature uncollaborative and unprogressive: they cannot take form as sciences because they assign excessive weight to individual action and judgment and are incapable of growing by their own internal strength. The philosophers and scientists and magicians of the Renaissance had, it is true, energetically insisted on the value of "experiments," as against the bookish culture of late Scholasticism, and had underlined the practical value of all research. But they had continued to conceive the work of science as the fruit of solitary labor, as the privilege of exceptional personalities, as the product of collaboration by the "enlightened" which required special and secret means of communication and mysterious initiations. Della Porta, Cardan, Agrippa, and Paracelsus moved on this terrain. Bacon proposed a different portrait of the scientist, founded on a different conception of science. Science is not a series of thoughts jotted down, but methodical and systematic thought. It is not a simple appeal to experience, it is not only rejection of the authorities, it is not only observation. Science is not the intuition of a solitary genius, but is research and the institutionalizing of research in specific social and linguistic forms.

(3) The course of history was profoundly changed, according to Bacon, by mechanical inventions. His protest against the sterility of the traditional culture appears to be founded on the contrast between the mechanical arts and speculative philosophy. The sciences, he writes in the *Novum organum* (I, Preface), have remained unchanged for two thousand years almost, while the mechanical arts, as if pervaded by a vital spirit, continually grow and advance. In the dialectical exercises of the medieval schools, in the rhetorical exercises of the humanists, every assertion remained what it was, unchanged; and every question remained unresolved, as if transfixed. The intellectual sciences stood like statues worshipped and celebrated, while the progress of the technical arts is so swift that it even surpasses the desires of men. This progress depends on the fact that in the mechanical arts there is no room for the dictatorial power of an individual: in these arts the minds of many collaborate. The figure of the master is replaced by that of the inventor, the image of the sage by that of the investigator who adds something to the work of those who preceded him (*De augmentis. . . , Works*, I, 457–58). The Baconian revaluation of technology and the mechanical arts, central to the new culture, entailed the rejection of that conception of science which, though cracked in a thousand places, had remained alive and operative for centuries:

a science which is born only when the necessities of life have already been procured and which then develops into a disinterested contemplation of truth. In a very large sector of European thought, during antiquity and the Middle Ages, the distinction between slaves and free men was identified with the contrast between manual labor and intellectual work, between practical knowledge and rational knowledge, between technology and science. Thus the Baconian distinction between "ancients" and "moderns" takes on, from this point of view, a more exact meaning; to fall under the spell of tradition means to accept one of the characteristic dogmas of the past: the transformation of one's own inadequate technique into a theory of being. The ancients put "beyond the bounds of possibility . . . whatever is beyond their own or their master's knowledge or reach" (*Novum organum*, I, 75). The Aristotelian philosophy of nature was constructed on the basis of inadequate and insufficient instruments of control and guidance. To the "thus far and no further" of the ancients Bacon opposes the "there is more beyond" of the new science; the "inimitable thunderbolt" (*inimitabile fulmen*) can now be imitated. Taking the mechanical arts as a *model for culture*, it is then possible to bring to birth a type of learning which, unlike the ancient kind, is capable of progress. But Bacon never thought of reducing science to technology. In the new culture the work of the mechanics and empirics was to unite with that of the theorists so that "the kind of Mechanics often merely empirical and operative" would be surpassed (*De augmentis . . . , Works*, I, 572). In any case, collaboration between science and technical arts was to take the place of chance and gross observation. For more than twenty years the Lord Chancellor drove home a double critique, for which he fought, so to speak, "on two fronts": against the inadequacies of the work of the empirics and against the arbitrariness of the doctrines of the rationalists. The transformation of reality and the instauration of the *regnum hominis* cannot be entrusted solely to the fire of the laboratories and the work of the shops, but must depend on reason capable of operating with the aid of instruments. As he writes in the *Cogitata et visa:* "In both the arts and sciences there is a universally accepted cleavage into the Empirical and the Rational or Philosophical." But in Bacon's view these twin attitudes have not up to now been properly mingled and combined. The Empirics are like ants; they gather and consume. The Rationalists are spiders spinning webs out of themselves. But the bee combines both functions. It gathers its material from flowers of garden and field, and digests and transforms them by a faculty of its own.

This is the type of true philosophy. It takes the matter furnished by natural history and mechanical experience and stores it in its memory, but not before it has been transformed and wrought upon by the understanding. Bacon is, of course, aware that some Empirics disclaim the title of Empiric pure and simple, and some Dogmatists are ambitious to be thought determined and intelligent experimentalists. But, whichever group they belong to, these pretensions are only evidence of their wish to have a reputation above their fellows. In fact the divorce between the two activities, speculation and experiment, has always obtained. But if the two could be joined in a closer and holier union, the prospects of a numerous and happy issue are bright indeed.

(4) The new logic of the sciences (*novum organum scientiarum*), as Bacon conceives it, is not only a method of inquiry. The interpretation of nature (*interpretatio naturae*), which is founded on induction and its method of elimination and which aims at the determination of forms, is closely linked with the *expurgatio intellectus* whose task it is to liberate the human intellect from the prejudices (*idola*) deriving from the spontaneous and uncontrolled operations of reason, language, and traditional philosophies. Many commentators, beginning with Hegel in his *History of Philosophy,* have identified the whole work of Bacon with the second book of the *Novum organum,* which contains the famous doctrine of the Tables (*tabulae*) and Instances (*instantiae*). But rather than expound that doctrine it will be more useful to set out some considerations of a general nature touching the Baconian method. Bacon held that one of the essential tasks, if not indeed *the* task, of scientific inquiry was to remedy the poverty of factual information. The draft of a logic of scientific inquiry, at which Bacon had worked since 1603 and which found expression in the second book of the *Novum organum,* was interrupted because he was convinced that the construction of perfect tables was the decisive element for the advancement of science. The fourth part of the *Instauratio magna,* which was to carry out the work of ordering the varied contents of natural histories, came to seem to Bacon more important than his new logic itself. The gathering of materials for research seemed to him more urgent than any perfecting of the theoretical apparatus of the sciences. But Bacon had reached these conclusions in a special historical setting. Replacing the traditional collection of rhetorical topics, applying the art of memory to ends different from the traditional, conceiving the *tabulae* as a means of ordering with whose help memory prepares an organized reality for intellectual work, and making use of Ramus' rules in the endeavor to determine forms, Bacon introduced into his logic of science many elements drawn from the

dialectico-rhetorical tradition of the Renaissance. From the viewpoint of his method he was much closer than he realized to the conceptions of dialectic entertained by Ramus or Melancthon when they conceived it as the means for the orderly disposition of ideas, establishing order in a reality which presents itself as something chaotic. The Baconian conception of scientific method, despite all that is distinctive about it, still moves on the terrain of the Ramist definition of *dispositio* as *apta inventarum rerum collocatio*. Method, for Bacon, is a means of ordering and classifying natural reality. It is not a matter of chance that Bacon described it as a thread (*filum*) capable of guiding man through that forest (*silva*) and intricate labyrinth called Nature. The chief limitations of the Baconian method derive no doubt from the fact that Bacon had a very meager awareness of the function of hypotheses, abstractions, and mathematics in scientific research. But even this want of understanding, which led him to value "mechanics" like George Agricola higher than "theorists" like Copernicus and Galileo, is closely connected with the image of logic as the means of putting order into the natural "forest." The Platonic and Galilean image of a world logical and mathematical in structure, created by a "geometer God" who carried out the creation by number, weight, and measurement (*numero, pondere et mensura*), was undoubtedly to be more fertile for the development of modern physics than the Baconian image of Nature as a labyrinth in which man moves with toilsome difficulty, uncertain whether the constructions of his mind correspond to the structures of reality. The Platonic image of nature and the doctrine of the economy and simplicity of nature led to a type of questioning which was much more fruitful than the Baconian, which operated on the basis of models taken from the tradition of rhetoric.

(5) Natural history, for Bacon, is a history at once of free nature and of nature modified and transformed by the hand of man. Making the history of techniques an integral part of natural history, Bacon rejected the traditional opposition of *nature* and *art*. Art is not an "aping" of nature, and the products of art are not essentially different from the products of nature. The progress of science and the amelioration of the condition of mankind demand therefore, according to Bacon, that the knowledge of the technicians, excluded by age-old tradition from the field of science and natural philosophy, be imported into that field. The methods, the procedures, the operations, the language of the mechanical arts have been maintained and perfected outside the world of the official culture, in the circles of the engineers and architects and skilled artisans and makers of machines and instruments. These methods, these procedures, these operations, these languages

must become subject-matter of reflection and study. Only in this way, with the help of academies and scientific societies, can the *experientia erratica* of the mechanics, the limited observations of the artisans, the daily labors of those who transform nature with their hands be rescued from chance and pure empiricism and lead to a unitary, systematic *corpus* of knowledge.

III

The reflections presented by Bacon in *De sapientia veterum* (1609) and *De augmentis* (1623) on the wisdom of the ancients, on the fables of the poets, on language and poetry were to exercise a decisive influence on the *Scienza nuova* (1725–44) of Giambattista Vico, work which was meant to be an "application to human affairs" of Bacon's method. The Baconian theses concerning symbols and real characters were to have an audible echo in the English theorists of universal language, from John Wilkins to George Dalgarno, and subsequently in the linguistic doctrines of Condillac. The doctrines on methods of communicating style for scientific works were profoundly to influence English prose. But above all the grand themes of Bacon's philosophy—the criticism of tradition, the idea of progress, the revaluation of technology, the project of a history of the arts—were to inspire some of the chief spokesmen of European thought. The new science as separate from religion, as renunciation of the endeavor to determine essences, as "historical," descriptive, and phenomenal knowledge of the world, as outcome of the conjunction of theory with the practice of artisans, as human instrument for the domination of the world: on these typically Baconian themes Mersenne and Gassendi, Boyle and the "virtuosi" of the seventeenth century join hands. To become fully aware of the powerful influence exerted by Bacon's doctrines, it suffices to read the pages devoted by Gassendi to natural history (*Exercitationes*, in *Opera*, Lyons [1658], III, 107b) or the *Considerations touching the Usefulness of Experimental Natural Philosophy* of Robert Boyle (in *Works*, London [1774], III, 392ff.), in which the anatomy-theater and the workshop of the artisans are contrasted with the libraries of the humanists. In 1653, writing to Peiresc, Mersenne proposed an academy which, founded on the ideal of cooperation among the wise, should gather together all the learned of Europe. The advancement and progress of the sciences through collaboration—this was the common goal appealed to by the first modern scientific academies: The Accademia del Cimento (1657), the Royal Society (1662), the Académie des Sciences (1666). And to this vision of vast collaboration, of a self-nourishing research growing through the work carried on in a whole series of scientific institutions, Fontenelle and Pascal conjoined a new conception of history as product of a common labor, as resultant of the efforts of many generations, as a slow accumulation of experience always further integrable and perfectible. In a famous page of John Wallis' describing the first meetings in London of the cultivators of natural philosophy (1641), the name of Bacon is already linked with that of Galileo as one of the two founders of the "new and experimental philosophy" beginning to be cultivated in Italy, France, Germany, and England. Among the first tasks of the Royal Society we find the compilation of faithful records of all the works of nature and the arts, and the study of the effect of experiments on the manual trades. The rejection of the sterility of the old philosophies coincided with the demand for a simple, clear, accessible language. That "Verulamium design" about which John Beale had written to Robert Boyle in July 1666 (Boyle, *Works*, London [1774], VI, 404) gathered even more numerous adherents throughout Europe. Not only in England but everyone in France, Germany, and Italy who was working on a new science invoked the name of Bacon. The *Initia et specimina novae generalis pro instauratione et augmentis scientiarum*, a work of Leibniz, reveals in its very title its unmistakable Baconian inspiration; in this work Leibniz urges the necessity of gathering up in one organic body of knowledge the piecemeal "know how" of technicians and artisans (*Die Philosophische Schriften von Gottfried Wilhelm Leibniz*, ed. C. I. Gerhardt, 7 vols., Berlin [1875–90], VII, 69). And in his *Discours touchant la certitude et l'art d'inventer* (ibid., 181–82), Leibniz explicitly revives the project of a great encyclopedia of the arts, based on a conception of science and progress which challenges Descartes' willful "solitude" and recalls Bacon for support. But the appeal to Bacon was also significant and important with respect to method because despite all the criticisms that can be levelled against the scientific methodology of the *Novum organum*, one very obvious thing must not be forgotten: the science of the seventeenth and eighteenth centuries was at once Galilean *and* Baconian *and* Cartesian. Boyle's law on the volume and pressure of a gas at constant temperature and Galileo's law of falling bodies seemed to be "truths" independent of the different methods employed in determining them. The "romance of Cartesian physics," as Christiaan Huygens called it, continued to wield its influence in European culture for more than a century. Boyle, the founders of the Royal Society, Gassendi on the continent, and Newton himself felt themselves to be followers of Bacon and continuing his lead. When Newton, in opposition to Descartes and Galileo, regarded mathematics not as "the queen of the sciences" but as a method and instrument for the clarification of experi-

ment, and when he rejected the vision of Nature as mathematical in essence, he revived, though on a very different level, some very characteristic Baconian positions. In any event, the distinction between the so-called two methods of scientific research (the mathematico-deductive and the experimental-inductive) was felt to be as real in the seventeenth and eighteenth centuries. The "myth" of Bacon, it is well to remember, was not an invention of nineteenth-century historians but an operative reality for the British scientists and the French *philosophes* of the Age of Reason—even though, in point of fact, the distinction was not invariably pure and clear; some passages in Descartes and Galileo on the two methods remind one very much of Bacon, and Bacon himself provides a fair number of examples of "hypotheses" or "anticipations of nature." Finally, it ought to be remembered by excessively severe critics of Baconianism that the progress of modern anatomy, embryology, botany, zoology, and mineralogy was intimately associated with a Baconian insistence on observation and experiments, and with a conviction that the immense variety of the forms of nature can be ordered, classified, and described. Here too, of course, the need to formulate hypotheses soon became clear. The Baconian identification of science with experiments was seen to be one-sided. Nevertheless, the demand for experiments and the mistrust of audacious hypotheses played a historical role of crucial importance.

The taste for observations and experiments, the triumph of experimental over theoretical physics, the slackening of interest in geometry, and the inadequacy of Cartesianism—all these contribute to explain the extraordinary prestige of Baconianism among the men of the Enlightenment, even though there were fundamental differences between the judgments of D'Alembert, the firm Baconianism of Diderot, the scrupulous analyses of Alexandre Deleyre in his *Analyse de la philosophie du Chancelier François Bacon* (Amsterdam and Paris, 1755), the judgments of Voltaire. In the twelfth of his *Lettres Philosophiques* Voltaire proffers a very acute judgment, that Bacon erected the grand edifice of modern science with the help of a scaffolding (the *Novum organum*) that seems today no longer usable. In point of fact the Bacon of the Encyclopedists is not the theorist of method. He is the philosopher who first proclaimed the cultural value of technology, who destroyed the prejudices against the mechanical arts that (as Diderot wrote under the heading *Art* in the Encyclopedia) filled the cities with indolent contemplators and the countryside with ignorant petty tyrants. Bacon becomes the theorist of the necessary interdependency of the sciences and the technical arts, the author of the first great encyclopedia of modern times, the philosopher who first grasped with clarity the necessary union of theory and practice, the social function of scientific knowledge, its power to transform the world, to enlighten men, and to make them happier.

The reaction in romantic and spiritualist circles to the Enlightenment's exaltation of Bacon came in tones of decided asperity. Joseph de Maistre, for example, saw in Bacon the spiritual father of all the enemies of humankind. But it was especially the appraisal of the spiritualist chemist Justus von Leibig (1863) that determined subsequent evaluations of Baconism. Many of his hasty and superficial judgments (for example, his judgment of Bacon's attitude to Copernicus) became commonplace. But the prestige of Bacon perhaps reached its lowest level when, on the basis of an identification of the history of ideas with the history of the problem of knowledge, the whole of the works of Bacon was reduced to Book II of the *Novum organum*. Bacon came then to be seen only as the constructor of a vast logical machine destined to remain unused, or only as the precursor of the inductive logic of John Stuart Mill. In a historiography of Hegelian ancestry, which proceeded by way of successive self-transcendings and saw in English empiricism only the preparation for the *Critique* of Kant, it was not difficult to come quickly to a judgment of Baconian bankruptcy.

Baconianism occupies a peculiar position, too, in that species of romantic exaltation of science known as positivism. Instead of a real resumption of the great themes of the philosophy of Bacon one finds in Comte an attempt to make of Bacon a clever but confused anticipator of the positivist philosophy. Baconism is identified with empiricism and utilitarianism. Whewell and Mill, on the other hand, limit themselves to proposing corrections of the logic of the *Novum organum*. Very much more sustained and stimulating is the discussion undertaken by the pragmatists. There is hardly need to recall the Baconism (not always, however, sufficiently recognized) of John Dewey, and his insistence upon the social nature of science, his conception of modern thought as originating in the adoption by inquiry of the procedures and aims of productive labor, his conception of a "reconstruction in philosophy" as a realized expression, in modern times, of the aspirations which were the aspirations of Bacon. Dewey, different in this from less discerning pragmatists, sees clearly the inadequacies of every interpretation of Baconism as utilitarianism. To see in the Baconian exaltation of "works" the expression of a utilitarian position means in fact to leave altogether out of account the thesis, many times formulated by Bacon, of a full and total coincidence between truth and working;

it means not to take seriously his repeated affirmation that *only truth* is capable of producing fruit and works. *Opera ipsa pluris facienda sunt, quatenus sunt veritatis pignora, quam propter vitae commoda* (*Works*, III, 612): to ask whether scientific truths depend upon the procedures employed to determine them or upon their fecundity is for Bacon a meaningless dilemma: a scientific truth is always fecund and its fecundity depends exclusively upon its truth. A practicality without truth is for Bacon arbitrary and chance-dominated, incapable of progress and development. What concerns him is that theoretical progress and the general "advancement" of the condition of humanity should not be considered separately or even as flatly opposed to each other, as had been the case in philosophy ever since the days of Plato.

The thesis of a Bacon "vulgarly utilitarian," propounded by reactionary nineteenth-century thought, has been restated in this century, in much subtler form, by the proponents of the "critical theory of society." Taking up again the themes of Husserl's criticism of Galileo in *Krisis*, Adorno and Horkheimer (*Dialektik der Aufklärung,* 1942) saw in Baconism the typical *animus* of modern science, indistinguishable from technology, intent upon the exploitation of nature and total instrumentalization. According to these writers, it is the scientific and technological enthusiasm of the Lord Chancellor that lies back of the materialism, the mercantilization of culture, that leads to modern industrial society, realm of alienation and conformism and standardization and the destruction of all human values. Once again Bacon is reduced to a *symbol*, and the reduction, once again, is carried out at the cost of an extreme simplification: since for Bacon the foundation of the *regnum hominis*, the restoration of the dominion of man over nature had meaning only if realized in a definite religious, political, moral, and cultural context. Even today it can be a salutary lesson to recall the central ideas of Baconianism—and so prevent the analysis of the alienating and inhuman aspects of the contemporary world from issuing in a decadent and pessimistic revulsion from work and civilization, or in a mystical awaiting of a mythical future in which the "pleasure principle" will have triumphed at last over the "reality principle."

A good many criticisms of modern industrial society, science, and technology appear to rest on the conviction that man can realize himself *without* dominion over nature. Many of these criticisms resolve themselves often in an exaltation of subjectivity, a plaint for the primitive and mythical, a nostalgia for the days of a "wisdom" or "total knowledge" founded on metaphysics, theology, or the practices of shamans. Many of these critics, who in point of fact derive their ideas from Heidegger, are fond of referring to the texts of Karl Marx. They too easily forget that Marx applauded not only the radical criticism of civilization of Rousseau's first *Discours* but also the celebration of work and technical skill in Francis Bacon's *New Atlantis*. Bacon never believed that science and technology, *as such*, represented the salvation of man. The liberation of man—and in this too he is modern—can be painfully achieved (by ways far more complicated than he was able to imagine) only through the labor, the works, the well-being of the whole of humanity.

BIBLIOGRAPHY

The Works of Francis Bacon, eds. R. L. Ellis, J. Spedding, D. D. Heath, 7 vols. (London, 1857–59). *The Letters and Life of Francis Bacon, Including All His Occasional Works*, ed. J. Spedding, 7 vols. (London, 1861–74). Among the bibliographical works: R. W. Gibson, *Francis Bacon, A Bibliography of his Works and of Baconiana to the Year 1750* (Oxford, 1950). For the period 1800–1956: P. Rossi, "Per una bibliografia degli scritti su Bacone," *Rivista critica di storia della filosofia*, **12**, 1 (1957), 75–89. The best biography is by M. Sturt, *Francis Bacon: A Biography* (London, 1932). Also useful is the commentary of Th. Fowler on the *Novum organum* (London, 1878). Outlines of the influence of Bacon: G. Sortais, *La Philosophie moderne depuis Bacon jusqu'à Leibniz* (Paris, 1922). On the Rhetoric, Science of Man, style, and prose of Bacon: K. R. Wallace, *Francis Bacon on Communication and Rhetoric* (Chapel Hill, 1943); *Francis Bacon on the Nature of Man* (Urbana, Ill., 1967); B. Vickers, *Francis Bacon and Renaissance Prose* (Cambridge, 1968); W. S. Howell, *Logic and Rhetoric in England: 1500–1700* (Princeton, 1956). Two quick sketches are very significant: P.-M. Schuhl, *La Pensée de Bacon* (Paris, 1949), and B. Farrington, *Francis Bacon, Philosopher of Industrial Science* (New York, 1949). On the first period of Bacon's activities: B. Farrington, *The Philosophy of Francis Bacon: An Essay of its Development from 1603 to 1609* (Liverpool, 1964). The best study on Baconian logic is that of T. Kotarbinsky, "The Development of the Main Problem in the Methodology of Francis Bacon," *Studia Philosophica* (1935). Among the recent works on the whole of Bacon's philosophy: F. Anderson, The *Philosophy of Francis Bacon* (Chicago, 1948); P. Rossi, *Francis Bacon: From Magic to Science* (London and Chicago, 1967). On the idea of progress and value of technology: P. Rossi, *Philosophy, Technology and the Arts: in the Early Modern Era* (New York, 1970). On the Encyclopedia: R. McRae, *The Problem of the Unity of Sciences, Bacon to Kant* (Toronto, 1961). On special aspects: Marie Boas, "Bacon and Gilbert," *Journal of the History of Ideas*, **12**, 3 (1950), 466–67; E. Moody Prior, "Bacon's Man of Science," *Journal of the History of Ideas*, **15**, 3 (1954), 348–70; P. H. Kocher, "Bacon on the Science of Jurisprudence," *Journal of the History of Ideas*, **18**, 1 (1957), 3–26. On the religious theme: P. Rossi, "Bacone e la Bibbia,"

Archiwum Historii Filozofii (Warsaw, 1966). Among the few works on Bacon's influence: H. Dieckmann, "The Influence of Francis Bacon on Diderot's *Interprétation de la Nature*," *Romanic Review*, **24**, 4 (1943), 303–30.

PAOLO ROSSI

[See also **Ancients and Moderns**; Crisis; Positivism; Pragmatism; Progress; **Renaissance Humanism**; **Technology**; **Work**.]

BALANCE OF POWER

THE IDEA of balance of power initially envisaged the relations between two states (and, by extension, two groups) as comparable to a pair of scales, with the possibility of intervention by a third party either to restore the equilibrium or to tip the balance in favor of one of the two. Later, the notion was extended, first to three states, then to an entire congeries of states, poised against one another, any substantial change in the mass of one of the units requiring a regrouping amongst the rest if the equilibrium was to be maintained. All this has developed into a wider theory of international politics which makes the preservation of the equilibrium an object (even sometimes the overruling object) of policy for the purpose of preventing the indefinite expansion of a predominant member of the system; and which, by its regard for the diagram of forces, tends to base foreign policy on considerations relating to power.

I. THE ANCIENT WORLD

Classical antiquity carried political thought to a considerable depth while it discussed the problem of the state as though only one example existed in the world; but its intellectual achievement is disappointing in the field of interstate relations. The notion that a government should ally itself with the power that it fears the less against the power that it fears the more, and the idea that a state, when confronted by an aggressor who is superior in strength, should seek an ally, hardly rise above the level of banality. Neither the view that small states should combine against a threatening giant, nor the habit of shifting alliances as circumstances change, can be regarded as more than the raw material of human experience, familiar long before the rise of Athens. It is only too easy for us to read into such elementary phenomena a complicated notion of equilibrium which has become second nature to modern man.

179

Thucydides, though he does not envisage an actual balance, may be said to adumbrate a number of maxims which would have been recognized in the eighteenth century as part of the complex of ideas which the theory embraced, e.g.:

You, Spartans, are the only people in Hellas who . . . instead of crushing an enemy in its infancy, wait until it has doubled its strength (I.69).

Athens is capable of standing up against the whole of our coalition and is superior to any one of us individually; so unless we go unanimously to war with her, both as a body and as individual states and peoples, she will find us divided and will overcome us, one by one (I.122).

The only assured basis for an alliance is for each party to be equally afraid of the other; for the one who wants to attack is deterred when the odds are not on his side. . . . [Athens] was able to lead the stronger states against the smaller, leaving the former to be dealt with last of all, after they had lost its allies and had become more easy to deal with (III.11).

Some writers have asserted that Polybius gave "classic" expression to the principle of the balance of power. But we must take him at his word. He wrote that "it is never right to help a power to acquire a predominance that will be irresistible" (Book I, Ch. 83, 4). Though David Hume tried to argue that the idea of the balance goes back to the ancient Greeks, he discovered situations which provide analogies for a modern student, rather than the concept itself, present in men's minds as a fertilizing thing. Observing how the Hellenistic governments failed to prevent the rise of Rome, he had to admit his disappointment at the fact that no ancient writer reproached them for their neglect of the balance of power.

The Indian writer, Kautilya, who seems to have lived three or four centuries before the beginning of the Christian era, has sometimes been thought to have had an idea of the balance of power. But one Indian commentator has rightly called attention to the "scholastic elaboration" of some of his teaching and has mentioned other intricacies in his diplomacy which "had apparently much interest to kings and politicians in ancient India, though to us they appear dreary and obscure." Another Indian commentator and translator tells us that "the text is hard and capable of several interpretative twists." The *Arths'āstra*, which must be of the greatest interest when related to its proper intellectual context, offers dangerous temptations to the twentieth-century student who seeks to achieve rapid results and reads the present into the past. Some of its concrete maxims seem absurdly trite, while some seem to reveal a mind comparable to that of Machiavelli; but some seem not even consistent with the idea of the balance of power. Kautilya could say: "When a weak king is attacked by a powerful enemy, the former should seek the protection of one who is superior to the enemy. . . . In the absence of a superior king, he should combine with a number of his equals who are equal in power to his enemy." But even a passage like this makes one unsure about his appreciation of the notion of balance.

II. THE RENAISSANCE

When the idea of the balance of power actually emerged it did not even come as something deduced by the modern scholar from ancient history. Few political concepts have been so definitely the fruits of modern man's experience—so definitely the result of reflection on things as they happened and on vicissitudes actually suffered. We cannot trace the genealogy of it through a succession of books, as though it were a theory simply passed like a torch from one author to another, but receiving fresh fuel at each change. It grows rather with the development of diplomatic practice, with increasing reflection on things that happen in the world, with the emergence of other concepts in associated fields, and with the achievement of more systematized views on international affairs.

In the fifteenth century it would appear that Italy provided almost ideal conditions for the formulation of the concept. Here, at the Renaissance, a number of closely interacting states formed a miniature system, within which alliances often changed, and governments seemed carefully to calculate the weights and counterweights. At the beginning of the fifteenth century, the Florentines are reported as having become convinced that Venice, while working to prolong their conflict with Milan, in the hope of weakening both the combatants, was anxious to prevent either party from securing such aggrandizement at the expense of the other as would make it a threat to Venice itself. Vespasiano da Bisticci describes Cosimo de' Medici as being afraid of the aggrandizement of Venice, but as having achieved peace after the mid-century through the skillful policy of "bringing the Italian powers to an equality of strength" (*Renaissance* . . . , p. 232). In 1498 Bernardo Rucellai specifically speaks of Italy's being "balanced" and attributes this to Lorenzo de' Medici, though Alessandro de' Pazzi in a Discourse of 1522 imputes the success of this "balancing" to good fortune, i.e., the states in Italy were so nearly equal in actual power and the states outside Italy were unable at that time to invade the peninsula (Albertini, pp. 87–88).

Machiavelli is disappointing in the field of diplomacy, though he was able to learn so much from the ancients about military matters and the conduct of war. He repeatedly deals with the question whether a state should remain neutral when its neighbors are at war, and he is aware that the result of the war itself may be the aggrandizement of one of the belligerents. If he presses the policy of intervention, however, this is not out of consideration for the balance, but because in his view the neutral loses the respect of both sides—he treats the problem as a question of prestige. He sees that a state in this intermediate position may be able to tip the scales in favor of one of the belligerents rather than the other. But where he has the opportunity of suggesting which of the two sides to opt for, he does this without regard for the general balance, though he is affected by the fact that one state (for internal reasons) may be more aggressive in spirit than the other.

At a later date, 1537, Francesco Guicciardini surprises us with a passage in the early pages of his *History of Italy* which might well stand as one of the "classical" formulations of the balance of power. He describes how the chief rulers of Italy—those of Florence, Naples, and Milan—felt that they had more to lose than to gain from any disturbance of the status quo, so they formed an alliance which checked aggression in spite of the fact that the partners were far from sincere with one another. It was a curious kind of balance that resulted, since Guicciardini tells us that most of the minor principalities of Italy joined the alliance too. But in other respects the passage was wonderfully predictive, for it vividly described how the very jealousies between the states made the peace more stable, each power keeping an unremitting watch on the movements of the rest, so that none was able to steal a march on any of the others. This nervous tension became a marked characteristic of the later balance of power system; but Guicciardini, envisaging the constricted area of the Italian peninsula, would be far ahead of his time if he were held to be recommending in this passage a formula of general policy. It is more likely that he was merely the historian diagnosing acutely a situation that seemed unique.

If we envisage not merely Italy but Western Europe as a whole, it is clear that, until this date, men were fumbling their way to a notion of balance—exposing their deficiencies by the random nature of their experiments. It was not yet possible to envisage a European system, with its internal interactions. Philippe de Commynes could picture France as the rival of England, England as set off against the Scots, Spain as confronting Portugal, Bavaria as opposed to Austria—each of these states watching its opposite number—while still being unable to transcend these partial and local observations and combine them in an overall system. Nor would the situation of the Continent, or the international politics of the time, have authorized such a synthetic view. Even when he is

speaking of Italy, he sees states in couples, and regards God as having imposed upon each of them a "contrary" to keep it humble—the Venetians set against the Florentines, for example, while both Naples and Milan are tormented by the problem of rival dynasties. In these circumstances it is little wonder that the emergent notion of balance is an incipient one, based merely on the analogy with a pair of scales.

It must not be assumed that, even so, the maintenance of the equilibrium was necessarily regarded as the object of policy. A monarch who claimed to hold the balance might merely be advertising the fact that he was worth purchasing, because he could tip the scale in favor of whichever party he joined. Also, men seem easily to recognize and resent a state's "predominance" without realizing that this should entail a positive notion of "equipoise." If a certain amount of diplomatic reflection took place during the period of the Renaissance, and if the first firm result of this was to lead to a notion of the balance of power, ideas on this subject as yet rose little above the level of banality, save in the case of Guicciardini. And, still, as throughout the previous centuries in both the Christian and the Islamic worlds, the books that were written for the guidance of princes, though they could contain considerable sections on the conduct of war, and even deal with the rise and fall of states, would show little concern for diplomacy and the conduct of foreign affairs.

The long conflict between France and the Habsburg dynasty in the sixteenth and seventeenth centuries made it more possible for men to envisage a great part of Europe in a single survey. The impression of omnipresence given by the Habsburgs, who were in Austria and Spain, in Italy and Hungary, in the Netherlands and Germany, was calculated to induce people to take something more like an overall view. It also provided the French with the basis of their claim that this dynasty was seeking "universal dominion," while they themselves were fighting to save the smaller states of Europe as well as their own country. The idea of a balance of power may have been implicit in such a situation though it is surprising to see how rarely it receives explicit formulation in the sixteenth century. And if England or Savoy sought to reap benefit from the conflicts between their greater neighbors, we may be too ready to read modern ideas of the balance of power into their attempts to snatch some advantage out of other people's quarrels. What was important was the fact that most of Europe was coming to appear more like a states-system, and many states conducted their foreign policy with reference to the main conflict between France and the Habsburgs. Also the world learned to fear the threat of "universal dominion." **181**

III. THE ASSEMBLY OF THE
CONSTITUENT IDEAS

It was important that, by the end of the sixteenth century, Machiavelli was coming to have his most significant period of influence. He was no longer entirely disreputable, for men like Justus Lipsius (who was so influential amongst both Protestants and Catholics) were separating the results of his dry, scientific, and realistic approach from some of his political maxims, which were still too crafty and cruel for acceptance in respectable circles. Henceforward, even those who were far from being governed by wishful thinking in the matter were ready to learn from Machiavelli that the state is associated with force, and that politics must be envisaged as power politics. The very men who deplored the fact were now ready to recognize a certain unanswerability which makes force so formidable a matter. People who in the twentieth century deprecated the notion of the balance of power on the ground that it regarded international politics as too much a game of power politics were really addressing themselves to this point. At the same time the wider recognition of the role of force meant the provision of something that was vaguely measurable, and it opened the way to the notion of Europe as a diagram of forces—indeed to a type of thought somewhat more analogous to the scientific.

After 1600 the references to the balance of power become more numerous, and at least the language is less clouded by ambiguities. Francis Bacon, by 1612, describes Henry VIII, Charles V, and Francis I as having been nervously in equilibrium; like Guicciardini, he notes the need for unremitting vigilance and talks of princes "keeping due sentinel." For much of the seventeenth century, however, it is the dissemination rather than the actual development of the idea that strikes the eye. The age is chiefly important for the emergence of both the political conditions and the type of thinking that were to lead to a more sophisticated view of the matter; also for the production of single ideas that were to be involved in the final synthesis.

Quite early in the century the peculiar anxiety about the problem of menacing war led to some thinking that paid attention to Europe as a whole. In a different realm, but with similar preoccupations, Grotius produced a significant advance in modern international law. Apart from this, one can see that diplomacy itself was becoming an object of serious reflection among some of the people who were practicing it. This meant, not the adoption of the teaching of Machiavelli but the application of the method in a field where Machiavelli himself had not pursued it very far. An impressive example of this in the second quarter of the century is Cardinal Richelieu, who recognized his debt to the Italian writer.

Richelieu shared the main preoccupation of the theorists of the balance of power when he put to his monarch the alternative of a reforming policy at home or an active policy abroad, while insisting that the adoption of the former would mean the sacrifice for an indefinite period of any chance of checking the hegemony of Spain. By the conscious confrontation with the problem which the conflict with Spain then presented to a genuine Catholic, he set out the terms for what we today would call a "non-ideological" foreign policy—a policy that was indispensable to a mature theory of the balance of power. Grasping the crucial distinction, he regarded it as a desperate necessity to check the menace of Habsburg dominion, but also he resolved (and tried to keep to his resolution) that his Church should suffer as little as possible from this. He adopted a parallel attitude to the Huguenots inside France, whom he determined to destroy insofar as they were an armed "state within the State," though he would tolerate their religion and hoped that this example of charity would be conducive to their ultimate voluntary conversion. The later theorists of the balance of power realized the importance to their system of the processes which helped to bring Europe out of the fanaticism of the wars of religion; and there is something in the diplomatic ideas of Richelieu which extracts matters of faith from the objectives of diplomacy and war, and even hints at the idea of war for limited purposes only. He preached, furthermore, that negotiation should never cease, that states should negotiate even when there was no issue between them and simply for the cultivation of good relations. It is surprising that at least the theorists of the balance of power should not have followed him in his further injunction: that diplomacy should not be abandoned even in time of war.

Only after about the middle of the century, however, do the references to the balance of power itself begin to come in something like a flood, bringing the suggestion that the topic has awakened general interest. The prelude to this is found, in the 1640's, in the despatches of Richelieu's successor, Mazarin—despatches which show that the practicing diplomats are now having to pay attention to the matter. The idea is associated with Venice, and this means that it is treated as having special implications. Mazarin regards Venice as making a fetish of the balance of power because she has an interest in seeing that the status quo shall be preserved. Mazarin himself is willing to adopt the policy where it has the same implications; and in a treaty of alliance which he concluded with Denmark in 1645, there is a clause which says that since the interests of commerce require the maintenance of the status quo in the Atlantic, the North Sea, and the Baltic, the two powers will "work to secure that this ancient and salutary equilibrium shall be maintained without any alteration." The balance of power is interpreted as the policy of those who want to keep territorial arrangements as they now stand.

After all that has been said, it still remains true that it was the decades of Louis XIV's personal rule (i.e., the period after 1660) which were the most important for the idea of the balance of power, producing the remarkable developments and the extraordinary currency of the idea. And now, at last, it seems that the maintenance of the equilibrium comes to be regarded as the supreme object of international politics. The significance of the idea was greatly heightened by the fact that, in this period, governments paid considerable attention to propaganda in time of war, and the conflicts associated with Louis XIV's reign provoked in various countries many pamphlets and topical treatises. Both in its origin (which one can trace back through Partition Treaties) and in its course, the War of the Spanish Succession reveals the degree to which the policy of states was now being determined by consideration for the balance. The European settlement at Utrecht involved a redistribution of territory in which that consideration was paramount; and if the idea of balance had put England at first on the side of the Habsburg candidate, the same idea helps to explain how Britain could accept a Bourbon candidate when a change in the situation of the Habsburg made him, in turn, a possible threat to the equilibrium. By this time the doctrine was repeatedly appearing in diplomatic despatches, state papers, treaties of alliance, and treaties of peace.

But the very notion of balance had suffered a great transmutation by this time, achieving a pattern of which Guicciardini and Bacon themselves can have had perhaps only a glimpse. In writings of considerable importance in the seventeenth century, the main conflict between France and the Habsburgs had still been the main theme, and what was envisaged was, even at that stage in the story, something analogous to a pair of scales. Still, as in the sixteenth century, it was said by some writers that the British represented the "tongue" of the balance, and by others that this was the role of the Dutch.

The reign of Louis XIV added a new chapter to the history of man's modern experience; and, if the appropriate conclusions were soon drawn from it, we might say that whenever they have been forgotten since that date, the world has been the loser. It became clear that, after fighting for so long against the threat of "universal dominion" from the Habsburgs—fighting often on behalf of smaller states as well as on her own behalf—France herself had emerged as the aggressor and the dominating power, and Louis XIV now appeared as the continental bogy. The truth was not recognized as early as it might have been, and historians have sometimes noted that certain governments persisted too long in the view that Spain was still the general enemy. In time, however, even long-standing alliances came to require readjustment; and, towards the end of the seventeenth century the principle of the balance of power was being used as a weapon against France. Official circles in that country tended therefore to disapprove of the idea.

But, in a famous case, it becomes evident that the true consequences were drawn from reflection on the fact that Spain had been the menace in one age while France was the aggressor in another. Fénelon (François de Salignac de la Mothe), a representative of the dissidents in this latter country, did not rest content with the answer that the Spaniards had been wicked at one time, the French at another time. He produced the thesis which was the most essential of all for the mature doctrine of the balance of power in the eighteenth century. He insisted that it was the disposition of forces which made Spain the menace in the sixteenth century and France the aggressor at a later date. If a state were allowed to rise to a position of predominance, one would no longer be able to rely on its good behavior, no matter how moderate it had hitherto been in its policy. It might have struggled for the balance of power and defended the interests of small states—it might even have combated the whole idea of "universal dominion"—but once it found that it could do what it liked with impunity, it would throw overboard the old inhibitions, and no longer confine its purposes within accustomed channels. Indeed the very process of resisting the predominant power of today would be likely to generate the new aggressor, who, demanding more and more securities against the enemy, might slide imperceptibly into lust for "universal dominion."

As a consequence of all this, Fénelon not only insisted on the importance of the balance of power but held that its claims were of an overriding nature, the equivalent of an overruling law. Even the laws which prevailed in the interior of a country—the rules governing the succession to the throne, for example—should give way, he said, to "the right that so many nations had to security." Also, a nation which had no quarrel on its own account with a predominating power had the right to take precautionary measures against it for the sake of European liberty in general, though care must be taken to limit one's objective, and never seek the destruction of a power under the pretence of curbing it.

183

Supposing the objection were made that a state might find itself lifted to a predominant position at a moment when it was being directed by a virtuous ruler, Fénelon had his answer ready. Such a state might conduct a moderate policy for a single reign, he said, but its merit could hardly endure longer than that. Important factors in the situation itself would produce the wrong policy or bring the wrong kind of ruler to the top.

IV. THE EIGHTEENTH CENTURY

1. The Eighteenth-Century Theory of International Politics.

The general treaties of Westphalia (1648) and Utrecht (1713) had made it more easy, and more a matter of habit, to see a considerable part of Europe as an integrated system. These were days when the parallel ideas of a balance of trade and the equipoise of the English constitution had already been gaining currency. The world had become familiar with parallelograms of forces, and in various human studies, as well as in different branches of science (zoology, for example), the mind seemed to be taking a mechanistic turn. Henry Brougham pointed out in the *Edinburgh Review* in 1802–03 that the theory of the balance of power had been unknown to the ancient Greeks and had arisen from the progress of science and the peculiar circumstances of modern Europe. The development of a Baconian kind of reflection amongst even the practitioners of diplomacy, as well as the incidental comments of international lawyers like Grotius, had brought out more sophisticated ideas, some of which came together in the work of Fénelon. And the ideas of Fénelon helped to give a moral basis to the resulting combination; for if the virtue of governments depended somewhat on the distribution of power, it followed that in a well-balanced Europe the ambitions of all rulers would be moderate, for all would grow accustomed to feeling that only marginal aggressions were feasible. In the last struggles with Louis XIV the balance of power became a system fully conscious of itself and "quite as comprehensively and carefully worked out as the mercantilism of the seventeenth and eighteenth centuries" (Gulick, p. 299). It now graduated as a general theory of international politics.

On this mature theory, Europe was seen as almost a parallel to the system of Newtonian astronomy. The various states—whether great or small—exerted a pull or a pressure on one another, and this bore some relationship to their respective masses and to their distances from one another. If the mass of any one of them was substantially altered, this would be likely to destroy the equipoise unless the distances were corrected, the alliances changed, the states regrouped. In a world in which governments could recognize their real interests, or could envisage long-term results instead of being governed by momentary desires and prejudices, the readjustments would be rapid and might be regarded as automatic. But since states could be shortsighted, the idea of the balance of power might not always be a theory of what actually happens. It might become a policy that governments were urged to pursue; and so it might be turned into a matter of precept.

The object of the system was to prevent the emergence of a power so predominant that it could misconduct itself with impunity and march to something like "universal dominion." It was assumed that all states had the latent desire for aggression, even the small ones indulging in conquest if local circumstances provided the opportunity. So long as they were powerless, the tendency to this would be merely latent, and, where there was an equilibrium, it would become second nature to keep one's ambitions at a moderate level. It was not held that under the system of the balance of power the tendency to aggression would be abolished altogether, however. On the contrary it was assumed that once a state found that the way was open for such a thing, it would move forward to "universal dominion."

The great requirement was that the others should see the danger, and adjust their alliances in time, so that vigilance and farsightedness were necessary. It might be too late if one awoke only when the aggressor had already made a great advance—too late if one even waited for him to show his hand. It had already been a matter of controversy as to whether it was permissible to attack a state merely because it was a potential menace—i.e., before it had committed any actual offence. Some writers were in favor of even this preventive policy, though Grotius had disapproved of the idea.

An objector might argue that it was better to allow a hegemony to be established—better to have something like a Roman Empire which would secure peace throughout the system. Before the end of the eighteenth century the writers on the balance of power were addressing themselves to this argument. They claimed that here were the only two alternatives—either a states-system which made the map of Europe look like a patchwork quilt, or a "universal dominion" that embraced the whole continent.

They were well aware that when a supremacy of power has been conceded, the beneficiary can do anything that he likes with it—the chance of controlling him, or making him keep any promise that he has made, is lost. But they were prepared to confront the problem at a higher level still. Against the idea of a universal empire, which would end by producing a widespread uniformity, they pressed the case for a European civilization enriched by the variety of its national manifestations. If initially they needed a congeries of states because they insisted on having a distribution of power, they proceeded to advance further still, and argue that small states had in fact an intrinsic value. The system was claimed to be the only one which (in a world that was somewhat at the mercy of force) could secure the actual existence of small states.

The balance in fact secured not only their existence but also their autonomy, their power of independent action. Any defect in the balance would tend at least to deprive them of a genuine foreign policy, reducing them to the position of satellites. Richelieu had once complained that, in his own day, small states were able to have greater freedom of action than the larger ones, and we in the latter half of the twentieth century can see how this might be the case. In a certain sense the system of balance itself might depend on the small states, who could shift their allegiance if a power which had been their friend was turning into a general menace. The system was capable of providing, therefore, something like an actual diplomatic role for smaller states.

Indeed, before the end of the century, it had come to be realized that the system of the balance of power was directed to the maintenance of liberty rather than to the prevention of wars. It assumed (or enjoined) the adoption of the view that the ultimate object of a state was its survival or its independence; and sometimes this was taken to imply that survival was the constant motive, that all conflicts should be treated as a question of survival—in other words, all policy should be subordinated to the issue of the distribution of power. This was perhaps an abuse of the theory, since it was sufficient to say that the question of survival, the question of the distribution of power, should never be allowed to fall out of sight. The effect of the abuse was to turn policy sometimes into an arid kind of *raison d'état*.

The really important thing, as the *Edinburgh Review* repeated in 1802, was that there should be unremitting vigilance, for danger might arise from changes taking place at the other end of the map. The point was made, however, that the acquisition of territory by one power did not mean that others must make a similar expansion or that actual war would be necessary to restore the balance. The more mature theory recognized that, at the heart of the whole argument, was the idea of restoring the equilibrium by readjustments in alliances. It was realized that an internal development—a great economic advance—might alter the power of a state as much as the acquisition of territory, and this was to be counterbalanced in the same way.

It came to be seen, therefore, that the whole system assumed or acquired a high degree of flexibility, and that traditional alliances, sentimental associations, dynastic marriages, and established commercial channels might obstruct the response to changing situations, and clog the whole machine. Above all, the apostles of the balance of power feared anything like what we should call "ideological" diplomacy and "ideological" war. There was a further thing which they repeatedly said must never be allowed to happen again; and that was the fanatical "wars of religion."

As the century proceeded, the theorists tended more and more to exalt equilibrium as such, and to make it the highest objective of foreign policy, insisting that the egotism of advancing states, or even the punishment of a defeated aggressor, should not be carried to the point at which the international system itself was overthrown. And if it was sometimes said that the balance of power, while assisting the cause of liberty, tended to make conflicts more numerous (tended even to make them general), the same teaching did imply at least a doctrine of warfare for limited purposes, and a preference for the kind of peace treaty that produced only marginal cessions for the adjustment of the balance. An essential feature of the system was the realization that the enemy of today may be required as an ally tomorrow and that excessive concessions made to a monarch who happens to be virtuous may benefit his successor, who will make an evil use of them. In any case, war for the actual destruction of a state was anathema, for it meant the creation of a vacuum which would serve the purpose of a potential aggressor better than anything else.

The "war of religion" (or the "ideological" war) was recognized to be the extreme antithesis to the system. It ignored the balance of power, and it rendered a policy of compromise too difficult. It came to be understood that the system of states depended in fact on an underlying unity of culture, a common sense of values and a preexisting community of tradition and custom. The international order itself, and the balance within it, depended on the assumption that all the participants were like members of the same club. A theory that was far from denying the egotism of states, called at times therefore for loyalty to the club itself and asked that egotism should stop short of any threat to the international order.

2. The Operation of the Balance. In the first half of the eighteenth century the Continent was not yet integrated and it was customary to say that there were two systems—a more southern or "European" one, and another which was described as "Northern." In 1709 there was a momentary fear that they might come together—the War of the Spanish Succession combining with the Great Northern War in a struggle that would be really general. England had separate Secretaries of State for the North and the South, and when A. H. L. Heeren produced his *Handbuch* on the European states-system in 1809, he devoted a long narrative to "the balance of the South," and a separate one to "the balance of the North." After this the two came to be combined, for, after 1763, Russia had become more definitely a part of the European system, though France was still disposed to regard not only Russia but also Britain as an outsider. It was held, however, that, within the general equilibrium of Europe, there were also local or regional balances—one in the north, one in the south, and perhaps a separate one for Germany. Also, there were some people who thought that overseas colonies might affect the calculation of the balance.

Down to 1789 people were able to pride themselves that neither in the main part of the Continent nor in the Baltic was there a power capable of making a bid for "universal dominion." This might be attributed to the fact that power itself was fairly evenly distributed; but both F. von Gentz and Talleyrand (Charles Mauriel de Talleyrand-Périgord) insisted that the balance of power did not require nations to be roughly equal in size—in their view the equilibrium might be more difficult to achieve if one had a world of exactly equal states. Frederick the Great and Edmund Burke noted that the effect of the system was to make wars general, and they, along with Edward Gibbon, held that it made a plan of large-scale conquest no longer feasible. In the Seven Years' War, the enemies of Frederick the Great planned the destruction of Prussia as a power, but the representatives of Louis XV's "secret" diplomatic system—the ablest school of diplomats that the century produced—made this an additional reproach against the alliance with Austria in 1756. They complained that such a war objective was a breach of the code and that a victory in the war would have been worse than the defeat that was actually suffered. The destruction of Prussia, they said, would have restored the Habsburgs to their former predominance.

The career of Napoleon produced, amongst his enemies, a further insistence on the theory of balance, and in 1809 Heeren suggested that, in the long run, the system might become a global affair. The peace treaties with France at the end of the wars were an excellent demonstration of the effects of the theory. And, in the crucial cases, the Congress of Vienna showed that it was more attached to the balance of power than either to dynastic rights or to nationalism.

It has often been asserted that the balance of power was responsible for the partition of Poland; but it has been said equally often that it was responsible for the preservation of the Ottoman Empire. This raises the issue of the local versus the continental balance; and there has never been a more intensive application of the balance than between Russia, Prussia, and Austria in eastern Europe after 1763. Perhaps it has always been true that where these bitterly rival powers could come to an agreement about anything, there existed no counterpoise in Europe that could hold them in check in their own region. At any rate, France and England could not have stopped the partition of Poland, and this might be imputed to the lack of a wider "general balance" at that moment. France and England were able to defend the Ottoman Empire against Russia because—partly through their maritime opportunities—they were in a position to make the general balance effective.

V. SINCE 1815

The theory of the balance of power reached its climax during the conflict with Napoleon, whose enemies may have lacked the required flexibility; all the same, to meet the threat from France, they gave Prussia an important position in the Rhineland. Some of the theory had passed into the teaching about the states-system at the University of Göttingen, and lay behind Ranke's famous essay on "Die grossen Mächte"; and there remained at least the conviction that one could not risk allowing any country to acquire a predominance, and one must never quite ignore the question of the distribution of power. In this sense the old rules—which were directed to the preservation of the states-system—served to set limits to policy, showing the point beyond which governments ought not to go in promoting either their interests or their ideals. Soon there came to be less talk of a states-system, however; for, from 1815, a group of five or six Great Powers acquired the leadership in Europe and the balance was regarded as existing between them. These indeed may have been carrying the eighteenth-century ideas a stage further when, as members of the same club, they tried to turn the balance into a harmony and establish what was called the Concert of Europe. The maxims associated with the states-system were probably contravened less in the nineteenth century than in the eighteenth, and if Bismarck was an exception when he took Alsace-Lorraine from France in 1871 such an exception confirms the rule, for Germany soon had reason to regret it. But the maxims and rules seem to have been carried into the subconscious realm, for the tradition of formulating them—the literature of the states-system—seems to have come fairly soon to an end. One might say that all the rules were broken in the course of the First World War and though it could be argued that this was unavoidable, its consequences have confirmed the old predictions.

Even in the eighteenth century, the theory had had to accommodate itself to existing ideas of "legitimacy," i.e., the normal recognition of dynastic rights and the principle of hereditary succession. It had circumvented the difficulties by resorting to those "Partition Treaties" which were so common for a period of about a century and were feasible in the days when, for the majority of people, the local landlord or noble mattered so much more than the question of who might be king. Diplomacy found it less easy to adjust itself to a new kind of "legitimacy" which came to prevail and which conceded much more to the idea of the self-determination of peoples. But it was not impossible to adjust the balance of power even to this; and if Britain, after the Napoleonic wars, insisted on the union of Holland and Belgium to strengthen the barrier against France, she gave way on this point in the 1830's.

The partiality which the Congress of Vienna (1815) had had for the balance of power helped to make liberal opinion in Europe hostile to the principle as well as to the work of the Congress. Felix Gilbert has shown that in a nontechnical way the *philosophes* of the eighteenth century had attacked the current ideas, calling for a new "diplomacy" that in a certain sense anticipated Woodrow Wilson. The French Revolution introduced something like the "ideological" element in diplomacy, though the younger Pitt conceived his war with France as directed purely against the international offenses of that country, while Fox, in opposing the war, had brought out the same principles of the balance of power—he thought that Pitt, like Burke, was making the conflict "ideological."

After 1815, first England and then France broke with the policy of Metternich, which regarded revolution as an international menace, to be countered by international action. At the end of 1826, George Canning announced that he had "called the New World into existence to redress the balance of the Old." French revolutionaries in 1830 and 1848 called for a foreign policy that would promote the cause of liberalism, particularly against reactionary Russia. The foreign policy of the Second French Empire and of contemporary England showed a certain degree of sympathy with the nationalist aspirations of the Italians. The idea of the balance of power lost its presidential position, as public opinion made itself felt in international affairs; but it remained (where perhaps it ought to remain) in the background of the minds of statesmen. At least, the balance was not overturned, and the liberal Frenchman of the first half of the century would

have been shocked to see how, for its sake, the young Third Republic made alliance with Tsarist Russia. The greatest embarrassment for the principle of the balance of power occurred after 1900 when Germany came to be seen as so immediate a danger that men forgot Russia—a danger calculated to be still more formidable but as yet more remote—the predicament presenting the kind of problem which it is the function of diplomacy to solve.

After 1919 the reaction against what was called the "old diplomacy" led to a widespread condemnation of the idea of the balance of power. To that idea—rather than to the cupidities which it was intended to keep in check—were imputed the aggressive policies which had led to war. The view was understandable in that the theory fixed attention on the diagram of forces and was sometimes understood to mean the subordination of everything to the question of the distribution of power. Also there existed after 1919 a kind of "messianism"—the belief that a new world had been born, and a new diplomacy was needed.

The situation after the Second World War left room for no such illusions; and the significance of the European balance was never more patent than at the moment when the balance was destroyed—destroyed apparently in just that irretrievable manner which the eighteenth-century theorists had most feared. The language of the balance of power became current again even when the equilibrium had to be envisaged on a global scale and as a system comprising, for a time, only two giant members. It is only in recent years, however, that, amongst the students of international politics, the question of the balance of power has been again the subject of that semi-scientific treatment which was so characteristic of the eighteenth century. But it is interesting to see that the modern thought in this field does not make a development from the point which the eighteenth century had reached, for the work of that century had been long forgotten. It is difficult not to believe that in certain modern writers some of the formulations would have been different if the pre-1815 theories had been known.

It is sometimes suggested that the nuclear weapon has made the notion of balance out-of-date, since, when two powers are both in a position to destroy one another, the superiority of either of them becomes an irrelevancy. But the competition for support in the Third World—and the part which the uncommitted states have been able to play in diplomacy—would suggest that nuclear calculations are not supreme, and that, in one contingency and another (in diplomacy if not in actual war) the consideration of the balance of power may still be a factor in the case. Since the

187

system prided itself on its assurance of an independent foreign policy to smaller states (and indeed depended on this) it had to allow for these latter choosing neutrality, and it relied on their being converted to an alliance when they realized the necessity for taking part.

BIBLIOGRAPHY

R. v. Albertini, *Das florentinische Staatsbewusstsein im Übergang von der Republik zum Prinzipat* (Bern, 1953). F. Bacon, "Of Empire," *Works*, ed. J. Spedding, et al., 7 vols. (London, 1857–59), VI, 419–23. Vespasiano da Bisticci, *Renaissance Princes, Popes, and Prelates*, trans. W. G. and E. Waters (New York, 1963). Henry, Lord Brougham, "The Balance of Power," *Contributions to the Edinburgh Review* (London, 1856), II, 3–80. H. Butterfield and M. Wight, essays on "The Balance of Power," *Diplomatic Investigations* (London, 1966), pp. 132–75. L. Dehio, *Gleichgewicht und Hegemonie* (Krefeld, 1948), trans. F. Fullman as *The Precarious Balance* (London, 1963). F. de S. de la Mothe Fénelon, Supplement to "L'Examen de Conscience sur les Devoirs de la Royauté," *Oeuvres* (Paris, 1824), XXII, 306–15. F. v. Gentz, *Fragmente aus der neusten Geschichte des politischen Gleichgewichts in Europe* (St. Petersburg, 1806), trans. as *Fragments upon the Balance of Power in Europe* (London, 1806). Felix Gilbert, "The New Diplomacy of the Eighteenth Century," *World Politics*, 4 (1951). E. V. Gulick, *Europe's Classical Balance of Power* (Ithaca, N.Y., 1955). A. H. L. Heeren, *Handbuch der Geschichte des europäischen Staatensystems und seiner Colonien*, 2nd ed. (Göttingen, 1811), trans. as *A Manual of the History of the Political System of Europe and its Colonies* (London, 1834). D. Hume, "The Balance of Power," *Essays and Treatises* (new ed., London, 1770), II, 112–24. E. Kaeber, *Die Idee des europäischen Gleichgewichts in der publizistischen Literatur vom 16 bis zur Mitte des 18 Jahrhunderts* (Berlin, 1906). Morton A. Kaplan, *System and Process in International Politics* (New York and London, 1957), e.g., pp. 22–43. Kautilya, *Arthas'āstra*, trans. R. Shamasastry (Mysore, 1951), pp. 289–348. E. W. Nelson, "Origins of the Balance of Power," *Medievalia et Humanistica* (1942), Fasc. 1, 124–42. G. Ostreich, "Justus Lipsius als Theoretiker des neuzeitlichen Machstaates," *Historische Zeitschrift*, 181 (1956), 31–78. A. Rein, "Über die Bedeutung der überseeische Ausdehnung für das europäischen Staatessystem," *Historische Zeitschrift*, 131 (1927), 28–90. Max Savelle, "The American Balance of Power and European Diplomacy, 1713–78," in R. B. Morris, ed., *The Era of the American Revolution* (New York, 1939), pp. 140–69. A. J. Toynbee, *A Study of History*, 12 vols. (London and New York, 1934–61), III, 304–06, 345 n.

HERBERT BUTTERFIELD

[See also **Machiavellism;** Nationalism; Nature; **Peace, International; State;** War and Militarism.]

BAROQUE IN LITERATURE

THE TERM "Baroque" is today generally applied to the literature of the seventeenth century. The transfer of this term from the fine arts is, however, of rather recent origin. The etymology of the word itself has been the subject of a long debate. Two derivations have been proposed: one from the Portuguese word *barroco*, a jewelers' term for the irregular, odd-shaped pearl first brought from Goa to Portugal in the sixteenth century, and in the early eighteenth century used in French as an adjective meaning "bizarre" or "odd"; and the other, from *baroco*, the name of the fourth mode of the second figure in the scholastic terminology of syllogisms. ("Every P is M, some S are not M, hence some S are not P," or to give an example: "Every fool is stubborn, some people are not stubborn, hence some people are not fools.") This type of argument was early felt to be sophistical: e.g., Luis Vives, in 1519, ridiculed the Professors of the University of Paris as "sophists in *baroco* and *baralipton*." Montaigne (in *Essais*, Book I, Ch. XXV) says *C'est Barroco et Baralipton qui rendent leurs supposts ainsi crottez et enfumez.* The phrase *ragioni barrochi* can be documented in Italian since 1570 and apparently the Italian *barocco* is derived from it. In the eighteenth century the two terms seem, independently of each other, to be applied to the art and architecture of what the century felt to be the "bad taste" of the preceding age. The third edition of the *Dictionnaire de l'Académie* (1740) defines "baroque" as *irrégulier, bizarre, inégal* while the *Dictionnaire de Trévoux* (1771) speaks of *un goût baroque, où les règles des proportions ne sont pas observées, où tout est représenté selon le caprice de l'artiste.* J. J. Rousseau in the *Dictionnaire de Musique* (1768) states: *il y a bien de l'apparence que ce terme vient du Baroco des Logiciens* but apparently the etymology from the jeweler's term has also played a role. In Quatremère de Quincy's *Dictionnaire historique de l'architecture* (1783) baroque is defined as *une nuance du bizarre.* Francesco Borromini and Guarino Guarini are considered models of the baroque. Francesco Milizia's *Dizionario delle belle arti del disegno* (1797) takes over this definition: *Barocco è il superlativo del bizzaro, l'eccesso del ridicolo.* Jakob Burckhardt stabilized its meaning in art history as referring to what he considered the decadence of the High Renaissance in the florid architecture of the Counter-Reformation in Italy, Germany, and Spain. Quite casually the term was transferred to literature, first by Giosuè Carducci in a *Prolusione* in 1860, where he refers to the *Barocco dei secentisti* (*Opere*, Edizione Nazionale, Bologna [1941], V, 520) and in Spain, when Menéndez y Pelayo, in *Historia de las ideas estéticas* (1886) spoke of *barroquismo literario* of the seventeenth century, in discussing a Portuguese critic of the eighteenth century (Santander [1947], III, 488). In the meantime Burckhardt's younger colleague at the University of Basel, Friedrich Nietzsche, in *Menschliches Allzumenschliches* (1878, *Aphorism* 144), suggested that "the Baroque style arises every time at the waning of every great art." It chooses themes and motifs of the highest dramatic tension, it indulges in the eloquence of strong emotions and gestures, of the ugly-sublime, of great masses, in general of quantity as such, as it is announced in Michelangelo, the father or grandfather of the Italian baroque artists. Nietzsche sees a parallel in the present state of music alluding to Richard Wagner and speaks of the frequent recurrence of a baroque style since the time of the Greeks, in poetry, in eloquence, in prose style, in sculpture as well as in architecture. This transfer to antiquity seems to have been common. Nietzsche's foe, Ulrich Willamowitz-Moellendorf wrote about "ancient Baroque," i.e., Hellenistic art, as early as 1881 and L. von Sybel, in his *Weltgeschichte der Kunst* (1888) includes a chapter on ancient Roman Baroque.

But Heinrich Wölfflin's *Renaissance und Barock* (1888) is a real turning point in the history of the term, not only because it gave a first thorough analysis of the development of the style in Rome in appreciative terms, but also because it contains a few pages on the possibility of applying the term to literature and music (see pp. 83–85). Wölfflin suggests that the contrast between Ariosto's *Orlando Furioso* (1516) and Tasso's *Gerusalemme liberata* (1584) could be compared to the distinction between Renaissance and baroque. In Tasso he observed a heightening, an emphasis, a striving for great conceptions absent in Ariosto. The images are more unified, more sublime; there is less visual imagination (*Anschauung*) but much more mood (*Stimmung*). Wölfflin's positive evaluation of baroque art was soon followed by a proliferation of studies, particularly in Germany, by art historians such as Cornelius Gurlitt, Alois Riegl, and Georg Dehio and in Italy by Giulio Magni and Corrado Ricci, but Wölfflin's attempt to transfer the term to literature remained for a long time unheeded.

Occasional scattered usages of the term applied to literature occur especially in the old Austro-Hungarian Empire and in Italy where baroque art and architecture are much in evidence. In 1893 a Polish scholar, Edward Porębowicz, put the word "baroque" in the title page of his monograph on a seventeenth-century Polish poet, Andrzej Morsztyn (Cracow, 1893). A well-known Italian essayist, Enrico Necioni, published an essay "Barrochismo" in *La Vita italiana nel seicento* (Milan, 1894) which, impressionistically, related the

arts and poetry of the age. In the introduction to a reissue Gabriele D'Annunzio, oddly enough, referred to it as "Del Barocco" (see *Saggi critici di letteratura italiana*, Florence [1898]). In 1899 J. W. Nagl and Jakob Zeigler devoted a long chapter of their *Deutschösterreichische Literaturgeschichte* to *österreichische Barocke und deutsche Renaissance-literatur*. There the style is described (I, 656) as "decorative and symbolic" and seen as an expression of the Counter-Reformation. In 1914 a Danish scholar, Valdemar Vedel, published a paper *den digteriske Barokstil omkring aar 1600* (in *Edda*, **2**, 17–40) in which he draws a close parallel between Rubens and French and English poetic styles between 1550 and 1650.

Baroque literature is, like the art of Rubens, decorative, colorful, emphatic. Vedel lists favorite themes and words in literature which he considers applicable to the art of Rubens: grand, high, flourish, red, flame, horses, hunt, war, gold, the love of show, bombast, mythological masquerade. But Vedel's article, probably because it was written in Danish, was completely ignored. Also Karl Borinski's treatment of the history of conceptist theories (see below) in Spain (e.g., in Baltasar Gracián) and his sketch of the history of the term in a learned book, *Die Antike in Poetik und Kunsttheorie* with the subtitle for the first volume, *Mittelalter, Renaissance und Barock* (1914) does not reflect Wölfflin's suggestions, though Borinski was his colleague at the University of Munich.

All this was preparation for the enormous and sudden outburst of studies of the baroque and the use of the term "baroque" for literature in Germany. In 1915 Wölfflin published a new book, *Kunstgeschichtliche Grundbegriffe*, in which Renaissance and baroque are contrasted as the two main types of style and criteria for their distinctions are worked out concretely. This book made a tremendous impression on several German literary historians struggling with the problem of period style. It seemed to invite transfer to literary history. In 1916, without mentioning Wölfflin, Fritz Strich made a stylistic analysis of German seventeenth-century lyrical poetry which he called "baroque" (in *Abhandlungen zur deutschen Literaturgeschichte: Festschrift für Franz Muncker*, Munich). Oskar Walzel in the same year claimed that Shakespeare belonged to the baroque, applying one pair of Wölfflin's fundamental concepts, "closed" and "open form" to the contrast between Shakespeare and French classical tragedy ("Shakespeares dramatische Baukunst," reprinted in *Das Wortkunstwerk*, 1926).

The enormous vogue of the term "baroque" outside academic scholarship is however due to the sudden interest in seventeenth-century German poetry after the first World War. Several anthologies of seven- 189 teenth-century German poetry, called *Die deutsche Barocklyrik*, or similar titles, were immensely successful in the 1920's. Scholars discussed the hitherto neglected literature in awe-struck terms, looking for its underlying philosophy. Arthur Hübscher was the inventor of the slogan of the *antithetische Lebensgefühl des Barock* (in *Euphorion*, **22** [1924]) which has found much favor and suggested a number of books which all describe baroque in terms of one opposition or of a number of oppositions. Herbert Cysarz's *Die deutsche Barockdichtung* (1924) was the first bold synthesis to operate largely with the concept of a tension between the classical form and the Christian ethos and sentiment of baroque literature. Since then interest in the German seventeenth century has risen steadily, and produced a large literature permeated by the term "baroque." The reasons for its immense success are obvious: Germans after the first World War felt in sympathy with the period of the Thirty Years War. Expressionism with its turbulent, tense, and torn diction and tragic view of the world seems to have been anticipated in an earlier century dominated by a similar crepuscular mood. The new understanding of the baroque was, no doubt, often based on an unhistorical parallel but it was also the expression of a genuine change of taste, a sudden appreciation of an art despised before because of its conventions, its supposedly tasteless metaphors, its allegories, its morbid or sensual themes.

German scholars soon applied their newly found criterion to other European literatures. Theophil Spoerri was, in 1922, the first to carry out Wölfflin's suggestions as to the difference between Ariosto and Tasso in *Renaissance und Barock bei Ariost und Tasso. Versuch einer Anwendung Wölfflin'scher Kunstbetrachtung* (Bern, 1922). Ariosto is shown by Wölfflin's criteria to be Renaissance; Tasso, baroque. Marino and the Marinists appeared baroque. Spain was also easily assimilable, since "Gongorism"—the involved style of Luis de Góngora (1561–1627)—and conceptism—a style characterized by ingenious and precious conceits, of which Francisco Quevedo (1580–1645) and Baltasar Gracián (1601–58) were the main representatives—presented parallel phenomena which had but to be christened "baroque." But all other Spanish literature, from Guevara in the early sixteenth century to Calderón in the late seventeenth century, was soon claimed as baroque. Wilhelm Michels in a paper on "Barockstil in Shakespeare und Calderón" in the *Revue Hispanique*, **85** (1929) used the acknowledged baroque characteristics of Calderón to argue that Shakespeare also shows the same stylistic tendencies. There seems to be only disagreement among the German writers as to the status of Cervantes: Helmut Hatzfeld as early as 1927 had spoken of Cervantes as *Jesuitenbarock*

in *Don Quixote als Sprachkunstwerk* (Leipzig [1927], p. 287) and had argued that Cervantes' world view is that of the Counter-Reformation. In a later paper, "El predominio del espíritu español en las literaturas del siglo XVII," in *Revista de Filología Hispánica* (**3** [1941], 9–23), Hatzfeld tried to show that Spain is eternally, basically baroque and that it was historically the radiating center of the baroque spirit in Europe. The permanently Spanish features, which are also those of baroque, were only temporarily overlaid by the Renaissance. Ludwig Pfandl, however, limits baroque to the seventeenth century and expressly exempts Cervantes. (See *Geschichte der spanischen Nationalliteratur in ihrer Blütezeit*, Freiburg im Breisgau [1929], p. 289.) Both Vossler and Spitzer, however, consider even Lope de Vega baroque (in spite of Lope's objections to Góngora). (See Karl Vossler, *Lope de Vega und sein Zeitalter*, Munich [1932], pp. 89–105 especially; Leo Spitzer, *Die Literarisierung des Lebens in Lopes Dorotea*, Bonn [1932].)

French literature was also described by German scholars in terms of the baroque. Neubert and Schürr talked, at first somewhat hesitatingly, of baroque undercurrents and features in seventeenth-century France. (See V. Klemperer, H. Hatzfeld, F. Neubert, *Die romanischen Literaturen von der Renaissance bis zur französischen Revolution*, Wildpark-Potsdam [1928]; Friedrich Schürr, *Barock, Klassizismus und Rokoko in der französischen Literatur. Eine principielle Stilbetrachtung*, Leipzig [1928].) Schürr claimed Rabelais as early baroque and described the *précieux*, the writers of the sprawling courtly novels and of burlesques, as baroque, a style which was displaced by the new classicism of Boileau, Molière, La Fontaine, and Racine. Others advocated the view that these French classics themselves are baroque. Leo Spitzer endorses it with some qualifications. In a brilliant analysis of the style of Racine ("Klassische Dämpfung in Racines Stil," in *Romanische Stil- und Literaturstudien*, Marburg [1931], I, 255n.), he has shown how Racine always tones down baroque features, how Racine's baroque is tame, subdued, classical. Though Hatzfeld does not completely deny the obviously striking distinctions of French classicism, he is the one scholar who most insistently claims all French classicism as baroque. In an early paper, "Der Barockstil der religiösen klassischen Lyrik in Frankreich" (*Literaturwissenschaftliches Jahrbuch der Görresgesellschaft*, **4** [1929], 30–60) he discusses the French religious poetry of the seventeenth century, showing its similarity to Spanish mysticism and its stylistic similarities to general baroque. In a long piece in a Dutch review, "Die französische Klassik in neuer Sicht. Klassik als Barock" (*Tijdschrift voor Taal en Letteren*, **23** [1935], 213–81) he accumulated many observations to show that French classicism is only a variant of baroque. French classicism has the same typically baroque tension of sensuality and religion, the same morbidity, the same pathos as Spanish baroque. Its form is similarly paradoxical and antithetical, "open," in Wölfflin's sense. The discipline of French classicism is simply a universal characteristic of the "rule over the passions," furthered by the Counter-Reformation everywhere.

English literature, even outside of the attempts to claim Shakespeare as baroque, was also soon brought in line. Friedrich Brie's *Englische Rokokoepik* (Munich, 1927) is the first attempt of this sort. There Pope's *Rape of the Lock* is analyzed as rococo, but in passing a contrast to the baroque of Garth and Boileau is drawn. F. W. Schirmer in several articles and in his *Geschichte der Englischen Literatur* (Halle, 1937) used the term for the metaphysicals, Browne, Dryden, Otway, and Lee, excluding Milton from the baroque expressly. This was also the conclusion of Friedrich Wild in his "Zum Problem des Barocks in der englischen Dichtung" (*Anglia*, **59** [1935], 414–22), where he called even Ben Jonson, Massinger, Ford, and Phineas Fletcher baroque. The idea of an antithesis of sensualism and spiritualism in English seventeenth-century poetry was in the meantime developed by Werner P. Friederich's "Spiritualismus und Sensualismus in der englischen Barocklyrik," in *Wiener Beiträge*, **57**, Vienna (1932).

The view that all English seventeenth-century civilization is baroque has been pushed farthest by Paul Meissner in *Die geisteswissenschaftlichen Grundlagen des englischen Literaturbarocks* (Munich, 1934). He includes also Milton and has devised a whole scheme of contraries covering all activities and stages of the English seventeenth century. In a piece which stresses the Spanish influence in England, Hatzfeld goes so far as to call Milton "the most Hispanized poet of the age, who to the foreigner appears the most baroque" (*Revista de Filología Hispánica*, **3** [1941], 22). Bernhard Fehr finally has extended the frontiers of English baroque by finding it in Thomson and Mallet and even tracing it in the verse form of Wordsworth. (See "The Antagonism of Forms in the Eighteenth Century," *English Studies*, **18** [1936], 115–21, 193–205, and **19** [1937], 1–13, 49–57.) Thus all literatures of Europe in the seventeenth century (and in part of the sixteenth century) are conceived by German scholars as a unified baroque movement, e.g., in Schnürer's *Katholische Kirche und Kultur der Barockzeit* (Paderborn, 1937), in Spain, and Portugal with Camões, in Italy, France, Germany, and Austria, but also in Poland, Hungary, and Yugoslavia.

The idea of a baroque age in literature was taken up soon by scholars of other nationalities. In 1919 F.

Schmidt-Degener published a piece on "Rembrandt en Vondel" (*De Gids*, **83** [1919], 222–75). A German translation by Alfred Pauli was published as *Rembrandt und der holländische Barock*, in *Studien der Bibliothek Warburg*, No. 9 (Leipzig, 1928), in which Rembrandt is identified as an opponent of baroque taste, while the poet Joost Van Den Vondel, Flemish by descent and a convert to Catholicism, is presented as the typical representative of the European baroque. The author looks with distinct disfavor on the baroque, its sensual mysticism, its externality, its verbalism in contrast to the truly Dutch (and at the same time universal) art of Rembrandt. With Heinz Haerten, *Vondel und der deutsche Barock* (1934) found in *Disquisitiones Carolinae. Fontes et Acta Philologica et Historica* (ed. Th. Baader, **6**, Nijmegen [1934]), the revaluation of baroque has also triumphed in Holland. There Vondel is claimed as the very summit of Northern, Teutonic baroque. In general, seventeenth-century Dutch literature seems to be now described by the Dutch themselves as baroque.

The next country to succumb to the lure of the term was Italy. Giulio Bertoni had reviewed Spoerri without showing much interest, in the *Giornale storico della letteratura italiana* (**81** [1923], 178–80); Lionello Venturi early expounded Wölfflin in an article "Gli schemi del Wölfflin," in *L'Esame* (**1** [1922], 3–10). But late in 1924 Mario Praz finished a book, *Secentismo e Marinismo in Inghilterra* (Florence [1925], cf. pp. 94, 110n., 113), which, in its title, avoids the term baroque; in its text, which is actually two monographs on Donne and Crashaw respectively, it freely refers to baroque in literature, and to the literary baroque in England. Praz studied especially the contacts of Donne and Crashaw with Italian and neo-Latin literature, and he knew the work of Wölfflin.

In July 1925 Benedetto Croce read a paper in Zurich on the concept of the baroque which was then published in a German translation by Berthold Fenigstein as *Der Begriff des Barock. Die Gegenreformation. Zwei Essays* (Zurich, 1925). It is practically identical with Chapters 2 and 1 of *Storia dell' Età barocca in Italia* (Bari, 1929). There he discusses the term without, it seems, much consciousness of its newness in literature, though he vigorously protests against many of the current German theories, and pleads for a revival of the original meaning of baroque as a kind of artistic ugliness. Though Croce tried again and again to defend his negative attitude to the baroque, he himself adopted the term as a label for the Italy of the seventeenth century. His largest book on the period, *Storia dell' Età barocca in Italia*, has the term on the title page. After 1925 he discussed even his beloved Giambattista Basile in terms of baroque. (See his introduction to

Basile's *Lo Cunto de li Cunti*, 2 vols., Bari [1925]. The paper on Basile in *Saggi sulla Letteratura Italiana del Seicento*, Bari [1910] did not yet use the term. The English translation by N. M. Penzer, introducing the *Pentamerone of Giambattista Basile*, 2 vols., London [1932], conflates the two pieces.) Baroque thus seems victorious in Italy.

1927, the tercentenary of Góngora's death, established the term in Spain. An anthology of Góngora spoke of him as a baroque poet. (See Gerardo Diego, ed., *Antología poética en honor de Góngora*, Madrid [1927]. It was reviewed by Dámaso Alonso in *Revista de Occidente*, **18** [1927], 396–401.) Dámaso Alonso published an edition of the *Soledades* (Madrid [1927], especially pages 31–32) which has a page on Góngora's *barroquismo* with an express recognition of the novelty of the term. In the same year, Ortega y Gasset, in reviewing Alonso, called "Góngorism, Marinism, and Euphuism merely forms of baroque." "What is usually called classical in poetry is actually baroque, e.g., Pindar who is just as difficult to understand as Góngora." (See "Góngora, 1627–1927," in *Espíritu de la Letra*, Madrid [1927], quoted from Ortega y Gasset, *Obras*, Madrid [1943], II, 1108–09.) Another famous Spanish scholar, Américo Castro, also began using the term "baroque," first for Tirso de Molina, but also for Góngora and Quevedo.

France is the one major country which has resisted longest, though there are a few exceptions. André Koszul called Beaumont and Fletcher baroque in 1933, and referred in his bibliography to some of the German work. (See "Beaumont et Fletcher et le Baroque," in *Cahiers du Sud*, **10** [1933], 210–16.) A French student of German literature, André Moret, wrote a good thesis on the German baroque lyric, adopting the term as a matter of course in *Le Lyrisme baroque en Allemagne* (Lille, 1936). See also his "Vers une solution du problème du baroque," in *Revue Germanique* (**38** [1937], 373–77.) Gonzague de Reynold's *Le XVIIe Siècle: Le Classique et le Baroque* (Montreal, 1944), however, is the first French book to make much of the term. M. Reynold recognizes a conflict between the baroque and the classic in seventeenth-century France: the temperament of the time, its passion, and its will seem to him baroque; Corneille, Tasso, and Milton are called so, but the actual French classicists appear as victors over something which endangered their balance and poise. One should note that Gonzague de Reynold was a professor at Fribourg, where Schnürer was his colleague, and that he taught for years at the University of Bern, to which Strich had gone from Munich. Most French literary historians, such as Baldensperger, Lebègue, and Henri Peyre have raised their voices vigorously against the application of the term to French literature. (See Fernand Baldensperger, "Pour une Révaluation littéraire du XVIIe siècle classique," *Revue d'histoire littéraire de la France*, **44** [1937], 1–15, especially 13–14; Raymond Lebègue, *Bulletin of the International Committee of Historical Sciences*, **9** [1937], 378; Henri Peyre, *Le Classicisme français*, New York [1942], cf. pp. 181–83.) Then, on the other hand, Marcel Raymond in a volume in honor of Wölfflin tried to distinguish Renaissance and baroque elements in Ronsard with subtle, though extremely elusive, results. Madame Dominique Aury edited an anthology of French baroque poets which elicited a fine essay by Maurice Blanchot, entitled "Classique et baroque dans la poésie de Ronsard," which appeared in *Concinnitas: Festschrift für Heinrich Wölfflin* (Basel, 1944). Other essays are those by Dominique Aury, *Les Poètes précieux et baroques du XVIIe siècle* (Paris, 1942), and by Maurice Blanchot, "Les poètes baroques du XVIIe siècle," in *Faux Pas* (Paris [1943], pp. 151–56).

Not until the fifties did the term "baroque" take hold in French literary history. The discovery by Alan Boase, an Englishman, of Jean de Sponde, a late sixteenth-century poet, the reprinting of the almost forgotten La Ceppède, and several anthologies of French poetry, unearthing little-known poets between Ronsard and Malherbe, established a consciousness that there existed in France a fine poetic tradition which was neither Renaissance nor classical, and can be best described as baroque. In French scholarship Jean Rousset's *La Littérature de l'âge baroque en France* (Paris, 1953) and a new book by his teacher Marcel Raymond, *Baroque et renaissance poétique* (1955) finally carried conviction. Both Rousset and Raymond use Wölfflin's categories as their starting point: Rousset devises a new dichotomy: Circe and the Peacock, the principle of metamorphosis and the principle of ostentation. Still, while the term and concept is used now in France very freely, the French have resisted the attempt to extend it to French classicism itself. A careful account of the struggle between baroque and classical elements in Racine is the work of an Englishman Philip Butler, entitled *Classicisme et baroque dans l'œuvre de Racine* (Paris, 1959).

Baroque as a literary term has also spread to the Slavic countries with a Catholic past. It is used in Poland widely for the Jesuit literature of the seventeenth century, and in Czechoslovakia there has been a sudden interest in the half-buried Czech literature of the Counter-Reformation which is now always called baroque. The editions of baroque poets and sermons and discussions became especially frequent in the early thirties. There is also a small book by Václav Černý (1937) which discusses the baroque in European poetry, including in it even Milton and Bunyan. Julius Kleiner, in *Die polnische Literatur* (Wildpark-Potsdam, 1929), uses the term, e.g., of Casimir (Sarbiewski), the neo-Latin poet, in studies and editions by J. Vašica (e.g., *České literární baroko*, Prague [1938], p. 15, V. Bitnar, Zdeněk Kalista, F. X. Šalda, Arne Novák, etc.; Václav Černý, *O básnickém baroku*, Prague [1937]). The term is used in Hungarian literary history for the age of Cardinal Pazmány (1570–1637), and by Yugoslavs to characterize Ivan Gundulić (1588–1678) and his epic *Osman*.

In England and America the term, as applied to literature, appeared late, much later than the revival of interest in Donne and the metaphysical poets. Herbert Grierson and T. S. Eliot do not use it. A rather slight essay by Peter Burra, published in *Farrago* in 1930, is called "Baroque and Gothic Sentimentalism" (reprinted privately, London, 1931), but uses the term quite vaguely for periods of luxuriance as an alternative for "Gothic." The more concrete literary use seems to come from Germany: J. E. Crawford Fitch published in London a book on Angelus Silesius in 1932 which uses the term occasionally, and in 1933, the philosopher E. I. Watkin, a student of German Catholic literature, discussed Crashaw as baroque, in a work entitled *The English Way: Studies in English Sanctity from St. Bede to Newman*, edited by Maisie Ward (London [1933], pp. 268–96). Watkins must have known the book by Mario Praz, mentioned above. Crashaw is again, in 1934, the center of a study of the baroque by T. O. Beachcroft in an article called "Crashaw and the Baroque Style" (*Criterion*, 13 [1934], 407–25). In 1934 F. W. Bateson published his little book, *English Poetry and the English Language* (Oxford [1934], pp. 76–77), where he applied the term baroque even to Thomson, Gray, and Collins. Since then the term baroque occurs in English scholarship more frequently. F. P. Wilson in *Elizabethan and Jacobean* (Oxford [1945], p. 26) used it to characterize Jacobean in contrast to Elizabethan literature, and E. M. W. Tillyard in *John Milton, Private Correspondences and Academic Exercises* (Cambridge [1932], xi) applied it in passing to Milton's epistolary prose.

In English literary histories the term is today usually confined to a few authors. Thus David Daiches, in his *Critical History of English Literature* (London, 1960) refers only to Giles Fletcher, to Sylvester's translation of Du Bartas, and to Crashaw as being baroque. Miss M. M. Mahood applies it to Milton and Odette de Mourgues, in a book in English, *Metaphysical, Baroque and Précieux Poetry* (Oxford, 1953) uses it as a term of disapproval limited to Crashaw. But on the whole, in England, the term "metaphysical" has predominated.

In the United States, as early as 1929, Morris W. Croll christened a very fine analytical paper on seventeenth-century prose style "baroque," calling it "The Baroque Style in Prose." It appeared in *Studies in English Philology: A Miscellany in Honor of Frederick Klaeber*, edited by K. Malone and M. B. Ruud (Minneapolis [1929], pp. 427–56). It was reprinted with other papers in *Style, Rhetoric, and Rhythm* (Princeton [1966], pp. 207–33). Earlier, in several papers on the history of prose style, he had called the same traits of the anti-Ciceronian movement "Attic," a rather obscure and misleading term. Croll knew Wölfflin's work and used his criteria, though very cautiously. In the following year George Williamson, in his *Donne Tradition*, singled out Crashaw as "the most baroque of the English metaphysicals," and calls him a "true representative of the European baroque poet, contrasting with Donne therein" (Cambridge, Mass. [1930], pp. 116, 123). Williamson, of course, had read Mario Praz. Since then Helen C. White in her *Metaphysical Poets* (New York [1936], pp. 84, 198–99, 247, 254, 306, 370, 380) used the term for Crashaw, and Austin Warren's book on Crashaw has the subtitle: *A Study in Baroque Sensibility* (Baton Rouge, 1939).

Baroque, in the United States, has not caught on very widely in academic literary scholarship. It is usually, as in England, limited arbitrarily to a few authors: thus Tucker Brooke uses "Baroque glory" as a label for Donne's prose, and for Thomas Browne and Jeremy Taylor in Albert C. Baugh, *Literary History of England* (New York [1948], pp. 613–23). Douglas Bush calls the younger Giles Fletcher's *Christ's Victorie and Triumph . . .* (1610) "the chief monument of baroque devotional poetry" but elsewhere insists that Crashaw is "the one conspicuous English incarnation of the 'baroque' sensibility. The simplest definition of baroque is to him "poetry like Crashaw's." (See *English Literature in the Earlier Seventeenth Century*, Oxford [1945], pp. 86, 140–41, 362.) Two scholars, Imbrie Buffum in a book on Agrippa d'Aubigné (1951) and in *Studies in the Baroque from Montaigne to Rotrou* (New Haven, 1957) and Lowry Nelson, Jr., in *Baroque Lyric Poetry* (New Haven, 1961) have made concrete analyses of French, English, and Spanish poetry in order to arrive at new characterizations of the baroque. More daringly Wylie Sypher, in his *Four Stages of Renaissance Style* (Garden City, N.Y., 1955) elaborated a parallel between Italian painting and the history of English poetry in which the baroque is represented by Milton and late baroque by Dryden and Racine. Sypher analogizes often extravagantly as does Roy Daniells. In *Milton, Mannerism and Baroque* (Toronto, 1963) Daniells tries to describe Milton's development in terms of the change from mannerism to baroque in the visual arts.

193

The term is also used for the echoes of English seventeenth-century literature in America. Austin Warren identified the newly discovered early eighteenth-century American poet, Edward Taylor, as Colonial baroque. (See "Edward Taylor's Poetry: Colonial Baroque," *Kenyon Review*, **3** [1941], 355–71, reprinted in *Rage for Order*, Chicago [1948], pp. 1–18.) Thus baroque is widely used today in discussing literature.

This sketch of the spread of the term may have suggested the varied status of baroque in the different countries—its complete establishment in Germany, its recent success in Italy and Spain, its slow penetration into English and American scholarship, and its late success in France. It is possible to account for these differences. In Germany the term succeeded because it found a vacuum: terms such as the first and second Silesian school, which were used before, were obviously inadequate. Baroque has become a laudatory term in the fine arts and could easily be used for the literature whose beauties were discovered during the change of taste caused by expressionism. Furthermore, the general revolt against positivistic methods in literary scholarship enhanced interest in period terms. Discussions as to the essence of the Renaissance, romanticism, and baroque occupied German literary scholars tired of the minutiae of research and eager for sweeping generalizations. In Italy there had been long recognized the phenomenon of Marinism and *secentismo*, but baroque seemed a preferable substitute, as not being associated with a single poet and as not a mere century label. In Spain baroque has also superseded *góngorismo, culteranismo, conceptismo*, as it is a more general term, free from associations with a single style or with some peculiar critical doctrine or technical device. In France baroque was, at first, rejected, partly because the old meaning of "bizarre" was still felt very vividly, and partly because French classicism was a distinct literary movement inimical to the ideals of contemporary baroque movements in Spain and Italy. Even Helmut Hatzfeld, who is no doubt right in stressing some affinities with the general European Counter-Reformation and some concrete influences of Spain on French classicism, has to speak of the French "Sonderbarock" in "Die französische Klassik in neuer Sicht. Klassik als Barock," (found in *Tijdschrift voor Taal en Letteren*, **23** [1935], 222), a prefix which seems to weaken his thesis considerably. The *précieux*, whatever their affinities with Spain and Italy may have been, are also clearly distinct in their lightness and secularity from the heavier, predominantly religious art which one associates with southern baroque. In England the reluctance to adopt the term has somewhat similar reasons: the memory of Ruskin's denunciations of seventeenth-century taste seems to be lingering in English minds, and this distaste cannot be corrected by the sight of any considerable baroque architecture in England. The term "metaphysical" is too well established (though admittedly misleading), and today it is too honorific to be regarded as in any serious need of replacement. As for Milton, he seems too individual and Protestant to be easily assimilated to baroque, still associated in most minds with Jesuits and the Counter-Reformation. Besides, the English seventeenth century does not impress the historian as a unity: its earlier part up to the closing of the theaters in 1642 is constantly assimilated to the Elizabethan Age; its later part from 1660 on has been annexed by the eighteenth century. Even those who would sympathize with the view that there is a continuity of artistic tradition from Donne and Chapman to the last writings of Dryden cannot overlook the very real social changes of the civil wars, which brought with them a considerable change of taste and general "intellectual climate." In the United States nothing hinders the spread of the term.

In analyzing the meanings of the term we must, first of all, draw the important distinction between those who use baroque as a term for a recurrent phenomenon in all history and those who use it as a term for a specific phenomenon in the historical process, fixed in time and place. The first use belongs to a typology of literature, the second to its history. Croce, Eugenio d'Ors, and many Germans consider it a typological term. Croce argues that the term should be returned to its original meaning, "a form of artistic ugliness," and that the phenomenon can be observed among the Silver Latin poets as well as in Marino or in D'Annunzio. Croce, however, abandoned this use and preferred to call baroque only "that artistic perversion, dominated by a desire for the stupefying, which can be observed in Europe from the last decades of the sixteenth to the end of the seventeenth century" (*Storia dell' Età barocca in Italia*, pp. 32–33). In Germany, Walzel used baroque as an alternative term for Gothic and romanticism, assuming an underlying identity of all these periods opposed to the other sequence of classical antiquity, Renaissance, and neo-classicism. This is found in his *Gehalt und Gestalt im Kunstwerk des Dichters* (Wildpark-Potsdam [1925], pp. 265ff., 282ff.). Eugenio d'Ors called such pervasive stylistic types "eons" and saw baroque as a historical category, an *idée-événement*, a "constant" which recurs almost everywhere. He draws up a table of the different variants or subspecies of *homo barocchus* in *Du Baroque* (Paris [1935], pp. 161ff.), where we find an archaic baroque, a Macedonian, an Alexandrian, a Roman, a Buddhist, a Gothic, a Franciscan, a Manuelian (in Portugal), a Nordic, a Palladian (in Italy and

England), a Jesuit, a rococo, a romantic, a *fin-de-siècle*, and some other varieties of baroque. In his view it pervades all art history from the ruins of Baalbek to the most recent modernism, all literature from Euripides to Rimbaud, and all other cultural activities including philosophy as well as the discoveries of Harvey and Linné. Half of the world's history and creations are baroque, all that are not purely classical. The term thus used becomes so broad and vague when cut off from its period moorings that it loses all usefulness for concrete literary study. The historian of literature will be interested far more in baroque as a term for a definite period.

Even as a period term the chronological extension of its use is most bafflingly various. In England it may include Lyly, Milton, and even Gray and Collins. In Germany it may include Fischart, Opitz, and even Klopstock. In Italy, Tasso as well as Marino and Basile; in Spain, Guevara, Cervantes, Góngora, and Quevedo as well as Calderón; in France, Rabelais, Ronsard, Du Bartas, the *précieux*, but also Racine and even Fénelon. Two or even almost three centuries may be spanned; or at the other extreme, the term may be limited to a single author in English, Richard Crashaw, or to a single style such as Marinism or Gongorism. The term baroque seems, however, most acceptable if we have in mind a general European movement whose conventions and literary style can be described concretely and whose chronological limits can be fixed narrowly, as from the last decades of the sixteenth century to the middle of the eighteenth century in a few countries. Baroque points out that Sir Thomas Browne and Donne, Góngora and Quevedo, Gryphius and Grimmelshausen have something in common, both in one national literature and all over Europe.

BIBLIOGRAPHY

René Wellek, "The Concept of Baroque in Literary Scholarship," in *Journal of Aesthetics and Art Criticism,* **5** (1946), 77–106, with full bibliography; reprinted with a "Postscript 1962," in *Concepts of Criticism* (New Haven, 1963), pp. 69–127. The following works are arranged by date of publication. Carlo Calcaterra, "Il problema del Barocco," in *Problemi ed orientamenti critici di lingua e di letteratura italiana,* ed. A. Momigliano (Milan, 1949), III, 405–501. Václav Černý, "Les origines européennes des études baroquistes," in *Revue de littérature comparée,* **24** (1950), 25–45. András Angyal, "Der Werdegang der internationalen Barockforschung," in *Forschungen und Fortschritte,* **28** (1954), 377–84. Giovanni Getto, "La Polemica sul Barocco," in *Letteratura e critica nel tempo* (Milan, 1954), pp. 131–218. Giuliano Briganti, "Barocco: storia della parola e fortuna critica del concetto," in *Enciclopedia universale dell'Arte,* (1958), 2, 346–59. R. A. Sayce, "The Use of the Term Baroque in French Literary History," in *Comparative Litera-*

ture, **10** (1958), 246–53. Otto Kurz, "Barocco: storia di una parola," in *Lettere Italiane,* **12** (1960), 414–44. Helmut Hatzfeld, *Der gegenwärtige Stand der romanistichen Barockforschung,* Sitzungsberichte der Bayerischen Akademie der Wissenschaften (Munich, 1961), Heft 4. Bruno Migliorini, "Etimologia e storia del termine 'barocco,'" in *Manierismo, Barocco, Rococò, Convegno internazionale* (Rome, 1962), pp. 39–49. Helmut Hatzfeld, *Estudios sobre el Barroco* (Madrid, 1964).

RENÉ WELLEK

[See also Classicism in Literature; **Expressionism in Literature; Gothic;** Renaissance Humanism; Romanticism; **Style.**]

THEORIES OF BEAUTY TO THE MID-NINETEENTH CENTURY

THE OPINION of many historians and philosophers is that the concept of beauty, like other universal ideas (for instance, nature, truth), is a vague and empty abstraction. Yet, beauty has often been defined. During many great cultural periods, artists who created works and critics who established the norms and the theory of these works stated what beauty is, and it seems preposterous to assert that those who have felt to be in the presence of beauty deceived themselves. Undoubtedly the person who has this feeling or inner certitude not only means something which is very relevant to him, but also something which he believes to be inherent in the object thus characterized. On the other hand, it is equally certain that the peculiar quality called beautiful is not the same at all times and for all persons; nor can we deny that a variety of subjective and objective factors influence our opinion that something is beautiful. A brief survey of the types of answers that have been formulated on this issue may illustrate its relevance.

In English the term beauty goes back to the French *beauté,* which in turn is derived from a conjectured vulgar Latin *bellitatem,* formed after the adjective *bellus,* which neither originally nor properly designated something beautiful; *pulcher* and *formosus* had this function. *Bellus* was a diminutive of *bonus* (good) and was used first for women and children, then ironically for men. Its affectionate overtones are said to explain why *bellus* (and not *pulcher*) was adopted in the Romance languages, where it survived either alone or jointly with *formosus.* The German *schön* carries in its oldest forms the meaning of bright, brilliant, and also striking, impressive.

It is uncertain whether the adjective or the noun was used first. Whenever the issue *is* decided, it will be done not on historical but "philosophical" grounds. Empiricists and positivists claim priority for the adjective, metaphysicians for the noun. Homer, who is often cited in the controversy, uses the adjective *kalos*. He applies it to men, women, garments, weapons, cattle, and dogs and seems to refer to a pleasing, sensuous characteristic; occasionally he takes *kalos* in the general sense of good, proper, designating a high achievement or the full realization of a potential. It is doubtful whether Homer means personified beauty when he uses the noun *kallos*.

To be sure, neither the etymology nor the early history of a term designating a universal idea can explain the later uses of the term, but it is not without interest for the student of the long and intricate history of beauty to see that the ambivalent use of beauty and goodness, beauty and light or radiance, goes back to the very origin of the concept, and that already in Homer's time the term was used comprehensively.

In the following we shall deal with the fundamental approaches to the question of beauty and with the factors that enter into the judgment of beauty. No claim is made to have found a logical classification for the material, nor for proceeding systematically. We have tried to be clear and coherent in our necessarily succinct summaries, and we hope to have established an intelligible pattern.

I. THE FUNDAMENTAL POSITIONS

1. The Objective Existence of Beauty. For Plato the individual forms of beauty partake in Absolute Beauty which transcends them. Beauty as Idea is a Being by itself, beyond the limitations of space and time, and independent of relativities; it reveals the Ideal and the Universal. It also has the metaphysical property of reconciling the finite with the infinite, and it manifests itself in proportion and symmetry, in the harmony of the parts in relation to the whole, and in measure. The individual, single judgment stating that something is beautiful ultimately refers to an underlying, general quality of beauty. If it does not, it only expresses the fact that something pleases us.

The notion of symmetry and due proportions moreover links beauty with the Good, and inasmuch as beauty reveals Being, it is related to Truth. This link can also be defined by saying that Truth guarantees Beauty or gives Being to Beauty.

Beauty's relationship to Being is expressed in terms of light and of making it appear, making it visible. Beauty is light in that it manifests Being. Measure, proportion, light are not understood to be simply inherent characteristics, but are meant to have an effect upon the soul and the mind.

The soul before entering into life contemplates Being; the soul cannot behold Truth or the Good, but it can behold Beauty, and it remembers the vision when it sees individual beauty in this life. In this conception of remembrance is the root of the Platonic idea of ascent from sensuous beauty (beauty appearing in color, sound, and form) to inward and intellectual beauty, and thence to the ultimate vision.

There remains, however, the question whether beauty has, so to speak, a substance of its own, or whether it only makes qualities appear, qualities which are also those of Truth and the Good. Plato did not answer this question clearly. It is, however, certain that he does not refer to art in his metaphysics of beauty.

Some of the ideas set forth here can be found also in the writings of the Pythagoreans and pre-Socratics, in Hesiod, Polykleitos, and Xenophon. For a further discussion of Plato, see below Section II, Paragraph 1, *Metaphysical Foundation*.

Although Aristotle did not establish a theory of beauty and although he neither deduced the principles of the arts from the idea of the beautiful, nor tried to determine the idea of the beautiful as a fundamental problem of art, he made a major contribution to this issue: he separated the beautiful from the good and linked on principle the beautiful with the creation of works of art. The component elements of beauty are, according to him, order, symmetry, and definiteness.

In his *Poetics* Aristotle also uses formal relationships as a foundation of beauty; the mimesis of action in a story must represent an integrated whole, i.e., there must be the multiple, the parts or incidents, and the unity, a connection so close "that the transposal or withdrawal of any one of them will disjoin and dislocate the whole" (Ch. 7). Beauty is thus defined in terms similar to those of Plato; at the same time these terms are used in a way which is opposed to Plato, for a work of art is no longer twice removed from the truth of things, but is the image of a reality which fulfills nature's unachieved possibilities or intentions. The world of appearance which the artist creates is no longer judged by the standards of the truth of Being (with regard to which it is inferior) but is judged by the standards of the perfection of form.

A conclusion *not* drawn by Aristotle, but implicit in his ideas, is that the artist who follows the norms of beauty (order, symmetry, and definiteness) and observes the formal relationships will create a form of beauty which corresponds to objective criteria; however, these are not metaphysical.

Plato's conception of beauty is at the origin of much of Western aesthetic thought; however, it often was not the original conception which exerted an influence, but the modified form which Plotinus and Saint Augustine gave to it. Plotinus dealt with the ideal of beauty, not only as a problem of metaphysics (as Plato did), but also as a fundamental problem of art (which Plato did not). His combination of the two perspectives considerably influenced the interpretation of Plato's ideas in the subsequent centuries.

The starting point of Plotinus' theory of beauty is the dualism of mind and matter, or form and matter. Matter is metaphysically described as a principle of privation; matter is undetermined, indefinite; it is non-Being. This negative definition is made, however, with regard to Being, i.e., it implies that matter is the want of form, order, determination.

When the mind penetrates matter, it imposes form upon it, i.e., order, number, proportion, quantity, quality. With regard to our topic, it is particularly significant that Plotinus called the determining principle, which he conceives as a forming force, beauty, and that he called matter, which is amorphous, ugly. (The connotations of beauty and light, respectively matter and darkness, are equally important.) In this way Plotinus introduced a dialectics of beauty and ugliness and conceived of beauty as creativity and a plastic force. The notions of harmony, order, measure, and proportion establish the link between the beautiful and the good. Inasmuch as the objects which we perceive participate in form, they are beautiful, and their beauty is an image of the ideal form. This notion of participation is important in Plotinus; he emphasizes at times that beauty does not consist in symmetry, proportion, and the relationship of the part to the whole, for if it did, beauty could be identified with it and would be sensuous. Beauty is, however, an idea which, being one, creates unity; by their participation in the *idea*, things are beautiful. With regard to the arts this means that the artist's mind must ascend toward the vision of the beautiful, where he finds the model for his creation. This vision, however, is not the highest degree of which the *soul* is capable. The highest degree is reached in the intuition of the intelligible, an intuition through which the image of the intelligible is formed and created within the soul itself.

For Saint Augustine God as the absolute beauty is the principle and source of all that is beautiful in this world. All that exists does so through form, measure, and number; God has ordered all according to inalterable proportions. Unity, order, and proportion are the elements of beauty.

Saint Augustine conceives of God not only as unity, but also as multiple in His infinite virtues. With regard to beauty this means that the unity of beauty admits variety, a variety subjected to divine measure.

Saint Augustine follows Plato in adopting the dialectical method of ascent; he differs, however, in the conception of the stages; the mind rises from the sensuous appearance of beauty, an appearance to which Saint Augustine gives full significance, to the contemplation of the soul; from there to measure and proportion, to the idea, and ultimately to God. Of great significance is the context in which these ideas are developed. In *De Trinitate* the idea of beauty is connected with the Word. É. Gilson gives a concise account of the pattern of ideas:

Thus it is in the Word that we find the root of unity and being; moreover we can find in it the root of the beautiful. When an image equals that of which it is the image, it brings about a perfect correspondence, symmetry, equality, and resemblance. There is no difference between the model and its image, hence no discrepancy, no inequality; the copy corresponds in every particular to the original; hence its beauty and the name of form (*species*) by which we designate it. Now this original beauty based on resemblance is to be found again in all the partaking beauties. The more the parts of a body resemble one another, the more beautiful the body. In general, it is order, harmony, proportion, i.e., unity produced by the resemblance which engenders beauty (Gilson, 1929).

In Augustine's *De musica* we find detailed discussions of meter, rhythm, intervals, and more generally, of numerical relationships which are the source of musical delight. Throughout many of his writings, Saint Augustine dwelt on the beauty in color and sound as well as on the fitness and loveliness of the spectacle of nature. The importance which he gave in his thought to the question of beauty is still further emphasized by the fact that he composed, as he informs us himself, a work entitled *De apto et pulchro* ("On Fit Proportion and the Beautiful"), a work which was lost.

The pronounced religious character of Plotinus' ideas on beauty and Saint Augustine's renewal of Plato's thought, as well as his fusion of the Platonic tradition with Christian doctrine, played a decisive role in the continuity of the thought of classical antiquity in reflections on beauty.

It has been asserted that the conception of beauty as developed in classical antiquity and the post-classical period dominated Western thought throughout the Middle Ages and the Renaissance up to the beginning of the eighteenth century, when there occurred a radical shift in the manner of raising the issue. This statement is valid only as far as the key concepts and the fundamental positions are concerned; they remain constant. There exist, however, variations of meaning and stress. Saint Thomas Aquinas' triad of integrity (perfection), consonance (fit proportion, proportion of the parts and the whole), and clarity (the radiance of form communicated to matter) summarizes Saint Augustine's ideas; still, the *resplendentia formae* is emphasized and becomes a highly significant feature of the beautiful.

During the Renaissance, the rapid and glorious development of the various arts, the detailed elaboration of art theory and literary theory, the accentuation of the role of the artist as creator and of nature as his model, led to a close connection between speculation on beauty and art theory. Though the metaphysical and objective idea of beauty is in essence maintained, it undergoes important modifications. We cannot trace these here, since they can be studied only in their specific forms. Instead we shall deal briefly with three authors who maintain the objective and ontological conception of beauty at a time when the shift in perspective took place.

Père André's *Essai sur le beau* (1741), a defense of the objective existence of beauty, is written against the Pyrrhonians, i.e., those who make the idea of beauty depend upon prejudice, upbringing, imagination, and caprice of individual liking. Rejecting the question: What things are beautiful? and asking: What is beauty? Père André follows Saint Augustine and through him Plato, and sees in unity, order, proportion, and symmetry the essence and form of beauty. Then he goes beyond his models and distinguishes three orders of beauty: an essential beauty which is absolute, i.e., not instituted; a natural beauty, which exists in the world and depends on the *will* of the Creator, but is independent of human taste or opinion; a beauty instituted by man and arbitrary to a certain degree, since it depends on custom, individual or national taste, and manners of representation in the arts. The variations in judgment, feeling, and standards of taste (the main tenets on which the skeptical arguments are based) apply only to the third type of beauty.

All three types of beauty are considered with regard to the mind and its creations, to morals, and to the body. The chapters dealing with this application contain many detailed observations which are original, pertinent, and sensitive.

The *Essai sur le beau* had a marked influence on the eighteenth century and also, through Victor Cousin's new annotated edition in 1843, on the nineteenth century. It renewed the metaphysical and ontological conception of beauty at a time when the very foundation of this conception was being undermined. The Cartesian elements of the *Essai* may have contributed to this effect, but there is no doubt that Père André's conception of the *beau géométrique*, his high evaluation of structure, his analysis of light and color, and in connection with it his praise of Newton, strongly appealed to his contemporaries. Père André admirably combined a metaphysical foundation and structure

with empirical analysis and a sense for relativism. Last but not least, the fact that he sharply criticized the Pyrrhonians and yet included the *beau arbitraire* in his system proved that he considered a reform of the theory of beauty necessary and that he tried to reconcile the Ancients and Moderns.

Francis Hutcheson's influential *Enquiry into the Original of Our Ideas of Beauty and Virtue* (1725) offers a striking example of the attempt to reconcile an objective conception of beauty with the theory that beauty is a subjective, inward experience. He emphasizes that "the word *beauty* is taken for the idea raised in us," and "a *sense of beauty* for our power of receiving this idea" (I, 9), that by his term of absolute or original beauty (i.e., beauty in an object without relation to anything beyond it), he does not understand "any quality supposed to be in the object which should of itself be beautiful, without relation to any mind which perceives it." Beauty, like other sensible ideas, "denotes the perception of some mind" (I, 16). He concedes, using John Locke's distinction of primary and secondary qualities, that "the ideas of beauty and harmony being excited upon our perception of some primary quality may have a nearer resemblance to objects than sensations in our mind," but hastens to add: "were there no mind with a sense of beauty to contemplate objects," they could not be called beautiful (ibid.). The fluctuation in these statements between two different views—(a) that beauty is not a quality in the object and (b) that every statement on beauty presupposes a perception of the mind—is apparent.

We notice the same incertitude in the definition of the sense of beauty: it is called an internal sense, but is different from our other senses; it receives "those complex ideas of objects which obtain the names of beautiful, regular and harmonious" (I, 8). Although Hutcheson calls the internal sense "a natural power of perception, or a sense of the beauty of objects," "antecedent to all custom, education or example" (VII, 1), he conceives of it as "a *passive* power of receiving" (VI, 10; italics added). The remark on the antecedents is directed against those followers of Locke who maintained that in the absence of innate ideas only utility, custom, and education can form the basis for our judgment of beauty. The followers of Locke play for Hutcheson a role similar to that which the Pyrrhonians played in Père André's essay. There is, however, this difference, that Hutcheson accepts Locke's sensationalism, his rejection of innate ideas, and the principle of starting from the beginning, i.e., from the generally, naturally human. The polemics as well as the acceptance account for Hutcheson's stress on immediacy and his insistence that the internal sense is in its nature a sense like the others.

Although pleasure may accompany the perceptions

of the external senses, the pleasure which accompanies perceptions made by the inward sense is higher. This notion of higher pleasure is linked to the fact that the internal sense is capable of perceiving a compound of simple perceptions produced jointly. The pleasure attached to the perception is immediate (it does not presuppose a process of cognition), and disinterested.

That which excites in the internal sense the pleasant idea of absolute beauty is, according to Hutcheson, "a real quality in objects" (I, 9); Hutcheson identifies it as uniformity amidst variety; the more variety the better, provided uniformity ties it together. This is the foundation of the beauty we perceive in nature generally; in individual things in nature proportion of the parts (the integrated whole) also is a source of beauty. The perception of unity amidst variety is to be found as well in theorems and in the laws of nature, e.g., gravitation. Relative beauty springs from imitation of original beauty, when a conformity or unity is discovered between the idea (perception) of the imitated object and that of the original; the latter may also be some established idea. With regard to relative beauty—Hutcheson adds rather oddly—it is not necessary that there be any beauty in the original. There also exists relative beauty derived by means of comparison.

The *qualitas* which elicits the perception of beauty in us and constitutes the foundation of all judgment on beauty is, as Hutcheson stresses, objective and real; it is there, even when it does not appear, and it is universal. In addition to uniformity amidst variety, it is called proportion, order, harmony, and symmetry. The action of eliciting comes from the outside, and the process of eliciting is strictly empirical; the internal sense functions immediately and necessarily; our mind receives necessarily ideas from the presence of objects (VI, 10).

Uniformity amidst variety, order, harmony, and symmetry have, as shown above, originally an ontological meaning and can only be "perceived" by a discursive, rational process. Hutcheson employs the concepts with the full prestige of their traditional meaning (it is significant in this context that he speaks of *qualitas* when he means relationship), but disavows this meaning by his principle of empirical foundation and his axiom of immediate sense response. Nowhere does he show by what operation the beautiful is constituted and why the sensation of "greater pleasure," of "a positive delight," accompanies it. What we experience through our senses as a different kind is said to be objectively different. Since the object that arouses the pleasant idea of beauty is *sui generis*, Hutcheson must introduce a special sense.

The mixture of subjective and objective, empirical and ontological elements is fully apparent in Hutcheson's *Enquiry* and permits us to seize directly what in other authors is concealed by vague or brilliant terminology. One may say that Hutcheson can no longer combine the various elements of the aesthetic content, nor can he keep them apart.

In only one case does Hutcheson mention a mediating factor: in the case of a kind of beauty which is neither absolute nor relative in the sense of imitation. It is the beauty "arising from correspondence to intention," which we can observe in nature when the mechanism of the various parts "seems adapted to both the perfection of that part and yet in subordination to the good of the whole" (IV, 7). The intention we recognize is that of the author of nature, who thus mediates the relationship and our response in the judgment of beauty.

Hutcheson's *Enquiry* and Père André's *Essai* are the starting point for Denis Diderot's article "Beau" in Volume II of the *Encyclopédie* (published early in 1752). The full title of the article is "Recherches philosophiques sur l'origine et la nature du Beau." Only the central issue of the article can be presented here, omitting the historical sections, and also the many reflections on the difficulties encountered, according to Diderot, by all those who seek to define beauty, including himself. The article is a major contribution on the present subject.

Diderot is more radical than Hutcheson on both the subjective and objective aspects of beauty; he rejects the obscure notion of a sixth sense and briefly traces on empirical and pragmatic grounds the genesis of the concepts of relation, order, proportion, symmetry, and unity. They are formed when we begin to exercise our faculties and to provide for our wants. If we call our perception of a judgment on beauty immediate, or believe it to be a spontaneous feeling, we forget or ignore the long history of the formation of our ideas.

Considering not our response but beauty itself, Diderot asserts that we can define it as that which rouses in our mind the idea of relations (*rapports*). Beauty is a notion of the mind, accompanied by pleasure, but a notion founded on something real, existing outside of us. The concept of relations comprises those of order, symmetry, proportion; it is a general and abstract concept, but only such a concept can comprise all the various appearances of beauty. The relations can be real, or perceived by the mind, or formed by it; they can be considered with regard to the parts of one object or with regard to several objects, or with regard to nature, the arts, or ethics; they differ quantitatively and vary according to their nature. The specifically beautiful is thus a matter of differentiation, the differentiation of a universal formative law.

It is apparent that Diderot's concept of relations is very close to the meaning given that term in the mathematics and physics of his time; however, it is not simply copied from the sciences. Diderot uses the term in the aesthetic-scientific sense for the first time in his *Mémoires sur différents sujets de mathématiques* (1748), where in a discussion of the general principles of acoustics, he deals with the parallelism between the mechanical relations (number of vibrations and length of a chord) and the relations in music that please us by their beauty.

Structure, symmetry, proportion, conceived as special instances of relations, no longer have a metaphysical meaning in the article "Beau"; however, they acquire through the association with the mathematical sciences a new ontological significance, for, in the same way in which, according to eighteenth-century scientific thought, relations and proportions make us understand nature in its objectivity and real character, so the *rapports* are for Diderot the objective foundation of the *beau réel* and our judgment on beauty. By using the principle of *rapports* in an analysis of specific works of architecture, painting, music, and literature, Diderot gives an illustration of the insights into structure, form, and beauty to be gained by the application of a principle, which is general and abstract only in its definition.

Many more instances of the use of formal and structural characteristics in the definition of beauty can be quoted from older or more recent authors. During the modern period the characteristics are generally either rationalized or brought into a scientific context. We must omit them here and can do so since they are only variants of the uses we have mentioned. It must be decided in every individual case whether a metaphysical or ontological meaning is implied in the use of the characteristics.

2. The Objective Conception of Beauty in Artistic Representation. Inasmuch as beauty is considered to be the result of artistic achievement, it is subjective; but inasmuch as the artist does not express his individual, personal feelings and ideas, but follows a model and applies criteria established independently of him, beauty is objective.

We find a striking example of this conception of objective beauty in the *ars poetica* of seventeenth-century French classicism, which influenced classicism in Europe and can thus be chosen as a model structure. Some of its criteria (proportion, harmony, perfection, form, and the idea of the model) were derived directly or indirectly from the speculations on beauty discussed in our first section. Beauty is considered to be the object or aim of art; in order to achieve it the artist must imitate nature and follow the rules. Nature is not understood to be the sum of sensuous data, but "general nature" or ideal nature, selected, ordered, arranged by

reason. Philosophically speaking, nature is an order of Being, manifest in eternal, fundamental laws. The rules which the artist follows are also ultimately founded on reason and must be justified by reason. René Bray expressed succinctly this interrelationship of the concepts in the *doctrine classique*:

. . . eternal reason, universal beauty, unchanging rules, the three terms are closely linked. The perennity of reason imposes that of beauty, since if beauty were to change, reason, which is the judge of beauty, would change also. It imposes likewise the permanence of the rules, of which it is the foundation (Bray, 1927).

To the modern historian it is obvious that the norms of classicism are in part not timeless and universal, but related to a specific intellectual, historical, and social structure; however, as far as the classical theory is concerned, this relativity does not affect their normative value and hence the objective character of beauty.

The rules or norms are also related to the literary or artistic genres; if the rules are satisfied, the genre attains perfection, and the work is beautiful. One might say that it is ultimately the link with the idea of perfection and the conception of beauty which explains the great value attributed to rules and genres in classical literary and art theory.

The rules, most of which were derived from Aristotle (or his Renaissance interpreters) and Horace, are moreover sometimes justified by the model character of classical antiquity; the rational and the historical justification are generally linked together.

The works of classical antiquity are also considered to be by themselves a guarantee of the objectivity of beauty. They were said to be close to nature or to represent the major and most probable occurrences of life and the fundamental aspects of human nature. Their perfection and beauty, their presentation of what is essential and lasting had been tested by the unanimous judgment of centuries. In the domain of plastic arts J. J. Winckelmann's (1717–68) enthusiastic and eloquent praise of the exemplary beauty achieved in Hellenic art (it embodied the very norm of beauty) is a famous instance of the founding of beauty on the art works of classical antiquity, an instance which was all the more influential as Winckelmann wrote an epoch-making history of the art of that period. His perceptive, novel, and ingenious interpretations became justly famous, and the two criteria "simplicity and serenity," which he added to the already established norms of beauty, were still echoed in nineteenth-century classicism. It was Nietzsche who later opposed the Dionysian element in Greek art to Winckelmann's Apollonian vision; and the expression of profound, universal emotion, as well as the sublime, to the beauty of appearance and illusion.

3. Other Instances of the Objective Conception of Beauty. We find a simpler and often empirical notion of objective beauty in the idea that the artist who wishes to present perfect beauty selects out of many examples the most beautiful parts of each, since one cannot find one person whose every part is perfect. The argument occurs already in Xenophon's *Memorabilia of Socrates* (III, x, 1). In several cases this view is modified by the principle that the sculptor, painter, and poet must avoid the imitation of the individual with his characteristic peculiarities and present a composite image, formed after a model created in the mind.

The relationship between the beautiful and the useful is defined in a variety of ways. The critics of beauty as an innate idea, as a form of Being or, more generally, as a metaphysical or ontological idea, often consider the useful to be the foundation of beauty; empirical and pragmatic reasons are to replace the so-called obscure and vague notions.

Usefulness or utility is, however, also taken in the sense of fitness and appropriateness, meaning the aptitude of proportion, form, or structure to the end proposed. When the full realization of a potential in human beings and the fitness of the parts to the design for which each thing is formed are called beautiful, no pragmatic or utilitarian idea is involved. The use of utility by the Earl of Shaftesbury shows that the concept can find a place even in a metaphysics of beauty:

The same features which make deformity create incommodiousness and disease. And the same shapes and proportions which make beauty afford advantage by adapting to activity and use. Even in the imitative or designing arts the truth or beauty of every figure or statue is measured from the perfection of Nature in her just adapting of every limb and proportion to the activity, strength, dexterity, life and vigor of the particular species or animal designed. Thus beauty and truth are plainly joined with the notion of utility and convenience, even in the apprehension of every ingenious artist, the architect, the statuary or the painter (*Characteristics* . . . , II, 267).

In all these instances the beautiful does not depend upon the useful and is not derived from it, but is linked or coexists with it. For a further discussion of Shaftesbury, see below, Section II, Paragraph 1, *Metaphysical Foundation.*

4. The Subjective Approach to Beauty. As observed by several historians of aesthetics, a decisive shift of perspective in the analysis of beauty occurred towards the end of the seventeenth and the beginning of the eighteenth century. Beauty is no longer self-subsistent, an essence, an objective nature, or a relation. Its foundation is in the response of our feelings, emotions, or

our mind. The starting point of our reflections on beauty is in our experience of a particular kind of agreeableness. Two statements by David Hume show this approach in its extreme form:

Beauty is no quality in things themselves: it exists merely in the mind which contemplates them; and each mind perceives a different beauty. One person may even perceive deformity, where another is sensible of beauty; and every individual ought to acquiesce in his own sentiment, without pretending to regulate those of others (Hume, *Essays* . . . , I, 266).

And "pleasure and pain, therefore, are not only necessary attendants of beauty and deformity, but constitute their very essence" (Hume, 1886). But these pseudo-precise pronouncements were not Hume's last words on the matter. On the other hand it must be said that pronouncements of this sort have obscured the fact that the subjective approach may consist simply in a careful analysis and description of the nature and causes of our aesthetic feelings and the way the effect is achieved, without any claim being made that there is nothing outside of us which corresponds to the effect produced.

The subjective approach was to all probability prepared by the emphasis on emotional appeal in works of art, an emphasis which is one of the manifestations of the currents of *sensibilité* in the eighteenth century. Already Fénelon associated the beautiful with the moving when he observed in his *Letter to the Academy* (1716):

According to Horace, it is little for a poem to be beautiful and brilliant; it must be moving, pleasing, and consequently simple, natural and passionate.
Non satis est pulchra esse poemata; dulcia sunto.
Et quocumque volent, animum auditoris agunto.
The beautiful which is only beautiful, that is, brilliant, is but partly beautiful. It must be an expression of the passions in order to inspire them. It must take hold of the heart in order to turn it toward the rightful aim of a poem.

The criticism of the merely brilliant occurs repeatedly in the aesthetics of classicism. In this passage it is connected, however, with a stress on the moving and emotive power of poetry. Still, we should not overlook the connotations of simple, pleasing, and natural in Fénelon's statement, nor that the passage appears in a criticism of *bel esprit* and contrived style.

The logical, rational, and metaphysical components of the idea of beauty, as well as the corresponding notions of formal relationships, proportion, objectivity (*adequatio rei*), of perfection, goodness, truth, of variety and unity, all of which are intellectually perceived, are gradually replaced by beauty's direct appeal to our sentiments, affections, and passions. In order to distinguish the specific aesthetic appeal from the general effect, some authors have recourse to the conception of a special inner sense. The most consequential and influential statements on the identity of the beautiful and the moving, as well as on the aesthetics of feeling, are to be found in the *Réflexions critiques sur la poésie et sur la peinture* (1719) of the abbé Jean-Baptiste Du Bos.

The fact that the discussion of beauty is often connected in the eighteenth century with that of taste is a consequence of the subjective approach. This connection had, however, a curious result: several authors, who are ready to assert that beauty is a subjective impression, are reluctant to do so in the case of taste. The objective criteria which they defend in the latter case are no longer based on reason, but on consensus and on history (e.g., the universal and continuous acknowledgment of the art and literature of classical antiquity). It is this recognition which in many cases leads to conflicts with the subjective approach to beauty and thus to revisions of this approach.

In a more general way one might see in the shift to the subjective approach an example of the passing of aesthetic speculation from a method of synthesizing ideas (Truth, Good, Beauty, Perfection, Unity, Harmony, Proportion), fitting them together, unifying, systematizing, and objectifying them to a disjunctive method of dissociating ideas and reflecting on their origin in sense perceptions and in the working of the mind.

"Aesthetic" is used intentionally in connection with the subjective approach. The term was introduced only in 1750 by A. G. Baumgarten, who rooted the new "science" of aesthetics in psychology and epistemology, but the notion existed already at the beginning of the eighteenth century and is the result of the shift in perspective we have mentioned. When our responsiveness to beauty became the center of interest, both the faculty and the nature of responsiveness were made the subject of analysis. We find a striking example of this in Joseph Addison's articles in *The Spectator* (1712) on "The pleasures of the imagination." Addison was conscious of the novelty of his approach when he set off imagination as the proper organ of the response, distinguishing it from that of the senses and the understanding, and observed that the "pleasures" were elicited not only by what is beautiful but also by that which is great and novel or uncommon (*The Spectator*, Nos. 409, 412, 415), and that the causes for the pleasure were to be found in nature, literature, and the representative arts; in history, the sciences, and even in the activity of the mind. Such latitude was clearly incompatible with the traditional criteria of beauty. More important still was the fact that the new values of the sublime and the picturesque were put next to beauty or were esteemed more highly than beauty. Even ugliness ceases to be simply a negation of beauty and finds a place in aesthetics. Its relationship to beauty is no longer antithetical, but becomes dialectical, when the subjective responses of pleasure—pain, pleasing—displeasing were substituted for the objective opposition: beautiful—ugly. Edmund Burke shows that pain and sorrow can become agreeable sensations and that the ugly, when it is "united with such qualities as excite strong terror" (Burke, 1958), evokes the feeling of the sublime. Using one of the most fruitful principles in the analysis of pain and pleasure, viz., conversion, Hume demonstrates how the feelings of distress, terror, and anxiety are transformed into pleasing emotions ("Of Tragedy").

It is not surprising that Burke, when he developed in his essay on the sublime and beautiful a coherent theory of the sublime, attacked and ridiculed the traditional principles of beauty: proportion, fitness, harmony, and perfection. He also opposed the close connection between or unity of the True, the Good, and the Beautiful and attributed beauty wholly to qualities in objects: smallness, smoothness of surface, variety of outline, delicacy and brightness as well as softness of color, qualities which act mechanically through the *senses*. Beauty had clearly lost its supremacy. Even when its former criteria were maintained, as in William Hogarth's *Analysis of Beauty* (1753), variety was considered to be the most important one and to include the others. The line of beauty was the serpentine line, which by its curves delighted the eye and gave play to the imagination.

The conception of beauty also profited, however, from the subjective approach, above all in the inquiries into the working of the human mind, when it is faced with aesthetic experience. The rapid development of British empirical psychology in the eighteenth century played the major role in these inquiries. Particularly fruitful were the studies of the role which the mind's capacity for association and transference played in generating the feeling of beauty. By the analysis of the response of our faculties to order, symmetry, succession, as well as to the interplay of uniformity and variety, and by the study of the mental connections which are provoked by resemblance, contiguity in space or time, and repetition (or parallelism) in cause-effect relations, a link was established again between the operations of our mind and the conception of objective beauty. Archibald Alison's inquiry into the associations connected with angular and curved forms, and his observation that the combination of uniformity and variety is a natural tendency of our mind and is represented by the winding line (*Essays on the Nature and Principles of Taste*, 1790), and Henry Home's (Lord Kames) discussion of the beauty of different geometrical forms and the relation between the beauty of motion and the flow of our perceptions are examples of associationalist responses to form.

Inasmuch as Kant deals with the phenomenon of beauty not directly, but in the perspective of the foundation and validity of our aesthetic judgment, his approach is subjective; he considers only the relation in which the object stands to us. On the other hand, his search for an *a priori* principle of the faculty of pleasure and pain leads him to a criticism of the subjective elements in the theories of his predecessors and to a new conception of subjectivity, objectivity, and universality. In his methodological starting point Kant is close to Home's statement: "Beauty which for its existence depends on the percipient as much as on the object perceived, cannot be an inherent property of either" (Home, 1788). He rejects the notion that beauty is a power in the object and distinguishes the aesthetic pleasure, which is disinterested, from other kinds of pleasure. A pure aesthetic judgment is possible only when we are free from the compulsion of want or need and indifferent with regard to what is serviceable in actual life, i.e., when we are at play. Kant also dissociates the idea of perfection from that of beauty and states that the beautiful is not subject to a rationally definable end.

Beauty created by art is free; it is not bound by the rules of understanding nor by those of practical reason. On the other hand, beauty does not give us knowledge of things in themselves, i.e., of the transcendental world of Reason.

And yet, Kant observes, we seem to perceive a certain purposefulness in beauty; the objects of our aesthetic judgment seem to be designed to stimulate our faculties of apprehension to harmonious interaction, to unify understanding and senses in the working of imagination. Out of this harmonious cooperation of our faculties springs the feeling of beauty. In the judgment on beauty, there is also contained the idea that others will concur with our feeling of beauty. This conception of a universal voice has nothing to do with empirical or statistical evidence; it can be fully achieved only in the ideal. It is a postulate based on the fact that all men share the same faculties, and it is an imperative to transcend the subjectivity of pleasure and the mixture of the good and the beautiful, and to free ourselves from individual limitations. Here Kant

transforms the former objective universality of beauty, which was rejected by empirical psychology and is incompatible with his transcendental method, into a subjective one.

His distinction of free and dependent beauty, often criticized in the nineteenth century, may have a renewed meaning in the modern period: free beauty exists only in idyllic nature, in flowers and in arabesques, i.e., in the purposeless play of forms; dependent or appendant beauty presupposes the concept of what the object should be in its perfection.

Kant's ideas on the significance of our aesthetic judgment for the mediation of the sensuous and the intelligible, the phenomenal and noumenal worlds, on the role of imagination, and on the free play as well as harmony of our faculties, exerted a deep influence on Goethe, Schiller, and German romanticism and idealism. The two schools of thought, in turn, contributed many ideas to English and French writings on beauty. Kant's denial of the cognitive function of beauty was rejected, however, by several of his followers. F. W. J. Schelling was one of the first to claim that beauty gives to us a symbolic knowledge of the world of the Mind and is the presentation of the Absolute in the sensuous particular, an idea which is at the root of later theories concerning the higher insights granted to us by beauty.

Friedrich Schiller places the question of beauty into the perspective of the harmonious development of human nature and the formation of our "true humanity." The beautiful does not result from the effect of objects upon us, nor does it exist as a quality outside of us; its origin is within us. One might say that Schiller considers beauty to be an imperative, something which we must achieve. Only after having fulfilled this task, can we receive beauty. However, we cannot fulfill it once and for all; there remains an "ideal" of beauty as well as of achievement. Beauty is the result of the harmonizing of the demands of man's sensuous and rational nature, of the two fundamental motive impulses, the material drive (*Stofftrieb*) and the form drive (*Formtrieb*); or, to put it differently, beauty is neither mere life nor mere form, but living form. The experience of living forms was decisive in the development of Schiller's idea of beauty; it pointed to a reconciliation of the realm of nature and that of freedom.

Schiller uses the term "drive" intentionally, for as long as reason is taken to be a pure intellectual faculty and to be radically different from the senses, no mediation is possible, whereas a sensuous and a rational drive can act reciprocally. When they work in harmony, a new impulse, the play impulse, results.

Play, a state in which we are free from the straining

of our will and from all pursuits that are directed towards a specific goal, is of all man's conditions the one that unfolds both sides of his nature at once and makes him whole (Schiller, 1967). The realm of play is not that of reality, but of semblance (*Schein*), a realm in which man creates his own world, that of beauty and the arts. (This presupposes that not only the practical world, but also reality and the metaphysical connotation of beauty, truth, are dissociated from beauty.) We might say that beauty has its origin in and is the object of the *Spieltrieb*, the aesthetic play-drive, inasmuch as the latter is the balanced unity between the material drive and the form drive. Although play presupposes a state of superfluity in man as in society, its great import in man's life saves it from becoming a sign of luxury and frivolity.

The refinement and ennoblement of the senses, the connection of the idea of freedom with our aesthetic formation, and the harmonization of man's faculties, a harmonization which we achieve through our striving for beauty and which in turn we receive from beauty, have their effect also on ethics (by *disposing* us toward moral conduct) and on our relationship to others. Schiller's idea of the aesthetic education of man could easily be extended to the unfolding of our feelings of sympathy and social affections. This broader application exists already to a certain extent in the last of Schiller's letters on aesthetic education.

Herbert Spencer adopted Schiller's idea of the play-impulse and transformed it to mean a new outlet of man's energy in the state of leisure, after the use of man's energy in maintaining life and the race has been satisfied. Play of all kinds is for Spencer "this tendency to superfluous and useless exercise of the faculties that have been quiescent" (Spencer, 1887).

Charles Darwin also was interested in the play impetus and in the ethical as well as social connotations of Schiller's idea of beauty. However, Darwin regards play and beauty as natural phenomena, whereas Schiller relates them to the world of freedom. Spencer and Darwin, moreover, reject the limitation of the sense of beauty to the world of human beings and find this sense also among the animals.

The ideas on aesthetics of Hegel and Schiller have in common the method of dialectical reconciliation of opposites, the method of historical-philosophical construction in their exposition of the realization (succession and development) of individual art forms of beauty, and the principle of identity; as far as the idea of beauty is concerned, both place beauty in art above beauty in nature, in the same way as they place mind above nature. For Hegel beauty in nature is, however, only a dialectical *moment* in the development of the ideal of beauty in art; one might say that natural beauty is the reflection of beauty of mind, and that it is art which gives to phenomenal appearances a higher reality, i.e., a reality born of mind. This conception (as also Schelling's idea that the beautiful is a symbolic representation of the infinite) confirmed the "romantic" dissociation of the world of art and beauty, from the finite world, the world of our common experience, which became the prosaic, trivial world, deficient in all beauty and poetry.

In the unfolding of the absolute spirit (the identity eternally subsisting in itself and returning to itself), art is the contemplation of the absolute spirit and comes before religion and philosophy; however, art is ultimately surpassed by the two others. One notices, moreover, in the early stages of Hegel's account of the process of unfolding, a close relationship between the development of art and religion, as well as the presence of religious meaning in the working out of the particular aesthetic concepts.

In the process of the Absolute passing into self-manifestation, beauty is the realization of the Absolute in the relative; beauty discloses itself in the manifold development of a formative power and in the life that animates a perfectly developed form. In Hegel's discussion of the forms which beauty assumes, we find again the principles of fitness of relation, definiteness of proportion, and unity of the manifold. Yet beauty in art is not for Hegel the expression of abstract ideas, of a relationship, or of laws, but a concrete idea. Inasmuch as the degree of beauty depends upon the degree to which an object expresses the presence of the Spirit and not merely the relationship to a subject, Hegel can be said to reintroduce the conception of an objective and definite existence of beauty.

Hegel's conception of beauty as a creation of the *Geist* ("Mind" or "Spirit") transcended the difference between beauty as objectively founded and beauty as resulting from a response of our faculties. The way was open to consider beauty as a manifestation in objective sensory form of man's mind and consciousness, or, more generally, of his creativity and his deep-seated unconscious forces. Beauty is defined as the complete expression of and participation in the fullness of life. In dialectical materialist aesthetics this rather comprehensive notion is made more specific by the theory that beauty is a product of historical and social forces. As an outcome of the former, it will have a different content in different periods and will reflect given historical conditions; being the creation of man as a social being, beauty will express changing social conditions and play a decisive educational role in society. The objective and productive character of beauty is stressed in this conception, and is identified with the idea of realism. Although beauty will still be manifested predominantly in works of art and artistic images, it will also be expressed in life itself (as the realization of the creative capabilities of all men) and in the creation of social and economic conditions (in the revolutionary reconstruction of society) which will permit to all a full ability to appreciate and enjoy beauty. In this conception the view that art is more perfect than life is reversed; compared to the inexhaustible wealth of life and its creativity, art is a poor second and can be justified only inasmuch as it becomes one of the expressions of this life.

II. MODES OF PERCEPTION AND RESPONSE

The last section of this article, dealing with man's inner disposition towards beauty, with the faculties that perceive beauty, and with the effect of beauty, is related to the preceding section. Some of the points discussed before will be touched upon again; they will be placed, however, into a different context. We limit ourselves, as previously, to the fundamental positions.

1. Metaphysical Foundation. The most famous and influential account of the apprehension of beauty is in Plato's *Symposium* and *Phaedrus*. The primary theme of the former work is love, and beauty is discussed in this perspective. Plato describes the way in which the love of beauty is kindled and how it develops in a sequence of steps. He seems to think that to proceed in a sequence is essential. At the beginning is the admiration of beauty in a human body; one advances to the love of inward beauty, from there to the contemplation of the beautiful as it appears in observances, laws, and knowledge, and thence to the study of the beautiful itself, "so that in the end he comes to know the very essence of beauty" (*Symposium* 211), which is absolute, always the same, and of which the multitude of beautiful things partakes. In his *Phaedrus* Plato speaks of the "kind of madness which is imputed to him, who, when he sees the beauty of the earth is transported with the recollection of the true beauty," which he saw once, before passing into the form of a human being (249–50). This reminiscence is the reason for our yearning after beauty and explains the awe and reverence we feel in the perception of beauty. Love seeks beauty, and beauty in turn inspires love, so that love becomes creative of beauty.

The ideas of a right process and of an ascent in our knowledge of love (Plato uses the image of the ladder which we climb, leaving the lower rung beneath us), of a state of rapture and frenzy accompanying the intellectual vision of the highest beauty, and of the essential creativity of the love of beauty have formed a powerful tradition; we find the themes again and

again, either singly or together, either in their original form or modified, in later theories of beauty. In the eighteenth and nineteenth centuries the renewal and transformation of Plato's ideas in Shaftesbury's thought is of fundamental importance.

For Shaftesbury the *conditio sine qua non* of our response to beauty is that our perception be disinterested, i.e., unselfish and without bias. Our knowledge of the beautiful is contingent—as in Plato—on the ascent from sensuous to intellectual perception; the process is stated, however, in different terms and is connected, in sharp contrast to Plato, with art.

The artist who wishes to bring perfection into his work must have "the *idea* of perfection to give him aim." He must be above the world "and fix his eye upon that consummate grace, that beauty of Nature, and that perfection of numbers [harmony] which the rest of mankind, feeling only by the effect whilst ignorant of the cause, term the *je ne sçay quoy*, the unintelligible . . ." (*Advice to an Author*, in *Characteristics* . . . , I, 214).

In *The Moralists* the steps of ascent are defined; from the admiration of beautiful objects we rise to the insight that it is art, the beautifying, which is beautiful; from the love of beautiful bodies we pass to the recognition that their beauty is founded not in the body qua body, but in a forming power (or inward form), in action and intelligence, i.e., in the mind. Ultimately, we understand that the mind, in turn, is fashioned by the principle which is the very source and fountain of all beauty (ibid., II, 132–33).

Among the kinds of beauty formed by man are also his sentiments, resolutions, principles, and actions. Beauty, in turn, provokes and furthers our social and sympathetic emotions, quickening a pulsation of balanced, harmonious feelings.

Shaftesbury's emphasis on beauty as a creative force in man, an emphasis which is even stronger than in Plato, the strong bond which he establishes between our feeling for beauty and the forming of the personality of the "virtuoso," the fact that he relates the principles of order, harmony, and proportion on which beauty is founded to the principles of the new mathematical sciences, as well as the link between these ideas and the "high strains" (II, 129) of creative enthusiasm, make Shaftesbury's conception of our apprehension of beauty and the effect of beauty on our life a unique and highly influential combination of the ancient and the modern.

The idea of the harmonizing effect of beauty has been developed further by several thinkers and linked with the inner state achieved in the contemplation of Being: the restlessness and uneasiness of our inquiring, searching mind, the strain and intricacy of discursive thinking, our volitions and desires, all are resolved and come to rest when we behold beauty. In its contemplation our faculties are attuned in free and harmonious interplay; we find fulfillment in self-forgetfulness and abandon.

2. Immediate Perception. The frequent occurrence of the idea that beauty is perceived *immediately* can be attributed probably to the common observation that both the effect of and the response to natural beauty are direct and are not based on the recognition of prolonged application and preparation, or of achievement and action as is the case with virtues and abilities. To some extent this observation holds true even for the response to beauty in art. In aesthetic speculation immediacy is, however, interpreted and justified in a variety of ways.

According to empirical theory the eye and ear perceive beauty as soon as the object or color, shape, and sound are presented to them. The theory varies, however, as to whether beauty is placed into the object itself or is considered to be the result of our sense perception. There is further divergence in the explanation of the process leading to the result. We find the empirical conception occasionally even in metaphysical theories of beauty; the perception is then considered to apply to simple natural beauty (a faint shadow of true beauty) and to be the first unreflected step in our knowledge of beauty. The immediate perception may be also an intuition ascribed to a special sense or faculty, or to direct (not analytical or discursive) knowledge.

The direct response to beauty is accounted for also in terms of inner causation, as in the rousing of subconscious, latent, deep-seated forces or emotions, which cannot be analyzed. The argument of immediacy, moreover, is used polemically against theories that beauty is no primary datum, but is the result of secondary factors, such as utility, education, habit, or custom.

3. The Process of Knowledge. Opposed to the argument of immediate apprehension is the theory that the notion of beauty is the result of a cognitive process, in which quantity, quality, modality, and relation have to be determined by comparison, by determination of size and distance, and by the use of judgment. The factors involved in the process vary according to the conception of beauty. The faculty of judgment is predominant when norms, rules, and conformity form the basis. Most of those who maintain the argument of rational knowledge, posit a basic, direct response of pleasure and emotion, which precedes, stimulates, and accompanies the forming of knowledge.

There exists finally the opinion that owing to prolonged exercise of our aesthetic faculties and application as well as cultivation of talent, the cognitive

process escapes notice, and we or others *believe* our apprehension of beauty to be immediate.

BIBLIOGRAPHY

1. Sources: Père André, *Oeuvres philosophiques du Père André*, ed. Victor Cousin (Paris, 1843). Aristotle, *Metaphysics*, III, 13; *Problemata*, XVII, 1. 915b; *Poetics*, Chs. 6–8. Saint Augustine, *City of God*, X, 14; *Confessions*, IV, 13, 15; X, 27; XI, 18; *De musica; De Trinitate*, VI, 10; VIII, 6; X, 1; *Epistolae*, I, 3. René Bray, *La formation de la doctrine classique en France* (Paris, 1927), p. 127; translated by Herbert Dieckmann. Edmund Burke, *A Philosophical Enquiry into the Origin of our Ideas of the Sublime and Beautiful*, ed. J. T. Boulton (London, 1958), p. 119. Denis Diderot, *Oeuvres esthétiques*, ed. Paul Vernière (Paris, 1965). Étienne Gilson, *Introduction à l'étude de Saint Augustin* (Paris, 1929), pp. 272–73; translated by Herbert Dieckmann. Georg Wilhelm Friedrich Hegel, *Aesthetics* (1835). Henry Home (Lord Kames), *The Elements of Criticism*, 2 vols. (Edinburgh, 1788), I, 208. David Hume, *Essays moral, political and literary*, ed. T. H. Green and T. H. Grose, 2 vols. (London, 1882), I, 268–69; idem, *A Treatise of Human Nature, The Philosophical Works*, ed. Green and Grose (London, 1886), II, 96. Francis H. Hutcheson, *An Enquiry into the Original of our Ideas of Beauty and Virtue* (1725). All quotations are from Treatise I: "Of Beauty, Order, Harmony, Design." Immanuel Kant, *Kant's Critique of Aesthetic Judgment*, trans. J. C. Meredith (Oxford, 1911). Plato, *Hippias Major*, 289–98; *Phaedrus*, 249–55; *Symposium*, 199–212; *Philebus*, 25–26, 51–66; *Nomoi*, II, 665a. Plotinus, *Enneads*, I, 6; II, 4; III, 6; V, 8. Friedrich Schiller, *On the Aesthetic Education of Man . . .* , ed. and trans. E. M. Wilkinson and L. A. Willoughby (Oxford, 1967), XV, §7; a bilingual edition. Earl of Shaftesbury (Anthony Ashley Cooper), *Characteristics of Men, Manners, Opinions, Times, . . .* , ed. John M. Robertson, 2 vols. (London, 1900). Herbert Spencer, *The Principles of Psychology*, 2 vols. (New York, 1887), II, 630.

2. Further Readings. Bernard Bosanquet, *A History of Aesthetic* (London and New York, 1892). E. F. Carritt, *The Theory of Beauty*, 6th ed. (London and New York, 1962); idem, *What is Beauty?* (Oxford, 1932). Katharine E. Gilbert and Helmut Kuhn, *A History of Esthetics* (New York, 1953). Walter J. Hipple, Jr., *The Beautiful, the Sublime, & the Picturesque in Eighteenth-Century Aesthetic Theory* (Carbondale, 1957). H. R. Jauss, ed., *Die Nicht Mehr Schönen Künste. Grenzphänomene des Aesthetischen* (Munich, 1968). William A. Knight, *The Philosophy of the Beautiful*, 2 vols. (New York, 1898). Charles Lalo, *Introduction à l'esthétique* (Paris, 1912); idem, *Notions d'esthétique* (Paris, 1960). Charles Lévêque, *La Science du beau*, 2 vols. (Paris, 1872). George Santayana, *The Sense of Beauty* (New York, 1896). K. H. von Stein, *Die Entstehung der neueren Ästhetik* (Stuttgart, 1886). Robert Zimmermann, *Geschichte der Aesthetik als Philosophischer Wissenschaft*, 2 vols. (Vienna, 1858). The translation of Fénelon is by the author of this article.

HERBERT DIECKMANN

[See also Art and Play; **Beauty;** Creativity; Neo-Platonism; **Platonism;** Romanticism; Sublime; Taste.]

THEORIES OF BEAUTY SINCE THE MID-NINETEENTH CENTURY

DESCENDANTS of nearly every older theory about beauty can be traced in the late nineteenth and early twentieth centuries, and due notice of these will be taken below. The main purpose of this article, however, is to give an account of new ideas or emphases that have emerged.

I. BEAUTY IN DECLINE

The difficulty of discerning conceptual similarities and differences underneath terminological differences and similarities can be pointed up by an interesting contrast. Like other Hegelian idealists of the nineteenth century, Bernard Bosanquet, in his *History of Aesthetic* (London and New York, 1892), defined "Aesthetic" as the "philosophy of the beautiful." He also defined "the beautiful" as "that which has characteristic or individual expressiveness for sense-perception or imagination, subject to the conditions of general or abstract expressiveness in the same medium" (Ch. 1). Bosanquet noted that he was proposing a broader concept of beauty than that sanctioned in ordinary usage, or even in typical philosophical usage, but he claimed that his formula embodied the most profound insight into beauty that the "aesthetic consciousness" of man had yet reached. For he saw the whole history of aesthetics as a progressive intellectual development, from the first classical view of beauty as harmony and symmetry, or as unity in variety, to the recognition, first of the sublime and later of other qualities as having aesthetic significance, such as the grotesque, the graceful, the violent (Ch. 15). Thus we might say that in Bosanquet's view beauty swallows up the whole of aesthetic value; and that few later aestheticians have given such centrality and generality to beauty.

On the other hand, Frank Sibley's significant and highly influential essay on "Aesthetic Concepts" (*Philosophical Review*, **68** [1959])—though it discusses a variety of qualities, such as grace, elegance, delicacy, garishness—refers to beauty only in a final footnote, as merely one (perhaps not the most interesting or important) of those qualities. And in his later Inaugural Lecture at the University of Lancaster (1966), in which he calls upon philosophers to undertake far more extensive analyses of the varied terms in the critic's rich vocabulary, he suggests that too much effort has centered on a very few terms, including "beautiful." Here we might note an extreme compression of the scope of beauty, as contrasted with its expansion by Bosanquet, and say that in the intervening half-century beauty has itself been swallowed up by the broader concept of expressive quality.

Yet would this contrast be more than a verbal one?

If Bosanquet simply defines "beautiful" so that it includes all aesthetic qualities, and Sibley defines it so that "beautiful," "powerful," "elegant," and "gay," for example, now mark coordinate species, it might be argued that they are in fact saying nearly the same thing in different words. Of course, it is still of historical interest that the word is being used in a different sense, but perhaps that fact belongs to philology, not philosophy—the history of words, not the history of doctrines.

The contrast between Bosanquet and Sibley is indeed less significant, historically, than their similarity, for Bosanquet marks a turning point. In the nineteenth century, the Romantic and Victorian poets, the Transcendentalists, those who cultivated art for art's sake, ascribed to beauty the highest value, even a kind of divinity; and they would feel that beauty has not fared well in the twentieth century—even if they agreed that Robert Bridges' *Testament of Beauty* (Oxford, 1929) is one of its greatest poetic monuments.

First, beauty—the central topic in aesthetic theory from the Greeks through the German idealists—was displaced by the concept of expression. Benedetto Croce's *Estetica come scienza dell'espressione e linguistica generale* (Milan, 1902) developed a new view of artistic creation and aesthetic experience based on the double formula that "art equals expression equals intuition," and ended by defining beauty as simply "successful expression"—or rather "*expression* and nothing more, because expression when it is not successful is not expression." "Expression and beauty are not two concepts, but a single concept," he remarks in his *Breviario di estetica* (Bari, 1913), Lecture II. Croce's system was the dominant influence in aesthetics for three decades, and has left its mark even on the thinking of those who repudiate his basic doctrines. Not that the implications of his highly paradoxical statements have been found to be unequivocal: if art is identical to expression, and beauty is also identical to expression, then, it might be argued, beauty is the essence of art. But expression and intuition are for Croce the basic concepts in terms of which the aesthetic is to be understood. One consequence was that the way opened for recognizing a much wider range of aesthetic qualities than had ever been recognized before. It is noteworthy that the two most influential twentieth-century writers on the fine arts, Clive Bell (*Art*, London [1914]; New York [1958], pp. 20ff.) and Roger Fry (*Vision and Design*, London [1920]; Middlesex [1937], pp. 236ff.) contrasted beauty, at least in its ordinary senses, with "significant form," which was for them the important feature of visual art.

Second, the twentieth century has seen the most violent repudiation of beauty by some creative artists themselves—not merely by Dada, black theater, the "theater of cruelty," "op art," and similar minor movements, but by more serious artists, such as expressionist painters and ideological playwrights who have felt that the achievement of beauty is not the most important aim of art, and may interfere with the intensification of experience or the radicalizing of the perceiver. This conflict first appeared sharply among the French nineteenth-century realists and naturalists— Flaubert and Zola felt it, in their very different ways, and were prepared to dispense with beauty to achieve their visions of truth. The twentieth-century avant garde is more likely to speak in the voice of Henry Miller's *Tropic of Cancer* (Paris [1934]; New York [1961], pp. 1–2): "This is not a book, in the ordinary sense of the word. No, this is a prolonged insult, a gob of spit in the face of Art, a kick in the pants to God, Man, Destiny, Time, Love, Beauty."

Third, the twentieth century is perhaps the first century in which the very existence of beauty has been categorically denied. "Terms such as Beauty are used in discussion for the sake of their emotive value," said one of the earliest manifestoes of the modern linguistic movement in philosophy, C. K. Ogden and I. A. Richards' *Meaning of Meaning* (London and New York, 1923). According to their early version of what later came to be developed—notably by Charles L. Stevenson in *Ethics and Language* (New Haven, 1944)—into a much more sophisticated one, genuine empirical statements, whether objective ("This is red") or subjective ("I feel sad"), are couched in "referential language," but the statement "That is beautiful" (like other value judgments) is "emotive language," and amounts to no more than an exclamation of approval ("Oh, ah!" "Mmmmm!") in the presence of an object. On this view, the noun "beauty," though deceptively like the noun "booty," refers to nothing, since there is nothing for it to refer to, and hence all statements about beauty or about things being beautiful are, strictly speaking, meaningless.

II. CONCEPTS OF BEAUTY

The history of beauty is probably best conceived not as the history of a single concept selected and favored by the historian because of his own aesthetic theory, but as the history of a *term* (or set of more or less synonymous terms in different languages) designating a cluster of concepts whose distinctions and connections are of equal philosophic interest. Though not dominant in recent and contemporary aesthetics, the term "beautiful" has figured in a variety of theories and in a variety of inquiries, and these can best be understood if we first sort out the main senses in which the term has been, and is being, used.

It is safe to say that throughout its history "beautiful"

has always embodied both descriptive and appraisive elements: it has been used both to characterize works of art or nature and to judge them. Aestheticians have often commingled the two senses, or weaved back and forth between them, without being very clear about the distinction. In recent years these hazards have somewhat diminished (though not disappeared), largely owing to the influence of analytic or linguistic philosophers, whose high standards of rigor both in definition and in argument, and whose concern to keep clear the distinction between normative and nonnormative discourse, have led many aestheticians to adopt one or the other sense, either by stipulation or by an appeal to what they take to be ordinary (i.e., established nonphilosophical) usage. A fundamental difference among recent philosophers is between those who use "beautiful" appraisively as the most general term of aesthetic approbation and those who use it descriptively as a *ground* of aesthetic approbation.

In the first sense, "beauty" becomes synonymous with another widely-used term, "aesthetic value": to say that an object is beautiful is not to report any facts about it, but simply to praise it from the aesthetic point of view. This usage is not uncommon; it is, for example, that of Harold Osborne in his *Theory of Beauty* (London [1952], Ch. 1), where he defines "beauty" as "the proper or characteristic excellence of a work of art," though he also acknowledges that "beauty" is widely used as a "descriptive" term. Stephen Pepper (*Aesthetic Quality . . .* , New York [1937], Intro.) equates beauty with "positive aesthetic value"; Bosanquet's *Three Lectures on Aesthetics* (London, 1915) insists that to equate beauty with "aesthetic excellence" is "not merely convenient but right." Most aestheticians now avoid this use, since in effect it wastes a word that is needed for more specific purposes, and tends to add to the existing confusion in the use of "beauty."

In the second sense, beauty becomes a *ground* of aesthetic approbation, that is, a property that may properly be cited in a reason to justify that approbation. We may then say the music is good *because* it is beautiful; its beauty makes, or helps to make, it good. This is the usage chosen for the present article.

It is useful to distinguish between the *monists*, who hold that beauty is the sole ground of aesthetic value, and the *pluralists*, who allow that other properties may also count in favor of an object, when considered from the aesthetic point of view.

Those who treat beauty as a ground of aesthetic value, whether monists or pluralists, divide further into two groups, according to the sort of property they single out as legitimate grounds and describe as beauty. The term "beauty" is used affectively and attributively.

In the Affective use, to say "X is beautiful" means

the same as to say "X gives (or is capable of giving) a certain sort of pleasure or satisfaction" (call it "kalistic satisfaction"). In Chapters 3 and 4 of *What is Art?* (1896), Tolstoy, after reviewing a large number of statements about beauty (some definitions, some descriptions, some theories), concluded that when the "objective-mystical" ones are set aside, the rest amount to defining beauty as pleasurableness. Occasionally the word "disinterested" is added, though, as Tolstoy remarked, this is redundant. The distinctively aesthetic feature of kalistic pleasure has been found in its immediacy or sensuousness or its relative stability and permanence (Harry Rutgers Marshall, *The Beautiful*, London [1924]). Ethel Puffer (Howes) argued that to be beautiful is to possess the "permanent possibility" of giving an experience characterized by a "union of stimulation and repose" or "equilibrium" of "antagonistic impulses" (*The Psychology of Beauty*, Boston [1905], Ch. 2). C. K. Ogden, I. A. Richards, and James Wood called this equilibrium "synaesthesis" (*Foundations of Aesthetics*, London [1922]). Perhaps the best-known suggestion is that of George Santayana in *The Sense of Beauty* (New York [1896], Part I): that "Beauty is pleasure regarded [that is, experienced] as the quality of a thing," or "pleasure objectified."

A more fundamental difference among Affective uses is that between relativistic and nonrelativistic ones. Beauty may be defined *nonrelativistically* as the capacity to provide kalistic satisfaction. John Ruskin, for example (*Modern Painters*, London [1846], I, i, 6), says, "Any material object which can give us pleasure in the simple contemplation of its outward qualities without any direct and definite exertion of the intellect, I call in some way or in some degree, beautiful." Again, W. D. Ross in *The Right and the Good* (Oxford [1930], Ch. 4) states clearly and defends ably a view "which identifies beauty with the *power* of producing a certain sort of experience in minds, the sort of experience which we are familiar with under such names as aesthetic enjoyment or aesthetic thrill" (p. 127). It is in this sense that he holds beauty to be objective, for it is a property of (a capacity in) the object. On this view, the question whether a particular painting is beautiful is a straightforward question, whether someone can be found who derives kalistic pleasure from it, or whether there is reason to believe that in time such a person will appear. The nonrelativist position has been defended by Stephen Pepper, *The Work of Art* (Bloomington, Ind. [1955], Ch. 2).

The alternative view is that when a particular person, A, says "X is beautiful," he is to be understood as saying that X actually does give, or has given, pleasure to him (whether or not among others); and of course when B says "X is beautiful" he is saying that

X gives pleasure to him. Thus if A and B enter into a dispute about the beauty of X, one affirming and the other denying that X is beautiful, it may turn out that they are not in fact contradicting one another, for A is saying that X pleases A and B is saying that X does not please B. A *relativistic* definition of beauty is one that permits such a situation to arise, i.e., one according to which two persons who verbally disagree about the beauty of an object can both be speaking the truth. The view of beauty proposed by Samuel Alexander in *Beauty and Other Forms of Value* (London [1933], Ch. 10) is relativistic in this sense. Though Alexander initially proposes a capacity-definition—"Beauty . . . is that which satisfies . . . the constructive impulse used contemplatively, and is beautiful or has value because it pleases us after the manner so described" (pp. 179–80)—he allows beauty to have value only when it "satisfies a standard mind," or those who "possess the standard aesthetic sentiment," and since the standard varies with the society, "It follows that there is no fixed or eternal standard of the beautiful but that it is relative to age and people" (pp. 175–77). Another notable defense of relativism is that in C. J. Ducasse, *Philosophy of Art* (New York and Toronto [1929]; rev. ed. [1966], Ch. 15, §§ 10–16).

The questions whether there is a peculiar species of satisfaction or pleasure properly called "aesthetic," and whether works of art provide such satisfaction, and whether the provision of such satisfaction is a legitimate ground of aesthetic value, are all important questions. But there seems little warrant for introducing the term "beauty" into such discussions. Beauty of course can be enjoyed, can give us pleasure; but when we say that it is the beauty that pleases us we cannot be understood to mean anything so empty as that what pleases us is what pleases us. Therefore many aestheticians avoid the Affective use of the term "beauty."

The alternative is to regard beauty as a property of perceived things (of sunsets and precious stones as well as of sonnets and landscape paintings). To hold this Attributive view is not necessarily to be committed to any far-reaching metaphysical or epistemological position—but only to say that when a painting is seen, its seen beauty is a phenomenally objective character of it, in the same way its colors and shapes are, and that beauty can be heard in sound—though whether it can also be tasted and smelt is a question that goes back a long way in the history of aesthetics, and is still subject to dispute (see, for example, Francis J. Coleman, "Can a Smell or a Taste or a Touch be Beautiful?" *American Philosophical Quarterly*, **2** [1965]).

The position of G. E. Moore (*Principia Ethica*, Cambridge [1903], Ch. 6) may be cited as an example of the Attributive view. For though he thinks it best to

209

define beauty as "that of which the admiring contemplation is good in itself" (p. 201), he holds that the "beautiful qualities" of objects—"that is to say any or all of those elements in the object which possess any positive beauty"—is such that their mere existence has *some* intrinsic value, though it is the *enjoyment* of beautiful objects and the pleasure of personal relationships that are "by far the most valuable things, which we know or can imagine" (pp. 188–92). (See also a very good defense of this view by T. E. Jessop, "The Definition of Beauty," *Proceedings of the Aristotelian Society*, 1933.)

Those who regard beauty as a property divide on the question whether it is a natural property, explainable in psychophysical terms, or a nonnatural property, supervening upon the object, but having a transcendent status, like a Platonic Idea. The nonnatural view, despite its ancient tradition, has practically disappeared from the scene, outside the schools of Neo-Scholasticism (for example, Jacques Maritain, *Art et scolastique*, Paris [1920]; trans. J. F. Scanlan, New York [1930], and also by Joseph Evans, New York [1962]; and Étienne Gilson, *The Arts of the Beautiful*, New York [1965]). The naturalist view is defended by D. W. Prall, *Aesthetic Judgment* (Cambridge, Mass., 1929). He holds that beauty may be called a "tertiary quality" of objects, but strictly speaking it occurs only in "transactions" between objects and human organisms, its occurrence being dependent on both organic and external processes.

Naturalists and nonnaturalists alike also divide on the further question whether beauty is complex or simple.

What may be called the Definist view is that beauty is a complex property, capable of analysis into more elementary features of a formal kind. This view, coming down from Platonists, Neo-Platonists, Stoics, Augustinians, and others, makes a key use of various pregnant terms: harmony, measure, proportion, symmetry, order. Traditional philosophers who searched for a definition of beauty were presumably sometimes searching for a successful formula of this sort, but such proposals have seldom stood long against the proper tests to determine whether the proposed properties are both necessary and sufficient for beauty.

The Nondefinist may argue that very simple things (single colors or tones) can be beautiful, though they have no harmony, symmetry, etc. He may argue that even if all well-proportioned things are beautiful, well-proportionedness cannot be identified with beauty, for one causes, or explains, the other. For him, beauty is a simple quality, like yellow or the taste of sugar, and it is incapable of being analyzed into simpler constituents. Many inquiries that are described, perhaps even by the inquirer, as a search for the "definition of beauty" are better understood as a search for the *conditions* of beauty: i.e., those features of objects whose presence insures (or aids) the presence of beauty. Among those modern aestheticians who have concerned themselves much with problems about beauty, the Nondefinist view has generally prevailed.

But Nondefinists themselves divide on what is evidently the next question: What are the conditions of beauty? Broadly speaking, there are those who hold that the conditions of beauty are internal properties of the object that is beautiful (we may call them Objectivists) and those who hold that the conditions of beauty lie, *at least in part*, outside the object itself.

Objectivism may be characterized in general as commitment to a principle defended by G. E. Moore: that given two objects with the same "intrinsic" properties, if one is beautiful, the other must be equally so. But Objectivism can be formulated in two different ways, and it is important not to lose sight of the distinction, though for convenience we can discuss them together. Affective Objectivism is the position that adopts an Affective definition of beauty and proceeds to inquire into the perceptual conditions of kalistic satisfaction; Qualitative Objectivism regards beauty as a quality and inquires into its perceptual conditions. A proposed answer to the question, "What are the objective conditions of beauty (considered as either kalistic satisfaction or as a quality)?" is a genuine *theory* of beauty, i.e., a theory about what makes an object beautiful. Two types of theory have figured largely in the history of aesthetics, and are still alive today. Each makes the old and much-disputed distinction between the form and the content of an object; each selects one of these aspects as the exclusive (or at least primary) determinant of beauty. Let us call them Formalism and Intellectualism.

Formalism is the theory that the beauty of an object (or the kalistic satisfaction it provides) is a function solely of its formal features. For example, "*Any* formal organization or pattern which is intrinsically satisfying may be said to possess beauty" (T. M. Greene, *The Arts and the Art of Criticism*, Princeton [1940], Intro.). Here measure, proportion, order, etc., may be invoked again; or the theorist may attempt to work out more refined conditions, such as the good *Gestalt*, the Golden Section, Hogarth's "line of beauty," "dynamic symmetry." Some contemporary theorists have proposed to apply information theory to art and calculate optimum levels of redundancy that can explain the beauty of a melody or a visual design.

Intellectualism is the view that beauty (or kalistic satisfaction) is a function of cognitive content: a concept, or an Idea (in the Hegelian sense), embodied in sensuous form, shines in appearance and gives a thing its beauty. Philosophers have been won to this view by reflecting that certain great beauties are difficult to account for by formal perfection alone, and also by its systematic suitability to their other metaphysical and epistemological positions. (See, for example, W. T. Stace, *The Meaning of Beauty*, London [1929]. For a sustained and interesting defense of the view that beauty is "that in which we see life as we understand and desire it, as it gives us joy," see N. G. Chernyshevsky, *The Aesthetic Relation of Art to Reality* [1855], trans. in *Selected Philosophical Essays*, Moscow [1953]; cf. A. G. Kharchev, "On the Problem of the Essence and Specifics of the Beautiful," trans. in *Soviet Studies in Philosophy* [1962–63].)

Formal and Intellectualist elements have been combined in various ways. For example, Friedrich Kainz—*Vorlesungen über Ästhetik* (Vienna, 1948), trans. H. M. Schueller, *Aesthetics the Science* (Detroit, 1962)—who treats beauty Affectively, holds that it depends on both content and form (though sometimes he speaks of "beauty of form" and "beauty of content" as distinct). He discusses at length various formal and cognitive features that contribute to the production of beauty (see Ch. 4, §3; Ch. 2, §8): for example (on the side of content), conformity to type and Idea, "perceptual perfection," "plenitude of life," "animation"; and (on the side of form) symmetry, proportion, "agreeable rhythmic structure," "eusynopsy and complexibility" (which seem to constitute organic unity).

Other aestheticians, while often agreeing that the beauty of an object has something to do with its formal features (and perhaps sometimes agreeing that it has something to do with its cognitive content), have come to doubt that beauty can be fully accounted for in these terms alone. They have been struck by, and have sharply called attention to, the enormous apparent variability of taste in beauty, from person to person, age to age, culture to culture. What one person finds beautiful in women, in clothes, in buildings, in sculpture, in music, may not appear beautiful at all to another who is older or younger or is from a different ethnic group or "subculture." This fact (often incorrectly called "relativism") has been stated very frequently and very emphatically in recent decades, and its recognition has done much to undermine confidence in the Objective Theory. Nonobjectivism is widely maintained.

Objectivists have pointed out that variability does not necessarily disprove objectivism. Certainly the variability of taste must be accounted for, insofar as it exists. If the Ubangi bride appears beautiful to her husband, but not to a Miss America judge, then the capacity to perceive beauty, at least under certain conditions, must depend on subjective factors. But it does not follow that the beauty is not there merely because it can be overlooked by those who are culturally deprived in some relevant way; a Westerner may not be able to hear the beauty of Chinese music simply because he has not yet learned the musical system. Moreover, variability of taste may have been exaggerated. Do we really know what the Ubangi husband sees in his wife? Just because he chooses her and cherishes her, we cannot infer that she looks beautiful to him; he may be interested in something besides beauty, just as many architects who design ugly buildings know that their clients care less for beauty than for ostentatious display of wealth or a fashionably "modern" look.

Although a piece of cloth looks red to some and gray to others, we do not hesitate to say that it is "really" red, even though a person who is color-blind cannot perceive its redness. We regard the redness of the object as a function of its physical properties (wavelength of reflected light), even though the *experience* of redness is a function of both the object and certain necessary conditions in the perceiving organism. Similarly, the Objectivist wants to regard beauty as a function of objective features. But the Nonobjectivist asks whether, in this case, the functional relationship is so obscure and the variability of perception so great that the analogy with color cannot be maintained. This problem has proved to be a continuing cause of puzzlement and dispute.

A number of factors, both personal and social, have been investigated to explain divergencies in the perception of beauty. For one example, the modern movement of functionalism, a descendant of the old view that beauty depends in some way on utility, has sometimes been interpreted as holding that what makes an object beautiful is its being designed to fulfill a purpose in the simplest and most efficient way. Many plausible examples, of course, can be given, and functionalists have taught us to be willing to see beauties to which we had been blind or indifferent—in machines and tools. But Edmund Burke pointed out long ago that the snout of a pig may be just as efficient for its purpose as the body of a racehorse—which does not make it beautiful. Thus functionalists generally fall back on a qualification: the object must not only fulfill its function well, but "express" its function; however, this may not lead to beauty but to some other desirable aesthetic quality.

III. STUDIES OF BEAUTY

The main work that has been done in the twentieth century on the concepts of beauty may conveniently be sorted into four lines of inquiry: (1) the philosophical analysis of beauty, (2) the phenomenology of beauty, (3) the psychology of beauty, (4) the sociology and anthropology of beauty. These will be described briefly.

1. Philosophical Analysis. The distinctions made in Part II of this article are the product of philosophical analysis by many mid-twentieth-century thinkers, a number of whom have already been referred to. Philosophical analysis consists of various procedures designed to elicit and make explicit the nature of a concept: e.g., is it simple or complex? If complex, what are its constituents? Does it have necessary and sufficient constituents, or is it really a family of concepts with overlapping sets of criteria? Analytic methods have contributed to progress in every branch of philosophy, including aesthetics. It is safe to say that, at the very least, the distinct issues involving beauty and the reasonable defensible resolutions are better understood today than in any previous period.

2. Phenomenology. The phenomenologist is concerned with the characteristics of experience itself, including its "intentional objects." His aim is to remain wholly faithful to what is given, without importing extraneous presuppositions or illegitimate inferences— to discriminate and expose the subtle differences between closely allied experiences, and fix their essential natures. To ask what is the difference in experience between beauty and grace or prettiness, for example, is a phenomenological question. What distinguishes contemporary phenomenology as a particular school or movement is the systematic formulation of its program (despite many differences among its practitioners) and the immense sensitivity and thoroughness with which inquiries have been carried out.

Phenomenologists (including those sometimes referred to as existential phenomenologists) have contributed to several branches of aesthetics. Some understanding of their methods and results can be provided by a brief account of two phenomenological essays, among the few that deal directly and in detail with concepts of beauty. The first is "Der Ursprung des Kunstwerkes," by Martin Heidegger (Holzwege [1950]; trans. by Albert Hofstadter, as "The Origin of the Work of Art," in Hofstadter and Richard Kuhn, eds., *Philosophies of Art and Beauty*, New York [1964]). Seeking for the essential "workly" character of the art-work (in contrast to the "thingly" character of mere things and the "equipmental" character of useful objects), Heidegger finds it in "the setting-itself-into-work of the truth of what *is*." Thus in Van Gogh's picture of the peasant shoes (i.e., of certain pieces of equipment), the being of the shoes (their "truth") is "unconcealed." In its capacity to suggest something of the life of the peasant—his toil, poverty, toughness—this painting

"discloses a world"; as a physical object, exploiting and exhibiting the qualities of a medium, it "sets forth the *earth*." The art-work is a field of conflict between world, which strives for openness, and earth, which has a tendency to withdraw and hide; in this conflict, the truth of being is laid open, and this happening is beauty: "Beauty is one way in which truth occurs as unconcealment."

The second essay is *Truth and Art*, by Albert Hofstadter (New York, 1965). According to Hofstadter, beauty, "the central aesthetic phenomenon," is "a union of power and measure, a dynamic or living harmony" that is "the appearance of truth—not of any truth at random, but of truth of *being*"—which is the kind of truth that "comes about when a being projects and realizes its own being." In certain natural phenomena—the snowflake, the color gold, the form of the horse—Hofstadter discerns this self-realization; e.g., "the horse's visual appearance makes it *look* like life-will—energy, vitality, mobility—come to perfect realization" (Ch. 7). In the experience of beauty we are seized by the "rightness" or "validity" of the object, which appears in its highest form in works of art (Ch. 8).

3. Experimental Psychology. The systematic experimental study of aesthetic responses is generally regarded as having been initiated by Gustav Fechner, in his *Vorschule der Aesthetik* (Leipzig, 1876). He has been followed by a large number of investigators, among whom Richard Müller-Freienfels and Max Dessoir are especially noteworthy. Psychological aestheticians have studied reactions to elements of visual, musical, and verbal design (colors, lines, sounds of words), and to combinations of elements (rhythm, meter, pictorial balance); they have used the "method of paired comparisons" to discover what kinds of object certain people call beautiful, and what kinds of people call certain objects beautiful—and why. They have learned a great deal about preferences in these matters, e.g., that it is not the Golden Rectangle, but proportions close to it, that are preferred in playing cards, etc.; that the popularity of red among American children declines after age six; that British children find beauty in nature before they become aware—about age ten—of beauty in art; that when photographs of several men or women are superimposed to produce a "profile-picture," it is judged more beautiful than the originals. Much of this work is reviewed in A. R. Chandler, *Beauty and Human Nature* (New York and London, 1934), and C. W. Valentine, *The Experimental Psychology of Beauty* (London, 1962).

It is not always clear at what point psychological aesthetics casts light on the nature of beauty. Valentine holds—and offers experimental evidence (in Chs. 7 and

13) to show—that the appreciation of beauty is not the same as the enjoyment of pleasure, though typically accompanied by it; yet "It has been found more convenient in such psychological experiments to ask persons the question, 'Do you like this, and if so, why?' or 'Do you find this pleasing?' rather than "Do you think this beautiful, and why?'" (p. 6). But different questions, however convenient, are likely to evoke different answers (cf. H. J. Eysenck, *Sense and Nonsense in Psychology*, Baltimore [1957], Ch. 8).

The problem of explaining our perception of beauty (or our experience of kalistic pleasure) has tempted few psychologists, and is generally thought to remain unsolved. During the first decades of this century, the Empathy Theory was widely accepted. First expounded by Theodor Lipps in his *Aesthetik* (2 vols., Hamburg and Leipzig, 1903–06), the theory was developed and popularized by Vernon Lee (Violet Paget), in *The Beautiful* (Cambridge and New York, 1913) and Herbert S. Langfeld, *The Aesthetic Attitude* (New York, 1920). The primary purpose of the Empathy Theory was to explain the expressiveness of visual forms in terms of the unconscious transference of the perceiver's activities to the object (something in the mountain as seen activates our tendency to rise, and so we see mountain as "rising"); when the empathic response is highly unified and quite uninhibited and unchecked, beauty is experienced. The hypothesis was never verified, and serious difficulties were raised as a result of some experiments. The satisfaction taken in perceiving ordered patterns of visual stimuli has been explained by the Gestalt psychologists in terms of phenomenal "requiredness" and "good gestalts" (see, for example, Kurt Koffka, "Problems in the Psychology of Art," in *Art: A Bryn Mawr Symposium*, Bryn Mawr, Pa., 1940); but Gestalt psychologists have generally not given special attention to beauty.

4. Social Science. When beauty is considered in the context of a whole society or culture, a number of significant questions suggest themselves: What are the social causes and effects of people's ideas of beauty or experience of beauty? How is the capacity to appreciate a certain kind of beauty, or the preference for it, associated with other cultural traits, or with social class, role, or status? Though the pioneering sociological thinkers of the nineteenth century, for example, Jean-Marie Guyau, *L'Art au point de vue sociologique* (Paris, 1889), began to consider such questions, even today it cannot be said that we have obtained very conclusive answers. This is partly because the specific questions about beauty have been sunk into more general questions; there are many studies of the variability of taste, of connoisseurship, of artistic reputations, etc., but it is not clear in many cases what

light they shed on the social aspects of beauty. Adolf S. Tomars, for example, begins his *Introduction to the Sociology of Art* (Mexico City, 1940) by marking out the "phenomena of art" as those referred to in making the judgment "this is beautiful" (Ch. 1). And he defends a relativistic account of beauty, which he holds to be required by the scientific character of his investigation (Ch. 12). But for the most part, beauty drops out of his inquiry into relations between characteristics of art ("styles") and types of community, social class, or institution. Vytautas Kavolis (*Artistic Expression; A Sociological Analysis*, Ithaca, N.Y. [1968]) discusses many discoveries about preference: for example, according to the Lynds' study of "Middletown," homes of lower middle-class urban families in the 1920's "were more likely than those of other class levels" to have Whistler's portrait of his mother (Chs. 3, 7); and highly ethnocentric people prefer regular, balanced designs (B. G. Rosenberg and C. N. Zimet, 1957). But Kavolis himself does not use the term "beauty" at all.

Cultural anthropologists have made a beginning in the investigation of beauty (again almost always approached through aesthetic preference, especially in view of the linguistic difficulties), with cross-cultural comparative studies, and intercultural functional studies. There is evidence to support two generalizations.

First, "the appeal of what a people consider surpassingly pleasing, beauty as an abstraction, that is, is broadly spread over the earth, and lies deep in human experience—so wide, and so deep, that it is to be classed as a cultural universal" (Melville J. Herskovits, in *Aspects of Primitive Art* [1959], p. 43). This is seen, for example, in the Pakot (Kenya) distinction between the "good" milk pot and the "beautiful" lip of the pot's rim or the severely critical attitude of the Tlingit audience toward their dancers, and in the artistic activities of Australian aborigines: "aboriginal art is predominantly nonmagical, i.e., used in the secular and ceremonial life by men, women, and children, to satisfy an aesthetic urge or to portray their beliefs" (Charles P. Mountford, in Marian W. Smith, ed., *The Artist in Tribal Society*, New York [1961], p. 8). Herbert Read, commenting on this paper, however, suggested that "tribal art in general is vital rather than beautiful" (ibid. p. 17).

Second, there is a significant cross-cultural convergence in standards of beauty, despite evidence that some standards of judgment applied by experts in one culture are not applied in others. "I believe that there are universal standards of aesthetic quality, just as there are universal standards of technical efficiency," wrote Raymond Firth (*Elements of Social Organization*, London [1951]; 3rd ed., Boston [1963], p. 161). Irvin L. Child and various collaborators in a number of studies have provided evidence against the earlier prevalent view among ethnologists that taste is completely variable. They found, for example, significant correlations between BaKwele and New Haven judgments of beauty (or aesthetic likeability) in BaKwele masks (I. L. Child and Leon Siroto, 1965).

SUMMARY

Though displaced from their central or dominant position in the aesthetician's field of concern, the concepts of beauty have continued to be of interest, and indeed have been the subject of numerous books and smaller studies, especially in English, French, German, and Italian. Philosophers have carefully explicated the distinctions, and the logical connections, among these concepts, and have proposed solutions to the philosophical problems about beauty. To a lesser extent, other researchers have investigated the empirical problems about beauty. But it has not lost its capacity, evident from the beginning of aesthetic inquiry, to tease and puzzle thought.

BIBLIOGRAPHY

Raymond Bayer, *Traité d'esthétique* (Paris, 1956). M. C. Beardsley, *Aesthetics from Classical Greece to the Present* (New York, 1966), Chs. 11, 12; idem, *Aesthetics: Problems in the Philosophy of Criticism* (New York, 1958). E. F. Carritt, *The Theory of Beauty* (London, 1919; 5th ed., 1949). Katherine Gilbert and Helmut Kuhn, *A History of Esthetics*, 2nd ed. (Bloomington, 1959), Chs. 16–19. Horace Kallen, *Art and Freedom*, 2 vols. (New York, 1943), Vol. II. Guido Morpurgo-Tagliabue, *L'esthétique contemporaine* (Milan, 1960). Thomas Munro, "The Concept of Beauty in the Philosophy of Naturalism," *Toward Science in Aesthetics* (New York, 1956).

MONROE C. BEARDSLEY

[See also **Beauty to Mid-Nineteenth Century**; Empathy; **Form**; Idea; **Naturalism in Art**; Relativism in Ethics.]

BEHAVIORISM

INTRODUCTION

IT IS SOMETIMES said that La Mettrie, or Hobbes, or even Aristotle was the first behaviorist. But such claims ignore the cardinal point that behaviorism was essentially a methodological movement in psychology which can only be understood in the historical context of the early twentieth century. Its basic tenet, proclaimed by John B. Watson, its founder, was that psychology could only become a science if it based itself on the sort of objective observations and measurements that were made by natural scientists and biologists. This claim had point because it was made at a time when introspective psychology had run itself into the ground with abortive controversies about imageless thoughts and when, by contrast, the study of animal behavior, which had received great impetus from Darwin's theories, was advancing rapidly. The time, therefore, was ripe for Watson's polemical suggestion that the only way to advance the scientific study of human beings was to adopt the same sorts of observational techniques that had proved so successful with the study of animals. This was the kernel of behaviorism and, incidentally, about the only doctrine which was common to all those who later called themselves behaviorists.

Connected with this claim about the appropriate data of science was a view about the proper function of science. Watson held that the function of science was not so much to explain events but to predict and control them. Behaviorism therefore had close affinities with certain aspects of American pragmatism as represented by John Dewey, Charles Peirce, William James, and fitted in well with the general American tendency to believe that the obvious way to improve the condition of man was to manipulate the external environment which was regarded as the main determining influence on his behavior.

What, then, has led people to claim that previous figures in the history of psychology, such as Hobbes and Aristotle, might be termed behaviorists? Partly, perhaps, the fact that many others before Watson had approached the study of man *objectively*, but without, in fact, relying much on introspective reports; for there were previous thinkers who had proceeded more or less in this way without erecting it into a methodological doctrine. More important, however, was the fact that there were other doctrines espoused by Watson which fitted well with his methodological directives, and previous thinkers had advanced these doctrines.

Watson, like many other behaviorists, held a tacit or an implicit metaphysical doctrine about the sort of entities that there are in the world. He was a *materialist* who believed, for instance, that thought was identical with movements in the brain and larynx. Connected with his materialism was his view about the sort of concepts that were appropriate in developing a science of psychology. Like Hobbes before him and Hull after him he believed that the concepts should be *mechanical* in character. This belief was shared by many later conceptual behaviorists who were not prepared to take up any position on metaphysical issues which, they claimed, lay outside the province of science. Finally Watson was an *associationist* in his theory. He believed that simple reflex arcs were linked together in behavior by principles of association. In this respect his theory was quite unoriginal: for he merely transferred to the sphere of simple bodily movements a theory which had previously been put forward to account for the links between simple ideas. He stressed the importance of peripheral connections between stimuli and minimized the role of central processes. He thus founded what has come to be called the S-R (Stimulus-Response) theory of learning.

When, therefore, assertions are made about the more remote historical origins of behaviorism these usually relate not so much to the methodological doctrine, which was central to it as a movement in psychology, as to other aspects of Watson's thought, which not all behaviorists shared—to his materialism and to his use of mechanical concepts and of associationist principles. There was also the less self-conscious use of objective methods by many before who studied human behavior.

This brief analysis of what was distinctive of behaviorism suggests a convenient method of treating it as a phenomenon in the history of ideas. A few key figures in the history of psychology will first be introduced to substantiate the position here defended that only in rather contingent respects could they be regarded as precursors of behaviorism. This will pave the way for the exposition of the more closely connected antecedents of behaviorism as a movement in the history of psychology.

I. THE INTELLECTUAL ANCESTRY OF BEHAVIORISM

1. Aristotle. Many things in the history of thought have been traced back to Aristotle with varying degrees of appositeness, but there is almost nothing apposite in tracing back behaviorism to him. To credit him, for instance, with taking up a position on the central methodological issue of the use of publicly observable data, as distinct from introspective evidence, in studying human beings would display a gross lack of historical perspective; for the distinction between the private world of the individual's own consciousness and the public world, which all could observe, was alien to the Greeks. Indeed there is a sense in which the Greeks had no concept of consciousness in that they did not link together phenomena such as pain, dreams, remembering, action, and reasoning as exemplifying different modes of individual consciousness. The concept of consciousness was largely a product of individualism, of the various movements such as Stoicism, Epicureanism, and Christianity, which supplied types of conceptual schemes that were very different from those which were appropriate to the shared life of the city-states. The coordinating concept of individual consciousness was not made explicit until it found expression in the systems of Saint Augustine and Descartes. The use of introspection as a technique for investigating consciousness went along with such systems of thought, and behaviorism can only be understood as a reaction against such a technique. It would, therefore, be absurd to search for hints of the central doctrine of behaviorism in a thinker such as Aristotle, whose way of thinking about human life antedated the conceptual schemes which permitted such questions to be raised.

What can be said about Aristotle is that, being a marine biologist by training, he was the first to approach the study of human beings in an objective and systematic way. He developed a classificatory system which included plants, animals, and man as belonging to the same genus of living things. He sent his research workers all over the known world to provide him with facts, not only about the different species of living things but also about the different types of customs and systems of government under which men lived. This was all recorded and fed into the classificatory system that he developed at the Lyceum.

When, however, we turn to Aristotle's *Metaphysics* and *De anima,* and study the conceptual scheme which he thought appropriate for describing and explaining human behavior, we find not just that his doctrine of form and matter was incompatible with the materialism espoused by many behaviorists but that, in his psychology, he was an explicit critic of the mechanists of his day.

Aristotle held that a living thing is a "body with a soul," "soul" designating the self-originated tendency of living things to persist towards an end. This tendency can be exhibited at the nutritive and reproductive level as in plants, at the level of sensation and movement as in animals, and at the rational level as in man. Aristotle accused mechanists such as Democritus and Empedocles of the all-pervading mistake of concluding from the fact that the soul is the cause of movement, that it is itself moved. He maintained that the soul moves the body "by means of purpose of some sort, that is thought." Thinking is not a sort of motion any more than desire or sensation are. His predecessors had misunderstood the sort of concept that "soul" was. Insofar as it is a capacity, how could it be moved? A capacity is not the sort of thing that can be moved. Insofar as it is an exercise of a capacity, such as thinking, it is manifest in a process that cannot adequately be described as a change in motion. Aristotle deployed many ingenious arguments to substantiate this criticism of mechanical theories, many of which are similar to those which can be found in the work of modern philosophers such as Ryle (Peters [1962], pp. 102–04; Ryle [1949]).

There are thus almost no grounds for linking Aristotle with behaviorism either in respect of its central doctrine or in respect of its more peripheral ones. If Aristotle is to be linked with any school in twentieth-century psychology the obvious one would be that of the "hormic" (purposive) psychology championed by William McDougall. For here too we find behavior studied objectively, an exaltation of purpose as the most important explanatory concept, and a vehement attack on the mechanists of his day, namely J. B. Watson and the reflexologists. Indeed McDougall's indebtedness to Aristotle is explicitly acknowledged at many points.

2. Hobbes. There would be more plausibility in attempting to trace behaviorism back to Hobbes than to Aristotle. To start with, Hobbes was one of the great thinkers of individualism and wrote at a time when the private world of the individual was both recognized and valued—and threatened by tendencies towards absolutism. Hobbes himself regarded man's capacity to form "phantasms" or images as one of his most miraculous powers. "Of all the phenomena or appearances which are near to us, the most admirable," he says "is apparition itself, τὸ φαίνεσθαι; namely, that some natural bodies have in themselves the pattern almost of all things, and others of none at all" (Hobbes [1839a], p. 389). It was man's mysterious power to register within himself what was going on around him and to store up his impressions for use on further occasions that awakened Hobbes's passionate curiosity. How could this mysterious power be explained? This was the problem that lay at the heart of Hobbes's psychology and theory of nature.

Thus Hobbes's starting point in psychology reveals both the conceptual possibility of behaviorism for him and also the absurdity of thinking that, in the most important respect, Hobbes was in fact a behaviorist; for no behaviorist could regard the problem of imagery as the most important phenomenon for a psychologist to explain. It is also difficult to see how much could be done about explaining it without constant resource to introspection.

On the central question of the appropriate data for a science of human behavior Hobbes was, as a matter of fact, absolutely explicit. In his Introduction to *Leviathan* he wrote:

But let one man read another by his actions never so perfectly, it serves him only with his acquaintance, which are but few. He that is to govern a whole nation, must read in himself, not this or that particular man; but mankind: which though it be hard to do, harder than to learn any language or science; yet when I shall have set down my own reading orderly, and perspicuously, the pains left another, will be only to consider, if he also find not the same in himself. For this kind of doctrine admitteth no other demonstration (Hobbes, 1839b, Introduction).

Hobbes not only extolled introspection as the appropriate method for investigating mankind; he also pointed to the unreliability of inferences made on the basis of the observation of others. Since Hobbes accepted the use of introspective evidence, why has his linkage to behaviorism seemed so plausible to so many? There are, first of all, some underlying assumptions which are common to the views of Hobbes and modern behaviorists, and these are so deeply embedded in modern thought that we tend to take them for granted. The first is the assumption that there is some reliable method for advancing knowledge. Hobbes was one of the many "new men" of the post-Renaissance period who believed that knowledge of nature was available to anyone who was prepared to master the appropriate method. He thought that Copernicus and Galileo had revealed the method for investigating the natural world, that Harvey had applied this to the study of the body, and that he, Hobbes, was showing how this method, the resoluto-compositive method of Galileo, could be applied to psychology and politics.

Hobbes's early contact with Francis Bacon, for whom he had worked for a period as a kind of literary secretary, had also convinced him that knowledge meant power. Hobbes's psychology and politics were constructed with a very practical end in view—the preservation of peace, and he thought that there was no hope for England, in the throes of civil war, unless those who had some influence on the course of events, could be persuaded to accept the logic of his demonstrations concerning man and civil society. This practical concern underlying his theorizing, which was later to be applauded by Marxists, was another underlying link between Hobbes and the behaviorists.

A much more explicit link between Hobbes and the behaviorists was his materialism, and his attempt to extrapolate the concepts and laws of Galileo's mechanics to the human sphere. "For seeing life is but motion of limbs . . . what is the heart but a spring; and the nerves but so many strings; and the joints but so many wheels, giving motion to the whole body, such as was intended by the artificer" (Hobbes, 1839b, Introduction). Desires and aversions are motions towards and away from objects. Thinking is but motion in some internal substance in the head and feeling is movement about the heart. Imagery, which he found so wonderful, was to be viewed as a kind of meeting place of motions. The phenomena of perception and imagination could be deduced from the law of inertia. In order to make such deductions Hobbes postulated infinitely small motions, which he called "endeavours," in the medium between the object of sense and the brain, and he had recourse to them also to explain how movements coming from outside bodies are passed on through the body so that they eventually lead to the gross movements observable in desire and aversion.

Within behaviorism it is customary, following Tolman, to distinguish between molecular and molar theories of behavior. A molecular theory, such as that of Clark Hull, is one which starts from postulates at the physiological level and attempts to deduce the movements involved at the molar level, e.g., the gross movements of the body, from them. Hobbes anticipated such molecular theories to an astonishing extent (Peters and Tajfel, 1957). But such anticipation had nothing to do with behaviorism in a strict sense. It was rather the consequence of applying the hypothetico-deductive procedure of Galileo, together with his mechanical concepts and laws, to the realm of human behavior. Hull, combined this Galilean approach to psychology with the restriction of data to what could be publicly observed, which was the central feature of behaviorism (Hull, 1943). Hobbes, therefore, can properly be regarded as the father of mechanistic theories in psychology rather than of behaviorism; for not all behaviorists were mechanists, and Hobbes himself relied on introspection in the psychological sphere.

3. Descartes. It would be more absurd to regard Descartes as a behaviorist than Hobbes; for he was notorious for the dualism of mind and matter which he postulated. But, as a matter of fact, both his dualism and his assumptions about scientific method did much to create the climate of opinion which made behaviorism possible, if not almost inevitable.

Descartes held that there are two sorts of substances in the world, mental and physical. If the behavior of these substances was to be scientifically studied, assumptions about them had to be made explicit and exhaustively analyzed until clear and distinct ideas were arrived at, which were simple in the sense that no further analysis of them was possible. In the case of ideas about material objects, for instance, the scientist eventually arrived at the simple ideas of extension, figure, and motion. If certain of these simple ideas were combined, relationships could be grasped between them which served as postulates for a deductive system, as in geometry. Thus the understanding of bodies and of minds respectively rested upon clear and distinct ideas which had no features in common. Descartes' problem about the relationship between mind and body derived from the fact that, though in our confused everyday experience we are aware of interaction, as when our limbs move because of our intentions, no clear and distinct idea can be formed of the manner of this union. Such perspicuous ideas are only forthcoming in the spheres of the mental and the physical when they are proceeding independently of each other—as in logical reasoning on the one hand or in reflex movements on the other.

Descartes' dualism and his assumptions about scientific method thus gave rise to two traditions of enquiry which came to be pursued more or less independently of each other. On the one hand the human body, which was regarded as functioning mechanically right up to the level of instinctive behavior and simple habits, becomes a fit subject for objective study. Harvey had made a splendid advance in this field with his mechanical theory of the circulation of the blood. On the other hand, the mind, by which Descartes meant mainly the higher thought processes and the will, could only be studied introspectively. The consequence of Descartes' dualism was, therefore, the school of mechanistic biology and reflexology on the one hand and the introspective school of psychology on the other, which reached its culmination about 250 years later in the laborious experimental work of Wundt and Titchener.

It was against the assumptions of the introspective school that Watson revolted—their assumptions about both introspective method and the "stuff" of consciousness which he claimed they were trying to study by this method. And when he revolted he fell back on the other tradition stemming from Descartes: mechanistic biology and reflexology. All he did was to attempt to extend its domain to the level of thought and action which had previously been regarded as "mental" and hence to be studied by introspective methods. And when Watson theorized about behavior he was unwittingly Cartesian in his approach. He thought that the complex phenomena of behavior could be explained by analysis into clear and distinct units of behavior—simple reflexes.

4. Reflexology. Descartes' dualism involved the assumption that the behavior of the body, below the level of willed action, could be explained mechanically. He had, however, a crude idea of how the body works. He thought of it as a statue or machine made of earth and was much impressed by the feats which mechanical manikins could be made to perform in the gardens of the aristocracy by arranging water-pipes within them. They could be made to move their limbs and even to produce sounds like words. He thus pictured the nervous system as a piece of intricate plumbing. The nerves were thought of as tubes along which "animal spirits," which occupied an indeterminate status between the mental and the physical, flowed continuously. Changes in the motion of these spirits cause them to open certain pores in the brain. When this happens the motion of the animal spirits is changed and they are "reflected" into the muscles which move the body. For he thought that many movements of the body are not brought about by conscious intention, but by an *undulatio reflexa*, or a movement of rebound in the animal spirits at the meeting of the sensory and motor channels at the pineal gland, where the mind could also influence the body by means of images. The

217

automatic reactions of the body, which were not under voluntary control, were thus called reflexes.

Little was done to refine this conception until 1811 when Charles Bell published a paper entitled "An Idea of a New Anatomy of the Brain," which he communicated to the Royal Society in 1821, and in which he claimed that the nerves, which are connected with the spinal centers by anterior roots, are employed in conveying motor impulses from the brain outward, and that the sensory nerves are connected with the posterior roots of the spinal cord. This was confirmed by Magendie in 1822. In 1833 Marshall Hall demonstrated clearly the existence of reflex action which proceeded independently of conscious volition, and in the latter part of the nineteenth century the antics of animals deprived of their higher brain structure were a commonplace. In 1851 Claude Bernard pioneered physiological work on the influence of specific nerves on the blood vessels and the consequent changes throughout the sympathetic system, thus helping to understand the connection between the brain and the viscera and other changes involved in emotional and motivational states. Evolutionary theory, especially that of Herbert Spencer, led Hughlings Jackson to postulate different levels of evolution in the nervous system from the less to the more organized, from the automatic to the voluntary.

From the point of view of the history of behaviorism the crucial step forward was taken by Pavlov, whose particular interest was in the digestive system. In 1897 he published a book on *The Work of the Digestive Glands*, in which he noted that there are certain irregularities and interruptions in the work of these glands, which he attributed to psychic causes, e.g., that sometimes the glands would start to work before food was given to a dog, when the dog saw the man who usually fed it. In 1902 he embarked on a long series of experiments to study such phenomena. He concentrated on salivation, rather than on gastric secretion, because it was more accessible to experimental analysis. A dog was strapped in a test frame, with elaborate experimental controls, and a bell (conditioned stimulus) was repeatedly sounded before food (unconditioned stimulus) was placed in the mouth to produce salivation (unconditioned response), until eventually the sound of the bell brought about salivation (conditioned response) before the presentation of the food. Pavlov also found that the conditioned stimulus becomes generalized, in that the dog comes to respond to a wide range of stimuli. He found, too, that dogs could be taught to discriminate between stimuli by rewarding responses to one stimulus, such as a circle, but not to another, such as an ellipse. If the difference between the stimuli was gradually reduced a point would be reached where

the dog's behavior evinced all the symptoms of acute neurosis. The concept of "reinforcement" was invented to refer to this process in which the conditioned stimulus is presented in close juxtaposition to the unconditioned stimulus. Many have commented on the similarity between this concept and that of Thorndike's "reward," central to his law of effect. But the two concepts emerged from very different theoretical backgrounds and their differences are as important as their similarities (Wolman [1960], pp. 53–55).

Pavlov was unrepentantly a physiologist and he linked his experimental findings with a theory about irradiation and processes of excitation and inhibition in the brain. He expressed contempt for psychology and refused to take sides in psychological controversies. Nevertheless his influence has been nugatory in physiological theory but vast in psychology, because the behaviorists later seized upon his findings. His contemporary, Bekhterev, on the other hand, who also popularized the conditioned reflex, was more catholic in his interests. In 1907 he published his *Objective Psychology* in which he proclaimed that the future of psychology depended upon objective, external observation. He envisaged excluding introspective data and mentalistic concepts and basing psychology on physical and physiological findings. In this respect Bekhterev harped back to La Mettrie and the materialistic tradition in psychology. In his conditioning experiments he did not confine himself to reactions such as salivation but met with some success in conditioning motor responses as well. He also took an interest in speech, as also did Pavlov towards the end of his life.

Watson embarked upon his behavioristic program in ignorance of the physiological studies of Pavlov and Bekhterev, but he gradually incorporated them into his theory when he became familiar with them through translation. Thus Watson's reflexes functioned in his theory as the direct descendants of Descartes' "simple natures" in the bodily sphere. The links between them, however, namely the principles of association, and the assumptions about how generalizations could be arrived at about such links, came from another source—the empiricist tradition. A brief exposition of the leading ideas of this tradition will complete the account of behaviorism's intellectual ancestry.

5. The Empiricist Tradition. The other aspect of Descartes' thought, the interest in the contents of consciousness, was developed by both rationalists and empiricists alike. The empiricists, like the rationalists, were really preoccupied with problems of knowledge. As John Locke put it, they were concerned with the "original, extent, and certainty" of human knowledge. They held, however, that knowledge was based on experience, not in the unexceptionable sense that however we come to obtain beliefs about the world, their truth or falsity must be tested by comparing them with what can be observed, but in the much more dubious sense that our ideas about the world *originate* in our own individual sense-experience. Therefore, questions about the extent and certainty of knowledge tended to resolve themselves into speculations about how ideas originated; for followers of what was called "the way of Ideas" held that genuine ideas must be tracked back to impressions of sense. The result was that philosophical questions about the meaning of terms and about the grounds of knowledge were systematically confused with questions in genetic psychology about their origin. It was not until the nineteenth century, when F. H. Bradley proclaimed that "In England we have lived too long in the psychological attitude" (Bradley [1922], 1, x) that this confusion, which persisted from Locke to James Mill and Alexander Bain, began to be systematically exposed.

The net result of this confusion was that the work of the empiricists contained both a philosophical theory about the grounds and acquisition of knowledge and a psychological theory about the working of the mind. The philosophical theory came straight from Francis Bacon. To obtain knowledge, it was held, a start had to be made with simple uninterpreted data, or impressions of sense. There must be no premature hypotheses or "anticipations of Nature." Generalizations had to be made which reflected regularities in the data. Bacon elaborated tables of co-presence, co-absence, and co-variation of instances to ensure that these generalizations were well-founded. These were later elaborated by Mill in his celebrated methods of experimental enquiry. It was of cardinal importance in this process of "induction" that generalizations should not go beyond the data and that no recourse should be made to unobservables. Laws expressed correlations between what could be observed.

The psychological theory which developed *pari-passu* with this philosophical theory about the grounds and acquisition of knowledge had two main features. Firstly it maintained that the experience, thought, and consequent action of the individual is caused from without. The environment causes simple ideas (Locke) or impressions (Hume) to arise in the individual. The individual's body was also regarded as part of the external world which gives rise to impressions of reflexion—e.g., of pleasure and pain—which enter the mind through different types of receptor. (This was later on called "the inner environment" by behaviorists.) Secondly it was held that the ideas arising from these two environmental sources become linked together by principles of association such as contiguity and resemblance. Action is initiated by an idea that

has become linked with pleasure or pain. Thus food, for instance, gives rise to an idea in the mind, which has become linked to the idea of eating, which in its turn has been linked with the idea of pleasure. This brings about the action of eating the food. This account of the initiation of action can be found in Hobbes, though he did not give much prominence to the association of ideas in his account of thinking. He stressed the importance of plans deriving from desire.

The history of empiricism is largely the history of the elaboration and sophistication of these basic ideas. In the philosophical and methodological sphere there were three main derivative doctrines. Firstly the notion of "data" was gradually sophisticated into modern theories of sense-data, which can be found in the work of philosophers such as G. E. Moore, Bertrand Russell, and A. J. Ayer. In the scientific sphere Kant did much to popularize the idea that the domain of science was coextensive with the domain of the measurable. It became important, therefore, for scientists to obtain data which were as precise and pure as possible by devising various forms of measurement. In psychology the nineteenth-century concentration on psychophysics, stemming largely from the work of Weber and Fechner, bore witness to this search for measurable data—the notorious just noticeable differences.

Secondly, a theory of meaning developed which has come to be known as "logical empiricism." This maintained that only those terms are strictly meaningful that can be cashed by reference to what can be observed. The language of morals and of poetry is, strictly speaking, meaningless (or has merely "emotive meaning") because it cannot be tied down in this way to observables. Scientific terms have either to be "operationally defined" or related indirectly to observation by a process of "logical construction." In the early twentieth century P. W. Bridgman's book *The Logic of Modern Physics* (1927) popularized this view of scientific terms. Its leading ideas were applied to psychology by C. C. Pratt in *The Logic of Modern Psychology* (1939) and exerted a considerable influence on B. F. Skinner, a leader of modern behaviorism.

The third development was the attempt to formulate precisely the methods for arriving at well-founded generalizations and to get clearer about the theory of probability which was presupposed. The works of J. S. Mill, W. E. Johnson, and J. M. Keynes were classics in this tradition.

The psychological theory which was favored by most of the empiricists was given an ambitious start by David Hume who pictured himself as the Newton of the sciences of man. Simple impressions were regarded as mental atoms and the principles of association were postulated as performing, in the mental sphere, the same function of uniting them together as was performed by the principle of gravitational attraction in the physical sphere. David Hartley developed an even more ambitious version of this type of theory; for he held that the psychological principles of association paralleled the mode of operation of physiological disturbances in the substance of the nerves, spinal marrow, and brain, which he called "vibrations." It was left to James Mill, however, to free associationism from Newtonian pretensions and physiological speculation and to attempt to formulate soberly and prosaically the basic principles in terms of which ideas were thought to be connected. Most of the subsequent work in the nineteenth century of the British associationist school consisted in criticism, refinements, and simplifications of Mill's edifice.

In France, largely through the infectious cynicism of Voltaire, British empiricism came to exert an influence that was more mundane, and less theoretical. It encouraged thinkers to observe more carefully and more objectively how men in fact behaved. Diderot's *Lettre sur les aveugles* and *Lettre sur les sourds et muets* were classics of their kind—concrete case studies of individual lives. Similarly Condillac approached Locke's problems in a more concrete, if more imaginative way, by creating the fiction of a statue endowed only with the faculty of smell. And Cabanis, a vehement critic of Condillac, began his psychophysiological writings in 1795 with an attempt to answer the concrete, if depressing question, of whether the victims of the guillotine suffer any pains after decapitation. His theory, which attacked Condillac's starting point of imagining a being capable of sensation in isolation from the structure of the organism as a whole, was diametrically opposed to the atomism of the associationist tradition. But it was a theory based on actual observations of men from childhood to maturity. Similarly, La Mettrie, who elaborated Hobbes's thesis that man is a superior type of machine, developed his theory not as an imaginative extrapolation from Galilean mechanics but partly as a result of his medical studies under Hermann Boerhave, and partly from direct observation of his own experiences during a fever. And in the nineteenth century Taine, who represented very much the antimetaphysical, positivistic school in France, scrambled together, in his *De l'intelligence* (1870; trans. as *On the Intelligence,* 1871), reports from asylums, physiological facts, and references to Mill's *Logic!*

It would be tempting to suppose that this interest in the concrete behavior of men, and the attempt to study it objectively, which was so characteristic of French empiricism, was one of the formative influences in the development of behaviorism. There is, however,

little plausibility in this suggestion. For the rise of behaviorism is to be explained partly as a methodological reaction to introspective psychology and partly as a consequence of the success which was being attained in the study of animals. Almost the last thing which the behaviorists actually came to study was the concrete behavior of men. Let us now pass, therefore, to the immediate origins of behaviorism.

II. THE IMMEDIATE ORIGINS OF WATSON'S BEHAVIORISM

J. B. Watson was by no means the first to see the importance for psychology of the objective study of behavior. William McDougall, in his *Physiological Psychology* in 1905, had defined psychology as "the positive science of the conduct of living creatures" and had resisted the tendency to describe it as the science of experience or of consciousness. In 1908, in his *Introduction to Social Psychology,* he explicitly introduced the term "behavior" claiming that psychology was "the positive science of conduct or behavior." He maintained that psychology must not regard introspective description of the stream of consciousness as its whole task. This had to be supplemented by comparative and physiological psychology relying largely on objective methods, the observation of man and animals under all possible conditions of health and disease. Similarly in 1911 W. B. Pillsbury, a pupil of Titchener, published his *Essentials of Psychology* in which he claimed that psychology should be defined as "the science of human behavior." But neither McDougall nor Pillsbury put forward a puritanical or restrictive position. They were merely arguing that the objective study of animals and of physiology had a lot to contribute to psychology. It was therefore unwarranted to give a definition of psychology which excluded their findings from the outset.

What was distinctive about Watson's view of psychology was what it excluded rather than what it included; for McDougall himself was a devotee both of physiology and of animal studies. Watson was determined to rule out introspection as a legitimate method of obtaining data and to banish "consciousness" and other mentalistic terms from the conceptual scheme of his new science. What led him to this methodological puritanism?

1. Animal Psychology. From the time of Darwin's *Origin of the Species* (1859) and *Expression of the Emotions in Man and Animals* (1872) there had been a growing interest in the behavior of animals, birds, and insects in order to test his hypothesis of the continuity between animals and man. In 1872, for instance, Spalding had studied swallows in order to determine whether they learnt to fly by imitation or whether they had an inborn tendency to do so. Between 1879 and 1904 Fabre had made a long series of observations on insects to determine how much of their behavior was due to instinct. The thesis that intelligence is continuous between animals and men was examined by Romanes, Lloyd Morgan, and Loeb on the basis of observations of animal behavior. But the decisive step, from the point of view of the rise of behaviorism, was taken when in 1896 E. L. Thorndike introduced cats, dogs, chickens, and monkeys into the laboratory and carried out experiments on them in order to determine how they learn. From the gradual, though irregular, improvements in the learning curves Thorndike inferred that the animals could not learn by "insight" or by reasoning. Imitation was ruled out by experimental controls. "Trial and error" seemed the only possibility left. The animals, he suggested, went through a variety of responses. Gradually the unsuccessful responses were eliminated and the successful ones were stamped in.

Thorndike believed that there were two basic laws which explained this process. The law of exercise maintained that connections were strengthened by use and weakened by disuse; the law of effect maintained that connections, which were rewarded and thus led to satisfaction, were strengthened. This was not a particularly original theory, as the principles employed were a commonplace in the associationist tradition. What was original was his application of such principles to the connections between stimulus and response and the experimental evidence from his laboratory which he provided to support his view.

Watson, significantly, started his academic career in philosophy, but switched to psychology during his period of graduate study at the University of Chicago, and devoted himself to animal psychology. In 1908 he became professor of psychology at Johns Hopkins University and in 1912 he launched his polemic in some public lectures which were eventually published in 1914 in his book entitled *Behavior*. The vehemence of his attack was to be explained partly by his resentment of the grudging and slightly condescending attitude of most orthodox psychologists of the day towards animal studies. Instead of putting a reasoned case, as did McDougall and Pillsbury, for the importance of animal studies and physiology for psychology, Watson pointed a derisive finger at the state of introspective psychology. "Today" proclaimed Watson "the behaviorist can safely throw out a real challenge to the subjective psychologists—Show us that you have a possible method, indeed that you have a legitimate subject-matter" (Watson [1924], p. 17). This jibe was occasioned by the "imageless thought" controversy amongst introspectionists and other examples of divergent results obtained in different laboratories by well-trained introspectionists. Watson confidently asserted that psychology could only become a science, instead of a debating society, if the methods were used which had proved so successful in animal laboratories.

2. *Inductivism.* The second positive starting point of behaviorism was the view about scientific method which Watson shared with the introspectionists whom he attacked. Wundt and Titchener, the giants of the introspective school, had been vehement in their ambition to base psychology on properly controlled experiments. The general appeal to look into oneself in order to decide upon psychological questions, which one can find, for instance, in the controversies between Locke, Berkeley, and Hume, was not good enough. Introspective observers had to be carefully trained. Moreover Titchener argued that they had to be trained to distinguish pure experience as "existences" from the "meaning" which it has for men in their ordinary lives. Unless this could be done psychology would never arrive at any pure data on which a science of mind could be created.

This presupposed a certain view of scientific method, dating back to Bacon, which is often called "inductivism" or "observationalism" (Popper, 1962). The leading idea of this conception can be summed up in Titchener's own words: "We are agreed, I suppose, that scientific method may be summed up in the single word 'observation'; the only way to work in science is to observe those phenomena which form the subject-matter of science" (Titchener [1908], p. 175). Watson himself had basically the same conception of scientific method. To quote him: "You will find, then, the behaviorist working like any other scientist. His sole object is to gather facts about behavior—verify his data—subject them both to logic and mathematics (the tool of every scientist)" (Watson [1924], p. 7). Watson's basic objection to introspectionism was that it was an attempt to form a science on very unreliable data about which experimenters could reach no agreement, and which purported to reveal facts about a nonexistent subject matter, namely consciousness. If psychologists were to start from data provided by rats in mazes they would at least have a chance of developing a science on the basis of publicly observable data.

When it came to making generalizations Watson again showed his inductivist allegiance; for the Baconian view was that generalizations should never go beyond the data. They should simply record correlations between observables. Thus Watson was as uninterested in physiological speculation about intervening processes as he was hostile to any recourse to unobservable mental entities or processes to explain what could be observed. One should, of course, quantify the data if possible and operate mathematically on it. But this was merely a way of arriving at correlations.

3. *Associationism.* The correlations which Watson discerned were again part and parcel of the introspectionist tradition, namely, the laws of association. He did not reject the postulate of instincts, but accorded them less and less importance in comparison with the influence of the environment via learning. In his theory of learning he rejected Thorndike's law of effect because the concept of "satisfaction" was mentalistic. He relied on the law of exercise under which Thorndike had subsumed the old principles of association such as frequency and recency. He also minimized the importance of the brain and of central processes in learning. All behavior, he believed, was sensori-motor, consisting of stimulus-response units. It was initiated by the stimulation of a sense organ and terminated in a muscular or glandular response.

Thorndike produced conclusive evidence to demonstrate the inadequacy of the law of exercise as a sufficient explanation of learning, but Watson kept his head above water by incorporating into his theory the postulate of the conditioned response which Pavlov had first put forward in 1902. This, together with the concept of reinforcement, gave a more acceptable account of the type of strengthening of connections which Thorndike had covered by his mentalistic law of effect. But it was only gradually that the work of Pavlov and of Bekhterev, who put forward a similar theory of associated reflexes at about the same time, became known in America. It seems as if Watson was familiar with the Russian work from about 1914 onwards but he only gradually grasped its importance for his theory. By 1924 he had come to entertain the view that the conditioned response might afford the key to all habit formation. Other behaviorists, however, took over the conditioned response with alacrity. Indeed, in a modified form, it kept their theory going for about a quarter of a century as will later be explained.

If Watson had stuck rigidly to what could be externally observed he would have severely restricted his "subject-matter." However he claimed that thinking could also be studied because it consisted in implicit speech reactions or in subvocal talking. The implicit behavior, which constitutes thinking, becomes substituted for overt manipulation. The child begins by learning to name things that he is doing while he is doing them, speech being a series of conditioned responses. He then learns to do this inaudibly and as a substitute for doing them. Thinking is therefore surrogate behavior.

Watson also contrived to include emotions within his subject matter by claiming that they consisted in implicit visceral reactions. He espoused the James-Lange theory, while disregarding the introspective feelings which James claimed to be consequent on the visceral changes. In his actual studies of emotion, however, he rather ignored their visceral source and concentrated on their overt manifestations. He singled out three emotions—rage, fear, and love—as being innately determined, and suggested that all others are acquired by conditioning. He achieved some fame, or notoriety, by showing how small children can be conditioned to develop aversions to harmless animals like rabbits and white rats, if their appearance is associated with a noxious stimulus such as a loud noise.

Thus on the slender basis of the conditioning of reactions such as salivation and simple movements, of a bizarre and quite dubious theory of thinking, and of a few interesting experiments in conditioning children's emotional reactions, Watson made optimistic claims for what could be achieved in education and social life generally by a process of systematic and benevolent conditioning. His doctrine fitted well with the thinking of a nation one of whose basic problems was to create American citizens out of a multitude of immigrants of diverse origins, and who, in their approach to life combined a pragmatic outlook with a high level of technical skill, and a friendly extroverted disposition with an optimistic attitude towards the future.

III. THE DIFFERENT TYPES OF BEHAVIORISM

It has been argued that behaviorism was basically a methodological movement in psychology which laid down restrictions on the data on which a science could be properly based. In the case of its founder, J. B. Watson, this central doctrine was supported by an inductivist view of scientific method flanked by the metaphysical doctrine of materialism and by the associationism of a peripheralist, or S-R, type as a psychological theory. Few of the later behaviorists shared all these assumptions. In commenting, therefore, on the main features of their theories special attention will be paid to their adherence to or departure from these other tenets of Watson which have come to be loosely associated with behaviorism.

1. *Early Materialists.* Some of Watson's more immediate contemporaries had more in common with his bold, metaphysical brashness, than his later followers. Albert P. Weiss, for instance, published a book entitled *A Theoretical Basis of Human Behavior* in 1925 in which he banned consciousness and introspection from psychology and claimed that all behavior could be interpreted in terms of physiochemical processes. Nevertheless he argued that what is distinctive of a human being is that his environment is social. Psychology is therefore a bio-social science which is particularly concerned with the impact of the social environment on a biological organism. Weiss was particularly interested in child development and learning, but he never seriously tackled the conceptual problems facing his reductionism, of how features of the social environment, such as commands, promises, and moral exhortation can be analyzed in purely physical terms.

Another early behaviorist, who showed equal naiveté about the environment, was W. S. Hunter. He held that consciousness or experience for the psychologist is merely a name which he applies to what other people call "the environment." This suggestion epitomizes the epistemological innocence of most of the early behaviorists, against which Koffka reacted so strongly. Hunter, however, distinguished himself in other ways. He thought that the new look in psychology deserved a new name and attempted, without any success, to substitute "anthroponomy" for "psychology." He also was the first to use the temporal maze for the study of motor learning.

A more ingenious and interesting theorist of early behaviorism was E. B. Holt. He was one of the first to try to deal with Freudian phenomena within a behavioristic framework and his *The Freudian Wish and its Place in Ethics* (1915) is a classic in this tough-minded tradition, which was later to include O. H. Mowrer, J. Dollard, and N. E. Miller. Holt also developed Watson's idea that thinking is subvocal talking and theorized about the connections between language and conditioning. He thus anticipated later much more ambitious, if abortive, attempts to exhibit language as a system of conditioned responses.

Karl S. Lashley was a pupil of Watson's who made distinguished contributions to the physiology of the nervous system. This, however, did not prevent him from making pronouncements about the subject matter of psychology and about its methods, for instance, that introspection is "an example of the pathology of scientific method" (Lashley, 1923). His physiological findings, however, as expressed in his *Brain Mechanisms and Intelligence* (1929), did not support other doctrines of Watson. His postulates of equipotentiality—that one part of the cortex is potentially the same as another in its capacity for learning, and of mass action—that learning is a function of the total mass of tissue, favored a centralist theory of learning rather than Watson's peripheralist theory. He became very critical of S-R theories which postulated a simple connection between stimulus and response and which ignored the role of intervening cortical processes. The simple switching function accorded by Watson to the brain, which he inherited from Descartes, was denied.

Lashley, however, never departed from Watson's materialistic standpoint. Like Weiss and Hunter he believed that ultimately behavior could be describable in the concepts of mechanics and chemistry. It is also significant that all these early behaviorists shared an inductivist view of scientific method. They thought of the different sciences as having different subject matters and as consisting of generalizations about them derived from reliable data drawn from these subject matters. In this respect they shared not only Watson's methodological recipes but also the view of scientific method from which these recipes arose (Peters, 1951).

2. E. C. Tolman. One of the most influential and forceful converts to behaviorism was E. C. Tolman; for he was calling himself a "purposive behaviorist" as early as 1920, though his definitive work entitled *Purposive Behavior in Animals and Man* did not appear until 1932. He aligned himself with the behaviorists because he accepted their central methodological doctrine about the sort of evidence on which a scientific psychology should be based. He did not indulge, like Watson and Weiss, in metaphysical assertions about the sorts of entities which there are in the world; he admitted that, at a common-sense level, men introspect and manage well enough with mentalistic terms. What he doubted, however, was the adequacy of this terminology for scientific purposes. "Raw feels" are scientifically useless, and mentalistic terms can be translated into the language of observable behavior. Tolman, in other words, was a conceptual behaviorist rather than a materialist, as well as being a behaviorist in his explicitly stated methodology.

In the conceptual sphere Tolman made at least three contributions, two of which were of permanent importance. Firstly he called himself a purposive behaviorist because he maintained that the concept of purpose was irreducible. As has been mentioned (sec. I, 2), he distinguished between the *molecular* and the *molar* level of behavior, whose unity as segments of behavior is provided by the ends towards which movements persist and in the attainment of which they are docile. He accused Watson of not distinguishing clearly between the molecular and the molar levels of analysis and maintained, against Hull, that behavior at the molar level is an "emergent" which has descriptive and defining properties of its own. Descriptions of it cannot be reduced to or deduced from analyses at the molecular level.

Secondly Tolman made rather bizarre attempts to translate mentalistic terms, which had application at the molar level, into a behavioristic type of terminology. "Consciousness" became "the performance of a 'sampling' or 'running-back-and-forth' behavior." He even suggested that Freudian personality mechanisms can be translated into this type of terminology.

223

Thirdly, Tolman introduced into psychological theory the notion of intervening variables. Terms like "instinct" had previously been used, e.g., by McDougall, not simply to postulate that certain purposive behavior patterns were unlearned; they also had a metaphysical dimension to them—a suggestion of Aristotelian entelechies, of dynamic mental atoms activating behavior. Tolman argued that it was perfectly legitimate for a behaviorist to use a term like "drive" which did not denote an unobservable entity, but which was a shorthand symbol for stating a correlation between antecedent conditions, e.g., food-deprivation, and variations in behavior, e.g., eating.

This conceptual clarification helped to set psychology free to theorize without fear of metaphysics. It led on to the use of hypothetical constructs, which did commit theorists to postulates about unobservables usually of a physiological sort. (For this distinction see MacCorquodale and Meehl, 1948.) Tolman thus contributed to ridding psychology of the inductivist myth, shared by the early behaviorists, that scientists must never go beyond what is observed. In fact, however, the postulation of unobservables to explain the observed has been one of the most potent sources of scientific advance.

In the details of his psychological theory Tolman was eclectic. He stressed the importance of both demand variables and cognitive variables in behavior, and attempted to state more precisely assumptions of the sort which McDougall had incorporated in his theory of instincts, i.e., of innate dispositions to pay attention to and behave in specific ways towards objects of a certain class.

In his account of the demand variables Tolman distinguished first-order drives, which are linked with specific antecedent physiological conditions and consequent states of physiological quiescence (e.g., food-hunger, sex-hunger) from second-order drives (e.g., curiosity, constructiveness) which are not so obviously linked. This distinction, which was later to become that between biological and acquired drives, was important in the history of behaviorism. On the cognitive side Tolman postulated "means-end readinesses" for "means-objects" which are innate but docile relative to the success of the organism in attaining its goal. Also in his account of "behavior supports" he tried to escape the sensory atomism of stimulus-response psychology. He also developed the concept of the "sign-Gestalt expectation" to incorporate the findings of Gestalt psychology into his assumptions about the organism's perceptual field.

Although Tolman emphasized the importance of innate appetites and aversions in behavior he was equally emphatic on the importance of learning, in which he stressed the role of cognitive variables. He argued, also, that the evidence of latent learning was inconsistent with Thorndike's law of effect. In trial and error learning a refinement of sign-Gestalts takes place. A kind of cognitive map develops of the different possibilities as the various alternatives are explored.

Motivational variables are, of course, important in learning in that they determine which aspects of a situation will be emphasized. But learning depends primarily on the expectancy of achievement and on confirmations of the expectancy. In learning animals and men make predictions and the maps which they use to do this are refined more and more as experience confirms or falsifies them. As Tolman developed his theory he became more and more interested in and convinced of the importance of cognitive variables. It is therefore understandable that behaviorists became increasingly embarrassed by Tolman's claim that he was one of them.

3. C. L. Hull. Behaviorism was basically old philosophy masquerading as a new scientific theory. In the 1930's philosophers began to be extremely critical of the old inductivist view of scientific method, which most of those in the empirical tradition had accepted, though Whewell in the nineteenth century had been an acute critic of this view. The role of hypothesis and deduction in science, which had been so prominent in the work of Galileo, was emphasized. Psychology began to be influenced by this change of emphasis in the philosophical climate. It was suggested, notably by Kurt Lewin and by Clark Hull, that psychology was in a state of disarray, split into warring factions, because it had not yet entered its Galilean phase. Lewin, a Gestalt psychologist, wrote a detailed methodological polemic to this effect in his chapter on "Aristotelian and Galilean Modes of Explanation" in his *A Dynamic Theory of Personality* (1935). He envisaged the use of the resoluto-compositive method of Galileo to erect a field theory in psychology employing postulates taken from dynamics.

Clark Hull, unlike other prominent behaviorists, was not trained in an animal laboratory. He had established a reputation for himself as an ingenious and talented designer of experiments in concept formation, hypnosis, and suggestibility. He next turned to Pavlov's laws of conditioning, and Hull's love for mathematics led him to set up a hypothetico-deductive model of learning. He became more and more ambitious and revived Hobbes's dream of a mechanical system in which the laws of human behavior could be deduced from postulates about "colorless movements" at the physiological level. He accepted Tolman's distinction between molecular and molar behaviorism, but differed from Tolman in thinking that behavior at the molar level could ultimately be explained in terms of movements at the molecular level. In 1943 he set out his ambitious program in his *Principles of Behavior,* and in 1951 he published a revised and more formalized version of his system in his *Essentials of Behavior.*

There was little original in the actual content of Hull's system save the appearance of exactitude created by his technical constructs and mathematical form of expression. Hull started from the biological postulate of self preservation and maintained that the organism is in a state of need when there is a deviation from optimum conditions for survival, e.g., lack of food, water, air. These needs are reduced by adaptive actions. The pattern of actions which lead to a reduction of a need becomes reinforced—as in Thorndike's law of effect. A stimulus which leads to a need-reducing action may become associated with another stimulus in accordance with principles of conditioning, though Hull believed that there is no conditioning without need-reduction.

Hull acknowledged the importance of what Tolman had called "intervening variables" in theory construction, and also took over his concept of "drive." He regarded needs as producing primary animal drives, which enabled him to correlate observable antecedent conditions—e.g., of food deprivation with the energy expended in behavior, e.g., in eating. He classified drives on the Darwinian principle of whether they tended towards survival of the individual organism or of the species. Whereas, however, Tolman only postulated such drives in order to explain the activation of behavior patterns, Hull postulated them to explain their acquisition as well, and their consolidation into habits. Tolman, as has already been explained, was critical of the law of effect. Hull, on the other hand, tried to provide a mechanical theory to explain its operation. He also rejected Tolman's emphasis on cognitive variables and claimed that they could be derived from his fundamental postulate of stimulus-response association. Like Watson he was basically a peripheralist and an associationist in his orientation. He merely attempted to formulate these assumptions more precisely as part of a mechanical system.

Hull said that his book had been written "on the assumption that all behavior, individual and social, moral and immoral, normal and psychopathic, is generated from the same primary laws; and that the differences in the objective behavioral manifestations are due to the differing conditions under which habits are set up and function" (*Principles of Behavior,* Preface, p. v). This was programmatic. In fact his definitions and postulates were not well rooted in physiological findings, and precise deductions to the level of motor behavior were never made—if indeed they ever

could be made. Unobservables, such as drive-stimuli, drive-receptors, etc., which were meant to fill in the mechanical picture of the workings of needs and drives, functioned more as hypothetical constructs relating to entities whose existence was shadowy and whose interrelations were highly obscure. The main value of his work was to formulate assumptions about animal learning at the motor level in a precise enough way to be refutable. And most of his assumptions were in fact refuted, e.g., by Hebb, Young, Harlow, and others. His system, however, became popular. Needs and acquired drives proliferated which lacked even the pretence of being anchored to physiological moorings (Peters [1958], Chs. 4 and 5). Drive-reduction became a classic example of twentieth-century metaphysics.

4. E. R. Guthrie. Hull had been content to state empirical laws at the molar level in terms of actions such as "biting the floor-bars" and "leaping the barrier" on the assumption that laws at this level of description could eventually be deduced from physiological postulates. E. R. Guthrie, on the other hand, a contemporary of Hull, eschewed physiological speculation and attempted to reduce behavior at the molar level to movements such as muscle contractions and glandular secretions, between which correlations could be stated. He claimed that all such correlations were derivable from the old associationist law of contiguity namely that stimuli acting at the time of a response tend on their recurrence to evoke that response. He was an S-R theorist par excellence.

Guthrie was one of the few behaviorists to stress the difference between acts and movements. An act, he claimed quite rightly, is a movement, or a series of movements, that brings about an end and acts are classified in terms of the ends which they bring about. Learning, he argued, deals with movements, not with acts. Thorndike's law of effect concerns acts, not movements. It does not therefore deal with the basic laws of learning which state correlations between movements—e.g., between the stimulation of a sense organ and a muscular contraction. In a famous experiment which he did with Horton (Guthrie and Horton, 1946) he placed a cat in a box, release from which was obtained by touching a pole in the middle of the floor. It was demonstrated that the cat tended to repeat the posture in which it first touched the pole and obtained release. This experiment at least showed that contiguity is an important principle of learning; it did not establish that it is the only principle and later experiments (e.g., by Seward) showed that improvement in learning was brought about by providing an additional reward. Whether Guthrie's experiment showed anything about the wider issue of the importance of movements in learning as distinct from acts

225

is quite another question. It is significant that Guthrie had to go to extreme lengths in constructing a situation where no intelligence was required to escape from the box, in order to make his reduction look in the least plausible. Nevertheless Guthrie was an important figure in the history of behaviorism because he at least saw the importance of the distinction between movements and acts, and because he saw it as an obstacle in the path of any reductionist program.

5. B. F. Skinner. Skinner is the last survivor of the great men of the behaviorist era, but in many ways he is the most old-fashioned of all of them in his methodology; for in Skinner we encounter the pure strain of the inductivist doctrine of scientific method. Skinner believes that a scientist must start from empirical data and gradually move towards making inductive generalizations or laws. Then, at some later stage, he may be in a position to formulate a theory which unites the laws. He must therefore be very careful to start from reliable public data. Skinner admits that men have "inner lives" which are of importance to them as well as to novelists, as Skinner himself portrayed in his novel *Walden Two.* But data drawn from this source can never form a reliable basis for a science. Skinner's polemics against other psychologists, such as Freudians, who based generalizations on data drawn from this inner realm, have been as forceful as Watson's polemics against the introspectionists.

Skinner has also accepted the inductivist warning that a scientist must never go beyond the observable in order to explain the observed. He has had no more use for physiological speculation about what goes on inside the organism than he has had for mentalistic constructs. He accords a limited importance to Tolman's intervening variables such as "drive" provided that it is clearly understood that such terms are shorthand symbols for designating the operations by which the rate of responses can be measured. To speak of hunger as a drive, for instance, is to pick out the effects of operations such as deprivation on the probability of eating behavior.

Another significant feature of Skinner's approach is his operationalism, which has recently been fashionable as a theory about the language of science. (See I, 5 above and Peters, 1951.) To Skinner this meant "the practice of talking about (1) one's observations, (2) the manipulative and calculational procedures involved in making them, (3) the logical and mathematical steps which intervene between earlier and later statements, and (4) nothing else" (Skinner [1945], p. 270). This doctrine maintained that a term like "length" or "hunger" refers not to a characteristic of an object or to a state of an organism but to the experimenter's operations of observing, manipulating, and measuring

it. It was an offshoot of positivism and of the verificationist theory of meaning which came to the fore during the period between the two World Wars.

This theory of meaning has now been abandoned by most philosophers. But it lives on in the methodology of Skinner and some other behaviorists, where it has the added appeal of being in line with the emphasis on control and manipulation of the environment which was so characteristic of behaviorism in the Watsonian tradition. Behaviorism was in many respects an offshoot of American pragmatism. The experimenter has not got to trouble his head with theoretical questions about why organisms behave as they do, especially if reference might be made to recondite inner causes in order to answer them. It is sufficient to see what forms of behavior develop if one environmental variable is manipulated rather than another. This will lead to predictions which will eventually enable the experimenter to "shape" behavior.

Skinner claims that he has no "theory" of behavior but only notes correlations. But this, of course, is either naive or a matter of stipulation about the use of the term "theory." In fact his work has presupposed a biological theory of a Darwinian type in which conditioned reflexes are postulated as having survival value. In formulating the laws in accordance with which these "reflexes" are built up Skinner in fact revived many of the established principles of associationist theory.

In formulating these laws Skinner made an important distinction between "respondent" and "operant" behavior. This was facilitated by his introduction of the Skinner box, which enabled him to study instrumental conditioning in a much more controlled way than had been possible in Thorndike's puzzle box. In a respondent reaction there is a known stimulus, such as the ticking of the metronome, with which a reaction such as salivation can be correlated as in classical conditioning. In an operant response, however, such as lever pressing, there are no known stimuli with which the response can be correlated in this way. There may, of course, be some form of internal stimulation, but such speculations were ruled out by Skinner's operationalist approach. So operant responses must be regarded as functions of experimental conditions such as food schedules which can be manipulated by the experimenter. As behavior consists largely of such operant responses, which are instrumental in obtaining a variety of goals, Skinner thought that the study of conditioned operants and their extinction must provide the basic laws which would enable behavior to be predicted and controlled. One day a theory might be devised to unify these laws; but the scientist must proceed to such "interpretations" in a Baconian manner. He must not "anticipate" Nature by premature theorizing—especially if this involves speculations like those of Hull about the internal workings of the organism. Thus Skinner rejected the peripheralist approach of Watson but has remained agnostic about the central processes which mediate between stimuli and responses. Operant conditioning has been, in fact, another way of reformulating Thorndike's Law of Effect, in nonmentalistic terminology.

Like Watson, Skinner has not been averse to extending his conceptual scheme to cover other aspects of behavior. For instance in his *Science and Human Behavior* in 1953 Skinner made pronouncements about emotions, the names of which serve to classify behavior with respect to various circumstances which affect its probability. In spite, too, of his hardheaded positivistic approach in his *Verbal Behavior* (1957), he outlined an ambitious scheme for including language within the behavioristic framework. This work, however, was just about as programmatic as Hull's *Principles of Behavior,* and has been severely criticized by philosophers and linguists alike (Chomsky, 1959).

In recent times Skinner has been very much preoccupied with providing a technology of teaching in which skills and sequences of material are carefully broken down and the path of learning systematically shaped by positive reinforcement. However, his concept of "reinforcement," which has always been criticized for its obscurity and circularity, has undergone such changes that his recipes for teaching amount to little more than injunctions that material should be logically analyzed and students should be taken through it step by step in a way which minimizes the repetition of mistakes, and which supplies constant rewards for success. This type of procedure, as Skinner himself has admitted, could be devised without much reference to his elaborate laws of operant behavior.

IV. SUMMARY AND EVALUATION

It has been argued throughout this article that behaviorism, as an historical phenomenon, has been a loosely knit collection of doctrines and theories woven round a central prescription about the proper method to use in developing a science of psychology. Behaviorism, first of all, has often been associated with the *metaphysical* doctrine of materialism. Nowadays there is less reluctance to discuss metaphysical problems than there was in the heyday of behaviorism and of "the revolution in philosophy" (Ryle, 1956). Materialism has been revived, though it has few adherents amongst philosophers (Smart, 1963; Armstrong, 1968). One of its problems has been to state coherently what could be meant by saying that mental and bodily processes are identical (Hamlyn, 1964).

It would be difficult to maintain that, in the sphere of *scientific theory,* behaviorism has advanced the understanding of behavior in any major respect. The theory which was most widely employed was that of associationism which was as old as Hobbes, Hume, and Hartley. The behaviorists merely transferred this theory from the realm of ideas to the realm of movements. What occupied them most was disputes amongst themselves within this type of theoretical framework. There were two major issues which divided them. The first related to the importance of reward or reinforcement in setting up S-R connections. The second issue concerned the relative importance of central as distinct from peripheral processes. It was not really surprising that the behaviorists in fact contributed little in the way of theory to the understanding of behavior; for basically most of them were not interested in explaining behavior or even learning for that matter. They were interested in conditioning. Even at the animal level it is extremely doubtful whether rats, dogs, cats, and monkeys in fact learn much by conditioning in a normal environment. Ethological studies certainly cast grave doubt on the omnipresence of this type of learning. It is probable that this type of learning is an artifact of the situations in which animals have been confined. The extrapolation of this type of learning to the human level, where the pattern of life is determined largely by social rules and purposes, was largely programmatic. However, behaviorists showed that associationist principles might well apply to the learning of simple reactions and motor habits. Little more could in fact be claimed for their contribution to psychological theory.

Many of the defects in behavioristic theorizing, especially their programmatic extrapolations to the human level, derived from their lack of clarity about such *concepts* as stimulus, reinforcement, and response. Underlying these particular confusions were fundamental confusions about the concept of behavior itself, due to their aversion to assuming the existence of consciousness. Guthrie was most sensitive to this difficulty. He made the distinction between acts and movements and tried to arrange an experiment which dealt only with movements; for he realized only too well that descriptions of behavior at the molar level are in terms of acts and not in terms of mere movements. And we identify their acts by reference to what human beings have in mind when they make certain movements. For example, an act involving the same movements of the arm is identified as either signalling to a friend or fanning the face (Hamlyn, 1953).

Skinner, in his distinction between operants and respondents, actually hit upon a distinction which is crucial for getting clearer about the concept of action. Respondent reactions like salivations and eye-blinks, which can be dealt with reasonably well by classical conditioning theory, are indeed reactions which can be correlated with stimuli. But they are not, strictly speaking, actions; they are events that happen to us. When, however, we pass to Skinner's operants, to things done as instrumental to an end, we are entering the sphere of action proper. Such actions, at the human level at any rate, cannot either be described or explained as mere movements exhibited at the reflex level. For an action is not simply a series of bodily movements; such movements as are necessary to it are done for the sake of something, as Aristotle pointed out in his criticism of the mechanists of the ancient world. They are classed as belonging to an action because of their assumed relevance to an end (*telos*).

Similarly, on the perceptual as distinct from the motor side of behavior, the importance of consciousness is inescapable. Human beings, and probably animals as well, do not often simply react to stimuli in terms of their purely physical properties, as the Gestalt psychologists pointed out in their distinction between the psychological and physical or geographical properties of the environment. They see things as meaning something; they respond to features of situations which are interpreted in terms of their understanding of them. Skinner, for instance, was grossly misleading when he claimed that what we call emotions are names for classifying behavior with respect to various circumstances which affect the probability of the behavior's occurrence; for the circumstances are those which are *interpreted* by the subject in a certain light, e.g., as dangerous in the case of fear, as involving somebody else having something which we want in the case of envy. The relationship between circumstances and the subject is not one of purely physical causality (Peters, 1965).

In brief even what the behaviorists called "behavior" includes a range of phenomena between which there are very important distinctions, let alone other purely mental phenomena such as remembering and dreaming, which may have no overt expressions and which may lead to no overt actions. Many more distinctions than these can be drawn which would complicate the picture even further. But this would not affect the two cardinal points that need to be emphasized: first, that it is impossible to make such distinctions without reference to consciousness and, second, that behaviorists tend to think that the form of description and explanation applicable at the lowest level of reflex behavior can be extrapolated to explain the much more complex phenomena at higher levels.

About the *methodological* doctrine that was the kernel of behaviorism—that psychology should base itself as a science on the type of publicly observable data that biologists use when theorizing about animals—the first point to make is that it is an example of the long-standing delusion that success in science depends upon following a particular method. A study of the history of science gives no support for the belief that science has in fact been advanced by following any particular method, if this is interpreted as meaning following a particular procedure for making discoveries or arriving at laws. It is impossible to formulate any method for arriving at hypotheses; all that can be done is to lay down general rules about testing them.

Is there then anything to be said for the behaviorists' prescription as a procedural rule relating to the testing of hypotheses rather than to their formulation? If they had been concerned solely with animal behavior their prescription would have been unexceptionable but otiose; for there is no possibility of obtaining introspective reports from animals. Insofar, however, as they studied animals partly with the intention of making extrapolations to human behavior, their prescription seems to be very much a self-denying ordinance, for in science it is advisable to obtain all the evidence available. Also the sort of observations which are appropriate depends upon what is being studied. If it is reactions such as salivation, knee-jerks, and simple motor skills, which were the main field of interest amongst behaviorists, introspective reports may not be of great significance. If, however, hypotheses about dreams, perception, delusions, remembering, emotional phenomena, or moral development have to be tested, it is very difficult to see how much relevant evidence could be accumulated without recourse to reports by the subject. And it simply will not do to say that the experimenter is then relying on another form of behavior, namely verbal behavior. Furthermore, this move by behaviorists is a form of *conceptual* behaviorism. The methodological doctrine, which is distinctive of behaviorism, would evaporate if a subject's reports were re-admitted as evidence because they too were regarded as forms of behavior.

Historically, therefore, behaviorism was a salutary corrective that was pushed to inordinate extremes. At a time when psychology was largely preoccupied with examining the minutiae of a subject's introspections there was some point in drawing attention to what could be publicly observed. But this injunction unfortunately was not accompanied by any suggestion of new hypotheses that might be tested. It functioned mainly as a new recipe for continuing the old associationist program. The widespread implementation of this recipe, however, had very important consequences for psychology generally. It enhanced the status of psychology as a science amongst the scientific community. Psychologists could now wear lab-coats like biologists and be admitted to the Faculty of Science. Although behaviorism was basically a philosophical movement psychologists were now able to part company with philosophers and set up on their own.

Whether this separation has been beneficial in advancing our understanding of human behavior is another question; for the basic problem in the central spheres of action, motivation and emotion, perception, learning, remembering, etc., is to decide what is a psychological question. In the sphere of learning, for instance, in which behaviorists evinced most interest, how much depends upon the conceptual and logical relationships involved in what has to be learnt and how much depends on general empirical conditions about which psychologists might reasonably test hypotheses? The work of theorists such as Jerome Bruner and Jean Piaget, who have been concerned with human learning and development in a concrete rather than a programmatic way, raises such problems in an acute form. But it is difficult to see how much progress can be made until issues of this sort are squarely faced. But to face them would involve a revolution in psychology as radical as the methodological movement which Watson himself initiated.

BIBLIOGRAPHY

This bibliography includes works referred to in the text as well as important works of reference.

D. M. Armstrong, *A Materialist Theory of Mind* (London and New York, 1968). F. H. Bradley, *The Principles of Logic*, 2nd ed. (London and New York, 1922). N. Chomsky, Review of B. F. Skinner, *Verbal Behavior, Language*, 35 (1959), 26–58. E. R. Guthrie, *The Psychology of Learning* (New York, 1935); idem, and E. P. Horton, *Cats in a Puzzle Box* (New York, 1946). D. W. Hamlyn, "Behaviour," *Philosophy*, 28 (1953), 132–45; idem, "Causality and Human Behaviour," *Proceedings of the Aristotelian Society*, Supp. Vol. 38 (1964), 125–42. E. R. Hilgard, *Theories of Learning*, 2nd ed. (New York, 1956). T. Hobbes, *De corpore, Works*, Vol. I, ed. W. Molesworth (London, 1839); idem, *Leviathan*, Vol. III (London, 1839). C. L. Hull, *The Principles of Behavior* (New York, 1943). K. S. Lashley, "The Behaviorist Interpretation of Consciousness," *Psychological Review*, 30 (1923), 237–72, 329–53; idem, *Brain Mechanisms and Intelligence* (Chicago, 1929). K. MacCorquodale and P. E. Meehl, "On a Distinction between Hypothetical Constructs and Intervening Variables," *Psychological Review*, 55 (1948), 95–107. R. S. Peters, "Observationalism in Psychology," *Mind*, 60 (1951), 43–61; idem, and H. Tajfel, "Hobbes and Hull: Metaphysicians of Behavior," *British Journal of the Philosophy of Science*, 7 (1957), 30–44. R. S. Peters, *The Concept of Motivation* (London and New York, 1958); reprint New York, 1965); idem, ed., *Brett's History of Psychology*, rev. ed. (London and New York, 1962); idem, "Emotions, Passivity and the Place of Freud's Theory in Psychology," in B. B. Wolman and E. Nagel, *Scientific Psychology* (New York, 1964). K. R. Popper "On the Sources of Knowledge and Ignorance," *Conjectures and Refutations* (London, 1962; New York, 1963). G. Ryle, *The Concept of Mind* (London and New York, 1949). G. Ryle et al., *The Revolution in Philosophy* (London, 1956). B. F. Skinner *The Behavior of Organisms* (New York, 1938); idem, *Science and Human Behavior* (New York, 1953); idem, *Verbal Behavior* (New York, 1957); idem, "The Operational Analysis of Psychological Terms," *Psychological Review*, 52 (1945), 270–77. J. J. C. Smart, *Philosophy and Scientific Realism* (London and New York, 1963). C. Taylor, *The Explanation of Behavior* (London, 1964). E. B. Titchener, *Lectures on the Elementary Psychology of Feeling and Attention* (New York, 1908). E. C. Tolman, *Purposive Behavior in Animals and Man* (New York, 1932). J. B. Watson, *Psychology from the Standpoint of the Behaviorist* (Philadelphia, 1919); idem, *Behaviorism* (New York, 1924; Chicago, 1958; also reprint). B. B. Wolman, *Contemporary Theories and Systems in Psychology* (New York, 1960). R. S. Woodworth, *Contemporary Schools of Psychology* (New York, 1931; 1943).

R. S. PETERS

[See also Baconianism; Education; Historical and Dialectical Materialism; Idea; **Man-Machine;** Pragmatism; Psychological . . . .]

BIOLOGICAL CONCEPTIONS IN ANTIQUITY

THE ANCIENTS did not distinguish between being alive and having a soul, which was conceived in various ways as something that organizes and controls the body. Lacking optical instruments, they had no concept of the living cell, nor did they think of flesh or wood as possibly different from the constituents of nonliving things. Life was given by the soul, both in animals and in plants. Biology, as the study of the living, is a modern concept; when we speak of ancient biology, we mean the study of the ensouled. At the same time, the difference between living and nonliving things was less marked, because the ancients tended to assume that all matter possesses power and mobility and is quasi-alive (the assumption that the material world is alive is known as "hylozoism").

The early biological conceptions seem to originate in pre-philosophical reflection upon everyday experience. A great deal of data was available concerning husbandry, stockbreeding, hunting, nutrition, medicine and poisons, childbirth and dying, to which was added special information from Persian game reserves, from the wild animals of India, Egypt, and Libya, from the Babylonian gardens where the fertilization of fig and

229

palm was practiced, from augury and sacrifices, and from ritual crafts like root-cutting for drugs. From this variety of data there arose certain common ideas which can be conveniently grouped under the topics of the four elements (Earth, Air, Fire, Water), the mysterious extra element (aether), heredity, species, classification, and teleology. But these ideas did not acquire precision until philosophical argument came to sharpen them. Agriculture and medicine were conducted by traditional rule of thumb. It was the early philosophers who used these data to illustrate and justify their own cosmological arguments, and thereby evolved biological theories which were then taken over by the agricultural and medical writers (especially the Hippocratics). The theoretical influence therefore ran mostly from philosophy to biology rather than the other way. Zoology and botany were not separated from cosmology until Aristotle departmentalized the sciences; and even he did not set up autonomous principles in biology, but applied a conceptual framework from his general philosophy. The earlier biological theories therefore need to be understood in the context of larger physical theories. Inevitably Greek philosophy is the best place to study these ideas. Not that the other ancient civilizations lacked biological speculation; but we do not find there any major biological idea that does not also appear in the richer and fuller Greek discussions.

I. THE FOUR ELEMENTS

The soul was traditionally associated with blood, breath, semen, the warmth of life, and the persona. Each of these retained significance as theorizing developed. The most universal was the conception of vital warmth, which was regarded as one aspect of the role played by heat in the cosmos. Here the early cosmologists combined three traditional ideas: vital warmth; the seasonal powers of hot, cold, wet, and dry; and the four world-masses of fire, air, water, and earth. Vital warmth was extended from warm-blooded animals to all animals and even to plants. It clearly meant more than temperature, for pine wood (which is not hotter to touch than other timber) was thought to contain more heat and therefore to burn better. Hotter plants have better fruit; hotter animals are more intelligent. Animal droppings may still contain the warmth of life, enabling them to generate maggots. This is the concept of heat as a stuff, not merely a quality and not necessarily perceptible, which survived into the eighteenth-century theory of phlogiston. It was common ground among ancient scientists, even those who did not consider heat to be an element. The atomist Democritus, for instance, who argued that heat is merely a sensation, nevertheless gave it an objective basis by saying that it is the round atoms that feel

hot and that form the soul; that the heart contains the fire of life; that stags grow horns because their bellies are hot and send the nourishment upwards; that the owl sees in the dark because she has fire in her eyes. These views are typical of the age.

As heat is necessary to life, so cold brings death: it is not mere absence of heat, but a stuff with its own powers. Wet and dry also figure in early theorizing, more commonly than other powers, as being necessary in various forms of liquid and solid. These four were assimilated to fire, air, water, and earth. The two sets do not exactly match, but Aristotle eventually reconciled them by a formula of cross-pairing: fire is hot plus dry, air is hot plus wet, and so on. He held that hot, cold, wet, and dry are the primitive qualities of matter but cannot exist in isolation, while fire, air, water, and earth are the simplest separable elements, capable of transformation into each other.

Some medical theorists at first opposed the concept of four elements, arguing that there are other equally basic powers in the body, such as the sweet, bitter, salty, acid, astringent, insipid, and that the body contains separate essential liquids (later "humours" from the Latin translation). After controversy the humors were agreed to be four—blood, black bile, yellow bile, phlegm—which were accommodated to Aristotle's elements by similar cross-pairing: blood is hot plus wet plus sweet, phlegm is cold plus wet plus salty. . . . Each humor was associated with a season and a human temperament. This systematization lasted through the Middle Ages.

Heat always seemed the chief active force. Its characteristic action was to concoct materials, to bring them to fruition, to energize, sometimes to volatilize or dissolve. Cold caused condensing, coagulation, solidifying. When Aristotle called hot and cold the chief instruments of nature, he was expressing a universal view, whose details clearly originated from kitchen and garden. Water and earth were the materials upon which hot and cold worked; Aristotle analyzed them into various kinds of liquid and solid.

The importance of a fruitful balance among elements, a harmony of opposites, impressed the Greeks perhaps more than other peoples, and came from them into medieval European thought. The idea of symmetry and proportionate blending dominated their medicine, their art and architecture, their social and political thinking. The cosmologist Alcmaeon, who was also a physician, made it his first cosmic principle under the political metaphor *isonomia* ("equality of rights"). When applied to mixtures of materials, it led the way from a qualitative assessment towards a quantitative chemistry. But the ancients did not go far in that direction. Aristotle held that if the proportions of a mixture were upset, one ingredient could master (*kratein*) the others. Wine and water can form a mixture; but a single drop of wine, put into an ocean, would be overcome and would lose its nature entirely. Both concepts, proportion and mastery, are important in his biology, particularly in genetics.

II. PNEUMA

The notion of a mysterious extra element in the living body began to appear in Aristotle's time, especially among those inclined towards a materialistic explanation. Aristotle believed in a special fifth element, the *aether*, but he confined it to the heavens. In biology he uses a concept of innate breath (*pneuma*), which is mingled with vital heat and is present even in nonbreathing animals. It transmits sensation, and is the conveyor of soul in the semen. At one point he compares its generative power with the *aether*, but otherwise he defines it as warmed air, which the body replenishes by respiration.

After Aristotle the *pneuma* concept spread widely, with different applications according to the different philosophical positions. Among medical writers it was the residuary legatee of unattributed functions, psychic and sensory. The Stoics equated it with the divine *Logos* that permeates nature, identifying *pneuma* and *aether* (which remain confused in the medieval concept of the fifth element or *quinta essentia*). Even the atomists posited a special kind of atom to account for the soul, which Epicurus said consists of atoms of fire, air, wind, and a nameless fourth kind—thus reducing his opponents' *pneuma* to wind but replacing its mysterious functions with a new mystery.

Aristotle's predecessors had debated whether the brain or the heart is the center of sensation, and whether the heart or the liver is the source of the blood. He decided for the heart in both cases. But in the third century B.C. the Alexandrian anatomists distinguished arteries from veins, and isolated the nervous system with the brain as its base. This led to an elaboration of *pneuma* theory: venous blood is formed in the liver, where it is charged with the lowest grade of *pneuma* (Latin *spiritus naturalis*, "natural spirits" in Renaissance medicine); some venous blood flows to the heart, where it is mixed with "*pneuma* necessary for life" ("vital spirits") and so becomes arterial blood; this flows to the brain, where its *pneuma* is purified into "*pneuma* used by the soul" (*spiritus animalis*, "animal spirits"). To explain the blood's route, Galen in the second century A.D. postulated minute passages leading from right to left ventricle in the heart, for which later anatomists searched in vain. After Harvey had demonstrated the circulation of the blood, the whole hypothesis of *pneuma* was gradually discarded.

III. GENETICS

It was an ancient question whether the male or the female contributes the seed which grows into the embryo; the answer to it partly determined a society's view of blood-kinship and legal inheritance. In classical Greece the father was thought to be the primary contributor, but they disputed whether the mother provides merely nutrition (as in the dramatic decision in Aeschylus' *Oresteia*) or a second seed which unites with the father's. Aristotle's analysis of current theories in his *Generation of Animals* shows that discussions were particularly lively in this field, where much evidence was quoted, some seriously misleading—for example, that fishes swallow the milt, or that wound-scars have been inherited (*G.A.* I. 17–18, III. 5, IV. 1). He himself opposed the concept of female seed, but it was accepted by Galen, Avicenna, and the Renaissance scientists, until finally it was superseded by Von Baer's demonstration of the mammalian ovum. Among many diverse theories held by the atomists, "pangenesis" was important: that seed is drawn from every part of both parents' bodies, to account for resemblances. Another was "preformationism": that every part of the embryo must preexist in the seed ("for how could hair grow from non-hair?" said Anaxagoras). Some argued that males must develop from the father's seed and females from the mother's; others attributed sex-differentiation to differences of heat or position in the uterus. Multiple births, monstrous growths, superfetation, sterility, were regularly quoted in evidence: to some they suggested disproportion between two seeds, to others they suggested excess or deficiency of heat.

A Persian tradition connecting the semen with the brain and spinal marrow was followed by those who held the brain to be the center of psychic activity. Those who held the heart to be the center argued that semen must come from the blood. A Greek tradition associated it with foam (*aphros*, as in Aphrodite). Aristotle rationalized this idea in terms of *pneuma*, which emulsifies the semen, being present in it as the vehicle of soul.

Aristotle gathered together these trains of thought in a formulation based on his own theory of matter and form. The male seed transmits soul, which is form and movement; but its somatic part is sloughed away. The female contributes only the material (the catamenia). Among his arguments, he points out that fishes' eggs do not develop unless sprinkled with the milt, yet this does not change them quantitatively; and that certain insects (as he thought) can receive the male impulse without a transmission of seed. Using his concept of "mastery" he argues that family likeness depends upon the extent to which the male impulse controls the female material. Malformations, redun-

231

dancies, sterility, are due to disproportion of materials.

After Aristotle, the concept of female seed was revived by the Alexandrian anatomists, who demonstrated the genital connections of the ovaries and concluded that these are channels for seeds coming from the blood. Later Galen demonstrated the oviduct in sheep; but instead of moving to a concept of mammalian ovum, he tried to reconcile this new datum with Aristotle's view, arguing that the female seed contributes only nutrition and the allantois, while the male seed forms the other embryonic membranes (chorion, amnion) and bodily parts.

It was a universal belief (until Pasteur) that many insects and plants grow out of rotting materials without seed. The early cosmologists used this to argue that life must have begun in that way. A typical account occurs in the *History* of Diodorus Siculus in the first century B.C. In the primeval mud (that is, *cold dry* earth mixed with *wet* rain and the sun's *heat*) there appear membranes containing embryo animals of every kind, which grow up and then reproduce themselves sexually. There was no ancient theory of evolution out of simpler forms, and therefore one problem was to explain how young animals, having appeared spontaneously, could survive in the mud long enough to become mature.

Those like Aristotle, who held that the universe had no beginning, still had to account for spontaneity. He argued that *pneuma* containing vital warmth is sometimes present in water and earth mixed; a foamy bubble is then formed, out of which may arise eels and certain of the fishes, testaceans and insects. He would not however allow that rottenness is a cause, for rottenness is disintegration whereas only concoction by heat can generate new life.

IV. SPECIES

In folklore the animals and plants had clear-cut natures, including moral characterizations such as we find in Aesop and in the Oriental and African fables. The ancients believed that some types regularly metamorphose into each other, for example, cuckoo hawk and hoopoe interchange, and wheat can become darnel. By this they meant a change of identity, not an ambiguity between these types, nor a seasonal change (as stoat to ermine).

Plato was the first to apply a philosophical technique to the conception of animal types. According to his theory of Forms, we identify natural qualities by comparing them with ideal qualities which may not appear exactly in nature but are known directly to the mind. The animal type is an aggregate of characters which approximate to ideal Forms. The Forms therefore are an absolute reference point.

Aristotle inverts this analysis, by taking the animal type as the exact object of knowledge, while its characters vary in precision. Some characters are essential, some not (for instance, the eye may be essential, and an eye must have a color, but its actual color is inessential and imprecise). The animal type, namely its species, is a unified pattern of essential characters and functions. It is identical in all members of the species. The variations between individuals are due to their material makeup, not to their form.

There have been so many conceptions of species in modern times that it is perhaps useful to say what Aristotle's conception is not. It is not a statistical average, not a population, not an approximation, not an arbitrarily selected type-specimen. On the other hand, it is not a form imposed by God. It is a type-pattern that exists in nature as an objective datum: it is there to be detected within individuals. It differs from any one individual as absolutely as the mathematical circle differs from a drawing of a circle. It is this species-pattern that Aristotle believes to be eternally reproduced in nature, for that is the nearest that sublunary beings can get to the eternal cyclic movement of the stars. The fact that it may never be exactly reproduced does not affect his point, which is that nature tends to reproduce it.

This conception could easily become a belief in fixed species, but Aristotle did not consider that point; there was in fact nothing in his biology that was incompatible with an evolutionary theory, had the question ever arisen. He accepted reports of new species resulting from miscegenation (he quotes dog and fox, dog and wolf, several fishes and birds). He makes only the proviso that interbreeding is limited to animals that are alike in species, size, and length of gestation, and that in any case there could not be indefinite production of new species, because that would defeat nature's teleology (meaning that there would be no goals, for the goal is the reproduction of the parent's form). He emphasizes that the ladder of nature is continuous, and that many types overlap the borders of classifications. Moreover his theory of reproduction is aimed at explaining how the father's form is transmitted and how the family likeness may come to be disturbed: the precise goal is that the animal should "beget another like itself," and its specific form is something wider that is only latent in it. There is a contradiction in his doctrine here: for he says theoretically that species is the object of science while individual differences are due to matter and are unknowable, but in practice he brings to scientific account many characters that are below specific level—not only family likeness but inessential attributes such as coloration and voice. Just occasionally he suggests that individuals differ not only in matter but in form too, since the materials that individualize them could be stated generally; but he does not follow this up. (It was followed up by some medieval scholastics, who thereby removed this difficulty from his theory of individuation.)

Aristotle therefore could have accommodated an evolutionary theory of species; but he had no need of it. He had no paleontology, no obsolete species to consider; similarity of species could be covered by his theory; and believing that the world had no beginning, he had no problem of the origins of species. By the third century A.D. some Stoic and Neo-Platonist theologians had developed the idea that forms and species are thoughts in the mind of God. It was this idea, rather than Aristotle's theory, that led later scientists like Linnaeus to posit the fixity of species.

V. CLASSIFICATION

Animals were traditionally grouped into Birds, Beasts, and Fishes, air, land, and sea creatures, and some of them into subgroups like cloven-hoofed, horned, carnivorous. Plants were grouped as trees, shrubs, fruiting, leguminous, and others that Theophrastus reports. Popular classification did not go far, and was unsystematic in that some classes cut across each other.

Plato developed in several dialogues the logical technique of "Division," whereby a large concept is analyzed into its varieties—for example, the concept "living on land" is divisible into walking and flying, and walking is further divisible into quadruped, biped, and polypod. With it he combined the complementary technique of "Collection," whereby data are sorted into groups by common concepts, and these groups are further grouped under more general concepts; for example, biped and quadruped share the concept walking, and walking, flying, and swimming share the concept locomotion. Collection is the inductive process which Division follows and confirms deductively. Plato's aim was to "track down" and identify concepts by showing their relationships in a Division.

Plato intended his method to reveal the actual divisions in nature, but when applied to animal characters it split up natural groups. Aristotle therefore took as initial data not characters but animal types (which have multiple characters). Class the species by likeness, then class the classes by more general likenesses, until you arrive at the class Animal itself. Then reconsider what are the most significant distinguishing characters, and re-divide the classes accordingly down to the individual species again. You now have an orderly hierarchy of genera and species, enabling you to define species by group-characters, to classify new species as they appear, and to predict characters not yet observed. This is the same conception that Ray and Linnaeus successfully developed, but Aristotle lacked enough data to make it workable. He also handicapped it unnecessarily by laying down that within a genus the member-species must have characters differing only in degree (for example, wings of various shapes), whereas between genera the comparison must be one of "analogy" (as wing to fin). He began with a division of Animal into "blooded" (that is, red-blooded) and "bloodless," and divided these into (1) man, viviparous quadrupeds, oviparous quadrupeds, cetaceans, birds, fishes and (2) crustaceans, testaceans, mollusks, insects. But he points out that this scheme omits some types (snakes, sponges), and that below this level the natural subgroups cut across each other: for example, the classes solid-hoofed, hornless, ruminant are defeated by the "overlapping" types pig and camel.

He therefore preferred to arrange the species in an order of "perfection." This too was inspired by Plato, who had set out a rough *scala naturae* running downwards from man, through bipeds, quadrupeds, polypods, serpents, to fishes; his indices were intelligence and posture. Aristotle took vital heat as his index of perfection, as shown not only by intelligence and posture but also by respiration, method of reproduction, and state at birth. This method better suited his view that nature is continuous from plant to animal (the testaceans and sponges being in both categories). In his actual practice he often argues from this order of perfection, but makes almost no use of genus-species classification.

VI. TELEOLOGY

Teleological explanations in ancient biology are of several kinds. They have in common the basic meaning that natural processes occur *for the sake of* their consequences; they tend towards goals. Traditional religion ascribed this tendency to the gods, who send rain to make the crops grow. This conception of providential teleology could vary from its strong form in Judaic monotheism to the quite unsystematic religious beliefs of the Greeks. Opposing the popular ideas of providence, the early Greek cosmologists claimed to account for all phenomena by "necessity," that is by automatic causes like the hot and the cold. But within their naturalistic theories there was room for teleology of another kind, no longer implying providence or purpose. Anaxagoras included "Mind" among his natural causes, to account for nature's orderliness; Empedocles included "Love and Strife" to account for complexity; Diogenes held that the cosmic Air is intelligent, to account for nature's tendency towards goals. They were opposed by the atomists, who held that all three features—orderliness, complexity, and directiveness—

could be explained by random movements of atoms. These features have remained the chief talking-points in the debate over teleology, which has continued into modern times.

Plato argued that the cosmologists merely analyzed the material constituents of things, and failed to account for the characters of whole entities as such: for a whole has a character which is not found by adding together the characters of its parts. He also criticized Anaxagoras for not making proper use of his concept of Mind, for he did not explain how things tend towards "the best," nor what "the best" means. Plato's own concept was a world-soul distinct from the material elements. He believed in an overall teleology, namely that nature is coordinated so that the "best" for an individual cannot be distinguished from the good order of the cosmos; but control by the world-soul is not complete, for there is much failure and evil due to irrational material.

This dualism disappears in Aristotle's analysis. He still uses Plato's double explanation—material necessity on the one hand, directiveness or "the final cause" on the other hand—but he emphasizes that both coexist in natural movements. Living things contain their own sources of motion and directiveness. There is no world-soul or divine providence outside them. The "Unmoved Mover" (God) which he posits as the sustaining cause of motion in the universe, does not elicit the individual "beginnings of motion" which are all the time occurring in nature; nor does God originate or comprehend nature's forms and species. Again, within nature itself there is no overall design nor coordinating agency, no quasi-conscious purpose. In his explanations of animal structures the goal is the animal's own complete state, nothing beyond. For convenience he personifies "nature who does nothing at random, but always does what is best out of the available possibilities," and speaks of it as a prudent housewife who "apportions" the materials and "uses" the necessary movements of the elements. In so speaking, he formulated several principles of nature's economy which were adopted by later teleologists, such as: one function to one organ, no duplication of defenses, use of by-products from one tissue in another. But if taken literally, these expressions would have to imply an overall purposiveness in nature, for which there is no foundation in his philosophy. They must therefore be rhetorical. His frequent comparison between nature and craftsman helps to analyze teleological sequences but does not imply a craftsman in nature. Lucretius the atomist uses even more colored language about *natura creatrix*, which he could not possibly mean. The one or two occasions when Aristotle seems to suggest that one animal's advantage is sacrificed to the good

of other species probably mean no more than a general balance of nature. He never speaks of "purpose" in nature. His expression for the final cause is "the end for the sake of which the development occurs," and this end is the individual's perfection and reproduction.

The source of directiveness in an animal or plant is its soul. Aristotle did not agree with Plato that the soul is a separable entity, but argued that it is the form of the single body-soul entity. It is both the structural pattern of the living body, and the motive force which makes it grow into that pattern. This difficult conception is closely related with his conception of directive nature. It is natural for the elements to act according to their simple properties; but it is equally natural for them to combine and become organized in complexes, and in so doing to act against the simple properties. He takes this development from simple to complex as a datum, for which he offers no extra-physical cause. Even where he posits the soul as the cause of development, this soul is not something over against the complex of materials: it is the form of the whole complex, its essential nature as a unity. Where Plato regarded necessity and directiveness as arising from separate sources, Aristotle regarded them as arising simultaneously within nature. An animal is a process (a "road to nature" in his words) consisting of many movements, all natural, which by natural coordination tend towards the animal's complete form.

There is therefore no "extra factor" such as modern teleologists posit, no "conatus" (innate striving) irreducible to the laws of physics. Aristotle's physics no doubt made it easier to accommodate directiveness, for he was some way from the concept of an exactly quantitative science, nor had he the theory that bodies are naturally inert. He may also have been unconsciously influenced by traditional hylozoism, which represented nature as behaving like a living being. At any rate, soul is not enough to account for all of nature's directiveness, for Aristotle explicitly says that nature proceeds without a break from the soulless to the ensouled (*P.A.* 681a 12, *H.A.* 588b 4).

When he defends teleology he does not argue primarily from directiveness, like later teleologists, but from the fact that forms and species exist; from this fact he then infers directiveness. The object to be explained is a living animal and its structures. If it were an artifact—for example a chair—it would not be enough to define it as "something made of wood," but its form must be included. In an animal there is the further point that it is able to function (for a dead man's hand is no longer strictly a hand). Therefore the first thing to grasp is the form and function of the whole living animal, and only then can one understand its growth. The parts are "for the sake of the whole"; and just as a whole differs from the sum of its parts, so an end differs in kind from the process leading to it. From the fact that nature regularly produced these forms, he infers that natural processes tend towards them.

After Aristotle the Epicurean atomists produced a counter-theory to make teleology unnecessary. Atoms have all kinds of shapes, and those that happen to fit together must tend to interlock when they meet in random collisions. In this way complexes can be formed, which may grow very large. Within them movements will necessarily become restricted to certain patterns. Having been formed by pure chance, such a system will become stabilized, so long as it does not conflict with neighboring systems. For as atoms continually flow in and out of it, a successful system will automatically perpetuate itself by rejecting atoms of incompatible shape, while retaining those that fit. Furthermore, if a complex part of the system comes away, it will consist of atoms linked in the same conformation as in the parent system. One such system will be an animal. Innumerable unsuccessful animals will doubtless be formed, lacking essential organs and so unable to feed or defend themselves. But sometimes a successful one will appear, able to survive. Its offspring will naturally be of the same conformation. Teleological explanations are therefore vacuous: the eye is not produced for the sake of sight, but having been produced by chance it then creates its own use.

This hypothesis of course could not be an inference from data; spontaneous generation was the only supporting evidence available. It was a theoretical construction designed to show that random atomic movements would originate complex and stable systems, which would then reproduce themselves. The atomists' explanation of the survival of the fittest systems was indeed a conception of random natural selection. It was not, however, linked with an evolutionary theory, though it would have readily lent itself to one if it had been suggested.

A new kind of teleology appeared in Stoicism, which was a materialistic theory of divine providence. The divine *pneuma*, consisting of warm air, is a continuum that permeates the whole of nature. Not only souls, but all forms and abstract constructions, are parts of the divine, and are somatic; they penetrate natural objects and hold them in tension. Hence every detail in nature is continuously controlled by providence, which coordinates all goals in a predestined design. In such a conception Aristotle's primary defense of teleology (that forms cannot be explained by material causes) is irrelevant. The Stoics based their case on directiveness, and it was therefore important to account for every detail teleologically. Galen's exhaustive

treatise *On the Use of the Parts* (second century A.D.) shows the difference from Aristotle's conception. Writing under Stoic influence, Galen analyzes bodily structures to the smallest detail of tissue and arrangement, to show their uses. Where some detail carries a disadvantage, he shows that it is for an ulterior advantage (for example, the skull's thinness aids the brain's efficiency); positive evils, like disease, are there for moral training. Aristotle on the other hand depends upon conceiving the animal as a coherent pattern of activity, not upon piecemeal explanations of utility, and he recognizes that "while many things are for the sake of ends, much else occurs of necessity": if you have bone for the sake of rigidity, you must expect it also to be breakable.

In this way the Stoics contributed the first thoroughgoing conception of providential teleology, within a naturalistic philosophy. This at once creates a problem of evil; in biology it means that all the inessentials and imperfections which Aristotle could attribute to "necessity" must now be shown to be purposed. The Stoic answer to this problem was unsatisfactory (as were their answers to the allied ethical problems of free will and wrongdoing). They confused the issue by trying to equate providence and nature. And by trying to treat immaterial things (such as abstract ideas) as if they were material, they confused design and directiveness. Subsequent developments, however, clarified the real issues in the teleological arguments.

The first step was the return of Stoicism to a nonmaterialistic theology. With the Neo-Platonists of the third century A.D., they held that forms are thoughts in God's mind, from which they emanate into matter or are imposed upon it. Hence nature exhibits a rational design which is blurred by matter's intractability. This was a return to Plato's view and restored the distinction between abstract and material. The next step was due to the impact of Judeo-Christian theology, which introduced the idea (not found in Greek philosophy) that God is not part of the universe, is omnipotent, and has created the universe out of nothing. From this it follows that matter of itself is inert, and its motion is imparted to it. Natural and supernatural were now categorically distinguished. Providential design could no longer be confused with a natural directiveness. At first indeed Aristotle's conception of natural teleology seemed impossible, for all movements in nature must be imparted by God alone. The problem of evil now became critical, but was answered at this stage by theological doctrines (such as the Fall of Man) which do not concern teleology. But as the concept of inertia developed in physics during the later Middle Ages, a contrast came to be drawn between the automatic orderly movements of physical bodies and the supernatural guidance leading to goals. This brought out a distinction which had been latent but obscure in Greek physics, between orderliness and directiveness. The orderliness of nature had been claimed in evidence both by Aristotle and by his opponents, the atomists. But now, and especially after Newton, it seemed to support only the anti-teleologists: they now developed a concept of nature working like a machine by the "laws" of physics, while teleologists had to produce evidence of God's interference in the causal nexus. Then in the nineteenth century the Epicurean conception of random natural selection appeared anew in association with the Darwinian theory of evolution. The concept of rigid laws of nature became modified into a concept of statistical probability. Teleologists opposed the notion of randomness, but began to argue less from design and more from directiveness, so moving closer to Aristotle's natural teleology. But modern teleology still differs from his insofar as it relies upon directiveness first, rather than upon forms, and insofar as it posits an "extra factor" that is not reducible to physics and chemistry. It is therefore less simple, and to that extent less rational, than Aristotle's. But although teleology has taken so many different forms, and has been opposed on different grounds, nevertheless the debate has in a way always been between the same contestants.

BIBLIOGRAPHY

A. L. Peck's editions (Loeb Classical Library, London and Cambridge, Mass.) of Aristotle's *Parts of Animals* (1955), *Generation of Animals* (1953), and *Historia Animalium* (1965) contain expository introduction, English translation and notes, including a short bibliography of modern secondary literature on ancient Greek biology. E. Lesky, *Die Zeugungs- und Vererbungslehren der Antike und ihr Nachwirken* (Vienna, 1950) describes ancient genetic theories. O. Keller, *Die antike Tierwelt*, 2 vols. (Leipzig, 1909–13) collects information under each animal. Ernest H. F. Meyer, *Geschichte der Botanik*, 4 vols. (Königsberg, 1854–59) discusses authors chronologically from classical times. E. L. Greene, *Landmarks of Botanical History*, Smithsonian Miscellaneous Collections 54 (Washington, D.C., 1909) and A. Arber, *The Natural Philosophy of Plant Form*, (Cambridge, 1950) analyze Greek views, especially of Theophrastus. F. S. Bodenheimer, *The History of Biology* (London, 1958) includes English translations of ancient non-Greek texts.

D. M. BALME

[See also **Atomism;** Causation; Chain of Being; Classification of the Sciences; **Evolutionism; Genetic Continuity;** God; Platonism; Stoicism.]

BIOLOGICAL HOMOLOGIES AND ANALOGIES

Introduction. In his study of evolution, or arrangement of organisms into taxa, the systematic biologist makes continual use of the concepts of homology and analogy. The historical development and current meanings of these concepts are of interest both because they help show how the science of systematics is done, and because of the intriguing frequency with which philosophically mistaken arguments have intruded into the science.

The fundamental aim of taxonomy is to classify organisms into groups in a biologically meaningful way. The Linnean hierarchy, built along lines formally proposed by Aristotle, is the familiar result. A major purpose of evolutionary biology is to discover the actual diverging sequences of organisms, commonly described by phylogenetic trees, and the causes of those divergences.

Historical Development of the Concept of Homology. It is in the light of these goals and difficulties that one should consider the prevalent evolutionary definitions of homology and analogy. According to G. R. De Beer, "The sole condition which organs must fulfill to be homologous is to be descended from one and the same representative in a common ancestor." G. G. Simpson also defines homology in terms of common inheritance: "Homology is resemblance due to inheritance from a common ancestry." Usually, this evolutionary sense of homology is contrasted with analogy, resemblance due to common function. A frequent example of homology is the relation between a bird's wing and a mammalian forearm; of analogy, the relation between the wing of a bird and of an insect.

It has recently been claimed by several authors that the evolutionary definition of homology is viciously circular, for "in order to show that a part of one organism, x, is homologous with a part y of another organism, it must be shown that they are derived from a part z in a common ancestor. But homology itself is invoked in identifying parts x and y with part z" (Jardine, 1967). It will be argued below that the circularity of De Beer and Simpsons' definition is not at all vicious, but whether it is or not, the circularity points up the priority of a nonevolutionary, phenotypic sense of homology, defined solely in terms of phenotypic similarity, and logically independent of criteria of descent.

A nonevolutionary sense of phenotypic homology was widely utilized prior to Darwin. In 1818, Geoffrey

St. Hilaire, in his *théorie des analogues* (where *analogue* is roughly equivalent to phenotypic homology), argued that animals conform to a common type; the analogy of parts was to be established by showing that they occupied corresponding relative positions in different animals—the *principe des connexions*. Owen, in his *Lectures* . . . (1843), defined homologue as "The same organ in different animals under every variety of form and function." In 1847 he distinguished special homology "the correspondence of a part or organ, determined by its relative position and connections, with a part or organ in a different animal," from general homology, "a relation in which a part or a series of parts stands to the fundamental or general type." Several authors in addition to Owen, most notably the poet Goethe, advocated this Platonic idealism of fundamental types, or common bauplans (construction plans) of which diverse organisms were seen as imperfect realizations.

Darwin himself utilized Geoffroy St. Hilaire's concept of homology in the *Origin of Species* . . . (1859): ". . . If we suppose that the ancient progenitor, the archetype as it may be called, of all mammals, had its limbs constructed on the existing general pattern, for whatever purposes they served, we can at once perceive the plain signification of the homologous construction of limbs throughout the whole class." Darwin, of course, thought homology evidence *in favor of* evolution, but he utilized a nonevolutionary, phenotypic concept of homology.

Both the Platonic idealism of fundamental types, and the nonevolutionary sense of homology soon came under attack. In 1870, E. R. Lankester argued that St. Hilaire's and Owen's use of homology "belongs to the Platonic school. . . . Professor Owen . . . would understand by homologue 'the same organ in different animals under every variety of form and function'. . . . But how can the sameness (if we may use the word) of an organ under every variety of form and function be established or investigated? . . . to settle this question of sameness, an ideal 'type' or a group . . . had to be evolved from the human mind, . . . then it could be asserted that organs might be said to be the 'same' in two animals" ("On the Use . . . ," pp. 34–43). In the place of this idealist, purely phenotypic concept of homology, Lankester proposed a definition resting in part on common ancestry. "Structures which are genetically related, in so far as they have a single representative in a common ancestor, may be called homogenous" (idem). The term "homogeny" was not accepted, but its definition was used to define "homology" in the evolutionary sense later advocated by Simpson, De Beer, and others.

Are Lankester's points well taken? It is true that Owen's and Goethe's fundamental type or common bauplan has the features of a Platonic Ideal of which all organisms of the type were imperfect realizations. Their major motivation for the supposition of a fundamental type was the belief that in order to class a group of organisms together, the organisms must jointly share some common features, the fundamental type.

This understanding of the nature of universals has been criticized by the philosophers Ludwig Wittgenstein and (more recently) Morton Beckner. Wittgenstein points out that we apply the concept "game" to diverse objects which share different attributes in partially overlapping ways but have no single attribute in common. Classification of objects together requires only that we have repeatable criteria for their classification. Thus phenotypic homology need not lead to idealism.

Furthermore Lankester's definition of homogeny (homology) failed to meet his own criticisms of Owen, for to establish that two structures have a single representative in a common ancestor requires showing that the two structures are homologous to that single ancestral representative; and the only criterion of homology to which Owen can allude is phenotypic homology. If phenotypic homology inevitably led to idealism, then Owen's redefinition of homology would fail to escape the disaster.

There were, however, more valid grounds for the introduction of Lankester's sense of homology. It was argued that evolutionary theory provided a criterion by which to distinguish "true" from accidental homology. Because the traits of organisms overlap in complex ways, phenotypic clusters can be made discrete only somewhat arbitrarily. Hence, phenotypic homology is somewhat arbitrary. However, evolution of organs in one species took place, presumably, in only one way. By utilizing the criterion of descent of two structures from the same representative in a common ancestor, evolutionists like Simpson and De Beer felt they were providing a less arbitrary and more biologically meaningful sense of homology. With the wide adoption of this evolutionary sense of homology, the meaning of the term had changed. In its new sense, homology required the theory of evolution for its definition. This is one of many cases in science in which a theory built in part with data described by one concept, later is used to change the meaning of that concept itself.

But the clarity of aim of the evolutionists to introduce a concept of homology which overcame the arbitrariness of mere phenotypic homology does not completely attain its goal. To establish that two structures are homologous, in Simpson's sense, requires showing that a phylogenetic hypothesis is true. But part of the evidence that the hypothesis is true stems from phenotypic resemblance of structures in fossil and living organisms. And that phenotypic homology suffers from the arbitrariness which the evolutionist hoped to avoid. Nevertheless what the evolutionist does do is to construct and attempt to verify phylogenetic hypotheses on the basis of *all* the available information, including not only phenotypic homology but also temporal relations among structures in the fossil record, as well as considerations about possible sequences of change in structures, which minimize the total number of changes which must be supposed to have occurred. For the evolutionist, the statement that two structures are homologous is the result of a great deal of theory building. Because the evolutionist utilizes other criteria in addition to phenotypic similarity in asserting that two structures are homologous, he is able to say that two phenotypically dissimilar structures are homologous; for example, the bones of the mammalian middle ear and their homologues in fish.

The evolutionary sense of homology has held sway for nearly a century. It is currently facing vigorous attack by systematists who wish to substitute a purely phenotypic sense of homology. The argument is not merely semantic, for it expresses very different convictions about how best to do systematics.

The pheneticists (who wish to classify organisms on the basis of clusters of phenotypic traits) raise three major arguments against the traditional evolutionary taxonomist. 1. The evolutionary sense of homology is claimed to be viciously circular, for homology must be utilized to show that two structures are descended from the *same* representative in an ancestor. 2. The pheneticists argue that the traditional evolutionist has poorly defined criteria for asserting the phenotypic similarity of organisms. 3. Worse, it is argued, the traditional taxonomist interjects speculative phylogenetic hypotheses into his very phenotypic classification schemes, thus rendering them biased and unscientific, and rendering suspect any purported *evolutionary* homologies derived from the data.

In place of these putatively objectionable practices, the pheneticist, and in particular, the numerical taxonomist, wishes to substitute less biased, more reliable methods (Sokal and Sneath, 1963); therefore, they have introduced "operational homology" (Sokal and Camin, 1965). Unit characters, such as eyes: red, blue, green, etc., are chosen (Colless, 1967); and, on the basis of a set of such characters and their "states" for each organism in a sample, similarity among groups of organisms is computed. Many techniques of calculation of similarity have been generated (Sokal and Sneath), depending upon whether each unit character is considered of equal or differing weight. Diverse functions on these characters are computed as measures of similarity or "distance" between organisms, and diverse types of cluster and factor analysis are utilized to generate clusters.

The claims for scientific respectability of these techniques are: 1. The criteria by which organisms are judged similar are explicit and repeatable, in contrast, the pheneticists allege, to the unclear criteria by which traditional taxonomists talk of similarity among organisms. 2. The phenotypic clusters found by these techniques are supposed to be free of phylogenetic speculations, or, more strongly, free of theory, and unvarnished data on which to build theory.

Can these arguments be maintained by the pheneticist against the traditional evolutionary taxonomist? First, the circularity ascribed to the evolutionary sense of homology also applies to the purely phenotypic sense of homology. The evolutionist's homology is circular because of his reference to the "same" ancestral structure; but that "same" is just the circle the phenotypic sense of homology requires. If it is a vicious circle, both evolutionist and pheneticist would be trapped, but the circle is benign. Many concepts can only be defined by reference to a self-defining set of terms. For example, "homologus," "similar," "resembling," "almost the same," . . . etc. Benign circles are not limited to biological concepts, a "rule" cannot be understood without the ideas of "correct" and "wrong," nor they without it.

The pheneticist's hope for a "theory-free" operational homology is illusory. No operation is completely free of theory; measuring the same ear length again requires a theory about measuring rods not changing length in these circumstances. Nor are the pheneticists' similarity measures free of phylogenetic bias. Different choices of unit characters or different computation schemes will yield different phenetic clusters consistent with diverse phylogenetic sequences. Suppose the pheneticist deduced from his clusters a presumptive phylogenetic sequence which happened to be inconsistent with the temporal relations in the fossil record. Faced with disconfirming evidence, he might doubt the deductions, doubt the fossil record, or doubt the adequacy of his clustering techniques or choice of unit characters. If he were willing to consider altering his unit characters or clustering techniques, then he would be doing what he accuses the traditional evolutionist taxonomist of doing, namely, redefining his phenotypic classification scheme to fit with other phylogenetic data or hypotheses. If he would never change his clustering technique, he might be asked to justify his position, and would find it hard to do so.

Finally, the pheneticist is wrong in asserting that

the traditional evolutionist taxonomist must be unscientific since he cannot make explicit and simple the criteria by which he judges organisms similar. An art critic can correctly recognize a Picasso, but would probably be unable to make all his criteria explicit and simply measurable. While the numerical taxonomist's measures are probably more repeatable, and perhaps more easily learned than those of the traditional taxonomist, numerical methods nevertheless are not necessarily more meaningful measures of phenotypic similarity than the traditional evolutionist methods.

In brief, the differences between those who support a phenotypic and those who favor the evolutionary sense of homology is not as great as the furor of current debate makes it appear. Both utilize a phenotypic sense of homology. The pheneticist must admit that his operational homology is neither theory-free nor unbiased with regard to phylogenetic hypotheses, and that the evolutionary taxonomist is not necessarily unscientific for his lack of simple measuring operations.

Serial, Sexual, and Genetic Homology. While the evolutionary and phenotypic senses of homology are the most fundamental, several derivative senses of the term are commonly utilized. Serial, sexual, and genetic homology apply to entire organs; amino acid sequences in proteins and base sequences in DNA allow the application of homology at the molecular level.

Serial homology refers to more or less identical, repeating structures in an organism, for example, the vertebrae or teeth. The criteria for serial homology include phenotypic homology of different structures in the same adult, phenotypic homology of structures in the embryo, similarity of connections of the repeating parts, and phylogenetic arguments. The phenotypic similarity of teeth, vertebrae, ribs, etc. of an adult mammal are obvious. Even if vertebrae in the adult were grossly different, however, their claim to serial homology might still be made on the basis of the serial homology of the embryonic somites from which they arose. Thus, ontogenetic data can be utilized to demonstrate serial homology. Similarity of connections of the humerus and femur help establish them as serially homologous structures. Even if structures were very different, if they could be shown to have evolved from structures which were themselves serially homologous, then the derived structures might also be said to exhibit serial homology.

The occurrence of serially homologous structures provides an important clue about both evolution and ontogeny. It appears that it is relatively easy to evolve by changing the number of repeating units which occur in an organism. Unfortunately, very little is known about how repeating structures are generated, or how their number is controlled.

Sexual homology refers to structures which differ between the two sexes of the same species, but which derive from a common embryonic rudiment. For example, the mammalian penis and clitoris are homologous structures deriving from the same region of the genital ridge. The criteria for sexual homology are therefore the phenotypic homology of embryonic parts and careful comparative anatomy of the stages of embryonic development in the two sexes.

In its original sense, genetic homology meant that if structures in two organisms were the consequence of the action of the "same" gene in both organisms, then those structures were homologous. The homology of the structures was a consequence of the homology of the gene(s). Unfortunately, there is no simple correspondence between the genotype and phenotype of an organism. Alteration of a single gene may have effects on many phenotypic traits, and alteration of each of many genes may have the same effect on a given phenotypic character. A consequence of this complexity is the great difficulty in trying to prove that a given phenotypic character in two organisms is due to the action of the "same" gene(s) in both. It is the common experience of geneticists that if two initial populations undergo an identical selection regimen which successfully maximizes some trait, then the gene modifications which underlie that change in the two populations can differ, and usually do differ strikingly. Application of the notion of genetic homology in such instances is useless. Because of these difficulties, genetic homology is not widely utilized.

Ontogenetic criteria of homology had wide application when the Recapitulation Theory was accepted. If ontogeny recapitulates phylogeny, then to establish the evolutionary sense of homology between two organs—that they were derived from the same part in a common ancestor—it was sufficient to show they had the same origin in ontogeny. In 1870, Karl Gegenbaur stated that special homology is the relationship between two organs which have had a common evolutionary origin, and which, as a corollary, have arisen from the same embryonic Anlage. However, E. B. Wilson (1895, p. 101) and De Beer (1958) have shown cases of homologous adult structures derived from different embryological origins. Such a straightforward application of ontogenetic criteria no longer suffices to prove that two adult structures are homologous in the evolutionary sense.

Molecular Homology. In the 1950's and 1960's the notion of homology has begun to be extended to the molecular level, to the comparison of nucleotide sequences in the DNA's of different organisms, and to the comparison of amino acid sequences in proteins from different organisms. If the work to establish molecular homology is great, so too are the conceptual rewards. One of the most difficult handicaps of classical genetics and evolutionary studies is, as we have noted, the lack of a simple relation between the genotype and phenotype of an organism. A consequence of this complexity is that if two classes of organisms exhibit a certain degree of phenotypic difference, one cannot usually determine the extent of genotypic difference between the two classes. Thus, from classical genetics we can usually know neither the extent of genotypic change underlying the observed phenotypic alterations in evolution, nor, therefore, the rate at which the genotype changes in evolution.

These difficulties are partially overcome by considering nucleotide sequences in DNA and amino acid sequences in proteins. Since the nucleotide sequence of the DNA is the genotype, comparison of nucleotide sequences in different organisms is the most direct means of assessing the extent of genetic change in evolution, and genetic homology between species. However, such an assessment is not as straightforward as one might have hoped. In the first place, direct analyses of truly long sequences of bases in DNA are not currently available. Estimations of similarity of nucleotide sequences between DNA's utilize indirect techniques which only establish approximate homology, not identity of sequence. These techniques will be described later.

Even were it possible to obtain quite detailed nucleotide sequences for the DNA of two organisms, say bacteria, estimation of the extent of genotypic difference between the two would remain difficult. The concept of the extent of genotypic difference is ambiguous. Ambiguity resides in the dual reference of "genotype" to the actual physical structure of the DNA, the sequence of bases, and also to the DNA as the carrier of genetic information. If one is referring to the physical genotype, then the extent of difference between two genotypes is simply the number of homologous loci at which the nucleotides differ. Alteration in the informational genotype is related in rather complex ways to alteration in the physical genotype. Amino acids are coded for by triplets of nucleotides; most amino acids are coded for by two or more codons. Thus, some nucleotide substitutions change a codon to a second codon for the same amino acid. Such a substitution alters the physical genome, but leaves the informational genotype unaltered. Physical genotypes different at many loci can be the same informational genotype. Conversely, nearly identical physical genotypes can be radically different informational genotypes. This possibility is a consequence of the fact that codons are triplets, and an amino acid sequence is specified by a sequence of triplets in which the nucleo-

tides are "read" from a specific starting point, three at a time. A deletion of a single nucleotide can cause a "reading frame shift" in which all codons downstream from the deletion are misread and a large number of incorrect amino acids are incorporated into the protein. A small change in the physical genotype yields a large change in the informational genotype. If one is concerned with the extent and rate of alteration of the informational genotype in evolution, one must view with caution data derived from estimates of physical homology of the DNA's of various organisms.

Indirect physical techniques to study the extent of base sequence homology of the physical genotype depend upon the DNA's duplex structure whose complementary strands may be separated and caused to recombine. Since single-stranded DNA components from different origins may also be induced to form "hybrid" structures, a means is afforded by which to assess genetic relationships among organisms. It can be shown that duplex formation between single strands derived from DNA of the same or nearly identical species occurs readily, but fails to occur if the strands are derived from very different organisms.

Results of such studies (Bolton, p. 77) indicate that phenotypically similar animals have very similar DNA base sequences. Furthermore, ". . . the similarities and differences in polynucleotide sequences quantitatively indicate the extent of the taxonomic category to which the systematist refers. Thus, among the primates, a superfamily distinction means that about one-quarter of the polynucleotide sequences are different, half are different for subordinal separation, and about three-quarters for ordinal distinction." Bolton also notes that "the quantitative similarities in polynucleotide sequences among vertebrates can be related to the time at which the lines of organisms in the present diverged from one another in the geologic past according to the paleontologist's judgment." Bolton's figure shows a linear decrease in the logarithm of DNA similarity with time.

While Bolton's data gives a good indication of the rate of alteration of a physical genome in evolution, it remains difficult to relate the results to the extent and rate of change of the informational genotype in evolution.

A conclusion reached by Britten and co-workers (1968, p. 529), is that many nucleotide sequences occur repeatedly in the DNA of higher organisms, there being many DNA families, each with many nearly identical copies of one sequence. The existence of these homologous DNA sequences renders the rela'' n between the physical and informational genotype even more complex, for the functional significance of the redundant DNA is not known. Britten's data also casts doubt on

Bolton's conclusion about DNA homology among species, for Bolton probably measured only highly redundant DNA sequences.

In contrast to changes in nucleotide sequences which may occur without alteration of the informational genotype, changes in amino acid sequence are evidence, by definition, of alteration of the informational genotype. With the exception of substitutions of nucleotides which do not change the amino acid specified, substitution of a single nucleotide results in the substitution of a single amino acid at a locus in the polypeptide. Since the assignment of codons to amino acids is now fairly well established, it is now possible to say which amino acid substitutions can occur by substitution of a single nucleotide in a codon. Some amino acid substitutions cannot be made by altering a single nucleotide, but would require the simultaneous alteration of two or three nucleotides; or else, since nucleotide substitutions must usually occur one at a time, intermediate proteins with an amino acid different from both the first and final form, must have existed.

Partial or complete sequences of amino acids have now been worked out for several sets of homologous proteins in different organisms, for example, hemoglobin and cytochrome C (Fitch and Margoliash, 1967). By utilizing arguments about minimal possible changes causing sequences of amino acid substitutions, coupled with assumptions about nonreversal of changes, it is possible to arrange contemporary proteins into presumptive branching phylogenetic sequences (ibid.).

Evidence supporting the *deduced* branching phylogenetic relations can be sought in the fossil record. The form of argument utilized is closely similar to that noted by E. O. Wilson in 1965 for deducing consistent possible phylogenies based on gross phenotypes of contemporary organisms. Utilizing such techniques on cytochrome C, Fitch and Margoliash (1967) have produced a phylogenetic tree linking fungi, yeasts, nematodes, fish, birds, and mammals, which is very similar to phylogenetic trees proposed by classical zoologists. The number of amino acid substitutions, coupled with time estimates derived from the paleontological record, can give an estimate of the rate of mutation of the informational genotype. It will be of particular interest to compare the rates for proteins performing diverse functions, for the rate must depend in part upon the strictness of selective constraints on workable amino acid sequences.

The extent of homology in amino acid sequence for some proteins is enormous; neurohypophysial peptide hormones hardly differ from man to shark (Acher, 1969). Other proteins exhibit far less homology, differing in many loci in many different ways. The occurrence of such proteins, all performing the same function in different animals, has led some biologists to suppose that some amino acid substitutions do not affect protein function and are therefore not subject to selection. By random drift, large numbers of such substitutions are claimed to accumulate, so that these homologous proteins differ at many loci but continue to function.

Amino acid sequence homology is also utilized to help establish possible common evolutionary ancestry for different proteins. For example, the alpha, beta, delta, and gamma chains of hemoglobin have long identical sequences (Fitch and Margoliash, 1967). This argues strongly that the four protein chains were derived from some single gene, perhaps by its endoreplication to form the sort of redundant DNA of which Britten has spoken, and then the further evolution of the four genes.

Clearly, the extension of the concept of homology to the molecular level promises to be exceptionally rewarding.

Analogy. Analogy is commonly defined as similarity of function, and is opposed to the evolutionary definition of homology in terms of common ancestry. It is often unclear whether analogy is meant to be restricted to nonhomologous structures. The source of this unclarity rests, in part, upon uncertainty whether the evolutionary, or a phenotypic notion of homology should be utilized. Granted the evolutionary sense of homology, it becomes possible to distinguish similarities between organisms which are not due to homology; thus, a bird's wing and a butterfly's wing are not homologous despite phenotypic similarity. If we utilize only a phenotypic concept of homology, it is unclear how we are to distinguish similarities between organisms which are homologous from similarities which are not homologous but analogous. A virtue of the evolutionary concept of homology, therefore, is that it allows us to discuss ways in which distinct (nonhomologous) phylogenetic lines have become phenotypically similar. The notion of analogy facilitates descriptions of phylogenetic convergence.

The notion of analogy can be extended to the molecular level. One can consider different molecular structures performing the same function, for example, different oxygen carrying pigments, or structurally different enzymes capable of catalyzing the same reaction. The matter is of great importance, for it would be helpful to have some estimate of the number of diverse ways in which any chemical (catalytic) job might be accomplished in order to gain insight into the difficulty which evolution faced in finding at least one workable mechanism, or in evolving new ones. Despite its importance, little work has been done in this potentially interesting area.

241

In summary, homology and analogy are working tools with which the biologist attempts to classify organisms into hierarchically nested taxa, formulate phylogenetic hypotheses, discuss evolutionary forces, describe ontogenetic similarities, and, in short, carry on his science.

BIBLIOGRAPHY

R. Acher, "Évolution des Structures des hormones Neurohypophysaires," *La Spécificité zoologique des Hormones hypophysaires et leurs activités*, Éditions du Centre National de la Recherche Scientifique, No. 177, (Paris, 1969). M. Beckner, *The Biological Way of Thought* (Berkeley, 1968). E. T. Bolton, "The Evolution of Polynucleotide Sequences in DNA," *Mendel Centenary: Genetics, Development, and Evolution*, ed. R. M. Nardone (Washington, D.C., 1968). R. J. Britten and D. E. Kohne, "Repeated Sequences in DNA," *Science*, **161** (1968), 529. D. H. Colless, "An Examination of Certain Concepts in Phenetic Taxonomy," *Systematic Zoology*, **16** (1967), 7. C. Darwin, *On the Origin of Species by Natural Selection* (London, 1859; many reprints). G. R. De Beer, *Vertebrate Zoology* (London, 1928); idem, *Embryos and Ancestors*, 3rd ed. (Oxford and New York, 1958). W. M. Fitch and F. Margoliash, "Construction of Phylogenetic Trees," *Science*, **155** (1967), 279. K. Gegenbaur, *Grundzuge der Vergleichenden Anatomie*, 2nd ed. (Leipzig, 1870). R. Goldschmidt, *Theoretical Genetics* (Berkeley, 1955). N. Jardine, "The Concept of Homology in Biology," *British Journal for the Philosophy of Science*, **18** (1967), 125. E. R. Lankester, "On the Use of the Term Homology in Modern Zoology," *Annals and Magazine of Natural History*, **6**, series 4 (1870), 34–43. R. Owen, *Lectures on the Comparative Anatomy and Physiology of the Invertebrate Animals* (London, 1843); idem, "Report on the Archtype and Homologies of the Vertebrate Skeleton," *Report of the British Association for the Advancement of Science*, **16** (1847), 169. J. M. Rendel, *Canalization and Gene Control* (London, 1967). E. G. St. Hilaire, *Philosophie Anatomique* (Paris, 1818). G. G. Simpson, *Principles of Animal Taxonomy* (New York and London, 1961). R. R. Sokal and P. H. A. Sneath, *Principles of Numerical Taxonomy* (San Francisco, 1963). R. R. Sokal and J. H. Camin, "The Two Taxonomies: Areas of Agreement and Conflict," *Systematic Zoology*, **14** (1965), 176. E. B. Wilson, "The Embryological Criterion of Homology," *Biological Lectures, 1894, Marine Biological Laboratory* (Woods Hole and Boston, 1895). E. O. Wilson, "A Consistency Test for Phylogenies Based on Contemporaneous Species," *Systematic Zoology*, **14** (1965), 214. L. Wittgenstein, *Philosophical Investigations* (Oxford, 1958).

STUART A. KAUFFMAN

[See also **Analogy in Early Greek Thought; Biological Conceptions in Antiquity;** Evolutionism; Game Theory; **Genetic Continuity; Recapitulation.**]

BIOLOGICAL MODELS

THE MAKING of models, so much a part of all the natural sciences, and increasingly of the social sciences, has been a central feature of the development of biology. Indeed, modern biology springs from that ur-model, the *bête-machine*, described in 1637 by René Descartes:

If there were a machine that had the organs and the external features of a monkey, or some other dumb animal, we would have no way at all of knowing that it was not, in every aspect, of the very same nature as those animals (*Discours de la méthode*, Part V).

For Descartes, even man would be indistinguishable from such an automaton if it were not for his power of communicating and apprehending complex thoughts by means of speech. Even this exception to the machine model of living organisms was challenged early in the history of biology with the publication of La Mettrie's *L'Homme machine* (ca. 1750).

The machine-animal, and its extension the machine-man, are more than simply examples of model and metaphor in biology; they are at the basis of all model-making, for they are a statement of an underlying relation between effects and causes in living organisms. It was precisely the element of will and the infinite variety of personal and idiosyncratic response to external conditions that led Descartes to exempt man from the constraints of such a model. Animal behavior seemed to him stereotyped, without variety, and totally predictable from external conditions, so that for beasts the relation between cause and effect was unbroken. Not so for man, whose essential nature lay in his free will. It seems reasonable, on the other hand, that it was La Mettrie's Jansenist training, with its heretical denial of free will, that made possible his inclusion of man in the realm of automata. As we shall see, the Cartesian view of cause and effect, while an integral aspect of model-making for a large part of modern biology, has been replaced, for some problems, by a weaker form of relationship among events. These are the so-called "stochastic" theories in which the relationships between events are described by probability statements rather than by exact one-for-one correspondence. The influence of Cartesianism is very strong, however, and stochastic theories are admitted only slowly, grudgingly, and with a certain condescension toward those "inexact" fields of biology that seem to require them. As in nineteenth-century physics, some feel that uncertainty in a system is a reflection of epistemological rather than ontological properties so that with the aid of a "Laplace's demon" it would be possible to reformulate stochastic theories in completely deterministic form. Thus, after 300 years, Descartes' original metaphor maintains its powerful influence on model-making in biology.

WHAT IS A MODEL?

Biologists, like other scientists, use the notion of model in a host of ways. At one extreme they may mean a scaled-up, three-dimensional wire and plastic representation of a cell. At the other, they may mean an abstract structure such as a "mathematical model" of evolution which may consist only of a set of differential equations. In what sense can the wire and plastic cell be said to be the same kind of structure as a set of differential equations? And in what sense are they like a mouse, which is said to be a "model organism" for the study of certain physiological or genetical problems?

The similarities of these models can best be understood by beginning with the most abstract. The basic theory of evolutionary genetics is well worked out, based on a detailed knowledge of the mechanics of inheritance and certain empirical information about the biology of reproduction and survival of a variety of organisms. This theoretical superstructure is sufficiently complex that quantitative predictions of the outcome of evolutionary changes cannot be made by inspection. In order to find out what is entailed by the theory in any particular case, a model is built. First, the theory is abstracted and is framed in terms of a logical flow diagram involving dummy variables and logical relations among these variables. Then this logical structure is realized by a program for a computer, or a set of matrices and matrix operators, or a system of difference or differential equations. All these realizations are isomorphic with each other and with the original logical structure.

A second possibility is that a series of resistors, capacitors, and other electric and electronic devices is used to make a physical model such that these electrical elements produce a set of electrical quantities (current, voltages) that behave isomorphically with the dummy variables of the abstract system. Alternatively, a "model organism" may be employed, like the fruit fly, *Drosophila*, which is thought to be a specific realization of the same general principles as are expressed in the abstract representation of the original theory. In fact, with a physical analogue as complex as a "model organism," the explicit construction of the abstract system that served as the pattern for the mathematical realizations may never be made. Rather, the model organism is assumed to embody the general properties of the system being modelled and, in fact, the general theory of evolutionary genetics supposes

that all organisms embody certain general relations which are the subject of investigation. A model organism can then be used, and often is, in the absence of a well worked-out theory of a biological process on the assumption that general biological similarities between the systems will guarantee isomorphism with respect to the specific aspects under investigation.

The differences between the mathematical model, the electronic model, and the model organism as realizations of the underlying abstractions, are of great importance. The physical entities in the latter two kinds of models carry with them certain intrinsic properties that are different from those in the original being modelled. That is, these physical realizations are *metaphorical* and their iconic elements can be a source of serious difficulty. The physical realizations were chosen because some set of their properties was isomorphic with some set of properties of the original system or theory. In the case of the electronic analogue, the theory of capacitors, resistors, and vacuum tubes is so well understood and the empirical properties of these objects are so different from the system being modelled that there is no danger of confusion from the metaphorical elements. That vacuum tubes glow, get hot, break when jarred, make a tinkling sound when knocked together, will in no way confound the biologist since he is unlikely to confuse these properties with the properties of evolving organisms. In the case of model organisms, however, the danger is very great, because the metaphorical elements introduced by these organisms are in some cases so subtly different from the properties being modelled, that they cannot be distinguished, yet they produce great distortions.

Moreover, since such metaphors are often introduced without an explicit laying out of the abstract system of which the model should be a realization, there is no clear way of differentiating relevant from irrelevant from obfuscating properties of the model. For example, *Drosophila* was used for a long time as the model for the genetic mechanism of sex determination in man, because of a general similarity of genetic mechanisms between flies and man. But this has turned out to be completely wrong, and the conclusions that arose from this model were erroneous. This danger does not arise only from using complex organisms as realizations. The "digital computer" model of the central nervous system has been one of the most misleading and possibly harmful examples of allowing metaphorical properties to intrude. In this case such properties as redundancy checks, topological relationship between physical elements and conceptual elements, and the bit structure of information characteristic of electronic digital computers, although all metaphorical, were taken to be

243

isomorphic with the elements of the central nervous system, whereas they certainly are not. It is for this reason that an explicit abstraction of the original system, followed by a realization of that abstraction in either an abstract or physical form is much preferable to modelling by generalized and "felt" analogy.

There is some confusion in biology between "models of" and "models for." The isomorphisms with particular biological systems are "models of." But models in the sense of ideals or patterns, like the "model of a modern major general," are also found in the biological literature. The essential difference is in their epistemological status. "Models of" are not intended, especially when they are abstract, as contingent. They are analytic isomorphs of some phenomenon or system. They may be good or bad models as they are perfect or imperfectly isomorphic, but they cannot be said to be true or false. On the other hand, "models for" like the logistic model of population growth or the Lotka-Volterra model of species competition, or the gradient model of development, are taken as statements about the real world, as contingent, and are in fact assertions about the way organisms really behave. Sometimes such models (patterns) are introduced as examples of how nature *might* be, but they very soon become reified by biologists. Such "models" are most common in those branches of biology where there is little or no theoretical basis. In these cases it is quite proper to speak of "testing the model" since it is not really a model but a hypothesis. Unfortunately, confusion between these two senses of "model" sometimes results in an attempt to test a "model of" which always results in a vacuous "confirmation" of the model. Since the model is analytic, it must be, and always is, confirmed. Some such "tests" of analytic models go on in population biology, where a model organism is placed under extremely well controlled experimental conditions so that it realizes a mathematical structure that has been solved. If the mathematics has been done competently, the model, which is a living computer, confirms it. But, of course, no "test" (except of the competence of the investigator) has been performed.

FUNCTIONS OF MODELS

Model-making in biology serves much the same set of functions as in any science. The special complexity of many biological systems and the apparent diversity of biological phenomena place a rather different weight on various functions of modelling in biology than in the physical or social sciences.

1. Models have an *experimental convenience*. Fruit flies are easier to breed than man, and the giant axon of the squid is easy to manipulate in neurophysiological experiments. The very great delicacy of many biological materials and especially the idiosyncrasies of each species, make the search for "model organisms" in which particular features are convenient for investigation one of the outstanding features of research strategy. Most important advances in biology depend upon finding just the right "model organism" or "model system" for investigation. The best known example is the dependence on the use of bacteriophage for the development of molecular genetics (Cairns, Stent, and Watson, 1966). This case also shows how unique aspects of the model system itself, its metaphorical content, can distract attention from the central features of the realization. A great deal of the research on bacteriophage is now concerned with the peculiar properties of this parasite interacting with its host, properties that are irrelevant or even misleading for general genetical problems. At the present time a determined search is under way for a model organism for the study of the molecular and micro-anatomical basis of central nervous system function, based on an explicit list of desirable model properties.

2. Second in importance for models in biology is the function of *computation*. An increasing number of biological theories are framed in terms of numerically quantified variables. Even when the variables are themselves qualitative ("on" vs. "off" in nerve firings, "male" vs. "female," "gene A" vs. "gene a"), many theories are probabilistic and provide only probability distributions for the states, even for fixed inputs. The computation of such probability distributions cannot be carried out by observing nature since only single realizations of particular input sets exist. It is not possible, for example, to build and check a quantitative theory of population extinction by observing actual populations becoming extinct. Extinction is reasonably rare in nature and no two populations have the same starting conditions or environments. A theory of extinction is expressed in terms of a very large number of variables including certain stochastic inputs from the physical environment. Such theories are modelled by analogue or digital computer programs in which there is no metaphorical element and the model is isomorphic, with stochastic variables introduced to provide an empirical probability distribution of results. An alternative has been to create large numbers of controlled populations in the laboratory or on islands.

3. Of lesser importance to biology is the function of *reification*. In physics, inferred entities like electrons and constructs like the photon are reified in macroscopic models, presumably because one cannot "understand" or "comprehend" them otherwise. Most of the entities of biology are either macroscopic or can be visualized with optical devices. As molecular biology has grown, however, with its concept of gene as molecule and with its preoccupation with the mechanical interactions between molecules, there has been an increase in macroscopic modelling. Molecular models of metal or rubber in which atoms and chemical bonds are represented by three-dimensional objects with exactly cut angles and shapes are now common in biology. Most of these models are built in order to "have a look at" a complex biological molecule because it is felt that somehow its three-dimensional structure will provide some intuition about its function. Closely related to this kind of comprehension is a form of weak hypotheses testing that accompanies reification. When J. D. Watson and F. H. C. Crick were investigating the molecular structure of DNA, they built metal realizations of their hypothetical structures, based on numerical information from X-ray crystallography. A number of those did not fit together too well (one is described as a "particularly repulsive back-bone model") while the final, correct solution looked right ("Maurice [Wilkins] needed but a minute's look at the model to like it"). The fact that many of the structures seemed strained and tortured while the one model had an elegant and easy-fitting look was important in reaching the final conclusion about the correct molecular configuration (Watson, 1968).

4. Slowly, biological model-making is coming to serve as a function of *unification*. Biology has been marked in the past by particularism, by the notion that most generalizations are only trivially true, and that what is truly interesting and unique about biological systems is their variety and uniqueness, arising from their complexity. Even a great generalization like Darwinism allows for such a vast variety of forms of natural selection and variation, that evolutionists for many years concentrated on individual patterns of evolutionary change. This has been even truer of ecology, which has remained anecdotal and particularist in the extreme. Abstract models usually framed in logical and mathematical terms with little or no iconic element, have come into use in an attempt to unify large areas of biological investigation. Computer simulations especially have shown that a model involving only a few genes and a fairly simple set of assumptions about the environment will predict a great variety of possible evolutionary outcomes depending upon the initial state of the population that is evolving. Models of coupled harmonic oscillators appear to be predictive of events in the central nervous system, embryonic development, and physiological rhythms, and may indicate an underlying general mechanism for all these diverse phenomena.

5. Unification of diverse phenomena can be accomplished by increasing complications of models. A sufficiently complex model will be homomorphic with (structurally similar to) a vast variety of phenomena, but trivially so. But models in biology are increasingly being used for *simplification* as well. A new technique in the investigation of problems in community ecology is to make a series of models with fewer and fewer entities, variables, and syntactical rules in an attempt to find the "simplest" model that will give a satisfactory account of the observations. While this seems a commonplace description of how science in general is done, it has not been true of community ecology in the past. The explicit program of R. MacArthur and R. Levins (1967) to express the ecological niche in terms of a very small number of abstract dimensions sufficient to explain the numbers of organisms of different species coexisting, is a radical departure in ecology and one not universally approved. The opposite approach, that of "systems analysis" (Watt, 1968) is to build a model so complex that it approaches as closely as possible an isomorphism (one to one correspondence) with the natural systems. In part, this difference in approach reflects a difference in intent. The systems analytic model is designed for the control of particular pest organisms, or the management of wildlife. As such it is concerned with a particular organism in a particular circumstance. The minimal model is esteemed chiefly for its elegance and is viewed as a part of the general program of natural science—to explain as much as possible by as little as possible.

DETERMINISTIC AND STOCHASTIC MODELS

Descartes' machine has been the meta-model on which most biological models have been patterned. It is a clockwork machine designed so that a fixed input will result in a fixed output. The input-output relation is one-one or many-one, but never one-many. A perturbation at any point in the structure results in an exactly predictable response (including no response) at every other part of the structure. This meta-model is widely accepted in biology and molecular biology. The program of molecular biology is identical with the program described by Descartes in Part V of the *Discourse on Method*. The present description of the action of genes in controlling protein synthesis, which is the core of molecular biology, is isomorphic with the description of an automobile factory including quality control, inventory control, assembly lines, and the like. There is even a conscious exclusion of ambiguities when they appear in experimental data, because of the *a priori* certainty that the correct model is a Cartesian one. For example, the present picture of the action of genes is that each triplet of bases in the DNA molecule specifies a particular amino acid to be added to the protein. The experimental results that established the correspondence between triplet and amino acid showed that a particular triplet could cause the incorporation of several amino acids *in vitro*, but one more than others. It was assumed that this ambiguity was an experimental artifact and that genes are more exact than chemists. In general, molecular biologists deal with all-or-none concepts, with switchings-on and switchings-off of genes, with repression and de-repression. While the methods and data of this kind of biology are quantitative and continuous, the interpretations are qualitative and discrete. It is not accidental that statistics and probability, the fitting of curves, and the estimation of parameters, is not part of the apparatus of modern molecular biology.

A quite different world view is reflected in the models constructed for the analysis of population phenomena like evolution and ecology. The models are Laplacean rather than Cartesian. Chance elements are built into the models, although this does not imply that the phenomena being modelled are themselves really uncertain. That is, most biologists adhere to a deterministic view of phenomena but assume that a large number of small deterministic effects that cannot and need not be analyzed, give an apparent indeterminacy to phenomena at a higher level.

In stochastic or probabilistic models the correlative statements connecting variables are of the form "If X takes the value x then Y takes the value y with probability $f(y|x)$." That is, each rule becomes a table of probabilities of y given x, or a function for generating those probabilities. Realizations of such models then require generations of "random" sequences, or, more usually, *pseudo-random* sequences, which are indistinguishable from randomness by nearly any criterion, yet are produced by an analytic rule.

Such stochastic models can then be set in motion over and over again to produce empirically an array of outcomes for any given input, since the random sequence generator never repeats itself. For example, in primitive populations, marriages are contracted according to certain age, clan, and relationship preferences. These rules are not rigid, however, but can be expressed as probabilities. If a village has a small population size, the subsequent history of marriages, births, and deaths cannot be exactly given but various histories may occur with different probabilities. It is relatively simple to simulate the history of such a village in a computer program and then to run hypothetical village histories over and over again from which an array of growth rates, pedigrees, total birth and death rates will be produced. This array is a picture of the probability distribution of outcomes predicted by the theory.

While this kind of stochastic modelling is very common in population biology and ecology, it raises a serious problem. Since a range of outputs will occur for a given input, only the weakest kind of comparison with nature is possible. There is only one primitive tribe with a unique history. Is this history "explained" by the theory that has been modelled, when that model produces an array of results among which the observed history may very well lie? What kind of observed history would be at variance with a model that produces an array of results? About the best that can be done in those areas of biology is to say that a given observation in nature is reasonable under the theory, that it is not surprising given the hypothetical structure. The method of making such judgments is the method of statistical testing. The model is used to construct a calculating engine which produces a probability distribution of outcomes, given the hypothesis. The actual case is compared with this probability distribution, and if it is very improbable, the hypothesis is rejected as an explanation of the natural event. The difficulty is that many theories, especially in evolutionary genetics, when modelled, turn out to give such a broad array of results that almost any observation is compatible with them.

Modelling serves a function that becomes apparent in biology, but not in the physical sciences. If theories contain a stochastic element and if only unique realizations of particular cases occur, model building may be used to show that *no choice among theories can be made at some levels of theory making*. These conditions, which apply in much of population and evolutionary biology, may also turn out to have the same effect in social science.

BIBLIOGRAPHY

For a detailed categorization and bibliography of models in biology, see W. R. Stahl, "The Role of Models in Theoretical Biology," *Progress in Theoretical Biology*, **1** (1967), 165–218. See also M. W. Beckner, *The Biological Way of Thought* (Berkeley, 1968), Ch. III; R. B. Braithewaite, *Scientific Explanation* (Cambridge, 1953), Chs. III, V; J. Cairns, G. S. Stent, and J. D. Watson, *Phage and the Origins of Molecular Biology* (Cold Spring Harbor, 1966); H. Freudenthal, ed., *The Concept and the Role of the Model in Mathematics and Natural and Social Sciences* (Dordrecht, 1961), 1–37, 163–94; R. MacArthur and R. Levins, "The Limiting Similarity, Convergence and Divergence of Coexisting Species," *The American Naturalist*, **101** (1967), 377–85; A. Rosenblueth and N. Wiener, "The Role of Models in Science," *Philosophy of Science*, **12** (1943), 317–20; J. D. Watson, *The Double Helix* (New York, 1968); K. E. F. Watt, *Ecology and Resource Management* (New York, 1968).

R. C. LEWONTIN

[See also **Biological Homologies;** Evolutionism; **Genetic Continuity;** Man-Machine; Recapitulation.]

BUDDHISM

1. The Founder. Buddhism is the religion which was founded by a historical person in India, who was later called "the Buddha." The founder of Buddhism was a man known as Gotama Siddhattha (in Pāli) or Gautama Siddhārtha (in Sanskrit). Although his date is not clearly ascertainable, he is the first man in Indian history whose date can be assigned to a limited period with any degree of certainty. There is a minor difference between Northern and Southern traditions concerning the dates of the life and death of the Buddha. Southern Buddhists, following the Ceylonese tradition, accept the year 544 B.C. as the year of his death, and on that basis celebrated the 2,500th anniversary in 1956. European scholars have rejected this chronology as incompatible with the dates of the Indian kings who were contemporaries of the Buddha. Thus a somewhat later date is sought.

Many Japanese Buddhists accepted a Northern tradition conveyed to China by a monk called Saṅghabhadra in A.D. 489, according to which they celebrated the 2,500th birthday in 1932. However, the Jōdo, Shin, and Nichiren sects did not join with them since the founders of these sects had adopted the legend that the year of the Buddha's death was 949 B.C., as fixed by the Chinese priest Fao-lin (A.D. 572–640). Needless to say, even the followers of these sects do not believe this legend literally nowadays. Hakuju Ui, the late Buddhist scholar of Japan, comparing the legends set forth in Sanskrit, Tibetan, and Chinese versions of the scriptures, fixed the date of the Buddha as 466–386 B.C. The dates of King Aśoka, on whose life Ui based his computations, have been altered by recent research, so the correct dates for Buddha would be 436–383 B.C., if his arguments are to be accepted. Even though there is no agreement concerning the exact chronology, Japanese and Chinese Buddhists were glad to collaborate with Southern Buddhists in their 2,500th-year ceremonies honoring the Buddha.

Gotama the Buddha was born at Kapilavastu in what is now Nepal near the border of India, the son of a nobleman of the Sākya clan. When about twenty-nine years of age, he left his wife, his little son, and his father, and renounced the world. As an ascetic he became a disciple of several teachers in succession, but did not find satisfaction in their teaching and resolved to seek truth for himself. Finally, at the spot now known as Bodh-gaya in Bihar, he attained Enlightenment at the age of thirty-five; he is therefore called the Buddha "the Enlightened One" or "the Awakened One." From this time until his death at the age of eighty, he spent his life in teaching his disciples, constantly traveling, except in rainy seasons, in the area along the River Ganges to deliver sermons to people. He died quietly, surrounded by his disciples, at a place called Kuśinagara near the border between Nepal and India.

2. Historical Development. In the latter half of the third century B.C., Buddhism spread rapidly during the reign in India of King Aśoka, who supported the Buddhist order and sought to extend the teaching of the Buddha throughout his empire. He sent missionaries to the various countries known at that time, such as Ceylon, Burma, Macedonia, and Egypt. A bilingual edict by Aśoka in Greek and Aramaic has been found in Afghanistan. Since that time Buddhism has become a world religion, with Ceylon as the center for the spread of Southern Buddhism. Meanwhile, in India the Buddhist order came to be divided into two schools, Conservative (*Theravāda*) and Liberal (*Mahāsaṅghika*), finally subdividing into about eighteen schools in the second century B.C. Some of these schools showed liberal tendencies in thought and discipline towards reform, and towards adaptating themselves to social changes. The most important of these schools is the Sarvāstivādins.

The social movements of liberal Buddhists in India, coupled with new ideas and practices, developed gradually, and found their culmination in the creation of a new Buddhism called the Mahāyāna ("Great Vehicle") in contrast with the traditional, conservative Buddhism, which was depreciated as the Hīnayāna ("Lesser Vehicle"). The rise of the Mahāyāna system is probably to be placed in about the first and second centuries A.D. The new, reforming sects called themselves Mahāyāna because they thought of their system as (1) large and vast, (2) one which can save *many* living beings, and (3) a system which is *superior.* Mahāyāna believes that the teachings of Buddhism will vary according to the different climatic and cultural situations in which it finds itself, that they will change and develop through the years, and that even at the outset not all of the Buddha's teachings were included in the canon. Mahāyāna advocated salvation by grace of Buddhas and Bodhisattvas (aspirants to Buddhahood), who were ardently worshipped and invoked. Among the followers of Mahāyāna there were many merchants and traders, some of whom had become very rich due to their trade with the Hellenistic world or with the Roman empire. The unit of Indian gold coins, i.e., dīnāras, was exactly the same as that in Rome, i.e., denarius, in terms of appellation and weight. The prestige of some traders almost surpassed that of kings. Until the tenth century Hīnayāna and Mahāyāna thrived side by side in India. Huge temples and monasteries with luxurious halls and elaborate carvings were built by rich lay believers to accommodate monks and nuns. The images of Buddhas and Bodhisattvas were made. A great number of philosophical treatises, hymns, religious stories, etc., were composed.

There were two philosophical schools of Mahāyāna; the Mādhyamika school founded by Nāgārjuna (ca. A.D. 150–250) and the Yogācāra school founded by Maitreyanātha (ca. A.D. 270–350) or Asaṅga (ca. A.D. 310–90). The Mādhyamika school advocated the philosophy of Voidness (śūnyatā); that everything is devoid of abiding substance and that Voidness gives the basis for ethical and religious practice. The Yogācāra (or Vijñānavāda) school advocated a sort of idealism, saying that everything manifests itself as the manifestation of Store Consciousness (ālaya-vijñāna), the fundamental principle of representation of all phenomena. Its philosophy is identified with the "Representation Only" or "Ideation Only" theory (vijñaptimātratā).

Buddhism could not completely eradicate the popular beliefs of Hinduism current among common people. These tended to become predominant from the fourth century on, with the decline of the trader class due to the suspension of commercial interchange with the West, so that from the eighth century on Buddhism was greatly influenced by Hindu popular beliefs. Some Buddhists came to practice esoteric, mysterious rites. This form of Buddhism was called "Esoteric Buddhism" (Vajrayāna, "Diamond Vehicle").

The Muhammedan conquest of North India (1193–1203) caused the downfall of Buddhism, which was finally uprooted in India. While Hinduism, which had taken to its grassroots, could not be easily destroyed, Buddhism, which had been supported by many kings, merchants, and landowners, was extirpated at one blow by the Muhammedan army. Temples and monasteries were destroyed; monks and nuns were killed. Buddhism did not revive again on the soil of India until it was re-introduced from Buddhist countries in the twentieth century.

Owing to the efforts of Buddhist missionaries, Buddhism was introduced, in about the first century A.D., to Persia, Afghanistan, and Central Asia (Kuccha, Khotan, etc.), and then to China. It was then introduced to Korea in the latter half of the fourth century, and to Japan in the sixth century, first via Korea, and later directly from China. Buddhism, especially in the form of Esoteric Buddhism, came to Tibet in the seventh century; Tibetan Buddhism is called Lamaism by foreigners. ("Lama" means a spiritual leader.)

In China and Japan thirteen major sects came into existence, of which Zen is one. Zen is the Japanese equivalent of ch'an in Chinese, and of dhyāna ("meditation") in Sanskrit. Zen Buddhism is a sect, which, while having its roots in Indian dhyāna, gradually

moved away from the quiet and imaginative Indian contemplation to a specifically Chinese religious practice, and became highly influential in Japanese culture. Another noteworthy sect in China was the Pure Land (Ching-t'u) sect which stressed the worship of Amitābha Buddha (Amida in Japanese, "the Buddha of Infinite Life and Splendor") who was supposed to be located in the Pure Land (or "the Extremely Pleasant Land") in the western direction from this earthly world. Among present-day Chinese Zen and Pure Land Buddhism have been amalgamated into one. In Japan the latter has been the most popularly influential sect, whereas Zen Buddhism was influential among the upper classes such as samurai and landowners.

3. Buddhism Today. The estimates as to the number of Buddhists in the world today range all the way from 200 million to 850 million. By United Nations estimates (1967) there are over 1 billion 300 million people in the countries in which Buddhist influence is an important factor—Burma, Ceylon, Thailand, Cambodia, Laos, Vietnam, Nepal, Sikkim, India, Korea, Mongolia, Japan, and China. If China (650 million) is omitted from that figure, on the ground that it is very difficult to estimate the influence of Buddhism in Communist China, there are 650 million people in the remaining Buddhist countries. Of that number, at least 50 million are followers of Southern Buddhism (Theravāda), and about 125 million are avowed followers of Northern Buddhism (Mahāyāna).

The whole Buddhist world can be divided into two, Southern and Northern Buddhism. The former is Conservative Buddhism, and the latter is a newly developed form of Buddhism, which appeared after the Christian era. The former is now ardently adhered to in South Asiatic countries, i.e., Ceylon, Burma, Thailand, Laos, and Cambodia. These Buddhists call themselves "Theravādins," those who profess Theravāda, which appellation means "the Way of the Elders" (vāda means "school," "way," or "ism"; thera means "the elder.") This is the Buddhist school based on the canon written in the Pāli language. It asserts that it follows insofar as possible the practices and teachings of the time of the Buddha, although there have been considerable changes since then. In the past there were some other schools of Conservative Buddhism besides Theravāda, which have now almost all vanished.

Northern Buddhism calls itself Mahāyāna ("Great Vehicle") because it claims to save a great many people by the altruistic activity of its followers. Mahāyāna is now prevalent in Nepal, Sikkim, Tibet, Mongolia, China, Vietnam, Korea, and Japan.

Southern Buddhism has preserved the original features of early Buddhism rather intact. The attitude of its followers is conservative and traditional. Mahāyāna has, on the other hand, been apt to adapt itself to the climatic and social environment in which it has spread. Theravāda claims itself to be the genuine form of Buddhism, having preserved the true doctrine of the Lord Buddha, whereas Mahāyāna, which has always been in close contact with the common people, has vehemently attacked the Hīnayāna Buddhists for their self-complacent and self-righteous attitude. However, there is some unity in the two divisions, for Mahāyāna has also treasured much of the teaching which has been preserved in Conservative Buddhism. Theravāda has maintained a high degree of consistency in teachings and practices, while great diversity has grown up in Mahāyāna due to its more liberal and elastic attitude.

In India today, there is no Buddhist sect extant, although Buddhist influence by tradition can be noticed in the daily life of the Hindus. The revival of Buddhism which occurred recently, from the end of the nineteenth century on, has been chiefly due to the efforts of the members of the Mahabodhi Society, which started under the auspices of Ceylonese Buddhists. Conversion to Buddhism in India is nowadays most conspicuous among the Untouchables. The number of Buddhists increased rapidly from 180,800 in 1951 to 3,250,000 in 1961.

In the South Asiatic countries there is now only one form of Buddhism, Theravāda. In Central Asia Buddhism has almost vanished. In Nepal and Sikkim, Buddhism only prevails in the form of Esoteric Buddhism (Vajrayāna). In Tibet, Lamaism, which is an amalgamation of Esoteric Buddhism with popular faiths, prevails with Lamas as spiritual leaders, although their spiritual prestige has greatly declined due to the Communist invasion in 1959.

Uniformity in Buddhism is established in China, Korea, and Vietnam, where Zen (*Ch'an*) Buddhism, fused with Pure Land Buddhism (and with Taoism, in China) is now the only remaining sect. The traditions of all the rest of the sects have almost gone out of existence. In Japan, by contrast, there still exist approximately thirteen major traditional Buddhist sects, many of which can no longer be found in China or in India. However, the ways of living followed by Japanese priests, who are mostly married, are highly worldly and secular.

Challenged by Western culture and by changing forms of society, Buddhism has been forced to reform itself. There are many signs of vitality in the new educational institutions, the new research projects, philanthropic activities, etc., of Buddhist groups. The movements of Buddhist reformers have become culturally influential, and international activities by Buddhists have become more and more widespread.

4. Scriptures. The scriptures of Buddhism are called "the Three Baskets" (*Tipiṭaka* in Pāli; *Tripiṭaka* in Sanskrit). Both Southern and Northern Buddhists have always esteemed the scriptures as the supreme source of knowledge, the standard by which everything should be judged. The only notable exception to this reliance upon the scriptures has been in Zen Buddhism, with its emphasis upon direct insight and its assertion that only silence avoids violating the truth. And even Zen does not entirely reject the scriptures. In Southern Buddhism also there are some teachers who emphasize meditation virtually to the exclusion of study of the scripture, but the general pattern throughout all Buddhism has been one of great reliance upon the scriptures. The decision as to which of the scriptures will be accepted as authoritative differs with sects. Even though almost all Buddhists will base their faith on the scriptures, there is no one scripture which is accepted as having the same authority for everyone who calls himself a Buddhist, and very few are accepted equally throughout all the Buddhist world.

However, there is one formula which is universal. That is the formula by which one expresses one's faith in the three refuges (which are called "the Three Jewels," *tiratana* in Pāli), the Buddha, the Teaching (*Dhamma*), and the Brotherhood (*Saṅgha*). It runs as follows: "I put faith in the Buddha. I put faith in the Teaching. I put faith in the Brotherhood." This formula is recited in the Pāli language in South Asiatic countries, and in the language of the people concerned in North Asiatic countries. In Southern Buddhism the scriptures in the Pāli language are accepted as the final authority; in Northern Buddhism the corpus of scriptures contain many more commentators' texts, which were mostly composed after the Christian era.

5. The Fundamental Attitude. Buddhists should follow the path which was prescribed by the Buddha. For this purpose faith is indispensable, but it is only a preliminary requirement for one's practicing the way. According to Buddhism faith should not be in contradiction to reason. The Buddha was described as one who has reasoned according to the truth rather than on the basis of the authority of the Vedas or tradition. Buddhists have accepted two standards for the truth of a statement: it must be in accordance with the scriptures and must be proved true by reasoning.

Buddhism presupposes universal laws called *dharmas*, which govern human existence and may be known by reason ("dharma" means etymologically "the one that keeps"). Personal relations should be brought into harmony with the universal norms, the universal laws which apply to all existence, regardless of time and space. Buddhism claims to be the Path which is regarded as the universal norm for all mankind, conformity to the nature of the universe. A Buddha is simply one who has trodden this Path and can report to others on what he has found. Buddhism theoretically admits the existence of many Buddhas.

On the other hand, metaphysical speculation concerning problems not related to human activities and the attainment of Enlightenment is discouraged—e.g., problems such as whether the world is infinite or finite, whether the soul and the body are identical with, or different from, each other.

6. The Main Teachings. Buddhism has asserted the following: life is suffering; the struggle to maintain individuality is painful. It asks: Why do we suffer? The answer is, because of the transiency, the impermanence of human existence. There is no substance which abides forever. Suffering is caused by desire, since what we desire is impermanent, changing, and perishing. These desires are caused by ignorance. We are ignorant concerning our true nature and the nature of the universe in which we live. And we may be freed from our ignorance by following the Path. Through the wisdom which comes from reflection on the transitoriness of life, by following the Path taught by the Buddha, everyone can attain Enlightenment, which characterizes Nirvāṇa, the ideal state.

The teaching of Non-ego has been regarded as characteristic of Buddhist thought. The Buddha clearly told us what the self is not, but he did not give any clear account of what it is. He did not deny the soul, but was silent concerning it. He did not want to assume the existence of souls as metaphysical substances, but he admitted the existence of the self as the subject of action in a practical and moral sense. He seems to have acknowledged that the true self in one's existence will appear in our moral conduct conforming to universal norms. To make clear the teaching of Non-ego, Buddhists set forth the theory of the Five Aggregates or Constituents (skandhas) of our existence. Individual existence is made up of these Five Aggregates or Constituents as follows:

1) Corporeality or Matter (rūpa),
2) Feelings or Sensations (vedanā),
3) Ideation (saññā in Pāli, saṃjñā in Sanskrit),
4) Mental formations (saṅkhāra in Pāli, saṃskāra in Sanskrit),
5) Consciousness (viññāna in Pāli, vijñāna in Sanskrit).

None of the Five Aggregates is the self or soul (attā in Pāli, ātman in Sanskrit), nor can we locate it in any of them. On the other hand, as early Buddhism did not deny the self in the ethical sense, later Mahāyāna developed the theory of "the Great Self."

We are always distressed by cravings, thinking that there is something real in satisfying these desires in the mundane world. This mistake about the true essence of reality is the cause of all the sufferings that affect our lives. Ignorance is the main cause from which false desires spring. Ignorance and false desires are the theoretical and the practical sides of one fact. So when knowledge is attained and cravings are quenched, suffering comes to end. This state is called "Nirvāṇa," which means the "cessation" of selfish desires or ignorance.

Between ignorance and suffering, Buddhist thinkers found and formulated several intermediate steps, and this formulation was called "Dependent Origination" or "Origination through Dependence" (Paṭiccasamuppāda in Pāli, Pratītyasamutpāda in Sanskrit). In Mahāyāna philosophy this term came to mean "Interrelated Existence of all Things." It asserts that nothing can exist separately from other things, and that all things are interrelated.

In ancient India, belief in rebirth or transmigration was generally current, and this conception was associated with the doctrine of karma (meaning "act," or "deed"), according to which good conduct brings a pleasant and happy result, while bad conduct brings an evil result. The karma committed with previous intention will come to fruition, either in this life or in afterlives after death. However, the acceptance of this belief by Buddhists gave rise to a difficult problem: How can rebirth take place without a permanent subject to be reborn? The relation between existences in rebirth has been explained by the analogy of fire, which maintains itself unchanged in appearance, yet is different in every moment. In order to meet this vulnerable point, some Buddhists later assumed a sort of soul, calling it by different names. This assumption gave rise to the conception of the fundamental consciousness (ālaya-vijñāna) of the Yogācāra (or Vijñānavāda) school in Mahāyāna.

7. The Universe. Buddhism declares that everything has causes; that there is no permanent substratum of existence. There is general agreement that the only true method of explaining any existing thing is to trace one cause back to the next, and so on, without the desire or need to explain the ultimate cause of all things. The universe is governed by causality. There is no chaotic anarchy and no capricious interference.

The belief in karma and rebirth led to the assumption of good and bad places to which people could be born according to their deeds. The three spheres, or planes, are (1) the immaterial plane where pure spirits live, (2) the material plane where beings with subtle bodies live, and (3) the plane of desire which corresponds to our natural world, and in which the six classes of living beings—gods, men, departed spirits, animals, demons, and infernal creatures—live. Zen Buddhism in China and Japan, however, has been rather indifferent to the problem of the structure of the universe. Moreover, Buddhist intellectuals who have been educated in modern science, however devout they may be, do not believe this traditional cosmology.

Buddhism does not admit God as the creator of the universe. It asserts that the universe is without beginning and end, although one period of the universe consists of the four periods; origination, duration, destruction, and annihilation. These succeed one after another in cyclic change.

8. Buddha. The person who has attained Wisdom or who has realized universal norms (dharmas) is called the Enlightened One (Buddha). Theoretically there can be many Buddhas. Mahāyāna Buddhism developed the idea of the Threefold Body of the Buddha: (1) "the Body of the Law" (dharmakāya) is Voidness, the formless reality beyond our words and thoughts; (2) "the Body of Enjoyment" (sambhogakāya) means the void and absolute reality which, enjoying virtues as results of merits, has taken a merciful vow to live amid the empirical world, and to save it by leading it into wisdom; (3) "the Body of Transformation" (nirmāṇakāya) is a corporeal, preaching Buddha revealed in our empirical world, such as Sākyamuni Buddha.

9. The Institution of Buddhism. The Buddha established a religious order which has continued to the present day as one of the oldest and most influential orders of religious brethren in the oriental world. The Buddhist order (saṅgha), and the kindred religion called "Jainism," have survived longer than any other institutions. "Saṅgha," the appellation of the Buddhist order, means "congregation." In the days of the Buddha saṅgha in the political sense meant "republic," and saṅgha in the economical sense meant "guild." So various ways of managing guilds or republics, such as decision by voting, secret ballot, etc., were incorporated in the rules of the Buddhist order.

It is noteworthy that the Buddha organized the order of nuns also, in addition to that of the monks. Consequently the whole body of the Buddhist order consists of four kinds of followers: (1) monks (bhikkhu in Pāli, bhikṣu in Sanskrit), (2) nuns (bhikkhunī in Pāli, bhikṣuṇī in Sanskrit), (3) laymen (upāsaka), and (4) lay women (upāsikā). The central role of the order has been played by monks in South Asiatic countries and in China, where monks and nuns spend a celibate life in monasteries or nunneries.

In Tibet many monks have practiced celibacy; they belong to the Ge-lug or Yellow Hats sect. But others (the Nyng-ma or Red Hats sect) live a married life. In Nepal and Japan some Buddhist leaders are celibate and follow monastic disciplines, but many are married and live the life of a householder. Korean priests have observed celibacy very strictly for a long time, but in recent years some Korean priests have imitated the Japanese priests and have married. In an effort to get rid of everything Japanese, the Korean Government has been expelling married priests from the temples.

Monks are known as bhikkhus in South Asiatic countries, this term meaning "one who lives on alms." In Burma they are often called "Phongys" (phon means "great," gyi means "glory"). In South Asiatic countries monks are greatly respected and worshipped. Monks, when saluted, do not return salutation to laymen, even to kings and prime ministers, according to the traditional disciplines of their order. They take food, after seeking alms, which they may do only in the morning.

In Japan, the religious leaders are called by the Japanese equivalents of "priests," "monks," or "ministers," and are often given the honorary title of "Reverend." The English term bonze is a corruption of the Japanese word bōzu, which means "the head of a monastery," and was formerly an honorary title, but in the 1960's it came to be used in a derisive sense.

In Buddhism monks and priests are responsible for the spiritual guidance of laymen, and laymen are responsible for the support of the religious orders.

In Thailand, Cambodia, and Laos, all Buddhist laymen are expected to spend some time in a monastery receiving instruction in Buddhism; it is possible to be ordained as a monk and then return to lay life. Some remain as monks in monasteries for life. In Burma it is not uncommon for laymen to spend some time in monasteries, but they do not customarily receive ordination unless they intend to remain. In all other Buddhist countries, the practice of returning to lay life after receiving ordination is not usually approved.

The ceremony of ordination according to the rules of the Book of Discipline (Vinaya) is followed in South Asiatic countries. According to the Book of Discipline, a monk is dismissed when he commits one of the following four Major Offences: (1) sexual intercourse, (2) taking what is not given to him, i.e., theft, (3) claiming in public that he has already become a Holy Man, although he has not yet attained that state, and (4) killing a human being. The rules of discipline in Conservative Buddhism were for a long time the custom in Mahāyāna countries also. However, there was another informal self-vow ordination, practiced by some Mahāyānists—the Bodhisattva ordination—which became overwhelmingly prevalent in Japan. In Esoteric Buddhism the ritual of ordination by anointment with water is followed.

Throughout all the Buddhist world, the Buddhist community has never been organized around a central authority which could decree doctrines or practices which must be observed by all followers. Buddhists have been comparatively individualistic and unwilling

251

BUDDHISM

to submit to a rigid authority. Agreement as to the doctrines to be held and the practices to be followed has been reached by discussion within the community, guided by the scriptures accepted as a basis for their faith. In Southern Buddhism there is great unity, with the different sects playing only a minor role. In Tibet, although there are several sects, Buddhists there are united in most matters. In China the sectarian differences of the past have blended into one general form. Some writers say that Buddhism is practically extinct in Communist China. Only in Japan are there marked sectarian differences, but the authorities of the extant sects are not coercive. Collaboration among different sects is well performed.

10. The Mission of Buddhism. Throughout the long history of Buddhism covering almost twenty-five centuries, Buddhists have recognized their mission to spread the teachings of the Buddha throughout the world. Soon after the founding of the order, the Buddha sent out his followers on missionary journeys to spread the teaching "for the profit and good and happiness of the world" (*Mahāvagga* I, 6, 8, etc.).

The Buddhist teachings were considered universal and all-comprehensive, to be made known to all men for their enlightenment. This spread of Buddhism was marked by the devotion of monks and laymen, and conversion took place only by persuasion. There is no known case of conversion to Buddhism by the use of force. Even King Aśoka, under whose reign Buddhism spread as a universal religion in many countries, renounced the use of force.

However, Buddhist mission work, generally speaking, declined throughout the Buddhist world from the tenth century on. Under the impact of the spread of Christianity and communism, some Buddhist leaders have come to be enthusiastic in mission work; they have established some international organizations.

11. Ethics. The way of the Buddha is called the Middle Path because it avoids the extremes of the pursuit of worldly desires or the practice of several asceticisms. It must be adjusted to the infinitely varying circumstances of actual life. Evil actions are to be avoided by following the Middle Path or ethical practice. Only Pure-Land Buddhism has been an exception, with its belief that all living beings are sinful and are saved by the compassionate grace of Amitābha Buddha.

The fundamental principle of Buddhist ethics is that all men should develop an attitude of compassion (*maitrī*, literally "true friendliness"). If we allow the virtue of compassion or love of neighbors to grow in us, it will not occur to us to harm anyone else, any more than we would willingly harm ourselves.

The laymen should obey the five precepts which admonish him (1) not to kill, (2) not to take what is not given, (3) to refrain from unlawful sexual intercourse, (4) not to tell lies, (5) not to drink intoxicating liquors. (But in Tibet and Japan the fifth precept is often not observed.)

The duties which are stressed are those between parents and children, husband and wife, pupils and teachers, friend and friend, master and servants, and laymen and monks. The virtues stressed are (1) generosity, (2) benevolence, (3) cooperation, (4) service; these four are regarded as the fundamental ones for social life. Courtesy, sympathy, and honesty, etc., are also encouraged.

From the time of the Buddha, Buddhism has stressed the equality of man. The Buddha said: "For worms, serpents, fish, birds, and animals there are marks that constitute their own species. There are differences in creatures endowed with bodies, but amongst men this is not the case; the differences among men are nominal only" (*Suttanipāta* 602–11). There was no discrimination among the monks in the early Buddhist order. This sense of equality has been theoretically preserved throughout most Buddhist orders, although it has often been impaired due to political reasons.

12. Buddhism and the Polity. Buddhism came to flourish in each country under the patronage of rulers from Aśoka (third century B.C.), to Prince Shōtoku (sixth to seventh centuries A.D.) in Japan. On the other hand a hostile government led to the extermination of Buddhism in India. It was persecuted by the three emperors called Wu in China, and also was opposed on several occasions by the government of Japan, especially in the beginning of the Meiji era (1867–1912). The Communist government has greatly affected Buddhism in China and Tibet, to keep it under control.

In early Buddhism, the rights of a king were not considered to be sacred or conferred by the gods; the sovereignty of the kings was delegated to them by the people in ancient times. The Buddha said: "Kings are like venomous serpents. You should not make them angry. It is better not to come into contact with them" (*Saṁyutta-Nikāya* I, 69). It is said that the Buddha extolled a republican form of government realized among the Vajjis and other tribes. Such an unpolitical attitude could not be maintained, however, and as time went on both Conservative and Mahāyāna Buddhism were drawn into the political sphere. Frequently the state controlled Buddhism for its own purposes and such control was often detrimental to Buddhism.

In Tibet, the unique amalgamation of Buddhism and political power continued as the final authority, until the communist invasion by the Chinese army in 1959. Buddhism is the state religion of Thailand, Laos, and Cambodia. Many Buddhists in Burma and Ceylon argue that it should be the state religion in their countries.

252

In Japan, the Nichiren sect, and some of its new off-shoots (Shinkō Shūkyō), hold that the state and religion should be identified, and that the teaching of Nichiren alone should be adopted. Most of the other Japanese sects prefer noninterference on the part of the government. On the proper relation between Buddhism and the state, diversity of opinion exists in both Southern and Northern Buddhism.

In countries where Buddhism has flourished it has had considerable influence upon the administration of justice. In some countries of ancient India capital punishment and mutilation had been abolished due to the teaching of compassion. In Japan in the Heian era (the eighth to the twelfth centuries), when Buddhist influence was strong, there was no case of capital punishment. In Tibet, the thirteenth Dalai Lama abolished capital punishment and extreme mutilation. Generally speaking, when Buddhist influence was strong, punishment was lenient, and rarely cruel.

The use of military force by the state was renounced by Aśoka after he became a Buddhist, and there have been many Buddhist emperors since his time who have tried to govern by persuasion rather then by force. The Tibetans and Mongolians were transformed from fierce warlike nomads to a peaceful, friendly people by the acceptance of Buddhism. Some Confucians and scholars of Japanese classics criticized Buddhism on the ground that its emphasis on compassion tended to make poor soldiers. On the other hand, the samurai class in Japan once adopted meditative disciplines of Zen Buddhism as a part of their training to become brave warriors.

In China, Korea, and Japan, from about the sixteenth century on, Buddhism became separated from the ruling class, and the priests were obliged to turn to the populace for support, as the ruling class became materialistic. By contrast, in the countries of Southern Buddhism the laymen in the ruling class have still held to their Buddhism and have influenced the policies and culture of their countries.

Buddhist orders have not been strong enough in financial, administrative, and military power to oppose aggression by the secular, military power of kings of communist governments. And if they were to rebel, they would be easily suppressed.

In the 1960's democracy was observed in free Buddhist countries and totalitarianism abhorred. Buddhist monks and nuns were allowed to take part in politics. In communist countries Buddhist orders have been tolerated, although the lands once owned by them have been confiscated; still some expenses for their maintenance are met by the communist governments in China, Mongolia, etc. In the Soviet Union Buryat Mongolians remained Lamaists even in the 1960's.

The traditional pacifistic attitude of Buddhists can be noticed in such a political leader as U Thant, the third Secretary-General of the United Nations.

13. Ethics of Commerce. Buddhism at the outset arose in cities and especially won the support of kings and merchants. In ancient India, for example, it spread along the trade routes.

A hundred years after the demise of the Buddha a controversy occurred on ten topics, and the whole Buddhist order was divided into two groups. One topic at issue was whether monks could accept money as a gift by laymen. Conservative monks did not permit such gifts, but liberal monks did. The first attitude has been practiced by Southern Buddhists; the second by a sect called the "Mahāsaṅghika," and in later days by the Mahāyāna. Early in the Christian era some temples in India became very rich, being endowed with huge areas of land, and with funds which were donated by lay believers. The temples used the funds to develop small industries, and with the gains from these, and the rents from their lands, support was derived for the monks.

In Southern Buddhism monks were not permitted to engage in commercial activities. They were forbidden to cultivate land or to be involved in profit-making. They were not allowed even to keep any coins; they lived only on alms. In China most monks lived in the same way, but in Zen monasteries monks came to engage in raising food and in all sorts of manual labor to maintain themselves. The spirit of labor and service was encouraged. This way of life was introduced into Japan. In Japan today priests are not prohibited from engaging in commercial activities.

The Buddha also admonished laymen not to waste money on extravagant and passionate pleasures. Liquor and gambling were forbidden; frequenting the streets, visiting fairs, idleness, and associating with evil companions were discouraged. Consequently Buddhists in Southern Asia even today do not drink liquor. In China lay Buddhists drink, but monks do not. In Japan and Nepal most Buddhists do not prohibit drinking.

On the other hand, the virtue of diligence has been encouraged. By diligence and thrift one may accumulate riches.

> To him amassing wealth, like a roving bee
> Gathering its honey (and hurting naught),
> Riches mount up as an ant-heap growing high.
> When the good layman has so amassed wealth
> Able is he to benefit his clan.
> In four portions let him divide this wealth.
>
> .   .   .
>
> One portion let him spend and taste the fruit.
> To conduct his business let him take two (portions).
> And the fourth portion let him reserve and hoard;

So there will be wherewithall in times of need (*Sigālovādasutta* 26, trans. C. A. F. and T. W. Rhys Davids, slightly amended in collation with the Pāli).

Buddhism never denounced the accumulation of wealth; however, riches should be accumulated only by lawful means, and all people should benefit from it. Throughout all the Buddhist world there has been no thought of forbidding interest on loans. A reasonable interest rate has been regarded as permissible.

In China some monks engaged in philanthropic activities; they formed groups of Buddhists to lend money to people in need. In Japan some monks, in a similar philanthropic spirit, constructed rest-houses and hospitals, roads, ponds, bridges, and harbors.

In Indian Buddhism all vocations were permitted except selling slaves, weapons, and liquor. This ban on weapons and liquor was not observed in Japan.

15. *Buddhist Attitudes Towards Non-Buddhists.*
Tolerance has been an outstanding moral characteristic of Buddhism from earliest times. Buddhism has attempted to arrive at the truth, not by excluding its opposites as falsehood, but by including them as another form of the same truth. Buddhists are generally noted for their liberal attitude toward other religions, whether polytheistic, monotheistic, or atheistic. Buddhists admit the truth of any moral and philosophical system, whether primitive or developed, provided only that it is capable of leading men at least part way toward their final goal. Although Buddhism has been predominant in many Asiatic countries, there is no record of any persecution by Buddhists of the followers of any other faith. They have waged no religious war.

Buddhism has tolerated the various pagan faiths native to some countries of Asia which lack any clear religious doctrine. In South Asiatic countries, many Hindu gods and goddesses have been included in the religious ceremonies of the Buddhist community, and many Buddhists still observe festivals and customs associated with goblins or demons (*nats*) and other nature spirits of each country.

In China, Buddhism had actually been amalgamated with many Taoist beliefs and practices; many shrines were semi-Buddhist and semi-Taoist. Chinese legendary sages were worshipped in temples. The same tolerance brought about a blending of the various Buddhist sects in China producing one mixed form of Buddhism. The situation is similar to the condition of Buddhism in Korea.

In Tibet, Buddhists assimilated with Bonism, the native religion of Tibet, by incorporating many of its gods and goddesses into the lowest grade of Guardian Deities, without affecting the doctrinal integrity of Buddhism. The animal sacrifices were replaced with symbolic worship, and inner purification was taught in place of black magic.

In Japan, the indigenous gods and goddesses of Shintoism were dealt with in the same way. Till the eighth century they were assigned rather low positions, but later their positions became gradually higher and higher; they were regarded as incarnations of Buddhas and Bodhisattvas. The Japanese people very often do not distinguish between Buddhistic divine beings and Shintō gods. In the past in Japan there were very few shrines that did not have shrine-temples built in their confines, where Buddhist priests performed the morning and evening practices of reciting Sutras and served the shrine gods and goddesses together with Shintō priests. The majority of the Japanese pray before the Shintoist shrines and at the same time pay homage in Buddhist temples, without being conscious of any contradiction. A devout Buddhist is very often a devout Shintoist at the same time. Buddhist authorities do not interfere with Buddhists who go to Christian churches or attend Christian colleges to learn English or Western culture.

The relation between the Buddhists and the Hindus is viable insofar as Hindus regard Buddhism as a branch of Hinduism.

15. *Buddhist Influence on the West.* Evidence of any direct influence of Buddhism on the West in the period before Alexander the Great is dubious. It is still a matter of controversy whether the attitude of indifference and nonattachment which Pyrrhon of Elis (ca. 360–270 B.C.) showed towards his drowning teacher Anarxarchos, was derived from any knowledge of the Buddhist ideal of the Holy Person (Arhat). However, historical investigations have shown that many Greeks or other Europeans, living in the Middle East in the Hellenistic period, after the invasion of India by Alexander the Great in 327 B.C., professed Buddhist or Hindu faith. King Milinda, whose name is found in the title of the celebrated book in Pāli literature called *The Questions of King Milinda* was identified with Manandros, the Greek King, who ruled Western and Northern India in the latter part of the second century B.C. This book states that he was converted to Buddhism. He may indeed have been a devout Buddhist according to inscriptions, and because of the statement by Plutarch that the relics of the king were distributed for worship among eight tribes.

Apollonius of Tyana, a Neo-Pythagorean (first century A.D.) made a peregrination in search of the wisdom of the Brahmins. He is mentioned as a Buddhist in an Indian classical work, *Jagadgururatnamālāstava* by Brahmendra, an Advaita-Vedāntin, and in a commentary on this work, as shown by M. Hiriyanna (*Indian Historical Quarterly*, **2** [1926], 415–16). Some scholars say that Plotinus was influenced by the teachings of Buddhism, e.g., E. Benz, in *Indische Einfluss auf die Frühchristliche Theologie* (Wiesbaden, 1951). There are many similarities between the philosophy of Neo-Platonism and that of Mahāyāna Buddhism.

There is an hypothesis that Buddhism had spread to the islands of Britain before the introduction of Christianity, judging from a statement by Origen and the similarity of the images of the Celtic Cernunnos to those of the Indian Virūpākṣa and Śiva. British archaeologists officially reported (e.g., Sir John Marshall in *Taxila*, 3 vols. [1951], I, 22), that Buddhist sculptures of Gandhāra style were discovered in the ruins of ancient Roman cantonments in England. Buddhist images were also discovered in ruins in Sweden.

Scholars like James Moffatt (J. Hastings, *Encyclopaedia of Religion and Ethics*, Edinburgh and New York [1908–27], V, 401; XII, 318–19), say that the ascetic practices observed by the Essenes, who lived around the Dead Sea in the second century B.C., contained some Buddhist elements. Celibacy, vegetarianism, and a life of meditation practiced in monasteries in Egypt before the birth of Christ are held by some to be evidence for the influence of Buddhism.

A number of analogies have been pointed out between the life stories of Christ and Buddha, and also between precepts and parables in the Bible and the sutras. Scholars such as Arthur Christy (1932, pp. 255–56) and Richard Garbe in his *Indien und das Christentum* (1914; trans. 1959), assert that these analogies are not mere coincidence, but represent borrowing by the writers of the Bible. There is little doubt that the life stories given in apocryphal gospels seem to be modifications of the life of Buddha.

Gnostics were greatly influenced by Buddhism. Some scholars, following Ernst Benz, say that Basilides (second century A.D.) advocated an altruism based on the standpoint of Mahāyāna and held an idea of transmigration in the Buddhist sense. By recent studies Buddhist influence has been traced in the philosophy of Manicheism, and is found in the second and third centuries in the works of Pantaenus, Bardesanes, Clement of Alexandria, Origen, and Philostratus. It seems that the first Western philosopher who expressly referred to Buddhism was Clement of Alexandria (d. 215 A.D.). He says (*Stromateis* I, p. 305 A–B, as also Megasthenes, frag. 43), that some Indians worship *Boutta* (i.e., Buddha). The pyramid-worship he refers to in this connection apparently refers to the Stūpa-worship prevalent among the Indian Buddhists.

It was probably in the sixth or seventh century A.D. somewhere in Eastern Iran or Turkestan that the legend of Barlaam and Josaphat originated. "Barlaam" is a corruption of the Sanskrit word *bhagavān*, an epithet

for Buddha, and "Josaphat" derives from the Sanskrit word *bodhisattva*. This legend is a copy of the life of the Buddha made by some Christian missionaries for the purpose of facilitating Christian propaganda among people living in Buddhist countries. This story came to be very popular in the medieval West. Both Barlaam and Josaphat were venerated for a time as saints in the Catholic Church. Some of the Jātaka tales, parables, and other stories given in Buddhist scriptures find their counterparts in the Western world in more or less revised forms.

With the advent of Westerners to Eastern countries in the beginning of the modern age, Eastern languages and literatures came to be directly known to Europeans. A great many Eastern religious and philosophical works have been translated into Western languages. However, in the Renaissance period and in the European literature and philosophy of the seventeenth century little influence of Buddhism could be traced. What chiefly influenced Europe then was Chinese thought, especially Confucianism in a form rationalized and idealized by Western intellectuals. It was only in the eighteenth century that the influence of Buddhism could be seen in European literature and philosophy.

In the efforts to introduce Eastern thought Friedrich Max Müller (1823–1900) was a leading scholar of wide influence. He edited many Buddhist texts, and also a 50 volume series of translations called "Sacred Books of the East," which included various Buddhist texts of great importance. He was effective in spreading Buddhist thought. J. Estlin Carpenter developed comparative religion, by continuing the scholarship of F. Max Müller.

Thomas William Rhys Davids (1843–1922), with his wife, Mrs. C. A. F. Rhys Davids, established the Pāli Text Society in London (1881) to publish texts of early and Southern Buddhism in the Pāli language, and this set the line of Buddhist studies. American scholars such as Henry Clarke Warren and Franklin Edgerton (toward the end of the nineteenth century) made remarkable contributions in this field.

In the field of philosophy Schopenhauer expressly identified the essence of his philosophy with that of the Upaniṣads and Buddhism, as well as with that of Plato and Kant. His idea of "blind will" is related to the Buddhist concept of "Nescience" (*avidyā*). The philosophy of the "Unconscious" of Eduard von Hartmann derived from this line of thought. Along with Schopenhauer, Karl Christian Friedrich Krause, a mystical thinker of the early nineteenth century, was also influenced by Indian thought. He called his philosophical standpoint "Pan-en-theism." Schopenhauer's admirer, Paul Deussen, devoted his whole life to the study of Indian philosophy, especially Vedānta. He was the first scholar who ventured to write a comprehensive history of Eastern and Western philosophy entitled *Allgemeine Geschichte der Philosophie* (6 vols., Leipzig, 1906f.). His *Elemente der Metaphysik* (1877) was a reflection of the influence of Buddhist philosophy in the Western world.

Count Hermann Keyserling especially drew the attention of Westerners to the East. At the end of his unique work, *The Travel Diary of a Philosopher* (Darmstadt, 1919), he said that only the Bodhisattva ideal would save the whole world from confusion and destruction.

Karl Jaspers examined the significance of the philosophical views of various Buddhist thinkers. Albert Schweitzer, although he overtly criticized Buddhism, was influenced by its idea of the respect for life.

Buddhism as a religion was examined from the viewpoint of a sociologist by Max Weber to demonstrate his assertion that Buddhism could not contribute to the rise of capitalism as Calvinism did in the West. Rudolf Otto and other scholars of comparative religion recognized parallel developments between two world religions, Christianity and Buddhism. The studies of these scholars resulted in giving up the idea, held in general by Western intellectuals, that Christianity is the only true religion.

Eastern philosophy was introduced into America by Ralph Waldo Emerson, whose transcendentalism was greatly influenced by the philosophy of brahman in the Upanisads as well as by Buddhist philosophy. Henry David Thoreau tried to live a solitary life like a Yogin or a Buddhist recluse. In the 1950's and 1960's Aldous Huxley incorporated principal ideas of Vedānta and Zen in his writings. Critics and writers who show Buddhist influence include Alan Watts, Christopher Isherwood, and others. The standpoint of Charles Morris is somewhat similar to that of Early Buddhism, as he himself says. Irving Babbitt translated the *Dhammapada* with respect for the spirit of Buddhism, humorously criticizing his contemporary civilization.

The increasing interest in Eastern philosophy on the part of Western thinkers gave rise to "comparative philosophy." Paul Masson-Oursel (1882–) of France was probably the first scholar to use the term, in his *Philosophie comparée* (1923; trans. 1926). The East-West Philosophers' Conference has been held four times at Honolulu, since 1939, with philosophers of Eastern and Western countries participating, and the journal, *Philosophy East and West*, specifically directed to this kind of studies, with most of the issues under the editorship of Charles A. Moore, has been published by the University of Hawaii. The *Journal of the History of Ideas*, under the editorship of Philip P. Wiener, has in recent years included topics relevant to Eastern philosophy. A great many eminent philosophers, such

as William Ernest Hocking, Filmer S. C. Northrop, Van Meter Ames, Archie Bahm, Abraham Kaplan, Edwin A. Burtt, Georg Misch, Dale Riepe, and others, have engaged in studies of comparative philosophy. Such specialists of Indian and Buddhist studies as Helmuth von Glasenapp, W. Norman Brown, Daniel H. H. Ingalls, Walter Ruben, Constantin Regamey, Jean Filliozat, and others have published relevant works. All these scholars agree that Western philosophy is not the only philosophy of mankind, and that any philosophy which will develop in the future must also take note of Eastern, especially Indian and Buddhist, philosophy.

In the field of literature, many German writers of the nineteenth and twentieth centuries, such as Richard Wagner, Eduard Grisebach, Josef Viktor Widmann, Ferdinand von Hornstein, Max Vogrich, Karl Gjellerup, Fritz Mauthner, Hans Much, Albrech Schaeffer, Ludwig Deinhard, Karl Bleibtreu, Hermann Hesse, Adolf Vogel, and many others, wrote novels, poems, and dramas, clearly influenced by Buddhist or Eastern *Weltanschauung*. Significant for English readers, *The Light of Asia* (1879), a long poem on the life of Buddha, by Sir Edwin Arnold, was still widely read in the twentieth century.

Western thinkers influenced by Buddhist teachings did not accept the role of God as the Creator. A religion without the idea of God was something new in the eyes of Westerners, and they were attracted by the Buddhist ideal of Compassion which is supposed to permeate all living beings.

A Buddhist temple was established in 1924 in Berlin by Paul Dahlke; in London there has been a Buddhist Society since 1906. In North America there were about 174,000 Buddhists in the 1960's. Many Buddhist churches in America and Canada are mostly supported by Americans and Canadians of Japanese origin, but their influence has spread among others. *The Gospel of Buddha*, (1894), by Paul Carus, was warmly welcomed in America as a good introduction.

Japanese culture reflecting Buddhist influence was diffused internationally by the literary works in English of Lafcadio Hearn (1850–1904), a journalist from America who became a Japanese citizen, and by the writings of Wenceslau de Moraes (1854–1929), a Portuguese diplomat.

Zen Buddhism has come to be well known to Westerners through works by Japanese scholars. Daisetz Teitaro Suzuki wrote many works on Zen (chiefly Rinzai) in English, and lectured at various universities in the West. Shigatsu Sasaki and in 1930 Mrs. Ruth Sasaki established the First Zen Institute of America in New York. Nyogen Senzaki exerted influence in California. Books on Sōtō Zen in English have been published by that sect in Japan.

Some Americans welcome the practical and non-metaphysical character of Zen. The irrational and anti-traditional attitude of some Zen masters of the Sung Period of China appealed directly to American "beatniks" for the justification of their non-deferential and eccentric behavior. Some Americans observe the Buddhist life of solitude.

Pure Land Buddhism is becoming known to Americans, first because of the efforts of Buddhist missionaries such as Itsuzō Kyōgoku, and also from the evaluation by the scholars who took an interest in it, such as Paul Tillich, Robert H. L. Slater, and Kenneth W. Morgan.

The political ideal of Buddhism, as it was set forth by its leaders, is making an impression in world politics because it is observed by U Thant and some Buddhist statesmen of international significance. They abide by the Buddhist principles of pacifism and the unity of mankind.

BIBLIOGRAPHY

1. On Buddhism in General. P. V. Bapat, ed., *2500 Years of Buddhism* (Delhi, 1959). Edward Conze, *Buddhism, Its Essence and Development* (London, 1951; New York, 1959). Charles Eliot, *Hinduism and Buddhism: An Historical Sketch*, 3 vols. (London and New York, 1954). Kenneth W. Morgan, ed., *The Path of the Buddha: Buddhism Interpreted by Buddhists* (New York, 1956). Hajime Nakamura, *Ways of Thinking of Eastern Peoples*, rev. and ed. Philip P. Wiener (Honolulu, 1964). Junjiro Takakusu, *The Essentials of Buddhist Philosophy* (Honolulu, 1947).

2. On Indian Buddhism. S. B. Dasgupta, *An Introduction to Tantric Buddhism* (Calcutta, 1958). Nalinaksha Dutt, *Early Monastic Buddhism*, 2 vols. (Calcutta, 1941). Étienne Lamotte, *Histoire du bouddhisme indien, des origines à l'ère Saka* (Louvain, 1958). T. R. V. Murti, *The Central Philosophy of Buddhism* (London and New York, 1955). Govind Chandra Pande, *Studies in the Origins of Buddhism* (Allahabad, 1957). *Sigālovādosutta*, see *Dialogues of the Buddha*, trans. from the Pāli of the Dīgha Nikāya, by C. A. F. and T. W. Rhys Davids (London, 1957), Part III, p. 180. Th. Stcherbatsky, *The Central Conception of Buddhism* (London, 1924); idem, *The Conception of Buddhist Nirvāna* (Leningrad, 1927; reprint New York, 1965); idem, *Buddhist Logic*, 2 vols. (1930; many reprints). Edward J. Thomas, *The History of Buddhist Thought* (London, 1953). Maurice Winternitz, *A History of Indian Literature*, Vol. II (Calcutta, 1927).

3. On Chinese Buddhism. Wing-tsit Chan, *Religious Trends in Modern China* (New York, 1952). Yu-lan Fung, *A History of Chinese Philosophy*, trans. D. Bodde, 2 vols. (Princeton, 1952–53).

4. On Japanese Buddhism. Masaharu Anesaki, *History of Japanese Religions* . . . (1930; London, 1953; Tokyo and New York, 1963). Charles Eliot, *Japanese Buddhism* (London, 1935).

5. On Zen. Heinrich Dumoulin, *The Development of Chinese Zen* . . . , trans. Ruth F. Sasaki (New York, 1953); idem, *A History of Zen Buddhism* (New York, 1963). Daisetz Teitaro Suzuki, *Essays in Zen Buddhism* (London, 1926; New York, 1961).

6. On East-West Relations. Van Meter Ames, *Zen and American Thought* (Honolulu, 1962), contains an extensive bibliography. Arthur Christy, *The Orient in American Transcendentalism* (New York, 1932). Richard Garbe, *India and Christianity: The Historical Connections Between Their Religions*, trans. Lydia G. Robinson (La Salle, Ill., 1959).

7. Bibliography. *Bibliographie Bouddhique* [since 1928] (Paris). Shinso Hanayama, *Bibliography on Buddhism* (Tokyo, 1961).

HAJIME NAKAMURA

[See also Causation; **China;** Cycles; **God; Religion, Ritual in;** Sin and Salvation.]

CASUISTRY

THE WORD casuistry (literally "concern with individual cases") has been used in three different, if connected meanings. In its widest sense, it has described a mentality which pays closer attention to the concrete instance than to abstract generalities. In a narrower sense, it has been employed to characterize legal systems like those of the Anglo-Saxon countries under which all-inclusive norms are derived from judgments in particular lawsuits, instead of being laid down beforehand in rationally elaborated codes. In its narrowest sense, it refers to the use of subtle definitional distinctions in the handling of ethico-legal or purely ethical problems with the aim of drawing fine dividing lines between what is permissible and what is not. As this technique has at times been applied in order to excuse crimes and sins and to exculpate criminals and sinners, this last usage of the term (at present the most widespread) has contracted a definitely pejorative undertone.

In its best sense casuistry is opposed to inflexible, literal, or legalistic interpretation of moral rules; indeed casuistry rejects any attitude which absolutizes a general and abstract norm and insists on its all-round unyielding and quasi-mechanical application, while at the same time denying any abatement or adjustment to changing contingencies.

The historical appearance of casuistry has always been dependent on the existence of its opposite—ethico-legal or purely legal absolutism. It is in its nature a movement with the aim, first, of bridging the gap between the abstract and the concrete, the general norm and the individual case, and, second, of mitigating the rigor of the laws which must produce hardness and hardships if they are not made somewhat elastic in their application to particular problems. It was

257

because legalism was well-nigh lacking in Greece that casuistry, too, was largely unknown. A sharp distinction between the Is and the Ought was alien to the ethos of the Greeks; the grand aim of education was to inculcate the moral rule, or rather a moral character, in the heart of the individual; correspondingly, there was no formulation of moral codes which would confront man from the outside, as something essentially alien to him; and therefore there was no desire to wriggle out of the clutches of a law, be it law in the narrower sense of the word or moral law. Everything was, so to speak, elastic. In an atmosphere of this kind, casuistry does not unfold; there is just no call for it.

Everything was radically different in the orbit of Judaism. Here it was part of the unconscious metaphysic of the nation to assume that there was a sharp and thoroughgoing opposition between the Is and the Ought, and that therefore the Ought must confront the Is as something superior and demanding, indeed, as something absolute and unyielding, for (it was thought) it was only in this way that the required minimum of law-abidingness could be secured. The doctrine of original sin was the starting point, and the promulgation of the Torah or Sacred Law was the answer to it. The Law, as laid down in the Pentateuch, was both too abstract to be immediately applicable in most cases, and, especially in its ceremonial regulations, too minute and too full of perplexities not to generate a desire to make it, on occasions, less stiff and burdensome. Both facts stimulated the evolution of casuistical thinking, even in the earlier stages of Hebrew history. Later on, both legalism and its unavoidable adjunct and opposite, casuistry, received new impetus. When the Jews lost their freedom for a time during their Babylonian captivity, and when they forfeited it finally under Titus, the Law became the very Palladium of national existence. To let go of it, would have meant to lose everything. Therefore the dominance of the Law was greatly enhanced. It became inflexible and formal, and the result was that life, in an understandable counterstroke, fashioned casuistry as its logical and political complement and corrective. The development of Muhammadanism was somewhat similar. The Koran embodied law which claimed to be divine, i.e., of a validity beyond doubt and discussion. Yet it was too simple not to need specification, and when its rule was extended over larger areas, it was not easily applied to all the circumstances which it encountered. Law schools appeared, and had to appear, which prepared the universal imperatives for local use, and in the process they added a very rich and varied case law to the original revelation. The science which they founded and greatly developed was thoroughly casuistical.

Under the Christian dispensation, the area in which casuistry first made its appearance, was, not surprisingly, the activity of the Church which comes closest to the function and the practice of the law—the exercise of discipline, more concretely, the punishment of sins and sinners. From the third century onward, a certain casuistical content is increasingly characteristic of Christian literature. Writers like Gregorius Thaumaturgus and Cyprian give information about the penances which it is meet and right to impose where definite faults have been committed, and from these beginnings sprang the penitential books of later times. Irish and Anglo-Saxon texts spread far and wide and predominated between the sixth and tenth centuries. These early Christian casuistical publications aroused far fewer misgivings than their later—late medieval and early modern—pendants. The reason for this lies not only in a greater willingness to accept and to undergo the rigors of a stern law, but also in the fact that the ecclesiastical tribunals were, in every essential detail, very much like the secular ones. The bishop's sentence was seen as parallel to the judge's; in fact, he *was* the judge in his diocese. His activity in dealing with penitents was plainly legal. But in the application of laws casuistical practices and procedures were, and were seen to be, entirely justified, indeed, unavoidable. Everybody knew and realized that, as the Roman lawyers had taught, the salient act of the man on the bench was *subsumptio*, i.e., the subsumption of a concrete case under a general rule. Cases therefore had to be carefully distinguished; before *subsumptio*, there had to be *constructio*, an identification of their distinguishing marks. It must be remembered here that the old penitential procedure was public and formal. That alone made it similar to the state's jurisdiction and covered its methods with the mantle of legitimacy.

Much changed when the locus of penance shifted and the *forum externum* was replaced by the *forum internum*, i.e., when the treatment of sinners became more private and less formal. When auricular confession developed, the main function of the father confessor was no longer to sentence the sinner, though an element of this quasi-legal action unavoidably remained; it was rather to win him over to more moral modes of thought and action, to educate him. The emphasis was less on the past, the deeds done, than on the future, the conduct to be expected. This alone tended to soften the Church's penitential practice, and to make it more flexible, understanding, and patient. Furthermore, in many genuine penitents, an unreasoning fear of hell was found to be present which produced a psychological condition of great discouragement with consequences which were far from good in any sense of the word. This pushed the confessional practice further in the direction of what is sometimes called laxity. We can see how and why the word casuistry received the particular coloring with which it is now connected. But a further factor intervened. The father confessor was also a spiritual director. The laity had recourse to him, not only after a sin had been committed and had to be counterbalanced and atoned for by an apposite penance, but even before certain morally difficult decisions, for instance, when one of the faithful found himself puzzled as to what the correct action would be in the given circumstances. The conflict of different duties, to give but one example, would send a man to church to ask guidance of the priest. These were the famous "cases of conscience" whose discussion fills the later literature. Many of them, owing to the complexity of the human condition, were very knotty indeed. The dog-Latin word *casus cnusus* for a besetting problem which seems insoluble and yet has to be solved was coined to describe such torturing problems. Thus there arose all that was needed to give birth to a whole science, the science of casuistry: a social need, a group of men who had to fulfil it (the confession-hearing and guidance-giving clergy), and a host of questions difficult enough to arouse lively interest and to demand sustained ratiocination. We find its precipitate in the great *Summae casuum* or *Summulae confessionales* which were written after the Fourth Lateran Council of 1215 had decreed that every Christian was in duty bound to go to confession at least once a year. The *Summa de vitiis* of the Dominican Guielmus Peraldus, was one of the first; Raimundus de Pennaforte's *Summa de poenitentia et matrimonio*, another Dominican work, of similar date (before 1238), came to join it, and the Franciscan Astexanus d'Asti added his *Summa de casibus conscientiae* around the year 1317. The matter was abstruse enough in itself, but the well-known Scholastic passion for distinction-making made it much more so. The busy priests needed commodious handbooks for quick information rather than learned tomes, and such a one was provided when the *Summa Silvestrina* of the Dominican Silvester Prierias (ca. 1515)—a work arranged according to alphabetical headings—was put on the shelves next to the *Summa Raimundiana* and the *Summa Astesana* which had been the main standbys before and remained so for a considerable time.

In the hands of these writers the old legal casuistry of the primitive Church changed into a moral casuistry which offered a rather different face to the world. While the casuistical method is, as we have pointed out, impeccable in the field of law, it appears, in ethics, easily as an illicit bending of general principles, if not indeed as a playing fast and loose with sacred imperatives. This must be so especially if "accommo-dation"—the adjustment of a firm law to the needs of an individual law-breaker, a "tempering of the wind to the shorn lamb," to use a common phrase—becomes in practice the guiding principle. The basic problem lies in the fact that the confessional is a tribunal of love as well as a tribunal of law. The end pursued in it is less the conviction and the condemnation of the sinner than his reclamation and reconciliation. To confront him with the letter of the law and to refuse to make allowances in his personal, perhaps attenuating, circumstances would always mean to discourage and often to lose him. On the other hand, to give way to special pleading, to set aside obligations and commandments which must needs be binding on all men, would lead to a catastrophic undermining of human discipline and morality. The casuists tried to do their job without falling either into excessive hardness (legalism in the bad sense of the word) or into excessive softness (casuistry in the bad sense of the word). Hence the ambiguous, problematical reputation which is theirs. Love and law can never be totally reconciled in their conflicting claims. A synthesis must be attempted in every age without ever being achieved or even achievable. The classical casuistic literature of the later Middle Ages was one attempt in this direction.

The permanent character as well as the further development of casuistry was deeply influenced by the ethical doctrines of Saint Thomas Aquinas which are set out in the second part of his *Summa theologica*. His moral system, deeply influenced as it is by Plato and Aristotle, centers on the concept of "right relations," of a *justitia generalis*, the realization of which would bring human society into an ordered and satisfying (even morally satisfactory) condition. According to Aquinas, all virtues can, in a manner, be reduced to the basic virtue of righteousness and/or justice. These two key words—righteousness and justice—suggest a legal, if not, indeed, a legalistic turn of mind, and there can be no doubt that in one sense all human relationships, insofar as they approach the ideal, are conceived as norm-informed and norm-determined. Yet there is another aspect which must not be missed. Right and just relationships are not only right and just in the minimal sense, in the cold sense, so to speak, they are also right and just in the full, the maximal sense, the sense of closeness and warmth, indeed, of love. If this is not always obvious on the face of the texts, because Thomas sports a sober mode of expression, it is yet the inner substance of his social and moral philosophy. Law is for him the form, while love is the appropriate content. *De facto* relations which fully coincide with the relations which are expected and demanded *de jure*, will spontaneously generate a spirit of *caritas*, for there is, for Thomas as for Aristotle, a drift in reality which, by its own power, leads upward towards the summit of perfection. All tends towards God. God is indeed the source of all law, but He is also the source of all love. Law appears therefore in the last analysis as essentially a means to an end, and the end is the vision of, and the union with, God, the Value of Values. The practice of the confessional, from which casuistry sprang, and which it, in turn, shaped, was in line with these conceptions. The quasi-legal and casuistical side of the priest's dealings with the penitent, the *constructio* of his failings and their *subsumptio* under the appropriate norms, was merely a preparation for the prodigal's reconciliation with his outraged father, i.e., the reestablishment of a condition of love.

It is only if it is seen within this framework, that the essence of casuistry can be recognized and the whole phenomenon duly appreciated. Nothing but error can result if it is considered in isolation. The inclusive system of moral philosophy which emerged in and through the great *Summae* was bipolar. It consisted of Ascetics on the one hand, and of Casuistics on the other, and the two belonged together like light and shadow, or like the two sides of a coin, each being meaningless without the other. The ascetic element loomed less large in the bulk of the literature, but not because it was considered of minor importance; the reason was rather that, with its simple and lapidary pronouncements, it did not need so much space as its casuistical opposite whose fine-spun and detailed distinctions needed a lot of room for their due display. Ascetic morality represented a kind of classics, having come down from the Old Testament (the Ten Commandments) and the early rigorists such as Tertullian or Saint Augustine, whereas casuistical morality regarded itself as its modern, developmental completion. The discipline of Ascetics represented a striving for moral perfection; it formulated the moral maximum, as it were; Casuistics, for its part, showed in contrast a search for the moral minimum; it tried to draw the lowest acceptable line between ethical and nonethical, e.g., egotistical conduct, for instance, in economic or market dealings. Ascetics formulated its concepts and commands *in terminis*, whereas Casuistics was, and had to be, much more tentative and vague. One reason for this difference was that Ascetics, in majestic isolation from reality, issued absolute propositions which time and space would not, should not, and could not modify, whereas Casuistics was in the closest contact with reality, with the everyday dealings of human beings with each other, and tried to cope as best it might (often greatly hampered by the ascetic tradition with which it was yoked together) with the myriads of situations and incidents which were encountered from day to day. Because of its whole nature, the ascetic

tendency excluded from its statements and developments every trace of sentiment; it tended to be rationalistic; it conceived its doctrines to be truth in the same sense as mathematical propositions are the truth. Between Is and Ought it saw the same difference as between black and white. It was not in these terms that the casuistical authors speculated. They saw a world of grey hues, some rather dark in complexion, others rather light, and they believed in the possibility of diminishing the black ingredient in the mixture and increasing the white. This was to be achieved by a clever strategy, by elasticity, understanding, forebearance, patience, and all similar tactics, but also (this must in fairness be emphasized) by persistence and perseverance. If the ascetic moralist was a quasi-mathematician, the casuist was a kind of medical man. He aimed at providing the right treatment which, by slow improvements, would nurse a sickening soul back to robust health so that it could feed again on the hard fare of ascetic morality.

Considered in this fashion, the system of the *Summae* represented a microcosm of all ethical philosophizing. Max Weber, for instance, divided moral philosophy into the ethics of principle, absolutizing ethics (*Gesinnungsethik* as he called it—Kant's categorical imperative as archetype), and the ethics of accommodation, relativizing ethics (*Erfolgsethik*—Bentham's utilitarianism as archetype). The former embraced the maxim "Let justice prevail though the world perish" (*fiat justitia, pereat mundus*); it was pure and august and majestic, but it was essentially divine rather than human, a manifestation of the noumenal world, with the result that it would be denied what its weaker and less impressive other self secured, namely success in practical affairs. The latter rejected the formula "all or nothing" and was satisfied with a little step here and again a little step there; it was of the phenomenal world in which we live, afflicted with its impurities, by no means endowed with a grandiose and distant impressiveness, but a workable technique securing ever anew petty improvements. In a word, the latter variety of ethics based on consequences (*Erfolgsethik*) was a kind of moral Machiavellism, and this is precisely what casuistry was in the framework of the Catholic doctrinal system. We can describe it so, provided of course we remember that the ultimate aim of the Florentine was also the moral regeneration of his city and country.

To the Catholic thinkers themselves, the contrast which we are trying to draw and within which alone the essence and the historical achievement of casuistry can be fairly assessed, presented itself in other, though parallel, terms. Their thought was theological. God could either be conceived as king or judge, or he could be conceived as father or friend. To the one conception he was distant, stern, even unapproachable, to the other near, loving, and easy to approach. Correspondingly there were two basic psychological conditions with regard to the human attitude to the divinity, fear of God on the one hand and love of God on the other. This love of God was not necessarily destroyed, though it was unavoidably affected, if a sin was committed, especially a relatively harmless or "venial" sin. (The distinction between venial or mortal sins was therefore a constant preoccupation of Catholic moral theology in general and the casuistical morality which formed an integral part of it in particular.) The soul besmirched by sin had to be cleansed, and that cleansing was the task of the confessional. In the confessional, Ascetics was not of so much use as Casuistics was, as *Gesinnungsethik* was not of so much use in the outer, wider world as was *Erfolgsethik*. The ascetic approach threatened, at least in all probability, to shake, abash, and frighten the sinner and thereby to inhibit the striving towards the good which he might still bear within him. The casuistical treatment, however, promised, or at least raised the hope, that he would be soothed, comforted, encouraged, and elevated, and thereby given the energy for a new and more successful effort towards reintegration in the society of the righteous and just. To these differences in basic attitude corresponded a contrast of more practical importance. The priest's formal absolution of the sinner was conditional on his repentance, but in the framework of ascetical absolutism repentance for the love of God (*contritio*) was demanded, whereas in the context of casuistical strategy and education repentance for the fear of God (*attritio*) was deemed sufficient. We have here a curious, but entirely logical, crossing of the lines of thought. Contrition, the more perfect form of repentance, sees sin as an offense against the loving God, the father and friend; here Ascetics works with a concept in other ways more congenial to Casuistics; attrition, however, the less perfect form of repentance, with which the "laxist" casuists were invariably satisfied, was inclined to define sin as an insult to the highest lord, the legislator and judge of the world—it borrowed the theological core-conception of Ascetics. This proves again that the two halves of the theology and morality of the *Summae* form a whole which cannot be severed without destroying both.

The close systematic connection between ascetic and casuistic moral theology would seem to demand, ideally, an equally close and systematic cooperation. In principle, the practical counsels of casuistry should be derived, by a process of logical deduction, from the theoretical propositions of Ascetics. There should, in other words, be a flawless and faultless descent from the universal to the specific. If this had been so, casu-istry could never have broken away from its ascetic corrective. On the other side, the firsthand experiences of the practitioners of casuistry should have been reported, for the purposes of reconciliation with, and incorporation into, the canons of absolute morality, to the representatives of dogmatic ethics who would then have avoided all possible estrangement from ongoing reality. There would thus have been an ever-renewed ascent from the specific to the universal. As it was, this highly desirable cooperation of the two branches was only very partially achieved, and the looseness of their coherence and coordination brought many and serious evils in its train. The ascetic, absolutistic, theoretical part of the system was not sufficiently enriched and refined by experience, the casuistical, relativistic, practical part was not sufficiently kept in contact with the direction-giving, standard-ensuring securities of ultimate principle. In the end there appeared a real danger in the domain of casuistry—the possibility that, in its hands, the specification and specialized application of general rules essential to social control and the moralization of everyday life would turn into their dissolution—differently expressed, that casuistry which up to then had been a relativized absolutism would degenerate into an absolute relativism. The trouble was partly due to the social factor. Ascetics, in other words, moral theory, was mainly cultivated by men more or less divorced from the world, by monks at first, by professors later on. Casuistics was in the hands of others who were perhaps too much in contact with the world, the parish clergy, who under the pressure of the needs of their care and cure of souls might easily drift away from the high canons which they had learned in the seminaries during their youth. This would not have been too serious, if the world had been and remained static. As it was, the pace of development was greatly speeded up during the fifteenth century and so the two branches, which should never have lost the closest contact, tended to be divided by a gap ever increasing in width and depth. It was especially economic and industrial development which created a kind of no-man's-land between the two: partnership agreements and the dissolution of partnerships in trade, the division of profits and inheritances, problems arising from the complexities of the slowly forming insurance business, with all its uncertainties and temptations and the like, required serious theoretical thinking through and equally serious practical solutions. As it was, the traditional science of Ascetics had become too hard and set in its thought ways, too enclosed in its inherited questions and answers, to move with alacrity and effectiveness into this new and broadening field. There were notable exceptions. The Dominican Saint Antoninus of Florence, for instance, who died in 1459, showed a deep understanding of the new realities in his writings. But, on the whole, the area was left to the casuists for cultivation, with the result that the voice of the Church became somewhat uncertain, and rigorists raised increasingly sharp criticisms which contributed their mite to the impending Reformation movement.

It is certainly a very significant historical fact that Martin Luther, when he burnt the papal bull of excommunication directed against him, also threw a current casuistical text, a copy of the so-called *Summa Angelica* (1486) of Angelus de Clavasio, into the flames. In its first stages (though, as we shall see, only in its first stages), the Reformation was decidedly anticasuistical. In this respect, the attitude of Calvin far outdistanced that of Luther. With his associated doctrines of the total perversion of man and the incomprehensible majesty of God, he banned, and had to ban, all ideas of a possible accommodation of God's commands to the needs of man: man was simply too low and mean, too near to zero in value and importance to deserve consideration, while God was too high up and too far away to concede it. Thus Calvinism became thoroughly, indeed passionately, rigorist in moral theory and practice. This had the understandable and unavoidable consequence of driving Catholicism in the opposite direction. In the great competition of the confessional groups for the adherence of men which ensued, Calvinism tried to impress by the sternness of its moral code, the extremity of its disciplinary commands, while Catholicism strove to attract by the mercifulness of its methods, by its willingness to build golden bridges for the repentant sinner and keep the Church's doors ever open for him. In the realm of social education, nothing is more characteristic of the contrast between the two variants of Christianity than the fact that Calvinism returned to open confession and open condemnation (the stool on which the culprit had to stand to hear his failings discussed before and by the congregation became almost symbolical), whereas Catholicism made confession ever more easy and ever more private (the confessional box with its division between priest and penitent who communicated in darkness through a grille was now introduced). While the Church of Rome as a whole thus moved away under external pressures from the rigorist toward the laxist, casuistical pole in moral theology, developments took place within her own house which further strengthened this tendency and created in the Jesuit Order a powerful internal vanguard of an even more extreme laxist and casuistical movement. Calvinism, with its harking back to the stark ascetical conceptions of Saint Augustine, aroused an echo in parts of the Catholic camp, and the community known to history as the Jansenists came into being. One of them, Antoine Arnauld, pub-

lished a treatise on the *Morale pratique des Jésuites* (Vol. I, 1669, Vol. II, 1683) strongly upholding the rigorist point of view; another Jansenist and even greater writer, Blaise Pascal, launched in his famed *Lettres provinciales* (1656–57) a blistering attack on the Jesuits and on all casuistry. But this attack failed. Such works as Hermann Busenbaum's *Medulla theologiae moralis* (1645) and Antonio Escobar y Mendoza's *Liber theologiae moralis* (1644) did much more than merely maintain themselves in the market: they became widely predominant, not to say dominant, handbooks of Catholic moral guidance. The former ran through twenty-three editions during Busenbaum's lifetime (1600–68), the latter through forty. Busenbaum's text reached in the end more than two hundred printings! The two treatises mark the earlier climax of casuistry in the Catholic Church.

Meanwhile the rigorism of the Protestant theologians was undergoing very considerable modifications. At first, rid of the need to hear confessions and to give absolution, Luther and the Lutherans could easily maintain their original attitude of "no truce with sin." But this changed as soon as some of them became advisers to princes and thus found themselves in the same positions, or rather the same quandaries, as their Catholic counterparts. When Luther himself had to help Philipp von Hessen in his marital complications, he fell back on a typical casuistical device, the making of fine distinctions: he counselled that the *Landgraf* should not publicly announce his second clandestine marriage, for there was, he argued, a difference between a public "yes" and a confidential one. Indeed, he moved even deeper into casuistry. In the parochial sermons there is a passage where he goes so far as to turn the tables on the Catholics. The monks, he pronounces, describe all lying as sinful, but there are cases, such as those of *Nutzlüge* and *Lieblüge* (lying for the sake of a good cause or for the sake of love), which are not to be subsumed under the concept of sinning, if they spring from a good heart. In due course, there appeared a fairly substantial Lutheran literature on casuistry which paralleled the works of Busenbaum and Escobar y Mendoza in most things, even laxity. We might mention Johann Friedrich König's *Theologia positiva acroamatica* (1664) and Johannes Olearius' *Introductio Brevis in theologiam casuisticam* (1694) as prime examples. Even in the Calvinist fold, something like a casuistical approach made its appearance. Somewhat stricter, more penitential in tone and more edificational in design, it is yet a proof of how widespread casuistical moralizing was in the age, and how real the need for some such bridging of the gap between the simplicity of abstract rules and the multiplicity of concrete needs is in any age. Three English works, all by William Perkins, illustrate Calvinist casuistry: *A Case of Conscience* (1592), *A Discourse of Conscience* (1597), and *The Whole Treatise of the Cases of Conscience* (1606). Perkins' disciple, William Ames, wrote *De conscientia et eius jure vel casibus* (1630) which could serve as a manual and enjoyed for a time considerable circulation.

Prima facie, one would expect that the transition from the age of faith to the age of reason would have diminished the relish for casuistical disquisitions, but on closer inspection the opposite is seen to be the case. The reason for the survival, nay continuing vigor, of casuistry lies in the cause which has ever produced casuistry as its effect: the formulation and propagation of a strongly absolutist, ascetical system of morals. The conquering rationalism of the eighteenth century tended to bring forth precisely such a system and in Immanuel Kant we find it perfected and classically expressed. The imperative on which his ethics rests as on a *rocher de bronze* is a categorical, not a hypothetical, imperative. True, even Kant, though his contact with life was tenuous, had at least on one occasion to fall back, under the pressure of circumstances, on a technique, the practice of which was a standing reproach to casuists: the use of somewhat less than univocal statements in order to defend higher values. When, after his conflict with the Prussian government, he promised to abstain "for the future" (*fernerhin*) "totally" (*gänzlich*) from lecturing on religion, he cleverly addressed this declaration to "your royal majesty" (*Ew. Königlichen Majestät*), in the intention that the restrictions he had thus taken upon himself would, by the form of words chosen, be confined to the lifetime of King Friedrich Wilhelm II. Absolutist in ethics though he was, he employed here the current casuistical distinction between a government which remains within its legitimate rights and thus can demand absolute candor of its subjects, and one which goes beyond them and may under certain circumstances be treated differently.

The vogue of Protestant and later secularized rationalism and the often underestimated spread of Jansenist rationalism, which took in rulers like Joseph II of Austria, but other formally Catholic princes and princelings as well, evoked in the eighteenth century a new and last flowering of casuistry in the person of Saint Alphonsus of Liguori. Alphonsus, the founder of the worldwide Redemptorist Order, can best be understood as a representative of the pre-romantic movement which protested against the prevalence of rationalism in thought and human relationships and called for a "religion of the heart" to replace the "head-religion" which controlled orthodoxy and led to a progressive drying-up of the spiritual life, especially prayer-life, but which also affected the handling of sin and sinners in the confessional. The parallel between him and the Wesleys is obvious. As a moral theologian, Alphonsus strove to transmute cold justice into warm charity. He had, however, been trained as a lawyer and tried to carry out his grand design, not by pushing aside the laws which were in force, but by softening them up, so to speak, from within by introducing into their practice principles and policies of love and accommodation, with the result that a highly profiled system of casuistry flowed from his pen. The slogan of the later so-called sociological school of law was also his: through the law, *always* through the law, but beyond it! Formally, his system, as laid down, for instance, in his *Theologia moralis* (1756), was a modernized version of Busenbaum's *Medulla;* in substance it was both richer and deeper. As Busenbaum had been the chief target of Protestant polemics, so Alphonsus of Liguori became that of the Enlightenment. He was said to have no principles at all, but to be prepared to use any sophistry to transmute unacceptable into acceptable, unethical into ethically innocuous actions. A cooler assessment of his work, however, shows that his casuistry, as all casuistry, was in the last resort still rooted in ascetical thinking. To give but one example: he allowed, in certain desperate cases, the use of ambiguous statements. We may think, for instance, of a political prisoner under interrogation by a secret police in the shadow of rack and rope. Most moralists, indeed, most upright men, would, in these circumstances, permit even downright lying. Not so Alphonsus. The use of ambiguous statements was precisely meant to obviate the need to lie. The victim was advised, not to deceive, but to allow the persecutor (who, morally, had no right to torture or perhaps even to question a fellow-man) to deceive himself. Respect for truth was in a manner preserved by such a stratagem. It is obvious from this illustration how the casuistics of Saint Alphonsus strove to help in the individual case without hurting general law.

With Alphonsus of Liguori, whose *Theologia moralis* was declared unexceptionable by the Congregation of Rites in 1803, who was canonized in 1839 and pronounced a *Doctor Ecclesiae* in 1871, and who thus marks the later climax of casuistry in the Catholic Church, the main history of this variant of moral theology comes to a close. Casuistical works continued to appear throughout the nineteenth century, but confessional practice, while still applying the insights of the casuists, moved more and more into the middle of the stream of moral philosophy, trying to avoid at the same time the Scylla of a loveless rigorism and the Charybdis of an overindulgent laxity.

In this century, in recent decades, casuistry has regained some interest. It was, implicitly and explicitly, subjected to a new kind of criticism. If it was, in the past, accused of betraying the abstract and general in the interest of the concrete and individual, it was now said to be itself far too abstract and generalizing in attitude. A leading case is, after all, a kind of genus. What the casuists did was (though on a lower level of generalization) exactly what the legalists did, namely, to subsume an individual instance under a universal, or near-universal, at least potentially universal, concept. But, it was argued, moral philosophy is, or should be, concerned with the absolutely unique, for not only is every human soul unique, but every situation in which a soul finds itself when it encounters a moral quandary is, in principle, unique also. Moral solutions to moral problems, so "situational ethics" pleaded, must spring from the unrepeatable decisions of unrepeatable personalities in unrepeatable situations. The problem of this new movement in theoretical ethics would seem to be largely identical with that with which the classical casuists tried to grapple: how to extricate men from the clutches of a law which is, and must be, alien to them, if for no other reason, then simply because it is a law meant for all and thus not understanding enough for the needs of any one. As for casuistry in the traditional sense of the word, the new discussion has shown up one of its distinguishing marks, namely to be—in spite of the fact that it is, in such thinkers as Saint Alphonsus of Liguori, an attempt to introduce kindness, and indeed emotionalism, into the legal sphere—itself to some extent a form of legalism and rationalism.

BIBLIOGRAPHY

Joseph Mausbach, *Catholic Moral Teaching and its Antagonists*, trans. A. M. Buchanan, from the 6th revised and augmented German ed. (New York, 1914). Joseph Klein, "Ursprung und Grenze der Kasuistik," *Aus Theologie und Philosophie*, Festschrift für Fritz Tillmann (Düsseldorf, 1950), pp. 229–45. Richard Egenter, "Kasuistik als Christliche Situationsethik," *Münchner Theologische Zeitschrift*, **1** (1950), 54–65. Paul Ramsey, *Deeds and Rules in Christian Ethics* (New York, 1967).

WERNER STARK

[See also Education; **Equity;** God; Justice; Law; Love; Rationality; Reformation; **Right and Good;** Sin and Salvation.]

CATHARSIS

THE GREEK word for purgation, cleansing, and purification is a word that has become part of the learned vocabulary of scholars. It is derived from *katharein*, a Greek word meaning "to cleanse." It has come down to contemporary discourse by way of religious, medical, and learned traditions.

In religious history cathartic rules and behavior are recorded in different cultural environments. In order to escape from unclean influences man had to purify himself and also objects around him. Uncleanliness originated from actions that were not permitted. To disturb a taboo made a man "unclean." Purification is an action to remove uncleanliness resulting from a violation of the taboo. The cleaning can be performed by means of water, blood, change of garment, wine, fire, or sacrifice. In the Old Testament catharsis was accomplished by means of washing and bathing. Uncleanliness was believed to exist in menstruation and leprosy. The purification was performed in the Temple. In the New Testament purification was performed by means of baptism.

In the Greek tradition cathartic actions are noted in the Homeric poetry, in poems by Hesiod, and later on in the mystery cults at Delphi and Eleusis. The cathartic actions were performed in disciplines or rituals, aimed at a spiritual and moral cleansing of sins.

Closely related to religious purification is the medical concept of catharsis or purgation. Religious and moral sins were associated with disease. Purification and purgation were means of getting rid of disease and plague. A plague was considered a retribution due to individual or collective behavior that was in violation of the laws of God or Nature. This is seen in Sophocles' *Oedipus Rex*, for Oedipus has broken a taboo against incest, and a plague punishes Thebes. When Oedipus is also punished, the plague is removed, and Thebes is cleansed.

In the medical practice of Hippocrates and his school, and later in the Asclepian therapy, there are studies of the cathartic processes of diarrhoea, vomiting, and menstruation. It is difficult to trace a precise borderline between religious purification and medical purging. Catharsis can be considered to be mainly the removal of uncleanliness in order to establish a healthy harmony and correct relationship between men and the gods.

In the philosophical theories of literature, the concept of catharsis plays a central role, for example, in the writings of Plato and Aristotle. Obviously, Aristotle's famous definition of tragedy in the sixth chapter of the *Poetics*, and particularly the final ambiguous words about pity, fear, and catharsis, have influenced posterity in a number of more or less probable interpretations.

Aristotle mentions catharsis at the end of his *Politics* in connection with music, and this important text can be used in order to understand his controversial definition of tragedy in the *Poetics*. Aristotle explains the catharsis of music in this way:

We say, however, that music is to be studied for the sake of many benefits and not of one only. It is to be studied with a view to education, with a view to a purge [catharsis]—we use this term without explanation for the present; when we come to speak of poetry, we shall give a clearer account of it—and thirdly with a view to the right use of leisure and for relaxation and rest after exertion. It is clear, then, that we must use all the scales, but not all in the same way. For educational purposes we must use those that best express character, but we may use melodies of action and enthusiastic melodies for concerts where other people perform. For every feeling that affects some souls violently affects all souls more or less; the difference is only one of degree. Take pity and fear, for example, or again enthusiasm. Some people are liable to become possessed by the latter emotion, but we see that, when they have made use of the melodies which fill the soul with orgiastic feeling, they are brought back by these sacred melodies to a normal condition as if they had been medically treated and undergone a purge [catharsis]. Those who are subject to the emotions of pity and fear and the feelings generally will necessarily be affected in the same way; and so will other men in exact proportion to their susceptibility to such emotions. All experience a certain purge [catharsis] and pleasant relief. In the same manner cathartic melodies give innocent joy to men (*Politics* VIII:7; 1341b 35–1342a 8, trans. J. Burnet).

As is well known, Aristotle did not explain what he meant by "catharsis" when he came to speak of poetry in the *Poetics*. He mentions catharsis twice. One instance is not very elucidating. He refers to Orestes in connection with the purification ritual, but he does not at all explain what is meant by catharsis in connection with the arts. The other instance is the end of the definition of catharsis in the sixth chapter. To support the interpretation of this instance, there is a discussion of catharsis in the *Politics*. But it is of little help, since Aristotle admits that he has to explain the term more carefully.

In his definition of tragedy Aristotle says:

Tragedy is an imitation of an action that is serious, complete, and of a certain magnitude, in language embellished with each kind of artistic ornament (rhythm, harmony, and song) being found in separate parts of the play, in form of action, not of narrative (*Poetics* VI, 2).

Immediately after these words follows the final qualification of a tragedy—that there is pity and fear and a catharsis in a tragedy.

The translation of these last words is difficult not because we do not know the meaning of pity and fear and catharsis but because we do not know how they are related to each other. The final words of the definition are ambiguous. This ambiguity has created one of the most important bodies of exegetical literature.

From the point of view of quantity it can be compared with biblical exegeses. Philologists have tried to find a reasonable meaning of the words, but there is no agreement at all. The meaning of catharsis has been elucidated by means of comparisons with the religious uses of the word, by comparative research in other cultures, by the study of medical uses of the word, or by conjectures trying to prove that there is a real meaning of catharsis that is moral, or psychotherapeutical, or aesthetic. In a situation of this kind the scholar is not too easily convinced of one final interpretation. He has to exert a kind of skeptical *epokhe* in order to find a balance of probabilities.

The first step in understanding Aristotelian catharsis is to discuss the connection between pity and fear and catharsis. First of all, it is evident that "pity" according to Aristotle is not "pity" in the sense of our ordinary usage. By "pity" we mean a sympathetic and humane consideration, a state of mind that is commendable, but Aristotle meant by "pity" a state of mind that is occasioned by undeserved misfortune. It is evident that Aristotle did not consider it a desirable state of mind, but a disturbance of the mind. Aristotle seems to think that pity has a connection with fear, but if the fear is too great pity cannot exist. Those who are in panic are incapable of pity because they are preoccupied with their own emotions and cannot recognize other persons' emotions. So "pity" is a state of mind affected by other persons' distress. Pity is mentioned often by Aristotle in connection with fear. Pity and fear seem to be a specific complex reaction—understanding another person's distress and then projecting the possibility of this distress happening to us.

In order to understand Aristotle, the translators have proposed that pity or fear (or just one of them) existed in connection with catharsis. Another proposal has been that Aristotle meant that pity and fear and other similar emotions accompany catharsis. But presumably Aristotle intended to say that catharsis is to be found in connection with the complex reaction of pity and fear.

It is important to stress this last point because one line of interpretation of catharsis has exaggerated the moral significance of the word "pity." This misinterpretation has its source in the change of language due to the Christian vocabulary. In his *Confessions*, Saint Augustine sketched an explanation of the paradox of tragedy—the paradox that we enjoy the expression of painful passions in a tragedy—by referring to the pleasure of sharing a sympathetic pity. This explanation was re-echoed by many thinkers in the eighteenth century: Adam Smith, Lord Kames (Henry Home), Bishop Hurd, Edmund Burke, Alexander Gerard, Hugh Blair, and George Campbell. It was an attractive interpretation because of the close relationship between artistic achievement and Christian ethics. David Hume opposed this interpretation; that we enjoy exerting sympathetic pity. If this were the case, he said, a hospital would be preferable to a ball. It is not only a bad solution of a topical problem in aesthetics, but it is also misinterpreting Aristotle's word. The cause of this misinterpretation is the change in meaning of the basic vocabulary.

What role does catharsis play in relation to pity and fear? Aristotle gives many possibilities of interpretation. The mind can be clear of harmful emotions such as pity and fear, according to one possibility. Another possibility is that the mind is purified by means of pity and fear. A third possibility is that the harmful elements of pity and fear are removed and a valuable calm will pervade the mind. Violent passions can subside into steady calmness. It is difficult to get a final understanding here because of the risks we take in forcing our psychological distinctions on Aristotle's words.

These preliminary remarks will be more meaningful when we have discussed the problem of locating the texts in which catharsis is found. If we follow the discussion of catharsis in connection with music in Aristotle's *Politics*, it seems as if catharsis is located in the mind of the person who listens to music, not in the music itself. It has been thought that catharsis in connection with tragedy is experienced by the audience. However, in 1957 Gerald F. Else introduced a learned and elaborated interpretation of Aristotle's text saying that catharsis is to be found in the actions of the drama, and in the plot. This means that pity and fear and catharsis are to be found in the tragedy and not in the audience. This interpretation has stimulated much current discussion. There has been a great amount of controversy in the literature on Aristotelian catharsis since Else's view appeared. The main objection to Else's view, however, is that the text of the *Politics* does not support such an interpretation. It does not seem probable that Aristotle has one meaning of catharsis in his *Politics* and another in his *Poetics*.

This controversy can be clarified if we consider that catharsis was to occur in connection with the performance of a tragedy. It seems as if Aristotle saw tragedy as a communication to the audience from a creative artist (writer or actor) by means of a stage production. In the passage from the *Politics* quoted above, Aristotle has the same idea of artistic suggestion as in the seventeenth chapter of the *Poetics*. We can support this doctrine of suggestion or communication from actor to audience if we refer to the doctrine of inspiration in Plato's *Ion*. Inspiration creates the same kind of emotion in the poet, in the actor, and in the audience.

This is a predominant opinion in antiquity: "Similia similibus. . . ." Distress in the Homeric hero produces distress in the rhapsodist, Ion, and may produce the same distress in the audience. If we accept this premiss, then the problem of where pity and fear and catharsis are to be found can more easily be solved.

Pity and fear and catharsis are to be found in the actions and plot of the tragedy; and, by means of the stage performance, the actor and the audience are links in the chain of emotional communication. The same state of mind is communicated through these links. If so, there is no necessary contradiction between Else's interpretation and the conventional interpretation. If we take away the tendency to regard the two views as excluding each other, they can work together inside the accepted frame of interpretation. If catharsis is in the plot of tragedy, it is in the actor and in the audience as well.

The main discussion of the meaning of catharsis is, however, the most crucial part of the group of issues connected with Aristotle's definition of tragedy. Did Aristotle follow the religious or the medical use of catharsis when he related it to tragedy? In the *Politics* Aristotle associates religious music with medical therapy. However, the catharsis of tragedy is not necessarily to be understood as religious or medical catharsis. In the *Poetics* we have no supporting passage for either interpretation. It seems possible that Aristotle used the term in a metaphorical way. But how are we supposed to understand the metaphor? In chapter seventeen of the *Poetics* Aristotle refers to religious purification in Euripides' *Iphigenia in Tauris*. But this is not sufficient to maintain that Aristotle meant that the catharsis of a tragedy is simply a religious purification. The discussion of his theory in antiquity does not lend support to this purely religious interpretation.

The French critic, Charles de Saint-Denis de Saint-Évremond wrote in his *De la tragédie ancienne et moderne* (1672) "Aristotle was sensible enough . . . in establishing a certain purgation which no one hitherto has understood, and which in my opinion he himself never fully comprehended." This is an exaggeration. If Aristotle used the word catharsis, he gave the word a specific meaning in the context; but it is difficult for us to understand him because of the change of cultures and because of the fact that many of Aristotle's writings are lost or damaged. The *Poetics* is a fragmentary book. There has been discussion as to whether it was written in his early or in his later career. It is possible that the text is not a fragment of a book that Aristotle intended to publish, but a work that he had in progress under revision, and that was used as notes for teaching.

It has been maintained that catharsis is a religious purification of the mind. We have to take into account that Greek drama was a religious or ritual drama. Aeschylus, incidentally, was born in Eleusis, the place of the mysteries. To be initiated in Greek mysteries was to pass through different kinds of purifications. To enter a Temple, a man had to be cleansed by means of water. The tragic hero in the drama was the scapegoat who took upon himself sins and pestilence in order to restore divine harmony in society. In fact, he was responsible for the weather, wind, and a good harvest in an agricultural society. The religious ritual resembles tragedy. Although Aristotle lived in the century after the culmination of Attic tragedy, it is probable that his interpretation of tragedy was not, in fact, completely secularized.

Another interpretation of catharsis is based on the medical meaning of purgation. It has been maintained that Aristotelian catharsis presupposes the Hippocratic doctrine of the four "humors." The balance of the body and the mind had to be maintained by purging the evil humors. Melancholy was derived from the black bile, and the musical arts were used for purging such a disturbance of the mind and body. John Milton interpreted catharsis in this way in his preface to *Samson Agonistes* (1671). Tragedy has the power, according to Milton, "by raising pity and fear, or terror, to purge the mind of those and such like passions, that is, to temper and reduce them to just measure with a kind of delight, stirred up by reading or seeing those passions well imitated." Milton adds this interpretation: "Nor is Nature wanting in her own effects to make good this assertion; for so in physic, things of melancholic hue and quality are used against melancholy, sour against sour, salt to remove salt humours." In fact, John Milton applies the old medical principle, *Similia similibus curantur* ("similars cure the similar"). You will cure a disease by giving the same kind of disease. The pain of the hero of the tragedy will cure and purge you from pain. Measure for measure.

Is this a correct interpretation of Aristotle's use of catharsis? Earlier than Milton, Antonio Minturno had made a similar interpretation in 1564 in his *L'Arte poetica*, and later on, Thomas Twining in 1789 and H. Weil in 1847 made similar medical interpretations of catharsis. But these were the interpretations of a learned minority. Since Jakob Bernays contributed new arguments to the medical interpretation in 1857, it has met with increasing interest among scholars. According to this interpretation, tragedy gives the public a therapeutic stimulation of the passions and will lead the audience to an emotional crisis. Afterwards relief and calm pleasure are experienced. Aristotle's words in the *Politics* support such an interpretation. This therapy is mainly a mental one, but it acts in a manner that is analogous to bodily purgation.

However, since the Renaissance, the moral or ethical interpretation of catharsis has dominated, and has for support Aristotle's use of "pity" in connection with catharsis, but we have seen that this support is illusory. There are, of course, moral qualities in both religious purification and in mental and bodily therapy. It is good to live in peace with the gods, to be in good health, to enjoy mental harmony. To separate individual morality from religion and health is difficult, and for Aristotle it must have been more so than for us.

Aristotle's *Nicomachean Ethics* does give, however, support to a specific ethical interpretation of catharsis. In the opening books we read that virtue and character are connected with pleasure and pain, and pleasure and pain are the result of successful or thwarted activities. Activities are, in Aristotle's teleological philosophy, movements toward a desired end. Thus nothing is more important in the education of character than training to rejoice and to feel pain in the right way, to do the right things at the right times, and to the right extent. It is not reasonable or right to be afraid of nothing, or to be angry at nothing. There are things the wise man should fear and at which he should be angry. There are, according to Aristotle, reasonable fears.

In the *Nicomachean Ethics* he says furthermore:

If it is thus, then that every art does its work well—by looking to the intermediate and judging its work by this standard (so that we often say of good works of art it is not possible either to take away or to add anything, implying that excess and defect destroy the goodness of works of art, while the mean preserves it; and good artists, as we say, look to this in their work), and if, further, virtue is more exact and better than any art, as nature also is, then virtue must have the quality of aiming at the intermediate. I mean moral virtue; for it is this that is concerned with passions and actions, and in these there is excess, defect, and the intermediate. For instance, both fear and confidence and appetite and anger and pity and in general pleasure and pain may be felt both too much and too little, and in both cases not well; but to feel them at the right times, with reference to the right objects, towards right people, with the right motive, and in the right way, is what is both intermediate and best, and this is characteristic of virtue (Book II, Ch. 6, trans. W. D. Ross).

The moral or ethical interpretation of catharsis applies these words to the understanding of the final qualifications of a tragedy according to Aristotle's definition. Catharsis will produce a reasonable moderating of the passions, the just mean, or the relieving balance. This is what a qualified tragedy is able to produce in the wise man, a kind of harmony after an excess of emotions. Reason and wisdom are thus connected with the passions.

This interpretation has a long tradition. Corneille, Racine, and Lessing formulated different solutions, but they agreed that the catharsis made the experience of tragedy a moral one, and made the public morally wiser. With the support of the *Nicomachean Ethics*, we dare say that there is an ethical or moral element in catharsis, a kind of passionate experience when dominated by moderation and by a kind of insight and wisdom.

A psychological interpretation of catharsis is difficult to maintain in isolation, but all the interpretations of catharsis have to provide psychological observations concerning the mixture of pain and pleasure, and concerning the change from intense passionate response to an experience of relief and calmness. In the eighteenth century the paradox of tragedy, formulated by David Hume in his essay "Of Tragedy," in his *Four Dissertations* (1757), was a discussion of this effect of tragedy. Tragedy arouses painful and violent passions, but the artistic character of the tragedy causes the experience to induce a calm and pleasant state of mind.

This kind of interpretation has reached a new position through later psychology. Arthur Schopenhauer, Friedrich Nietzsche, and Sigmund Freud have shown how pleasure and pain are connected with each other—in the way Plato and René Dubos have pointed out—and that men do not act to sacrifice pleasure according to the pleasure principle of hedonism. In fact, Schopenhauer, Nietzsche, and Freud insist that men desire to take risks, to be shocked, to suffer pain, not in order to obtain pleasure subsequently. Of course, the actual uses of tragedies—writing of new tragedies and stage directing and interpreting old tragedies—have been biased by this change of psychology.

Of special interest is the connection between Aristotelian catharsis and Freudian psychoanalysis. In fact, in the 1890's Sigmund Freud and Josef Breuer initiated their therapeutical methods and designated them the "Cathartic therapy." Jakob Bernays, in Bonn, who formulated a modern medical interpretation of Aristotelian catharsis, was the uncle of Sigmund Freud's wife, and Freud was well aware of the medical interpretation of catharsis.

Psychological interpretations are too subtle to be used in reconstructing the original meaning of Aristotelian catharsis, and they are too vague to explain how tragedies are experienced. There are different ways of experiencing a tragedy, and these different experiences do not admit the assumption of one normal way of doing so. The ways of experiencing a drama have changed from antiquity to our time. It is too risky to impose the practice of psychoanalysis on the interpretation of Aristotelian catharsis.

Another interpretation of Aristotelian catharsis is the aesthetic one. David Hume came close to such an interpretation in his essay on tragedy, and so also did Gerald Else. Hume maintains that the true pleasure given by a tragedy flows from its perfection of form.

These different interpretations of Aristotelian catharsis must be combined with the analyses of pity and fear. Many possibilities will appear by means of such a combination. In the fourteenth chapter of the *Poetics* Aristotle said that we must not demand of tragedy any and every kind of pleasure, but only that which is proper to it. The proper pleasure of tragedy may be a cathartic reaction from pity and fear and provide a kind of intellectual harmony. Another alternative is that the reaction may be changed so that it is not a reaction away from a dominating pain, but towards a culminating pleasure.

Another possibility occurs when catharsis provides relief from disturbances such as pity and fear. Catharsis can be explained, again, to the extent that pity and fear are not totally withdrawn from the mind, but will still be in the mind, though changed. Another type of explanation is, finally, that pity and fear will be the means to relieve the soul from other emotions, and this relief is the catharsis.

The combination of different passions with the different explanations of catharsis shows many refined shades of psychological analyses. These different interpretations have isolated and clarified parts of Aristotle's doctrine. However, no one single interpretation is clearly better or more probable than another.

The reason is that we cannot find sufficient evidence for distinguishing a religious, a medical or therapeutic, a moral or ethical, a psychological or psychiatric, or an aesthetic interpretation in isolation from one another. The proper pleasure or purpose of tragedy is vague because of the absence of definite explanations by Aristotle. Perhaps he took his words as sufficiently good explanations, or perhaps his explanations have been lost.

Our modern distinctions impose definite borderlines where there were no borderlines in Aristotle's time. We should not only read Aristotle's texts and interpret them by means of supporting texts from antiquity, but we should also reconstruct Aristotle's own cultural situation and be aware of the difficulty of using our cultural distinctions in interpreting those texts.

Plato's writings provide a background to the Aristotelian use of catharsis. In *Phaedo* and in *Phaedrus* Plato connects virtue and mystery and uses the word "catharsis" for purification in this connection. Empedocles and his pupils distinguished the madness arising *ex purgamento animae* from the madness due to bodily ailments, according to E. R. Dodds. In his study *The Greeks and the Irrational* (1951), Dodds has stressed the connection between purification, purgation, and religious mysteries. The Dionysiac ritual was essentially cathartic. Dancing mania and other manifestations of collective hysteria were relieved by a ritual outlet. Music was considered good for states of anxiety, according to Plato and Theophrastus. Democritus denied that a great poem could be written *sine furore*. Poetry, music, and dance were strictly connected with each other as ritual means to purification and purgation. The Pythagoreans used music to induce harmony of the soul. For them music was a medicine. Hippocratic medical practice provides a background connecting ritual catharsis and therapeutical catharsis with the arts. It is difficult to distinguish between religion and medicine in this tradition, both close to the practice of the arts.

We also need to examine the Asclepian tradition, a medical and religious practice that was close to Aristotle's time and to his own situation. Aristotle's father was the Asclepian physician Nicomachus. We also know that Aristotle admired Sophocles' *Oedipus Rex*, and Sophocles was the first Asclepian priest in Athens. Sophocles dedicated an altar to Asclepius and wrote an Asclepian Hymn. In the therapeutic methods and case studies of the Asclepian center in Epidaurus we find the use of drama and music, and there was a practice of psychiatric as well as of chirurgical character. Shock treatment and athletics were important in the therapy. Catharsis was a key word in this medicine and religion—but we cannot say whether the catharsis was a purification or a purging. At times the moral interpretation applies, at other times the psychological, and very often the religious as well as the medical.

It seems as if we cannot give an exact interpretation of the ten words at the end of Aristotle's definition of tragedy. Gerald Else has declared: "The controversy over catharsis has revolved—for some years 'spun' would be a better term—on its own axis for so long, and with so little determinate result, that one sometimes wonders if it should not be declared officially closed or debarred" (p. 225).

Ulrich von Wilamowitz-Moellendorff said in his work on the Greek tragedy that catharsis is one of the words over which rivers of ink have run and, nevertheless, there is no agreement on its interpretation. He observes that the word was not very much discussed in antiquity. In connection with Aristotle's writings, Proclus and Iamblichus mention catharsis but do not give an elucidation. Purification is a key word in the Christian religion, and when interest in Aristotle's *Poetics* was reviewed during the Renaissance, the interpretation of catharsis was affected by the religious use of "catharsis." The word was interpreted and re-

interpreted, perhaps fruitlessly, but these discussions for more than four hundred years have been a stimulation to psychology, aesthetics, and dramaturgy.

The links connecting drama, religious ritual, and medical therapy are manifest in this discussion. In Molière's *Le Malade Imaginaire* we find catharsis presented in a farcical situation: *Clysterium donare, Postea seignare, Ensuita purgare* ("With a clyster deterge, then let the blood spurge, and finally purge").

From the discussions of scholars the word "catharsis" has come into the common vocabulary. Enjoying a tragedy we refer to our experience as a catharsis. We think that we know what we mean. But we may not know exactly the meaning of this positive qualification. Jakob Bernays said that the word is a pompous expression that the educated person has at hand but that no thinking person will know precisely what it means. Else says: "We have grown used to feeling—again vaguely—that serious literature is hardly respectable unless it performs some 'catharsis.' 'Catharsis' has come, for reasons that are not entirely clear, to be one of the biggest of the 'big' ideas in the field of aesthetics and criticism, the Mt. Everest or Kilimanjaro that looms on all literary horizons" (Else, p. 443).

The importance of the word and the importance of the efforts of the scholars stand in contrast to the difficulties in coming to a precise interpretation of the Aristotelian use of the word. It is still more ironic that M. D. Petrusevski in Skoplje, Yugoslavia, has given good reasons for the opinion that Aristotle never used the word "catharsis" in the definition of tragedy in the *Poetics*. This is one of the boldest conjectures of our time and it has been overlooked in contemporary literature. His study was published in *Ziva Antika*, Vol. 2 (Skoplje, 1954), with a detailed summary in French. The thesis is that the terminal words in the definition are not *pathematon katharsin* ("catharsis of feeling") but *pragmaton systasin* ("action brought together"). The argument for the thesis is rather detailed. First of all, there are different readings of the manuscripts. Instead of *pathematon* there is an alternative reading of *mathematon* which is nonsensical. Secondly, there is the ambiguous wording in the definition of tragedy which is against Aristotle's rules of definition. Thirdly, there is a switch from objective to subjective qualifications, which is also against Aristotle's rules of definition. Fourthly, there is a commentary in the *Poetics* on the different parts of the definition, but catharsis is not included.

Professor Petrusevski has identified these words as *pragmaton systasin*, and the meaning is then that the tragedy has pity and fear in the actions that are brought together. These words are commented on by Aristotle in the later chapters of the *Poetics*. The explanation of a misreading is that Aristotle's writings were damaged and then edited by copyists who made the emendation because they had read in the *Politics* that Aristotle intended to explain catharsis in the *Poetics*. But in the definition he did not use the word "catharsis." In fact, there is, according to Professor Petrusevski, not a tragical catharsis, only a musical catharsis. In the *Poetics* Aristotle discussed the music of a tragedy, but these parts are lost. Presumably catharsis was discussed in this missing passage of the *Poetics*.

This is a bold and valiant conjecture. It assumes, however, that Aristotle could not fail to follow his own rules of definition. The conventional reading of the terminal words of the definition of tragedy forces us to give three different meanings of "pathematon"—an objective genitive, a separative genitive, a subjective genitive. It seems improbable that Aristotle was so clumsy a writer. This clumsiness is most likely to be due to a copyist. The misreading existed when Iamblichus and Proclus were reading Aristotle's text in late antiquity.

If Professor Petrusevski is right, the discussion of the meaning of catharsis seems to imply that an immense and erudite controversy was created by a mistake of a copyist. The serious discussion of tragedy is thus changed into a learned absurdity. Although this article has made serious efforts to contribute new interpretations to Aristotle's use of catharsis, the author is inclined to believe in Professor Petrusevski's conjecture. But it may be that his suggested change of the text will not be accepted very soon by other scholars. It is almost too elegant and too reasonable to be accepted at once.

BIBLIOGRAPHY

The exposition of the meaning of catharsis is concentrated on Aristotelian catharsis and its different interpretations. A more detailed argument is to be found in Teddy Brunius, *Inspiration and Katharsis* (Uppsala, 1966), together with references to the literature. The interpretation of M. D. Petrusevski is in *Ziva Antika, Antiquité Vivante*, **4**, 2 (Skoplje, Yugoslavia, 1954). A detailed summary is given in French. Petrusevski's arguments are partly derived from Heinrich Otte, *Kennt Aristoteles die sogenannte tragische Katharsis?* (Berlin, 1912). The latest text of the *Poetics* of Aristotle is edited by Rudolf Kassel (Oxford, 1965). For the *Nicomachean Ethics*, see the Oxford translation by W. D. Ross (Oxford, 1925), Vol. 9. A good bibliography and commentary is given in D. W. Lucas, *Aristotle's Poetics. Introduction, Commentary and Appendixes* (Oxford, 1968). The interpretation of Gerald F. Else is to be found in his *Aristotle's Poetics: The Argument* (Cambridge, Mass., 1957). The relation between Platonic and Aristotelian catharsis is discussed in G. Finsler, *Platon und die aristotelische Poetik* (Berlin, 1900). Cathartic traditions are described and discussed in Louis Moulinier, *Le Pur et l'impur dans la pensée des Grecs* (Paris, 1952). Theodore Waechter discussed early cathartic ritual in *Religionsgeschichtliche Versuchen und Vorarbeiten* (1910), Vol. X. Asclepian therapy is found in Rudolf Herzog, *Die Wunderheilungen von Epidauros, Philologus*, Supplementband **22** (Leipzig, 1931), and by Emma and Ludwig Edelstein in *Asclepius*, Vols 1 and 2 (Baltimore, 1945). Important contributions to the interpretation of Aristotelian catharsis have been made by E. P. Papanoutsos, *La Catharsis des Passions d'après Aristote* (Athens, 1953), by Wolfgang Schadewaldt, *Hellas und Hesperien* (Zürich and Stuttgart, 1960), pp. 346–88, and H. D. F. Kitto, "Catharsis," in *The Classical Tradition, Studies in Honor of Harry Caplan*, ed. L. Wallach (Ithaca, 1966), pp. 133–47. The connection between psychoanalysis and Aristotelian catharsis is discussed by Eva Berczeller in "The Aesthetic Feeling and Aristotle's Catharsis Theory," *The Journal of Psychology*, **65** (1967), 261–71.

TEDDY BRUNIUS

[See also Harmony or Rapture in Music; **Health and Disease;** Pythagorean . . . ; **Religion, Ritual in.**]

CAUSATION

THE VIEWS of causation among the literate peoples of the ancient world exhibited the almost universal tendency of antiquity as well as of modern pre-literate cultures, to interpret natural phenomena in terms applicable only to the arrangement of human society, or at least to the actions of intelligent agents. Such, at any rate, seems to be the judgment of the best students of ancient Mesopotamian and Egyptian civilizations. These views have been called "mytho-poeic" and "socio-morphic" accounts of the natural world because they are myths in categories devised either to explain who brought about the present state of the cosmos or to explain the regular or periodic routine of nature. For example, the alternation of seasons and the position and movement of the heavenly bodies were thought to be the result of decrees and arrangements made by the gods. These divine decrees or arrangements were conceived in close analogy to the regular arrangement of society or the edict of a law giver. The clear and sharp distinction between personal and impersonal or the difference between nature and society, so familiar to modern man, did not seem to exist for the ancient world at that time. In particular, the systems of retributive justice were applied to explain the phenomena of nature. The details of this view of the universe and its regularity have been discussed in a number of treatments of ancient Mesopotamian and Egyptian civilizations (Frankfort, Wilson, and Jacobsen, 1949).

Early Greek philosophy reveals the survival of such notions especially in fragments of Anaximander, Parmenides, and Heraclitus. That some kind of retributive justice holds things to the right order is indicated in a number of places, e.g., Anaximander's statement that "things pay penalty and retribution to one another for their mutual injustice according to the decree of time" provides one such survival (Diels, *Fragmente*, 12A). Heraclitus' statement that the handmaids of justice watch over the sun in his courses (ibid., 94B), and Parmenides' doctrine that justice holds fast what exists in fetters, provide others.

Although there are other such vestiges of pre-philosophic ideas among earliest Greek philosophers, Greek philosophy's formal beginnings succeeded in making considerable advances beyond this style of thought. There is some evidence that the Milesian and other early schools conceived the ultimate source of all things as being something divine. There was a tendency to de-personalize this divine being, and with this came an absence of caprice, that is, the regularity of natural phenomena was made to depend on a regularity in the operation of their cause or causes. Moreover, the analogies drawn from observation tend to be drawn from natural and observable connections. Anaximenes, for example, explains the different states of matter in terms of rarefaction and condensation. This explanation is radically different from anything like a mytho-poeic or socio-morphic category. Of course, mythic explanations continue to be found, but even they take on a different character.

The problem of causality explicitly appears at the beginning of the fifth century B.C. The first philosophers of Greek antiquity were concerned with genuine scientific and philosophic problems: What is the substance from which all things arise and to which they return? What is the nature of change? It was soon discovered that it is impossible to believe that the universe consists of a single simple substance and that change can also occur. The difficulty received its classic formulation from Parmenides. Being or that which is, cannot arise from nonbeing; and what is, cannot cease to exist. From this came the celebrated maxim that *ex nihilo nihil fit*. At first, this maxim, that nothing can come from nothing, was applied to justify a material substratum, but when the pluralistic systems of Anaxagoras and Empedocles were developed, the maxim was applied not merely to the eternity of the elements, but also to the eternal elemental forces which served to combine and separate the eternal elements. In this way, causal principles were introduced: events require both underlying permanent substances and forces to explain the various combinations and arrangements of things. The primary beliefs in a causal and substantival order were elaborated into fundamental principles of philosophy. The first explicit statement was made by Melissus of Samos (fl. 440 B.C.), "That which was, was always and always will be, for if it had come into being, it necessarily follows that before it came into being, nothing existed, but if nothing existed, in no way could anything come into being out of nothing" (Diels, 1B). The verbal character of Melissus' originality will not escape the modern reader. To say that X *comes from* nothing is to say of "nothing" what can be significantly asserted of something. It is true that an empirical proof of this maxim was attempted much later by Epicurus and his followers, but the earlier attempts to argue the point are entirely nonempirical in character. But however it was established in ancient Greek philosophy, the principle was accepted almost without challenge until the eighteenth century.

The belief in the pervasive character of the causal nexus can be found also among the medical writers of the fifth century. In the Hippocratic medical writing, *The Art* (Loeb, Vol. II), we read that everything which occurs does so through something, so that "spontaneity" is a mere name and has no reality.

The first full expression of principles of causation can be found in the writings of Plato and Aristotle. Plato expresses his views on the necessity of causation in several places. In the *Timaeus* 28A; also in the *Laws* 895, in the *Philebus* 26, and in the *Parmenides* 138, he asserts that "whatever becomes must necessarily become, owing to some cause; without a cause it is impossible for anything to achieve becoming." Since the Forms are eternal and unchangeable, they require no causal explanation. (There is only one passage which is inconsistent with this. It occurs in the *Republic* 597.) But the realm of physical objects including organisms, is derivative in two different ways and therefore requires a cause of change. Physical objects and organisms are copies of Forms and are always changing and being thus insufficient, require causes of their generation. However, it is impossible to discover what Plato means by the *necessity* of a cause. Plato also retains a counterpart of the material from which things are composed, the so-called Receptacle. We can thus discern some of the prototypes of Aristotle's four causes in these views.

One feature of Plato's thought about causation deserves a special mention. This is the element of teleology—the idea that natural changes were intelligently directed by an intelligent and divine agent had never been completely eliminated from early Greek speculation. The attempt of the Sophists radically to distinguish between nature and society, had it been successful, might have led the way to a completely mechanical account of natural processes. Indeed, suggestions of such an account are perhaps indicated by the views of the Greek Atomists. The one remaining statement of Leucippus and what we can reconstruct from the views of Democritus as well as the revival of Atomism by the Epicureans, show that the Greeks were capable of conceiving of natural processes in purely mechanical terms. But the philosophy of Plato and Aristotle so completely overshadowed this attempt that it is fair to say that the teleological explanation dominated European thought until the seventeenth century. Plato's teleology, to be sure, was considerably different from that of Aristotle. According to Plato, the order and arrangement of the world resulted from the action of a divine Artificer who, looking to the Forms as a model of perfection, fashioned the world out of some kind of pre-existing eternal but recalcitrant stuff.

The most elaborate treatise of causality in Ancient Greek thought, is to be found in Aristotle. In the first place, he distinguished four senses of "cause": the material out of which things come; the form which things eventually have when they are perfected; that which brings about this completion, the moving cause; and finally the purpose or function of such things, the final cause. Thus there is a teleological interpretation of causal transactions but it is a teleology of a very special sort. For these ends or purposes, which are realized by natural objects when they achieve their perfection, are not imposed from without but rather arise from their intrinsic natures. All things naturally tend toward intrinsically determined goals. The ultimate cause of this tendency or natural striving is God, who moves things by being the object of their desire. This tendency has gone on from eternity and will go on without end.

Some important details of Aristotle's views on causation must now be discussed. Like Plato, Aristotle maintains that the cause of change must be assumed as an absolute necessity. Everything which undergoes change is made to do so necessarily by something (*Physics* 7, 241b, 25). This necessity of a cause of change is explained in the following way: motion is the process of actualization of what is capable of being so moved. What undergoes change is what has a potency or capacity to do so (*Physics* 251a, 12). Now this actualization of potency by definition requires an actual agent (*Physics* 257b, 9). Nothing which has a capacity to undergo change can bring about that change by itself (*Metaphysics* 107b, 29–31). All these statements, as is obvious, really depend on the definition of change as the actuality of potency, so that the necessity that change be effected by something distinct from what undergoes change, depends on the definition which Aristotle gives. It is true that Aristotle provides

considerations which he thinks ought to induce us to accept such a characterization of change, but the repeated insistence that these principles are necessary plainly depends on his definition. From this definition of change a number of special causal principles are derived. First, it is clear that similar changes require similar causes and conversely, similar causes will always give rise, if there is no interference, to similar changes. (There is an exception to the second of these principles in the case of free agents so that the principle must be qualified so as to apply only to what Aristotle calls irrational potencies, 1046b, 5–6; 1048a, 8 et passim.) Furthermore, the cause and the effect must be alike either ostensibly or covertly (1049b). It is for this reason that Aristotle denies what Mill later called the "plurality of causes." Since each of two effects of the same kind must resemble its cause, the causes will be identical in species or in genus. This is the rationale behind Aristotle's discussion of the point in *Posterior Analytics*, Book Two, Chs. 16–18.

To summarize, every change requires a cause that resembles the change in question and such causal transactions (with the exception noted above) occur with regularity if there is no interference. The discovery of particular causal routines depends ultimately on the direct observance of repetitions in the natural world. By induction from the observance of particular cases, we infer universal propositions which formulate these routines. Aristotle nowhere explicitly provides the ground for such inductive inferences from particulars to the general case, but his medieval successors suggest the following argument: what happens always or for the most part, cannot be due to chance; therefore, if we see in a number of cases that under condition A, an object of the kind C is attended by changes of the kind E, we can take this as a clear indication of the universality of the principle.

Another important feature of Aristotle's views on causation requires mention. Causal connection is simultaneous determination (*Metaphysics*, Book 5, Ch. 2, 1014a, lines 20f.). It is not easy to see how this doctrine, that cause and effect are mutually simultaneous, can be made consistent with any temporal succession of events in the world.

The Stoics and Epicureans are as insistent as their predecessors about the necessity of a cause for every change. According to the Stoics "Nothing takes place without a preceding cause" (Plutarch, 11, 574) "... this determining cause acts by necessity and any apparent chance or apparently causeless event is due to a hidden cause" (ibid., 7, 572). The Stoics are well known for their deterministic view of the universe which they find not a little difficult to reconcile with the apparent facts of human choice. A peculiarity of the Epicurean view of the causal principle deserves mention. Epicurus maintains that nothing comes into existence from what is nonexistent. Otherwise, he holds, anything would have come from anything since it would have no need of a proper and appropriate origin or seed (Diogenes Laërtius, X, 39). His argument is stated in detail by Lucretius (*De rerum natura*, I, 160). The argument seems to be something like the following: if the principle *ex nihilo* were false, then anything would have come from anything and if anything would have come from anything, then the resemblance between parent and offspring in the case of both plants and animals would be exceedingly rare or absent. But on the contrary, the resemblance in question is an absolute rule so far as observation informs us; therefore, the principle "from nothing, nothing comes" is justified. Whatever may be thought of the weakness of this argument, it is at any rate an empirical argument for a principle which in earlier thought had been largely urged for nonempirical reasons and, in this respect, is almost unique.

The Greek skeptics raised serious doubts about the principles of causation which we have already encountered. But it is worth noting that none of their arguments is anything like the critical considerations about the nature of causal connections which are associated with the name of Hume. It is true that some of the views about our knowledge of substance can be traced to the skeptic Carneades and it is also true that the contention that we have only probable cognition about things and processes in the world came from the same source. But the skeptical arguments which Hume used to such great effect, cannot be found in any of the discussions of the skeptics of antiquity.

We come now to Neo-Platonism. The principal contribution which the Neo-Platonists made to the concept of causal connection is this: that effects not only resemble their causes and causes resemble their effects, but also that the effect has some kind of pre-existence in its cause and conversely, that the cause has some kind of post-existence in its effect. The Neo-Platonic doctrine that all things emanate from a single ineffable source, that these things therefore pre-exist in and emerge from this source lies at the foundation of their view of the causal nexus. This view is associated with many of the medieval discussions of the subject. Even those philosophers and theologians who do not accept the main contention of the Neo-Platonists, viz., that all reality emanates from an inexhaustible fountain of existence, nevertheless do accept some form of the principle that the effect has some kind of pre-existence in the cause.

The intellectual tradition of antiquity was largely assimilated by medieval Jewish, Christian, and Muslim philosophers. Augustine, for example, assumes without argument that every event must have a cause and argues for it in a somewhat simplistic way. In Chapter 17 of Book 2, *On the Free Will*, he holds that nothing can give itself form because nothing can give itself what it does not have. So that if it does not have form at the outset and cannot receive from itself what it does not possess, it must receive this from something other than itself. The pre-existence of all things in the ultimate cause, God, is conceived in semi-Platonic terms: the Archetypes or Exemplars of all finite beings exist in the mind of God. Many statements of the necessity of causation can be found in Augustine's writings (*De ordine, De Trinitate, De genesi contra Manicheos*) and his views are echoed by a number of medieval Christian theologians of the early medieval period. For example, Anselm in *The Monologium*, Chapter 3, holds that it is altogether inconceivable that anything could exist without a cause.

The Muslim philosophers developed a conception of causality largely dependent on Aristotle and usually modified by Neo-Platonic doctrines. This was largely due to the fact that some pseudo-Aristotelian writings circulated among them and partially due to the further circumstance that some of them, for example Al-Farabi, found the philosophy of Plato and Aristotle to be mutually harmonious. Al-Kindi, Al-Farabi, Ibn-Sina (Avicenna), and Ibn-Tofail all accept as self-evident the principle that whatever exists after not having existed needs some producing cause. The tenth-century system of Avicenna is especially important both as a complete representation of philosophy in the Near Eastern world of the eleventh century and because of its influence on Christian thought in the early thirteenth century. He adopted an elaborate form of the Neo-Platonic emanation-theory in terms of which the genesis of the universe from the Godhead was conceived as necessitated. The first Being is absolutely necessary (in fact it is called the "necessary being of existence," *ens necessarium*). All other realities emanating therefrom are possible beings considered in themselves, but necessary beings considered in terms of their cause. The universe in this concept is an organic system in which causal interrelations of all things are strictly observed. In the System of Al-Kindi, the causal influence of everything upon everything else is emphasized following earlier Neo-Platonic suggestions so that a kind of universal harmony is achieved. This is carried to such an extent that Al-Kindi maintains that a complete knowledge of any single thing would reveal the nature of the entire universe.

The first medieval critique of the maxims of causality comes from the school of orthodox theologians founded by Al-Ashari. This school defended the doctrine that

God is the only cause and that the ordinary regularities in the natural world are only the result of God's usual mode of action. The most detailed defense of this medieval Occasionalism is to be found in the writing of Al-Ghazali (1058–1111), *The Incoherence of Philosophers*. In this attack on the philosophical system of Avicenna, Al-Ghazali argued that there was neither empirical nor logical warrant for ascertaining the existence of causal connections among any finite things. He asks why philosophers hold that fire is the cause of combustion, say of a piece of cloth. The philosopher can give no reason for this except the observance that combustion occurs on contact of a flame with the cloth. But this shows only that the combustion occurs together with the contact but not as a result of it. In other words, the empirical observation of the concomitance of two events reveals no causal interaction. Moreover, the connection between the so-called cause and its alleged effect is not necessary. There is only one kind of necessity, viz., logical necessity and no logical necessity can exist between two distinct things or events. For if one of these is distinct from the other, the affirmation of one does not include that of the other nor does the negation of one include the negation of the other. The only reason that there appears to be any logical connection between distinct events or objects is because the description of one of the two includes reference to the other. But this is purely verbal, and in no wise proves a real connection of the events.

The reader will immediately recognize the resemblance between Al-Ghazali's criticisms of causality and that of Malebranche and Hume. (No evidence exists to establish an historical connection here.) Al-Ghazali's critique of causality as well as his attack on other aspects of philosophy practically terminated any original philosophical speculation in the Muslim world of the Near East. His work was elaborately examined much later by Ibn-Ruschd. Ibn-Ruschd (Averroës) was perhaps closest to Aristotle of all the Muslims. In his attack on Al-Ghazali, *The Incoherence of the Incoherence*, and in other writings, he correctly points out that a denial of the principle of causality between finite events, cuts the ground entirely from any attempt to prove the existence of a god, for without any empirical evidence of causal connection among finite beings, there is no way left for us to infer the existence of the unobserved from that of something observed. In this, Ibn-Ruschd was perfectly correct, but he does not really succeed in answering Al-Ghazali's criticisms.

The only distinctive contribution to the subject of causality among the medieval Jews was made by Ibn-Gabirol (Avicebron). According to his doctrine, the only truly efficacious force in the universe is the will of God which holds matter and form together through-out the universe. As we proceed from God down through the hierarchy of things, this force is debilitated so that in the world of corporeal objects, we find beings incapable of exerting any efficacy whatever. The other philosophers among the Jews maintain views on causality which are sufficiently similar to those already mentioned and merit no special attention.

The translations of the major works of Aristotle into Latin during the twelfth and the thirteenth centuries, as well as translations from Jewish and Arabic philosophy made at the same time, provided a new impetus to philosophical speculation in Christendom. In one of the earlier discussions of the subject by Robert Grosseteste, *On Potency and Act*, we find the characteristic Aristotelian doctrine that everything which is caused is caused by something similar to itself either in species or according to some analogy. From this, it follows that the act of any potency precedes it and this act is like the potency it actualizes either specifically or analogically.

The most detailed discussion of causality is to be found scattered through the writings of Aquinas. Aquinas' discussions are enriched by the development of logic from the twelfth century onward, and by the fuller understanding of Aristotle's views. Aquinas maintains all of the familiar Aristotelian doctrines. Everything which is brought into actuality from potency requires a cause which is like the potentiality it actualizes, and all changes require causes, and this requirement is one of absolute necessity. Finally that this necessity is logically conceived is put beyond all question by Aquinas' argument in the *Summa theologica* (Part I, Qu. 44, Art. 1). Here Saint Thomas is arguing that everything excepting God Himself, must be created. Now some people have maintained that since any given kind of being does not involve the notion of *being caused* as a part of its definition, there is no reason why any member of such a kind may not exist without being created. To this, Thomas replies that, although a connection with a cause is not a part of the definition of the kind of thing which is caused, this connection still follows from some aspect of its nature. For from the fact that something exists by participation in Being, it does follow that it must be caused by something other than itself. A similar consideration taken from Thomas' proof for the existence of God (ibid., Part I, Qu. 2, Art. 3) shows that the relation between things and their causes is logically necessitated. There Thomas argues to the necessity of a cause of every change from the Aristotelian definition of change. Since change is the actualization of a potency, anything which undergoes change must be actualized by something, and since nothing can actualize itself, the change must be effected by something other than the object undergoing it. Thomas insists that all finite beings have their own appropriate capacities both to undergo and to induce change. This doctrine is held to be consistent with the view that God cooperates with His creatures whenever any of them exercises its own proper causal efficacy.

A crisis in medieval Christian philosophy occurred in the last quarter of the thirteenth century. The expositors of Aristotle in the Faculty of Arts at the University of Paris insisted on their obligation to expound Aristotle's natural philosophy even on points where it conflicted with the tenets of Christian dogma. Accordingly, they held that in natural philosophy, creation from nothing is impossible. Every new being must be generated from a pre-existing matter. Also there is no exception to the regular and characteristic activities of natural objects, so that there is no room in the natural world, as conceived by Aristotle, for any miracles. Again, the causal dependence of accidents on their substrata admits of no exception. Now all this was in patent conflict with Christian dogma. The doctrine of creation from nothing, the miraculous suspension of the causal powers of natural objects, and the existence of accidents without a material substratum in the Eucharist to all of which Christians were committed could not be reconciled with Aristotelian natural philosophy. Accordingly, serious adjustments were required. Of course, this had been realized by the scholastics before the great condemnation of strict Aristotelism in 1277, but the matter did not assume critical proportions until that time.

These adjustments took several forms. In Duns Scotus, the essentially Aristotelian view about causal connection is generally maintained with one important qualification. Instead of holding that finite creatures will exercise causal efficacy whenever circumstances are appropriate, Duns Scotus maintained that these beings are so constituted that they will exercise their powers if and only if God cooperates. So we cannot say that causal connection is inevitable, but only that finite things are naturally apt to act in their characteristic ways.

A somewhat more radical view can be found in Ockham and his successors. While it is very clear that Ockham believed in the efficacy of natural causes, his epistemological reservations concerning our knowledge of causal connection paved the way for the radical skepticism which is characteristic of some of the fourteenth-century theologians. According to Ockham, the only way in which we can establish any causal connection between one thing and another is the observation that when one of these occurs, the other also occurs at the same time and at or near the same place. Since it is logically possible that God may at any time per-

form a miracle, it is impossible to provide absolute evidence for any causal transaction (Sentence II, 8–5). Sufficient evidence however, for causal transactions, can be found in the aforementioned criterion of spatio-temporal concomitance. What is important however, is that Ockham insists that this is the *only* way to establish causal connection. Once we have established such a connection in a single instance, we can infer the proposition that this connection holds for all cases of the kind, by the self-evident proposition that all things of the same kind produce effects of the same kind in appropriately disposed objects under the same circumstances.

A more radical view of the subject was expounded by Nicholas of Autrecourt. He has been called a medieval Hume, and his right to this title is based on some letters to a certain Bernard of Arezzo. In these letters, he maintained that all certitude is based on and reducible to the immediate evidence of experience and the Principle of Contradiction. But there is no absolute evidence derived from experience that any natural causes operate. Moreover, it is a consequence of the Principle of Contradiction that in every valid inference the consequent simply restates all or part of what was stated in the antecedent. Hence from the fact that one thing is known to exist, it cannot be inferred with the evidence of the Principle of Contradiction that another and different thing exists. From this, it follows that effects cannot be logically inferred from alleged causes nor conversely. Thus, though there may be a probability for causal connection, there can be no certainty that any natural causes exist. Neither experience nor logical reasoning can provide such certainty. Nicholas' views were hotly contested by his contemporary, John Buridan, but his criticisms of Nicholas fall short of the mark. The influence of Nicholas of Autrecourt extends into the next century, for we find his arguments used by Cardinal Pierre d'Ailly and others. Many other authors in the fourteenth century exhibit similar critical tendencies concerning the great metaphysical questions of causality, substance, and the like, but the majority of scholastic writers continue to maintain views similar to those of the great thirteenth-century scholastics.

The philosophy of the Renaissance represents revivals of antiquity's theories or the continuation of medieval doctrines on the subject. Neo-Platonic, Stoic, and Epicurean doctrines all find their champions at this time. Even ancient Greek skepticism found its early modern representative in the fifteenth and sixteenth century, but nothing distinctively new emerged until the period of the great discoveries in physical science of the seventeenth century.

One of the main modifications of medieval views about causal connection depends on the new conception of inertia introduced by Galileo and Descartes. In accordance with this notion, it is no longer necessary to assume a cause in order to explain continuation of motion or rest. Nevertheless, philosophers and scientists continue to maintain the necessity of a cause for every new event. In some cases, novelty involves either a change in velocity or direction. Nonetheless, causes are always presupposed. In Descartes, we find the assertion that everything which exists requires a cause (Reply to the Second Objections: Axiom I). Moreover, the principle that causes must be adequate to their effect is applied by Descartes in a new way; even the content of our ideas requires adequate causes and it is this principle which Descartes employs in his main proof for the existence of God. Descartes' radical dualism between mind and matter introduced a special problem: How can there be any causal interaction between things so very different as mind and extension? The causal interactions within the physical realm are explained exclusively in terms of the communication of motion. But since motion is conserved, there is a difficulty in explaining how human volition can in any way modify the actions of bodies. Either Descartes or his immediate successors supposed that human volition could modify the direction of a motion without changing the total amount of motion in the universe. But many of the successors of Descartes were unsatisfied with this explanation and introduced the doctrine of Occasionalism. The best known of the Occasionalists was Malebranche. In his *De la recherche de la vérité* (*The Search for Truth*, 1674), he defined a real cause as something between which and its effects, the mind perceives a necessary connection. Now since only the Infinite Being is one between whose will and its effects the mind perceives necessary connection, God is the only real cause. He supports this view in two ways: (1) we see no necessary connection between any finite being and its alleged effects; and (2) observation reveals only succession and no genuine causation. Consequently, all events are caused by but one being, namely God. Other Occasionalists such as Cordemoy and LaForge, used other arguments to support the same conclusion.

In Britain, Hobbes maintained a strictly materialistic account of all causal interaction, and Francis Bacon attempted to formulate the methods by which causal connections could be discovered. Even there, some skepticism about the discernment of causal connection is expressed by a number of authors. Newton's teacher, Isaac Barrow, in his *Mathematical Lectures* (ed. W. Whewell, 1800) held that only in mathematics can any necessary connection be established so that no connection of an external efficient cause with its effect can

be established by logical considerations. Joseph Glanvill in *The Vanity of Dogmatizing* (1661) expressed similar doubts.

Locke, both in his *Essay Concerning Human Understanding* and in his controversy with Stillingfleet, maintained that the proposition, "Whatever has a beginning has a cause," is a principle of reason which can be justified simply by the analysis of the meaning of the terms "beginning" and "being caused." The idea of power is derived, according to Locke, from our expectation of the constant concomitance of two events, but he nowhere explains satisfactorily how this concomitance reveals anything more than regularity in the occurrence of events. It is true that he finds direct evidence of activity in the action of the mind which is immediately observed, but how this direct observation of mental activity is connected with any physical changes, he leaves entirely unexplained.

Berkeley's philosophy introduced an idealism which tried to refute the materialistic interpretation of the world external to ("without the") mind. The only place where activity is directly encountered is in the activity of our own spirit. The ideas which are the content of mind are causally inefficacious. Yet Berkeley assumes without question and without discussion, that there must be some cause (ultimately God) of those ideas which are not the result of human volition. So on the one hand, the regularity of our experience does not imply the relation of cause and effect; but on the other hand, the existence in us of ideas which we did not ourselves produce, indicates some other cause which Berkeley construes as divine activity.

On the Continent, the two great systems of the seventeenth century were those of Spinoza and Leibniz. Spinoza conceives causal interaction essentially in two different ways: on the one hand, every event in the universe is a necessary consequence of the divine nature so that cause and logical ground are identified; on the other hand, the finite chains of events which constitute the regularities of nature, though somehow dependent upon the necessary causality of God, are not satisfactorily integrated into his system. The problem of the causal interaction of mind and matter is resolved by Spinoza in terms of an identity theory. Mental and physical occurrences are two aspects of the same event so that the Cartesian problem of interaction is resolved. Leibniz denied any causal or spatio-temporal relations among the monads or centers of energy (*vis viva*) which constitute his universe. Instead of causal connection, he postulated a "pre-established harmony" among the monads in terms of which the states of any given substance correspond to the states of all the other substances in the universe. This correspondence was established by the deity at the beginning of creation because God selected just those substances whose successions of states would exhibit this harmony. There is, however, a real causality within each monad, for in each monad, the later states emerge from the earlier according to the law of succession which determines the life history of each monad (as a mathematical function determines the relations of the elements of an algebraic series). Moreover, all the monads are causally dependent on the deity at each moment of their several existences.

The most important contribution to the subject of causal connection in modern philosophy was made by David Hume. Although Hume's arguments were anticipated by the medieval Muslim Ash'arites, Al-Ghazali, and by Nicholas of Autrecourt and others in the Middle Ages, and to some extent by the French Occasionalists of the seventeenth century, Hume's way of putting these arguments as well as his explanation of necessary connection, was a distinctly novel contribution. According to Hume, logic is incapable of providing a foundation in reason for the several received maxims concerning causal connection. That every beginning must have a cause, that like antecedents will always be followed by like sequents, and that a cause must be like its effect had, in the great majority of Hume's predecessors, been regarded as principles for which reason could provide an absolute justification. Hume rejects all this by a series of brilliant criticisms of all the traditional attempts in this direction, and he concluded that the belief in causal connection has an entirely different foundation. We observe nothing but the regular succession of events. This repetition in our experience produces a felt expectation which Hume calls "an impression of reflection." This impression is projected onto the objects revealed by sensation and so we mistake a feeling in us ("felt expectation") for a connection of objects with one another. The idea of necessary connection is thus derived from habitually felt expectation and has no other foundation. A cause is nothing but an object precedent to and contiguous with some other object and such that objects like the former stand in a similar relation of precedence and contiguity to objects like the latter. Causation considered as a natural relation has the further aforementioned feature of habitually felt expectation which is contributed by the mind of the observer and is in no way a constituent of the objective situation. The uniformity of nature according to Hume, does in fact exist, but our belief in it is a matter simply of customary expectation and it can have no foundation in reason; nor does the so-called principle of the "uniformity of nature" have even any probability since all probable

arguments presuppose this principle and thus can never be used as its justification.

Hume's psychological explanation of causal belief seemed to constitute a threat to the foundations of natural science. Immanuel Kant, while accepting Hume's negative critique of previous *a priori* views of necessary connection in causality, nevertheless regarded Hume's theories of the genesis and nature of causal belief inadequate. Since Kant believed that natural science was firmly established—especially with Newton's universal laws of physical phenomena—he felt obliged to give another account of causal connection as well as of all our experience of physical objects, and he thought that he discovered this new account in the original constitution of human cognition. According to Kant, our minds so operate as to construe the congeries of sensation in substantival and causal ways. The necessity for causal connection is thus dependent on the structure and function of the human mind. The principle of causality is valid for all human experience because the human mind construes experience ineluctably in causal ways. It was by this means that Kant supposed that he could rescue natural science from the skepticism of Hume. The principle of causality has absolute and objective validity as applied to the entire range of experience. Kant's principal argument is to be found in "The Second Analogy of Experience," in his *Critique of Pure Reason*. There he argued that the objectivity of succession can be explained only in terms of the way all human minds construe the succession of events revealed in sensation.

Several quite different developments constitute the subsequent history of reflections about the nature of causal connection. The absolute idealists, particularly Hegel, account for the connections of things with one another by a radical modification of logic which they substitute for the logic of contradictories—the logic in which the questions of causality had been discussed in almost all earlier philosophy. Hegel introduced the dialectic of contraries. This innovation made it possible to connect distinct things by virtue of their very distinctness. Earlier philosophers had raised the question "How can different things be causally related?" But Hegel's dialectic converted this question into another one, viz., How can distinct things fail to be connected? In other words, the very difference of distinct aspects of reality required their interconnection and ultimately their interdependence. All reality so construed becomes one systemic whole in which all the parts are interdependent. This doctrine achieved the result which was desired but at the great cost of replacing standard logic with what Hegel called dialectical logic but what was in reality an entirely new metaphysic.

277

The principal contribution to the subject from the nonidealist side was made by Maine de Biran, who argued that we have a direct experience of causal efficacy in the actions of our own consciousness. A later and somewhat different form of this view was championed by A. N. Whitehead. He distinguished between two radically different kinds of perception—perception in the mode of presentational immediacy and perception in the mode of causal efficacy—and maintained that the latter revealed to us direct and unmistakable evidence of causal interaction. The main difficulty with contentions of this kind had already been anticipated by Hume. Even if there is some unique feature of experience which we are inclined to regard as a direct evidence of efficacy, it would serve in no way to guarantee the existence of repeatable causal routines in nature. Yet, it is the repeatability of succession that is an essential ingredient in any useful notion of causal connection and this, the alleged perception in the mode of causal efficacy does not and cannot guarantee.

The development of natural science since the seventeenth century has tended to emphasize functional determination, for example, as expressed in the generalizations of physics and chemistry, rather than regularities of succession, and the equations of physics provide little or no basis for the layman's belief in causal connection as conceived by earlier philosophical discussions of the matter. While it is still true that in the less advanced sciences, laws of succession continue to play some role, the possibility of the ultimate explanation of these laws by derivation from the generalizations of the more exact sciences, renders any ultimate concern with these laws of succession relatively unimportant.

Some final consideration must be given to the discoveries in the realm of physics concerning Heisenberg's Principle of Indeterminacy. Whatever ultimate interpretation may be given to this principle, it appears at present that strict and unexceptional regularity in the occurrence of events in the subatomic realm must be given up and statistical rather than nomic generalizations—laws asserting necessary connection—accepted as the best characterization of the relation of events at this level.

The conviction that some kind of uniformity governs the play of events in the natural world has been one of the most influential beliefs of man since the beginning of human reflection. Attempts of various kinds, as we have seen, were made to base this conviction on the deliverances of reason. In particular, the belief that the causal maxims could be established by purely logical considerations, dominated almost the entire history of the subject. The criticisms of this rationalistic view of causal connection gradually undermined these convictions so that today it is not too much to say that they have been abandoned by a considerable number of philosophers and are in no way operative in the practice of scientists.

BIBLIOGRAPHY

There are standard editions of major authors and the following selected works are also helpful.

Primitive Period. Henri Frankfort, Mrs. Henri Frankfort, John A. Wilson, and Thorkild Jacobsen, *Before Philosophy* (Harmondsworth, 1949). Hans Kelsen, *Society and Nature* (Chicago, 1943). R. B. Onians, *The Origins of European Thought* (Cambridge, 1951).

The Greeks and Romans. Cyril Bailey, *The Greek Atomists and Epicurus* (Oxford, 1928). F. M. Cornford, *Plato's Cosmology* (London, 1937). Diels-Kranz, *Die Fragmente der Vorsokratiker*, 5th ed. (Berlin, 1951–54). S. Sambursky, *Physics of the Stoics* (London, 1959). F. Solmsen, *Aristotle's System of the Physical World* (Ithaca, 1960). Léon Robin, *Pyrrhon et le scepticisme grec* (Paris, 1944).

The Medieval Period. Léon Baudry, *Lexique philosophique de Guillaume d'Ockham* (Paris, 1958), article "Causa." M. Fakhry, *Islamic Occasionalism* (London, 1958). Erich Hochstetter, *Studien zur Metaphysik und Erkenntnislehre Wilhelms von Ockham* (Berlin, 1927). Michalski Konstanty, "Le criticisme et le scepticisme dans la philosophie du XIVe siècle," *Bulletin International de l'Académie Polonaise des Sciences* (1919–25). Francis Meehan, *Efficient Causality in Aristotle and St. Thomas* (Washington, D.C., 1940). J. Obermann, "Das Problem der Kausalität bei den Arabern," *Festschrift Joseph R. von Karabacek* (Vienna, 1916), pp. 15–42.

The Modern Period. Maine de Biran, "Essay upon the Foundations of Psychology," *The Classical Psychologists*, ed. Benjamin Rand (Cambridge, 1912). Standard editions of René Descartes, *Meditations* and *Principles of Philosophy;* Thomas Hobbes, *Works;* David Hume, *Treatise of Human Nature* and *Enquiry Concerning Human Understanding;* Immanuel Kant, *Critique of Pure Reason.* G. W. Leibniz, *Leibniz's Philosophical Papers and Letters,* trans. Leroy Loemker (Chicago, 1956). Standard editions of John Locke, *Essay Concerning Human Understanding;* Nicolas Malebranche, *Recherche de la vérité.* J. S. Mill, *System of Logic* (London, 1949). Bertrand Russell, *Human Knowledge* (London, 1948); idem, *Mysticism and Logic* (Garden City, 1957), "On the Notion of Cause." Moritz Schlick, "Gesetz Kausalität in der gegenwärtigen Physik," *Die Naturwissenschaften* (Berlin, 1931). Arthur Schopenhauer, *Über die vierfache Wurzel . . .* (1813), trans. as *The Fourfold Root of the Principle of Sufficient Reason* (London, 1907). Benedict Spinoza, *Ethics* and *Correspondence,* standard editions. A. N. Whitehead, *Symbolism* (New York, 1927); idem, *Process and Reality* (New York, 1929).

JULIUS WEINBERG

[See also Analogy; Atomism; **Causation in Islamic Thought; Causation, Final Causes;** Chance; Dualism; God; Hegelian . . . ; **Indeterminacy; Necessity;** Neo-Platonism; Pre-Platonic Conceptions.]

CAUSATION IN HISTORY

ALTHOUGH the topic of historical causation has occupied philosophers and historians from early times, the discussions to which it has given rise have not conformed to any single continuous pattern or theme. Like other matters that have been the focus of perennial theoretical controversy and dispute, and particularly those falling within the sphere of the human studies, it has been approached from a variety of directions and examined in the light of a number of different perspectives and interests; as a consequence debates on the subject have not infrequently been bedevilled by misunderstanding and confusion. One broad division within the field may, however, be introduced at the outset, its being convenient for the purposes of the present article to apply a familiar contemporary distinction and to consider the principal issues raised beneath two main headings.

Under the first we shall discuss substantive theories of causation, such theories being concerned, in one way or another, with determining the actual forces operative in history and with trying to elicit the factors ultimately responsible for historical development and change. Theories of this type are often associated with the speculative writings of classical philosophers of history; but they have also found expression—whether explicitly or implicitly—in the works of practicing historians, informing their methodology and influencing the manner in which they have approached the empirical data confronting them. Under the second heading we shall be concerned with a type of theory that is of more recent origin and which is of an analytical or critical character. Here the questions involved have been of a conceptual rather than a factual nature, having to do with the notion or category of causality as it is commonly employed within the context of historical thought and discourse: the problems raised by this kind of investigation have not been related to the workings of the historical process itself but have pertained instead to the explanatory concepts and linguistic devices in terms of which historians are accustomed to interpret the events of which it is composed. Yet, as will emerge in the course of this survey, the two types of enquiry have not evolved independently of one another, there being in fact significant connections discernible between them.

I. SUBSTANTIVE THEORIES

What, if anything, underlies the course of history as a whole? What are the fundamental or real determinants of historical change? Can any one factor be picked out as being of preeminent importance? Is it possible to formulate causal laws that hold universally throughout the domain of historical experience? What is the role of human thought and decision in history, and how far is it justifiable to impute moral responsibility for their actions to individual historical figures? Is it legitimate to regard accident or chance as playing a significant part in deciding the direction taken by historical events? Is historical determinism true, and if so what are its implications? These constitute some of the questions that have been asked by theorists preoccupied by the problem of giving an account of causality as it manifests itself within the field of the human past. Not only have they generated a host of diverse and often conflicting answers; they have also been raised at different levels of enquiry and with distinguishable considerations in mind.

Theological and Metaphysical Conceptions. It is not, for instance, the case that the causal agencies regarded as determining the sequence of occurrences have always been conceived to be empirical factors lying within the historical process. On the contrary, it has sometimes been assumed that the clue to all that happens must ultimately be located in something that lies outside that process, such as the will of a divine or transcendent being. One potent source of speculation has been the belief that the pattern of historical events represents the unfolding of some overall purpose or design, views of this sort originating in religious notions of the universe and of man's place within it. Thus, early in the Christian era, certain of the Church fathers were already reacting against Greco-Roman views that pictured history in terms of recurrent cycles, seeking to substitute a conception of linear movement wherein the intentions of a sovereign providential power were clearly discoverable; while by the fifth century Saint Augustine had given articulate philosophical expression to a directional view which presupposed a providential order and which was to prove immensely influential. Augustine's ideas admittedly diverged widely from the cruder hypotheses of his predecessors; moreover, he was notably reticent about the possibility of interpreting the details of terrestrial history in a providential manner, implying for the most part that such things fell outside the range of human cognizance and concern. The same cannot, however, be said of some later writers who looked back to Augustine for inspiration, and least of all of the seventeenth-century French historian, J. B. Bossuet. Bossuet's *Discours sur l'histoire universelle* (1681) was indeed remarkable for the confidence displayed by its author in his capacity for penetrating the workings of the divine intelligence insofar as these impinged upon the affairs of men. It was not merely that he took pleasure in offering examples of the retribution visited by God upon erring nations and individuals; he further professed to know

279

that even the most (apparently) fortuitous occurrences had been "contrived by a higher wisdom, that is to say, in the everlasting mind who has all the world's causes and all the effects contained in one single order."

The modern development of historical enquiry as a firmly established discipline in its own right has been—not unnaturally—accompanied by a marked decline in the tendency to try to explain the general course of history by reference to a governing agency external to it. It is true that some latter-day theologians, for example, Reinhold Niebuhr, have spoken as if certain forms of providential interpretation remained feasible: but the proposals put forward have usually been so tentative and heavily qualified, so imbued with a desire not to trespass upon areas occupied by professional or "technical" historians, that to treat them as strictly comparable with the ambitious programs of earlier periods would be a mistake. Nevertheless, the view that the totality of historical events can and should be understood as composing an intelligible teleological sequence has been a persistent one in human thinking, and in the eighteenth and nineteenth centuries this found expression in systems in which the purposive element stressed by previous theological writers was, so to speak, absorbed within the historical process itself. Thus various attempts were made to portray history as moving in a determinate and meaningful direction, but without thereby positing a transcendent entity which could be regarded as ultimately responsible for the direction it took; the providential principle was regarded as being immanent in world history rather than as deriving from an extraneous source.

Some such thought underlies the theories of history propounded by Vico, Kant, and Hegel. Despite their considerable differences on other counts, these philosophers at least shared the common assumption or methodological postulate that what happens in the historical sphere possesses an inner "logic" which can be regarded as being intrinsic to the course of events. By this they did not mean that the actual participants in the process were always aware of the long-term significance of their actions: on the contrary, they implied that the historical purposes served by particular agents were obscure or even unknown to the agents themselves; it was only in retrospect—and from a vantage point that transcended the contingencies of immediate occasion and circumstance—that the deeds of individuals could be seen as contributing towards the realization of a state of affairs which was in some sense implicit from the beginning as a final goal or end. At the same time, they did not wish to be understood as recommending a kind of applied theology. When Vico, for instance, spoke of there being an "ideal

eternal history . . . whose course is run in time by the histories of all nations" (*Scienza nuova*, §114), he expressly repudiated the suggestion that he was postulating a divine "potter who molds things outside himself." It was man who made his own history; he did so, however, in a fashion such that each stage of social development could be interpreted as having a part to play in a sequence that, taken as a whole, displayed a necessary teleological structure. Likewise, Kant was insistent upon the possibility of conceiving history in a way that portrayed the conflicts and vicissitudes to which men are subject by virtue of their own activities as representing the means whereby the human species progressively realized the capacities originally implanted in it by nature and thus moved towards the fulfilment of its earthly destiny. The case of Hegel is more complicated, since his conception of history was impregnated with conceptions deriving from a comprehensive metaphysical system that encompassed every aspect of human experience; yet here, too, a similar theme may be discerned. For history, along with everything else, exemplified the unfolding of a rational principle or "Idea" that was destined to realize itself in time. Hegel admittedly spoke of the operations of a "World Spirit" (*Weltgeist*) in history, but he does not seem to have envisaged this as an independent agency; rather, it expressed itself directly in the activities of historical individuals and was nothing apart from these. So understood, the historical process moved inexorably forward, one phase giving way to another in a dialectical progression that culminated in a form of social life which—as the embodiment of freedom—constituted its ultimate objective, being referred to by Hegel as "the final cause of the world at large."

Hegel himself sometimes gave the impression that his interpretation of history could be regarded as a "hypothesis" that both accounted for and was grounded upon the empirical data at his disposal. And a major attraction, indeed, of teleological theories of the type to which his may be said to belong has been the feeling that, unlike explicitly theological conceptions, they do not in the end require for their support anything other than the attested facts of historical experience. Such a feeling is understandable. For what, from one point of view, the historical teleologist can be considered to be doing is making a claim to the effect that a certain trend or tendency has manifested itself in human affairs; and such a claim, it would seem, is one fully capable of being confirmed or disproved by experience alone. It is, however, one thing to assert that events have, as a matter of fact, exhibited a particular tendency or direction; it is another to say that it was necessary that they should have taken the course that they did: and it is another again to seek to confirm this necessity by reference to the state of affairs in which they have issued or to which they eventually led. To argue that certain things had to happen if something else was to happen is not in itself to explain why the earlier events in the series occurred as they did; the most that would be shown is that the occurrence of the prior events was a necessary condition of the occurrence of the sequel. The situation would, of course, be different if, on independent grounds, it could be demonstrated that the end-product of history was in some manner intended or preordained from the start and, moreover, that there was only one route by which such a consummation could be attained. But it remains hard to see how such an additional assumption could be established, or even assigned a clear meaning, in the absence of anything over and above the facts of man's past as determined by ordinary historical investigation. For this reason, among others, a number of empirically-minded theorists, such as Saint-Simon and Comte, were led to look elsewhere in their search for an explanatory key with which to unlock the secrets of historical evolution and change.

The Quest for Causal Laws. One factor which, from the Enlightenment onwards, exercised a pervasive influence upon the development of historical speculation was the progress of the natural sciences. The discoveries of men like Galileo, Kepler, and Newton had apparently opened the way to unlimited advance in the exploration of nature, showing how ranges of physical phenomena, often of the most diverse kinds, could be systematically accommodated and unified within schemes of vast explanatory and predictive power. It was, furthermore, a feature of the theories and laws propounded that they had been evolved within the setting of a mechanistic rather than a teleological conception of the universe: enquiry was guided by the aim of determining the detectable conditions under which phenomena occurred, the uniformities of sequence which they exhibited in precisely specifiable circumstances, rather than by considerations involving the supposition that they were activated by purposive principles mysteriously embedded in the structure of the cosmos. It is not surprising that the possibility of applying similar approaches and techniques to the study of psychological and social phenomena should have occurred to thinkers to whom it appeared unreasonable and obscurantist to assume the existence of an absolute gulf separating the realm of nature from the realm of mind. Why should the thought and behavior of human beings not be subject to universal and necessary regularities comparable to those that governed physical reality? At the individual level this attitude was to find expression in such "materialist" works as Holbach's *Système de la nature* (1770) and

La Mettrie's *L'Homme machine* (1748), as well as in the "associationist" psychological doctrines of eighteenth- and nineteenth-century British empiricism. Its most spectacular and influential manifestations, however, took place within the province of social theory: here a determined effort was made to lay the foundations of a historical science which would not only rival the natural sciences in richness and scope but would also provide a firm theoretical base from which to conduct large-scale projects of social reorganization and reform. The practical advantages that would accrue from a proper understanding of the fundamental determinants of history were seldom far from the minds of those who undertook to achieve it.

If causal laws were operative within history, what form did they take and how were they to be discovered? As a number of recent critics have been at pains to point out, the enthusiastic advocacy of a scientific approach to human affairs was not always matched by a corresponding grasp of the actual nature of scientific method and inference. Thus some theorists were apt to rely upon a rather naive mode of induction by simple enumeration in arriving at their conclusions; one consequence of this was a proneness to overlook or leave out of account possible counter-examples to the principles or generalizations they supposed themselves to have established. Again, it is arguable that the interpretations they put upon certain crucial concepts were on occasions open to objection. Karl Popper, for instance, has maintained that the term "law" was not infrequently used incorrectly, being misappropriated to apply to what were in fact no more than particular trends or long-term processes; insofar as these were regarded as possessing some sort of inherent necessity, it was perhaps partly due to the survival of teleological preconceptions which, though openly repudiated, nonetheless continued to exert a covert influence. Yet another persistent feature of scientifically-inspired theories of history was the restriction they imposed upon the range of conditions considered to be basically or "decisively" relevant: it was assumed that the fundamental laws of historical development should be formulable in a manner that gave priority to factors of some specific type—race, environment, and the growth of knowledge or technology being among those variously accorded this privileged status. As a result many of the theories in question were monistic in character, presupposing a sharp contrast between, on the one hand, merely superficial or "apparent" causative agencies and, on the other, deeply-lying forces to whose operation the general shape and direction taken by significant social phenomena must in the last analysis be ascribed. Yet here, once more, it was often far from clear what justification, empirical or otherwise, had been offered for introducing distinctions and limitations of the kind referred to. Some of these tendencies, and their accompanying difficulties, are illustrated in the works of two nineteenth-century thinkers, whose writings made a profound impact upon their age: H. T. Buckle and Karl Marx.

Buckle had been impressed by his reading of Auguste Comte and J. S. Mill, themselves both wedded to the conception of a social science, and he regarded it as a scandal that so little had previously been done "towards discovering the principles which govern the character and destiny of nations." In particular, he heaped ridicule upon doctrines—such as those ascribing to men a power of undetermined free choice—which in his view had hindered the creation of a genuinely scientific interpretation of history. Against obfuscatory and "metaphysical" dogmas of this kind he affirmed the "undeviating regularity" with which human actions followed upon antecedent circumstances, and he set out to provide a detailed account of the fashion in which what he called "three vast agents"—climate, food, and soil—combined to determine the original character and evolution of different peoples and cultures. Buckle's erudition was considerable and his deployment of it to substantiate his claims was not devoid of value, leading other historians to take seriously matters that had not received the attention they deserved. Yet what he said can hardly be considered to have fulfilled his own ambitious aspirations. His generalizations were conspicuously lacking in precision, and his denial that such factors as government and religion could properly be regarded as "prime movers of human affairs" functioned more as a prejudice than as an argued thesis. Moreover, having proved to his satisfaction that a particular condition was necessary to the production of some social outcome, he was liable to pass without further ado to the conclusion that it was sufficient as well. Thus his conduct of the enterprise he had undertaken seemed often to be vitiated by logical confusions in addition to the methodological inadequacies it displayed.

Marx's conception of history was subtler, and in general has proved to be far more fertile in its consequences for historical writing and research. Roughly speaking, it involved the contention that the final determinant of historical movement was to be found, not in the ideas men entertained, but in their material activities and methods of production; it was the manipulative interaction between man and his environment—the ways in which men worked upon it in order to create their means of subsistence and to satisfy their developing needs and wants—that was responsible for the course taken by human affairs, necessitating the form assumed by phenomena in other departments of social life and experience. Marx and his followers were thereby led to distinguish between the economic "base" of society (consisting in the productive forces together with the class alignments these forces gave rise to) and the ideological "superstructure" (comprising religion, ethics, political institutions, systems of law, and so forth), the latter being essentially the product of the former. History could thus be seen as owing its momentum to changes that took place in human productive techniques and to corresponding movements and conflicts within the social structure: as Marx and Engels wrote in their *German Ideology* (1845–46), "men, developing their material production and their material intercourse, alter, along with this their real existence, their thinking and the products of their thinking" (p. 38). Such a theory possessed a challenging originality and economy; it appeared both to illuminate hitherto uncharted ranges of historical phenomena and also to set in a new light, at times even to undermine, such traditional modes of explanation as those that emphasized individual plans and projects and the beliefs or ideals that inspired them. Yet, despite the insights it undoubtedly embodied, the very comprehensiveness and neatness of the Marxian interpretation was felt by some to mask a variety of problems concerning its validity and its application in practice to the material it was designed to explain. How far, for example, was it possible to describe or identify the factors assigned to the economic base or "foundation" without introducing considerations of a political or juristic nature? What exactly were the grounds for asserting that ethical or political doctrines were essentially expressions of the interests of economically determined classes, and how was such an hypothesis to be empirically tested? Or again, was it legitimate to treat the role of individual personalities in history as cavalierly as Engels, in particular, sometimes implied? More generally, could it not be argued that the progressivist optimism, implicit in the Marxian notion of history as moving inexorably forward towards the creation of social forms that would render possible the complete realization of human potentialities, owed more to the postulates of the Idealist metaphysic Marx had absorbed in his youth than to any entailed by a strictly scientific methodology? It was one thing (such critics protested) to stress the importance of economic factors and to show how these might exert an unsuspected but nonetheless crucial influence upon historical change; it was surely quite another to suggest that, once their significance had been appreciated, the entire historical process would present itself as conforming to a necessary pattern in such a way that future phases of its development could be unerringly predicted.

Pluralistic and Antinomian Views. Ideas like those of Buckle and Marx brought to the fore issues that have not always been clearly distinguished. Thus the question of whether history is interpretable by reference to some unitary principle (whether teleological or causal in character) has sometimes been identified with the question of whether history can be said to form an intelligible field of study, susceptible to rational understanding and elucidation. The twentieth-century historian Arnold Toynbee has, for example, suggested that in the absence of such a principle, history would amount to no more than a "chaotic, fortuitous, disorderly flux"; while others have spoken as if the sole alternative to regarding historical phenomena as ultimately determined by some specific set of material or social forces was to relegate them to the sphere of the merely random and contingent. Alleged dilemmas of this kind may be challenged, however, on the grounds both that they exploit ambiguities inherent in such notions as *intelligibility* and *contingency* and that at the same time they presuppose a too restricted model of acceptable explanation. It can be maintained, for instance, that a pluralistic conception of historical causation—one, that is, which ascribes causal efficacy to a variety of independent factors without according paramount status to those of any single type—is in no way incompatible with the belief that historical events and developments can be rendered intelligible in a perfectly straightforward sense; it has, indeed, been argued that such a conception accurately reflects the practice of the majority of working historians, few of whom would admit that they were thereby committed to the view that their subject matter was in some fashion radically incoherent or intractable. Nor, likewise, need a historian think that history is the product of arbitrary caprice, or even that it is essentially (in Carlyle's famous phrase) "the biography of great men," if he subscribes to the opinion that the characters and decisions of individual figures often play a central and irreducible role in determining what occurs. In this connection it is interesting to observe that the Marxian theorist G. V. Plekhanov (1857–1918), himself an avowed adherent to the "monist view of history" and insistent upon the stringent limits that social conditions and "general causes" imposed upon the capacity of individuals to affect the course of events, was nonetheless prepared to allow that personal disposition and talent, as expressed in the activities of individuals, could make a real difference to what happened in certain historical contexts. Any theory (he held) which tried wholly to dispense with a consideration of individual factors would assume an implausible "fatalistic" appearance, just as one that by contrast attributed everything to these would end, absurdly, by depicting history as an inconsequential and wholly fortuitous series of happenings.

A further source of difficulty and confusion has been the tendency to conflate issues of the kind discussed with others relating to the place of freedom in history and to the general status of determinism. As Buckle correctly noted, a powerful motive for resisting deterministic or scientifically orientated conceptions of historical development has been the conviction that their acceptance is inconsistent with a belief in human free will and responsibility. One characteristic reaction to such theories has accordingly taken the form of emphasizing the decisive contributions made by outstanding individuals and of arguing that if, for example, Napoleon or Lenin had not been born, European history might have followed a markedly different course. But the claim that the deeds of particular personalities have often had profound long-term effects does not by itself entail that the historical process cannot be regarded as constituting a causally determined sequence. All that the determinist postulates (it may be objected) is that, given any historical event, an explanation of the occurrence of that event could in principle be provided in terms of causally sufficient conditions. And this in no sense contradicts the contention that "great men" or "world-historical individuals" sometimes exercise a decisive influence upon what happens; what it states is that, if and when they do, their choices and actions must themselves always be susceptible to a complete causal explanation.

Somewhat similar considerations apply to the claim that the obtrusion of accidental or chance happenings into history represents a refutation of deterministic assumptions. It is, of course, quite true that historians are apt to employ the notions of *chance* or *accident* in the course of unfolding their narratives and explanations: this was a feature strongly underlined by the British historian J. B. Bury. However, as Bury himself pointed out in a well-known essay entitled "Cleopatra's Nose," it is a mistake to conclude from that that the use of such concepts presupposes "the intrusion of a lawless element" into history. It would appear rather that, when a historian refers to something as having happened by chance, he implies that its explanation lies—in a manner admittedly not easy to characterize with precision—off the main track of his enquiry or concern. An event that is described as fortuitous or accidental in the context of one set of interests may take on a different aspect when it is surveyed from another standpoint, being seen there as intrinsically related to the historian's principal theme or subject: in neither case, though, need the suggestion that it has no causal explanation be present. Bury himself, echoing the account provided by A. Cournot in his *Considérations sur la marche des idées et des événements dans les temps modernes* (1872), referred to chance as involving the "valuable collision of two or more independent chains of causes." As a definition this may not be impeccable, but it at least avoids the pitfall of presuming that, in talking of chance occurrences, the historian is irrevocably committed to some form of indeterminism.

II. ANALYTICAL APPROACHES

An examination of substantive theories of historical causation shows that many of the problems raised by them tend to shade into others that concern, not so much matters of fact, as the meaning and implications of various key terms or ideas. This aspect of the subject first began to attract widespread attention during the latter half of the nineteenth century, when a certain skepticism regarding the feasibility of large-scale interpretations of the historical process on allegedly scientific lines set in, and when it was felt to be necessary to consider more carefully the actual structure of the concepts by which the explanation of historical phenomena was customarily attempted. It was clear, for instance, that the program of elevating history to scientific status presupposed that historical events could be subsumed beneath laws and hypotheses of the type that had been employed with success at the level of natural phenomena. How far, though, was such an assumption really justified? Was it not conceivable that the whole notion of explanation and understanding within the field of the human studies precluded the adoption of such an approach, with the consequence that some of the grandiose attempts which had been made to set history upon the "sure path of a science" could be regarded as mistaken in principle, the products of a profound categorial confusion? In any case, was it not reasonable to investigate the logical character of the explanations which historians in practice used before embarking on projects whose relevance and applicability to the subject matter of historical enquiry had been taken for granted not critically ascertained?

The Notion of Cause. The original stimulus of much modern controversy concerning the nature of historical thought and understanding derived from the work of writers who were themselves deeply opposed to the suggestion that the explanatory procedures appropriate to the human studies (or *Geisteswissenschaften*) were not significantly different from those typically adopted in the natural sciences. For both the German philosopher, Wilhelm Dilthey, and the Italian, Benedetto Croce, it was the dissimilarities rather than the similarities between historical and scientific conceptions of enquiry that were important and striking. Thus each tended to emphasize the individuality or uniqueness of historical phenomena and to lay stress upon the need to regard the events of history in a light that presented them as integrally related to the specific periods and social milieus within which they took place: human nature was not conceived to be something static, the

subject of omnitemporal laws or regularities, but was viewed as involved in a continual process of change, finding expression in forms of thought and feeling that were in turn reflections of diverse patterns of life or culture. Moreover, the concept central to history was identified as that of human agency, and the understanding or inner recognition of what it is to be an agent, pursuing purposes or adhering to practical principles and beliefs, was held to bring into play a variety of explanatory concepts and modes of exegesis that were without analogue in disciplines whose province was the nonhuman world. Many of these themes were adumbrated with exceptional clarity and force by the British philosopher, R. G. Collingwood, and it was largely through his persuasive writings that they subsequently came to achieve wide currency in Anglo-Saxon circles. Collingwood was especially insistent upon a proper appreciation of the role played by thinking in determining historical phenomena: "all history," he once affirmed, "is the history of thought" (*Idea of History*, pp. 214–15). He went on to argue in accordance with this dictum that the notion of cause was employed in the historical sphere with a distinctive meaning, a meaning that rendered misconceived and futile attempts to assimilate history to natural science. For him, the cause of a historical event was "the thought in the mind of the person by whose agency the event came about," the historian's understanding of such an event therefore consisting in the reconstruction or "reenactment" of the process of thinking from which it issued. Such a model of the historian's procedure was to be sharply contrasted with the mode of explanation Collingwood attributed to the scientist, whereby particular occurrences were shown to be intelligible in virtue of their exemplifying generalizations correlating them with other events of a specific type.

The conception of historical understanding illustrated by the work of Collingwood has not been without its critics, many of whom have considered his claim that such understanding is radically different in form from scientific kinds of explanation to be unwarranted. What has come to be known as the "covering law model," which was developed in the thirties and forties of the present century by a number of logical empiricists and which—so far as history is concerned—has achieved classic expression in the work of Carl Hempel, explicitly rests upon the contention (resisted by Collingwood) that any adequate explanation of a causal type must necessarily exhibit the event to be explained as instantiating some general law or laws; when strictly interpreted, this was held to imply that the explanandum should be deducible from a set of premises consisting, on the one hand, of statements descriptive of initial or boundary conditions and, on the other, of further statements expressing well-confirmed universal hypotheses. Proponents of the view in question, which in its general outline conformed to the account of causality originally suggested by Hume, argued that historical explanations, when their basic structure was fully revealed, displayed no significant divergences from those used in other fields of enquiry; indeed, it was only on an analysis along the lines proposed that the historian's manner of making the past understandable could be appreciated as implying an inherently rational procedure, subject to the sort of check and verification that was a precondition of the respectability of any empirical discipline. Talk of empathetic projection into the minds of historical agents, such as was indulged in by theorists like Dilthey and Collingwood, might have value as signifying a heuristic aspect of the historian's method of arriving at his explanations: so far, however, as the problem was one of elucidating the fundamental logic of these, it amounted to little more than a mystifying irrelevance.

Despite its initial plausibility, and notwithstanding the ingenuity and pertinacity with which its supporters have sought to defend it, the covering law analysis has in its turn encountered criticisms, two of which may be mentioned here. Thus from one standpoint it has been contended that the explanations historians actually provide simply do not measure up to the stipulations embodied in the proposed model: the average historian would be hard put to cite the universal hypotheses upon which the meaning and validity of his causal propositions allegedly depend. The model would therefore seem to require (at best) considerable qualification and amendment if it is to serve as an adequate framework within which to characterize how historians in fact proceed. From another standpoint it has been urged that the presentation of historical events as rationally intelligible in the light of the motives, aims, and beliefs of the agents involved constitutes an intrinsic and ineliminable feature of historical understanding, and that this feature cannot be satisfactorily accommodated within the limits set by the covering law theory. Hence there has been a tendency on the part of some recent writers—notably, W. H. Dray—to try to reformulate what they hold to be the essential points of Collingwood's antipositivist position in a way that shows them to be both epistemologically unmysterious and empirically sound. Among other things, it has been suggested that a crucial characteristic of the causal accounts offered by historians consists in demonstrating that the actions of which they treat were rationally justified or required from the point of view of the agents concerned, rather than that they were occurrences to be expected or predicted on the basis

of inductively established uniformities. Whether, if it is to be finally adequate, an interpretation of this kind can really dispense with an appeal—at least at some level of the analysis—to the notions of law or generalization remains a disputed question, the answer to which would appear partly to depend upon the resolution of wider and still controversial issues in the philosophy of mind.

Freedom and Determinism. An advantage that is sometimes claimed for the approach favored by Collingwood and his modern followers is that it does not imply that there is any incompatibility between regarding an action as explicable and treating it as a free one. For it is argued that to explain what a historical agent did by referring to the good, or even compelling, reasons that he had for doing it does not commit the historian to maintaining that the agent's recognition of these reasons rendered his action inevitable. And this result may be contrasted with the consequence of adopting a covering law analysis. In the case of the latter, it is held, an action is said to have been explained if and only if it has been shown to have followed necessarily, as a law-governed effect, upon the fulfilment of specific initial conditions. Thus the covering law theorist, insofar as he considers historical events to be capable of explanation, cannot avoid adopting a deterministic position.

One reply to this has been that accounts of historical causation often take the form of indicating certain necessary, as opposed to sufficient, conditions for the occurrence of an event, and that a covering law theorist can without difficulty adapt his analysis to accommodate explanation in this sense. On this (modified) view, his adherence to the postulate that historical events are explicable need not be interpreted as carrying deterministic implications. But it has also been suggested that there is in any case no justification for holding that the acceptance of determinism logically excludes belief in human freedom; even if a historian assumes all human behavior to be susceptible in principle to explanation in terms of sufficient, and not merely necessary, conditions, he is not thereby debarred from supposing that the subjects of his enquiries sometimes acted as free and responsible agents. Thus the traditional fear of determinism, which (as was seen earlier) often helped to inspire resistance to certain speculative theories of history, is based upon an illusion that largely derives from an illegitimate identification of causation with such notions as those of coercion and external constraint: it is possibly with this argument in mind that the contemporary British historian, E. H. Carr, has written that the "logical dilemma about free will and determinism does not arise in real life," human actions being "both free and determined" (*What is*

History?, p. 124). There are, however, others—among them Isaiah Berlin—who have found it unconvincing and who have felt that all attempts to analyze concepts like *freedom* and *moral responsibility* in such a way as to make their employment compatible with a thoroughgoing causal determinism ultimately fail to do justice to the implications of ordinary thought and language. In their view, moreover, the fabric of the historical studies, as we customarily know and understand them, is shot through with libertarian and evaluative conceptions to a degree that has not always been adequately appreciated. Hence those who have contended that a commitment to unrestricted determinism in human affairs would entail sweeping revisions of the vocabulary and categories the historian normally brings to the interpretation of his material have been substantially right. Though this is not of course positively to affirm that a thoroughgoing determinism is untenable, it is to claim that for the most part historians habitually write and think as if it were untenable. And that is a point which, if correct, cannot be lightly brushed aside.

BIBLIOGRAPHY

Substantive Theories. J. B. Bossuet, *Discours sur l'histoire universelle* (Paris, 1681; reprint, 1925). H. T. Buckle, *The History of Civilisation in England*, 2 vols. (London, 1857–61). G. W. F. Hegel, *Vorlesungen über die Philosophie der Geschichte* (Berlin, 1837); trans. J. Sibree as *Lectures on the Philosophy of History* (New York, 1944). I. Kant, "Idee zu einer allgemeinen Geschichte in weltbürgerlicher Absicht" (Berlin, 1784); trans. W. Hastie as "The Idea of a Universal Cosmo-Political History," in Kant, *Eternal Peace and Other International Essays* (Boston, 1914). K. Marx and F. Engels, *Selected Works*, 2 vols. (Moscow, 1950); idem, *The German Ideology* (1845–46), ed. R. Pascal, trans, W. Lough and C. P. Magill (London, 1938; reprint, 1965). J. S. Mill, *A System of Logic* (London, 1843), Book VI. G. V. Plekhanov, *In Defence of Materialism*, trans. A. Rothstein (London, 1947). A. Toynbee, *A Study of History*, 10 vols. (Oxford and New York, 1934–54; also reprints). G. Vico, *Scienza nuova*, 3rd ed. (Naples, 1744); trans. T. G. Bergin and M. H. Fisch as *The New Science of Giambattista Vico* (Ithaca, 1948; 1968).

Critical and Analytical Works. I. Berlin, *Historical Inevitability* (Oxford, 1954). J. B. Bury, *Selected Essays* (Cambridge, 1930). E. H. Carr, *What is History?* (New York, 1962). Morris Cohen, *The Meaning of Human History* (Lasalle, Ill., 1944). R. G. Collingwood, *The Idea of History* (Oxford, 1946). B. Croce, *Teoria e storia della storiografia* (Bari, 1917); trans. D. Ainslie as *History—Its Theory and Practice* (New York, 1921). W. Dilthey, *Gesammelte Schriften* (Stuttgart, 1957–60); extracts from Dilthey's writings on history are in *Meaning in History*, trans. and ed. H. P. Rickman (London and New York, 1961). W. H. Dray, *Laws and Explanation in History* (Oxford, 1957). P. L. Gardiner, *The Nature of Historical Explanation* (Oxford, 1952). C. G. Hempel, "The Function of General Laws in History," *The Journal of Philosophy*, 39 (1942). Ernest Nagel, *The Structure of Science* (New York, 1961), esp. Chs. 13–15. K. R. Popper, *The Poverty of Historicism* (London, 1957); idem, *Open Society and its Enemies*, 4th rev. ed., 2 vols. (Princeton, 1963), esp. Vol. II. M. White, *Foundations of Historical Knowledge* (New York, 1965). P. Winch, *The Idea of a Social Science* (London, 1958).

Anthologies. W. H. Dray, ed., *Philosophical Analysis and History* (New York, 1966). P. L. Gardiner, ed., *Theories of History* (Glencoe, 1959). S. Hook, ed., *Philosophy and History: A Symposium* (New York, 1963). H. Meyerhoff, ed., *The Philosophy of History in Our Time* (New York, 1959).

PATRICK GARDINER

[See also **Causation;** Chance; **Determinism in History;** Free Will; Hegelian; **Historicism; Historiography;** Necessity; Positivism; Progress.]

CAUSATION IN ISLAMIC THOUGHT

IN AN ENDEAVOR to safeguard what it regarded as the Qur'anic concept of divine omnipotence, the dominant school of Islamic theology (*kalām*), founded by al-Ash'arī (d. 935), adopted the occasionalist doctrine that causal efficacy resides exclusively with the divine will. The Ash'arites denied the concept of "natural" causation, that is, that action proceeds from an existent's very nature or essence. They thus rejected the Aristotelian concept of natural efficient causality, subjecting it to criticism on logical and empirical grounds. They also rejected Aristotle's theory of eternal matter, advocating a metaphysics of contingent atoms and accidents that are created ex nihilo, combined to form bodies, and sustained in temporally finite spans of existence by direct divine action. Accordingly, the orderly flow of these events has no inherent necessity, being no more than a habit ('*āda*), decreed arbitrarily by the divine will. Hence when God creates a miracle, that is, when He disrupts the habitual course of nature, no contradiction obtains. As for human volitions, acts, and cognitions, the Ash'arites regarded these also as temporal events (*ḥawādith*), the direct creation of God.

This doctrine, held with individual modifications, became widely accepted and represents the most distinctively Islamic causal concept. The history of its development reflects two main phases: (1) an early phase where it is primarily concerned with doctrinal questions within *kalām;* (2) a later phase, initiated by Ghazali (al-Ghazālī; d. 1111), where it directs itself more explicitly against the necessitarian metaphysics of the Islamic Neo-Platonists, Alfarabi (al-Fārābī; d. 950) and Avicenna (Ibn Sīnā; d. 1037).

I

Ashʿarite causal doctrine was at first adopted largely in opposition to fundamental tenets of the most important of the earlier schools of kalām, the Muʿtazilite. This school attained the height of its influence in the first half of the ninth century, a period caught in the throes of the first wave of the transmission of Greek philosophy and science to the Arabs. Although greatly influenced by Greek thought, the Muʿtazilites remained essentially dogmatists, selecting and reformulating philosophical ideas to serve theological ends. Now the Islamic version of atomism that underlies Ashʿarite causal doctrine had its origin with the Muʿtazilite school, many of whose members adopted varying occasionalist views. There was, however, no consensus of opinion among the Muʿtazilites on causal questions, their differences betraying the difficulties they encountered in reconciling the concept of divine omnipotence with the two cardinal principles of their theology, those of divine unity and justice. Ashʿarite causal doctrine meant the rejection of these principles.

The first principle denied the distinction between God's eternal attributes and His essence. This raised a question concerning the concept of divine will in relation to the doctrine of the world's temporal creation. Most of the Muʿtazilites rejected Aristotle's theory of the potentially infinite divisibility of substance, adopting atomism as the only view consistent with the Qurʾanic statement that God knows the determinate number of all things. Moreover, they transformed Greek atomism into a doctrine of transient atoms and accidents, created ex nihilo, constituting a world created in time. The doctrine of the world's eternity, they maintained, deprived God of will. It meant the simultaneity of cause and effect which only obtains, as in natural causes, when the effect is necessitated by the agent's nature or essence. Here, however, their principle of divine unity faced a major difficulty: if the divine will is conceived as an eternal attribute and hence not distinct from the divine essence, God's acts become in reality essential, not voluntary. This led many Muʿtazilites to argue that the divine will itself is created—a doctrine vulnerable to the Ashʿarite criticism that such a will requires another created will to create it and so on ad infinitum.

The principle of divine justice posed further difficulties. Based on the premiss that some acts have intrinsic moral value, it asserted (a) that God performs only the just act and (b) that He performs it because it is in itself good. Al-Naẓẓām (d. ca. 848) argued that it is impossible for God to act unjustly. Other Muʿtazilites, rejecting this view as a denial of divine omnipotence, held that God has the power to perform unjust acts, but in fact never does. How then were they to account for evil without implicating God? In one attempt to solve this problem, Muʿammar (d. ca. 825) maintained that God creates only bodies, imprinting on them specific natures: accidents (bad or good) are either the necessitated effects of these natures or the effects of voluntary agents like man. This latter point entailed the doctrine of man's freedom of the will, universally endorsed by the Muʿtazilites who argued that a just God can only judge men for acts they themselves initiate. They agreed that man "creates" his acts, but disagreed as to whether the human will is effective in the outer world. Is man the real author of "the generated acts" (al-afʿāl al-mutawallida), the events in the outer world normally regarded as the effects of his action? Some affirmed this either wholly or with qualifications; others denied it. Among the latter, some held that the generated acts are necessitated by the causal properties in nature; others, denying natural causes, attributed them to direct divine action. A curious position was attributed by Muslim writers to Thumāma Ibn al-Ashras (d. 828) who was alleged to have argued as follows: since it is possible for a person to will an act and then die before the consequent generated acts, and since action is not attributable to the dead, generated acts cannot be attributed to man. Nor can they be attributed to God, since they may be evil. Hence, generated acts have no author.

These inconsistencies, the Ashʿarites argued, arise from the erroneous Muʿtazilite principles of unity and justice. The eternal attributes, they argued, are "additional" to God's essence and include His will. It is thus that God's acts are voluntary, not necessitated by His essence. As for the second principle, all acts, the Ashʿarites argued, are in themselves morally neutral. An act is just simply because God performs or commands it; unjust, because He prohibits it. Divine decisions are not conditioned by any intrinsic values in acts and the question of whether God has the power to act unjustly is redundant. Men do not create their acts. Human acts, like all other events, are created directly by God. To avoid identification with the Islamic determinists (al-mujabbira) who held that human acts are "compelled" by God, the Ashʿarites resorted to the proverbially enigmatic doctrine of "acquisition" (al-kasb). They distinguished between a compulsory act, like a spasmodic bodily movement, and a deliberate act. While both kinds of acts are created in man by God, the second is created together with the "power" (al-qūwa), which exists only with the act, not before

287

it. They also seem to have held that whatever is normally regarded as the effect of man's deliberate act is also created by God simultaneously with the power, so that both "power" and "effect" are acquired by man from God. In other words, the relation between man's "created power" and the "created effect," as in all sequences in the world, is that of mere concomitance. (But this point has been interpreted differently; see Bibliography).

II

Initial Ash'arite repudiation of natural causation, as we have seen, arose out of doctrinal disputes within *kalām*. The arguments, as far as the available sources indicate, are mainly theological and metaphysical. A second phase in the history of the Ash'arite causal theory is marked by a more explicit attack on the Aristotelian theory of necessary efficient causality as adapted to the emanative metaphysics of Alfarabi and Avicenna. Here we encounter two developments: (1) an emphasis on the purely epistemological argument that necessary causal connection is provable neither logically nor empirically; (2) an attempt to uphold the Aristotelian *method* of scientific demonstration and its claims of attaining certainty, on occasionalist, non-Aristotelian, metaphysical grounds. Both these developments are largely due to Ghazali. Elements of the epistemological argument are found in earlier Ash'arite writings, but it was Ghazali who gave this argument its most forceful expression and who first attempted an occasionalist reinterpretation of Aristotelian demonstrative logic.

Ghazali's criticism of necessary efficient causation pervades his *Tahāfut al-Falāsifa* (*The Incoherence of the Philosophers*), directed mainly at Avicenna's emanative metaphysics. Avicenna described the efficient cause as that "which brings about an existence other than itself." In natural science, he held, this existence represents motion in one of its forms. For the metaphysician, however, and here we note his Neo-Platonism, the efficient cause is also productive of existence as such. In Avicenna's cosmogony, the world emanates eternally from God as a chain of necessitated and necessitating existents, terminating in the world of generation and corruption. In this sublunar world, for the effect to follow from the efficient cause, the material, formal, and final causes must also exist. The efficient natural cause must be the proximate cause and there must be no impediment. Agency, in a natural cause, is "an essential attribute," hence productive of one specific kind of act. Action is also determined by the specific nature of its recipient. When such causal conditions obtain, the effect follows by necessity.

Ghazali attacked Avicenna's concept of divine causality as a negation of the divine attributes of life, will, and power. Only inanimate beings, Ghazali argued, are said to act by necessity. By definition, a necessitated act is not a voluntary act. Ghazali also opposed Avicenna's scheme on the grounds that it does not allow God to act directly in the world of men, but only through the mediation of other causes. Since the chain of existents proceeding from God is necessarily connected, there can be no disruption of its order. Miracles, defined by the Ash'arites as the disruption of nature's habitual order, are thus impossible and a prophet proclaiming their occurrence becomes a deceiver. It is in arguing for the possibility of miracles that Ghazali levelled his epistemological argument against the concept of necessary causal connection:

> The connection between what is habitually believed to be the cause and what is habitually believed to be the effect is not necessary for us. But in the case of two things, neither of which is the other and where neither the affirmation nor the negation of the one entails the affirmation or the negation of the other, the existence or non-existence of the one does not necessitate the existence or non-existence of the other; for example, the quenching of thirst and drinking, satiety and eating, burning and contact with fire, light and the rising of the sun, death and decapitation. . . . On the contrary, it is within God's power to create satiety without eating, death without decapitation, to prolong life after decapitation and so on in the case of all concomitant things. [Trans. by the author.]

He then argued that necessary causal connection is never observable in nature: when, for example, cotton is brought in contact with fire, all that is seen is the occurrence of burning "with" (*ma'*) the contact, not the burning of the cotton "by" or "through" (*bi*) the fire. The one who enacts the burning, he asserted, is God.

Ghazali did not deny that events in the world are ordered in sequences of priority and posteriority, temporal and ontological, ordinarily regarded as causes and effects and on the basis of which scientific inferences about nature can be drawn. He denied, however, that these latter are real causes and that their order is inherently necessary. He endorsed Aristotle's method of scientific demonstration, but sought its interpretation in occasionalist terms. He thus used Avicenna's argument to justify the principle of nature's uniformity, but drew from it a different conclusion. Avicenna (basing himself on Aristotle, *Physics* ii. 5. 196b 10–15) had argued that mere observation of past uniformities does not suffice to give us the certainty of their future continuance; in addition, there is the "hidden syllogism" to the effect that if these had been accidental or coincidental, "they would not have continued always or for the most part." Ghazali endorsed the argument to this point, but unlike Avicenna, who concluded that the uniformity derives from the natural necessary connection between things, Ghazali maintained it derives from God's arbitrary decree. For Ghazali, God creates in man knowledge that the world is orderly, but also that its order is contingent and disruptible. When a miracle occurs, God refrains from creating in man the expectation of the uniform event, creating instead knowledge of the miracle. Ghazali did not elaborate on this latter point, leaving unanswered serious questions arising from it.

III

In *Dalālat al-Ḥā'irīn* (*The Guide of the Perplexed*), of which a Latin version, based on a Hebrew translation, was known to Christian scholastics early in the thirteenth century, Moses Maimonides (d. 1204) discussed the occasionalist atomism of *kalām*, criticizing it mainly on the metaphysical level. Averroës (Ibn Rushd; d. 1198), in his *Tahāfut al-Tahāfut* (*The Incoherence of "The Incoherence"*), answered Ghazali's *Tahāfut*, quoting almost all of it; a Latin translation of Averroës' work was first made in the fourteenth century. These translations have raised the question of a possible Islamic influence on parallel criticisms of causation in Europe, particularly that of Nicolaus of Autrecourt (d. 1350) whose writings suggest acquaintance with Maimonides' account of Islamic atomism. For the history of the concept of causation in Islam, however, Averroës' *Tahāfut* is of special interest. In this and other shorter works Averroës was attempting to check the spread of Ash'arism, particularly in North Africa and Muslim Spain. The attempt, however, was abortive, and Aristotelian causal theory, though it continued to be held in Islam, remained on the defensive.

BIBLIOGRAPHY

Pertinent medieval Arabic sources in translation include al-Ash'arī, *Kitāb al-Luma'*, trans. R. J. McCarthy (Beirut, 1953); Averroës, *Tahāfut al-Tahāfut*, trans. S. Van Den Bergh (London, 1953), particularly the 3rd and 17th discussions; Avicenna, *La Métaphysique du Shifā'*, French translation by M. M. Anawati, mimeographed edition (Quebec, 1952), particularly, Book IV, Ch. 1; al-Ghazālī, *Tahāfut al-Falāsifah*, trans. S. A. Kamali (Lahore, 1958); Ibn Khaldūn, *The Muqaddimah*, trans. F. Rosenthal, 3 vols. (New York, 1958; 2nd ed., 1967), Vol. III, Ch. IV, Sec. 14; al-Khayyāṭ, *Kitāb al-Intiṣār*, reprint of M. Nyberg's Arabic edition with a French translation by A. N. Nader (Beirut, 1957); Maimonides, *The Guide of the Perplexed*, trans. S. Pines (Chicago, 1966), Chs. 73–76.

A basic historical account of Islamic occasionalism with a philosophical discussion defending a Thomistic approach to causality is M. Fakhry's *Islamic Occasionalism and its Critique by Averroës and Aquinas* (London, 1958). For an interpretation of Ibn Khaldun's discussion of causality, see H. A. Wolfson, "Ibn Khaldun on Attributes and Predestination," *Speculum*, **34** (October, 1959), 585–97, reprinted in H. A. Wolfson, *Religious Philosophy: A Group of Essays* (Cambridge, Mass., 1961). For a detailed discussion of Ghazali's attempt at interpreting Aristotelian demonstrative logic in occasionalist terms, see M. E. Marmura, "Ghazali and Demonstrative Science," *Journal of the History of Philosophy*, **3** (October, 1965), 183–204. On *kalām* theories of free will and ethical value, see M. Fakhry, "The Mu'tazilite View of Free Will," *The Muslim World*, **42**, 2 (April, 1953), 95–109; G. F. Hourani, "Two Theories of Value in Medieval Islam," *The Muslim World*, **50**, 4 (October, 1960), 269–376; A. N. Nader, *Le Système Philosophique des Mu'tazila* (Beirut, 1956); W. M. Watt, *Free Will and Predestination in Early Islam* (London, 1948). For an interpretation of the doctrine of *kasb* differing from ours that allows a measure of genuine efficacy in deliberate human action, see R. M. Frank, "The Structure of Created Causality according to al-Ash'arī," *Studia Islamica*, **25** (1966), 13–75. On Islamic atomism, see S. Pines, *Beiträge zur Islamischen Atomenlehre* (Berlin, 1936). For the question of a possible Islamic influence on Nicolaus of Autrecourt, see J. R. Weinberg, *Nicolaus of Autrecourt* (Princeton, 1948). For general accounts of Islamic theology, see L. Gardet and M. M. Anawati, *Introduction à la Théologie Musulmane* (Paris, 1951); D. B. Macdonald, *Development of Muslim Theology, Jurisprudence and Constitutional Theory* (New York, 1903), outdated but still pertinent; W. M. Watt, *Islamic Philosophy and Theology* (Edinburgh, 1962).

MICHAEL E. MARMURA

[See also Atomism; **Causation;** Causation in Law; **God; Islamic Conception;** Necessity; Neo-Platonism.]

CAUSATION IN LAW

WHILE CAUSATION is an idea of general consequence in religion and philosophy, it is a term of more specialized meaning in science, in history, and in law. In science, causation is largely a principle of explanation and prediction. For history, when admitted at all, it is a vast abstraction that succeeds only minimally in ordering the complexities of observed human behavior. In law, the idea is at once highly theoretical as the most general justification for the imposition of liability, and severely practical as a means for assigning legal responsibility in the individual case. Law views causation as related both to the order of nature and to the nature of justice. In the first, causation plays a central role in the determination of legal facts; in the second, causation emerges as a leading component of the idea of responsibility. Each of these roles is indefinitely complex. Their combination is the history of the idea of causation in law.

Law and Religion. Causation is a leading motif in most religions: the ways in which the world comes into existence and is sustained, and the modes by which man may discharge religious obligation. Each notion involves a theory of causation. A religion's cosmology issues in its science, primitive or advanced; the obligations imposed on man by his religion are his first law. All the ramifications of the idea of causation in religious history have this dual character. Causation is either physical or purposive, according as its referent is nature or human conduct. Causation in law retains the two strands, though its concern is much more with human action than with the order of physical events.

In the history of Western religion, God is said to have caused the world to come into existence and to govern it through his laws (note the legal reference). In the Bible, the cosmogonic account of the origin of the universe is scant and primitive; the laws governing man are detailed and sophisticated, so much so that the original document comes to be known as the Book of the Law (Torah, in Hebrew). There was an early development of a widespread casuistic activity which has never ceased to occupy the Hebraic religions. Religious law concerns itself with the limits of human obligation or responsibility, and inherent in all such legislation or decision is a notion of causation. It is usually assumed that a man is responsible for the state of affairs which he has caused. The extent to which he may be held responsible for events he has not caused is a matter of deep and continuing perplexity.

Out of this religious practice grew one major strand of the idea of causation in law. And since law becomes separated from religion, if at all, only in the late maturity of religion, it is easy to see how important religious beliefs in the matter of causation are to legal development. In brief, religion bequeaths to law the notion of moral responsibility for man's interventions in the regular course of nature and for impositions of his will upon nature and society. It may or may not hold him responsible for what he does in a state of divine madness, *atē, karma,* or fate. "Not I was the cause of this act," said Agamemnon, "but Zeus and the Erinys who walks in darkness: they it was who in the assembly put wild atē in my understanding, on that day when I arbitrarily took Achilles' prize" (Dodds, 1957). A modern pleader might say, "Not guilty be*cause* of temporary insanity."

Law and Philosophy. All philosophical systems subscribe to some central idea of causation. In philosophy as in religion, the notion of causation is either physical or purposive, or both. At times a mechanistic or deter-

ministic theory of causation is held applicable to the whole of nature, including man. At others, nature is seen as a total purposive or teleological structure. In the philosophic beginnings of Western culture, that is to say, in the teachings of the Pre-Socratics, there is much evidence that the order of nature is seen as a regime of legal obligation. ". . . Anaximander's doctrine of the systematic justice of the universe reminds us that the most important idea in the new philosophy, that of Cause (*aitía*) was the same as the idea of Retribution and was transferred from legal to physical terminology" (Jaeger, 1945). Justice rules the world and the seasons must repay their just debts.

In classical antiquity, apart from the materialistic atomists, man and nature are clearly separated and the emphasis shifts from a philosophy of nature to a philosophy of human nature. Theories of causation become full-fledged, and philosophy starts on the task of amplifying an account of this process which it has never wearied of. Aristotelian and Stoic ideas of moral obligation entered into Roman cultural life and indirectly exerted a great influence on the course of the development of the Roman Law. Apparently, however, Greek philosophical notions of causation had little effect on Greek legal practice, which indeed never developed a system of general jurisprudential ideas. "Why were Greek philosophy and Greek law so little influenced by each other?" (Jones, 1956). Indeed, even Roman jurists, as distinguished from the philosophers, appear to have resisted philosophic "indoctrination" until the end of the classical period (Schulz, 1953).

The Aristotelian doctrine of causation went over into the medieval religious systems, both Jewish (B. Cohen, 1966) and Christian (Wigmore, 1912) and entered intimately into ecclesiastical law, clerical and lay, partly through the Canon Law and partly in medieval Jewish philosophy and rabbinical practice.

Modern philosophical theories of causation have had a large though usually indirect effect on modern jurisprudence, especially after the separation of law from theology on the Continent, and in the theories of physical and psychological causation of Hobbes, Bacon, Locke, and Hume in England. The rationalistic epistemologies (Descartes, Spinoza, Leibniz) tend toward ethical determinism (Spinoza) or barely rescue freedom of will by a palpable device (Descartes). In Leibniz, trained lawyer and diplomat, the problem of legal "conditions" was a matter of early concern, and in Christian von Wolff (1679–1754) the whole deductive apparatus of rationalism was taken over bodily and applied to the law. Strangely enough, the rather sophisticated theories of ethical determinism developed by the rationalists found an echo in the primitive theory of legal liability that a man acts at his peril, and that while religion may look tolerantly on the ignorant sinner, the early law shows him scant indulgence. Its motto was: *Qui inscienter peccat, scienter emendet* ("Who unknowingly sins, knowingly makes amends").

Of British empiricism, Hume's view of causation as based on custom was most congenial to the common law jurists. Returning to the continent, the Kantian theory of causation has had but little effect on theories of causation in law. When we come to the nineteenth-century philosophical movements, we find that theories of causation, particularly those of the philosophers of science (e.g., Bentham, Comte, Mill, Spencer) reach the daily practice of the law, if at all, only through the screen of philosophy of law or of jurisprudence. In sum, philosophy enables the legal philosopher or jurisprudent to amplify and adapt philosophical theories of causation to general systems of jurisprudential thought. These in turn stimulate legal specialists or commentators and eventually the ideas filter down into legal practice.

In contrast to philosophic origins of causation, law more often takes account of ideas and sentiments of causation as popularly conceived, even when the law does not find it necessary to deal directly with causation as a general juristic idea. And at all times the law is busily engaged in creating the materials out of which a body of learning on causation can be created. Beginning with the nineteenth century, this body of theory comes into existence and jurisprudential ideas of causation enter directly into the everyday life of the law.

Cause as a Term of General Significance. The legal word "cause" and the Roman law *causa* are terms of ancient usage (Plucknett, 1956a). These terms meant (and still mean) variously the right which the injured party asserts, or the form of judicial redress, or the justification by either party for his course of conduct. Indeed, this idea of cause, whose essence is caught up in the ordinary word "because," is the primary and ubiquitous meaning of "cause" (Plucknett, 1956b). The plaintiff or petitioner pleads his "cause of action." The defendant is called on to "show cause" why the machinery of the law should not move against him. In the Civil Law and vestigially in the Common Law, the plaintiff may be required to establish a good "cause" why a promise should be enforced, as for example in a gift made in contemplation of death (*causa mortis*). "Without just cause" is a legal catch phrase traditional with many forms and modes of judicial process.

Needless to say, these are pristine and basic meanings of the term "cause." When, late in the development of both matured systems of law (common and modern civil law), students of legal theory attempted to form a comprehensive theory of causation in law, they framed the idea of causation from three familiar factors. These are physical causation; the subjective state of mind of the agent in pursuing a goal or purpose; and the policies of the law underlying its decisions in awarding or withholding redress. These three elements may be stated as part of the plaintiff's *prima facie* case. He must show physical causation by the defendant. In addition, he may be called on to show that the defendant intentionally or negligently caused the harm. Finally, he may have to demonstrate that it is the law's policy to regard the defendant's behavior as just "cause" for redress.

The mode by which legal causation is differentiated from causation as a philosophical idea can be illustrated simply. In law, if you cause an injury, you may be held responsible. Conversely, if you happen to be held legally responsible, the law is apt to say you "caused" the injury. Most of the apparently limitless debate on the nature of legal causation originates in this simple conversion of the idea. There is little scholarly agreement on the nature of legal causation. Opinion ranges all the way from the assertion that causation underlies all legal phenomena to the denial that causation is a necessary or even a defensible notion in the realm of legal liability. In between these extremes, causation theories proliferate, and their examination and defense continues to be the subject of a vast literature in the present century.

Causation in Law in Historical Perspective. We have seen that highly advanced systems of law such as the Greek and Roman were able to get along with only the most primitive theories of causation. This invites a word of explanation. Greek juristic practice was at all times at the mercy of the vagaries of oratorical appeal. Causation as a logical and integral part of legal responsibility received scant attention. The Roman law, like the Common law, was a legal system whose theoretical ideas were shaped mainly in practice and largely dependent on the exigencies of the available forms of action. All that Roman jurisprudence seemed to need in terms of a general idea of causation was the rule that injuries that were compensable under the *Lex Aquilia* had to be "direct" (Thayer, 1929). All else was taken care of in the more informal procedures of the edictal law.

The early common law is believed to have been a system of strict liability where the question of whether the defendant intended the harm he caused or was in a negligent state of mind is irrelevant. Hence, only physical causation seems to be in issue. Such defense is exceptional. The absence of physical causation would plainly show that the plaintiff did not know what he was about or was ignorant of who or what caused his injuries. Primitive systems of law are apt to be particularly harsh on one who starts up the machinery of law and does not prevail. Hence, physical causation, while always relevant, could largely be taken for granted. Nor do the primitive systems of law take much account of purposive causation, that is, the question of whether the defendant intends the series of consequences which flow from his act or is culpably negligent in initiating them. Indeed, the whole question of causation is blanketed in primitive law either by the rigidity of its procedures or by the overwhelming importance it attaches to responsibility as flowing solely from immemorial and therefore unexceptionable custom.

In the matured systems of law of the Western world, legal liability begins in tort and crime, which are scarcely distinguishable. Legal capacity and responsibility rest in the collective unit of the kin. It alone is recognized as a legal entity and it is responsible for the harm caused by its members. Causation, therefore, is in the kin.

When the legal unit became the adult male citizen or freeman the notion of "collective" causation or responsibility was continued. For the head of the patriarchal family was responsible for a numerous retinue of human beings who themselves had only limited legal personality. A large body of legal impositions developed against many who could in no reasonable interpretation of the term be held to have "caused" the harm.

Causation in Modern Law. In modern law, legal personality has expanded to include almost all adult human beings, but liability is curtailed in comparison with the broad coverage usually attributed to primitive law. Today, common learning states that defendant cannot be charged with responsibility for a wrong unless his conduct has physically caused the wrong and unless the law deems this cause to have been *proximate*. The use of the idea that among all the physical antecedents of an event, one or a few may be discerned as "proximate" is apparently due to medieval philosophers, notably to Saint Thomas Aquinas. Its use in English law is usually laid to Sir Francis Bacon: "The law looks to the proximate, and not to the remote cause" (*In jure non remota causa, sed proxima spectatur; Maxims*, Reg. I [1596]).

In the nineteenth century, English and American law used the idea of causation, primarily in tort law, as a means of restricting responsibility for the growing rate of accidents and the large amount of property damage accompanying the industrial revolution. In the early cases, causation and other devices, especially the doctrines of intervening cause, contributory negligence, and voluntary assumption of risk, served to relieve from liability many of those who in a simple agricultural system would normally be held responsible for loss of life or damage to property that resulted from their acts. Naive ideas of physical causation alone would have saddled growing industry and transportation with most of the responsibility for the harms flowing from these activities. It was in this emergency that notions of *proximate* causation and intervening cause were invoked, and harmful behavior which normally might be taken as the physical cause of injury was increasingly held not to have caused the injury "proximately" or not to have been a "substantial factor" in the injury or not to have been the "natural and probable consequence" of the defendant's acts. Hence arose the important distinction between physical causation and legal causation which has been the subject of thousands of decisions in all the advanced industrial countries and particularly in England and in the United States.

The idea of physical causation has been enriched by scientific learning on the nature of cause. In the eighteenth century, the idea of physical cause and effect as a phenomenon of probability made itself felt in the law. Particularly in the matter of proof, the law began to accept the notion that a given cause can never unequivocally be assigned as the responsible agent of an effect, but at best only a probability judgment can be made. This learning was revived in the twentieth century and cases and commentaries began to state physical causation in terms of probability theory.

At best, physical causation came to be recognized as only a *conditio sine qua non* of liability. If plaintiff is unable to establish physical causation, then this view holds he is subject to non-suit. If plaintiff does establish physical causation, then he must go on to show that the defendant's harmful conduct was the "proximate" or "legal" cause of the injury. Causation in law thus became a matter of legal policy, a device for selecting out those chains of physical causation to which liability would or would not attach. Causation in law came to be frankly recognized as legal policy; not causation at all but judicial policies respecting liability.

Examination of cases shows that for the same series of acts, liability may be held to be based on causation or not, depending upon whether the defendant is found to have intended the harm, has been negligent, or is innocent of any wrongful state of mind. This seemed to show not causation, but a judicial policy of assessing liability on the state of mind of the defendant rather than on the chain of causation set up by his conduct. Numerous other policies, such as liability for ultrahazardous activities, or for faulty products are cast in terms of causation.

Contemporary learning on causation has a very extensive examination in a recent work called *Causation in the Law* by H. L. A. Hart and A. M. Honoré. The authors espouse the theory that causation in law is an essentially nonphilosophical, profession-oriented device, heavily charged with common sense ideas on current meanings of causation. Paradoxically, it takes a philosophical theory (the "ordinary language" philosophical outlook) to establish this thesis. The idea itself is old, and arises not only from a general antiphilosophical bias extant from Roman law times, but in the nature of the case from the way in which philosophical ideas become homogenized with a discipline that absorbs them. We should not take too seriously the protestations of experts in the field of causation in law that their special doctrines have little to do with philosophy. "The lawyer cannot afford to adventure himself with philosophers in the logical and metaphysical controversies that beset the idea of cause," says Sir Frederick Pollock (1887). However, we must remember that it is the normal fate of philosophy as the parent of the sciences to suffer repudiation by its children.

A very sophisticated formulation of the nature of legal causation relying explicitly on the philosophy of science is found in the work of Morris and Felix Cohen (Cohen and Cohen, 1951). Of peculiar interest is Felix Cohen's application of field theory and cultural relativity to the notion of causation in law (1950).

Legal causation is concerned not only with the question of who or what caused harm, but also with the *extent* of harm to be attributed to the defendant's act. A man's careless toss of an unextinguished match may burn down an entire ship and her cargo. Since almost all modern theory on legal causation has centered on the law of negligence, the issue comes to be framed as one of determining whether the defendant should have foreseen that he was creating an unreasonable risk of harm. This thought construct, "the reasonable man," is created and endowed with a set of physical, psychological, and moral awarenesses and responses that correspond to average opinion, as seen by courts and commentators, on how a reasonably prudent person of ordinary ability should conduct his affairs.

At times, this reasonable man turns out to be singularly obtuse; at others he is charged with almost divine prescience. Writers on legal causation attempt both to shape the course of legal decision on the basis of a rich conglomerate of causation theories, and, after the fact, try to analyze out of the cases principles of decision which they offer as guides to future developments of the law.

The law of negligence is the birthplace of all modern sophisticated theories of causation. From there, the theories diffuse throughout the rest of the law of torts, thence to contracts, particularly on the question of *extent* of damage to be attributed to a breaching defendant, and to the law of crimes, where, not the extent of harm, but the relation between the forbidden harm and the criminal conduct is the issue (Hall, 1947).

Conclusion. Millennia intervene between the death of a boy accidentally impaled on a javelin hurled by Olympic games athletes in ancient Greece and a modern spectator struck on the head by a flying puck in a hockey arena. But the determination of legal causation is still as difficult in either case. Today the spectator at the hockey game is said to have "legally" caused his own harm by "voluntary assumption of the risk." The Greeks said the boy caused his own death by running upon the javelin.

Modern doctrine attempts to ease the burden of the individual human being immediately or directly causing injury by shifting loss on those more able to pay or more likely to be able to pass the loss on by insurance and thence ultimately to the consuming public in the form of higher prices.

Thus we see that while physical causation is still thought to be basic, it is the notion of purposive causation, and of legal policy (the law's purposes) that modern lawyers think of when the idea of legal causation comes to mind.

BIBLIOGRAPHY

B. Cohen, *Jewish and Roman Law* (New York, 1966), Vol. II, Ch. XVII, "The Principle of Causation." F. S. Cohen, "Field Theory and Judicial Logic," *Yale Law Journal,* **59** (1950), 251–59. M. R. Cohen, *The Meaning of Human History* (LaSalle, Ill., 1947), pp. 105–61. M. R. Cohen and F. S. Cohen, *Readings in Jurisprudence and Legal Philosophy* (New York, 1951), pp. 233–68. T. A. Cowan, *Essays in the Law of Torts* (Newark, N.J., 1961), pp. 12–18. E. R. Dodds, *The Greeks and the Irrational* (Berkeley, 1951). K. Engisch, *Die Kausalität als Merkmal der strafrechtlichen Tatbestände* (Tübingen, 1931). L. Green, *Rationale of Proximate Cause* (Kansas City, Mo., 1927). Nicholas St. John Green, "Proximate and Remote Cause," *American Law Review,* **4,** No. 2 (Jan. 1870), 201–16. J. Hall, *General Principles of Criminal Law* (Indianapolis, 1947), pp. 256–66. H. L. A. Hart and A. M. Honoré, *Causation in the Law* (Oxford, 1959). W. Jaeger, *Paideia: The Ideals of Greek Culture,* trans. Gilbert Highet, 3 vols. (New York, 1939–44), Vol. I (2nd ed. 1945), p. 158. J. W. Jones, *The Law and Legal Theory of the Greeks: An Introduction* (Oxford, 1956), p. 292. F. H. Lawson, *Negligence in the Civil Law,* with Introduction (Oxford, 1950). C. Morris, *Torts* (Brooklyn, 1953), Ch. VII. E. Nagel, *The Structure of Science* (New York, 1961), Ch. X. C. S. Peirce, "Proximate Cause and Effect," in Baldwin's *Dictionary of Philosophy and Psychology* (London, 1901–05), II, 373. T. F. T. Plucknett, *A Concise History of the Common Law* (Boston, 1956a); idem, "Law," *Encyclopedia Americana* (New York, 1956b), 17, 89. R. Pound, *Jurisprudence,* 5 vols. (St. Paul, Minn., 1959), IV, 508–25, has extensive references. W. L. Prosser, *The Law of Torts,* 2nd ed. (St. Paul, Minn.,

1955), Chs. 8 and 9. F. Schulz, *History of Roman Legal Science* (Oxford, 1953), pp. 69, 135, 295. Saint Thomas Aquinas, *Summa theologiae*, Ia, 14, 13. J. B. Thayer, *Lex Aquilia* (Cambridge, 1929). J. Wigmore, *Select Cases on the Law of Torts* (Boston, 1912), I, 764ff.

THOMAS A. COWAN

[See also **Law,** Ancient Roman, **Common; Legal Responsibility.**]

CAUSATION IN THE SEVENTEENTH CENTURY

IN BOOK I, Part III, Chapter XIV, of *A Treatise of Human Nature* (1739), David Hume, having proposed his now famous definitions of "cause," stated what he took to be a corollary of his view. According to Hume, it should have been clear from the foregoing discussion that "all causes are of the same kind. . . ." Part of his intention in making this statement was to make explicit his opposition to the Aristotelian and scholastic doctrine of four kinds or genera of causes. "There is no foundation," he went on to say, "for that distinction . . . betwixt efficient causes, and formal, and material, . . . and final causes"; and he indicated clearly in this passage that, on his view, all bona fide causal statements were about efficient causes. Although the originality of Hume's discussion of causation has been acknowledged, this contention has not usually been singled out for attention. Commentators seem to have assumed that, in declaring that all causes were of the same kind, Hume was simply generalizing a maxim that antischolastic advocates of the mechanical or corpuscular philosophy had proposed and followed in their investigations of nature and that he displayed his originality in his analysis of the meaning of the causal terms used in science and in daily life. Both parts of this assumption would be difficult to defend. Among antischolastic and (in Robert Boyle's inclusive sense of the term) "corpuscular" philosophers in the seventeenth century, there was a wide variety of reactions to the traditional doctrine of fourfold causes; and there was no agreement, in theory or in practice, that the discovery of efficient causes was the exclusive aim, or indeed the principal aim, of investigations of nature. A survey of views about causal explanation in the seventeenth century also shows that Hume's questions about force and necessary connection had been raised and that his own analysis of the meaning of certain causal expressions had been proposed. The following survey, by no means exhaustive, includes some pre-Newtonian philosophers in England; Descartes and some of his followers on the Continent; and the giants of the end of the century, Newton and Leibniz.

I. PRE-NEWTONIAN PHILOSOPHERS IN ENGLAND

The methodological discussions of Francis Bacon, Thomas Hobbes, and Robert Boyle are of special interest because they exhibit a variety of reactions among advocates of the new science to the traditional distinction of four kinds of causation. Professedly and more or less heatedly antischolastic, they shared the corpuscular view that the phenomena of nature were to be explained by the motion of small particles or corpuscles. Yet each of them made use of scholastic terms in distinguishing kinds of causal explanations.

In the classification of sciences in Book III, Ch. IV, of *De augmentis scientiarum* (1623), Bacon distinguished four kinds of causes. The investigation of nature was divided in two parts: physics was to be concerned with efficient and material causes, while metaphysics was to deal with final and formal causes. Explaining this classification, Bacon cautioned his reader that, although he was continuing to use traditional terms, he felt free to alter their senses; and it is clear that his view differed from that of his scholastic contemporaries in at least three important respects. First, metaphysics, which was distinguished from first philosophy and natural theology, was a part of natural philosophy; and to metaphysics he assigned what he took to be the most important and productive part of his new science—the investigation of forms or formal causes. Second, although the investigation of final causes was also within the province of metaphysics, it, unlike the investigation of forms, could provide no knowledge of physical causes. Although it made sense to assert "that the firmness of hides in animals is for the armour of the body against extremities of heat or cold," such an explanation did not specify the actual physical cause of the phenomenon; and it was, according to Bacon's frequently cited condemnation, "barren and like a virgin consecrated to God produces nothing" (Book III, Ch. V). Third, the term *forma* underwent a sea change in Bacon's philosophy. Aware of Platonic and Aristotelian connotations, he explained in *Novum organum* (1620) that, when he used this term to refer to what was to be discovered in the productive part of metaphysics, he did not mean "abstract forms and ideas, either not determined in matter at all, or ill determined" (Book II, Aphorism xvii). His forms could be discovered, and could be precisely determined, by "true induction," i.e., by the method of "rejection or exclusion." An investigation of the form of heat, for example, showed that it was a species of motion: specifically, a motion that was "expansive, restrained, and acting in its strife upon the smaller particles of bodies" (Book II, Aph. xx).

Although motion of this kind was said to be the cause of heat, Bacon carefully distinguished this cause from what he called the "efficient cause" of heat. The term "efficient cause" was reserved for the results of investigations of a quite different and less fundamental nature that were to be a part of physics, namely, investigations of the ways in which bodies could be heated. Holding that heat could be produced in a body in various ways, he maintained that the efficient cause was variable or, in J. S. Mill's terms, that there was a plurality of efficient causes of heat. By contrast, what was discovered by "rejection or exclusion" was universally present in all hot bodies; and Bacon seems to have called this species of motion the "form" or "formal cause" of heat because he thought that, in making this discovery, he had discovered what heat really was—its nature or essence—and not something that was distinct from heat and, in Hume's terms, was "constantly conjoined" with it. In a passage in which he was concerned to explain precisely what he meant, and what he did not mean, when he asserted that heat was a species of motion, he expressed this thought quite clearly. He did not mean, he explained, that "motion generates heat"; rather, his conclusion was that "Heat itself, its *quid ipsum*, is Motion and nothing else . . ." (Book II, Aph. xx). Although Bacon was not always as clear as he was in this passage about the nature of conclusions reached by "rejection or exclusion," the view that he was attempting to formulate in this passage was, in more recent terminology, that the most basic laws of science were contingent statements of identity; and he carefully distinguished these laws from conclusions of lesser consequence about efficient causes and also material causes.

Examining the metaphysicians' view of causation in *De corpore* (1655), Hobbes claimed that the only tenable distinction within the fourfold classification was that of efficient cause and material cause (Part II, Chs. IX and X). What the metaphysicians classified as final causes and formal causes—ends and essences, respectively—were, according to Hobbes, really efficient causes. Ends, he maintained, could be ascribed only to what had sense and will; and the end of a desire was the object desired. On his view, however, the object desired was the efficient cause of the motion that constituted the desire; and, whereas it seemed "as if we draw the object to us," what was really the case was that "the object draws us to it by local motion" ("Short Tract on First Principles," Appendix I in *The Elements of Law*, ed. F. Tönnies, Cambridge, 1928). Taking the scholastics' view about formal causes to be that "the essence of a thing is the cause thereof, *as*

to be rational is the cause of man . . . ," there is little wonder that Hobbes deemed the view unintelligible. Yet he was not prepared to deny that essences functioned as causes: "knowledge of the *essence* of anything," he maintained, "is the cause of the knowledge of the thing itself; for, if I first know that a thing is *rational*, I know from thence, that the same is *man . . .*" (*De corpore*, Part II, Ch. X). Essences were *causae cognoscendi*, but Hobbes insisted that, as such, they were efficient causes, or rather parts of the efficient causes, of the knowledge that resulted from knowledge of them.

Hobbes retained the terms "efficient cause" and "material cause" to mark a distinction within what he called the "entire cause" or "cause simply." Anticipating Mill's view about a philosophical sense of "cause," the entire cause was for him "the aggregate of all the accidents both of the agents how many soever they be, and of the patient put together; which when they are all supposed to be present, it cannot be understood but that the effect is produced . . . ; and if any one of them be wanting, it cannot be understood but that the effect is not produced" (Part II, Ch. IX). Since, on his view of bodies, there was no substantial change, every change was a change of an attribute or accident of a body; and the cause, or "entire cause," included all of the many attributes of the agent and patient bodies that were necessary and jointly sufficient for the occurrence of the change. Realizing that not just one condition but many were necessary and that the term "cause" was usually used to refer to only one of these conditions, he distinguished the "entire cause" and the cause *sine qua non* and tried to state the criterion used in the selection of one of the many conditions as the "cause," in the ordinary sense of the term, or cause *sine qua non*. In this attempt, he seems not to have been successful, but he did make clear what he (if not others) meant by "material cause" and "efficient cause." The totality of conditions necessary for the occurrence of a change included attributes of the body acted upon, for instance, dryness of wood that was ignited, as well as attributes of the agent body or bodies. The former were the material cause, and the latter the efficient cause.

When Hume claimed that all causes were of the same kind, he seems to have been aware of one of the distinctions that Hobbes made. In the passage quoted, he claimed to find no basis for a distinction "betwixt efficient causes, and causes *sine qua non*. . . ." Holding himself that "the same cause always produces the same effect, and the same effect never arises but from the same cause" (*A Treatise* . . . , Book I, Part III, Ch. XV), he seems not to have been aware of the problem that Hobbes discovered in the discrepancy between a defi-

295

nition of "cause" in terms of necessary and sufficient conditions and the ordinary use (Hume's included) of this term.

Boyle was more hospitably disposed toward explanations in terms of final causes than Hobbes or Bacon. Concluding his discussion of final causes in *The Usefulness of Experimental Natural Philosophy* (1688), he maintained that "as to animals, and the more perfect sorts of vegetables, it is warrantable, not presumptuous, to say, that such and such parts were preordained to such and such uses, relating to the welfare of the animal (or plant) itself, or to the species it belongs to. . . ." Yet he exhorted the true "naturalist" not to "let the search or knowledge of final causes make him neglect the industrious indagation [i.e., investigation] of efficients," and he implied that the naturalist's principal aim was the discovery of efficient causes. This supposition in Boyle's discussion of methodology does not seem to accord with the Baconian way in which he stated the conclusions of his investigations of the "origin" of certain qualities. His investigation of heat, for instance, revealed its "nature"; and this way of stating his conclusion suggests that, like Bacon, he thought that he was discovering what heat really was—its nature or essence. The apparent inconsistency can be explained if we attribute to Boyle a view like John Locke's in *An Essay Concerning Human Understanding* (1690), in which the term "heat" was used equivocally to refer both to heat as it existed in bodies and to heat as it existed in us. (Cf. Book II, Sec. viii, of the *Essay*.) Using "heat" in the first sense, Boyle could represent the conclusion of his investigation as the discovery of the nature of heat. Since what was discovered was also thought to be the efficient cause of heat in the second sense, he could also represent the conclusion of his investigation as the discovery of the efficient cause of heat. That Boyle used terms like "heat" in two senses is evident from his seemingly contradictory statements about color: color was not "an inherent quality of the object," yet whiteness—for Boyle, a color—could be "considered as a quality in the object" and, as such, "depended on the asperity of the superficies of the body" (*Robert Boyle on Natural Philosophy*, ed. M. B. Hall, pp. 255–56). Like Locke and unlike Bacon, Boyle did not think it important to distinguish two kinds of investigations of the phenomenon of heat; and the conclusion of any investigation was alternatively about the nature of heat as it existed in bodies or about the efficient cause of heat, i.e., about a power in bodies to produce heat in us, and also in other bodies. For this reason, and because he did not think that the nature or cause of heat was directly observable, there was no temptation to characterize the aim of causal inquiry in Humean terms as the discovery of constant conjunctions between kinds of objects or events. In the case of "forms and qualities," it was the discovery of their "origin."

II. DESCARTES AND HIS SUCCESSORS

Though it is customary to contrast Hume's empiricism with the rationalism of Descartes and the Continental philosophers whom he influenced, their discussions of causal explanation had certain important features in common. One was concern about the notion of force. Descartes and the occasionalists, attacking what they took to be animistic conceptions of forces in nature, raised questions about the origin of the idea of force; and Nicolas Malebranche, employing arguments like Hume's, reached essentially the same conclusions as Hume did—much later in a nontheological manner—about causal statements in science and in daily life. A second common feature was the view that physics was concerned with efficient causes and not with final causes. While Descartes was prepared to admit that there were causes other than efficient causes—for instance, that created things could be viewed as serving God's purposes, and also that God as *causa sui* was not, strictly speaking, the efficient cause but rather the formal cause of His existence—he insisted that in physics only efficient causes were to be investigated. Spinoza, also imposing this restriction, rejected outright the doctrine of final causation and also rejected Descartes' distinction of God's formal causation of Himself and efficient causation of the universe.

In *Principia philosophiae* (1644), Descartes, laying down the rule that efficient and not final causes were to be investigated (Part I, Princ. xxviii), was concerned to banish several kinds of explanations in physics. Although he thought that ends or purposes could be attributed to creatures having a soul or mind and also to God, "God's purposes . . . seem to be hidden in the abyss of His inscrutable wisdom"; and, while some parts of nature served our purposes, to say that they were created for this reason would have been conjecture and not an expression of genuine knowledge. Proposing this rule, Descartes also had in mind certain kinds of statements and explanations that he found in scholastic manuals, for example, that heavy bodies sought the center of the earth. To say that heavy bodies sought the center of the earth was to impute to these bodies characteristics that, according to Descartes, could only be ascribed to beings having a soul or mind.

In letters to the Princess Elizabeth (May 21 and June 28, 1643, in *Correspondance*, ed. Adam and Milhaud, V, 289–92, 322–25), he distinguished four primitive notions under which all of our ideas could be subsumed and pointed out what he took to be misapplications of certain ideas, or category mistakes, in scholastic physics. In addition to (1) ideas that were applicable to any conceivable entity—e.g., being, number, and duration—there were (2) ideas that could be applied only to bodies, namely, ideas of their extension, shape, and motion; (3) ideas under the category of thought that pertained only to souls or minds; and (4) ideas applicable to the union of soul and body in a human being, including an idea of the "force that the soul has of moving the body." When, according to Descartes, the scholastics explained the behavior of heavy bodies by asserting that their weight made them seek the center of the earth, they misapplied ideas of the third and fourth categories. They conceived of weight as an unextended entity that was supposed to be in some way attached to an extended body yet could also be removed if the body ceased to be heavy. This quasi-substantial unextended entity, or "real property," was, as it were, a small soul; and the animism of the scholastics consisted in part in their imputing to inanimate objects entities with characteristics of the third category that could only be applied to beings having a soul or mind. They also thought of the weight of a body as exerting force and acting on the body; and, so doing, they misapplied an idea of the fourth category—namely, of the force that the soul has of moving the body—to entities that were to be described exclusively in terms of their geometrical properties and motion and rest.

Although Descartes took exception to what he thought was an animistic or anthropomorphic conception of force in scholastic physics, he made use of terms like "force" in his own physics. Stating his principle of inertia, for instance, he maintained that "once a body has begun to move, it has in itself a force to continue its motion . . ." (letter to Mersenne, October 28, 1640). In attributing an inertial force to moving bodies, he did not think that he was imputing to them the kind of force experienced in voluntary action; for, as he carefully explained, the force that he attributed to a moving body—its "quantity of motion"—could be defined in terms of the clearly and distinctly perceived properties of motion and (ultimately) volume.

Commentators have raised questions about Descartes' attempt to explain what he meant by terms like "force" and "tendency to move" by reference to motion and rest and the geometrical properties of bodies. In his physics, he distinguished the motion that a body tended to have from its actual motion; and, making this distinction, it seems that he could not consistently identify force, or quantity of motion, with the product of mass or volume and actual motion. In the last year of Descartes' life, Henry More raised an objection of this kind: he was unable to reconcile Descartes' contention that motion, like shape, was a mode or state of a body and his assertion that motion could be transferred or communicated from one body to another. In his reply, Descartes found it necessary to make a distinction. Motion, in the sense of translation from place to place, was, like shape, a mode or state of a body. But this was to be distinguished from a body's moving force (vis movens), which he explained "can be God's, conserving the same amount of motion in matter as he placed in it from the first moment of creation; or also that of a created substance, such as our mind; or that of any other thing to which God gave the force of moving a body" (August, 1649, Correspondance, VIII, 264). This explanation left the question open as to whether God had bestowed this force on bodies themselves. But Descartes added that he had not discussed the matter in his published writings for fear of giving the impression that, on his view, God was the soul of the world; and he implied, though he did not clearly assert, that the moving force of bodies was not to be attributed to bodies but to God. It seems that, when More pointed out an ambiguity and Descartes found it necessary to make a distinction, it was difficult for him to say unequivocally where the force that he had distinguished from motion was located. If he attributed it to bodies, he would have been imputing to them a property admittedly other than motion and extension, and his own view would have been subject to the kind of objection that he had raised regarding the forms and qualities of the scholastics. Yet he needed the notion of a body's force, or quantity of motion, to explain its behavior. His last words on the subject expressed an inclination to consign this putative property of bodies to God.

In his published writings, Descartes had claimed that God was the primary and universal cause of motion (Principia, Part II, Princ. xxxvi), and he had explained that, but for God's imparting motion to matter in the beginning and continuing to impart motion by his "ordinary concourse," matter would have been a homogeneous substance undifferentiated by the motion of its parts. He was clearly on record that the divine concourse, or God as causa secundum esse, was a necessary condition of the motion of bodies. Accepting this view, the occasionalists employed a variety of arguments to show that God was also the sufficient condition of a body's moving, and that a body of itself lacked the power to continue its motion or to communicate it to other bodies. In Méditations chrétiennes et métaphysiques (1683), Malebranche argued that, in conserving a body from moment to moment, God must continue to will either that it exist in the same place or that it exist in different places. If He willed that it exist in the same place, the body was necessarily

297

at rest. God's will was inviolable, and nothing could make a body move that He had willed to be at rest. In similar fashion, if God willed that a body exist successively in different places, nothing could keep it from moving to those places. Since the motion or rest of bodies was determined necessarily by the will of God, Malebranche concluded that bodies could not move themselves or other bodies and that the moving force of bodies was the will of God.

To Malebranche, the inefficacy of bodies—and indeed of any "second cause"—seemed to be a direct consequence of Descartes' doctrine of divine conservation. But he also supported his conclusion in other ways. In *Éclaircissement* XV, appended to his *De la recherche de la vérité* . . . (1674–75), he maintained that we could not form a clear idea of the putative force in bodies nor indeed of the force allegedly exercised in human volitions. He held that, when we consulted our clear and distinct idea of the essence of a body, we discovered that it was necessarily extended, divisible, and movable; but, in consulting this idea, we could not discover the force that it was supposed to have to move itself or other bodies. If such a force could be discovered from an investigation of an idea of a body, it would have been possible to determine *a priori* and without recourse to experience how it would move. It would have been possible, for example, to determine *a priori* and without recourse to experience that, when a billiard ball in motion came in contact with another ball that was at rest, the second ball would move off in a certain direction. There was, however, no necessary connection between the motion of the first ball and that of the second, and the behavior of the second ball could not be determined *a priori*. It was only from experience that we learned that the second ball would move in a certain way. Since our experience of regularities in the behavior of moving bodies was abundant, the mind moved with great facility from the thought of the first ball coming in contact with the second to the thought of the second ball moving; and, as a result, we tended to think that there was a necessary connection and that one event was the true cause of the other. This, however, was a mistake. The two events were distinct and not necessarily connected; and, for Malebranche, the only necessary connection to be discovered between distinct events was between the volition of an omnipotent being and its execution.

In similar fashion, Malebranche argued against the efficacy of human volitions. To show that we lacked a clear idea of the mind's alleged power to move the body, he maintained that there was only a contingent connection between a volition and movement of the part of the body that was willed. Moreover, the effort that we sometimes experienced in attempting to move

a part of our bodies did not provide us with an idea of efficacy or necessary connection, for effort of this sort was not always successful. Like Hume, he also appealed to our ignorance of the cerebral mechanics required to move parts of the body and to our failure to understand how a volition could bring about motion of physical particles in the brain.

Although Malebranche proclaimed that God does everything (*Dieu fait tout*), he did not deny outright or unqualifiedly that bodies or minds were causes. Following the precedent of Géraud de Cordemoy in *Le Discernement du corps et de l'âme* (1666), he distinguished the real or true cause, on the one hand, and the occasional or particular or natural cause, on the other. When one billiard ball came in contact with a second and the second moved, the impact of the first ball could be called the occasional cause of the second ball's moving. To say that it was the cause in this sense was simply to say that the second ball moved on the occasion of contact with the first ball and that events of the one kind regularly followed events of the other kind. About the analysis of causal statements of this sort, Malebranche and Hume were of the same mind. Hume was aware of this similarity, but he chose to stress the difference between his view and that of the occasionalists. The occasionalists distinguished two kinds of causes; whereas, according to Hume, "all causes are of the same kind . . . ," and there was "no foundation for that distinction . . . betwixt *cause* and *occasion*." It is fair to say that, in rejecting this distinction and claiming that all causes were of the same kind, Hume expressed what was truly original in his view about causation.

Benedict Spinoza, rejecting the Cartesian distinction of God and nature, also took exception to certain Cartesian views about causation. While Descartes banished final causes from physics on the ground that they were unknowable, Spinoza, in the famous Appendix to Part I of his *Ethica* (published posthumously, 1678), maintained that the notion of final causation in nature or in God was rationally indefensible. To suppose, he argued, that God acted for certain ends entailed that He sought something of which He was in need, and this consequence was incompatible with the divine perfection. Earlier, in Part I of the *Ethica,* he had also argued that the supposition of God acting for an end could not be reconciled with divine omnipotence or, properly interpreted, divine freedom. Rejecting the view that things in nature were created to serve our ends, he maintained that everything followed of necessity from the divine nature; and, contrary to Descartes, he claimed that God was cause of Himself in the same sense in which He was cause of all other things, namely, as efficient cause. It has been noted, however, that

Spinoza's conception of an efficient cause was unlike Descartes' and also Hume's. While agreeing with Descartes that an efficient cause need not be temporally prior to its effect, he conceived of God as *causa immanens*, that is, as not producing anything outside of, or distinct from, Himself; and, though he anticipated Hume's view that all causes were of the same kind, Spinoza's God and also the fixed and eternal things causing individual mutable things were not temporally prior to, nor in reality distinct from, their effects.

III. NEWTON AND LEIBNIZ

"Mechanism" is sometimes defined as the view that the phenomena of nature are to be explained by the motion of bodies having only geometrical properties. In this sense of the term, neither Isaac Newton nor G. W. Leibniz can be said to have advocated mechanism or subscribed to the mechanical philosophy. Both distinguished motion and change of motion from the forces required to bring them about; and, though they thought that these forces were measurable, they did not attempt to identify them with the properties by which they were measured. Nor, in their accounts of the nature and properties of bodies, were they prepared to reject in its entirety the scholastic doctrine of fourfold causation, though both excoriated attempts to explain particular phenomena by invoking occult qualities and forms.

Defining "force" as the "causal principle of motion and rest," Newton attributed to bodies an internal force—*vis insita* or *vis inertiae*—"by which existing motion or rest is conserved in a body, and by which any being endeavors to continue in its state and opposes resistance" ("De gravitatione et aequipondio fluidorum," *Unpublished Scientific Papers of Isaac Newton*, ed. Hall and Hall, p. 148). This force was listed as one of the essential properties of bodies and was distinguished from external forces and active principles, such as the force of attraction or gravity. Although Newton did not include gravity, along with *vis inertiae*, among the essential properties of bodies, he thought that it was a universal property; and, when the charge was raised that gravity was an occult quality, enjoying the same dubious status as the forms and qualities of the scholastics, Newton insisted that it was a "mathematical force," the existence of which was attested by experience. He also denied that, in positing this force, he had attempted to explain, or give the cause of, gravity. On this point, Leibniz, seems to have misunderstood him; for, like Leibniz, he thought that the notion of bodies acting on one another at a distance was unintelligible, and he professed ignorance of the means, physical or spiritual, by which gravitation was effected.

Attacking the Cartesian view that the essence of bodies was simply extension, Newton adapted scholastic terminology in presenting his own view. Space or extension, of which God was *causa emanativa* and which was coeternal with God, was the *materia prima* on which God, in creating bodies, imposed impenetrability and form; and "that product of the divine will is the form or formal reason of body denoting every dimension of space in which body is to be produced" ("De gravitatione . . . ," p. 140). Newton hastened to add, however, that his notions of *materia prima* and substantial form differed from the nebulous notions of his predecessors.

Leibniz, also rejecting the Cartesian conception of matter, contended that the simple substances or monads of which bodies were constituted were unextended centers of force. By "force," he explained, he meant "something between the capacity and action, something which includes an effort, an act, an entelechy . . . [and] passes of itself into action, in so far as nothing hinders it" (Leibniz, *Philosophischen Schriften*, ed. C. I. Gerhardt, IV, 472). Motion and geometrical properties, like the sensible properties—heat, color, etc.—were appearances or well-grounded phenomena (*phaenomena bene fundata*). According to Leibniz, each monad mirrored the universe from a particular point of view, and there was harmony or correspondence in the states of the various monads. But these correspondences did not result from, nor constitute, efficient causation among monads. Each state or property of a monad followed from its given nature; and, though it was not incorrect to speak of causation among monads, this was "final" or "ideal" causation based on God's having formed monads in advance in such a way that they accommodated themselves to one another. In his metaphysical system, Leibniz found a place for each of the traditional four genera of causes, distinguishing *materia prima* and substantial form and arguing for the compatibility of explanations by efficient and final causes. He was more charitably disposed toward the scholastics than other corpuscular philosophers: they were not, he observed, entirely to be despised, though they erred in attempting to explain particular phenomena by forms and qualities.

The distinction of kinds of causation, along with the Leibnizian conception of force, was rejected by Hume in the *Treatise*. Correspondences, in the sense of constant conjunctions of temporally successive and spatially contiguous objects or events, were *ipso facto* causal relations; and all explanations and inferences concerning matters of fact were based on relations of this kind. To many philosophers of an empiricist or positivist persuasion, Hume's criticisms of traditional views and formulation of a regularity theory of causation have seemed an impressive and lasting achievement. Some recent opinion has been more critical. Concerning the explanation of human behavior, it has seemed important to distinguish reasons and causes; and it has been suggested that, as there are different types of causal inquiry, there "may not be a single conception of causation but rather a cluster of related concepts" (H. L. A. Hart and A. M. Honoré, *Causation in the Law*, p. 17).

BIBLIOGRAPHY

Francisco Suárez's influential *Disputationes metaphysicae* (1597) contains an extended presentation and discussion of the scholastic doctrine of fourfold causation. See Disputations XII–XXXIII, in Vol. II, 323ff., and Vol. III of the recent Latin and Spanish edition (Madrid, 1960–64). The interesting and revealing controversy between Descartes and More is to be found in Vol. VIII, 90–107, 121–39, 154–85, 204–17, 240–52, and 261–67 of *Descartes: Correspondance*, edited by Charles Adam and Gérard Milhaud (Paris, 1963). Newton's anti-Cartesian tract "De gravitatione et aequipondio fluidorum" was published by A. Rupert Hall and Marie Boas Hall in *Unpublished Scientific Papers of Isaac Newton* (Cambridge, 1962), pp. 89ff. The following books and articles, representing a very small part of the literature, have been particularly useful: Yvon Belaval, *Leibniz, critique de Descartes* (Paris, 1960); M. H. Carteron, "L'Idée de force mécanique dans le système de Descartes," *Revue philosophique de la France et de l'étranger*, **94** (1922), 243–77, 483–511; R. W. Church, "Malebranche and Hume," *Revue internationale de philosophie*, **1** (1938), 143–61; Étienne Gilson, "De la Critique des formes substantielles au doute méthodique," *Études sur le rôle de la pensée médiévale dans la formation du système cartésien* (Paris, 1951), pp. 141–90; Marie Boas Hall, *Robert Boyle on Natural Philosophy* (Bloomington, 1965); Peter Hoenen, *Cosmologia* (Rome, 1949); Max Jammer, *Concepts of Force* (Cambridge, Mass., 1957); Alexandre Koyré, "Galilée et la loi d'inertie," *Études galiléennes*, Vol. III (Paris, 1939); idem, "Newton and Descartes," *Newtonian Studies* (London, 1965), pp. 53–200; David Kubrin, "Newton and the Cyclical Universe, Providence and the Mechanical Philosophy," *Journal of the History of Ideas*, **28** (1967), 325–46; Maurice Mandelbaum, *Philosophy, Science, and Sense Perception* (Baltimore, 1964); Richard McKeon, "Causation and the Geometric Method in the Philosophy of Spinoza," *The Philosophical Review*, **39** (1930), 178–89 and 275–96; Paul Mouy, *Le Développement de la physique cartésienne, 1646–1712* (Paris, 1934); idem, *Les lois du choc des corps d'après Malebranche* (Paris, 1927); Joseph Prost, *Essai sur l'atomisme et l'occasionalisme dans la philosophie cartésienne* (Paris, 1907); P. P. Wiener, "The Experimental Philosophy of Robert Boyle," *The Philosophical Review*, **41** (1932), 594–609.

WILLIS DONEY

[See also Atomism; **Baconianism; Causation, Final Causes;** God; **Man-Machine;** Nature.]

CAUSATION IN THE SEVENTEENTH CENTURY, FINAL CAUSES

I. THE CRITICS OF FINAL CAUSES

EVEN THOUGH we find at the core of seventeenth-century culture teleological conceptions (final causes or end-purposes as explanations), almost all the important philosophers of the time criticized them. Some philosophers, like Boyle and Leibniz, who wished to retain final causes, found it necessary to change their significance. To criticize teleology was equivalent to asserting that (a) nature is to be studied by itself and through its own principles (*juxta propria principia*), disregarding all purposes (final causes) external to the scientific sphere; (b) this study assumes that nature proceeds according to mechanical laws, and hence ignores or denies any final causes internal to nature; (c) only man can provide ends, for nature has no purposes, but if anyone wishes to say that science has a goal, that end is man. In other words, teleology (finalism) can have only an artificial aspect (or, in the language of that era, it belongs to the arts) and eventually a moral meaning, but neither a physical nor a metaphysical one.

The refutation of teleology is best seen in the context of the culture of the times. In the seventeenth century man asserts in various ways his faith in technique and his mastery over nature; the new science implies a change in the conception of nature and of man's relations to nature. In order to control nature man detaches himself from her and gives up anthropomorphism and metaphysical anthropocentrism, the essential characteristics of teleological ideas. Man still remains, indeed, at the center of the universe, but that is due to his own activity and not simply to a Providence that has ordered everything for man's benefit. Only man is active while nature is completely passive and material. Now only after establishing these presuppositions is it possible to reintroduce a universally valid theory like the mechanical theory which treats man in the same way as it treats Nature, interpreted not in terms of final causes except to consider the ends inserted by man in nature, that is, in technics and morals. The critics of teleology almost exclusively attack Aristotle and the Scholastics. Their criticisms were aimed chiefly at the metaphysical principles that justified the application of final causes in natural philosophy; however, except in rare cases, the criticisms lack detailed applications. Perhaps, this lack is explained by the fact that final causes had already been abandoned in scientific practice; in any case, the discussion was focussed on the domains of metaphysics and natural theology. Moreover, scholastic doctrine easily permitted discussion to concentrate on its principles. Indeed, it was assumed that all ends have to be desired, and they can be desired according to the wishes of God or of man. Now nearly all philosophers are agreed that man actually desires certain ends in ethics and in the arts, and that God desires ends in all that is created. But while it is admitted that man's ends are marks of man himself, it is denied that God's ends are marks of man and that it is legitimate to consider these ends in natural philosophy; no longer is this science to study final causes, but theology can do so only in so far as they can be revealed to man.

As we shall see, criticism generally denied the knowability of God's ends but not their existence. Spinoza alone denied that God could have ends. His was the most radical critique, however; the other philosophers, on the contrary, tried not to compromise the ideas of providence and free will, traditionally linked to final causes. Four factors made possible and facilitated the work of criticism: (a) the dissolving of the idea of form; (b) the prior criticisms of the use of final cause in natural philosophy and its ever more widespread abandonment; (c) the spread of the mathematical method; (d) the new theories about the unity of the sciences.

(a) The idea of form was essential to Aristotelian teleology because the actualization of form represented exactly the end of a process. That idea comes to be criticized at length in the sixteenth and then in the seventeenth century, e.g., by Bernardino Telesio, Francis Bacon, and Pierre Gassendi.

(b) The idea of end no longer had any importance in mechanics. In biology, on the other hand, it was preserved but there were a few authoritative voices raised against it, e.g., that of Jean-Baptiste van Helmont (1577–1644).

(c) Spinoza and a few others after him—e.g., Christian August Crusius (1758–1831)—saw in the geometric method a singular enemy of teleology.

(d) The theories formulated in the seventeenth century on the unity of the sciences presupposed empirical sciences treated in separation from one another except for a preconstituted general vision of the universe. The reconstruction of their unity not only presupposes their separation but respects, within certain limits, the autonomy of the sciences. In that way the continuous presence of God as the ultimate end was no longer noticed inside a science (which had developed autonomously) but came to be considered separately in a more general perspective, globally comprehending the relations between God and the universe. A far-reaching element noticeably enters into the factors that have facilitated the critique of final causes, viz., the new resurgence of the philosophy of Lucretius (first century)

which yielded fruit in Michel de Montaigne, Pierre Charron, and Francis Bacon.

Charron (in the footsteps of Montaigne) not only combatted teleological anthropomorphism and anthropocentrism but also reduced the concept of human ends by regarding human nature as an end in itself, without need of a final cause entering from outside, that is, from God, for insertion in universal nature. Hence in naturalistic ethics there is lacking the idea of a transcendent highest good, which constitutes in a religious ethics the supreme end of human actions. Thus the concept of end came to be transformed with regard to ethics. Paradoxically a more extreme idea than that of Charron, viz., to mathematize ethics leaving aside the idea of end, seemed to insinuate itself even in Mersenne who was Charron's great enemy. However, this tendency was to find its outlet partly in Hobbes and completely in Spinoza.

Fundamental for almost all the seventeenth-century philosophers were Francis Bacon's criticisms based on the distinction between philosophy and theology, and between human science and natural science. Bacon believed that the idea of final cause compromises this distinction and consequently the progress of natural philosophy. The latter in fact can be known only by means of the natural light of reason, while theology on the contrary requires revelation; the two methods of knowledge are not to be confused, and neither are the two disciplines. God may wish to have final causes in nature, but then they are to be studied where God's will is studied, viz., in metaphysics, not in physics, otherwise impiety sets in. If the study of final causes has improperly penetrated natural philosophy, the reason is, according to Bacon, that man believes himself the measure of all things and attributes to nature laws which are peculiar to him exclusively. Now the study of final causes is proper for ethics and the arts, but to introduce them into nature is anthropomorphism. The use of final causes in natural philosophy is doubly to be condemned, that is, for being both illegitimate and sterile. Science aims at the control of nature and demands the very progress which an unwarranted use of final causes obstructs. On the other hand, final causes clearly have their place in ethics because the end of actions furnishes the criterion of moral behavior.

Galileo's criticism was developed within the context of the attack on the geocentric conception of the universe; it was directed, above all, at the anthropocentric character of final cause and was rather moderate. Galileo maintained that a concept, according to which the one and only end of the universe is man, depreciates the omnipotence of God. Moreover, to reason with final causes means to consecrate the sort of ignorance which accompanies anthropocentrism.

Criticism is linked with a new idea of the relations between man and nature: man is no longer at the center of the universe, nor is what is advantageous to man the criterion of scientific reasoning for either God or man (God foresees, but this consideration escapes scientific discourse).

Descartes' position is similar to Bacon's and Galileo's if limited to the fact that he rejects the use of final causes from natural philosophy; but he is more wary in other disciplines and does not deny that God possesses final ends, or even that man can know them with the natural light of reason alone. Descartes' discourse never goes beyond this point, and he does not develop ideas that he simply hints at; for example, that final causes say nothing about the nature of the scientific object. He has nonetheless insisted on criticizing anthropocentrism, anthropomorphism, and the impiety of those who claim to know final causes (for such a person claims to know God's purposes and is therefore vain). On the other hand, final causes have their function in ethics, but it is only a charitable and merely conjectural function without ever being able to warrant the status of scientific knowledge. In particular, his criticism of anthropocentrism serves Descartes as a subsidiary argument in criticizing geocentrism. Naturally it is possible for God to reveal his purposes, but the philosopher in the absence of such revelation has at his disposal only the natural light of reason which permits him to consider only efficient causes. None of this prevents Descartes from admitting the intervention of God in the creation, but he takes this into consideration only when he speaks of very general principles.

Although Descartes' arguments show no particular originality, they have enjoyed a very important role historically. Following their master's suggestions the Cartesians found themselves free to choose between two roads: on the one hand, to subordinate to continuous and special divine intervention the possibility of explaining a more or less large number of natural principles (but sufficiently general always); or else render that intervention as something so general as to make it practically of little interest. Generally the first road was the one chosen.

There is no longer any talk of final causes in physics (some concessions occur at times in biology) but they still survive in metaphysical discourse, even though in more general terms than those used by the Scholastics. In ethics final causes succeed in prevailing undisputed, but also beyond discussion was the condemnation of anthropocentric and anthropomorphic conceptions. These Cartesians bring no new argument against final causes; as an exception, there is Jan de Raei (d. 1702) who develops in an original manner the charge of impiety against Aristotelian final causes, guilty (ac-

cording to Raei) of having deified nature. Moreover, the Cartesians reevaluate final causes somewhat. The following are a few specific cases.

Henricus Regius (1598–1679) influenced by the Calvinist doctrine, develops a deterministic view of final causes, limited to theology and metaphysics, and remaining mechanistic in physics and biology.

Johann Clauberg (1622–55) explains the body-mind relation by taking recourse to the will of God as the primary basis of final causation.

Lambert van Velthuysen (1622–85) accepts from Calvinist theology the viewpoint of a determinism of final causation (analogous to the viewpoint of Regius, Velthuysen's is limited to theology and to the general consideration of the relations of God to the world, while natural philosophy remains mechanistic). He denies that there is real contingency in the world by maintaining that contingency is only an external denomination arising out of our ignorance (a reason deepened by Spinoza).

Arnold Geulincx (1624–69), although opposed to final causes in natural philosophy, brings them back in ethics, theology, and metaphysics; he appears to be generally more moderate than Descartes, and yet we find him rejecting any anthropocentric character from final causes. Furthermore, even though he excludes the consideration of final causes from natural philosophy, he nonetheless puts all the natural sciences under the insignia of final causation by maintaining that though the origin of things is still to be studied according to the criteria of the mechanical philosophy, their use is to be considered in relation to the final end which can be no other than God (occasionalism).

Nicolas Malebranche remains mechanistic in physics but has reassessed the relevance of final causation in other fields quite profoundly. His view of purposes as causes, however, has nothing to do with that of the Aristotelians, as is shown by his clear refutation of substantial forms. In biology he restored final causes seeking, however, not to expel mechanism but rather to find a way of accommodating both; for example, he considers the world of organic creatures as preformed according to teleological criteria but their growth and development follow mechanical laws. In that way there is left open to mechanism a sphere in which final causes operate from outside but without violating the mechanical order. (The general attitude of Leibniz was to be essentially the same.) Malebranche maintains that God is the ultimate end by his own nature, and that he orders the whole of creation with his own ends in view; therefore, it is possible to state the primary as well as secondary ends that God has put in the universe, including the purposes of scientific research which, however, proceeds in accord with the laws of mechanism. Thus the viewpoint of final causes originates in the domain of metaphysics and theology and not in the physical realm. What we have here is not an anthropocentric view of final causes but a theocentric one. And teleology does not reign undisputed in ethics; although the morality of an act resides in its end-purpose, the cause of this purpose or end is not to be found in the end but in "self-love" (*amour propre*) and in the desire to be happy. The study of this cause is not teleological.

Quite different are the criticisms of final cause by Thomas Hobbes and Baruch Spinoza. Hobbes is more explicit than his predecessors in reducing the final cause to an efficient cause, and this he does not only in natural philosophy but also in ethics based on the principle of self-preservation rather than on the good as the end willed. Moreover, by denying that the highest good (*summum bonum*) can be attained in this life (with respect to what he calls "the so-called felicity and ultimate end"), Hobbes intended to preclude the possibility of fusing naturalistic ethics with religious ethics, that is, with any concession to a transcendent end. There is no lack of criticisms in the works of Hobbes directed against anthropocentrism and anthropomorphism, for example, in defending the principle of inertia. The important thing to note is that these criticisms run up against the source of religious belief in the ignorance which induces men to believe the world to be governed providentially, that is, by God's purposes and for man's benefit.

We find the same criticism again in Spinoza, but put more radically. He has not merely denied the knowability of final causes but absolutely denied their existence and their putative origin in God. Man, according to Spinoza, believes that everything (God, nature, man himself) acts through final causes (ends, purposes) because he does not know the true causes and refers all natural phenomena to himself; that is, as if nature were directed to man's benefit (anthropocentrism) by God, who is imagined to be a sort of superman (anthropomorphism). But in nature everything happens according to necessity and not freely. Final causes do not help science and knowledge in general because they induce man to refer every event to the inscrutable will of God. Besides, belief in final causes tends to destroy divine perfection because it deems God to have created the world in order to assimilate it; we should have to admit that God, lacking things in the world, has need of them and is therefore imperfect. Spinoza extends his criticism of final causes to the belief in providence and miracles by maintaining that God never acts against the laws of nature which he himself sanctions. Final causes, thus excluded from God and from nature (that is, from metaphysics, natural philosophy, and also

theology which has no cognitive value for Spinoza), they are also routed from ethics. There are final causes or end-purposes considered in his ethics but with the premiss that they are illusory and not reliable instruments of knowledge, even if they are objects of knowledge. This teleological illusion is an inherent part of human nature and justifiable only as ignorance of the chain of efficient causes which determine human conduct. Spinoza also criticizes the idea of good understood as the final cause of moral acts; he moreover denies that such a good resides outside of human nature. Man's task is to follow the laws of his own nature and thus attain the maximum of knowledge and consequently of blessedness. Every person acts through an innate tendency to persevere in his own being (*conatus in suo esse perseverandi*). This principle is as much a scientific one and as little a teleological one as the principle of inertia.

II. DEFENDERS OF FINAL CAUSES

Final causes had followers among the Scholastics, among the biologists in the Aristotelian and Galenic tradition, among the Neo-Platonists, and among those philosophers in whom we customarily see the basic features of the baroque period. Final causes were also welcomed by other parties, e.g., by some of the atomists despite the fact that they were strongly influenced by Epicureanism. Sébastien Basson (ca. 1600) and Pierre Gassendi were teleologists. Gassendi defended his own views against those of Descartes by opposing them on religious grounds, and by maintaining the applicability of final causes in natural philosophy, especially in biology. Furthermore, Gassendi insisted on the necessity of final causes that would demonstrate the existence of God and his presence in creation.

Similar religious preoccupations guided Leibniz and Boyle in their attitude toward final causes. Leibniz maintained that Descartes' antifinalism led to Spinoza's determinism (we may recall that in the Scholastic tradition of final causation the ideas of free will and providence were linked together; however, we have also mentioned the finalistic determinism of the Calvinists). Leibniz argued for the subordination of mechanical to final causes; in addition, he tended to inject final causes also into physics, and believed he had succeeded in doing so by dealing with an argument in optics (light rays in refraction follow the path of least action, a problem solved by the calculus of minimal paths or "economy of action"). But he did not succeed in going much farther, and in any case his treatment of final causes did not rest on any structure used by Aristotle to justify final causation. Still Leibniz did speak often in favor of substantial forms and of Plato's teleology. Religious concerns motivated him

303

and also convinced him that a mechanical explanation of the universe was inadequate.

Robert Boyle insisted on the necessity of investigating the ends or purposes of those things which were studied according to the criteria of mechanism, but that we ought not to ignore Divine providence. However, he did believe it illegitimate to deduce from alleged ends consequences otherwise unknown.

Despite all the attempts to restore final causes they indeed received a very severe blow, particularly in natural philosophy.

BIBLIOGRAPHY

Robert Boyle, *Works*, ed. Thomas Birch, 6 vols. (London, 1772). R. B. Braithwaite, "Teleological Explanations," *Proc. Aristotelian Soc.* N. S., **47** (1947), i–xxi. Enrico de Angelis, *La critica del finalismo nella cultura cartesiana. Contributi per una ricerca* (Firenze, 1967). W. Heitler, *Der Mensch und die naturwissenschaftliche Erkenntnis* (Braunschweig, 1962). Paul Janet, *Les causes finales* (Paris, 1876). G. W. Leibniz, *Monadology*, in *Leibniz Selections*, ed. P. P. Wiener (New York, 1951). Ernest Nagel, *The Structure of Science* (New York, 1961), pp. 401–28. R. B. Perry, "A Behavioristic View of Purpose," *Journal of Philosophy*, **18,** 4 (Feb. 1921), 85–105. B. Spinoza, *Ethics & The Improvement of the Understanding*, ed. James Gutmann, trans. William H. White (New York, 1953). E. C. Tolman, *Purposive Behavior in Animals and Men* (New York and London, 1932).

ENRICO DE ANGELIS

[See also **Causation;** Free Will; God; **Nature;** Progress; Right and Good.]

CERTAINTY IN SEVENTEENTH-CENTURY THOUGHT

THE PROBLEM of the certainty of knowledge was not new in the seventeenth century. In the preceding century the Reformation brought to the fore the question of the reliability of religious knowledge, particularly the question of which church—Catholic or Protestant—could provide the best guarantee of the truth of its doctrines. The revival of learning in the Renaissance brought to the attention of the learned of the time the writings of the ancient Greek skeptics, particularly of Sextus Empiricus (ca. A.D. 200). Most deeply affected by this discovery was Michel de Montaigne who in his *Apology for Raymond Sebond* extended the arguments of the skeptics to raise questions about the reliability of all our knowledge. The issue involved in the resurgence of skepticism was the question of how certain one can be of what he believes. The skeptic claims

one can have no knowledge at all; at best one must remain in doubt and suspend judgment. If the structure of nature is complex, if the senses sometimes deceive, if one's thought processes do not match the structure of nature, then nothing is certain. Montaigne asks: If the senses cannot be trusted how reliable is scientific knowledge? If reason errs how reliable are claims to know of God's existence and nature? If moral principles cannot be justified then how seriously ought one to pursue the good life or try to do what is right?

If the problem of certainty was not new for the seventeenth century, the solutions to it were. In addition to the suspension of judgment counselled by such skeptics as François de La Mothe Le Vayer, Pierre Charron, and François Veron, two alternative views were developed. First there was the extreme opposite view, that of dogmatism. Francis Bacon argued that by furnishing the senses with mechanical aids and the mind with a new method of inquiry one can gain certain knowledge about nature. René Descartes argued that by grounding all knowledge on clear and distinct ideas of the self and of God, completely certain knowledge can be gained about self, God, and the world. The second major alternative to skepticism was the claim that a middle way could be found between the extremes of skeptical uncertainty and complete certainty, thereby forming a perspective which later became the foundation of what we now call the "scientific" temperament. This view has been called "constructive skepticism." On the Continent this view was initially worked out in the context of science by Marin Mersenne and Pierre Gassendi. In England it was formulated in the context of theology by a liberal Anglican, a convert from Catholicism, William Chillingworth, and later systematized and applied to the theory of science by such early members of the Royal Society of London as John Wilkins and Joseph Glanvill. It was applied in the sciences by such men as Robert Boyle and Sir Isaac Newton. Finally, it received its definitive expression in the philosophical writings of John Locke. However, it was not completely assimilated into the mainstream of European thought until the dogmatism of Descartes was dealt its final blow by David Hume.

Francis Bacon, the reputed father of modern experimental science, was one of the first to formulate a way out of the skeptical crisis. Though his emphasis upon experimental procedures and on the utility of science for the benefit of human life won him acclaim in his own century, it was not his views on the certainty of the results of scientific inquiry that were the decisive ones in the shaping of the views of early members of the Royal Society and of the scientific temperament.

The best known and perhaps most serious attempt to solve the skeptical crisis of the seventeenth century was formulated by René Descartes. He was aware that the Reformation, the new developments in science, and the resurgence of skepticism had thrown all accepted claims to knowledge into question. He was personally acquainted with such skeptics as Mersenne and Veron and knew the arguments of Montaigne and Charron. The view he found among his immediate acquaintances was that everything was subject to doubt. Probability was the most that could be claimed for anything. Descartes realized that if there are only probabilities, then there is no secure foundation for truth; for then there is no adequate criterion by which to distinguish truth from falsity. The strategy of his position is to follow the arguments of the skeptics to their conclusion, to reject everything as false, and in the depths of uncertainty to find truth and a criterion of truth. This criterion is then tied to the goodness of God.

In the *Discourse on Method* (1637) Descartes had formulated a "natural method" to assure certainty in the sciences. The first rule of this method was ". . . to accept nothing as true which I did not clearly recognize to be so . . . to accept . . . nothing more than what was presented to my mind so clearly and distinctly that I could have no occasion to doubt it." Ten years before publishing the *Meditations* (1641) he came to realize that all knowledge was under attack and therefore the criterion would have to be applied more extensively. Indeed, it became a very definition of knowledge: to know is to apprehend without any possibility of error. The *Meditations* begins with a rehearsal of basic skeptical arguments from the fallibility of the senses and problems about being awake or asleep. In rehearsing such arguments he is claiming nothing particularly new; these were the standard weapons of the skeptics. To accept them was to admit that the senses were unreliable sources of knowledge of the nature of the external world. Descartes realized that to overcome skepticism he had to go all the way. Hence he formulates an argument more critical than any presented by any preceding skeptic: the argument based on the possibility that there is an evil demon whose sole business is to make us believe true what may in fact be false. Unless this serious doubt is overcome, skepticism will always triumph, for there is then no dependable criterion of truth. Unless one can exorcise the evil demon no criterion is possible; what appears as self-evident may in fact be false. Even such simple matters as that a square has four sides or that three plus two is equal to five may be erroneous. Given the possibility of the evil demon all evidence and the rational processes of interpreting it are subject to error. Hence what can be known? Descartes suggests that his use of skeptical arguments differs from that of the skeptics' use of them. Whereas they used them to show

that nothing can be known he is using them to show precisely that truth and a criterion for its discovery can be found. Descartes finds the answer to doubt in the famous *cogito ergo sum* ("I think, therefore I am"). In formulating the most critical of the arguments of skepticism one discovers something true, his own existence. This follows not as the conclusion of an argument but as the conclusion of a doubt.

Having found this one truth Descartes has also found the criterion by which to distinguish truth from falsity: whatever is as clearly and distinctly perceived as the *cogito* is true. This criterion enables him by the light of natural reason to recognize the truth of several causal principles with which, in conjunction with the idea of a perfect being, he can demonstrate the existence of a perfect being, God. This being serves two functions: first, being perfect he would not allow man always to be deceived, thus exorcising the evil demon; and secondly, he guarantees the correctness of the criterion. In short, the criterion is rooted in the goodness of God. From this point Descartes proceeds to establish the reliability of the senses and prove the existence of the physical world. On this metaphysics of self, God, and matter, together with the criterion of clarity and distinctness, he then rebuilds the scientific description of the world around us. What we find in Descartes, then, is the recognition that "The Reformation, the revolution in science, and the onslaught of scepticism had crumbled the old foundations that used to support the entire framework of man's intellectual achievements. A new age required a new foundation to justify and guarantee what it had discovered. Descartes, in the tradition of the great medieval minds, sought to provide this basis by securing the superstructure, man's natural knowledge, to the strongest possible foundation, the all-powerful, eternal God" (Popkin, p. 179).

By Descartes' criterion—not to accept anything as true unless it is clearly and distinctly perceived—not only is one subjectively certain that something is true, but he is certain that it actually is so. Without the goodness of God there is always room for doubt. In working out this solution to the skeptical problem Descartes has offered, as Popkin argues, a Reformation solution to an epistemological problem concerning our secular knowledge. The Reformers and their opponents had shown each other that their views were without rational justification. The Reformers, particularly the Calvinists, had then argued that by a direct insight they were privileged to see true principles of faith and by an act of divine grace to see that these principles agree with the rule of faith, the Scriptures. What Descartes offers is the same kind of argument for all, not merely theological, knowledge. We perceive truth directly,

305

which in turn reveals a criterion; and by the criterion one can discover the goodness of God which guarantees the reliability of the criterion.

Descartes' solution to the skeptical crisis brought him immediate acclaim, not only by his defenders but also, and more particularly, by such critics as Mersenne, Gassendi, and Hobbes. But in spite of the severity of the attacks on his views, his solution to the skeptical crisis pushed out of sight an alternative to it, a solution which in the long run triumphed over his own.

Constructive skepticism—the lasting contribution of the seventeenth century to the "scientific attitude" and to contemporary philosophy—admits the full force of the skeptical attack on necessary and certain knowledge, but allows for a lesser knowledge about appearances. Mersenne and Gassendi on the Continent and Chillingworth in England first formulated the view later worked out by some early members of the Royal Society of London and fully articulated by John Locke but not accepted until the collapse of the dogmatism of Descartes.

Marin Mersenne was trained at the Jesuit school at La Flèche and later joined the Order of Minîmes. A great part of his life was devoted to publicizing the "new science." His writings are an attempt to show the importance of science despite the attacks of the skeptics. His book, *La Vérité des sciences* (1625), argues that even if the skeptic cannot be refuted we have a wealth of knowledge suited to our purposes in life. Such knowledge consists of information about appearances: hypotheses can be made about the connections of events and predictions made of the future course of experience. Science and mathematics do not yield knowledge about any transcendent reality or make any metaphysical claims or depend upon any such claims, as both Bacon and Descartes had maintained.

Mersenne is fully conscious of the skeptics' attack on knowledge. His position is not that we do not know anything but only that some things are unknown. Appearances and effects can be known, though we do not know their real causes. Our senses do not inform us about the real natures of things but this does not prevent formulation of laws—such as those of refraction—which enable us to predict future experiences and account for observed events. Despite the disagreements men have, which Mersenne cannot but acknowledge, there are many agreements among them too, and it is this that the skeptic overlooks.

Against the claim of the skeptic that everything is a matter of controversy Mersenne replies that many things are never disputed. Against the claim that all arguments lead to an infinite regress (in the search for premises to support premises) Mersenne claims that

there are some self-evident premises and that predictions can be checked empirically to determine the accuracy of the argument. In reply to the skeptic's claim that syllogistic reasoning is unreliable because there is no guarantee that any set of premises guarantees its conclusion, he answers that we do judge of the truth of premises and accept conclusions.

Mersenne's avowal of the extent of our knowledge is not itself a claim that complete certainty can be attained. Indeed, in his *Les Questions théologiques* (1634) he presents his own skeptical views. First, he shows that knowledge of eternal truths is not possible. All we know is subject to doubt. There is no body of demonstrative knowledge. He accepts the antimetaphysical claims of the skeptic but also argues for the truth of science. The reliability of knowledge does not depend on discovering the grounds of all certainty. In this sense both the dogmatist and the skeptic are mistaken—the one for claiming that metaphysical knowledge is possible and actual, the other for claiming that it is not. Both are mistaken in assuming that science depends upon a metaphysics and that metaphysical knowledge must be completely certain. Both the dogmatist and the skeptic are undermined. Between their positions lies a constructive path: doubting the grounds but accepting the structure of knowledge.

Not unlike the views of Mersenne were those of Pierre Gassendi. Known best as a critic of Descartes, Gassendi actually rivalled him in popularity as a scientist and philosopher of science. Well-read in the arguments of the skeptics, Gassendi rejected them as defeatist and negative because of the advances made in the sciences in his own times. He is credited with introducing the distinction between primary and secondary qualities of objects into modern philosophy, thereby attacking the Aristotelian view that scientific knowledge can both be based on sense perception and be necessarily true. If the observable properties of things are not their real properties, there can be no necessarily true empirical knowledge. All we know are the appearances of things. As a disciple of the skeptical tradition Gassendi holds that all claims to knowledge about the real world are unfounded and that appearances are the basis for all knowledge. By experience we cannot discover any general principles because we may always discover a negative instance. We observe only the appearances of things, not their real structures; hence we can make no inferences from appearances to reality. However, to account for these phenomena Gassendi reconstructed a version of Epicurean atomism—not as a metaphysics but as a set of theoretical constructs to account for appearances, a view which Robert Boyle later characterized as the "corpuscularean hypothesis." Such knowledge as we have about appearances does not yield certainty about the real structure of nature, though it gives a certainty sufficient to make predictions about future experiences. It is practically useful though not completely certain.

The views put forward by Mersenne and Gassendi were generally not understood by their contemporaries; further, they were overshadowed by the forcefulness of Descartes' position. It was not until a view somewhat like theirs was developed in England that their solution to the intellectual crisis of the time could make its impact.

During the second and third decades of the century there arose in England what has become known as "the Rule of Faith controversy," an outgrowth of the Reformation controversy concerning the adequacy of each church for salvation. Each side used a battery of arguments from the arsenal of skepticism to show that the other side could not guarantee its claim to religious knowledge and truth. The Catholic polemicists argued that their opponents had no way of determining which book is the Bible, what it says, or what one ought to do about it. Protestants argued that the appeal by Catholics to tradition and authority was unreliable, and that the average man had no way of determining infallibly what the tradition was, the reliability of its authority, nor even who was Pope.

Out of this controversy grew a form of constructive or mitigated skepticism that was able to deal with the issues. The view is offered that theoretically it might not be possible to eradicate or overcome the doubts raised about the possibility of religious knowledge, but that there was a type of assurance that was sufficient for practical religious purposes. By using the standards of common sense and practical life one could attain a limited amount of certainty—as much as the case admits of—a certainty that is beyond any "reasonable doubt" and sufficient for any "reasonable man."

One of the leading contenders in the Rule of Faith controversy was the young Anglican clergyman, William Chillingworth, whose once famous book, *The Religion of Protestants, a Safe Way to Salvation* (1638), deals with the theological issue of whether Protestants have any assurance of salvation outside the Catholic Church. His opponents had argued that there are only two alternatives with respect to religious knowledge: either absolute certainty of the truths of faith or none at all. With respect to the first, Chillingworth argues that such certainty is not humanly attainable in religious matters, though possible in mathematics and metaphysics. Skeptical arguments against the senses and reason preclude such certainty. He is also unwilling to accept the second alternative, skepticism; for such arguments, if taken too seriously, can destroy all belief. He proposes instead that one can be reasona-

bly certain of the doctrines necessary for salvation. The assurance of common sense about everyday affairs is made the standard for solution to perplexities about religion. The reasonable solution to any problem is to examine such evidence as is available and to proportion assent to it. It became a cardinal principle to proportion assent to evidence: to each kind of evidence there corresponds a kind or degree of assent, and as the evidence is greater or less so should be one's certainty.

In his description of the kinds of certainty a person can have of the truth of a statement Chillingworth is not systematic. In the main he distinguishes three levels with their subclassifications or degrees: (1) absolutely infallible certainty, (2) conditionally infallible certainty, and (3) moral certainty. The first of these— presumably the kind of certainty Descartes sought in his *Meditations*—Chillingworth regards as beyond human reach. Such certainty excludes every possibility of doubt, a condition not attainable by mortal man. Conditionally infallible certainty is the highest attainable by man; it is based upon such evidence as excludes, for all human purposes, the possibility of error, but does not exclude it completely since all experiences may, for example, really be dream events. This kind of certainty occurs whenever one has knowledge, that is, in those instances in which, upon knowing the meanings and connections of the terms involved, assent is compelled rather than voluntary. Because such mathematical truths as "the whole is greater than any of its parts" and "twice two is four" are of this kind, the certainty one has of their truth is called mathematical certainty; similarly the axioms of metaphysics are said to be metaphysically certain. Such infallible certainty is possible not only for simple statements of the kinds mentioned, but for demonstrations also, provided the rules of deductive inference are correctly applied.

The third kind of certainty is moral certainty, the certainty one has of what is believed but not known. This is the certainty of everyday life about matters of fact and is based on such evidence as excludes the possibility of error for all practical purposes. The certainty one has when traveling that he is on the right road and that the book one is reading is the work of the person whose name appears on the title page are of this sort. Moral certainty is described as the certainty a sane, reasonable, and thoughtful person has after considering all available evidence as fully and impartially as is possible and giving his assent to that side on which the evidence seems strongest. Since belief is based upon a different kind of evidence than knowledge, and is therefore less certain, the possibility of error is increased. As in conditionally infallible certainty the dream hypothesis prevents absolute certainty from being attained, so in moral certainty a skeptical doubt also operates, for "seeing the generality of men is made up of particulars, and every particular man may deceive and be deceived, it is not impossible, though exceedingly improbable, that all men should conspire to do so" (Chillingworth, pp. 203–04). If this possibility were taken seriously life would soon fall apart. If on grounds of possibility of error alone one refused to accept the testimony of witnesses the trial of criminal cases would soon become a shambles. Rejection on similar grounds of the reports of travelers and chroniclers would soon turn history into fiction. Although such possibilities exist, they are not destructive of the everyday activities of life; such beliefs as one has of matters of fact—of routes, the reliability of witnesses, and so on—suffice to get one through the day. Many things of which one is only morally certain may be true, but since the available evidence does not warrant a claim to knowledge one need and can be only as certain as the evidence allows. Unlike mathematical certainty, moral certainty admits of degrees because the strength of the evidence varies. Precisely where the lines are to be drawn between the several degrees of moral certainty, however, and what the standard is by which the degrees are measured, are not made clear.

The theoretical justification for accepting moral certainty is that some things by their very natures do not admit of more than a specific kind and amount of evidence and therefore it is unreasonable to demand more, e.g., mathematical proof for a matter of fact. The practical justification, stated with respect to religious belief, is that moral certainty suffices to turn the sinner from the ways of darkness to the path of light.

This view of the nature of certainty was developed in the next generation by several early members of the Royal Society of London who were also clergymen, among them John Tillotson, Joseph Glanvill, and John Wilkins. As so developed, especially by Wilkins and Glanvill, the theory was secularized, i.e., stated and applied in the context of scientific knowledge. Wilkins' views are particularly instructive, for in them is found a formulation in the context of religion which was applied to scientific procedures by Royal Society members and which later received full expression in the writings of John Locke. Its application to scientific procedures was due largely to Wilkins' influence in founding the Royal Society and in formulating its policy.

After taking a degree at Oxford in 1634 Wilkins took orders and rose rapidly in the Church of England—in part because of political influence. One of his major interests was in science. Though not of the prominence of such of his friends as Boyle, Hooke, Wallis, and Barrow, he nevertheless took a keen interest in several of the particular sciences. More important than his role as an amateur scientist was his association with the Royal Society. It is known that he attended scientific meetings of the Invisible College in London as early as 1645, and that he initiated a new series of meetings in Oxford when he moved there. Later, in 1660, he presided over the meeting in which formal action was taken to establish a society. He held offices in and was active in the Royal Society until his death.

Wilkins' major work, *Of the Principles and Duties of Natural Religion*, was published posthumously in 1675. In it he sees knowledge characterized by the same extremes as had Chillingworth, absolute certainty and extreme skepticism. He acknowledges the ideality of the first but realizes that it cannot be attained because of the limitations of the human faculties. The second alternative is at all costs to be avoided, because acceptance of "the cavils of Sceptical captious Men" would put an end to the certainty of religious and scientific belief and of the beliefs of everyday life, none of which Wilkins is willing to forego. He is not willing, as was Descartes, to reject everything for which the conditions of falsity can be stated; such skepticism leads to nihilism and is therefore rejected as absurd. Wilkins admits at the outset that the structure of reality cannot be completely understood by the human mind, but does not take this as a reason for despair.

The antiskeptical theme is an important one in his book on religion, in which the major question for consideration is, how can religious belief be justified without capitulation to the arguments of the skeptic? Wilkins' solution is a development of the theory of probable certainty stated earlier by Chillingworth. In general, he disregards the arguments of the skeptic and bases his theory of religious knowledge on the fact that ordinary people are not seriously affected by such arguments. In their daily and practical affairs people do claim certainty and base it on evidence. He tries to discover what kinds of certainty they claim, together with the corresponding kinds and levels of evidence. In his classification, a scheme later used by Locke in his *Essay Concerning Human Understanding* (IV, xiv–xv), two levels of assent are distinguished. On the one hand there is knowledge, ". . . which doth arise from such plain and clear Evidence as doth not admit of any reasonable cause of doubting" (Wilkins, p. 5). Three subclassifications are made: physical, mathematical, and moral certainty. On the other hand there is probability, ". . . which doth arise from such Evidence as is less plain and clear" (Wilkins, p. 8). Beneath these, where the evidence is such as to warrant neither affirmation nor denial, there is simply hesitation or suspension of judgment.

On another scheme of classification, which follows Chillingworth's text more closely, three levels of certainty are distinguished: absolutely infallible certainty, conditionally infallible certainty, and indubitable certainty. The first is the prerogative of God. The second comprises both physical and mathematical certainty and is the greatest humanly possible (revelation possibly excepted). Such certainty presupposes fulfillment of two requirements, that "our faculties be true, and that we do not neglect the exerting of them" (Wilkins, p. 9). Wilkins sets down their fulfillment as a postulate without which knowledge is impossible. The third level, indubitable certainty, which is the same as moral certainty, is not as strong as infallible certainty for, although the same suppositions are made, the evidence is less strong and thus provides only an assurance "which doth not admit of any reasonable cause of doubting."

Each of these kinds of certainty is clarified by an examination of the evidence to which each is supposed to be correlated. In doing this Wilkins tries to be precise and so defines his crucial terms, though his meanings are not always clear. He begins with the senses and distinguishes the external from the internal. The senses are the source of the highest certainty of which man is capable, physical certainty, but they are not infallible. Wilkins admits that he does not know how the senses operate, but claims that this is no argument against the genuineness of the knowledge derived from them. The causes of sense perception are one thing, the results another, and difficulties about the one do not necessarily bode ill for the other.

The second kind of evidence Wilkins considers— evidence from the nature of things—relates to the function of the understanding and (at its best) gives rise to mathematical certainty. Mathematical certainty is the kind of assurance one has of the propositions and demonstrations of mathematics and other abstract sciences. Upon knowing the meanings of the terms involved no one could deny without contradiction that the whole is greater than the part or that three plus three equals six. There occurs here what Wilkins calls "natural necessity"; one could no more deny this sort of proposition than he could avoid feeling hungry or sleepy. Denial of such propositions as these would be self-contradictory for it would be to deny meanings already accepted. Evidence from the nature of things occurs "when there is such a Congruity or Incongruity betwixt the Terms of a Proposition, or the Deduction of one Proposition from another, as doth either satisfy the mind, or else leaves it in doubt and hesitation about them" (Wilkins, p. 4).

Moral or indubitable certainty follows mathematical certainty. Of the three major kinds of certainty Wilkins recognizes this is the most important since of most things said to be known one can at best be only morally certain. By it he runs the middle course between absolute certainty and complete uncertainty. Moral certainty is the assurance one has of anything for which there is no ground for a "reasonable doubt." In making reasonable doubt the distinguishing feature of moral certainty Wilkins is making an appeal to common sense. In the context of religion in which he is writing the skeptic and dogmatist are both unreasonable, the one for making the bare possibility of doubt a sufficient reason for withholding assent, and the other for demanding a kind of evidence not open to any doubt whatever. Wilkins makes an appeal to what the man in the street believes, and makes this the standard by which to solve his problems: whatever is unacceptable to the common and reasonable man is probably not true. This appeal is made in two ways. First, the examples he uses are drawn from the ordinary affairs of life: the reports of travelers, merchants, and the like. "I appeal to the common judgment of mankind," says Wilkins. Secondly, the kind of certainty appealed to is that of the reasonable man. What an ordinary person, possessed of all his faculties and judicious in his use of evidence, would accept as true is for Wilkins the standard of truth.

The principle of reasonable doubt leaves open the possibility that what has been proved may be otherwise than the evidence indicates; however, this is not a sufficient reason for withholding assent. "Who is there so wildly skeptical as to question," asks Wilkins, "whether the Sun shall rise in the East, and not in the North, or West, or whether it shall rise at all?" No one can doubt such things without abandoning rationality. Acceptance of less than infallible certainty is a principle so strong in human nature that if it were otherwise reason would be a torment to mankind. Men would be soon driven to insanity if the mere possibility of error were a suitable basis on which to establish one's doubts or beliefs.

The evidence giving rise to moral certainty is that of the senses or of the nature of things when the senses are not adequate to give rise to higher levels of certainty. Particularly relevant to belief in matters of fact beyond one's immediate experience is testimony. The testimony of witnesses to a crime, of an explorer to the customs of a distant country, or of an historian to events in the past are all adequate bases for belief, provided that the witnesses are authoritative and credible. The criteria for determining competence are not, however, spelled out by Wilkins.

In laying the groundwork for his discussion of natural religion Wilkins proceeds, after considering the kinds of evidence and certainty, to establish their relationship more closely. One point he makes is that there are no degrees of truth; truth does not admit of more or less. Historical and geographical statements are as true as those of mathematics and metaphysics. The problem is that the same kind of evidence cannot be produced for each. But to deny the truth of an historical proposition because it cannot be immediately verified in sense experience or by demonstration (and thus not infallibly certain) would involve the gross error of supposing that because all truths are on a par the evidence must be so too. Wilkins cites in this connection a passage from Aristotle's *Nicomachean Ethics* (I, 3) in which it is pointed out that where there are differences in the subject matter to be proved the kind of evidence must be expected to differ. Paraphrasing Aristotle, Wilkins points out that it would be absurd to use a rhetorical speech to prove a mathematical proposition and equally out of place to use a demonstrative argument to arouse the emotions of an audience. This principle is Wilkins' ultimate justification for accepting less than infallible certainty in religion and the sciences. So long as any proof is good in its kind and suited to the subject matter, its conclusion is justified.

The account of constructive skepticism worked out by Chillingworth and Wilkins with respect to religious knowledge was not restricted to that domain. There is evidence to show that even in Wilkins' writings an effort is made to extend it to scientific knowledge as well. The writings of several of his contemporaries contain views on evidence and certainty remarkably similar to those Wilkins held. In the "experimental philosophy" of the Royal Society scientific conclusions are not taken to be absolutely true but as probable only. Such conclusions are subject to revision upon discovery of new evidence. The ideal of science as a deductive system is recognized for what it is, an ideal not attainable in practice because of the limitations of our faculties and the complexity of nature. Science does not make known the real structure of things but formulates hypotheses to account for what is observed—a redevelopment of the account put forward by Mersenne and Gassendi.

This account of certainty as applied to scientific conclusions was detailed by such early members of the Royal Society as Joseph Glanvill and Robert Boyle. Whereas Glanvill was primarily concerned with the theory of science, Boyle applied this account of certainty to his own scientific conclusions. However, much of Boyle's exposition of the theory is still in the context of religion; the majority of his comments on the nature and extent of knowledge occur in his theological writings. In the writings of Isaac Newton the situation is somewhat different. Here there is little discussion of a theory of knowledge though a theory is assumed in his scientific writings. Whereas most of his contemporaries in the Royal Society had been explicit in their views on the limitations of knowledge and the levels of certainty, Newton has little to say on these points. According to him there are some things the scientist finds beyond the reach of intellect and whose natures must be acknowledged as unknown, particularly the natures of light and gravity and of physical bodies, though speculative hypotheses can be formulated to account for them.

In his early contributions to the *Philosophical Transactions* concerning the analysis of light Newton says that his views are certain; however, it is an account only of the rays of light as they appear to the observer and not as they are in themselves. "But, to determine more absolutely, what light is, after what manner refracted, and by what modes or actions it produceth in our minds the Phantasms of Colours, is not so easie. And I shall not mingle conjectures with certainties" (*Phil. Trans.* No. 80 [19 February 1671/72]). To give an account of the nature of light would be to formulate a speculative hypothesis, a conjecture which has no role in the presentation of the results of scientific inquiry. Though he sought to discover the nature of light he was not successful in doing so. Hence he limited himself to a descriptive account of how light is bent, refracted, and so on.

As in the case of light, so also the force of gravity is unknown. In spite of this Newton did manage to formulate some significant laws describing the motions of bodies as affected by gravity. That such significant results can be achieved, it should be noted, is an application of the perspective taken earlier by Mersenne and Gassendi. Again, our knowledge of bodies is limited to an acquaintance with their secondary qualities, not their real natures. Shapes, colors, tactile qualities, and the like can be observed but "their inward substances are not to be known either by our senses or by any reflex act of our minds" (Newton, *Mathematical Principles . . .* , p. 546). The world of primary qualities is beyond our grasp, though one can formulate an hypothesis about them. Newton's hypothesis is not unlike the atomism of Boyle and Gassendi.

Newton's predecessors and contemporaries in the Royal Society had delineated with care several levels of certainty, each corresponding to a particular kind of evidence. At the summit was usually the certainty of immediate sense perception or that of mathematics or metaphysics. Next were the several degrees of morally certain propositions, which class usually contained those of science and religion. At the bottom was mere probability. Boyle, for example, works out such an hierarchical view. One can never be completely certain of the conclusions of the sciences because of the limitations of our abilities and because of the possibility that God may change the course of nature (as occurs in miracles) at the very moment we formulate laws. Scientific conclusions for Boyle give rise to physical certainty when all conditions are at their best, but this is an ideal seldom achieved. Generally, such conclusions are only morally certain. Both of these kinds of certainty, he says, are "but an inferior kind or degree of certainty." He regards the attempt of Descartes and other physicists, for example, to prove that certain comets are not meteors on the ground and that their parallax is less than that of the moon, to have only a moral certainty for they have not themselves made the relevant observations.

Newton is much less explicit in his presentation, distinguishing only mathematical propositions from those that are physically certain, and pointing out that scientific statements are not mathematically certain. What the scientist regards as true may in fact turn out to be false since his conclusions are based upon merely human principles. Science cannot provide an explanatory account of the real structure of nature but must limit itself to a descriptive account of what is observed to occur, and its conclusions are less than absolutely or demonstratively certain. In his controversy with Robert Hooke concerning the nature of light he admits his conclusions are only physically certain because of limitations in the evidence. One begins with evidence that can be expressed in mathematical formulae and from these deduces the existence of other phenomena to be observed. The conclusions of one's inferences are no more certain than the premises from which one begins; if these are inductive generalizations one's conclusions have no greater certainty.

Newton's account of what can be known is applied by him to religion as well as to science. One of the features of the movement in English thought that we have been tracing concerns the close relation between evidence for religious and for scientific propositions. In Chillingworth's writings references to scientific knowledge occurred only incidentally; in Wilkins' writings such references were of fundamental importance. The point was often made that the canons of evidence which held for one also held for the other. In Newton's thought the relation between religion and science also plays a significant role. Indeed, for him the pursuit of scientific truth has as one of its ultimate justifications insight into religious truth. The first of his letters to Richard Bentley begins with the comment that the complexity of nature can be accounted for only by reference to a deity with mathematical ingenuity. In one of the Scholia to the *Mathematical Principles of Natural Philosophy* (1687) he notes, "And so much concerning God, to discourse of whom from

the appearances of things, does certainly belong to Natural Philosophy" (Newton, p. 546). Newton's point seems to be that if the evidence for scientific and religious propositions is of the same kind, then the certainty for each will be the same also.

Such then is the reply of the seventeenth-century mind to the crisis of skepticism. Two major alternatives are worked out: the dogmatism of Bacon and Descartes on the one side and the constructive skepticism of Mersenne, Gassendi, Chillingworth, and the early members of the Royal Society of London on the other—a view which, after the middle of the eighteenth century, became the accepted account of certainty in all domains of knowledge. In the final decade of the seventeenth century John Locke formulated an account of the extent and certainty of knowledge which articulates for all knowledge—not merely scientific and religious knowledge—the constructive skepticism we have been examining. But Locke's theory of the certainty of knowledge also included some elements of the Cartesian epistemology, a blending which gave rise to a new series of problems for eighteenth-century thought.

BIBLIOGRAPHY

Francis Bacon, *Novum Organum*, in *The Works of Francis Bacon*, eds. J. Spedding, R. L. Ellis, and D. D. Heath, 15 vols. (Boston, 1861). William Chillingworth, *The Works of William Chillingworth, containing his book The Religion of Protestants, a Safe Way to Salvation* (Philadelphia, 1844). John Dewey, *The Quest for Certainty* (New York, 1960, reprint). René Descartes, *The Philosophical Works of Descartes*, eds. E. S. Haldane and G. R. T. Ross, 2 vols. (New York, 1955). John Locke, *Essay Concerning Human Understanding* (1690; London and New York, 1924; many reprints). Marin Mersenne, *La Vérité des sciences contre les sceptiques ou pyrrhoniens* (Paris, 1623); idem, *Les Questions théologiques, physiques, morales et mathématiques* (Paris, 1634). Isaac Newton, *Mathematical Principles of Natural Philosophy and his System of the World*, trans. A. Motte (1729); rev. by F. Cajori (Berkeley; 1946). *The Philosophical Transactions of the Royal Society of London*, eds. C. Hutton, G. Shaw, and R. Pearson, 18 vols. (London, 1809). Richard H. Popkin, *The History of Scepticism from Erasmus to Descartes* (New York, 1961). Henry G. Van Leeuwen, *The Problem of Certainty in English Thought 1630–1690* (The Hague, 1963). John Wilkins, *Of the Principles and Duties of Natural Religion* (London, 1699).

HENRY G. VAN LEEUWEN

[See also **Appearance and Reality;** Axiomatization; Baconianism; Causation; **Certainty since the Seventeenth Century;** Faith; Indeterminacy; **Necessity; Newton on Method; Rationality;** Reformation; Sin and Salvation; Skepticism.]

CERTAINTY SINCE THE SEVENTEENTH CENTURY

AFTER THE seventeenth century, questions about the certainty of knowledge agitated those who wanted to understand and improve the lot of man on earth more than those anxious to safeguard religious truth. Science rather than religion became recognized as the realm of the most venerable truths, and questions about the character of scientific knowledge dominated discussions about certainty.

The new context for these discussions was set by the Scots philosopher, David Hume, who, unlike earlier skeptics, did not merely emphasize that the human intellect was imperfect, but denied that it had any demonstrable link with the order of the universe. Whereas Hume was able to reconcile philosophical uncertainty with accepting other certainties, his successors looked for a more secure relationship between man and a cosmos made of alien stuff, and they hoped to discover such security by redefining rationality. This led them, with the exception of Hegel and his followers, to narrow the meaning of rationality by circumscribing either the objects that could be known or what could be said about them or the act of knowing, ending in a radically revised understanding of knowledge that attached certainty to acts of will rather than intellect.

Hume's denial that man's reason gave him insight into the rational order of the universe was inspired by his opposition to the doctrine that moral perfection consisted in the triumph of reason over passion. Instead of dividing human nature, as previous accounts had done, between a higher part, reason, that connected man with God, and a lower part, passion, which men shared with animals, Hume proposed that man was simply a bundle of perceptions, all of whose ideas were merely copies of sense impressions. Although some of Hume's successors were to fasten on sensation as the source of certainty, for Hume perceptions were a flow of unconnected particulars which could not in themselves constitute knowledge because that had to do with relations and general ideas. Far from denying that men possessed well articulated, valid structures of general ideas, Hume insisted upon it. He not only admired Newton's work and accepted the laws of physics established by him, but argued against miracles on the ground that they violated the laws of nature. The credentials of the belief in necessary connections between perceptions had to be examined precisely because it was intrinsic to human life.

Hume divided the connections men made between ideas into two kinds—relations of ideas and of matters of fact. Of the former, he considered mathematical reasoning the most obvious example. Mathematical truths, Hume believed, depended on comparing a finite set of ideas with one another, the criteria for making these comparisons correctly being given by a system which is complete in itself and has no reference to the outside world. "That the square of the hypotenuse is equal to the sum of the squares of the other two sides" has to be accepted by anyone who understands what the terms of the proposition mean. But there were no such well-defined criteria for propositions about matters of fact. How then did men come to believe not only that fire burns, but that it always burns?

If the traditional explanation that we have insight into the nature of fire were correct, Hume argued, the belief that fire burns should arise after observing only one instance. Instead we require repeated experiences of a connection between cause and effect before believing that one necessarily follows the other. As there is nothing in several resembling instances absent in one of them to explain why two events must be joined, the addition must come from the mind. The necessary connection we discover is therefore "an internal impression of the mind, or a determination to carry our thoughts from one object to another" (*Treatise*, Sec. XIV, "Of the Idea of Necessary Connexion," p. 165). Belief in necessity is nothing more mysterious than a feeling attached to certain ideas and is produced by repeated experiences of a conjunction between two ideas, or, in other words, belief arises from custom.

Hume gave a similar explanation of abstract ideas such as those of space and time. Here he followed the suggestion made by Newton's critics, such as Leibniz and Berkeley, that space and time were not independent realities but a way of understanding the coexistence or succession of objects. After repeatedly experiencing the coexistence of patches or points of color, Hume argued, we separate the idea of this coexistence from particular perceptions and think of it as the abstract idea of space or of time. General ideas arise in the same fashion, from the custom of associating a number of objects with the idea of one of them.

The mind then consists wholly of sensations or feelings, reflected in ideas, which appear to the mind in certain relations. From these relations a natural instinct of the mind leads men to conclude that objects exist and that events are related as cause and effect. Our justifiable certainty about the attributes of objects and causal relationships has not been reached by grasping the simple, unitary nature of a thing or event. Everything we know is a compound of perceptions that become something more than a heap only thanks to a propensity of the mind to recognize resemblances and connections and to reflect on this propensity. Hume confessed that he had not accounted for the person who did the perceiving, recognized resemblances, and made connections. He had nevertheless suggested a radically different character for human knowledge.

The result was a picture of knowledge that resembled a pointillist painting. There are no sharp outlines, no definite shapes or solid blocks of color. Yet, the circus performer on her horse can be seen perfectly distinctly. Anyone who looks closely can discover that she is made of points of paint. But it is impossible to know whether these dots are mind or matter. Whether they constitute appearance or reality of the painting is a meaningless question. The painting consists of nothing but the dots arranged as they are.

As there is in Hume's view of knowledge no realm of eternally fixed essences or forms to be distinguished from the transitory world of sensations, no line can be drawn between "knowledge" (of reality) and "opinion" (about appearances). None of the connections men make among their perceptions of the outside world is a necessary one, for its contrary is always conceivable without contradiction. Man cannot then aspire to anything but "opinion" in the ancient sense. (Hume reserved the name "knowledge" for reasoning about the relations of ideas but made it clear that this was not the "knowledge" of the ancients. He also sometimes spoke, in the ordinary fashion, of "knowledge" about matters of fact, but without meaning to suggest that such knowledge was anything more than probable, and therefore "opinion" in the ancient sense.)

Yet some things could be known with more assurance than others. We feel that our assertions are less probable when

... we have not observed a sufficient number of instances, to produce a strong habit; or when these instances are contrary to each other; or when the resemblance is not exact; or the present impression is faint and obscure; or the experience in some measure obliterated from the memory; or the connexion dependent on a long chain of objects; or the inference derived from general rules and yet not conformable to them ...

(ibid., p. 154). There is no ground for denying that further experience may remove this lack of certainty. But where uncertainty persists—and Hume was inclined to believe it would in some matters—it arises not from any contingency in the operation of cause and effect but "from the secret operation of contrary causes" (ibid., p. 132) too minute or remote to be discovered. But there are also other kinds of assertions, "proofs," which are about cause and effect and yet "entirely free from doubt and uncertainty" (ibid., p. 124). It is impossible to establish that the sun must necessarily rise tomorrow; yet men are and should be certain that it will rise. Such certainty is not merely a practical aid to living, nor just an approximation to truth good enough for ordinary purposes, nor merely a conclusion that we have not the power to contradict. It is a genuine certainty in the sense that there are no grounds for doubting its truth, even though its contrary is conceivable.

What justifies the certainty about tomorrow's sunrise is the experience not merely of countless sunrises and sunsets, but of a whole concatenation of events and the relations men have discovered among them. From this broad intricate pattern of experience, men have come to believe in the uniformity of nature and this belief has become linked in a complicated fashion with a series of other beliefs which constitute what men think of as natural laws. In other realms of experience as well, men have over the years built up elaborate compositions of observations and general propositions issuing in certain beliefs. None of these is necessarily true yet each is certain until its falsity is established.

As there is no ascent from appearance to reality, there is no hierarchy of knowledge in the ancient sense, nor is there any reason for assuming that men can build a single logically coherent system encompassing all knowledge. Although Hume did not explore the precise relations of different kinds of knowledge, he indicated how he thought about the question. He never doubted that men can and should be as certain about the truth of Newton's laws as about the evil of murder. On the other hand, when a man thinks philosophically, he can become certain that there are no demonstrably necessary grounds for believing any proposition about matters of fact. But each of these "certainties" has a different character. None has an exclusive claim to our attention or respect, nor can it constitute, as Hume's predecessors might have argued, the perfect consonance of mind with the architecture of the universe. Each certainty is arrived at differently, through different kinds of procedures, rules, discriminations, and is related differently to other propositions within its own realm of knowledge. There is not a single system of knowledge, but a number of differently organized accounts of human experience, related to different points of view.

By recognizing a variety of kinds of knowledge, Hume saved men from being sentenced to irresolution and perplexity. Uncertainty belonged only to the philosopher's study. There the philosopher learned that the grounds upon which human beings had to judge and choose were made entirely by men in the course of building civilization. But if God or Reason did not guarantee any human truth, that was no reason to deny that there was a human truth, upon which men could base firm decisions and assertions, whether in science, morals, or politics.

This human truth made it possible also to understand that error arose from an inclination to confuse one kind of resemblance with another, to pass from one idea to a similar one without noticing the change (ibid., pp. 60, 61). Therefore the problem common to all knowledge is that of discriminating correctly among resemblances, distinguishing true or relevant resemblances from false and irrelevant ones. Long chains of reasonings or conjunctions or objects are more likely to include errors than simpler propositions. But making such discriminations correctly can be helped by the general rules that civilized men have come to accept. These draw our attention to regularities or differences that may be obscured by the peculiar circumstances or disposition of the moment. Thus we come to realize that although an object moved to a greater distance from us appears to be smaller, it has not decreased in size. Similarly, in morals and aesthetics general rules help us to correct improper or crude internal sensations of approval or disapproval by helping us to distinguish what appears to be one sensation into a number of associated ones, or to recognize similarities that are easily overlooked because they are associated with striking differences.

And, indeed, without such a correction of appearances both in internal and external sentiment, men could never think or talk steadily on any subject; while their fluctuating situations produce a continual variation on objects and throw them into such different and contrary lights and positions (*Enquiry Concerning the Principles of Morals*, par. 185).

Although he had made it impossible to anchor human knowledge to the order of the universe, Hume believed that language and knowledge corresponded to the constitution of the universe. For there exists "a kind of pre-established harmony between the course of nature and the succession of our ideas" (ibid., par. 44). How this correspondence comes into being, what maintains it, or how exact it is, Hume put beyond human power to know. And with this limitation Hume bade men to be content. For such was "the whimsical condition of mankind."

The boldest answer to Hume was given in Germany by Immanuel Kant. He was concerned, as Leibniz and Descartes had been, with establishing that the truths of both physics and religion were certain. But Newton's development of experimental physics, combined with the questions raised by Hume, had given the problem a new turn. Hume had undoubtedly proved that necessary truths could not be derived from experience. Yet Newton's laws were, Kant believed, necessarily true and unqualifiedly certain, and had been established with the aid of experiments, not by pure reason. Unless he could find a way of reconciling these two convictions, Kant was obliged to deny either that Newton's

laws were certain or that their discovery in any way depended on experience. He was troubled besides by another conflict: Newton had revealed a nature entirely subject to inescapable laws; yet men were conscious of being free from such determination and had built their moral life on such freedom. The certain truth of experimental physics had then to be reconciled with human freedom as well as with Hume's argument against experience as a ground for certainty.

Instead of inquiring, as Hume had, into the validity of our belief in the necessary connection between cause and effect, Kant started from the certainty that the principle of causality was necessarily true and set himself to accounting for it. He found the clue to his answer in revising Hume's view of mathematics as identical with logic and consisting only of relations between ideas. Kant argued that mathematical propositions correctly describe the external world of experience and are accordingly synthetic, not analytic. But as they are obtained through construction, not observation, they are *a priori*, that is, not derived from experience. It followed that mathematical truths constitute a kind of proposition that philosophers had not previously distinguished from others, propositions that were valid about experience but reached independently of experience. Unlike empirical propositions that are drawn from experience, synthetic *a priori* propositions could be necessarily true. They therefore held the solution to the problems raised by Hume's demonstration that experience could not yield necessary truths. If Newton's laws were based on synthetic *a priori* propositions, the certainty of scientific knowledge could be saved without denying its connection with experience. It remained to explain how men could construct synthetic propositions without referring to experience.

Kant found that when all content that might be derived from experience had been removed from mathematical judgments, there remained the notions of space and time. He concluded that space and time "are therefore pure intuitions that lie *a priori* at the basis of the empirical" (*Prolegomena*, par. 10). Further analysis produced other concepts that were the presuppositions of experience but not drawn from it. And finally Kant connected these concepts into a logical system, enabling him to say "that these, and this exact number only, constitute our whole cognition of things from pure understanding" (ibid., par. 39). These categories formed the framework of knowledge common to all human beings. They were the formal conditions of experience, the sorting and ordering machinery for sense intuitions whereby such intuitions become empirical judgments. Without them, no experience would be possible.

Experience had then to be understood as a construction the mind imposed on sensation. This construction had the shape of an inverted pyramid resting on synthetic *a priori* concepts, upon which the mind built a hierarchy of rules, rising from general and necessary to particular and accidental. Perceptions are channelled through these categories and so made to constitute experience. In acquiring knowledge, the mind moves downwards from empirical consciousness of particular and accidental rules to pure consciousness of its *a priori* concepts. Whereas common sense is aware only of the more superficial rules without discriminating carefully among them, the scientific mind disentangles the necessary from accidental connections among perceptions so as to make explicit this basic structure. The answers science produces come from the same source as its questions, for the mind discovers what the mind had originally made. It operates in the manner of the mathematician who first constructs a figure and then learns what he has put into it. Nature is then nothing but the order framed by the mind. Thus Kant rejoined the knower to the known.

The role played by experience in Newtonian physics could now be made clear: Newton had abstracted from accidental appearances until he arrived at hypotheses about the necessary conditions of those experiences. But it was only when he found no exceptions to these hypotheses in experience, that he could be sure he had arrived at the basic laws. Without making experiments, Kant insisted, we cannot know whether our concepts are truly concepts of the understanding or merely imaginary. Without constructing hypotheses beforehand, we cannot know how to question experience or how to make our accidental observations yield a necessary law.

As there was no pure content of the mind distinct from the mental processes which made experience possible, consciousness became identical with an act of judgment. The mind forced experience to take up a position within its own framework and by its own constructive action produced knowledge. Knowing was then no longer an activity of reception but a creative organizing activity.

The certainty of knowledge had been secured, but at the expense of a severe restriction on its domain. Because we know by imposing our own categories on experience, we can know things only in relation to ourselves. What we know are the sensible effects of things on us or what Kant called their "appearances" or *phenomena*. To know "things in themselves" or *noumena,* that is, what ultimately causes them to affect us as they do or what governs their existence or constitutes their essence, we should have to possess some direct insight into their nature. This power, Kant was as reluctant as Hume to grant to men. Reason in Kant's view provided a framework that rendered experience

intelligible without offering any way of penetrating the objects of experience: "For our understanding is not a faculty of intuition, but of the connexion of given intuitions [i.e., sense impressions] in experience" (ibid., par. 34). Knowing things as part of nature, as *phenomena,* means knowing that they exist and how they are related to other things as parts of chains of causation, but not why these causal chains are so or that they must be so. Nevertheless we can be certain that the sensible world exists in the form it presents to us. Kant even believed that he could demonstrate the reality of the outside world, and he severely reprimanded philosophers who argued, as Hume did, that it had to be taken on faith.

But for all the certainty that Kant could promise about our knowledge of the sensible world, the restriction of human knowledge was crucial for him. It enabled Kant to reconcile the world of mechanical necessity revealed by science with freedom of the will and moral life. As there were two distinct ways of knowing things, he could both defend the legitimate claims of science against its enemies and reject its arrogant attempts to encompass the whole of reality. He could even insist on the possibility of discovering universal laws of history without denying human freedom. For just as men can know the appearances of other things, they can know themselves as objects of sense subject to the same laws as other objects.

But by separating certain knowledge of appearances from insight into things-in-themselves and into men as moral beings, Kant set up an opposition between certainty and the aspiration after ultimate or higher truths. Certainty pertained only to what might be called "technical" knowledge of how things work as opposed to knowing why they work so.

As all appearances are in one mind, they are known only insofar as they are organized into one connected world by that mind. The failure to put things in their place in the mind's organization, Kant explained, is what we mean by idiocy or madness. The search for knowledge is therefore identical with the search for some way of connecting all phenomena into a logically coherent system. But unlike the disciples of Leibniz and C. von Wolff, Kant never attempted to deduce all truth from the principle of unity. He regarded it rather as the basic regulative principle, guiding reason in its organization of the data of experience by indicating what problems it must solve. It is the assumption that stimulates every intelligence to find a way of reconciling apparent inconsistencies by discovering the underlying unity.

Reason cannot, however, think this systematic unity, Kant argued, without giving it an object. This object is the concept of God. As experience cannot directly display the object of its unity, there is no way of establishing the existence, as in physics, of an object corresponding to the conception of God. Nevertheless God must be postulated in order that men may understand the connection of things in the world of sense as if they had their ground in such a being. Reason has then shown both that the concept of God must be assumed by reason and that it cannot be understood by reason. The belief in God is therefore justified but belongs to the realm of faith. In this fashion, Kant supported religious faith while denying the rationalists' extravagant pretensions to knowing things beyond experience.

By acknowledging that men had ideas of "the higher world of reality," even though he denied any possibility of knowing it, Kant suggested that reason was capable of operations other than discovering the laws of nature. But just how such operations affected the conception of reason as a whole was not made clear. For generally Kant equated rational knowledge with the construction of a system of laws. He described the understanding as a "faculty of rules" occupied with investigating appearances "in order to detect some rule in them" and "rules so far as they are objective and therefore necessarily depend upon knowledge of the object, are called laws" (*Critique of Pure Reason*, A127). The whole had to be constructed from the parts, but when completed, the form of the whole would be the same as if the parts had been deduced from a single principle. Its parts would be related to one another in the manner of a mathematical demonstration and this would be the mark of its certain truth. Although Kant had denied that mathematics was identical with logic, he tied certainty to the logic of mathematical reasoning. Certain knowledge in his view is always and only a system of laws in which the more particular ones are "only special determinations of still higher laws, and the highest of these, under which the others all stand, issue *a priori* from the understanding itself" (ibid.). There is no variety within the realm of knowledge such as Hume's picture permitted. In history as in physics, what was knowledge had to have the order of a system.

Kant saw no reason why all of experience should not eventually come completely under the reign of law. Although natural science, even after Newton, still contained an area of "endless conjecture" (ibid., A481, B509), there could be no retrogression in knowledge. Logic was already complete because "since Aristotle it has not required to retrace a single step, unless, indeed, we care to count as improvements the removal of certain needless subtleties or the clearer exposition of its recognised teaching, features which concern the elegance rather than the certainty of science" (ibid., B viii). Whatever laws had been established were established forever.

Moral knowledge must be just as certain as any other—"we must not venture upon an action on the mere opinion that it is *allowed,* but must know that it is so" (ibid., A823, 851). Because the unity of the self is the only ground for certainty, we strive to impose on our own lives a rational order and unity such as we discover in nature and this is what we mean by morality. We achieve morality by submitting all our thoughts and actions to universal precepts and that is the only way human lives can become stable and dignified. Any principle that cannot provide such universal precepts, as for instance the principle of happiness, is deficient as a moral principle.

Instead of varieties of knowledge, there are in Kant's view only degrees of conviction, ascending from opinion, which is known to be objectively deficient but is subjectively satisfying, through belief to knowledge. Even opinion, however, is somewhat dependent upon certain knowledge. For we must never presume to "opine" without knowing with certainty what connects that opinion to truth, as well as the law governing that connection, which although not complete, is yet more than arbitrary fiction. Otherwise, "I have nothing but opinion; it is all merely a play of the imagination, without the least relation to truth" (ibid., A823, B851).

To affirmations that are justified only by the peculiar character of the individual subject, Kant denied any validity whatsoever. An affirmation worthy of being a conviction must have some degree of objectivity, and objectivity was for Kant strictly synonymous with being universally valid. He never vacillated, as Plato did, between understanding objectivity as what those engaged in a particular enterprise can agree upon and regarding objectivity as utterly independent of circumstances or person and the same for all men at all times. Only the latter meaning was recognized by Kant for whom universal validity was inseparable from truth. But it is sometimes easier, Kant pointed out, to get universal agreement than to demonstrate universal validity. Universal agreement might therefore be used as "the touchstone whereby we decide whether our holding a thing to be true is conviction or mere persuasion" (ibid., A820, B848, cf. B4). By connecting in this fashion the idea of certainty with that of agreement, Kant suggested the possibility of making agreement among men the criterion of truth.

But within his own philosophy, certainty is the essence of any knowledge. It is equated with rationality and endowed with its most comprehensive meaning, from which later philosophers were to abstract some aspect and reconstruct upon that a more limited version of certainty.

What was thought about the question of certainty after Hume and Kant can be understood as variations on the themes they constructed. But two new subordinate motifs were added by opponents of Hume—the common sense philosophers, and by an avowed disciple, Jeremy Bentham.

The so-called common sense philosophers, Thomas Reid and James Beattie, wanted above all to refute what they took to be Hume's denial that anything could be known, and Berkeley's denial that matter existed. Reid and Beattie refused to indulge in the inordinate metaphysical reasoning and sophistry of their predecessors and proposed instead to discover a new ground for certainty in the constitution of human beings. This was in keeping with the fashion established by the end of the eighteenth century of contrasting the hard truths of "common sense" with the fantasies of philosophy. But the suggestion for a theory of common sense had in fact appeared earlier in Shaftesbury's philosophy and had been developed somewhat in Hume's theory of moral sentiments.

The only way to escape an infinite regress of grounds for holding any truth and the uncertainty it produced, Reid and Beattie argued, was to recognize that knowledge was based on self-evident truths which, though impossible to prove, are also impossible to disbelieve. Otherwise there could be no reasoning because "All reasoning must be from first principles; and for first principles no other reason can be given but this, that by the constitution of our nature we are under a necessity of assenting to them" (Reid, *An Inquiry into the Human Mind* [1823], p. 77). What identified these intuitive first principles was

. . . an instantaneous and instinctive impulse; derived neither from education nor from habit, but from nature; acting independently of our will, whenever its object is presented, according to an established law, and therefore not improperly called Sense; and acting in a similar manner upon all mankind, and therefore properly called Common Sense

(Beattie, *An Essay on the Nature and Immutability of Truth*, 8th ed., p. 34). Why we must trust to our constitution or why it may not deceive us or lead to contradiction could not be explained. Men had to be satisfied "to take things as they find them," and "believe Nature upon her bare declaration, without suspecting her of any design to impose upon them" (ibid., p. 38).

Only prejudice or "inveterate opinion" might be rendered more evident by reasoning or argumentation; the truth of common sense could only be displayed. The crucial distinction then is not that between contingent and necessary truths, but between reasoned and self-evident truths. Some truths of common sense are however necessary because their contraries are inconceivable, and these include the first principles of morals along with the axioms of geometry. But other self-evident truths command assent rather than conviction, because the contrary of "I do not feel this hard body"

is equally conceivable. Beattie further distinguished degrees of moral assent descending from the highest "moral certainty" through several stages of opinion, to "that suspense of judgment which is called doubt." We may "without absurdity," Beattie insisted, speak of probable truth as well as of certain truth. For a probable truth can be known to be probable with the same certainty as a certain truth is known. It can be as "universal" and "permanent" because it is also a truth which "a rational being is determined by . . . his nature to admit" (ibid., p. 25). For all their antipathy to Hume, the common sense philosophers followed him in separating certainty from necessity and equating certainty with "belief beyond doubt," so that they were able to include within its magic circle synthetic propositions as well as purely formal propositions without encountering Kant's problem of having to justify synthetic *a priori* propositions.

Implicit in the common sense philosophies are the main assumptions of later attempts to escape from the problems raised by Hume without recourse to metaphysics or to *a priori* knowledge. The starting point of all speculation was made the whole of consciousness, within which, by careful reflection, one could distinguish the foundations from the superstructure. The direct object of thought was taken to be not, as Locke, Hume, and Berkeley had maintained, the contents of the mind which mediated between the knower and the external world, but the external object itself. This direct relation between thought and the external world suggested a new ground for certainty without recourse to the pure reason of Kant.

Quite another avenue to certainty was laid out by the utilitarian followers of Hume, who emphasized the shortcomings of common sense. Jeremy Bentham was concerned with the practical problem of how to make life more pleasurable for more human beings rather than with any speculative questions about how men come to formulate and judge knowledge or truth. His thinking began from a translation of Hume's description of ideas as reflections of sense impressions into the postulate that all human thoughts and actions could be traced back to sensations of pleasure and pain. Confusion, fostered by language that obscured the pains and pleasures inspiring or produced by some course of action, Bentham was convinced, caused all the difficulties and injustices afflicting men. Any statement about human beings that could not be reduced to pleasures and pains felt by someone must be rejected, and a rigorous application of logic would make the references of words perfectly clear. Human endeavors that could not be subjected to such analysis were delusive, fraudulent, and dangerous.

Bentham accordingly devoted himself to constructing an utterly clear, technical vocabulary for politics and law, as well as to making exact definitions of crucial concepts and formulating rules for combining words and sentences without obscurity. This was to be the foundation for a rational system of law entirely derived from a single principle and its corollaries, that would need no interpretation and could, with but minor adjustments, do for all nations. Although he himself never completed his code of laws, Bentham's equation of certainty with unambiguity, reached through analysis of language and precise definition of basic terms, set a pattern taken up later by analytical philosophers.

In the nineteenth century, the new meanings given to the idea of certainty were the work of social reformers who had either professional or amateur interests in the natural sciences and hoped to find more reliable answers to social problems by applying the assumptions and methods of the natural sciences to social phenomena. There was a model for them in the efforts of the French Encyclopedists to make a new social science continuous with the natural sciences. A number of different schemes were proposed: P. H. D. d'Holbach emphasized the reign of necessary laws in all realms which made it as easy to construct a system of ethical and political values on material grounds as a system of physical laws. É. B. de Condillac hoped to reach exact knowledge by discovering the simple primary facts upon which purely logical operations could build generalizations about the human mind. The most clear-cut justification for expecting certain truth about human affairs was given by a mathematician, M. J. de Condorcet, whose ideas became influential in England through the work of Auguste Comte.

Condorcet rested all his hopes on the calculus of probabilities. There was no essential difference between the natural and social sciences, he argued, because all laws about experience are no more than probable. Where the observation of facts is more difficult, as in the social sciences, the truth will be less probable, yet there can be certainty about probable truth because probability theory makes it possible to evaluate mathematically all statements and to reach a certain estimate of their reliability by applying the calculus of probability. It should even be possible to discover, Condorcet believed, under what conditions the decision of an assembly or a tribunal could be guaranteed to be more truly representative. Thus although certainty was to be had only about the probability of truth, certainty remained the criterion of acceptable knowledge and mathematics, the paradigm of certainty, and at the same time social as well as natural sciences were rendered valid.

The English attempts to produce a unified science were not quite so simple. Bentham's outstanding disci-

ple, John Stuart Mill, wanted to build a system embracing all aspects of human life and exhibiting the unbroken chain of causality from natural to mental effects on utilitarian principles. But he recognized that there were special difficulties about moving correctly to a general theory from simple facts for which the ordinary logic had no remedy, and he became absorbed in what is now known as the problem of induction.

This problem had already been carefully discussed by a distinguished scientist, William Whewell, with a better claim to be heard on the character of scientific discovery. Whewell had argued that logic could not bring certainty into science because discovery depended ultimately on personal genius and not on impersonal correctness of method, and that the progress of science would draw attention to different aspects of reality rather than ascend to some one set of permanent truths. But Mill promised more. He was convinced that the key to correct induction lay in logic—"the laws of the investigation of truth by means of extrinsic evidence whether rationative or inductive" (*Letters*, Sept. 28, 1839). His "Four Methods of Experimental Inquiry," described in his *Logic*, were designed to make induction safe, and to guarantee that scientific truth was unquestionably valid even if not demonstrably certain.

Many of the leading scientists in the nineteenth century shared Mill's dream of accounting for all natural and mental phenomena in a single theory. They regarded science as a growing collection of certain truths that could now go further to provide what T. H. Huxley recommended as "a complete theory of life, based upon a clear knowledge alike of its possibilities and of its limitations" (*Essays*, III, 143). But the pattern of their theories was different from Mill's. It had more in common with the positivist philosophy of Auguste Comte, in whom Mill had found his inspiration although he had rejected Comte's social philosophy.

Suggestions for a unifying theory, that reduced the most complex things to combinations of the most primitive ones, came from both biologists and physicists. A number of different lines of biological and geological research converged in Darwin's *Origin of Species*, which reduced superficial resemblances to blood relationships explained by a purely mechanical process of chance variations and natural selection. From this Huxley drew a conclusion that became widely accepted—that the difference between the lowest plant and the highest animal was one of degree not kind, and depended solely on the division of labor. The physicists suggested another synthesis in terms of matter and energy that made it seem reasonable to hope that physics would one day deduce "Hamlet" from the molecular forces in a mutton chop. The grandest attempt to generalize the results of science was made by Herbert Spencer. His philosophy of evolutionism explained all scientific laws, social as well as biological and physical, as variations on a single fundamental law: that the universe and everything in it were moving towards a state of equilibrium in which all forces in the world would be perfectly balanced. Although he relegated questions about the origin of things or the existence of God to the "Unknowable," he believed that the answers to all other questions, whether political or mechanical, could be found in his theory.

Those who were influenced by Spencer's faith in scientific synthesis, even when they disagreed with his version of it, were confident that as long as they dealt in scientific terminology and renounced excursions into the "Unknowable" they were dealing in certainties. The diversity of prescriptions based on supposedly scientific ideas, such as the struggle for survival, did not prevent Sidney and Beatrice Webb, along with other social reformers, from recommending the political organization that they favored as an indisputable scientific truth. But beyond agreeing on the impropriety of metaphysical speculation and the exclusive validity of the experimental method of science, none of these reformers endeavored to explain how scientific truths were discovered or justified.

The idea that had inspired the scientific syntheses— that the truth about the universe would be discovered when men could construct a system that displayed the connection of all phenomena with some ruling principle—had been suggested by Hegel. He had adapted Kant's principle, that truth was guaranteed by logical completeness, to a system that was designed not only to include *noumena* as well as *phenomena*, but also to reveal that the whole was but the unfolding of all the potentialities of Spirit in the course of history. Unlike most of Hume's other successors, however, Hegel recognized a variety of truths and certainties. Absolute Truth is to be found only at the stage of Systematic Science (represented by Hegel's philosophy) when it has become possible to survey the whole and to see how and when each new phase of experience emerged. Nevertheless each of these phases, Hegel emphasized, remains a permanent and distinct part of human life. Knowledge has a variety of moments and the moments assume the form of modes of consciousness, each of which contributes to the whole. The certainty of sense-experience is different from the certainty of moral self-consciousness or of demonstrative reasoning. To questions such as when Caesar was born, how large a space is, or how the hypotenuse and sides of a right-angled triangle are related, it is proper to give exact answers. But philosophic truth has a totally

different character and must therefore take another form. Each certainty is appropriate in its own sphere, and makes a distinctive contribution to the whole. In Hegel's view it became most important to recognize the partial character of all knowledge short of Absolute Truth, and the question, "Can human knowledge be certain?" could have no single answer.

This variety of certainties was ignored by the philosophies that took their stand on an opposition to Hegel. For G. E. Moore and Bertrand Russell, Hegel's attempt to show that the cosmos and man were made of the same spiritual stuff seemed to deny the reality of everything that common sense believed in, above all that there is an external world independent of experience yet perceived as "facts." Truth, according to Moore and Russell, consisted in the correspondence of thought to the external world. Since Hegel described the relation between thought and its objects differently, they concluded that Hegel had rejected the possibility of discovering any truth.

Moore reaffirmed the certainties of common sense. He claimed that he knew a great number of propositions without a possibility of doubt, such as that he had two hands or was standing up and speaking. These were, he admitted, not necessary but contingent propositions, which were neither known *a priori* nor tautological and could be denied without contradiction. They were nevertheless "absolutely certain." But the self-evident truths of common sense were not enough for Russell, who more than any other modern philosopher shared Kant's passion for discovering a realm of pure certainty. He required besides that the ground for certainty be totally independent of human beings. In Russell's world men were only puny inhabitants of a remote corner of the universe, not the center or apex of creation. If what men knew were wholly derived from themselves, it could reveal nothing significant about a universe that was vastly more nonhuman than human. Yet the traditional sorts of impersonal knowledge were ruled out. On the one hand Russell was committed to the empiricist belief that sensation was the ultimate ground of knowledge, and he could not therefore look to a metaphysical reality. But on the other hand, neither could he accept an empiricist solution such as Hume's because he wanted above all to establish that men could discover certain truth about reality.

Russell began his search for certainty where Kant had, by considering mathematics, but in order to disprove Kant's view that mathematics depended on human construction. He hoped to derive all of mathematics from a few basic logical principles, which were, if not literally Platonic Forms, at least analogous insofar as they constituted a "region of absolute necessity, 319 to which not only the actual world, but every possible world, must conform . . ." ("Study of Mathematics," in *Philosophical Essays*, p. 82). This dream of a perfect logical structure on foundations independent of human thought was broken when Russell discovered a number of contradictions in his system that could be removed only by more or less clumsy makeshifts. It was ended finally by Wittgenstein, who convinced him that mathematics was after all, as Hume had argued, entirely tautological. From the philosophy of mathematics, Russell turned to seek a more modest kind of certainty in science which "is at no moment quite right but it is seldom quite wrong. . . . It is, therefore, rational to accept it hypothetically . . ." (*My Philosophical Development*, p. 17).

Although he no longer believed in the real existence of logical concepts, Russell kept his faith in logic as an instrument for achieving certainty. By logic he meant the kind of analysis used in the *Principia Mathematica* to break up complex propositions into their components. Its success in reducing the whole of mathematical knowledge to a more systematic unity confirmed the validity of logical analysis for Russell. But he had already declared his allegiance to it when he had rejected idealism, and with it the tenet that made analysis useless—that the world of human experience is an organic whole and therefore more than the sum of its parts. From this it followed, Russell believed, that nothing could be known about a part in isolation from the rest because anything short of complete knowledge about an organic whole is an abstraction and necessarily falsifies the relation of the part to the whole. As human beings could never become omniscient, idealism implied that men could know nothing for certain. Anyone looking for certainty had to turn to a totally different conception of the universe—as an agglomeration of discrete packets that can be bundled together or undone into smaller ones without affecting the character of the parts. If, as Russell assumed, the language of common sense and science mirrored this agglomeration, then every complex proposition or set of propositions could be resolved into smaller, more basic elements which might provide a perfectly secure foundation for the rest.

Russell began by analyzing common sense beliefs to discover whether there was "any knowledge in the world which is so certain that no reasonable man could doubt it" (*Problems of Philosophy*, p. 9). He found that although we can question the existence of material objects such as a table, we cannot doubt "the existence of the sense data which made us think there was a table" and he concluded: "Whatever else may be doubtful, some at least of our immediate experiences seem absolutely certain" (ibid., p. 27). Two questions

had then to be answered: What constitutes data? How do we move from such data to knowledge, i.e., to our belief in material objects and finally to the laws of physics?

At first Russell hoped to establish an absolute distinction between a pure, luminously certain, nonhuman source of truths that he described variously as "data," "hard data," "primitive knowledge," "knowledge by acquaintance," all indicating the hard core of knowledge as opposed to inferred or derivative knowledge where error arose. Analysis would arrange knowledge in "a hierarchy of dubitables" which would make clear the certain, sensory core along with the succession of inferences based on it so that their correctness could be checked and rendered more certain or appropriately graded for lack of certainty. But the notion of data was gradually enlarged. Even at the outset, Russell included within it what he called "universals" ("yellow" as opposed to "this yellow ball"; relations of before and after, up and down, resemblance), as well as general propositions of logic. Later he added "perceptions," "beliefs," and "propositions," as he found that he could not eliminate but only "whittle away the element of interpretation" (*Inquiry into Meaning and Truth*, p. 124). He had in the end to conclude that once anything was said, even if only "there is a chair," the speaker was necessarily making generalizations and inferences because the pure datum could not be articulated. The notion of "data" became a limiting concept that at most "we can approach asymptotically" (ibid., p. 124).

In much the same fashion inference also lost its purity. There appeared to be different kinds of inferences, the most primitive being those of common sense which men were obliged to make by biological necessity. But inductive inferences yielded at best only probabilities which "are not disproved when what they show to be probable does not happen" (ibid., p. 317), and thus seemed more likely to produce falsehood than truth when not corrected by common sense. And finally Russell felt obliged to declare that induction rested on "*a priori* non-demonstrative forms of inference [such as the principle of causality] which experience can neither confirm nor confute, but which we regard, in some circumstances, as more certain than the evidence of the senses" (ibid., p. 317). There was no mistakeproof method for building up knowledge, even if an indestructible foundation for it had been discovered. Knowledge had no simple structure with sharply defined parts but rested on many mutually supporting piers.

When he could discover no "set of beliefs which are never mistaken" nor any test which "will always enable us to discriminate between true and false beliefs"

(*Analysis of Mind*, p. 268), Russell's faith came to rest on reducing the risk of error. If doubtful inferences and unproved assumptions could not be altogether eliminated, some could be avoided or translated into less doubtful propositions by the technique of logical construction. This was suggested by the theory of descriptions developed in the *Principia* which distinguished two kinds of subjects in propositions: proper names representing something that can be directly perceived, and incomplete symbols denoting something that may never have existed and gets its meaning only from the context in which it appears. Russell found that incomplete symbols could be replaced by an enumeration of qualities and were thus shown to be merely linguistic devices summing up a collection of particulars. As Russell dissolved more and more "proper names" into descriptive phrases, he came to believe that although common sense sees the world as composed of things having certain qualities, it would be more precise to speak only of qualities existing in a particular place and time (that there is "redness," "squareness," "heaviness" here, and not "there is a red *table* here"). For qualities alone are known to experience. The subject to which they are ordinarily attributed cannot be experienced and is therefore unknown and unknowable, indeed nothing but a fanciful and pointless imposition on what is known.

In his early enthusiasm over the technique of logical construction, Russell hoped that he might be able to purify science of any entities that could not be analyzed into perceptions of qualities. But later he admitted that at most the number of such entities could be reduced, that scientific concepts such as "light waves" were built up not only of perceived events but also of "unperceived aspects" of reality. (Cf. Schilpp, pp. 707f.) Objects of perception were only part of the subject matter of physics, and it was irrelevant to the truth of physical laws whether all that they described could be perceived.

He also modified his view of what scientific truth was about. Science gave an account not of the whole of reality, but only of its "structure." By "structure" Russell meant a recurring pattern of relations in time and space among events whose causes or subjects are unknown to us. He understood it as analogous to the form of a proposition which the logician discovers by replacing the actual words of a sentence with symbols or variables related in the same way so as to show how sentences saying different things have in common the same logical form. At other times Russell likened the "structure" of reality to a map that indicates the spatial relations between points without telling us anything about the nature of things indicated by those points. Because of its formal character, i.e., because it indi-

cated possible relations without specifying the character of particular things, the structure revealed by science seemed to share somehow in the certainty of purely formal or analytical truth. Yet it was, Russell insisted, just as real as the real world, only it left out "that essence of individuality which always eludes words and baffles description, but which, for that very reason, is irrelevant to science" (*Introduction to Mathematical Philosophy*, p. 61).

With what might be called his "empirical formalism," Russell granted science something less than the certainty established by Kant. Nor could he refute the skeptic, "whose position must remain logically unassailable," as he could affirm only that the congruence between reality and the causal laws discovered by science "must be regarded as a fortunate accident and how long it will continue we cannot tell" (*Analysis of Mind*, p. 271). Still, he had made truth more nearly independent of human creation and will, and had shown that science could achieve "definite answers" and "successive approximations to the truth in which each new stage results from an improvement but not a rejection of what had gone before" (*A History of Western Philosophy*, p. 789).

But Russell had extracted this promise of progress "towards the unattainable ideal of impeccable knowledge" (*Analysis of Mind*, p. 271) by renouncing much of what has been commonly taken to be knowledge. Although he followed Hume in giving knowledge the character of a painting made up of many points, he did not conclude, as Hume had, that we must resign ourselves to a mystery about how the dots of paint produce the figure on the horse. Instead Russell insisted that we concentrate wholly on describing in mathematical terms the relations among the colored points in space. About that, he believed, men could be almost certain. The rest, which was bound to be seen differently by each observer and might even be an illusion, he preferred to ignore.

A more tenacious effort to carry out Russell's original program for certainty was made by the Vienna circle of logical positivists, who took their stand on the doctrine suggested by Russell and developed in Ludwig Wittgenstein's *Tractatus* (1922), that there were elementary statements corresponding to simple facts. In *The Unity of Science* (1934), Rudolf Carnap declared that the "protocols" of "given direct experiences . . . constitute the basis of the entire scientific edifice" (*Unity of Science*, pp. 76, 93). Far more reluctant than Russell to give up the search for an infallible sensory core to knowledge, the positivists became engrossed in the difficulties of explaining why one man's certainty, if derived from his sense experience (as they insisted it must be) should be valid for any other.

When they could find no way of avoiding the conclusion that knowledge was either unverifiable or subjective, the logical positivists retreated from seeking certainty into arguing that there was no way of establishing a correspondence between knowledge and fact. The possibility of discovering any reasonable ground for believing in a relationship between words and the world seemed to have been destroyed by Wittgenstein's *Philosophical Investigations* (1953). The only certainty left was the possession of language and the linguistic analysts devoted themselves to analyzing the use of language without committing themselves to any beliefs about the nature of reality.

A curious reflection of the positivist progress from the certainty of protocol statements to linguistic analysis is to be found in the development of the arts in the twentieth century. The early dadaists hoped to find the objective stuff of art by ridding themselves of all social and aesthetic restraints and giving a free rein to the unconscious or chance. Their more recent successors, such as the so-called "new novelists" of France, have been more inclined to look for the unadulterated truth in impersonal and detailed accounts of objects, gestures, movements stripped of comment and interpretation. But all these efforts have come to the conclusion that order and truth are merely conventional, and therefore fraudulent, and that reality is nowhere to be found. The artist is left with nothing to do but to reflect on the nature of his creative acts and to proclaim the only certainty remaining—that he can destroy what he makes.

While the positivists were attempting to find certainty by making knowledge independent of human will, others were returning to the Kantian emphasis on the intervention of the knower. They did so in a variety of ways, but all refused to regard physical science as the model of final truth.

The phenomenology of Edmund Husserl reaffirmed the power of reason to intuit the content as well as the form of truth and restored respectability to the hope for certainty about the nature of being. There is in Husserl's work an echo of Goethe's scientific passion and his search for the *Urpflanze* (the fundamental or ideal form of the flower) as well as of his criticism of the natural scientists for their indifference to Truth. But whereas Goethe had insisted on the unity of man and nature, Husserl maintained that we know only what is present to our consciousness which is a continuous whole. It is meaningless therefore to speak of "reality" or "noumena" outside consciousness. By methodically analyzing consciousness, we can however discover within it the "essences" of the objects of consciousness, that is, what is necessarily true about an object as distinct from the accidental and changing

qualities attached to it by custom or prejudice or evident only in some of its individual manifestations.

Every object of consciousness, whether the color red or a horse, real or fictitious, has an essence if it can be clearly distinguished from what is essentially something else. Each kind of essence must however be described in a different manner. The essence of mathematical concepts may be described "exactly" because it is unchanging; other objects of consciousness can only be described "strictly," that is, narrowly enough to distinguish absolutely and necessarily between one essence and another. The essence of science is to arrive at complete certitude. This aim is implicit in all science, and yet cannot be realized by any positive science which concerns itself with how things act, and not with what they are. To discover the essences of scientific concepts is the task of philosophy and it is therefore the only true science, the science of the sciences.

A description of an essence is valid when it could not be otherwise for anyone else studying the object. But there is no proof of phenomenological truth, only the hope that others will see things in the same way. Neither is there a system growing out of one fundamental principle into which each essential truth must fit, nor can the truth about one essence be derived from knowledge of another. Each must be examined by itself and verified in itself and the edifice can never be complete. But with the help of correct phenomenological analysis, scholars can discover, and know with certainty, the essences of those things about which men have been speaking since the beginning of time.

Some of the scientists, however, as a result of the new quantum theory developed in the twentieth century, were denying that certainty was the essence of science. Quantum theory united two conceptions that had formerly been thought to be mutually incompatible—the wave theory and the corpuscular theory of energy. When quantum theory declared both of them to be equivalent and equally fundamental for explaining microphenomena, the reality of scientific truth seemed to be put in doubt. Besides, it was found impossible to determine precisely both the energy and the position of an electron. The state of atomic particles appeared to be altered by the measurement of them, so that the precise state of a particle after measurement could not be told from the measurement and the repetition of the experiment under apparently identical conditions might produce different results. Instead of one exact description of microparticles, quantum theory yielded only packets of possible values for the variables in question, that is, probabilities. This limitation on the degree to which the state of microparticles could be precisely determined was summed up by Werner Heisenberg in the Uncertainty Principle; moreover, the uncertainty of position and momentum was only one of many uncertainties intrinsic to quantum theory. Nevertheless quantum theory successfully explained a great deal and made a major revision of physics.

Some scientists saw in the Uncertainty Principle nothing more than an expression of the limits of human knowledge and the crudeness of measurement which did not rule out the possibility of discovering an entirely new explanation, free from the restrictions of quantum theory. But Heisenberg concluded that quantum theory had shown elementary particles to be always in only partially defined states, thus endowing nature with a random or free quality. The assumption of classical physics—that nature obeyed fixed laws unaffected by human observation—was therefore false. Physics, as Heisenberg came to see it, did not describe an independent nature but only our relationship with nature.

That science does not establish certain truth has been the thesis also of Karl Popper, but for quite other reasons. Nor is Popper's argument based on the other common ground for denying the certainty of science, that it yields only probable truth. Such an assertion, he believes, confuses two senses of probability, "verisimilitude" and "the calculus of probability." If the latter is meant, then there is nothing uncertain about the results obtained from the calculus of probability. One need recognize only that the answers obtained pertain to a range of events rather than to a single event. If verisimilitude is meant, then scientific theories should not have a high degree of probability.

Indeed "it can even be shown that all theories, including the best, have the same probability, namely zero" (*Conjectures and Refutations*, p. 192). For the truth of a theory depends not on its being irrefutably established, but on its having been submitted to rigorous attempts to refute it that have failed. The less content a theory has, the more difficult it is to refute and the more likely that it will not turn out to be false. If probability of truthfulness were the only criterion, the ideal scientific theory would be a tautology. Valuable scientific theories, however, have a high content because they attempt to explain a great deal, and are therefore more likely to be refuted. The heart of science, according to Popper, is refutation; what matters is not the "probability" of a theory, but what it can explain and the degree to which it has survived severe tests or been "corroborated": "For us therefore science has nothing to do with the quest for certainty or probability or reliability" (*Conjectures and Refutations*, p. 229).

Popper bases this un-Kantian view of the uncertainty of science on a theory of knowledge in some ways resembling Kant's; both Kant and Popper escape the need to justify induction by denying that induction takes place. Instead of trying to eliminate interpretation and theorizing from science, as Russell had done, Popper considers the invention of theories the object of science, making observation a test, not a source of scientific laws. There is neither an *a priori* basis for knowledge nor any certainties based on sensation such as atomic facts or propositions. As in Hume's picture, man remains a stranger in the universe, but a stranger who is continually making guesses about the nature of his world. The scientist attempts systematically to test these guesses. Logic, mathematics, scientific imagination combine to suggest connections among guesses established as true until a coherent body of scientific theory is built up. At any given moment, some parts of this knowledge will be better corroborated than others; failures of corroboration may lead to minor or to more basic revisions either in the theory being tested or in the methods of observation. Although, in any given test, some part of existing scientific theory must be assumed to be true, no scientific truth is permanently proof against refutation. It always remains possible that a new test will overthrow it. Nor is there any certainty about whether the facts taken currently to be basic or essential will continue to be so. For today's basic facts may be resolved into more basic elements by tomorrow's theory.

Nevertheless, as in Russell's view, the reality of an external world (and the relation to this reality) remains the final arbiter of truth, and the scientist may believe that an accepted scientific theory truly describes reality. Science aims at truth without ever being certain.

What appears to be the most radical condemnation of the quest for certainty was made by John Dewey. The foundation of his pragmatic instrumentalism—that every idea is a design for manipulating experience—had been used differently by C. S. Peirce and William James. Dewey's interpretation made both truth and certainty irrelevant to knowledge.

Dewey was disturbed by the cleavage between theory and practice, knowledge and action that made some lives and activities seem worthier than others, and put science into conflict with moral values; such a cleavage suggested that men had to choose between scientific and moral progress. These were spurious dichotomies, he argued, based on the belief that there was a realm of pure rational activity which could hope to achieve certain knowledge about immutable Being. By contrast, practical activity that dealt with perishable, changing things and was therefore full of risk and uncertainty was bound to be considered low and irksome. Men were consequently always trying to escape from practical activity into the safer realm of theoretical certainty and they neglected the real possibilities for putting themselves in stable possession of the worthwhile things of life. But the success of the experimental method of science, by installing doing as the heart of knowing, has helped to break down these misleading distinctions. They disappear altogether once it is recognized that there is no higher, fixed truth or good, indeed nothing but constantly changing events and their interactions.

Living means interacting with one's environment. In the course of their interaction with the outside world, men encounter conflict, confusion, discomfort. When a man becomes aware of something troublesome, "he can make a change in himself either by running away from trouble or by steeling himself to Stoic endurance; or he can set to work to do something so as to change the conditions of which unsatisfactoriness is a quality" (*The Quest for Certainty* [1929], p. 222). If he tries to solve the problem, he will imagine "hypothetical solutions" and then test them. When his "inquiry" is successful, the original "indeterminate situation" is transformed into a "unified whole" (*Logic* [1938], pp. 104f.). The final solution is a "warranted assertion," which Dewey proposed as a more precise name for knowledge.

Human life is not then divided between thinking and doing, but between needs, problems, hopes, fears, aversions and the responses to these—ideas, inquiries, hypotheses, solutions. There is nothing purely mental or theoretical because "nothing merely mental can actually resolve doubt or clarify confusion. At most it can produce only a *feeling* of certainty—something best obtained by withdrawing from the real world and cultivating fantasies. . . . In principle, the correspondence of what we do when a situation is *practically* unsatisfactory with what happens in the case of intellectual doubt is complete" (*Quest for Certainty*, pp. 221–22). Thought is not separate from action, but ". . . a mode of directed overt action. Ideas are anticipatory plans and designs which take effect in concrete *reconstructions of antecedent conditions of existence . . .* their worth has to be tested by the specified consequences of their operation" (ibid., p. 160). Science cannot conflict with the values men cherish, because it is their most effective instrument for changing their outer conditions so as to secure what they prefer. The problem of knowledge is only the problem of discovering how to redirect events and is "never ended, always in process; one problematic situation is resolved and another takes its place" (ibid., p. 281).

That this was a correct view of being and knowledge was moreover corroborated by the latest scientific achievement, Heisenberg's principle of uncertainty or indeterminacy, as Dewey called it: "The principle of indeterminacy thus presents itself as the final step in the dislodgment of the old spectator theory of knowledge. It marks the acknowledgement, within scientific procedure itself, of the fact that knowing is one kind of interaction which goes on within the world . . ." (ibid., p. 195). Natural laws are shown to be not statements about immutable properties but "a way of transacting business effectively with concrete existences, a mode of regulation of our relations with them" (ibid., p. 198). It is made obvious that nature is being understood "not by a mind thinking about it from without but by operations conducted from within, operations which give it new relations summed up in the production of a new individual object" (ibid., p. 205–06).

Thus Dewey translated Kant's prescription for reaching certainty, through eliminating intellectual contradictions and producing a logically perfect whole, into a prescription for achieving security by removing tensions in the practical world so as to organize it into an organic unity. He thereby drew out the most extreme implications of Kant's suggestion that certainty depended on what the knower constructed, and made explicit a new understanding of knowledge that has become widely accepted in the twentieth century, even by opponents of pragmatism such as existentialists. The object of knowing is no longer to grasp that which is, but to create and securely establish what is wanted. Man overcomes his strangeness in the universe by transforming it to fit the image he invents, and the perfection of knowledge that once was thought of as certainty becomes the unceasing reconstruction of the world.

BIBLIOGRAPHY

James Beattie, *An Essay on the Nature and Immutability of Truth in Opposition to Sophistry and Scepticism* (London, 1812). Jeremy Bentham, *An Introduction to the Principles of Morals and Legislation* (1776; Oxford, 1948; various reprints). Rudolf Carnap, *The Unity of Science* (London, 1934). John Dewey, *Logic, The Theory of Inquiry* (New York, 1938); idem, *The Quest for Certainty* (New York, 1929; reprint 1960). David Hume, *A Treatise of Human Nature* (1739; reprints New York, 1941, Oxford, 1951); idem, *Enquiry Concerning Human Understanding* (1748; various reprints); idem, *Concerning the Principles of Morals* (1751; various reprints). T. H. Huxley, *Essays*, 9 vols. (London, 1893–94; New York, 1894–1908). Immanuel Kant, *Prolegomena* (Chicago, 1933); idem, *Critique of Pure Reason* (1781; 1787; London, 1929; New York, 1934). John Stuart Mill, *System of Logic*, 2 vols. (London, 1843; 8th ed. 1872; New York, 1929); idem, *Letters*, 2 vols. (London, 1910); idem, *Auguste Comte and Positivism* (London, 1865). George Edward Moore, *Philosophical Papers* (London and New York, 1959).

Karl Popper, *Conjectures and Refutations* (London, 1963; New York, 1968). Thomas Reid, *An Inquiry into the Human Mind on the Principles of Common Sense* (1764; London, 1923). Bertrand Russell, *Analysis of Mind* (London and New York, 1921); idem, *A History of Western Philosophy* (London and New York, 1946); idem, *An Inquiry into Meaning and Truth* (London and New York, 1940; Baltimore, 1963); idem, *Introduction to Mathematical Philosophy* (London, 1919; New York, 1963); idem, *My Philosophical Development* (London and New York, 1959); idem, *Philosophical Essays* (London, 1910; various reprints); idem, *The Problems of Philosophy* (London and New York, 1912). P. A. Schilpp, ed., *The Philosophy of Bertrand Russell* (Chicago, 1944). William Whewell, *History of the Inductive Sciences*, 3rd ed. (1857; reprint, 1968). Ludwig von Wittgenstein, *Philosophical Investigations* (Oxford, 1953); idem, *Tractatus Logico-philosophicus* (London, 1922; a new trans. by D. F. Pears and B. F. McGuinness, London, 1961; New York, 1963).

SHIRLEY ROBIN LETWIN

[See also Causation; **Certainty in Seventeenth-Century Thought;** Necessity; Positivism; **Pragmatism; Probability.**]

CHAIN OF BEING

THE IDEA of a Chain of Being, or Scale of Creatures, is one of the guiding threads of interpretation of the universe worked out in Western science and philosophy. Like all ideas developed through a process of elaboration lasting centuries, it can be defined only by retracing its historical development in all its varied and often contradictory complexity. It will suffice to point out here what is constant in its many changing formulations. The Chain of Being is the idea of the organic constitution of the universe as a series of links or gradations ordered in a hierarchy of creatures, from the lowest and most insignificant to the highest, indeed to the *ens perfectissimum* which, uncreated, is yet its culmination and the end to which all creation tends.

This idea entails, as we shall see in the sequel, a series of essential component ideas in the history of Western metaphysics—the principles of gradation, of plenitude or fullness, and continuity, along with the principle of sufficient reason—and also defines man's place in the cosmos with psychological and moral, and sometimes even political, implications of fundamental importance for intellectual history.

I

1. The Ontological Basis for the Gradation of Existing Things. Historically we may trace the conception of a Chain of Being to the Platonic Idea of Ideas, or Idea of the Good, discussed in the seventh book of the *Republic*. This Idea is in fact the summit of the hierarchy of knowable things, for not only do they owe to it the quality of their being knowable, but derive from it their very existence by participating in various degrees in its nature (509b). Thus, the supreme Idea provides the logical basis of a world of sensibilia conceived as graded with respect to perfection. The Idea of the Good, however, is no more than a logical foundation, insofar as no active element or agent intervenes yet; instead, this element of activity is made an intrinsic feature of the Demiurge, introduced by Plato in the *Timaeus*. The Demiurge creates the sensible world modelled on the intelligible one (27d–29c). He cannot fail to generate things in that way since, being without jealousy, his very nature is to desire that all things approach as closely as possible to himself (29d–30a). Fecundity is thus an essential element of divine perfection. Self-sufficient perfection is at the same time self-transcendence in the sensible world. Thus God becomes at once the logical and ontological foundation of the world's multiplicity and variety.

This quality of generative self-transcendence of the supreme Being finds its most radical expression in Plotinus. It is of the very nature of the One in its perfection to "overflow," producing in its exuberance the "other" (*Enneads* V, 21). All beings, then, participate in the nature of the Good in such measure as they may, according to their individual capacity.

2. The Chain of Being as a "plenum formarum" or Plenitude of Forms. It is again in the *Timaeus* that we must seek the source of what Lovejoy has called the "principle of plenitude": the idea that in passing from the eternal order to the temporal, from the ideal to the sensible, there must be realized a fullness of forms in which every possible form becomes actual. If creativity is essential to the very perfection of the supreme Being, existence cannot be begrudged any manner of things, whatever their grade of perfection. Moreover, the supreme Being creates after the likeness of an intelligible model: for every idea there must be a corresponding perceptible object; every possibility will have its corresponding reality.

It follows—and Plotinus draws this consequence in all its import—that the divine self-transcendence, or inexhaustible power of the One, must in its creative necessity reach the extreme limits of the possible. There is a kind of chain of delegated productive powers: every hypostasis in this generative scale is involved in this productive necessity, and its creativity must proceed out of itself to the extreme limit of the possible. Nothing may be barred from existence, which is to say, from more or less participation in the nature of the Good (*Enneads* IV, 8, 6).

What is full obviously cannot admit any discontinuity. Thus in the Chain of Being the principle of continuity is associated with the principle of fullness and is often confused with the latter. Aristotle had already observed that in the world of living things the different orders overlap. In the classification of animals according to habitat—terrestrial animals, animals inhabiting air and water—there are many intermediate forms irreducible to one or another of these classes. The passage from the inanimate to the animate is so gradual that continuity makes the boundary between the two orders imperceptible. It is the same for the passage from the order of plants to that of animals, so that for many living forms it is hard to establish to which of the two classes they belong (Aristotle, *History of Animals* VII. 1. 588b).

It is easy to see that such considerations should have reinforced the principle of plenitude—even though this was not authorized by the Aristotelian teaching on potentiality and actuality, according to which there do exist possibilities which have not yet come into existence (*Metaphysics* III. 1003e 2; XII. 1071b 13).

II

1. The Principle of Plenitude and Christian Theology. The idea of an inexhaustible divine productivity which cannot but create all possible forms, thus establishing a full and continuous chain of existing things, was transmitted to Christian philosophy from Neo-Platonism, chiefly through the medium of Augustine and the Pseudo-Dionysius. And it gave rise immediately to a series of antinomies at the heart of Christian thought. The first of these (in order of importance) was the question of reconciling this divine self-transcendence, this constitutional inability not to create every possible thing without exception, with the divine attribute of liberty.

The problem is clearly presented, for example, by Abelard (*Intro. ad theologiam*, III). The Good can produce nothing but good; to imagine there are good things He might create, but does not, can only be to imagine a jealous and unjust God. Thus goodness becomes a necessary divine attribute, limiting His freedom: being good, He could not have failed to produce the world, nor could He have produced a better one than the one He did produce. To the objection that God acts, then, out of necessity rather than free choice, Abelard answers that a certain necessity is inherent in His nature. His goodness is so great that He does spontaneously what it is impossible for Him not to do. The "Spinozism" of this position has been clearly pointed out by Arthur O. Lovejoy ([1936], pp. 71–72); the connection between this problem and the theodicy of Leibniz is no less evident.

Thomas Aquinas had to face the same problem, once having accepted the principle of plenitude. God wills the multiplicity of things inasmuch as He wills His own essence and perfection, which indeed contains in itself all things (*Summa contra gentiles* I, 75). And yet it cannot be said that He acts out of necessity—and here Thomas introduces the notion of consistency: the divine choice is such that He chooses that which is consistent with His perfection without, however, His being constrained by it (ibid., I, 81). But now it is clear that this idea of the contingency of creation, which depends on the divine choice, contradicts the principle of plenitude previously affirmed (ibid., II, 45; III, 71; *Summa theologica*, I, q. 25, a. 6).

It is not surprising, given these difficulties, that the official teaching of the Church tended to silence the Platonic conception of a self-transcendent deity compelled to create all possibilities. In general the "Christianization" of the Platonic doctrine of participation involved a denial of emanationism, for the quality of liberty had to be attributed to the Creator; and the multiplicity of the forms of being flowing from the free act of creation reflected, but did not modify or condition the richness and perfection of the Divine Being.

But if the idea of fullness, which requires the coincidence of the possible and the real, involved Christian thought in the difficulties we have seen, the application of the idea of the biological continuum went far more smoothly: it was in fact used repeatedly in praise of that interconnectedness of things (*connexio rerum*) by which nature passes only by steps from one kind to another. The notion of continuity was amply used even in psychology. In the nature of man different grades of being meet: as microcosm, he recapitulates the continuity of orders inherent in the scale of nature. He is a workshop of all created beings (*creaturarum omnium officina*), and also stands as the union of all creatures (*medietas atque adunatio omnium creaturarum*). Not independent of any creatures (*nullius creaturae expers*), in common with the angels he has intelligence, with animals he shares sensibility, with plants the vegetable life, and with stones simple being. These are recurrent motifs in, e.g., Albert the Great, John Scotus Erigena, William of Conches; and also in Thomas Aquinas, who places in the human soul the boundary between corporeal and incorporeal things (*Summa contra gentiles* II, 68).

2. Gradation in Nature and in the Sciences, ("scala naturae" and "scala scientiarum"). If the ascending way is placed before the Christian as an itinerary of moral edification, the same way is also, until the Renaissance, the route that science must follow in reconstructing that universal plan expressed precisely in the Chain of Being. This methodical ideal of an upward orientation is very evident, for example, in Raymond Lully's (or Lull) construction of the tree of knowledge—hence it was transmitted, thanks to the continuity of tradition set by Lully, to Renaissance encyclopedism, and to the pansophic ideal of the first half of the seventeenth century.

"The likenesses to the divine nature," writes Lully in his *Compendium artis* . . . , (in *Opera*, Mainz, [1721–24], III, 74), "are imprinted upon every creature according to that creature's receptive capacities, greater or less in each case . . . thus every creature carries, more or less, the sign of its Maker." Whence the ideal of a way of knowing that proceeds by signs (*per vestigias*) towards the reconstruction of the scale of beings, of the hierarchies of the cosmos: from stone to plant, to animal, to man, to the heavens, to the angels, to God (cf. *Liber de ascensu et descensu intellectus* [1304]). Whence also, the full construction of the "trees" of an encyclopedic knowledge that comprehends, in one organic picture of the universe, not only sensible nature but also the ethico-political life of man, the structure of the heavens, the divine hierarchies, all the way to the *arbor divinalis*, which is the culmination of the cosmic hierarchy. All things are contained in Lully's sixteen trees; and in them, taken together, we have another example of the continuity of the Scale of Being—for every tree participates in the nature of all the preceding ones, so that each is a kind of compendium of the natures below it, and contiguity is established between preceding and succeeding orders.

This ideal of knowledge as an ascent through the grades of perfection of creatures is kept alive, and is even renewed, through all of the Renaissance. For example, Giordano Bruno, in the *De umbris* (1582), says that all things have an orderly and connected structure, and for that reason man should keep this scale of nature clearly before his eyes, and make the effort to climb from multiplicity to unity. It is this ideal that animates all Renaissance encyclopedism, and is still quite alive at the birth of the new science—as the ideal of a reconstruction of the universe that shall exhibit the qualities of comprehensiveness, gradation, and continuity—alongside the experimental method and its collection of more or less unconnected and scattered scraps of information. The program of the Royal Society, for example, as formulated in 1669 by Thomas Sprat (*History of the Royal Society*, p. 110), is witness to this symbiosis of the techniques of experimental research and the idea of a full and hierarchical universe. It is precisely the task of science to retrace the steps of this universe: the program proposed "to follow all the links of this chain [of the diverse orders of creatures], till all their secrets are open to our minds.

. . ." The pages of the *Philosophical Transactions* are a body of minute experimental data, offered to the attention of men of science for no more than what they are worth as disparate experimental findings; and yet, for example, the various universal language plans drawn up by certain eminent members of the Society (John Wilkins being among the most notable) are based precisely on the notion of a hierarchical classification that holds good both ontologically and logically—for nature as well as for science.

III

1. The Principle of Plenitude and the Plurality of Worlds. According to Lovejoy ([1936], Ch. IV), the Renaissance idea of a plurality of inhabited worlds in a physical universe infinite in space owes more to the persisting force of the principle of plenitude than to the new Copernican astronomy. The doctrine of an infinity of worlds, as put forward most notably by Giordano Bruno, is associated with his interest in the new astronomy; but it is equally true that this doctrine, as well as the hypothesis that there is life on these worlds, could not be deduced from astronomical data alone. The argument of which Bruno avails himself is clearly a development of the principle of plenitude. We may not think that a finite effect comes from an infinite cause; in God, and therefore in the temporal order that derives from Him, the possible and the real coincide. Divine power cannot remain idle, divine goodness cannot but be infinitely diffused, being infinitely communicable. God, then, is a fertile father (*padre fecondo*), endowed with an illimitable generative capacity (*capacissimo di innumerevoli mondi*), as found in *De l'infinito universo e mondi* (1584), Dial. I.

Descartes' authority, in the course of the seventeenth century, lends support to this rejection of the idea of the universe as a finite and self-contained sphere; and the idea of a plurality of inhabited worlds is given great currency in Fontenelle's *Entretiens sur la pluralité des mondes* (1686).

2. The Full Universe of Leibniz. The diffusion of the idea of a Chain of Being in eighteenth-century thought was certainly and decisively aided by the success of Leibniz, a great advocate of the principle of plenitude and continuity, which he posited as a correlative of the principle of sufficient reason. Leibniz, in one of his letters to Samuel Clarke (1715–16), writes:

The least corpuscle is actually subdivided infinitely, and contains a world of other creatures, of which the universe would be deprived, if that corpuscle were an atom, that is, a body of one entire piece without subdivision. In like manner, to say that there is a vacuum in nature would be to attribute to God a most imperfect production; it would be to violate the great principle of the necessity of a sufficient reason . . . (*Leibniz Selections*, p. 236).

And elsewhere (*De synthesi et analysi universali*) the principle of sufficient reason, whence flows, among other things, the fullness of the universe, is defined as one of the greatest and most fertile truths of human cognition, since it assures us that all truths, even the most contingent, have an *a priori* proof, i.e., a reason for which they are rather than are not. This bond had already been established by Leibniz in the *Elementa philosophiae arcanae* (1676): the principle of the harmony of things requires that there exist the greatest possible quantity of essence. There is no gap among forms; it is not possible to find an empty space or time. Every particle of matter contains infinite creatures (cf. also the so-called First Truths, *Primae veritates* [1686]).

The argument is drawn out at length in two other writings of Leibniz: *De rerum originatione radicali* (1697) and the *Principes de la nature et de la grâce* (1718, posthumous). "Not only in no one of the singular things"—writes Leibniz in the first of these, "but neither in the whole aggregate and series of things, can one find a sufficient reason for their existence (*nam non tantum in nullo singulorum, sed nec in toto aggregato serieque rerum inveniri potest sufficiens ratio existendi*). The world's reasons must therefore be sought in something extra-worldly, different from the succession of states, or series of things, the aggregate of which constitutes the world (*rationes igitur mundi in aliquo extra-mundano, differente a catena statuum, seu serie rerum, quarum aggregatum mundum constituit*)." We must go back, then, from the physical necessity of things to their metaphysical necessity—which would be precisely their sufficient reason. Leibniz goes on:

In possible things, or in their very possibility or essence, there is an exigency to exist, or (so to speak) claim to exist; in a word, . . . essence of itself tends towards existence. Whence it follows that all possible things . . . tend with equal right towards existence in proportion to their quantity of essence or reality, or according to the grade of perfection they contain; for perfection is nothing but the quantity of essence.

Thus, given only that there is a reason for the passage from possibility to actuality, it will follow that a maximum of reality will be actualized. In other words every possibility has an "impulsion (*conatus*) to be real"; and the sole restriction in the passage from the possible to the actual is that imposed by the criterion of "compossibility," the reciprocal compatibility of possibilities. From the conflict of all the possibilities which severally seek existence, the result will be the existence of the maximal series of all possibilities.

The argument is taken up again in the *Principes*, in relation to the problem of the monads. All is full in nature; every monad is a living mirror that reflects the universe; and there is an infinity of degrees in monads, *les unes dominant plus ou moins sur les autres* (ibid., pp. 3–4). The sufficient reason for the existence of the universe cannot reside in the series of contingent things, but only in God, from whose perfection it follows that from the impulse towards existence proper to all essences, the most perfect of possible worlds will result. Without that we should be unable to say why things are, and why they are as they are (ibid., pp. 7–10).

3. Ethico-political Consequences of the Idea of the Chain of Being in the Eighteenth Century.

It is Leibniz, as we know, who draws from the idea of a Chain of Being, and particularly from the principle of plenitude, those optimistic consequences already implicit—consequences which for that matter did not escape others before him, for example, Giordano Bruno (cf. *De immenso* [1591], II, 13). Already in the *De rerum originatione radicali* (1697), Leibniz passes from the principle of sufficient reason to the perfection of the world:

. . . from what has been said it follows that the world is most perfect, not only physically, or, if one prefers, metaphysically, because that series of things has been produced in which there is actually a maximum of reality, but also that it is most perfect morally. . . . The world is not only the most admirable mechanism but insofar as it is composed of souls, it is also the best republic, through which the greatest measure of happiness and joy is conferred upon these souls, in which their physical perfection consists (*Leibniz Selections*, p. 351).

Experience seems to show the opposite: particularly if we consider the conduct of mankind, the world seems rather chaotic than ordered by a supreme wisdom. But, objects Leibniz, it is not fair to judge the whole by the part. We know only a small part of an eternity infinitely extended, namely the extent of the memory of a few millennia handed down by history. And yet from such scant experience we rashly judge what is immense and eternal. It is as if we were to examine a tiny portion of a painting and discern there nothing but a confused mass of colors without design and without art. In the universe, in short, the part can be disturbed without prejudice to the whole, which will inevitably escape whomever, like man, has only a partial vision of things. The theme is taken up again by Leibniz on many occasions in the *Théodicée* (1710) and in the *Principes* (1718).

We have seen how the principle of plenitude—by virtue of which all possible things pass into actual existence (the criterion of compossibility being the only limiting factor)—was connected, in Leibniz, with that of sufficient reason. Of this latter principle Lovejoy ([1936], pp. 145–49, 165–80) gives an interpretation intended to show its affinity with Spinoza's kind of determinism. According to Lovejoy, the principle of sufficient reason, with its criterion of compossibility as sole restriction in the passage from the possible to the actual, is not substantially different from the universal necessity of Spinoza; and absolute logical determinism would then be characteristic of the thought of both.

This interpretation of the principle of sufficient reason and of the consequent justification of moral and physical evil helps clarify the special nature of Leibnizian "optimism," and in general of eighteenth-century optimism of Leibnizian derivation; and also helps explain how it could coexist with a description of man's place in the universe which certainly does not seem, at first, to encourage an optimistic vision of the human condition. It was not a question of denying the existence of evil but rather of showing the necessity for it—and this was done in the face of the most dismal and grim descriptions of a natural and moral reality in which this same passage from possibility to reality shaped up as a struggle for existence. This is a recurrent motif in the theological and moral writings of the time, and there is an echo of it in Pope's *Essay on Man* (1734), a great popularizer of the idea of the Chain of Being and its implications. The contrast between such avowed optimism and this taste for the grimmest descriptions of the human condition did not escape Voltaire, the most famous critic of the optimism of his day: *Vous criez "Tout est bien" d'une voix lamentable*, he observed; and he invited his adversaries to cease proposing the immutable laws of necessity as explanation of evil.

In this plan of a perfect universe in which outrageous (and necessary) afflictions of individuals are embraced and given a new value in the law of universal harmony, a not inconsistent feature was the idea that man, far from being the king of creation and the measure of all things, was a mere link in the Chain of Being, infinitely farther from the highest grades of creation than he is above the lowest of creatures. This too is a recurrent motif in the literature of the time.

An argument in favor of political conservatism followed from all of this: if the perfection of the divine plan requires a universe ordered in a hierarchy of beings, each destined to occupy a place in the scale of creatures so that all gradations are filled, then the same law should prevail in the world of men, or the moral universe: the norm of behavior should be to live in keeping with one's condition, without subverting any order of society which, like a microcosm, reflects the very order of the universe.

IV

1. Two Objections. There seems to have been only two dissident voices in this ideal climate, namely, those of Dr. Johnson and Voltaire. Samuel Johnson (in 1757) applied Zeno's argument to the Chain of Being.

The Scale of Existence from Infinity to Nothing cannot possibly have Being. The highest Being not infinite must be . . . at an infinite Distance below Infinity . . . and in this Distance, between finite and infinite, there will be Room for ever for an infinite series of indefinable Existence. Between the lowest positive existence and Nothing, . . . is another chasm infinitely deep; where there is room again for endless Orders of subordinate Nature. . . . Nor is this all. In the Scale . . . there are infinite Vacuities. At whatever Distance we suppose the next Order of Being to be above Man, there is room for an intermediate Order of Beings between them; and if for one Order, then for infinite Orders; since every Thing that admits of more or less, and consequently all the Parts of that which admits them, may be infinitely divided . . . (A *Review of a Free Inquiry into the Nature and Origin of Evil*).

Johnson's argument, as we see, strikes directly at the foundation of the Chain of Being—the principle of plenitude. Still, with a moment's reflection, we see that it is not really pertinent: the Chain of Being is, so to speak, the cosmological translation of Zeno's paradox, and its fullness is predicated precisely upon the "fault" Johnson finds with it, namely, that infinite divisibility which affords the insertion between one order and another of "endless orders."

Voltaire, on the other hand, questions on the basis of empirical observation whether it can be held that there is a gradation of created beings (*Dictionnaire philosophique* [1764], s.v. "Chaîne des êtres créés"). It is gratifying to the imagination, he says, to contemplate that imperceptible passage from the inanimate to the organic, from plants to zoophytes, to animals, to angels, all in ascending grades of perfection up to God Himself. This hierarchy pleases the *bons gens*, who believe they recognize in it the Pope, followed by the cardinals, archbishops, and bishops, followed in turn by the curates, vicars, and simple priests, deacons and sub-deacons, lastly by friars and capuchins. But there is an essential difference between the cosmological and ecclesiastical hierarchies: whereas in the latter the humblest member can be Pope, in the former not even the most perfect of creatures can become God. And with this apparently jesting observation Voltaire catches an essential feature of the Chain of Being—its immobility: if the principle of plenitude requires that every grade be filled by an order of creatures, this hierarchy must necessarily be static, for we cannot admit a passing onto higher orders which would leave holes in the universal fabric. And in any case between

329

even the most perfect of creatures and God an infinite hiatus must remain (*il y a l'infini entre Dieu et lui*).

But Voltaire's objection regards, above all, the principle of continuity, which is nowhere evidenced in nature: let the proof of that be that there are extinct species in both the animal and vegetable kingdoms. It is probable that even among men there are extinct species; and between apes and men there is clearly a gap. As for spiritual substances, Christians believe in them because faith teaches that these substances exist; but what reason had Plato for believing so? And finally how can there be in empty space a chain that binds all? Here Voltaire catches another difficulty in the idea of a continuum, namely, one owing something to the philosophy of Newton, who had affirmed the existence of a vacuum—something rejected by Leibniz in favor of the plenitude hypothesis.

Of the two criticisms presented above, Johnson's in its logical strictness misses the mark because he challenges the principle of plenitude precisely on the basis of the idea that makes it possible, namely the infinite divisibility of matter. Voltaire's is the more interesting because it reflects the debates current in the biological sciences of his day, and especially the discussions of the notion of species, which, as we shall see, were to be decisive in the development and eventual dissolution of the Chain of Being.

2. Kant's Criticism and the Chain of Being. In the *Allgemeine Naturgeschichte und Theorie des Himmels* (1755), Kant takes up the Leibnizian argument of the coincidence in God of the possible and the actual: creation is surely commensurate with the power of an infinite being, and it would be nonsense to say that God allows only a minimal part of his creative potential to pass into actuality. It is more reasonable to suppose that divine creativity does not unfold all at once but gradually, that creation has indeed a beginning but no end. In the formation of worlds, the first elements of chaos already bear the signs of that completeness that is of the very nature of their origin, since their nature can only be a consequence of the eternal idea of the divine intelligence. Matter itself has within it the tendency to organize itself, through natural evolution, in always more perfect forms.

Here, as we see, Kant gives us what Lovejoy ([1936], Ch. IX) later called a "temporalized" version of the Chain of Being, in which creation takes the form of a natural development starting from the divine idea; and it comes about step by step, filling up space with worlds in the process of eternity. It is an evolutional ebb and flow in which worlds are formed and dissolved; but the production of ever new worlds guarantees the fullness and infinite variety of the whole. If in its temporal variations a system exhausts all the variety of which it is constitutionally capable, it becomes a useless member of the Chain of Being, and so performs its last act in the vicissitudes of cosmic change, paying its tribute to mortality.

The problem of the Chain of Being is taken up in very different terms in the *Critique of Pure Reason* (1781), and precisely in the Appendix to the Transcendental Dialectic. Here Kant examines the principles of plenitude and continuity still operative in the sciences of the time, in order to reduce them to "ideas of the Reason" (transcendental ideas), which as such have no "constitutive" use but a purely "regulative" one, that is to say, they are capable of directing the Understanding to a certain aim, conferring upon its concepts the greatest unity and extension. Even lying quite outside the limits of possible experience, the ideas of the Reason constitute the systematic unity of knowledge. By virtue of this "transcendental presupposition" we may assume a homogeneity in the apparent infinite diversity of nature, a unity of its fundamental properties. This is the scholastic principle of Ockham, "entities are not to be multiplied more than are necessary" (*entia praeter necessitatem non esse multiplicanda*); and it is the foundation of logical classification. Beside this principle, which Kant calls the "principle of homogeneity," and which allows the reduction of the various species to subsumption in a few genera, also at work in the reason is the "principle of specification," which requires a multiplicity and difference among things in spite of their grouping in a same genus. Each genus requires diverse species, and each species diverse subspecies; and

as none even of these subspecies is without a sphere . . . reason in all its extension requires that no species should in itself be considered as the lowest, since the species being always a concept containing only that which is common to different things, . . . it must always subsume other concepts or subspecies. This principle of specification might be formulated thus: *entium varietates non temere esse minuendas* ("the variety of things is not to be minimized").

What Kant calls the law of specification is precisely the principle of plenitude. Inasmuch as it is an ideal of the reason it cannot be inferred from experience, since empirical specification goes no farther than observable multiplicity; but it is a regulative principle of experience, since it invites reason to seek the "distinctive and to presuppose it ever anew, although not immediately manifest to the senses." From the two foregoing principles—homogeneity and plenitude—there also arises the principle of the continuity of forms, which provides a continuous transition from species to species by means of a gradual building up of differences. Since

. . . there is no void in the entire sphere of all possible concepts, and as nothing can be discovered outside this sphere, there arises the principle *non datur vacuum formarum*, that is to say, there are no different original and first genera, isolated and separated from each other, as it were by an intervening void, but all the different genera are divisions of only one supreme and general genus. From that principle springs its immediate consequence, *datur continuum formarum*, that is, all the differences of species border upon one another and admit of no transition from one to another *per saltum*. . . . This logical law of the continuum of species (*continuum specierum*) presupposes a law of continuity in nature (*lex continui in natura*), which however remains only thinkable, not knowable: This continuity of forms is a mere idea, for which it is not possible to find a corresponding object in experience, not only because the species in nature are actually divided, and must form, each by itself, a discrete quantity (*quantum discretum*), . . . but also because we can make no determinate empirical use of this law, since it does not offer the least criterion to tell us how and how far we ought to seek for different grades of affinity; the law of continuity tells us only in general that we ought to seek for them. . . .

In short, there is no empirical use of the principle of continuity; it has only a regulative use: as simply an idea, it serves only to alert us in general that a series should be sought in nature.

The same can be said, Kant goes on, of the "famous law" of the Scale of Creatures, consequence of the two principles in question. The notion of a Chain of Being is not objectively verifiable by observing nature: "the steps of this scale, so far as we are able to know them by experience, are much too far apart, and the (putatively) small differences in nature itself are ordinarily crevices so vast, that such observations cannot be relied upon. . . ." Even the idea of a Chain of Being, then, is a regulative principle only, a "method" according to which we seek order in nature—but a method that "goes too far for experience or observation to match."

Thus the Chain of Being is reduced, in Kant, to one of those ideals for which there is no empirical application, and which indeed, in their empirical use, can produce only imaginary knowledge and hence eternal contrasts and contradictions. And with that an essential aspect of the Chain of Being is wanting: its function, namely, as a scheme of nature that observation is supposed to fill in gradually by reconstructing it empirically. Such a reconstruction, for Kant, is not possible: it would indeed constitute an example of the dialectic of appearance. In these same decades, and no doubt independently of the Kantian criticism, the biological sciences produced a profound transformation in the idea of a Chain of Being; and at the end of this process the conclusion emerges that it is impossible to reconstruct in a scientific way the hierarchical

structure of the universe. In this way that fixed structure loses all objective validity and is no longer one of the constitutive principles of scientific research.

V

1. Crises of the Chain of Being: The Controversies over the Notion of Species. We have said that for Kant the empirical use of ideas such as that of continuity and of the plenitude of forms (*plenum formarum*) was illegitimate and could only make for contradictions and controversies. His conclusion seems to be, and indeed is, in part, a commentary on the eighteenth-century discussions of continuity and plenitude in the biological world.

At first the new instruments of scientific research do not seem to contradict the idea of a Scale of Creatures. Indeed, the already widespread use of the microscope makes it possible to observe the world of the infinitely small; and in 1739 the discovery of Trembley's *Hydra* is hailed as the discovery of the missing link between the vegetable and animal worlds. Even the skeptical "Pyrrhonism" of men of science, or their awareness of the limitations of experimental research, echoes Leibniz' vision of a universal "plenum" of which we have a partial vision only. No, it is rather the debate over the notion of biological species that challenges the foundations of the Chain of Being, and in particular the principle of plenitude. In order to salvage this principle it was necessary to attribute only a conventional, not real, value to biological classifications: subdivision into species would in fact have created in nature a too nicely spaced series, letting precisely those imperceptible gradations escape which assure continuity and plenitude in the natural world.

The conventionality of species is affirmed in Buffon's *Discours sur la manière d'étudier et de traiter l'Histoire naturelle*, which prefaces the first volume of his *Histoire naturelle* (1748). The methods or "systems" of classification are, to be sure, indispensable but artificial: as against the nuances of natural reality we have an arbitrarily articulated series. The error of all classification rests on the inability to grasp the processes of nature, which are always realized by degrees, by imperceptible nuances, thus escaping all division. In short, only individuals exist in reality; genera or species do not.

But Buffon wholly reversed his position in the course of his research, prompted by the now general recognition of species as a genetic entity. In fact, in Volume XIII of the same work (1765) he affirms that the only true beings in nature are species and *not* individuals.

Robinet, a firm advocate of the principle of plenitude, was quite clear about the dangers inherent in classifications: if we accept the separation of nature into orders of this kind, the Chain of Being is fatally broken (*De la nature* [1766], IV, 4–5). Doubtless the introduction of the idea of species as a genetic entity contributed decisively to this crisis of the principle cf plenitude: since two individuals are said to belong to the same species if they are capable of producing a fertile offspring and of transmitting to it their own hereditary characteristics, it is hard to imagine a "full" concatenation among the diverse species. Actually, in the second half of the eighteenth century, the notion of species is already established and operative in the biological sciences. The controversies—accelerated by the always growing body of empirical data, and particularly by the data of the new science of paleontology—had to do rather with the fixity or nonfixity of the species (taken now as established entities).

2. Crisis of the Chain of Being: Permanence and Becoming in Nature. In a world hierarchically arranged, such as the one described by the great metaphor of a Chain or scale of beings, orders of creatures had to be considered fixed *ab aeterno* with their essential and thus unalterable characteristics. In the third decade of the century Réaumur wrote: "The author of nature wanted our earth to be populated with a prodigious number of species of animals, and has given the earth those species fit for it to possess. . . ." And again: "One must start from the principle that the species of insects are—no less than those of animals—invariable in form" (*Mémoires pour servir à l'histoire des insectes* [1734–42], II, XL–XLI). The physician Antonio Vallisnieri (1661–1730) affirmed on anatomical grounds that it was impossible for carnivorous habits to be acquired: it is no accident (only to regret it afterward) that God, immutable and omnipotent, wanted herbivores to be so different from carnivores: such difference is but another proof of the unalterable structure of that great theater that is nature (*Opere fisico-mediche*, I, 315A). In general all adaptation phenomena should be interpreted not as chance environmental mutations but as providentially preordained laws (ibid., I, 137B). The fixity of species is also basic to Linnaeus' *Philosophia botanica* (1751).

Faith in the permanence of nature (required by the idea of the Chain of Being) and the affirmation that there is evolution in nature are clearly contradictory: mediating between them was a theory of the preexistence of seeds—already diffuse, beginning from the last decades of the seventeenth century—according to which every living thing would exist already formed in all its parts in the seed, and all seeds, created *ab initio*, would simply be transmitted and developed in reproduction. With such a doctrine—adopted by Fontenelle and Leibniz among others—one could conceive of the history of nature as explication and development of all those possibilities already foreseen *ab aeterno* as essential parts of the world's structure.

This transformist view afforded a reconciliation of the idea of plenitude with that of the perfectibility of nature. And in this sense it is used, for example, by Robinet in his *De la nature* (1761–68). In a word, natural development, if seen as development of maturation of preexisting seeds, adds nothing really new to creation but simply explicates its original productivity. Nature is continuously working itself out, and the principle of plenitude is manifest in this temporal process.

Yet just this transformism was bound to challenge, explicitly or implicitly, the notion of the fixity of species and thus precipitate a crisis in the hierarchical image of the cosmos. But for that matter numerous and grave objections to the fixity of species were being raised by the necessity to give some plausible account of hereditary and adaptation phenomena, which require the intervention of variation and of environmental determination. Remarkable how Maupertuis in his *Essai de cosmologie* (1750), precisely by reflecting upon adaptation phenomena and the natural selection that implies, was led to draw the same conclusion that Kant was to draw some years later, in regard to the illegitimacy of the empirical use of the principles of plenitude, of homogeneity, and of continuity. Only those species that have certain adaptable relations (*rapports de convenance*) with nature may survive.

One would say that chance has produced an incalculable multitude of individuals; a small number happened to be so constructed that the parts of each creature were capable of satisfying its needs; in another number, infinitely larger, there was neither adaptability nor order; such species have all perished . . . and the species that we see today are the tiniest part of all a blind destiny has produced (*Essai*, in *Oeuvres* [1756], I, 11–12).

The continuity of the natural world can never be, then, an empirical statement: uniformity is (as we may say) a spiritual exigency and has no exact counterpart in experience: Continuity pleases our mind, but does it please Nature? (*Elle plaît à notre esprit, mais plaît-elle à la Nature?*—ibid., 51). The Chain of Being, thanks to which we may imagine a universe so constituted that the beings that fill it can only be the perfectly juxtaposed parts of the whole, was perhaps broken up by some telluric cataclysm; however that may be, it cannot now be reconstructed on the basis of observation. And it is for this reason that Maupertuis, in the third part of his *Essai*, presents it as pure conjecture.

But even more telling than Maupertuis' *Essai* of the new philosophy of nature is his *Système de la nature* (first ed., in Latin, 1751), wherein we witness the dissolution of that bond between natural forms and divine creativity which had, from the *Timaeus* on, formed the basis of the Chain of Being. To suppose that all individuals were made by the divine will on one and the same day of creation, says Maupertuis, means to have recourse to a miraculous rather than physical explanation. The laws at work in nature, which are the only object of science, operate to conserve and also to transform natural forms (French edition [1756], sections XI–XLIX).

The importance of this new conception of the relations between God and nature is certainly the decisive element in the dissolution of the Chain of Being. As Roger has observed ([1963], pp. 486–87), Maupertuis, rejecting the preexistence of seeds, the notion of God as "maker," and the fixity of forms, was led to study the life of natural forms in time, introducing duration into biological sciences as an essential element. This general temporalization of nature is a particular example of what Lovejoy has called ([1936], p. 242) the "temporalizing" of the Chain of Being. According to the traditional conception, the Scale of Creatures was static and the temporal process brought no enrichment. In the new "temporalized" version the *plenum formarum* was conceived instead "not as the inventory but as the program of nature, which is being carried out gradually and exceedingly slowly in cosmic history" (ibid., p. 244).

VI

1. The Principle of Continuity in the Philosophy of Becoming. We have seen from the beginning how the idea of the Chain of Being was founded on two basic principles: the principle of plenitude and that of continuity. In the history of the idea, as we have been reconstructing it, these two principles not only go together but at times indeed coincide. But we should not forget that they have completely different and independent origins. The principle of plenitude—of Platonic origin—was born of an essential attribute of the Demiurge or Creator God, and that is His superabundance and necessary creativity; it is therefore bound up with the principle of sufficient reason, as Leibniz tells us quite explicitly. The principle of continuity, on the other hand, is a biological one, arising from the observation that there exist beings hardly reducible to one or another of the great classes into which all natural things seem to fall. Now the different origin of these two principles should be borne in mind in retracing the dissolution of the Chain of Being.

The question of the existence or nonexistence of species in nature ended up in a crisis for the principle of plenitude: if one acknowledged the real, objective existence of those genetic entities called species, it was hard to picture nature except as a series of distinct units—which of course contradicted the principle of plenitude. It was not however impossible to imagine a continuity in the series—a continuity subsisting

somehow between the inorganic and the organic, between the vegetable and animal worlds: witness, for example, the position of Buffon. We have seen that he had come in the course of his research to reverse his first denial of the existence of species, indeed to the point of affirming that they are the only natural reality; and yet he never denied the unity and continuity of nature. And this in the name of the experimental method, which should always remind us of the abstract character of definitions, and distinguished the name from the thing. Once a definition is accepted, writes Buffon in Chapter VIII of his *Histoire des animaux* (1749), it is imagined that the word is a line of demarcation among the products of nature; that, for example, all above a certain line "should be really *animal*, and that everything below be nothing but *vegetable*. . . . But as we have already said many times, these lines of demarcation do not exist in nature." The same continuity—unity between inorganic and organic, between animal and man, unity in the perpetual flux of things—is amply witnessed in the writings of Diderot in the *Rêve de d'Alembert:* "All creatures merge into one another . . . all in perpetual flux. . . . Every animal is more or less a man; every mineral is more or less a plant; every plant is more or less an animal. There is nothing precise in nature." (*Tous les êtres circulent les uns dans les autres . . . tout est dans un flux perpétuel. . . . Tout animal est plus ou moins homme; tout minéral est plus ou moins plante; toute plante est plus ou moins animal. Il n'y a rien de précis dans la nature.*) Even Robinet, in the name of the principle of continuity, denies that the organic and the inorganic are quite different, to the point of attributing a kind of rudimentary reason to matter even in its inorganic phase. According to La Mettrie nature seems to proceed, so to speak, by trial and error towards greater and greater organization, and it is just this that assures its unity: there is a kind of "imperceptibly graduated scale" in the sensory faculties, from plant to animal to man; and nature "passes through all gradations without skipping a single one in all its various productions" (*L'homme-plante* [1748], in *Oeuvres* [1796], II, 69). J. T. Needham too, rejecting the fixity of natural forms, considers the gradation in nature as the result of a progressive organization (cf. the *Philosophical Transactions of the Royal Society*, 45 [1748], no. 490). Robinet and Bonnet debate at length the problem of reconciling the idea of a Chain of Being with that of the evolution of forms. In general, then, a latent vitalism, introducing the idea of a teleology inherent in matter, tends more to fill than to accentuate the breaks among the different orders of natural reality.

In the second half of the eighteenth century, then, the temporalization of the natural sciences disparages but does not eliminate the idea of a biological continuum which, as we have seen, persists as a recurrent *topos* in the scientific thought of the time. It persists however, in a very different formulation from the traditional one: not as gradation and contiguity of natural forms, but as (temporal) continuity in the organizational process of nature. And as such it goes well beyond the eighteenth century, surviving in the biological vitalism of the following century, up to Bergson's *élan vital*. In general we might say that in all philosophies of becoming—vitalism, post-Kantian idealism, evolutionism—continuity is adopted as (to use Kant's term once more) a "regulative ideal," capable only of assuring the unity of becoming. Even the doctrine of evolution can be understood as a temporal translation of the continuity principle. It is no accident that one of the most recent theorists of evolution avails himself of it, not only as criterion for the interpretation of nature but as the foundation of a "new humanism." Writes Julian Huxley: ". . . all aspects of reality are subject to evolution, from atoms and stars to fish and flowers, from fish and flowers to human society and values—indeed . . . all reality is a single process of evolution. . . ." The biological process "takes place in a series of steps or grades, each grade occupied by a successive group of animals and plants, each group sprung from a preexisting one and characterized by a new and improved pattern of organization." This assures the kinship of man with nature: "he now knows that he is not an isolated phenomenon, cut off from the rest of nature by his uniqueness. Not only is he made of the same matter and operated by the same energy as all the rest of the cosmos, but . . . he is linked by genetic continuity with all the other living inhabitants of his planet" ("The Evolutionary Vision," in *Evolution after Darwin*, 3 vols., Chicago [1960], III, 249–53).

But this survival of the principle of continuity is by itself not enough to guarantee the survival of the Chain of Being, even in its temporalized form. Of independent origin, the idea of continuity contributes to the development of the idea of the Chain of Being only insofar as continuity is associated with, or indeed fused with, the principle of plenitude. And, surviving the principle of plenitude (though in a profoundly changed way), the idea of continuity also survives the idea of a Chain of Being, which was grounded essentially in the principle of plenitude.

2. From the Chain of Being to the Tree of Life. As should be clear from the foregoing, the frequent references to the concatenation of creatures in eighteenth-century science (with, perhaps, an exception for Robinet) appeal rather to the principle of continuity than to that of plenitude. Now although continuity is an idea implicit in that of plenitude, the

converse is not true. That nature makes no jumps—and no scientist in the second half of the eighteenth century appeared to doubt it—does not in fact mean that nature realizes all those possibilities implicit from all eternity in the act of creation. The world's continuity, in other words, is due to the action of laws and forces and not to a necessity inherent in the divine nature. And with that the very foundation of the principle of plenitude, namely, its connection with the principle of sufficient reason stressed by Leibniz, is broken down.

Typical in this sense is, once again, Buffon's position, when he places the principle of sufficient reason among moral entities (*êtres moraux*), created by man on the basis of arbitrary relations which can produce "*rien . . . de physique et de réel*," and can never become a "physical reason" for things. It is therefore illegitimate to ask ourselves the "why" of nature (*Histoire des animaux*, Ch. V). Science no sooner rejects the principle of sufficient reason than it does the principle of plenitude, that is, the very foundation of the Chain of Being. The principle of continuity which, as we have seen, survives the process of temporalization, is by itself not enough to guarantee the survival of the Chain of Being. And the best epitaph, at the conclusion of this sketch, might be one from the same Buffon: *le vivant et l'animé, au lieu d'être un degré métaphysique des êtres, est une propriété physique de la matière* ("Animated life, instead of being a metaphysical grade of being, is only a physical property of matter," ibid., Ch. I).

The succession of living forms appears explainable now on the basis of the working of physical laws or of an activity inherent in nature: nature, as La Mettrie says, is "neither Chance, nor God" (*ni Hasard, ni Dieu*). The certainty of this descending process, from God to the natural world, fails; and with that is lost too the presumption that science can reconstruct the plan of creation in all its fullness by working its way back *per vestigias*.

Now we may say that the divorce between the two ideas, that of continuity and that of plenitude, is complete, even though they appear associated once more in romantic philosophy: in Schiller's dialectic of *Formtrieb* and *Stofftrieb;* in Fichte's conception of the Ego as infinite activity; in the philosophy of nature of Schelling; in the ethico-political ideal of the reaching of moral perfection through an indefinite progress; and in the conception of aesthetic progress as infinite productivity.

In science, the metaphor of the Chain of Being was to continue to circulate long after its "crisis"; the English paleontologist James Parkinson, still in the second decade of the nineteenth century, saw in it an obstacle to the correct interpretation of the data of the new science (Greene [1959], p. 122). But in general, in nineteenth-century science, another metaphor gains currency, one that keeps the quality of continuity but not of plenitude. It is the tree of evolution, published by Lamarck in the *Philosophie zoologique* ([1809]; reproduced in Greene, p. 163), which represents a series branching off in an irregularly spaced but uninterrupted way. It is what Darwin calls the "Tree of Life" (*Origin of Species* [1859], Ch. IV).

The affinities of all beings . . . have sometimes been represented by a great tree. I think this simile largely speaks the truth. The green and budding twigs may represent existing species; and those produced during former years may represent the long succession of extinct species. At each period of growth all the growing twigs tried to branch out on all sides, and to overtop and kill the surrounding twigs and branches, in the same manner as species and groups have at all times mastered other species in the great battle for life. . . . As buds give rise by growth to fresh buds, and these, if vigorous, branch out and overtop on all sides many a feebler branch, so by generation I believe it has been with the great Tree of Life, which fills with its dead and broken branches the crust of the earth, and covers the surface with its ever-branching and beautiful ramifications.

BIBLIOGRAPHY

The historian of the idea of the Chain of Being is Arthur O. Lovejoy. The present article is predicated upon his exemplary study, *The Great Chain of Being. A Study of the History of an Idea* (Cambridge, Mass., 1936; 1961).

We cannot here provide a bibliography for all the authors touched on and for all the different themes involved in one way or another with the idea of the Chain of Being. However, the following are certain studies to which (although they may not deal specifically with the subject in question) the present article is indebted for clarification and useful suggestions.

For the influence of the *Timaeus* and the continuity of Platonic thought to the Renaissance: H. Lyttkens, *The Analogy between God and the World* (Uppsala, 1953; 1955); T. Gregory, *Anima mundi* (Florence, 1955); E. Garin *Studi sul platonismo medievale* (Florence, 1958); R. Klibansky "The School of Chartres," *Twelfth-Century Europe and the Foundation of Modern Society* (Madison, 1961).

For the connection between the Scale of Nature and the classification of the sciences from the Middle Ages to the Renaissance: T. Carreras y Artau and J. Carreras y Artau, *Historia de la filosofía española* (Madrid, 1939), I, 233–640; J. Carreras y Artau, *De Ramón Lull a los modernos ensayos de formación de una lengua universal* (Barcelona, 1946); P. Rossi, *Clavis universalis* (Milan and Naples, 1960).

Fundamental for knowing the background of the developments of the Chain of Being in scientific thought from the late Renaissance to the late eighteenth century are: J. Roger, *Les sciences de la vie dans la pensée française du XVIIIe siècle* (Paris, 1963), esp. Part III ("La science des philosophes," pp. 457–761); *The Forerunners of Darwin*, ed.

B. Glass (Baltimore, 1959; 1968), containing among other things an essay of Lovejoy on Buffon ("Buffon and the Problem of Species," pp. 84–113). There is something on the Chain of Being in S. Toulmin and J. Goodfield, *The Discovery of Time* (London, 1965). See also: *Roots of Scientific Thought*, ed. Philip P. Wiener and Aaron Noland (New York, 1957), Pt. 4; C. Greene, *The Death of Adam: Evolution and its Impact on Western Thought* (Ames, Iowa, 1959); and *Leibniz Selections*, Philip P. Wiener, 2nd ed. revised (New York, 1966).

LIA FORMIGARI

[See also Conservatism; Continuity; **Creativity;** Evil; Evolutionism; God; **Hierarchy; Macrocosm;** Neo-Platonism; Perfectibility; Romanticism in Post-Kantian Philosophy; Theodicy.]

CHANCE

So FAR as we can judge, primitive man does not conceptualize his world of experience in any comprehensive way. To him, some events just happen; some he can control himself; some he can influence by sympathetic magic; for some he can enlist the aid of the unseen world of spirits which surrounds him. He knows of no general laws; and hence he knows of no absence of general laws. If he ever thought about the matter at all he might, perhaps, have considered that many events happen simply because they fall that way; and their falling so (Old French *la cheance*, from Latin *cadere*) was in the nature of the world, as we should say today, "just one of those things."

The emergence of more organized thought and language was slow to change essential ideas about happenings. As man collected his experiences, formed and named his concepts, and began to perceive regularities in the heavens and on earth, he developed the idea of cause and effect, and as time went on, it seemed to him that more and more events were causally linked. But whether every event had a cause was a question which he was late in asking (and for that matter, has not yet answered). Some events were explicable in a straightforward way; but others were equally certainly inexplicable, and many more had to be explained in terms of minor deities invented for the purpose. In polytheistic societies, such as the Egyptian, the Greek, and the Roman, it was held possible to influence events by enlisting the aid of some superhuman being, with sacrifice, donation, or even punishment (as when tribes thrashed their idols); but these beings themselves were not omnipotent and it would seem—though the records are, not surprisingly, silent on such questions—that a

335

great part of the manifestation of the world was regarded as proceeding blindly without direct intervention of God or man, or without being subject in all its aspects to law.

Nevertheless, nature proceeded in a manner which man perceived more and more to be orderly. We now encounter one of those peculiar dichotomies of which history affords so many instances: the emergence of gambling, on the one hand, and the employment of fortuitous events for divination, on the other. The gambler deliberately threw his fortunes at the mercy of uncontrolled events; the diviner used uncontrolled events to control his future.

The Germans of Tacitus' time, for example, decided many of their tribal procedures by a random process. The priests would write a number of runes on slips of bark, offer a prayer for guidance, choose one haphazardly, and follow the advice which it gave (or, at any rate, gave according to their interpretation). The Jews made important choices by lot. The Romans had their Sybilline books and their Etruscan custom of haruspication (divination from entrails). To modern eyes such procedures would look very like settling a doubtful issue by tossing up for it, but that was not how it appeared to the ancients. It was their way of interrogating their Deity, of referring the decision to a Better Informed Authority.

At the same time, gambling became widespread. One of the oldest poems on record, in the Rig-Veda, is a Gambler's Lament, in which the poet bewails the loss of all his possessions but, unfortunately for us, says nothing about the kind of game he was playing. In very early settlements there occur deposits of huckle bones (small bones in the foot of sheep or goat) which were assembled by man, almost certainly for playing some kind of game. These "astragali" have four clearly defined surfaces and were probably the antecedents of the ordinary six-faced cube or die, specimens of which are datable as far back as 3000 B.C.

The Greeks thought poorly of dice-playing. For them it was an amusement for children and old men. This, among other things, may be the reason why no Greek writers other than Aristotle and Epicurus showed any interest in chance, and as far as is known, none arrived at any idea of the statistical regularities embodied in series of repetitive events. The Romans were inveterate gamblers, especially in Imperial times; the emperor Claudius wrote a treatise on dice, which unfortunately has not survived. The Germans were even worse and an individual would on occasion gamble himself into slavery. We know a little about the type of dice-playing which was indulged in. It was almost certainly the ancestor of the medieval game of hazard, itself the ancestor of the American game of craps. (The word

"hazard," from Arabic *al zhar*, "the die," was probably brought back to Europe by the Crusaders. It was the name of a game, not a concept of random occurrence.)

Just how much the ancients knew about calculating chances is doubtful, but it cannot have been very exact knowledge, even though a gambler can hardly fail to have formed some notion of regular occurrence "in the long run." Early examples exist of loaded dice, which indicates that some persons at least were not content to leave things in the lap of the goddess Fortuna. But anything approaching a calculus of chances was not even adumbrated.

The advent of Christianity, and later of Islam, brought about a number of important changes, both in the philosophical concept of chance and in moral attitudes towards gambling. To the monotheist every event, however trivial, was under the direction of the Almighty or one of his agents. In this sense there was no chance. Everything happened under the divine purpose. Hence there grew up the belief that events which we describe as fortuitous or random or subject to chance are no different from any other happenings, except that we do not know why they happen. Chance, then, became a name which man gave to his own ignorance and not a property of events or things.

This belief has endured until the present day. Saint Augustine, Saint Thomas Aquinas, Spinoza all held it. The physicists of the nineteenth century mostly subscribed to it, though not necessarily for theological reasons. The more Nature was discovered to be subject to law (or, if one prefers it, the more man shaped his concepts into regular patterns to correspond with observation), the more it became evident that "chance" events appeared as such only because something remained to be discovered or because their causality was too complex for exact analysis. In the first half of the twentieth century we find a distinguished French probabilist, Paul Lévy, remarking that chance appeared to him to be a concept invented by man which was unknown to Nature; and Einstein, notwithstanding developments in subatomic physics (see below), never accepted chance as an essential unanalyzable element of the universe.

We return to the effect of Christianity on the concept of chance. Augurs, sybils, diviners, prognosticators generally, were frowned on by the Church from early times. This was not merely because the new priesthood could tolerate no competition from the old. Under the new religion it was impious to interrogate God by forcing Him, so to speak, to disclose His intentions. Moreover, gaming soon became associated with less socially tolerable activities—drinking, blasphemy, violence—and as such was sternly discouraged. We still possess a sermon of Saint Cyprian of Carthage against gamblers; more than a thousand years later, Saint Bernardino of Siena was inveighing against gambling and its vices to the same tune. None of this, of course, arrested gaming for very long. The number and frequency of the edicts issued against gaming are sufficient evidence of its prevalence, on the one hand, and its persistence, on the other. However, ineradicable as gambling proved to be, the official attitude of the Church was probably strong enough to prevent any serious study of it.

Up to the middle of the fourteenth century the main instruments of gaming were dice. The Western world then invented or acquired playing cards, whose precise origin, numerous legends notwithstanding, is still unknown. Cards began to displace dice, but more slowly than might have been expected, probably on account of their cost. It was not until the beginning of the eighteenth century that dice began to lose their popularity in favor of cards. Roulette wheels and one-armed bandits are, of course, products of modern technology.

It might have been supposed that, after playing with astragali, dice, and cards for several thousand years, man would have arrived relatively early at some concept of the laws of chance. There is no evidence that he did so much before the fourteenth century, and even then, after faint beginnings, it was three hundred years before the subject began to be understood. The earliest European record of any attempt to enumerate the relative frequency of dice-falls occurs in a medieval poem *De vetula* (dated somewhere between 1220 and 1250), one manuscript of which contains a tabulation of the ways of throwing three dice. It is an isolated contribution and for the next recorded attempt at the calculation of chances we have to notice a treatise on card-play by the gambling scholar, Girolamo Cardano. This remarkable man, part genius and part charlatan, was an inveterate gambler and a very competent mathematician. His book, written perhaps in 1526 but published only posthumously (1663), contains a clear notion of the definition of chances in terms of the relative frequency of events and of the multiplicative law of independent probabilities. A translation into English and a biography of Cardano by Oystein Ore appeared in 1953.

So far as concerns extant literature, Cardano's work is also isolated. Some Italian mathematicians of the sixteenth century considered a few problems in dice-play, and in particular, we have a fragment by Galileo (about 1620), in which he correctly enumerates the falls of three dice. Undoubtedly there must have been much discussion about chances, especially in those countries where men of science mingled freely with men of affairs; but little or nothing was published. The calculus of chances as we know it first became the subject of

general mathematical interest in France at the closing half of the seventeenth century, in the form of correspondence between Pascal and Pierre de Fermat. The time was ripe for a rapid expansion of the mathematical theory of chance. The first book on the subject, by Christiaan Huygens, was published in 1657. In 1713 there appeared the remarkable study by James (Jakob or Jacques) Bernoulli called *Ars conjectandi* in which he derived the so-called binomial distribution and raised the fundamental question of the convergence of proportions in a series of trials to a "true" chance. Once so launched, the mathematical theory advanced rapidly. A little over a hundred years later appeared a major masterwork, Pierre Simon de Laplace's *Théorie analytique des probabilités* (1812). The subject was by now not only interesting and respectable, but applicable to scientific problems and, before long, to commercial and industrial problems. It has been intensively cultivated ever since.

In one respect commerce took advantage of chance events. Some Italian shops of the fifteenth century would have a sack full of small presents standing by the counter and would invite customers to take a lucky dip. This *lotteria* developed into the present-day system of raising money by selling chances on prizes. The system spread over Europe but lent itself so readily to fraud that it was either forbidden or, in most countries, conducted as a state monopoly.

The subject which was formerly called the Doctrine of Chances, and is now more commonly but less accurately called the Mathematical Theory of Probability, is mostly a deductive science. Given a reference set of events and their probabilities, the object is to work out the probabilities of some contingent event; e.g., given that the chance of throwing any face of a die is $\frac{1}{6}$, find the probability that all six faces will appear in a given number of throws greater than six. Interesting as the subject is to the mathematician and useful as it may be to the statistician, it is not of concern in the history of ideas except insofar as its results are required, as we shall see below, in scientific inference.

Once again we must go back a little in time. At the end of the seventeenth century the philosophical studies of cause and chance, and the mathematics of the Doctrine of Chances were poles apart. They now began to move closer together. It was not long before the events of the dice board and the card table began to be seen as particular cases of fortuitous events of a more general kind, emanating in some rather mysterious way which conjured order out of chaos. In short, it began to be realized that chance, which conceptually was almost the negation of order, was subject to law, although to law of a rather different kind in that it admitted exceptions. The English savant, Dr. John

Arbuthnot, for example, became interested in the equality of the sex ratio at birth and saw something of Divine Providence in the phenomenon by which the apparently random occurrence of the individual event resulted cumulatively in a stable sex ratio. Thirty years later, J. P. Süssmilch, an honored name in the history of statistics, reflected the same thought in the title of his *magnum opus* on the divine order: *Die Göttliche Ordnung* (1741). In one form or another the idea has remained current ever since. There are few people who have reflected on the curious way in which random events have a stable pattern "in the long run" who have not been intrigued by the way in which order emerges from disorder in series of repeated trials. Even events which recur relatively infrequently may have a pattern; for example, the nineteenth-century Belgian astronomer and statistician Adolphe Quételet, one of the fathers of modern statistics, was struck by *L'effrayante exactitude avec laquelle les suicides se reproduisent* ("The frightening regularity marking the recurrence of suicides").

During the eighteenth and nineteenth centuries the realization grew continually stronger that aggregates of events may obey laws even when individuals do not. Uncertain as is the duration of any particular human life, the solvency of a life insurance company is guaranteed; uncertain as may be the sex of an unborn child, the approximate equality of numbers of the two sexes is one of the most certain things in the world.

This development had an important impact on the theory of chance itself. Previously chance was a nuisance, at least to those who wished to foresee and control the future. Man now began to use it for other purposes, or if not to use it, to bring it under control, to measure its effect, and to make due allowance for it. For example, errors of observation were found to follow a definite law, and it became possible to state limits of error in measurements in precise probabilistic terms. In the twentieth century we have seen similar ideas worked out to a high degree of precision: in the theory of sampling, where we are content to scrutinize only a subset of a population, relying on the laws of chance to give us a reasonably representative subset; or in the theory of experimental design, in which unwanted influences are distributed at random in such a way that chance destroys (or reduces to minimal risk) the possibility that they may distort the interpretation of the experiment. Man cannot remove chance effects, but he has learned to control them.

In practice, there is little difference of opinion among the experts as to what should be done in any given set of practical circumstances affected by random influences. But, though they may agree on procedure and interpretation, there underlies the theory of chance

and probability a profound difference of opinion as to the basis of the inferences which derive from probabilistic considerations.

We must now draw a distinction between chance and probability. To nearly all medieval logicians probability was an attitude of mind. It expressed the doubt which a person entertained towards some proposition. It was recognized (e.g., by Aquinas) that there were degrees of doubt, although nobody got so far as to suggest that probability could be measured. It was not necessarily related to the frequency with which an event occurred. Saint Thomas would have considered the word "probability" as equally applicable to the proposition that there was a lost continent of Atlantis as to the proposition that next summer will be a fine one.

The Doctrine of Chances, on the other hand, was related to the relative frequency of occurrence of the various modalities of a class of events. The two ideas have been confounded over the centuries, and even today there are strongly differing schools of thought on the subject. One school takes probability as a more-or-less subjective datum, and would try to embrace all doubtful propositions, whether relating to unique or to repetitive situations, within a probabilistic theory of doubt and belief. The other asserts that numerical probabilities can be related only to relative frequency. Both points of view have been very ably expounded, the main protagonists of the subjective viewpoint being Bruno de Finetti and L. J. Savage and those of the frequency viewpoint, John Venn (1866) and R. von Mises (1928). The two are not, perhaps, irreconcilable, but they have never been successfully reconciled, at least to the satisfaction of the participants in the argument. The nearest approach, perhaps, is that of Sir Harold Jeffreys (1939).

To modern eyes, the matter becomes of critical importance when we realize that all science proceeds essentially from hypotheses of doubtful validity or generality through experiment and confirmation, to more firmly based hypotheses. The problem, then, is whether we can use probability theory, of whatever basic character, in the scientist's approach to forming his picture of the universe. The first man to consider the problem in mathematical detail was Thomas Bayes, a Methodist parson whose paper was published posthumously (1764) and whose name is now firmly attached to a particular type of inference. Shorn of its mathematical trappings, Bayesian inference purports to assign numerical probabilities to alternative hypotheses which can explain observation. It can do so only by assigning prior probabilities to the hypotheses, prior, that is, in the sense that they are given before the observations are collected. Here rests the conflict between the Bayesians and the anti-Bayesians. The former like to express their degree of doubt about the alternative hypotheses at the outset in terms of numerical probabilities, and to modify those probabilities in the light of further experience; the latter prefer to reserve their initial doubts for a final synthetic judgment at the conclusion of the experiment. The course of thought during the nineteenth century was undoubtedly influenced by Laplace, who accepted Bayes's treatment, although recognizing the difficulty of resolving many practical situations into prior alternatives of equal probability.

The basis of the controversy may be set out in fairly simple terms. A naïve statement of an argument in scientific inference would run like this:

> On a given hypothesis a certain event is to be expected;
>
> We experiment and find that the event is reasonably closely realized (or not realized);
>
> We accept (or reject) the hypothesis, or at any rate regard it as confirmed (or not confirmed).

Such an enunciation requires some sophistication. The question is whether, if we interpret "to be expected" in terms of probability in the sense of the Doctrine of Chances (e.g., on the hypothesis that a penny is unbiased the chances are that in 100 tosses it will come down heads about half the times), we can, so to speak, invert the situation and make numerical statements about the *probability of the hypothesis*. Bayes saw the problem, but to attain practical results, he had to assume a postulate to the effect that if a number of different hypotheses were exhaustive and all consonant with the observed event, and nothing is known to the contrary, they were to be supposed to have equal prior probabilities. This so-called Principle of Indifference or of Nonsufficient Reason has been warmly contested by the anti-Bayesians.

There seems to be no decisive criterion of choice between the Bayesian and non-Bayesian approaches. As with attitudes towards frequency or nonfrequency theories of probability, a man must make up his own mind about the criticisms that have been made of each. Fortunately, in practice conclusions drawn from the same data rarely differ—or if they do it appears that the inference is entangled with personal experiences, emotions, or prejudices which are not common to both parties to the dispute.

Until the end of the nineteenth century, chance and probability, however regarded axiomatically, were still considered by most scientists and philosophers alike as expressions of ignorance, not as part of the basic structure of the world. The fall of a die might be the most unpredictable of events, but its unpredictability was due to the fact that we could not compute its trajectory with any accuracy; given enough information about initial conditions and sufficient mathematical skill we could calculate exactly how it would fall and the element of chance would vanish. Notwithstanding the philosophic doubts raised by Hume and his successors about causality, the world was (and still is) interpreted by most people in a causal way. The laws of chance were not *sui generis;* they were the result of the convolution of a multiplicity of causes. As A. Cournot put it, following Aristotle, a chance event was the result of the intersection of many causally determined lines.

This edifice began to crack with the discovery of radioactivity. Here were phenomena which appeared to generate themselves in a basically chance manner, uninfluenced by pressure, temperature, or any external change which man could induce in their environment. It has even been suggested that a truly random sequence could be generated by noting the intervals between impacts in a Geiger counter. It began to look as if chance behavior was part of the very structure of the atomic world, and before long (ca. 1925), P. A. M. Dirac, Werner Heisenberg, and others were expressing subatomic phenomena as waves of probability.

We are still fairly close to the period in which these ideas were put forward, and in assessing them we have to take into account the general cultural and psychological environment of the times. Immediately after the First World War there was an upsurge of revolt against the repressive society of the later nineteenth century, and any idol which could be shown to have feet of clay was joyfully assaulted. Scientists, whether natural or social, are no more immune than poets to such movements. The warmth of the reception given to the theory of relativity (far more enthusiastic than the experimental evidence justified), to the quantum theory, and to Freudian psychology was in part due to this desire to throw off the shackles of the past; and the elevation of chance to a fundamental rule of behavior may have embodied a similar iconoclastic element. It is too soon to say; but now that the honeymoon period is over there are some who would revert to the older view and consider that perhaps it is our ignorance again which is being expressed in the probabilistic element of modern physics.

There remain, then, several important questions on which unanimity is far from being reached: whether a theory of probability can embrace attitudes of doubt of all kinds, whether chance phenomena are part of the basic structure of the world, what is the best method of setting up a theory of inference in terms of probability, whether all probabilities are measurable. Perhaps these questions may not be resolved until a great deal more knowledge is gained about how the human mind works. In the meantime the theory of probability continues to develop in a constructive manner and is an important adjunct to man's efforts to measure and control the world.

BIBLIOGRAPHY

J. Arbuthnot, "An Argument for Divine Providence, Taken From the Constant Regularity Observ'd in the Birth of Both Sexes," *Philosophical Transactions of the Royal Society,* **27** (1710), 186–90. T. Bayes, "An Essay Towards Solving a Problem in the Doctrine of Chances," *Philosophical Transactions of the Royal Society,* **53** (1763), 370–418. Jakob (Jacques) Bernoulli, *Ars conjectandi* (Basel, 1713, posthumous; Brussels, 1968). Rudolf Carnap, *Logical Foundations of Probability* (Chicago, 1950; 2nd ed. 1962). A. A. Cournot, *Essai sur les fondements . . .* (1851), trans. M. H. Moore as *Essay on the Foundations of our Knowledge* (New York, 1956), Chs. IV, V, VI. F. N. David, "Studies in the History of Probability and Statistics, I. Dicing and Gaming," *Biometrika,* **42** (1955), 1; idem, *Games, Gods and Gambling* (London, 1962). Bruno de Finetti, "La Prévision: ses lois logiques, ses sources subjectives," in *Annales de l'Institut Henri Poincaré,* **7** (1937), 1–68; trans. H. E. Kyburg, Jr., in *Studies in Subjective Probability* (New York, 1964). Sir Harold Jeffreys, *Theory of Probability* (Oxford, 1939; 3rd ed. 1961). M. G. Kendall, "On the Reconciliation of Theories of Probability," *Biometrika,* **36** (1949), 101; idem, "Studies in the History of Probability and Statistics, II. The Beginnings of a Probability of Calculus," *Biometrika,* **43** (1956), 1; ibid., V. "A Note on Playing Cards," *Biometrika,* **44** (1957), 260. J. M. Keynes, *A Treatise on Probability* (London, 1921). Pierre Simon, Marquis de Laplace, *Théorie analytique des probabilités* (Paris, 1812); is found in *A Philosophical Essay on Probabilities,* trans. F. L. Truscott and F. L. Emory (London and New York, 1902; New York, 1951). Oystein Ore, *Cardano, The Gambling Scholar* (Princeton, 1953). L. J. Savage, *Foundation of Statistical Inference,* 2nd ed. (New York, 1964). J. P. Süssmilch, *Die Göttliche Ordnung in den Veränderungen des menschlichen Geschlechts aus der Geburt, dem Tode und der Fortpflanzung desselben verwiesen* (Berlin, 1741). Isaac Todhunter, *A History of the Mathematical Theory of Probability . . .* (Cambridge and London, 1865). John Venn, *The Logic of Chance* (London, 1866). R. von Mises, *Wahrscheinlichkeit, Statistik und Wahrheit* (Vienna, 1928); trans. as *Probability, Statistics and Truth* (London, 1939; New York, 1961).

MAURICE KENDALL

[See also Causation; Chance Images; Epicureanism; Fortune; Free Will and Determinism; **Game Theory; Indeterminacy;** Number; **Probability.**]

CHANCE IMAGES

IMAGES MADE by chance (or chance images, for short) are meaningful visual figurations perceived in materials—most often rocks, clouds, or blots—that have not been, or cannot be, consciously shaped by men. An awareness of such images is probably as old as mankind itself; evidence of it has been found in the art of the Old Stone Age. The thoughts stimulated by this awareness, however, are not recorded before classical antiquity. As a chapter in the history of ideas, these thoughts have become the subject of investigation only very recently, so that the following account cannot be more than provisional in many respects.

Strictly speaking, an image made by chance is an absurdity. Explicit, fully articulated images, our experience tells us, must be the result of purposeful activity, which is the very opposite of chance in the sense of mere randomness. The dilemma can be resolved either by (1) attributing a hidden purpose to chance, which thus becomes an agency of the divine will personified under such names as Fate, Fortune, or Nature; or by (2) acknowledging that chance images are in fact rudimentary and ambiguous, and are made explicit only in the beholder's imagination. The former view, characteristic of prescientific cultures, is akin to all the beliefs based on the "ominous" meaning of flights of birds, heavenly constellations, the entrails of sacrificial animals, and countless other similar phenomena. It was prevalent until the Renaissance and has not entirely lost its appeal even today. The latter view, although adumbrated in classical antiquity, found adequate expression for the first time in fifteenth-century Italy; it has been adopted and verified by modern scientific psychologists who made it the basis of projective tests such as the ink blot series named after Hermann Rorschach. Both views, however incompatible, are strongly linked with past and present ideas concerning the nature of artistic activity, in theory as well as in practice.

I

Classical antiquity seems to have confined its attention to chance images of three kinds: those in rocks, blots, and clouds. For the first two, our earliest source is Pliny's *Natural History,* although his references to these phenomena are clearly derived from Greek (probably Hellenistic) literature. He tells of an image of Silenus found inside a block of Parian marble that had been split open with wedges (XXXVI, v) and of "the agate of Pyrrhus on which could be seen Apollo with his lyre and the nine muses, each with her proper attribute, rendered not by art but by nature, through the pattern of the spots" (XXXVII, i). The context from which Pliny lifted these passages cannot be reconstructed; the images, absurdly perfect down to the last iconographic detail, are apparently cited as evidence of the miraculous generative powers of Nature, superior to any man-made artifact. Somewhat more illuminating is Pliny's story about a panting dog in a picture by the famous Hellenistic painter Protogenes (XXXV, x). The artist tried in vain to represent the foam issuing from the mouth of the animal until, in a rage, he hurled a sponge at his panel and thereby achieved the desired result. This dog, Pliny states, "was wondrously made," since the natural effect was the work of *fortuna*. The same story, he informs us, is told of another famous painter, Nealces, with a horse taking the place of the dog. A variant of the latter version, substituting Apelles for Nealces, occurs in the sixty-fourth oration of Dio Chrysostom, which deals with the workings of *fortuna*. Here again the chance image is so perfect as to surpass any human intention. The inference to be drawn from the sponge story, it would seem, is that Fortune reserves such "strokes of luck" only for the greatest of artists, as if on occasion she took pity on their ambition to achieve the impossible.

It must have been these accounts of incredibly perfect chance images that provoked the following skeptical rejoinder from Cicero:

Pigments flung blindly at a panel might conceivably form themselves into the lineaments of a human face, but do you think the loveliness of the Venus of Cos could emerge from paints hurled at random? . . . Carneades used to tell that once, in the quarries of Chios, a stone was split open and the head of a little Pan appeared; well, the bust may not have been unlike the god, but we may be sure that it was not so perfect a reproduction as to lead one to imagine that it had been wrought by Scopas, for it goes without saying that perfection has never been achieved by accident (*De divinatione* I, xiii).

This early hint at the rationalist explanation of chance images corresponds to the classicistic taste that dominated Roman art of the late Republic and the Augustan era (note the references to classic Greek masters). The story of the sponge-throwing painter, in contrast, reflects an admiration for spontaneity, for inspired groping by a great individual as against an impersonal ideal of perfection. If *fortuna* favors only artists of the stature of Protogenes, Nealces, or Apelles, is she not just another name for genius? Such an unclassical (one is tempted to call it romantic) attitude seems to have existed in Hellenistic art, although it cannot be documented from surviving examples. An echo of it may be found in another passage of Pliny's *Natural History* (XXXV, cxlv) that speaks of painters whose unfinished pictures were sometimes even more admirable than their completed work, because they still showed the lines of the original sketch and thus revealed the working of the artist's mind.

The agate of Pyrrhus, too, although obviously mythical, has a bearing on artistic practice. Greeks and Romans greatly admired carved gems of varicolored semiprecious stones, as attested by the large number of preserved specimens. In many of these, the design takes advantage of, and may indeed have been suggested by, the striations of the material. Thus the value of a gem stone was probably measured by its potential in this respect even more than by its rarity, and those that lent themselves particularly well to carving would have been looked upon as miraculous "images made (or at least preshaped) by Nature." How far human skill has been "aided by Nature" in any given case is of course difficult to assess after the carving is finished, although certain gems indicate that the artist wanted to suggest that such aid had been considerable.

The ancient marble sculptor's interest in chance effects, suggested by the tales of images found in cracked blocks, is even harder to verify. One widespread feature of later Greek and Roman decoration, the foliage mask (Figure 1), may have originated in this way. Ladendorf has proposed that it developed from the acanthus ornament crowning Attic grave steles, which sometimes tends to assume the appearance of a human face (Figure 2). This physiognomic effect is so unobtrusive that, in the beginning at least, it could hardly have been intentional. A stele (an upright stone slab or pillar) evokes the image of a standing figure, and its upper terminus thus may be viewed as its "head." Perhaps this notion was unconsciously present in the carver's mind. In any event he must have become aware at some point of the face hidden among the foliage, and from then on the effect was exploited quite explicitly. The foliage mask, then, could be termed an "institutionalized chance image."

Figures that are seen in clouds are noted by Aristotle (*Meteorology* I, ii) and briefly mentioned in Pliny's *Natural History* (II, lxi) and other ancient authors. Because of their instability and remoteness, however, they were not given the significance of the miraculous images made by Nature or Fortune in rocks and blots, and their origin rarely excited speculation. An exception is Lucretius (*De rerum natura* IV, 129ff.), who found them a challenge to his theory that all images are material films given off by objects somewhat in the manner of snakes shedding their outer skin. Since cloud figures are unstable, there cannot be any objects from which these image films emanate; Lucretius therefore postulates the spontaneous generation of such films in the upper air—an ingenious but hardly persuasive solution. By far the most interesting analysis of the phenomenon, linking it for the first time with the

341

FIGURE 1. Foliage Mask. Baalbek, Temple of Bacchus. Second Century (AFTER WEGNER)

FIGURE 2. Acroterium, Grave Stele of Thutimos. Late Fourth Century B.C. EPIGRAPHIC MUSEUM, ATHENS

process of artistic creation, occurs in a memorable dialogue in Philostratus' *Apollonius of Tyana* (II, 22). Apollonius and his interlocutor, Damis, agree that the painter's purpose is to make exact likenesses of everything under the sun; and that these images are make-believe, since the picture consists in fact of nothing but pigments. They further agree that the images seen in clouds are make-believe, too. But, Apollonius asks, must we then assume that God is an artist, who amuses himself by drawing these figures? And he concludes that those configurations are produced at random, without any divine significance; it is man, through his natural gift of make-believe, that gives them regular shape and existence. This gift of make-believe (i.e., imagination) is the common property of all. What distinguishes the artist from the layman is his ability to reproduce his mental images in material form. To Philostratus the difference between cloud figures and painted images would thus seem to be one of degree only: the artist projects images into the pigments on his panel the way all of us project images into the random shapes of clouds, but he articulates them more clearly because of his manual skill. Although this view clearly reflects the growing ascendency of *fantasia* over *mimesis*—of imagination over imitation—that had been asserting itself in the attitude of the ancients toward the visual arts ever since Hellenistic times, it retains the traditional conception of painting and sculpture as crafts or "mechanical arts" as against the "liberal arts." That the artist might be distinguished

342

from the nonartist by the quality of his imagination rather than by his manual training did not occur to Philostratus. If it had, he would have anticipated an achievement of the Renaissance by more than a thousand years. Nor did ancient painters think of the pigments on their panels as a "hunting ground" for images analogous to clouds; they seem, in fact, to have been repelled by clouds—the skies in ancient landscapes are devoid of them, and even where the subject requires them (as in *The Sacrifice of Iphigenia*, Naples) they appear as the merest wisps. This aversion was clearly a matter of aesthetics, not of disability. Ancient painters commanded all the illusionistic techniques for rendering clouds, and bequeathed them to Early Christian art, where clouds are conspicuous.

II

The Middle Ages inherited most of the classical accounts of chance images, but did not respond to all of the three types discussed above. The "lucky blot," known from Pliny's story of Protogenes, seems to have evoked neither repetition nor comment. References to cloud figures occur as a rhetorical device in theological writings, stressing their instability and lack of substance, as when Anselm of Canterbury (*Cur Deus homo*, ed. F. S. Schmitt, Darmstadt [1960], p. 16) compares certain fallacious arguments to "figments painted on clouds" (perhaps indirectly echoing Philostratus); Michael Psellus, in a similar vein, says that demons can change their appearance as easily as the ever-changing configurations of clouds, which may resemble the shape of men, bears, dragons, etc. Albertus Magnus seems to have been the only one to attribute material substance to cloud figures, although his explanation differs from that of Lucretius: exhalations from the earth, he claims, if aided by heavenly constellations, can form in the clouds perfect though lifeless animal bodies, which may actually drop from the sky (*On Meteors*, III, iii, 23, citing Avicenna).

Elsewhere he also records the chance images inside blocks of marble, stressing their miraculous character; he even reports that he himself once saw the head of a bearded king on the cut surfaces of such a block that had just been sawed in two (*On Minerals*, II, iii, 1); all who witnessed the event agreed that Nature had painted this image on the stone. Both of these accounts of "natural miracles" were given popular currency toward the end of the Middle Ages by Franciscus de Retza, who cited the animal body dropping from the sky as well as the head in the marble as arguments for the Immaculate Conception in his *Defensorium inviolatae virginitatis Mariae* (ca. 1400). The scenes were even illustrated in an early printed edition (Figure 3).

By far the most widespread chance images, however, were those of the "agate-of-Pyrrhus" type. The ancients' love of gems continued undiminished throughout the Middle Ages; indeed, these stones were the only artistic relics of the pagan past to enjoy continuous and unquestioned appreciation. Thousands of them were incorporated in medieval reliquaries and other sacred objects, regardless of their pagan subject matter, and reports of chance images recur in treatises on mineralogy from the lapidary of Marbod of Rennes to Ulisse Aldrovandi and Athanasius Kircher. (The accounts of these *pierres imagées* have been collected and analyzed by Baltrušaitis.) Their effect on artistic practice, however, is difficult to measure. One clear-cut —and so far unique—instance was discovered by Ladendorf: the tiny faces hidden among the striations of the multicolored marble columns on the canon table pages of the Gospel Book from Saint Médard, Soissons (Figure 4). The artist who painted these columns in the early years of Charlemagne's reign may have seen such faces in early Christian manuscripts, or he could have "discovered" them in his own brushwork while he was at work. In either case, his intention must have been to characterize the material of these columns as miraculous and uniquely precious—and hence worthy to frame the words of the Lord.

A certain propensity toward chance images seems to have existed throughout medieval art, even though the subject is far from fully explored. Thus, in the Nativity scene of an early Gothic German Psalter, there are no less than three faces on the ground in the immediate vicinity of Saint Joseph (Figure 5). The one farthest to the left appears to have been developed from a piece of drapery; the other two fill interstices between clumps of plants. Perhaps the most plausible explanation for them is that the artist "found" (i.e.,

FIGURE 3. Chance Image in Stone, after Albertus Magnus, from Franciscus de Retza, *Defensorium inviolatae virginitatis Mariae*, Speyer, 1470

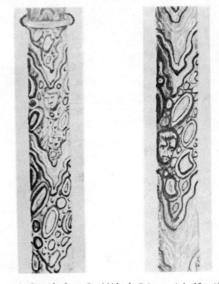

FIGURE 4. Gospels from St. Médard, Soissons, fol. 12v. (detail). Late Eighth Century. BIBLIOTHÈQUE NATIONALE, PARIS (AFTER KOEHLER)

Figure 5. Nativity, *St. Blasien Psalter*, fol. 7v. (detail). German, ca. 1230–35. COLLECTION H. P. KRAUS, NEW YORK. PHOTO COURTESY HARRY BOBER

Figure 6. Foliage Mask on a Console of the "Rider." Bamberg Cathedral. ca. 1230. PHOTO COURTESY HEINZ LADENDORF

Figure 7. Detail, *Hours of Catherine of Cleves*, p. 268. Dutch, ca. 1440. THE PIERPONT MORGAN LIBRARY, NEW YORK

projected) them in the process of copying an older miniature whose stylistic conventions he did not fully understand. His readiness to interpret unfamiliar details physiognomically suggests that he knew the "institutionalized chance image" of the foliage mask, which had been revived at least as early as the twelfth century and was well-established in the repertory of Gothic art (Figure 6). Since these masks sometimes carry inscriptions identifying them as images of pagan nature spirits or demons, the faces in our Nativity may have

been intended to evoke the sinister forces overcome by the Savior.

That Gothic art continued to be receptive to chance images even in its final, realistic phase is strikingly shown by the *Hours of Catherine of Cleves*, a Netherlandish manuscript of ca. 1435–40 distinguished for its elaborate painted borders. One of these consists of butterflies, rendered with painstaking attention to the colorful patterns of their wings. Among them is a butterfly (Figure 7) whose wing pattern resembles a cavernous human face, like that of a decaying corpse come back to life. There can be no question that the effect is intentional, yet it could hardly have been planned from the start; in all likelihood the artist became aware of it only in the process of painting, and then chose to elaborate upon it so that the beholder could share his experience. What made him do so, we may assume, was not only an interest in chance images (there is evidence of this on other pages of the same manuscript) but the role of the butterfly as a symbol of *vanitas*, which associated it with death. Despite such links with orthodox iconography, there is a strong element of playfulness in medieval chance images. The purest instance of this is a drawing of 1493 by the young Albrecht Dürer, one side of which shows a self-portrait, a sketch of his left hand, and a pillow, while six more pillows appear on the other side (Figure 8). Ladendorf was the first to recognize the purpose of these pillows: a search for faces hidden among the folds. Most easily recognizable is the one in the lower left-hand corner—a bearded Turk with a huge turban. Turning the sheet upside down, we also discover that the pillow in the upper left-hand corner contains the craggy face of a man wearing a pointed hat. Since these are the only image-bearing pillows we know of in the history of art, Dürer presumably discovered their physiognomic potential by accident, perhaps while sketching a pillow in preparation of a print or a painting. What enabled him to play this game, however, must have been a familiarity with chance images in other, more traditional materials such as stone. He might indeed have looked upon his pillows as "malleable rocks" from which such images could be elicited by manipulation. Yet he seems to have kept his discovery to himself, so that the pillow-faces never became "institutionalized."

III

The Renaissance phase in the history of our subject begins with the opening sentences of Leone Battista Alberti's treatise *De statua*, written about 1430. Here the origin of sculpture is described as follows:

Those [who were inclined to express and represent . . . the bodies brought forth by nature] would at times observe in tree trunks, clumps of earth, or other objects of this sort certain lineaments which through some slight changes could be made to resemble a natural shape. They thereupon took thought and tried, by adding or taking away here and there, to render the resemblance complete.

Before long, Alberti adds, the primeval sculptors learned how to make images without depending on such resemblances latent in their raw material. This passage is the earliest statement of the idea that what sets the artist apart from the layman is not his manual skill but his ability to discover images in random shapes, i.e., his visual imagination, which in turn gives rise to the desire to make these images more explicit by adding or taking away.

How did Alberti arrive at this astonishing insight? Classical art theory provides no etiology of sculpture, and its etiology of painting is purely mimetic: the first artist traced a shadow cast by the sun. Moreover, in contrast to the agate of Pyrrhus and the heads supposedly discovered in cracked blocks of marble, the chance images in Alberti's tree trunks and clumps of earth are rudimentary rather than miraculously complete. Perhaps the key to the puzzle is the fact that Alberti postulates wood and clay, not stone or marble, as the sculptor's aboriginal materials. If he started out by wondering what the earliest statues were made of, he

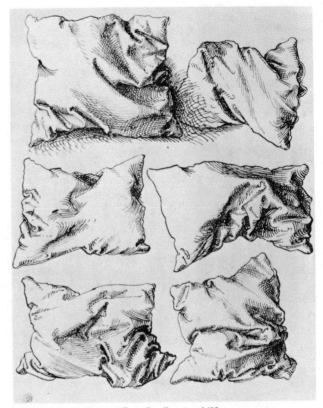

FIGURE 8. Albrecht Dürer, *Pillows*. Pen Drawing, 1493. COLLECTION ROBERT LEHMAN, NEW YORK

could have found an answer in Pliny (XII, i), who concludes a discussion of the central importance of trees in the development of religious practices by stating that the statues of the gods, too, used to be *ex arbore*. In view of the anthropomorphic shape of certain trees, reflected in such myths as that of Daphne turned into a laurel, this must have seemed plausible enough. Another early work of Alberti, the dialogue *Virtus et Mercurius*, has Virtus complaining of persistent abuse at the hands of Fortuna: "While I am thus despised, I would rather be any tree trunk than a goddess," a notion suggestive both of the Plinian tree deities and of the tree trunks in *De statua*. This "truncated" Virtue-in-distress was translated into visual terms by Andrea Mantegna (Figure 9), whose image of her might almost serve as an illustration of the *De statua* text. It also resembles actual idols such as the pair of tree-trunk deities carved by a Teutonic contemporary of Pliny and recently unearthed in a bog near the German-Danish border (Figure 10).

Like many another explorer of new territory, Alberti did not grasp the full significance of what he had

345

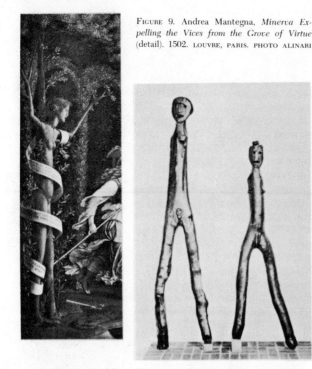

FIGURE 9. Andrea Mantegna, *Minerva Expelling the Vices from the Grove of Virtue* (detail). 1502. LOUVRE, PARIS. PHOTO ALINARI

FIGURE 10. *Idols.* ca. 500 B.C.–A.D. 500. LANDESMUSEUM, SCHLESWIG

discovered. His chance-image theory is subject to two severe limitations: it applies to sculpture only, and to the remote past rather than to present artistic practice. In his treatise on painting, written a few years after *De statua*, he merely cites the ancient shadow-tracing theory but adds that "it is of small importance to know the earliest painters or the inventors of painting." When he mentions the chance images in cracked blocks of marble and on the gem of Pyrrhus recorded by Pliny, he does so in order to fortify his claim that painting is a noble and "liberal" activity, since "nature herself seems to take delight in painting." He also explicitly denies that painting is comparable to the kind of sculpture "done by addition," even though the painter works by adding pigments to a bare surface.

This puzzling gulf that existed in Alberti's mind between the two arts reflects the singular importance he attached to scientific perspective as the governing theory of painting. His treatise focuses on painting as a rational method of representing the visible world, rather than as a physical process, and hence leaves little room for the chance-image etiology he had proposed in *De statua*. We do not know who first applied it to painting and to present-day conditions. The earliest

explicit statement occurs in the writings of Leonardo, but the passage strongly suggests that he learned it from older artists:

If one does not like landscape, he esteems it a matter of brief and simple investigation, as when our Botticelli said that such study was vain, because by merely throwing a sponge full of diverse colors at a wall, it left a stain . . . where a fine landscape was seen. It is really true that various inventions are seen in such a stain. . . . But although those stains give you inventions they will not teach you to finish any detail. This painter of whom I have spoken makes very dull landscapes (*Leonardo's Treatise on Painting*, ed. and trans. Philip McMahon, Princeton [1956], I, 59).

Apparently Leonardo here records an experience he had about 1480, shortly before his departure for Milan; Botticelli, then at the height of his career, plays the role of an "anti-Protogenes" whose views Leonardo turns to his own advantage. In another passage, Leonardo recommends that painters look for landscapes as well as figure compositions in the accidental patterns of stained walls, varicolored stones, clouds, mud, or similar things, which he compares to "the sound of bells, in whose pealing you can find every name and word you can imagine." The spotted walls, clouds, etc., here obviously play the same role as the tree trunks and clumps of earth in *De statua*. Leonardo, moreover, states more clearly than Alberti does that chance images are not objectively present but must be projected into the material by the artist's imagination. While he presents his idea as "a new discovery," there can be little doubt that he did in fact derive it from Alberti, whose writings are known to have influenced his thinking in a good many instances.

That Leonardo should have transferred the chance-image theory from the remote past to the present and from sculpture to painting is hardly a surprise in view of his lack of interest in historical perspectives and his deprecatory attitude toward sculpture. At the same time, the reference to Botticelli (whose remark may well have been aimed at Leonardo himself) suggests that there was some awareness among early Renaissance painters of the role of chance effects in actual artistic practice before Leonardo formulated his chance-image theory of pictorial invention.

That such was indeed the case may be gathered from some visual evidence which in point of time stands midway between Alberti's *De statua* and "Botticelli's stain." Interestingly enough, these are images in clouds, rather than in the more palpable substances that had yielded chance images in medieval art, thus indicating a new awareness of the unstable and subjective character of chance images. The best-known instance is the tiny horseman (Figure 11) in Mantegna's *Saint Sebastian* in Vienna, which has resisted all efforts to explain it in terms of the overt subject matter of the panel. Not only is the image so unobtrusive that most viewers remain unaware of it; it is also incomplete, the hind quarters of the horse having been omitted so as not to break the soft contour of the cloud. Did Mantegna plan it from the very start, or did he discover the horseman only in the process of painting that particular cloud and then, like the primeval sculptors of *De statua*, added or took away a bit here and there in order to emphasize the resemblance? Be that as it may, we can only conclude that he must have been taken with the idea of cloud images, and that he expected his patron, too, to appreciate the downy horseman. This patron would seem to have been a passionate admirer of classical antiquity, for the panel is exceptionally rich in antiquarian detail; the artist even signed it in Greek. Apparently the horseman is yet another antiquarian detail, a visual pun legitimized by the discussion of cloud images in Greek and Roman literature. It has been kept "semi-private" so as not to offend less sophisticated beholders. If this view is correct, the horseman need have no connection at all with the chance images of Alberti, even though Mantegna must have been well acquainted with Alberti's writings.

We know rather less about a second cloud image, contemporary with Mantegna's horseman, that occurs in the *Birth of the Virgin* by the Master of the Barberini Panels. Here a cloud assumes the shape of a dolphin (Figure 12). A possible clue to its meaning is the flight of birds next to it, which may be interpreted as a good omen for the newborn child according to Roman belief. Since the scene takes place in a setting filled with references to pagan antiquity, an "auspicious" flight of birds would be in keeping with the rest; and the cloud-dolphin would then be a further good omen (dolphins having strongly positive symbolic connotations), whether the image was planned or accidentally discovered. Flights of birds as a means of divination are mentioned so frequently in Roman literature that they must have been well-known among fifteenth-century humanists.

These early cloud images, however small and unobtrusive, are the ancestors of a wide variety of figures made of clouds in sixteenth-century painting. Mantegna himself institutionalized the technique in his late work (*Minerva Expelling the Vices from the Grove of Virtue*, 1501–02, Paris, Louvre), Raphael introduced cloud-angels in his *Madonna of Foligno* and *Sistine Madonna*, and Correggio depicted the amorous Jupiter as a cloud in his *Io* (Figure 13). Even the human soul, hitherto shown as a small figure with all the substance of living flesh, could now be given a cloudy, "ectoplasmic" shape, as in El Greco's *Burial of Count Orgaz* (Figure 14). What began as a semi-private visual pun

FIGURE 11. Andrea Mantegna, *St. Sebastian* (detail). ca. 1460. KUNSTHISTORISCHES MUSEUM, VIENNA

FIGURE 12. Master of the Barberini Panels, *Birth of the Virgin* (detail). ca. 1450–75. METROPOLITAN MUSEUM OF ART (ROGERS AND GWYNNE M. ANDREWS FUNDS, 1935), NEW YORK

had become a generally accepted pictorial device for representing incorporeal beings.

It would be fascinating to know whether Leonardo practiced what he preached. If he did, no evidence of chance images derived from spotted walls or similar sources has survived among his known works. A *Madonna and Saints* by one of his Milanese followers indicates that Leonardo's advocacy of chance images was not confined to the theoretical plane. The group is posed against an architectural ruin among whose

FIGURE 13. Correggio, *Jupiter and Io.* ca. 1532. KUNSTHISTORISCHES MUSEUM, VIENNA

FIGURE 14. El Greco, *The Burial of Count Orgaz* (detail). 1586. SANTO TOMÉ, TOLEDO. PHOTO ANDERSON

FIGURE 15. Milanese Master (Bernardo Zenale?), *Madonna and Saints* (detail). ca. 1510–20. SAMUEL H. KRESS COLLECTION, DENVER ART MUSEUM

crumbling stones we discern the face of a bearded man wearing a broad-brimmed hat (Figure 15). Evidently the artist, alerted by Leonardo's teachings, felt that no ancient wall surface was complete without a chance image. The influence of Leonardo's chance-image theory can be seen also in the work of the Florentine painter Piero di Cosimo, who according to Vasari was in the habit of staring at clouds and spotted walls,

"imagining that he saw there equestrian combats and the most fantastic cities and the grandest landscapes." Some of Piero's pictures show extravagantly shaped willow trees with pronounced chance-image features (Figure 16) but based on a close study of actual trees, which he must have gone out of his way to find. Finally, Leonardo's discussion of chance images may have inspired a curious pictorial specialty that flourished mainly in Florence from the late sixteenth to the eighteenth century. These paintings are done on the polished surfaces of agates or other strongly patterned stones in such a way that the colored veins become part of the composition, providing "natural" backgrounds of clouds, landscape, etc., for the figures. They were prized as marvels of nature no less than of art (a description cited by Baltrušaitis terms them "an interplay of *ars* and *natura*") and tended to accumulate in the cabinets of royalty. Linked with the legendary gem of Pyrrhus, they might be defined as elaborated chance images were it not for the fact that the painter's share always remains clearly distinguishable from nature's. Apparently a real merging of the two spheres was deemed aesthetically undesirable.

Despite his interest in unorthodox techniques—confirmed by recent studies which show that he often painted not only with brushes but with his fingers—Leonardo did not favor homemade chance images such as "Botticelli's stain." Nor does he reveal how the images found in spotted walls, etc., are to be transformed into works of art. Apparently he thought of this process as taking place in the artist's mind, rather than on the surface of the painting, where the task of "finishing the detail" would be impeded by the inherent vagueness of images resulting from thrown sponges. His ideal of objective precision, inherited from the early Renaissance, gave way in sixteenth-century art theory to values more attuned to the concept of genius. Among them was *sprezzatura*, a recklessness mirroring inspired frenzy at the expense of rational control, which meant a disregard of accepted usage in literature and a rough, unfinished look in the visual arts. The story of the sponge-throwing Protogenes could now provide a supreme example of such recklessness, as it does for Montaigne (*Essays*, I, xxiv, xxxiv), who cites it to illustrate the close relationship between chance (good luck, *fortuna*) and inspiration.

IV

The chance images discussed so far all have one feature in common—the artist finds them, or pretends to find them, among the random shapes of the outside world. He does not create them but merely discovers them and "makes the resemblance complete" while leaving the identity of the matrix (stone, foliage, pillows, clouds, etc.) untouched. This limitation may help to explain why Leonardo's advice to painters, even though enshrined in the text of his *Treatise on Painting*, had little practical effect until the dawn of the modern era. At that time it was suddenly revived, with appropriate modifications, by the British landscape painter and drawing teacher Alexander Cozens, who in 1785–86 published an illustrated treatise entitled *A*

FIGURE 16. Piero di Cosimo, *The Discovery of Honey* (detail). ca. 1498. WORCESTER ART MUSEUM

New Method of Assisting the Invention in Drawing Original Compositions of Landscape. It describes "a mechanical method . . . to draw forth the ideas" of artists, which consists of making casual and largely accidental ink blots on paper with a brush, to serve as a store of compositional suggestions (Figure 17). Cozens recommends that these blots be made quickly and in quantity, and that the paper be first crumpled up in the hand and then stretched out again. The next step is to select a particularly suggestive sheet of blots, place a piece of transparent paper over it and make a selective tracing; the author cautions us to "preserve the spirit of the blot" by not adding anything that is not suggested by it. The drawing is then finished by adding ink washes.

Cozens cites Leonardo's words about the images to be seen on dirty walls, etc., but adds proudly that he thinks his procedure an improvement, since it permits the artist to produce his chance images at will, without having to seek them out in the world of nature. Oddly enough, he fails to quote the Leonardo passage dealing

FIGURE 17. Alexander Cozens, Blot Landscape, from *A New Method* . . . , London, n.d. 1784–86. METROPOLITAN MUSEUM OF ART (ROGERS FUND, 1906), NEW YORK

FIGURE 18. Grandville, Satire of Romantic Painting, from *Un autre monde*, Paris, n.d. 1844.

350

with "Botticelli's stain," which anticipates his own procedure so closely that one wonders if he was really ignorant of it. The ink blots of Cozens' *Method*, however, are not meant to be entirely accidental; he defines them as "a production of chance, with a small degree of design," since the artist is expected to think of a landscape subject in general terms while producing them. His own sample of such a "blotscape" is clearly a work of art, displaying a highly individual graphic rhythm. Its purpose, he makes clear, is to free the artist from involuntary servitude to conventional schemes of landscape composition by making him relinquish deliberate control of his movements as much as possible in the beginning; the selective tracing of the blots is intended to redress the balance.

To his contemporaries, on the other hand, Cozens' blots seemed sheer chaos, and an occasion for endless ridicule. Neo-classic taste was so opposed to the ideas implicit in the *Method* that it rejected even the hallowed story of Protogenes. In a critique of the pictures shown at the Paris Salon of 1783 (*Le Triumvirat des arts, ou dialogue entre un peintre, un musicien et un poète*, published anonymously as a pamphlet) the poet ridicules one painting by pronouncing it a masterpiece *à la manière de Protogène*. Henry Fuseli notes that "many beauties in art come by accident that are preserved by choice," but is quick to add that these have nothing in common with the sponge of Protogenes or "the modern experiments of extracting compositions from an ink-splashed wall," an obvious reference to Cozens (*Aphorism 153*). Yet Cozens' very notoriety kept his *Method* from being forgotten. Its liberating effect on Constable and Turner, the great Romantic landscape painters of the early nineteenth century, must have been profound.

That Cozens anticipated a general trend toward free, spontaneous brushwork transcribing the artist's creative impulse more directly than before, is amusingly attested by a French cartoon of 1844 (Figure 18) which shows the Romantic painters, with Delacroix in the foreground, as simian virtuosos who do not even bother to look at their canvases while they paint. The *Method* also seems to be the ancestor of the Rorschach ink-blot test. A parlor game based on it enjoyed a certain vogue in England and may have helped to popularize it on the Continent, especially among amateurs. Elaborated blots are to be found in the drawings of Victor Hugo, and in the 1850's the German physician and poet Justinus Kerner produced *Klecksographien*, ink blots on folded paper which he modified slightly to emphasize the chance images he had found in them (Figure 19). He wrote little descriptive poems based on these images and collected this material in his *Hadesbuch*, which remained unpublished until 1890. The belated rediscovery of Kerner's *Klecksographien* makes it likely that they were known to Hermann Rorschach, who used the same folded-paper technique for his tests but substituted oral for graphic interpretation of images.

Meanwhile, Alberti's hypothesis about the origin of sculpture was also being put to the test. In the 1840's Boucher de Perthes, one of the pioneer students of Paleolithic artifacts, collected large numbers of oddly shaped flint nodules which he claimed had been treasured by the men of the Old Stone Age because of their accidental resemblance to animal forms. As evidence he adduced what he regarded as efforts by these primeval sculptors to modify the shape of these "figure stones" so as to make the likeness more palpable. His discovery caught the imagination of other students of "antediluvian antiquity," and figure stones soon turned up in England as well (Figure 20), while the skeptics denounced Boucher de Perthes and his followers as self-deluded or fraudulent. The skeptics eventually won out, but the issue may never be fully resolved; after all, the men of the Old Stone Age might have prized these nodules for their image-bearing quality even if there is no proof that they modified their shapes. Nor was the controversy useless, for it probably alerted students of the Paleolithic to the existence of modified chance images in the cave art of Spain and the Dordogne, which was discovered a few decades later.

The aesthetic attitude of the Romantics not only favored impulsiveness at the expense of rational control; it also undermined the classic view that "painting is mute poetry" by enthroning music as the highest of the arts. To those who espoused this belief, the subject of a picture was little more than a peg on which to hang attractive combinations of form and color. Their most articulate spokesman, James Whistler, began in the early 1860's to call his works "symphonies," "harmonies," "nocturnes," or "arrangements," in order to stress his conviction that descriptive values in painting are as secondary as they are in music; the subject proper was mentioned only as a subtitle, for the benefit of the ignorant public.

Whistler's attitude toward chance effects, far more radical than Cozens', became a matter of public record during his famous libel suit against John Ruskin, who had charged him with "flinging a pot of paint in the public's face." In painting a Nocturne, Whistler stated, "I have . . . meant to indicate an artistic interest alone . . . , divesting the picture from any outside sort of interest which might have been otherwise attached to it. It is an arrangement of line, form and colour first, and I make use of any incident of it which shall bring about a symmetrical result." By "incident," he clearly meant accidental, unforeseen effects, and "symmetrical" to him was a synonym for "harmonious." Some

FIGURE 19. Justinus Kerner, *"Klecksographie,"* from *Das Hadesbuch.* 1857.

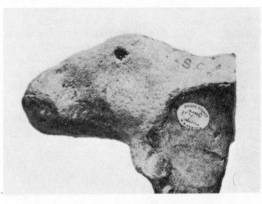

FIGURE 20. Figure Stone. Collection W. M. Newton. AFTER JOURNAL OF THE BRITISH ARCHAEOLOGICAL ASSOCIATION, MARCH 1913

of Whistler's works are indeed so divested of "outside interest" that without the aid of the subtitle we would be hard put to recognize the subject. How much accident went into the painting of them is impossible to say, for we are approaching the point where chance and intention become inseparable.

Unlike Cozens, who still wanted his blots to yield recognizable images, Whistler solicits chance effects for the sake of "symmetry"; representation, taken for granted as the aim of art from the beginning of time, is about to give way to a new primary reality, that of the brush stroke itself, and when this happens we lose the frame of reference that enables us to differentiate between accident and purpose. The nonfigurative art of the twentieth century is strikingly forecast in Whistler's thinking (and to a lesser extent his practice).

The retreat from likeness that began with Impressionism would seem to leave no room for the concept of images made by chance. Not surprisingly, the subject is disregarded—as extra-aesthetic, we may assume—in theories keyed to Cubism and abstract art. Still, an awareness of it persisted, as evidenced by the following story, which Picasso told to Françoise Gillot. During the most austere phase of "Analytical Cubism," when he and Braque were working in closely related styles, Picasso one day went to look at his friend's latest work. Suddenly, he became aware that there was a squirrel in the picture, and pointed it out to Braque, who was rather abashed at this discovery. The next day Braque showed him the picture again, after reworking it to get rid of the squirrel, but Picasso insisted he still saw it, and it took yet another reworking to banish the animal for good. Whatever its literal truth, this anecdote suggests that the artist's imagination remains basically iconic, and hence ready to find images where none were intended, even under the discipline of an abstract style. Picasso's own later work, from the 1930's on, abounds in chance images of every sort. The most striking cases occur among his sculpture, such as a bull's head composed of the seat and handlebars of a bicycle, or a monkey's face made of a toy automobile (Figure 21). Making the resemblance explicit here involves, in the first instance, no more than putting the bicycle parts together in a novel way; in the second,

the artist forces us to share his interpretation of the toy automobile by constructing the rest of the animal around it. Perhaps it was visual adventures of this kind that made him recall the story of Braque's squirrel some thirty years after the event.

During the interval, the artistic climate of the Western world had been thoroughly transformed by Dada and Surrealism, which acclaimed chance as the basis of aesthetic experience. As early as 1916–17, Hans Arp was producing compositions of torn bits of paper which he claimed were "arranged according to the laws of chance"; later, he wrote eloquently in praise of "the Muse of Chance." Marcel Duchamp, the most influential member of the movement, was an equally persuasive advocate and practitioner of chance effects. What the Dadaists sought to elicit was not chance images so much as "chance meetings"—unexpected juxtapositions of objects which by their very incongruity would have a liberating effect on the imagination. The creative act to them was a spontaneous gesture devoid of all conscious discipline. Surrealism supported this outlook with an elaborate theoretical framework invoking the authority of Sigmund Freud for its view of the unconscious. It also invented a number of new pictorial techniques, or variations of older ones such as ink blots, for soliciting chance images, its orientation being unabashedly iconic. Nor was this reversal of the retreat from likeness confined to the Surrealists; the same trend can be found among artists independent of or only loosely linked with the movement. The result has been a renewed awareness of the link between chance and inspiration. The sponge-throwing Protogenes, were his story better known today, would be the ideal hero of many mid-twentieth-century artists.

V

The history of our subject in Western civilization has a close parallel in the Far East, although the evidence is even more fragmentary and its frame of reference difficult to interpret. As early as the eighth century, toward the end of the T'ang dynasty, there were Chinese painters using procedures astonishingly similar to Cozens' *Method*. Their style, called *i-p'in* ("untrammeled"), is known only from literary accounts such as that concerning one of them, Wang Mo:

Whenever he wanted to paint a picture, he would first drink wine, and when he was sufficiently drunk, would spatter the ink onto the painting surface. Then, laughing and singing all the while, he would stamp on it with his feet and smear it with his hands, besides swashing and sweeping it with the brush. The ink would be thin in some places, rich in others; he would follow the shapes which brush and ink had produced, making these into mountains, rocks, clouds, and water. Responding to the movements of his hand and

FIGURE 21. Pablo Picasso, *Baboon and Young* (detail). 1951.
MUSEUM OF MODERN ART (MRS. SIMON GUGGENHEIM FUND), NEW YORK

following his inclinations, he would bring forth clouds and mists, wash in wind and rain, with the suddenness of Creation. It was exactly like the cunning of a god; when one examined the painting after it was finished he could see no traces of the puddles of ink (S. Shimada, 1961).

Such a display of *sprezzatura* was surely an extreme manifestation of the *i-p'in* style. Yet Wang Mo and the other "untrammeled" painters had a catalytic effect upon the development of Sung painting analogous to that of Cozens on the Romantics. Their works may not have survived for long, but descriptions of their methods did, providing future artists in both China and Japan with a model of the creative process stressing individual expression and an exploratory attitude toward the potentialities of ink technique.

There are later accounts, ranging from the eleventh to the nineteenth century, of painters soliciting chance images in ways comparable to those of the *i-p'in* pioneers. None of the surviving examples, however, approach the freedom of Cozens' "blotscapes." It is hard to say, therefore, how accurately the literary sources reflect actual practice. One recurrent element in these accounts is the claim that the work—almost invariably a landscape—looks as if "made by Heaven" or "brought forth with the suddenness of Creation," rather than like something made by man. Such terms of praise imply that the picture in question seems completely effortless and unplanned; a work of nature, not a work of art. This aesthetic ideal must have led the Chinese to the discovery that certain kinds of veined marble could be sliced in such a way that the surface suggested the mountain ranges and mist-shrouded valleys characteristic of Sung landscapes. The marble slabs would be framed like paintings and supplied with an evocative inscription (Figure 22). Since they were small,

durable, and produced in large quantities, it seems likely that some of them reached the West with the expansion of the China trade in the eighteenth century. If so, these Far Eastern chance images may have helped to stimulate the train of thought that produced Cozens' *Method*.

BIBLIOGRAPHY

Jurgis Baltrušaitis, "Pierres imagées," *Aberrations, quatre essais sur la légende des formes* (Paris, 1957). Ernst Gombrich, *Art and Illusion* (New York, 1960). H. W. Janson, "After Betsy, What?", *Bulletin of the Atomic Scientists,* **15** (1959), 68ff.; idem, "The 'Image Made by Chance' in Renaissance Thought," *De Artibus Opuscula XL, Essays in Honor of Erwin Panofsky* (New York, 1961), pp. 254–66. Ernst Kris and Otto Kurz, *Die Legende vom Künstler* (Vienna, 1934). Heinz Ladendorf, "Zur Frage der künstlerischen Phantasie," *Mouseion, Studien . . . für Otto Förster* (Cologne, 1960), pp. 21–35. John Plummer, *The Hours of Catherine of Cleves* (New York and London, 1966). Patrik Reuterswärd, "Sinn und Nebensinn bei Dürer," *Gestalt und Wirklichkeit, Festgabe für Ferdinand Weinhandl* (Berlin, 1967), pp. 411–36. Karl Schefold, "Zur Frage der künstlerischen Phantasie," *Antike Kunst,* **4,** No. 2 (1961), 79. S. Shimada, "Concerning the I-p'in Style of Painting—I," *Oriental Art,* n.s. **7,** No. 2 (1961), 3–11. Osvald Siren, *Chinese Painting,* 3 vols. (New York, 1956), I, 216.

H. W. JANSON

[See also Chance; China; Fortune, Fate, and Chance; **Genius;** Iconography; Mimesis; *Virtù.*]

CHINA IN WESTERN THOUGHT AND CULTURE

LIKE THE West itself, China possesses an ancient civilization of great complexity that is difficult to comprehend quickly and fully.

Before 1514, Europeans learned of China mainly through intermediaries, a few travelers, and luxury imports. In the sixteenth century China was thought to be a "Mightie Kingdome," technologically more advanced than Europe. The Europeans of the seventeenth century were told by the Jesuits that China had a rational society of great antiquity and continuous development that would have to be incorporated, by one means or another, into their Christian, monogenetic view of the world. Both the Jesuits and the *philosophes* of the Enlightenment saw China as a model of Enlightened Despotism. Artists and connoisseurs of the eighteenth century were intrigued with China as the source of exotic *objets d'art* and as the home of

FIGURE 22. Landscape of Veined Marble. Chinese, ca. 1800(?)
PRIVATE COLLECTION, NEW YORK

an imaginary, happy people who came to life in the paintings on porcelain. The reaction against China as a rational model and as a source of exotic delight came in the nineteenth century. While Sinologists sought to understand the China of historical reality, other Europeans esteemed Chinese poetry and culture as being aesthetically superior, and worthy of study and imitation. There were Westerners who also derided China as a stagnant, inferior society that had nothing to offer the West but problems. The modernizing, nationalizing, and communizing of China produced the contemporary fear of China as a nemesis of Western culture.

I

In antiquity China gradually received a delineation in Western thought which set it apart from the rest of Asia, especially India, as an independent civilization. Trade on an important scale convinced the Romans of China's advanced technical capability, but the ideas of China, even in arts and crafts, left few deep or lasting imprints upon Roman culture. From the fourth century A.D. to the return of Marco Polo to Venice, nearly a millennium later, medieval Europe almost lost sight of China as an independent civilization and it again became an undifferentiated part of a vague or mythical Asia.

The restoration of overland communications by the Mongols from 1215 to 1350 permitted Christian missionaries and merchants to visit China (Cathay) and enabled them to prepare accounts of their experiences there. But even commentators as acute as Marco Polo and Odoric of Pordenone were unable to provide insights into Chinese thought, probably because they did not command the language. What the European reporters of the Mongol era accomplished was to re-awaken interest in China as an advanced, wealthy, and independent civilization. It was not until the establishment in the sixteenth century of permanent relations by the sea routes that Europe began to acquire a sense of the depth and sophistication of Chinese thought and culture.

The sea passage opened to India by the Portuguese in 1499 was extended to the coast of south China by 1514. With the establishment of direct intercourse the Portuguese and their associates in Europe eagerly sought information on the merchandise, military potential, religion, and customs of the Chinese. Their concern to learn about religion and customs was originally inspired by the fear that the hated Muslims might be firmly entrenched in China, as they were in India and southeast Asia. The Portuguese were quick to learn, however, that the obstacles to intercourse with China were not created by the Moors but by the Chinese themselves. The Ming policy of isolation severely restricted foreign intercourse, but a few Europeans still managed to penetrate China illegally. The earliest reports to reach the West based upon direct experience came from Europeans who were prisoners in China.

In Europe the accounts of the Portuguese prisoners were used as sources by the chroniclers of the discoveries, Fernão Lopes de Castanheda and João de Barros. The chroniclers also garnered whatever information they could from the oral reports of European merchants and sailors and natives coming from China itself, or from Eastern ports where information on China was current. Barros had a Chinese slave who read and abstracted materials for him from Chinese books that had been expressly collected for this purpose in the East. The Portuguese chronicles, like most of the previous accounts, are limited to descriptions of the physical aspects of life, political institutions, and history, and the most striking and obvious social practices.

Observers and writers of the Catholic orders provided the first glimpses of China's religious and intellectual life. The Portuguese Dominican, Gaspar da Cruz, after spending several months in south China in 1556, presented in his *Tractado . . .* (Evora, 1569) a rounded and detailed account of life in China. In obedience to orders from Pope Gregory XIII, the Spanish Augustinian, Juan González de Mendoza, completed his comprehensive *Historia . . . del gran Reyno de la China* (Rome, 1585). It was quickly translated into most European languages and soon became one of the best selling and most widely quoted books of the day. The first systematic Jesuit work in which China figures prominently is the compendium of Giovanni Petri Maffei entitled *Historiarum Indicarum libri XVI* (Florence, 1588). Maffei's sketch of China is based in large part upon the manuscript descriptions prepared by Alessandro Valignano, the notable Jesuit Visitor to the Asian mission. Richard Hakluyt in his *Voyages* (1599) published, in English translation, a small discourse prepared by the Jesuits in China which summarized briefly what the missionaries had learned of Chinese civilization to that time.

In their descriptions of China the sixteenth-century religious observers in the field and the compilers in Europe show a fresh and lively interest in Chinese language, customs, arts, thought, and religious practices. The Jesuits are the first to undertake the systematic study of the Chinese language, the tool essential to the penetration of learning. Aside from describing the peculiarities of the Chinese language, certain of the more sophisticated commentators begin to speculate on the possible relationships between Chinese pictographs, Egyptian hieroglyphs, and the Amerindian languages of the New World. Chinese books on ceremonies, laws, sciences, arts, and history were collected and sent to Europe. Excerpts from some of these books were translated in the Philippines and then relayed to Europe. Mendoza, apparently on the basis of such translations, seeks to give a complete list of the names, chronological limits, and great achievements of the Chinese dynasties. All of the writers comment admiringly on the architectural monuments, great cities, and excellent social organization of the Chinese. Close attention is paid to Chinese methods and organization in education and to the examination system for state offices. The religious writers comment favorably on the treatment of women, and on the maintenance by the state of almshouses and hospitals. While their admiration in these cases is genuine, it should also be remembered that the religious commentators were always writing for the edification of their European readers.

Certain of the sixteenth-century religious writers are highly critical of the content of Chinese learning. More than once the Europeans remark with disdain on the unsophisticated character of Chinese astronomy, mathematics, and geography. The knowledge of the Chinese in these fields is judged to be limited to empirical observations of the sort that people everywhere make. Chinese science is esteemed to be in the same primitive state that the European sciences were in before Aristotle organized them and before Christianity enlightened them.

In their social life the Chinese are said to suffer from gross superstition, inhumane tortures, unnatural practices, and excessive preoccupation with pleasures of the flesh. Their three principal religions—Confucianism, Buddhism, and Taoism—do little, in the estimation of the Christians, to raise the moral tone of Chinese personal life. Confucianism, with its stress upon attaining the five virtues and an orderly society, approaches truth more closely than the other two faiths. Buddhism, which teaches a primitive notion of immortality, is otherwise fraught with obvious errors that are easily refuted. Neither the Taoists nor the Buddhists show any interest in learning and their priests are reviled for their evil and servile behavior.

To the Europeans of the sixteenth century, China was a "Mightie Kingdome" whose major art was government, or the effective political and social organization of a large and heavily peopled nation. Its civilization was admired for longevity, continuity, and cohesiveness. In the arts and crafts it was thought to be as advanced as Europe, perhaps even more so. Its limitations in theoretical science, in personal morality, and in appreciation of religious truth were attributed to its ignorance of Christianity. Once China had been evangelized, the inference is clear that it would necessarily become worthy of emulation by Europe.

II

The Jesuits of the last generation of the sixteenth century had directed their efforts toward the development of a policy and program that would help them to penetrate the Chinese mainland and establish relations with the highest levels of cultivated society. On the basis of their experiences at Macao, the Jesuits under Valignano's leadership decided to pursue a policy of "accommodation," or cultural compromise. It was in this conciliatory spirit that the Jesuits began to study seriously Chinese language, customs, and learning. Matteo Ricci, an Italian priest, appeared on the Chinese mainland in 1583, established cordial relations with Chinese officials and scholars, and ultimately made his way to the imperial court in Peking.

Ricci resided at Peking from 1601 to his death in 1610. During that decade he won the confidence of the Ming Emperor and the Confucian literati through his gracious and dignified bearing, his polite and intelligent absorption in Chinese learning, and his sincere and sophisticated efforts to explain Western science and Christian teachings in terms that could be appreciated and understood by the learned and tolerant. While writing of Western thought and religion in Chinese, Ricci composed a manuscript history of the introduction of Christianity to China. His Italian text, and references from his *Journals*, were translated into Latin by Father Nicolas Trigault while on a sea voyage from China to Europe. Trigault published Ricci's work in five books under the title *De Christiana expeditione apud Sinas* . . . (Rome, 1615). This account was quickly accepted throughout Europe as the official, best informed, and most recent exposition on China and the progress of Christianity there. Within a few years after its appearance, translations were issued in French, German, Spanish, and Italian. The first and the last of Ricci's books deal with China; the others are mainly concerned with the history of the mission.

Ricci, unlike Mendoza, was a close student of China's thought and religions. Since he lived in China at a time when Buddhism and Taoism were degenerating, his works exhibit forthright scorn for them. Especially repellent are Buddhist practices which appear to be devilish parodies of Christian rites. The "delirium" and "ravings" of the Taoists about Lao-Tze he attributes to the inspiration of the devil. Confucianism, the official thought of the literati, is much more to Ricci's taste. Confucius he sees as the equal of the best pagan philosophers of antiquity and superior to many of them. The emphasis in Confucianism upon morality, rationalism, public order, and teaching by precept and ex-

355

ample appeal to Ricci as being in accord with Christian principles. He points out further that the Confucianists have no idols, believe in one God, and revere the principle of reward for good and punishment for evil.

The Chinese literati convinced Ricci that Confucianism was not a competing faith but rather a set of moral precepts which was used for the proper government and general welfare of the state. Ricci was also led to believe that Confucianism "could derive great benefit from Christianity and might be developed and perfected by it" (Gallagher, p. 98). It was Ricci's simplistic presentations of early Confucianism, uncomplicated by the subtleties of later exegesis, that led several generations of Jesuits to believe that China could best be won by close study of the Confucian Classics, by alliance with a native literati devoted to its moral precepts, and by conversion of the leading lights of the realm and the emperor himself to Christianity. To the Jesuits at home such a program seemed congenial and likely, for it paralleled closely the educational, social, and conversion policies that they were then following in Europe.

The Jesuit successors of Ricci in China included a number of mathematicians and scientists who continued to advance the cultural mission. Reports on their progress began to appear in Europe at mid-century. Alvaro Semedo, a Portuguese Jesuit, published at Madrid in 1642 a work on the empire of China in which he pays far greater attention to secular affairs than Ricci had. He also gives the text of and explanatory notes for the Nestorian monument found at Sianfu in 1625. He informs Europe about the wars being fought between the Ming and the Manchus. More material on the calamitous events taking place in north China was provided with the publication of Father Martin Martini's De bello Tartarico historia (Rome, 1654). In the following year Martini published his Novus Atlas Sinensis (Amsterdam), the first scientific atlas and geography of China and one that remains a standard reference work. In 1658 Martini published at Munich his Sinicae historiae, the first history of China written by a European from Chinese annals. In the meantime Father Michel Boym had returned to Europe to announce in 1654 the conversion to Christianity of members of the expiring Ming family and court. Far more important for European science and thought was the publication of Boym's Flora Sinensis (Vienna, 1656), a work comparable in intellectual merit to Martini's Atlas.

The Jesuits also published Latin translations of selected Confucian Classics. Prospero Intorcetta issued the translation by Ignatius da Costa of the Ta Hsüeh ("Great Learning") in his Sapientia sinica (Goa, 1662). At Paris in 1673, Intorcetta published his own transla-

tion of the Chung yung (Doctrine of the Mean). Fourteen years later a group of French Jesuits headed by Philippe Couplet published the Confucius Sinarum Philosophus (Paris) and dedicated it to King Louis XIV. It contains translations of the Classics previously published as well as the Lun Yü ("Analects"). Francisco Noël in his Sinensis imperii libri classici sex (Prague, 1711) republished the earlier translations and added to them his own version of the Meng-tzu ("Mencius"), the Hsiao ching ("Filial Piety"), and the Hsiao hsüeh ("Moral Philosophy for Youths"), a small work of interpretation by Chu Hsi (1130–1200) that was then used in China for elementary instruction in the Classics. The Classics selected by the Jesuits for translation were those which had been given new prominence by Chu Hsi and the Neo-Confucianists of the orthodox school then dominant in China.

While the Jesuits provided scholarly treatises and translations of the Confucian Classics, the merchants and diplomatic emissaries of Europe supplied by their accounts a less sophisticated and a more impressionistic documentation on China and its people. The Dutch, who had been sailing directly to the East since 1595, became particularly aggressive in the 1620's as they sought to secure a monopoly of the trade with China. In connection with these efforts they established a fort and settlement in southern Taiwan in 1624. But with the dynastic troubles that swept China, Dutch hopes for an expanded trade were quickly disappointed. Once the Ch'ing dynasty took over at Peking, the Dutch tried to negotiate directly at the capital. But the embassies sent to Peking in 1656, 1667, and 1685 produced few concrete results, and so no further efforts were made to establish legitimate trading relations with China.

The Dutch produced a number of independent accounts of China that were published in Europe between 1644 and 1670. Isaac Commelin issued a collection of early Dutch travel accounts in 1644 that was followed two years later by the publication of William Bontekoe's Journal. These reminiscences paint a picture of the Chinese that is far different from the glowing and adulatory image of an ancient, rational society created by the Jesuits. To the Dutch observers the Chinese were sinister, devoid of all virtue, and experts in treachery. The Dutch emissary, Johann Nieuhof, in his account of the embassy of 1665, presents a more balanced view of China based both on the Jesuit writers and his own experiences. Olfert Dapper, a Dutch physician, compiled in Holland the reports of the second Dutch embassy to Peking, and in 1670 issued an encyclopedic compendium on China gleaned from the embassy descriptions and a wide range of other sources. His book, entitled Atlas Chinensis in its English translation, is often erroneously attributed to Arnoldus

Montanus. The Dutch accounts share a distrust of the Chinese and a skeptical view of China's vaunted civilization. The Dutch also provided Europe with its first comprehensive descriptions of the Chinese island of Taiwan, and of the widespread ruin produced on the mainland by the dynastic wars.

III

The Jesuits were meanwhile faced with a crisis of their own, the Rites Controversy. In its origins this bitter struggle within the Catholic Church can be traced to Ricci's view, which stressed the idea that no essential conflict existed between Confucianism in its pristine form and the tenets of Christianity. The original doctrines of Confucius, according to Ricci, taught monotheism and possibly even contained a primitive knowledge of Jehovah. Corruption of ancient Confucianism had taken place over the centuries as was clearly demonstrated by the growth of Taoism and the successful introduction of Buddhism into China.

Father Nicolas Longobardi, the Jesuit successor of Ricci at Peking, was himself skeptical that the ancient Chinese had knowledge of the true God. The Dominican and Franciscan missionaries, who began to evangelize in south China in the 1630's, were hostile to "accommodation" in any form. They branded all the Chinese sects as idolatrous, and initially made no serious efforts to study the language or to understand Chinese civilization. The two methods of evangelizing quickly came into conflict, as each group embarrassed and outraged the other. It was not long before the issue was joined in Europe as well as in the East.

At first the controversy raged over the question as to whether or not the ancient Chinese had a conception of the true God. Soon this debate led to the more practical question of the Chinese term best suited to render in its full significance the Christian conception of God, a problem that the Jesuits had earlier resolved in Japan by introducing the Latin word *Deus* into Japanese. But in China, where the Jesuit linguists knew that new terms could not so readily be added to the language, and where the Jesuits held that there already existed a primitive conception of Jehovah, the question of terminology could not be so adroitly handled. A host of other Christian terms, "soul" and "spirit" for example, could not easily be given Chinese equivalents that would carry with them the overtones that these words and concepts necessarily must have for believers. To the Dominicans and Franciscans the Confucianists for all their learning were simple atheists or agnostics who taught a materialistic doctrine inimical to the Christian faith. They were particularly outraged when the Jesuits permitted their Christian converts to continue performing ancestral rites. The Jesuits, following the logic of their original position, held that these rites were social and political rather than religious ceremonies.

The controversialists first appealed to Rome for an opinion in 1645. Pope Innocent X took a position that was critical of the Jesuit policies. But in 1656, Pope Alexander VII took a benign attitude on the question of the "Chinese rites" and granted that they should be permissible under certain conditions. The Dominican, Domingo Fernández Navarrete, then assumed leadership in the struggle against the Jesuits. In China, where he was superior of the Dominican mission from 1664, Navarrete gathered a mass of data relating to the "terms" and "rites" questions. On the basis of these he prepared two imposing and authoritative volumes called *Tratados historicos, politicos, ethicos y religiosos de la Monarchia de China* (Rome, 1674). While it was a powerful attack upon the Jesuit position, Navarrete's book was also an excellent compilation of observations on Chinese life, customs, and practices.

At this juncture the authorities in Rome became understandably confused and disturbed over the Rites Question. The Congregation of the Propaganda in Rome decided to include the China question among the problems of general missionary activity and procedure then under investigation. The learned of Europe were consulted and began to take sides on the question. The *Missions étrangères* in Paris, which had increasingly become critical of the Jesuit effort to dominate the mission field, urged the Holy See to dispatch an Apostolic Vicar to China. Charles Maigrot, sent to China in this capacity, stood firmly in his mandate of 1693 against the practices being followed by the Jesuits. In Europe the Jansenists joined forces with those who denounced the Jesuit practices in China. The faculty of the Sorbonne in 1700 condemned the view advanced by the Jesuit, Louis Le Comte, that the primitive Chinese had practiced morality while the rest of the world still lived in corruption. The Rites Controversy, as it became involved with the Jesuit-Jansenist debate, threatened to produce an irreparable split within the Church.

In a dramatic effort to investigate and resolve the controversy, Pope Clement XI sent a special legate to China in the person of Charles de Tournon, Patriarch of Antioch. The De Tournon legation arrived at Canton in 1705 to begin its investigation. The atmosphere blackened quickly when, in 1706, De Tournon roundly denounced the Chinese, including the emperor, as atheists. Opposed on all sides for his ignorance and intolerance, the legate was condemned and arrested by the Chinese. De Tournon died in China in 1710 without retracting. In Europe the Papacy forbade further controversy, and in 1715 issued the constitution *Ex illa die* which clearly condemned the Jesuit position.

357

Controversy nonetheless continued, both in Europe and China, until a strong papal pronouncement, *Ex quo singulari,* was issued in 1742 requiring the Jesuits in China to take a special oath to abide by the papal decisions.

IV

Étienne de Silhouette, a pupil of the Jesuits, wrote in his *Idée générale du gouvernement . . . des Chinois* (Paris, 1729) that the controversies over the Chinese Rites "have given rise in the minds of everyone to a desire to know China" (Rowbotham, p. 145). He might also have observed that the question of the Rites and the religious, philosophical, linguistic, and social questions linked to it, had long been of deep interest and concern to intellectuals both inside and outside the Society. The compilation of Athanasius Kircher, *China Illustrata* (Amsterdam, 1667), an important work by a Jesuit scholar who had never been to China, inaugurated for the last generation of the seventeenth century the European age of erudition on things Chinese. Kircher's huge tome, with its numerous illustrations, was quickly reissued in Dutch, English, and French translations, and it thereafter became the starting-point for those who wrote or thought about China. Kircher's distinction as a scholar, his interest in the comparative study of languages, his analytical presentation of the Nestorian monument, his perceptive comments on flora and fauna, and his incorporation of authentic and numerous engravings of Chinese persons and scenes all combined to produce a work of enduring value and persistent influence.

The Chinese language with its peculiar system of characters had intrigued the earliest commentators. Sample characters began to appear in European publications of the late sixteenth century. While a practical knowledge of Chinese was acquired by most of the missionaries to China, the scientific study of the Chinese language in Europe emerged in the seventeenth century through diverse routes. Jacob Golius in the Netherlands first became interested in the Chinese language by way of his Arabic and Persian studies. Students of Near Eastern languages were given an even better starting-point when Kircher published parallel columns of Syriac and Chinese (also Romanizations) copied from the Nestorian monument. Andreas Müller, the provost of Berlin and a student of Near Eastern languages, was one of the first to use the Nestorian inscriptions and other available materials in his fruitless efforts to produce a key for the easy understanding of Chinese. His contemporary in England, John Webb, published in 1669 a book in which he sought to prove that Chinese was the primitive language spoken from the time of Adam to Noah, and that it had remained in a petrified condition ever since.

When Father Philippe Couplet brought two Chinese converts to Europe in 1685, the Jesuit and one of his charges were quizzed by linguists at Oxford, Berlin, and Vienna about the nature of the Chinese language. Another Chinese convert remained in Paris to work on a dictionary that the French Jesuits were preparing as a tool for missionaries in the field. By 1700 European scholars had learned from their investigations of Chinese something about the differences between the literary and spoken languages; the tonal system and dialects of the spoken tongue; the monosyllabic nature of the characters; the absence of grammar and inflection; the historical evolution of the characters; and the various styles of calligraphy. They were not able, however, to produce the key either to Chinese or to the hieroglyphs of Egypt, which a number of them vainly sought.

European interest in the Chinese language was originally linked to the general Renaissance concern with Hebrew and Egyptian as primitive and emblematic languages; to the efforts of the rationalists to discover the primitive language from which all others were supposed to derive; to the hopes of certain optimists who sought to find a language more universal than Latin, and to the ambitions of others to construct an artificial and perfected philosophical language for use in the arts and sciences. Chinese appealed to language theorists because the characters, they believed, were based on concepts rather than arbitrary 'sounds. Seventeenth-century linguists thought this conceptual basis essential to the construction of a universal language.

Some interested scholars thought of Chinese as the lost language of Noah, or as the primitive language of all mankind; others persisted in holding the belief that the revival of Chinese would restore the languages of the world to that perfect condition which had obtained before Babel. Leibniz hoped to use elements from Chinese in developing a philosophical language that would replace Latin and help to make direct communication possible among the intellectuals of the world.

Closely related to the confusion of tongues was the problem of China's antiquity and history, and its relationship to orthodox Christian and Western beliefs in monogenesis. The publication of Martini's *Historiae sinicae* (1658) set the stage for a fundamental controversy over historical chronology which was finally to shatter Western concepts based upon the Bible. Issac Vossius, an eminent Dutch scholar who was avowedly an ardent admirer of the Chinese, published his *Dissertatio de vera aetate mundi . . .* (The Hague, 1659), the first essay to examine the implications of Martini's historical data for Western thought. Martini's book, according to Vossius, showed that China's history antedated the universal deluge, that its civilization was continuous, and that its historical records took no notice of the Flood. Vossius, casting Christian tradition aside, proceeded directly to the conclusion that the history of man was fourteen hundred and forty years older than it was commonly supposed to be. The reason for the error in the West was the tendency of the Christian chroniclers to rely upon Hebrew texts rather than upon the Septuagint version of the Old Testament. Vossius likewise concluded that, because the Flood is not mentioned in the Chinese annals, the probability is that it was not universal but simply an event in the history of the Jews. Vossius, on the basis of his faith in the Chinese annals, thus reduced the Bible to a book of local history (Pinot, p. 205).

The critics of Vossius, especially Georg Horn, stressed his rashness in accepting uncritically the evidence of the Chinese annals. They also attacked the authenticity of China's historical traditions and the accuracy of Martini's chronological calculations. A tendency gradually developed, however, to effect a reconciliation of Chinese and biblical history through numerous elaborate devices, including the use of the Septuagint chronology suggested by Vossius. The Chinese annals were thought to be at best distorted renditions of the events related in Genesis. The Chinese, it was surmised, could recall their antediluvian history through remembrances preserved for them by Noah's family. The sage emperors of China were identified with Adam, Cain, Enoch, and Noah. Once such identifications had been established, it became possible to argue that the Chinese annals provided verification for the historical authenticity of Genesis.

The Jesuits, in part because of their position in the Rites Controversy, were compelled to uphold the veracity of the Chinese annals. In 1686 Philippe Couplet published a *Tabula chronologica monarchiae sinicae* . . . (Paris), an effort at reconciling Chinese and Christian chronologies by trying to show that concord existed between the Septuagint and the Chinese records. In so doing he added fourteen hundred years to the period between creation and the life of Abraham. But this solution failed to satisfy either the intellectuals of Europe or the missionaries in China. The Bible was hereafter used historically by the missionaries in China mainly for the purpose of filling in gaps or of explaining obscure references in the Chinese annals. In Europe the Bible as a source for world chronology increasingly fell into desuetude. Even in the 1970's we are required to use concordances to reconcile Chinese and European dates.

In their conception of the beginnings of the world the Europeans were committed to a search for common origins. The ancient civilizations of Persia and Egypt were familiar to the writers of antiquity and the Bible,

and so could be brought into universal history through these channels. China raised an almost insoluble problem because its civilization developed in isolation, its history was uninterrupted, and its chronology conflicted with Western conventions based on the Bible. Theories had to be devised consequently to account for the repopulation of China after the Flood. Egypt, because of its antiquity and the affinities of the hieroglyphs to Chinese characters, was identified by some as the center from which the great postdiluvian migration to the East began. The people of Pre-Columbian America, who likewise wrote in pictographs, were thought to be descendants of the earliest wave in the great eastward migration. But such a theory of development upset the traditional periodization of the world based on the "four monarchies": Chaldean, Persian, Hellenistic, and Roman. In the light of the new knowledge this old geographical and political scheme of periodizing gave way completely, and was supplanted by periods based entirely on chronology, i.e., ancient, medieval, and modern. It was only by this device that China's history could be correlated with classical and later Western historical periods.

The most ingenious and tortuous effort to reconcile Judeo-Christian and Chinese traditions was advanced by a small group of Jesuits in China who have been called "Figurists." They claimed to find evidence in the Confucian classics and in other Chinese works that would support a theory of the common origin of mankind and the law. The Figurists held that the Ancient Law given by God to man was originally in the hands of a supreme lawgiver: Enoch in the Hebrew tradition, Zoroaster in Persia, Fu Hsi in China. Shem, the son of Noah, carried the pure *Logos* to China after the Flood. Fu Hsi, following the precepts of Enoch, promulgated the law in three forms: pictographic concepts and folk heroes for the simple people, more complex symbols for scholars and religious leaders, and mystical symbols for the sages. A source of mystical symbols of great import was thought to be the *I Ching* (*Book of Changes*), one of the most cryptic of the Chinese classical books. Once they had concluded that the mystical figures (trigrams and hexagrams) of the *I Ching* were symbols of eternal verities they tried to decipher them. While nothing came of these attempts at cryptography, the Figurists by their enthusiasm and ingenuity did help to elevate China and its civilization to a place of primary importance in the deliberations of those intrigued with theories of common origin and universal kinship.

The first and greatest of the European thinkers to come under the spell of Figurist ideas was Leibniz. The German philosopher, who had long been fascinated by the revelation of China's great civilization, became a correspondent of Father Joachim Bouvet, one of the leading Figurists. Around 1701 Leibniz was won over to the idea that the "hieroglyphics" of the *I Ching* were the creations of Fu Hsi and were mystical symbols that represented the Infinite and the Chaos from which God had rescued mankind. For a time he himself experimented with the trigrams, and sought through the analytical use of his binary arithmetic to show that they had a coherence and order about them which indicated that they might be a key to all the sciences. A successful deciphering of these symbols might lead, Leibniz thought, to the establishment of a firm scientific basis for the story of Creation and for the history of the antediluvian epoch. André-Michel Ramsay and Montesquieu were also intrigued by the ideas of the Figurists, but they made no serious efforts to help the Jesuits document their fantastic claims. However, they were impressed, as Leibniz was, by the Chinese Classics as sources which provide evidence for the homogeneity of human thought and for the objective existence of universality.

European religious and lay thinkers of the seventeenth century, under the influence of the debates attending the Rites Controversy, began to speculate as to whether the Chinese were materialists or spiritualists, atheists or deists. The freethinker François La Mothe le Vayer in his *De la vertu des payens* (Paris, 1642) placed Confucius in Paradise with other great pagan thinkers. He also asserted that the Chinese, from time immemorial, have recognized but one God, and he then deduced that the Chinese ethical system is based on reason and the law of nature. Pascal believed that the Chinese were God-fearing people whose religious beliefs could be understood only allegorically. In the *Pensées* (1670) he wrote: "China obscures, but there is clearness to be found; seek it." Pierre Bayle suggested that Spinoza's pantheism owed a debt to Confucian concepts of God. But Bayle, while praising the tolerance of China, like many other rationalists unhesitatingly branded the Chinese as atheists, and his opinion was to have influence well into the eighteenth century. Herbert of Cherbury, a precursor of the English Deists, looked upon the Chinese as proponents of natural religion. Antoine Arnauld, the Jansenist lawyer and articulate foe of the Jesuits, saw nothing but iniquity in the Confucian ideas. Christian Thomasius, the Protestant educator of Halle, viewed Chinese religion as blind faith in the authority of dogma. Malebranche, the Oratorian philosopher, in his *Conversation between a Christian Philosopher and a Chinese Philosopher on the Existence of God* (1708) tried to refute the Chinese idea that matter is eternal. He, like Bayle, saw points of similarity between Spinoza's philosophy and Chinese thought.

Leibniz was the only secular philosopher of the later seventeenth century to support the Jesuits in the Rites Controversy and in their interpretation of Chinese religion and thought. In his diverse writings Leibniz shows himself to be convinced that the ancient Chinese were monotheists who conceived of God as being both spirit and matter. This Chinese God he sees as an entelechy similar to his own Supreme Monad. In the practice of their religion the Chinese worship God in the virtues of particular objects. But they are not idolaters, for they worship the spiritual rather than the material essence. In ancestral worship, he contends, there persists a concept of the immortality of the soul; rites are performed before the ancestors to remind the living to act so as to deserve the recognition of posterity. Leibniz' interpretation of Chinese religion was more than faintly reminiscent of the leading ideas in his own *Monadology*.

Like the Jesuits themselves, Leibniz rejoiced openly in the edict of toleration for Christianity promulgated in 1692 by the K'ang-hsi emperor. He congratulated the Jesuits on this success and heralded it as a vindication of their understanding of how best to reconcile Christian and Chinese thought. In 1697 he published his *Novissima Sinica* as a call to Protestants to emulate the example of the Jesuits and to dispatch a mission to China. He was even encouraged to hope, after the conclusion in 1689 of the Treaty of Nerchinsk between Russia and China, that the land route to Peking might be reopened and regular communications established through Russia between learned groups in China and Europe.

V

The Jesuits took seriously Leibniz' advice to send more useful objects and practical information to Europe from China. They also continued throughout the eighteenth century, even after the suppression of the Society in 1773, to publish detailed information on Chinese life ranging from the history of the Jews in China to brief essays on Chinese games. The *Lettres édifiantes et curieuses*, an intentional popularization, were issued in printed form beginning in 1702, and were later compiled and reissued in twenty-six volumes at Paris between 1780 and 1783. J. B. Du Halde, one of the editors of the *Lettres édifiantes*, published in four volumes his encyclopedic *Description de la Chine . . .* (Paris, 1735) which was translated into English and Dutch in the following year. In following the encyclopedic tradition which they helped to inaugurate, the Jesuits published at intervals from 1777 to 1814 what were called *Mémoires concernant les Chinois* (Paris). Unlike their earlier publications, the Jesuits, who were now generally in disrepute, here issued in sixteen volumes, with but few editorial comments, a wide variety of translations of Chinese materials. Contemporaneously, Father Mauriac de Mailla published in 1778 a translation in twelve volumes of the *Tung-chien, kang-mu* ("The Outline and Details of the Comprehensive Mirror"), a twelfth-century version of Chinese history prepared under the direction of the philosopher Chu Hsi.

What most impressed the Jesuits and Leibniz about China, was its superiority to Europe in the establishment and maintenance of a rational social order. Leibniz fancied from what he read that the K'ang-hsi emperor was a model ruler who governed his subjects firmly but with great respect for law and the advice of his counsellors. So great was Leibniz' admiration for the government, social stability, and moral system of the Chinese that he confessed:

. . . we need missionaries from the Chinese who might teach us the use and practice of natural religion, just as we have sent them teachers of revealed theology (trans. in Lach, *Novissima Sinica*, p. 75).

To Leibniz and the Jesuits, the morality of the Chinese was inseparable from government. The Chinese, it was alleged, have no concern with abstract questions of morality but are interested only in applying to daily life the teachings of Confucius regarding the duties of men. The morality of the Chinese is seen to be a set of prescriptions designed to procure and assure individual, familial, and social happiness. The successful organization of the Chinese monarchy, as opposed to the European states, is based on the fact that the emperor applies and adapts to the administration of the state the principles which obtain in individual and family life. Political means are used in China to achieve a more perfect morality. The end of life, society, and government in China is happiness, here and now. Abstract religious virtue, with its invisible and other worldly rewards, is of no interest to the Chinese. China flourishes as a great and virtuous empire without the aid of revealed religion.

Among the earliest of the philosophical popularizers to propagate to the learned public the Sinophilism of the Jesuits was Christian Wolff, the follower of Leibniz. In a lecture delivered at the University of Halle in 1721 before the combined faculty and student body, Wolff proclaimed the excellence of Chinese moral philosophy and its correspondence with his own teachings regarding the efficacy of human reason in meeting the problems of daily life. Duty and virtue, the difference between good and evil, and the imperative to right action may be learned from nature as well as revelation, according to both the Chinese and Wolff. While Wolff contends that no conflict exists between this doctrine of lay morality and Christian teachings,

his Pietistic colleagues at the university remained unconvinced. In their determination to end what they thought of as Wolff's heretical teachings, the Pietists prevailed in 1723 upon King Frederick William I of Prussia to banish Wolff from his territories.

From the sanctuary of the University of Marburg Wolff continued thereafter to write about and teach his "practical philosophy." Others continued to write polemical tracts about Wolff and his interpretations of Confucian morality and Chinese statecraft. In 1730 at Marburg Wolff delivered a lengthy lecture on China as the outstanding working example of an enlightened government. His views of the "Real Happiness of a People under a Philosophical King" did not go unnoticed by Voltaire and the young Frederick whom he was tutoring at Rheinsberg. Within German university circles the moral philosophy and Sinophilism of Wolff continued to be a subject for learned debate until the last generation of the eighteenth century. Wolff's major pronouncements on Chinese morality and government were greeted with great cordiality by the Jesuits. In the *Description* of Du Halde, issued five years after Wolff's lecture at Marburg, emphasis continued to be placed upon the natural morality, rational religion, and enlightened statecraft of the Chinese.

The first systematic treatise on the science of statecraft published in Europe was Montesquieu's *L'esprit des lois* (*The Spirit of the Laws*, 1748). For his information on China Montesquieu used the merchant accounts as well as the adulatory statements of the Jesuits, but preferred the merchants as the less biased observers. The merchants, as we have seen, were as unanimous in their condemnation of the treachery, deceit, and dishonesty of the Chinese as the Jesuits were in their praise of China's natural morality and good government. In response to the conflict in his sources, and in harmony with the thesis of his book, Montesquieu concluded that a wide gulf separates theory from practice in the governing of China. Peace and tranquillity are assured by patriarchal repression and by the dominion of fear. An attack upon a magistrate becomes an attack upon the entire system, hence dissent and liberty are nonexistent and reform of evil impossible. As long as the elements are cooperative, the people industrious, and the state not too repressive, life in China is satisfactory. But nature is not often benign and so disruptions occur. And, since reform of the state is not possible, the individual Chinese make out as best they can by resorting to artifice. The state, handcuffed by its own system, tolerates deception while eschewing reform. China, because it is governed by the rod, is classified as a despotism in which honor and virtue are little more than theoretical objectives. Nonetheless, by the attention he gave to China, Montesquieu recog-

361

nized that study of its laws and institutions is necessary to any objective examination of the principles of government and similar questions of universal import.

Rousseau, in his *Discourse on Political Economy* (first printed in the *Encyclopédie* in 1755) likewise experienced the need to reckon with China in propounding his generalizations. The emperor of China he sees as being exemplary in unswervingly following the dictates of the "general will" in resolving disputes between the officials and the people. Rousseau approvingly noted that it is "the constant maxim of the prince to decide against his officers" without delay or investigation, and concludes that since the "public outcry does not arise without cause" the Chinese emperor finds "seldom any injustice to be repaired." He also praised the fiscal system of China "where taxes are greater and yet better paid than in any other part of the world." The reason for this, in Rousseau's estimation, is that food grains are free of taxes, and the heavy duties levied on other commodities are paid by the ultimate consumer, or by those who can afford to pay.

Voltaire in his historical works, especially in the *Essai sur les moeurs et l'esprit des nations* (1756), measured China's civilization against the achievements of other peoples. China occupies the place of honor in his *Essai* and is the first civilization he considers. The Chinese are especially successful, in Voltaire's eyes, in using government to protect civilization. The emperors of China, comparable to philosopher-kings, for centuries maintained a stable, tolerant, and wise regime. Their benign, patriarchal rule, reinforced and aided by a corps of dedicated mandarins, served the people well. Society, following the Confucian principles, was built on respect for the Golden Rule, mutual toleration, and public service. In upholding the Confucian ideals, the Chinese produced throughout history an intelligent, rational, and deistic ruling class which set an example to the rest of society by cultivating virtue, refined manners, and an elevated style of life. But the Chinese system, for all of its moral and political virtue, could do nothing to encourage the expansion of the arts and sciences. Superstition, ancestor worship, and the character system of the language were persistent deterrents to advancement. The consequence was that China did not develop the arts and sciences as it might have done. That China's ancient civilization was overtaken by the European in the mid-seventeenth century is best documented by the fact that "even" the Jesuits were able to teach the mandarins something from their first arrival on the Chinese scene.

If Voltaire's Sinophilism was qualified, a number of political theorists of the mid-eighteenth century were convinced that Europe had more to learn from China than it had to teach. In Germany, a leading cameralist writer of the day, J. H. G. Justi published in Berlin in 1762 *Vergleichungen der europäischen mit den asiatischen und andern vermeintlich barbarischen Regierungen*. In this comparative work, as well as in several of his other writings on political economy, Justi concentrates on China as the foreign state most worthy of study. He is particularly attracted by China as an example of enlightened monarchy in which the unlimited authority of the ruler is effectually combined with moderation in its exercise. Moral restraint in the monarch is inculcated in China by careful education of the prince in humility, industry, respect for human life, reverence for learning, and concern for agriculture, the main occupation of the people. Like Leibniz, he believed that the Chinese emperor is constrained to virtue by his desire to receive the favorable judgment of history. While subjects have the duty to remonstrate with the ruler, he sees in China no formal constitutional restrictions on the emperor. Systematic training in civil morality is taught to the people by the mandarins, who are themselves selected, rated, and promoted by a civil service institution. No hereditary nobility exists in China, and elevation to high rank comes only through excellent performance in public service. The censorate, which acts as the eyes and ears of the emperor, is the surveillance institution that guarantees integrity and efficiency at all levels of government. Administration by boards rather than by individuals alone also helps to check license and despotism among officials. Most impressive of all is the fact that the Chinese system is internally so well balanced and its administrative machinery so wisely constructed that it works *automatically* to insure the general welfare. In China, Justi clearly thought he had found a working example of the kind of enlightened despotism that he and others were advocating for the German states.

In France the ideal of an enlightened and rational absolutism was most fully articulated by the Physiocrats. The Physiocrats were especially critical of state economic policies which overstress commerce and neglect agriculture. In China they saw a government vitally concerned with agriculture, as was symbolized dramatically by the annual spring rites at which the emperor, or his deputy, turned the first furrow. The most characteristic of the Physiocratic writings which elevated China to a model for Europe was François Quesnay's *Le despotisme de la Chine* (Paris, 1767). Quesnay sees the government of China as one in which the ruler through legal despotism enforces the natural economic laws. Authority is rightly invested in an emperor who is impartial, tolerant, and constantly careful to protect the public welfare. Since China is an agricultural nation, the ruler correctly pays special attention to problems relating to the land and the cultivator. He does not lay arbitrary taxes, but follows the Natural Law by requiring as payment "a portion of the annual produce of the soil" (Maverick, p. 290). He does not tolerate monopolies, but does his best to encourage free and natural competition in all economic enterprises. He demands regular accountings of public funds and swiftly punishes malversations. The perpetuity of China's government is attributed to the stable natural order enforced by the ruler. China's greatest problem is overcrowding of the land with the result that too many of its people live in poverty or slavery.

VI

With the beginning of direct intercourse in the sixteenth century, the artists and craftsmen of Europe had become intrigued with Chinese textiles, porcelain, and lacquer ware. A pronounced taste for Chinese art objects was widespread in Europe by the time tea was introduced to Restoration England. The motifs on the Chinese products were widely copied in Europe both in imitations that were made of the products themselves and in other art forms. Europeans were successful by the late seventeenth century in producing an acceptable and competitive lacquer ware. A generation later they had learned to make true hardpaste porcelain. Along with the art products themselves, the Europeans sought to obtain information on Chinese techniques. Books and articles on Chinese arts were collected and read by interested amateurs and professionals as the China vogue spread from France to the other European countries, and from the nobility to the lowest classes in society. Never before had Europe received so powerful and varied an artistic stimulus from a distant civilization.

The craze for Chinese art objects reached its peak in the early and middle years of the eighteenth century. Royalty, nobility, and men of substance collected Chinese cabinets, chairs, tables, screens, fans, hangings, porcelains, and lacquered bowls. Interiors were paneled with lacquer or wallpapered with Chinese designs. In the palaces a special chamber was often designed to house the porcelain collection of the owner. Many of the items collected were prepared in China especially for this vast European market and were designed to appeal to the European taste for the exotic. As a consequence they often reflected more about the Chinese conception of European taste than about Chinese art itself. Parasols, pagodas, and mandarins were depicted on the wares made in China as the Europeans conceived of them rather than as they actually looked. European artists, who incorporated these contrived designs into their own works, were often copying Chinese people, objects, and scenes that were born in the minds of those European artists and artisans afflicted by Sinomania.

"Chinoiserie" (meaning bizarre tricks or monkeyshines in modern French usage) is a term descriptive of the eighteenth-century European view of China as a place of escape from the trials of daily life, as a haven of leisure and luxury, as a utopia where laughter is always gay. In this conception China is remote in distance rather than in time. Its "Golden Age" is not in the past or future, but in a perpetual and glorious present. Its landscapes are always green, its waters clear and cool, its skies sunny. The Chinese people are graceful, delicate, and colorful; they love beautiful gardens, quiet ponds, tinkling bells, and happy society. They are the gay Chinese of the porcelains who have almost no relationship to the wise Chinese of the Jesuits and philosophers or the wicked Chinese of the merchants. They are the untroubled people who live under the reasonable and tolerant rule of an enlightened and prosperous king.

The playful, and sometimes wistful, spirit of chinoiserie is best reflected in the visual arts. To Europeans, weary of Renaissance adulation of the staid art of antiquity, the strange objects of China provided welcome relief. Frivolous courtiers and serious artists at Versailles in the time of Louis XIV were among the first to bring the light spirit of chinoiserie into the established arts of Europe. Perhaps as a reaction against the classical plan of the park at Versailles, an exquisite pleasure house, the *Trianon de porcelaine*, was erected in the gardens in 1670. This was but the first of many such pavilions that would dot the classical and landscape gardens of Europe in the following century. But, as was often the case, the Trianon was a building whose basic architecture was uncompromisingly French and baroque. It was only the surface ornamentation which gave it a bizarre, Chinese appearance. As a general rule, the Chinese taste was incorporated into baroque art by the addition of exotic ornaments and motifs to forms that remained fundamentally European both in conception and structure alike.

The rococo art of the Regency period in France lent itself especially well to exotic treatment. Antoine Watteau in his drawings and paintings was the earliest and most influential of the creators of rococo chinoiseries. His mandarins, temples, and parasols became hallmarks of decoration *à la Chine* and were copied by lesser artists all over Europe. Monkeys came frequently into his fantastic decorations and they were regularly added to chinoiseries for exotic effects. The increased use of watercolors in painting probably owed a debt to the porcelain pictures. François Boucher, a painter and a designer of tapestries, stressed the charms of Chinese pastoral and village life, and his people began to look like real Chinese in face and figure. Jean-Baptiste Pillement, draughtsman and painter to Louis XIV, drew chinoiseries for engravers that were even more fantastic and vivacious than the paintings of Watteau. The drawings of Pillement were copied everywhere, and are still considered to be the best examples of chinoiserie at the height of its refinement. While the artists themselves were not influenced by the conception of China found in the *philosophes*, there is no doubt that the popularity of the chinoiseries owed a debt to the high reputation which the savants gave to China. The ordinary person could readily draw the conclusion that these happy people lived under a philosopher-king.

In the eighteenth century it was generally agreed that the English landscape garden, as it then evolved, owed a substantial debt to the art of Chinese gardening. Sir William Temple, a critic of classical, formal gardens, noted in 1685 that the Chinese in their gardens seek to reproduce natural effects by following schemes based on "Sharawadgi," his own rendition of a Chinese or Japanese term meaning "studied irregularity." On the basis of Temple's remarks the conviction grew that the Chinese example was more important to the evolution of the landscape garden than were Roman prototypes, the semi-formal garden, or a new attitude towards nature in its wild state. Naturalism as an end in itself was not enough to satisfy Sir William Chambers, who believed that an inanimate, simple nature was too insipid and that gardens required "every aid that either art or nature can furnish" (Bald, p. 318).

It was as such an aid that the chinoiserie form was used. But because European garden architects had almost no direct knowledge of Chinese garden design, art historians today generally hold that the Chinese example had no influence upon what has been called the Anglo-Chinese garden. The case for Chinese influence has usually been supported exclusively by reference to the large number of garden buildings, pagodas, and bridges which were included in the new gardens by their designers or added by their owners. Whatever else it was, the Anglo-Chinese garden was certainly another art form which came under the influence of the vogue for ornamenting through chinoiseries.

From the arts of gardening and architecture, the revolt against classical rigidity stimulated by the idea of "Sharawadgi" speedily passed to the other arts. Chinese persons or scenes were introduced into baroque novels to provide gallant, grotesque, or fantastic elements, as in C. W. Hagdorn, *Aeyquan, oder der Grosse Mogul* (1670). Romances were based upon Oriental tales to lend them an idyllic and exotic air. Utopian writers cited China as an example of a tolerant

society. Books on Chinese designs as exhortations to adopt the new taste are typified by Thomas Chippendale's *The Gentleman and Cabinet Maker's Director* (1754). Writers of fictional travel accounts, sometimes called extraordinary voyages, provided thumbnail sketches of Chinese people and places.

The *sage chinois*, who represented in literature the idealized Chinese of the *philosophes*, was frequently used as a literary spectator of and commentator upon the European scene. The Marquis d'Argens dedicated his *Lettres chinoises* (The Hague, 1755) to the shade of Confucius, "the greatest man the world has yet produced," and he speculated that Confucius and Leibniz were holding frequent conversations in another world. Oliver Goldsmith in his *Chinese Letters*, which appeared in *The Public Ledger* between 1760 and 1762, put his critical observations of European society into the mouth of Lien Chi Altangi out of deference to the prevailing fashion. Voltaire in his play of 1755 called *L'Orphelin de la Chine* (or "Confucian morals in five acts") actually utilized as the basis for his plot the translation of a Chinese drama that had been published by Du Halde. Voltaire's play, which was extremely popular on the contemporary stage, celebrates the triumph of Chinese civilization over the barbarous Mongols. Voltaire's drama was also an indirect attack upon Rousseau's adulation of the primitive and unspoiled society. The essayists of the *Encyclopédie* wrote at length on Chinese customs and compared them to those prevailing in Europe and in other parts of the world. In most of these comparisons China's practices almost always win high honor for their rationality, refinement, and good taste.

VII

Beginning in the mid-eighteenth century disillusionment with China as a model of rationality, good government, and the gay life was expressed with increasing frequency and greater vigor. The hostility in Europe towards the Society of Jesus, its expulsion from a number of countries, and its formal dissolution by the Papacy in 1773 led many contemporary observers to be more than a bit skeptical about the veracity of the glowing Jesuit reports of China. The growing criticism of rationalistic thought and enlightened absolutism also produced a reaction against a China which had been elevated to a model society by rationalistic social, economic, and political theorists. The more effective closure of China to European trade had the practical result of eliminating regular intercourse and of forcing Europe's attention to turn to other more hospitable places. The outbreak of the French Revolution and the continental wars brought an end to almost all European relations with eastern Asia. England, which managed to retain a degree of independence from continental involvements, turned the major share of its attention to India. The United States, where the China craze imported from Europe began just after the revolt against Britain, was one of the few places in the Western world where disenchantment with China had not set in by the end of the eighteenth century.

The intellectual and artistic foes of rationalism and classicism stood in the vanguard of those who attacked the China of the *philosophes* and the rococo painters. The young Rousseau in his *Discourse on the Arts and Sciences* (1750) raised two fundamental questions. What advantage, he asked, has China "reaped from the honors bestowed on its learned men?" Can it be, he goes on satirically, "that of being peopled by a race of scoundrels and slaves?" Or is the reward for holding learning in honor the defeat of the empire by "rude and ignorant Tatars?" Dr. Samuel Johnson, who had been an ardent admirer of China in his earlier years, came to look upon the Chinese as barbarians who had no art other than "pottery" and who had never advanced sufficiently to possess an alphabet. Baron F. M. Grimm, who castigated the Jesuits in his literary correspondence for deceiving Europe with false reports, branded China an unenlightened despotism with the Confucian moral code fitting precisely a "herd of frightened slaves" (Reichwein, p. 96). The young Goethe, who had read the *Analects* as well as Montesquieu and Rousseau, had no patience with the "knickknacks" of chinoiserie and was inclined to regard China itself as possessing a hybrid, overrefined, superficial, and sick civilization.

As ideas about China during the Enlightenment were subjected to a more intimate inspection, the tendency grew to stress the static quality of its civilization. Enlightenment philosophers of progress generally concerned themselves with the advance of reason in the West and rarely referred in their considerations to other parts of the world. Voltaire and other rationalists were primarily intent upon revealing the universality of reason and were content with simply finding a place for China in their cosmic designs. In doing so, even some of the greatest admirers of China posited a civilization that was unchanging, unprogressive, and being rapidly overtaken by the West. None of the enlightened writers, not even the authors of universal history from Bossuet to the Göttingen school, undertook seriously to bring China into their considerations of historical process.

Adam Smith in his *Wealth of Nations* (1776) asserted that the poverty of China's lowest classes is far greater than anything to be found in Europe. Like Montesquieu, Smith was inclined to accept the travelers' view of China and to put aside that of the Jesuits as suspect. "The accounts of all travelers," he noted, "inconsistent in many respects, agree in the low wages of labor, and in the difficulty which a laborer finds in bringing up a family in China" (Book I, Ch. VIII). Since the travel accounts from Marco Polo to those of his own day describe China in essentially the same terms, Smith concluded that China "seems to have been stationary" (ibid.). But though China appears to stand still, "it does not seem to go backwards" (ibid.). Its towns and cultivated lands are not deserted or neglected. China's failure to develop economically, despite its acknowledged wealth in people and resources, he ascribed to its neglect of international trade. Failure of the state to encourage trade and provide security for investors and workers produces a bipolarization of Chinese economic life by which "the oppression of the poor must establish the monopoly of the rich" (Book I, Ch. IX).

J. G. von Herder, in his earliest writings, conceived of China as an agrarian country dominated by a paternalistic government which inhibits the growth of the intellectual and creative capacities of the people. In his *Ideen* (1791) Herder self-consciously attempted an objective appraisal of Chinese civilization in an effort to let it fit itself into his universal historical conception. He reviewed China's natural environment and history and concluded that its physical isolation and rigid institutions prevent the growth of dynamism and creativity. The descent of the Chinese from barbaric Mongols left a heritage of coarse habits and unrefined tastes. Natural growth is repressed by the false stress placed upon filial piety and obedience to authority. The civilization that evolves in stubborn isolation from other world cultures is stultified, artificial, and unimaginative. "The empire," he asserted, "is an embalmed mummy inscribed with hieroglyphics and wrapped in silk." Later in life Herder modified this view and praised the Chinese for their tolerance, patience and enlightened government.

T. R. Malthus in *An Essay on the Principle of Population . . .* (1798) analyzed the incentives to and checks upon the increase of China's population. He estimated on the basis of Du Halde's figures that China's population in the early eighteenth century was almost 240,000,000; at the end of the century Sir George Staunton, the British emissary to Peking, estimated it at about 334,000,000. Malthus accounted for China's vast numbers and their rapid increase by reference to the productivity of the land, its intensive cultivation, the government's concern for agriculture, the industriousness and relatively high social position of the farmer, and the encouragement given to marriage by the religious and social systems. He also noted that despite its vast area, China had a population density of thrice to twice that of France, a deplorable situation brought on mainly by the cultural imperatives encouraging marriage. But limits are set upon the operation of marriage as an incentive to increase of population by the large number of priests, monks, scholars, servants, and slaves who remain single and childless. Disease, especially among children, is a positive check but not as important as might be expected in such an overcrowded country. Infanticide by exposure and drowning is common but it varies with abundance and scarcity. Frequent crop failures from drought, floods, or plagues of insects produce devastating famines that, because of China's isolation, cannot be relieved by outside help. Unrelieved scarcity results in riots and wars, which with widespread famine act as the most powerful check on population increase. Malthus saw little prospect for China to improve the lot of its people through manufacture and the encouragement of foreign trade. Its wealth, based on cultivation, had already reached its zenith and little hope for relief could be envisaged either through greater agricultural or industrial productivity. In terms of material development China seemed doomed to stagnation and predestined to suffer a staggering burden of overpopulation and grinding poverty.

The thesis that China was a static and unprogressive civilization received its classical formulation in Hegel's *Philosophy of History* (1830–31). Hegel was a close student of the critical merchant and Protestant accounts of China as well as of the adulatory writings of the Jesuits. China, like other Oriental states, possesses for Hegel a civilization in which nature terrorizes man and in which progress is limited by geographical and racial contradictions. While China has its own *Volksgeist*, it has never advanced beyond the initial stages in the realization of freedom. The only free individual is the despot; for others freedom under the state has never been realized and no sense exists of the infinite worth of the individual.

Hegel saw Confucius as a moralist, not a systematic or speculative philosopher. The sage prescribed principles for action, and made morality for the individual identical with the emperor's will and law. It is this prescriptive quality of Chinese morality which accounts for the unchanging, despotic character of Chinese society and for the failure of the Chinese to have an interest in abstract knowledge for itself. Since China's civilization does not progress, it is relatively certain that China was not better off in antiquity than at present. Study of prevailing conditions might then be assumed sufficient to unlock the secrets of China's past. Hegel, who was also a close student of Voltaire's idea of universal history, explicitly rejected the uniformity of nature and placed the stagnant Orient,

including China, at the bottom of his ladder of linear history which culminates in freedom's self-realization in the Europe of his day. But by this scheme Hegel did not succeed in explaining how universal history itself progressed from its first "unchanging" phase to the Greek stage in which a greater degree of freedom somehow developed.

Marx's concept of Asia, as spelled out in his writings of the 1850's, was based essentially on the views of the classical economists, especially John Stuart Mill. Both Marx and Engels embraced the then current belief in an Asiatic society that was unique in possessing peculiar systems of land ownership and production which definitely set it apart from the agrarian societies of classical antiquity and feudalism in the West. Climate and geography necessarily made artificial irrigation the basis of Asian agriculture. The Asiatic state came into being to control waterworks spread over vast territories where the people, living in dispersed, self-supporting villages, depended upon strong central authority to organize and control irrigation. In China the economy rests upon a combination of small agriculture and domestic industry in which the state consumes almost totally whatever surplus value can be produced. The Asiatic mode of production thus made the state the real landlord, and it maintains in perpetuity a condition of general slavery for the masses.

China, Marx and Engels thought in 1850, was the "oldest and most unshakeable empire of the world" (Lowe, p. 19), isolated and rotting. But, at about this time, China began to be forced out of its shell of isolation by imperialist attacks from the West. The best evidence for China's loss of stability was the outbreak of the Taiping rebellion in the 1850's and the changes that it threatened. Faced by the reality of a China in decline, Marx and Engels had to fit China into their theoretical framework as a changing element. China, it was concluded, under pressure from industrial capitalism, would leap over antiquity and feudalism to the capitalist and ultimately to the socialist modes of production. Marx and Engels saw changes in China of the kind they expected to see in the West. In their preoccupation with Europe they failed to notice indigenous reasons for change. In their concern with a changing China, they abandoned their efforts to fit China into their unilinear scheme of universal history as they tried to understand what influence it might have upon the world transition from capitalism to socialism.

VIII

Professional study of China, especially of language, literature, and history, made rapid progress in the early nineteenth century. In the eighteenth century a few compendia, grammars, and dictionaries had been produced, such as G. S. Bayer's *Museum Sinicum* (St. Petersburg, 1730) and Étienne Fourmont's *Grammaire chinoise* (Paris, 1742). The Society of Jesus, which was revived in 1815, continued to provide the scholars of Europe with raw materials from the field. The Jesuits issued translations as well as essays on Chinese and its relation to other Asian tongues. J. P. Abel Rémusat, who in 1814 became professor of Chinese at the Collège de France, inaugurated serious study of Taoism and Chinese medicine, and translated novels of romance and family life. He also participated in the organization of the *Société asiatique* in 1822. J. H. Klaproth, an associate of Rémusat, published the *Asia Polyglotta* (1823) in which he divided Asian languages into twenty-three groups and indicated how comparative studies might be undertaken. Sir William Jones, the father of modern Sanskrit studies in the West, studied Chinese language and history in his efforts to understand India's early relations with China.

The Protestant missionaries, who started evangelizing China in 1807, compiled dictionaries in English, studied dialects seriously, and established educational institutions and printing presses in southeast Asia and China. Robert Morrison, the first Protestant missionary in China (1807), published between 1815 and 1823 a six-volume *Dictionary of the Chinese Language*. W. H. Medhurst published between 1832 and 1837 his *Dictionary of the Hok-kien Dialect of the Chinese Language*. Both of these early dictionaries were published at Macao as were other early vocabularies and encyclopedias designed for the use of missionaries. The Chinese themselves began around 1875 to prepare dictionaries for the use of Westerners. But the English-speaking world owes its greatest debt to the British scholar Herbert A. Giles who published at Shanghai in 1892 his *Chinese-English Dictionary*, designed for merchants and missionaries. He provided as well a system of transliteration which Western students still depend upon in working with the Chinese language. In the nineteenth century Chinese dictionaries were also prepared for Portuguese, French, German, and Russian users.

As comprehension of Chinese improved, translations of popular literature, classics, histories, and documents became more numerous. Dramas, poems, and short stories were translated into English and French. As the Protestant pastors and their families steadily grew in number, they came to exercise an enormous influence upon the growth of scholarly knowledge and upon the formation of public opinion and policy in their homelands. Elijah C. Bridgman the first American missionary to China, launched a periodical called the *Chinese Repository*, published in China from 1832 through 1851, which was designed to inform foreigners about China's past and present. Bridgman also translated the Bible into Chinese (with M. S. Culbertson), published in 1862. S. Wells Williams, an American missionary-scholar, lectured on China and compiled an encyclopedic two-volume study, *The Middle Kingdom* (1848), which remained a standard reference work until the end of the nineteenth century. Many of the missionaries or their children acted as interpreters in diplomatic negotiations with China or returned home to teach in the universities, advise the government, or work in export businesses. In the learned societies devoted to the investigation of Chinese affairs the views of the missionaries commanded respect.

Knowledge of China produced a practical impact upon the agriculture and administration of the enterprising West. Serious projects were undertaken in the United States during the mid-nineteenth century to compete with China in raising silk and tea, and experiments were performed to adapt Chinese plants and animals to the needs of American agriculture. T. T. Meadows, a British diplomat, published *Desultory Notes on the Government and People of China* (1847) in which he described the civil service system of China and urged the institution in Britain of a comparable examination system for the recruitment, rating, and advancement of civil servants. Through his statement the problem was aired, and in 1855 Britain created its first civil service commission. Most of the civil service systems now in existence, including those started before the British system, owe an incalculable debt to the Chinese example.

James Legge, in the 1850's, undertook the translation into English of the Confucian and Taoist texts, and became the first professor of Chinese at Oxford. His pioneer translations, worked out with the aid of a Chinese assistant, have been criticized by modern scholars as being ethnocentric and inaccurate. Nonetheless, they still remain the standard English versions. In France the Marquis d'Hervey Saint-Denys published a valuable anthology of T'ang poetry in 1852 that was influential among the literati of Europe. The Berlin Orientalist, Karl Arendt, rendered into German in the 1870's a number of selections from Ming novels the themes of which inspired poets and dramatists of the following generation. Continental Sinologists also wrote at length on Chinese administration and international affairs with increasing reliance on Chinese sources. H. B. Morse in the early twentieth century organized for the English-speaking world the international relations and commercial administration of the Chinese empire, mainly on the basis of Western sources.

The study of China in relation to its continental neighbors was given its present structure in the works

367

of Sir Henry Yule. In 1871 he published *The Book of Ser Marco Polo the Venetian* with a complete scholarly apparatus. His documentation, drawn from his personal travel experiences as well as from the best available literary sources, set a new standard for Eurasian studies. He also edited the works of other medieval travelers and his studies were continued and augmented by Henri Cordier, a French diplomat and scholar. It was Cordier who compiled the *Bibliotheca Sinica* (1904–08) which remains the standard bibliography of Western works on China. Paul Pelliot, the founder of the leading scholarly journal *T'oung Pao* (1890–), continued the Yule tradition but with a greater attention to monographic research. René Grousset, a French popularizer of Asian studies, sought more self-consciously than his colleagues to reinforce the literary sources with materials derived from study of the visual arts.

The Protestants, originally hostile to Buddhism for its outward resemblances to Catholicism, began seriously by the end of the century to translate and study its texts. Much of the growing interest in the study of Asian religions historically and on their own terms was due to the inspiration of Max Müller, the editor of the *Sacred Books of the East* (1875–1900). In this collection he presents, side by side with other Oriental books, most of the Chinese philosophical and religious texts in careful translations. The availability in English of this repository of material inspired serious historical and comparative studies of world religions.

Max Weber in his lengthy essays on *Confucianism and Taoism*, first published in 1916, brought China into his sociology of religion and more specifically into his theoretical considerations about the relationship between the Protestant ethic and the spirit of capitalism. These essays, which consider the social and economic as well as the religious foundations of Chinese society, constitute one part of a series of comparative studies designed to throw light on the general question as to why rational bourgeois capitalism became a dominant phenomenon *only* in the West. In China, as in other Asian societies, Weber concludes that the dominant religious traditions did not possess an "economic ethic" compatible with capitalistic growth. He concedes that traditional China possessed the materialistic potential for capitalistic development, but contends that Confucianism lacked the dynamism of ascetic Protestantism since it stressed rational adjustment to the world as given rather than rational mastery of it. Taoism he sees as a conservative and negative force which stressed passive acceptance rather than innovation and activism. In his analysis of the structure and function of Chinese society, Weber provides startling insights into the roles of the bureaucracy, literati, and the kinship system, which have inspired numerous recent investigations in depth by specialists in social history. For comparative religion, his examinations of Confucianism and Taoism still constitute empirical starting-points for generalized typological concepts.

IX

In the early nineteenth century the reaction against China as a model state led to a more positive interest in the Chinese as human beings. The sources for this new interest were found in the translations of popular literature, especially poetry, which had become increasingly available. A precursor of this trend was Ludwig Unzer, the German poet, who published in 1773 an elegy entitled *Vou-ti bey Tsin-nas Grabe, eine Elegie im chinesischen Geschmack*. In this poem, which the young Goethe criticized as contrived, Unzer sought to depict the feelings of a Chinese who is bereaved at the death of his beloved. Unzer's allusions to Taoist beliefs and other Chinese attitudes are naive, but his poem is important as the first European effort to show that the individual Chinese is subject to the same emotions as others when facing death.

Goethe, who had satirized the Chinese in his youth, was in the final decade of his life to express open admiration for the Chinese attitude towards nature, the self-discipline and refinement of the people, and the aesthetic qualities of Chinese literature. He was particularly moved by the Chinese poems which were published in English translation in Peter Perring Thoms' *Chinese Courtship* (1824). He rendered a few of Thoms' translations into his own poetic language and epitomized others in his set of lyrical poems called *Chinesisch-deutsche Jahres- und Tageszeiten* (1827). Friedrich Rückert published in 1833 his imitation in freely paraphrased odes of the *Shih-ching* ("Book of Poetry"). The German romantic poets thus deepened, personalized, and beautified Europe's conception of the Chinese. In their vision of Chinese imaginative life they fused an admiration for the intellectual resources of the Chinese with a sensitivity to Chinese creativity that was not appreciated in the eighteenth century.

But not all of the German poets shared Goethe's enthusiasm. Heinrich Heine, at the beginning of the third book of his *Romantische Schule* (1833), used one of the stories of Chinese beauties, translated by Thoms, to lend color to his own attack upon the grotesque character of German romanticism. Others in the romantic and Young German movements saw in China nothing but dry pedantry and tiresome automatism in government. The Liberals of the 1830's regarded China as a model of the police state that they so heartily despised (see Rose, p. 314). The American Transcendentalists, like the British romantic poets, were concerned more with Indian than with Chinese thought.

But the ethical teachings of Confucius appealed to Emerson, particularly the emphasis on the duty of the individual to assume social responsibility. Tennyson expressed the Victorian exasperation with a static and unprogressive China by proclaiming: "Better fifty years of Europe than a cycle of Cathay" ("Locksley Hall," line 184).

In France, Théophile Gautier, influenced by the China specialist G. Pauthier and the novelist René Bazin, became at mid-century a propagandist for Chinese literature and art. He wrote stories and verses on Chinese themes, collected Chinese art, and talked about Oriental subjects with Flaubert, Baudelaire, and Victor Hugo. His daughter, Judith Gautier, who studied Chinese with a tutor, translated Chinese poems into French verse in the Livre de jade (1867). Her intention was to transmit poetic quality rather than linguistic accuracy, a goal which has been retained by most Western translators of Chinese poetry ever since. She also wrote several novels about China and collaborated with Pierre Loti in preparing a Chinese play entitled La Fille du Ciel. Edmond and Jules de Goncourt, who were more interested in Japan than in China, were among the first to point out the debt of Japanese literature and art to China. Among those who fell under the spell of the Goncourts was Émile Guimet, an industrialist and founder of the Paris museum of Oriental art that still bears his name. Georges Clemenceau, while not active in politics, prepared just at the beginning of the twentieth century a play about China that was inspired by his study of the Chinese classics and his reactions to the Boxer Rebellion.

Collection of Chinese art became popular in Europe after 1860, the date of the sacking of the summer palace in Peking. The Boxer expedition of 1900 also brought a windfall of Chinese art into the West. But while individual connoisseurs and museums built up impressive collections of all forms of Chinese art, Western artists have so far not been inspired to imitate Chinese painting and sculpture. The influence of Chinese art in the West has been limited to a continuation of the popular vogue for chinoiseries and the decorative arts. This is particularly surprising in the light of the attraction that Japanese color prints, architecture, and furnishings have had for Western artists. The visual arts have also had but a small interest as sources for China's social and intellectual history. Only in recent years, and especially in the works of C. W. Bishop and H. G. Creel, have the findings of archaeology been used in the West as aids in the reconstruction of China's ancient past.

The dispatch of Chinese students to the West on Boxer fellowships and other grants helped at the beginning of the twentieth century to stimulate a new interest in Chinese thought. Irving Babbitt at Harvard early evinced an interest in the humane and moderate qualities in Buddhism and other faiths as they were practiced in China. The Imagist poets, particularly Ezra Pound and Amy Lowell, were attracted to Chinese poetry for its compact portrayal of universal wisdom. In Germany, O. J. Bierbaum, one of the leaders of impressionist art and culture, wrote novels and poems on the basis of his own renditions of Chinese themes. He stressed the erotic elements and burlesqued the pompous characters of his Chinese literary sources. More accurate translations of the meaning and spirit of Chinese poetry were provided in Germany by Richard Wilhelm, in America by Florence Ayscough, and in England by Arthur Waley. Through the efforts of both poets and translators, Chinese poetry, mythology, and history became a source of inspiration for creative writers in the contemporary West.

X

The industrial development of Europe and its expansion overseas in the mid-nineteenth century had the general result of forcing an end to the seclusion of both China and Japan. China was opened to Western penetration by the wars of 1839–42 and 1856–60, and by the treaties which followed. Japan was opened by the "black ships" of the Americans in 1853–54 and thereafter by a series of treaties with the Western powers. It was this train of events, observed and commented upon by Marx and Engels, which transformed quickly the belief in China's stagnation into a positive assertion of Europe's superiority. In his essay "On Liberty" (1859), John Stuart Mill envisaged China as a nation victimized by despotic custom. China's failure to improve over the millennia he attributed to the success of the Chinese in repressing individuality and mental liberty, and in impressing uniformity of thought and conduct through education and state control. The yoke of conformity to maxims and rules weighs so heavily upon society that, in Mill's view, if China is "ever to be farther improved, it must be by foreigners."

The Protestant missionaries were initially scornful of Chinese society, thought, science, and religion. Unlike the scholarly Jesuits, the conservative Protestants of the Victorian age saw little but vice and deprivation in China. The work of the missionary, they thought, was to bring the light of Christ to the heathen Chinese in order to save them from eternal damnation. But preoccupation with Chinese language and literature gradually brought a more enlightened generation of missionary scholars into being in Europe and America, a generation which took a more tolerant view of Chinese civilization. For example, James Legge, the missionary linguist, concluded in 1867 after long study

369

of Confucius that he was unable to regard the sage as a great man; but by 1893 he admitted: "The more I have studied his character and opinions, the more highly have I come to regard him" (Mason, p. 204, n. 33).

In the mid-nineteenth century the vast majority of Europeans held widely divergent and contradictory views on Chinese society. Both missionary and secular writers praised the Chinese for mildness, docility, and adaptability. They were also thought of as industrious, shrewd, and practical, but with a penchant for lying and deceit without conscience. Chinese of all social levels were considered to be extremely polite, urbane, and courageous in facing personal adversities; but they were also thought to be cruel, sensual, and licentious. "Of the earth earthy," in Legge's words, "China was sure to go to pieces when it came into collision with a Christianly-civilized power" (Dawson, p. 139).

The "scientific" historians of the nineteenth century, in their preoccupation with national and European history, rejected China even for comparative purposes. Leopold von Ranke in his *Lectures on World History* (ca. 1830–48) pronounced as "unhistorical" Hegel's postulation of the eternal stagnation of the Orient, and classified the Hindus and Chinese as living eternally in a state of *Naturgeschichte* of a completely secular and unreligious character. Ranke then went on to exclude China from history proper by asserting that the Chinese sources are mythical, unreliable, secondary, or unavailable to one who does not read Chinese. Jakob Burckhardt prized the Western heritage so highly that he completely excluded China from his lectures in the fear that alien infiltrations might muddy the limpid stream. Ernest Lavisse, who shared Burckhardt's high regard for the West and his fears for the future, grimly prophesied in 1890: "All strength gives out; the ability to maintain the lead in history is not a permanent attribute. Europe, which inherited it from Asia three thousand years ago, will perhaps not always keep it" (*Vue générale de l'histoire politique de l'Europe*, p. 239).

The potential wealth of China in natural resources was spelled out for the West in three large volumes and an atlas published between 1877 and 1885 by Baron Ferdinand von Richthofen. In his *China*, Richthofen gave for the first time a geographer's systematic estimate of China's economic resources. He called attention to the rich oil fields of Shantung and Manchuria and to the huge reservoirs of capable labor available in China. The prospect envisaged by Richthofen of an industrialized and modernized China was shortly transmuted in the West into the specter known as the "Yellow Peril."

The threat of China to white, Christian supremacy was raised repeatedly in the last third of the nineteenth century by missionaries, racists, and military theorists. Count Arthur de Gobineau who theorized on the superiority of the white over the yellow and black races, warned of the dangers to white dominance from excessive intermingling with inferior breeds. Blood pollution was identified by Houston Stuart Chamberlain as a threat to the superiority of the Teutonic supermen. Kaiser William II of Germany and Tsar Nicholas II of Russia corresponded after 1895 about "the Defense of the Cross and the old Christian European culture against the inroads of the Mongols and Buddhism . . ." (Levine, *Letters from the Kaiser . . .*, p. 10). The British publicist, C. H. Pearson, prophesied in 1893: "We shall wake to find ourselves elbowed and hustled and perhaps even thrust aside by peoples whom we looked down upon as servile and thought of as bound always to minister to our needs" (*National Life and Character*, p. 85). In the United States, the Hearst press warned at the end of the century that more adequate defenses were needed to protect the American way of life against the floodtide of Oriental emigration. The ghosts of the theorists were given flesh and bones by the startling military victory of Japan over Russia in 1905 and by the swift rise thereafter of strong nationalist and anticolonial sentiment throughout the Far East.

XI

While it was generally alleged in the West that the Chinese were scientifically inept and militarily weak, it also gradually became apparent after 1860 that China had staying-power as well. How was it possible that the Chinese with all their adversities continued to go their own way and to remain singularly unimpressed with the material superiority of the West? Chinese immigrants proved to be industrious, willing, and honest workers who adapted successfully to new environments. The Chinese of the treaty ports were also quick to learn the ways of the West. The government in Peking, despite its obvious weakness, showed a remarkable ability to play off one Western power against the other to preserve China from partition. Nationalist demands for the reform of the Manchu government and the development of an embryonic industrial base in the Yangtse valley during the 1860's provoked Westerners to begin probing for the sources of China's seemingly unquenchable vitality.

The basis for this new vision of China was not found simply in the increased knowledge and understanding that resulted from closer contact. It also emerged from the belief that there was something to discover in Chinese culture that the West did not possess at all or possessed only to a lesser degree. Growing disillusionment with the nationalistic, materialistic, capitalistic, and individualistic society of the West drove leading thinkers to seek for new values and directions. Joseph Ferrari, an Italian parliamentarian, wrote a comparative study called *La Chine et l'Europe* (1867) which denies that China is barbarous, static, or isolated and asserts that its civilization merits attention as an historical counterpoise to Europe. Eugène Simon, a French agricultural expert and consul in China, published *La cité chinoise* (1885; cf. Fustel de Coulanges, *La cité antique*, 1864), which idealizes China as a peasant society where liberty in all its forms—political, economic, religious, and intellectual—is realized. Simon's book, which was very popular, prophesied that all European attempts to subject China to industrialization, colonization, or modernization would fail because of the astounding vitality of the rural nation and its naturalistic civilization. On contemporaries, Simon's book, along with Richthofen's of about the same period, had an impact out of all proportion to its intrinsic importance. Paul Ernst, the German poet, was inspired by Simon to adulate the collectivist peasant culture of China for giving a higher place to spiritual than to material values. Later in life Ernst took most of his illustrations and inspirations from his study of Chinese art, poetry, and Taoism. He eventually concluded that China offered the rest of the world a unique metaphysical revelation.

Tolstoy began to take an interest in China following the religious crisis he experienced in 1884. He read widely, especially in the books of T. T. Meadows and Eugène Simon, on the political and social organization of China. Like Simon he was intrigued with Taoism and the peasant society of China and in his publications he urged the Chinese not to follow the way of the West. He discerned a spiritual kinship among China, Russia, and the other great agrarian countries which set them apart from the industrialized, materialistic West. He was especially attracted by the Taoist doctrine that men by their own efforts achieve harmony with nature and that the role of government should be kept to a minimum. He also responded affirmatively to Confucian theories about the moral and immoral effects of music. Tolstoy so greatly admired China that he asserted just before his death in 1910: "Were I young I would go to China" (Bodde, p. 29).

John Dewey first lectured at Peking in 1912, and again after the First World War. Along with his pupil, Hu Shih, Dewey was disturbed by the popularity of "isms" in China. He urged Chinese and Westerners alike to study the problems themselves, propose workable solutions, and avoid the panaceas of socialism, anarchism, or bolshevism. Dewey was convinced that socialism could have no roots in China because of its low level of industrial development. Bertrand Russell,

a devoted pacifist in World War I, spent one year lecturing in China during 1920. Although he was known internationally as a socialist, Russell felt that industrialization in China could best be promoted by a partially nationalized system of capitalism. In the articles which he wrote for *Dial* and the *Atlantic Monthly* in 1921, Russell unabashedly asserted that the Chinese were more "laughter-loving than any other race," not self-assertive either nationally or individually, avaricious for money for enjoyment rather than power, and socialist and scientific rather than capitalistic and mechanistic in temperament. R. H. Tawney, the British historian and member of the League of Nations Commission (1931–32) on the reorganization of education in China, likewise held a romantic notion of the historical isolation of China and its effects upon the growth of institutions, ideas, and practices.

While disenchantment grew in the twentieth-century West over China's inability to solve its own political and economic problems, inquiring minds nonetheless continued to examine China's past institutions for fresh ideas. Henry A. Wallace, as a progressive American student of agriculture, was inspired by studying the economic principles of Confucius to advocate experimenting in the United States with the "ever-normal granary" idea of the Chinese. When Wallace became Secretary of Agriculture in 1933, he continued to work for a program that would provide a constant supply of grain at all times without serious price fluctuations. In 1938 Wallace's program became part of the Agricultural Adjustment Act, a piece of legislation that owed its direct inspiration to Chinese ideas and practices. At the end of the Second World War Wallace called for the internationalization of the "ever-normal granary" idea as a necessary step on the road to world recovery. In response to Wallace's suggestions and the pressing needs of the time, the United Nations created a World Food Bank to establish and manage a world food reserve. Heavy political attacks from various nations quickly brought an end to this scheme.

Twentieth-century efforts at world history have self-consciously sought to make room for China and to integrate its civilization into the totality of history. H. G. Wells, in his *Outline of History* (1920) deplores the fact that Chinese culture has received such a minimal treatment in world history. While he strives to bring China into his work at each appropriate point, his isolated paragraphs on China are sketchy to the point of being unintelligible. Oswald Spengler's *The Decline of the West* (1918–22) treats Chinese civilization as an organism with a life cycle of its own that, after an initial flowering, fell into decay and putrefaction. Arnold Toynbee in his monumental *A Study of*

History (1934–61) assigns Chinese civilization a philosophical equivalence to Europe. But the actual amount of space devoted to Chinese civilization is nonetheless relatively slight. Toynbee's ideas about the origins of the Yellow River civilization as a response to a challenging environment and his chronological divisions of Chinese history have been severely attacked by specialists. In William McNeill's *The Rise of the West* (1963), China is for the first time integrated intelligibly into the history of the human community by the stress that is placed on its relationship to rather than its isolation from other centers of civilization.

Academic study of China in the West during the twentieth century has mainly been characterized by greater attention to command of the language, to internal developments, and to case studies of village life, social classes, bureaucracy, and the effects of modernization and Westernization. Translations from popular literature have focused upon the novels and dramas of social and individual discontent. Western literary creations about China, especially those of Alice Tisdale Hobart and Pearl Buck, glorified the sturdiness of the common man in meeting adversity and the satisfactions found by Chinese of all classes in the fullness and vitality of the ancient culture. The resistance of China to Japanese aggression reawakened interest in the study of China's relations with its neighbors and in the nation's ability to survive in spite of foreign depredations and internal political divisions. To the end of World War II the belief was commonly held that the social and cultural ties of traditional China were still solid enough to withstand fundamental changes.

XII

Lenin, originally wedded to the Marxist idea that China suffered from the system of production and governmental despotism peculiar to Asia, gradually began by the First World War to shift to the view that China might become a future center of revolution and social democracy. In his writings of the war years, Lenin dismissed as irrelevant the peculiar character of Asiatic society and sought to demonstrate that elimination of private property would lead everywhere to the victory of socialism. But in the 1920's he advocated a closer union between the Western proletariat and the Eastern toilers in their common struggle against traditional bondage and capitalistic imperialism.

Trotsky, a close student of Chinese affairs, saw in the economic backwardness of China a positive incentive to creative revolutionary action. In his theory of permanent revolution Trotsky envisaged China as one of the leading elements in the movement towards global revolution and rapid social and economic progress. While he did not believe that the peasantry

as a class was devoted to international revolution, he was convinced by 1927 that a socialist revolution would succeed in China. The undirected political radicalism of the Chinese would be swept towards socialism by world revolutionary trends too powerful to be resisted.

Stalin, once Lenin's influence was removed, began to emphasize the "feudal" character of China's agrarian society and bureaucratic government, and to deny the common interests of the peasants and workers. Of the three types of class societies described by Stalin (slave-holding, feudal, and capitalist), Nationalist China was to become the prototype for latter-day Marxists of the "feudal" or "semi-feudal" society. Until his death Stalin remained convinced that the followers of Mao Tse-tung were "margarine Communists" and that revolution based upon the peasantry would fail. In 1950, the leading lights in Oriental studies in Russia declared the complete "rout of the notorious theory of the 'Asiatic mode of production'" (Wittfogel, p. 5).

Karl Wittfogel, a close student of the Marxists and Weber, finds the source of *Oriental Despotism* (1957) in what he defines as the hydraulic society. The total power characteristic of Asian states derives in his eyes from governmental management of the large-scale works of irrigation and flood control necessary to the development and nurturing of agriculture. The class that manages the government, not the property-owners or the workers, constitutes the dominant elite in such societies. Agrarian despotisms, such as China, suffer from landlordism, capitalism, and domination by a gentry inspired and sustained by the administrative bureaucracy. Social stagnation is characteristic of hydraulic societies, and fundamental social changes in them have been affected historically only through the impact of external forces. The endurance of the Confucian tradition in China is a cultural expression of the staying power of the monopoly bureaucracy which upheld it as the official credo. Even in Communist China a managerial order has been retained which, while differing from the old bureaucracy in structure and intent, owes a substantial debt to the agrarian despotism of traditional China.

The victory of communism in China in 1949 brought sympathy and affection in most Western powers to a swift end. The treason of China to the West, and to Western expectations, set up a formidable, and through the 1960's, irreducible barrier to communication and understanding. Communist China is seen by those who fear it as a growing industrial and nuclear power as nothing but a belligerent and implacable foe. Respect persists for its ancient culture; but fear of a united, efficient, and totalitarian China as the leader of Asian communism has come to override almost all other considerations.

Throughout the history of modern Western thought, China and its civilization have been subject to a variety of interpretations. The number increased with the passage of time, but no one interpretation was ever completely lost. At all periods the West remained undecided as to how best to evaluate and relate to Chinese civilization as a totality. A fascinating ambiguity constantly appears between the Westerner's view of objective conditions in China, and his own vision of European society in its relations to other civilizations. While the West's changing conception of China strongly reflects the main currents of Western intellectual history, occasions arise when objective conditions in China impress themselves upon the current image. To our own day China is still conceived of as being at once remote and fantastic, wise and admirable, backward and inferior, and fearful and dangerous. While it is conceivable that these paradoxical characterizations are entirely of the West's own creation, they are also reflections of the distortions that inevitably occur whenever spokesmen of one civilization take a fixed position from which to look at or generalize upon an alien civilization of great longevity and complexity. The total impression which Westerners possessed at every period derived from the prevailing intellectual conditions at home, the stereotypes inherited from the Western past, and the objective conditions in China itself.

BIBLIOGRAPHY

William W. Appleton, *A Cycle of Cathay. The Chinese Vogue in England during the Seventeenth and Eighteenth Centuries* (New York, 1951). R. C. Bald, "Sir William Chambers and the Chinese Garden," *Journal of the History of Ideas*, **11** (1950), 287–320. H. Belevitch-Stankevitch, *Le goût chinois en France au temps de Louis XIV* (Paris, 1910). Henri Bernard-Maitre, *Sagesse chinoise et philosophie chrétienne* (Paris, 1935). Derk Bodde, *Tolstoy and China*, No. 4 in The History of Ideas Series (Princeton, 1950). Raymond Dawson, *The Chinese Chameleon: An Analysis of European Conceptions of Chinese Civilization* (London, 1967). Eleanor von Erdberg, *Chinese Influence on European Garden Structures* (Cambridge, Mass., 1936). Louis J. Gallagher, *China in the Sixteenth Century: The Journals of Matthew Ricci* (New York, 1953). Hugh Honour, *Chinoiserie, The Vision of Cathay* (London, 1961). G. F. Hudson, *Europe and China: A Survey of Their Relations from the Earliest Times to 1800* (London, 1931). Harold R. Isaacs, *Images of Asia: American Views of China and India* (New York, 1962). Donald F. Lach, *The Preface to Leibniz' Novissima Sinica. Commentary, Translation, Text* (Honolulu, 1957); idem, *Asia in the Making of Europe*, Vols. I and II (Chicago, 1965; 1970); idem, "The Sinophilism of Christian Wolff," *Journal of the History of Ideas*, **14** (1953), 561–74. Isaac D. Levine, *Letters from the Kaiser to the Czar* (New York, 1920). Donald M. Lowe, *The Function of* "China" in Marx, Lenin, and Mao (Berkeley, 1966). Arthur O. Lovejoy, "The Chinese Origin of a Romanticism," in A. O. Lovejoy, *Essays in the History of Ideas* (New York, 1960), pp. 99–135. Mary Gertrude Mason, *Western Concepts of China and the Chinese, 1840–1876* (New York, 1939). Lewis A. Maverick, "Chinese Influences upon the Physiocrats," *Economic History*, **3** (1938), 54–67. J. M. Menzel, "The Sinophilism of Justi," *Journal of the History of Ideas*, **17** (1956), 300–10. Joseph B. Needham and Wang Ling, *Science and Civilization in China*, 4 vols. (Cambridge, 1954–65). C. H. Pearson, *National Life and Character. A Forecast* (London, 1893). Virgile Pinot, *La Chine et la formation de l'esprit philosophique en France: 1640–1740* (Paris, 1932). Adolf Reichwein, *China and Europe: Intellectual and Artistic Contacts in the Eighteenth Century*, trans. J. C. Powell (London, 1925). Ernst Rose, "Paul Ernst und China," *Modern Language Quarterly*, **4** (1943), 313–28. Arnold H. Rowbotham, *Missionary and Mandarin: The Jesuits at the Court of China* (Berkeley, 1942). Ernst Schulin, *Die weltgeschichtliche Erfassung des Orients bei Hegel und Ranke* (Göttingen, 1958). Raymond Schwab, *La renaissance orientale* (Paris, 1950). Elizabeth Selden, "China in German Poetry from 1773 to 1833," in Vol. XXV (1941–44) University of California Publications in Modern Philology, Berkeley, 1942. Oswald Sirén, *China and Gardens of Europe of the Eighteenth Century* (New York, 1950). Ssu-yü Têng, "Chinese Influence on the Western Examination System," *Harvard Journal of Asiatic Studies*, **7** (1943), 267–312. Ed. Horst von Tscharner, *China in der deutschen Dichtung bis zur Klassik* (Munich, 1939). Edwin J. Van Kley, "Europe's 'Discovery' of China and the Writing of World History," *The American Historical Review*, **76** (1971), 358–85. Karl A. Wittfogel, *Oriental Despotism: A Comparative Study of Total Power* (New Haven, 1957).

DONALD F. LACH

[See also **Buddhism;** Enlightenment; **Islamic Conception;** Language; **Marxism;** Romanticism; Socialism.]

CHRISTIANITY IN HISTORY

Christianity: the religion which grew out of the Jewish faith as transformed by the worship of Jesus Christ after the Resurrection, and which, by combination with Greek culture and the conversion of a great part of the Roman Empire, took a systematized form as "historical Christianity," having its chief basis in Europe and presiding over the development of Western civilization until recent centuries.

I. THE EARLY CHURCH

1. Judaic Christianity. The disciples of Jesus, if they appeared ready to confess their despondency and even weakness at the time of the Crucifixion, made a recovery so rapid that it puzzles the historians. It altered the course of history; for though, as a result of it, they did not exactly announce a new religion to their fellow countrymen, they proclaimed an "event" which brought the older faith to its culmination, shattering its traditional framework and calling for a host of new interpretations. It would seem that, during the lifetime of Jesus, they may have followed Him without properly understanding the drift of His teaching; and it would appear to have been the vividness of their belief in the Resurrection that transformed the situation for them, enabling them to feel that now everything could be fitted into place. It had in fact convinced them that Jesus was the fulfilment of the famous prophecies on which the Jews had been relying for a long time; and that, if the truth had been so difficult to recognize, it had been because those prophecies—and particularly the notions of the Messiah and the divine Kingdom— had been construed in too mundane a manner. Once this basic insight had been reached, a remarkable work of intellectual synthesis was quickly achieved, and there followed an amazing missionary endeavor, which required considerable bravery at first and cannot be plausibly accounted for by reference to mundane vested interests. It is clear to the historian, and it was amply admitted at the time, that the dynamic behind all this was the conviction that the beloved Leader has risen from the dead. There was a strong expectation that He would quickly return.

It has always been a matter of the greatest difficulty for Christianity—and perhaps for any similar form of faith—to secure by peaceful means and sheer missionary endeavor the wholesale conversion of a people already dominated by an exclusive form of supernatural religion. The Holy Land was in this position, and though Judaism was in a fluid and interesting state, the disciples produced only what appeared to be an addition to the multitude of sects and parties there— some of these latter being impressive on the spiritual and ethical side, and some of them so similar in one way or another that the tracing of influences among them is a delicate affair. The Church for a few decades was predominantly Judeo-Christian, its members still attending the Temple and conforming to the Law, but meeting also in private houses or the Upper Room for instruction, prayer, and the breaking of bread. Until the war which led to the destruction of the city in A.D. 70, it was the group in Jerusalem (with James, the brother of Jesus, at its head) which was the leader.

It seems to have been quickly recognized that converts from paganism were admissible; and pagans were encountered in great numbers when the gospel was carried to the virtually Greek cities, such as Caesarea, on the Palestine coast. Communities were soon established also in Damascus and the Hellenistic city of

Antioch, beyond the frontier; and Antioch, where the term "Christian" came into use, became the center for a wider missionary campaign in the Greco-Roman world. But also, at this early stage in the story, Christian missions (following previous ones on the part of the Jews) spread eastwards to Transjordan and into Arabia, and they were pushed forwards to the upper Euphrates and the Tigris. Here, churches using the Aramaic tongue became important during the earliest centuries. Some difficulty arose over the question whether the pagans should be made to conform to the Jewish law and this may have created additional difficulty for Paul, the Apostle to the Gentiles, as Jewish nationalism became more intense, more exacting. But the extension into the Greco-Roman world, together with the destruction of Jerusalem, brought the Christian faith a higher degree of autonomy, a further scope for development; and it opened to Christianity the possibility of becoming a world-religion. The early need for exposition in the Greek language, the marriage with Greek ideas, and the contact with a highly developed culture were to prove important in this connection. "Historical Christianity"—the religion as we have actually known it in its concrete development through the centuries—comes in some respects as a Greco-Jewish synthesis, owing part of its power to the combination of two such highly different systems. It would be interesting to know how the religion would have developed if, in its early generative period, it had combined with a different culture.

The historian is hampered because the Christians in their very earliest period produced so little in writing, or at least preserved so little. Their leaders knew what was needed at the time, however, and the whole future question of authority in the Church would seem to have been decisively affected by the fact that (for the immediate purpose) so much was realized to depend on the evidence of eyewitnesses, and the primacy was naturally given to these. Perhaps it is for similar reasons that one glimpses the importance of certain relatives of Jesus in the earliest days at Jerusalem; and, of course, Saint Paul was accepted as an Apostle because his particular vision of the risen Christ was regarded as giving him first hand knowledge. Once the eyewitnesses had passed off the scene, it was natural that a certain primacy should be conceded to those who had been closest to them—those to whom they had communicated most; and the objective was the preservation of what had originally been delivered at first hand—what in the course of time could only appear in a less cogent form as "tradition."

The attempt to secure uniformity in the Church would seem to go back to the jealousy with which the Judeo-Christian leaders in Jerusalem regarded the

"Hellenizers"—some of these latter being Jews who had been affected by Hellenization or pagans who (before becoming Christian) had been converts to Judaism. When the "Hellenizers" carried the gospel to pagans in the Greek coastal cities of Palestine or in Syria, it would appear that the Church at Jerusalem would send a "Hebrew" to check on the result of their work. But, in spite of the care that was taken, there were aberrations even amongst the Christians in Palestine; and in Samaria, which had already been heterodox in its Judaism, an irregular form of Christianity slid away and became the origin of Gnosticism—this after A.D. 70, when the failure of Jahweh to grant victory in an apocalyptic war helped to produce a movement partly directed against the Old Testament deity. Henceforward, the rise of Christianity was paralleled by the multiplication of Gnostic sects which, in spite of their fantastic character, proved imposing. Now, more than ever, it was necessary to safeguard the original doctrines of the Church.

2. *The Church in the Roman Empire.* The Christians would appear in the empire as a strange small sect and for a time their recruits were perhaps chiefly amongst the lowly, though churches for which the epistles of Saint Paul were written can hardly be regarded as unimpressive. In the Roman Empire the believers might be hated because they were confused with the Jews or because the Jews incited the pagans against them; but in the first two centuries they suffered from the hostility of the populace rather than the intolerance of the emperors. After the fall of Jerusalem it was in Asia Minor that they came to appear most numerous, most lively, and most capable; and for a long time this was the most impressive seat of the Church. In various parts of the empire the teaching in the apostolic period itself would tend to vary, at least in its emphases, and the tradition came to develop on differing lines. Also, as time went on, one great region (almost as a matter of temperament) would be preoccupied chiefly with doctrine while another concentrated on asceticism and another became interested in organization.

From the middle of the second century, Hellenization—which found its climax in Alexandria—had captured the mentality of churchmen, who, instead of appearing as a mere sect came out into first-class controversy with leading intellectuals. They had taken Platonic ideas into their own system, but they set out to show where pagan thought had gone wrong, and claimed that Christianity was the culmination of Greek culture, the real heir of ancient philosophy. While this was happening, and the Church was settling down to a long-term role in the world, there arose in Asia Minor the Montanism which in a sense implied a reversion to the primitive spirit, the exultant early days. It meant a wave of "prophesyings," a reawakening of more immediate eschatological hopes, a severity in disciplinary matters and something like an actual thirst for martyrdom. Dealing with these problems was part of the larger process by which a sect that had envisaged an imminent eschatological climax gradually turned into a sedentary Church, realizing what it needed if it were to exist on a permanent footing. Controversies in the third century about penance, about relapses in time of persecution, about the validity of baptism by heretics, and about the rights of bishops, were part of the consequences of this transition.

Christians were beginning to develop a larger world view; scholarship was accumulating; the interest in history was rising. Confronted by the multiplicity of theological opinions, towards the end of the second century, Irenaeus had insisted on the steadying influence of bishops, who were still regarded as the repositories of the original apostolic tradition. In spite of the varieties at a certain level, an impressive uniformity and consistency had been made possible by such procedures as the communication from one region to another of the decisions made by local councils of bishops. At the same time, the heads of great sees attempted on occasion to secure the support of Rome in a doctrinal controversy, and this was capable of being construed later as an appeal to Rome. The church in Rome, very much a church of foreign colonists at first, was for a long time cosmopolitan—consisting of groups that had brought their local traditions and customs with them. Like Christianity itself, all new sects, all heresies, all novel teaching sought to reach the capital of the empire; and the bishop of Rome would have to meet early at a local level the challenge that these were later to present to the Church in general. When Christians from further east brought to Rome their different dates for the celebration of Easter, he was in a position to be highly aware of the inconvenience of this anomaly. Perhaps because he was inclined to be less speculative than the bishops of the Greek-speaking East, and more concerned for tradition and order, he not only met problems early but seems often to have commanded respect by his actual decisions. In the remarkable period in which the universal Church was developing its organization, he gains in importance, though all his claims do not go unchallenged. To us it might appear that the leadership which he asserted was likely to become due to him by reason of his merits. At the same time, it was still recognized that the authority of a bishopric—or a local tradition—depended primarily on the distinction of its apostolic origin. Rome could claim to go back to Peter and Paul.

375

In the middle of the third century the expansion is remarkable in Africa and in Western Europe, as well as in the lands to the east of the Mediterranean. Further east again, the missionary work pushes across Iraq, though its effect is to be gravely limited from this point by a Persian dynasty that is committed to Zoroastrianism. At a time when the Roman Empire was coming under pressure on the frontiers and was moving towards a grim development—while in any case this empire held hosts of *déracinés*, people feeling lost, not quite at home in the world—the older paganism was coming into decline. Oriental mystery cults attempted to answer the need for a salvationist faith with its mysticisms and forms of sacrament; philosophy outside the Church was running to religiosity. By the second half of the third century the Church had become an imposing body and a powerful influence in the empire, with important government and court officials amongst its members. Amongst its assets in the great conflict of religions were the possession of a sacred book; the attachment not to a mythical figure or a demiurge but to a Person who had walked in the world and could be identified in history; the assistance of an imposing organization; and the fact that this religion, besides producing its martyrs and issuing in an expressive kind of devotion, had become intimately connected with the moral life and works of charity. The Church was beginning perhaps to suffer even from its prosperity, and, to some, the rise of heresies seemed to come as a retribution for this. Already the controversies had opened which led to the long conflicts over the Holy Trinity and the Person of Christ.

Christianity had profited from the meeting of Jewish religion, Greek philosophy, and the Roman Empire—a conjuncture that seemed to coincide with the Incarnation. It had profited from the defects of all three—Jewish legalism, the tendencies of Greek philosophy at this late period, and the frustrations and distractedness of the Roman world. It had appeared at an advanced date in that long period in which much of the ability and the yearning of the human race in Asia, and now even in Europe—the result of a great anxiety about man's destiny—had been directed to the exploring of the possibilities of the spiritual realm. At a turning-point in the history of man's religious consciousness, Christianity, moreover, had moved into a highly civilized world which had an advanced form of urban life—a world which could support it with a certain refinement of intellect.

Its success was bound to affect the mentality of men—bound to alter their way of experiencing life, their attitude to nature, their posture under the sun, and their notions of human destiny. Since Christians believed in the Incarnation, they were bound to deny the gulf which the pagans had so often presumed to exist between God and Nature—bound to reject the view that matter is evil and that salvation must consist in escape from the body. They could not believe that in an eternity of cyclic repetitions Christ would go on dying over and over again for sinners; so they were released from extreme cyclic theories, while the Old Testament presented history as moving forward, moving to an objective, an unrepeatable and irreversible thing. The Old Testament indeed, forced them to look at history and regard it as important, and it cannot have been without significance that in Europe, for generation after generation, men could not learn about their religion without turning to what was really very ancient history. Instead of a great emphasis on Fortune, Christianity gave currency to the notion that the hand of Providence was in everything and (as had already happened) this might mean that retrospective reasoning could ultimately make sense of that kind of history-making which goes on over people's heads, overriding their conscious purposes and their predictions. Christianity stressed the sanctity of human life, the importance of the family, the inadmissibility of sexual license and the evil of such things as gladiatorial contests and the murder of infants. It regarded suicide as wicked. It insisted that man's life had a spiritual dimension, but it combined a high view of personality and its potentialities with an insistence on man's universal sin. It must have affected the world—the very conception of a human being—when, week in and week out, in numberless localities, men were reminded to reflect on their own sins, on forgiveness, humility, mercy, and love.

3. *The Christianized Empire.* After the failure of a great persecution and a tyrannical development of the empire, the Emperor Constantine granted to the Church in A.D. 313 full freedom of worship and the restitution of confiscated goods. Henceforward, he increased his favors to the Christians, and the Church began to move into a privileged position. It could be argued that his interests as an emperor would recommend an alliance with an institution that carried power; but there are signs that he was a sincere believer, though pagan in his manner of believing—too sure that the Christian God was the one who was victorious in battle and helped him to outwit his enemies. All this came as the climax of the Christian interpretation of history that had been developing—with the Hebrews regarded as the fathers of civilization, their language the original one, the language of God; Christianity being the return to the original religion of mankind, the one from which the Jews had lapsed (only to be partially rescued by Moses) while the Greeks had declined still more—the Church being the heir of the wisdom of both Jews and Greeks, however, and the Incarnation coinciding neatly with the

establishment of the Roman Empire, the era of peace. It seemed that, at this culminating moment, when the empire itself was becoming Christian, churchmen were willing to attribute to a Christian emperor the kind of divinity that they had refused to concede to his predecessors.

Henceforward it became almost consistently true that all who wished to gain imperial favor or to hold office or to make their way in society would have every motive for joining the Church; and the conversion of the Roman Empire—hitherto a matter of persuasion and not without its risks—was to be continued by the strong arm of the state. This was almost bound to introduce corruptions in the Church itself, and to increase the danger of a formal Christianity, mixed with paganism and thinking in pagan terms—the danger also of official compromises with paganism. It was perhaps natural, but it was unfortunate, that when there were parties in the Church, one or more of these (not merely the orthodox, but sometimes the heretical) should appeal to the emperor, even when he was not inclined to intervene. This had its special dangers, for in A.D. 325 Constantine himself, having called the first ecumenical council at Nicaea, put himself behind the decree of that Council, condemning the Arian heresy, but within less than three years was induced to change his mind.

Stranger still, men so convinced that they spoke for the right religion—and so sure that government and power should be at the service of God—were soon advocates of persecution; and the process in this case was so understandable that nobody today can feel sure that, living in the same period and sharing the same assumptions about religion, he would have decided differently. Some who were slow in their conversion to the practice appear to have been brought over when the victims of persecution declared later in life that they were now glad that they had been coerced.

Already, in the reign of Constantine, there arose issues which were to trouble the Church for a long time. One of them was the Donatist schism, which arose out of the later persecutions and was directed against bishops who had consented to the handing over of sacred books to the magistrates. It led to the erection of a counter-church in Africa—bishop confronting antibishop—with violence, persecution, atrocities, self-immolation, and streaks of the revolutionary and the apocalyptic. An extravagant, though serious and understandable, religious issue received tremendous leverage from social discontent and possibly a sort of nationalism, and from hostility to the Roman establishment. The trouble lasted for a century, almost until the barbarians overran the province.

Shortly before 325, Arius, who wished to guard the sovereignty of God the Father, and may not have been far enough from paganism to reject all ideas of subordination in the deity, produced a doctrine which, while asserting the divinity of the Son, secured a clear reduction of status for Him. The controversy tore the Church apart until A.D. 381, and it is perhaps not too much to say that for a longer period than this a great deal of the ecclesiastical conflict lay between men who wished to assert both the complete divinity and the complete humanity of Christ, but could not agree on the formula that would ensure the one without depleting the other. The formula adopted at Nicaea, homoousion (consubstantial with the Father) had already been rejected in a part of the eastern Church that had reacted against a heresy of an opposite tendency. It was uncongenial to some because in any case it could not claim to be scriptural. Various shades of the Arian and Nicene formulas were attempted by one party and another, who suggested "like the Father" and "of like substance with the Father," though there emerged one group that diverged further than Arius and declared that there was no likeness at all. The emperors provided a complicating factor—now hesitating, now changing their minds, now plumping for a form of Arianism. The West remained firm in its support of the Nicene formula, but subtle differences arose when technical terms had been translated into Latin, and the West was later than the East in confronting the earlier heresy that had constituted the opposite danger. At a moment when a great work of reconciliation was being achieved, there emerged an emperor who was a Westerner and a pious man, and he clinched the matter by an edict in 380, and a second ecumenical council, that of Constantinople, 381, which confirmed Nicaea.

If the Church had become more worldly and more contentious, its power to inspire renunciation and the life of the spirit was reasserted in the development of monasteries. There had been analogies to this in other parts of the globe, but Christianity had had from the first an ideal of chastity and poverty, and the sufferings of the martyrs had kept its self-denying aspects alive. The Egyptian anchorites are anterior to the victory of the Church in the empire, and, when they appear, they have strange features, particularly their obsession with the battle against the vast multiplicity of demons—a battle which could only be won by the repudiation of the world, a tremendous disciplining of the body, and a conquest of all ordinary emotions. It was a battle not to be won by the man who lived as a citizen in society; and, though prayers—sometimes repeated in what seems to be an incredibly mechanical manner—contributed to the objective, the movement was one which needed the greatest care by the Church. Nor is it clear how much of its deeper Christian character may not have been contributed retrospectively by the influential literature that it provoked. We are told, however, that Saint Anthony, when he went to a solitary life in the desert in A.D. 271, was moved by the injunction: "Sell all that thou hast and give to the poor and follow me." The Egyptian desert offered a remarkable opportunity, and great numbers followed his example. Something that almost seems like a competition in asceticism may have developed here and there—and warnings against spiritual pride in this connection appear early in Egypt—but out of his very loneliness the hermit was to contribute something of rare quality to the inner life of the Church.

The anchorites came to rudimentary forms of grouping for certain purposes, but it was Saint Pachomius who, in about A.D. 320 or 323, brought to the problem an essentially organizing mind and established the community principle. He prescribed rules for a whole order of monasteries; and, now not only renunciation but also obedience was important, while, besides vigils, readings from the Bible, prayer, and contemplation, there was greater emphasis on manual labor. The hermit was to have a significant history in Palestine and Syria, but Saint Basil the Great, from about A.D. 357, produced a community ideal which superseded this and became current throughout the Greek world. Before the middle of the century the news had reached the West and very soon ascetic groups were being founded there, though it was not until something like two hundred years later that Saint Benedict established his famous Rule that became the guide for Westerners. The whole movement, the literature that arose from it, and the spiritual teaching it produced had a great effect on the Church in general; and in the fourth century important people, including a surprising number of the leading intellects, associated themselves with it, at least during part of their lives. In its ultimate extension, it was to have by-products of an unpredictable kind—especially its contributions to cultural and even economic life. It may have been in one sense a protest against the growing worldliness of the fourth-century Church, or an attempt to find a new pattern of renunciation, in some cases perhaps even an escape from civic obligations. But it became, from the religious point of view, an eminently creative thing.

It is a whole Christian version of civilization that comes to the front in the fourth century. Biblical scholarship has advanced and become a technical affair. Eusebius not only reconstructs the story of the Church but has an interpretation of world history. The ancient culture receives a Christian shape, and the transmutation sometimes shows originality. The greatest intellects of the time, and some of the most imposing Christian figures of any age are the Fathers of the Church

who cluster in the latter half of the century—almost all of them highborn, enjoying the best education of the time, and trained in the monastic movement, yet emerging also as great men of the world—Saint Basil, Saint Ambrose, Saint Jerome, Saint Augustine, and many more. In a period of influential bishops, particularly Saint Ambrose in Milan, the reign of Theodosius I (379–95) saw paganism forbidden, heretics pursued by the government, Catholic orthodoxy the official religion of the whole empire, and the spiritual authority boldly asserting its right against the temporal. The piety of the lower sections of society made itself evident in the further development of the cult of martyrs and the veneration for relics, as well as in the eagerness for pilgrimages.

Early in the fifth century, Saint Augustine had to meet an important accusation from the paganism that still asserted itself, particularly in some of the aristocracy. Barbarian raiders had even reached the city of Rome. The tragedy that was falling upon the West was being ascribed to the desertion of the pagan deities. Augustine answered the charge in his *City of God*.

II. THE MIDDLE AGES

1. The Church and the Barbarian Invaders. Between the fifth and the tenth centuries, the downfall of the Roman Empire in the West, the eruption of barbarian hordes from Asia, the establishment of Teutonic monarchies and the long period of wars and migrations threw the map of the European continent into the melting pot, until it finally emerged with a general pattern that is still recognizable today. From the seventh century, the rise of Islam and the expansion of the Arabian Empire produced a drastic and permanent division in that Mediterranean world which had been the seat of the Greco-Roman civilization and had formed the original Christendom. In the eastern half of the ancient Roman Empire, the imperial system maintained itself at Byzantium, and, though it lost to Islam most of its territory bordering on the eastern as well as all the southern Mediterranean, it retained its cultural continuity (and preserved Christianity in Constantinople) for a further period of something like a thousand years.

In a sense it is now the history of Europe that really opens, and this Europe is to emerge as the new form of "Christendom" though it is only very slowly that the northern part of it becomes Christianized. The centuries of upheaval produced a grave decline of culture even in the south, and much of what had been subtle and profound in classical thought—much even of the scholarship and science—was to disappear for a long period. Henceforward, there is a separate history of the West and we trace the rise of a Western civilization from a comparatively early stage at which society itself has returned in many respects to primitive forms. Compared with the Byzantine world, and even later with the rapidly developing culture of Islam, the West appears as a backward region for a long time, its backwardness illustrated by the appalling collapse of its city-life, at a time when Constantinople, and later Bagdad, were of tremendous prestige and size. For special reasons this Western civilization at its formative period, when everything was still malleable, found itself under the presiding influence of a Christianity that had acquired greater power over mundane affairs than ever before.

Some of the Teutonic invaders had become Christianized before their eruption into the Roman world, but they had been converted by Arians and had received the faith in a heretical form. This would seem to have created difficulties with the populations they subjected, for no Arian dynasty survived, though, in the case of Spain, the Visigoths maintained themselves by going over to Catholicism. The Frankish invaders of Gaul may have owed some of their success to the fact that their dynasty was converted only after their migration into the Roman Empire, so that from the very first, they adhered to the Catholicism of their Gallo-Roman subjects. For centuries the reigning dynasties were to have an exceptional part to play in the shaping of the map, the history and the culture of Europe, and it was they who brought their peoples over to Christianity in those more primitive conditions under which it was inevitable that religion should be regarded as the affair of the group.

If Christianity had won its way in the Roman Empire through individual conversion, it owed its spread over Europe sometimes to mass-conversion, i.e., to the decrees, perhaps the example, sometimes the pressures and persecuting policies, of those who held the government. It was to be extended further in the north of Europe in subsequent centuries by movements from both the Catholic West and the Orthodox East, so that, when the thirteenth century opened, only a small wedge of paganism remained, near the point where the southern coast of the Baltic turns north. Lithuania resisted longest of all, balanced for a considerable period between the influence of Rome and the influence of Byzantium. From the western side the advance was sometimes made through military conquest and colonization policies, particularly in the east of what the modern historian knows as Germany. Here the warfare between Christian and pagan might be of a brutal kind, down to the time when, in the thirteenth century, Prussia was "converted" by the Teutonic Knights.

A considerable part of Europe was Christianized,

therefore, by methods not unlike the ones by means of which a similar area was brought over to communism in the twentieth century. As in the case of communism—though with greater effect in those earlier stages in the history of society—the Christian control of education, the procedures of indoctrination, and the withholding of knowledge about possible alternative systems (or the treatment of all alternatives as merely disreputable) ensured the maintenance of the authoritarian creed in subsequent centuries, without the need to continue perpetually the forcible methods that had been required for its installation. Granted the conditions of the time, one could say, however, that those countries which became Christian were fortunate. The existing alternatives would hardly have been more happy for them. Indeed, it was their conversion that brought them into the orbit of civilization.

In the Byzantine East, Roman Emperors, continuing a regime that had developed from the time of Constantine, were able to exercise in some respects (though perhaps less than was once thought) a species of "caesaropapism." But in the West the Roman Emperor had disappeared, while the bishop of Rome maintained his spiritual ascendancy amongst Christian believers and acquired during the invasions even a certain leadership in some secular matters. Pope Gregory the Great (590–614) was fervent in his religious duties, extending his influence over western countries, directing the conversion of England, and asserting the spiritual supremacy of Rome as the see of Saint Peter. But in default of anybody else, at a time when Byzantine authority in Italy had become inert, he was compelled to negotiate with the Lombard invaders of Italy and to administer Rome as a governor, inaugurating the temporal power of the papacy. It almost seemed as though the Church in the centuries before the barbarian invasions had unwittingly been developing an organization exactly calculated to survive, and to preserve the faith, through just such a period of cataclysm as had now occurred.

In a world where civilization had suffered such a recession, Christianity itself shared in the "barbarization," coming closer sometimes to those pagan superstitions that governed primitive minds. Neither the spiritual life nor examples of saintliness were impossible, but the intellect was ready to accept magic and legend even more easily than before; and, since ancient thought itself was now imperfectly known and imperfectly understood, something of superstition was run into the interstices, and there was produced an outlook which entangled the material with the spiritual, making religion more earthy, in a way, and nature herself a field for the miraculous.

On the other hand, whatever may be said about the

way in which the new nations of Europe were converted, there was a sense in which the spread of Christianity was the kind of conquest that justifies itself retrospectively. The most impressive part of the story is the tremendous internal missionary work which the Church conducted in the succeeding centuries in the countries into which it spread—work calculated to bring religion home to the individual, and to make it gradually more genuine and profound, even if it had been shallow and unreliable at first. It was not merely a case of eliminating all the superstitions that could not be harnessed to Christianity or preventing lapses into paganism, but also teaching the belief that had been handed down, influencing manners and morals, and deepening sincerity, deepening the appreciation of the faith. Part of the curious charm of Bede's *Ecclesiastical History* (including those papal letters which provide guidance for the conversion of England and prescribe special consideration for those who need careful weaning from paganism) lies in an amazing gentleness that stands out (early in the eighth century) against a background of violence; in it also is found a combination of high ideas at the spiritual level with crude notions about the universe, a simple love of amiable miracles. The great support of the Church in the Middle Ages was to be the sheer fidelity of the mass of the people to their beliefs, and whether the faith were superstitious or not, its genuineness was in the last resort the real weapon that popes were to have against kings.

During its earliest centuries, the Church had developed in a highly civilized world, and its theological teaching had come to require a considerable degree of sophistication. The literature to which it was attached, and its own insistence on the continuity of its doctrinal tradition, gave it a vested interest in the preservation of the Greco-Roman culture. It could not prevent a serious relapse even within its own ranks; but in a sense it had from the first been particularly organizing itself for the preservation of a creedal system; and this—indeed the maintenance of the whole tradition—called for a staff of trained ecclesiastics. These latter, precisely because of the education that was so essential for them, were to become indispensable also in the work of secular government. The attachment to the Scriptures made the Christian Church the enemy of illiteracy at a crucial stage in the development of peoples; and the need to have translations for missionary purposes secured that it might even be the chief agency in the development of a literary language.

The whole situation, in fact, imposed upon churchmen the tasks of educating the "barbarians" and they became the principal instrument by which the culture of the ancient classical world was transmitted to the Teutonic peoples who had acquired the predominance in Europe. In the most violent days the monasteries stood like fortresses, preserving the tradition of learning—preserving, sometimes without knowing it, the manuscripts of classical works that went out of circulation for centuries. And for centuries it was churchmen—people with minds primarily shaped by their religious beliefs and religious training—who took the lead in the gradual recovery and deepening appreciation of the thought and learning of antiquity. The ancient materials were now envisaged in a framework of Christian ideas. It was as though, in Western Europe, a civilization was being constructed from old materials but to a new architectural design. There emerged in the Arabian Empire a parallel culture, closely connected with that of ancient Greece, but under the presidency of the Islamic faith. These two imposing examples of a culture which developed in a religious setting almost under the eye of the historian, offer promising material for a resort to the comparative method.

During centuries of tumult and upheaval, however, the framework of medieval culture (like the pattern on the map of Europe itself) was slow in taking shape. There was a period in the eighth century when England and Ireland seemed to be the last refuge of civilization, and missionaries particularly from Northumbria (often in the tradition of Bede) carried the light back to the continent, converting parts of Germany that had never been Christianized, and contributing to the emergence of the "Carolingian Renaissance" at the end of the century. At this latter date, a long alliance between the papacy and the predecessors of Charlemagne had resulted in the re-creation of an "empire"—one in which Charlemagne was able to exercise a sort of "caesaropapism," controlling the Church even in essential matters and expecting from it spiritual support—as though the function of the laity was to fight the battles while the function of the clergy was simply to assist the warfare with their prayers. A "Carolingian Renaissance," which did not itself open out into a long-term cultural development, established, through the emperor's edicts, the enduring principle that monasteries and cathedrals should accept the responsibility for education.

Then further waves of invasion in Europe—and even in Britain—in the ninth and tenth centuries brought a renewed period of turbulence; and in the tenth century the papacy, having no longer an emperor to protect it, came to "the saddest period in its history" when it met something worse than "caesaropapism," becoming the victim and the plaything of the local Roman aristocracy. The danger from violence of this immediate sort was doubled by the spread of the doctrine that the lord of the soil had the ownership of all the land, even the land that was devoted to religious use. David Knowles (in a paper, "Some Trends of Scholarship, 1868–1968, in the Field of Medieval History") has described how

The ownership and control of all churches, not excluding monastic and canonical foundations, passed gradually into the hands of individuals who, whether laymen or ecclesiastics, were lords of the land. Thus from the eighth century onwards there was gradually established in western Europe the regime of the private or proprietary church, of which the lord enjoyed many of the fruits and to which he appointed a priest (or abbot or bishop) of his choice, and which he could give, sell or divide like any other real property. When the system was linked at the summit to the extreme claims [of] the emperors to appoint bishops and even popes, there existed in perfect form the "church in the hands of laymen."

2. The Establishment of the Medieval Order. The real recovery of Europe from what can justifiably be regarded as "Dark Ages" dates from the latter half of the tenth century, when the Germans halted the Magyars, nomadic hordes from Asia, who had carried their raids across the length and breadth of the continent. Henceforward the west of Europe was guarded against the worst of its dangers by the consolidation of Germany and the establishment of the Magyars in a sedentary Christian state in Hungary, as well as the development also of Christian monarchies in Poland, Bohemia, and Scandinavia. The establishment of a "Roman Empire" under Otto I in 962 opened at last a period of comparative stability, and there emerged something like the shape of the Western Europe we know—a Europe which by 1053 had lost a great deal of its connection with the Orthodox Church. Trade and industrial production increased again, and the Mediterranean, which in 972 "like the Baltic, was a hostile sea," saw important developments which brought Venice, Genoa, and Pisa to the front. The period between 1050 and 1150 was to prove one of the most creative epochs in European history, and its great achievement was that it established the real bases of the medieval system. In this period intellectual influences from the more highly developed Islamic world provided an important stimulus; but it was only one factor in the case. The intellectual leadership had passed to the northern part of France and to Lorraine. The promotion of the study of logic (which goes back to Gerbert in Rheims, A.D. 972, and was based at first on the writings of Boethius) became "the most important feature in the advancement of learning in northern Europe."

But from the time of Otto I the Church had become still more the prey of the laity and a low-water mark was reached when the Emperor Henry III (1039–56) deposed three popes and installed his own nominees. From the Church's point of view, the main problem to be solved was the question of the independence of the spiritual authority; for the existing system led to many abuses and obstructed any attempt to bring the clergy under discipline. A monastic reform which started in Cluny in 910, though it did not attack this problem, established centers of piety over a very wide area. Another such movement in Lorraine can be seen from 1046 making a specific call for the absolute independence of the spiritual authority. The demand for change arose in the provinces therefore, and it was a band of people connected with the Lorraine movement who brought this latter program to Rome and became influential in that city. They supported their cause by a study of the canon law, and if on the one hand they made use of what we know as the "False Decretals" (produced two centuries earlier in the province of Tours) they also found more imposing evidence, including documents from the time of Gregory the Great.

Perhaps their labors would have been ineffectual if the Emperor Henry III, though nominating popes, had not appointed some worthy people to the Holy See. Their efforts at a time when the next emperor, Henry IV, was a minor, led in 1059 to a crucial decree which excluded the laity—whether the emperor or the Roman aristocracy—from any part in the appointment of a pope and prescribed an independent election by cardinals. A great development of ecclesiastical litigation and an increasing number of appeals to Rome may have represented another way in which action from the provinces helped to elevate and transform the papal office. The Lorraine reformers had been equally anxious—indeed, it would seem to have been their initial anxiety—that local ecclesiastical authorities should be liberated from subservience to a powerful laity. During the pontificate of Gregory VII (1073–85) the zeal of the pope for the reform of the Church at large, and particularly the Church in Germany—the determination to get rid of such evils as simony—led to that conflict between papacy and empire which was to form one of the great themes of medieval history. In any case, the essential system of the Middle Ages now took shape.

At first it was a controversy as to whether the monarch should choose his own bishops and invest them with the insignia of the spiritual office. And here the Church was faced with problems that arose out of the character of its new entanglement with the world. Bishops in Germany had vast temporal possessions and might be the heads of considerable principalities. An emperor could not be indifferent to the appointment of such formidable dignitaries. What was called the "Investiture Contest" was in fact open to compromise, and one pope, in what seems like a fit of absent-mindedness, accepted the interesting idea of turning the bishops into purely spiritual officers—a thing which had no chance of being tolerated by the German episcopate. The pope possessed weapons—he could use discontented magnates, or incite foreign powers, or foment public opinion, against an emperor. Before long, pope and emperor were presuming to depose one another.

There can be little doubt that the assertion of the independence of the spiritual authority, and the resulting conflict between "spiritual" and "temporal," were amongst the factors that were to give to Western history its remarkable dynamic quality. The controversy directed the thought of men to the question of the origin and basis of government, whether secular or ecclesiastical, and produced a literature that has little parallel in the history of Byzantine Christianity. At times it led to a confrontation between the theory or the assumptions of the canon law and the principles that lay behind Roman Law. The fervor for political theory in Europe in the centuries from the time of the Renaissance may owe something (just as medieval thought itself owed something) to the influence of the ancient world. But many of the modern ideas rise more directly out of the politico-ecclesiastical controversies of the Middle Ages. This point became a great feature in the historical thinking of Lord Acton, who summed up the matter by saying that Saint Thomas Aquinas had been "the first Whig."

In the age of the Reformation many of the medieval patterns of thought are still visible, whether in the theory of the divine right of kings, or the notion of a contract between king and people, or the idea of constitutional limitations on monarchical authority, or the controversy over tyrannicide. At a later period still, it is possible to trace the actual secularization of what had once been politico-religious ideas. Without what under various forms was an epic conflict between the secular authority and the spiritual, a Western Europe under a predominant religious faith might have hardened into something like the Byzantine or oriental systems.

Gregory VII and the restored papacy stood for the idea of a Christian Commonwealth—not a "state" but a "religious society" existing for the glory and the service of God. The whole was to be managed by a secular arm and a spiritual arm, and these were supposed to cooperate with one another. Often the two did cooperate, the Church not only offering its prayers and its spiritual services—not merely giving a vague support to the whole order of things—but allying with

the monarch because, for example, it had an interest in preserving the larger territorial unit from disruption. The ecclesiastics might introduce the monarchy to ideas of law, notions of property, the use of written deeds—techniques of an older civilization which they were in a position to remember, and perhaps to need for themselves. Monarchs in turn defended and endowed the Church; and at a desperate moment an emperor had helped to produce that reformed papacy which was to harass his successors. When the two clashed, it was almost in the logic of the medieval system that the conflict should be long and that the spiritual arm should ultimately prevail, but only to its own detriment. Already, for Gregory VII, the pope represented Christ, the real governor of the world, and it was for him to guide the destiny of the "religious society," directing and coordinating its larger purposes. The most signal illustration of this in the latter half of the eleventh century was the way in which Gregory VII and his successor took up the idea of a Crusade assuming that Rome should have the role of inspirer and director. At a time when monarchs were in revolt against the Holy See, and Germany in particular withheld its support, it was the pope, not the emperor, who launched the First Crusade (1096–99) and showed himself the leader of Western Europe.

3. *The Culmination of the Middle Ages.* What was now in the process of formation was a Christian culture based on the universal acceptance of the faith and typified in the twelfth century by the rise of scholasticism, the great cathedral building, and the gradual transition to what we call universities. Behind it lay the revival of Western economic life in the eleventh century; the growth of towns; the emergence of something like city-states in Italy; the development of Mediterranean trade by some of these as Moslem power in that sea declined; the success of the First Crusade; the wider view of the world; the contacts with Arabian civilization; and the recovery of important areas of ancient thought—all these, together with the fact that both men and society had come to the stage of general intellectual awakening, or had found the kind of exhilaration which lights the spark. Starting from the discovery of Aristotelian logic—and greatly relishing this—while lacking the concrete knowledge of the world and nature which Aristotle had possessed, men ran to a great amount of deductive reasoning from little material; and, as the more scientific work of Aristotle emerged, they accepted virtually his whole system of nature, which became to them an inherited "authority," almost like the Bible—an authority all the firmer because it was in schools that medieval thought developed. The great achievement was the degree to which the natural science and the philosophy of Aris-

totle were combined with the Christian faith, to produce a "scholasticism" which was bound to have a character of its own, if only because the philosophy (always remembering theology in the background) tended to concentrate on such problems as the existence of God, the immortality of the soul, the question of free will.

The pontificate of the statesmanlike Innocent III (1198–1216) sees the "religious society" of Western Europe in all its majesty, and it is this that sets the stage in the thirteenth century for the development of scholasticism to its culmination in Saint Thomas Aquinas, the renewed cathedral building, and the spread of universities—the climax of that Christian culture which, a century after Innocent, was to produce a Giotto and a Dante. Innocent more than once chose an emperor, and he forced Philip Augustus of France to recognize as a queen the first wife whom he had tried to divorce. He had the kings of Aragon, England, Portugal, Castile, Denmark, and Sicily as his vassals. He launched two crusades against the infidel, as well as a third against the heretics in the south of France. He also dominated the whole European diplomatic situation. His Lateran Council of 1215 was attended by over 1200 bishops, abbots, and priors (including representatives from Armenia and the Latin churches that the crusaders had established in Syria and the Balkans) as well as many other people from European countries—proctors from the Emperor at Constantinople, for example, and from the kings of France, England, Hungary, and Poland. In other words, it was "like a representative Parliament of all Christendom." It was entirely the pope's council and it passed judgment between rival candidates for the empire, and between King John of England and his barons. It also allotted the major part of the county of Toulouse, besides taking measures for the reform of the Church, and planning a new crusade.

The activities of the papal curia and its agents were now undergoing a great expansion. The multiplicity of the appeals to Rome and the constant despatch of delegates from Rome to all parts of Europe secured the authority of the canon law throughout the system, and kept the papacy in touch with all regions. The increasing organization and the increasing circulation of money assisted the development of papal finances and enabled Innocent to draw on the great wealth of the Church.

This mundane success had its darker side, and, indeed, for some time the protests against the worldliness of ecclesiastics had been rising—protests that took shape as heresies. In the case of the Cathari, who had brought Manichaeism from the East and had captured much of society in the south of France, as well as spreading into neighboring regions, the class of austere *perfecti* were a reproach to the Church, while the ordinary *credentes* were allowed excessive license, and the whole movement could be regarded as a threat to society itself. The menace was so formidable that the idea of the crusade was now directed to the conflict against the heretic as well as against the infidel. A cruel suppression took place and the Inquisition was gradually developed to cope with the aftermath.

In the case of Peter Waldo and his followers who from about 1170 took to poverty and began to draw doctrine straight from the New Testament, the suppression of the unauthorized preaching drove a band who had erred only through their enthusiasm, into revolutionary ways and actual heresy. When Saint Francis dedicated himself to poverty in 1208, Innocent III took care not to repeat the error, though Francis and his followers had found their own way of imitating the apostolic life and they, too, had preached without license. They were harnessed to the Church, and the organization of the movement was gradually taken out of Saint Francis' hands. The monastic system, based on poverty, chastity, and obedience, was adapted to the purpose of men who went out into the world to preach; and so the friars found their way into the medieval landscape.

Similarly, Saint Dominic in 1215 received permission to establish an order which should meet heresy with argument and learning, and the members of this order were particularly trained for a preaching and teaching role. These new orders of wandering friars, who served under the direct command of the pope and constituted his special sort of army, quickly became important and numerous. They brought religion home to the people and acquired a popularity that sometimes weakened the position of the parish priest. They recruited brilliant men, some of the Dominicans leading in the development of scholasticism; and they came to acquire an important place in universities. The Franciscans soon carried their missionary work into northern Europe and North Africa. Before long they were in China.

This was a period when religion was so imposing in the way in which it was handed down and presented to people—and was so powerful in its forms of current expression—that, in spite of some strange deviations, it hardly occurred to the great mass of human beings (even to the rebels and the powerful intellects) that there was the alternative of disbelief. A religion that has soaked itself into the minds of men, and almost become second nature to them, can work like a chemical in society, inspiring original thought, giving wing to the imagination and inciting the believer to strange adventures, curious experiments in living. In the Middle Ages a certain marriage of Christianity and the world—Christianity with the whole mundane order—produced a supra-national religious society that was itself an amazing structure and can now be envisaged as a work of art. If we have in mind all the external apparatus of the religion as it existed at that time—its symbolism and its ceremonial, its biblical personalities and famous saints, its associations with a peculiar pattern of the cosmos, even its view of the hand of God in history—we can entertain the hazardous idea of a "Christian civilization," which, culminating in the thirteenth century, affected the landscape of town and country, governed the calendar of the year, touched the home, the craft guilds, the universities, and even put a stamp of its own on the most idle superstitions. This civilization carried its own ideas about the nature of personality and about the right posture to be adopted by human beings under the sun. It provided the conditions for the development of piety and the inner life—for the deepening of religious thought and religious experience—and for the expression of all this in cathedrals, in painting, and in poetry.

Even the papacy, which can seem so unattractive to us as it asserts its claims against powerful monarchs, stood in many ways as a beneficent influence, insisting on certain standards, raising the quality of the clergy, checking forms of tyranny, providing antecedents for modern international law, and directing governments to objects that transcended the ambitions of secular rulers.

4. The Beginning of Decline. However, in this whole medieval order of things Christianity was gravely entangled with the systems of the world, its bishops, for example, being great landholders and feudal lords. Even if men in general had been more otherworldly, the conditions in the terrestrial sphere itself were bound to suffer changes as time went on. Because even the ecclesiastics (by the very character of the situation) were not sufficiently otherworldly, the Church itself came under the operation of some of the laws which govern other religions—govern human systems generally. In a sense it became the victim of the remarkable success that it had achieved in the preceding period. To the upholders of the existing order of things, the changes that were brought about during the fourteenth and fifteenth centuries were bound to appear as a decline; and in certain respects the medieval synthesis can be seen to be breaking down. But the story of religion—even the story of the state as essentially a "religious" society—had by no means come to its end. The downfall of the old order is difficult to disentangle from the interesting movements that were reassembling the materials and bringing about the creation of a new one. In some respects

the medieval period moved into what we call modern times on its own momentum, as a result of impulses within itself. Amid much confusion, we see deeper lines of continuous development, as though the logic of events were working itself out.

It was in the realm of thought—indeed, it was at the heart of scholasticism itself—that the most fateful changes occurred. And these changes were calculated to affect the actual character of religion, not merely the relations between Christianity and the world. Saint Thomas Aquinas, by his reexposition of Aristotelianism, had provided believers with a philosophy which explained the cosmos and was crowned by a theology; but the result had been to make philosophy an autonomous affair. Even while he was at work there were men who were more down-to-earth, more prepared just to hold their Aristotelianism neat; and perhaps a certain worldly-mindedness made them a danger not only to an ecclesiastical system but also to religion itself. Others who were not worldly-minded or unbelieving tended to argue their way behind the tradition of classical philosophy itself, and to question its basis—to doubt even the possibility of metaphysics. It meant denying the ability of the human mind to reach the kind of truths that were associated with "natural religion," or to reason in any way about God.

Under the influence of William of Ockham a great section of the academic world went over to a system which, without denying the revelation, cut away the forms of rationalization hitherto current, making religion a matter of pure fideistic acceptance. Even the difference between right and wrong was removed from the domain of reason—it came to be held that a thing was good because an arbitrary God had decreed it so. If scholasticism itself had emerged too directly out of a passion for logic, and had lost something by its development in an abstract realm, too remote from life and from general culture, the fourteenth-century developments increased the gulf and helped to make the whole system curiously arid. Even the content of religious thought came to be altered, for reflection was now concentrated on the absolute power of a God who was beyond man's reason, and who, from a state of unconditioned freedom, settled all things by sheer arbitrary decree. The will of God, the power of God, became the great theme, and the result was by no means the same as when the emphasis is placed on the thesis: "God is love." Even in the discussion of human beings, attention was fixed on the role of man's will and that of God's grace in the work of salvation.

These preoccupations help to explain some of the peculiar emphases and developments in the sixteenth-century Reformation. In any case, the separation between faith and reason was bound to create difficulty—

belief itself now appearing more farfetched and more unreal, God himself more remote—a situation which could encourage secularism and religious indifference.

Perhaps more dramatic at the time, however, were the changes in the relationship between the Church and the world, and even the appearance of a tremendous controversy concerning the nature of the Church itself.

At the beginning of the fourteenth century the papacy both presumed too much on the success that it had achieved, and discovered what it had lost by the discomfiture of its chief rival, the empire in Germany. Henceforward, it had to confront the rising national monarchies without the powerful assistance which, ideally, should have come from the ancient partnership between pope and emperor. In the bull *Unam Sanctam* of 1302, Pope Boniface VIII (1294–1303), relying on the assertions and on the victories of his predecessors, issued too high a challenge to monarchs—claiming too boldly the right to direct and judge them even in the exercise of their temporal power. The resulting conflict, in which the French government accused him of appalling crimes and demanded his trial before a general council of the Church, brought him to humiliation in 1303 at the hands of a body of desperadoes, and he died within a few weeks after he had been released.

In 1305, an archbishop of Bordeaux who was elected as Pope Clement V proved to be a creature of the French king; and, besides creating many French cardinals, he took up his residence at Avignon, which was then just outside the frontiers of France. Owing partly to the political confusion of Italy, a return of the papacy to Rome proved impracticable for a long time. Gregory XI went back there in 1377, but he died in the following year and then the cardinals in Rome elected a pope, but another was elected in Avignon. Now, therefore, the system reached its *reductio ad absurdum,* two successors of Saint Peter making concurrent claims and exercising concurrent power. Nothing could have been more injurious to the Church and more damaging to prestige than the existence for over thirty years of the Great Schism—some parts of Europe attaching themselves to a pope in Avignon, others to a pope in Rome, with the further complication of overlappings here and there, so that a diocese might not be sure which of two rival claimants was its duly appointed bishop. There now arose the question: What means of rescue were open to a Church that seemed to have been struck at its very heart?

5. The Conciliar Movement. It was natural that there should be some tension in the Middle Ages between the idea of the Church as the entire community of believers, collectively sustained and inspired by the Holy Spirit, and the notion of a clerical hierarchy, imposed from above, and deriving a special authority from outside the system, i.e., direct from Christ. It had been noted that if Peter had received the power of "binding and loosing" (in Matthew 16:18–19) this particular prerogative had been extended after the Resurrection to all the Apostles (in John 20:22–23); but though the effect of this was to widen the basis of authority in the Church, it did not in reality override the prevailing view that the bishop of Rome, as the representative of Saint Peter, had the effective power of government. The term "Roman Church" was ambiguous—it could mean the local church of the city of Rome but also it could signify the entire congregation of the faithful. It was the latter that was supposed to be preserved against error, not in the sense that lapses here and there were impossible, but in the sense that the Church in its entirety would never go astray—there would never be heresy in all its parts at a single time.

Even this stress on the wide-ranging community of believers, was not taken to mean that the community as such could carry on the work of government without the directing hand of the papacy; and those who glorified General Councils of the Church normally assumed that the pope himself would actually summon these bodies and lead them—that, indeed, his own authority came to its maximum when he worked through a General Council. On the other hand, it was possible to consider that, though the church in Rome had played a distinguished part in the establishment and maintenance of orthodoxy, the pope as a man might fall into error; and if he notoriously supported what had long been regarded as heresy, his authority would be *ipso facto* at an end. It came to be asserted that the same would be true if he were publicly and obviously guilty of serious crime.

The possibility of such contingencies raised the question of the part which the College of Cardinals or General Councils might have to play at the moment when the incapacity had to be declared. It has been pointed out that in canonist writers of about A.D. 1200 are to be found anticipations of all the main assertions of the Conciliar Movement. Yet this was the time when the papacy under Innocent III was making the highest possible claims and asserting that all other jurisdictions in the Church were only a derivation from Rome.

In the thirteenth century, however, the development of the kind of canon law which treated the Church as a corporation tended to increase the possible leverage of conciliar ideas. There now appeared more of the suggestion that a corporation is the source of the authority of its head, that all members of a corporation should take part in decisions which affect the whole body, that a corporation could survive as a unity if it lost its head, and could take the necessary measures to rectify the default in the leadership. Such ideas were able to develop at the very time when papal publicists, for their part, were continuing the line of thought which had brought the authority of Innocent III to its height. Amongst writers hostile to the papacy the idea arises not only that the cardinals could act on behalf of the pope when he himself was defaulting in some way, but also the idea that in serious matters the pope should always act in consultation with the cardinals—and moreover the idea that the cardinals had the authority to summon a General Council.

In all this we find the insertion of what the modern student would regard as "constitutional" ideas into canonist reflections on Church government. The supporters of the Conciliar Movement at the beginning of the fifteenth century could feel that they were by no means innovators—that, indeed, they were following principles with a long and respectable ancestry, principles essentially orthodox.

In any case, the Great Schism—the scandal of two lines of successive popes reigning contemporaneously and dividing the West—made it necessary to turn to just that kind of thinking which envisaged the Church's power of self-rectification during a failure in the supreme leadership. The Schism lasted for nearly thirty years, and, though almost all of the popes elected during this period had sworn to resign if their departure would help the cause of unity, the promises were not kept. If either of the rival popes summoned a General Council it could only be a party affair and the two colleges of cardinals failed in their attempts to persuade their respective popes to issue a joint invitation to a Council. When in 1409 a Council was called by cardinals at Pisa, its legality was doubtful, and though it pretended to depose the two existing holders of the papal office and secure the election of a third, the real effect of this was to make the situation worse—there were now three claimants to the dignity instead of two. It is understandable if such an impasse provoked much discontent with the general condition of the Church, and stimulated a great deal of thinking about the position of both popes and General Councils.

The situation was aggravated by the fact that the nation-states were now becoming more important and governments that had the choice of adhering to one pope rather than another acquired more power over their national churches. Their diplomacies (particularly during the Hundred Years' War between France and England) affected their ecclesiastical loyalties (the English disliking a pope at Avignon, for example); and when the Emperor Sigismund combined with one of

the rival popes to summon the more imposing Council of Constance, it was through diplomacy conducted with various national governments that he secured a broad basis for the assembly. This body attacked the papal problem in 1415, and began by deposing the successor of the pope who had gained office as a result of the Council of Pisa—they struck at the very pope who had joined Sigismund in summoning the new Council. The resignation of another claimant was then secured; and, though the pope at Avignon refused to give way, the diplomacy of Sigismund prevented his having the support of reigning monarchs.

The Great Schism was for practical purposes healed and a new pope, Martin V (1417–31), was appointed—a man who, once in authority, opposed the conciliarist ideas then prevalent. The cry had gone up that a General Council was superior to the pope and it was decreed at Constance that a Council should be summoned at least every ten years. There were some who urged that even laymen should have a place in such a Council, which was being regarded as a representative body. Another Council which assembled at Basel in 1431 refused to be dissolved at the command of another pope, and it brought absurdity to a higher degree than before, for it threatened a renewal of schism by presuming to depose the pope and to appoint another one. The excesses of the radicals frightened some of the moderates into conservatism, however, and in any case it was the pope rather than the Council who had the power to execute a policy effectively.

In 1439 a rival Council which the pope had summoned to Ferrara decreed that a Council was not superior to a pope; and though a dwindling body went on meeting at Basel, they came to terms in 1449, abandoning their adhesion to the man whom they had presumed to appoint to the papal office. They had humiliated a supreme pontiff and compelled him to treat with them after he had decreed their dissolution; but they brought the whole Conciliar movement to a miserable end.

6. The Transition to a New Order. In the meantime new forms of heresy had been arising, and they gained additional strength from the abuse that was being made of such things as indulgences, from the jealousy felt toward ecclesiastical property, and from national feeling against the intrusions of papal power into one country and another. From about 1374 John Wycliffe in England was preaching against the excessive wealth of the Church and claiming that the monarch should decide how much of this should be retained—a gospel that brought him the patronage of a powerful and covetous nobility. He lost some of his humbler allies when he attacked the problem of the eucharist, declaring that Christ was present spiritually but that the bread and wine retained their former substance. Emphasizing the absolute power of the will of God—a form of emphasis which the influence of Saint Augustine as well as contemporary movements in philosophy encouraged—Wycliffe ran to predestinarian views which were calculated to lessen the role of church offices in the work of salvation. He encouraged the reading of the Bible (and its translation into the vernacular) because the Scriptures were of higher authority than the traditions of the Church.

Some analogies to the later Protestantism are apparent in all this; but the first Lancastrian monarch of England, Henry IV (1399–1413), desired the Church's recognition of his title to the throne of England, and his parliament carried a new statute, requiring the burning of heretics—a statute which was severely executed during the reign of his son. The "Lollard" followers of Wycliffe, some of whom had tended to revolutionary ideas, could survive only as ineffectual secret heretics.

Partly under the influence of the English movement, John Hus led a similar revolt against ecclesiastical evils in Bohemia, and, though he avoided some of Wycliffe's doctrinal innovations, he was burned in 1415 by the Council of Constance, which wished to show that at least it did not tolerate heresy. Some of Hus's associates came nearer to the ideas of Wycliffe, and there emerged a popular radical movement which attacked monasticism, the adoration of saints, purgatory, indulgences, etc., on the ground that these things were not authorized by the actual words of Scripture. And here, as in England, a powerful and richly endowed Church, rife with obvious abuses, was challenged by a dangerous picture of Apostolic Christianity—the concept that the clergy should be poor men leading a simple life as they guarded their flocks.

In 1419 the Czechs revolted and their religious grievances, which gave the conflict at times something of an apocalyptic character, combined with a tremendous national hatred against the Germans, who had acquired a strong position at court, in the university of Prague, and in the industry of the towns. Successive campaigns against the rebels came to disaster, and though the extremists were defeated in 1434, an agreement had to be made with the moderates which put the Bohemian church in a special position (e.g., in regard to the reception by the laity of communion in both kinds). Bohemia remained, indeed, a region of potential revolt, potential heresy.

It might have been argued that the fifteenth century had a special need for the Christian religion at its best, since deep forces in society were producing a great secularization of life—producing indeed a society that increased the mundane claims on human beings. The growth of industry and commerce, the development of high finance, the increasing importance of a bourgeois class, and the blossoming of virtual city-states in Italy, Germany, and the Netherlands provided a new dynamic for the secular activities of men. The resulting erosion of the traditional feudal forms of society was bound to produce disorder in the period of transition, and the Church had tied itself unduly to the older order of things—the very pattern of its organization ceased to correspond with the systems that were developing in the world. The exile of the papacy in Avignon, the ensuing Great Schism and the Conciliar Movement had increased the tendency of separate regions to look after their local religious affairs, and the national governments were growing in strength and importance, legislating against papal interference or making their own terms with the popes.

The principle of nationality was itself receiving recognition, even in the organization of General Councils and universities. The Renaissance in Italy and the more effective recovery of the thought of antiquity, assisted a secularization which, however, had also been showing itself in the development of vernacular literature and its advance to high artistic status. And the secularization showed itself within the great development of the visual arts, especially in Italy—perhaps also in the tendency of some scholastic writers to move over to science, to problems of celestial mechanics, for example.

But all this—and the palpable abuses in the Church itself—did not mean that Christianity was coming to its terminus or that there had been a serious decline of religious faith as such. The very revolts against the Church were born of religious zeal—themselves signs of a questing kind of religion that gets behind the conventions and seeks the original fountain of the faith. The interesting eruptions of spontaneous life are not antireligious but are more like a groping for fresh adventures in religion, longings for an almost noninstitutional kind of piety, as though it were felt necessary to cut through the artificialities and go direct to the essential things. Most significant of all are the devotional movements, that press for contemplation and austerity, or seek a mystical apprehension of Christ. And the *Imitation of Christ* which has been the inspiration of both Protestants and Catholics—written in the mid-fifteenth century, and more widely published and translated than anything in Christianity except the Bible—contains hardly a reference to the Church in spite of its devotion to the Eucharist. An interesting feature of the new age is the involvement of the laity in the new religious movements, and the association of these with municipal life.

387

III. THE REFORMATION AND
COUNTER-REFORMATION

1. The Pre-Reformation Church. The Church at the beginning of the sixteenth century confronts us with the variety which we should expect to find when we look at the manifold life of a whole continent. There were abuses and disorders—indeed an unusual number of grave scandals at certain levels—but also in many places even deep piety and reforming zeal. The Renaissance itself could bring attempts to enrich the Christian outlook with the new humanism, projects for a further alliance between Platonism and religion, and a fresh interest in the ancient texts—the Scriptures and the Fathers of the Church. Even in Italy there were many localities that had their religious revivals, some of them medieval in character, popular and even perhaps superstitious, though the one associated with Savonarola in Florence captured some of the famous figures of the Renaissance. The monastic system, from its very nature, was subject to ups-and-downs, especially as its rules took for granted a certain intensity of spiritual life. But if in some regions monasteries had sunk into immorality, there had been a number of reforming movements, some of them emerging from within and arising spontaneously. There had been educational developments—the religious schools under the Brethren of the Common Life in the Netherlands, for example, and the founding in fifteenth-century Germany of universities under the patronage of the clergy or the pope. Many of these movements were local in character, arising from below. Even a wicked pope would normally have no reason for checking them, or for discouraging piety as such.

On the other hand, the leading officers of the Church could be too remote from these things and ordinarily too indifferent in respect to them. It is doubtful whether the directors of the Catholic system took even the minimum measures that were required to maintain their guidance over religious life or ensure the survival of the system as a whole. In some regions the state of the priesthood and the work of the pulpit had sunk so low that a prince who wished to plunder the Church had only to open the door to the missionaries of Protestantism, who might bring an awakening or a revolt without meeting with an adequate reply. Too much of the burden of the Church had come to be borne by a lower clergy who seemed sometimes hardly trained to realize the nature of their own religion, and had every reason to be discontented with their lot. A surprising number of them (and particularly of those who belonged to the minor and mendicant orders) were to become Protestants, and some of those who had been unsatisfactory before their conversion were by no means contemptible after it. It would appear that there

was often too much of what might be called paganism or superstition still mixed into the popular Christianity of the period—too great a readiness on the part of the authorities to exploit the willingness of ignorant people to rely on wonders that were mechanically operated, salvation-devices that had lost their connection with the inner man.

Apart from the more technical controversies at a higher level the Reformers were to attack in the world at large the attitude which the lowest classes were encouraged to take towards images, relics, indulgences, the invocation of saints, and the like. There were now too many people who were coming to be too mature for this; and the Reformation (which could have achieved nothing without the success of its preaching) came in one aspect as a religious revival, a call to a more personal faith, a demand for a more genuine "Christian society." The Reformation was to have its dark sides but it was to secure its successes because so many people were ready to be earnest, ready (when called upon) to bring religion home to themselves and to feel that they had some responsibility in the matter. In a sense the Reformation occurred because (on a long-term view) the medieval Church had done its work so well, producing out of barbarian beginnings a laity now capable of a certain self-help, a certain awareness of responsibility. And as the Church of Rome, once it had been provoked into reexamining itself, was to recover its hold on people by its own preaching and its spiritual intensity, the opening centuries of modern times see the reassertion of religion both in the individual and in society.

The Reformation was to be helped at the same time by what on the one hand was a colossal envy and covetousness, and on the other hand a great resentment. The abuses in the ecclesiastical organization itself were sufficient to provoke a revolt, and if they offered an opening for zealous reformers they presented too great a temptation to monarchs and magnates. In the Middle Ages there had been serious opposition to the development of the power of the papacy in particular—the capture of the spiritual prerogatives into a single center and the insertion of papal authority into every corner of the European system. At a certain stage in the story the process had been understandable; the papacy had often stood as the most beneficial agency on the continent; abuses, disorders, and lapses into superstition had tended to occur in the regions which the hand of the pope could not reach.

But the centralization did not prevent benefices, offices, indulgences, dispensations, etc., being used as a means of making money, and new offices being created in order that they could be sold—the Church, and particularly Rome, being saddled with dignitaries who had to find the means of recouping themselves for the initial outlay. Early in the sixteenth century the position of the papal states was so difficult that the pope, as the ruler of a principality, had a desperate need for money; and he used his spiritual prerogatives in order to procure it—an evil that was liable to show its consequences throughout the length and breadth of Western Christendom. A higher clergy who were too often like the sharers in a colossal spoils system did too little for the earnest people, though they seemed to stamp very quickly on any enterprise that might threaten their own profits. The Church lost much, therefore, through the nature of its entanglement with the world; and its vested interests—the mundane possessions that were supposed to guarantee its position—became in fact a terrible weakness, an abuse to some people, and, to others, the primary object of cupidity.

2. The Reformation in Germany. The Reformation is to be regarded as essentially a religious movement and all our history becomes distorted unless we see it as arising primarily out of the spiritual needs and aspirations of earnest men. Social conditions might place certain sections of the population in a favorable position for hearing propaganda or for welcoming it—rather in the way that townsmen may be more ready than peasants to open their minds to a new thing—and such factors might have an effect on the social or geographical distribution of a new religious system. The current forms and the current needs of society might affect that fringe of ethical ideas and practical precepts in which a new form of faith works out some of its more mundane implications.

In history, everything is so entangled with everything else that for many students the political or economic consequences of the Reformation might appear more momentous than any other aspect of the movement. But religion is the stone that is thrown into the pool, the agency that starts all the ripples. In the Reformation itself we are dealing with people for whom religion was not merely a matter of opinion or speculation, leaving an opening for alternatives. They were people who superstitiously feared the powers of hell, and reckoned the afterlife as clear a vested interest as anything in the world—people, also, who believed that only one form of religion could be right, and regarded it as a matter of eternal moment that God should be served and propitiated in the proper way.

Martin Luther, while still a young man, and a member of the Augustinian order which was to produce so many supporters of the Reformation, became remarkable through the intensity of his inner experience and his exaggerated attempts to secure the salvation of his soul by his own works and religious exercises. In this whole endeavor he would seem to have over-

looked certain aspects of theological teaching that had not been lost in the Middle Ages, and he was brought into the predicament of Saint Paul—powerless to achieve the good that he so greatly wanted to achieve. After a distressing time, the help of his own superior and the study of the Epistle to the Romans brought him further light, and he came to the view that man is justified by faith alone, but that the Catholicism of his time was preaching salvation by "works," even by religious exercises.

In reality historical Christianity had always excluded as Pelagianism any idea that a man could save himself by his own efforts; and Luther, though he had seized on something that had been part of the Church's tradition—going back to certain aspects of Saint Augustine and Saint Paul—went to the opposite extreme, insisting on the corruptness of man and his inability to have a part in his own salvation, so that he ran to predestinarian ideas which were later systematized by Calvin, and which gave the Reformation an antihumanist aspect. The later Middle Ages had seen a concentration on the problem of both freedom and the will in both man and God; and it seems clear that unfortunate consequences followed from too intent a consideration of the power and sovereignty of God, if these were regarded as separate from His love.

In a sense Luther's views sprang from the intensity of his own spiritual experience and his feeling about what had happened in his own case; and they answered to what many people throughout the ages had felt to be their own experience—the sense of being drawn by a power greater than themselves, pulled into salvation by forces which they tried in vain to resist. Luther therefore had been open to the criticism that he inferred too much of his theology from his personal experience.

In Wittenberg he was one of those people who promoted a local religious revival, and his immediate superiors were encouraging him in his work, advancing him to a professorship so that his influence would be enlarged. He was a mountain of a man, capable of great profundities and giant angers, but possessing a vein of poetry, and, at times, the heart of a little child. But he was liable to be intellectually erratic, and when in 1517 the abuses of indulgence-selling led him to offer his ninety-five theses as a debating-challenge, he enlarged the issue by his theological assertions and provided his enemies with a basis for attack. Instead of calmly reasoning with him, they too set out to enlarge the issue, driving him from one logical conclusion to another and into positions that he had not anticipated. And he—incited by the wave of feeling that he had aroused in Germany as well as by his own mighty passions—was glad to be provoked, moving forward 389 until he had denied the authority of popes and councils, and denounced the condition of the whole Church.

Carefully measuring his power, he enlarged the whole campaign in 1520, setting out to undermine the sacramental system of the Church which contributed to the power of priests. He called in the secular authority to carry out the work of reform which the Church seemed unable to achieve for itself. Against the power of a vast organization that had long had the governments of Europe behind it, he asserted what he called "the liberty of a Christian man." Soon he was attacking the monastic system to which he had once been devoted. And he convinced himself that the pope was Anti-Christ.

He was helped by a certain religious dissatisfaction and by the anger, particularly in Germany, against ecclesiastical abuses that were associated with Italy. He was enabled by the printing press, and by his own prodigious energy, to conduct what was perhaps the first really large-scale publicity campaign of the kind that makes its appeal to general readers.

An enormous factor in the case was the weakness in Germany of the Emperor Charles V, who was distracted by the problems of the many countries over which he ruled, and by the princes of the separate states in Germany who sought to aggrandize their authority and were sometimes ready to see the advantage of an alliance with Lutheranism. The Emperor was to be held up still further by the advance of the Turks, which made it necessary for him to postpone the solution of his German problems. When the cause of the Reformation came to be preached—in the cities of South Germany for example—it found an eager reception; and for a considerable time even regions like Bavaria and Austria—regions that later became renowned for their Catholicism—seemed to be moving over to Protestantism.

In reality Luther seems to have been a man of conservative and perhaps authoritarian disposition. He had been moved to action because he could not bear the manner in which the Church was tolerating both practical abuses and misrepresentations of the faith. But in the period of the great revolt he put forward certain theses which were to be remembered as the great Reformation principles, and were to have a broader historical influence than even his theology. They asserted the right of the individual to interpret the Scriptures; the priesthood of all believers; and the "liberty of a Christian man." When others took these theses according to their obvious meaning but at the same time came to conclusions that were different from his, he made it plain that he could not tolerate their individualism, and that indeed he had no use for rebels. There was one interpretation of Scripture, and that

the true one; and only sheer perversity could induce a man to read anything else into the text. Neither the Roman Catholics nor the Zwinglians nor the Anabaptists were free to interpret the Scriptures for themselves. And when Luther came to the construction of his own system, he showed himself in many respects a conservative at heart. Clearly it had not been his desire to divide the Church, but his theological teaching—and his persistence in it after it had been condemned—was almost bound to produce that result. The general historian of Europe would have to say that the most momentous consequences of the Lutheran revolt were things of which Luther would have disapproved.

Lutheranism itself remained essentially Teutonic, and, outside Germany, it established itself at the time only in Scandinavia. There was a moment when it seemed likely to sweep over Germany, a politico-religious upheaval of the kind that can create a nation. Once it failed to carry the whole country however, it was bound to have the opposite effect, creating a new, confessional division, in some respects more bitter than any of the others, more difficult to overcome. It resulted in one important contribution to the German nation, however—Luther's translation of the Bible into a language which was to prevail over local dialects and to have a unifying effect. But, though Luther, when he called for the aid of princes, thought of them as servants of the Church, bound by duty to serve the lofty cause, he produced a situation in which princes had the power to choose between competing systems and so acquired great authority in religious matters. His pessimistic ideas about man and the world may have had the effect of diminishing the role and the influence of religion in the political realm, making Lutheranism too uncritical an ally of monarchy.

In the period immediately after his condemnation at the Diet of Worms (April 1521), Luther was in hiding at the Wartburg castle, and during his absence more radical developments began to take place. In Wittenberg itself, Andrew Karlstadt (or Carlstadt) promoted a further movement against the Mass and, on the strength of the Old Testament attacked images and called for a stricter sabbatarianism, so that signs of the later Puritanism were already visible. This, in March 1522, provoked Luther's return to Wittenberg, for he did not give the same authority to Old Testament law, and, in regard to the things that the populace loved, he deprecated a destructive policy conducted without sufficient previous explanation. In the meantime the reform movement had been establishing itself in towns where the social conflict had made the situation almost revolutionary; and by the spring of 1521 Thomas Müntzer had combined the religious cause with civic revolt in the town of Zwickau. Before the end of the year he had proclaimed in an apocalyptic manner the downfall of the Church; he insisted that a scriptural religion was not enough since the voice of God spoke directly within the believer, and he threatened the opposition with punishment at the hands of the Turk. Also some of the other "prophets" of Zwickau moved in 1522 to Wittenberg, where they produced trouble for the Lutherans. Soon the objections to infant baptism became significant.

Forms of apocalypticism and mysticism had made their appearance in various regions in the later Middle Ages, and in Germany not only the peasantry but the lower classes in the towns provided promising soil for these movements. Now, as so often in history, religious radicalism could quickly lead to political extremism and to the feeling that the time had come for the destruction of the godless. Thomas Müntzer came to be connected with the Peasants' Revolt in 1525, and, when speaking to the rebels about the enemy, could say: "They will beg you, will whine and cry like children. But you are to have no mercy, as God commanded through Moses." Yet he is deeply moving when he writes of his spiritual experience and the voice of God in the believer: "Scripture cannot make men live, as does the living Word which an empty soul hears." The sects for which Luther so unwillingly opened the way did not know how to apply the brake, and when they captured Münster in 1534 they established polygamy, while in Moravia they experimented in communism. It was they who carried the seeds that were to be so important to the far future—the insistence that God regarded men as equal, that Christ had made them free and that there was an Inner Light which men had to obey. The twentieth century has shown that even the apocalypticism can be deeply ingrained in man and admits of being secularized. It goes back to biblical times, but (at least when the pattern has once been established) it can exist without a supernatural religion.

3. Calvin. In the Swiss Reformation the city-state made its last contribution to history; for it communicated to a nascent church something of the pattern of its own organization (and particularly government by councils) as well as something of its spirit, so that the secular and the spiritual seemed to have kinship with one another, just as the development of the Catholic hierarchy had fitted neatly into the feudal world. Here, moreover, the transformation that occurred was more radical—organized Christianity reshaped itself, producing a palpably different landscape.

Signs of this are apparent in the case of Zwingli, the original leader of the revolt within the Swiss Confederation. The initial breach occurred on matters of discipline, but the changes in doctrine and thought were more radical, more rationalistic than in the case of the Lutheran Revolt. Here, however, the identification of the movement with the political ambitions of Zürich turned the Reformation into a politico-religious affair—a patriotic cause—Zwingli meeting his death in battle.

What we might regard as the international Reformation is associated with John Calvin and with Geneva—a city which was not yet part of the Confederation, and which belonged to no country, though it stood at the point where France, Germany, Italy and Switzerland came together. After trying to establish himself in the city from 1536 and being driven out in 1538, Calvin from 1541 gained the mastery, and held it till 1564, though this involved the expulsion of many of the ancient families and the granting of citizenship to hosts of refugees from abroad. At the beginning of this period, the Reformation itself had arrived at a critical stage. Many people had become weary of the conflict, and there were distinguished intellects as well as political leaders who had come to desire ecclesiastical reunion. Under Melanchthon, the Lutherans seemed to be trying to discover how far they could go towards a reconciliation with Catholicism. After the Peasants' Revolt in Germany in 1525 there had been the spectacle of the revolutionized city of Münster in 1534, and this had shown what could happen if religious rebellion was not restrained. Calvin represented a new generation, and an important part of his work was the stabilizing of the Reformation—conceiving it as an international affair, and erecting it if possible into an international order comparable to the Catholic one of the Middle Ages.

In 1536, by the first version of his *Institutes of the Christian Religion* (which was to prove the best-seller of the sixteenth century), and then, in the following year, by his part in the "reunion" discussions in Germany, he had been qualifying himself to become an international leader. In 1539 his *Letter to Cardinal Sadoleto* had proved to be the most successful of the popular defences of the Reformation. The wheel had come into full cycle, and he saw that what was needed was the reestablishment of ecclesiastical authority. He realized that the situation called for three important things: a confession of faith, a doctrine of the Church, and an ecclesiastical discipline. His originality lay not in the generation of new doctrines but in the better coordination of received ones, and their adaptation to the purpose of achieving a coherent system. Difficulties concerning the question of the "real presence" in the Eucharist prevented a union with the Lutherans, who preserved something of the Catholic point of view, and, for a long time, also, with the Zwinglians, who treated the sacrament as rather a symbol and a remembrance

391

of Christ. These latter began to be reconciled, however, from 1549.

It is in Calvinism that the Reformation, at least in externals, begins to wear the aspect of almost a new type of religion—like a new style in art or, as some would think (perhaps unfairly) a change from poetry to prose, if not a reaction against aestheticism itself. It becomes clear now that religion is a very serious matter; the preaching holds a great importance; and, under the tighter authority that is possible in the city-states, there arises a severer control of private life. Calvin was ready (as Zwingli had been) to follow the Bible more consistently than Luther, and this was bound to give an increased importance to the Old Testament. He put the idea of the sovereignty of God at the center of his whole system, whereas Luther might be said to have been preoccupied by the idea of Grace. The emphasis on sovereignty had its counterpart in the demand for obedience from the human side. Here was the basis for a firm authoritarianism—an insistence that the Christian life should be a severe discipline.

It has been said that Catholicism is the religion of priests, Lutheranism the religion of theologians, and Calvinism the religion of the believing congregation. In spite of its inaccuracies, this comparison throws light on the Calvinist system in which, theoretically at least, the Church was the congregation of believing Christians, independent of mystery and ceremony and external paraphernalia. The system governed through assemblies, synods, consistories; pastors were elected by congregations; and all pastors were equal, just as all churches were equal. The layman was given a part to play in ecclesiastical affairs; and the ministers were to have no special immunities, no territorial lordships, and they were to pay taxes like anybody else. The ecclesiastical system was to have no prisons, no instruments of mundane power; their sole weapon against the offender was to be exclusion from the Lord's Supper. In other words, sacerdotalism was at an end; and it was Calvin rather than Luther who broke the power of priests. It was all congenial to the pattern of a city-state, and suggests a Christianity that is being reshaped in the context of a more modern world.

Yet it was authoritarian, and only with the greatest difficulty did Calvin impose it on an unwilling city. Coming later than Luther, and having a more remorselessly logical mind, he did not pretend that the individual might interpret Scripture for himself. If congregations elected their ministers the qualifications of these had to be approved, and their ordination carried out, by other ministers, and in Calvin's time the congregation would be provided with a nominee; all it could do was to give or refuse its consent. In

reality, the system was governed by an oligarchy which recruited itself by cooptation and closely superintended its members, entering private houses, and exercising control over private life. It was even something like a police-state, with spies, informers, and occult agents, and with neighbors and members of families betraying one another—the culprit being handed over to the civil magistrate, who carried out the requirements of the Church. If the influx of foreign exiles enabled Calvin to clinch his mastery of Geneva, it also provided him with the means of extending his influence abroad. The city became like a modern nest of international revolution, where the foreign guests received their training, and then departed to continue the work in their home country.

Though he repressed freedom of conscience and personal liberty, and, like Martin Luther, gave the individual no right to rebel, he did allow disobedience to rulers who commanded what was contrary to the word of God, and he gave currency to a theory of resistance to monarchy which was to be of great importance in the subsequent period. Individuals had no right to rebel but representative institutions (the States-General in France, the Parliament in England, for example) were justified in fighting the king. The doctrine was quoted from Calvin by the early Whigs and debated by the nascent Tories in seventeenth-century England and it had already been significant in other countries. It inaugurates the modern theory—the modern paradox—of "constitutional revolution" where the organ of revolt (as in France in 1789) is the representative system itself.

It happened that, in various countries, Calvinism spread originally in opposition to government, and its leader approved of these movements and guided them. Calvinism, in fact, often emerged in the attitude of rebellion, and Calvin's warnings against this were not always heeded, if indeed he himself was quite consistent about the matter. It is not an accident that liberty extends itself in the modern world via Holland, Great Britain and the United States—countries where political rebellion was allied to Calvinism.

4. The Counter-Reformation. The Catholic revival of the sixteenth century has two aspects. On the one hand, like the Protestant Reformation itself, it can be regarded as a religious revival, a reaction against the ecclesiastical abuses that had been accumulating, and a protest against the secularization of Church and society. In this sense, if it ran parallel to the Lutheran movement, it had in fact begun at an earlier date. And one of its important features had been a purification of the Church in Spain—a remarkable reform of monasteries for example—before the end of the fifteenth century, that is to say, under Ferdinand and

Isabella, and chiefly through the piety of the latter. One result of this was the fact that even the "Renaissance" in Spain had a peculiar character—it was largely a regeneration of ecclesiastical scholarship, and for a time it gave Erasmus a considerable influence on the religious life of that country. In their program for the New World the Spaniards gave a high place to the idea of transplanting Christianity and a Christian civilization to the other side of the Atlantic. Spanish monks, using the Bible, canon law, and scholastic writings, assisted the transition to modern international law by their works on the laws of war and the rights of the native population, as they related to the overseas empire. At the same time, the fanaticism and intolerance of the Spaniards seems to have been an acquired characteristic, a product of history. At an earlier date they had been reproached by other Christians for their laxity, their resort to infidel doctors, their visits to Moorish courts, so long as the Muhammadans remained in the peninsula. The enduring conflict with the infidel, and the religious propaganda connected with it, helped to make Spain more firmly Catholic, more intolerantly orthodox, than any other country.

On the other hand there was a Counter-Reformation in a stricter sense—the reaction against the Protestant movement, which, to a Catholic was the greatest of the disorders of the time. There was a moment when some men were able to feel that the Catholic revival might combine with the Lutheran movement, especially when more radical revolts had broken out and a section of the Lutherans had taken a conservative turn. A group of important Catholics were even sympathetic to a certain form of the doctrine of justification by faith; and when the accession of Pope Paul III brought something of a turn towards a reformation at Rome itself, the appointment of a number of cardinals in the year 1534 was significant in the story, for a handful of these belonged to this more liberalizing group, including Cardinal Contarini and the Englishman, Cardinal Pole. The years 1537–41 saw the failure of reunion negotiations which had been promoted in France as well as Germany, and, from that time, the men who had seemed prepared to broaden the basis of the Church were in disrepute—indeed, more than one of the Cardinals involved in this aspect of the reforming movement was himself in danger from the Inquisition.

The years 1540–43 have special importance in the history of the Counter-Reformation. In 1540 the Society of Jesus was formed, and quickly attained an influence, though its widespread results were only to be apparent in the second generation. In 1541 came the failure of conferences between Catholics and Lutherans at Ratisbon, so that the movement for comprehension

and reunion was now virtually at an end. And though at this time there were disturbing manifestations of Protestantism in a number of localities even in Italy, effective action was now taken against the movement. In 1542, Cardinal Contarini, the leader of the reformist group died, and at about this time the stronger members of that party passed off the stage, leaving Cardinal Pole—a less effective personality—in the leading position. In 1542, moreover, a General Council of the Church was summoned; and, by this time, it had become apparent that it would not represent an opposition to Rome in the way that the conciliar movement of the fifteenth century had done. It would itself be under the leadership of Rome.

Some controversy has been caused by the question how far the leadership of Spain was responsible for the turn which the Counter-Reformation took. Everywhere—in the peninsula itself, in Africa, in the Mediterranean and in America—Spain's enemy seemed to be the infidel and the championship of orthodoxy had become a major part of the national tradition. The Jesuit Order was founded and organized by Spaniards and its first generals were Spaniards. The new form of papal Inquisition was influenced by the more powerful and modern form of Inquisition that had been established in Spain. The pope's chief assistants and advisers at the Council of Trent, particularly on theological questions, were Spaniards. In the latter half of the sixteenth century the Catholic party in the French Wars of Religion and the supporters of Mary Tudor in England looked to Spain, and the Counter-Reformation came to be identified with the aggressive policies of Philip II.

At the same time one must not overlook the determined manner in which the popes set out to hold the leadership in the Counter-Reformation. They were not Spaniards; they were often anti-Spaniards, and now, as in the past, they tended to be hostile to the Spanish preponderance in Italy. The severest of the anti-Protestant popes, Paul IV (Caraffa) had been a Dominican and his religion may have been affected by his residence in Spain at an earlier period in his life. But even as Pope he found himself at war with Philip II, and Spanish troops besieged him in Rome, where he was defended by Lutheran mercenaries. The popes were even a little hostile and jealous in their attitude to the Jesuit Order at first, and this was partly because that order seemed so closely connected with Spain. The popes indeed would have liked to see the reform of the Church carried out through committees and commissions in Rome, where in 1552 Julius III established a Congregation of Reform.

Important sections of the Catholic world, headed by the Emperor Charles V, had long wanted the summoning of a General Council of the Church to reform abuses, particularly the abuses in Rome. On various occasions—in Germany early in the 1520's and in France early in the 1550's—there had been threats of a National Council of the Church to bring about ecclesiastical reform within a single country. When the Council met at Trent it made sure that its decrees should reserve the rights of the pope, and should be subject to his confirmation; also that he should have the sole right of interpreting them. Throughout the proceedings (which took place in three sessions between 1545 and 1563) papal diplomacy proved to be remarkably effective. Perhaps the great dynamic features of Protestantism, as it developed in later centuries, lay in the way in which it confronted a man with the Bible and allowed him to seize upon the things which he internally ratified, the things which in his spiritual experience he grasped as living and true; the way also in which it could cut its way to the original sources, and, by returning to the fountain of the faith, disengage Christianity from the accidents of a long period of intervening history.

Perhaps the great stabilizing feature of Catholicism has been that it sought rather to preserve a tradition of doctrine, so that a man did not just think out the things he was to believe—he sought to discover the teaching which had united Christians throughout the centuries. On this system, at least one did not persecute on behalf of doctrines that one had only recently worked out for oneself. The impressive feature of the Council of Trent is the way in which doctrine, instead of issuing from some brilliant book by an individual theologian, was threshed out by commissions that sought to discover what had really been the tradition of the centuries. On questions of dogma, a conservative position was maintained. Against Luther's teaching about the interpretation of the Bible it was agreed that the Bible must be interpreted by the tradition and conscience of the Church. And the authoritative version was the Vulgate, which had been related to the development of Church doctrine through so many centuries. The Bible in the original languages was available for academic work, but the decision of the Church's doctrines was not to be transferred in a spirit of literalism to the experts in philology.

Luther's doctrine of justification by faith was condemned at the first session of the Council in 1545, but an opening was still left for the resurgence of the tradition of Saint Augustine in the Jansenism of the seventeenth and eighteenth centuries. The doctrine of predestination was condemned, but the Church had never tolerated Pelagianism, and there was still room in Catholicism for long quarrels between the Jesuits and the Dominicans about the proportion to be attrib-

uted to Divine Grace and to a man's free will in the work of salvation. And though transubstantiation was confirmed there was still room for controversy within Catholicism about the interpretation of even this doctrine. In regard to an important dispute concerning the question whether bishops held their power direct from God or only through the pope—a controversy in which the Spanish bishops were hostile to the papacy—the Council failed to come to a clear decision.

In order to have a picture of the Counter-Reformation, however, it is not sufficient to see what was happening at headquarters and in the central institutions of Catholicism—one must have some impression of what was taking place in the world at large. One thing that was involved was the revival of preaching, and in this connection some of the Observantine section of the Franciscans, who reformed themselves in 1525 and became known as the Capuchins, become important amongst the common people in Italy, France, and Germany. During the numerous outbreaks of plague that occurred in Italy, their fidelity and courage made a great impression.

The Jesuits attacked the problem at a different level and became important at first through their teaching and influence in universities, though later they became powerful at royal courts. Even in Spain where they gained most adherents, and in France, where the supporters of Gallican claims and particularly the Parlement of Paris had special reasons for jealousy, they suffered some opposition at first. When they went to Cologne in 1544, some said that the urgent need was rather for good bishops and parish priests. Just after the mid-century, not only were many of the German bishops still worldly-minded and indifferent to the religious cause, but there were regions where it was impossible for good Catholics to be served except by priests who were actually married or living with concubines, and preaching semi-Lutheran ideas. In the 1550's, however, the famous Jesuit, Canisius, began the important work which saved the city and university of Vienna from the Protestants who had come to acquire almost absolute control. His influence extended to Prague as well as to Ingolstadt, which became the great Catholic educational center in the next generation. The same Canisius was responsible for the issue of a catechism which was to be of great importance in Catholic teaching. At the humblest level of all, moreover, great efforts were made to inspire and nourish popular piety.

Even so, it is difficult to see how the new influences could have found a footing if they had not been patronized by princes, particularly the Wittelsbachs in Bavaria and the Habsburgs in Austria. The papacy was wise enough now to make concessions to princes who might have become Protestant for the sake of the spoils; and the Bavarian princes were to acquire a good deal of revenue from ecclesiastical sources on which they were now permitted to draw. For a few years from about 1563 the Duke of Bavaria sought to bring his principality back to Catholicism but this imposed upon him a difficult conflict with his parliamentary estates and with the nobility. He succeeded in restoring the Church only by high-handed measures and by making encroachments on ecclesiastical jurisdiction himself. In general, the restoration of the clergy and the care for the educational work were calculated in themselves to have a great effect, and even in Bohemia, a traditional home of heresy, Catholic preaching and Catholic saintliness began to exercise their influence again.

5. The Results of the Reformation. It is more clear to the twentieth century than it was to the sixteenth that a great deal of the evil and the suffering which arose from the Reformation—a great many of the wars, atrocities and crimes that came to be associated with it—arose from the beliefs that the various parties had in common. The world had changed greatly since New Testament days, and all were agreed that religion was not a matter for the Individual only; that the uniform "Christian Society" was the important thing; and that only one form of faith could be true, the rest standing not merely as errors but as diabolical perversions. It was the duty of rulers to support the true faith and there were precedents for the view that when all else failed—when the ecclesiastical system was too decadent to rectify itself—the secular arm should reform the Church. Luther, Zwingli, Calvin, and the Anabaptists sought to capture the government—if only the government of a city-state. And this only highlighted the fact that the papacy needed the support of the secular authority too.

Many of the results of the Reformation—particularly the more paradoxical results—sprang from the fact that neither the papacy, on the one hand, nor Luther (or any other Protestant leader) on the other, was able to secure a total victory that would have reestablished unity in the West. This itself contributed to the power of princes, for it left them the choice in matters of religion, so that they tended to become masters rather than servants at the most crucial point of all. A monarch like Henry VIII of England could evade the alternatives before him, simply setting up a system of his own.

Furthermore, besides confiscating much of the property of the Church, they became accustomed to controlling religious affairs—even (in the case of Lutheran princes and Henry VIII, for example) replacing the pope as the superior over bishops. Each state tended to become its own "Christian Society," and authority—being now closer at hand—was liable to become more tyrannical than before. Although the tendencies were already in existence and may have contributed to the growth of an antipapal movement, the Reformation gave a fresh stimulus to the rising power of kings, and the development of nationalism. It was a great blow to such international order as had previously existed.

A revival of religion had occurred, and both published works and private letters bear evidence of inspiring thought and deep sincerity—a tremendous reexploring of Christianity. But it was also a revival of religious passions, religious hatreds and religious wars, and it showed what a scourge a supernatural religion could be to the world if it were not tempered by the constant remembrance of the dominating importance of charity. In sixteenth-century Europe the rivalry between one set of doctrines and another, and even the negotiations between the parties—indeed all the transactions which related to doctrinal tests—inaugurated a period in which the confessional issue was too momentous, and there was too hard an attitude toward intellectual statements of belief.

In the long run, the very conflict of authorities was bound to leave a greater opening for individualism—even a tendency to see all the religious parties with relativity. But the process to this was slower than one would have imagined and for nearly two centuries the conflict had a politico-religious character. In a given country the Reformation, particularly in its Calvinist form, was likely to arise in the first place amongst a minority; and there were signs of it even in countries that were to remain Catholic—signs in Italy and even Spain, and a formidable movement in France. The irrepressibility of these nonconformists, even when they failed to capture the government, added a dynamic quality to the history of a number of states, particularly England. Yet for the most part it was due to their predicament rather than to their theology that the dissenters made their great contribution to the modern world. They wished to capture the whole body politic; and because they failed they were in the mood for opposition to the Establishment, both Church and State; and they could better afford to judge society and government by reference to Christian principles and fundamental ideas.

The elevation of the Bible by the Protestants, and particularly the Calvinists—what has been called the bibliolatry of the sixteenth century—was to have important and widespread consequences. Even the translation of the book had a wide general significance, especially in France and Germany. In an age when everything is being thrown into the melting pot, it becomes more easy to note the equality of men before

God, the Christ who makes men free, the idea of communism in the New Testament. One of the effects of the concentration on the Bible was the unprecedented importance which the Old Testament acquired in the sixteenth and seventeenth centuries. In some respects it replaced the volumes of canon law which Luther had burned, and it proved less flexible than the canon law, to which Luther objected, partly because of the development that had taken place in it; he objected not to its prohibition of usury but to the loopholes which it had come to admit. Now, economic regulations, political theories, ethical ideas—and even science, even one's views about the physical universe—would be taken from the Old Testament, which was more relevant for these mundane purposes than the New. Monarchy itself found its justification there and Luther's view of what we should call the state was Old Testament rather than medieval—the king having the power while being expected to listen to the prophet (the Reformation leader) at his side. And over and over again the early Protestants would refer to their monarch as the King Josiah, who had reformed the Church after discovering the books of the Law.

The conception of the covenant, which was so familiar amongst the ancient Hebrews, was now revived and seems to have played its part in the development of the Social Contract theory. When the Pilgram Fathers went to America, they signed what they called a "covenant," in which they constituted themselves as a body politic. Amongst the Puritans the prohibition of images may have tended to the discouragement of the visual arts. In England, Sundays (which had at first been deprecated, along with the excessive number of saints' days) came to be equated with the Jewish Sabbath. The Old Testament provided textual bases for witch-burnings, which multiplied at this period, as well as for religious intolerance and severe theories of persecution, including the view that heretics should be destroyed as blasphemers.

It has been held by Max Weber and others that something in the nature of Protestantism itself played an important part in the rise of capitalism, and the advance of England and Holland (together with a decline in Belgium and a backwardness in Spain and Italy) has lent plausibility to this view. But capitalism and the spirit of capitalism were highly advanced in Italy and the Netherlands before the Reformation, and the famous Fugger family in Germany was Catholic. Luther, joining in the hostility that had already arisen against it—said that the greatest misfortune of the German nation was the traffic in usury, and he blamed the pope for having sanctioned the evil. Calvin, coming at a later date, recognized the changed condition of the world and attacked the Aristotelian view that

money is "barren" but he was a little troubled lest this should assist the capitalists and encourage usury. He would have liked to drive the latter out of the world, but since this was impossible, he said that one must give way to the general utility. He sought to prevent the evil which explained the antipathy of agricultural societies to usury—namely, the practices which took advantage of the misfortunes of the poor—and to him Venice and Antwerp were an exposure of the mammonism of the Catholics.

In fact the traditional medieval policy was pursued in Geneva in Calvin's day; and, after his time, the prejudice against usury continued in that city, where, indeed, business life proceeded as formerly, without receiving any great impetus from the religious movement, and in 1568 the influences of the Calvinist parties prevented the formation of a bank. In Amsterdam the biggest capitalists belonged to families that were working on a large scale before the Reformation and it was the poor who became the most fanatical Calvinists. It was preached that everything beyond a reasonable subsistence should be set aside for the poor, and disciplinary action was taken against bankers—the old prejudices continuing until the middle of the seventeenth century. So long as a religious revival retains its character, it is not in its nature to encourage mammonism, a point which even the Puritans of seventeenth-century England illustrate.

The view that a believer should praise and serve God in his daily avocations should not be strange in any religion; and the Middle Ages (as well as the Jesuits later) began wisely to adjust their ethical precepts—their views on commerce and man's daily tasks—to the needs of a changing world. It is surprising that anybody should hold the view that capitalism was encouraged because the Reformers separated salvation from "works"; for the Puritans were far from representing an easy view of Christian conduct, though they held that a man did not win salvation by the effort. When Baron von Hügel read Bunyan he said that the book was "curiously Catholic in its ideas . . . certainly very strong about the necessity of good works." Puritanism encouraged work, reprobated waste of time in idle talk and mere sociability, and held that leisure was equivalent to lasciviousness. It also reprobated luxury and promoted virtues like thrift, no doubt giving religious sanction to qualities that were particularly useful in the capitalistic world that had been developing. It is therefore open to the charge of regarding the making of money as laudable while the spending of it was a vice.

John Wesley, when he drew up his first printed rules for Methodists in the eighteenth century, condemned usury on biblical grounds and had to be made to see that this was demanding the impossible, so that he retreated and prescribed only a moderate rate. He sketched out the view that the very virtues of Christians might lead to prosperity and thence to a decline of religion. But it is only very late in the day that Puritanism is in any sense the ally of mammonism.

Apart from the fact that Protestantism could spread more easily in town than in country, it provided an example of a new movement in religion which, in its formative period, when so many things were malleable, confronted what men were recognizing to be a new economic world. Besides its theological doctrine, it was bound to acquire an attendant social outlook—a fringe of more mundane prejudices and associations—and these showed it in the first place bitterly hostile to capitalism. But, as time went on, it was almost bound to give the support of religion to the ethical ideas which corresponded to the needs of the new social world. Catholicism had fixed many of its principles in a different state of society, and was likely to be less malleable, though it, too, made its adjustments (perhaps more slowly) as society changed. Late in the day, and almost as ratifying a *fait accompli*, Puritanism did perhaps become the support of a capitalist society; and, even so, it was a Protestantism that had changed its character; in a sense it was not religion but a decline in religion, or an injection of secularism which had this result.

Protestantism, more than Catholicism, tended to change its general character as the centuries passed; it moved from its initial sixteenth-century form and preoccupations, and at least presented a different spectacle and assumed a different role. It was at a later stage that it became consciously and avowedly the ally of individualism, liberty, rationalism, capitalism, and the modern kind of state.

IV. THE MODERN WORLD

1. The Age of the "Wars of Religion." The principle of *cujus regio ejus religio* (religion is determined by the ruler) prevailed from 1559, not because the aspiration for a "universal" Church, a single form of Christianity, had been surrendered, but because something of a stalemate had been achieved. The various states now blossomed out as differing forms of "Christian Society"; and it might be the accidents of history and geography (rather than any antecedent national "spirit") that led e.g., England and Scotland or the two halves of the Low Countries to diverge from one another. It might be the form of confession then adopted which, for the future, conditioned the developing character and tradition of a country. The process of nation-making was still continuing, and religious differentiations still tended to play a considerable part

in this. With the breakdown of the medieval "universal" idea, the overall picture became more disturbing; Europe had very slowly to find its way to a new kind of international order, a new conception of the society of states. For the time being, a momentous religious issue had arisen to complicate the relations between governments and to embarrass European diplomacy. For nearly a century the world was torn by a succession of wars in which religion (however closely it might be combined with other factors) was the primary motor, or the real source of the fanaticism and bitter feeling.

But monarchs—though they were greatly elevated under the system of *cujus regio ejus religio*—were not always masters of the situation. Mary Queen of Scots was unable to prevent Scotland from being Calvinist, and the rulers of England could not prevent the Irish from remaining Roman Catholic. In the northern provinces of the Low Countries a minority of Calvinists, using sometimes almost gangster methods, captured the magistracies in the cities and reduced a majority of Catholics to the status of "second-class" citizens, during the rebellion against Philip II. By the end of the sixteenth century, the humane and scholarly tradition that was associated with Erasmus had asserted itself in this region, and brought distinction to the University of Leyden. There emerged the Arminian movement, which sought to soften the severities of predestinarianism amongst the Calvinists, and this was supported by a burgher aristocracy whose culture acquired a leading position in Europe in the first half of the seventeenth century. The movement was resisted, however, by the populace, who were incited by the intransigeance of the Calvinist ministers and supported by the House of Orange. The defeat of Arminianism was registered in 1619 at the Synod of Dordrecht, which was attended by representatives of so many foreign countries that it almost looked like a Calvinist attempt at a General Council of the Church.

Because religion was such a momentous matter in those days, and was supported by such grim sanctions, it had the capacity to bring public opinion to new importance in the state, and it often increased the tensions within the body politic. In countries like England and Bohemia the resistance of a religious minority represented virtually the beginning of modern political opposition to the reigning monarch. Calvinism in particular was no more willing than Catholicism to be checked by the power of the king.

This being the general situation, the peculiar predicament of France was to give this country a significant role in the transition to a new order of things. Here, the action of the government against heretical movements at home had been delayed, partly by one king who had patronized certain Renaissance groups, partly by another who had had a political quarrel with the pope. When serious attention came to be given to the problem in 1559, it transpired that the Reformers had become too strong to be dealt with by any ordinary police methods. In a way that often happened, an unhappy social position made sections of the nobility particularly ready for refractoriness in religion, and these not only took up the cause of the Calvinists but endowed it with a military organization. The whole issue became involved in further disputes concerning the rights of princes of the blood and the question of the Regency during a royal minority. On the whole—and especially in the desperate days of Catherine de' Medici—the government would try to maintain itself by holding the balance between the overpowerful Catholics and the overpowerful Huguenots. For *politique* reasons, it was prepared, in a time of great danger, to adopt a policy of toleration which was anomalous for a Catholic ruler, and which in any case nobody would have regarded as the ideal.

In these circumstances, not only did repeated civil wars occur, as the one side and the other attempted to capture the government, but the two religious parties would look abroad for allies, the ardent Catholics working with Philip II of Spain. At a time when France needed to safeguard herself against the predominance of Habsburg Spain, those who were governed principally by love of their country might be inclined to a *politique* foreign policy too—an alliance with Dutch and German Protestants, for example. In these circumstances the extreme Catholics, looking to Philip II, tended to behave rather as a hostile force—a kind of "fifth column"—within the country itself. In France, therefore, the problems of the age of religious conflict took an extreme form, and came near to ending in the destruction of the state.

Religious toleration begins to emerge as a *politique* policy, and some of its upholders recognize that it contravenes the whole ideal of the state as a religious society. They argue, however, that the killing has gone on too long and that the body politic itself is being too radically disrupted. It was as though a terrestrial morality was being used to challenge an alleged supraterrestrial morality, and at first it was unscrupulous rulers, like Catherine de' Medici, and not the pious ones, like Mary Tudor, who were prepared to allow religious dissidence. The members of a persecuted religious party might protest against the intolerance, but even so, they sometimes made it clear that their objection was not to persecution as such but to the persecution of the right religion by the wrong one. Only the Socinians in Poland in the latter half of the sixteenth century proclaimed toleration as a principle,

and that was because they could claim to be preaching a religion without any dogma.

Given the structure of society as it existed in those days, toleration itself did not always imply what it means today. It could involve giving the nobles a free hand to force their tenantry to a change of religion. And only very gradually did the various Reformation parties learn to tolerate one another.

Early in the seventeenth century both Catholics and Protestants could hope that, by a special effort, they might turn the balance in their favor (particularly in Germany and the imperial territories). There are signs of anxiety and a special fear of war, as though one were already conscious of the looming shadow of the coming conflict—the struggle that was to last for thirty years. Plans for the establishment of perpetual peace or a remodelling of the map of Europe, the inclination of the Lutherans to work for appeasement, and the similar policy which helped to make James I so unpopular in England, are features of the time which seem to show the effect of these apprehensions. Projects for the reunion of Protestants and Catholics were brought out by Grotius in Holland, John Drury in England, and later by Leibniz in Germany.

2. The Characteristics and Controversies of Revived Catholicism. The intellectual advances of Catholicism, its successful missionary work in Europe and elsewhere, and the victories of the Habsburg supporters of the papacy in the early stages of the Thirty Years' War, brought about a fine feeling of exultation in Rome when the new basilica of St. Peter's had been completed there, and was consecrated in 1626. This "greatest architectural wonder of the world" still remained the real center of artistic activity in Rome which, under Urban VIII (1623–44) and his two successors, was turned into a baroque city. The sculptor and architect, Lorenzo Bernini, and the painter, Pietro da Cortona, had a great part in this; and the new style—which came to be associated with the Jesuits—imprinted its character on the city more strongly than any previous style had done. It was dynamic and sought dramatic effects, loading churches with ornament and gilding, colored sculptures and sensuous curves. It spread from Rome to Spain, Portugal, Austria, Catholic Germany, and Poland; though its influence seems to have been smaller in France. This whole form of art still seems to convey to us something of the exuberant spirit of the Counter-Reformation. Here, therefore, Christianity, entangling itself once again with the world, presents pictures and scenic displays quite different from the religious landscape of England and Holland.

In France there emerged in the seventeenth century a "Catholic Renaissance" which helped to enhance the role of that country in the history of religion and of Europe in general. The intellectual strength of the movement is illustrated by the fact that the clergy moved over so naturally to the leadership of the state itself in peace and war. From 1624 to 1642 Cardinal Richelieu was the effective ruler, and he surrounded himself with priests and monks—a cardinal becoming a general, while an archbishop was made admiral—the most intimate counsellor, especially in diplomatic matters, being the famous Father Joseph. The new spirit showed itself in charitable foundations, attempts at reform and Christian missions to the native peoples of French Canada; and the beneficent work of Vincent de Paul was perhaps the most characteristic feature of the revival. Also there began, amongst the congregation of St. Maur, that scholarly work which was to bring so much distinction to the Benedictines in the seventeenth century.

Richelieu himself illustrates the way in which France, through her special problems and special position, was mediating the passage to a new order of things in Europe. In spite of his severities in desperate times, he was a pious man and he gave the *politique* policy a turn which made it more admissible for the Christian. He destroyed the military establishment by means of which the turbulent Huguenots had secured their position within France; but he continued the religious toleration which this party had been enjoying since 1598, and he seems to have been sincere in his hope that this example of generosity would be conducive to their ultimate voluntary conversion. In respect of foreign policy, he judged that France would be eclipsed for an indefinite period if Spain were not checked; so he gave priority to the policy of war against the Habsburgs, though, again, he seems to have been sincere in his determination to see that this should do as little harm as possible to the cause of Catholicism. In both these cases his formulas more carefully pinpointed the valid role of force and discriminated between the objectives of foreign policy, imposing at home and abroad the idea of warfare for limited ends. It was a stage in the formation of a different kind of international order and in the transition by means of which even earnest Christians could find their way out of the Wars of Religion. It was to end in the virtual abstraction of religion from the game of power-politics.

If the Western Church had come to a tragic cleavage at the Reformation, however, and if the Calvinism of the Dutch had later been brought to a serious crisis by the emergence of Arminianism, it is interesting to note that the seventeenth century saw great conflicts within the revived Catholicism—conflicts, moreover, on patterns already familiar—and that the chief arena for these should have been France. Firstly there came

to the forefront again that assertive spirit of nationality which had been refractory to the papacy before the close of the Middle Ages, and which had then been a factor in the Reformation itself. "Gallicanism" was medieval in origin, and it stressed the national character of the French Church—stressed the authority of the French bishops as something more than a mere delegation from Rome. The movement also had its internal constitutional aspect, and regarded the French king as holding his temporal authority direct from God, and therefore as not amenable to the pope in his exercise of it. In a sense, the king was the protector of the French bishops against the pope, but they were his subjects and if they gained ground from Rome, he himself stood out more clearly as their leader and chief. Also the Gallican cause was assisted by the fact that, since the Council of Constance, the king had more than once settled the position of the French church in separate agreements with the papacy. It had come to be easy to see that church as a national affair, to be conducted for the most part by French bishops under the French king; and even the idea of a national ecclesiastical council had been used as a possible weapon against the pope. The Spanish Church had already acquired a remarkable independence, and the French became the chief mouthpiece of the nationalist program, though a parallel form of protest against Rome distinguished the Venetians, particularly at the beginning of the seventeenth century.

From the fifteenth century, the French enemies of the Gallican principles were beginning to be known as "Ultramontanes," and, after the Counter-Reformation, it was the Jesuits who distinguished themselves in this capacity. In the period of the "Catholic Renaissance" the propaganda campaign involved an interesting development of politico-ecclesiastical thought; but Gallicanism rose to a new height when, firstly the monarchy came to its climax under Louis XIV, a king who received continual incense from a great part of the clergy, and, secondly when the movement became associated with the famous name of Bossuet, who tried to hold it within reasonable limits. A "Declaration of the French Clergy" in 1682 asserted the principles: that the king's temporal sovereignty was independent of the pope; that even in matters of faith the papacy needed the concurrence of the bishops; that a General Council was superior to the pope; and that the ancient Gallican liberties (e.g., the exclusion of papal bulls and briefs that had not received the consent of the king) were to be regarded as sacrosanct. The result was a violent conflict with the papacy at a time when Louis XIV was beset by other serious difficulties, and the Declaration was formally withdrawn. Its tenets continued to prevail in France, however, and Gallicanism was still to play a great part in the country, as well as setting an example for nationalistic aspirations elsewhere.

The posthumous publication in 1640 of *Augustinus* by Cornelius Jansen (1585–1638) was to have tremendous and far-reaching effects for a long period in France and neighboring countries. The work tried to show that Saint Augustine's teaching conflicted with that of the seventeenth century (and particularly that of the Jesuits); and by stressing the helplessness of man it moved to predestinarian ideas, though an admixture of Catholic doctrine still distinguished it from Calvinism. The cause was taken up by theologians at the Sorbonne, and then by important scholars as well as the nuns of Port-Royal-des-Champs. When five propositions were condemned by Pope Innocent X in 1653, the French leader of the movement agreed that the propositions were heretical and that the Church had the authority to condemn them; but he denied that they were contained in Jansen's *Augustinus* and claimed that this was a historical point on which the pope's ruling was not authoritative.

The whole controversy flared up again at the beginning of the eighteenth century, when a number of theologians at the Sorbonne claimed that absolution need not be refused to a priest who maintained this distinction between questions of doctrine and questions of fact. Pope Clement XI denounced this thesis in 1705 and, as he had the support of Louis XIV, the campaign against Jansenism was a powerful one, culminating in the bull *Unigenitus* which in 1713 condemned 101 propositions. Jansenism, which had spread widely amongst the people and the lower clergy, was supported at times by the Sorbonne and the *Parlement* of Paris, and for some years the Archbishop of Paris refused to submit to the bull *Unigenitus*. The persecution aroused great passions and led to an enlargement of the area of the controversy, its victims appealing, for example, for a General Council of the Church. Under desperate pressures the movement tended to change character, claimed to produce miracles, and had convulsionist manifestations. It turned into a broader kind of opposition to Church and monarchy in the eighteenth century and achieved at times an almost revolutionary atmosphere.

At the same time a great number of French Jansenists fled to Holland where a permanent schismatic organization was established in Utrecht. The movement spread to North Italy and the system which it established at Pistoia was condemned by Pope Pius VI in 1794. The "Jansenism" which was supposed to influence the ecclesiastical policy of the French Revolution had departed far from the original movement, and involved Gallican ideas and democratic claims in respect of the rights of the lower clergy. It has been suggested that "Jansenism" in North Italy in the nineteenth century became transmuted into a kind of secular religion.

3. The Transition to the Age of Reason. Because the practice of the right religion was considered so important, and because there was such a conviction that only one form of religion could be right, it was only by a very slow process (and by certain changes in the very structure of Christian thinking) that toleration could come to be itself a religious ideal. In the middle of the seventeenth century it seems to come almost as a "discovery" to some people that the other man's creed, instead of being the product of perversity, might be as much a case of conscience as one's own; and perhaps it required the standing presence for a considerable period of rival sects to produce the persuasion that, though a man may hold his own faith as an absolute, he must treat the matter with a certain degree of relativity in his relations with other men, who have the same right to follow their conscience.

Some progress was made through pondering on the current doctrine that ethics required the granting to others of the treatment one expected to receive from them. It was more easy for the various branches of Protestantism to adopt this attitude towards one another than to give Roman Catholics the benefit of it. When sects were multiplied—as in Puritan England— and when religious variety had become a standing phenomenon, it was more easy to see that the individual judgment had come to have preponderant significance; and some sects were individualistic, some highly insistent about the Inner Light. It meant a kind of intellectual revolution, but when one came to see that voluntariness of belief was itself an essential thing (and that the quality of belief even had some relation to its voluntariness), Christians in the course of time could come to wonder why they had ever permitted persecution at all. Protestants came to feel that diversity itself might be enriching for Christendom, that truth might be served by the clash of controversy, and that the right could be brought to prevail in the long run by force of mere persuasion.

But the laymen played a great part in the coming of toleration. In England, a certain religious indifference—or a reaction against fanaticism—was visible from the 1650's. There may have been an increasing squeamishness about the infliction of suffering for religious reasons and a feeling that extravagant sects had exposed the pretentions of authoritarianism. The settlement in the Treaty of Westphalia in 1648, the need for manpower in Germany to aid in the work of economic recovery after the devastation of the Thirty Years' War, the growing importance of the laity in society and the decline in the general prestige of the clergy—these, as well as special political conjunctures—have their part in the coming of a toleration which still left dissenters penalized in some ways. As the eighteenth century proceeded a country like England ceased to have the appearance of a "Christian Society" and the Church of England became more like a privileged "Establishment" in a secular state. In both England and Ireland, the Catholics were still harassed by cruel penal laws. In 1685 Louis XIV revoked the Edict of Nantes, and deprived his Protestant subjects of the toleration they had enjoyed for nearly a century.

In the meantime, however, other factors had been altering the place of religion in society and in life, and making the survival of religious intolerance all the more anomalous. Christianity had successfully confronted the superior culture of Greco-Roman antiquity. In the Middle Ages it had subjugated Aristotle to its own purposes and had survived the contact with what had been in some respects the higher civilization of the Arabs. At the end of the seventeenth century it was to find itself more seriously embarrassed by a scientific movement which sprang in a sense from its own bosom—a movement absolutely and uniquely European, rising from the traditions of the Western world itself. The scientific movement of the seventeenth century carried human thought beyond anything that ancient Greece or ancient China had ever given the promise of producing, and the student of its antecedents would find himself carried back to some of the subtle thinking of the scholastic writers.

The movement was promoted to a considerable degree by men who often believed that, by concrete enquiries into history and nature, they were glorifying the Creator and illuminating the work of Providence. It was one of its essential principles that men should turn away from the discussion of final causes and the ultimate essence of things, topics which had hitherto proved so tantalizing and distracting. They should observe how one particular thing in the natural world acted upon another, and by reflection and inference upon the observed results, they should climb to a range of important intermediate generalizations. So they freed their minds for a more specialized form of research, freed science itself from its compromising entanglement with "natural philosophy." Some of them were looking for laws before they properly knew how to discover them, and were seeking to embrace everything in the realm of law—leaving no gaps in the clockwork universe—before they had found the clue that might lead them to such a system. And they said that they were vindicating the rationality of God the "Creator," a God whom they could not believe to be guilty of arbitrariness or caprice in his arrangement of the cosmos.

It was Sir Isaac Newton who, when he had established the automatic working of the solar system, was seized with misgiving, because he realized that instead of leading to the greater glory of God, it might tempt men to think that a deity was henceforth a superfluity. At this point he seemed to show an uncommon anxiety to find some loopholes in the system that he had produced. The inferences from the system itself, and the victory of the mechanistic (or, as it called itself, the "geometrical") kind of thinking that now became fashionable—the overall result of the seventeenth-century revolution in science—opened the door to a "deism" which allowed the existence of a Creator who, after setting everything in motion, had become the complete absentee.

The Church confronted the crisis at an unfortunate moment, a moment when religion in general had come to an exceptionally low state. Fanaticism had continued until the middle of the seventeenth century and it had added to the bitterness of war in Europe, as well as the constitutional struggles in England. The Puritan regime in England had been followed by the relaxation and license that is associated with the reign of Charles II. The religiosity of the latest period of Louis XIV's reign was followed by a similar reaction—the levity and the laxity of the subsequent Regency. The concession of religious toleration in England at the end of the seventeenth century coincided paradoxically with the decline of the body who were to have been its main beneficiaries—the Presbyterians—some of whom began to move into Unitarianism. Only the advent of John Wesley put an end to what had been a serious religious setback in the country at large. The conflict between the Protestant and the Catholic versions of religious authority would seem in any case to have had the effect of undermining confidence in any kind of claim to authoritativeness.

The results of the scientific revolution were sometimes popularized and transmuted into a new world view by men like Fontenelle in France, who had caught skepticism not really from science itself but from the writings of classical Greece. The wider knowledge of the globe, the writings of travellers, the study of primitive peoples and distant civilizations, and developing notions of comparative religion, made it possible to reckon with cultures that had never been touched by Greece and Rome, and to envisage the traditions of Christendom as not in any sense universal, not necessarily even central, but something of a regional phenomenon. On this view, all religions were merely the effect of an original and basic "natural religion" which in every place had come to be overgrown with peculiar local accretions, local mythologies, local legends.

When Sir Isaac Newton clinched the success of the seventeenth-century scientific revolution, there was a sense in which, in any case, the authority of both the Middle Ages and the ancient world was at last overthrown. Also the secularization of life was proceeding rapidly; and at the end of the seventeenth century the intellectual leadership passed to the regions which were industrially and commercially the most advanced —England, Holland, and France, particularly the Huguenot part of France. The learned world had lost its leading position; the arbiters in the realm of thought were a wider reading-public, a bourgeois class that prided itself on a worldly-minded kind of common sense.

4. The Eighteenth Century. From this time we see the spread of unbelief amongst the intelligentsia, and in the latter part of the eighteenth century the deism is sometimes changing into atheism, though it is too easily forgotten that the nineteenth century was still to be a great epoch in the history of religion and that, in England, for example, the churches still had a great hold on the masses at the beginning of the twentieth century. From this time, too, the Church—and particularly the Catholic Church—came to be afraid of science and discovery, beginning what was to be a long and unhappy rearguard action against the forces of modernity. In France, where the *philosophe* movement brought the Age of Reason to its climax, the conflict between the Roman Catholic and the liberal or progressive sections of society seems to have produced an almost permanent sundering of the national tradition. In England the antithesis in the eighteenth century was less severe, partly because the churchmen there proved to be no mean antagonists, and partly because the influence of nonconformity helped to bridge the gap between religious conservatism and secular liberalism. In Methodism a strong desire to awaken the social conscience of the country was balanced by a moderate political outlook which is sometimes regarded as having helped to save the country from the turmoil of a French Revolution. Protestantism, moreover, proved more flexible than Catholicism at the critical period. There emerges now a Protestantism in many ways radically unlike that of the sixteenth century. It claims to be the ally of humanism, rationalism, individualism, and liberty.

At this point in the story a significant part was played by that interesting figure, the "lapsed Christian"—the man who has thrown overboard the theological dogmas, but has not been able to jettison a host of assumptions, mundane evaluations and ideals, views about personality and the structure of the human drama, which had been associated with the Christian tradition. One aspect of the eighteenth century is the more or less unconscious attempt to provide a counter-system to Christianity—at least to fill the gap which was left when the Church was taken out of the picture. It showed itself in minor writings, provincial move-

ments, local activity—an interesting attempt for example to teach a secular morality, a kind of public spirit, and to promote virtue by rewarding it with civic prizes.

Sometimes the rivalry became conscious and the enemies of the Church would claim that they were the better Christians; they were solicitous for the humble and poor, while the church-people were intent on mere ceremonies. Sometimes the critics were justified in their accusations and it would seem that they themselves, by breaking with the Church, had disembarrassed themselves of conventions which hindered the realization of what Christian charity really did require. One enemy of the Church still made the curious note that it would be good for men to meet once a week for a homily on morality. And the famous "philosophies of history"—the attempts to lay out the shape of the whole course of centuries—were (down to the time of Hegel) a curious reflection of earlier Christian attempts to lay out the plan of world history, the design of Providence. A number of ideals—liberty, democracy, egalitarianism, socialism, communism— had been caught first from biblical sources and Christian principles by religious dissidents who, as a minority, could more easily dare to follow principles to their logical conclusion. But the real battle for their actual realization was often fought either by non-Christians or by religious nonconformists, and by a curious paradox the official church sometimes seemed to be the principal enemy that had to be fought. In this realm, too, the churches too often committed themselves to a lengthy rearguard action. Having imagined that Christianity could not survive the destruction of the Aristotelian cosmos, they easily convinced themselves that it might not survive the destruction of a particular kind of regime. In other words, they had tied their religion too closely to various types of mundane systems. And the course of history drove them to enquire more deeply into the question: What was the essential thing in the Christian faith?

Protestantism fared better than Catholicism in the eighteenth century; for in Britain's American colonies the earlier half of the century saw a religious awakening in which Jonathan Edwards was a central figure; it might be said that the Seven Years' War (1756–63) decided that the northern continent of America should be predominantly Protestant; and the rise of Prussia and Russia added great weight to the non-Catholic part of Europe. Even in the religious and devotional life, it was Protestantism that showed itself the more dynamic throughout the period. On this side, the story illustrates the point that one can hardly put limits to the conditions which provoke a religious revival. The thing can come by surprise at the moment which seems the most unfavorable; and the weather that withers the routine of religion in official churches may be just the kind to bring out a spontaneous growth, a development outside the recognized program.

In the later decades of the seventeenth century (just as deism was coming to the front) there emerged in Germany a pietism which may have had antecedents in the later Middle Ages, and which, as it spread to neighboring countries, may have owed something to English Puritanism and to movements in Holland. It first became important in the Lutheran church in Germany, but in the Netherlands and then in Germany it spread to the Reformed churches, and its influence was increased by the ascendancy that it acquired in the university of Halle. A similar movement was that of the Moravians, who were established in the lands of Count Zinzendorf and extended their influence abroad, even to England and America; John Wesley was one of the people who acknowledged a debt to them.

Evangelicalism in the English-speaking world is in fact a parallel phenomenon. It was an essential feature of the movement that mere membership in organized churches and the routine participation in the offices of these were not sufficient for the authentic Christian. The nominal believer still needed to be properly "converted" and to bring the matter home to himself; and the "conversion" should come after he had been seized with a vivid conviction of his sinfulness. No great interest was shown in theological discussions and dogmatic controversy—there was just an insistence that a man should be born again, and that he should have a personal experience of Christ. At the same time Bible reading was emphasized, there was a great love of hymn singing, great importance was attached to philanthropic work. One might remain a member of the state-church, but in any case one would join little informal groups which were meant for fellowship, study, and prayer.

An important feature of eighteenth-century Protestantism was the formation of religious societies, some of which would comprise members of various denominations—societies which would promote foreign missions, educational work, the care of the poor, or a particular measure of reform, and which became more numerous as the century drew to its close. From evangelical circles in England there arose the demand for an improvement in prisons, the attack on slavery and the slave-trade, and the later cry for industrial legislation. And from laymen who had been trained by their activity in religious groups there emerged some of the working-class leaders of the nineteenth century.

5. Roman Catholicism and the State, 1760–1815.
In the closing decades of the eighteenth century the

secular character of the state was becoming more clear, and the Enlightenment itself, which acquired particular prestige amongst monarchs and statesmen, seemed almost to take the place of religion as the fountain of influence at royal courts. There now occurred a series of dramatic attacks by the modern state upon the Roman Catholic system; and the church, which in any case was hardly in a condition to meet the challenge, was badly crippled by an initial strategic blow in the 1760's, when the Bourbon courts of France, Spain, Naples, and Parma (following the example of Portugal) expelled from their European and overseas dominions the Jesuits who had once wielded so much power as the confessors of kings. It was easy to raise suspicion against them because of their alleged views on tyrannicide, or their casuistry, or their recent commercial operations, or the antinational character of their constitution; but their impressive importance now was due to the virtues of their educational work, which made Frederick the Great of Prussia and Catherine of Russia delighted to receive the exiles.

By this time the governments of Europe were exercising immediate influence on papal elections, and in 1769 they secured the elevation of Clement XIV, who could be expected to abolish the order, and who signed the Brief of Suppression in 1773. The pope was now in the position of having to protest against a Protestant state and a schismatic empire that gave the Jesuits a field in which to work; but, though he induced the Prussians to secularize them, he had to agree to a subterfuge which enabled the order itself to continue in Russia and even to recruit novices (in spite of its formal suppression), its members being needed for the care of Catholic subjects taken over by Russia in the first Partition of Poland.

In 1763 an important and influential work by Nikolaus von Hontheim combined the teaching of the Conciliar and Gallican movements in the program known as "Febronianism" and made Germany a significant field of conflict; but similar writings in Italy, the Netherlands, and even Austria reveal the tremendous change of outlook that had been taking place in the Catholic world. Even Maria Theresa of Austria (the one great ruler who had been unwilling to see the destruction of the Jesuits) was ready, in spite of her piety, to take action against a monastic movement that had run to excess. But in 1780 she was succeeded by her son Joseph II—himself a sincere Christian though in so many ways a disciple of the *philosophes*—and it is astonishing to see the speed and consistency with which he not only excluded the authority of the pope and controlled a movement of ecclesiastical reform, but established what was virtually a national church, in which he decided the character of the training in ecclesiastical seminaries, prescribed the spiritual functions of the priesthood, attacked images, etc., in churches, and insisted on an austere type of piety quite different from the baroque piety that he regarded as idolatrous.

In Austria, as elsewhere, what was called Jansenism implied Conciliar and Gallican ideas but also a stress on devotion and on works of charity and a genuine desire to raise spiritual standards. At the same time, the ecclesiastical work of Joseph II was a remarkable anticipation by a "benevolent despot" of the attempt by the French Revolution at an overall reconstruction of the Church. An ecclesiastical congress in Germany in 1786 produced the Punctuation of Ems, a program for which Joseph II lost his enthusiasm when he saw that the powers it took from the pope might serve to aggrandize the metropolitans and bishops of Germany rather than the secular authority. A synod of 234 clergy held at Pistoia in the same year under the patronage of Joseph's brother, Leopold, the Grand Duke of Tuscany, combined the tenets of the Jansenists with those of Gallicanism and called for the abolition of all religious orders founded since the time of Saint Benedict. But the great mass of the population refused to follow Joseph II in his religious policy; and the extension of this to his Belgian territory led in 1786 to a revolt of students at the nationalized seminary of Louvain—a revolt which was to prove the prelude to a wider rebellion. And though Joseph's brother, Leopold, was more careful of public opinion, his religious reforms led to a popular upheaval in Florence in 1787.

All this was only the prelude to the cataclysm of the French Revolution. In view of the existing distress and the bankruptcy of the state, it was not easy for the French after 1789 to treat as property dedicated to God a great deal of the wealth which had for so long supported luxury and immorality amongst the clergy. Church property was nationalized on 2 November 1789, and then the state, which proposed to take the responsibility for clerical stipends, thought to rationalize the whole system in the interests of the taxpayer and the public in general, dissolving religious orders that had no utilitarian function, rearranging bishoprics, fixing stipends, and regulating discipline. The Church, under this Civil Constitution of July 1790 was to retain its communion with Rome, but the pope, who had not been consulted about the reforms, was no longer to invest bishops with their spiritual authority, and bishops and clergy were to be selected by popular election. The clergy were required to accept this Civil Constitution on oath, but, though the new system greatly improved the financial position of the lower clergy, half of the *curés* refused to conform. The

government was committed therefore to a policy of persecution, and the revolution was jeopardized by a first-class religious conflict which helped to provoke a civil war. Early in 1798 the French invaders of Italy established the revolution for a short time in Rome itself, and in 1799 Pope Pius VI died an exile and prisoner of France.

Napoleon Bonaparte, as First Consul, was determined to make capital out of the errors of the revolution, which had reorganized the Church without consulting the pope and had brought on itself the trouble of a religious war. He determined to secure the credit for restoring the Church, and this in fact enabled him to put greater pressure on the papacy, which was anxious for such a settlement. By his Concordat of 1801 he saved essential features of the revolutionary settlement, and acquired for these the assent of the pope, while recognizing Catholicism as "the religion of the great majority of French citizens." But when he followed this by unilateral action in his 77 Organic Articles, which asserted Gallican principles and the predominance of the state over the church, the pope and the French Catholics could do little unless they proposed to destroy the effect of the whole settlement. From 1806 the spread of the Napoleonic Empire brought a conflict with the pope as a temporal prince; because of his spiritual primacy, he felt unable to put his territories at the service of the French in their war against England. The conflict became a dramatic one, and in 1809 Napoleon decreed the end of the temporal power and declared Rome a Free Imperial City. Very soon, Pope Pius VII was himself a prisoner.

6. *The Nineteenth Century.* A course of curriculum history which concentrates on governmental affairs and on the writings of the intellectuals in eighteenth-century Europe may do less than justice to the ordinary life of town and country, and the mood of a great part of society. It is easy to forget the famous hymns which the eighteenth century produced, the choral music of Bach, Handel's *Messiah*, the tremendous momentum of the Methodist movement, and the way in which religion itself could even come to terms with the new outlook. At the same time, human needs, which the hard, dry thinking of the Age of Reason failed to satisfy, are to be recognized in the quasi-religious aspirations of Rousseau and in certain aspects of that romantic movement which was sometimes associated with the nostalgias of lapsed Christians—even (particularly in Germany) lapsed sons of the manse. Almost at the very time when Napoleon was realizing the political capital that he might gain within France itself from a Concordat with the papacy, Chateaubriand, in his *Génie du Christianisme* (1802) registered a new mood which was capable of reviving the power of religion, and his influence seemed to be increased by the fact that he gave more place to sentiment than profound reasoning.

At the same time the cataclysms of twenty-five years were calculated to revive both a religious awe and a distrust of human systems; and, after 1815, it became easy (while, for many, it was a matter of high policy) to preach that the writings of the *philosophes* had been responsible for the recent tragedies, and that the human race cannot afford to turn its back on history. The new situation helped to increase the significance of history and—particularly when combined with the romantic mood—it tended to alter the character of the historical endeavor, creating a disposition to turn it into what was much more a study of the past for its own sake. One result of this was the awakening of interest in the Middle Ages and a discovery of the achievement of the medieval Church; and this was initially the work of Protestant scholars, though it became a source of considerable stimulus to Roman Catholicism. After the example had been set in England by Edmund Burke before the end of the eighteenth century, the cause of tradition in both the political and the religious field came to find its expositors amongst the European intelligentsia, and conservatism itself acquired a more imposing intellectual support. These factors help to explain why, in the nineteenth century, religion again became a power in the world, and why also the most remarkable features of the story were the revival of Roman Catholicism and the emergence in the 1830's of the Oxford movement.

Yet, to a considerable degree, the movement against Christianity increased in power, and the hostility to ecclesiastical systems now turned more definitely into an attack on religion as such. The formidable character of the secularizing forces helped in fact to provoke a counter-movement (to alarm the Tractarians in Oxford, for example) and the conflict between belief and unbelief became a more profound and serious affair. It is interesting to see that in France, where the hostility to Rome and to Christianity itself was still so strong, the growth and the assertiveness of Catholic piety became particularly evident; and the very power which the state acquired over the church in the Napoleonic settlement drove Catholics to recognize the papacy as their true support, the old Gallican prejudices giving way to Ultramontanism.

The century saw the continued enlargement of the power and the scope of the state—a state now by necessity increasingly engrossed by secular preoccupations—and this became irksome at times even to Protestants, irksome even to sections of that highly national body, the Church of England. Precisely because the state was so obviously no longer a "religious society," virtually coextensive with a church, Christians were thrown back on the idea of the Church as a separate body, functioning for special purposes and existing by virtue of a divine commission. Something of the resulting aspiration for autonomy is visible not only in the Oxford movement but even in Germany, where princes in the period after 1815 still had great power over their churches, and were able to bring about the unification of the Lutheran and Reformed systems in many regions.

At the same time the natural sciences, and the outlook that was associated with them, began to present more serious difficulties. In the 1830's and 1840's geology challenged the book of Genesis, though progressive Christians were able to meet the difficulty by reverting to more flexible ideas about biblical inspiration—ideas which had been held before, and the resort to which was coming to be necessary for other reasons. But the doctrine of evolution, particularly as developed by Charles Darwin in the *Origin of Species* (1859), seemed to involve a more radical change in one's views about the nature of man, the character of the universe, and the potentialities of science. All the while the development of biblical study and the application of the historical method in that field—including a closer analysis of the Gospels—was producing equally disturbing results, especially in the work of the Tübingen school, for example the *Life of Jesus* (1835) by David Friedrich Strauss. Some people met all this with blind conservatism, some left the Church, and from memoirs, biographies, and fiction we can see how often this was accompanied by great heart-searching, carried out as though it were itself a religious act. Some kept the old belief that in the long run religion would become compatible with both science and history, and were driven to think more deeply about the essential nature of their faith.

Apart from the ferment of the liberal and democratic ideas which had come down from revolutionary France and had been disseminated over Europe through the victories of Napoleon, the rise of industrialism, the emergence of vast urban concentrations, and the plight of the new working classes resulted in an environment more hostile to religion, more refractory to ecclesiastical teaching. For many centuries it had been almost too easy to be a believing Christian. Now, it was not so easy, and those who adhered to the faith had to think more deeply about the nature of it and revise their notion of the duties that it carried with it.

Roman Catholicism may have gained considerable strength from the fact that it set itself so consistently against the very things that were to become the prevailing tendencies of the nineteenth century. It seems to have acquired internal depth and spiritual intensity from the fact that it stood so firmly by its ancient teaching and was so assured in its dogmatic claims. Its revival had begun before 1815, and it produced a restoration of religious orders (including the general reestablishment of the Jesuits in 1814); also an intellectual revival in Germany which made Munich an exhilarating city before the middle of the century. The creation of an unprecedented number of congregations, societies, etc., meant that the activity and support of the laity as well as the clergy were recruited, as never before, for the care of the distressed, the carrying of the gospel to neglected areas in the towns, and the missionary work abroad.

Attempts to reconcile the religion and the authority of the papacy with a program of modern democratic ideas were firmly suppressed, however. For a little while after his elevation in 1846 Pope Pius IX tried to cooperate with liberalism in the Papal States; but the drift to extremism, and the crucial demand that he—a prince of peace—should turn "nationalist" and help to drive the Austrians from Italy, showed the impossibility of this. In 1864 his Syllabus of Errors made clear how Rome had been setting itself against the encroachments of the state in ecclesiastical matters, including education; it was also against the views of liberals on toleration, and against any qualification of the claim that Roman Catholicism was the single true religion. There was specific condemnation of any suggestion that the Supreme Pontiff either could or ought to reconcile himself with "progress, liberalism, and modern civilization." If the year 1870 saw the great humiliation of the pope—his loss of Rome and his disappearance as a temporal power—it saw also the Infallibility Decree of the First Vatican Council and the explicit recognition of his supremacy in the spiritual realm.

All this would have been impossible if he had not now found in faithful Catholics throughout Europe a support more reliable than his predecessors had received from actual governments, and if there had not been a widespread resolve to rescue the traditions and doctrines of the Church from current, fashionable, intellectual movements. On the theoretical side, the conservative attitude itself became imposing through the reassertion and reexposition of the scholastic teaching of Saint Thomas Aquinas. Before the end of the century Pope Leo XIII encouraged French Catholics to cooperate with the French Republic, but this did not prevent the complete separation of Church and State and further attacks on the religious orders in that country. In the ten or fifteen years from 1893 an effective resistance was made to the Catholic "Modernist" movement, which attempted to take account of achievements in biblical scholarship and historical criticism (and in particular to introduce the more flexible views of biblical inspiration now familiar amongst the Protestants). Though there were features in this Modernism which disturbed even enlightened Protestants, the radical nature of its suppression lent color to the view of Baron von Hügel that the Curia was carrying reaction too far.

In England and Germany the Pietistic and Evangelical movements went on increasing their power. In England the nonconformists had been growing rapidly in numbers, embracing a quarter of the population at the beginning of the nineteenth century. Their expansion became still more remarkable from this time, especially in the newly industrialized regions, and it was now that "the nonconformist conscience" became a formidable affair. From 1833, however, when as a result of the Reform Bill it was less easy than before to regard Parliament as the lay assembly of the Anglican Church, and when the Whigs seemed particularly menacing, the Oxford movement reasserted the idea of the Church as a separate, divinely constituted body to be governed by bishops who held authority as the successors of the Apostles. Still more, they wished to reassert the Catholic side of the Anglican tradition, to revive the spiritual life that had been manifested in the ancient saints and to restore the beliefs and ceremonies of earlier times. The very episcopal authority which they invoked declined on the whole to tolerate them, and in this predicament some of their distinguished representatives—men like Newman and Manning—moved over to Rome. Like the nonconformists, the Oxford Tractarians had an influence that extended far beyond their own circle, and in their case it was an influence out of all proportion to their numbers.

Germany, on the other hand, not only saw a quickening of religious life, but also acquired a remarkable intellectual leadership in the Protestant world. The predominance that she had achieved in philosophy and historical science gave her resources for adventurous attempts to vindicate the Christian outlook, and made Lutheranism more creative than it had been since the days of its founder. The German thinkers tried to meet the challenge of the age by examining the bases of religion itself—some grounding theology on inner experience, some insisting on a creatureliness and a feeling of dependence in man, some stressing the direct apprehension of the divine, some holding that all thinking should start with Christ and the Gospel. Certain writers raised the question whether the surrender of Christianity to Greek thought in the early centuries of the Church had not been a misfortune. Others carried further than ever before the study and criticism of the Bible, the examination of the early Church, and the history of Christian dogma.

Protestantism became more splintered than ever in the nineteenth century; but even more than Roman Catholicism it expressed itself in movements to assist the distressed classes, to reform society, to carry religion into neglected areas, and to enlarge the missionary work abroad.

The nineteenth century was important in the history of religion, partly because it saw advances in thought on both the Catholic and the Protestant sides, and partly because the conflict with secularism and unbelief had become so formidable. In spite of the great secessions that took place, both Catholicism and Protestantism appeared stronger at the end of the century than at the beginning, besides involving far greater numbers of their adherents in a clearer act of affirmative decision, and stimulating greater activity in the laity. In both great sections of the Church, the clergy, in their combination of earnestness, intelligence, and training, may have reached a general standard rarely known in the history of the Church. It would not be easy for people today to realize the degree to which, down to 1914, the local church was for most people the hub of their social life—the place that often provided the only societies, sporting clubs, festivals and parties, informative lectures, and musical evenings—the place where men met their sweethearts and gathered their circle of friends. A tremendous foreign missionary endeavor from the 1790's, particularly in Protestantism (and facilitated to some degree by the opportunities open to colonialist nations), had far exceeded all precedents and had carried Christianity into every quarter of the globe.

In the United States the number of Christians and the percentage of the population that were church members, at the beginning of the nineteenth century, were remarkably low and ecclesiastical systems did not possess the privileges that they so often enjoyed in the European states. The material preoccupations of a pioneer society, and the industrial and urban developments as the century proceeded, would have seemed calculated to check the development of religion; yet a tremendous internal missionary work made the advance of the churches in the United States more remarkable than in the Old World. This missionary work accompanied the westward movement, and the peculiar needs of the frontier and of pioneer conditions helped to produce "revivalist" methods, camp-meetings, circuit riders, and travelling evangelists—techniques of mass-conversion often supported by the fervor for "Gospel hymns" and negro "spirituals." The effect of all this was to alter the balance of forces and in general to change the physiognomy of American religion. Victory came to the denominations that had missionary ardor and the ability to offer the kind of message that could reach the people. Within Protestantism it was now the Baptists and Methodists who multiplied, swamping the Congregationalists, Presbyterians, and Episcopalians, who had predominated at the beginning of the century.

Roman Catholicism from being one of the smallest became the largest single religious body in the country, partly as a result of the great number of immigrants. Protestantism now acquired a remarkable "popular" shape which corresponded to the "popular" side of Catholicism, though it bore a vastly different character, which contributed similarly to the cause of intellectual conservatism in the churches. The whole movement led to a great splintering of the older denominations and the founding of new ones, particularly Mormonism in 1830, the Seventh Day Adventists, organized in 1863, and the Church of Christ Scientist in 1879. In the nineteenth century and the early decades of the twentieth there was a vast increase in the percentage of the population that was actively connected with some church, and, by the close of that period religion—with its Social Gospel and its colossal philanthropies—had done much to shape the American outlook, helping first to generate the American ideal and then, perhaps, to fasten Christianity itself within the limits of that ideal.

7. The Twentieth Century. In the twentieth century two World Wars, centered at the heart of European Christendom, shook the earth and made history more dynamic. Christianity was faced by organized systems such as Communism and Nazism, which constituted a more powerful threat to it, and cleared away more of the traditional fabric of society, than anything hitherto known. The acceleration of scientific progress, the resulting change in one's notions of the physical universe, the great power that man had acquired over nature, the enormous advances of educational systems that were essentially secular, and the influence of the popular press, radio, and television in the dissemination of a new world view—all these produced a greater intellectual challenge than religion of any sort had ever had to meet before. Now, also, the ethical ideas of society, though so many of them still carried the marks of Christian influence, came to conflict in an unprecedented way with some of the longest and most consistent traditions of the churches. The fact that the churches had so often been engaged in a rearguard action—sometimes against liberty, sometimes against science itself—became a disadvantage, since it left (as an additional obstruction to the hearing of the Gospel) a resentment in intelligent people, even a fear lest the Church should ever recover its power. In other continents, the great missionary endeavor (in which man may sometimes have tried unthinkingly to tie Christianity to the values and the manners of Western civilization) came to be charged understandably, but unjustly, with having sought to provide cover for imperialist purposes.

The resulting issues are as momentous as in the days when the faith of the first disciples had to confront the culture of the Greco-Roman world, and it is not easy to say what will be the long-term effects of the new situation on the intellectualization of the faith and the attempt to run it into a new world view. The actual experiences of the human race, as it develops the implications of its current systems, may affect the story; and it is not clear that Christianity may not have to confront a world somewhat similar to the one which the early Church had to face in the Roman Empire—a hostile world, but suffering strange nostalgias and harassed by competing forms of faith.

In some respects the churches may have drawn in upon themselves as though determined not to lose anything essential in their ancient heritage. A liberalism which, before and after the First World War, may have been too directly rationalistic, soon came to appear "dated," and even Protestants—even nonconformists—became somewhat more interested in their tradition. The situation of the world may help to explain why Karl Barth in 1918 began to present the "theology of Crisis," directly attacking liberalism and reviving some of the profounder aspects of early Lutheranism. But historiography raised radical problems, especially when from 1919 the teachers of *Formgeschichte* examined the shape which the early Church had given to the packets of oral tradition that lay behind the Gospels. History emerged again as a crucial issue for an "historical religion" in the much controverted work of Rudolf Bultmann. He called for "de-mythologizing" and presented existentialist ideas which threw light on some aspects of Christianity if not also on history itself.

The Bible retained its influence even amongst people (including Roman Catholics) who had accepted the kind of criticism that could be described as central. In the United States the churches retained their high membership and remarkable vigor for further decades, the country acquiring a recognized leadership in the Protestant world. But, even amid technological progress and booming prosperity, influential teachers issued their moral challenges, took their stand on the Bible, and reasserted the pessimistic view of human nature. The spectacular scandals and crimes in certain sections of society did not nullify that compassion and that American idealism which owed so much to an ultimate Christian influence.

It was natural that, in the new situation, the various sects and denominations should lose much of their former fanaticism and hostility, and should come to feel one another as allies against a world of hostile forces. To a considerable degree it was coming to be the case that, within Protestantism, the differences between the liberals and the conservatives in the various churches were deeper than the differences between one denomination and another. Even in the decades after 1914, it became an important consideration that the work of foreign missions was being hampered by the divisions within Christianity. Unions between denominations and cooperation for special objects, though not unknown before, now became much more frequent and significant. The Ecumenical movement was a natural development of this and a typical feature of it was the preparation in 1938, and the official constitution at Amsterdam in 1940, of the plan for a World Council of Churches. The work of Pope John XXIII and the Second Vatican Council of 1962–65 stand as one of the most remarkable features of the twentieth-century story—a significant change in the relations between Catholic and Protestant, who (in spite of rivalries and hostilities) had never, throughout the centuries, quite ceased to exert a beneficent influence on one another.

Lord Acton once remarked that he saw Providence in general history (saw it in the march of "progress," as he explicitly stated on a number of occasions); but he added that he did not detect it in the history of the Church. His attitude is understandable, for ecclesiastical systems have not been exempted from scandals and crimes; and (at least in those tangible things which the secular historian has chiefly in mind) they would seem to have been subject to the laws which govern other religions, including that of the Old Testament. Acton may have been misled because he tended to be interested in the kind of history that deals with "public affairs" and perhaps saw the historical Church too much as a politico-religious institution. All the same, he must have known in his heart that its essence lay in the spiritual life which presumed the immediacy of divine activity, though it might be unrelated to "progress"—a spiritual life which might be at least as profound in the fifth or the fifteenth century as in the twentieth. He was prepared also to see all history as the development of the scope and the quality of the human conscience, this conscience being a key to progress itself and the effective dynamic behind even modern revolution, in his view. The enlarged scope for the individual conscience had been achieved by the influence of Christianity, making the great contrast with classical antiquity where, he said, man's duty had been prescribed to him by the state.

Mazzini regarded the French Revolution as the climax and fulfilment of Christianity which, by making every human being a value incommensurate with anything else in the created universe, could be regarded as working throughout the centuries for the principle of "individualism," working for it at times even when ecclesiastical systems were resisting it. On this view a Christian civilization operates (as Acton believed) to produce a regime of freedom, and the effect of its advance is to bring about a greater differentiation in personalities, a world in which each man decides the object he will work for and the God whom he will serve. Mazzini was not content with this, however, and insisted that a new stage had been reached—a stage at which the individual ought to give way to the "organic People." And this is perhaps the great issue; whether men shall be organized, and even herded like cattle, to carry out a single all-consuming purpose that is imposed on everybody.

There are elements or patterns of Christian thought that appear in a more or less secularized form in a Voltaire, a Rousseau, a Hegel, a Mazzini, a Ranke, and a Marx; and perhaps they come to an end there. From the middle of the twentieth century, the world moves on its own momentum to new patterns of thought, new notions of the enterprise of living, new realms of human experience. Behind the technological age and the attempt to explore the outer universe, and behind the permissive society are elements which were part of the Christian outlook, but which, having become autonomous, have moved far forward on their own account. Perhaps the great compassionateness now visible in contemporary society will stand as the most palpable result of fifteen hundred years of Christian predominance in Europe. And now, perhaps, for the first time during those fifteen hundred years, Christianity returns to something like its original state—a world in which it cannot be objected that, for the great majority of people, things are unfairly disposed in favor of conventional or habitual or hereditary belief.

V. THE ORTHODOX CHURCH

In the Byzantine or Orthodox Church of the East the situation was seriously affected by the fact that the culture, the imperial system and religion itself enjoyed a continuity which the barbarian invaders had badly broken in the West. The Eastern Emperor remained still in a sense the Pontifex Maximus; he could virtually choose the Patriarch of Constantinople, he legislated on ecclesiastical matters, initiated such legislation, and could behave tyrannically on occasion. It gradually became explicit that the ordinary administration of the Church was regarded as shared by the five Patriarchates of Rome, Constantinople, Antioch, Alexandria, and Jerusalem; though a place of special honor was conceded to Rome, and, from the eighth

century it was true for the most part that the Patriarchate of Constantinople covered the area effectively ruled by the Eastern emperor.

Elements of an earlier democracy continued in the ecclesiastical system, the laity having a part in the election of a priest, the lower clergy in the choice of a bishop. The laity—and perhaps, in particular, the mob in Constantinople—were a force in religious affairs, and were not regarded as incapable of holding views on theology. They were greatly under the influence of the lower clergy and the monks, and able to resist even a Patriarch, even an emperor. Perhaps the most effective practical difference from the West came from the continuance of secular education in the Byzantine Empire: the fact that high civil servants might be more cultured than the bishops and might be appointed to high ecclesiastical office. On doctrinal matters Constantinople was disposed to have respect for Rome, but in the East, the final authority in this field was an Ecumenical Council, and there was a greater desire not to allow minute differences of doctrine to ruin charitable relations with other parts of the Church. Greater value was attached to mysticism, and there was less suspicion of it, than in the West, the emphasis being more definitely on the otherworldly aspect of religion.

When the Church had settled down after the Iconoclastic controversy in the eighth and early ninth centuries, the missionary work amongst the Slavs was taken up, and with it went the general civilizing influences of Byzantium, producing a distinct differentiation in culture between the two halves of the whole continent. Soon after 860 Cyril and Methodius carried to the swollen Moravian empire the Slavonic literary language which they had constructed apparently on the basis of a dialect in Macedonia. Both here and in the conversion of Bulgaria the competition between the Eastern and the Latin church is visible, and it brought out a tendency to mutual criticism, but did not produce anything like the serious schism once associated with the name of Photius.

Over a century later the conversion of a Russian prince and his marriage to a Byzantine princess heralded the Christianizing of Russia and brought that country into the orbit of Byzantium, though Latin missionaries had appeared there at an earlier date. Earlier than all this the rule of Byzantium in southern Italy, and the policy of taking over for the Orthodox church that region, together with Illyrium (which had been part of the Roman Patriarchate), had begun to lead to serious trouble. Furthermore the conquests by the Normans in southern Italy in the eleventh century, together with their threat to move into the Balkans, complicated still further the relations between Latin

409

and Greek. The troubles of 1054, however, did not produce the real schism or the enduring estrangement that the Western church later alleged to have taken place. Political events and purely ecclesiastical rivalries and disputes would lead to polemical quarrels between Rome and Constantinople over points where each side had often been content to allow differences. The emperors in Constantinople, however, often needed help from the West, and tended to be an influence on the side of reconciliation.

The chief difficulties had reference to some things which had received general recognition in the Western church only comparatively recently, so that in a sense they were the result of the separate life that had been developing. This was true of the most serious theological difference, the famous *filioque* clause, the Western view that the Holy Spirit proceeds from the Son as well as from the Father. Fundamental differences in mentality and language between the Greeks and the Latins obstructed any agreement on this; but in any case the East had a still stronger hostility to the Western policy of adding to the creed without reference to a general council.

The reform of the Western church and the tremendous advance of papal claims in the latter half of the eleventh century (at a time when conditions in Rome for a long period had led Easterners to have a low opinion of the papacy) provided a substantial cause of further alienation, especially as the claims involved the right to appeal to Rome from ecclesiastical courts in Constantinople. For the rest the Orthodox Church tended to feel strongly about the comparatively recent development which had brought the West to the use of unleavened bread in the sacrament. And, once hostility was awakened, there were numerous differences in custom that could be turned into debating points against the West—the fasting on Saturdays, the clerical shaving of beards, the question of the celibacy of the clergy, etc.

Though the first Crusade was an answer to a call for help from Constantinople, it increased the estrangement. The establishment of a Latin bishop of Antioch, while the Orthodox one went into exile, produced a real schism in one of those eastern Patriarchates that had hitherto tried to avoid participation in the quarrels between Rome and Constantinople. The Fourth Crusade, involving the sack of Constantinople and the establishment for a time of a Latin empire there, made the estrangement enduring and profound, and marks the fundamental breach.

From the thirteenth century Byzantine culture was brilliant, as the empire declined. The Emperor Michael VIII Palaeologus in 1273–74, hoping to stave off another attack from the West, overbore both the Patriarch and the Synod and, in an agreement for ecclesiastical union, admitted the full primacy of the Roman See. But the Church refused to hold to this. The teaching of Gregory Palamas, which gave Orthodox mysticism a dogmatic basis and was adopted as official doctrine, provided a new obstruction to union; but the need for help against the Turks made the issue a live one in the fourteenth century and the Conciliar Movement in the West produced a situation somewhat more favorable to the policy. Representatives of Byzantium appeared at the Council of Constance. In 1439 a union was achieved at the Council of Florence. The Russians rejected this; however, the Byzantines were unreconciled; Constantinople fell in 1453; and in 1484 the agreement was formally repudiated there.

Before 1453 a great part of the flock of the Patriarch of Constantinople (in Asia Minor, for example) had been living under Turkish rule and the Patriarchates of Alexandria, Antioch, and Jerusalem had long been under the infidel. After the conquest, the Christians were allowed to exist as a separate nation, governing their own affairs according to their own laws and customs, the Patriarch being responsible for the administration, the securing of the payment of taxes, and the maintenance of a proper attitude towards the government. The Turkish government itself was not hostile but the local authorities in Asia seem to have been more intolerant than those in Europe. Also, in their reduced position, the Christians were unable to keep up their educational system, and the church suffered disastrously for this, though before long some use was being made of facilities in Venice.

The Russians were more passionately Orthodox than the Greeks, and more hostile to other forms of Christianity, so that they regarded the fall of Constantinople as the punishment for the union attempted with Rome. The Christians under Turkish rule might have a Patriarch, but they no longer had the leadership of a Christian emperor, and as the rulers of Russia increased in power—becoming Tsars from 1480—they saw themselves as heirs of the Byzantine emperors, Ivan III having married the niece of the last of these in 1472. They appointed their own Metropolitan of Kiev (after a nominal election) and though Ivan III had declared that the Patriarch of Constantinople had no authority in Russia, the Metropolitan acknowledged the superior position of the latter. The Russian clergy came to have a certain contempt for the Greeks, and the Tsar claimed to be the royal leader of Orthodoxy. In 1587 Constantinople recognized Moscow as a Patriarchate.

After the Time of Troubles, the first Romanov Tsar, Michael, made his able father Patriarch, and from 1610 to 1633 these two ruled together, to the great advantage of the Church. Orthodoxy had suffered a great loss during the troubles, however, because the whole of the Ukraine, including Kiev, had passed to Poland, which was attempting to impose upon it a Uniate system, agreed upon in that country in 1595. This involved the recognition of papal supremacy but the retention of the Orthodox liturgy, marriage of the clergy, etc. Between 1652 and 1658 Nikon, the Patriarch of Moscow, made a thorough reform of the Russian church, and even pressed ecclesiastical authority in the spirit of the medieval papacy. Peter the Great saw the danger, however, and, from 1700, he and his successors refused to nominate a Patriarch.

Relations with the West are illustrated by the fact that Cyril Lucaris, who was Patriarch of Constantinople from 1620 to 1635 and in 1637–38, put out a distinctly Calvinistic "confession of faith." Before 1640, Peter Moghila, Metropolitan of Kiev drew up (in Latin) a similar "confession" which showed a curious sympathy with Catholic doctrine. From 1672, Dositheus, the Patriarch of Jerusalem, was working to secure the production of a "confession" which should at least avoid these aberrations. In the eighteenth century progress was limited by the fact that in Constantinople the lay intelligentsia acquired the leading position amongst the Greeks, while Catharine the Great in Russia tended to elevate free-thinkers to high ecclesiastical appointments. In 1774 Russia created trouble for the future by securing treaty-recognition of her right to intervene on behalf of Orthodox subjects of the Ottoman Empire.

The prosperity of the Phanariots, the great influence they acquired over the church in Constantinople and their dream of a revival of Greek imperialism brought embarrassment to the Patriarchs; and the opening of the Greek revolt—which the Patriarch could not bring himself actually to denounce—led to the execution of the head of the church, two metropolitans, twelve bishops, and all the leading Phanariots in 1821. The Patriarchate never recovered from this blow and began to lose many of the features that had made it generally important in mundane affairs. With the establishment of a Greek kingdom not only the Orthodox Greeks of the country itself but also those in Turkey tended to look towards the Metropolitan of Athens. The twentieth century has seen an important squeezing out of Orthodoxy in Turkey and Egypt, and this has been helped in both cases by the departure of so many of the Greeks from these two countries. The See of Antioch has become much more important because it contains along with the Patriarchate of Jerusalem, the main Arabian section of Orthodoxy, and has itself been in Syrian or Lebanese hands throughout the present century. The Orthodox church in Europe became closely associated with nationalism in the Balkans, and

this worked to the detriment of the Patriarch of Constantinople, who, however, was perhaps too Greek to be truly ecumenical. It was even Arab-speaking members of the Orthodox church who played a leading part in the rise of Arabian national movements.

The Church has suffered of late from the secularizing, tendencies of the modern world, and in the 1960's it has in the Middle East only a fifth of the numbers it had fifty years ago. Though the Patriarch of Constantinople has only a small immediate flock, the very misfortunes of the office seem to have freed it for a more ecumenical role, especially as the Orthodox in Western Europe, in America, and in Australia are under its jurisdiction. And at least, in spite of all that has happened in recent centuries, the Church has maintained its spiritual power and its ability to play a part in the ecumenical movements of the present day.

BIBLIOGRAPHY

General. F. L. Cross, *The Oxford Dictionary of the Christian Church* (Oxford and New York, 1957). Adolf von Harnack, *Outlines of the History of Dogma*, 3rd ed. trans. Neil Buchanan, 7 vols. (London, 1894–99). K. S. Latourette, *A History of the Expansion of Christianity*, 7 vols. (New York, 1938–45).

The Early Church. N. H. Baynes, "Constantine the Great and the Christian Church," *Proceedings of the British Academy*, **15** (1929), 341–443. Henry Chadwick, *The Early Church*, Vol. I of *The Pelican History of the Church* (Harmondsworth, 1967; London, 1968). Jean Daniélou and Henri Marrou, *The First Six Hundred Years*, Vol. I of *The Christian Centuries: A New History of the Catholic Church*, ed. L. J. Rogier, et al. (London and New York, 1964). E. R. Dodds, *Pagan and Christian in an Age of Anxiety* (Cambridge and New York, 1965). Louis Duchesne, *Early History of the Christian Church. . .* , trans. Claude Jenkins (from the 4th French edition), 3 vols. (London, 1920–24). W. H. C. Frend, *The Donatist Church . . .* (Oxford and New York, 1952). A. H. M. Jones, *Constantine and the Conversion of Europe* (London, 1948; New York, 1949). J. N. D. Kelly, *Early Christian Creeds*, 2nd ed. (London and New York, 1960); idem, *Early Christian Doctrines*, 4th ed. (London, 1968). D. Knowles, *Christian Monasticism* (New York and Toronto, 1969). M. J. Lagrange, *Histoire ancienne du Canon du Nouveau Testament* (Paris, 1933). Hans Lietzmann, *A History of the Early Church*, trans. B. L. Woolf, 4 vols. in 2 (New York, 1961). A. Momigliano, ed., *The Conflict between Paganism and Christianity in the Fourth Century* (Oxford and New York, 1963). James M. Robinson, *A New Quest of the Historical Jesus* (London and Naperville, Ill., 1959). Albert Schweitzer, *Von Reimarus zu Wrede: eine Geschichte der Leben-Jesu-Forschung* (1906), trans. Montgomery as *The Quest of the Historical Jesus* (London, 1910).

The Middle Ages. A. Fliche, *La Réforme grégorienne et la Reconquête chrétienne*, 1057–1125, Vol. 8 of *Histoire de l'Église*, ed. A. Fliche, et al. (Paris, 1934–   ). André Forest, F. van Steenbergher, M. de Gaudillac, *Le Mouvement doctrinal du XIe au XIVe siècle*, Vol. 13 of *Histoire de l'Église*, op. cit. (Paris, 1934–   ). É. Gilson, *History of Christian Philosophy in the Middle Ages* (London and New York, 1955). E. F. Jacob, *Essays in the Conciliar Epoch* (Manchester, 1943). D. Knowles, *The Evolution of Medieval Thought* (London and New York, 1962). V. Martin, *Les Origines du Gallicanisme*, 2 vols. (Paris, 1939). G. Mollat, *The Popes at Avignon, 1305–78*, trans. from the 9th ed. (London and Camden, N.J., 1963). J. R. H. Moorman, *A History of the Franciscan Order . . . to the year 1517* (Oxford and New York, 1968). H. St. L. B. Moss, *The Birth of the Middle Ages, 395–814 A.D.* (Oxford, 1935). Steven Runciman, *A History of the Crusades*, 3 vols. (Cambridge and New York, 1951–54). K. M. Setton, ed., *A History of the Crusades*, 2 vols. (Philadelphia, 1955–62). R. W. Southern, *The Making of the Middle Ages* (London and New Haven, 1953; London, 1967). B. Tierney, *Foundations of Conciliar Theory* (Cambridge and New York, 1955). W. Ullmann, *The Growth of Papal Government in the Middle Ages*, 2nd ed. (London, 1962; New York, 1963); idem, *The Origins of the Great Schism* (London, 1948).

Reformation and Counter-Reformation. R. H. Bainton, *"Here I Stand." A Life of Martin Luther* (London and New York, 1951). H. Boehmer, *Road to Reformation* (Philadelphia, 1946). E. Doumergue, *Jean Calvin*, 7 vols. (Lausanne, 1889–1927). H. O. Evennett, *The Spirit of the Counter-Reformation* (Cambridge and New York, 1968). H. Jedin, *A History of the Council of Trent* (London and New York, 1957), Vol. I. M. Philippson, *La Contrerévolution religieuse au XVIe siècle* (Brussels, 1884). E. G. Rupp, *Luther's Progress to the Diet of Worms, 1521* (London, 1951); idem, *Patterns of Reformation* (London, 1969). R. H. Tawney, *Religion and the Rise of Capitalism* (London, 1926). M. Weber, *The Protestant Ethic and the Spirit of Capitalism*, trans. Talcott Parsons (New York, 1930).

Modern Times. R. Aubert, *Pie IX*, Vol. 21 of *Histoire de l'Église*, op. cit. (Paris, 1952). R. W. Church, *The Oxford Movement* (London, 1891). R. E. Davies, et al., eds., *A History of the Methodist Church in Great Britain* (London, 1965), Vol. I. A. L. Drummond, *German Protestantism since Luther* (London and Naperville, Ill., 1951). E. E. Y. Hales, *Revolution and Papacy, 1769–1846* (London and New York, 1960). K. S. Latourette, *Christianity in a Revolutionary Age*, 5 vols. (New York, 1958–62; London, 1959–63). E. Préclin and E. Jarry, *Les luttes politiques et doctrinales aux XVIIe et XVIIIe siècles*, Vol. 19 of *Histoire de l'Église*, op. cit. (Paris, 1956). H. Welschinger, *Le Pape et l'Empereur, 1804–15* (Paris, 1905).

Byzantine Church. F. Dvornik, *Byzance et la primauté romaine* (Paris, 1964), trans. as *Byzantium and the Roman Primacy* (New York, 1966). G. Every, *The Byzantine Patriarchate* (London and New York, 1962). J. M. Hussey, *Church and Learning in the Byzantine Empire* (Oxford, 1937). Steven Runciman, *The Eastern Schism . . . the Papacy and the Eastern Churches during the XIth and XIIth Centuries* (Oxford and New York, 1955); idem, *The Great Church in Captivity: A Study of the Patriarchate of Constantinople*

from the Eve of the Turkish Conquest to the Greek War of Independence (Cambridge, 1963; New York, 1968).

HERBERT BUTTERFIELD

[See also **Church as Institution;** Gnosticism; **God;** Heresy; Millenarianism; Myth in Biblical Times; **Religious Toleration;** Sin and Salvation.]

CHURCH AS AN INSTITUTION

THE WORD "Church" (in German, *Kirche;* Dutch, *kerke*) probably derives from the Greek κυριακόν, meaning "belonging to the Lord" or "the Lord's house." It is likely that the term was first acquired by Germanic invaders of the Roman Empire before their conversion to Christianity; for otherwise it would seem that they would, on their conversion, have adopted from their Christian teachers some form of the word ἐκκλησία (Latin, *ecclesia*), which was in current use for the "Church." It has been suggested that the heathen Germanic peoples got their term from the Christian buildings ("belonging to the Lord") which, as invaders, they pillaged and destroyed.

The word ἐκκλησία, which was first used by the primitive Greek-speaking Christians, meant in secular speech an assembly, primarily of citizens in a self-governing city (the Acts of the Apostles, 19:39, in its original Greek text preserves an instance of this meaning in so describing the assembly of the citizens of Ephesus). But for the early Christians ἐκκλησία already had a sacred significance, since it was used in the Septuagint (the Greek translation of the Hebrew Scriptures, dating from the second century B.C., which the early Christians used) for the assembly or congregation of the Israelites. The Hebrew word *kāhāl*, which the Septuagint rendered as ἐκκλησία, meant, however, more than a physical gathering or assemblage: it signified the nation of Israel as the Elect People of its god Yahweh, and it implied a covenant relationship with Yahweh that marked Israel off from all the other nations or "Gentiles." Another word used in the Septuagint which had an equivalent meaning to ἐκκλησία was συναγωγή ("synagogue"), which translated the Hebrew term ʿēdhāh; but "synagogue" came increasingly to be applied to local congregations of Jews formally gathered for worship. As the Book of the Revelation to John shows (2:8, 9; 3:7, 9), already by the end of the first century, Christians were employing the word *ekklēsia* for their own body (i.e., the Church), in counterdistinction to *synagōgē* for Jews or Judaism.

However, the emergence of the idea of the Christian *ekklēsia* or Church, as a distinct and different entity from Judaism, was a more complicated process than appears in the New Testament writings. For example, in the Gospel of Matthew (16:18; 18:17) Jesus is represented as both declaring his intention to "build my Church (*ekklēsian*)" and implying that the Church was already in existence in his lifetime. But it is the general opinion of New Testament scholars that these two passages reflect the anachronistic belief of the Christian community for which the Matthean Gospel was written about A.D. 80–85, i.e., some fifty years after the death of Jesus. The Acts of the Apostles (1:8, 2:1ff.) presents a different suggestion, namely, that the Church was miraculously founded fifty days after the Crucifixion.

Recent research into Christian origins has shown, however, that the idea of the Christian Church as a distinctive body, divinely authorized and with a worldwide mission, emerged only after the Roman destruction of Jerusalem in A.D. 70. Since this date is climacteric in the evolution of Christianity, it is important to appreciate the transformation that was consequently wrought in the movement that had stemmed from the life and teaching of Jesus of Nazareth in Judaea some forty years earlier.

So far as it is possible to reconstruct the beginnings of Christianity, as a historical phenomenon, from the extant evidence, it would seem that Jesus inaugurated a Messianic movement aimed at preparing Israel for the coming of the Kingdom of God. This apocalyptic program involved a reformation of the sacerdotal aristocracy that controlled the cultus of the Temple at Jerusalem, and it implied the end of the Roman suzerainty over Israel. In other words, the movement as conceived by Jesus was concerned essentially with the apocalyptic destiny of Israel. Jesus was recognized as the Messiah of Israel by his followers, and it is probable that he made this claim himself. He was executed by the Roman governor, Pontius Pilate, for sedition against the Roman government in Judaea, which fact should have terminated his movement. But the subsequent belief of certain of his chief disciples, that God had raised him from the dead and that he would shortly return to earth, with supernatural power, to complete his Messianic role of "restoring the kingdom to Israel" (Acts of the Apostles, 1:6, Revised Standard Version), revived the movement. Jerusalem, instead of Galilee, then became the center of the movement, the aim of which was adjusted to persuade the Jews to accept Jesus as the Messiah *redivivus* and prepare for his second coming. The movement continued to be essentially Jewish in practice and outlook. The Jerusalem Christians, organized as a community by pooling their economic resources, worshipped regularly in the Temple and zealously practiced the ritual Law. Their two distinctive customs were the baptism of converts, as an initiatory rite of purificatory significance, and a common meal, commemorative of the Last Supper of Jesus. They were distinguished from their fellow Jews only by their recognition of Jesus as the Messiah of Israel; and this faith had the effect of making them more zealous for the Mosaic Law (Acts 21:20). They clearly never contemplated their faith in Jesus as constituting a new religion, distinct from Judaism. The Qumrân community, known to us through the Dead Sea Scrolls, affords an interesting contemporary parallel. The peculiar beliefs of these "Covenanters" caused them to live in the inhospitable desert by the Dead Sea, and, like the Jewish Christians, they were critical of the Jewish authorities who ran the Temple; but they, too, remained within the fold of Judaism, hoping for a reformed and purified Israel.

There is some obscurity, doubtless due to apologetical reasons, in the New Testament documents about the organization of the Christian community at Jerusalem. It would seem that for a short while Peter, the chief disciple of Jesus, was recognized as the leader or spokesman of the community; but he was soon replaced by James, the brother of Jesus. This fact is significant, for it, too, attests to the essentially Jewish nature of the Christian movement at this stage, James being the next male successor to the founder. On the execution of James by the high priest Ananus in 62, the succession went to Symeon, a cousin of Jesus (Eusebius, *Ecclesiastical History*, III, xi). The position of James, according to the Epistle to the Galatians 2:12 and Acts 15:13, 19, appears to have been monarchical; he seems to have been assisted by elders (*presbyteroi*), but they evidently had a subordinate role (Acts 21:18). The movement remained strongly centralized in Jerusalem, and the community there, which comprised the original apostles of Jesus presided over by James, constituted the unchallenged source of authority and discipline. Thus, emissaries from Jerusalem were sent to order the affairs of new communities at Samaria and Antioch (Acts 8:14ff., 15:22ff., Galatians 2:12–13), financial contributions were required from the daughter communities (Galatians 2:10; Epistle to the Romans 15:25–26; II Epistle to the Corinthians 9:1ff.), and the Apostle Paul had to report back to Jerusalem on his missionary work in various places in the Greco-Roman world, "lest somehow I should be running or had run in vain" (Galatians 2:2; Acts 21:17–19).

The evidence indicates, accordingly, that, at this initial stage, the Christian movement, although conscious of itself as a distinct community of believers in the Messiahship of Jesus and organized as such, saw its mission strictly in terms of the destiny of Israel.

A reminiscence of this limitation of outlook is preserved in a saying of Jesus recorded in the Gospel of Matthew 15:24: "I was sent only to the lost sheep of the house of Israel." Consequently, when certain Gentiles, resident in Judaea, desired to join the movement, according to the Acts of the Apostles 10:1–11:17, Peter was only persuaded to accept them for baptism after a special revelation from God, and even then he encountered the criticism of some of his fellow Christians. In the narrative of the Acts, this incident is followed by an account of how certain Jewish Christians, who were not natives of Palestine but of the Diaspora of Cyprus and Cyrene, "preached the Lord Jesus" to Greeks living in Antioch, the capital of Syria, with considerable success (Acts 11:19–21). This action constituted a notable departure from what had hitherto been the aim and outlook of Christianity, and it is unfortunate that the text of the Acts at this point is essentially obscure. It is, for example, difficult to understand what is meant by preaching "the Lord Jesus" to non-Jews. In Greek the word "Lord" (*kyrios*) had a wide range of meaning, and it is crucial to know in what sense at Antioch Jesus was thus presented as *Kyrios*. It is, however, significant that such a term is used instead of "Messiah." For it indicates an acknowledgment that Jesus could not be presented to Gentiles as the Messiah of Israel such as he was conceived as being by his original Jewish disciples, and such as he probably claimed himself to be. Such a presentation to Gentiles, if it were indeed understood by them, would have been essentially offensive unless they were prepared themselves to become Jews. This step meant, for male Gentiles, being ritually circumcised as well as observing the Mosaic Law. It was a condition that was, indeed, demanded by a significant body of Jewish Christians. The sequel is obscure, owing to the conflict of interests in the relevant documents: it seems that some kind of compromise was arranged, but it is obvious from Paul's Epistles that the circumcision of Gentile converts remained a disputed issue.

But whatever was the form in which Christianity was first presented to the Gentiles, the real and effective change from the original Jewish form of Christianity was due to Paul of Tarsus. In his Galatian Epistle (1:11–17), Paul claims that his gospel or version of Christianity was directly mediated to him by God for propagation among the Gentiles; and he vigorously asserts that he was wholly independent of the Jerusalem Christians at this critical juncture in his career. According to Paul, there were two versions of Christianity: one for the Jews, which he calls the "gospel to the circumcised," and that with which he was divinely entrusted, namely, the "gospel to the uncircumcised" (Galatians 2:7). The general content of this latter "gos-

pel" can be pieced together from Paul's writings, although he gives no systematic presentation of it.

Paul, who was a Hellenistic Jew and not an original disciple of Jesus, conceived of Christianity as a universal salvation-religion, and not as a form of Judaism that identified Jesus as the Messiah of Israel. He presents Jesus as a preexistent divine being, whom God sent into the world in human form to rescue mankind from their state of spiritual perdition. This state of perdition he refers to under various images, e.g., as enslavement to daemonic forces, associated with the planets, who ruled this lower world (I Corinthians 2:6–8; Galatians 4:3–10; Colossians 2:13–15, 20), as deliverance from the wrath of God (Romans 1:18ff.). But what is especially important in the present context is that, as the basic presupposition of his soteriology, Paul envisaged the whole of mankind, both Jew and Gentile, as being in this fatal state of perdition and as needing a common savior, who is Jesus. The death of Jesus, at the hands of the Romans, Paul lifted completely out of its historical setting, ascribing it to the daemonic powers that ruled the lower universe (I Corinthians 2:8). Hence in Paul's "gospel," Jesus is presented as the divine savior of mankind, who saves by his death and resurrection; on this evaluation, the Jesus presented by the Jerusalem Christians as the Messiah of Israel was a subsidiary, if not an irrelevant, equation.

In turn, Paul's conception of the Church is correspondingly universalist in scope and vocation. Thus he writes in his Epistle to the Galatians (3:27–28), picturing initiation into the Church as mystical incorporation into Christ: "For as many of you as were baptized into Christ have put on Christ. There is neither Jew nor Greek, there is neither slave nor free, there is neither male nor female; for you are all one in Christ Jesus." Although he saw Christianity in this universalist context, Paul still remained by feeling and upbringing a Jew, and he keenly felt the problem inherent in the fact that the majority of the Jews continued to reject Jesus. How was this rejection to be reconciled with the long-cherished belief in Israel's Election as the People of God? The solution that Paul found was destined to have a profound effect upon the later conception of the Church. Invoking the prophetic idea of a "Godly Remnant" of the nation that constituted the "True Israel," whatever the apostasy of the rest, Paul identified this True Israel with the Jews and Gentiles who had accepted Christianity (Romans 9:22ff.). In other words, the Church was the true heir to the promises, recorded in the Hebrew scriptures, which God had made to the Hebrew patriarchs. The full implications of this identification were not worked out by Paul, but they remained for later Christian theologians to draw. Paul's outlook, so far as the future of the Church was concerned, was limited by the current eschatological expectations of the original Jewish disciples of Jesus. He believed that Christ might suddenly return at any moment, "then we who are alive, who are left, shall be caught up together with them [i.e., the resurrected dead], in the clouds to meet the Lord in the air; and so we shall always be with the Lord" (I Thessalonians 4:17). Consequently, although he speaks exaltingly of the Church, as an institution he sees it as having but a brief duration in this world, as indeed he regarded the world itself as fast approaching its end. Together with this universalist and transcendental conception of the Church (*ekklēsia*), Paul also spoke of local communities of Christians, for example, at Corinth and in Galatia and Judaea (I Corinthians 1:2; Galatians 1:2, 22) as churches (*ekklēsiai*), and he even refers to the church (*ekklēsia*) in the house of two distinguished Christians, Aquila and Prisca (I Corinthians 16:19).

Paul's version of Christianity, however, was not accepted by the members of the Mother Church of Jerusalem. They quickly saw that Paul's teaching, namely that the whole of mankind, both Jews and Gentiles, were in a common state of perdition and alike needed a savior, negated the unique spiritual status of Judaism, which was the basic tenet of their religious faith. And this teaching not only conflicted with their own version of Christianity; it endangered also their position and prospects with their fellow Jews in Judaea. Indeed, reports came back to Judaea that Paul was undermining the foundations of Judaism by teaching the Diaspora Jews not to circumcise their children. The reports were a distortion of Paul's actual teaching; but they gravely compromised and endangered the position of the Jerusalem Christians with their compatriots. Consequently, the leaders of the Mother Church of Jerusalem repudiated Paul as an accredited apostle and teacher of the faith. This they were easily able to do, since Paul had not been an original apostle of Jesus and an eyewitness of his life; to implement this repudiation, they sent out emissaries to inform Paul's converts and to present the Jerusalem gospel as the authentic form of the faith. Paul was in a fundamentally weak position; for, whereas he had to recognize the authority of the Jerusalem leaders as the original apostles of Jesus, he could only base his own authority upon his private conviction that he had been divinely commissioned to preach his version of Christianity to the Gentiles. His position became increasingly untenable, and he finally went to Jerusalem to try to effect some *modus vivendi* with James and the other leaders. They compelled him to give proof of his Jewish orthodoxy in the Temple. The sequel was disastrous for Paul: set upon by a Jewish mob in the Temple, he was rescued by the Roman garrison from the nearby Antonia fortress; rather than have his case tried in Judaea, he then invoked his rights as a Roman citizen to be tried in Rome. He was sent there, but then disappears from history without record of his ultimate fate, except in later legend (Acts 21:17–28:30). However, from a farewell speech attributed to him in Acts 20:17–38, and from other evidence, it is patent that his reputation suffered eclipse for a time, and that his version of Christianity would doubtless have disappeared but for political events in Judaea.

Proper appreciation of the environment of primitive Jewish Christianity, by which it was profoundly influenced and its fate decided, has been achieved only in the last two decades. This has been due chiefly to the acquisition of a better understanding of the essentially religious character of Zealotism, the patriotic "resistance" movement against the Roman government of Judaea, especially through the excavation of the Zealot fortress of Masada. Also there has been a more critical evaluation of the evidence of the Jewish historian Josephus, and circumstantial evidence from the Dead Sea Scrolls and the excavation of the Covenanters' settlement at Qumrân. This evidence, in turn, has placed the trial and execution of Jesus of Nazareth by the Romans in a new context; it has helped to explain the execution of his brother James, the head of the Jerusalem Church, in the year 62, and it has made intelligible the complete disappearance of that Church after the destruction of Jerusalem by the Romans in A.D. 70. This destruction came as the disastrous climax of the Jewish revolt against Rome which began in the year 66. In this revolt, which was religiously inspired and led by the Zealots, the Jerusalem Christians must surely have joined and perished in the final overthrow of their nation. This new interpretation of the nature and fate of the original Christian movement is a subject for continuing specialist research and debate, since the assessment of the relevant evidence is a difficult and complicated task; but what, in the context of the present article, is beyond dispute is the fact that after the destruction of Jerusalem in A.D. 70, the Mother Church of Christianity ceased to exist and a completely new situation succeeded. Thus, whereas before A.D. 70 the Christian movement was directed and controlled by the Jerusalem community, which constituted the unique source of authority in faith and discipline, after that date Christian life is organized and directed from churches in a number of Gentile cities, namely, Rome, Antioch, Ephesus, Alexandria.

This transformation of the Christian organizational situation was reflected in a new conception of the Church and its vocation. Christianity ceased to be a Jewish Messianic movement, aimed at preparing the Jewish people for the second coming of Jesus as the

415

Messiah to "restore the kingdom to Israel"—a movement to which was attached, awkwardly and illogically, a body of Gentile converts largely through the activity of Paul. Instead, Paul's idea of Christianity as a universal salvation-religion was rehabilitated in consequence of the obliteration of the original Jewish form of the faith. It was rehabilitated, however, in a modified and amended form, owing to a variety of causes, the chief of which was the disappointment of the primitive apocalyptic hope that the Second Advent of Christ was imminent.

While Christians believed that the world was shortly coming to a catastrophic end, the Church correspondingly was seen as having a limited existence here. To Paul it was the community of those reborn in Christ by baptism to a new transcendental life (Romans 6:2ff.), who would shortly be caught up to meet the returning Christ in the sky (I Thessalonians 4:17). The upheavals occasioned by the Jewish revolt in 66, the Roman civil war consequent on the death of the Emperor Nero in 68, and finally the signal destruction of Jerusalem and the burning of the Temple, greatly excited the eschatological expectations of the Christians, as is seen, for example, in the thirteenth chapter of the Gospel of Mark. But, as the years continued to pass after A.D. 70 and Christ did not return, a new orientation of outlook, which profoundly affected the evaluation of the Church, gradually began to emerge. Instead of being the temporary community of Christ's redeemed in a world on the brink of destruction, the Church was now seen to have an enduring role in a world that strangely continued to endure. Consequently, it came to be evaluated as a divinely instituted society, entrusted with a twofold long-term mission. Since Christians, after their baptism, had to continue to live in the midst of a pagan world that both tempted them from their allegiance to Christ and persecuted them for their loyalty to him, they needed spiritual help and guidance. Accordingly, the Church gradually developed a sacramental system through which such help was given. Baptism, which Paul had already made into a rite of spiritual rebirth in Christ, and the Lord's Supper (in time to be known as the Eucharist or Mass), became the two great sacraments, to which five other so-called Lesser Sacraments were gradually added. This developing sacramental system went together with a gradual evolution of a hierarchy of ministers endowed with specific spiritual powers and authority. The three major orders of this hierarchy, in ascending order, were those of deacon, priest, and bishop. The bishop came to be regarded as having a plenitude of spiritual power as a successor of the Apostles of Christ, and gradually a doctrine of Apostolic Succession emerged. According to this doctrine, it was believed that the spiritual authority and power which Christ had originally given to his Apostles was passed on through a ritual laying-on of hands, in a service of ordination to the particular office concerned. With this sacramental system, and the hierarchy that managed it, there went also a system of discipline. Approved forms of faith, practice, and conduct were laid down as consistent with orthodoxy, and deviation from these standards had to be confessed and atoned for by a prescribed form of penance. In cases of heinous transgression and refusal to submit to correction, a Christian could be officially excommunicated from the Church and denied its sacraments and ministrations.

To give spiritual guidance and help to the faithful, the Church was regarded as having also a teaching role. But the teaching of the faith also meant the defining of the faith. Since Jesus had given to his disciples no written systematic exposition of his doctrine, from the beginning Christian doctrine consisted of the interpretation put by those disciples upon what they remembered and understood of his life and teaching, and the significance of his death. As was noted above, the evidence of Paul's writings shows that within some twenty years of the death of Jesus two different versions of Christianity were current within the Church: the "gospel" of the Jerusalem Christians and that of Paul. The evolution of Christian doctrine after A.D. 70 was a gradual process, whereby a kind of synthesis between Paul's concept of the divine savior and the tradition about the historical Jesus, which was first achieved in the Gospel of Mark, was assimilated and interpreted by Christian thinkers educated in the concepts and terminology of Greek philosophy. Out of much conflict of opinion, sometimes involving bitter controversy, the great dogmas of the Church, such as those of the Trinity and the Nature of Christ, gradually emerged. They were ultimately defined and proclaimed at councils of bishops, of which those held at Nicaea (325) and Chalcedon (451) are the most notable. These dogmas were held to constitute the orthodox Catholic faith, and, after the Church won the patronage of the Roman Emperor Constantine (288–337), acceptance of these dogmas was enforced by imperial power. Those who dissented were excommunicated from the Church as heretics, and were often punished by civil penalties. The ideal of Catholicity, as characterizing the faith and practice of the Church, was laid down by Vincent of Lérins (died *ante* 450), in his *Commonitorium* (II.3) as *quod ubique, quod semper, quod ab omnibus creditum est* ("what has been believed everywhere, always, and by all")—a formula, incidentally, that described an ideal rather than historical reality.

The Church was regarded, from the beginning, as being divinely commissioned to preach the Gospel of

416

Christ to all nations, and it has continued down the centuries faithful to this charge. The obligation is a logical corollary of Christian soteriology: that Christ was incarnated, died, and was resurrected to save mankind from a state of perdition from which its members could not save themselves. The logic of this doctrine was absolute, and it was uncompromisingly stated by Saint Augustine of Hippo (354–430): *nulla salus extra ecclesiam* ("no salvation outside the Church"; *De baptismo* IV:17). The Church, accordingly, was regarded as the only divinely instituted means for saving the fallen human race from eternal damnation. All other religions and philosophies were rejected as either inadequate, as in the case of Judaism, or as inventions of demons as were the cults of the Greco-Roman world, or as a pernicious heresy as was Islam. In order not to condemn the Old Testament saints, such as Abraham, to this fate, it was believed that, before his resurrection, Christ had descended into Hades to rescue those godly Hebrews who had lived before his coming. The fate of pious pagans, such as Socrates and Plato, also puzzled some Christians; a solution was found by inventing the idea of *limbo*, a special compartment of Hades where they dwelt without torment, but also without hope of salvation.

In consequence of their need to defend the Church against pagan attack, early Christian thinkers gradually formulated a philosophy of history to explain the Church's place in the scheme of divine providence. They were particularly embarrassed by pagan taunts about the newness of Christianity, compared with the ancient cults of the Greco-Roman world. They sought, therefore, to show that the Christian Church had its roots in a remote antiquity. Paul had prepared the way for this by identifying those Jews and Gentiles who accepted Jesus as the True Israel, as was noted above. This identification meant, in practical effect, that the Church considered itself entitled to take over the Jewish Scriptures (in their Septuagint form), as its own inheritance, and to interpret them according to its own views. In process of time (by the fourth century) the Church produced its own sacred scriptures, which were embodied in the corpus known as the New Testament, in theological distinction from the inherited Jewish scriptures which were designated the Old Testament. The idea implied in this nomenclature was that God had originally made a covenant or testament with Israel, which was superseded by the new covenant or testament made by Christ through his own sacrifice on the Cross. This conception of there being two stages in the unfolding of divine providence for the salvation of mankind found expression also in chronology. From 525 the custom arose of reckoning time from the Birth of Christ as *anni Domini*, "years of the Lord"; and,

although the practice of designating the period preceding that event as "Before Christ" (B.C.) did not start until the eighteenth century, the idea of a *Praeparatio Evangelica* was prevalent from the first century as Paul's Epistle to the Galatians 4:4 and the Epistle to the Hebrews 1:1–2 attest.

The development of the Church during the first millennium of its existence was closely related to the fortunes of the Roman Empire, into which it was born and within which its formative years were spent. From the reign of Constantine I, the Roman Empire, from being its persecutor, became the Church's supreme patron and protector. But the moving of the imperial capital by Constantine from Rome to Constantinople, and the subsequent division of the Empire into eastern and western parts, followed in time by the collapse of the Western Empire centered on Rome, had profound repercussions for the Church. The bishop of Rome, who had long enjoyed a unique status by virtue of his location in the metropolis of the Empire, inherited much of the prestige of Rome after the last Western Emperor was deposed in 476. On the ruins of the Western Empire the new states of Europe were gradually established, and, on conversion to Christianity, they naturally looked to Rome and its Pope as the ordained center and head of the Christian world. In the Eastern Empire, which survived until the capture of Constantinople by the Ottoman Turks in 1453, a very different situation prevailed. The Patriarch of Constantinople remained subservient to the Emperor, who had a quasi-sacred character. The political separation of East and West soon involved a cultural and religious separation, which was finally consummated in the schism of 1054, when the authorities of each Church excommunicated one another. Although in agreement on the fundamental doctrines of Christianity, the Eastern (or Orthodox) Church has continued to be different from the Western Church in ethos and character. It is essentially a mystical hierurgical institution concerned with the salvation and divinization of man. Owing to the fact that those lands in which the Eastern Church was established fell victim to the onslaught of Islam, it suffered much loss and persecution, and for centuries was isolated from the progressive culture of the West. The Church of Russia, which became the most influential of the national Orthodox Churches after the fall of Constantinople, suffered a great diminution of power and influence from the Bolshevik Revolution of 1917.

It was in the Papal-controlled Church of Western Europe that Christianity achieved, in the Middle Ages, its greatest power and influence. That achievement finds its classic expression in the Gothic cathedral, the *Summa theologica* of Saint Thomas Aquinas and the

417

Divina commedia of Dante. The Church was conceived as being tripartite in its constitution, until the Second Coming of Christ. The visible Church Militant here on earth comprised the body of the faithful, striving to live the Christian life amid the perils and temptations of this world. Beyond this world was an invisible Church, which had two divisions: the Church Expectant, containing the souls of the faithful departed undergoing purification in purgatory, and the Church Triumphant of the saints, who enjoyed already the Beatific Vision of God. This situation would continue until a final apportioning of destiny was made at the Last Judgment, consequent on the Second Coming of Christ.

The Church Militant, as organized in this world, was regarded as Christendom; and in theory it reflected the feudal structure of medieval society, with Christ presiding as King. The idea stemmed from Saint Augustine's great work *De civitate Dei* ("The City of God"), in which he virtually identified the Church as the Kingdom of God on earth. In the medieval conception of Christendom, Christ's authority was delegated to two representatives on earth: the Pope and the Emperor of the Holy Roman Empire. This latter office was created in 800, when Pope Leo III crowned Charlemagne, the king of the Franks, as "Emperor of the Romans." Theoretically the Pope was the Spiritual Head, and the Emperor the Secular Head of Christendom. The history of medieval Europe, however, was much concerned with the subsequent struggle for supreme power between Pope and Emperor. A notable manifestation of the idea of Christendom was the Crusade of Christian armies against the Islamic powers for the recovery of the sacred places of the Holy Land; in reality the Crusades epitomized both the idealism and the moral defects of medieval Christendom.

The monolithic structure of the medieval Church was shattered by the Protestant Reformation of the sixteenth century. The movement drew its strength from various sources: abuses of Papal government and ecclesiastical practice, new nationalist aspirations, new modes of thought generated by the Renaissance. Protestantism was essentially a centrifugal force, and, despite the efforts made at consolidation and control by the major Protestant authorities (Lutheran, Calvinist, Presbyterian, and Anglican), subdivision into small independent sects continued in all lands where Protestant Christianity became established. Most of these churches and sects have, each, their own peculiar conception of what the Church should be.

Since World War II most Christian bodies, including the Roman Catholic Church, have shown an active desire for the reunion of the Church in some form. Many conferences have been held and much mutual good will expressed. Although cooperation in good works and some ecumenical participation in worship have been achieved, it remains to be seen whether the major denominations will be able to overcome their basic doctrinal differences and reestablish a truly united Christian Church.

BIBLIOGRAPHY

There is a vast literature on the nature and mission of the Church, and on its history. Much of this is from the point of view of the allegiance of each writer. The following books may be reasonably regarded as objective studies, and give extensive bibliographies. Standard reference works include: *Encyclopaedia of Religion and Ethics*, ed. J. Hastings, 12 vols. (Edinburgh and New York, 1910), Vol. III, article "Church" by J. Oman; *The Oxford Dictionary of the Christian Church*, ed. F. J. Cross (London and New York, 1958), many relevant articles; *Religion in Geschichte und Gegenwart*, 3rd ed. (Tübingen, 1959), III, 1296–1339; *Reallexikon für Antike und Christentum*, ed. T. Klauser (Stuttgart, 1959), IV, article "Ekklesia"; *Dictionary of the Bible*, rev. ed. J. Hastings (London and New York, 1963), article "Church"; *Dictionary of Comparative Religion*, ed. S. G. F. Brandon (London and New York, 1970), many relevant articles.

Among books, the following are especially pertinent: G. Barraclough, *The Medieval Papacy* (London, 1968). S. G. F. Brandon, *The Fall of Jerusalem and the Christian Church*, 2nd ed. (Naperville, Ill., 1957); idem, *Jesus and the Zealots* (New York, 1967–68); idem, *History, Time and Deity* (New York, 1965). A. G. Dickens, *Reformation and Society* (New York, 1966). A. A. T. Ehrhardt, *Politische Metaphysik von Solon bis Augustin*, Band II (Tübingen, 1959); idem, *The Apostolic Succession* (London, 1953). M. Goguel, *The Birth of Christianity* (New York, 1953); idem, *The Primitive Church* (New York, 1964). A. Harnack, *History of Dogma*, 7 vols. (reprint, New York, 1961). F. Heer, *Aufgang Europas* (Vienna and Zürich, 1949). N. D. Kelley, *Early Christian Creeds* (London and New York, 1950). S. Runciman, *A History of the Crusades*, 3 vols. (New York, 1954). N. Zernov, *Eastern Christendom* (New York, 1961).

S. G. F. BRANDON

[See also **Christianity in History; Church, Modernism in the Christian;** God; Heresy; Hierarchy; **Prophecy; Reformation; Religion, Origins of; Ritual in;** Sin and Salvation.]

MODERNISM IN THE CHRISTIAN CHURCH

1. Introduction. The term "modernism," when used in the context of the history of religions, refers most precisely to the cluster of critical, philosophical, and ecclesiological ideas advanced by a number of European Roman Catholic intellectuals in the period

1890–1910, and especially to the systematic condemnation of these ideas by Pope Pius X in 1907. It also denotes the liberal (broad) and radical movement for reform in the Church of England which began in the late nineteenth century and reached its peak in the years after World War I. The term has also served very loosely and without precise theological reference as the opposite of fundamentalism, or the equivalent of liberal Protestantism, especially in the United States. Even more generally the attempts of all traditional religions, including those of the East, to come to terms with the secular and scientific culture of the modern Western world have been described as modernism.

The words "modernist" and "modernism" were originally negative and polemical in meaning. To be a modernist was to be a heretic. For three generations in Roman Catholicism "the taint of modernism" effectively destroyed careers and ended serious consideration of new ideas. In what follows the word "modernism" is used to refer to the papal synthesis, and the word "modernist" is restricted to the ideas of men directly involved in the condemnation. It must be understood, however, that the terms have also been used by participants in it and by sympathetic historians of the movement (Houtin, 1913; Petre, 1918; Vidler, 1934, 1970). And it should be clear that for many contemporaries of the crisis, inside and outside the Church, the ideas of *all* nonscholastic or more generally, non-Curial thinkers, from J. A. Mohler of Tübingen to Cardinal Newman of Oxford and Maurice Blondel of Aix, were suspect for several decades.

Two tasks concerned the handful of Roman Catholic clerical and lay intellectuals who were to emerge as the central figures of the crisis at the turn of the century. The first was the development of a biblical criticism which was both scientific by the standards of nineteenth-century historiography and supportive of the essentials of Catholic teaching. The second was the creation of a new philosophical language which would provide Catholicism with an apologetic tool suited to men of the twentieth century. Two principles controlled both efforts. The first was the conviction that if change was to come to Roman Catholicism in either criticism or theology it would have to come from within: the new ideas must be introduced by men whose loyalty and personal faith were above criticism. The second was that the Catholic faith and culture could be shown to be complementary to the vision of man and society which modern thinkers had developed since the Reformation.

In "reconciling" traditional Catholicism and the modern world these intellectuals drew deeply on several major currents of thought. First was the tentative tradition of liberal Catholicism. Two attempts had already been made to break the intellectual and political isolation of the intensely ultramontane church. Félicité de Lamennais and his followers during the 1830's, and then Marc-René, marquis de Montalembert, Johann Joseph Ignaz von Döllinger, and Lord Acton in the 1860's served as examples of Catholics generating a more vigorous approach to their religion, as well as examples of the personal dangers such an effort entailed. For the Italian modernists in particular the social concerns of early liberal Catholicism were to be influential; but both Alfred Firmin Loisy and George Tyrrell cite in their autobiographical writings the great impact of reading books by Lamennais, Montalembert, and J. B. Henri Lacordaire. And more recently there was the great figure of John Henry Newman, whose idea of development seemed to have been at least indirectly endorsed by his elevation to the cardinalate by Leo XIII in 1879, and the work of American Catholics like John Ireland and Thomas Hecker.

French Catholic intellectuals interested in applying nineteenth-century historical techniques to the Bible could find a model in their own church: Richard Simon, the tireless critic who had been politically, if not intellectually bested by Bishop Bossuet. But there were more contemporary stimulants in Germany. The long "quest for the historical Jesus" which Albert Schweitzer was summarizing in his 1906 study, *Von Reimarus zu Wrede* had produced new techniques for studying the new and old testaments, as well as a variety of scandalously "naturalistic" interpretations. These made Christian revelation subject to Kantian, Hegelian, and Darwinian concepts and produced several major *bêtes noires* for the polemicists, notably D. F. Strauss, and the high priest of scientism in France, Ernest Renan. More recently attention had come to focus on Albert Ritschl and Adolf Harnack, and exegetes like J. Wellhausen, J. Weiss, and H. J. Holtzmann.

By the end of the century the ferment of German Protestant theology and criticism had produced two images of Jesus Christ, and by implication, of the Church, with which Catholic scholars would have to come to terms. The first and better known was the liberal Protestant image of Jesus as the God-enlightened founder of an ethical and moral kingdom. On this idea had been built an interpretation of the Church as the embodiment of human progress. The approach was initially very attractive to some Catholic critics of their church's social backwardness. The second image was quite different. Called the radical or consistent eschatological school, it presented the Jesus of the Gospel as a messianic figure who preached a kingdom completely at odds with that of the world and who died to force it into life. This second version

419

of the gospel brought those who adopted it to an impasse. Though initially stimulating it offered a poor foundation for building an apologetic for the century of science, progress, and bourgeois order. Theologically, it demanded a demythologization—or in terms of the day, a "symbolic" approach—not only to the gospel but to the whole Catholic tradition: and that undertaking called for a new language, one which also could be found in German thought.

Thomism, of course, was the official philosophy of the Catholic Institutes started in response to Leo XIII's call for a revival of Catholic learning, but by the mid-1890's the new or revitalized Catholic journals and reviews were responding to the stream of French translations of German philosophers, and some early enthusiasts of the new scholasticism were agreeing with Marcel Hébert who declared in 1881 that "Kant had the great distinction of giving to philosophical minds a powerful impulsion." In 1885 the Thomist Society in Paris heard Hébert's paper on "Thomism and Kantianism": in the succeeding decade the roster of names evaluated in the more progressive publications grew to include Schopenhauer and Nietzsche. The major channel through which German thought reached the progressive wing of the French Catholic community was the work of Maurice Blondel, who drew major elements of his complex philosophy of action from Spinoza, Fichte, and Schelling as well as from Kant and Hegel, after finding these writers sympathetically discussed at the École Normale by his teacher Émile Boutroux and his friend Victor Delbos.

At the same time other currents of thought were moving over Europe and even across the Atlantic. Baron Friedrich von Hügel in England was reading the neo-Kantian Rudolf Eucken and recommending his books; Englishmen and Frenchmen were learning neo-Hegelianism from the popular works of John Caird; Frenchmen and then Englishmen were enthusing over the mixture of Schleiermacher and evolutionary thought in Auguste Sabatier's *Outlines of a Philosophy of Religion* (1892). Besides drawing on the Germans Blondel could point to an indigenous alternative to scholasticism in the works of Ollé-Laprune, and much earlier, Maine de Biran and Ravaisson. All these intellectual exchanges were among those committed to one form or another of traditional Christianity, but they were paralleled by a remarkable renaissance of interest in religion among secular intellectuals which began in the mid-1890's. The philosophies of intuition and pragmatism developed by Henri Bergson and William James had their impact, but the "neo-Christianity" of the 1890's was fostered more dramatically by the novels of Paul Bourget, whose *Le Disciple* (1889) dramatized for many the "bankruptcy

of science," even as the editor of the influential *Revue des Deux Mondes*, Ferdinand Brunetière, was announcing, after a visit to the Vatican, that the time had come for intellectuals to recognize the great power for moral order which was embodied in Catholicism. With republican anticlericals suddenly criticizing Taine and Renan and finding good words to say for the pope, the moment for a Catholic offensive into the learned world had come.

2. *Criticism and Dogma.* The question of the Bible and a new apologetic for Catholicism were most dramatically broached in the work by the French scholar Alfred Loisy. Loisy was a critical autodidact, who escaped from rigid scholastic and Gallican seminary teaching into the study of Bible languages, the French liberal Catholics, Newman, and the German critics, especially the exponents of the consistent eschatological school like Johannes Weiss. Alfred Loisy's critical work had radical theological implications which he was not afraid to draw out in his teaching, unlike the more politic Louis Duchesne, another pioneer in scientific historiography, under whose sponsorship Loisy came to the newly-founded Institut Catholique in Paris. Dismissed from his post at the Institute in 1893, for denying the inerrancy of scripture, and indirectly censured in Leo XIII's encyclical (*Providentissimus Deus*) on Bible study in the same year, Loisy developed a general theory of cultural and religious evolution, and presented it in the form of an antiliberal Protestant polemic, *L'Évangile et l'église* ("The Gospel and the Church," 1902), a refutation of the French edition of Harnack's popular Berlin lectures, *The Essence of Christianity* (1900). Loisy claimed that he was not a theologian but simply a Catholic and a critic though he believed, contrary to the progressives who welcomed his work, that the Church could not merely translate its old formulas into a modern language but needed to completely revise its cosmology. He insisted on the necessity of this undertaking because he saw the Church as the major premodern manifestation of man's spiritual evolution, and a guarantee as well of social order.

In his modernist works Loisy argued that Harnack was wrong to see the fatherhood of God and the brotherhood of man as the essential Christian gospel obscured by the later development of Catholicism. The original gospel, as a rigorous but Catholic criticism revealed it, was not the source, but the product, of the faith of the first followers of Jesus. Its message was exclusively messianic and eschatological. Jesus, who entered history as man, not as God, felt himself to be the Messiah and died for his belief. But if he announced the kingdom, it was the Church which came. The "impulse of will" or "soul of Jesus," originally expressed in the messianic teaching, was given new forms. The theological formulations of Paul, who was "compelled to explain, since he could not narrate," and of the fourth Gospel, and the whole rest of the history of Christian doctrine were successive symbolical representations of the original mystery, which is itself inaccessible to the historian. "The Church can fairly say that, in order to be at all times what Jesus desired the society of his friends to be, it had to become what it has become; for it has become what it had to be, in order to save the Gospel by saving itself" (Loisy [1912], p. 151).

The theologian and the man of faith could make larger statements than the historian. The raw materials of historical science did not reveal transcendence any more than did the rest of the natural world. "God does not show himself at the end of the astronomer's telescope. The geologist does not find him in his samples, nor the chemist at the bottom of his test tube. God may very well exist through all the world, but he is in no way the proper object of science" (Loisy [1903], p. 9). These public statements paralleled a more pantheistic personal religious stance: Loisy's historicism was apparently Christian to those of his readers who admired the emergence of a sophisticated (and polemically antiliberal Protestant) critical mind, but for himself, the personal incarnation of God was "a philosophical myth," and not simply because human philosophy had not yet developed a more adequate notion of personality than those of the Fathers and the Councils. "More pantheist-positivist-humanitarian than Christian" in 1904 ([1930–31], II, 397), Loisy still insisted in 1936 that there was a "moral and spiritual supernatural" reality at work in human history, and he hoped for a new religion, "crown of the Christian religion and of every other," concentrated "on the perfecting of humanity in the life of the spirit, that is, in communion with God" (1950, p. 32).

Loisy's ideas were the focus for a complex critical and theological debate long before the condemnation of 1907. While his works were officially censured and he engaged in a cat-and-mouse game of conditional retraction with the authorities, enthusiasts for a radical freedom in critical matters like Baron von Hügel (himself a Bible student, but better known for his writings on mysticism and his correspondence with the leading figures of the crisis) defended Loisy's work. Exegetes who appreciated the dangers of historicism, but who wished for more and better critical work (Pierre Battifol of Toulouse, and Marie-Joseph Lagrange of the *École biblique*), tried to separate the two. The majority of Loisy's critics rejected the techniques along with the evolutionary and culture-relative religious philosophy implicit in his use of them.

3. Philosophy and Belief. Although his writings were never censured, the work of Maurice Blondel stood at the center of the controversies over the possibility for a new Catholic apologetic. Blondel's thesis, *L'Action* (1893) was criticized by his Sorbonne examiners, partisans of Renan's scientism, for its religiosity. His approach was long rejected by Roman theologians as religiously insufficient: the "method of immanence" was seen as a device for infiltrating agnosticism and fideism into Catholic doctrine. Blondel irritated both camps because he wished to draw the attention of all philosophers away from abstract thought to personal commitment and action. He argued that man's need to know stems from the dynamism of his will as it faces life situations. Once man has intellectually mastered the world of phenomena a new act of will is demanded. Either he must settle for the reality around him, or assume a stance which is open to religious experience. Blondel held that there was sufficient testimony to the ultimate transcendence of human action to make the hypothesis of a supernatural gift of life philosophically necessary for true freedom. "I must be involved to run the risk of losing all; I must be compromised. . . . Head, heart, and hand, I must give them willingly or they will be taken from me. If I refuse my free dedication, I fall into servitude" (Blondel [1893], pp. viii–ix).

The implications of what Blondel styled "the method of immanence" for Christian faith were developed in his "Letter on Apologetics" in 1896, in which he argued that while philosophy could not prove the truth of any religion, much less the superiority of one over another, it was central to a modern apologetic which would help the autonomous mind to recognize through the method of immanence the reality of revelation. Blondel insisted that Christian faith was a gift and not something immanent in man's nature; what was immanent was the ability of mind to understand its need for transcendence. To have faith "as issuing from ourselves" alone is not to have it at all. Blondel's eagerness to preserve the transcendence of Christian faith—especially the mystery of Christ's divinity in the face of the critic's focus on the Jesus of history—led him into a complicated correspondence assessing Loisy's critical work.

Some of the letters formed the basis of the essay *History and Dogma* (1905) in which Blondel attacked both the historicists—i.e., Loisy, who argued that criticism had made it clear that if religion was to survive it must be as an evolving expression of man's spirit in relation to an unknowable force without—and those he dubbed "extrinsicists," that is, the orthodox Roman theologians who believed that the Christian revelation was completely trans-historical and arbitrary, the unchallengeable (and inexplicable) foundation of a dogmatic fortress normative for all times and all societies. Blondel rejected those who argued that "the Bible is guaranteed *en bloc,* not by its content, but by the external seal of the divine: Why bother to verify the details?" (Blondel [1964], p. 229). He proposed, in place of the excesses of Loisy and of his ultra-orthodox critics, a new emphasis on the Church as a living tradition. Blondel believed that his idea of "a concept of tradition obtained with the help of a philosophy of action" would lead to a Christianity "both more concrete and more universal, more divine and more human, than words can express" (ibid. p. 286).

The need for a new philosophical approach to religion was directly associated with the critical question by an essay entitled "Qu'est-ce qu'un dogme?" ("What is a Dogma?") published in 1905 in the progressive Catholic journal, *Annales de philosophie Chrétienne* by the mathematician and layman Édouard Le Roy, who was in fact more a student of Bergson than of Blondel. Le Roy's article became the center of a controversy second in intensity only to that provoked by Loisy's *The Gospel and the Church.* Le Roy argued that dogma was simply "unthinkable" for modern man "because it is imposed by simple fiat and because it is conceived as a function of outworn systems, reaffirming those anthropomorphic notions which make it unacceptable to the mind." The moral meaning of a dogma must be placed before its speculative meaning: the latter only functions negatively to establish the minimal parameters of belief. Le Roy interpreted the dogmatic propositions on the personality of God as meaning "practically" that man must deal with God as he would with another human person; the resurrection of Jesus meant that "he still mediates and lives among us, and not at all merely as a thinker who has disappeared and left behind a rich and living influence . . . he is literally our contemporary" (Le Roy [1918], p. 70).

Blondel's closest disciple was the oratorian Lucien Laberthonnière who developed similar ideas in a specifically religious context in his *Essai de philosophie religieuse* (1903), and in *Le réalisme chrétien et l'idéalisme grec* (1904), and who was silenced in 1914 for his polemical battle with the ultraorthodox Catholic defenders of the *Action Française.* Laberthonnière wrote that dogmas were not "simply enigmatical and obscure formulations which God has promulgated in the name of his omnipotence to mortify the pride of our spirit. They have a moral and practical meaning; they have a vital meaning more or less accessible to us according to the degree of spirituality we possess" (1903, p. 272). Le Roy and Laberthonnière both insisted that their concern with action and practice was completely traditional; Le Roy cited, as did Blondel and

J. Semeria (the Barnabite priest who disseminated Blondelian ideas in Italy), the Gospel principle: *qui facit veritatem venit ad lucem.* All those who sought a new understanding of the dynamic character of Christian teaching opposed the tyranny of Aristotelian categories, especially the dominant intellectual tradition of neo-scholasticism.

For all of these men the Thomistic revival encouraged by Leo XIII in the encyclical *Aeterni Patris* (1879) was no more helpful than the categories of Gallican theology. It was especially inadequate to deal with the problems raised by biblical criticism in Christology. There was considerable difference of position among the philosophical modernists on the questions of Christ's nature and knowledge. In 1903 Laberthonnière wrote that Blondel, von Hügel, and he had the same goal in their reconsideration of Catholic teaching: ". . . a Christ truly real and truly human" (Blondel [1961], p. 161). Blondel wrote that "as humanity grows, Christ rises above the horizon," but he rejected von Hügel's argument that Christ's knowledge of his messianic mission developed in time. In his turn, von Hügel tended to side with Loisy in insisting that history has to set the canons for the philosophy of tradition and action, and he criticized Blondel's tendency to attribute to Christ an entirely time-transcending human consciousness.

The extrinsic, static, excessively rational character of Catholic intellectual life was vigorously attacked by the Irish convert Jesuit George Tyrrell, whose books were the second source, after Loisy's work, for the papal synthesis of modernist teaching. Tyrrell was a combative and eloquent writer of apologetic, who had developed a unique pastorate among English Catholic intellectuals; his independent development was reinforced by his friendship with von Hügel. The influence of Matthew Arnold and of his own personal brand of Thomism was soon overshadowed by that of Loisy's critical works, by the consistent eschatology of Weiss, and by "the method of immanence" presented by Blondel and Laberthonnière.

In his mature work, Tyrrell developed a philosophy of religious knowledge which emphasized his belief that revelation was a deposit of faith which was first a law of prayer and life, and second, a law of belief. "Devotion and religion existed before theology, in the way that art existed before art criticism, reasoning before logic, and speech before grammar" (1907, p. 105). Tyrrell feared (and sometimes hoped) that if the Church really accepted the implications of development as well as the eschatological reading of the gospel, she would be absorbed by modern rational and material culture just as she had once absorbed the Hellenic world view. He searched for an interim theological formulation which would preserve the gospel and the church Loisy had sundered. He argued that there was a revelation: there was a transcendent reality and it was manifest in Jesus Christ; but everything the Catholic believed was "an analogue of metaphor" substituting for an original experience of the divine, given to the apostles, but now "withdrawn from view." The evident impasse reached by making dogma and theology equivalent as relative conceptual devices or analogies for transcendence—thus fixing an apparently unbridgeable gap between the revelation of transcendence in Jesus Christ and the faith of the believer—was overcome first by Tyrrell's conviction that "the spirit of Christ has lived and developed in the collective life of the faithful," and later by his belief that the "religious sense" operated immanently in men who were open to it: the soul of every man was *naturaliter christiana*. This religious sense, or "consciousness," was universal: it was not a moral principle, but the ability to respond to God, and the force which linked "the life of religion with the rest of our life," proving that "the latter demands the former."

Knowledge of God through immanence was to be seen as intimately bound up with knowledge of him through the historical revelation of the gospel. Growth occurred in the former, and thus preserved life in the latter, even though it remained fixed in the apostolic era. The correlation between the revelation of immanence and that of history in Jesus Christ, was made by the consensus of the "people of God" (*consensus fidelium*), and of "theoreticians" like the modernists, not of the theologians of Rome. The followers of Jesus must evolve new symbols, sacraments, and institutions to express the notion of immortality—the linking beyond time of man with the transcendent—which was taught by Jesus when he preached the kingdom, and which was entirely dependent on the example of his life and death and resurrection. Thus all dogmas, all theologies, were "symbols of the transcendent." Christians faced with modern life needed hope, rather than faith. "Our best God is but an idol, a temple made with hands in which the Divine will is as little to be confined as in our Hell-Purgatory-Heaven schematization" (Tyrrell [1912], II, 416).

4. Condemnation of Modernism and Extension of the Crisis. The argument of the magisterium, later developed by Catholic scholars, was synthetic. The modernist was seen in the encyclical letter *Pascendi* (1907) as a "type" who "sustains and includes within himself a manifold personality; he is a philosopher, a believer, a theologian, an historian, a critic, an apologist, a reformer" (Sabatier [1908], pp. 236–37). Modernist ideas were traced to the Reformation and to the Enlightenment. According to the pope, philosophical modernism taught that man could not know God by reason and that what sense he did have of the transcendent came through the "vital immanence" of the divine in the human. Theological modernism held that religion was an expression of the collective consciousness of mankind which expressed itself in purely symbolic dogmas. Historical modernism maintained that all ideas and institutions evolved and could only be understood relative to their epoch. Modernist apologetic was castigated for daring to associate these ideas with Catholic tradition. And finally the modernist as reformer was condemned for advocating an end to fasts and to clerical celibacy, demanding seminary reform, the purging of popular devotionalism, complete freedom of church and state as an ideal, and the democratization of the government of the Church, especially the Curia.

The papal condemnation of 1907 was followed by a series of excommunications, most notably those of Tyrrell and Loisy, the censuring of works of Le Roy and many others, and by the institution of an antimodernist oath in September, 1910. The body of bitter polemical literature already generated by the *affaire Loisy* and by the writings of the Blondelians was now enlarged through the efforts of a secret antimodernist society, the *Sodalitum pianum* or *Sapinière*, whose members, known as Integrists, devoted particular attention to the links between modernism and Christian democracy, as in Marc Sangnier's *Sillon* movement. (Integrism in its excessive zeal was in turn censured by Pope Benedict XV in 1914.) Some "progressive" or "liberal" thinkers—as such they described themselves—rejected the notion of a "modernist" heresy as (in Loisy's phrase) a "figment of the papal imagination." Anticlericals competed with orthodox publicists in exaggerating the extent of the "infection." One journal estimated that modernist ideas had captured 15,000 priests in France alone. Tyrrell, who defended his version of modernism in two long letters to the *Times* of London, said 20,000 would be a better figure. Loisy said 1,500 was more accurate than 15,000. Anonymous publications presented counter-systems and demands; in Italy, *The Program of the Modernists* and *Letters of a Modernist Priest* (Buonaiuti, 1907, 1908); in America, *Letters of a Modernist to Pope Pius X* (Sullivan, 1909). A *Revue Moderniste Internationale* was only one of several short-lived journals which sprang up to advance the cause of reform, if necessary against the Curia, explaining ideas the Pope had "improperly understood and wrongly condemned."

The condemnations of 1907 had in fact brought to a head a crisis of belief which had roots antedating any of the condemned works and which continued long

423

after the crisis was over. Many priests, disillusioned by the obstinacy of the magisterium in the face of minimal pleas for autonomy in scholarship, or overwhelmed by a loss of personal belief in anything but the most broadly symbolic understanding of Christian faith, left the Church. Others hid their true views. Notable in their impact in the years when Loisy's critical work was first coming to notice were Marcel Hébert, a dynamic Parisian priest and teacher whose dialogue, *Souvenirs d'Assise* (1889), stated the dilemma of many who gave up faith reluctantly ("I am not agnostic, because I affirm the Divine: but what is the Divine?"), and Albert Houtin, the major contemporary historian of the general crisis of faith and knowledge who wrote as a Catholic long after he had abandoned orthodoxy—as did Loisy.

Italians involved in the crisis tended to persist in their efforts after the rationale for their work had been destroyed. Antonio Foggazzaro had called for a revival of mysticism and a reform of church polity in his tremendously popular novel *Il Santo* ("The Saint," 1905); in spite of censure he helped to found the modernist review *Il Rinnovamento* in 1907. This journal was the organ of the group of national liberal Italian reformers who tried to reconcile Catholicism and modernity by discussing intellectual freedom, the need for an accommodation with post-Kantian subjectivism, the involvement of the laity in the life of the Church, and a new approach to church-state relations. Such efforts at synthesis were paralleled by two other thrusts in Italian modernist circles.

On the other hand, a small number of priest-scholars took their lead from the French thinkers who were intermediaries of the ideas of Baron von Hügel, and sought to develop an apologetic less concerned with Protestant and rationalist science. There were also priests and laymen who were primarily socially and politically motivated, and who moved beyond officially sanctioned activities like the *Opera dei congressi* toward Christian democracy. Of the former group the most prominent figure was the church historian and polemicist Ernesto Buonaiuti; of the latter, the political leader Romolo Murri, founder of the *Lega democratica nazionale* (Scoppola, 1961).

The crisis made little impact in Germany. Nineteenth-century German Catholic scholarship had developed in a more realistic relationship to Protestant and secular thought. Anti-ultramontanism was the major dimension of reforming movements before and after the condemnation, motivated in part by resentment against Roman distrust of German thought, reflected in the excommunication of Döllinger in 1871 and the more recent censuring of the liberal Hermann Schell, in part by zeal to express Catholic solidarity with the nation in the wake of Bismarck's *Kulturkampf*. Periodical literature was the major German contribution, in particular, the *Zwanzigste* (1909: *Neue*) *Jahrhundert*.

In England Maud Petre, a friend of Tyrrell and his executor, refused to take the antimodernist oath and predicted the eventual recognition of the validity of much of modernist apologetics. Two other Englishmen, both friends of Tyrrell, mediated much of Catholic modernist thought into the separate evolution of Anglican modernism; Alfred Lilley through his *Modernism: A Record and a Review* (1908), and Alfred Fawkes in his *Studies in Modernism* (1913). But the complicated, highly institutionalized, and long-lived movement of modernism in the Church of England developed mainly out of two indigenous sources, nineteenth-century liberal theology (especially the work of F. D. Maurice and H. F. D. Hort) as well as the new critical currents from Germany. Just as in Roman Catholicism, Anglican modernism was a clerical and intellectual effort at providing an apologetic for Christianity which would foster its appeal to the middle classes drifting away from orthodoxy. Defenders of the established church could claim with some justice that "we have never yet met a Modernist kitchen maid" (Pryke [1926], p. 1). Through the Modern Churchman's Union (1898), the periodicals *Liberal Churchman* (1904–08) and *Modern Churchman* (1911–56), and annual conferences the modernists had a considerable effect on the establishment, especially in prayer-book reform. The theology and history of the Anglican movement and its connections with the Catholic crisis was assessed by H. D. A. Major, one of several critics who in the years after World War I have extended universally the movement by defining it as "the claim of the modern mind to determine what is true, right, and beautiful in the light of its own experience . . . whether in religion, ethics, or art" (1927, p. 8). A comparable dilution of the term occurred in America in the wake of the crisis, most notably in the liberal-fundamentalist controversy, but also closer to the Catholic tradition in the writings of William L. Sullivan.

A dense web of correspondence among men involved in the new ideas, the personal activity of Baron von Hügel, who traveled continuously and who had connections in the Vatican, and a flood of short-lived periodicals boasting the defense (and orthodoxy) of the components of the condemned system created the appearance of an international modernist movement. In fact one secret meeting of leading figures did take place, in the Italian mountain town of Molveno in 1907, but little came of it except fuel for Integrist paranoia.

5. Historiography and Conclusion. The history of the idea of crypto-modernism in the Church since 1910 is an index to the dismal ramifications of the condemnation. Léonce de Grandmaison, editor of the Jesuit periodical *Études* during the crisis, summarized the liberal-progressive view of the crisis when he defined the modernist as one who believes that there could be a conflict between "the traditional and modern positions" in Christian teaching, and who, faced with that conflict, decided that it was "the traditional view which must be adapted to the modern, by retouching, or, if necessary, radical alteration or abandonment" (*Études,* **176** [1923], 644). The progressives argued that the modernist error did not necessitate the abandonment of the vital work of bringing the truth of tradition into contact with the truth of modernity. They wanted development in Christian teaching, defined by Blondel as "a continuous creation starting from a germ which transubstantiates its nourishment," as opposed to evolution, which he saw as change resulting only from "external pressures" (Marlé [1960], p. 129). They rejected historicism and, in Wilfrid Ward's phrase, they called for "not less, but more, and better, theology." The progressive—by the standards of 1929—historian of the crisis, Jean Rivière, said that the modernist effort was a revolution, not a reform, which "ended in destroying the objective fundamentals of Catholic dogma," but he regretfully noted that the most visible result of the "odious and deplorable campaigns" of the Integrists was to panic bishops and people, polarize opinion, render the loyal suspect, and thus make "more difficult the already hard task of those who were exerting themselves to combat modernism effectively on its true ground" (1929, col. 2041).

What should be noted in conjunction with these three opinions is that Grandmaison was himself suspect, that a special papal document from Pius XII was necessary to remove all taint of heterodoxy from Blondel's name as late as 1944, and that Rivière was regarded as a crypto-modernist and officially limited in his teaching. In fact the literature and correspondence of the period is a vast set of criss-crossing efforts to indict or to exculpate figures seen as heterodox by Roman theologians, including Newman before the crisis, and Teilhard de Chardin after it. The sad human dimension of the crisis and the subsequent repression of intellectual life in the Church were summed up in the advice given by a veteran of those days to a church historian in the 1950's: "If you ever treat of the modernist crisis, do not forget to tell how much we suffered." Recent historians, most notably Émile Poulat, have attempted to approach modernism and integrism sociologically (1960, 1962, 1969), and with an eye on the tumult in the Church in the wake of Vatican II (O'Dea, 1968).

Seen from the general perspective of intellectual history in the modern period the modernist crisis in Catholicism is an example of the imperfect transfer of ideas between two cultures which, in spite of a common heritage, were quite distinct by the opening of the twentieth century. Protestant and scientific thought, the secular national state and the transformation of its class structures and ideologies through industrialization and world commerce created a world alien in almost every principle to the Catholic universe encapsulated within it, even as the Rome of the popes was circumscribed and sealed by the modern Italian state. Roman Catholicism was perceived by its defenders as a closed and perfect system of belief and action. From time to time concessions were made to the epiphenomena of modernity and the perennial tradition of mysticism, but generally the magisterium insisted that "the human intellect could know God from his effects, that the historical proofs of Christ's divinity were perfectly proportioned to the minds of men of all times, that there was an objective supernatural order adequately defined by the Church's doctrine" (O'Dea, p. 86). Accustomed to the use of power by centuries of political experience, the magisterium found it natural to use power to suppress and thus negate the existence of an intellectual upheaval which was evident disproof of the fundamental premiss of its life: the unthinkableness of an alternative cosmology and another language of theological and philosophical discourse for any man shaped in its ways.

It was the argument of most modernists that they had *not* been deeply influenced by currents of thought outside the Church, but had simply drawn out the logic of Catholic tradition. Thus Loisy insisted on the originality of his own work in part because once the statement was made that his teaching was "German rational-Protestant theology translated into French" his work would no longer be studied seriously, and his usefulness for change within the system would end. Similarly Tyrrell polemicized violently against liberal Protestantism, not only because he felt that he had been too attracted by liberal Protestantism in his early writing but because he knew that once an idea could be labeled Protestant, or worse, Kantian, it was automatically refuted. The dilemma of the modernists in relation to contemporary thought was intensified by the fact that they were in revolt against the rationalism of the post-Tridentine Catholic Church *and* the rationalism and materialism of secular thought. They also tended to ignore their dependence on the modern culture they sought to manipulate. Thus Loisy's work was often naively historicist, and Tyrrell was utopian in his scheme for a science of religion. This occurred because, as "latecomers to the Enlightenment," in

Gentile's phrase, they were overwhelmed by the out-pourings of the Pandora's box of ideas which had been closed to Catholic thinkers for so long. The confusion of themes in modernist books puzzled the Pope: in the encyclical the modernists were condemned both as rationalists and as anti-intellectuals.

In their turn, many of the modernist intellectuals, overwhelmed by the attractions of scientism and historicism, saw the obstinacy of the magisterium as final proof that Catholicism as a syncretistic expression of man's moral evolution was as unacceptable in the modern world as the eschatological "late messianic Judaism" from which it had sprung. Institutional re-forms unimagined by the modernists have been ac-complished in the era of *Aggiornamento*. A theological revolution has grown out of the ecumenical movement many of them derided. Transformations in the scientific climate have weakened the attacks of the secular humanist. But the Catholic Church and ecumenical Christianity are still deeply challenged by dynamics of modern culture. The threat of the *religio depopulata* which this handful of religious intellectuals feared remains as the residues of "a religious past defined long ago" confront "a present which has found elsewhere than in it the living sources of its inspiration" (Poulat [1969], p. 5).

Émile Poulat's wide-ranging study of the first stage of the modernist crisis has been characterized as "sociological." Hopefully, further studies of individuals involved in the controversy will follow his example and attempt to locate the theological and philosophical issues in a social and political context. The separation of church and state, the rise of left Catholic political thought and movements, and the utilization of the modernist crisis for political purposes by the Catholic right, are important issues with which the history of modernism in France should be fully integrated. Recent work on Italian modernism (Scoppola, 1961), explores the larger context, but comparable work has not been done for modernism in England. The integrist position has been examined in the setting of social history by Poulat in the introduction to his edition of documents, *Intégrisme et catholicisme intégral* (1969). Of greater significance for the general history of ideas is the proc-ess whereby the currents of positivism and historicism were brought to bear on traditional Catholic thought. The lines of this development can best be traced through the reconstruction of the understanding of Protestant and secular learning held by Catholic writers, as has been done for the influence of German philosophical sources on the formation of Blondel's method and thought by J. J. McNeill in *The Blondelian Synthesis* (1966). The comparative analysis of modern-ist writings and the seminal works in the Protestant and secular scientific world can be complemented by tracing patterns of influence in reading and corre-spondence. The model for this kind of study is the examination, done by most students of the crisis, of Harnack's *Das Wesen des Christentums* (1900) and Loisy's *L'Évangile et l'église* (1902).

Finally, modernist ideas should be examined in the context of Catholic critical movements in the sixteenth and seventeenth centuries, and in conjunction with the emergence of radical Catholic theological currents in the 1960's. Comparisons of the two recent periods should prove particularly enlightening, since in both cases Protestant thought and scientific advance were major spurs to innovation. Students of the relationship between the crisis and the development of Catholic science in Germany should examine Edmond Vermeil, *Jean-Adam Möhler et l'école Catholique de Tubingue, 1815–1840* (1913).

BIBLIOGRAPHY

The recent works of Émile Poulat locate the modernist crisis in a sociopolitical context. His edition of the memoir of Albert Houtin and Felix Sartiaux, *Alfred Loisy, sa vie, son oeuvre* (Paris, 1960), contains an indispensable bio-bibliographical index of all major figures in the controversy; his *Histoire, dogme et critique dans la crise moderniste* (Paris, 1962) relates the periodical literature to the major works of Loisy and Harnack, discusses manuscript sources, and offers a comprehensive bibliography for the French and English aspects of the crisis; finally, his Introduction to *Intégrisme et catholicisme intégral* (Paris, 1969) assesses the antimodernist campaign, as does his article "'Modernisme' et 'Intégrisme'; du concept polémique à l'irénisme critique," *Archives de Sociologie Religieuse*, No. 27 (Jan.–June 1969). Other studies are evaluated by Roger Aubert, "Recent Literature on the Modernist Movement," *Historical Investi-gations, Concilium*, Vol. 17 (New York, 1966). For Italian modernism, Pietro Scoppola's *Crisi modernista e rin-novamento cattolico in Italia* (Bologna, 1961) is important. Alec Vidler, whose *The Modernist Movement in the Roman Catholic Church* (Cambridge, 1934) was the first study sym-pathetic to Loisy and Tyrrell to appear in English, writes about a few major and several minor French and English participants in *A Variety of Catholic Modernists* (Cambridge, 1970). The impact of modernism within the Anglican Communion is examined in H. D. A. Major, *English Modernism* (1927), W. M. Pryke, *Modernism as a Working Faith* (London, 1926), while the inter-war tendency to globalize the conflict of tradition and modernity in religion is clear in Victor Branford, *Living Religion* (London, 1924). For American echoes, see John Ratté, *Three Modernists* (New York and London, 1967). Thomas F. O'Dea's *The Catholic Crisis* (New York, 1968) is one of the many post-conciliar liberal attempts to reassess the crisis in the light of subsequent history; a useful collection of revisionist essays appeared in *Continuum*, 3 No. 2 (1965). Jacques Maritain takes a more traditional view in *Le paysan de la Garonne* (Paris, 1967).

Central sources for study of modernist ideas are the papal documents translated in Paul Sabatier's *Modernism* (New York, 1908); the works of Alfred Loisy, most notably *L'Évangile et l'église* (Paris, 1903; Eng. trans. New York, 1912), *Autour d'un petit livre* (Paris, 1903), *Mémoires pour servir à l'histoire religieuse de notre temps*, 3 vols. (Paris, 1930–31); Maurice Blondel, *L'Action* (Paris, 1893), idem, *The Letter on Apologetics and History and Dogma* (London, 1964), idem (with Laberthonnière), *Correspondance philosophique* (Paris, 1961); L. Laberthonnière, *Essais de philosophie religieuse* (Paris, 1903); Édouard Le Roy, *Dogme et critique* (Paris, 1907; partial Eng. trans. New York, 1918); René Marlé, ed., *Au coeur de la crise moderniste* (Paris, 1960), a collection of letters by Blondel, Loisy, von Hügel, and others; Baron Friedrich von Hügel, *Selected Letters, 1896–1924* (London, 1928); George Tyrrell, *Through Scylla and Charybdis* (1907), idem, *Christianity at the Crossroads* (London, 1908; New York, 1966), and George Tyrrell and Maud Petre, *Autobiography and Life of George Tyrrell*, 2 vols. (London, 1912).

Histories of the movement and the crisis which themselves form part of the explosion of ideas include Jean Rivière's article on modernism in the *Dictionnaire de théologie catholique*, Vol. X, Part 2, cols. 2010–47, his book, *Le Modernisme dans l'église* (Paris, 1929), the article on modernism in the *Dictionnaire apologétique de la foi catholique*, III, col. 592–637, and the classic pro-modernist accounts of Albert Houtin, *Histoire du modernisme catholique* (Paris, 1913) and Maud Petre, *Modernism, Its Failures and Its Fruits* (London, 1918).

JOHN RATTÉ

[See also Agnosticism; **Church as Institution;** God; Myth in Biblical Times; Reformation.]

THE CITY

I. ANCIENT CITIES

THE RELIGIOUS and cosmic symbolism of the city reaches back to the early stages of human culture. It seems that in none of the great archaic cultures have cities been understood simply as settlements, arbitrarily established at a certain place and in a given form; both the placing and the shape of cities were conceived as related, in a hidden or manifested form, to the structure of the universe. The most common form of this symbolism is the belief that the cities have astral or divine prototypes, or even descend from heaven; sometimes they were believed to have a relationship to the underworld. In both cases, however, they refer to an extraterrestrial reality.

Babylonian cities were believed to have their proto-

types in the constellations: Sippar in Cancer, Nineveh in Ursa Major, Assur in Arcturus. Sennacherib had Nineveh built according to the "form . . . delineated from distant ages by the writing of the heaven-of-stars." This model, situated in a celestial region, antedates the terrestrial city. The terrestrial city, usually with the sanctuary at its center, is a copy of the divine model, executed according to the command of the gods. This is still reflected in the *Wisdom of Solomon* 9:8—"Thou gavest command to build a sanctuary in thy holy mountain, and an altar in the city of thy habitation, a copy of the holy tabernacle which thou preparedst aforehand from the beginning."

Similar ideas are found in India. Royal cities are believed to have been constructed after mythical models. The relationship between model and copy sometimes implies an additional meaning: in the age of gold the Universal Sovereign dwelt in the celestial city; the earthly king, residing in the terrestrial city built after the celestial prototype, promises to revive the golden age.

Somewhat similar ideas are also found in Greek philosophy. Plato's ideal city also has a celestial prototype (*Republic* 592; cf. 500). The Platonic "Forms" are not patterned after the planets, but they, too, are situated in a supra-terrestrial, mythical region, and at times reference is made to astral bodies (*Phaedrus*).

In the Western tradition, the best known example of a city with a celestial prototype is Jerusalem. According to several sources it was created by God before it was built by men. The Syriac *Apocalypse of Baruch II* (4:2–7) suggests that the celestial Jerusalem, graven by God's own hands, was shown to Adam before he sinned. The Heavenly Jerusalem inspired the Hebrew prophets and poets (e.g., Isaiah 60ff.; Tobit 13:16ff.). Ezekiel is transported to a high mountain to be shown by God the city of Jerusalem (Ezekiel 40:2). According to the *Apocalypse* 21:2ff. the new Jerusalem actually descends from heaven. "I John saw the holy city, new Jerusalem, coming down from God out of heaven, prepared as a bride adorned for her husband." In later Jewish traditions the divine city was actually the starting point of creation. According to *Yoma*, "the world was created beginning from Zion," the holy city. Adam, too, was created and buried in Jerusalem, and therefore, according to well-known Christian traditions, the blood of the crucified Christ could drip down on him and redeem him.

The spot on which the city is placed may also have cosmic significance. In the Near East the city was sometimes believed to mark the meeting ground of heaven, earth, and hell. Babylon was a *Bab-ilani*, a "gate of the gods," for it was there that the gods descended to earth. But it had also been built upon

427

the "Gate of the *Apsu*"—*Apsu* designating the waters of chaos before Creation. In the Roman world, the *mundus*—i.e., the trench dug around the place where a city was to be founded—constitutes the point where the lower world and the terrestrial world meet. Macrobius (*Saturnalia* I, 16, 18) quotes Varro as saying that "when the *mundus* is open it is as if the gates of the gloomy infernal gods were open."

Another common form of granting significance to the city's location is to assume that it marks the center of the world. In some Indian cities the foundation stone is said to have been placed above the head of the snake which supports the world; in other words, it is placed exactly at the center of the world. The map of Babylon shows the city at the center of a vast circular territory bordered by a river, precisely as the Sumerians pictured Paradise. This belief persisted into later periods. It has rightly been said that the pilgrimages to holy cities (Mecca, Jerusalem) are implied pilgrimages to the center of the world (see M. Eliade).

The shape of actual ancient cities (as excavated in archaeological campaigns) does not always conform to the vast body of religious symbolism. Some basic concepts of city planning go back to the third millennium B.C. The earliest pattern of a planned city, the gridiron scheme (i.e., straight parallel streets crossing other straight parallel streets at right angles) is found, in a slightly irregular form, in India (Mohenjo-Daro, roughly 2500 B.C.). This pattern probably emerged from the practice of "orientation," i.e., the establishing of a connection between man-made structures and celestial powers. The grid pattern is also found in Mesopotamia, and in Egypt King Akhnaton followed it in building his capital (ca. 1370 B.C.).

In Greece, ideas on town planning do not appear before the fifth century B.C. The acropolis, the original nucleus of the Greek town, developed from a fortified place of refuge, and usually consisted of an accumulation of irregularly shaped and dispersed volumes. Greek architectural thought was focused, as most scholars agree, on the individual building rather than on the town as a whole. Similarly Greek artists were more deeply interested in the volume and structure of bodies than in the space surrounding the figures.

The decisive step towards a regular layout of the city as a whole is traditionally connected with Hippodamus of Miletus (active ca. 470–430 B.C.), a half-legendary "Homer of city planning." The "Hippodamic system" is basically the gridiron scheme with particular emphasis on space classification, and a tendency towards symmetry. Aristotle contrasts the "Hippodamic system" distinctly with the archaic procedure of building without plan. Originally the system may have been influenced by the mathematical thought of

the period, and perhaps also by some symbolic religious traditions; in the diffusion of the system, however, economic advantages and practical hygienic considerations seem to have played a more important part. In Greece, no ritual laws seem to have existed for the foundation and layout of new settlements.

The Romans evinced a deeper concern for the city as a whole, and made significant and lasting contributions to town planning. Roman towns developed mainly from the *castrum*, basically a gridiron pattern subdivided into four major parts by two main axes, the *cardo* and *decumanus*. A square was placed at the crossing of the two axes. Both the major buildings and the square proper had an axial location. In laying out military settlements with permanent fortifications, which were established along the expanding frontiers, the Romans followed the same pattern (the so-called *castra stativa*). Another characteristic feature of the Roman town is that it was set off from the landscape surrounding it (contrary to the transition from town to landscape in Greece).

Although functional considerations clearly played an important part in establishing this pattern, the town plan and the foundation of cities did not lose their symbolic significance. The historian Polybius and the geographer Hyginus Gromaticus (early second century A.D.) describe the standard layout of the *castrum* town, but also discuss in detail the "orientation" of the towns and the consecration rites of newly established settlements. According to Pliny, measurements and proportions of the *castrum* were based on "sacred numbers," but so far no conclusive archaeological evidence has supported his statement.

The major Roman contributions to city building, the feeling for strict regularity, the organization of the city in large areas, and the firm shaping of space (best expressed in the patterns of squares), declined with the decline of the Empire.

II. MEDIEVAL "ORGANIC" TOWN

The medieval approach to the city, emerging in a period in which urban culture broke down, is complex and ambivalent. One of the characteristic features of the early medieval attitude is a disconnection between the notions of the celestial and the terrestrial city. Probably the most explicit expression of this attitude is to be found in Saint Augustine's famous work, *The City of God*. In this work, the image of the city becomes highly metaphorical, the term denoting a community rather than a material city. Even in his metaphors Augustine rarely refers to the city plan, to architectural elements (walls, gates, squares, etc.), or to actual cities (with the exception of Rome and Jerusalem, both of which assume a highly symbolic significance). The basis of "cities" is moral values or metaphysical ideas: the foundation of the terrestrial city is the "love of self" while the celestial city is based on the "love of God" (XIV, 28; cf. XI, 1 and X, 25). The two cities, the terrestrial and the celestial, are not only unrelated to each other, but there is a contradiction between them. The City of God "is a pilgrim on the earth" (XVIII, 54); the citizen of the Heavenly City is "by grace a stranger below, and by grace a citizen above" (XV, 1); Cain is described (based on Genesis 4:17) as the founder of a terrestrial city, while Abel, who was conceived as a prefiguration of Christ, "being a sojourner, built none" (XV, 1).

Like the Near Eastern thinkers, Augustine conceived of a celestial and a terrestrial city. But while in the Near East the city on earth is believed to be a copy of the one in heaven, Augustine sees the two as alien to each other. In moral terms they are even mutually exclusive: one belongs to either one or the other. Thus the hostile attitude towards the (terrestrial) city, an attitude that was to play a major part in medieval thought, is already clearly articulated at this early stage.

This attitude may be understood as an expression of a broad historical process which is probably also reflected in the development of the actual medieval town, and in the iconography of the city in medieval art.

It is significant that in a period as permeated by symbolism as were the Middle Ages not much thought was given to the symbolism of the city plan, as far as actual cities are concerned. The organization of the town as a whole was, as a rule, neither understood nor desired by medieval builders. This lack of interest led to the well-known irregular shapes of medieval towns. Even in cities which developed from Roman towns, the additions and changes which originated in the Middle Ages were made without consideration for the original Roman layout. The medieval town thus provides an almost perfect example of the city that has "grown" versus the "planned" city. The narrow, winding streets (*ruelles, Gassen*) of medieval towns and their beautiful but unpredictable vistas could be taken as an expression of "organic life," as the writers of the romantic period, in fact, characterized medieval life.

"Organic growth" as an overall characterization of the medieval town is not radically challenged by the fact that, especially in the thirteenth century, some new cities (*villes neuves*) were built according to a preconceived plan, and do in fact display some regular features (e.g., Aigues-Mortes, founded in 1240 by Saint Louis; Montpazier, established in 1284 by Edward I of England). These "new cities" remained exceptions.

In contrast to the irregularity of actual medieval towns, the innumerable representations of the "Heavenly Jerusalem" and of other holy cities in the art of the Middle Ages frequently show a regularity and symmetrical arrangement which strongly suggest the image of a "planned" city. In early Christian representations (e.g., the fifth-century mosaics in Santa Maria Maggiore and in SS. Pudenziana), the Heavenly Jerusalem is reduced to a simple round wall, but in later renderings (see Santa Cecilia) it becomes more elaborate, sometimes adorned with towers, gables, and columns. However, in spite of the inclusion of such actual architectural elements, the overall shape of the sacred city retains a remarkable regularity. Thus, in a ninth-century mosaic in San Marco in Venice, the city of Bethlehem has a clear oval shape. Even when representing the earthly Jerusalem (representations which are certainly symbolic rather than documentary records), the medieval artists tended towards clearly laid out, regular forms.

The iconography of the city in medieval art has not yet been systematically studied, but a review of the rich material pertinent to this theme suggests that the hostile attitude towards the city has had a formative influence on artistic imagery. Since the eleventh or twelfth centuries the city is symbolically portrayed not only by architectural motifs (walls, gates, towers) but also by secular, inherently vicious figures and scenes, considered typical of urban life. The view of the city as a place of carnal temptation, debased entertainment, and avarice is visually portrayed by figures of jugglers and acrobats, loose women, misers, and, in the late Middle Ages, by scenes of gambling seen against an urban background. In medieval art, cities are often inhabited by demonic creatures. Such figures and scenes, sometimes appearing in the margins of sacred texts, frequently anticipate the specific realism of a burgher art.

III. RENAISSANCE IDEAS OF THE CITY

The city, both as a social reality and as an architectural environment, played an important part in Renaissance thought and art. This may be partly explained by the fact that Renaissance culture developed in cities, and was an almost completely urban phenomenon (even the newly discovered affection for the rustic life of the villa attests to its basically urban character). The acquaintance with ancient literary sources further intensified the interest in the city; the polis became an object of study and imitation. But although Renaissance authors often referred to the polis, they usually attributed its characteristics to the Italian city-states of their own period. Thus Leonardo Bruni, in his *Laudatio Florentiae urbis* as well as in other writings, describes Florence as a model of an ideal city of justice, a city well-ordered, harmonious, beautiful, governed by *taksis* and *kosmos*. Bruni proclaims that Florence is rational and functional in her institutions as well as in her architecture: "Nothing in her [Florence] is confused, nothing inconvenient, nothing without reason, nothing without foundation; all things have their place, not only definite but convenient and where they ought to be. Distinguished are the offices, distinguished the judgements, distinguished the orders." The architectural structure corresponds to the rationality of the social and political structure. The city is built along a river, a module of urbanism is consistently applied in her architecture. As in a polis, in the center of Florence are the Palazzo dei Signori and the "Temple," i.e., the Duomo.

In this early stage we encounter already a characteristic feature of Renaissance urbanistic thought: the ideal city can, at least in part, be identified with a real one. Historians have remarked that the fifteenth century, instead of producing utopias, gave rise to many *laudationes* of actual cities, investing them with all the virtues of utopian settlements. Venice and Florence were described as embodiments of the political thought of the ancients.

Probably the earliest expression of the Renaissance spirit in actual town planning is to be found in Leon Battista Alberti's *De re aedificatoria,* written between 1450 and 1472. Alberti's civic convictions as well as his aesthetic and moral values are clearly reflected in his treatise. The novelty of Alberti's method is that he proposes a scheme for the building of an entire town. Although he carefully considers the problems of architecture for private and for ecclesiastical purposes, in his city plan every detail is subordinated to the design of the town as a whole. He strongly criticizes the medieval habit of each family's building a palace and a tower of its own without any consideration of its neighbors, except that of rivalry (VIII, 5).

Alberti stresses rational and "functional" elements. The site of the town must be healthful, in temperate climate, conveniently placed for water supply, and easy to defend. Convenience and clarity are the ruling principles of his city plan. The town should be clearly laid out, and the main streets conveniently connected with the bridges and gates; the streets should be wide enough not to be congested but not so wide as to be too hot (IV, 5). The predominant aesthetic principle is that of symmetry, particularly visible in the relation of the shapes of the two rows of houses on both sides of the street (VIII, 6).

Although Alberti probably was the first modern author to articulate this attitude, similar tendencies can be discerned in actual Italian architecture of his period. In the Piazza San Marco in Venice, a standard design

had been repeated around a square, and a similar procedure can be found in the square in front of the SS. Annunziata in Florence. The same spirit also governs Pius II's plans for Pienza, and Nicholas V's idea for linking Saint Peter's with the Castel Sant' Angelo in Rome (but in the latter project Alberti was personally involved).

Closely related to Alberti, and probably influenced by him, is Filarete, whose *Trattato di architettura* was composed in 1460–64. It is written in a somewhat romantic form which, as scholars have noted, brings it into close relation to the *Hypnerotomachia polifili* (written a few years later), and on ground of which the author has sometimes been called a "romantic." Part of the treatise describes an imaginary city, Sforzinda. Filarete depicts the pageantry accompanying the founding of the city, the time of which is chosen according to astrological observation. But behind these "romantic" details there is a rational spirit which reaches its clearest expression in the outlining of the town plan.

Filarete's ideal city has the overall shape of an octagonal star with a round piazza at its center from which a radial system of streets emerges. Filarete is wholeheartedly antimedieval, i.e., he is a radical critic of the city that has merely "grown." In his treatise great emphasis is placed on regularity and on the importance of having large squares. To the author's mind, however, the proposed city is no artificial structure; Filarete believes that Sforzinda, the *ville radieuse* of the Renaissance, is "beautiful and good and perfectly in accord with the natural order." At the same time, Sforzinda is designed to meet the economic and social needs of the community. Moreover, the town plan of Sforzinda, although "perfectly in accord with the natural order," translates into stone the political and social order of the Italian city-states of the fifteenth century. Cosmic and religious symbolism appears in the central buildings of Sforzinda. The dome of the Cathedral is covered by a mosaic representation of God in the form of a "resplendent sun that lights all the dome with its rays of gold," surrounded by a hierarchy of angels and saints. On the pavement beneath the dome there is a map of "the lands and waters," surrounded by the symbols of the seasons and the elements (Book IX).

In several of his notes Leonardo da Vinci (who in this case was interested mainly in problems of engineering) sketches an interesting model of an ideal town: the healthful city is built near the seashore or along a river (so that the dirt may be carried away by the water), and is constructed on two planes connected to one another by stairs. On the upper level live the "gentlemen" (*gli uomini gentili*), on the lower level the poor (*la poveraglia*). Traffic and services are concentrated on the lower plane. The aesthetic principles governing the town plan are largely functional. The beauty of the city follows from its functional form and its mathematical foundations. Thus, a given proportion should dictate the height of the houses and the width of the streets. At the same time, the city should be built "according to human measure," a well-known concept in the Renaissance which, in the context of urban planning, is already found in Filarete's treatise, and was later fully expressed by Francesco di Giorgio.

In sum, then, in fifteenth-century thought the ideal city is, first of all, a rational structure (and even in studying ancient models the rational elements are emphasized). Further, Quattrocento thought of the model city, although containing some elements of cosmic symbolism, is mainly concerned with problems of civil life, of how to make justice and wisdom work effectively in the community and be clearly expressed by urban architecture. Finally, the ideal city of the fifteenth century is altogether on earth; it is neither merged with, nor juxtaposed to, a "heavenly" city.

In the sixteenth century urbanistic thought undergoes a significant transformation: different types of symbolism acquire a greater significance in the outlining of the town plan than they had in the fifteenth century, and the ties between the ideal and the real city are less close. Although this process takes place under the impact of the Counter-Reformation, there is no return to medieval attitudes or models. Humanistic symbols prevail, but they are often transformed, given a new meaning and transplanted into a new realm. The most original contribution of this period is found in utopian town planning. The cities described in the utopias are separated from real cities; they are not placed in heaven, but are located in distant regions. Geographical isolation is a persistent characteristic of utopian descriptions. Civic functions, although described in detail, are usually less important than symbolic aspects in the outlining of the overall shape of the utopian town plan. The architecture usually is of an abstract regularity.

Utopian literature abounds in references to the ideal town, but the most detailed description of the town plan is given in Tommaso Campanella's *City of the Sun*, written in 1602 and first published, in a Latin version, in 1623. Although Campanella was a monk trained in the Dominican convent of Naples, his utopian city (which he locates in a distant isle) is governed by a solar religion, and an astral cult performs in it. For both the town as a whole and the central building Campanella accepts the round form as the most perfect. The overall shape of the City of the Sun is round. The houses are arranged as circular walls, or *giri*, concentric with the central circle in which the

temple is located. The temple itself, Campanella says, "is perfectly round, free on all sides, but supported by massive and elegant columns. This dome, an admirable work, in the center or 'pole' of the temple . . . has an opening in the middle directly above the single altar in the center. . . . On the altar is nothing but two globes, of which the larger is a celestial, the smaller a terrestrial one."

The round form, an old symbol of perfection, has an interesting history in utopian town planning, and frequently occurs both in the form of a radiating center and as a concentric arrangement. Its immediate source in Renaissance and baroque periods is the central plan in religious architecture.

Campanella's City of the Sun is an encyclopedic system with a "celestial" principle of organization. On the walls of the temple are depicted all the stars of heaven with their relation to things below. The walls of the houses bear depictions of mathematical figures, animals, and the different occupations of man; on the outermost circle or wall are exhibited statues of great men, moral leaders, and founders of religions. The City of the Sun has indeed been understood (in accordance with Campanella's intentions) as a "book" and has had a significant influence on pedagogic thought. Comenius' *Orbis pictus* is clearly patterned after Campanella's *City of the Sun*.

Utopian thought in general has frequently been interpreted as implying a criticism of the society in which the utopia was written; what the author feels as bad, or as missing, in his own social environment is corrected, or supplied, in his utopia. This may also hold true of the utopian town plan. The rigidly planned and perfectly regular utopian town constitutes a criticism of the "naturally grown" cities in which the authors lived. The narrow streets and confused arrangement of most medieval cities are criticized by depicting their opposite as ideal and perfect. In this respect, utopian town planning represents another chapter in the history of the debate between the planned and the grown city.

The rational and easily comprehended plan of the imaginary town is also related to the authors' views on the desirable structure of society as a whole. Particularly in the case of Campanella, the city plan seems to express the perfectly regulated and completely centralized structure of society which he envisaged. The utopian town plan thus becomes a mirror image of the utopian society.

IV. MODERN CITY PLANNING

The hectic social transformations and the rapid increase in urban population in modern times led to a heightened awareness of the social and economic 431 problems of the city. There also emerged moral attitudes towards the urban settlement; it was criticized as a place of vice or hailed as the promise of a radiant future. Such thoughts and attitudes were expressed, and modified, in actual town planning.

The Enlightenment conceived of the city as a place of virtue. Voltaire considered London, the typical modern city of his time, as the fostering mother of social freedom and mobility as against the fixed hierarchy in rural society. He noticed that even the aristocracy, traditionally connected with land, moved into the cities, bringing culture to the hitherto uncouth townsmen. Adam Smith, whose attitude to the city was more ambivalent than Voltaire's, also defended the city in relationship to the country. But he did see some of the moral deficiencies of town life, particularly its "unnaturalness and dependence." The nostalgia for rural life that was to characterize significant parts of English social thought of the nineteenth century is already expressed by Adam Smith. In Germany, where no large cities existed, the radical humanists exalted the communitarian ideal of the Greek city-state; but also the medieval town appeared to the early romantics as a culture-forming agent, and as the seat of virtues like loyalty, honor, and simplicity. German thinkers of the early nineteenth century (Schiller, Fichte, Hölderlin) fused the characteristics of the Greek polis and the medieval town into the image of a burgher-city as a model of an ethical community.

In the town planning of the period the ideal of the "planned" city clearly prevailed, although in actual fact most cities were not built, or expanded, according to an overall plan. The emerging science of city planning was challenged to provide rationally for the necessities of a progressively more industrialized and mechanized society. This led to the conception that the city as a whole is "architecture." Its spatial relationships, its organization, and the forms and levels of activity in it require that a city be "built."

At a very early stage of the modern period the visionary architect Claude-Nicolas Ledoux (1736–1806) drew an elaborate plan for a "built" city. A project, begun in 1773 when he was asked to propose some improvements in the residential quarters of a small, salt-producing town, continued all his life and resulted in the publication of *L'Architecture considérée sous le rapport de l'art, des moeurs, et de la législation* (1804). Ledoux planned five volumes, but completed only one. Filled with enthusiasm for J. J. Rousseau and the hope for an improved social order, Ledoux envisioned his ideal city and drew plans for it, thereby boldly combining traditional patterns with original motifs. The shape of his ideal town is a semicircle, with the factory at its center and the important buildings on the rings.

He thus anticipated both Ebenezer Howard's "garden city" and Le Corbusier's *cité radieuse*. Ledoux's poetic gifts become particularly evident in his plans for individual buildings which, although designed in the form of simple geometric shapes, are permeated by a personal, subjective symbolism.

Ledoux's starting point was comparatively modern (the salt-producing plant of Chaux) but the solutions he proposed place him within the tradition of utopian town planning. Like Campanella and other authors of utopias he emphasized the principle of the "planned city" and like them he preferred the round form.

The vision of an ideal city continued to exercise its fascination in the later nineteenth century, but more attention had now to be paid to problems arising from economic and technical conditions. One specific type of "built" city was proposed by Ebenezer Howard (1850–1928), a London architect who was deeply influenced by an extended visit to the United States. In order to counteract the industrial congestion of modern cities (mainly in England), Howard evolved the concept of the garden city. He published his proposals in his work *Tomorrow: A Peaceful Path to Reform* (1892), reprinted as *Garden Cities of Tomorrow* (1902).

Howard envisaged a self-contained town of strictly predetermined size (approximately 35,000 inhabitants) and plan. A well-balanced proportion between the urban area and agricultural land is essential. Any increase in population would be met by the creation of satellites, none nearer than four miles to the original city. The town plan of the garden city owes much to Ledoux, and through him to the utopian tradition. Howard's imagined city is round; factories and houses are placed on belts of open land to combine town and country advantages. (In this particular feature Howard is perhaps preceded by some English and American industrialists who moved their factories into the country and established villages around them.) Of particular interest in Howard's plan is the fact that he paid attention to, and made provisions for, the specific joys of urban life. Thus, in a wide glass arcade (significantly called "Crystal Palace") near a large park, that kind of shopping is done "which requires the joy of deliberation and selection." Howard's garden city allows large space for nature (not more than one sixth of the general area should be covered by buildings), but it is a "built" town, with rigidly prescribed boulevards, distribution of buildings, etc. Even nature is planned, being fundamentally recreation ground. Howard's close relation to what is known as the "English garden" is obvious.

Town planning in the twentieth century, although it largely remains on paper, shows the profound changes in urbanistic thought. Most of the problems of contemporary town planning were anticipated by

Tony Garnier (1869–1914) in his first project for an industrial town, designed in 1901–04. In his further projects and commissions, and in his book *Une cité industrielle* (1917) he discusses his plans in great detail. Clearly distinguishing between the different functions of the city (living, work, leisure, education, traffic), Garnier undertakes to design a town which will fully serve the needs of man in an industrial age. A bold innovator in the use of materials and in the shape of individual buildings (preferring an ascetic geometry), he is also highly original in the disposition of the town as a whole: he separates vehicular and pedestrian traffic, designs a residential district without enclosed courtyards but featuring continuous green areas, and plans a community center that anticipates contemporary social centers.

Another architect and town planner who anticipated the problems and shapes of the modern city, Antonio Sant' Elia (1880–1916), was sometimes associated with the Futurists. Sant' Elia was greatly attracted by some features of North American civilization, particularly by the romantic aspects of its technical development and by the progressive expansion of an industrial metropolis. His grandiose project for a *Città Nuova* was shown in Milan in 1914. In the catalogue to the exhibition Sant' Elia published a manifesto on the need of breaking with the past. The "New City" should correspond to the mentality of men freed from the bonds of tradition and conventions. In his many drawings a major theme is the architecture of a metropolis which is the result of a technological and industrialized society. In designing towering buildings with exterior elevators, multi-level road bridges, and imaginary factories ("monuments of the city of the future"), Sant' Elia raised these modern forms to the level of symbols.

Garnier and Sant' Elia influenced Le Corbusier. Le Corbusier's work in urbanism consists of a large number of articles and books, and an impressive number of projects for town planning. Only a small part of these projects has materialized (of particular importance is the so-called Marseille Block of 1952). Le Corbusier took a decisive step beyond Garnier and Sant' Elia. While Garnier still thought of small towns, limited to 35,000 inhabitants who are all engaged in industry, and Sant' Elia's visions remained in bare outline, Le Corbusier planned in detail for a city of 3,000,000 inhabitants. From the outset he steered towards the problems of the "change-over town" (as he later called it), a metropolis with diverse functions which must be disentangled.

A significant part of Le Corbusier's theoretical inquiry into the urban problem is a critical appreciation of cities of the past, particularly of the recent past, and of the solutions that have been proposed to this problem. Without ever allowing himself to be moved by "local color" or aestheticism, he denounced the blemishes of modern cities, that is, those aspects of the city not well enough adapted to their various functions. He also rejected the utopian ideas of limiting the size of cities, and contrary to Frank Lloyd Wright, who advocated the diffusion of urban communities, was opposed to horizontal spreading of the urban complex.

Le Corbusier's work in urbanism bears the mark of both rationalism and a philosophical image of man. His rationalism leads to an analysis of the city's different functions, and to an allocation of distinct spaces to each function. The establishing of an orderly relationship between traffic lanes, on the one hand, and living and working zones, on the other, is of primary importance in this context. A famous result of this approach is Le Corbusier's famous hierarchy of roads (the 7 V system), starting with 1 V, an artery carrying international and inter-urban traffic, and ending with 7 V, a fine capillary system in the zone reserved for children and schools. The analytical character is expressed even in small details. "So great is Le Corbusier's need for logical organization that, having to lay out the vast capital of Candigarh, he divides the vegetation to be used into six categories, each of which receives a precise function" (F. Choay, p. 16).

Le Corbusier combines the analysis of the city's functions with a philosophical image of man, for whom the city is built. Although he emphasizes the specifically modern conditions of urban life (millions of inhabitants in one metropolis, the decisive role of traffic) and proposes specifically modern solutions (the "Cartesian skyscraper," the zoning of traffic), he is deeply indebted to the humanistic tradition. The thought of the utopians (especially of Charles Fourier) was of particularly great importance for his work. This is reflected even in his language: terms such as "radiant city," "architecture of happiness" are both frequent in his writings and characteristic of his ideas and attitudes.

In his work, both in individual buildings and in town planning, he tries to achieve an "adaptation to the human scale": in individual buildings by applying the "Modulor" (his own invention of a scale of architectural proportions related to the proportions of the human body), in the designing of the city as a whole by assuming an hour of walking as the basic unit of town planning. In his town planning he emphasizes the city's center: on a small scale it is a community center (as in St. Dié, 1945–46), on a monumental scale it is a capitol (as in Candigarh, the metropolis of Punjab, begun in 1950). Under Le Corbusier's influence the "Athens Charter" was published by the international architectural organization (CIAM) in 1933, set-

433

ting out data and requirements connected with the planning of modern cities under five headings (Dwellings, Recreation, Work, Transportation, Historic Buildings).

Le Corbusier's work makes it evident that in the twentieth century, as in former periods, town planning is not only a highly complex technical task but involves philosophical ideas and the creation, or application, of traditional, symbolic forms.

BIBLIOGRAPHY

1. General. Sir Patrick Abercrombie, *Town and City Planning* (London, 1944). Joseph Gantner, *Grundformen der europäischen Stadt* (Vienna, 1928). Pierre Lavedan, *Histoire de l'urbanisme*, 2 vols. (Paris, 1926, 1941). Lewis Mumford, *The Culture of Cities* (New York, 1938); idem, *The City in History: Its Origin, Its Transformations, and Its Prospects* (New York, 1961). Camillo Sitte, *The Art of Building Cities* (New York, 1945). Paul Zucker, *Town and Square: From the Agora to the Village Green* (New York, 1959). For bibliographies, see: George C. Bestor and Holway R. Jones, *City Planning: A Basic Bibliography of Sources and Trends* (Sacramento, 1962); Philip Dawson and Sam B. Warner, Jr., "A Selection of Works Relating to the History of Cities," in Oscar Handlin and John Burchard, *The Historian and the City* (Cambridge, Mass., 1963), pp. 270–90.

2. Antiquity. India and the Near East: B. B. Dutt, *Town Planning in Ancient India* (Calcutta and Simla, 1925); Mircea Eliade, "Centre du monde, temple, maison," *Le symbolisme cosmique des monuments religieux* (Rome, 1957), pp. 57–82; Henri Frankfort, *The Art and Architecture of the Ancient Orient* (Baltimore, 1959), with a good bibliography; Francis John Haverfield, *Ancient Town Planning* (Oxford, 1913); Stuart Piggott, *Some Ancient Cities of India* (London, 1945); Earl Baldwin Smith, *Egyptian Architecture as Cultural Expression* (London, 1933). Greece: Fustel de Coulanges, *Numa Denis: The Ancient City* (New York, 1955); M. Erdmann, *Zur Kunde der Hellenistischen Städtegrundungen* (Strasbourg, 1879); Knud Fabricius, "Städtebau der Briechen," in Pauly, *Realencyclopädie der classischen Altertumswissenschaft*, revised by Georg Wissowa (1929); A. H. M. Jones, *The Greek City from Alexander to Justinian* (Oxford, 1940); Roland Martin, *L'urbanisme dans la Grèce* (Paris, 1956). Rome: R. C. Bosanquet, "Greek and Roman Towns," *Town Planning Review* (1914); William Warde Fowler, *Social Life in Rome at the Age of Cicero* (London, 1908); Léon Homo, *Rome impériale et l'urbanisme dans l'antiquité* (Paris, 1951); Guido Kaschnitz-Weinberg, *Über die Grundformen der Italisch-Römischen Struktur*, 2 vols. (Munich, 1944, 1950).

3. The Middle Ages. R. Borrmann, "Vom Städtebau im islamischen Osten," *Städtebauliche Vorträge* (1914). A. E. Brinckmann, *Spätmittelalterliche Stadtanlagen in Süd-Frankreich* (Berlin, 1910). Edith Ennen, *Frühgeschichte der europäischen Stadt* (Bonn, 1953). Karl Gruber, *Die Gestalt der deutschen Stadt: Ihr Wandel aus der geistigen Ordnung der Zeiten* (Munich, 1952). Christoph Klaiber, *Die Grund-rissbildung der deutschen Stadt im Mittelalter* (Berlin, 1912). Achille Luchaire, *Les communes françaises*, 2nd ed. (Paris, 1911). Henri Pirenne, *Medieval Cities* (Princeton, 1925). Earl Baldwin Smith, *Architectural Symbolism of Imperial Rome and the Middle Ages* (Princeton, 1956); idem, *La città nell'alto medioèvo* (Spoleto, 1959).

4. Renaissance and Utopian Town Planning. Wolfgang Braunfels, *Italienische Städtebaukunst* (Berlin, 1950). André Chastel, "Cités idéales: Marqueteurs italiens du XVe siècle," *L'oeil* (Dec. 1957). Horst de la Croix, "Military Architecture and the Radial City Plan in Sixteenth Century Italy," *The Art Bulletin*, 42 (1960), 263–90. S. Lang, "The Ideal City from Plato to Howard," *Architectural Review*, 112 (1952). Robert Klein, "L'urbanisme utopique de Filarete à Valentin Andreae," *Actes du Colloque international sur les utopies à la Renaissance* (Brussels, 1963), pp. 209–30. Georg Münter, *Idealstädte: Ihre Geschichte vom 15.–17. Jahrhundert* (Berlin, 1957). Rudolf Wittkower, *Architectural Principles in the Age of Humanism* (London, 1949).

5. Modern. Giulio C. Argan, "Il pensiero critico di Antonio Sant' Elia," *L'arte* (Sept. 1930). Jean Badovici and Albert Morance, *L'oeuvre de Tony Garnier* (Paris, 1938). Françoise Choay, *Le Corbusier* (New York, 1960). Yvan Christ, *Projets et divagations de Claude-Nicolas Ledoux* (Paris, 1961). Gordon Cullen, *Townscape* (London, 1962). Frederick Gibberd, *Town Design* (London, 1953). Roland Rainer, *Städtebau und Wohnkultur* (Tübingen, 1948).

MOSHE BARASCH

[See also Astrology; **Enlightenment; Iconography; Organicism; Renaissance;** Romanticism in Literature; Technology; **Utopia.**]

CIVIL DISOBEDIENCE

I

THE PHRASE "civil disobedience" now used so widely for all cases of individual or group dissent from civil law appeared on the scene quite late. Henry David Thoreau is usually credited with coining the term, though it is not known for certain that he did or why he changed the title of his essay, later to become world famous, from "Resistance to Civil Government" to "Civil Disobedience."

The concept of civil disobedience, as distinct from the phrase, has a long and notable history, appearing already as the Antigone theme in Greek drama and in the antiwar motif of *Lysistrata,* where the women, in addition to deserting their men, seize the Acropolis and the Treasury of Athens. The conflict between civil law and conscience was sharply featured when the Jews passively resisted the introduction of icons into Jerusalem by Pilate, procurator of Judaea, and by Jesus in his dramatic purification of the temple, when he overturned the tables of the money changers and the seats of those who legally sold pigeons. The conflict has been highlighted in the history of English-speaking countries many times, though rarely more forcefully than when Milton refused to obey the licensing and censorship laws of seventeenth-century England and when the Abolitionists attacked the institution of slavery in nineteenth-century America. The most widely known cases of the conflict in the twentieth century are Gandhi's campaigns against colonial rule in South Africa and India, passive resistance campaigns against Nazi occupation governments during World War II, and the civil rights campaign against segregation in the United States starting in 1954. Civil disobedience attitudes and techniques also spread into attacks against the Vietnam War, draft laws, poverty, and the authoritarian structure of colleges and universities in the 1960's.

As the examples of it make clear, the concept of civil disobedience is extremely rich and diverse, not at all precise and specific—the way it is with most terms or ideas outside of a formal system. Yet much can be done to analyze and clarify the concept, though not formally define it, if attention is paid to recurring themes in the rich context of historical examples. An appreciation of these themes, without fixation on any one case, will, hopefully, make it possible to avoid the emotionally persuasive definitions of what civil disobedience "really" is, so popular at times as different groups try to put the phrase to work for *them*.

The concept of civil disobedience presupposes, first of all, some formal structure of law, enforced by established governmental authorities, from which an individual cannot dissociate himself except by change of citizenship. (Disobedience in the contexts of family, clan, church, lodge, or business does not count as civil disobedience.) It is not necessary, however, that an individual ultimately accept the governmental framework in which he acts disobediently; he may be accepting it only conditionally at a given time as a necessary but temporary fact of life or as a step in the direction toward the framework he ultimately accepts. To insist on the ultimate acceptance of the framework in which the act occurs, as some authors do, has the absurd consequence of denying that Thoreau, Tolstoi, and Gandhi engaged in acts of civil disobedience, since Thoreau and Tolstoi were anarchists and Gandhi was protesting colonial rule.

Civil disobedience, then, consists in publicly announced defiance of specific laws, policies, or commands of that formal structure which an individual or group believes to be unjust and/or unconstitutional. The defiance may also take the form of disobedience

of just laws if such disobedience appears to be an effective way to focus public attention on unjust laws. The defiance must be publicly announced, since the point of it is to bring the unjust and/or unconstitutional laws, policies, or commands to the attention of the public, for the purpose either of stirring its conscience or of frightening it into helping repeal the laws, change the policies, or mitigate the commands; or to get the attention of the courts so that their constitutionality can be judged. The defiance may take the form of doing what is prohibited (say, burning a draft card) or of failing to do what is required (say, refusing to report for induction). The defiance, moreover, must be a premeditated act, understood to be illegal by the perpetrator, and understood to carry prescribed penalties. Willingness to accept such penalties is a crucial part of that sort of civil disobedience which hopes to stir the public conscience, while eagerness to escape punishment is perfectly compatible with that sort of civil disobedience which aims to pressure and frighten the public. The defiance, finally, may be either nonviolent or violent and still count as civil disobedience. To restrict the concept of civil disobedience to nonviolent acts, as some authors do, ignores the difficulty of finding a precise dividing line between "nonviolence" and "violence" (Is *rigidly* blocking a doorway nonviolent?) as well as the facts of usage. Defiant acts of a violent sort, if they are focused, at least for the present, on specific laws, policies, or commands (and hence are short of unrestricted defiance of the whole government) and meet the above criteria, are in fact called acts of civil disobedience just as much as those which meet the same criteria but are nonviolent.

II

Assuming that the notion of civil disobedience is reasonably clear, the question immediately arises why anyone should be civilly disobedient. Is it ever legitimate? If so, under what conditions? The two most important justifications of civil disobedience traditionally have been the Higher Law doctrine and some version of Natural or Human Rights.

1. The Higher Law doctrine asserts that God's law takes precedence over civil law whenever it can be shown that the two come into conflict. Man is ordinarily duty bound to obey the civil law and magistrates since the benefits of orderly government are large indeed; on the other hand, man cannot, out of higher duty, obey the civil law or magistrates if they command him to break the word of God.

While the Higher Law doctrine was never wholly absent from thought and practice during most of the career of Western civilization, it was usually sporadic and individual in nature. For the most part, people were happy to accept the Higher Law concept without drawing its painful corollary of civil disobedience. The most sustained development of the concept and its most thorough application was the work of those nineteenth-century American abolitionists who owed their inspiration either to transcendentalism or to the pietistic, free-will Trinitarianism that came to dominate many branches of Protestantism early in the century.

According to the transcendentalists, the Law of God says that men are morally equal, while certain aspects of civil law in the United States either deny this or prevent its recognition. In view of this conflict, it becomes the duty of an honest man to follow God's law and defy Fugitive Slave Laws and other aspects of the civil law (the extent of violation depending upon whether or not one countenances violence, and to what extent). Not to do so is to be a "practical atheist"—that is, one who says he believes in God but does not follow his commands.

The transcendentalists, while united on the principle of Higher Law, certainly did not agree on how far to extend the commitment to civil disobedience. Emerson was reluctant to extend it very far because he felt that the only permanent solution to the evils of the world is a regeneration of men's souls. While he spoke sharply against slavery, it remained for transcendentalists like Theodore Parker and George William Curtis to be civilly disobedient and to answer effectively the critics of this activist policy.

The critic is wrong, Parker and Curtis said, in thinking that civil disobedience will lead to chaos or undermine the benefits of orderly government. Proponents of the Higher Law recognize the importance of stability and so are willing to obey many questionable laws; they claim only that some laws and policies are so thoroughly immoral that they must be publicly disobeyed as well as denounced else one renounces his own humanity. Moreover, the man of principle who will not obey a vicious law is that sort of person who can be counted upon as the strongest upholder of law in general since he will not break laws for selfish reasons or obey the law only when the constable is watching. Finally, a person who would obey *any* law just because it is a law is utterly immoral, for the vilest crimes are often committed on the excuse of following orders of a legally constituted superior. If the colonials had obeyed the law, they would never have thrown the tea into Boston Harbor and there would not have been a United States of America.

Henry David Thoreau is, no doubt, the most famous advocate of civil disobedience among the transcendentalists. It is well known that he refused to pay his poll tax by way of protest against the Mexican War and the expansion of slavery, and that he was turned out

of jail when friends paid it in his stead. The protest itself accomplished nothing, but for many people his act became highly significant as a symbol of passive resistance to injustice. There is little doubt that it can be so construed and that Thoreau so intended it. But the truly radical nature of his political beliefs is by no means adequately suggested by this standard interpretation, for Thoreau was essentially an idealistic anarchist who believed that all civil law that touched moral matters was an unacceptable encroachment on the rights of an individual. A majority vote, he thought, does not establish what is true or right. In the ideal state all individuals would act according to their own insights into Universal Truth and there would thus be no need of civil government at all, except for the exercise of practical affairs like garbage collection, road building, and other matters where decisions of conscience are not involved. Thoreau stated his anarchism succinctly by saying that if that government is best which governs least, then that government is absolutely best which does not govern at all.

The majority of antislavery activists owed their Higher Law inspiration to the pietistic, free-will Trinitarianism that flourished in the first half of the nineteenth century as a protest against both the theological and social conservatism of Calvinism. Although there were many differences, this "New Light" theology shared with the transcendentalists the notion of individual inner light that provides direct communication with God. When the law of God so obtained is violated by civil law, as in the case of slavery, the duty of the Christian is to be disobedient. The most interesting of this group, because they were the most radical and effective, were the Oberlinities, both the College and community, led by Asa Mahan, Charles Finney, John Keep, James H. Fairchild, and others. They ran a fabulously successful Underground Railway and participated in the famous Wellington Rescue Case that provided much important propaganda for the young Republican Party.

While the Oberlinites were thoroughly radical, they completely rejected the views of William Lloyd Garrison. Garrison was radical, they felt, in a completely useless way. He rejected both the Christian Church and the United States Constitution because they provided a framework that tolerated slavery. He believed that the only thing to do was for the North to secede and start over. The Oberlinites felt that this plan might help the consciences of some Northerners but would not help the slaves in the slightest. It was better, they felt, to make the Church militant (they helped organize the American Missionary Association); to work through the courts (they effectively nullified the Ohio Anti-Slave Law); to help create new political channels (they worked for the Free-Soil and Republican Parties); and, finally, to be civilly disobedient in an *effective* fashion (they never lost a slave to federal authorities).

2. The notions of "natural rights" and "human rights" are by no means identical since the former usually involves an absolutistic and rationalistic outlook in moral philosophy and is usually based on a theological foundation such as "God-given rights," while the latter does not usually entail such conceptions but leaves open the possibility, at least, of relativistic, voluntaristic, and humanistic foundations for man's basic rights. The concept of human rights is the one usually used these days, not simply because ours is a more voluntaristic and humanistic era but because this concept includes many social and economic freedoms which seem important to our age, along with the more traditional concept of freedom as "freedom from" various restraints. For example, the Universal Declaration of Human Rights, adopted by the United Nations in 1948, recognizes, among others, the rights to life, liberty, personal security, and equal protection of the law; freedom from slavery and degrading punishment; freedom of thought, conscience, speech, religion, and peaceful assembly; and the right to an education, choice of one's own employment, favorable working conditions, and protection against unemployment.

The concepts of natural and human rights, with all their differences, still have a core of common meaning, namely, that there are certain rights which belong to a man independent of his position in a civil society. Since society does not bestow these rights, it cannot justifiably take them away. This is the point in saying that such rights are *inalienable*. The function of society, far from interfering with these rights, is to sustain and protect them and to adjudicate conflicts that arise in the common pursuit of these rights. If a civil government subverts these rights in a wholesale fashion, it is not fulfilling its proper role and hence the people are justified in overthrowing that spurious government (with the least violence possible) and erecting a legitimate one in its place. It follows as a corollary of this general principle that if a government which on the whole respects its proper role nevertheless infringes or denies some specific rights, either to a majority or minority of people, then they have the right to civilly disobey the offending laws, policies, or commands (either nonviolently or violently, depending upon further arguments).

The notion of natural or human rights, it should be noted, strongly supports Thoreau's contention that a majority vote cannot decide what is right or wrong, and helps put the concept of democracy in its proper perspective. The notion of Popular Sovereignty espoused by Stephen Douglas in pre-Civil War days was supposedly the democratic answer to the problem of slavery in the territories. Let the settlers in each territory vote on whether or not to have slaves! This concept of democracy, of course, subverts the whole notion of human rights and is the rule of the majority to which Thoreau so strongly objected. The democratic principle envisioned by most of the architects of the Bill of Rights of the United States Constitution and of the Declaration of Human Rights of the United Nations is that the rule of the majority is the best way known to man of adjudicating the conflicts which inevitably arise in the common pursuit of their human rights by millions of people. It would have been shocking indeed to these people to have envisioned the democratic principle as deciding who is going to be allowed to have human rights.

The concept of human rights provides, no doubt, the most prominent justification of civil disobedience in the humanistically oriented modern world, and yet prudential considerations are sometimes offered by believers in the concept to soften the commitment to civil disobedience. These prudential considerations have always been with us (Bay [1968], p. 476). Thomas Hobbes represented the extreme position, of accepting the concept of natural rights and yet, out of fear of anarchy, rejecting not only civil disobedience but even dissent. David Hume provided a teleological, utilitarian approach to the relative limits of obedience and disobedience to civil magistrates and adopted "with considerable vehemence" a libertarian position in his *Treatise of Human Nature* (1739–40). Later, out of fear of anarchy again, he recommended "exact obedience" to the law of the land and the authority of its administrators. Jeremy Bentham saw no more point in these sweeping generalizations and anxieties about civil disobedience and anarchy than he did about generalizations in any other part of moral philosophy. On his view, each situation and political context should be carefully studied in its own right and the likely consequences predicted. If the prediction is for fewer overall mischievous consequences by disobedience than by submission, then it is the *duty*, not simply the right, of the conscientious citizen to resist the government.

To Bentham's counsel, the modern proponent of human rights who takes civil disobedience seriously adds that the cry of anarchy and civil disintegration is all too often unintentionally and at times even intentionally the mask of vested interests. There are, to be sure, genuine dangers in civil disobedience, well understood by its intelligent agents, but the dangers are to be *weighed* by a believer in human rights and not used as a rationalization for doing nothing when he has the security and someone else suffers the infringement of human rights. The point is simply this: if a person is so concerned about civil stability that he cannot conceive any conditions that would justify disobedience, then he really has abandoned any tenable concept of human rights.

III

Assuming that at least in some cases civil disobedience is justified, the question of what form it should take immediately arises. Should it always be nonviolent in nature or is the use of violence ever justified? And if violence is ever justified, what limits must be set upon it? Efforts to answer these questions form a large bloc of the literature on civil disobedience.

The defense of nonviolence has taken two radically different forms, one prudential in nature, the other a matter of principle. The prudential argument holds that if government forces are so strong and oppressive that they would retaliate tenfold against any violence, then they should be opposed only nonviolently or by "passive resistance." If the situation changes, if the strength of the oppressive government declines, then it may be violently resisted. There can be little doubt that this was the attitude of the valiant civilians in Norway and Denmark during the Nazi occupation whose campaigns of resistance are so vividly described in (and were influenced by) John Steinbeck's *The Moon is Down.* It was a grave offense to have a copy of this book in one's possession in any Nazi occupied country.

The most important defenders of nonviolence as a matter of principle were Leo Tolstoi, Mohandas Gandhi, and Martin Luther King, Jr. The principle usually invoked to justify nonviolence was the religious and moral belief that love is necessarily good and hence that violence by its very nature is evil; that only love of others brings happiness and the realization of a moral self, while anger and violence debase the character of the agent as well as wounding and killing others. There was a seriatim influence among Tolstoi, Gandhi, and King, though it must not be assumed that their concepts and campaigns of disobedience were identical simply because they agreed on these principles of nonviolence.

According to Tolstoi, man's conscience reveals to him a God that is the supreme Good, not a personal God but a God "within us." Jesus was absolutely right in saying, "Love thy neighbor as thyself," not, however, because he was the Son of God but because this is what is dictated by the conscience of man. Moreover, the goal of man is to achieve happiness and this can only be accomplished by getting rid of the greed and lust that continually breed trouble among men and by putting love in their place. Love precludes violence, which is wrong in every form, including the forms inherent in every form of government. The true Chris-

tian must refuse jury duty, conscription, and any state work, and he must likewise refuse to participate in any *violent* efforts to overthrow the state. Property, Tolstoi believed, is the private usurpation of what belongs to all men and is the source of most greedy activity and hence the root of violence. Tolstoi, in short, was a socialistic anarchist, though he never called himself an anarchist since anarchists frequently justify violence.

Gandhi called his own concept of disobedience the doctrine of *Satyagraha*, or "truth force." To him the concept of passive resistance came to seem inadequate to capture the full scope of nonviolence practiced as a matter of principle. One must not only resist passively the injustice of government but do so without feelings of animosity or hatred. Complete commitment to the love of fellow men is necessary not only as intrinsically right but as providing that "truth force" which is crucial to the success of civil disobedience. The adjective "civil" in the phrase "civil disobedience" meant for Gandhi peaceful, courteous, "civilized" resistance, and it is for this reason that some scholars have insisted that nonviolence is part of the very meaning of "civil disobedience." Admiration for Gandhi's views and campaigns, however, is not a good reason for making these views definitive of a network of views only more or less closely related. Such admiration is also not a good reason for overlooking the historically relevant use of the adjective "civil" in speaking of the civil government or the civil magistrate simply to distinguish them from ecclesiastical, military, and other authorities. Thoreau in the earlier title of his essay, "Resistance to Civil Government," surely did not wish to imply that the American government was distinctive in its courteousness.

Gandhi's formulation of civil disobedience was, in part, much like that of the Oberlin abolitionists. The lawbreaker should openly and quietly disobey unjust laws and suffer the consequences of such disobedience with dignity. However, Gandhi also felt it was legitimate to dissent from unjust policies and commands of a government by disobeying laws which were not themselves unjust provided that breaking these just laws did not itself violate principles of conscience. This addition to the Oberlin formula suggests that while the Oberlin community accepted the governmental framework in which it operated, though critically, Gandhi ultimately rejected the framework itself. And this suggestion, of course, is true in fact, for Gandhi was ultimately protesting the illegitimacy of colonial rule and not simply the injustice of certain laws within the English colonial system.

Martin Luther King, Jr. interpreted the Christian message as one of love and compassion and hence accepted the doctrine of nonviolence as a matter of religious principle. He was also much influenced by Gandhi's techniques of passive resistance, which he incorporated whenever possible into the civil rights movements, and by Gandhi's statement of the principle of civil disobedience. Like Gandhi he believed that unjust laws should be disobeyed quietly and the consequences suffered with dignity when they cannot honorably be avoided. He carefully defined the nature of the unjust laws against which Negroes were dissenting as the laws which a minority are forced to observe but which are not binding on the majority. However, in later years, after much civil rights legislation had been passed but either not enforced at all or only partly so, he emphasized that the root of racial injustice lay in a double standard of law enforcement—in short, in the unjust policies and commands of civil authorities rather than in unjust laws (King [1967], p. 82).

Many arguments have been offered against the view that nonviolent civil disobedience is always right in principle and that acts of civil disobedience therefore must always be peaceful (which is the common denominator in the thought of Tolstoi, Gandhi, and King). It should be borne in mind, of course, that arguments which claim to show that violence is not in principle wrong are not arguments to show that violence is always right or that any certain degree of violence is right but no other. When violence is justified and to what extent, are further questions that need to be answered by further arguments. Indeed, as we have seen, it is possible to believe that violence is not in principle wrong and still believe on prudential grounds that violence is not ever justified. The arguments against nonviolence-in-principle are too numerous to examine in detail here, but the general strategies involved are few and clear. Some people reject the pacifistic interpretation of Christianity and certain other world religions, while others reject entirely a religious viewpoint from which any moral position, pacifistic or otherwise, can be deduced. Still others reject the formalistic view of moral philosophy which gives rise to an absolute commitment to nonviolence. Others point out that a utilitarian justification of nonviolence is useless, since it would never yield the absolute quality necessary to the pacifist commitment. (It is also pointed out that unfortunately some of the most eminent proponents of nonviolence mix together, unwittingly, incompatible formalistic and utilitarian justifications.) Moreover, there are difficulties with an absolute commitment to love, since it implies an absolute commitment to forgiveness, as well as to nonviolence, which conflicts with that concept of justice which entails the need for punishment. Moreover, there are various crucial roles that anger and other emotions condemned by a nonviolence doctrine play in the psychological health of individuals and communities.

Finally, the argument is advanced that the absolute view of nonviolence is based on a mistaken view of man's present nature and future possibilities. The majority of men simply are not moral in nature and are incapable of responding to the call to conscience sounded by the advocates of nonviolent civil disobedience. Psychiatrists assure us that some people are *incapable* of the moral point of view because the affective tone of their emotional life is so dulled that they are incapable of fellow-feeling. Experience assures us also that many more people simply reject the moral point of view as a piece of outright foolishness; they are selfish as a matter of self-evident principle. Still others are selfish unwittingly, never having given any matter of principle a moment's thought. Certainly nonviolent civil disobedience is just so much chaff in the wind to all these people—and always will be. If anything will work it will be the use of pressure tactics. To be sure, pressure tactics are also irrelevant to those of seriously dulled emotions, but such tactics do have desirable effects on those who are selfish-on-principle or thoughtlessly selfish if they are reasonably enlightened. Such tactics may not convert these people, of course, but they will increasingly help justice be done as these people become convinced that their own welfare depends on it; and, hopefully, what they are at first pressured to do out of enlightened selfishness they will gradually out of habit come to regard as moral.

IV

Former Justice Abe Fortas offered a new justification of nonviolent dissent which does not view violence as necessarily wrong in all societies but as *unnecessary* in a free society like that in the United States of America. There is no *need* for disruption and destructive violence, he says, when there are constitutional and rational means of dissent in this society unparalleled in previous history. Universal suffrage allows the majority of people to express their dissent by voting out of office those officials whose policies and commands are objectionable. Moreover, individuals and groups are guaranteed the right to bring pressure to bear on their government by writing, speaking, organizing, picketing, and demonstrating, provided only that laws governing public safety, etc., are obeyed. They may also challenge unjust laws through the courts, claiming that the laws are unconstitutional as well as unjust. And when they sue the state or its officials, they are equals with the state in court and have the protection of elaborate procedural rights. This is possible because the courts are totally independent of the executive and legislative branches of government. This path of legal dissent was the one taken by the Negroes in their famous dissent over school segregation in *Brown v. Board of Education*, in which the Court ruled that state-maintained segregation of public schools was unconstitutional.

The nature of civil disobedience endorsed by Fortas is wholly procedural, and never violent, and always directed against specific laws. An unjust law which is judged to be unconstitutional is disobeyed so that a court test can be made. If the decision of the Court bears out the judgment of the dissenter he is justified and exonerated, but if the decision goes against him, he must accept the penalty of disobeying that law with dignity, the mark of his respect for the overall system in which he is operating. Furthermore, it is crucial that in disobeying a law which he judges to be unconstitutional the dissenter not violate laws which are clearly valid as a way of publicizing a protest and exerting pressure on the public.

A good example of this sort of admissible civil disobedience, Fortas thinks, is the work of Martin Luther King, Jr., who pledged that Negroes would disobey "unjust laws"—defined as laws that only a minority are compelled to obey—openly and peacefully, and that they would accept whatever penalties might result. "This is civil disobedience in a great tradition. It is peaceful, nonviolent disobedience of laws which are themselves unjust and which the protester challenges as invalid and unconstitutional" (Fortas [1968], p. 34). It is part of the valid framework of dissent and disobedience provided by the Constitution and constitutes a workable alternative to violence. Fortas concludes that "the experience of these past few years shows, more vividly than any other episode in our history, how effective these alternatives are." It has been "through their use—and not through the sporadic incidents of violence—that we have effected the current social revolution . . ." (p. 64).

This view of dissent and disobedience has many merits and is worthy of the deepest respect. One only wishes that it were the whole story, but, alas, it does not seem to be so. One writer has found as many as "nine fallacies" in Fortas' view (Zinn [1968], passim). There is, unfortunately, grave doubt that the sort of social revolution that Justice Fortas has in mind has in fact taken place, even though a legal one certainly has. A vast majority of school-age Negroes still go to segregated schools in the South in spite of the 1954 Supreme Court ruling, or attend de facto segregated and/or inferior schools in the North. Poverty funds have been frequently used for political purposes or, in any case, for something someone else thought would be good for the black population. Title VI of the 1964 Civil Rights Act, which allows federal withdrawal of funds in cases of discrimination, has been ignored in many cases of unequal treatment such as segregated

hospital facilities and used only sparingly in regard to schools. Under the 1965 Voting Rights Act only a pitifully small number of federal registrars have been sent to the South. And, most crucially of all, due to our computer revolution and the declining need for unskilled and semi-skilled workers, the employment situation of the Negro, in spite of feeble efforts to aid him, is worse than it was ten years ago.

Instead of a social revolution, one writer sees "little more than federally approved tokenism" and "a continuation of paper promises and ancient inequities" (Duberman [1968], p. 38). And Martin Luther King, Jr. in his later work sadly concluded that "there is a tragic gulf between civil rights laws passed and civil rights laws implemented." There is "a double standard in the enforcement of law and a double standard in the respect for particular laws" (King [1967], p. 82). King still offered universal love and nonviolence as the only answer to the new difficulties, but many black men found the old answer utterly irrelevant given these new revelations. The history of S.N.C.C. from "sit-ins" to militancy is instructive on this point. For better or for worse, black militants of all varieties marched in, and civil disobedience using various types and degrees of pressure is now very much part of the scene. Some have felt it necessary to go beyond civil disobedience to terrorism.

But it is not only in the civil rights area that a feeling of no progress and double-dealing has led to the fall of the "great tradition" in civil disobedience. In protests against the Vietnam War, the draft laws, poverty, and the authoritarian structure of colleges and universities, the same pattern of increasing militancy is exhibited. The common theme in the campaigns of the black man, the young man, and the poor man is that they want more participation in the decisions which are always being made for them by someone else. They want more "participatory democracy" because they feel that their "representatives" and "public servants" have produced sham progress and usually apply double standards. They ask pointedly: Are not those who refuse to implement laws just as civilly disobedient as those who disobey laws, with the crucial exception that there are severe penalties for the one but none at all for the other? It is not the American system and not the American judiciary that they are rejecting or have lost faith in, many militants say, but rather it is those who have been making their political, economic, and social decisions for them in whom they have lost confidence and now completely reject.

Rejection and alienation are frightening symptoms in the body politic as well as in the individual. Sometimes they are the result of deep understanding, other times of misunderstanding or ignorance; sometimes they are the result of deep injury, other times of fancied grievances; sometimes they are the result of righteous anger, other times of blind and selfish rage. It is most crucial at this point in history to distinguish more carefully than in the past these different origins and types of alienation so that they can be differentially and more effectively responded to than heretofore. No doubt, the wisest first move would be to take the clear-cut, deep grievances seriously and listen to what the oppressed themselves have to say. Not to do so is to run a grave risk of producing further "uncivil" disobedience.

BIBLIOGRAPHY

Consult the standard editions of the works of Sophocles, Euripides, Aristophanes, Hobbes, Milton, Hume, Bentham, Garrison, Emerson, Thoreau, Tolstoi, and Gandhi. This bibliography contains the less well-known historical figures mentioned in the text, anthologies, and contemporary articles and books where further bibliographical detail is to be found.

Christian Bay, "Civil Disobedience," *Encyclopedia of the Social Sciences*, ed. David L. Sills, 17 vols. (New York, 1968), 2, 473–87. Hugo Bedau, ed., *Civil Disobedience: Theory and Practice* (New York, 1969). Edward Cary, *George William Curtis* (Boston, 1894). Henry Steele Commager, *Theodore Parker: Yankee Crusader* (Boston, 1947; reprint 1960). G. W. Curtis, *Orations and Addresses*, Vol. I (New York, 1894). Martin Duberman, "Black Power in America," *Partisan Review*, **35** (1968), 34–48. James H. Fairchild, *Moral Science*, revised ed. (New York, 1892), pp. 172–81. R. S. Fletcher, *A History of Oberlin College* (Oberlin, 1943), I, 207–426. Abe Fortas, *Concerning Dissent and Civil Disobedience* (New York, 1968). Walter Harding, "Did Thoreau Invent the Term 'Civil Disobedience,'" *Thoreau Society Bulletin*, No. 103 (1968), 8; idem, *The Variorum Civil Disobedience*, annotated and with an introduction (New York, 1967). Martin Luther King, Jr., *Where Do We Go From Here: Chaos or Community?* (New York, 1967). Louis E. Lomax, *The Negro Revolt* (New York, 1962; 1963). Staughton Lynd, *Intellectual Origins of American Radicalism* (New York, 1968); idem, *Nonviolence in America: A Documentary History* (Indianapolis, 1966). E. H. Madden, *Civil Disobedience and Moral Law in Nineteenth Century American Philosophy* (Seattle, 1968). Asa Mahan, Series of articles on "Reform," *Oberlin Evangelist* (1844). Theodore Parker, *Speeches, Addresses and Occasional Sermons*, 3 vols. (Boston, 1852); idem, *Additional Speeches, Addresses and Occasional Sermons*, 2 vols. (Boston, 1855). Mulford Q. Sibley, ed., *The Quiet Battle: Writings on the Theory and Practice of Nonviolent Resistance* (Garden City, N.Y., 1963). Charles E. Silberman, *Crisis in Black and White* (New York, 1964). Howard Zinn, *Disobedience and Democracy: Nine Fallacies on Law and Order* (New York, 1968).

EDWARD H. MADDEN

[See also **Anarchism**; Constitutionalism; Democracy; Free Will; God; Individualism; Peace; **Protest Movements**; **Revolution**.]

CLASS

THE WORD "class" in the social sense is relatively new. It appears in the English and other Western European languages at the time of the Industrial Revolution. This article will emphasize English usage; French and German developments are roughly parallel. Before the 1770's, the ordinary use of "class" in English referred to a division or group in schools and colleges. In the late eighteenth century we first come upon "lower classes," to join "lower orders," which was a term used earlier in that century.

As a designation for workers, the terms "poor laborer" and "the poor" had been used synonymously since the sixteenth century, thus pointing to a relation between poverty and wage earning. By the eighteenth century a distinction was made between those not able to work, "the very poor" or "paupers," and those able to work, "the laboring poor." This term is widely used until and beyond the threshold of the Industrial Revolution and again suggests the connection between poverty and wage earning. But from the early nineteenth century on, as in the works of Malthus and Ricardo, the term now in common use is "the laboring classes" (the term "working class," or "classes," makes its appearance around 1815 in England and around 1830 in France). Function in the economic process replaces the earlier implicit focus on social rank and hierarchy of possessions.

Without going into detail regarding the designation of other social strata, it can simply be noted that "higher classes," "middle classes," and "middling classes" appear in the 1790's, and "upper classes" in the 1820's. The "upper middle classes" are first heard of in the 1890's and the "lower middle classes" in the present century.

The late appearance of the term "class" does not, of course, indicate that social divisions were not recognized earlier. But it indicates changes in the character of these divisions and in attitudes toward them, which came about with the Industrial Revolution. Class is a less definite and more fluid term than "rank" or "order," and the use of this less specific term subtly indicates the erosion since the Industrial Revolution of the earlier clear-cut hierarchical rank order which used to govern the English social structure and a shifting of focus from social status to economic criteria. Slightly later than in England, but roughly in the same period, the French terminology shifts from *état* to *classe* and the German from *Stand* to *Klasse*.

It is interesting to note in this connection that some of the new terms, such as "working" or "laboring classes," referred to functional contributions in industrial production; others, such as "middle classes" or "upper classes" still referred only to position in a hierarchy. The difference between classifications of people in terms of functional contribution or scalar positions will be dealt with presently. But before discussing modern conceptualizations of *class* a much older notion needs to be considered, i.e., the representation of societies as aggregates of people some of whom are above and others below. This notion can indeed be found throughout recorded history. It represents, in its various forms, the effort of social thinkers as well as of common men to come to grips with the stubborn fact of human inequality.

Ideas meant to explain or justify inequality among men are embodied in a variety of religious myths. In the Bible, for example, the offspring of Ham, who had been cursed by Noah, were condemned to eternal bondage in the service of Noah's descendants. Saint Augustine cited this in *The City of God* when he wished to show that slavery was justified, and medieval theologians used the same story to condone serfdom. According to the Koran, social stratification originates from the very will of Allah who has decreed, "We have exalted some of them above others in degrees, that some of them may take others in subjection" (Sura XLIII, 31). In the ancient Vedas, a vertical system of classes, or rather castes, was legitimated by way of an anatomical illustration. The Brahmins sprang originally from the lips of Brahma, the Kshatriya from his shoulders, the Vaishya from his thighs, and the Shudra from his feet. The notion of caste, which may be defined as "an endogamous and hereditary subdivision of an ethnic unit occupying a position of superior or inferior rank or social esteem in comparison with other subdivisions" (A. L. Kroeber, "Caste," *Encyclopedia of the Social Sciences*, New York, 1935), will not detain us here. While it is of central importance for Indian and other Asiatic societies, it is of but marginal interest in the context of the Western world. Note, however, that the relationship of American Negroes to the white majority has at least caste-like elements (John Dollard, *Caste and Class in a Southern Town*, New York, 1949).

Dichotomous Conceptualizations. While the image of society as some kind of vertical order is widespread, the specific forms in which such an order is conceived has varied considerably throughout history. Perhaps the most popular conceptualization is one which sees society as a dichotomous structure of top and bottom strata: the rich and the poor, the powerful and the powerless. Such conceptualizations are most frequently held by spokesmen for negatively privileged groups who wish to attack the prevailing system of inequality (though, as will be seen, these have no monopoly on such conceptions). For Gerrard Winstanley (fl. 1648–52), representing the extreme radical wing in the English Revolution, Cain becomes the forefather of the privileged landed oppressors of the common people. Cain against Abel; Ishmael against Isaac; Esau against Jacob—they stood to him and his co-thinkers for those who had illegally seized power and land and had turned their brothers into servants. The Levellers saw the Norman conquerors who had enslaved the English people as the symbolic heirs of Cain. More generally, every biblical case in which a good brother confronted a bad one was used to represent the dichotomous division of society between oppressors and oppressed, have and have-nots.

The concrete images of polar divisions between the top and bottom of society as they appear in history were, however, not uniform. At least three basic forms of dichotomy can be discerned, depending on what aspects of the privileges enjoyed by the upper classes are perceived as salient. Conceptualization differs depending on whether power, wealth, or relationships in the process of production are given central emphasis. Hence we get the dichotomous concept of rulers and ruled, of rich and poor, or finally, of exploiters and exploited. These variant formulations are, of course, not mutually exclusive but occur in a variety of combinations.

The primacy of the power dimension is expressed in such thinkers as Ibn Khaldun (1332–1406): "The possession of power is the source of riches" (*Les prolègomes*, Paris [1936], II, 339). Pre-Marxian and Marxian socialist doctrine reversed the relation between power and wealth by stressing that the possession of economic resources confers social power. The contemporary social critic, Ignazio Silone, attempted to come to grips with the characteristics of totalitarian, post-capitalist society and with the change in class relations resulting from power superseding wealth. He quipped, in his *The School for Dictators* (1938), that in contrast to the capitalist era which was dominated by *plutocrats* (rule by wealth), the totalitarian society had given rise to *cratopluts* (rule over wealth).

The relation between those who work and those who are idle, rather than seen as due to factors of ownership or power, was most clearly articulated by the rebellious underprivileged during the waning of the Middle Ages. "When Adam delved and Eve span," the impoverished queried, "Who was then a gentleman?" Such imagery is common in utterances during a variety of peasant revolts and *jacqueries* as well as in such writers as the Anabaptist leader of a Peasant War, Thomas Münzer (ca. 1490–1525). Shelley's formulation in his "Song to the Men of England" is but a reformulation of this theme:

Men of England, wherefore plough
For the Lords who lay ye low?

Wherefore weave with toil and care
The rich robes your tyrants wear?

Yet the use of the image of a dichotomous society was not limited to the spokesmen for the underprivileged. For the classical thinkers of antiquity, the basic division in the social structure was that between freemen and slaves, and this distinction was said by Plato and Aristotle to have a biological basis in human nature. Though Aristotle made more complicated distinctions when it came to the body of freemen, he was nevertheless certain that all physical work should be reserved for the slaves so that the legal division between free citizens and slaves would at the same time coincide with the economic division between nonlaborers and laborers.

In the writings of the early Church Fathers, e.g., John Chrysostom (329–89), Patriarch of Constantinople, in *Homilia*, 34, the major problem of social inequality was discussed not so much in terms of freemen and slaves or of masters and servants as in economic terms; social stratification was seen as based on relations of ownership. Rich or poor, owners and nonowners were seen as the two basic strata in society, no matter whether a specific Christian writer sided with the oppressed or was moved to defend the interests of the privileged.

Images of a dichotomous society are likely to conflict with everyday experience in societies that are at least as differentiated as those of the Greek *polis*. Such dichotomies clash with the perception that there are gradations of wealth and poverty—and not simply two classes, rich and poor—and that there are intermediate strata to be found between freemen and slaves or between nobles and commoners. Despite the inability of such dichotomies to encompass the totality of social differentiation, however, they have continued to be salient in the whole history of class societies. Among the reasons for such persistence may be mentioned the widespread psychological disposition to concentrate on extremes and to think in terms of polarities. But more important than such dispositions are those sets of circumstances which may favor the emergence or persistence of dichotomies.

In the first place, societies may in fact have a bipolar division so salient that finer gradations appear as of secondary importance. This is likely to be the case in slave societies, where, in view of the gulf between freemen and slaves, further differentiations within these categories, or the existence of strata—such as the Greek metics, who belong to neither side of the great divide—may not be given major emphasis.

In the second place, there are socio-historical circumstances which, no matter what the objective situation may be, make a dichotomous view of society agreeable to certain classes insofar as it can help promote their interests or contribute to the development of a strong sense of identity and historical mission. The particular antagonists with whom they are locked in combat seem to them to dominate society generally. For the serf, society is composed above all of serfs and lords; for the industrial worker, it is composed of workers and capitalists. The existence of other strata may be known, but they play no central part in the consciousness.

From the point of view of the privileged classes, dichotomous images are likely to be prominent when, as in an estate system, the contrast between the elite and the rest of the society appears so sharp that further differentiation between the underlying population can be safely ignored.

Finally, during periods of intensified class conflict, it might be to the advantage of rising classes to overlook intermediary positions and to focus attention on one basic cleavage. In 1789, all the divisions within the Third Estate were temporarily pushed into the background of the consciousness of its proponents. This cemented all those who fought against the aristocracy. A few years later, François Émile Babeuf divided the population of France into 24 million real producers and one million exploiters (*Pages choisies de Babeuf*, Paris, 1935)—totally neglecting those who were in intermediate positions. And Henri de Saint-Simon used the dichotomous division between the industrial class and the idle class for similar ideological purposes (Manuel, 1956). Similar dichotomous notions are frequent in the nineteenth-century socialist movement from Chartism (1830–48) to Louis Blanqui and Ferdinand Lassalle.

Tripartite Divisions. Despite the continued appeal of dichotomous conceptualizations of class structure, one has always had to contend with rival notions, viz., tripartite divisions or more complicated systems of multiple divisions and gradations.

Perhaps the best known of all trichotomous conceptualizations of class structure is the one Aristotle described in his *Politics* (Book IV, Ch. XI, 1295b): "In every city the people are divided into three sorts; the very rich, the very poor, and those who are between them." We encounter similar conceptualizations in the Church's interpretation of medieval society as divided into three basic estates, those who pray, those who defend the country, and those who toil. And in France, the image of Three Estates (clergy, nobility, commoners) dominated social perception till the eighteenth century, even though by that time what had once been conceived as distinctions along functional lines had already become overt distinctions of privilege. Finally,

443

as modern capitalistic society replaced the medieval and post-medieval hierarchy, Adam Smith, in his *Inquiry into the Nature and Causes of the Wealth of Nations* (1776), introduced a new trichotomous scheme referring to economic functions. The old trichotomy of priests, knights, and commoners became one of proprietors of land, proprietors of stock, and laborers. Society was now divided into those who lived by the rent of land, those who lived by profits, and those whose income was the wage of labor.

Thinking in terms of intermediary classes instead of dichotomies may have various consequences for the overall conceptualization of a particular thinker. There are at least two extreme positions in this respect, one of which is associated with Aristotle, the other with Marx. For the former, the middle class is—or rather should be—the basic class, with the rich and the poor simply deviations from the mean. "The best political community is formed by citizens of the middle class, and . . . those states are likely to be well-administered in which the middle class is large, and stronger if possible than both the other classes, or at any rate than either singly (*Politics*, 1295b; trans. B. Jowett, New York [1943], p. 191). For Marx, in contrast, and though he also at times used the trichotomous scheme of the political economists, the two fundamentally opposed classes are the basic classes; the middle class is less enduring and less stable. It typically is marginal in the sense that it allegedly will join with one or the other of the major classes when class conflicts are "inevitably" sharpened. For Marx, a dichotomous scheme is still dominant, and the trichotomous division is seen as a deviation which is "by its very nature" only temporary. The radical thinker tends to be drawn toward dichotomies even when he recognizes that reality does not correspond to this image. Conservative or liberal thinkers, however, when they think in trichotomies, tend to stress the virtues of middle strata as most conducive to the pursuit of moderate policies.

Multiple Divisions and Gradations. At the beginning of the capitalist era Alexander Hamilton still proposed a simple dichotomous model of class divisions: "All communities divide themselves into the few and the many. The first are rich and well-born and the other the mass of the people who seldom judge or determine right" (Speech [June 18, 1787], *Papers*, ed. H. C. Syrett and J. E. Cooke, 15 vols., New York [1961–68], IV, 185–200). But given the complicated and multifaceted class relations in nineteenth-century America as well as in Europe, and, in addition, the need to bring definitions of class relations into line with ideological justifications of the prevailing state of affairs, such dichotomous notions gave way to more complicated schemes among those whose social perceptions dominated the scene.

Among the types of perceptions of class relations that emerged in the nineteenth century—though we can find approximations much earlier—we may distinguish, following Stanislaw Ossowski (1963), between schemes of simple and schemes of synthetic gradations. In both cases, instead of viewing the class structure in terms of the fixed properties of two or more classes, the relation of higher and lower classes is based on the grading of some objectively measurable characteristics. In the case of simple gradation, concern is most commonly focused on gradations of wealth or income. In this view, relative wealth or income determines class membership, and assigns respective class positions in the vertical order. In contrast, ideas about synthetic gradations reject a simple gradation of classes in terms of economic criteria and combine these with the factors of education, occupation, social standing, and the like.

When diverse criteria are being used in the assignment of class positions, relatively low rank in one dimension, say income, may be compensated by relatively high rank in another, say education. Such ranking systems hence seem to have certain compensatory and consolatory functions, which cannot be performed by systems relying entirely on ranking in the economic order. When lack of education or inferior birth can be offset by economic standing, as among the "nouveaux riches," or when inadequate income can be compensated for by relatively high social status, as in the case, at least until recently, of college teachers, such arrangements or perceptions may help combat alienative tendencies in various sectors of society.

In similar ways, stratifying society into six or more layers may have additional compensatory functions for the people involved in all but the very lowest rank. The finer the gradations and the larger the number of dimensions used for establishing class position, the greater, it would seem, the conservative or stabilizing potential of stratification schemes.

However, it would be a mistake to explain the more complicated class schemes that have come to be used in the modern social sciences, as well as in popular consciousness, by ideological reasons alone. Modern industrial society has created so complicated a division of labor and so differentiated and fluid a status system that any simple classificatory scheme such as prevailed till the eighteenth century could no longer be adequate. Or, to put the matter differently, not even in so highly capitalist a society as that of the United States are economic criteria likely to be the only ones used in assigning people relative standing in society.

Max Weber's recognition that exclusive emphasis on economic factors as determinants of social class was insufficient to do justice to complex systems of stratification accounts perhaps for his current popularity among social scientists concerned with class analysis. Weber made distinctions between a variety of sources of hierarchical differentiation. Among the most important he selected class, status, and power. He reserved the term "class" to designate economic differentiations. A class, in his usage, was composed of people who shared common life chances or a similar situation in the market. Status, Weber's second major dimension of stratification, refers to the honor or prestige and hence the amount of deference accorded to individuals or positions. Status systems are linked to specific life styles and manners of living. Although Weber was aware that class and status positions in a given society are likely to be highly correlated, he performed the distinct service of highlighting those situations in which these correlations are less than perfect. For example, groups with higher status will be motivated to support manners and values that serve to perpetuate that status, no matter whether a particular holder of the status ranks high in an economic class hierarchy. In aristocratic or semi-aristocratic circles people will contend that their superior life styles entitle them to deference, regardless of their economic attainments. Thus, even in capitalist systems, money-making may be considered vulgar by those in superior status positions, and Boston Brahmins, just as East Elbian Junkers, may claim the rewards of high status, such as power, even though their rank in a purely economic hierarchy may be relatively low.

Just as at the dawn of the bourgeois era, merchants were wont to marry their daughters to the scions of aristocratic families, in effect exchanging the perquisites of class position for superior status, so in the contemporary world the "nouveaux riches" may, through marriage, education, philanthropy, or other means, attempt to acquire a status which is otherwise unobtainable.

Weber's third major dimension of stratification, power, was defined by him as the ability of a man or a group to impose its will on others even, if necessary, against their opposition. Power may flow from the possession of resources, be they economic or political. High position in both the status and the class system may confer power, as may commanding positions in religious, political, or trade union organizations. Power, then, is likely to be highly correlated with high positions in the other two dimensions, yet may also vary independently from them. In particular, as against the Marxist contention that the only basic source of power is the ownership of means of production, Weber argued that in the modern world commanding positions in a variety of administrative and bureaucratic hierarchies may confer social power on men whose purely economic power is minimal and who have but little social honor (Weber, 1946).

Since Weber's time, his list of three basic dimensions in the assignment of rank in modern societies has been further enlarged, and, depending on the interests and concerns of the investigators, increasing attention has been given to such factors as occupational prestige, education, kinship, ethnic group position, and the like. Though these dimensions of stratification tend to be highly interdependent, they nevertheless may vary independently from one another.

The picture that emerges from this simplified sketch of contemporary theory of stratification suggests a complexity of the class system that contrasts sharply with the stark simplicity of some of the earlier conceptualizations. Although there may be ideological reasons for the adoption of contemporary views, the major reason for their prevalence seems to lie in the fact that, because of their fluidity, contemporary class systems no longer lend themselves to the relatively simple categorizations that were more or less adequate for understanding earlier class structures. Ernest Hemingway was clearly wrong when, in answering Scott Fitzgerald's phrase, "The rich are truly different," he said: "Yes, they have more money." Whether in the world of the robber barons or in that of *The Great Gatsby*, in the world of Henry James or of Theodore Dreiser, no man has been simply assessed on the scale of wealth and income exclusively. Ossowski's synthetic gradations are hence likely to remain the most common way of conceptualizing the complex class relations of contemporary capitalist and postcapitalist societies.

Class Differentiation on the Basis of Social Functions. In addition to, and often accompanying, scalar conceptualizations of social class, functional conceptualizations are discernible from antiquity to the present day. Society is differentiated into a number of classes that fulfill different functions in the division of labor, and this distinctiveness of function determines the relations between these classes. The various classes generally are seen as complementary to one other and mutually interdependent. Some of these functional theories of stratification stress primarily the contribution this interdependence makes to the total society; others, particularly Marxian theory, focus on incompatibility of interests, antagonism, and conflict.

The functional conceptualization was self-consciously elaborated by Saint Thomas Aquinas, John of Salisbury, and other medieval Church spokesmen. They did not deny that society was full of inequalities; the equality that did exist was purely religious. These inequalities, however, as they appear in the relation of master to servant and in the differences in property or social standing, are legitimized by an ethic of "calling." It is the duty of every man to remain within his own class, and to serve others gladly. The teaching of

Saint Paul about remaining "in the calling to which one has been called" (II Corinthians 7:20) was now developed into a rational justification of inequality. The division of labor is the result of inequality in human endowment and capacities. It behooves man to accept the inequalities appointed by God, stay in his own order, and do his own work. Society is seen as an organic whole to which the various vocational orders make their peculiar contribution.

Luther's conception of the "calling" is essentially similar. To him, just as to Aquinas, men as they are variously placed within the social structure perform differing and yet complementary functions. One ought to live within his own class, according to the social standards of that class, and efforts at individual improvement of one's style of life or social position cannot be condoned. Obedient service in the calling is the first duty of the Christian.

One difficulty with these and similar functional conceptualizations arises from the fact that, as a contemporary sociologist, Ralf Dahrendorf has stated, "The notion of differentiation does not in itself imply any distinctions of rank or value among the differentiated elements" (Dahrendorf, p. 162). That is, an additional act of evaluation seems to be necessary if we are to move analytically from differentiations that are rooted in the division of labor to a rank order in a system of social stratification. Medieval social theory tends to obviate the difficulty by explicitly or implicitly accepting the rank order as it exists within medieval estate society. As Ernst Troeltsch puts it, "This actual situation, through its incorporation into the religious and organic theory as 'vocation,' is idealized and rationalized" (Troeltsch, I, 295). In the case of Lutheranism, likewise, and though there appear contradictory tendencies within it, by accepting the existing rank order it translated the ideal of a "cosmos of callings" into a conception of a desirable social hierarchy. Certain social theorists, more particularly Charles Fourier, deploring the lack of functional adjustment in their age, projected utopian images of a future society in which the specific contributions of differently constituted individuals would all blend harmoniously into an integrated whole.

The problem of how to move from the recognition of differing functional contributions of social classes to the establishment of a scalar hierarchy still besets modern sociological theory. It led functional theorists, such as W. E. Moore and K. Davis (see Bibliography), to claim that certain contributions are being judged more essential or "functionally important" for a society than others, and therefore need the rewards of high rank. They also claimed that, given the different degrees of complexity of different social tasks, those performing the more complex tasks require longer and more intensive preparations, and therefore need to receive greater rewards of power and wealth or income. As in the case of their medieval forebears, the suspicion is strong that they in fact but rationalize a given distribution of power and privilege. Moreover, when these theorists are asked how they establish which functions are more important than others, they tend to reply tautologically by pointing to those that receive greater rewards.

Moving from the facts of differentiation to the realities of hierarchy has been less serious a problem for the classical economists ever since Adam Smith enunciated his functional classification: proprietors of land, proprietors of stock, and laborers. Here tautological reasoning is avoided. Though these economists agreed that all three classes made functionally indispensable contributions to the well-being, stability, and development of the whole, they were also at one in according preeminence to the proprietors of stock, the new capitalists, who represented the dynamic principle of the new industrial order and the progress it promised.

Though by no means oblivious to conflicts of interests between various classes, the classical economists nevertheless tended to assume a fundamental identity of interests common to all classes. It is the rejection of this postulate which lies at the basis of Karl Marx's theory of stratification.

The Marxian Scheme. The rejection of all models of harmonious society, and their replacement by a conceptualization that lays utmost stress on the fundamental conflict of interests between classes is, of course, at the very core of the Marxian conception. According to Marx, ever since human society emerged from its primitive and relatively undifferentiated state, it remained fundamentally divided between classes whose interests are opposed and who clash in the pursuit of these interests; the whole of previous social history is a history of class struggle. With this overriding emphasis as a point of departure, Marx used a variety of class conceptualizations according to the context in which he wrote and the problem he dealt with.

Marx most frequently saw economic interests as being rooted in differing positions in the process of production. Here he integrated the categories of the classical economists with his basic concept of class conflict and viewed the relations between the classes of landowners, industrial capitalists, and wage earners as antagonistic rather than harmonious. Where the classical economists had seen this tripartite division as eternally given in the natural order of things, Marx, in tune with his relativizing historicism, saw such relations as typical only for specific historical periods, as a historically transient state of affairs. Though all previous historical periods were marked by class struggles, these struggles differed according to historical stages of production. In contradistinction to his radical predecessors, who had tended to see history as a monotonous succession of struggles between rich and poor, or between the powerless and the powerful, Marx maintained that, though class struggles had indeed marked all history, the contenders in the battle had changed over time. Though there might have been some similarity between the journeymen of the late Middle Ages, who waged their battles against guildmasters, and modern industrial workers, journeymen were yet in a functionally different situation from modern proletarians struggling with modern factory owners.

Although Marx used a functional analysis of classes in terms of position in the economic process, which was ultimately derived from the classical economists, he also wrote about class in a variety of contexts which show that this was by no means the only connotation of the concept. In particular, and in tune with the other great intellectual tradition to which he was indebted, that of German idealism, Marx used a notion of class in which class consciousness or class awareness became central. Here economic or social factors were supplemented by social-psychological ones. Though an aggregate of people, he argued, may all occupy similar positions in the process of production and hence have objectively similar life chances, they become a class as a self-conscious and history-making body only if they become aware of the similarity of their interests. An objective economic class, a *Klasse an sich* ("class in itself"), becomes a *Klasse für sich* ("class for itself") only if its members, through a series of conflicts with opposing classes, have acquired an awareness of the communality of their interests. And only such self-conscious classes can be said to be capable of changing the course of history; classes lacking such psychological bonds between their members remain impotent. (Marx expected that in time deprived classes would necessarily acquire such consciousness; *Communist Manifesto*, 1848, and passim.)

Most of the time Marx was drawn to a dramaturgical vision of society, a dichotomous conception in which two major classes preempted the center of the scene, even though an intermediary middle class might at times appear on the stage—only to be ground down by powerful grindstones: the two major class antagonists. Yet we encounter also different types of schemes. Sometimes, as in the final, uncompleted chapter of *Das Kapital* (1867–95) which represents his most self-conscious effort to present a theory of stratification, Marx adopted the trichotomous functional scheme of Adam Smith, e.g.: "the owners merely of labor-power, owners of capital, and landowners, whose respective sources of income are wages, profit, and ground-rent . . ." (*Das Kapital*, Vol. III, last chapter). Sometimes, more particularly in his historical writings, he adopted a multidimensional scheme, as when in his *Class Struggles in France* (1850) he distinguished between the class interests of the financial and those of the industrial bourgeoisie; or when in *The Eighteenth Brumaire* (1852) he talked about the class interests which divide the owners of capital and the owners of land. In addition, the rural population is sometimes seen as a specific class in Marx's historical writings, as is the *Lumpenproletariat* ("dregs of society"), so that we obtain an image of society, which, far from the usual dichotomic or trichotomic image, is differentiated into several strata with multiple interests. When Marx wrote as a propagandist, he used the stark imagery of a simple polarity of interests between two basic classes. When he wrote as a social analyst or historian, dichotomous concepts appeared inadequate and he used a more complex scheme which, though less serviceable as a means of energizing social consciousness, proved more in tune with actual complexities. The class schemes he used depended on the direction of his interests.

There are still other interpretations of class phenomena in the work of Marx. Although the major emphasis is on the separation between those who own the means of production and those who, owning no means of production, must sell their labor power, attention is sometimes focused on the opposition of those who work and those who do not, or of those who employ hired labor and those who do not. In the first case, a wealthy farmer who employs a few hired hands is not reckoned among capitalists; in the second, he is. Enough has been said to document the fact that the Marxian scheme of class analysis is by no means as uncomplicated or unitary as both proponents and adversaries of his theories have often made it appear.

Yet all such variations in Marx's scheme must not obscure the major difference between this and other theories of stratification. As distinct from all social theories that see society as a layer cake in which strata are simply superimposed upon one another, classes in Marx's view are essentially conflict groups. They gain their identity and the realization of the communality of their interests in confrontations and clashes with other, antagonistic, classes. Ultimately, then, classes are always power phenomena. The class struggle is a struggle for power between rulers and ruled, between oppressed and oppressing classes. Class relations, by their very nature, are asymmetrical relations in which those above and those below, exploiters and exploited, contend with each other for dominance. Man will truly come into his own, Marx contended, only when all class struggles which have so far characterized human history will culminate in a classless society in which the strife of classes will be replaced by an ultimate harmony of cooperatively producing men no longer divided by divergent interests.

The Fact and the Scandal of Inequality. Defenders of the status quo, when they did not have recourse to "functional" justifications, have most frequently used two strategies in order to cushion the impact of inequality on the underlying population. They have either referred to the transitoriness of human life and the promised righting of earthly imbalances in privileges and rewards in the afterlife; or they have attempted to show that social inequalities were but a result of natural differences in biological endowment.

Echoing, as he so often does, previous Christian conceptualizations in secular form, Diderot wrote in the article "Société" in the *Encyclopédie*, "There is no more inequality between the different stations in life than there is among the different characters in a comedy: the end of the play finds all players once again in the same position, and the brief period for which their play lasted did not and could not convince any two of them that one was really below the other." Yet without promise for rewards in the hereafter, such stress on the unimportance of class distinctions, *sub specie eternitatis*, was not very likely to command assent in the modern age.

A stronger impact and social efficacy was provided by theories of differences in natural endowment from the days of the ancient Greeks to Vilfredo Pareto and the prophets of the modern eugenics movement, such as Francis Galton and Karl Pearson, as well as their utopian forerunner Thomas Campanella.

Ever since the eighteenth century, opponents of the status quo have rejected the otherworldly justification of human inequality; their arguments are so well-known that they need not detain us here. As to the argument from biological inequality, social reformers, like the French disciples of Locke (Helvétius and Condillac), either contended that all men were biologically similar at birth, or, like Rousseau, argued for a sharp distinction between two kinds of inequality, natural and moral: "I perceive two kinds of inequality among men: one I call natural or physical . . . ; the other might be called moral or political" (Rousseau, *Second Discourse*). Denying that there were any necessary correlations between the two, he questioned "whether rulers are necessarily worth more than the ruled, and whether strength of body and mind, wisdom and virtue are always found in the same individuals, and found, moreover, in direct relation to their power and wealth . . ." (*Discours sur l'origine de l'inégalité;*

in *Contrat social*, new ed., Garnier, Paris, n.d., p. 39).

Rousseau posits the moral equality of men in the state of nature and contends that only upon leaving that state, through the emergence of private property, did class distinctions emerge in civil society. Not physical inequalities, such as those based on differences in health or bodily strength; only political inequalities were morally and socially relevant.

The stress on private property rather than human nature as the root of inequality remains central in the pertinent discussions from Rousseau to Marx. Thinkers in this general tradition do not differ so much in their views regarding the origin of class differences, which all of them seek in historical development rather than in biological or theological factors, but, rather, in their opinions as to their permanency. Conservatives such as Lorenz von Stein and liberals such as the British utilitarian political economists consider them an ineradicable feature of modern societies. In contrast, socialists and radicals envisage a future society, if only as a kind of asymptotic goal, in which distinctions of class and rank are abolished. Radical and socialist theories look upon the present order as merely transient and emphasize a dialectical tension between a provisional state of affairs and an ultimate classless future.

Equality of Opportunity. There is yet another position which needs detain us—if only because it has become a vital component of the common consciousness of modern America, and, though to variant degrees, of all industrial societies: the notion of equal opportunity within societies of unequals. This notion, though discernible among the forerunners of Saint-Simon, has been fully articulated by the master and his disciples. Saint-Simon retained what had been, despite Rousseau and radicals such as Morelly, the major eighteenth-century view that the maintenance of civilization required the preservation of inequality in wealth and status. But in contrast to his eighteenth-century ancestors who had argued that the inequalities were necessary to force men, indolent as they were by nature, to submit to the necessity of work and industry, he elaborated a distinctive defense of inequality: since men are unequal in their capacities a society is needed where each can function according to his ability.

In tune with the émigré traditionalists and such representatives of a new physiology and psychology as M. F. X. Bichat and P. J. G. Cabanis, Saint-Simon opposed the egalitarian tendencies of the disciples of Locke and stressed the existence of natural inequalities among men. The good society, he argued, was indeed, as the *philosophes* had said, a society congruent with what is natural in man—but what was natural was inequality rather than equality. The ideal society was seen as a harmonious association between men who were fundamentally different in their essential natures and capacities. Men fall essentially into three types: those with rational scientific capacities who will be the leaders and guides of society; those with primarily motor capacities apt mostly for manual labor; and those with sensory capacities who would be artistic and religious performers. Each man would express his own deeper nature and contribute to society in terms of his natural endowment.

Similar ideas about innate differences have, of course, been expressed by writers ever since Plato and Aristotle. What is new, however, is Saint-Simon's emphasis on the need to organize society in such a way as to "afford all members of society the greatest possible opportunity for the development of their faculties" (*Notice historique,* in *Oeuvres de Saint-Simon et d'Enfantin,* 47 vols., Paris [1865–76], I, 122). Equality of opportunity rather than equality of condition, equality at the point of departure in a man's adult life cycle rather than equality of status, is the hallmark of Saint-Simon's doctrine. This idea has become a major emphasis in Western social and popular thought. Whether in British liberal or Fabian thought of the nineteenth or early twentieth centuries, in Pareto's notion of the circulation of the elite, in similar conceptualizations by Mosca, or in contemporary sociological theories such as those of S. M. Lipset, the stress at the point of departure on openness of opportunity and equality has been pervasive. In America, in particular, equality of opportunity, whether as a description of what allegedly exists or as an ideal, has become part of an expected ideology which permits a reconciliation between ideals of individualistic achievement—in the tradition of the Protestant Ethic—and the tradition of political equalitarianism. Although men receive unequal rewards or goods and power, so it is argued, they have nothing to complain when, given equal opportunities, their differential positions express only their differential capacities.

In the mid-twentieth century all industrial societies continue to be class societies with sharp differentiations between top and bottom strata and a very large middle-class bulge, in which people are assigned to their class positions largely, though by no means wholly, in terms of imputed merit and achievement. Ascribed characteristics, such as those that come with birth and kinship, have receded in importance while achieved characteristics have gained ascendancy. Although Saint-Simon's ideal of a totally open society has not been attained, and although certain social strata, especially among American Negroes and some other minorities, still suffer from severe social disabilities, con-

temporary industrial societies both East and West have come so near the image of their desire that there must be great rejoicing in heaven among Saint-Simon and his disciples.

Whether the present stress on "meritocracy," to use Michael Young's telling phrase (1959, passim), might in due course be followed by a counter-tendency emphasizing a reduction or elimination of factual differences in power and reward, only the future can tell.

BIBLIOGRAPHY

Stanislaw Ossowski's seminal work, *Class Structure in the Social Consciousness* (New York, 1963) is a basic source, especially for the first part of this article. Other books covering aspects of the subject: Goetz A. Briefs, *The Proletariat* (New York, 1937); Ernst Troeltsch, *The Social Teachings of the Christian Churches,* 2 vols. (London, 1931); Ralf Dahrendorf, *Essays in the Theory of Society* (Stanford, 1969), esp. Chs. 6 and 7; Raymond Williams, *Culture and Society* (New York, 1963); Frank E. Manuel, *The New World of Henri Saint-Simon* (Cambridge, Mass., 1956); Michael Young, *The Rise of the Meritocracy* (New York, 1959); Hans Gerth and C. Wright Mills, trans. and eds., *From Max Weber: Essays in Sociology* (New York, 1946); Reinhard Bendix and Seymour M. Lipset, eds., *Class, Status and Power,* 2nd rev. ed. (New York, 1966). Cf. also K. Davis and W. E. Moore, "Some Principles of Stratification," *American Sociological Review,* **10,** 2 (1945); Melvin Tumin, "Some Principles of Stratification: A Critical Analysis," *American Sociological Review,* **18,** 4 (1953), and "On Inequality," *American Sociological Review,* **28,** 1 (1963). Also useful are the entries under "Stratification, Social" by Bernard Barber and Seymour M. Lipset, *International Encyclopedia of the Social Sciences* (New York, 1968), Vol. 15.

LEWIS A. COSER

[See also Economic History; Education; Equality; Hierarchy; **Ideology; Marxism;** Property; **Socialism;** Utopia.]

CLASSICISM IN LITERATURE

THE TERM "classicism" is comparatively new, particularly in English. Thomas Carlyle used it in 1831 for the first time, complacently and prematurely reflecting that "we are troubled with no controversies on Romanticism and Classicism," in his "Essay on Schiller" (*Critical and Miscellaneous Essays,* Centenary Edition [1899], II, 172). John Stuart Mill, in 1837, explained that the "insurrection against the old traditions of classicism was called romanticism" in France ("Armand Carrel," *Dissertations and Discussions* [1867], I, 233). Both these early uses refer to the Continental debate. But even there the term cannot be traced back very far. It seems to occur first in Italy, in 1818, during the discussion waged in Milan. Ermes Visconti uses *classicismo* frequently in a series of articles, "Idee elementari sulla poesia romantica" in the famous "blue sheet," *Il Conciliatore*. (See *Discussioni e polemiche sul romanticismo*, ed. E. Bellorini, Bari [1943], I, 436ff.) Stendhal picked up the term in Milan: he read and paraphrased Visconti whom he also knew personally, and then gave in *Racine et Shakespeare* (1823) the famous facetious definitions of classicism and romanticism. "Classicism is the literature which gave the greatest possible pleasure to our great grandfathers," while romanticism is the literature which gives us pleasure now.

But neither in France nor in England was the term widely used in the nineteenth century. In England rival forms which have since dropped out of use, occur occasionally. "Classicalism" appears, e.g., in Elizabeth Barrett (1839), in John Ruskin (1846), and in Matthew Arnold (1857). The alternate form "classicality" was used by Ruskin when he referred to the "vile classicality of Canova" (*Modern Painters,* Vol. I). In the atmosphere of the later nineteenth century generally hostile to the eighteenth century, the term "pseudo-classicism" emerged. James R. Lowell, in his essay on Pope (1871) speaks of a "pseudo-classicism, the classicism of red heels and periwigs" (*Literary Essays,* Boston [1891], IV, 8). In 1885 the word appeared for the first time on the title page of an American book. Thomas Sergeant Perry's *From Opitz to Lessing: A Study of Pseudo-classicism in Literature.* The neutral term "neo-classicism" emerges also toward the end of the nineteenth century and is still used widely to refer to the period of Dryden and Pope. But in that era "classicism" was even more successful. It occurs in Matthew Arnold's essay on Heine (1863). Walter Pater, in his essay on romanticism (1876), quotes the definition of Stendhal and literary historians increasingly refer to the age which used to be called "Augustan" as the "age of classicism." Louis Cazamian's *Histoire de la littérature anglaise* (1925) called a section "Classicism (1702–1740)" and his book was, in English translation, the standard English literary history for many years. Handbooks now contain chapters "The Rise of Classicism," "The Disintegration of Classicism," etc.

Similarly, in France, the term *classicisme* was rarely used in the nineteenth century. It is called a "neologism" as late as 1863 in Littré's *Dictionnaire.* Sainte-Beuve and Taine do not use the term. It spread more widely about 1880: Émile Deschanel, in *Le Romantisme des classiques* (1882) uses the term and Ferdinand Brunetière, in his review of the book ("Classiques et romantiques," in *Études critiques sur*

l'histoire de la littérature française, Paris [1890], Vol. III) picks it up. In 1889 Georges Pellisier's *Le Mouvement littéraire aux XIX siècle* contained an introductory chapter "Le classicisme." In 1897 Louis Bertrand put the term on the title page of his book, *La Fin du classicisme et le retour à l'antiquité,* a study of the late eighteenth-century classical revival in France. But Gustave Lanson's standard *Histoire de la littérature française* (1894) still avoids the term in the text, though two chapter captions use it casually. Louis Bertrand later belonged to the group of conservative critics who early in the twentieth century launched the anti-romantic campaign which accused romanticism of all the evils brought about by the French Revolution and the anarchy of our time. Charles Maurras, the editor of the *Action française,* Pierre Lasserre, the author of a violently antiromantic *Le Romantisme français* (1907), and the Baron Seillière who wrote many books attacking the romantic disease, made *Classicisme* a new slogan in France where it became also a political and philosophical war cry. In England T. E. Hulme drew heavily on the doctrines of the new French classicism: his paper "Romanticism and Classicism" (1913, published in *Speculations,* 1924) provided the most often quoted statement of the new classicism in England. T. S. Eliot proclaimed his classicism in the Preface to *For Lancelot Andrewes* (1928).

In Germany around 1800 the term "Romantik" became the battle cry of a whole group of writers. But the word "Klassik" occurs only in then unpublished notes of Friedrich Schlegel. In 1797 he jotted down the puzzling statements; *Absolute Classik also annihilirt sich selbst* ("absolute classicism thus annihilates itself") and *Alle Bildung ist Classik Abstraction* ("Every structure is classic abstraction") (*Philosophische Lehrjahre,* ed. E. Behler, Munich [1963], I, 23). "Klassizismus" seems not to be used at all until Hermann Hettner in his *Literaturgeschichte des achtzehnten Jahrhunderts* (6 vols., 1856–57) used it in referring to French classicism. In Wilhelm Scherer's standard *Geschichte der deutschen Literatur* (1883) the term occurs only in the Table of Contents. But about that time "Klassizismus" in Germany was slowly replaced by the term "Klassik." It seems to have been invented by Otto Harnack around 1887: in his *Goethe in der Epoche seiner Vollendung* (1887) he uses it first in quotation marks. He felt it to be an innovation as he explained in the preface to a later book, *Der deutsche Klassizismus im Zeitalter Goethes* (1906): "I could not this time avoid the unpleasant expressions 'Classicism' and 'classicist,' for which I usually substitute 'Klassik' and 'klassisch,' because usage has given the word 'klassisch' a special narrow meaning in relation to German poetry." Harnack draws a distinction between "Klassizismus," the imitation of antiquity, and "Klassik," a term designating the works of Goethe and Schiller. The new term replaced the older early in the twentieth century: Friedrich Gundolf, the most prominent literary historian of the circle around Stefan George, concluded his book, *Shakespeare und der deutsche Geist* (1911) with a chapter "Klassik und Romantik." In 1922 Fritz Strich attempted to apply the principles of Wölfflin's art history and his contrast between Renaissance and baroque to the conflict between classicism and romanticism in Germany in his *Deutsche Klassik und Romantik: oder Vollendung und Unendlichkeit.* The triumph of the new term was soon complete.

The reasons for its success are obvious. Classicism, in a sense resembling that of French classicism, is not a very appropriate term for most of the writings of Goethe and Schiller if one excepts the stages in their careers when they consciously aimed at the imitation of the ancients. The term "Klassik" resumes the old meaning of standard or model, while the association with the ancients almost ceases to be felt. It has become a term which pries the German classics loose from international classicism and yet resists the Western tendency to treat Goethe and Schiller as romantics.

The noun "classicism" and its variants are, of course, derivatives of the adjective "classical." *Classicus* first occurs in Aulus Gellius, a Roman author of the second century A.D. who in his miscellany *Noctes Atticae* (19, 8, 15) refers to *classicus scriptor, non proletarius,* applying a term of the Roman taxation classes to the ranking of writers. *Classicus* means there "first-class," "excellent," "superior." The term seems not to have been used in the Middle Ages but it reappears in the Renaissance in Latin and soon in the vernaculars.

The first recorded occurrence in French, in Thomas Sebillet's *L'art poétique* (1548) refers, surprisingly, to *les bons et classiques poètes français comme sont entre les vieux Alain Chartier et Jean Meun* (Paris [1910], Ch. II, p. 26). The names of these two medieval poets show that the word had then no association with classical antiquity and meant simply "standard" or "excellent." It remains to be found how the term became soon to be identified with the ancients, as in the phrase "classical antiquity." "Classical" came to mean Roman and Greek and still implied, for obvious reasons, superiority, authority, and even perfection.

"Classical" became also associated with the classroom, with the texts taught in schools, as the ancients were then the only secular authors studied and they were studied as models of excellence, both in content and form. The meaning "classical" and "classics," restricted in the sixteenth and seventeenth centuries to the ancients, was later extended to the vernacular literatures. In England George Sewell, in his introduc-

tion to Shakespeare's *Poems* (a part of Pope's *Shakespeare,* 1725) asked for careful editions of English authors which "we in justice owe to our own great writers, both in Prose, and Poetry. They are in some degrees our Classics." Sewell thought of Shakespeare as deserving and getting such treatment. Pope, in 1737, in the First Epistle of the Second Book of his *Imitations of Horace* said that "who lasts a century can have no flaw,/I hold that Wit a Classik, good in law."

The same expansion of the meaning occurred also in France, though surprisingly later than in England. Pierre-Joseph Thoulier D'Olivet, in his *Histoire de l'Académie* (1729) complains that "Italy had classical authors and we as yet have none" (ed. Livet, Paris [1858], II, 47). Years later Voltaire in a letter to the same abbé D'Olivet, proposed to edit the "classical authors" of the French, reserving Corneille for himself. Voltaire's own *Siècle de Louis XIV* (1751) put that age next to other golden ages: that of Leo X, of Augustus, and of Alexander. Characteristically, the age of Pericles is missing from the list. In all these discussions the implication of "classicity" as mode and standard is dominant. The remoter model behind the great modern writer in antiquity is assumed as a matter of course, but no more so than when Dante is considered a "classic" in Italy or when Spaniards speak of their Golden Age. The matter of style did not enter.

The decisive event for the development of the concept of "classicism" was the great romantic-classical debate waged in Germany by the brothers Schlegel. The transformation of the meaning of the word "classical" from a term of value to a term for a stylistic trend, type, or period in which differences of quality are allowed to exist, was the crucial turning point. The historistic revolution brought about an awareness of the existence, side by side, of at least two literary traditions. The Schlegelian dichotomy was first expounded in France by Madame de Staël in *De l'Allemagne* (1814) but a few months before the delayed publication of the book August Wilhelm Schlegel's *Vorlesungen über dramatische Kunst und Literatur* appeared in a translation by her cousin, Madame Necker de Saussure. In her Preface (1813) Madame Necker commented perceptively: "In Mr. Schlegel's work the epithet 'classical' is a simple designation of a genre, independent of the degree of perfection with which the genre is treated." Madame de Staël's book excited violent polemics in France. What had been a local German debate became a European one. The terms "classical" and "romantic" soon were discussed in every country of Europe and of the Americas.

The history of the term reflects the history of its meaning: at first, in the seventeenth and eighteenth centuries, a term for excellence, particularly in the

451

writings of antiquity, it changed under the impact of the romantic and historistic revolution, to a term for a style challenging opposed or parallel styles: romantic, realist, modern, etc. The exact value put on classicism will necessarily vary with the context and the polemical attitude of the writer. Often "classicism" is used pejoratively to refer to academic, conventional art. In other situations it assumes again the old meaning of superior value, perfection, and excellence as in the French classicist critics of this century or in their English counterparts, T. E. Hulme and T. S. Eliot. In different countries different ages are labeled "classical": the meaning shifts then from excellence, prescriptive greatness with an implied relation to antiquity, or even a claim of rivalling or surpassing antiquity, to that of a neutral, objective designation of a past style of art. The situation differs greatly in the main countries of Europe.

Italians speak of "classicism" today mainly as applying to what is usually called the Italian Renaissance, or speak of *neoclassicismo* in the eighteenth century: e.g., in the tragedies of Alfieri. But there is in Italy no particular feeling that Italy had its classical age, though Dante is the great classic in the sense of excellence. A series such as *Classici Italiani* includes simply writers of all epochs and styles of any eminence.

In France, the seventeenth century is considered the classical age: Corneille, Racine, Molière, Pascal, La Fontaine are the classics. Early in the nineteenth century beginning particularly with Chateaubriand, the French seventeenth century was exalted as the classical age in sharp contrast to the eighteenth century which to a modern literary historian may appear stylistically and in critical theory largely a direct continuation of the seventeenth century. But in the early nineteenth century the two periods were contrasted for reasons which can be called political: the seventeenth century appealed to the conservative reaction, while the eighteenth-century literature bore the stigma of having prepared and even caused the French Revolution. Désiré Nisard was, in his *Histoire de la littérature française* (4 vols., 1844–61), the most influential propounder of this conception. The French spirit, he assumes, reached perfection in the seventeenth century, while everything since appears as decadence. He regards the French classical age as parallel to that of the great Augustus while—as he had argued in an earlier book, *Études des mœurs et de critique sur les poètes latins de la décadence* (2 vols., 1834)—the age of Silver Latin corresponds to the French nineteenth century.

With the triumphs on the stage of the actress Rachel in seventeenth-century tragedies, and the great success of François Ponsard's tragedy *Lucrèce* in 1843, something like a comeback of classicism seemed assured.

Ponsard rather coyly pretended hardly to remember that one used to distinguish between "Classics and romantics, or people who were called something like that." But nothing came of this revival. The new enthusiasts for classical antiquity preferred to speak of the "pagan school" or named their style *néo-grec*. It was rather a new Hellenism which saw itself as very different from the tradition of French classicism. Sainte-Beuve's famous essay "Qu'est-ce qu'un classique?" (1850) must be seen in this context. While insisting on the Greco-Latin tradition Sainte-Beuve aims at enlarging the concept. He recognizes the existence of something transcending the French tradition: Homer, Dante, and Shakespeare are also classics, though they do not conform to the demands of what we would call French classicism. This kind of classicism, with its rules, Sainte-Beuve knows, is definitely a thing of the past. Still, he pleads, we must preserve the notion and the cult of the classics and at the same time widen it and make it more generous (*Causeries du Lundi*, Vol. III).

In England, the period generally referred to today as the Age of Classicism, has no comparable standing, because, in the later view, the age of Dryden and Pope was surpassed by the Elizabethan age and particularly by Shakespeare and Milton. The English classicists did not call themselves by that name. They spoke of the imitation of the ancients or the observance of the rules. Under the impact of the romantic movement their reputation declined early in the nineteenth century and they were looked upon as belonging to a bygone age, which was called variously the Augustan Age, the Age of Pope, the Age of Queen Anne, but not the Classical Age. Macaulay, in 1820, spoke of "the Critical School of Poetry"; others referred to it as "the French School," a disparaging term, as it implied that the English poets were derivative from France. This was the assumption behind Pope's well-known lines (from the First Epistle of the Second Book in *Imitations of Horace* [1737]):

> We conquer'd France, but felt our
>   captive's charms:
> Her Arts victorious trimph'd o'er our Arms.

English classicism was, it was assumed, the direct result of the Restoration of 1660 when the Stuarts returned from exile in France. This dependence of the English classics on the French has been since disputed: violently, e.g., by Thomas De Quincey, in 1851, who denied that "either Dryden or Pope was even slightly influenced by French literature" (*Collected Writings*, ed. D. Masson [1896], XI, 61) and more sensibly by modern scholars who pointed out the native elements in English neo-classicism (e.g., P. S. Wood, in *Modern*

Philology, **24** [1926], 201–08) and traced neo-classical theory in England to Ben Jonson.

This pushes the matter back into the past of the history of criticism, to the sources common to both French and English literature of the neo-classical, i.e., Aristotelian and Horatian theory, which was formulated in Italy late in the fifteenth and early in the sixteenth century and codified in Julius Caesar Scaliger's *Poetics* (1561) and by the Dutch humanists, Vossius and Heinsius. Ben Jonson paraphrased and translated these writers in his *Discoveries* (see J. E. Spingarn, "The Sources of Jonson's *Discoveries*," in *Modern Philology*, **1** [1905]) and French seventeenth-century critics were clearly influenced both by the Italians and the Dutch. (See also Edith G. Kern, *The Influence of Heinsius and Vossius upon French Dramatic Theory*, Baltimore [1949].) The direct influence of Boileau on Dryden and Pope is undeniable as is the influence of Molière on Wycherley. There were many other contacts, which should not, however, obscure the substantial originality of the great poets, Dryden and Pope, and of the greatest prose writer of the time, Jonathan Swift.

Still, the English eighteenth-century writers could never after 1800 assume the position of authority which the French classics of the age of Louis XIV or Goethe and Schiller assumed in France or Germany. In recent decades, with the general antiromantic reaction, much has been done to rehabilitate the "classical" English literature, particularly in scholarly circles. T. S. Eliot exalted Dryden (see *Homage to John Dryden*, 1924). Pope has found many defenders and admirers: even his translation of Homer has been reinstated as a triumph of the art of adaptation. Dr. Johnson has always had a following, mainly as person and sage. Scholarly efforts to revive the eighteenth century, particularly in the United States, are often motivated by a nostalgia for a time which is assumed to have been still a coherent society with its proper hierarchy of classes, a tranquil refuge from the stresses of our time. But the figure of the misanthropic Dean belies this conception. T. S. Eliot is right in saying that "we have no classic age, and no classic poet in English," though he reminds us that "unless we are able to enjoy the work of Pope, we cannot arrive at a full understanding of English poetry" (*What is a Classic?*, London [1945]).

Germans still recognize six *Klassiker*: Klopstock, Lessing, Wieland, Herder, Goethe, and Schiller (Wilhelm Münch, "Über den Begriff des Klassikers" in *Zum deutschen Kultur- und Bildungsleben*, Berlin [1912]), an extremely heterogenous group of which Klopstock today would appear to belong to what is usually called sentimentalism; Lessing, in spite of his polemics against the practices of French tragedy, is a rationalistic classicist who worshipped Aristotle; Wieland is

rather a man of the Enlightenment whose art strikes us often as rococo; Herder would seem an irrationalistic preromantic. It is difficult to see how a writer like Herder can be called *klassisch*. In 1767 he exclaimed "O the cursed word 'Classisch'" (*Sämtliche Werke*, ed. B. Suphan, I, 412) and he attacked Goethe's and Schiller's turning toward classicism as a betrayal of his teachings.

Goethe and Schiller did not call themselves *Klassiker* and actually had an ambiguous attitude toward the whole enterprise of establishing a classical literature. Goethe, in 1795, in an article, "Literarischer Sansculottismus" argued that no German author considers himself *klassisch* and that he would not desire "the revolutions which could prepare classical works in Germany" (*Sämtliche Werke*, Jubiläumsausgabe, XXXVI, 141). The paper was written when the French Revolution had not yet run its course: Goethe feared the dangers of centralization and the abolition of the little German states, with one of which (the Duchy of Weimar) he was closely identified, since "classical" meant to him writing which would express the unity of a nation. Only after the Schlegels had excited the great debate did Goethe use the term more freely, either denying the distinction and clinging to the older meaning of excellence or taking sides against the romantics. A letter in 1804 reports that Goethe rejected the difference between the romantic and the classic because "everything excellent is *eo ipso* classic" (Letter by Heinrich Voss, Jr., to L. R. Abeken, 26 January 1804, in Goethe's *Gespräche*, ed. von Biedermann, Wiesbaden [1949], p. 163). But later in 1829 Goethe made the famous pronouncement to Eckermann: "I call the Classic the healthy, the Romantic the sickly" (April 12, 1829, *Gespräche mit Goethe*, Houben ed., Leipzig [1948], pp. 263–64). Goethe was then disturbed by what he considered the excesses of the German romantics such as E. T. A. Hoffmann and he disliked the new French *roman frénétique*, particularly Victor Hugo's *Notre Dame de Paris* (1831). He had lost sight of the much wider meaning of the contrast, though, in a conversation in 1830 with Eckermann, Goethe claimed wrongly that the Schlegels merely renamed Schiller's distinction between the naive and the sentimental (ibid., 21 March 1830, pp. 322–23). Goethe himself always professed to stand above the battle. In *Helena* and particularly in the figure of Euphorion Goethe aimed at "reconciliation of the two poetic forms" (ibid., 16 December 1829, p. 299). While Goethe viewed the debate rather detachedly, he was, during his lifetime, fast becoming the German *Klassiker* or at least one of the two great *Klassiker*.

Goethe, after the great international success of the *Sorrows of Young Werther* (1774) fell into comparative **453** oblivion. Only the success of *Hermann und Dorothea* (1797) and the effect of the collection of epigrams, *Xenien*, written in collaboration with Schiller, gave him a commanding position in German literature. Goethe's towering reputation was secured first by the brothers Schlegel who played him up against Schiller yet did not consider either Schiller or Goethe classics. Friedrich Schlegel hoped as early as 1800 that Goethe would accomplish the task of "harmonizing the classical and romantic" (*Gespräch über die Poesie*, in *Kritische Schriften*, ed. W. Rasch, Munich [1956], p. 334). In August Wilhelm Schlegel's *Lectures on Dramatic Art and Literature* (1809–11) Goethe is discussed with the romantic drama written in the wake of Shakespeare. While Goethe's reputation as a great poet and sage steadily grew in the first decades of the nineteenth century and while his writings began to penetrate into the schools, neither he nor Schiller was considered a *Klassiker* or as representing "classicism" for a long time. The whole early nineteenth century in Germany, dominated as it was by Romantic theory and taste, would not have considered the term "classicism" flattering. Friedrich Schlegel, in 1800, referred contemptuously to the "so-called classical poets of the English: Pope, Dryden and whoever else" (*Gespräch über die Poesie*, ibid., p. 288).

August Wilhelm Schlegel's influential lecture courses treated all forms of classicism, French, English, and German with polemical harshness. The literary histories of the time avoided the terms "classicism" and "classical." Thus Gervinus in his standard *Geschichte der poetischen Nationalliteratur der Deutschen* (5 vols., 1835–42) never refers to Goethe or Schiller as *Klassisch* or *Klassiker*. Gervinus thought rather that the new edition of *Faust* (1808) put Goethe "in the vanguard of romantic trends" (Leipzig [1871–74], V, 789). The same is true of other histories such as A. F. C. Vilmar's popular *Geschichte der deutschen Nationalliteratur* (1857). Not until Rudolf Gottschall's *Die deutsche Nationalliteratur des 19. Jahrhunderts* (1854) were Goethe and Schiller called consistently *die Klassiker*. In 1867, when the privileges protecting the reprinting of the works of Goethe and Schiller were abolished, *Klassikerausgaben* began to proliferate. With the establishment of the German Empire the works of Goethe and Schiller assumed more and more the role of a national palladium: a cultural heritage surrounded by almost superstitious awe. The founding of the *Goethe-Gesellschaft* (1885), the publication of the 143-volume edition of Goethe's complete works known as *Weimarer Ausgabe* and the emergence of a new academic profession, *Goethe-philologie*, are symptoms of this victory. Only in the twentieth century did more detached views of the German classics become possible in Germany.

In retrospect it is obvious that the term "classicism" is a nineteenth-century term. It occurs first in Italy in 1818, in Germany in 1820, in France in 1822, in Russia in 1830, in England in 1831. In Germany about 1887 the new term *Klassik*, first used casually by Friedrich Schlegel in 1797, expelled *Klassizismus*. Clearly the terms have something in common: the reference to excellence, to authority, and to the relation to antiquity. In the countries we have discussed "classicism" refers however to three distinct bodies of literature: the French seventeenth century, the English late seventeenth and early eighteenth centuries, and the very late eighteenth-century German literature. They differ widely in their substance and form, their claim to authority and greatness, and even in their relation to antiquity. French classicism has preserved its immense prestige, but recent scholarship has minimized its debt to antiquity. Henri Peyre, in *Qu'est-ce que le classicisme?* (1935) has emphasized the distinctness and uniqueness of French classicism and argued that "the relations between French literature of the seventeenth century and that of antiquity were much looser than it is usually assumed" (*Le Classicisme français*, New York [1942], p. 32). English classicism has remained mainly a scholar's delight and preserve. The German classics, even if reduced to Goethe and Schiller, loom still large on the literary horizon. French and English classicism is far more "Latin" than German classicism which is more self-consciously "Greek." In a history of European styles of literature based on an analogy with art history, French classicism will appear as closely related to the baroque: it has many baroque features which are however, muted and subdued as Leo Spitzer has shown persuasively in "Die klassische Dämpfung in Racines Stil," found in *Romanische Stil- und Literatur-studien* (Marburg [1931], I, 135–268). English classicism seems most closely related to the Enlightenment, to realism, though on occasion it has affinities with what could be called rococo in its artistic style. This seems true of Pope's *Rape of the Lock* (Friedrich Brie, *Englische Rokoko-epik*, Munich [1927]). German classicism even in its most self-conscious stage appears often romantic or possibly nostalgic and utopian as did also the contemporary classicism elsewhere. The elegiac note is prominent in André Chénier and the painters and sculptors of the return to antiquity. David, Canova, and Thorvaldsen have a strong sentimental streak. The dream of the golden age is never far away (Rudolf Zeitler, *Klassizismus und Utopia*, Uppsala [1954]). The Empire style of Napoleon is classicistic: but Napoleon carried *Werther* and Ossian about with him.

The revival of classicism late in the nineteenth and early in the twentieth century was strongest and most articulate in France. Charles Maurras (1868–1952) proclaimed classicism as a slogan around 1894. "Classicism" with him and his followers was part of a general ideological scheme in which monarchism, belief in the Roman Church as an institution, a concept of history, of France and its past, were amalgamated into a coherent ideology which had strong political appeal. But the *Action française* became discredited by its collaboration with the Germans during the second World War. Many other contemporaries, often in violent disagreement with Maurras and his group, also embraced what they called classicism: Julien Benda, a violent anti-romantic polemicist, highly rationalistic in outlook, recommended classicism. For a time even André Gide considered himself "the best representative of classicism," as he told Émile Henriot in 1921. Its secret was "modesty," the tendency toward litotes, understatement. Gide argued that there are classics only in France, if one excepts Goethe; classicism is a French invention, elsewhere it remained artificial as the case of Alexander Pope shows. (See "Billets à Angèle" *Œuvres complètes* [1932], Vol. XI.) When the critic Jacques Rivière returned from German captivity after the first World War and assumed the editorship of *La Nouvelle Revue française* he promised, in his statement of purpose, to ". . . describe what seems to us to foreshadow a classical renaissance, not literal and purely imitative . . . but a deep, inner classicism" (*La Nouvelle Revue française*, 13 [June 1919], 8). Also Paul Valéry considered himself a classicist and defended even the most arbitrary rules and restrictions. Discipline, purity, form, restraint are classicist motifs in his poetics.

French neo-classicism radiated abroad. The two American neo-humanists, Paul Elmer More and Irving Babbitt drew on the earlier versions of French anti-romantic thought, particularly on Brunetière. Babbitt referred with approval to Maurras but was shocked to discover that Lasserre's book on romanticism was displayed in a bookshop in the Quartier Saint Germain along with books advocating the restoration of the monarchy. Babbitt remained a good American republican who had no use for "an impossible political and religious reaction" (Preface to *The New Laokoön*, Boston [1910]). Babbitt was T. S. Eliot's teacher at Harvard and must have influenced his literary ideology. Eliot read Maurras, dedicated his booklet on *Dante* (1929) to Maurras, and recognized the great influence of Maurras on his intellectual development (*Nouvelle Revue Française*, 11 [1923], 619–25). Eliot's "classicism" has however only a very general similarity with Maurras'. In describing modern classicism as "a tendency toward a higher and clearer conception of Reason, and a more severe and serene control of the emotions by Reason" he quotes a heterogeneous list of names: Sorel, Maurras, Benda, Hulme, Maritain, and Babbitt (*Criterion*, 4 [1926], 5). T. E. Hulme preceded

Eliot in his admiration for the French neo-classicism but could not have influenced Eliot as Hulme's essays, *Speculations*, were printed only in 1924; Eliot's position had been reached much earlier in the twentieth century.

In Germany there were also attempts to revive classicism: Paul Ernst (1866–1933) spoke in these terms, Hugo von Hofmannsthal showed such tendencies, as did the whole circle around Stefan George, but one cannot speak of a concerted movement. The same is true of Russia where the symbolist poet Vyacheslav Ivanov (1866–1949) was a classical scholar, and the group which called itself Acmeists resumed classical themes and forms.

Twentieth-century neo-classicism is and often was escapist and academic: in France it combined with xenophobia, with a violent nationalism conscious of its opposition to everything Nordic, German, and romantic. But the neo-classical movement provided also something of aesthetic importance: a resistance against the abolition of art and the rejection of beauty which culminated recently in pop and op art, concrete poetry, and electronic music. Neo-classicism may be a narrow taste and assumes a specific image of man but Phidias and Vergil, Raphael and Titian, Racine and Goethe will always provide a center of security, a point of stillness, an exemplification of what is art, or at least one kind of art, admired through the ages. In this sense the concept of classicism is likely to survive and is likely to be restored in the future. It is not merely a historical concept but a living idea.

BIBLIOGRAPHY

The history of the term has hardly been investigated. Some remarks are to be found in Pierre Moreau, *Le Classicisme des romantiques* (Paris, 1932); Henri Peyre, *Le Classicisme français* (New York, 1942), Ch II, "Le Mot Classicisme," deals with the word "classique" and has nothing to say about "classicisme" as a word; Ernst Robert Curtius, *Europäische Literatur und lateinisches Mittelalter* (Bern, 1948), esp. pp. 251ff.; Harry Levin, "Contexts of the Classical," in his *Contexts of Criticism* (Cambridge, Mass., 1957), pp. 38–54; Georg Luck, "Scriptor Classicus," in *Comparative Literature*, 10 (1958), 150–58; René Wellek, "The Term and Concept of Classicism in Literary History," in *Aspects of the Eighteenth Century*, ed. Earl R. Wasserman (Baltimore, 1965), pp. 105–28; also in *Proceedings of the IVth Congress of the International Comparative Literature Association: Fribourg, 1964* (The Hague, 1966), pp. 1049–67.

Most other discussions of "classicism" are analytical, ideological, or historical. Here is a small selection: P. Van Tieghem, "Classique," in *Revue de synthèse historique*, 41 (1931), 238–41, is purely analytical; Gerhart Rosenwaldt, "Zur Bedeutung des Klassischen in der bildenden Kunst," *Zeitschrift für Aesthetik*, 11 (1916), on page 125 contains a striking definition: *Klassisch ist ein Kunstwerk das voll-*

kommen stilisiert ist, ohne von der Natur abzuweichen, so dass dem Bedürfniss nach Stilisierung und Nachahmung in gleicher Weise Genüge getan ist ("A work of art is classical that is completely stylized without deviating from nature, so that the requirements of both stylization and imitation are equally well met"); Helmut Kuhn, "'Klassisch' als historischer Begriff," in Werner Jaeger, ed., *Das Problem des Klassischen und die Antike* (Stuttgart, 1933, reprint 1961), pp. 109–28; idem, *Concinnitas: Beiträge zum Problem des Klassischen. Heinrich Wölfflin zum achtzigsten Geburtstag . . . zugeeignet* (Basel, 1944); Kurt Herbert Halbach, "Zum Begriff und Wesen der Klassik," in *Festschrift Paul Kluckhohn und Hermann Schneider gewidmet . . .* (Tübingen, 1948), pp. 166–94; Heinz Otto Burger, ed., *Begriffsbestimmung der Klassik und des Klassischen*, Wege der Forschung, Vol. 210 (Darmstadt, 1971); W. Tatarkiewicz, "Les quatre significations du mot 'classique,'" *Revue Internationale de Philosophie*, **43** (1958), 5–11; E. F. Carritt, "Classicism," ibid., 23–36.

Fritz Ernst, *Der Klassizismus in Italien, Frankreich und Deutschland* (Zurich, 1924), is a thin sketch. Sherard Vines, *The Course of English Classicism from the Tudor to the Victorian Age* (London, 1930), is lively but confused. Two books on Goethe's fame are relevant: Reinhard Buchwald, *Goethezeit und Gegenwart* (Stuttgart, 1949), and Wolfgang Leppmann, *The German Image of Goethe* (Oxford, 1961), German version: *Goethe und die Deutschen* (Stuttgart, 1962).

Three encyclopedia entries merit attention: Antonio Viscardi, "Classicismo" in *Dizionario letterario Bompiani delle opere* (Milan, 1947), I, 22–43; Henri Peyre, "Le Classicisme," in *Encyclopédie de la Pléiade. Histoire des littératures* (Paris, 1956), II, 110–39; and W. B. Fleischmann, "Classicism," in *Encyclopedia of Poetry and Poetics*, ed. A. Preminger (Princeton, 1965), pp. 136–41.

RENÉ WELLEK

[See also **Ancients and Moderns;** Baroque; Criticism; **Enlightenment;** Historicism; Mimesis; Nature; Romanticism; Style; *Ut pictura poesis*.]

CLASSIFICATION OF THE ARTS

I. ANTIQUITY

THE HISTORY of the classification of the arts is complicated for several reasons but chiefly because the idea of art has changed. The classical idea differed from ours in at least two respects. First, it was concerned not with the products of art but with the act of producing them and in particular the *ability* to produce them; e.g., it pointed to the skill of the painter rather than to the picture. Second, it embraced not only "artistic" ability but *any human ability* to produce things so long as it was a regular production based on *rules*. Art was a system of regular methods of making

or doing. The work of an architect or a sculptor answered to this definition, but so did the work of a carpenter or a weaver, for their activities belonged in equal measure to the realm of art. Art by definition was rational and implied knowledge; it did not depend on inspiration, intuition, or fantasy. This conception of art found expression in works of Greek and Roman scholars. Aristotle defined art as the "ability to execute something with apt comprehension," and some centuries later Quintilian explained it as based on method and order (*via et ordine*). "Art is a system of general rules" (*Ars est systema praeceptorum universalium*), Galen said. Plato stressed the rationality of art: "I do not call art irrational work," he said. The Stoics placed greater stress on a fixed system of rules in the arts and simply defined art as a system. Aristotle stressed the idea that knowledge on which art is based is general knowledge.

This ancient conception of art is not foreign to us, but it appears today under other names: craft, skill, or technique. The Greek name for art was *technē*, and as a matter of fact our term "technique" suits the ancient idea of art better than our term "art," which is now used as an abbreviation for fine arts. The Greeks had no name for the latter since they did not recognize their distinctiveness. They grouped fine arts together with handicrafts, convinced that the essence of a sculptor's or a carpenter's work is the same, i.e., skill. The sculptor and the painter, working in different media with different tools and applying different technical methods, have only one thing in common: their production is based on skill. And so is the production of a craftsman; therefore a general conception which embraces fine arts cannot but likewise embrace the crafts.

The Greeks regarded both sciences and crafts as belonging to the realm of art. Geometry or grammar were indeed areas of knowledge, rational systems of rules, methods of doing or making things, and so they certainly answered to the Greek meaning of the term "art." Cicero divided arts into those which only comprehend things (*animo cernunt*) and those which make them (*Academica* II 7, 22); today we consider the first category as sciences, not as arts.

So "art" in the original meaning of the word embraced *more* than it does in our times, and at the same time it embraced *less*: it excluded *poetry*. Poetry was supposed to lack the characteristic trait of art: it seemed not to be governed by rules; on the contrary, it seemed to be a matter of inspiration, of individual creativeness. The Greeks saw a kinship between poetry and prophecy rather than between poetry and art. The poet is a kind of bard, while the sculptor is a kind of artisan.

The Greeks included *music* together with poetry in the sphere of inspiration. First, there was a psychological affinity between the two arts; both were comprehended as acoustic productions, and both were supposed to have a "manic" character, i.e., to be the source of rapture. Second, they were practiced jointly since poetry was sung and music was vocalized, and since both were essential elements of "mysteries."

Before the ancient idea of art became modern, two things were to happen: poetry and music were to be incorporated into art, while handicrafts and sciences were to be eliminated from it. The first happened before the end of antiquity. Poetry and music could indeed be considered arts as soon as their rules were discovered. This happened early so far as music is concerned: since the Pythagoreans found the mathematical laws of acoustic harmony, music has been considered as a branch of knowledge as well as an art.

It was more difficult to include poetry in the arts. The initial step was made by Plato: he admitted that there are two kinds of poetry; the poetry springing from poetical frenzy and the poetry resulting from literary skill, in short, "manic" and "technical" poetry. The second is art, the first is not. Plato however considered only the first as true poetry. Aristotle made the next step by supplying so many rules of poetry that for him and for his successors there could be no doubt that poetry *is* an art. It is an imitative art: "the poet is an imitator just like the painter or other maker of likenesses," Aristotle said (*Poetics* 1460b 8).

On the contrary, crafts and sciences were *not* excluded in the classical Greek era from the realm of the arts. Neither were they in the Hellenistic period, in the Middle Ages, and in the Renaissance—the early, classical idea of art survived for more than two thousand years. Our idea of art is a comparatively modern invention.

In antiquity numerous attempts were made to classify the arts; all of them classified the arts in the broadest sense of the word, by no means the fine arts alone. The first classification had been originated by the Sophists. Their work was continued by Plato and Aristotle and by the thinkers of the Hellenistic and Roman period.

1. The Sophists distinguished two categories of arts; arts cultivated for the sake of their *utility* and those cultivated for the *pleasure* they offer. In other words, they differentiated arts into those which are necessary in life and those which are a source of entertainment. This classification was widely accepted. In the Hellenistic epoch it appeared sometimes in a more developed form; Plutarch supplemented the useful and pleasurable arts with a third category, that of the arts cultivated for the sake of *perfection*. He regarded,

however, as perfect arts, not the fine arts, but the sciences (e.g., mathematics or astronomy).

2. Plato based his classification on the fact that different arts are differently related to real objects; some produce things, as does architecture, and others imitate them, as does painting. This opposition between "productive" and "imitative" arts became popular in antiquity and continued to be so in modern times. Another Platonic classification distinguished arts which produce *real things*, e.g., architecture, and those which produce *only images*, e.g., painting. For Plato, however, this classification was in fact the same as the former. Imitations of things are no more than images of them.

Aristotle's classification of the arts differed little from Plato's; he divided all arts into those which *complete* nature and those which *imitate* it. This was his excellent formula for the Platonic division.

3. The classification most generally accepted in ancient times divided arts into "liberal" and "vulgar." It was an invention of the Greeks, though it is known mainly in the Latin terminology as *artes liberales* and *artes vulgares*. More than any other ancient classifications it was dependent on social conditions in Greece. It was based on the fact that certain arts require physical effort from which others are free, a difference that to ancient Greeks seemed particularly important. It was the expression of an aristocratic regime and of the Greek contempt for physical work and preference for activities of the mind. The liberal or intellectual arts were considered not only a distinct but also a superior group. Note, however, that the Greeks considered geometry and astronomy as liberal arts, although they are now considered sciences.

It is doubtful whether it is possible to indicate who was the inventor of the division of the arts into liberal and vulgar; we know only the names of some later thinkers who accepted it; Galen, the famous physician of the second century A.D., was the one who developed it most fully. Later the Greeks called the liberal arts also "encyclic" arts. The word, almost a synonym of the modern word "encyclopedic," etymologically meant "forming a circle" and signified the circle of arts obligatory for an educated man.

Some ancient scholars added other groups of arts to liberal and vulgar arts; for instance, Seneca added those which instruct (*pueriles*) and those which amuse (*ludicrae*). In doing so he fused, in fact, two different classifications: that of Galen and that of the Sophists; his fourfold division was more complete, but lacked unity.

4. Another ancient classification is known from Quintilian. This Roman rhetorician of the first century A.D. (inspired by an idea of Aristotle's) divided the arts

457

into three groups. In the first group he included those arts which consist only in studying things. He called them "theoretical" arts giving astronomy as an example. The second group embraced the arts consisting solely in an action (*actus*) of the artist without leaving a product; Quintilian called them "practical" arts and gave dance as an example. The third group embraced the arts producing objects which continue to exist when the actions of the artist have ended; he called them "poietic," which in Greek means "productive"; painting served him as an example.

This classification had several variants. Dionysius Thrax, a writer of the Hellenistic epoch, added "apotelestic" arts, which meant "finished" or "carried out to its end": this was, however, only a different name for "poietic" arts. Lucius Tarrhaeus, the grammarian, added to the practical and apotelestic arts "organic" arts, i.e., arts which use instruments or tools (*organon* being the Greek name for tool), as playing a flute does. In this way he enriched the classification but deprived it of its unity.

5. Cicero used several classifications of the arts, most of them based on the old Greek tradition, including the one which seems to be relatively original. Taking as the basis of the division the importance of the various arts, he divided them into major (*artes maximae*), median (*mediocres*), and minor (*minores*). To the major arts, according to Cicero, belonged political and military arts; to the second class belonged purely intellectual arts, i.e., sciences, but also poetry and eloquence; to the third class belonged painting, sculpture, music, acting, athletics. Thus he considered fine arts as minor arts.

6. At the end of antiquity Plotinus undertook once again the task of classifying arts. This most complete classification distinguished five groups of arts: (1) arts which produce physical objects, as architecture does; (2) arts which help nature, like medicine and agriculture; (3) arts which imitate nature, like painting; (4) arts which improve or ornament human action, like rhetoric and politics; and (5) purely intellectual arts, like geometry. This classification, which may seem to be lacking a *principium divisionis* ("principle of division") is in fact based on the degree of spirituality in the arts; it forms a hierarchy, beginning with purely (as he supposed) material architecture and ending with purely spiritual geometry.

Let us summarize: Greek and Roman antiquity knew at least six classifications of the arts, most of them having several variants: (1) The classifications of the Sophists were based on the *aims* of arts; (2) the classification of Plato and Aristotle—on the *relation between arts* and *reality;* (3) the classification of Galen—on *physical effort* required by arts; (4) the classification of

Quintilian—on *products* of the arts; (5) the classification of Cicero—on *value* of the arts, and (6) the classification of Plotinus—on the *degree* of their *spirituality.*

All of these were general divisions of all human skills and abilities, none being just a division of fine arts. What is more, none singled out the "fine arts," and none divided arts in the broader sense into fine arts and crafts. On the contrary, fine arts were distributed, and divided into opposing categories.

(1) Thus, in the classification of the Sophists architecture was considered a useful art, while painting was an art cultivated for pleasure's sake. (2) Plato and Aristotle considered architecture a productive and painting an imitative art. (3) Liberal (encyclic) arts embraced music and rhetoric, but did not include architecture or painting. (4) In Quintilian's classification dance and music were "practical" arts, while architecture and painting were poietic (apotelestic) arts. (5) None of the liberal arts were considered by Cicero as major arts; only poetry and rhetoric were supposed to be median arts, and all other fine arts to be minor arts. (6) In Plotinus' classification fine arts were divided between the first and the third groups.

Consequently, antiquity never did face the possibility that fine arts could form a distinct group of arts. There may be a certain affinity between our notion of fine arts and the notion of liberal arts, of arts for entertainment's sake, of imitative arts, of "poietic" art; however, all these ancient notions were broader than the notion of fine arts and, at the same time, in some respects, narrower. Some of the liberal arts, some of the entertaining arts, and some of the productive arts, not all of them however, belonged indeed to the group we call "fine arts." Neither freedom, nor entertainment, nor imitation, nor productiveness were the properties by which arts in the modern, narrower meaning could be defined; imitation came relatively nearest to being such a property. The historian is tempted to believe that the ancients faced all reasonable possibilities of classifying the arts except the division into fine arts and handicrafts.

II. THE MIDDLE AGES

The Middle Ages inherited the ancient idea of art and made use of it theoretically and practically. Art was considered as a *habitus* of the practical reason. Thomas Aquinas defined art as an "ordering of reason" and Duns Scotus as "the right idea of what is to be produced" (*ars est recta ratio factibilium,* Col. I, n. 19), or as "the ability to produce based on real principles" (*ars est habitus cum vera ratione factivus; Opus Oxoniense,* I, d. 38, n. 5). Medieval art was indeed governed by fixed canons and by rules of the guilds. Hugh of Saint Victor said: "Art can be said to be a knowledge which consists in rules and regulations" (*ars dici potest scientia, quae praeceptis regulisque consistit; Didascalicon*, II). This medieval idea of art embraced handicrafts and sciences as well as fine arts. *Liberal* arts were now considered as the arts par excellence, the arts proper; "art" without an adjective meant: liberal art. The seven liberal arts were logic, rhetoric, grammar, arithmetic, geometry, astronomy, and music (including acoustics); they were—according to our understanding—sciences, not arts.

However, the Middle Ages were interested in non-liberal arts as well; they did not depreciate them any longer by calling them "vulgar" but called them "mechanical arts." Since the twelfth century Scholastics had tried to classify these arts and made a point of distinguishing seven of them, in symmetry with the seven traditional liberal arts, as did Radulphus Ardens in his "Speculum Universale" (see Grabmann). So also did Hugh of Saint Victor, who divided the mechanical arts into *lanificium* (supplying men with wearing apparel), *armatura* (supplying men with shelter and tools), *agricultura, venatio* (both supplying food), *navigatio, medicina, theatrica*. This was the major contribution of the Middle Ages to the classification of the arts. Two of those seven arts were similar to modern "fine" arts, namely *armatura*, which embraced architecture, and *theatrica* or the art of entertainment (a peculiar medieval concept).

Music was considered a liberal art, being based on mathematics. Poetry was a kind of philosophy or prophecy, or prayer or confession, and by no means an art. Painting and sculpture were never listed as arts, either liberal or mechanical. Still they certainly were arts, after all, as abilities based on rules; why then were they never mentioned? It was because they could have been classified only as mechanical arts, appreciated only when useful; the utility of painting and sculpture seemed insignificant. This shows the great change which has taken place since; these arts which we consider as arts in the strict sense, the scholastics did not think worthy of being mentioned at all.

III. THE RENAISSANCE

The classical idea of art and the traditional classifications of the arts were retained in the Renaissance. The philosopher Ramus, as well as the lexicographer Goclenius, repeated Galen's definition of art verbatim. Benedetto Varchi, a major authority on classification of the arts, in his *Della Maggioranza delle arti* (1549), divided the arts, as did the Sophists, into those which are produced by necessity, for utility, and for entertainment (*per necessità, per utilità e per dilettazione*); like Galen, into *liberali e volgari;* like Quintilian, into theoretical and practical (*fattive e attive*); like Seneca,

into entertaining, jocose, and instructing youth (*ludicre, giocose e puerili*); like Plato, into those which make use of nature and those which do not; like Cicero, into major (*architettoniche*) and minor (*subalternate*) arts.

However, the status of architecture, sculpture, painting, music, and poetry changed greatly: these arts were now so much more appreciated than other arts, that to single them out conceptually became a matter of course. In order to achieve this, it was necessary to realize not only what separates the arts from handicrafts and from sciences, but also what binds them together. This became a major achievement of the Renaissance: it was not a proper classification, but a preparatory operation, the *integration* of fine arts. It had to be carried out on several conceptual levels.

1. First, general ideas of particular arts had to be formed. Neither a general idea nor a general term of *sculpture* existed at the beginning of the Renaissance. The term "sculpture" had a narrower meaning, it meant only sculpture in wood. To denote those, whom we call "sculptors," Poliziano had to use five terms; *statuarii, caelatores, sculptores, fictores,* and *encausti,* meaning those who used, respectively, stone, metal, wood, clay, and wax. After 1500 the term "sculptor" already embraced all five of them. A similar integration occurred in painting and architecture.

2. A general idea of *plastic* art was also lacking. In antiquity and the Middle Ages architecture was considered rather a mechanical and utilitarian art and seemed to be unrelated to sculpture and painting. In the sixteenth century it was first noticed that all three of them are similarly based on drawing (*disegno*): G. Vasari as well as V. Danti started to consider them as one group and called them the *arti del disegno* ("arts of drawing").

3. A further integration was necessary to classify "arts of drawing" together with music and poetry. A general idea which would embrace all of them did not exist. The integration began in the fifteenth century, but it took time before the result was satisfactory. The affinity of those arts seemed certain, but the *principle* that would include all of them and exclude the crafts was lacking; since the Quattrocento diverse principles were suggested to fill this gap.

Ingenious Arts. The Florentine humanist of the fifteenth century, C. G. Manetti, suggested calling them ingenious arts because they are produced by the spirit (*ingenium*) and for the spirit. This suggestion did not, however, add very much to the traditional opposition of liberal and mechanical arts.

Musical Arts. Marsilio Ficino, the leader of the Florentine Academy, wrote: "It is music that inspires the works of all creators; orators, poets, painters, sculptors, architects." He continued to call those arts liberal arts, though in accordance with his idea the proper name would have been "musical arts." His idea was never published but only expressed in letters and therefore it never won a more general recognition.

Noble Arts. G. P. Capriano in his *De vera poetica* (1555) singled out the same group of arts, but applied a different principle; their nobility. They are "noble arts," he said, as they are the object of our noblest senses and because their products are durable.

Commemorative Arts. L. Castelvetro in his *Poetica d'Aristotele vulgarizzata* (1570) contrasted crafts with arts on a different basis. While crafts produce useful and necessary objects, the function of painting, sculpture, and poetry is to keep things in human memory.

Metaphorical Arts. On the other hand E. Tesauro, in *Cannochiale Aristotelico* (1655) tried to convince his readers that metaphorical speech, *parlare figurato,* constitutes the essence of these arts and distinguishes them from crafts. This was a point of view peculiar to the manneristic trend in aesthetics of the seventeenth century.

Figurative Arts. Some theoreticians of the seventeenth century supposed that the peculiarity of this group of arts consists rather in their figurative, pictorial character, since even poetry is *ut pictura.* Especially C. F. Menestrier in his *Philosophie des images* (1682), stressed that all these arts—poetry not less than painting and sculpture—*travaillent en images* ("work in images").

Fine Arts. The idea that such arts as poetry, painting, and music are distinguished by beauty was very seldom uttered before the eighteenth century (e.g., in the sixteenth century by Francesco de Hollanda, who called them *boas artes*). As the traditional idea of beauty was very broad, successful works of industry and handicraft were also called beautiful. However, the narrower meaning of the work permitted one to separate poetry, music, dance, painting, sculpture, and architecture as a peculiar group of *beaux arts,* "fine arts." This is often believed to be an achievement of the eighteenth century. But as early as 1675 the outstanding French architect F. Blondel, in his *Cours d'architecture* said that what these arts, called by earlier writers "noble," "commemorative," "metaphorical," etc., have in common is harmony.

Although harmony meant certainly the same as beauty, Blondel failed to call those arts beautiful. On the other hand, C. Batteux in his *Beaux arts réduits à un seul principe* (1747), used this term and included it in the title of his book. This was conclusive; the principle of beauty and the name "fine arts" were now generally adopted (though Batteux himself saw the common link of those arts not so much in their concern with beauty, as in the fact that their purpose is pleasure

and their method is imitation). However, a proper name came to be as important as a proper concept for the progress of aesthetic theory.

Elegant and Agreeable Arts. A few years earlier different names were proposed for beautiful arts. In 1744 G. B. Vico suggested "agreeable arts" and in the same year J. Harris recommended "elegant arts."

However, Batteux's terminology has prevailed. The "system of fine arts" was established, embracing poetry, music, theater, dance, painting, sculpture, and architecture. Since the fifteenth century it had seemed certain that these arts formed a peculiar group of arts. However, it took centuries before what unites this group and what separates it from crafts and science was made clear (see P. O. Kristeller [1951–52]). Paradoxically Batteux contributed to the acceptance of the "System of the arts" although his own system was different: he divided arts (in the broad, old sense) into mechanical arts, fine arts, and intermediate arts (architecture and oratory).

IV. MODERN TIMES

In about the second half of the eighteenth century there was only one major controversy (chiefly in Germany) concerning the arts: whether or not poetry belongs to the fine arts. Some writers contrasted *beaux arts* with *belles lettres*, considering them as two different fields of human endeavor. Still, Moses Mendelssohn in 1757 called for a common theory of both. This was done first by J. G. Sulzer in his *Allgemeine Theorie der schönen Künste* (1771–74). The agreement was not general. Goethe in his review of Sulzer's book (1772) ridiculed the linking of two things which, for Goethe, were very different (Kristeller [1951–52]).

By now new problems of classification arose and had to be solved. First, how is *all human activity* to be classified and what place do fine arts occupy in it? The classical solution was prepared by Francis Hutcheson and the Scottish thinkers such as James Beattie and David Hume, and eventually formulated in 1790 by Kant: there are three major human activities: the cognitive, the moral, and the aesthetic; fine art is the product of aesthetic activity.

The second problem was how to classify the narrower field of *fine arts*. Let us again take Kant as an example; he suggested that there are as many kinds of fine arts as there are ways of expressing and transmitting thoughts and feelings. There are three different ways, he said, and likewise there are three fine arts: using words, plastic images, or tones. The first way is used by poetry and oratory, the second by architecture, sculpture, and painting, the third by music. Kant suggested other classifications as well: he distinguished (following Plato) the arts of truth and the arts of appearance, architecture being an art of truth and painting an art of appearances. On the other hand, he divided fine arts into those which, like sculpture, deal with objects existing in nature and those which, like architecture, deal with objects possible only through art.

Classifications of the arts were continued in the nineteenth century. While the ancients attempted to classify arts in the broad sense of the word, the nineteenth century classified only fine arts. It did this in various and ingenious ways. It distinguished not only "free" and "reproductive" arts, but also "figurative" and "nonfigurative"; arts of motion and motionless arts; spatial and temporal arts; arts which require a performer (like music) and those which do not (like painting); arts evoking determinate associations (as painting or poetry do) and evoking indeterminate associations (as do music or architecture). These different principles lead after all to a similar classification of the arts. This result is demonstrated in Max Dessoir's table (1905):

Spatial arts Motionless arts Arts dealing with images	Temporal arts Arts of motions Arts dealing with gestures and sounds	
SCULPTURE PAINTING	POETRY DANCE	Reproductive arts Figurative arts Arts with determinate associations
ARCHITEC- TURE	MUSIC	Free arts Abstract arts Arts with indeterminate associations

Dessoir, the most expert aesthetician at the turn of the twentieth century, ended his review of art classification, however, with a pessimistic conclusion: *Es scheint kein System zu geben das allen Ansprüchen genügte* ("there appears to be *no* system that satisfies all claims").

Hegel's well-known division of the arts into symbolic, classical, and romantic had a different purpose: it did not differentiate branches of arts, poetry, painting, music, etc., but diverse *styles* of poetry, painting, music, etc. In classifying styles the nineteenth century was not less ingenious than in classifying arts.

In summary we may say that the *meaning* of the classification of arts has changed; in antiquity the classification of arts was a division of all human abilities; during the Middle Ages it was a division between purely intellectual (*artes liberales*) and mechanical arts; in the Renaissance attempts were made to divide arts into "fine arts" and others; since the eighteenth century it has been a division among fine arts themselves.

The problem seemed to have been settled, but in the twentieth century unexpected difficulties emerged. The established classification was based on three assumptions: (1) there exists a closed system of arts; (2) there is a difference between arts and crafts and sciences; (3) the arts are distinguished by the fact that they seek and find beauty. It took a long time and much effort to get this system accepted but eventually it seemed to be firmly established. However, we must observe that: (1) new arts were born—photography and cinema—which had to be included in the system. The same applied to those arts which have been practiced before but were not covered by the system, like town planning. Moreover, the character of arts included in the system has changed: a new architecture, abstract painting and sculpture, music in a twelve-tone scale, and the anti-novel have appeared. (2) Doubts arose whether one really ought to contrast crafts with arts. As recently as the end of the nineteenth century William Morris argued that there can be no nobler art than good craft. And ought one to contrast science with art? Indeed, many twentieth-century artists regard their work as cognitive, similar to science, or even science itself. (3) Finally, is it correct to assume that seeking beauty is essential in art and represents its *differentia specifica*? Is not the concept of beauty too vague to be useful in defining art? One can say of many works of art that beauty was not their objective. What one can say of them rather is that the reason for their creation was the artist's need of expression or his desire to excite and move other men.

Everything seems to speak for the need to define anew the concept of art. And, consequently, for the need to start afresh the classification of arts.

BIBLIOGRAPHY

The most important though indirect contribution to the history of the classification of the arts is: P. O. Kristeller, "The Modern System of the Arts: A Study in the History of Aesthetics," *Journal of the History of Ideas*, **12**, 4 (1951), 496–527, and **13**, 1 (1952), 17–46. W. Tatarkiewicz dealt with the subject in *The History of Aesthetics*, 3 vols. (Polish ed., Wroclaw, 1960–67; English ed., The Hague, 1970); idem, "Art and Poetry, a Contribution to the History of Ancient Aesthetics," *Studia Philosophica*, **2** (1939); idem, "Classification of the Arts in Antiquity," *Journal of the History of Ideas*, **24**, 2 (1963), 231–40.

Classical and medieval sources are: Radulphus Ardens, in M. Grabmann, *Geschichte der scholastischen Methode*, (1909), 1, 254. Aristotle, *Poetics*, passim, and *Physica*, 199a

15. Bekker, *Anecdota Graeca*, II, 654 (670). Cicero, *De oratore*, III, 7, 26. Galen, *Protrepticus*, 14, (Marquardt, 129). Isocrates, *Panegiricus*, 40. Plato, *Republic*, 601D; *Sophist*, 219A, 235D. Plotinus, *Enneads*, IV, 4, 31; V, 9, 11. Quintilian, *Institutio oratoria*, II, 18, 1. Hugh of Saint Victor, *Didascalicon*, II, in Migne, 176, cols. 751, 760. Seneca, *Epistolae*, 88, 21.

References for modern classification of the arts: C. Batteux, *Les beaux arts réduits à un seul principe* (1747). F. Blondel, *Cours d'architecture* (1675), pp. 169, 783. G. P. Capriano, *De vera poetica* (1555). L. Castelvetro, *Poetica d'Aristotele vulgarizzata* (1570); *Correzione d'alcune cose del dialogo della lingua de B. Varchi* (1572), p. 72. V. Danti, *Trattato della perfetta proporzione*, (1567), in P. Barocchi, *Trattati d'arte del Cinquecento*, Vol. 1 (Bari, 1960). D'Alembert, *Oeuvres* (1853), p. 99. M. Dessoir, *Ästhetik und allgemeine Kunstwissenschaft* (Stuttgart, 1906). M. Ficino, *Commentarium in Convivium* (1561). J. W. Goethe, review of Sulzer's paper, *Werke*, (Weimar, 1896), 37, 206. J. Harris, *Three Treatises* (1744), p. 25. G. W. F. Hegel, "Vorlesungen über die Ästhetik," *Heidelberg Lectures, 1818–29* (East Berlin, 1955). J. Hippisley, *The Polite Arts or a Dissertation on Poetry, Painting, Musick, Architecture, and Eloquence* (London, 1749), Ch. 2. I. Kant, *Kritik der Urteilskraft* (1790), p. 51. G. Manetti, *De dignitate et excellentia hominis*, (1532), 3, 131. M. Mendelssohn, *Betrachtungen über die Quellen der schönen Künste und Wissenschaften* (1757). F. Menestrier, *Philosophie des images* (1683). A. Poliziano, *Panepistemon* (1491). J. G. Sulzer, *Allgemeine Theorie der schönen Künste* (1771, 1774). E. Tesauro, *Canocchiale aristotelico* (1655), p. 74. B. Varchi, *Della maggioranza delle Arti* (1549), reprinted in P. Barocchi, *Trattati d'arte del Cinquecento*, Vol. 1 (Bari, 1960). C. Vasari, *Le vite*, ed. G. Milanesi (Florence, 1878, 1906), 1, 168. G. B. Vico, *Scienza nuova* (1744), p. 25. B. Weinberg, *A History of Literary Criticism in the Italian Renaissance* (Chicago, 1961), contains important references on the sixteenth century.

W. TATARKIEWICZ

[See also Classicism in Literature; **Classification of the Sciences;** Education; Mimesis; **Music and Science;** Music as a Divine Art; Naturalism in Art; Platonism; Renaissance Humanism; Rhetoric; **Style;** *Ut pictura poesis*.]

CLASSIFICATION OF THE SCIENCES

THE AIM of every classification is to establish order in things and in thought. When this operation is applied in the sciences at a given time in their evolution, it provides a faithful though provisional picture of the scientific knowledge at that time. By enabling us to take such an inventory of our knowledge, classification provides a sort of spatiotemporal cross section of the sphere of ideas and culture of a given period. The value

of classification, however, goes beyond a mere inventory or "table of contents," no matter how complete. The very fact that classification appeals to logical criteria which may possibly be subjective or objective in nature gives us an initial idea of the obstacles confronting the classifier, difficulties scarcely encountered in the preparation of a catalogue, properly so called. Consequently, a well conducted effort at surveying the history of the classification of the sciences may be valuable in leading us to discover the connections and analogies existing among the different fields of knowledge at a given time, and within the context of a particular type of civilization. However, history of any sort is not a static phenomenon, but follows an evolutionary course. We are obliged therefore to study the sciences and their classification considered essentially as an historical process subject to continuous development. We shall thus see the appearance of the great currents of ideas which have sometimes dominated many centuries and we can seek what is less apparent, namely, the structure underlying these ideas.

We can already discern among the ancients this need to classify and discover relationships and hidden connections in order to obtain a total view of reality and to explain the mechanism of the universe. Take Pythagoras, for example, whose life was described by Porphyry and Iamblichus, and whose teaching was addressed primarily to those initiated in his circle. According to Pythagoras, geometry, arithmetic (theory of numbers), and music (acoustics) lead to the discovery of the secrets of number and harmony; only the sage by starting with these principles is able to reconstruct reality (Stobaeus, *Florilège*, I, 62–63). Through Archytas of Tarentum, Plato had been introduced to the Pythagorean method, as can be seen in several places in the *Timaeus*, the Platonic dialogue on which Proclus wrote a commentary in four books.

Plato thought that ideas should be ordered according to their extension (denotation) in inverse relationship to their intension (comprehension): by starting from general and vague ideas, one should end up with more specific and clearer ideas. This dichotomy and progressive division of each idea into those ideas immediately below it, is expounded in the *Republic*. There is really a hierarchy made up of genus (γένη) and species (εἴδη), but for Plato, genus and species are inseparable. Besides, Plato applies the term *mathemata* (μαθήματα) not only to the exact sciences but also to the technical and mechanical arts and to the liberal arts like music and gymnastics, that is to say, to all the disciplines capable of educating a man. However, among these *mathemata* Plato bestows a privileged place on the sciences properly called mathematical. We must remember that geometry, arithmetic, astrology (in the sense of astronomy), and music belonged typically to Hellenic culture. In the *Laws*, Plato returns to this question in order to remind the reader that the first three sciences must be acquired by every free man (*Laws* VII, 817E).

It was not until Aristotle that we find the separation between species and genus, which was to become the basis of Aristotelian logic. The species is the specification of the genus; both appear in deduction, induction, and in the theory of definition (*per genus proximum et differentiam specificam*). We find this hierarchy again in all the later types of classification, however, the criterion of division by species and genus was later shown to be inadequate; for example, according to the theory of evolution zoological and botanical species have no stability. We must therefore take into account other criteria: such as the contrasting criteria of objectivity and subjectivity, criteria varying with respect to method, foundations, aims, and so forth. But, returning to Aristotle, who is generally more systematic in his ordering of the sciences, we note that for him there exist only three large groups of sciences: (1) theoretical sciences (physics and philosophy); (2) practical sciences (ethics and politics); (3) poetic sciences (aesthetics). We also note that for him all reality is knowable only through classification, but we must not forget also that for Aristotle all sciences have to be subordinate to philosophy. It is true that Aristotle's *Physics* comes exactly between mathematics and theology and is preceded by *Logic*, which is the structure of science and also the science of structure. *Physics* is followed by Aristotle's treatises *On the Heavens* (*De caelo*), and *Meteorology*. This plan is in conformity with the principles of classification which appear in several places of his work. We note three in particular. In Aristotle's *Topics* we read that science "is indeed called speculative, practical, and poetic, the differences depending on how each is related respectively to the theory, the production, and the action of something" (*Topics* VI, 6, 145a 15). In the *Nicomachean Ethics* (VI, 3–5) there is a brief passage concerning art (*technē*), science (*epistemē*), wisdom (*phronēsis*), philosophy (*sophia*), and intelligence (*nous*). There are longer passages in the *Metaphysics*.

"Physics is the theoretical science of material objects in motion . . . ; mathematics is a contemplative science, though certain mathematical entities are stationary" (VI, 1026a). Then farther on: "Theoretical sciences come before the practical ones and philosophy before the theoretical sciences . . . ; motion exists only in relation to quantity, quality, and place" (XI, 7 passim; XI, 12, 1068b).

Among Aristotle's pupils, Demetrius of Phalerum was a great encyclopedic mind and one of the organizers of the library in Alexandria, the center of scientists and philosophers. He deserves mention here for having introduced divisions and subdivisions of knowledge with the aim of permitting specialization in a given field of study. In the second century B.C., there was Posidonius of Apamea, the Stoic and polymath; he was later in Rome and Cadiz; his work also included all fields of learning, though unfortunately only some few fragments of his work are extant.

In the following century, in Rome, Marcus Terentius Varro expounded a whole program of studies extending from grammar to architecture (Varro was contemporary with Vitruvius), the program answering certain practical needs without being devoid, however, of a certain idealism. In Varro's *Disciplinarum* (ca. 50 B.C.), which may be regarded as the first illustrated encyclopedia, we find the following classification: grammar, dialectic, rhetoric, geometry, arithmetic, astrology, music, medicine, and architecture. It reflects perfectly the genius of his time and especially of his people; it owes nothing, in any case, to Aristotelian ideas. With respect to special disciplines, mention must be made of the works of the physician A. Cornelius Celsus and the *Natural History* of Pliny the Elder in 37 books, completed in A.D. 77, a true testament of ancient science and a model of classification within a branch of science. Pliny's work has come down to us in its entirety.

We know that the Arabs preserved Greek science, that they translated the works of the ancients, added commentaries, and not only left the imprint of their genius on these commentaries, but made some original contributions in every field of knowledge. Greek science, enriched by the Arabs' contribution, was introduced by the Moors into Spain, and then proceeded to penetrate other European countries. Within Islam there appeared during the seventh century the first seeds of the new sciences which were essentially religious; then a distinction was made between Arabic sciences (such as poetry and the art of oratory) and foreign sciences (astronomy, medicine, mathematics). Most of the "foreign sciences" came from the Greek heritage, thanks to the Syrian translations; there were also works translated from the Sanskrit via the Pali. A very distinct effort at classification is discernible among the Arabs, for example, in Al Farabi and Avicenna (Ibn Sina), an effort which had been preceded by the work of systematization. To be remembered are the names of Djahiz ('Amr Ibn Bahr Jahiz), an Iraqian scientist (died 868), author of a bestiary, or *Book of Animals* in seven volumes, in which we meet subjects going beyond the scope of the title. His contemporary Ibn Qutaibah wrote a treatise, *Adab al Katib*, containing an essay on classification (in the introduction).

463

In China and in India throughout the centuries, there are examples of classification in encyclopedic works. In China such works always enjoyed, more than elsewhere, an important role in education and in preparation for taking examinations for official positions. In the Han dynasty (second century B.C.) appeared a dictionary entitled *Erh-ya;* it was probably composed earlier. This work is divided into nineteen categories: explanation of definitions, definitions of concepts, explanation of words, degrees of affinity; then come the art of construction, tools, music, heaven, earth, hills, mountains, water, fields, forests, insects, fish, birds, quadrupeds, and domestic animals. Notice that this series is not devoid of a certain structure. During the same period there also appeared a classification in the dictionary of Liu Hsi (or Liu Hsieh), the *Shih-ming* or interpretation of concepts. The criterion applied is the way of passing from heaven to earth and from earth to man; it includes twenty-seven divisions. In the Ming era, which marked the first commercial contacts with the Occident, the number of schools and candidates taking examinations increased rapidly; in 1615, Mei Ying-tsu published the *Tzu-hui,* a dictionary which revolutionized the arrangement of words by ordering them on the basis of graphic analogies. A century later, by taking the *Tzu-hui* as a model, a new dictionary was published, the *K'ang-hsi tzu-tien,* (dictionary of the era of "splendid peace") which serves as the basis of modern Chinese encyclopedias.

In India, works embracing the whole of knowledge or bearing on a particular field have been traditional since ancient times. The language used in the beginning was nearly always Sanskrit. In the first centuries A.D. there were the *Dharmaśāstra* (Treatises of the Correct Order) in which there are ideas on cosmology, social rules, human functions, and law. In the eleventh century, the encyclopedic work of the Sanskrit author from Kashmir, Abinavagupta, and in the twelfth century Somadeva's work on the arts and techniques are worthy of notice. At the beginning of the nineteenth century, encyclopedic works multiplied constantly, at first in Sanskrit, then in the majority of the languages of India: Hindi (the government's language), Bengali, Marath, Gujrāti, Tamil, Malayālam, Telugu, Kannada.

Returning to the Occident, more precisely to the medieval Christian Occident, we find that for many centuries the regular study of the *Quadrivium* (arithmetic, music, geometry, and astronomy) was a required preliminary to the study of philosophy and theology. This rule, followed in Paris as well as in Oxford, had been the practice in Constantinople where a new branch of science was added to the list, namely, the art of "horse-matters" or veterinary art. In Paris, among the first masters of the Abbey of Saint-Victor,

which was one of the famous Parisian schools of the twelfth century, was the important scholar, Hugh of Saint-Victor. His chief work, the *Didascalicon*, contains a classification of the sciences and is a typical example of the cultural level of the high Middle Ages. The following are its main divisions, resulting from philosophy's encompassing all knowledge. Philosophy is subdivided into: (1) theoretical sciences (mathematics, physics, theology); (2) practical sciences (private or public); (3) mechanical sciences (navigation, agriculture, hunting, medicine, theater); (4) logic, including grammar and rhetoric. There is obviously a certain arbitrariness in the system proposed here, but nautical knowledge emerges as a new branch of science. Furthermore, cartography is soon to make its appearance—well before the era of great sea voyages and discoveries. As for Hugh of Saint-Victor, a curious mind and good pedagogue, he gave his readers the following advice: learn everything, you will see later that nothing is superfluous (*omnia disce, videbis postea nihil esse superfluum*).

In the thirteenth century, we see how Roger Bacon, continuing the work of Robert Grosseteste, placed mathematics at the base of the sciences of nature. His classification contains four large classes: (1) grammar and logic; (2) mathematics; (3) philosophy of nature; and (4) metaphysics and ethics.

We must now observe that the essays on classification mentioned above, though they provide us with a fairly faithful picture of the knowledge of an era and in a given country, have yet failed to yield any satisfactory connection among the scientific disciplines; they fail even more to furnish a theory of knowledge internal to the sciences which would enable us to take into account the great currents of thought in the sciences. It was not until the time of the Renaissance, more specifically, the end of the Renaissance, that a system of classification appeared which for the first time is logical, organic, and firmly structured with respect to aims, objects, and different groups of phenomena. It was the system proposed by Francis Bacon in his work on the worth and advancement of the sciences (*De dignitate et augmentis scientiarum*). The author applied psychological criteria, namely, Memory, Imagination, and Reason: history is constructed by memory, and may be either Civil History or Natural History; poetry flows from the fancy or imagination, and may be narrative, dramatic, or parabolic; finally, philosophy, which results from the use of reason, is divided into the sciences of the divine, of nature, and of man. The system of the classification of the sciences and arts by Francis Bacon was adopted, with a few modifications, by d'Alembert in the *Discours préliminaire des éditeurs de l'Encyclopédie.*

Locke and Leibniz make a clear distinction between natural sciences (of bodies and of the mind) and moral sciences (history and ethics). Locke introduced Semiotic or the science of language, and Leibniz gave logic a preponderant place. From the eighteenth century on, most philosophers and scientists who dealt with classification divided the sciences into two fundamental kinds: sciences of nature and sciences of the mind.

Towards the middle of the nineteenth century there appeared the system of Auguste Comte, which is based on a series of decreasing generality and increasing complexity of subject matter in the following order: mathematics, astronomy, physics, chemistry, biology, sociology. The order of the classes is inherently linear, and has several weak points. Comte pictured in it a "natural logic" which has nothing to do with the modern idea of axiomatic logic. He excluded the study of a spiritual or purely mental subject (it is true that he later added morals and introspective data); he included among the abstract sciences the concrete science of astronomy. His system was reshaped by T. Whittaker who separated the two orders of objective (physical) and subjective (psychological) sciences; unfortunately, this separation fails to take account of the historical development of the sciences.

It was the great physicist A. M. Ampère who proposed to make a comprehensive table of all the fields of science. In his first table, Ampère separated all knowledge into two domains and divided each domain into subdomains and branches; the first domain comprised the cosmological sciences and the second the sciences of the mind. In his second table, each branch is divided into sub-branches and into the primary sciences. In a third and final classification, he divided each science of the first order into sciences of the second and third orders, thus producing a sort of binary system which provided a total of $2^7 = 128$ names of disciplines. Ampère's system based on the content of the sciences, possesses a very dynamic internal structure; it takes into account the historical relations among different domains and it remains the most complete inventory of scientific knowledge for the mid-nineteenth century.

In 1851, A. A. Cournot worked out a system which introduced a separation between structural laws and historical criteria in all their forms by employing three great series of sciences, a theoretical, an historical, and a practical series, each composed of the following kinds of science: mathematical, physical, biological, mental or symbolical, and political. Every branch of science has its place in one of the three times five boxes in columns. This is clearly an advance on Comte's system in particular, even though, here again, logic remains a difficult science to place satisfactorily. (The question can again be raised whether each science does not have its own axiomatic structure or whether there might not be a common axiomatic structure underlying all the sciences.)

Not long after Cournot, Herbert Spencer started from the assumption that all knowledge varies with the object, and he classified the sciences according to their degree of abstraction in relation to the object. He thus obtained a linear series going from the abstract to the concrete, in which series there is the following order of succession: the abstract sciences, like logic and mathematics which are concerned with the form in which phenomena appear; the abstract-concrete sciences, like mechanics, physics, and chemistry which investigate the causes of these phenomena; and, finally, the concrete sciences which are interested only in results. There is a striking similarity between this division and the one in the passage from Aristotle's *Topics* quoted above.

It is in the *Manuel du libraire et de l'amateur de livres* ("Bookseller's and Book-Lover's Manual") of Jacques-Charles Brunet, and exactly in the introduction to Volume 6 (5th ed. 1865), that we find the first insight into a historical classification. The author examines many systems, including Konrad Gesner's, that of the Parisian publishers at the time of the Revolution, and Ampère's.

Several German and British philosophers and scientists dealt with the same problem of classification. Besides Schopenhauer, who distinguished between empirical (*a posteriori*) sciences and pure (*a priori*) sciences, there were Hegel, Helmholtz, Wilhelm Dilthey, Hugo Münsterberg, and later the psychologists Alfred Adler and Wilhelm Wundt. Wundt drew a sharp contrast between the sciences of the real and formal sciences. The chemist and Nobel laureate Wilhelm Ostwald divided the sciences into formal, physical, and biological. Paul Tillich considered three kinds: sciences of thought or the ideal, of being or the real, and of the mind or normative sciences. Among the British writers, classifications were made by Jeremy Bentham, John Stuart Mill, Karl Pearson, and Franklin H. Giddings. The American scientist and philosopher Charles S. Peirce (son of the mathematician and astronomer Benjamin Peirce) classified the sciences after investigating and writing on logic, psychology, mathematics, astronomy, optics, chemistry, and even technology. Peirce emphasized methods of inquiry in two essays "The Fixation of Belief" and "How To Make Our Ideas Clear" (*Popular Science Monthly*, 1877–78), which mark the beginning of American pragmatism, though he later preferred the term "pragmaticism" (as explained in the article "Pragmatism" in this *Dictionary*). Peirce's trichotomous classification placed Sciences of

Discovery first, followed by Sciences of Review and Practical Sciences in a descending order of importance. Sciences of Discovery included Mathematics (of logic, of discrete series, of continua and pseudo-continua), Philosophy (phenomenology, normative science, metaphysics), and Idioscopy (physical and psychical sciences). Peirce had a low opinion of Comte's and Spencer's attempts at synthesis which fell under Sciences of Review, and had even a lower opinion of the Practical Sciences which included a motley array of items such as etiquette, paper-making, wine tasting, etc. (Peirce, I, 77–137).

In 1920, Adrien Naville's *Classification des sciences* appeared, based not on nomenclature, strictly speaking, but on the leading ideas of the principal groups of sciences and their interrelations. Naville separated three great classes of science: Theorematics, science of laws; History, science of facts; and Canonics, science of normative rules. These three classes provide answers to three questions, respectively: What is possible? What is real? What is good? To Naville the science of laws (nomology) is fundamental. A law is a conditionally necessary relationship; law exists wherever resemblance dominates the scene. Hence, science must be concerned with general facts, thus recalling the statement of Marcelin Berthelot (1827–1907) in the Preface to the *Grande Encyclopédie* (p. v): "The classification of general facts is the classification of the sciences."

In the first class considered by Naville, following nomology are mathematics, physics, chemistry, somatic biology, psychology, and sociology. Natural history, the theory of evolution, and human geography belong to the second class. The sciences of normative rules are the work of the arts and of everything concerned with the beautiful, the true, and the useful for society as well as for the individual.

Among recent thinkers preoccupied with the problem of classification is the Soviet writer Bonifatii M. Kedrov whose system is a closed, cyclical, and tight structure based on principles of objectivity, subordination, and transition from lower to higher forms. The psychologist Jean Piaget has on several occasions investigated classification, its history, and its importance for the theory of knowledge. He has emphasized the increasing interpenetration of all the branches of knowledge, the role of linguistic structuralism, and the operational theory of intelligence. The system which he has proposed is not circular or closed, and even less a linear one, but rather takes the form of a constantly growing spiral. According to Piaget, the subject-object opposition and dualism must be eliminated, for there is a constant interaction and mutual exchange between the two.

The object is known only through actions of the subject and the subject is known only through the relations it has to objects, from which the twofold consequence is that in order to ground logic and mathematics we must really go back in one form or another to the subject, and in order to construct a science of the subject we must go back to biology, hence also to physics and mathematics (Piaget, p. 1159).

Lately a leading role has been assigned to language, to its mathematical structure, its axiomatic logic of grammatical categories, and to the logic of binary relations in linguistics. The linguistic problem is tied to the automatic (computerized) treatment of "information," which is a matter of interest not only to philologists, philosophers, and psychologists but equally as much to mathematicians, cybernetic theorists, and engineers. Logic, which has only with great difficulty found its place in the classification of the sciences, is not the sole basis of structural linguistics, for the latter depends on the psychology of form (*Gestalttheorie*) and on topology and graphs. Starting with language everything seems to converge on the unity of knowledge. This advance towards unity should perhaps be, after all, the primary aim of a new scientific humanism. A classification of the sciences which is free from the subject-object dualism and from an enslaving chainwork of values, and which takes into account the profound, intimate, and reciprocal relationships among all disciplines, would be the only classification fit to instruct us about the present state of our scientific knowledge.

BIBLIOGRAPHY

A.-M. Ampère, *Essai sur la philosophie des sciences, ou Exposition analytique d'une classification de toutes les connaissances humaines* (Paris, 1834). F. Bacon, *De dignitate et augmentis scientiarum* (London, 1623); *Advancement of Learning* (1605), *Novum organum* (1620); rev. English ed. with Introduction by J. E. Creighton (London and New York, 1900). R. Bacon, *The Opus Majus of Roger Bacon*, ed. J. H. Bridge, Vols. I and II (Oxford, 1897), Vol. III with revisions (London, 1900); idem, *The Opus Majus of Roger Bacon*, trans. R. B. Burke (Philadelphia, 1928). L. Baur, ed., "Die philosophischen Werke des Robert Grosseteste, Bischofs von Lincoln," in *Beiträge zur Geschichte der Philosophie des Mittelalters* (Münster, 1912). J. Bentham, "Essay on the Nomenclature and Classification of Arts and Sciences," in *Works*, 11 vols. (New York, 1962), VIII, 63–128. A. Comte, *Cours de philosophie positive* (Paris, 1830–42). A.-A. Cournot, *Essai sur les fondements de nos connaissances* (Paris, 1851); idem, *Des méthodes dans les sciences de raisonnement* (Paris, 1865). Jean le Rond d'Alembert, *Discours préliminaire de l'Encyclopédie* (Paris, 1751). Stewart C. Easton, *Roger Bacon and His Search for a Universal Science* (New York, 1952), has an extensive bibliography. G. Goblot,

Essai sur la classification des sciences (Paris, 1898); idem, *Le système des sciences* (Paris, 1922). H. von Helmholtz, *Über das Verhältnis der Naturwissenschaften zur Gesamtheit der Wissenschaften* (Brunswick, 1862). A. Hill, *Introduction to Science* (London, 1911). B. M. Kedrov, "La classification des sciences," *Actes du IIe Congrès de philosophie scientifique* (Zurich, 1954). G. W. Leibniz, *Nouveaux essais sur l'entendement humain,* Book IV, Ch. XXI, "De la division des sciences," in *Oeuvres philosophiques* . . . (Amsterdam and Leipzig, 1765), pp. 489–96. A. O. Lovejoy, "The Unity of Science," *University of Missouri Bulletin* (1912). R. P. McKeon, *Selections from Medieval Philosophers,* 2 vols. (New York, 1929), I, 259–314, contains excerpts from Grosseteste. A. Naville, *Classification des sciences* (Paris, 1920). K. Pearson, *The Grammar of Science* (London, 1911). C. S. Peirce, *Collected Papers,* ed. C. Hartshorne and P. Weiss, 6 vols. (Cambridge, Mass., 1935), I, 77–137. J. Piaget, "Classification des sciences et principaux courants épistémologiques contemporains," *Logique et connaissance scientifique* (Paris, 1967), esp. pp. 1149–1271. E. C. Richardson, *Classification, Theoretical and Practical* (New York, 1901). H. Spencer, *The Classification of the Sciences* (London, 1864). Paul Tillich, *Das System der Wissenschaften nach Gegenständen und Methoden* (Göttingen, 1923). UNESCO, *Cahiers d'histoire mondiale (Journal of World History),* **9,** 3 (1965); this number is devoted to encyclopedias from antiquity to the present in Europe and in other parts of the world. W. Whewell, *The Philosophy of the Inductive Sciences* (London, 1847). T. Whittaker, *The Metaphysics of Evolution, with other essays* (London, 1926).

PIERRE SPEZIALI

[See also Axiomatization; **Classification of the Arts;** Linguistics; **Pragmatism; Unity of Science.**]

SENSE OF THE COMIC

THE TERM "Comedy" designates certain traits of man's relationship with his fellows. More or less as fate is to the tragic hero, so society is to the comic hero. The idea of the comic, then, refers to some aspect of man's conflict with his group (political, familial, etc.) and its conventions, mores, ideals. But the same man is also part of that society; hence, in struggling with it he is apt to trip himself. Comedy, thus, is an ironic struggle with society.

Comedy involves the failure to live up to an accepted standard, a failure which usually elicits a smiling or laughing reaction. This article will not be concerned with theories of laughter but only with the form and content of the kind of action which awakens the sense of the comic.

The recorded lineage of comic action goes back to the *Margites* (ca. ninth century B.C.). Aristotle makes reference to comic plays enacted in fifth-century Megara. There are other early evidences of comic mimes who, in their little dramas, poked fun at mythological characters or at self-important citizens. Some scholars maintain that the comic tradition, beginning with these Greek sources, is continuous to modern times (cf. A. Nicoll, *Masks, Mimes, and Miracles,* 1963).

The relation of comedy to tragedy has, since the Greeks, appeared to be complex. In a famous passage of the *Symposium* (223D) Socrates argued that the art (τέχνη) of composing comedy is the same sort of thing as the art of composing tragedy. An ancient tradition ascribes to Aristotle an essay on comedy paralleling the *Poetics.* The *Tractatus coislinianus* (ca. 100 B.C.) may have drawn upon such an essay, for it formulates a definition of comedy closely analogous to the famous definition of tragedy in *Poetics* VI, only it remarks that comedy effects the catharsis of "pleasure and laughter." Perhaps an excessive or inappropriate pleasure or laughter was, by means of the comic action, thought to be rendered moderate, as measured by the political and rational nature of man. However, definitions of these terms and the theory explicating their usage have not come down to us. Other aspects of this Aristotelian tradition are mentioned by such writers as Iamblicus and Proclus; it has been elaborated in modern times by Lane Cooper (1922) and by Elder Olson (1968).

Comic writings are loosely organized compared to tragic writings; nevertheless, there is sufficient unity among them to warrant considering the form of comedy in a single section. The use of this form, however, is varied and will later be considered under several headings.

1. The Form of Comic Action. If, inclined by the tradition mentioned above, we accept the view that comedy is analogous in certain respects to the Aristotelian account of tragedy, then the discussion of the formal structure of tragedy, its beginning, middle, and end—and the reference of the end back to the beginning—will be relevant *mutatis mutandum* to comedy. However, certain differences should be emphasized. The principles of likelihood and necessity, which unite the episodes of tragedy, become the principle of comic likelihood. Comic likelihood is not without its own system, yet its logic may be quite different from, often the reverse of, tragic likelihood. It is usually related somehow to the socially actual, desired, or desirable, and by comparison with this standard its ridiculous, absurd, or naturally unlikely character emerges. For instance, a man for whom life has become intolerable jumps from a thirty-story building. On the way down he passes another man in a parachute. "Sissy," he murmurs.

467

Surely also the comic catharsis is significantly different from the tragic. Since the *Tractatus coislinianus* fails to develop definitions of "pleasure and laughter," it may be maintained that the purgation of folly by folly comes closer to describing the effect of actual comedies and comic situations. If the admired average of human kind is the careful worker or the grave professional man, both seriously concerned to act creditably within their social roles, then we must also suppose them at least occasionally to resent the discipline which their roles require and to be restive under the constant restraint which their reputations impose. Beneath the conformist, as Nietzsche insisted, there lives the satyr. Comedy tears off the foolish mask of conformity and indulges for a brief but relieving interval the equally foolish satyr. This catharsis yields an insight into the less respectable but ever present animal-like basis of the human being. Thus it purges folly by means of folly and brings man and his milieu into an easier and perhaps more fruitful harmony. Comedy deprecates the traditional mores, and by means of this permissive irreverence it preserves them. Comedy, like tragedy, is a self-corrective action. Hence John Meredith could speak of comedy as the "ultimate civilizer."

Guided by suggestions offered by Aristotle in the *Poetics*, F. M. Cornford (1914) holds that comedy, like tragedy, evolved from the ancient ritual slaying of the old king or scapegoat for the sake of the continued survival and fertility of the tribe. The agon between the old king and the young pretender, which often ended in the death or mutilation of the former, continued beyond the tragically relevant part usually to a triumphal procession (the *komos*), a feast, and a marriage. The procession, feast, and marriage comprised the portion which became the source of comedy. Or perhaps comedy is the whole ritual action perceived from the point of view of the *komos*, feast, or marriage. In any event, this account of the ancient ritual provides a likely story of the beginning of comedy, its continued preoccupation with political and sexual matters, and its ambiguous combination of opposites: cruelty and celebration, penance and festival, the serious and the irreverent. Comedy, then, is a forgetting of the tragic and bloody renewal in a careless, happy release. Yet a note of anxiety often still runs beneath its ridiculous and jovial surface.

Doubtless no human value is absolute, and no human act or role is as significant as it may at the time be thought to be. The insight of comedy is directed upon the meaningless aspect of human values and upon the absurdity inherent in all human acts, roles, and projects. Yet it is sometimes not without the suggestion of a vision beyond such foolishness.

Illustrating this comic pattern on the generic scale is Homer's *Odyssey*. Although the story begins with the tragedy of the Trojan War, the epic continues with Ulysses' journey back to Ithaca, his arrival disguised as a beggar, his energetic restoration of order, and his repairing to bed with Penelope. All these events come off in a manner basically in accord with the comic spirit; thus life was restored and traditional or ideal values were affirmed.

2. The Content of Comic Action. Taking comedy seriously for a moment, we can imagine the comic hero asking why man is involved in a Kafkaesque labyrinth of institutional red tape, conventional values, and conflicting ideals. The comic spirit responds that the evil of this situation is not an evil in itself. It is not a function of fate nor of cosmic order; rather it is a function of human and social order. Comedy manipulates this situation so that the hero appears as ridiculous (more or less harmlessly excessive) and could reform, or society appears as ridiculous and perhaps might be reformed, or the hero and his society become self-aware, self-critical, and appropriately reaffirm their common ideals. Comedy, thus, tends to adjust the individual toward the actual, or the actual toward the possible, or both toward the ideal. These three alternatives point to the three kinds of content which are enlivened by the comic vision of life. We shall briefly illustrate and consider each kind.

(a) Aristophanes often speaks strongly for an individual's accepting the ancient order of things. In the *Frogs*, for instance, he stages a kind of mock contest between Euripides, representative of liberal social reform, and Aeschylus, representative of traditional wisdom and order; although Aeschylus is pictured as laughably excessive in his traditionalism, he wins the contest hands down. And in the *Clouds*, Socrates is presented either as impiously searching out knowledge about the moon and clouds or else as teaching a destructive and rather foolish sophistry. In the end old Strepsiades, who had apprenticed himself to Socrates, returns chastened to the old ways and Socrates' "think-tank" is burned to the ground. Shakespeare is often moved to make comedy of excess and admonishment. The newly crowned King in the second part of *King Henry the Fourth* represses the irrepressible Falstaff and strongly suggests that he act his age. In *Measure for Measure* the good Duke gives over the rule to the self-righteous Angelo. Angelo sets up a Puritanical society, but then his ordinary human weaknesses get the better of him. His not unusual use of office for egotistical sexual ends is mercilessly exposed.

Molière is deeply devoted to the norms of his culture. Comedy for him is the "mirror of society" in which a man of his time could see the excesses for which society could and would make him suffer. Molière portrays the ridiculous attempts of the bourgeois "gentleman" to deck himself out in aristocratic finery, to acquire fashionable arts and wit, and to marry off his daughter above her station. In *L'Avare*, Harpagon sacrifices everything for money and in the end he gets only that, but only a little of that. Excessive anxiety about death, exaggerated fear of cuckoldry, misanthropy, religious hypocrisy, all these and more are limned by Molière against the backdrop of the honest normalcy of middle-class seventeenth-century mores.

Tom Jones, hero of Fielding's famous novel, lacks social prudence—"the duty which we owe to ourselves," as Squire Allworthy explains. Otherwise he is brimful of the most acceptable natural virtues. He is tricked by the hypocritical prig, Blifil, out of his name, his inheritance, and a possible fortunate marriage. As an outcast he wanders amiably but unthinkingly into various situations, mostly amorous. Finally he discovers himself apparently in the Oedipus predicament. In the end, though, the predicament proves to be illusory. Tom acquires a modicum of prudence, discovers his real parentage, and of course marries the girl. Blifil is unmasked and gets his due. The norms of good British society are once more reasserted and Fielding has realized his purpose of helping "to laugh mankind out of their favorite follies and vices."

The tradition of the clown, the fool, and the mime, though appearing in other comic roles, as a recollection of the Fool in *King Lear* will indicate, is often utilized by this species of comedy. The medieval clown, like the modern, possessed the usual human appurtenances and attitudes but to a laughably exaggerated degree. Punch, for instance, like many comic-strip characters, is berated and beaten for the thousand petty pretentions and foibles to which socialized man is heir.

(b) Comedy not only finds grist to its mill in the task of converting the deviant or the crackpot individualist into the reliable citizen; it also engages in the movement toward social betterment. Aristophanes' *Lysistrata*, written shortly after the disastrous Sicilian expedition, presents a simple plan for converting Athens from a warlike imperialist power into a peaceful city: the women plan to go on a sex-strike until the men agree to give up war. After some little difficulty in reaching unanimity among the ill-disciplined and lusty Athenian women, peace is achieved and all ends happily in bed.

Many of the Socratic dialogues are comic or utilize comic devices. The *Euthydemus*, to take one instance, offers the spectacle of two Sophistic clowns challenging the bystanders in the Lyceum to verbal battle. They easily defeat the boy, Cleinias, much to their delight, but then they seem to be unaware of being tripped and thrown by Socrates. In the *Meno*, Meno, a notable general, comes off less well in his dialectical struggle with Socrates than his slave boy. And at the end Anytus, taking the part of all right-thinking Athenian gentlemen, is offended upon being shown by Socrates that he knows nothing of the virtue to which he lays claim, and cares less. Socrates himself, with his unconventional manners, his appearance, and his ironic style, is as much a comic as a tragic character. Often, as in *Gorgias* (485ff.), by drawing ridicule upon his strange ways, he was able to turn it back upon popular conventions and values.

With gentle humor Chaucer set the men and women of his own day into contrast with a society or a life symbolized by the Canterbury Pilgrimage. And Rabelais, in a manner which Falstaff himself could not better, exploited the same contrast.

Much of English Restoration comedy expresses disgust with the customs of the times and a longing for reform. Jonson's *Volpone*, like his *Alchemist*, exposes the lust after gold which seemed to infect everyone with greed and duplicity, vices which are only thinly disguised by the ceremonies of civilized life. The elaborate plot and counterplot of *Volpone* are uncovered in the end not by the officers of justice but by the plotters themselves who fall to noisy recrimination. Moreover, the world, it is suggested, is as rapacious and as deceptive as Volpone himself. Wycherly's comedies likewise depict a life which is nasty, brutish, and if not short, certainly hypocritical. Indeed much of Restoration comedy may be characterized as the presentation of a consciously dissembling world. Its manners become the comic mask and, like Swift's bitter satire, suggest by negation a society quite opposite from the actual. No less does Huxley's *Brave New World* make the same suggestion.

Jean Anouilh's comedy, on the other hand, frequently takes the opposite tack. As if in opposition to an exaggerated and impractical idealism, Creon of Anouilh's *Antigone*, like the Grand Inquisitor of Dostoevski's *Brothers Karamazov*, freely admits that systematic injustice and clever manipulation, masked if need be by sophistry and ceremony, offer the only means to maintaining a modicum of social order. And in his *Waltz of the Toreadors* a due concern for forms and ceremony is said not only to keep society going but to provide a convenient and probably defensible screen for a modest self-indulgence. Still Anouilh's personages often seem more or less genuinely to long for an order where the ideal would be pursued for its own sake and where the individual and the common goods would be at one.

(c) Another species of comedy turns upon the point where the humorous and the tragic seem to blend and where the harsh actualities and deception of the world are somehow transformed by a lively faith. This point of turning is admirably illustrated in much of Chekhov. It is developed at length for their respective worlds by Dante in the *Divine Comedy* and by Goethe in the two parts of *Faust*.

More obviously, Cervantes' *Don Quixote* belongs to this species of comedy. The Don's foolish and romantic idealism needs to be brought low and awakened to the realities of the real world. But what is this real world? As embodied in Sancho Panza, it halfway credits the Don's imaginary realm, and in any event it is unwilling to risk losing the opportunity to profit from Don Quixote's possible discoveries. If the Knight of the Mancha is the wild adventurer and explorer, his squire is no less the egotistical exploiter. The gaming, criminal, ribald real world of Sancho Panza is quite as disproportionate in its own way as Don Quixote's. Society continually unhorses the Knight for his nonconformity, but this is such a society as needs to be spurred into movement. Still in the end Sancho Panza achieves some insight into his limitations and is resigned to being himself and to caring for his crops and his family. Likewise at his journey's end, Don Quixote acquires a certain wisdom. He sees that all men are equal in death, and are equally purged of their folly and illusions.

Nowhere, though, is this kind of comedy more clearly and beautifully set forth than in Shakespeare's later plays, the tragicomedies such as *The Winter's Tale* or *The Tempest*. The action in the latter play takes place on the island to which a tempest had borne the dispossessed Duke. Here Ariel balances Caliban; Prospero foils and forgives the unjust manipulations of his brother, and the magic of the world, its cloud-capped towers and gorgeous palaces, all give way to the young lovers. Prospero is a comic Lear; he calms rather than defies the tempest, and he gives himself to wisdom and his daughter to Ferdinand rather than both to death.

Recent tragicomedy is differently keyed. In Samuel Beckett's *Waiting for Godot*, two bums, reminiscent of Rouault's sad clowns, stand aside from the endless sadomasochistic spectacle of the passing world. They wait, for whom or what they know not. Call it Godot. They savor the passage of time, waiting absurdly for the unintelligible object of their faith. Time passes. They consider suicide. A tree buds. Is it the tree of life? Is it Godot himself? Who can say? At least they reach a vague recognition of their indeterminate plight.

The note struck by this kind of comedy is some sort of reconciliation. This is the comic spirit discovering in itself a tincture of seriousness and idealism. This spirit originated in the tragic world, but here it is caught at the moment at which it dissolves into comedy, even as the autumn moves around to vernal excess and as springtime moves on to the fall dance, feast, and festival. The two complement each other and form a unity. Perhaps indeed the seeming two arts of tragedy and comedy may at this point become parts of one and the same whole.

The comic sense, in sum, is an awareness of the ironic character of man's involvement in social evil. In form it may most briefly be described as the catharsis of folly by folly. Comic action has been regarded as a means for disciplining the foolishness inherent in pretentions to social respectability by exhibiting and indulging the foolishness of the "lower" and disreputable self. Consequently it depends upon the possible unity of the traditional duality of "that amphibious creature," man. This unity may be seen in the tendency of the comic sense to bring the deviating individual into accord with social norms, or to bring the deviating society to awareness of the ideal, or, finally, to reconcile the individual and his social milieu with the ideal by way of a productive and unifying insight into a more authentic vision of human possibilities.

BIBLIOGRAPHY

E. M. Blistein, *Comedy in Action* (Durham, N.C., 1964), biblio. pp. 131–39. A. Cook, *The Dark Voyage and the Golden Mean* (New York, 1949). L. Cooper, *An Aristotelian Theory of Comedy* (New York, 1922), biblio. pp. xv–xxi. F. M. Cornford, *The Origin of Attic Comedy* (London, 1914). M. Eastman, *The Enjoyment of Laughter* (New York, 1936). E. Lauter, *Theories of Comedy* (New York, 1964). A. Nicoll, *The Theory of Drama* (New York, 1931), pp. 175–243; suggestions for reading, pp. 245–56. A. Nicoll, *Masks, Mimes, and Miracles* (New York, 1963). E. Olson, *The Theory of Comedy* (Bloomington, Ind., 1968). H. T. E. Perry, *Masters of Dramatic Comedy and their Social Themes* (Cambridge, Mass., 1939), biblio. pp. 409–17. L. J. Potts, *Comedy* (London, 1948), biblio. pp. 168–71.

EDWARD G. BALLARD

[See also Art and Play; Catharsis; **Classification of the Arts;** Motif; **Satire; Tragic Sense;** Wisdom of the Fool.]

CONSERVATION OF NATURAL RESOURCES

THE WORD *conservation* has its origins in the Latin term *conservare*, meaning "to guard," and has been passed on to English through the Old French verb *conserver*. The dictionary definition equates it with preservation, guarding, protecting, or with the related word "conservancy." In its modern usage, however, and relation to natural resources, conservation has become a well-known idea only during the twentieth century and largely through the efforts of such men as Gifford Pinchot and Theodore Roosevelt in the United States (Pinchot, 1947).

During the twentieth century conservation has formed the basis for scientific, economic, and political attitudes toward man's environment. In the decade of the 1960's in particular it has attracted many supporters, each with a somewhat different idea of its meaning. The definition accepted in 1969 by the United Nations and the International Union for the Conservation of Nature is "the rational use of the environment to achieve the highest quality of living for mankind." This definition covers a wide range of ideas that could only be discussed in a long book. In this brief account, some of the development of these ideas in Western culture will be examined. However, conservation as an activity if not as a philosophy is to be found in all human cultures. It is of ancient origin.

Natural resources are variously defined in textbooks as "elements of the natural environment come into the service of man" (Smith, 1950); "uncaptured natural stores which are useful to mankind in any way" (Allen, 1959), or those natural "materials, areas, or living things considered useful or of value to a particular human culture" (Dasmann, 1968). This concept, like that of conservation, has had a shifting meaning over time. In 1969 resources are being equated with the sum total of the physical and biological environment for man on earth.

Concern over population increase or decrease is probably as old as mankind. Unquestionably at many times in human history, local populations exerted pressure upon local environments, and through this disturbance of the conditions of living endangered their own survival. The origin of primitive means for population control can be attributed to such recurring prehistoric dilemmas. However, concern for the dangers inherent in a worldwide increase of the human species can be considered of recent, probably eighteenth-century, origin, since it was at this time that the dimensions of the world and the potentials for human population increase were first well understood. Widespread apprehension over such dangers, and the concept of a "population explosion" followed World War II. The relationship between world population increase and world conservation appears to have been first defined and stressed in popular language by William Vogt (1948) and by Fairfield Osborn (1948).

It is impossible to identify the time when man first became aware of the consequences of excessive use or misuse of the resources of his environment, and took measures to protect himself and his habitat—measures that are today characterized as conservation. The evidence for such awareness is to be found, however, among most primitive peoples and among the historical evidences of man's use of the land. Edward Graham (1947) has reviewed some practices of the early Eskimo that fully qualify as conservation practices. Stewart Udall (1963) discusses the reverence felt by the American Indians for the lands on which they depended, and the skill with which they cultivated and fertilized their gardens. The adaptation of various primitive land-use practices to environmental realities is discussed in Carl Sauer (1952).

It may be generalized that primitive peoples learned those conservation practices that permitted their survival, although the abstract idea of conservation was probably neither understood nor stated. Man's early view of "natural resources" would necessarily be limited by his technology, and would at first include only those plants and animals useful for food or other purposes, water, and places in the environment suited to various needs. Much that is regarded today as a "natural resource," metallic ore, for example, would have no known value to primitive man. Much that he regarded as of great value, obsidian for spearheads, for example, would scarcely be considered a natural resource today except as a part of a broader environment.

In the written records of mankind the idea of conservation is closely related to man's view of the natural world and of his relationship with nature. It can be reasoned that the idea of nature or of a natural world did not occur until man, through civilization, had created an environment different from and in part separate from the surrounding world. But long before the obvious differences between the city and wild land had appeared, man had been modifying the environment in which he lived. Sauer (1952) has emphasized the role of Paleolithic man in changing his environment through the use of fire, and of his role in the extermination of the larger wild animals that had survived the Ice Ages. From the time when man first practiced agriculture and began to domesticate animals, the contrast between the tamed agricultural landscape and the wild, untouched country elsewhere must have been apparent. Clarence Glacken (1967) has pointed out that the contrast between man and nature observed by the Greeks and Romans was less the contrast between the city and the wilderness, for the latter was little known to them, than that between the city and the rural landscape of farms, pastures, and woodlands.

In the literature of the Western world a clear description of a conservation problem first appears in the writings of Plato. In *Critias* he attributes the decline in the fertility of Attica to deforestation, soil erosion,

471

and the consequent disruption of the hydrology of mountain watersheds.

A. O. Lovejoy (1936) attributes to the *Timaeus* of Plato the "principle of plenitude," an idea of major significance to modern conservation and to the science of ecology. Essentially this states that the world is better the more things and the more variety it contains; that there is a striving in nature toward diversity, toward the filling of all vacant niches in the environment with differing kinds of living things. The philosophy of those who today seek to preserve the maximum variety of living species may be traced back to this beginning. The writings of Charles Elton (1958) and Raymond Dasmann (1968) develop the more recent scientific basis for the ecological "principle of diversity."

Glacken (1967) has traced to such ancient Greeks as Anaxagoras, Anaximander, Empedocles, and Plato the general concept of a terrestrial unity in the midst of diversity, of an earth that is a fit environment for people and other forms of life. The Greek concept of the *ecumene*, sometimes translated as the inhabited or inhabitable world, is clearly related to the modern ecological concept of the biosphere—the thin film of air, water, and soil on the surface of the earth, upon which all life depends, and within which it exists.

Sound guides to land care based upon conservation principles appear by the third century B.C. in some of the writings of the Hellenistic period. Thus, *The Tebtunis Papyri* of Egypt includes instructions for the management of irrigated lands, for sowing, planting, and land care (Glacken, 1967). But long before this the Egyptians had been practicing empirically a high degree of sound conservation in their management of the lands of the Nile Valley. It is significant that these lands have supported civilization over five millennia, without serious impairment until recent times.

Some agricultural conservation with particular attention to the maintenance of soil fertility and the prevention of soil erosion was well established in Roman times and has been perpetuated in the writings of Cato, Columella, and Pliny. In Roman times also the movement of water over long distances to reclaim lands through irrigation had reached a level of development not to be equaled again in the Western world until the twentieth century. In this period also there is a forerunner of the controversies to be waged between the builders of dams and the conservationists of twentieth-century America. In the writings of Tacitus is an argument against the damming of rivers and the changing of their courses, pleading the loss of long-established farming lands. "Nature has made the best provision for the interests of humanity, when she assigned to rivers their proper mouths—their proper courses—their limits as well as their origins. Consideration, too, should be paid to the faith of their fathers, who had hallowed rituals and groves and altars to their country streams. Besides they were reluctant that Tiber himself, bereft of his tributary streams, should flow with diminished majesty" (Glacken [1967], p. 135).

The writings of Columella (first century A.D.) show great understanding of the relationship between misuse of the lands and their declining fertility. His descriptions of the ways in which soil fertility is derived and maintained under undisturbed conditions follows closely that of modern ecologists. Pliny carries this reasoning further, and recommends such practices as contour plowing to prevent loss of soils on the hillsides (Glacken, 1967). However, long before this time the Phoenicians had terraced the hills of Lebanon as a soil conservation measure.

Lewis Mumford (1961) has pointed out that in ancient Rome the full enormity of many of our modern problems of pollution had been recognized. Efforts to cope with them led to the construction of the great sewer, the *cloaca maxima*, of Rome, as a means for removing water-borne wastes, but this was at best a partial solution. The disposal of solid wastes remained a serious problem for all of the large cities of ancient times.

Perhaps because man's own existence was continually threatened in the European world that existed from the fall of Rome into the Middle Ages, there appears to be little writing relative to conservation. From the seventeenth century onward, however, with the agency of man on earth securely established and his hegemony reinforced by the growing industrial revolution, a concern for nature and for the growth of human populations becomes more apparent.

An interest in wildlife conservation, related to an interest in hunting, appears to be of great antiquity among the writings of mankind. Thus there is an inscription attributed to Sennacherib, describing the establishment of a wildlife sanctuary near Nineveh—an effort that would do credit to the best modern wildlife conservationists (Graham, 1947). Efforts to preserve game through regulation of human hunting and trapping of wildlife has a long history, but is related commonly to the desire to preserve suitable hunting grounds for royalty rather than any broad concern for wildlife as such. Aldo Leopold (1933) has traced the development of game laws from biblical injunctions through Greco-Roman times to the present British and American legal concepts. Graham (1947) in a similar review of the history of wildlife conservation points out that the American view of ownership and authority over wild animal life relates back to the British view that wildlife was the property of the Crown. Thus, fee-simple ownership of land in America includes the ownership of vegetation and underground resources, but not of the wild animals that live on the land.

Although there are many forerunners, a broad, modern view of conservation becomes most clearly apparent in two seventeenth-century works. John Evelyn, a founder of the Royal Society of London for Improving Natural Knowledge (1662), in his *Silva: or a discourse of forest trees . . .* (1664), provided a view of the consequences of deforestation in Great Britain, and recommended the establishment of forestry as a science and a concern of the Royal Society. His writings go beyond forest conservation to expound ideas of land management to create a landscape more pleasing as well as useful to people. He presents one of the early descriptions of the causes and consequences of air pollution, already a serious concern in London because of the industrial use of soft coal. At approximately the same time in France work was progressing under the leadership of Louis XIV's minister, Colbert, to produce the *French Forest Ordinance of 1669*. Motivated also by the evidence of increasing forest destruction and its consequences, the writers of this ordinance sought to present a plan for sound land management to be applied to all of France.

Increasing knowledge of natural history and biology, and an ever broadening view of the realities of the global environment gave greater scope to eighteenth-century ideas of conservation. The ability of G. W. Leibniz to define order in the midst of apparent chaos foreshadowed the work of modern technology and ecology. The establishment by Carolus Linnaeus of a philogenetic classification of living species provided a basis for describing and analyzing nature that permitted the development in the next century of Charles Darwin's evolutionary theory. It also paved the way for ecological understanding, and for greater human concern over the fate of wild species. Immanuel Kant analyzed the distinction between natural and man-made processes on earth, and recognized man as an agency causing change on earth comparable to a geological force (*Sämtliche Werke*, 8, 300). J. W. von Goethe showed an understanding of the relationships between organisms and environment that was later to be substantiated by ecologists. However, the works of Count Buffon and of Alexander von Humboldt reflect some of the major advances in thinking relative to conservation during the eighteenth and early nineteenth centuries.

Among his many accomplishments, including that of providing a basis for the science of biogeography, Humboldt was able to perceive the concept of a unity and prevailing order in nature, exhibiting itself in various environments in great variety and complexity.

He described with accuracy the major communities of vegetation on earth, the natural processes operating on them and the effects of man's activities, and provided a foundation for ecology and conservation.

Count Buffon brought together much of the knowledge of natural history available in his day. His interest lay in the agency of man on earth, rather than in wild nature as such. He distinguished the role of man in making the earth more fit for his own occupancy, and also his role as an exploiter and destroyer of natural resources. In one sense he can be considered a forerunner of those technologists who believe that through the application of science the earth can be made increasingly fruitful for ever increasing numbers of men.

The dangers inherent in the increase in human numbers on a limited earth exercised the thinking of many during the late eighteenth century. Noteworthy were M. J. de Condorcet, William Godwin, and Thomas Malthus. The argument in which they were engaged continues with similar vigor today. The Marquis de Condorcet foresaw an infinite perfectibility in human institutions. Although concerned with the potential for increase in human populations, he foresaw man's ability to cope with this problem when it arose. He was not unaware of the need for an ultimate limitation on the numbers of mankind but believed implicitly in man's future ability to limit his own increase and not to "encumber the world with useless and wretched beings."

Godwin had less faith in human institutions, but more in individuals. He could not foresee any real environmental limitations on either the numbers of man or his individual perfectibility. It was against Godwin in particular, but also de Condorcet, that the essays of Malthus were directed. In his view human perfectibility was a chimera, human population increase inexorable. Despite man's best intentions he was bound to run afoul of the limited capacity of the earth to provide for his sustenance. He foresaw a time of misery when populations would exert pressure upon the farthest boundaries of the earth. Only in the latter half of the twentieth century has the evidence in support of Malthus' thesis become widely available, but the argument continues to rage between those who see applied technology as the answer to population problems, and those who view dismally the limits of the earth.

It is necessary next to move to America to follow the trend of ideas relating to conservation, since it is in the United States that the concept has received its greatest development.

In the colonization of the New World the emigrants of Europe were placed in a position similar to that of primitive man. Wild nature was omnipresent; man's influence and power seemed insignificant. The issue at stake was survival for the fragile first colonies, not a concern for the preservation of nature. The concept of a relatively limitless continent with inexhaustible resources unquestionably dominated popular thinking during most of colonial times. Yet the danger of running out of some needed resource seemed apparent to certain individuals even at a time when overall space and resources were obviously vast. Thus, in the seventeenth century, in the earliest of colonial times, a concern for game preservation appears. In 1677, the colony of Connecticut provided for the regulation of hunting, and prohibited the export of game, hides, or skins (Graham, 1947). Protection of wildlife through regulation of hunting was established in twelve of the thirteen American colonies by the time of the revolution (Palmer, 1912). Forest conservation attracted attention at an even earlier date, so that by 1626 Plymouth Colony passed an ordinance prohibiting the cutting of timber on colony lands without official permission. In 1681 William Penn provided that one acre of forest land be left untouched for every five that were cleared. As early as 1799, the federal stake in forests was recognized when Congress provided for a forest reserve to supply ship's timbers to the Navy (Illick, 1939).

At a time when the American wilderness appeared endless and had scarcely been explored, a wilderness traveller, George Catlin, artist and student of the Indian, foresaw a time when wilderness might disappear. Witnessing the slaughter of buffalo, he could envisage their disappearance from the plains of America, and with them the Indians who depended upon them. In his journal for 1832 he proposed, for the first time, the concept of a national park in which the wild lands in all of their beauty, the animals, and the primitive Indians also, might jointly be protected for the ages to come. Several decades were to pass before Americans could accept the need for such a park.

The awakening of an American interest in the beauty of nature, the value of wilderness, and an appreciation of wildlife, owes much to the writings of such men as William Bartram, who explored the wild country of the East and South, and described it in his *Travels* (1791); James Fenimore Cooper, whose *Last of the Mohicans* appeared in 1826; and the writing and painting of John James Audubon, which began to appear in the 1830's. However, a broad philosophy of nature and man in America owes its origin in particular to Henry David Thoreau. Although a dweller in the rural woodlands rather than the Western wilderness, his appreciation of the values of the natural world transcended his geographical limitations. In his religion and philosophy he is indebted to his friend Ralph Waldo Emerson. Both saw in man and nature a mani-

festation of divine being. Thoreau saw in nature the possibility for true human freedom and spiritual enrichment. His oft-quoted phrase "in Wildness is the preservation of the World" reflects his philosophy, and was first stated in 1851. In 1858 he called for the creation of national parks in which wilderness could be preserved.

Thoreau's moral view of man's relationship with nature, recognizing an obligation toward it and a spiritual enrichment to be derived from it, is carried on by George Perkins Marsh whose *Man and Nature* (1864) is a scientific, comprehensive account of the worldwide impact of man upon the natural world, including the consequences of deforestation and watershed abuse. Marsh saw in the ruined lands around the Mediterranean the probable future of the new lands being recklessly misused in America. He called for a program of action to restore and rebuild the land, essentially the creation of a conservation movement. Unlike Thoreau, Marsh was practically oriented, and concerned with the use of natural resources under proper limits to improve the lot of mankind. He thus bridged the gap to arise later between utilitarian conservation and the believers in nature preservation as such.

It is worth noting that the thoughts and words of all who preceded Marsh had little influence upon the course of events in the world. Destruction of natural resources, encouraged by the decisions of political men and carried out by practical men of action, went on despite all that had been written. Early measures for conservation had little effect on man's behavior. Laws were seldom or poorly enforced. What was later to be known as America's federal department of conservation, the Department of the Interior, was established in 1849, but in its early decades it was far more concerned with the transfer of land and resources into private hands to encourage settlement than it was with their conservation. Government policy and private initiative operated on the understanding that nature was a force to be overcome, not an ally to work with and cherish. Yet, by the time Marsh's words appeared in print, the first steps toward arresting the degradation of natural resources had been taken.

The New York landscape architect, Frederick Law Olmsted, who had designed Central Park in New York City (1857–58), visited California in the early 1860's, and saw the grandeur of Yosemite Valley. Due to his influence, in part, Congress was persuaded, in the dying days of the Civil War in 1864, to pass a bill to preserve this area "for public use, resort and recreation." The significance of this act was scarcely realized by those who engaged in it, but the first step had been taken toward realizing the dream of Catlin and Thoreau.

Lacking at that time a federal organization to operate parks, Congress turned Yosemite over to California, as the nation's first state park.

In 1872, when Ulysses S. Grant was President, a bill that in Udall's words (1963) was "little-debated and little understood" passed Congress, and Yellowstone National Park was created in the wilds of Wyoming. This first unit in the national park system provided for the protection of wild nature, and had the greatest appeal to the followers of the Thoreau tradition. As a result of the influence of Stephen T. Mather, a Chicago businessman, the national parks were placed in 1916 under the administration of a special agency in the Department of the Interior, the National Park Service, which Mather was to head. Unfortunately, the act creating the Service contained wording that provided a built-in dilemma for those charged with the administration of the parks. They were told to provide for public use and enjoyment of the parks while at the same time leaving them "unimpaired for the enjoyment of future generations." With ever-growing use in the twentieth century the task of avoiding impairment has been at times impossible.

The late 1860's brought into the field men who were to contribute greatly in later decades to thinking about natural resources and their use. John Muir, a naturalist born in Scotland, came to California and began to explore the Sierra Nevada in 1868. In 1869 the American explorer and geographer, John Wesley Powell, began his descent of the Colorado River through the Grand Canyon. Muir deplored the despoiling of nature. In the tradition of Thoreau he worked for the preservation of great wilderness areas, not as storehouses of materials, but as sources of spiritual enlightenment and physical well-being for man. He became a battler for national parks, with Yosemite his special concern, and for wildlife and wilderness. With Thoreau he is a founder of the nature "preservationist" school of conservation thought. Although Muir's books, such as *Our National Parks* and *The Mountains of California* were mostly published after the turn of the century, his influence was felt strongly during the late nineteenth century.

John Wesley Powell's *Report on the Lands of the Arid Region of the United States,* published by Congress in 1878, did much to dispel the "myth of abundance" which had influenced the thought of pioneer America. Surveying the arid West, Powell recognized the limitations of its capacity to support either agriculture or grazing animals, and saw in its watersheds and their hydrology the key to its future. The reclamation of arid lands through irrigation became a theme which he pursued throughout his life, although his goal, a federal role in reclamation, did not become

realized until the creation, in the year of his death (1902) of a Bureau of Reclamation in the Department of the Interior. Powell, along with Marsh, recognized the role that scientific knowledge must play in any rational policy of land use. Through his influence the Geological Survey was established in the Department of the Interior in 1879, and still earlier the private American Association for the Advancement of Science was created. The followers of Powell's brand of conservation, however, were later to come into frequent conflict with those of John Muir, as we shall see below.

Under the administration of President Hayes, the Department of the Interior was headed by Carl Schurz. In 1877 his first report as Secretary scored the lumbermen for their depredations of America's public lands, and called for establishment of a system of federal forest reserves. It was not, however, until 1891 that President Harrison was influenced by Interior Secretary John Noble to establish such reserves. By a brief clause in a public lands bill, Harrison was authorized by Congress to establish by proclamation what was later to become the national forest system of the United States.

Because the last decades of the nineteenth and the first of the twentieth centuries in America saw the culmination of a long period of plunder of natural resources, and also the end of the frontier period in history, there was a widespread awakening of interest in conservation. However, much of this concern was directed toward the halt of further depredations of America's resources, and a belief that what was gone was forever lost. Only a few were thinking of possible restoration and repair through the operation of natural ecological processes—of the return of wildlife, the regeneration of forests, the long-term management of living resources based on recognition of rates of growth and of population increase. Ecology was a new science, and it was not until the appearance of Frederick Clements' book *Plant Succession* (1916) and Charles Elton's *Animal Ecology* (1927) that it became generally applied to natural resource management. Forestry was an exception, and America's first foresters were trained in Europe where ecological thinking was further advanced than in America.

Conservation as a national movement in America owes much to the influence of such men as Gifford Pinchot, a forester trained in France, and Theodore Roosevelt, a naturalist who became president. This early development of the conservation movement is described in Pinchot's *Breaking New Ground* (1947). In his view a "turning point in human history" occurred when Roosevelt called his Governors' Conference on conservation in 1908. Pinchot's point of view on forest conservation was use-oriented. Forests, he found, could be managed to produce crops of trees, restoring themselves through natural regeneration, or through man's aid in reforestation. Most lands could be managed to produce useful products as a "sustained yield" if care was taken to preserve the soil and a seed stock. Furthermore, any area of land could be managed to produce several kinds of useful products such as water, wood, and wildlife, an idea later to be formalized into the "multiple-use" concept adopted by Pinchot's Forest Service for management of national forest lands.

It was inevitable that the Pinchot view of conservation, like that of Powell, would clash with that of John Muir and his followers, who preferred nature in a wild and undisturbed state and were unattracted by useful products from former wilderness areas. This clash first attracted public notice when a proposal to construct the Hetch-Hetchy dam and reservoir in the Tuolumne Canyon of Yosemite National Park reached the attention of John Muir and his followers in his newly established Sierra Club. To Muir the Tuolumne was "sacred ground" not to be marred for utilitarian purposes. To the followers of Pinchot and to Roosevelt, it was not. Despite Muir's resistance, the dam was constructed.

It is significant that one of the more important contributions to the ethical and spiritual view of conservation since the time of John Muir came from a man who was himself basically in the Pinchot tradition of management for use. Aldo Leopold, who is credited by many as being the founder of modern, scientifically-based wildlife management, believed in producing game for the hunter's pleasure and table. His *Game Management* was the first textbook of wildlife conservation, and took into account the principles of animal ecology of Charles Elton. Nevertheless, he was a leading exponent of the preservation of wilderness for the same reasons as those that motivated Catlin, Thoreau, and Muir. In his *A Sand County Almanac* . . . (1949) he pleaded for the development of an *ecological conscience* to guide man's relationships with the land and his total environment, and for an extension of ethics to include a *land ethic* which might lead to a consideration of nature at least equal to man's consideration for his fellow human beings.

During the twentieth century, and in particular during its second half, the concept of conservation has steadily broadened to include all of those relationships between man and his environment, from the environment within cities, with their problems of crowding, congestion, and pollution, through to the preservation of rare species in remote wilderness regions. Starting with the works of Vogt and Osborn after World War II, conservation writings have become concerned with the problem of human population increase and its consequences. Ideas and practices of conservation developed in America have been widely accepted throughout the world. The international scope of the conservation movement was indicated by the formation in 1948 of what is now the International Union for the Conservation of Nature and Natural Resources. Recent views of the broad scope of conservation are available in such books as Udall's (1963) or Dasmann's (1968).

BIBLIOGRAPHY

The idea of conservation, related as it is to the man-nature theme, can be traced through Clarence Glacken, *Traces on the Rhodian Shore* (Berkeley, 1967). Glacken follows the theme of nature and culture in Western thought from ancient times up through the eighteenth century, and presents a comprehensive bibliography. William L. Thomas, ed., *Man's Role in Changing the Face of the Earth* (Chicago, 1956), is the transactions of a conference sponsored by the Wenner-Gren Foundation, and pursues many of the concepts basic to the idea of conservation. For the development of the conservation idea in America, Stewart L. Udall, *The Quiet Crisis* (New York, 1963), is particularly useful. It can be supplemented by Gifford Pinchot, *Breaking New Ground* (New York, 1947), and by Roderick Nash, *The American Environment: Readings in the History of Conservation* (Reading, Mass., 1968). A history of ideas on wildlife conservation is presented by Aldo Leopold, *Game Management* (New York, 1933), and Edward H. Graham, *The Land and Wildlife* (New York, 1947). The urban environment and the conservation problems related to it can be examined in Lewis Mumford, *The City in History* (New York, 1961).

The first books relating the world population problem to the problems of conservation are those of William Vogt, *Road to Survival* (New York, 1948), and Fairfield Osborn, *Our Plundered Planet* (Boston, 1948), covering the period of population crisis following the end of the Second World War. The modern scope of conservation is presented in Raymond F. Dasmann, *Environmental Conservation* (New York, 1968), and in Udall's book mentioned above.

Other references included in the discussion are: Shirley Allen, *Conserving Natural Resources* (New York, 1959). William Bartram, *The Travels of William Bartram* . . . (1791; various reprints). Georges Louis Leclerc, Comte de Buffon, *Natural History, General and Particular* (1749ff.; London, 1812). Frederick Clements, *Plant Succession* (Pittsburgh, 1916). M. J., Marquis de Condorcet, *Sketch for a Historical Picture of the Conquest of the Human Mind* (1795; New York, 1955). Charles Elton, *Animal Ecology* (London, 1927); idem, *The Ecology of Invasions by Animals and Plants* (London and New York, 1958). John Evelyn, *Silva: or, A Discourse of Forest-Trees, and the Propagation of Timber in His Majesty's Dominion* (1664; later reprints). William Godwin, *Of Population* (London, 1820). Alexander von Humboldt, *Cosmos: A Sketch of a Physical Description of the Universe* (1845–62; many editions). Joseph Illick, *An*

Outline of General Forestry (New York, 1939). Aldo Leopold, *A Sand County Almanac* (New York, 1949). Arthur O. Lovejoy, *The Great Chain of Being: A Study of the History of an Idea* (Cambridge, Mass., 1936). Thomas Malthus, *An Essay on Population* . . . (1798; various reprints). George P. Marsh, *Man and Nature, or Physical Geography as Modified by Human Action* (1864; Cambridge, Mass., 1965). John Muir, *The Mountains of California* (New York, 1894); idem, *Our National Parks* (Boston, 1901). T. S. Palmer, "Chronology and Index of American Game Protection, 1776–1911," U.S. Department of Agriculture, Biological Survey, Bulletin 41 (1912). John Wesley Powell, *Report on the Lands of the Arid Region of the United States* (Washington, D.C., 1878). Carl O. Sauer, *Agricultural Origins and Dispersals* (American Geographical Society, 1952). Guy-Harold Smith, ed., *Conservation of Natural Resources* (New York, 1950). Henry David Thoreau, *Excursions, the Writings of Henry David Thoreau* (1863; reprint Boston, 1893).

RAYMOND F. DASMANN

[See also Environment; **Environment and Culture;** Evolutionism; Nature; Perfectibility.]

CONSERVATISM

I. INTRODUCTION

1. Contemporary Usage. With the exception of Scandinavia, England, and a few countries of the British Commonwealth, no major national political party has officially labelled itself "conservative." Parties of the political "right" are, however, frequently called "conservative." Moreover, in the course of a general broadening of the political spectrum to the "left," the range of positions called "conservative" has become increasingly wider; however, it has become necessary to make a distinction between conservative and reactionary positions and policies. In everyday speech in the 1960's the term "conservative" seems to be more widespread than the contrasting terms "liberal" or "radical"; it denotes, as used by opponents mostly with a critical or pejorative tone, an attitude that attaches greater importance to the preservation and care of the traditional and enduring than to innovation and change. The typical conservative defends individual and collective material and cultural possessions, fears and resists revolution, and accepts progress only as a gradual development from the existing political system. This in turn places those who think and feel conservatively in a permanently defensive position from which they either incline to cultural pessimism or are obliged to demonstrate that "genuine," "true" conservatism is not really hostile to change, but is indispensable for the stability of a society with deep concern for the maintenance of continuity.

2. Etymological Summary. In Latin *conservare* means to protect, preserve, save; the noun of agency, *conservator*, appears as a synonym for the substantives *custos, servator*. Just as the Greek *Sōter* ("Savior") was adopted from the religious realm by the Hellenistic cult of the ruler, so too *conservator* is found among the Romans beginning in the Augustan era (as an epithet of both Jupiter and Caesar). Augustus appears as *Novus Romulus*, as protector of the *mos maiorum* and *pater patriae* to whom the Senate dedicated the coinage inscription *Parenti Cons* (*ervatori*) *Suo*.

In Christianity *conservator* appears along with the proper name for the Savior (*salvator*) on some occasions. Beginning in the thirteenth century, upon the acceptance of Roman law, *conservator* appears north of the Alps as a juridical and administrative term for an imperial, royal, or church functionary charged with the preservation or restoration of rights; in England they were predecessors of the "Justices of the Peace." In French *conservateur* is used roughly from 1400 to the end of the eighteenth century in the sense of an "official charged with the guardianship and protection of certain rights, of certain public property."

The political usage of "conservative" is derived from the French *conservateur*, and begins to appear only after the French Revolution, and then very hesitantly. In his *Reflections on the Revolution in France* (1790) Burke used the verb "to conserve," while his German translator, Friedrich Gentz, later spoke of the "tendency to conserve." In France *conservateur* in the sense of moderation and conservation may also refer primarily to *idées libérales*. In this sense it was used, among others, by Mme de Staël (1798) and by Napoleon on the 19th of Brumaire 1799: "Conservative, tutelary, and liberal ideas have come into their own by the dispersion of the factions which have been oppressing the Councils." The modern political meaning: "one who is a partisan of the maintenance of the established social and political order," derives from Chateaubriand's weekly newspaper *Le Conservateur* (started in 1818). ("*Le Conservateur* will support religion, the King, liberty, the Charter, and loyal, respectable people. . . .") "Conservateur" has never appeared as the official name of a party in France.

The characteristic political connotation of the English term "conservative" took final form in the 1820's in line with French usage. In 1827 Wellington expected from the *"parti conservateur"* of England the unity of all forces dedicated to the preservation of monarchical and aristocratic privileges in opposition to radical demands; in the struggles over the final version of the Reform Bill after 1830, "conservative" was often understood in the sense of "local, constitutional," and as the antithesis of "anarchic, radical." As the name of a party and as the expression of a changed conception of its own policies, "conservative party" appeared along with "Tory party" for the first time in 1830, though its meaning remained controversial. It was the personality of Peel that imposed an interpretation on the word "conservative" that may still count as valid to this day: defense of law and order, along with a willingness to reform any institution really in need of amelioration, but by gradual and deliberate steps.

II. NONIDEOLOGICAL CONSERVATISM

At all times and in all societies there are people—not only those who belong to the "establishment"—who desire the continuance of the value systems and milieu in which they have grown up or to which they have risen. Just to the extent that they fear departure from the familiar and prefer the certainty of the known to the risk of innovation, the traditional way of life will seem binding and sacrosanct to them, and imperiling it blasphemous. Much more so than those who see themselves as liberals, democrats, progressives, or socialists, and who have more or less conscious notions of what ought to be, conservatives perceive (and conduct) themselves within the framework of traditional value systems and models of behavior which are taken for granted rather than thought about; the ideological character of this is usually denied. Indeed, in the conservative's ideology and outlook on life there is hardly any distinction in the natures of religion, ethics, everyday morality, philosophy, politics, and understanding of the contemporary age. There is, instead, a reliance upon the individual and collective experience of living due to the superiority of age; upon historical development understood by analogy to the process of biological growth; upon an order that is not intellectually postulated but is imposed by nature, and upon the authority of persons and institutions whose legitimacy is considered to be self-evident rather than calling for critical examination. A conservative mentality is somehow a "natural" phenomenon, above all in established social groups: among the representatives and officials of traditional institutions as well as among the locally and professionally relatively stable portions of society (farmers, craftsmen). It also develops when upward social mobility has proved successful or when there is a readiness, following initial opposition, to identify oneself with the status claims and experience of family, occupation, or social group.

The criteria of value and taste corresponding to this mentality rely on preconceived judgments, on the "tried and true," and *eo ipso* a higher status is given

to the "eternal" values that are assumed to be independent of ephemeral fads and fashions. Intellectuality, rationalism, and criticism are indeed rejected as abstractions, but so are their opposites: extravagance of feeling, ecstatic self-abandon, and mystical withdrawal. In contrast to these the conservative mentality claims to be realistic and "practical," yet orients itself mostly by a pristine model that is thought to be perfect. Its reaction to the present is thus often defensive or selective, rejecting certain tendencies as destructive and affirming others as constructive and sound.

This "traditionalist" mentality remains latent so long as it is not provoked by encountering change or by an attack on vested rights and interests. When it is given expression, conservatism is thus almost always resistant and liable to react.

From this mentality forms of social behavior result that are determined by a sense of family, local and social stability, and the recognition of intrasocietal distinctions. The circle of marriages is kept relatively small, differences of faith and education are rarely overlooked, local usage and established class morals are heeded, and much is made of the authority of parents and the teacher's right to correct. Family and regional groups organized along corporative (*ständisch*) lines constitute the inner framework of conservative social conduct, so that individualism is as suspect as egalitarian collectivism; the concept of universal freedom is as incomprehensible as the concept of universal equality. The Church and its behests are approved and defended as social forces or factors; the standards of conduct and morality of earlier generations still possess the binding force of law. Social origin is assigned higher prestige than earned status; inherited property is more highly valued than acquired possessions; congenital qualities are given greater weight than those conditioned by and acquired in the environment. Conservative social conduct functions within the structure of a preconceived class and hierarchical order encompassing the whole of society, within which each man has his recognized station, and is protected in it by valid rights and by higher authority legitimized by its office (not democratically or by popular vote).

When placed on the defensive, conservative social action can easily turn into ideology and thereby achieve a consciously stylized veneration of past order in opposition to the present-day "fragmentation" and "destruction" of society. Aspects of this kind of attitude are still to be found everywhere even in contemporary egalitarian societies.

In its economic thought and action the conservative mentality is expressed in its attachment to traditional modes of labor and consumption, in its reluctant acceptance and almost rejection of industrialization and capitalistic competition, and in its inclination toward paternalism in business methods. The farmer, artisan, merchant are taken to be the basic types of working man; their attitude toward work (*Arbeitsethos*) is frequently preserved even in industrial society and is often idealized. If, as a result of changes in the economic structure and rationalization of production methods, certain branches of the economy are forced on the defensive, antimodernistic feelings often arise, including demands for a protectionist economic policy in which the interests of a specific group are blandly presented as being for the universal good; their preservation is justified not only for economic reasons but also for the well-being of society.

The conservative mentality does not distinguish between society and state, morality and politics. Society is controlled by vested rights and a leadership that is legitimized by religion, myth, and seniority: a reflection of what is assumed to be a universally valid divine and natural order. Within this order the claim to privilege has a role just as does the pursuit of simple self-interest to the extent that it can advance itself as the exercise of some "legitimately acquired" right. Naive political conservatism represents its notions of order as self-evident or obviously derived from nature and history. It rejects as impudent and utopian the belief in the possibility of a rational structuring of social and political conditions in order to achieve their conscious amelioration; generally it does not prohibit reforms, but remains convinced of the fundamental imperfection of man and of natural differences among their rights and duties, and therewith of the necessity of the leadership of the many by the few. It instinctively rejects not only the principle of democratic majority rule but also that of intellectual and bureaucratic elites. Leadership should be personally manifested; not however in the hands of one individual, but entrusted to the sounder part (*sanior pars*) of society; in practice, therefore, to a class accustomed to and experienced in leadership. The rulers are obliged to intervene to direct and order the lives of those classes not yet possessing discretion. The main task of legislature and judiciary is taken to be the safeguarding of vested interests; this, of course, applies to all, but in fact benefits the possessors, excluding the have-nots and making them the object of charity.

III. CONSERVATISM AS A
POLITICAL IDEA AND IDEOLOGY

1. Prerevolutionary Conservatism. In prerevolutionary, pre-industrial, and corporatively (*ständisch*) structured society a conservative social and political mentality was normal. It rested on the assumption that law is not made but discovered, and rulership is not legitimized by the consent of the governed, but by divine law. Changes in law, religion, and societal structure were therefore sternly rejected; their protagonists were found guilty of heresy, disturbance of the "natural" order, and *lèse-majesté* by the established powers. Conservative mentality is manifested, for example, in Cicero's standardizing of the old constitutional *res publica* and in the idealizing of the old Roman way of life by Roman historians, as well as generally in the exemplary lessons taught by history (*historia magistra vitae*).

It was on the basis of the same views, however, that reformers and rebels—among them Tiberius Gracchus, Cola di Rienzo, John Wycliffe, and the leaders of the German Peasant War—understood and justified their objectives as restoration (*renovatio, restauratio, reformatio*, Renaissance). Leopold von Ranke called Luther "one of the greatest conservatives who ever lived." The Glorious Revolution of 1688 was interpreted as the restoration of the traditional constitution proper to England. Only after "revolution" was understood as a deliberate total change in accordance with norms of universally valid rational and natural rights, as the elimination of abuse, and as a means of emerging from self-imposed infancy, could it no longer be represented as restoration. Instead, restoration became a conscious attempt to reverse revolutionary change, and conservatism became conscious opposition to revolutionary tendencies.

The change from a mood of predominant "standpattism" to one of reactionary opposition and of active defense of positions under attack, from habitual to conscious traditionalism, was not merely a consequence of political revolutions, but arose in opposition to criticism of and changes in the predominant mood, e.g., the Sophistic accusations against the Greek *polis*, the changed attitudes toward the ecclesiastical reformations of the sixteenth century, and also towards the Enlightenment.

The earliest translation of the antagonism between the defenders of the traditional social and ecclesiastical order and their adversaries into a party system of political conflict took place in England during the seventeenth century; it influenced the whole political thinking of Europe and North America. In England, the influence was due to political institutions (Parliament, State Church, common law) and societal factors (an aristocracy far from immune to panic, an ascending gentry, and an economically powerful bourgeoisie in London). Also the wide range of political positions, from the patriarchalism of Filmer via Hobbes, Hooker, Locke, and Milton to the radicalism of Winstanley, articulated during the fights between partisans of Stuart absolutism (closely connected with the Church of 479

England) and Puritan-Independent opponents in the English Parliament, which lasted for decades, gave the necessary impetus. The same basic political and ideological assumptions still shaped the fundamental principles of those Parliamentary groups which were called by their nicknames "Tories" and "Whigs" around 1679, though these parties gradually became guided by political conceptions during the eighteenth century.

The beginnings and core of the traditionalist defense and the formulation of a conservative position consisted in rejecting criticism of dogma, of the authority of ecclesiastical teachings, and of their influence in the realm of secular education which became increasingly independent. With the extension of this criticism to the whole hierarchical and aristocratic culture of the seventeenth century and to the traditional corporative and regional institutions of Europe, conservatism developed into a general social and political viewpoint opposed to the contract theory on which monarchy depended to support its centralizing administrative tendencies. The Enlightenment critics, the reform policies of progressive governments, and above all the French Revolution were the factors that led conservatism out of mere traditionalism and made it a political ideology. It did not, however, result in the dissolution of "pre-ideological" traditionalism.

Conservatism never attained the systematic unity and orthodoxy of Jacobinism, or of democratic radicalism, nor even that of liberalism. Down to the 1960's it remains an assortment of political ideas, a political credo that is more clearly delimited by what it rejects than by any positive program. The latter substantially depends on the degree of challenge at any given time. Thus conservatism is conceived of as antirevolutionary thought (Burke), as a counterrevolutionary appeal (de Maistre), as a "conservative revolution" (Hofmannsthal). Even when it supposes itself anti-ideological, this misunderstanding itself displays ideological traits. In an "age of ideology" conservatism has also not been able to escape ideological alignments; conservative ideologies, however, remain relatively unarticulated in any systematic theories; among the important representatives of political conservatism, then, are a large number of practical statesmen, while only a few can be named whose influence has been exclusively through their writings.

2. Antirevolutionary Conservatism. An antirevolutionary policy has by no means always been the aim of conservative political principles; in the vast majority of cases the objective of such a policy was rather a suppression of forces which, in the judgment of the rulers, threatened the existing order. The instruments used were (and are) press censorship, repressive laws governing association and assembly, and police regulations, but also school instruction, church sermons, and direct propaganda. Such a policy could always rely on the approval of those who view order, security, and a strong authority as the highest political values, even if this authority—by strictly conservative standards—is of dubious legitimacy. In fact, however, political conservatism has with increasing frequency since the eighteenth century found itself in a position where it could not rely on established authority—not only in those cases where it was put into power by the majority will of the sovereign people, but even under absolute monarchy—because that authority itself brought about changes in traditional social conditions and political institutions ("revolution from above," as expounded, for example, by Joseph II). With this weakening of the traditionalist components in conservatism naive support for traditional authority felt uncertain, and not infrequently released an unrealistic desire for restoration of that authority after it had been removed by revolutionary activity, thereby transforming in a democratic age the guiding image of monarchy into a version of the state as authoritarian, bonapartistic, presidential (when oriented toward a strong executive; *präsidial demokratisch*), or totalitarian.

Practical conservative politics, whether pursued by governments or by political groups and parties showed itself—simply because of its scarcely fixed ideological basis—to be extraordinarily adaptable. Only rarely (Metternich!) did conservatives understand their position by reference to abstract principle; in general they can be characterized as pursuing a policy along certain conservative guidelines in the interest of preserving the influence of the ruling classes who assumed their social and political position to be necessary for the functioning of their respective countries (Bismarck, Disraeli). It is on the basis of such an identification of group and state interests that conservative parties, above all rural interests, have ruthlessly pursued partisan politics.

It is difficult to trace the development of new ideas in the antirevolutionary politics of conservative governments, groups, and parties beyond adapting themselves to changing conditions in society. Conservative political philosophy in essence expresses uneasiness, and describes what is in principle a stable model of society that, without excluding change, permits changes only within the historical continuity of an order determined by the social nature of man. The conservative has always held firmly to this model in response to the challenge of social change and progressive political ideologies. Thus the speed and direction of the development of conservative ideas have been substantially determined by those forces that seemed to jeopardize this continuity. The only ones who moved away from a defensive position have been the romantic conservatives (A. Müller), the nationalistic conservatives of *Action Française* (Maurras), and the German neo-conservatives of the Weimar republic. But even here the positive values whose validity is claimed are at the same time negations of those principles which constitute the rationale of modern social philosophy and political thought; even so, as negations they are themselves rationalizations of mere traditionalism and of the naive conservative mentality.

Moreover, conservatism has not been able to isolate itself from the enlightened liberal ideas that dominated the political consciousness of the nineteenth century. The general feeling of progress and the power of the trend toward emancipation and egalitarianism were too strong for conservatism not to be drawn into their wake. On the other hand, an increasing number of liberals delimited the boundaries of progressivism because of the growing pressure of egalitarian democracy, and increasingly drew back from the ideas of bourgeois or social democracy. Thus an area of political thought was marked off in which conservative and liberal ideas drew so close as to be almost indistinguishable, above all in their joint approval of historical continuity, "organic" development, and "moderate" progress, in the rejection of revolutionary overthrow, in the recognition of the state as embodying the power to impose order on all classes and parties, and of the security of law and property as the foundation of society. Most political thinkers around the middle of the nineteenth century were active in this area: A. de Tocqueville, Robert Peel, F. J. Stahl, among them. Not until the late nineteenth century was there a shift; beginning with criticism of culture (*Kulturkritik*) and continuing in youth movements and the formation of elitist groups, political philosophies with antibourgeois and antiliberal as well as antidemocratic, antisocialistic, and anti-egalitarian viewpoints deliberately inscribed rejections of the nineteenth century on their banners, and after World War I coalesced into an ideologically authoritarian neo-conservatism.

IV. VARIOUS TYPES OF CONSERVATIVE THOUGHT

1. *Edmund Burke and Anglo-Saxon Conservatism.* Despite the relatively substantial unity and stability of its central values, conservatism displays a variety of nuances based on the different social experiences of its partisans at different times and in different countries. This was already apparent in the reaction to the democratic revolution of the late eighteenth century. Edmund Burke, who, as a critic of the French Revolution, gave the first (and to date most important) formulation of conservative political philosophy, vehemently rejected abstract political theories and efforts to found a constitution on them, because he esteemed as higher than the rationality of philosophers the reason that formed social and political institutions in accordance with natural and divine laws operating in the historical process. It is not the task of men to impose an order on things, but to recognize the order implicit in them and to act accordingly. With his practical political sense and philosophical inclination to identify nature and history Burke had too much respect for the traditional social order to be willing to cede its fate to the *ratio* and the deliberate plans of contemporary authors, and he was too skeptical a judge of men to have confidence in their original goodness (Rousseau) or in their rational foresight. He approved reforms, but rejected revolution because it destroyed tradition and continuity. He relied too heavily, moreover, on the foundations of a functioning English constitution to be able to understand the revolutionary challenge to conditions that had arisen historically in other countries.

Burke's ideas were of particular importance to European and American conservatism: he assigned priority to the historical accomplishments of generations rather than to the plans of individuals and the revolutionary acts of the masses; he did not acknowledge the separation of nature and history; he legitimized feeling and tradition as forces shaping the present, taking religion to be the "foundation of civil society," and provided an arsenal of arguments against revolution that appeared to have the weight of historical experience on their side.

2. *Restorationist Conservatism.* Burke's *Reflections on the Revolution in France* rapidly found an echo in Germany, where reception was prepared by the historicist opposition to radical enlightenment—above all in J. Möser, E. Brandes, A. W. Rehberg, and Friedrich Gentz. Though at first stamped by the Enlightenment, all of these found in Burke that mixture of political experience with concrete reflection, of assured consciousness of freedom with a skeptical attitude toward innovation and emancipation that could not have arisen independently under German conditions. Their rejection of revolution was not directed against Jacobin horrors alone. Because they recognized that it was no longer merely a question of a "change of regime" in the old manner, but of a "total revolution" (Gentz), even though executed by a part of the nation only, they denounced revolution as a "breach of the social contract" hostile to every order in society and therefore as an "amoral operation" (Gentz). To the claim of revolution to reconstitute society they opposed an equally comprehensive denunciation of revolution as a breach of law and as destructive of the foundations of the order of European society and state, but did not yet present any antirevolutionary counter-ideology, nor any program of restoration.

The former appeared in French aristocratic Catholic émigré circles from the pens of J. M., Comte de Maistre and L. G. A. de Bonald. They were consciously opposed to liberal enlightened thought, considered revolution as simply evil, and favored instead a retroactively purified "order" that was traditional, hierarchical, and springing directly from the will of the Creator; against revolutionary changes they offered the wisdom of history as the instructress of politics. A state could not be organized in accordance with rational constitutional principles: its form must derive from the history of a people, and the sovereign power that constitutes it originates in God, and so obtains its legitimacy. Written statutes are only the formulation of the unwritten, eternally valid laws; only those institutions can endure that are founded on religious conceptions. For de Maistre individual reason is presumption condemned to error, and philosophy is a destructive force. Since monarchy is for him the traditional ordering power and almost "natural," he wants it to be restored; not indeed in its absolute form, but in a patriarchal and decentralized manner commanding a society divided into corporations (*Stände*) and in the closest relation to the Catholic Church as the universal force for tradition and order. By setting the Church over the state, and the Pope over kings, de Maistre made them the most powerful instruments of counterrevolution and restoration, a barrier to enlightenment and individualism, and the prop of monarchy and corporative structure.

Even more clearly than de Maistre, de Bonald emphasized the view that only in society is human nature truly realized; he thereby gave expression to those anti-individualistic features of conservatism that enabled it to recognize the social problems of an industrial society in process of development and so to advance the social science. Bonald also formulated most clearly the differences between the individualistic and abstract versions of a republic (that could not achieve any important social objective) and a real "social" monarchy; his criticism became focal in conservative argumentation. Like de Maistre he sought restoration, but was not content with simply denouncing revolution; rather he presupposed its existence in order to derive from its abstract principles the concreteness of restorationist politics. The content and style of his thought later influenced the *Action Française*.

In central Europe restorationist conservatism found its most acute proponent in the Swiss, K. L. von Haller, who saw patriarchal leadership, the prerogative of civil law, and the corporate patrimonial state as "natural"

institutions; on the other hand, he viewed the entire development of the modern state as a path of error, and so won the approval of the Prussian conservatives close to Friedrich Wilhelm IV. Western and middle European restorationist conservatism found an echo in Russia and—together with ideas of mysticism, quietism, and romanticism—influenced Tsar Alexander I; the Holy Alliance, which was initiated by him and represented an antirevolutionary program, aimed at stability and was based upon the assumption of the solidarity of all Christian sovereigns and people.

3. Romantic Conservatism. While romantic conservatism in Germany was in practice drawn into restorationist politics, its ideas and intentions, however, were developed in dialectical opposition to enlightenment theories of the state and society as founded on rational laws, and in opposition to the politics of enlightened despotism. These theories and politics, and not primarily the revolution, were made responsible for the abandonment of the beautiful hierarchical order (family, corporate state, monarchy, church) that had been formed in the Middle Ages. The road to revolution had followed an inevitable path from the Reformation to rationalism and individualism, to administrative centralism and to the decline of corporative prerogatives. Rather than regard the revolution merely as a misfortune romantic conservatives understood revolution to mean that a soulless, nonreligious state and the presumptuous attempt to reconstruct it on substantially rational principles were doomed to failure. In opposition to this, they relied upon the old order and envisioned the better future of an idealized and harmonious Christian state (Novalis, A. Müller, F. von Baader). Since the evil reality of the present was viewed as a nonessential phenomenon the only escape was seen in the aesthetic reconciliation of opposites. Romantic conservative political thought in Germany was closely intertwined with historicism, with Schelling's philosophy of identity, and with the nationalist movement. The preference for vested rights over consciously sought "progress" and the conviction that every people must proceed along the lines of its own unique organic development, jointly produced in the educated classes a growing tendency to political conservatism. This attitude also penetrated the ranks of moderate liberalism in its increasing concern about radical and social democracy.

It was the reception of German romantic thought and its insistence upon history and *Volk* that formed the conservative component in the growing nationalism among the mainly democratic, educated classes of Eastern Europe. "The Society of Friends of Wisdom" (*liubomudry*, 1823) with its romantic-conservative nationalism and the circle surrounding N. V. Stankević were also shaped by ideas originating in Germany; both Muscovite groups were—despite a rather short existence—forerunners of the accentuated Russian nationalism during the second half of the nineteenth century.

4. Neo-conservatism. Since the late nineteenth century conservatism has in different ways moved away from being defensive as a result of the influence of industrialization and capitalism, of growing social mobility, of advances in scientific and technological thought, the liberalization of state and economy, and the secularization of thought and public life. Even then it has been easier for conservatives to determine what it is they are opposing than to design clear and realistic programs. The criticisms of civilization by Nietzsche, Renan, Taine, Dostoevski, and J. Burkhardt, among others, hardly fall under the rubric "conservative"; nonetheless they have furnished the political conservative with both a basic philosophy of civilization and a wide audience. The conservative "intellectual" has come forward to express the discontent felt for both the world of bourgeois capitalism and the programs of socialism; in his formulating new myths, forecasts, and schemes a skeptical, sometimes even nihilistic, accent has not been lacking. Appearing increasingly less aristocratic or class-oriented than intellectual and elitist, this type of conservative has attained his most widespread influence in conjunction with militant and integrative nationalism.

The best known phenomenon of this type was the *Action Française*, whose protagonists, Maurice Barrès and Charles Maurras, saw nationality as the inalienable distinction of man. Combining antisecular and anti-Semitic tendencies with ideas derived from Sorel they promoted an authoritarian conception of the state without undue scruples as to its legitimacy. Maurras demanded the establishment of an hereditary anti-parliamentary monarchy, hierarchically structured and corporatively organized, among whose firmest supporters should be the Catholic Church.

In Germany before World War I conservatism of this type was the program of small and isolated, though influential, groups. P. de Lagarde, with some bearing on romanticism, had demanded a state adequate to the character of the German people as well as a "German" religion, and based his hopes on a new elitist brand of education. J. Langbehn adopted this approach and developed it, amplifying its antimodernistic tendencies: homeland, *Volk*, nature, and art constitute a powerfully emotional ideological syndrome in Langbehn that had its effect on the youth movement.

This neo-conservatism was no longer "restorationist"; it sought not to preserve the existent, but to eliminate what had come to be; not to restore some medieval order, but to make room for a post-bourgeois,

post-capitalistic world. Its derivative conceptions of social order were by no means uniform; but there was substantial agreement among neo-conservatives to the extent that they were antiliberal, antidemocratic, and antisocialistic. The *Volk* must be ranked above the state, the nation above mankind, community above individual and society. The social organization of the *Volk* was conceived along occupational lines, the administration of the state as authoritarian: *Kultur* rooted in the soil was to be cultivated above cosmopolitan "civilization."

Neo-conservatism of this kind had its day on the continent of Europe especially after World War I. It was able to represent itself as a new national socialism (solidarity) and was used as the official ideology of national movements and national dictatorships, so that it sometimes came very close to fascism. One must, however, carefully distinguish between the "right" and fascism. The incorporation of elements of conservative thought in the wake of fascist movements and systems has been so damaging for the former that it is only with the greatest difficulty that a program of independent political conservatism can be formulated.

5. Conservatism in the United States. The position occupied by conservatives among the political viewpoints in any given country depends upon the political and social conditions obtaining in it. The attitudes and goals called "conservative" in the United States appeared to European eyes to be mostly rather "Whiggish." Until the 1960's it seemed even less easy in the United States to find a powerful national "right wing" of antirevolutionaries, restorationist legitimists, supporters of romantic and organic social doctrines, and antidemocrats than to find a precise counterpart of European liberalism. A radical left wing, on the other hand, has been almost nonexistent. Such facts made the dominant American credo look rather moderate; it may among other things be traced back to the working of its democratic machinery and to its antifeudal past, though its revolutionary break with feudal Europe was in a way justified by a restoration of colonial rights.

Despite that and despite the influence of Locke on American political thinking, political conservatism was manifested at the inception of the Union by the fathers of the Constitution. Their concern was for order and security to be attained by limiting the radical democratic tendencies found in the separate states, and thereby to strengthen the authority of the new federation. Suspected during the conflicts with the South from Calhoun to Little Rock, the defense of states rights—formerly the official position of radicals and liberals alike (Bill of Rights, Tenth Amendment), and adapted by Jefferson to the necessities of an expanding "empire"—was considered in the 1960's as conservative a policy as the insistence on laissez-faire economics. Once stock-in-trade of American capitalistic democracy it became the main argument of conservatives in the twenties (Herbert Hoover) against the modern welfare state.

A similar ambiguous attitude was displayed by the West. At first often expressing its outrage at economic and political supremacy of the East in terms of a radical and even egalitarian democracy, the rural West at the same time, and increasingly since the 1870's, displayed a rather conservative mentality. Strongly influenced by religious fundamentalism, its criticism of the megapolitan industrial East and its harking back to an authentic Americanism supplied the conservative cause with emotional arguments.

In America as well as in Europe liberal and conservative arguments often merged. What makes it so difficult for Europeans to draw a sharp line between liberals and conservatives in the United States is a missing guideline along strictly liberal or conservative terms; there is neither a Burke nor a Locke in the United States, which furthermore looked askance at any influence of the Catholic Church. The controversy between Hamilton and Madison seems to be reversed though both sides claim Jefferson to be in their camp. Even the often described tendency of Americans to solve their hardly articulated ideological conflicts "practically" tends to be conservative in itself and has led to almost schizophrenic attitudes toward social problems.

As a counterpoise to the social dynamism of a democratic society, conservatism in the United States has from time to time raised its head (for examples, Henry and Brooks Adams), just as it has recurred as the politics promoting the self-interest of social groups. While the most convincing American conservative of the nineteenth century was perhaps the Southerner John C. Calhoun, the development of new forms of conservatism independent of a certain area can be traced back to the end of the century. The social mobility of the American society at this time began to run out into horizontal movements whereas such ideals as the American "self-made" man were still worshipped. Asking for stability and a social equilibrium Americans formed a society with deep distrust of nonconformist behavior and change.

Further social and political changes in the last decades of the nineteenth century and particularly in the 1910's and 1920's, business reactions to certain New Deal measures, and above all antisocialism, the fear of communism, the "Cold War," and the hot ones in Korea and Vietnam together with latent prejudices and antimodernistic tendencies (Irving Babbitt) have induced a psychological and political situation which

was being spectacularly exploited by some conservative and right-wing American politicians about 1970.

CONCLUSIONS

The general expansion of the political spectrum to the "left" has had the result that many ideas and conceptions of social order and governmental organization that were initially promoted by liberal forces have not only found their way into conservatism, but themselves appear comparatively conservative. While liberal party politics in contemporary Europe is only very sluggishly active, conservatism has manifested itself as a stable counterweight to socialism; this has, however, been attained by a substantial surrender of its ideological substance. It has even been able to absorb some features of egalitarian democracy. It has come to an accommodation with representative democracy most readily in the Anglo-Saxon and Scandinavian countries. In Catholic countries it has not really appeared independently in political parties, but has animated the conservative clerical wing of Catholic People's parties. In the countries of the European continent, those with moderate conservative outlooks vote mostly for Christian Democratic parties (Italy, Germany, Austria, Belgium, Netherlands).

A special role has been played by de Gaullism, which has displayed features of the Bonapartism of the nineteenth and the nationalist presidential system of the twentieth century. Its success may be ascribed to the crisis of the parliamentary system and to national self-consciousness in France.

In the 1960's when radical critics denigrate even bourgeois liberals and social democrats as conservatives, the conservatives themselves are hardly able to articulate their position unequivocally and rationally. It is doubtful whether they are capable of offering a convincing alternative to the democratic welfare state with its liberal social character. They cannot halt the profound and comprehensive social changes which the modern world is experiencing. In this process conservatism seems to have the task of assuring continuity, to be a corrective against progress-at-any-price, and simply in this way to blunt reactionary tendencies.

BIBLIOGRAPHY

H. Barth, ed., *Der konservative Gedanke* (Stuttgart, 1958). R. Blake, *Disraeli* (London and New York, 1966). Crane Brinton, *Political Ideas of the English Romanticists* (Oxford, 1926; reprint New York, 1962). H. R. H. Cecil, *Conservatism* (London, 1912). Benjamin Disraeli, *Coningsby* (London, 1844); idem, *Sybil* (London, 1845); idem, *Tancred* (London, 1847). K. G. Feiling, *A History of the Tory Party 1640–1714* (London, 1924); idem, *What is Conservatism?* (London, 1930); idem, *The Second Tory Party 1740–1832* (London, 1959). H. Gerstenberger, *Der Revolutionäre Konservatismus*.

Ein Beitrag zur Analyse des Liberalismus, Sozialwissenschaftliche Abhandlungen 14 (Berlin, 1969). Stephen R. Graubard, *Burke, Disraeli and Churchill: The Politics of Perseverance* (Cambridge, Mass., 1961). M. Greiffenhagen, *Das Dilemma des Konservatismus in Deutschland* (Munich, 1971). R. Kirk, *The Conservative Mind. From Burke to Santayana*, revised ed. (Chicago, 1954). K. von Klemperer, *Germany's New Conservatism. Its History and Dilemma in the Twentieth Century* (Princeton, 1957). K. Mannheim, "Das konservative Denken. Soziologische Beiträge zum Werden des politisch-historischen Denkens in Deutschland," *Archiv für Sozialwissenschaft und Sozialpolitik*, **57** (1927), 68–142, 470–95. H. McClosky, "Conservatism and Personality," *American Political Science Review*, **52** (1958), 27–45. A. Mohler, *Die konservative Revolution in Deutschland 1918–1932. Grundriss ihrer Weltanschauungen* (Stuttgart, 1950). H. Muhlenfeld, *Politik ohne Wunschbilder. Die konservative Aufgabe unserer Zeit* (Munich, 1952). Michael Oakeshott, *Experience and Its Modes* (Cambridge and New York, 1933; reprint 1966); idem, *Rationalism in Politics* (New York, 1962). S. M. Osgood, *French Royalism under the Third and Fourth Republics* (The Hague, 1960). H. S. Reiss, ed. and Introduction, *The Political Thought of the German Romantics 1793–1815* (Oxford, 1955). H. Rogger and E. Weber, eds., *The European Right. A Historical Profile* (Berkeley and Los Angeles, 1965). C. Rossiter, *Conservatism in America: The Thankless Persuasion*, 2nd ed. revised (New York, 1962). P. Smith, *Disraelian Conservatism and Social Reform* (Toronto, 1967). R. Spaemann, *Der Ursprung der Soziologie aus dem Geist der Restauration. Studien über L. G. S. de Bonald* (Munich, 1959). E. C. Thaden, *Conservative Nationalism in Nineteenth-Century Russia* (Seattle, 1964). E. Troeltsch, "Konservativ und Liberal," *Die Christliche Welt* (1916), Nos. 33, 35. F. Valjavec, *Die Entstehung der politischen Strömungen in Deutschland 1770–1815* (Munich, 1951). Peter R. E. Viereck, *Conservatism: From John Adams to Churchill* (New York and London, 1956); idem, *Conservatism Revisited; The Revolt Against Revolt, 1815–1949* (New York, 1949). E. Weber, *Action Française. Royalism and Reaction in Twentieth-Century France* (Stanford, 1962). R. J. White, ed., *The Conservative Tradition* (London, 1950). E. L. Woodward, *Three Studies in European Conservatism. Metternich, Guizot, The Catholic Church in the Nineteenth Century* (London, 1929; reprint 1963).

RUDOLF VIERHAUS

[See also **Authority; Constitutionalism;** Historicism; Ideology; Liberalism; Nationalism; Revolution; Social Contract; Social Democracy; **State;** Totalitarianism; *Volksgeist*.]

CONSTITUTIONALISM

I

CONSTITUTIONALISM is descriptive of a complicated concept, deeply imbedded in historical experience, which subjects the officials who exercise governmental powers to the limitations of a higher law. Constitutionalism proclaims the desirability of the rule of law as opposed to rule by the arbitrary judgment or mere fiat of public officials. Thus Charles H. McIlwain has written that the essential quality of constitutionalism is that "it is a legal limitation on government; it is the antithesis of arbitrary rule . . ." (*Constitutionalism: Ancient and Modern*, p. 21). Another eminent scholar of constitutional law, Howard Jay Graham, has observed that "constitutionalism . . . is the art and the process of assimilating and converting statute and precedent, ideals and aspirations, into the forms and the Rule of Law—into a Fundamental and Supreme Law" (*Everyman's Constitution*, p. 6).

Throughout the literature dealing with modern public law and the foundations of statecraft the central element of the concept of constitutionalism is that in political society government officials are not free to do anything they please in any manner they choose; they are bound to observe both the limitations on power and the procedures which are set out in the supreme, constitutional law of the community. It may therefore be said that the touchstone of constitutionalism is the concept of limited government under a higher law.

This should not be taken to mean that if a state has a constitution, it is necessarily committed to the idea of constitutionalism. In a very real sense, every state has a constitution, if by a constitution is meant, in the words of Lord Bryce, "the aggregate of the laws and customs through and under which the public life of a State goes on . . ." (*Studies . . .* , I, 159). A constitution, Bryce asserted, is "a frame of political society, organised by and through law; that is to say, one in which law has established permanent institutions with recognized functions and definite rights" (ibid., 195). In this sense, every state may be said to have a constitution, since every state has institutions which are at the very least expected to be permanent, and every state has established ways of doing things. Even if the essence of the constitution is that the dictator exercises absolute or despotic powers, it may be said, for whatever it may be worth, that this is the constitution of the state. But no one would assert that in a despotically governed state the idea of constitutionalism has any place. In the absence of a commitment to limited government under the rule of law, it may be said that a state has a constitution without any constitutionalism.

Furthermore, even if a state does in fact possess a formal written document labelled "constitution" which includes the provisions customarily found in such a document, it does not follow that it is committed to constitutionalism, if in fact the document is a mere sham and not a statement of higher law which is actually followed and reasonably well enforced. Scholars have pointed up the distinction between "normative" and "nominal" constitutions. A good illustration of this point is the so-called Stalin Constitution of the Soviet Union. For a variety of reasons the Russian dictator found it desirable, in 1936, to adopt a written constitution. He was then trying to organize a collective security system against Hitler; this occurred in the popular front period when Stalin found it useful to try to win over the world's great body of democratic opinion. The Stalin Constitution was also intended to serve as a measure of progress for the Russian Revolution, and as the expression of goals for the future. It is also a testimony to the strength of the tradition of constitutional democracy that Stalin thought he would derive some political advantage from going through the motions of producing a written constitution in the democratic style. Even so, the Stalin Constitution does not purport to guarantee traditional individual freedoms in clear and unequivocal terms. For example, Article 125 declares that citizens are guaranteed freedom of speech, press, assembly, street processions and demonstrations, but only "in conformity with the interests of the working people, and in order to strengthen the socialist system. . . ." Furthermore, these individual freedoms are not in fact respected by the government of the Soviet Union, and even mild expressions of dissent from prevailing official policy are subject to police repression and severe punishment.

Communist China presents another example of a state which has a constitution without a commitment to constitutionalism. For example, Article 87 of the Constitution of the People's Republic of China (1954) provides: "Citizens of the People's Republic of China enjoy freedom of speech, freedom of the press, freedom of assembly, freedom of association, freedom of procession and freedom of demonstration." In actual fact, these freedoms do not exist in Communist China, and institutions and procedures are lacking for their effective implementation.

There is, however, a tradition in the history of political thought which describes a constitution in terms of a higher law which is an expression of the will of the people. In this view, the people are the ultimate source of all political power, and in promulgating a constitution they declare the supreme will of the state, binding upon all organs of the state. Thus, by definition, government is created by the constitution, and the constitution endows government with its powers and establishes limitations upon the exercise of those powers. Appropriate government officials may create statute laws, but the statute law must conform with the requirements of the higher law of the constitution. Implicit in this conception of the constitution is a basic distinction between the state and the government, and

between statute law and constitutional law. The state is created by and is organized by the people in the writing and adoption of a constitution, and government derives its authority, institutions, and procedures from this constitution. Statute law is law, but it is subordinate to the higher law of the constitution. These concepts are underscored by the fact that different methods are utilized to create constitutions and statutes. The higher law of the constitution is not subject to formal alteration by ordinary legislative procedures, and the constitution, unlike statutes, emanates directly from the whole body of citizens in the form of an organic document written and ratified in some special way which stresses that the people are the ultimate repository of political power, and that their enduring will must be obeyed by government officials.

This conception of a constitution was well stated by Bolingbroke when he wrote, in 1733: "By constitution we mean, whenever we speak with propriety and exactness, that assemblage of laws, institutions and customs, derived from certain fixed principles of reason, directed to certain fixed objects of public good, that compose the general system, according to which the community hath agreed to be governed." Similarly Thomas Paine maintained that any government which violates the constitution exercises "power without right." If the distinction between constitution and government is ignored, then, Paine argued, there being no check upon the will of the government, it follows that the state is a despotism. A true, written constitution, he held, was always antecedent to the actual government, for, in his words, "The constitution is not the act of its government, but of the people constituting a government" (*Basic Writings* . . . , p. 42). Generally speaking, this conception of the nature of a constitution prevails in countries committed to democracy and freedom. Where such a concept exists, it follows that constitutionalism is also concerned with freedom and the ultimate responsibility of government to the people. Thus in his classic treatment of this subject, McIlwain concluded his book with this sentence: "The two fundamental correlative elements of constitutionalism for which all lovers of liberty must yet fight are the legal limits to arbitrary power and a complete political responsibility of government to the governed" (*Constitutionalism* . . . , p. 146).

II

Some conception of a higher law will be found throughout the history of Western political thought. Thus in the very early Greek classical period Heraclitus taught that "all human laws are sustained by the one divine law, which is infinitely strong, and suffices, and more than suffices, for them all" (quoted in Andrews

[1968], p. 15). Generally speaking, however, the ancient Greeks made no distinction between the state and society. In their view the state is as old as human association itself, from which it followed that there was no natural law older than the law of actual states. For them, the law of nature merely meant the actual laws which were the same in all states. Furthermore, since the ancient Greeks had no concept that an unconstitutional law is unenforceable, they had no remedy for an unconstitutional act short of actual revolution. For them a revolution did not merely change the public law of the state; it changed the whole state and its institutions, which was a very compelling reason why revolution was so much feared.

Plato believed that human law was at best an imperfect reflection of an idea in the world of ideas. Contrary to the teaching of the later Stoics, he believed that the law of nature was merely an intellectual standard, a basis for comparison, and most certainly not a basis for actual judicial decisions. His ideal, or best form of government, as set forth in *The Republic,* was one ruled over by philosopher-kings who were not limited by law. But he came to believe that supermen with the necessary divine qualities were not and were not likely to become available. Accordingly, in his later thought, as expressed in *The Statesman* and in the *Laws,* Plato settled for constitutional government, but only as second best. The best sort of government would be one unhindered by law, but this was only an ideal, and he believed that actual states can only approximate the ideal. Whether the state had one or several rulers, his main point was that in a constitutional system government is limited by law derived from the uniformities of nature.

Aristotle, fully committed to the politics of moderation, rejected Plato's ideal state as a form of despotism, however benevolent. He was unwilling to vest unrestricted power in any particular individual or class, and insisted that those who exercise the powers of government must be guided by the law. Thus he favored constitutionalism in that the guiding principle of rulership was the rule of law, not force. He thought that governments must be responsible to the governed, and that freedom depends upon the right of men to have a hand in making the laws they are required to obey. The rule of law also meant for Aristotle that all men are equal under the law. The procedural aspects of constitutionalism were well developed in Aristotle's *Politics.* A constitution, he wrote, is "in a sense the life of the city." Thus he emphasized law, rather than human will, as the repository of the basic norms of the political society.

Natural law theory, which has been an essential element of concepts of constitutionalism, received its earliest significant development in the thinking of the Stoics of Greece and Rome after about 300 B.C. Thus Cicero made a characteristic statement of the nature of natural law in the following words:

There is in fact a true law—namely, right reason—which is in accordance with nature, applies to all men, and is unchangeable and eternal. By its commands this law summons men to the performance of their duties; by its prohibitions it restrains them from doing wrong. . . . To invalidate this law by human legislation is never morally right, nor is it permissible ever to restrict its operation, and to annul it wholly is impossible (Coker [1938], p. 151).

In accordance with this point of view, the Roman jurists established a basic distinction between public law (*jus publicum*) and private law (*jus privatum*). Furthermore, it was a basic principle of Roman jurisprudence that the ultimate source of all legitimate political authority in a state is the people, not the ruler.

This principle prevailed through the Middle Ages. That all political authority is limited by a higher law was a staple of medieval political thought. The medieval schoolmen regarded the origin of natural law as divine since they tied natural law to God. Illustrative of this view is the statement of Thomas Aquinas in the *Summa Theologica* that man as a "rational creature . . . has a share of the Eternal Reason . . . and this participation of the eternal law in the rational creature is called the natural law" (Pegis [1948], p. 618). Thus God and reason were fused. Above all, the natural law, along with the Church and the feudal nobility, limited the power of the king. This is suggested by the well-known observation of John of Salisbury in *Policraticus* (1159) that "there are certain precepts of the law which have a perpetual necessity, having the force of law among all nations, and which absolutely cannot be broken with impunity" (Sabine [1937], p. 247). John distinguished between a proper king and a tyrant in terms of whether the ruler obeyed the law.

For medieval England, *Magna Carta* (1215) strengthened the traditional view that the law is supreme. This supremacy was best stated in Chapter 39, which declared: "No freeman shall be taken or imprisoned or disseised or outlawed or exiled or in any way destroyed, nor will we go upon him nor send upon him, except by the lawful judgment of his peers or by the law of the land (*vel per legem terre*)." *Magna Carta* derived a great measure of its influence from repeated confirmations by later rulers (there were forty-four confirmations between 1327 and 1422), and from its revival and reinterpretation by Coke and other lawyers and judges in the conflict between parliament and the Stuart monarchy in the seventeenth century. Thus, in the words of Arthur Sutherland, "the Great

Charter was obviously a cherished standard, a welcome assurance that people could set some limitation on the arbitrary powers of the king" (*Constitutionalism in America*, p. 31).

Writing in the thirteenth century, Bracton, a justice of King's Bench in the reign of Henry III, and the most important English law writer before Blackstone, declared in *De legibus et consuetudinibus Angliae* that the law "is not anything rashly presumed by will of the king, but what has been rightly defined with the king's authorization on the advice of his magnates after deliberation and conference concerning it." In this philosophic treatise on the laws and customs of England, Bracton distinguished between "government," which was within the king's control, and "right," which was based on ancient custom, the elements of which, "since they have been approved by the consent of those using them and confirmed by the oath of kings, can neither be changed nor destroyed without the common consent of all those with whose counsel and consent they have been promulgated" (McIlwain [1947], p. 83). To put it somewhat differently, Bracton made a basic distinction between government (*gubernaculum*) and law (*jurisdictio*), and held that the king's absolute authority extended only to the former. The basic weakness of this concept, and indeed the fundamental inadequacy of all medieval constitutionalism, was that there was no way to combat violations of the law except by revolutionary violence or the threat of its use.

The supremacy of the law over government was greatly strengthened in England by the stirring events of the seventeenth century, culminating in the Revolution of 1689, which made the royal title dependent upon an act of parliament, the Act of Settlement of 1701, which gave the judges a tenure independent of the will of the king, and which established parliamentary control over the government. As Coke, one of the leading spokesmen of the resistance to Stuart claims to absolute power, declared in 1610: "That ligeance or obedience of the subject to the Sovereign is due by the law of nature: 2. That this law of nature is part of the laws of England: 3. That the law of nature was before any judicial or municipal law in the world: 4. That the law of nature is immutable, and cannot be changed." Speaking as a Justice of the Court of Common Pleas, Coke went so far in *Dr. Bonham's Case* (1610) as to declare that under certain circumstances the judges could refuse to enforce even an act of Parliament, "for when an act of parliament is against common right and reason, or repugnant, or impossible to be performed, the common law will controul it and adjudge such act to be void." Similarly, in his historic debate with James I, Coke asserted that "the King hath no prerogative, but that which the law and the land follows."

While Coke's contention that the judges have the power to refuse to enforce acts of Parliament which they deem to be contrary to the supreme law of the land, now known as the power of judicial review, did not prevail in subsequent English practice, his view that *Magna Carta*, later strengthened by frequent royal confirmations, was a compact between ruler and the ruled binding upon government, merged quickly into broad theories of social compact and natural law which contributed much to the modern history of higher law concepts.

The great natural law philosophers of the sixteenth and seventeenth centuries—such as Hugo Grotius, Samuel Pufendorf, Algernon Sydney, and John Locke—took God out of the law of nature and made it the basis for the modern secular constitutional state. For John Locke (*Second Treatise on Civil Government*, 1690), government was based on a social contract entered into in a preexisting state of nature operating under natural law, and for him natural law became the natural rights of the individual. Since the purpose of the social contract was to create government in order more effectively to protect man's natural rights, Locke, as the justifier of the Revolution of 1689, concluded that when government fails of its central purpose the people regain the right to create a new social contract. The state, therefore, is committed to constitutionalism, the terms of which are spelled out in a social contract which controls the acts of government.

III

American constitutionalism was derived, historically, from the views of the English common law lawyers and judges, and the natural law, social contract philosophers. During the period of colonial tutelage, the American colonists, in their perennial disputes with the government in London, looked for protection of what they regarded as their rights in the colonial charters, thus forming the habit of appealing to a higher law stated in documents. As the colonists moved from protest to revolution, American revolutionary doctrine was, on the whole, in line with English philosophy and historical precedents. Those who articulated the political theory of the revolutionary movement did not even claim that their ideas were original. On the contrary, speaking of "Revolutionary principles," John Adams declared that "they are the principles of Aristotle and Plato; of Livy and Cicero; and Sydney, Harrington and Locke; the principles of nature and eternal reason; the principles on which the whole government over us now stands" (*Works*, IV, 15). It is, of course, wholly understandable that the leaders of a revolution should appeal to familiar principles. The ideas of natural law and social compact spelled out in the Declaration of Independence found wide acceptance among the people precisely because they were thoroughly familiar ideas.

The keystone of American constitutionalism has been the written national Constitution of 1787, for this document is deeply rooted in a complex mythology which makes the American higher law doctrine truly meaningful and effective. To begin with, the Constitution was drafted in a special way, by a convention of delegates selected for this one purpose, and ratified in a special way, by conventions selected for this single function in the states. This is a far cry from the ordinary process of national legislation, which is in the hands of Congress and the President. In addition, there is a special method of amending the Constitution, by an extraordinary two-thirds vote of Congress plus approval by three-fourths of the states, which is altogether different and more complicated than the method available for amending legislation. These special procedures have the effect of highlighting the distinction between constitutional law and statute law. Other provisions of the Constitution underscore the supremacy of the former over the latter.

Thus the preamble recites the fact that "We the People of the United States . . . do ordain and establish this Constitution for the United States of America." This is consistent with the widely accepted notion that the people are the true and original source of all governmental authority, that government is their agent, not their master, that government is based on the popular will. In addition, Article VI declares that this Constitution "shall be the supreme Law of the Land," and goes on to say that "the Judges in every State shall be bound thereby, any thing in the Constitution or Laws of any State to the Contrary notwithstanding," and provides that all national and state officials must take an oath or affirmation to support this Constitution. Furthermore, all civil officers of the United States are, under the terms of Article II, Section 4, subject to impeachment if they betray the people's trust.

Finally, the Constitution achieves viability as a higher law through the practice of judicial review, which means that the judges, and ultimately the Justices of the United States Supreme Court, have the power to refuse to enforce legislative or executive acts found to be contrary to the Constitution. While the Constitution does not provide for judicial review in clear and unequivocal language, it was established early in the history of the document as a natural outgrowth of higher law doctrine and colonial experience. That courts have the power of judicial review was first established in the jurisprudence of the United States Supreme Court, in 1803, by Chief Justice John Marshall

in the celebrated case of *Marbury v. Madison* (1 Cranch 137). For Marshall the choice before the Court was a simple one: either the Constitution controls any legislative act repugnant to it, or, in the alternative, the legislature may change the Constitution by ordinary legislation. There is, he insisted, no middle ground between these alternatives.

The constitution is either a superior paramount law, unchangeable by ordinary means, or it is on a level with ordinary legislative acts, and, like other acts, is alterable when the legislature shall please to alter it. If the former part of the alternative be true, then a legislative act contrary to the constitution is now law: if the latter part be true, then written constitutions are absurd attempts, on the part of the people, to limit a power in its own nature illimitable.

John Marshall maintained that a written Constitution is intended to serve as the nation's "fundamental and paramount" law. He went on to say that

it is emphatically the province and duty of the judicial department to say what the law is. Those who apply the law to particular cases, must of necessity expound and interpret that rule. If two laws conflict with each other, the courts must decide on the operation of each. So if a law be in opposition to the constitution; if both the law and the constitution apply to a particular case, so that the court must either decide that case conformably to the law, disregarding the constitution; or conformably to the constitution, disregarding the law; the court must determine which of these conflicting rules governs the case. This is of the very essence of judicial duty. If, then, the courts are to regard the constitution, and the constitution is superior to any ordinary act of the legislature, the constitution, and not such ordinary act, must govern the case to which they both apply.

However the cogency of this reasoning may be challenged—and there have been challenges—this aspect of the Constitution as judicially-enforceable higher law has prevailed in subsequent American history. Judicial review by an independent judiciary, that is, a judiciary independent of the political branches of the government, is an indispensable element of American constitutionalism.

This aspect of constitutionalism has been stated and restated by many members of the United States Supreme Court. Thus, in the landmark case of *Ex parte Milligan* (4 Wall. 2), decided in 1866, the point was made that the Constitution is the supreme law of the land even in time of war. In this case, Justice Davis said:

The Constitution of the United States is a law for rulers and people, equally in war and in peace, and covers with the shield of its protection all classes of men, at all times, and under all circumstances. No doctrine, involving more pernicious consequences, was ever invented by the wit of man than that any of its provisions can be suspended during any of the great exigencies of government. Such a doctrine leads directly to anarchy or despotism . . . (4 Wall. 120).

The nature of the theory of constitutionalism was explained by Chief Justice Hughes in *De Jonge v. Oregon* (299 U.S. 353, 365), decided in 1937, in the following language:

The greater the importance of safeguarding the community from incitements to the overthrow of our institutions by force and violence, the more imperative is the need to preserve inviolate the constitutional rights of free speech, free press and free assembly in order to maintain the opportunity for free political discussion, to the end that government may be responsive to the will of the people and that changes, if desired, may be obtained by peaceful means. Therein lies the security of the Republic, the very foundation of constitutional government.

The concept of constitutionalism was spelled out from a different angle of vision by Justice Jackson in the Flag Salute Case of 1943, *West Virginia State Board of Education v. Barnette* (319 U.S. 624, 638), where he wrote:

The very purpose of a Bill of Rights was to withdraw certain subjects from the vicissitudes of political controversy, to place them beyond the reach of majorities and officials and to establish them as legal principles to be applied by the courts. One's right to life, liberty, and property, to free speech, a free press, freedom of worship and assembly, and other fundamental rights may not be submitted to vote; they depend on the outcome of no elections.

This statement goes to the very heart of the American concept of constitutionalism, that the constitution is a fundamental written law superior in obligation to all other forms of law. Indeed, there is a standard for measuring the justness of governmental acts which is not only binding upon all agents of the government, but which is independent even of the will of the current popular majority. While the American system is committed to majority rule as being preferable to rule by elites or by divine right, it is also committed to the proposition that government must be righteous and just, in spite of majority rule. These objectives are sought through a variety of devices, including judicial review by an independent judiciary, an enforceable Bill of Rights, the guaranty of equality before the law, the diffusion of governmental power through territorial federalism and functional separation of powers, checks and balances, and the subordination of military to civil authority. The government is obliged to observe the fundamental law, and the Constitution cannot be changed except in some special way.

American constitutionalism has been remarkably successful, if success is measured by such criteria as longevity and consensus. The American Constitution is the oldest written national constitution in service today, and mere survival is a benchmark of success in the difficult, complex world of government. Furthermore, age alone confers respectability, although the veneration of the United States Constitution is attributable to many other sources. Derived from the solid authority of "We the People," it was drafted by a convention which included many of the nation's most revered national heroes. It was not imposed upon the people by outside authority, but was, rather, an act of free will. In an age which believed that only a social contract created legitimate government, the Constitution, as a written document, was regarded from its inception as the very model of what a soundly conceived social contract should say.

The success of the American economy has been tied in with the success of the Constitution, the one interacting with the other. Above all, American constitutionalism has succeeded because it has been supported by a general popular consensus. This does not mean that the people have been in agreement on everything, since such agreement has never existed anywhere. But it does mean that there has been general acceptance of basic institutions and procedures that matter most, and that have the potentiality of becoming the sort of issues that men fight about. As a bare minimum, consensus as the underpinning of constitutionalism is possible only if there is very wide agreement on such vital matters as the regime itself, the form of government, the basic methods for making and unmaking policy decisions, and the fundamental goals of the society.

IV

There are many differences among constitutions from the point of view of both style and content. Indeed, Great Britain to this day has no single document labelled "Constitution," and for this reason it has become customary to describe the British Constitution as being an "unwritten" one. This is very misleading, since many parts of this Constitution are written, for constitutional status is invariably ascribed to such documents as *Magna Carta* (1215), the Habeas Corpus Act (1641), the Bill of Rights (1689), the Act of Settlement (1701), the Act of Union (1707), the Parliament Act (1911), and the successive Representation of the People, Judicature, and Local Government Acts.

All of these written documents, it is generally agreed, are parts of the British Constitution. But this Constitution includes much more, notably the rules of the common law, and well-established customs and conventions which deal with very basic matters, such as the principle of ministerial responsibility to the House of Commons, and which are observed as faithfully as the formal law itself. During the troubled and revolutionary days of the Cromwellian period, several efforts were made to reconcile the prerogatives of the ruler with the privileges of Parliament by the device of some sort of written constitution, but these efforts failed, and with the death of Cromwell the monarchy was promptly restored. Since then the limitations which the traditional parts of the English Constitution impose upon arbitrary rule have been so clearly delineated and so effective in operation that it has not been found necessary to state the basic constitutional law of the realm in the style of a formal written code. There is general agreement among students of government with the observation made by William E. Gladstone in 1878 that "the British Constitution is the most subtile organism which has proceeded from the womb and the long gestation of progressive history" (Wolf-Phillips [1968], p. 182).

A much more significant difference between the English and the American constitutions than mere matters of form and style is the existence in Britain of the principle of parliamentary supremacy. From the point of view of fundamental constitutional law, parliamentary supremacy means that the courts of the realm are legally incapable of refusing to enforce an act of Parliament on grounds of unconstitutionality. To be sure, the word "unconstitutional" is often used in Great Britain to describe an act believed to be contrary to the basic law of the country, but this does not have the legal significance which the term has in the United States. Parliament is supreme in the sense that all of its enactments have the quality of law. This does not mean that the English courts are powerless, since they have the responsibility of interpreting statutes. In view of the fact that Parliament legislates less than does the American Congress, and usually in more general language, the judicial power of statutory interpretation is not to be taken lightly.

Most of the new states of Africa and Asia have, in the twentieth century, felt that it was necessary to adopt formal, written constitutions, although the State of Israel has preferred to follow the English example. Israel has no formal constitutional document, and accepts the principle of parliamentary supremacy, for the Israeli courts do not have the power of judicial review. On the other hand, on the continent of Europe the practice has prevailed in modern times of having formal written constitutions, but usually without judicial enforcement. The 1948 Constitution of West Germany, however, created a Constitutional Court (*Bundesverfassungsgericht*) with judicial review powers, and the Supreme Court of Canada has such powers also. The de Gaulle Constitution of France (1958) created a Constitutional Council (*conseil constitutionnel*) with the power to declare *organic* laws of Parliament unconstitutional before enactment, and *ordinary* laws invalid if sent to it by the President or Parliament. But this Council is not a true court and is not part of the judicial system; private individuals and groups have no access to it, and it does not hear appeals from lower courts.

The absence of judicial review, however, as the English and Israeli examples illustrate, does not mean the absence of constitutionalism. An independent judiciary endowed with judicial review powers may exert a powerful influence as a limitation upon the exercise of governmental powers, but there are other instruments available to make constitutionalism a viable concept. These include periodic elections, a free press, opposition political parties, and various elements of political responsibility. As a protection against the exercise of arbitrary authority in Britain, for example, constitutionalism is a viable force because it is fully accepted by an informed electorate which has the power of voting out of office a government which would presume to ignore its requirements.

A constitution is more than a mere document, and even in judicial review countries, more than a mere law. It imposes restraints upon government, but at the same time it also legitimizes its power. It is a record of national experience and a symbol of the nation's aspirations. It serves the important function of articulating the ideals of the community, of stating its social and economic aims. It exerts a tremendous educational influence as a convenient, easily-read compendium of the nation's basic purposes and principles.

There are many differences among constitutions. Some are extremely detailed (e.g., the constitutions of India and Mexico), and some, like that of the United States, are very short. Some are judicially enforceable, while most are not. Some constitutions are "normative," while others are merely "nominal," not to be taken too seriously. Some are stable, others are fragile. Some are republican, while others are monarchical. Some create parliamentary systems of government, while others provide for presidential systems. Some establish federal systems while others, such as the American states, provide for unitary systems. Some are described as rigid, and others as flexible, depending upon the ease or difficulty of the processes of constitutional amendment. There are many other terms used to describe various constitutions—such as revolutionary, bonapartist, legitimist, programmatic, confirmatory—all suggesting aspects of world history.

Whatever particular form of government a constitution delineates, however, it serves as the keystone of the arch of constitutionalism, except in those countries whose written constitutions are mere sham. Constitutionalism as a theory and in practice stands for the principle that there are—in a properly governed state—limitations upon those who exercise the powers of government, and that these limitations are spelled out in a body of higher law which is enforceable in a variety of ways, political and judicial. This is by no means a modern idea, for the concept of a higher law which spells out the basic norms of a political society is as old as Western civilization. That there are standards of rightness which transcend and control public officials, even current popular majorities, represents a critically significant element of man's endless quest for the good life.

BIBLIOGRAPHY

The leading books on the concept of constitutionalism from the point of view of general history are by Charles H. McIlwain, *Constitutionalism and the Changing World* (New York, 1939), and *Constitutionalism: Ancient and Modern* (Ithaca, 1947). Other useful books on constitutionalism around the world are: Carl J. Friedrich, *The Impact of American Constitutionalism Abroad* (Boston, 1967); Leslie Wolf-Phillips, *Constitutions of Modern States* (London, 1968); William G. Andrews, *Constitutions and Constitutionalism*, 3rd ed. (Princeton, 1968); and Francis D. Wormuth, *The Origins of Modern Constitutionalism* (New York, 1949). Leading books on American constitutionalism which are well worth consulting include: Edward S. Corwin, *The "Higher Law" Background of American Constitutional Law* (reprint, Ithaca, 1955); Howard Lee McBain, *The Living Constitution* (New York, 1927); Arthur E. Sutherland, *Constitutionalism in America* (New York, 1965); Howard Jay Graham, *Everyman's Constitution* (Madison, 1968); and Charles G. Haines, *The American Doctrine of Judicial Supremacy* (New York, 1914). Useful essays will be found in James Bryce, *Studies in History and Jurisprudence* (Oxford, 1901), Vol. I, Ch. III, pp. 145–254, "Flexible and Written Constitutions," and Vol. II, Ch. XI, pp. 112–71, "The Law of Nature."

DAVID FELLMAN

[See also **Authority;** Democracy; General Will; **Law;** Legal Responsibility; Nation; Revolution; Right and Good; Social Contract; **State.**]

CONTINUITY AND DISCONTINUITY IN NATURE AND KNOWLEDGE

I. INTRODUCTION

CONTINUITY is a key conception in the history of ideas in many fields. A form of continuity, under one name

or another, is frequently attributed to processes or developments in mathematics, science, philosophy, history, and theology. In mathematics proper and its direct applications, especially to "exact" science, continuity is nowadays rigorously defined and unequivocally fixed. Also, in mathematical contexts continuity is sharply distinguished from neighboring concepts like uniformity, steadiness, constancy, etc., all of which have, in mathematical contexts, definitions of their own. But, by reason of its general nature, continuity is a sprawling concept. Outside of mathematics, it is ambiguously conceived and loosely applied, and mergers and fusions with neighboring concepts are really unavoidable.

Thus, the historical books of the Old Testament are a vast dissertation on the Lord's unceasing concern for his "Chosen People"; and a theologian may pronounce with almost no difference of meaning that the Lord perseveres in this concern with "continuity," or "steadiness," "constancy," "uniformity," etc.

In general history and theology imprecisions as to the meaning of continuity may be enriching rather than disturbing, but in descriptive science, in which imprecisions also occur, they may become outright embarrassing. A leading instance of such an embarrassment is the case of the hypothesis of uniformitarianism. The hypothesis asserts, for geology and biology, that there has been a certain continuity of evolution since the formation of the earth. But no satisfactory definition of this would-be continuity has been agreed upon, or is in sight. (See section V.)

Imprecisions as to the meaning of continuity may border on the very threshold of "exact science." A notable case is Isaac Newton's description of his absolute time, which runs as follows:

Absolute, true, and mathematical time, of itself, and from its own nature, flows equably [Latin: *aequabiliter*] without relation to anything external, and by another name is called duration [F. Cajori trans., p. 6].

Newton makes it clear that this pronouncement, which is made in an elucidating scholium only, is not meant to be a primary operational definition of absolute time but only a supplementary background description of it. The decisive ingredient of this description is the word "equably" (which does not occur in the immediately following description of "absolute space"), and it is meant to suggest that the flow of time is somehow intrinsically continuous and uniform. But this suggestion is tenuous and fugacious, and Newton's sentence about the nature of his time cannot be made into a truly informative definition.

Two thousand years before the *Principia*, Aristotle, in his great essay on time (*Physica*, Book 4, Chs. 10–14), performed much better than Newton. Aristotle's time is hierarchically anterior to events in it and even to our awareness of it; and Aristotle is much more persuasive than Newton in his expostulations that time is intrinsically continuous, and that this continuity is a preexistent standard by which to assess, for any "movement"—which, in Aristotle, stands for a general process in nature, more or less—whether it is continuous, discrete, or constant (Bochner, Ch. 4). Furthermore, already many centuries before Aristotle, a linguistic bond between time and continuity had been clearly present in Homer, and we are going to describe it briefly.

The Greek word for our "abstract" noun "continuity," as standardized by Aristotle, is the adverbial form *to synechés* (τὸ συνεχές), and the cognate verb *synechein* means literally "to hang, or hold together." It so happens that the Latin root of the English word *continuity* also means literally "hanging, or holding together"; but works on Indo-European linguistics do not assert that the Greek and Latin stem words for *continuity* had a common root in Sanskrit.

Now, the verb *synechein* and the adverb *synechés* occur already in Homer, but on different levels of abstraction. The verb occurs in *Iliad* 4, 133, in the expression: "The golden clasps of the belt were *held together*," in which its meaning is quite concrete. But the adverb, which is used twice, is both times used in a semi-abstract meaning, namely in the meaning of: *continually* (in time). The first occurrence is in *Iliad* 12, 25–26, thus: "Zeus made it rain *continually*"; and the second occurrence is in *Odyssey* 9, 74, thus: "There for two nights and two days we lay *continually*." Also, in the second passage the adverb *synechés* is reinforced, seemingly redundantly, by the adverb *aiei* (αἰεί) which means: *always, ever, eternally*. The Odyssey thus adumbrated a tripartite bond between continuity, time, and eternity, and this bond has been variously contemplated and exalted in general philosophy and theology since. This bond is nowhere stronger than in the Old Testament, but the extant canon of the Old Testament does not have a word whose functions would correspond to those of *synechés*.

Post-Hellenistically, this bond is also verified by the order in which the cognates of our English word *continuity* have come into use. According to the entries in the *Oxford English Dictionary*, our word *continual* (in time) was the first to emerge. It occurs already around A.D. 1340, in the phrase: "great exercise of body and continual travail of the spirit," in one of the so-called *English Prose Treatises* of the hermit Richard Rolle of Hampole (1290–1349). But for all other cognates of *continuity* the same dictionary quotes only from Chaucer, who wrote about half a century after Hampole, or from later sources, even much later ones. Thus, according to this dictionary, our adjective *continuous* gained currency in the seventeenth century only.

Continuity has many shadings of meaning and therefore also many antonyms. The leading antonym to "continuous" is "discrete"; other ones are: saltatory, sudden, intermittent, indivisible, atomic, particulate, and even monadic. A monad however, being a kind of synonym for unity and one-ness, may suggest both continuity and discreteness, at one and the same time. The monad of Leibniz, as presented in his *Monadology*, is apparently of such a kind; that is, it also suggests continuity, even if it is an irreducible ultimate unit, not only of physical structure but also of consciousness, cognition, and metaphysical coherence. In the thinking of Leibniz this simultaneousness is grounded in the all-pervading *lex continui*, which maintains that "all" basic constituents of the universe are somehow continuous, be they physical or metaphysical, elemental or rational.

Long before Leibniz, the outlines of a *lex continui*, and an involvement of unity with continuity, were already present in the great ontological poem of Parmenides (sixth century B.C.) from which we quote two passages (L. Tarán, p. 85).

Being is uncreated and imperishable, whole, unique, immovable and complete. It was not once, nor will it be, since it is now altogether, one, continuous (frag. 8, lines 3–6).

Nor is it divisible, since it is all alike. Nor is there somewhat more here, and somewhat less there, that could prevent it from holding together; but all is full of Being. Therefore it is all continuous, for Being adheres to Being (frag. 8, lines 22–26).

In sum, the Parmenidean "Being" is one, yet continuous; homogeneous, that is continuously distributed, yet indivisible; ungenerated, and imperishable, and atemporal. Such bold accumulations of divers attributes in one have been occurring in Western philosophy ever since. And Western science has been harboring self-dualities and near-inconsistencies, many of which affect continuity, from early Pythagoreans until our very day.

Our present-day intellectual discomfort, if any, over the contrast between the continuous and the discrete is an inheritance from the nineteenth century. Through the length of the nineteenth century there was a widespread predilection for continuity in all areas of knowledge, in mathematics, physics, earth-and-life science, general philosophy, and even in historiography. This predilection manifested itself in a tendency to subsume and subordinate the discrete under the continuous, even when the presence of the discrete was freely and fully acknowledged. In the twentieth century the Victorian outlooks on continuity have been modified and reoriented, some gradually and some vehemently; and the discrete has come into its rightful own, reaching a high-point in quantum mechanics.

II. PHYSICAL SCIENCE

The nineteenth century created the great doctrines of molecular chemistry, thermodynamics, and statistical mechanics, all of which take full cognizance of the fact that physical matter consists of discrete particles. Yet, in an overall sense, "Physical Science" of the nineteenth century gave decisive preference to "field" theory over "particle" theory, that is to continuity over discreteness.

Thus, in the beginning of the nineteenth century, Thomas Young and A. Fresnel rendered a decision, which was then long adhered to, that light is composed of waves and not of corpuscles. Secondly, D. S. Poisson, C. F. Gauss, and G. Green created field conceptions of "potential," with parallel mathematical properties, for electrostatics, magnetostatics, and gravitation. Thirdly, Maxwell's electrodynamics, as corroborated by Heinrich Hertz, was a field theory, and it is frequently viewed as the representative field theory of the century. Fourthly, mathematical physicists from Cauchy to Kirchhoff created and standardized the theory of mechanics of continuous media, which assumes that mechanical matter is distributed continuously, with a finite density point-by-point. This mathematical assumption runs counter to the indisputable hypothesis of basic physics and chemistry that matter is atomistic, or molecular; but, operationally, the theory of continuous media has been overwhelmingly successful and it is simply indispensable for many contexts. Finally, in statistical phenomena and theories, nineteenth-century physics was led to operate almost exclusively with the Gaussian law of probability, and this law represents continuous distribution par excellence.

Furthermore, within fluid mechanics, which is a part of the theory of continuous media, Helmholtz created a major theory of vortices. Lord Kelvin, his contemporary, was so impressed with it, that he hastily dashed off a theory of "vortex-atoms," in which individual atoms, even in their singleness, were made into continuously spread-out vortices à la Helmholtz. This attempt of Kelvin was so ill-advised that present-day physics has all but "suppressed" the memory of it (R. H. Silliman). Lastly, Helmholtz fully shared the general presumption that acoustics is a theory of waves, that is, a field theory, although it was he who pioneered in the discovery (for which he is justly famous), that, physiologically, there are discrete "tone atoms," that

is tones which the ear cannot "resolve" by physically subdividing them.

Physics of the twentieth century changed all this. It did not give up nineteenth-century insights but it refocused them. All field-like constructs of the preceding century were fully retained, and even enlarged and added to; but they were all balanced or complemented by the introduction of appropriate particle-like constructs of a dual kind. Thus, electric fields were balanced by electrons, light waves by photons, sound waves by phonons, and even gravitational fields were balanced by would-be duals which are hopefully called gravitons; conversely, and most importantly, all elementary particles of matter were balanced by undulatory counterparts, the so-called de Broglie waves. In the final outcome, the nineteenth-century link between physics and continuity was nowise weakened, but it was balanced by an equally viable link between physics and discreteness, and the whole structure of physics has been brought to rest on a duality between the continuous and the discrete. Except for sporadic and disjointed anticipations in philosophy of science (M. Jammer, p. 241), general philosophy of the late Victorian and even Edwardian era was unprepared and ill-equipped to cope with the novel postures in basic physics, and only very slowly is general philosophy accommodating itself to the stubborn fact that the duality principle in physics is here to stay.

A peculiar adumbration of our present-day duality between the continuous and the discrete may be discerned in the outlooks of the first atomists Leucippus and Democritus (fifth century B.C.). They recognized from the first that an atomic hypothesis does not only assert that physical matter is "granulated," that is, built up of particles which in a suitable sense are indecomposable, but also that these particles "interact" with each other across the "void" that separates them from one another. They interact unceasingly, and for the most part "invisibly." It is the mode and manner of these interactions which constitute the structure of matter, mainly in its microscopic properties, but also in its macroscopic attributes. Democritus saw this more clearly than most participants in the seventeenth-century "Revival of Atomism" (R. H. Kargon, 1966), and even chemists of the nineteenth century may have been lagging behind Democritus in this crucial insight. Democritus may have also known, in thought patterns of his, that even if an atomic theory intends to be "philosophical" rather than "physical" (van Melsen), it still has to establish its "legitimacy" by offering a context of physical explanations of some degree of novelty. Giordano Bruno, for instance, did not know this at all. He offered various atomistic and monadological statements, but they served no purpose in physics (K. Lasswitz, I, 391–92).

Aristotle, who lived about a life span after Democritus, was much concerned with the first atomists and their doctrine. He was opposed to atomism, but not because it assumed that matter consists of minimal constituents. In this assumption, Aristotle might have acquiesced. He was a biologist, and a very great one too, and as such he had it in his thinking that an organic tissue (like flesh, skin, bone, etc.) consists of "minimal" parts; just as in modern biology a tissue is composed of cells, which are ultimate units of life. What Aristotle could not accept for himself was the crucial assertion of atomism that, ordinarily, any two atoms are separated from each other by a spatial vacuity, which surrounds each of the atoms and extends between any two of them. Aristotle simply "abhorred" a vacuum, any vacuum, and he could do so with metaphysical justification. Firstly, even in present-day biology, cells are adjoined wall to wall, without biological interstices; and secondly, in physics proper, Aristotle was a thermodynamicist, and it is a fact of present-day physics, which Aristotle anticipated, that in a purely thermodynamical system an *absolute* vacuum is not allowed for. It is true that since the nineteenth century this kind of thermodynamics has been deemed compatible with an atomic, or rather molecular structure of the substances which compose the system (Bochner, p. 160). However, this reconciliation of apparent opposites has been brought about by statistical mechanics; but the basic attitudes of this doctrine were far beyond the reach of Aristotle, and of antiquity in general.

In spite of his opposition to atomism, Aristotle had a masterful grasp of the achievements of the Atomists, as evidenced, for instance, by the following passage.

Leucippus and his associate Democritus hold that the elements are the Full and the Void; they call them Being and Non-Being respectively. Being is full and solid, Non-Being is void and rare. Since the void exists no less than the body, it follows that Non-Being exists no less than Being. The two together are the material causes of existing things (*Metaphysica*, 985b 4–10; trans. Kirk and Raven, pp. 406–07).

This remarkable statement could serve as a motto for the polarity between particle and field and even for the de Broglie duality between corpuscle and wave. It is notable that Aristotle even "apologizes" for the Atomists for expressing the polarity between full and void in the quaint, and possibly misleading Parmenidean contrast between "Being" and "Non-Being," and Aristotle is reassuring the reader that the "Non" in "Non-Being" is only a *façon de parler* without any negative intent or force. And Aristotle's casual observation that "the two together are the material causes of existing things" is an oracle for the ages, for our age of physics, at any rate.

III. ATOMISM AND DISCONTINUITY
IN THEOLOGY

In the European West, atomism since Democritus has been persistently associated with forms of atheism, or at least with suspicions of it. But, as against this, in the Islamic Middle East, in the tenth and eleventh centuries A.D., when Islam's philosophy and theology were at their height, Islamic theologians—most of whom were of Persian extraction—based their orthodoxy, which was philosophically articulated, on a radical form of atomism and discontinuity in nature. (For a balanced recent account see M. Fakhry, Chs. 1 and 2.) From the Islamic approach it was the avowal of continuity which represented atheism, and the avowal of discontinuity which represented theism.

It is worth noting that a late Victorian scholar, a leading one, finds "Mephistophelian humor" in the fact that Islamic theists could embrace "atheistic" atomism. The scholar concludes that this came about because Aristotle had depicted Democritus so engagingly instead of warning theists against seeking refuge with him (L. Stein, pp. 331–32).

This Islamic doctrine, whatever its origin, was part of the so-called Kalam. Its intent was not so much to deny continuity as to deny causation, but it strongly correlated the two. And it denied causation, because any general law of causation would circumscribe, and even inhibit God's freedom of intervention and thaumaturgy. Thus, within this intellectual setting, the physical atomism of the Kalam became a scientific occasionalism of its philosophy.

A famous account of this atomism is incorporated in the *Guide of the Perplexed* (Maimonides, Part I, Chs. 71–75). As usual with Maimonides, his report is somewhat over-systematic, but the account seems very reliable and adequate. Now, according to this account, the Mutakallemim—that is, the professors of Kalam—atomized, or rather quantized (in the sense of our quantum theory) everything: matter, space, time, and motion.

Specifically they taught that the seemingly continuous locomotion of a body is in fact not really continuous but a succession of leaps between discretely placed positions; and they apparently took it for granted that there is a universal minimal distance between any two positions. Also, what is important, a leap from position A to position B consists of two interlocking subevents; the original body in position A ceases to exist, and an "identical" body comes into being in position B. This sounds surprisingly like the leap of a Bohr electron, when rotating around a proton, from one energy level into a neighboring one; except that in the Kalam, the second subevent follows on the first "occasionalistically," that is by an act of God, and not "causally," that is by a law of nature.

Somewhat more occasionalistic, but still compatible with our physics of today, was the insistence of the Mutakallemim that if a white garment turns red by being dipped into a red dye then it is wrong to say that red pigment has been transferred from the dye to the garment. Rather, by God's volition, an amount of red pigment ceased to be in the dye, and a corresponding amount of the pigment was created in the garment.

Most alien to our thinking is the "Hypothesis of Admissibility." It apparently asserted that anything which is "imaginable" is also possible. It is "imaginable" that man might be much larger in size than he is now, and he might indeed so be; in fact, he might be as large as a mountain. Fire usually goes upward, but we can "imagine" it going downwards, and so indeed it might go.

Even more striking than the atomistic pronouncements, were the accompanying occasionalistic theses, and the latter were displayed most dazzlingly in the work of the Iranian Muslim theologian al-Ghazali. Nevertheless, they were leading Islamic philosophical thought into a *cul-de-sac,* and it was very fortunate for the nascent medieval civilization on the European continent that the leading European schoolmen, Muhammadan, Jewish, and Christian, were refusing to be drawn into this blind alley. In the twelfth century, the Spanish Jew Maimonides was opposed to the occasionalistic doctrines of the Kalam, and so were also, very systematically, his contemporary Averroës (a Spanish Muslim), and, almost a century later, the Latin schoolman Thomas Aquinas in his *Summa contra Gentiles,* Book III.

It is regrettable, though, that this opposition to the Islamic occasionalism also kept the West from becoming generally acquainted with its scientific atomism. Saint Thomas, for instance, has very little about it. Almost a century after Aquinas, a Karaite schoolman, Aaron ben Elijah of Nicodemia (1300–69), who stood intellectually between West and East, made a last major attempt to keep Islamic atomism alive, but to no avail (Husik, Ch. 16).

It appears that the atomism of the Islam had been greatly influenced by the atomisms of Democritus and Epicurus, but it is not easy to say why the metaphysical and religious evaluations were so divergent. It has been suggested that Islamic philosophers were exposed to Indian influences (S. Pines), and also that a primitive atomism may have arisen within the Kalam indigenously (O. Pretzl). There are intimations that, from the beginnings of Islamic thought there had been reflections, naive ones, on the concentration of space and matter in elemental units. Also, the problem of the differences between Islamic and Greek atomism is compounded by the fact that there had been divergences of philosophy even between Democritus and Epicurus themselves.

It is reported that Democritus was of a serene disposition in his personal deportment. This serenity in manners may have corresponded to a determinism in scientific outlook which takes it for granted that, ordinarily, the physical constellation of today will determine the physical events of tomorrow. In the universe of Democritus, atoms were unceasingly in motion, by fixed laws and unchangeable rhythms. In the course of their motions atoms would combine to form "worlds"—which we may take to be solar systems, or galaxies, in our experience—and the worlds could also fall apart by dissolution of the combinations of atoms which constitute them. Also, by their structure, the worlds of Democritus were mostly (spiral) vortices, and once upon a time the vortices emanated from some kind of "turbulence," that is, from some kind of "primordial chaos" (Diogenes Laërtius).

All this sounds astonishingly "modern." Primordial turbulence, and spiral-shaped galaxies are giant-sized discontinuities in nature, the account of which fills the pages of any book on cosmogony of today; and it must not be held against the first atomists that they did not explain their provenance, because present-day cosmology cannot explain it either (J. H. Oort, p. 20).

The system of Democritus was not "atheistic" in a militant sense, but it was indifferent to divinity in a passive sense. Since everything in nature and life was presumed to follow predictably by laws and rhythms, there was apparently no need, or rather no room, for a Divine Providence that would affect the fate of man, or the course of the world, by acts of willed intervention and prodigy. Very much later though, mostly in response to Islamic occasionalism, the counterargument was fashioned that it is noncontinuity and indeterminacy which bespeak the absence of divine Providence; and that it is continuity and causality in nature which testify to a rule by Providence and perhaps even to an original creation by a divine resolve.

While the system of Democritus has the mystique of an incomparable classical creation, the atomic system of Epicurus, over a century later, bears the mark of an important but epigonic adaptation. It had a great appeal though. But the appeal was not due to the power of scientific inventiveness in Epicurus, who had set "Epicureanism" in motion, but to the beauty of

Lucretius' *De rerum natura* in which it is poetically enshrined. The latter work is not an essay in science but a poet's sweeping vision of the Great Chain of Being in its manifold manifestations; however, by some irrationality of inspiration, which has been a puzzle to many a poet and literary critic since, Lucretius transported his vision through the rather amorphous medium of Epicurus' system of knowledge, and thus immortalized Epicurus' variant on atomism in the process. Democritus had been a physicist, first and foremost, and very genuinely so. Epicurus however was first and foremost a moralist and a social critic, even if he elected to transmit his philosophemes in a setting of physical assumptions; and it was this humanism which attracted Lucretius to him.

With regard to discontinuity in the universe Lucretius avers, as did Democritus long before him, that, by conjunction and disjunction of atoms, numerous "galaxies" are formed and dissolved. He even alludes to a primordial turbulence (*nova tempestas*), but, regrettably, not to vortices (P. Boyancé, p. 273). Lucretius even seems to suggest, in words of his own—what is apparently not in the extant reports about Democritus—that the separate galaxies of the universe are likely to be distributed throughout the universe with a certain uniform frequency of occurrence (*De rerum natura*, Book II, lines 1048–66; C. Bailey, 2, 964–65).

Lucretius also has the significant report—which most regrettably does not occur in the extant remains of Epicurus himself, but has also been confirmed by Cicero, Plutarch, and others—that the atom of Epicurus was endowed with a so-called *clinamen* of his invention. It was a small-scale swerving motion of the atom, and Epicurus superimposed it on the large-scale rectilinear motion that had been advocated by Democritus. This *clinamen* was designed to temper the basic determinism of physics by an element of indeterminism; and as a suggestion in physics it was a remarkable adumbration of indeterminacies in the physics of our day. But Epicurus, and his followers ever since, went much too far in using it as a physical justification for indeterminacies in the science of man, namely as a justification for the freedom of human will and for man's self-mastery, in a moral, social, and theological sense.

Epicurus was adopted as the ancestral creator of the nineteenth-century Marxist doctrine that certain fixed assumptions in physics are an unfailing indicator of certain fixed attitudes in sociology. Thus, the *Dialectics of Nature* of Friedrich Engels, and, much more shrilly, the *Materialism and Empirico-Criticism* (1908) of V. I. Lenin, were proclaiming the doctrine that a philosophy which affirms the primacy of human freedom must be based on a certain kind of metaphysical "materialism," and that this materialism must more or less be predicated on a form of atomism.

Developments in twentieth-century science have been undermining the possibilities of such firm correlations. In the nineteenth century there were firm distinctions and separations between materialism and idealism, reality and imagination, phenomena and objects, experience and theory, experiments and explanations. But in the twentieth century, the spreading principles of duality for particle and field, for corpuscle and wave, and the progressive and unrelenting mathematization of all of theoretical physics, have been dissolving the scientific foundations for such distinctions and separations. Therefore, not only standard "Marxist" tenets, but also, many other Victorian and Edwardian correlations are losing their obvious justifications, and they will have to be re-thought from the ground up.

IV. MATHEMATICS

In mathematics, continuity is an all-pervading concept. Topology is a relatively recent major division of mathematics, and in the half-century 1890–1940 it was a vast exercise in continuity from a novel comprehensive approach. Also, this novel pursuit of continuity supplemented but did not supersede the study of continuity in "analysis," in which, knowingly or not, it had been a central conception since the fifth century B.C.

It will suit our purposes to distinguish, and keep apart two *aspects* of continuity in mathematics.

Aspect (1). Continuity of linear ordering. This aspect of continuity is suggested by, and is embodied in the intrinsic continuity structure of the so-called linear continuum of real numbers $-\infty < t < \infty$.

Aspect (2). Continuity of a function $y = f(x)$. The simplest, and still very important case of a continuous function $f(x)$ arises if x and y are both real numbers, and in this case a function is "equivalent" with an ordinary graph or chart on ordinary graph paper. In the general case, a function $y = f(x)$ is a "mapping" from any topological space $X:(x)$ to any other topological space $Y:(y)$.

Aspect (1) was envisioned by the Greeks, and they worked long and hard at elucidating it. Aspect (2) however eluded them. The Greeks had fleeting chance encounters with it, but they were not inspired to focus on it in any manner. This failure of the Greeks to recognize aspect (2) far outweighed their ability to identify aspect (1). By a purely scientific assessment, this failure greatly contributed to the eventual decline of Greek mathematics in its own phase.

Even in the recognition of aspect (1) the Greeks had two blind spots. Firstly, Greek mathematics never created the real numbers themselves. When the Greeks formed the product of two quantities that were represented by lengths then, conceptually, the product had to be represented by an area. Descartes may have been the first to state expressly, as he did with some emphasis at the very beginning of his *La Géométrie* (1637), that the product may also be represented by a length. The Greek substitute for our concept of real numbers was their quasi-concept of magnitude (μέγεθος; *megethos*), and the corresponding elementary "arithmetic" was the Greek theory of proportions, as presented in Euclid's *Elements*, Book 5.

The Greek magnitudes were a "substitute" for *positive* real numbers only; and we view it as a second blind spot of the Greeks that they did not even introduce a magnitude of value 0 (= zero), which, by continuity, would be the limiting case of magnitudes of decreasing (positive) values. Thus, Greek mathematics never had the thrill of conceiving that two coincident lines form an angle of value 0; and Greek physics of locomotion, as expounded in Aristotle's *Physica*, Books 5–8, always viewed "rest" (ἠρεμία) as a "contrary to motion" (κίνησις) and never as a motion with velocity 0.

In fact, the first outright criticism of this Aristotelian view is to be found only in Leibniz. It is strongly implied in his pronouncement that "the law of bodies at rest is, so to speak, only a special case of the general rule for bodies in motion, the law of equality a special case of inequality, the law for the rectilinear a subspecies of the law for the curvilinear" (H. Weyl, p. 161).

This pronouncement of Leibniz was part of a universal *lex continui* ("Law of Continuity") which runs through his entire metaphysics and science. Leibniz did not present the law in a systematic study of its own, but he frequently reverted to it, presenting some of its aspects each time. Leibniz recognized, reflectively, the importance of functions for mathematics. He coined the name "function" in 1694, and, what is decisive, he was well aware of our aspect (2) of continuity (Bochner, pp. 216–23). But he did not "create" functions in mathematics. As rightly emphasized by Oswald Spengler, the concept of function began to stir in the late fourteenth century, and its emergence constituted a remarkable difference between ancient and post-medieval mathematics. Also, as early as 1604, that is 90 years before Leibniz coined the name, Luca Valerio had *de facto* introduced a rather general class of (continuous) functions $f(x)$ to a purpose, and had operated with them competently in the spirit of the mathematics then evolving. However, it was Leibniz who was the first to assert, more or less, that functions and functional dependencies in nature are usually continuous. Thus he states the maxim of cognition that

"*when the essential determinations of one being approximate those of another, as a consequence, all the properties of the former should also gradually approximate those of the latter*" (Wiener, p. 187).

It is not easy to state the direct effect of Leibniz' Law of Continuity on the growth of mathematics and physics. In working mathematics, the meaning and role of continuity unfolded excruciatingly slowly in the course of the eighteenth and nineteenth centuries, through cumulative work of Lagrange, Laplace, Cauchy, Dirichlet, Riemann, Hankel, P. du Bois Reymond, Georg Cantor, and others, without any manifest reference to the metaphysically conceived *lex continui* or Leibniz. Of course, the "Law" of Leibniz may have been burrowing deep inside the texture of our intellectual history, thus affecting the course of mathematics. But to establish this in specific detail would be very difficult.

Mathematics of the nineteenth century elucidated basic facts about both aspects of continuity, for real numbers, and for real and complex numbers. These facts about continuity were intimately connected with facts about infinity, especially about the infinitely small. The efforts to elucidate these two sets of facts, severally and connectedly, had begun with early Pythagoreans and Zeno of Elea, and it took twenty-four centuries to bring them to fruition.

The twentieth century greatly widened the scene of continuity, especially of its aspect (2), by extending the conception of continuity from functions from and to real (and complex) numbers to functions from and to general point-sets, that is general aggregates of mathematical elements. In fact, a numerical function $y = f(x)$ is continuous if it transforms "nearby" numbers x into "nearby" numbers y. Therefore, in order to apply the notion of continuity to a function $y = f(x)$ from a general point-set $X:(x)$ to a general point-set $Y:(y)$ it suffices to know what is meant by the statement that points of X or points of Y are "sufficiently near" each other. Now, in the twentieth century this has been achieved by the introduction of a so-called topological structure on a general point-set. For any given topological structure it is meaningful to say when two points of the set are "near" each other, and when the two point-sets X and Y are each endowed with a topological structure of its own it thus becomes meaningful to say when a function $y = f(x)$ is continuous. The conception of a topological structure opened new vistas, and it has become involved in most of the mathematics of today.

V. GEOLOGY AND BIOLOGY

Continuity plays a major role in descriptive science, mainly in geology and biology, but also in psychology.

Aristotle's *Historia animalium* has already a renowned aphorism to this effect:

Nature passes little by little from things lifeless to animal life, so that, by continuity, it is impossible to present the exact lines of demarcation, or to determine to which of the two groups intermediate forms belong (588b 4–7).

Also, in Aristotle's system of psychology there may have been a hierarchy of souls corresponding to the hierarchy of living things (Tricot, pp. 492–93, note 2). Altogether Aristotle already envisioned the so-called Great Chain of Being, which reached a dominant position in the thinking of Leibniz and of the Age of Enlightenment (Lovejoy).

Leibniz took pains to expound that the Great Chain is indeed "great" in the sense that

All the orders of natural beings form but a single chain in which the various classes, like so many rings, are so closely linked one to another that it is impossible for the senses or the imagination to determine precisely the point at which one ends and the next begins (B. Glass, p. 37).

Also, in other contexts, Leibniz intensified, or diversified, the adjective "great" by equating it variously with "maximal," "optimal," "perfect," "complete," "continuous," etc.

Dr. Samuel Johnson, the redoubtable man of letters, termed the Great Chain of Being the "Arabian Scale of Existence," and he made a very pertinent observation about its "greatness." He compared this scale of existence to the mathematical linear continuum, which he probably knew from Aristotle's *Physica*, and he pointed out that, notwithstanding a superficial similarity, the two are very different from each other (Lovejoy, pp. 253–54). In fact, as stated by Aristotle in his *Physica* over and over again, the mathematical linear continuum is "everywhere dense," meaning that between any two elements of it there are always some other ones; in particular, no element of it is isolated. However, in nature's Chain of Being, biological and mineral, however great and complete it be, only a finite number of Links can be discerned. Thus, even if the Chain of Being has been made optimally great by filling in all possible gaps in it, there still is only a finite number of Links, all told. Because of that, each individual member of the Chain is isolated; meaning that there is a first neighbor that is hierarchically above it, and another one that is hierarchically below it.

Leibniz must have been aware of this unbridgeable difference between the Great Chain and the linear continuum. He must have even been aware of the fact that the linear continuum is not only "everywhere dense," as already known to Zeno of Elea and to Aristotle, but also "complete," in the sense that to any bounded sequence of real numbers which is mono-

tonely increasing or decreasing there corresponds a real number which is a limit of the sequence. The completeness of the linear continuum was properly established only in the nineteenth century by Dedekind and Cantor; but Eudoxus and Archimedes had, more or less, known it for their magnitudes, and Leibniz must have half-known it for real numbers too.

But Leibniz pretended to be undeterred by such differences. He desired to coalesce heterogeneous phenomena from exact science, descriptive science, and metaphysically oriented "moral" science into one comprehensive law of continuity. The latter was apparently also a law of optimality, and in this guise it was closely allied to a principle of contradiction and of sufficient reason. Yet, at other times Leibniz also acknowledged that heterogeneity cannot be forcibly overcome. Such an acknowledgment seems to be implied in the following statement in which Leibniz avows that his so-called labyrinth has two separate aspects.

There are two famous labyrinths where our reason very often goes astray. One concerns the great question of the Free and the Necessary, above all in the production and the origin of Evil. The other consists in the discussion of continuity, and of the indivisibles which appear to be the elements thereof, and where the consideration of the infinite must enter in (Leibniz, *Theodicy*, p. 53).

In the nineteenth century, a quest for continuity was particularly pronounced in geology and biology. As already mentioned in section I, the hypothesis of continuity peculiar to geology is called uniformitarianism; and its contrary was called catastrophism. Uniformitarianism was introduced in 1795 in a treatise by James Hutton (Gillispie, pp. 122–48; Albritton, chapter by G. G. Simpson), and it became generally known through a large-scale treatise of Charles Lyell, *Principles of Geology*, whose first edition appeared in three volumes, 1830–33.

In biology of today, the hypothesis of continuity is specifically the hypothesis of "transformism," that is the hypothesis that there is in operation an organic evolution of life which proceeds by a transformation of one species into another; the direct contrary to it would be the doctrine of "fixed species" which the French call "fixism" (P. Ostoya). Transformism as a biological hypothesis fully began with Lamarck, and evolution was assumed by him to come about by adaptation. Charles Darwin presented an impressive plea that evolution comes about by natural selection; and, "popularly," transformism is associated with this kind of evolution only. Yet in present-day biology, adaptation is not entirely ruled out, even if Natural Selection remains the prime cause.

Geologists nowadays greatly favor uniformitarianism over catastrophism, but it is easier to say what catastrophism asserts than what uniformitarianism actually is. Catastrophism maintains that manifest discontinuities in geological stratifications of mineral deposits and imbedded fossils are due to discontinuities in the physical processes which brought about the stratifications and perhaps even abrupt changes in the physical laws which produce the processes (Toulmin, Ch. 7). Uniformitarianism however wants to be a true contrary to catastrophism and not only a negation of it. A mere negation would only demand that important basic data and phenomena be continuous in time, and nothing more; there would be no need for anything to be a constant in time, say. Thus, the gravitational force need not have at all times the same Newtonian value $1/r^2$, but it might be a positive function of distance and time, provided that the dependence on all its variables is a continuous one. This however is not what uniformitarianism really wants to be. Its real aim is to avow that there is "uniformity" in nature; and this seems to imply that certain basic causes and laws are not only continuous in time, but also constant in time, and perhaps constant in some other parameters too. By the prevalent interpretations of uniformitarianism, certain leading attributes of nature are recognizably always the same, so that the "present determines the past" and, of course, the future.

It appears that our perception of "uniformity" and of "continuity"—in whatever form these concepts appear—is inseparable from our rational awareness of the flow of time. The awareness of time, in its turn, has come about by the presence of cyclical and recurrent phenomena in nature, although by cognitive structure time is rectilinear and, in fact, a mathematical linear continuum. It also appears that within our Western civilization man's capacity for specific rigorous knowledge has been awakened and shaped under the impact of lunar, sidereal, and planetary events in the external world which are recurring periodically (O. Neugebauer, Ch. 1).

Apparently in keeping with these basic ingredients of our rationality, the demand of uniformitarianism is a compound of constancy, continuity, and cyclicity; and the relative magnitude of these three components varies with the approach to the conception.

In the first half of the nineteenth century, in the thinking of Charles Lyell at any rate, the component of constancy was predominant; so much so that when Lyell was extending uniformitarianism from geological to organic matter, he had to give preference to fixed species over evolving ones. But in the second half of the nineteenth century, continuity proper was ever more outweighing constancy; and there was a rising

consensus that, contrary to the view of Lyell, uniformitarianism and transformism mutually condition and justify each other (Glass, pp. 367ff.). To Lyell, the transition from one species to a next following one, however short the distance, was a "catastrophe," and thus not admissible (de Beer, p. 104). To affirmers of general continuity however, a sufficiently close transition from species to species ceased to be a "catastrophe," that is a disquieting discontinuity, and became "progress," which bespoke the kind of continuity that arises in the optical merger of rapidly succeeding visual tableaus. (In the motion picture industry, "continuity" refers to the coherence of the scenario, and not to the flow of the optical illusion).

In the twentieth century, the continuity aspect of organic evolution has been somewhat beclouded by the fact that, genetically, evolutionary transition comes about by a so-called mutation of the chromosomic apparatus and that "the basis of spontaneous mutation remains one of the great unsolved problems of genetics" (McGraw-Hill *Encyclopedia of Science and Technology*, "Mutation"). Nevertheless, the fact that everything proceeds by mutations is no more damaging to the overall continuity in evolution than atomic and quantum spontaneities in basic physics are prejudicial to overall continuities in the foundations of modern physics and related science.

Strictly speaking, every event in nature is probably discrete, or a union of discrete subevents; that is, most likely, no one event actually proceeds as mapped on the mathematical continuum in its conceptual purity. But the "fiction" that most events are best described by continuous functions seems to be an operational necessity, and there is nothing to suggest that it will ever be possible to abandon it entirely. For instance, the principles of our engineering mechanics, as taught in engineering schools all over the world, were laid down in Victorian and Edwardian treatises, and it would be most cumbersome and inappropriate to make this entire mechanics, in all its parts, nuclearly discontinuous in accordance with some quantum field, or solid state theory of our day.

VI. PHILOSOPHY

Continuity enters into all parts of philosophy. A measure of continuity is involved in any conception or philosopheme of Plato's, be it about man or God, body or soul, memory or ideas, mathematics or morals, poetry or artisanship, state or citizen. Without an awareness of continuity there would have been no *City of God* or *Confessions* of Saint Augustine; no medieval problems about particulars and universals, creation and eternity, fate and free will, Faith and Reason. And yet, only in the philosophy of nature and of mathematics is the presence of continuity immediate and tangible; in other areas of philosophy the degree of its presence is not easy to verify and the importance of its role is not easy to determine.

Thus, Aristotle's *Physica* is full of concern for continuity, directly and emphatically, and it is easy to identify its presence in related treatises like *De caelo* and *De generatione et corruptione*. But there is, directly, very little about continuity in the *Metaphysica*, and almost nothing indirectly to stir one's imagination. Thus, at the beginning of Book 10 of the *Metaphysica*, continuity is mentioned, directly, as one of several meanings of Unity, but the context is philosophically indifferent and little known. And even the continuity in *Physica* deals, for the most part, only with the *linear continuum* of mathematics, which, from our retrospect, is a rather circumscribed topic, in a sense.

The first Western philosopher on record who tried to visualize the problem of continuity in its entirety, that is for philosophy in general, was G. W. Leibniz. He set out to spread his *lex continui* over the vastnesses of the theories of cognition, metaphysics, and sciences. He even asserted that the mission of the Law of Continuity is to affirm that "the present is always pregnant with the future," and he also implied that to deny the law would amount to denying the Principle of Sufficient Reason, whatever that be (*Leibniz Selections*, p. 185). Yet, whenever Leibniz attempts to be specific and to adduce some particular application of his general Law of Continuity, the application usually becomes a specific assertion within mathematics, or within natural philosophy, or within philosophy of mathematics. It is true that in his mathematical allusions Leibniz sometimes reaches out far into the future, but it is a future of professional mathematics and not of extra-mathematical philosophy.

After Leibniz, the eighteenth century contributed nothing notable to the comprehension of continuity in philosophy. This fully applies even to Immanuel Kant. To judge by the entries "Kontinuität," and "Stetigkeit" in a recent Kant dictionary (R. Eisler, *Kant-Lexikon*), Kant made no pronouncements on continuity that contributed anything new to what had been said by philosophers from Aristotle to Leibniz.

In the nineteenth century, in general philosophy, most pronouncements on continuity were likewise monotonous and uninspiring (R. Eisler, *Wörterbuch*). But a few philosophers did try to break out of the monotony; and by an odd coincidence, or perhaps concurrence, they designated continuity in philosophy not by names that are cognates to the Latin verb *continere*, but by names which they coined from the Greek verb *synechein*.

Thus, Johann Friedrich Herbart (1776–1841) has a section on "Synechology" in his *Metaphysics*. Next, Gustav Theodor Fechner (1801–87), co-founder of the famed Weber-Fechner law of quantitative psychology (intensity of sensation varies as the logarithm of the stimulus), the first of its kind, has, in an impenetrably obscure book of his, a section on the "synechological outlook versus the monadological outlook" (Fechner, p. 204). Finally, and most importantly, the American philosopher Charles S. Peirce (1839–1914), the leading architect of the algebra of relations in symbolic logic, denotes by "synechism" what, from a certain retrospect, was a revival of Leibniz' Law of Continuity. But Peirce made the *lex continui* genuinely universal, and he updated it in its scope and intent, so as to make it measure up to the exigencies of the late Victorian and Edwardian eras.

Herbart's synechology is a peculiar philosophical compound of realism and psychology. As a realist Herbart finds that data from natural philosophy like space, time, and matter exist outside ourselves. As a psychologist however he finds that all attributes of such data, continuity among them, are created by the psychological process which operates on the intuition through which such data reveal themselves to us. These two findings seem to be divergent, but Herbart somehow reconciles them.

In connection with this we wish to point out that a passage in Aristotle's *De anima* apparently argues against identifying the continuity of the process of thought with the continuity of data conceived by thought:

But the thinking mind is one and continuous in the same sense as the process of thinking. Now thinking consists of thoughts. But the unity of these thoughts is a matter of succession, that is the unity of a number, and not the unity of a magnitude. This being so, neither is mind continuous in the latter sense, but either it is without parts, or it is continuous in a different sense from an extended magnitude (407a 6–11).

Herbart has been lauded for the saying: "Continuity is union in separation, and separation in union" (Mauxion, p. 107). The saying is interesting enough, but there are plenty of similar statements in Aristotle. Also, after Herbart, in Fechner, there is a counterpart to Herbart's saying which seems more original. We translate it thus:

What is psychically uniform and simple comes out of physical variety; and physical variety contracts into something that is psychically uniform, and simple, or, at any rate, simpler (Fechner, p. 247).

Following this, Fechner asserts in a very difficult sentence of his that this "contraction" leads to a kind of "synechological" equidistribution in the world, which Fechner opposes to a "monadological" concentration at points, and, Fechner continues, of this equidistribution we have a divinely inspired awareness.

C. S. Peirce, finally, being a master of mathematical logic and also of philosophy of mathematics, knew about the importance of continuity for mathematics in considerable detail; he also knew how the conception of continuity, when fanning out from mathematics, was reaching into large areas of cognition. Being thus equipped, Peirce was elaborating aspects of continuity which are recognizably mathematical, and he was also endeavoring to establish a presence of continuity, under the name of "synechism," in most of philosophy.

It is however not clear from the statements in Peirce, and it may have never become clear to himself, whether synechism is indeed effectively present outside of areas of philosophy of mathematics, or whether, conversely, philosophy of mathematics extends into every precinct of metaphysics in which the presence of synechism is detectable. Peirce was one of the first of a species of philosophers who by trend, intent, or circumstances had been blurring the several demarcations between mathematics, mathematical logic, philosophy of mathematics, and general philosophy.

Being a logician by intellectual faculty, Peirce conceived his synechism within a logical setting. Peirce established a certain triad of metaphysical constructs which he called categories, in which he placed "Synechism" along with "Tychism" and "Agapism."

Peirce called his three categories "cenopythagorean": "Firstness, Secondness, Thirdness," and they recognizably corresponded to the triads in Kant's table of twelve categories, but also resembled the stages of Hegel's phenomenology of mind (Peirce, pp. 384ff.).

Now, "syn-thesis" means literally "putting-together," and in analogy to this, Peirce associated various aspects of Thirdness with "synechism," which means literally "hanging-together." And Peirce's aim becomes clear if one contemplates the actual content of his Thirdness, which a commentator of his has described thus:

Thirdness is mediation, generality, order, interpretation, meaning, purpose. The Third is the medium or bond which connects the absolute first and last, and brings them into relationship. Every process involves Continuity, and Continuity represents Thirdness to perfection (Freeman, p. 19).

Thus Peirce's design for his Synechism was even more ambitious than Leibniz' design for his *lex continui*, but Peirce was even less successful than Leibniz in carrying out his plans. Even friendly critics of Peirce, like Morris R. Cohen, were complaining that Peirce had been promising a vast philosophical system, but

had never been able to erect it. And a recent critic puts it thus:

The grand design was never fulfilled. The reason is that Peirce was never able to find a way to utilize the continuum concept effectively. The magnificent synthesis which the theory of continuity seemed to promise somehow always eluded him, and the shining vision of the great system always remained a castle in the air (Murphey, p. 407).

This harsh verdict against Peirce is true as to fact; and yet it can be mellowed by the fact that Peirce was reaching out for the impossible and stumbled over his own genius when attempting this. Peirce wanted a conception of continuity that would be philosophically as all-pervasive as Leibniz had envisioned it, and, at the same time, logically as rigorous as mathematics of his own day was capable of making it. But Peirce was striving after an impossibility. Mathematics cannot be thus fused with philosophy in entirety, and mathematics is in no justifiable sense sufficient to determine philosophy in its general scope. If a conception from general philosophy has been made mathematically rigorous, then it can wear the vestments of mathematical rigor to advantage only when moving about in areas of mathematics proper, or, at best, in border areas which mathematics is in the process of penetrating, but certainly not when moving about in areas which are well outside of mathematics' sphere of influence. There are differences between mathematics and philosophy which cannot be winked at with impunity. A. N. Whitehead and Bertrand Russell were frequently musing that it ought to be possible to trespass on philosophy proper with conceptions from mathematics. But they were prudent enough, especially Whitehead, not to become entangled in difficulties into which Peirce was stepping only too boldly.

VII. HISTORIOGRAPHY

Excepting simpleminded chronicles and listings, any historical work has a theme of continuity inside of it. The theme of the Old Testament, whatever the many digressions, is the gradual erection of the Israelite theocracy. Thucydides fused the two parts of the Peloponnesian war, which were separated by the peace of Nicias, into one continuous event. Aristotle created our academic field of the history of philosophy by conceiving a closely-knit continuity of development in natural philosophy from Thales to Democritus. Within this development he even created, rather forcedly, the subdevelopments of "monism" and "pluralism." Aristotle says himself that it may appear incongruous to create a continuity of transition from the "materialists" Thales, Anaximander, Anaximenes, to the "ontologists"

Parmenides and Melissus by calling them all "monists," but that he is going to do so anyhow (*Physica*, Book 1, Ch. 2). Aristotle also knew well that there had been a great difference between the four "roots" (= elements) of Empedocles and the infinitely many atoms of Leucippus and Democritus, but he subsumed them under the rubric of "pluralists" nonetheless.

Continuity as a methodology in history does not at all mean that all leading developments are presumed to be continuous, that is composed of accumulations of small-step events, let alone that developments are presumed to be always "progressive," that is positively accented forward advances.

After the Renaissance, under the spell of a widespread "idea of progress" (J. B. Bury), and lasting deep into the nineteenth century (Bochner, pp. 73–74), such presumptions sometimes did assert themselves. Thus, in the history of science, the inductivism of Francis Bacon presented such an idea of progress fairly closely. It presumed that science advances gradually from observation to theoretization, univalently, forcibly, unerringly. It also assumed that there are ways in science of deciding between right and wrong and that an experimenting and observing scientist can report on facts "faithfully" without at all rendering an opinion on them (Bochner, p. 62).

The twentieth century has become very critical of inductivism in the history of science, but it has not decided what to put in its stead. It is not properly known what brings about significant changes in science, and what the actual mechanism of change is. Sometimes a major change in science appears to be literally a "revolution" which came about in a single step, but at other times a major change, an equally significant one, may appear to be the sum of many relatively small changes in rapid succession. It is very difficult to find a rationale for difference of these two types of change or a schema common to both types.

The nineteenth century brought to the fore an interpretation of continuity in history which is much less naive than the ordinary belief in "inevitable progress," although it is deceptively similar to it. If we adopt the term "continuism" (Bochner, p. 61), its relation to the idea of progress may be seen as follows. Continuism also assumes that any event of today was directly preceded by some event which must have taken place yesterday. However, the event of today is not necessarily an "advance" over the event of yesterday, but it is only a "reaction" to it, and the reaction may be a positive or negative one. That is, the event of today may concur with yesterday's event and carry it forward, or it may disagree with it, and oppose it with something different.

An unmistakably continuist enterprise is evident in the large-scale work of Pierre Duhem in the history of science, which was achieved in the beginning of the twentieth century. In this work the author, unabashedly,

. . . forges what seems to be an unbroken chain of human links, from Thales to Galileo, clear across the entire Middle Ages, without omitting a single decade, or even a single year of them. He does not naively whiten out all the darknesses of the Middle Ages; but to Duhem the darknesses only indicate a certain lowering of the level of intellectuality, and not at all some chasmal rupture in the substance of the flooring (Bochner, p. 117).

Duhem's continuism is obvious and obtrusive, and therefore somewhat tedious; but subtler forms of continuism have been fully operative in many areas of academic activity since the early nineteenth century. Continuism has greatly influenced the routines of academic research, and it has been involved in an unprecedented growth of scholarship and of historically oriented analyses in many compartments of knowledge. Whether it be the study of the origins of the *Iliad* or the Old Testament, of Herodotus or Diogenes Laërtius, of a play of Shakespeare or the *Opticks* of Newton, there is always a strain of continuism involved in the investigation. Finally, like all methods in historiography, continuism had its distant roots in antiquity. In fact, Aristotle's conception of Pre-Socratic philosophy was entirely continuist, and has remained so since. After Aristotle, versions of continuism are identifiable in scholarship of any period, but it was the nineteenth century which made the most of it.

In the twentieth century a major challenge to straightforward continuism has come from the problem of the rise of Western civilization as a whole. It has long been recognized that in Western civilization in its total course there had been, at various stages of its growth, component civilizations with distinctive characteristics of their own. This finding by itself is not in conflict with continuism. But a conflict might arise if one posits that two component civilizations did not affect each other in a major way although they were temporally contiguous or even overlapping. And that there had indeed been such component civilizations has been proposed, respectively, by Oswald Spengler and by Arnold Toynbee. The novelty of such proposals is wearing off, yet the echo of them lingers on and is likely to persist.

Very intriguing is a certain "continuist" question relating to the origin of Western civilization in its Mediterranean littoral. The oldest components of this total civilization were the Old Egyptian and the Old

Mesopotamian civilizations. From the distance of our retrospect the two arose "almost simultaneously" in the fifth and fourth millennia B.C. This poses the problem whether there were any links between them, and, if so, what the links were. They both initiated the art of writing in a major way; and the absorbing problem is whether there was any "stimulus diffusion" (Toynbee, 12, 344ff.) from the one to the other, and also what it really was that made the Mediterranean littoral eligible for the rise of both.

BIBLIOGRAPHY

Al-Ghazali, *The Destruction of Philosophers* (Tahafut al-Falasifah), trans. A. Kamali (Lahore, 1958). This is his leading philosophical work. Aristotle, *History of Animals;* our text is adapted from D'Arcy W. Thompson's version in the Oxford translation of Aristotle's works under the general editorship of W. D. Ross (Oxford, 1910), Vol. 4. Averroës (Ibn Rushd), *The Destruction of the Destruction* (Tahafut al-Tahafut), trans. S. van Bergh (London, 1954); this is a refutation of al-Ghazali. Salomon Bochner, *The Role of Mathematics in the Rise of Science* (Princeton, 1966). Pierre Boyancé, *Lucrèce et l'Épicurisme* (Paris, 1963). J. B. Bury, *The Idea of Progress* (London, 1920; New York, 1932; reprint 1955). Florian Cajori, ed., *Sir Isaac Newton's Mathematical Principles of Natural Philosophy and his System of the World*, trans. Andrew Motte (1729) revised by F. Cajori (Berkeley, 1934; many reprints); the Latin title *Philosophiae naturalis principia mathematica* (London, 1687) is briefly identified as *Principia*. Gavin de Beer, *Charles Darwin* (London, 1963; New York, 1964). René Descartes, *La Géométrie*, original text, with an English translation by David Eugene Smith and M. L. Latham (Chicago, 1925). Diogenes Laërtius, *Lives of Eminent Philosophers*, 2 vols. (London and Cambridge, Mass., 1935), Book IX, secs. 28–51 on Leucippus and Democritus; Book X on Epicurus; II, 439ff. Pierre Duhem, *Études sur Léonard de Vinci*, 3 vols. (Paris, 1906–13); idem, *Le Système du monde. Histoire des doctrines cosmologiques de Platon à Copernic*, 10 vols. (Paris, 1913–59). Rudolf Eisler, *Kant-Lexikon* (Hildesheim, 1961); idem, *Wörterbuch der philosophischen Begriffe*, 4th ed. (Berlin, 1930), article, "Stetigkeit." Friedrich Engels, *Dialectics of Nature*, ed. C. Duff (New York, 1940). Majid Fakhry, *Islamic Occasionalism and its Critique of Averroës and Aquinas* (London and New York, 1958). Gustav Theodor Fechner, *Die Tagesansicht gegenüber der Nachtansicht*, 2nd ed. (Leipzig, 1904). Eugene Freeman, *The Categories of Charles S. Peirce* (Chicago, 1931). Charles Coulston Gillispie, *Genesis and Geology* (New York, 1960). Bentley Glass, *Forerunners of Darwin, 1745–1859* (Baltimore, 1958). Johann Friedrich Herbart, *Allgemeine Metaphysik* (Königsberg, 1829). Isaac Husik, *A History of Medieval Jewish Philosophy* (Philadelphia, 1916), Ch. XVI. Max Jammer, *The Conceptual Development of Quantum Mechanics* (New York, 1966). Robert Hugh Kargon, *Atomism in England from Hariot to Newton* (Oxford and New York, 1966). G. S. Kirk and J. E. Raven, *The Presocratic Philosophers* (Cambridge and New York, 1962). Kurd Lasswitz, *Geschichte der Atomistik . . .*, 2 vols. (Hamburg, 1892); Vol. I contains a scathing criticism of Bruno's atomism after a full account of its scope. Gottfried Wilhelm Leibniz, *Theodicy*, trans. E. M. Huggard (New Haven, 1953). *Leibniz Selections*, ed. Philip P. Wiener, revised ed. (New York, 1959). Arthur O. Lovejoy, *The Great Chain of Being: A Study of the History of an Idea* (Cambridge, Mass., 1936; New York, 1960). Charles Lyell, *Principles of Geology, being an attempt to explain the former changes of the Earth's Surface, by Reference to Causes Now in Operation* (London, 1830–33). Moses Maimonides, *Guide of the Perplexed* (Moreh Nebuchem, ca. 1170). Three leading translations are: (1) S. Munk, in French, with copious notes, 3 vols. (Paris, 1856–66); (2) M. Friedländer, 3 vols. (London, 1881–85, reissue 1 vol. 1925; reprint, New York, 1940), copiously annotated in English; (3) Shlomo Pines, in English also (Chicago, 1963), closer to the original than Friedländer's, and has important long introductions. Marcel Mauxion, *La Métaphysique de Herbart* (Paris, 1894). Murray G. Murphey, *The Development of Peirce's Philosophy* (Cambridge, Mass., 1964). Otto Neugebauer, *The Exact Sciences in Antiquity*, 2nd ed. (Providence, 1957; New York, 1962). Parmenides, *Works*, trans. Leonardo Tarán (Princeton, 1965). Charles S. Peirce, *Selected Writings* (New York, 1966). Shlomo Pines, *Beiträge zur Islamische Atomenlehre* (Berlin, 1936). Otto Pretzl, "Die Frühislamische Atomenlehre," *Der Islam*, **19** (1931), 117–30. Robert H. Silliman, "Smoke Rings and Nineteenth-Century Atomism," *Isis*, **54** (1963), 461–74. Solvay Institute, 13th Physics Conference. *Structure and Evolution of Galaxies* (New York, 1965). Oswald Spengler, *The Decline of the West*, trans. C. F. Atkinson, 2 vols. (New York, 1926–28). Stephen Toulmin and June Goodfield, *The Discovery of Time* (London, 1965). Arnold Toynbee, *A Study of History*, 12 vols. (London and New York, 1935–61). J. Tricot, *Aristote: histoire des animaux* (Paris, 1957). Andrew G. van Melsen, *From Atomos to Atom* (New York, 1960). Hermann Weyl, *Philosophy of Mathematics and Natural Science* (Princeton, 1960).

SALOMON BOCHNER

[See also Baconianism; Cycles; Historiography; Infinity; Platonism; **Pragmatism; Pre-Platonic Conceptions;** Progress; Pythagorean . . .; Revolution; **Uniformitarianism and Catastrophism.**]

COSMIC FALL

WITHIN THE CHRISTIAN tradition remarkably different answers have been given to the question: What was the extent of the damage wrought by the Fall of Man? On some accounts it was confined to human nature; on others, it was extended to other living beings, sometimes to the whole earth, and even to the cosmos at large. Some held that the damage was caused at the time of the Fall—once for all; and others that there is a continuing process of decay of the created world. Those issues were debated with unusual intensity in the late sixteenth century and the first half of the seventeenth century. The controversy is of importance to the historian of ideas, because among its participants were major writers in very diversified fields, literary, theological, philosophical, and scientific; and because the patterns of argument used in the debate have great intrinsic interest, arguments attempting to display the whole world (or large parts of it) as decayed, ruined, or as fecund and virile. The citation of empirical "instances," appeal to authority and metaphysical reasoning were supplemented by a lush and often eloquent use of metaphor, analogy, and imagery.

The controversy would scarcely have been possible, if the biblical accounts of the Fall and its effects had been free from ambiguity. What exactly was the "curse" elicited by sin, on the Genesis account? "Thorns also and thistles shall it bring forth to thee . . ." (Genesis 3:18). But was it only the ground and its cultivation that were affected—or the entire earth? The *Septuagint* and the *Vulgate* took Genesis 3:17 to mean "Cursed is the earth in thy work"—the whole earth (ἡ γῆ, *terra*). The *Authorized Version* (more correctly) has "Cursed is the ground for thy sake." This disparity added to possibilities for complex disputes.

The narrative of the Flood was a second obvious source for the view that human sin had results not limited to human affairs; though again the extent and duration of these results were disputable. We shall see that one of the last and most influential writings of the main controversy—Thomas Burnet's *Sacred Theory of the Earth* (Latin, 1681; English, 1684) attributed to the Flood nothing less than the formation of the chief features of the earth's topography as we know it.

Claims that the world is decaying, or is in its old age, could find some Old Testament support, if only in a few much-quoted texts, such as Psalm 102:25–26: ". . . the heavens are the work of thy hands. They shall perish, but thou shalt endure: yea, all of them shall wax old like a garment; as a vesture shalt thou change them. . . ."

To Saint Paul, the entire cosmos suffers and is in need of redemption: "The whole creation groaneth and travaileth in pain together" (Romans 8:22). The effects of human sin are not "insulated" from the rest of the world: it is too tightly integrated a unity. At least equal support, however, could be drawn from the Bible by writers who denied there had been any Cosmic Fall. They could make a strong case for claiming that in the dominant biblical view, nature continues to reflect the divine goodness, wisdom, and creative power; that "The heavens declare the glory of God; and the firmament sheweth his handywork" (Psalm 19:1), and that the world is not in decline or decay. God works *in* the world, and not only as judge or avenger. He "maketh the clouds his chariot" and "walketh upon the wings of the wind" (Psalm 104:3).

As will be apparent, the materials of the controversy were drawn from several traditions—not only from the biblical. Among Platonic themes, the Theory of Forms could be invoked to express a sharp and congenial contrast between the corruptible and defective objects of the spatiotemporal world and the perfection of the timeless archetypes and exemplars, the Forms themselves. In the cosmogony of the *Timaeus*, Plato's divine Craftsman exerts his creative power upon a nature that is recalcitrant in some degree. Although such a view could not ultimately be reconciled with the Christian doctrine of Creation, it had affinities with an account of nature as "fallen" and inhospitable to value; and these affinities were exploited.

Aristotelian materials were also prominent, especially the concepts of "privation" and of "contraries." We shall note how any lack of accord between what a thing is observed to be and what it ideally ought to be was to be taken by Goodman as a case of "privation," and the mechanism by which Decay proceeded was the conflict of contrary, discordant elements.

Lucretius, in Book II of *De rerum natura*, provided a story of cosmic deterioration, which was often alluded to in later literature: ". . . The ramparts of the great world will be breached and collapse in crumbling ruin about us. Already it is far past its prime." Once nature yielded of its own accord "smiling crops and lusty vines . . . which now can scarcely be made to grow by our toil. . . . Everything is gradually decaying and nearing its end, worn out by old age" (trans. R. E. Latham, Baltimore, n.d.). From another point of view, however, Lucretius' world-picture could not have been more different from that of the Cosmic Fall theorists. To him the universe was "certainly not created for us by divine power: it is so full of imperfections" (Book V).

Cosmic Fall theories repeatedly drew upon the imagery of a primeval Golden Age and a subsequent decline, symbolized by successively "baser" metals. For Christianity, this could not be a recurrent, cyclical movement, but a single irreversible decline. The stages were labeled in more than one way. "The Brasen-Age is now, when Earth is worne," wrote Fulke Greville (*Works*, ed. A. B. Grosart, 4 vols., New York [1870], III, 51f.). Philip Stubbes called this ". . . third and last age . . ." indifferently "the yron or leaden age" (*The Anatomie of Abuses*, 1583).

Martin Luther's *Commentary on the Book of Genesis* (1545) claimed that "The world degenerates and grows worse and worse every day. . . . The calamities inflicted on Adam . . . were light in comparison of those inflicted on us" (on Genesis 3:17–19). The Flood was an important crisis. "The whole face of nature was changed by that mighty convulsion"; and the trees and fruits of the present-day earth "are but miserable remnants . . . of those former riches which the earth produced when first created" (2:11–12).

Calvin, in his *Institutes* (1536), argued that if we fail to see God's glory in the created world, the failure is due not to that world's decrepitude but to men's own stupidity and inattentiveness. In his *Commentary upon the Book of Genesis* (1554), however, he wrote that "The inclemency of the air, frost, thunder, unseasonable rains . . . and whatever is disorderly in the world, are the fruits of sin" (3:19). Calvin denied that "The earth was exhausted by the long succession of time. . . . They think more correctly who acknowledge that, by the increasing wickedness of man, the remaining blessing of God is gradually diminished and impaired" (3:18). Calvin's conclusion is measured and balanced: "The order of the world is indeed disturbed by our vices . . . yet we perceive the order of nature so far to prevail, that winter and summer annually recur, that there is a constant succession of days and nights," and so on (8:22).

From the mid-sixteenth century, the idea of a continuing process of cosmic decay began to have an increasing imaginative influence—an influence extending far beyond technical theology. Current scientific observation could be interpreted as showing that not only the "sublunary" domain was involved in decay, but that the heavens too were not immune to corruption. For blemishes were observable on the moon; and there appeared the ominous "new star" of 1572.

"The antique world," wrote Edmund Spenser, in *The Faerie Queene* (1590–1609), "in its first flowring youth,/ Found no defect in his Creatours grace." But the world today, he lamented, "being once amisse growes daily wourse and wourse:" with all its "creatures from their course astray/ Till they arrive at their last ruinous decay" (II. vii. 16; V. Prologue i. 6).

In *The First Anniversary* (1611) and in his Sermons John Donne gave powerful expression to the theme of Decay. Donne saw man's mortality as due to the Fall: and he spreads the pathos of mortality over human life in general. "All our life is but a going out to the place of execution." Corruption and decay did not stop at man. "The noblest part, man, felt it first; and then/ Both beasts and plants, curst in the curse of man" (*The First Anniversary*, lines 199–200). "God hath put into [the world] a reproofe, a rebuke . . . sensible decay and age." Earth had been first created as a smooth sphere: now it is "disfigured" with "warts and pock-holes"—mountains and sea-depths. He instances too disorder in the seasons and the untoward appearing of new stars.

Despite his enthusiasm over the opening up of new lands and new routes, Samuel Purchas was also convinced that this is a decaying world, that no progress can be permanent, and that improvements in the human condition are merely providential interludes.

. . . the earth is accursed, whereby many things are hurtfull to mans nature, and in those which are wholsome, there is not such variety of kinds, such plentie in each variety, such ease in getting our plenty, or such quality in what is gotten. . . . Had not man sinned, there should not haue needed the death of beasts to nourish his life, which without such stay should haue beene immortall: the vse whereof was after granted, rather to supply necessitie when the Flood had weakened the Earth, then to minister a greater abundance then before it had (*Purchas his Pilgrimage*, 1613; 1626 ed., I, 14).

Sir Walter Ralegh's *History of the World* (1614) presented the image of a nature whose energies are all but exhausted: "Both the ages of men, and the nature of all things Time hath changed"—and changed for the worse.

Some interesting variations on (and hesitations over) Cosmic Fall doctrine can be found in Greville's poems. Sometimes Greville emphasizes the limits of change and decay: "Poor Earth, that dost presume to judge the skye;/ Cynthia is euer round, and neuer varies" (*Works*, III, 64). "Eternall Truth . . . [is] Onely exilèd from man's fleshly heart" (III, 126). Yet Greville can also say: "For as the World by Time still more declines,/ Both from the truth and wisedom of Creation:/ So at the Truth she more and more repines,/ As making hast to her last declination" (II, 30), and "Thy word incarnate, glorious heauen, darke hell/ Lye shadowed vnder man's degeneration" (III, 142).

The most detailed dispute on the whole issue of a Cosmic Fall is contained in the writings of Godfrey Goodman and George Hakewill. Goodman's *The Fall of Man . . .* was published in 1616. Hakewill's defense of an undecayed world, *An Apologie . . . of the Power and Providence of God . . .* appeared in 1627: its third edition, 1635, included arguments by Goodman, and further responses from Hakewill.

Goodman argued that to be aware of the vast extent of decay and disorder brought about by the Fall was essential to contrite and devout living. The world was originally well constructed to serve and to delight man, its centerpiece. Every feature of the world today that thwarts this purpose can be known, for that very reason, to be a result of the Fall. Nature as a whole is "directed to man" (*Fall*, p. 14); thus when man breaks "his owne bounds . . . it must necessarily follow, that all the rest of the creatures, which were bound or knit together in man, should likewise be inordinate" (p. 17). To Goodman again there would have been no mortality but for sin: "Obseruing the course and prouidence of nature, man should be exempted from death" (p. 331). Evil proliferates: while there is only one (precarious) state of health, there are innumerable forms of *ill*-health, countless ways to die. Man's intellectual powers are diminished; his passions conflict with his will; constant war is waged between man and the animals, and among the animals themselves. The rest of nonhuman nature is no less afflicted. Nature seems "more carefull of thornes, then of the best fruits" (p. 225, margin). "If God punish the earth with a great drought . . . it argues the barrennesse of our nature, in respect of good workes" (p. 92). Con⌐rariwise, when we want it dry, we are given harmfully wet weather—for instance, at harvesttime. Man cannot feel at home in a world, the greater part of which is wild and uninhabitable. Goodman attributes an important share in the disturbance of nature to the Flood: "This generall deluge was indeed the generall confusion of nature" (p. 281). The heavens are not exempt from decay: the sun's heat has diminished. The 1572 "comet" showed that change was occurring in the superlunary sphere where no change should be.

The Fall of Man . . . is a remarkable compendium of vilifying arguments and imagery. Because death terminates life, Goodman argues, "Our life is a kind of dying." As in the example from Donne, Goodman too spreads the emotion proper to dying over the activities of living as well. The further spreading of decay-and-senility language to the nonhuman world is justified in terms of the pervasive analogy between microcosm and macrocosm, and by the claim that disorder at the teleological center of the world cannot fail to infect all the rest, which is "bound or knit together in man."

Any skill that today requires study and labor to acquire, "must" have been possessed by man, innately, before the Fall, and required no laborious process of learning. Goodman's instances range from abilities like swimming (p. 88), to intellectual activity and human communication in general (e.g., pp. 305, 299). If it is possible to imagine ourselves as possessing an ability in a more perfect manner than we do, we can infer that, before the Fall, men did actually possess it in that way. Today "we (that is, our souls) doe not receiue the things themselues, but the *species* or images of things" (p. 46). "Were it not, that man is falne," we should be able to reason infallibly; the soul dealing "directly" with "intelligible objects" themselues (p. 48).

Goodman's view of the relations between God and nature are complex. For all his constant emphasis on the *corruptions* of nature, he does not deny that nature is in God's control. "God . . . hath so ordained nature, to worke His owne purpose" (p. 269). "Nature" and "grace" are not set in opposition: "both of them proceed from one fountaine," God being author of both (p. 10). But Goodman, in fact, oscillates between seeing nature (God-made, basically good) as God's obedient instrument for man's correction, and seeing it as itself horrifyingly involved in disorder and disintegration.

The decay of nature is not the work of specific and constant divine interventions. From the very beginning, there have been "contrary" elements in nature, capable of conflict, privation, and corruption. Before the Fall God prevented these destructive possibilities from being realized; but since the Fall, he prevents them no longer; although he does restrain the process from leading directly to the annihilation of the world.

George Hakewill's *Apologie* opposes Goodman's position in argument, attitude, and tone. Instead of the imagery of senescence and exhaustion, we find constant reference to new birth, growth, and virility. The curve of "decline" is repudiated. Hakewill combats Goodman's view not only by opposing instance to instance (he sees that appeal to cases cannot be decisive), but by attacking his use of the microcosm-macrocosm analogy, denying his general account of decay through the conflict of contraries, and arguing that the Cosmic Fall doctrine is incompatible with the demands both of theology and morality.

On the last point: Hakewill claims that the doctrine of decay tends not to be morally healthful, but "rather to breed sloath then to quicken industrie" (*Apologie*, p. 18). What is morally salutary is to contemplate God's wisdom and goodness, as these are still amply displayed in his creation. Not that Hakewill is an unbounded optimist, or takes human sin lightly. God will end the world, and there will be a final judgment. But to claim that God will act in these ways is altogether different from positing a running-down of the world. Both Scripture and reason lead us to expect "that the world shall bee by fire totally and finally dissolved and annihilated" (Book IV, Sec. 4).

Hakewill denies that human nature is deteriorating over the centuries. He compares the men of his own day with the Romans. Were the Romans braver? No: the corruption of their aggressive aims prevents us commending them as brave. (Hakewill, i.e., makes it a necessary condition of bravery that the action should be in a good cause.) Men today are freer from various kinds of lasciviousness, luxury, and vicious excess. We have not become more vulnerable to diseases: some diseases have in fact abated. There has been no general decline in length of life. Cases of unusual longevity among the ancients can be ascribed to special acts of 507

God for special purposes—such as the initial populating of the world. Whereas Goodman lamented a decline of intellectual powers, Hakewill reminds us of recent increases in knowledge and accomplishment, in the arts, in philosophy, science, and technology. In religion too Hakewill tells a story of progressive deliverance from superstition and idolatry, and from inadequate conceptions of God: there has been progress also in understanding the Christian faith.

With nonhuman nature, Hakewill again believes he can break the pattern of decline. The earth is no less fertile than in the past—though men may sometimes blunder in their cultivation. Goodman had been quick to point out areas where the land is becoming less hospitable to man: Hakewill alleged that the contrary pattern was no less prevalent—a compensatory restoration and improvement of conditions in other regions. The eroding of barren mountains is followed by the appearance of a fertile alluvial plain, rich for the plough and ready for new life. Hakewill is very willing to acknowledge mutability; but he makes a very sharp distinction between mutability and decay, a distinction essential to his whole case. In place of Goodman's pattern of steady change-for-the-worse, Hakewill thus sought to establish a cyclical pattern—a pattern of decay-and-restoration. Compensation or renewal can be counted upon to follow injurious events. Certainly, this pattern is not always empirically observable, but where it is not, Hakewill has a parable to meet the case. A human observer is like someone who studies the "end of a peece of Arras" and "conceives perhaps an hand or head which hee sees to be very unartificially made." But if he should uncover the whole, he "soone findes that it carries a due and just proportion to the body" (p. 96). The total pattern comes into view. So it is with any apparent decay in nature: if we could assume a synoptic view, that fragmentary pattern would be seen as part of a larger design, a design that involves "reciprocal compensation" (p. 28).

To consider finally the heavens: we are not entitled to infer decay from the evidence of the telescope. What the telescope reveals (e.g., spots on the moon) has always been so, though we have not been able to see it so clearly till now. The issue is not, in any case, to be settled empirically. Hakewill argues that there are no conflicting elements in the heavens that could make deterioration possible. He takes the question: Are the heavens in fact decaying? as equivalent to: Are they "in a naturall course . . . capable of such a supposed decay?" (p. 67). The heavens, furthermore, are moved by angels, and for that reason cannot "erre or faile in their motions."

To oppose Goodman effectively, Hakewill had to deny that the unhappy effects of human sin must necessarily "infect" the cosmic environment, and he argued that these effects are contained and confined within the little world of man. He claimed that, in general, there is no close and reliable set of correspondences between microcosm and macrocosm. The analogy, he believed, is a seriously misleading one, and to use it uncritically is to ignore important qualitative differences among the constituents of the world.

It should be clear that Hakewill did not counter Goodman's metaphysics with a "scientific" and anti-speculative theory. Hakewill, like other more scientifically-minded opponents of Cosmic Fall theories after him, certainly stressed the orderliness of nature. But he depended very heavily upon authority, on appeals to the supernatural and miraculous, and on eschatological doctrine. Further, as Goodman relied on a pervasive imagery of gloom, deterioration, and death, so Hakewill bombarded his reader with a selective and persuasive imagery of awakening life, vigorous growth, and fecundity. His aim was to "free the world from old age." The elements "by continuall generation each out of other renew their parts" (p. 109). The "slumbering drowzie spirit of the *Grecians* began againe to be revived and awakened" (p. 217). Medicine was "borne againe" under Galen (p. 226); and so on, through topic after topic.

If fecundity and growth are emphasized by Hakewill, so equally is *diversity*, as a basic positive value. Where his opponents tended to see diversified scenery (e.g., mountain-and-plain) as a declension from an original smoother, "perfect," topography, the diversity itself is seen by Hakewill as intrinsically good. The debate over nature's alleged decay was thus, in important measure, a contest between alternative criteria of aesthetic value.

Among other authors of the early seventeenth century who expressed views analogous to Goodman's was Robert Burton (*Anatomy of Melancholy*, 1621). "The virtue of all the vegetals is decayed," he wrote: men grow less in stature. Burton accepted the analogy between microcosm and macrocosm. He preferred nevertheless to raise questions rather than offer systematic answers on Goodman's lines. Some apparently disordered events may in fact be orderly, though not properly understood by us. He muses over the existence of marine fossils: Are these due to "Noah's Flood, as Christians suppose, or is there a vicissitude of sea and land?"

Drummond of Hawthornden (*A Cypresse Grove*, 1623) made liberal use of the imagery of cosmic decay. Inconstancy, he believed, is unlimited throughout the whole creation, the heavens included. In all growth the upward curve of youthful life is followed by a downward plunge to senility. Today universally the wheel is on that downward swing.

The central theme is tersely expressed in George Herbert's poem "Decay":

> I see the world grows old, when as the heat
> Of thy great love, once spread, as in an urn
> Doth closet up itself, and still retreat,
> Cold sinne still forcing it, till it return,
> And calling Justice, all things burn.

And to Henry Vaughan, man "drew the curse upon the world, and Cracked/ The whole frame with his fall" ("Corruption").

John Swan's *Speculum mundi* (1635) draws a sharp contrast between early times "when all things were in their full strength," and the present day, ". . . this weak age." Men today are "Pygmies"—"reeds compared to the Cedars of those times." The air is now "corrupted"; and the "fruits of the earth of a feeble nourishment" (4th ed. [1670], p. 457). The Flood wrought damage through the action of "the salt waters of the great deep," and also by way of "vapours or . . . Exhalations" (p. 458). Swan is not undiscriminating. Hills and mountains, for example, are not held to be the results of Cosmic Fall, but "were created in the beginning" (p. 37). He testifies to the "delectation and profit of the mountains, which do thereby . . . amplifie the goodness of God in his works" (p. 39). On the other hand, decay is active in the heavens: we read of dimming heavenly bodies and ominous signs of their corruption.

Not all Cosmic Fall theories were theories of a continuing process of decay. Decay is denied, for instance, in Jean F. Senault's *L'Homme criminel* (*Man Become Guilty, or the Corruption of Nature by Sinne*, 1650). Nature's order was damaged at the time of man's Fall: there was loss in beauty, fertility, harmony, and in the proper subordination of animals to men: the sun's light was diminished. But these were once-for-all changes, not signs of a continuing decline or waning of nature's powers. John Milton also rejected the language of old age and decline. The poem *Naturam non pati senium* (1628) denied that nature's face withers, "overgrown with furrowing wrinkles," her womb grown barren. Nor does "the never-ending hunger of the years . . . harry the stars."

In order to stress the enormity of the Fall of man, in *Paradise Lost*, Milton did describe cosmic upheaval. At the instant Eve plucked the apple, "Earth felt the wound" (IX.782). Then the sun was ordered to molest the earth with "cold and heat/ Scarce tollerable." Inclement seasonal change begins: "Else had the Spring/ Perpetual smil'd on Earth with Vernant Flours." War starts among the animals; ". . . To graze the Herb all leaving,/ Devourd each other; nor stood much in awe/ Of man." Although human morality goes on deteriorating, and Milton speaks of the "growing miseries which Adam saw/ Alreadie in part," the changes in nonhuman nature are not described in terms of a continuous process of decay (X.650–719).

In his poem "Upon Appleton House" Andrew Marvell claimed that the topography of the world today is dramatically different from its appearance at first creation. It is now a mere "heap," "together hurled;/ All negligently overthrown,/ Gulfes, Deserts, Precipices, Stone."

A most detailed and influential account of how the world changed for the worse was Thomas Burnet's *Telluris theoria sacra* (1681; *Sacred Theory of the Earth*, 1684). Burnet set out to prove that the topography familiar to us was largely determined by the cataclysm of the Flood. Originally the earth was "smooth" and "regular." "It had the Beauty of Youth and blooming Nature, fresh and fruitful, and not a Wrinkle, Scar or Fracture in all its Body." Below the crust were the "waters under the earth." Because of mounting pressure from vaporized water, the crust became weakened, and eventually fractured. "When the appointed time was come that All-wise Providence had design'd for the Punishment of a sinful World, the whole Fabrick brake, and the Frame of the Earth was torn in Pieces," mountains and sea-depths being formed. Burnet intended his account to be at once naturalistic and theologically acceptable; but the possibility of such a harmony looked less plausible as the implications of the theory were worked out. He could not defend his theory without being forced well away from any orthodox interpretation of Scripture.

If science and theory were in tension in Burnet, so also were two criteria of aesthetic value. On the one hand, the perfect earth was the *smooth* earth: all irregularity was subsequent deformity. On the other hand, the ruggedness and vastness of mountains had a fascination for Burnet, as his eloquence makes clear: terror and mystery often assume positive aesthetic value, both in Burnet himself and in the many writers who learned from him—among them Edward Young and Samuel Taylor Coleridge.

Among authors who weakened the case for a Cosmic Fall, Francis Bacon must have first mention. The development of the new sciences required attitudes to, and beliefs about, the relation between nature and man, very different from those we have been recounting in this article so far. Bacon rejected any adulation of ancient authorities, and repudiated the myth of a

509

Golden Age in the remote past. For science to be possible, men must come to understand nature, not exclusively as a background to the human drama, or as a participator in that drama, but in terms of its own laws and its own life. Hakewill drew upon Bacon in his polemic against Goodman; although Hakewill himself relied heavily upon appeals to authority.

John Wilkins (*Discovery of a World in the Moone*, 1638) suggested that the universe may well not be the nursery of human beings alone. There may even be life on other worlds, creatures on the moon perhaps; though we cannot tell of what kind. It was becoming increasingly hard to see the little world of man (as Goodman saw it) as a center from which malign influence would be expected to pass to the rest of the cosmos.

Cosmic Fall and Mutability themes appear in the writings of Sir Thomas Browne (*Religio medici*, 1642, written 1635; *Hydriotaphia*, 1658); but Browne did not consistently identify himself with the view that the world decays. In human affairs decay is acknowledged: and he can claim that "while we look for incorruption in the heavens, we finde they are but like the Earth" (*Hydriotaphia*, Ch. V). Yet he also affirms that the world is not in its old age or in progressive decline—though its end is not very distant (*Christian Morals*, III, Sec. 26).

The Cambridge Platonist, Henry More, makes very evident a growing tendency to look to nature not for signs of decay but rather for evidence of divine beneficence, wisdom, and design. In his *Antidote against Atheism* (1652), More adduces many instances of "things as might be otherwise, and yet are far better as they are." The structure of animals "is far more perfect then will merely serve for their bare existence" (*Antidote*, in *A Collection of Several Philosophical Writings* [1662], p. 5). On the alleged inhospitability of the world, More argued that it is necessary "there should be sufficient difficulty and hardship for all sensible and intellectual creatures to grapple and contest with" (*Divine Dialogues* [1668; 1743 ed.], p. 155). "The inclination of the *axis* of the earth is so duly proportioned for the making it as habitable as it can be, that the wit of man cannot imagine any posture better" (p. 162). The existence of wild animals is justified on two somewhat different scores—as a "ready instrument of Divine wrath . . . and a great enricher of the history of nature, which would be defective, did it not run from one extreme to another" (p. 196). More generally, in the biological world are "infinite examples of a steddy . . . acting according to skill and design" (pp. 22f.). Any appearance of malignity in nature is due to an inadequate and partial view of a world that in reality is glorious, diversified, and full.

The vitality and progress of the sciences in the mid-seventeenth century were taken increasingly as refuting claims about a general decay. Joseph Glanvill's *Vanity of Dogmatizing* (1661) argued on these lines, and so did Henry Power's *Experimental Philosophy* (1664). "This is the Age wherein all mens Souls are in a kind of fermentation, and the spirit of Wisdom and Learning begins to mount"—to mount, not to decay (*Exper. Phil.*, pp. 191f.). The earth is not physically the world's center, nor is there adequate reason to believe that man is the *raison d'être* of the universe. All nature is not directed to man, agreed John Spencer (*Discourse concerning Prodigies*, 1663–65): nature has its own laws, unvarying from the first creation of the world.

The replacing of a nature in decay by a well-designed nature was furthered by John Ray's *The Wisdom of God Manifested in the Works of the Creation* (1691). Like Henry More, Ray argued that man is not the sole center of value and significance, and that the other creatures have a life of their own. As well as wise contrivance, *fecundity* is one main criterion of divine creative power; and because of God's fecundity, we are entitled to infer, for instance, that "Every fixed star has [its] Chorus of planets." Decay is expressly denied in Ray's *Miscellaneous Discourses* (ca. 1692); and we are at the furthest remove, in these writings, from Goodman's picture of a disordered and sin-devastated world.

Cosmic Fall speculation (Burnet's in particular) was described as the product of poetic imagination, an "Ingenious Romance," by John Keil in his *Examination of Dr. Burnet's Theory of the Earth* (1698). Keil found no lack of mathematical and scientific muddle in Burnet. Burnet's account of the cracking of the earth's crust will not bear scrutiny: "The heat of the sun could never reach so far into so thick a Crust as to be great enough to raise water into Vapours (*Examination . . .*, pp. 175, 147ff.); nor would there have been "so much water in the Abyss as was sufficient to cover the face of the whole Earth" (p. 175). Keil concludes: ". . . never any Book was fuller of Errors and Mistakes in Philosophy, so none ever abounded with more beautiful Scenes and surprising Images of Nature" (pp. 175–76).

A succinct and forthright denial of any anthropocentrism can be found in Pierre Bayle. "If we had a proper conception of the universe, we should readily understand that the death or the birth of a Prince is such a small event—considering the nature of things as a whole—that it does not merit the concern of Heaven" (*Pensées diverses . . . à l'occasion de la Comète*, 1683).

Celestial phenomena, that is to say, are not primarily concerned with human weal or woe, nor are they to be explained in terms of these. Bayle's arguments are directed, not expressly against Cosmic Fall theory, but against the whole climate of thought in which these had flourished. One way of combatting the theory was by affirming the integrity of man, and *a fortiori* the integrity of nature. But equally well it could be countered, as here, by playing down the cosmic importance of man and deploring his vanity.

In the eighteenth-century literature of ideas Cosmic Fall controversy has not ceased. To take only one example: Voltaire devotes some words to a criticism of Flood-theories like Burnet's. Some writers, he says, have believed that "the world we inhabit is a mere ruin, and that such a fate befits guilty creatures like ourselves." But these writers are to be contrasted with those more enlightened philosophers who "discern a wonderful and necessary order in that seeming-confusion."

Voltaire realizes that there is enormous scope for divergent interpretations of the same data, depending on one's presuppositions and predilections. "To some, all seems disorder and vengeance; to others, design and goodness" (*Oeuvres complètes*, Paris [1879], 22, 549).

But straightforward error is also involved in those theories. Burnet and his fellow spirits, for instance, have vastly exaggerated the present irregularity of the earth's surface: considering the proportion of the height of mountains to the size of the earth, there is less irregularity than on the surface of an orange!

Essential to most theories of a Cosmic Fall was the analogy between microcosm and macrocosm—between the world of man and the greater world around him. Only if there were some necessary correspondence between the activities of man and events in the non-human world would it be at all plausible that man's Fall should have cosmic repercussions, or that the pattern of man's growth, maturity, and senescence would be doubled by the course of nature as a whole. This is, of course, a stronger claim than the claim that the creation of man was the culmination of God's work. And one could hold the latter while denying the former. A view like Burnet's, on the other hand, which tried to give a physical and natural explanation of the Flood and its effects, was not dependent on the analogy between microcosm and macrocosm.

Denials of the analogy were sometimes specific and direct, sometimes indirect and implicit. It could be argued, for instance, that God's glory was more fittingly manifested by his limiting the effects of sin to humanity itself and not allowing a universal decay. The analogy was indirectly challenged by any argument against man's central importance in the scheme of things, and by the increasing success of science in explaining events

by natural laws that make no reference at all to human affairs.

So long as the traditional distinction remained between the sublunary, corruptible realm and the supposedly incorruptible heavens, advances in astronomy (such as Galileo's observations of irregularities on the moon in 1610) could furnish new disturbing data for theories of a Cosmic Fall. But the same new science was simultaneously making untenable that distinction itself. When it had lost its authority, the Cosmic Fall theories had lost also their most dramatic demonstration of decay.

The New Science did not oust teleology: on the contrary, it gave a quite new popularity to the Argument from Design. In the writings of the Royal Society scientist-theologians, nature was seen as a single well-ordered system, mirroring the supremely intelligent divine Mind. All apparent disorder and irregularity could in the end be brought under the unity and simplicity of Newtonian law. There was an immense spate of writings that sought to exhibit the marvelous fitness and benevolent contrivance in the relation of organism and environment. But it is obvious how very different were teleological views of this general kind from the teleology which figured in the Cosmic Fall theories— theories that tended to see all nature as a stage-backcloth to the drama of man, and which proclaimed a radical *breakdown* of order.

The topic of nature's inhospitability to man, which we saw recurrent in the Cosmic Fall literature, reappeared in a variety of much later writings. One thinks, for instance, of J. S. Mill's essay, "Nature" (1874), T. H. Huxley's lecture, "Evolution and Ethics" (1893), and of writers such as Giacomo Leopardi and Thomas Hardy. (For an earlier eloquent statement one may study "Philo's" contributions in David Hume's *Dialogues concerning Natural Religion*, 1779.) But none of these posits a prior harmonious and hospitable state from which a Fall took place; and none is a defender of Christian theism.

It is interesting and instructive to bring the Cosmic Fall controversy into relation with the tradition of the Great Chain of Being. Ideas central to that tradition were invoked by both sides in the polemic. Argument for the fallenness of nature was facilitated by the claim that the whole of nature is a closely interconnected hierarchical system; it is a chain all of whose links must be intact, or else disaster ensues to the whole system. The thought of the chain in its original perfection provides an ironical counterpoint to Goodman's account of nature as it was in his day: only a grim caricature remains. (Compare also Sir Richard Barckley, who specifically likened the cosmos to a disintegrating chain—*The Felicitie of Man*, 1598.)

511

Opponents of Cosmic Fall theories, however, could appeal to other elements of the Great Chain tradition. That tradition saw the world as the work of divine fecundity: diversity and variety were supreme values. Better a world with all possible types of being (graded in value from God downwards) than a world with little variety, even though it contained other, high forms of value. Now, one who made that sort of value-judgment could easily be persuaded that the present-day earth with its varied topography was preferable to the smooth "perfection" of the imagined pre-Fall sphere. If preferable, then there is no sign that a catastrophe occurred: the world we see could be the world as God made it. Again the higher the value placed upon the infinite divine fecundity, the more difficult it was to believe that such a deity would permit his world to decay or to suffer "old age." The doctrine would argue against God's superabundant generosity and creative power. The Craftsman of Plato's *Timaeus* was not "grudging" in his creative work: likewise Hakewill argued, God could not be "niggardly or sparing. . . ."

The Great Chain tradition dealt with the problem of evil in several familiar ways. What we call evil is really imperfection—measured by distance from the summit of the hierarchy of being. For a hierarchy to be possible, there must be beings at all distances from the summit. Again, only a synoptic view of the world as a whole (which is beyond our capacities) could reveal the necessary place of apparently evil events in the good totality. On such a view there was no need to resort to the idea of a Cosmic Fall or a Decay of Nature, in order to account for the presence of evil.

Although theories of a Cosmic Fall were primarily and originally ventures in theology, they had implications, as we have seen, far outside the theological field. It made a great difference to a person's *aesthetic* experience of nature, for instance, whether he saw nature as a colossal ruin, a rapidly running-down world, or as manifesting divine splendor undiminished. The Fall of nature was widely admitted to involve an aesthetic Fall. The aesthetic repercussions of the Cosmic Fall were expressed not only in systematic statements like Goodman's and Hakewill's, but in countless brief, fugitive allusions in poetry and prose. The theory offered a rich stock of imagery; imagery of barrenness, old age, the proliferation of weeds and poisons, and fostered a sense that the earth had once possessed a beauty of which only a few hints now remained. So John Donne: ". . . the worlds beauty is decai'd, or gone" (*The First Anniversary*); and Fulke Greville: "Beauty growne sick; nature corrupt and nought" (*Works*, II, 52). Late in the controversy, as we noted in Burnet, the aesthetic quality of a ruined world became charged with an interesting ambiguity—evoking awe and fascination as well as dread.

Although rarely given prominence in twentieth-century theological discussions, Cosmic Fall speculation is not dead. One significant statement appeared in N. P. Williams' *The Ideas of the Fall and of Original Sin* (1924). According to Williams, there occurred a Fall in the "life-force" itself, "before the differentiation of life into its present multiplicity of forms and the emergence of separate species" (p. 523). This pre-cosmic vitiation of the whole "life-force" was responsible both for human evil and for the conflictful and wasteful aspects of nonhuman nature.

In some versions responsibility is placed upon a plurality of rebellious conscious beings other than man, beings whose Fall precedes man's. C. C. J. Webb thought it possible that "Superhuman evil wills exist and have injuriously affected the environment of humanity as a whole" (*Problems in the Relations of God and Man* [1911], p. 270). And in the mid-twentieth century Dom Illtyd Trethowan could claim from a Roman Catholic standpoint, that "sin . . . started with the angels." A result of their Fall, ". . . we may suppose, was a disorganization of the material universe, over which, according to a reasonable theory, the angels had charge" (*An Essay in Christian Philosophy* [1954], p. 128). Such theories are, of course, left with a serious problem over how to maintain God's unqualified omnipotence, and his perfect goodness and fairness to his creatures—in permitting this "disorganization." But the problem may be ultimately no more or less intractable, in this sort of theory, than in any other Christian treatment of evil.

Although the details of the Cosmic Fall controversies can appear remote and even grotesque to a reader today, such a reader cannot fail to be reminded also of certain deeply troubling issues of his own time. He may not speculate whether a deity has permitted the continuing process of decay of nature on account of man's disobedience; but he is aware of the problems of man's own despoliation of his planet, the rendering extinct of animal species, industrial pollution of air and water, open cast or strip mining, radioactive fallout. The idiom of discussion is a predominantly secular one, but there remain striking analogies in tone and attitude, between the statement of the old anxieties and of the new.

BIBLIOGRAPHY

Unless otherwise identified, translations are by R. W. Hepburn.

Godfrey Goodman, *The Fall of Man; or the Corruption of Nature* . . . (London, 1616). George Hakewill, *An Apologie or Declaration of the Power and Providence of God in* the *Government of the World* (Oxford, 1627). Victor Harris, *All Coherence Gone* (Chicago, 1949)—a study of the six-teenth- and seventeenth-century debate, to which this arti-cle is much indebted. Marjorie Nicolson, *Mountain Gloom and Mountain Glory* (Ithaca, N. Y., 1959).

R. W. HEPBURN

[See also Chain of Being; **Cycles;** Design Argument; Evil; **Hierarchy;** Macrocosm; **Primitivism; Sin and Salvation; Sublime.**]

COSMIC IMAGES

I

1. Astronomy may be broadly defined as any attempt at a logical explanation of celestial motions. For a long time this science was based essentially on calculation. Indeed, the distance of objects at first confined obser-vation within certain limits; the positive data acquired were limited to the study of positions and displace-ments. However, this descriptive knowledge was ex-tended naturally by scientific hypotheses. With the use of Galileo's telescope (1610) observation leaped for-ward as did speculation about the constitution of heavenly bodies. But astrophysics really began only with spectrum analysis (1859). Despite constant progress, our knowledge of astrophysics will probably remain, even in our time, indirect and limited; specu-lation and imagination will both probably continue to enjoy more or less an open field.

Imagination—the ability to elicit, forge, and connect a chain of images—is necessarily oriented and main-tained by preferences of taste and sensibility. We shall here consider imagination as a comprehensive faculty which involves the whole of our psychical life from the most intellectualized level to the depths of the unconscious. Now the field of astronomy makes a pow-erful appeal to this faculty or power of imagination. Nothing is more important to man than to have a view of the universe as a whole, because all life on earth depends on cosmic cycles and because the celestial world surrounding us seems to exert a compelling influence on man's destiny. The idea of a corre-spondence between Macrocosm and Microcosm strengthens the bonds between the mind of man and the Universe. In the view of philosophers, the cosmos, the whole of God's creation, is the very archetype of any harmonious construction of the mind and the pattern of any work of art. From the time when the Earth is no longer the fixed center of a closed world, the proportions in the mind's picture of the universe change; but as the Earth shrinks the importance of the

Universe grows. The idea that man makes of the world, therefore, affects on all levels that power of imagina-tion which we have said engages his whole mental life.

2. Let us start from the highest level. We owe to A. O. Lovejoy the idea of "metaphysical pathos"; we may prefer the more general term, "the pathos of abstract ideas." Certain ideas of this kind, despite their barren appearance, awaken in different temperaments various reactions of a specifically emotional resonance. No better definition of this phenomenon can be given here than that of Kant in his *Theory of the Heavens* (*Allgemeine Naturgeschichte und Theorie des Himmels,* 1755): "If the aspect of so perfect a totality stirs the imagination, a delight of another sort grips the intel-lect, all the more so when it considers how so many magnificent and grand consequences flow from a single general law. . . ." Kant's intellectual delight here was stimulated by a consummately abstract idea: the har-mony of a unified explanation.

Like this aesthetic emotion, to which it is closely allied, the intellectual emotion often originates on a level where obscure stimuli, difficult to bring to light, can yield only an incomplete explanation of their effects, so enriched are they by the development of culture and thought. However, certain cosmic hy-potheses appeal to unconscious predilections which are comparatively easy to detect: such are all dreams about genesis. In order to expose the origins of these imagi-native constructions we shall look to the undisputed gains of the main psychoanalytical schools (but without referring to any of the strictly orthodox among them).

Here, however, we shall adopt a working hypothesis: there exist families of minds, each corresponding to a type of cosmic imagination; furthermore, the manner in which a thinker conceives and imagines the universe is the best key to the character of his mind.

Since attempts at classifying minds according to ways of imagining the world have been made before, our course has already been charted. G. Bachelard has distinguished four types based on their respective modes of dreaming about the elements, and we shall meet them on the way. However, we prefer to follow the ideas of A. O. Lovejoy, A. N. Whitehead, M. H. Nicolson, and A. Koestler who have brought to light a certain polarity and classified minds in two opposing groups, which will be described below as the Parme-nidean and the Heraclitean. The works of these four authors, based on the study of scientific ideas and their reverberation in the poetic imagination, are to be joined to the conclusions of other inquirers whose starting point is different, namely, those who have been occupied with the idea of the baroque in the arts and literature: H. Wölfflin, E. d'Ors, and J. Rousset. There would then be two types of minds, one attracted strongly by permanence, the other by change. The first are usually called "classical," the second either "romantic" or "baroque." We prefer to follow Koestler's suggestion, and designate the two types of mind under the names respectively of two precursors of cosmogony: Parmenides and Heraclitus.

The Parmenidean places himself outside of time and takes the side of the eternal. Underneath his choice, one can detect perhaps a fear, a recoil from whatever is transformed, crumbles, decays . . . ; in short, he recoils from the biological laws which include decomposition as an integral part. Because he fears death, the Parmenidean does not love life. But there is something more: an aesthetic taste, a choice of an idea, and at times, a religious motivation.

The forms of cosmic pathos to which the follower of Parmenides is susceptible are those which have come to terms with the Eternal, attracted by the purity and rigidity of an incorruptible substance. Everything enters into a clear and stable harmony: the Pythagorean aesthetic of numbers and configurations, the circle and sphere as types of perfection; and as the divine type of motion a steady eternal rotation, equivalent to the unmoveable. With a greater degree of complexity, the Music and Dance of the planets appear in a harmony of numbers and combination of configurations in a similarly experienced duration and in strictly determined limits.

For this aesthetic of the Eternal is an aesthetic of the Finite: what is perfect or complete necessarily has limits. It is also the aesthetic of Discontinuity and of Hierarchy: the Scale of Being is fixed with distinct levels in the Parmenidean cosmos. Each thing has its place, and the thinking man enjoys the pleasure of feeling that he is in his right place. It is an aesthetic of immutable Unity, and not of a process of Fusion.

The Parmenidean thinker is more or less susceptible—and susceptibility varies in degree with each individual—to the pathos of Unity in explanation, of simplicity in basic assumptions, and of implacable rigor in formulated laws. There is also the pathos of ideal exactness in the appropriation and coherence of a well-knit network of logical correspondences and relations which take in the whole of creation and leave nothing out.

As for the Heraclitean, he is susceptible to the pathos of Becoming, and in order that it may unfold and reveal itself, he needs the Unlimited. If we seek any deep motivation, we discover a taste for life which accepts everything which life implies, including death as a condition for a new birth. There is a boldness in his outlook which rejects protection and authority, and

assumes a willingness to take risks of all sorts. The appeal of the Heraclitean kind of pathos to instinctive forces and to the Unconscious is naturally greater than it is in the Parmenidean family of minds.

The Heraclitean type includes everything arising out of the fascination of change, and transfers to the cosmic plane whatever is integral to the cycle of life. There are dreams of life's genesis: the pathos of Birth and its original freshness, the pathos of continuous Creation and its inexhaustible onward surge. There are dreams of life's evolution: the pathos of continuity and of the flow of the forms of life. Opposing the Parmenidean pathos of Unity is that of Variety: the taste for profusion and even disorder; the taste for the irregular, the original, the unique which will feed the dream of the plurality of worlds. In opposition to the joy of feeling satisfied with being "in one's place," there is the intoxication of being lost in the swarming proliferation of universal Being. In order to accommodate all these wonderful things, the true Heraclitean requires Plenitude, a fullness within the Infinity of space, akin to the infinity of God and to the unlimited capacity of the soul of man.

While the Parmenidean accepts hierarchy and its hemmed-in gradations, the Heraclitean, on the other hand, is alive to the pathos of absolute freedom; and in certain eras, he experiences the pathos of liberation, of transport, and of flight without thought of return. He is a traveler in the mind. Lastly, the science of motion for him is not mechanics but dynamics. Cosmic energies are absorbed in vital forces; he is receptive not to steady and completely smooth rotation, but welcomes the conflict of opposites, tension, and effort, so that his Universe tends to be polarized.

3. In practice it is not always easy to classify types of imagination because there are mixed forms. Sometimes the same myth can be sensed in two opposite ways, e.g., in the case of the idea of Eternal Return. There are, after all, pathological cases: obsessions which cannot be judged as preferences, but as feelings of disgust and terror; there also exist minds that are perverted or paralyzed by the dominant world view of their times. In fact, different sorts of individual characters are encouraged or modified by the spirit of the times. Philosophical influences play their role in the predominance of different types of imagination, e.g., whenever the Platonic influence is foremost, the heavens claim more attention; on the other hand, the Aristotelian influence turns the mind away from too eager concern about outer space. Furthermore, in the interaction of scientific research and cosmic dreams, the scale of science and imagination is displaced to the extent that the former makes itself independent

of the latter. Man's effort to confine science to involvement with his deeper wishes becomes more and more difficult, although never discouraged.

4. For we must take into account a phenomenon often noted but never explained: a sort of respiratory rhythm in history, a psychological balancing-wheel, which creates kinships between one epoch and another, separated by long intervals. According to E. d'Ors, a classical era is followed by a baroque era; in the cosmological imagination, a Parmenidean era is followed by a Heraclitean era. Intellectual rigor gives way to an insurgence of instinctive forces. There are wholesome but harsh disciplines (like Aristotelianism) which are obstacles to such revolts; then the day comes when the barrier collapses. It was maintained by timidity; all of a sudden fear has disappeared, and the attractive but disturbing doctrines regain their sway and release an enormous internal flood of images. These movements are difficult to explain, for social causation does not help; neither do the discoveries of new worlds or of Greek manuscripts. But they must be recognized and taken into account.

We can indicate summarily some of these intellectual rhythms. The triumph of scholastic philosophy in the thirteenth century inaugurated a Parmenidean era in cosmology. The Florentine Renaissance in the fifteenth century inaugurated a Heraclitean era which was joined with the Neo-Platonism of the first centuries; the new spirit kept growing stronger making possible the infinite worlds of Bruno's cosmology and the discoveries of Kepler and Galileo. The seventeenth century saw the opposition between classical French thought dominated by Descartes and British thought dominated by the appeal of the infinite. Newton reconciled temporarily the two tendencies by satisfying both. But the eighteenth century, in the main superficially classical, marked a return to the Renaissance, to a taste for magic and the occult; Leibniz' philosophy, whose influence was enormous, strengthened the renewed need for Plenitude, infinite Diversity, and creative profusion. And the nineteenth century, despite the steady progress of pure science, was to see, about every twenty years, a return of this Leibnizian intellectual outlook accompanied by the flourishing growth of the same dreams; for example, the plurality of inhabited worlds offered itself to a plurality of existing beings in a continuous ascent towards an unattainable Perfection.

The relations between imagination and astronomy will be studied here from two points of view: how imagination favors or obstructs the efforts of true scientists; and how, among nonspecialists, it takes possession of discoveries, distorts them, and supplements

them in its own way. We shall give only some attention to the second point of view.

II

1. We shall consider astronomy at the time when it began to stir, that is, when the sky was discovered to be observable, when the personality of astronomers and their relations to their cultural environment became more accessible to investigation. And we shall follow this intellectual adventure only until the first third of the twentieth century when the Einsteinian theory of relativity gradually brought to the uninitiated an unimaginable world. Individual psychology will be only a secondary consideration. (Kepler's psychology, for example, has been admirably studied by Nicolson and Koestler.) It is rather the turn of imagination characterizing a whole era which will be discussed here.

We start with the Ptolemaic cosmos, an improvement on Aristotle, whose reign, established in the thirteenth century, was soon to crumble. Ptolemaic astronomy provided a home for the Parmenidean imagination and satisfied both of its intellectual and aesthetic demands: a refuge secured by the closed-in cavernous Cosmos in which the stars, solidly attached to their spherical vaults of rigid ether, followed these spheres in their eternal rounds. It provided, with a sense of security, the intellectual satisfaction of simple mathematical relations and the aesthetic delight of a perfect harmony: circles and spheres, inserted within a single finite Sphere outside of which nothing existed except the world of pure minds.

It is true that this perfect image was merely a simplification, for the uninitiated, of a more heterogeneous and complicated view. There was the duality, unacceptable to a rigorous mind, of the incorruptible superlunar spheres and of the impure sublunar sphere of the Earth subject to change, this very Earth which paradoxically formed the center of the whole system, i.e., usurped what was, for the spontaneous imagination, the place of honor. Only astrological influences wove a network from one world to the other without succeeding in unifying them. There was also the increasing complexity of celestial mechanics accompanying progress in the observation of celestial movements, which required the refinement of Ptolemy's system; efforts made to "save the appearances" and to preserve the dogma of the Circle greatly compromised the simple harmony of the Great Dance. The aim of Copernicus' *De revolutionibus* (1543) was precisely to restore that simplicity, and to do it by returning to the heliocentric view of Pythagoreans like Heraclides of Pontus. Copernicus, as Koestler has

515

shown, was Parmenidean: to solve the mathematical problem of the world, Copernicus sought a more elegant solution than Ptolemy's and wished to repair the old clock by changing the arrangement of its wheels.

However, around Copernicus an intellectual ferment was taking place in which he did not seem to participate; and, as in times of crises, the two families of minds became self-conscious and opposed each other.

The return to favor of Neo-Platonism at the end of the fifteenth century contributed to the unification of the world. Marsilio Ficino explained astrological influences by the Spirit of the World (*Spiritus mundi*), a kind of vital fluid which came from the stars and planets to impregnate our earthly abode (*De vita libri tres*, 1489). Thinkers were thus prepared to accept the unity of substance between our Earth and the other heavenly bodies. Moreover, the Platonic cult of the divine Light and of the Sun as the image of the Idea of the Good, encouraged these thinkers to accept the central place which Copernicus was to assign to this orb, and he did so with visible satisfaction. In addition, they were prepared to accept the role of the Sun as the mover of the planets, a role which Kepler was later to attribute to it (*Astronomia nova*, 1609).

Moreover, a new state of mind was created: man took confidence in his powers to explore the world and to make use of it, affirming an idea that the world was put at his disposal by God. The outstanding work in which this assurance was expressed is the *Oration on the Dignity of Man* (1436) by Pico della Mirandola. For the first time Prometheus had a clear conscience. A new boldness inspired him: he no longer needed the safeguard of a protective shell; the rigid casement of the celestial spheres seemed like a prison to him, as did the infallible doctrine of Aristotle. A curiosity that was both more exact and more extended encouraged voyages of exploration, and in turn was developed by them. This curiosity extended to the celestial domain, where it was believed there was nothing more to discover. Finally, a fresh love of life led to the joyous acceptance of everything life brought with it: generation *and* decay. Alchemy contributed to this appraisal of the vital cycle that was thought to be realized in the alchemist's oven (*athanor*); and the incorruptible nature of the starry world lost its prestige. This cult of life and this explorer's sort of boldness found perfect expression in Galileo (*Dialogue on the Two Main Systems of the World*, 1632). In this work he proclaimed the superiority of the living over the static:

As for me, I hold the Earth as noble and admirable because of the numerous and varied alterations, mutations, and generative changes that take place in it.

And with regard to Aristotle's authority:

Only the blind need a guide, but anyone with two eyes in his head and with a mind should use them to guide himself.

However, this turn of mind had asserted itself much earlier. Thanks to it certain events in the sky—the outburst of new stars (the *Novae* of 1572 and 1604) and the passing of comets, introducing change in the immutable superlunar heaven—created a sensation and excited discussions. Concerning the Copernican clockwork, the followers of Heraclitus would maintain above all that the "Sphere of the Fixed Stars" had become useless because it no longer moved; it could dissolve and open out on the Infinite. It was thus that, before the crucial astronomical discoveries were made, G. Bruno (in his *Dialogues*, 1584) was able to put forth through the power of his imagination a typical Heraclitean cosmos: an infinite space, infinitely full, an inexhaustible, creative gushing of energy, an unlimited number of suns as centers of as many infinitely varied planetary systems, endless degrees of Perfection, an equilibrium in motion, a network of transformations and of perpetually new forms—all of it alive and giving birth to life. No hesitancy in Bruno; he trampled with the rapturous fury of an iconoclast over the ruins of the old cosmos, and the impulse of liberation and departure on his part was unattended by any apprehensiveness or by any looking back. From Bruno came the avid concern for the infinite which we find in British thought of the seventeenth century; following Bruno also, intoxication with life and variety was henceforth linked to the theme of the "Plurality of Worlds," a theme which would still be alive in the work of Camille Flammarion and in novels of the twentieth century.

2. Bruno will be remembered for a long time as a bold and audacious soul, gifted with an unusually fiery temperament. It was, however, by following the path of observation that astronomy leaped forward with Kepler and Galileo; the spirit of the times was all for observation. It was a novel thing to devote so much time and effort to determining the orbit of Mars, and especially to do what Kepler did, not without anguish, namely, to sacrifice doctrine for facts and the dogma of the perfect circle for the evidence of the ellipse. It would have been unthinkable, a half century earlier, to perfect, as Galileo did, a magnifying lens as a telescope directed towards unknowable celestial bodies, and to accept the facts of a moon with mountains, a sun soiled with spots, and celestial bodies woven out of the same elements as the earth.

However, the victory of the sons of Heraclitus was hotly disputed. What resisted change and the infinite was not primarily, as is commonly believed, the conservatism of the Church and the Aristotelian School-men, but rather a bundle of prejudices which occupied the framework of their inner lives. It is hard to understand today the moral collapse which the crumbling of the immutable Firmament signified for the sons of Parmenides. After losing the physical shelter and moral asylum of that deathless sphere towards which he could look for a refuge, man felt as exposed as a mollusk whose shell is broken. In the *Dialogues* of Bruno and of Galileo, the Parmenidean role is played by caricatured persons: "Where then is that beautiful order and that elegant hierarchy of Nature?" moans Bruno's critical interlocutor. Still the bewilderment and confusion of Simplicius and his like are natural and worthy of compassion. John Donne spoke the same language: ". . . all coherence gone." Even in the soul of the innovators opposing reactions conflict with one another and block progress.

The case of Kepler is typical. This great mind brought together within himself in tense opposition Heraclitus and Parmenides. He started from a dream of classical harmony, from a Pythagorean worship of numbers and shapes. He shied away from the Infinite, because nobody could locate any determinate place in it (*De stella nova*, 1606). He needed a hierarchy, a special nobility for the Sun and the Earth. His universe has a center, it remains spherical, and his proportions are based on the regular solids, perfect polygons, and musical harmonies (*Harmonice mundi*, 1619). Kepler made sure to integrate into this equilibrium the discoveries of his own calculations: the elliptical orbits of the planets and the inequalities of their motion.

But Kepler's geometric God is also an energetic God; the fusion of these two natures was achieved at the summit of Kepler's genius. The sun, image of the Father, is the source of life and motion; from the central astral body, there emanates a "moving force," an "immaterial substance" which draws the planets, an idea which came close to Newton's universal force of attraction. In Kepler's Pythagorean cosmos, we have the first model of a dynamic universe, the first hint of Energy.

3. A few years after Kepler's discoveries, mechanism triumphed over vitalistic dynamism in science and in the formulation of celestial motions.

Descartes was not an astronomer, but his cosmology wielded a powerful influence on thinkers in many countries as well as in France (*Principles of Philosophy*, Latin ed., 1644; French, 1647; *Treatise on the World*, posthumous, 1664). With respect to imagination Descartes's case is unique. He is undoubtedly classical in his preference for the simplicity of basic premises and for the inflexible Rigor of fixed Laws. Space was not absolute and the Void did not exist; Descartes started with an infinitely divisible and inert matter. Perfect motion, for Descartes, would be the kind that is determined by the principle of inertia, not in a circle but in a straight line. However, this motion is impossible in a Plenum in which no particle could be moved without displacing another—whence the Vortex, and whence by friction the formation of three kinds of particles. The most tenuous or subtle matter immediately fills all empty spaces; this dust forms the suns and their planets. In all this there is no scale of values or importance. So Descartes constructed, starting from an initial simplicity, a complicated, unstable system which was as stifling for an imagination in love with life and freedom as it was repugnant for the soul in love with harmony.

This system seemed, nonetheless, to satisfy both the rigorousness and the imagination of Descartes. The numerous images that he employed (eels twisted on the floor of a boat, straws in the eddies of a river) bear witness to his bias for minute displacements which reduce the universe to terrestrial models.

And yet Descartes did serve the cosmic imagination: he contributed greatly to the vogue of astronomy at the end of the seventeenth century. Since his was an unlimited universe, he satisfied those sensibilities that hungered for the infinite. As he brought in a great variety of vortices in perpetual combination and separation, he drew in his wake the lovers of change and diversity. He revived the great dream of the plurality of inhabited worlds. He created an impression of intimacy among these systems which come in contact with each other and modify one another. Finally, by introducing a cooling off of the sun or the impact of a comet, Descartes provided, in his lifeless cosmos, for death as a stage of the life-process. The end of the world, formerly considered a supernatural event, had now become Nature's threat; and it had to do with a theme of fascinating astronomical dreaming, as we shall see.

4. However, Newton's system of mathematical physics (*Philosophiae naturalis principia mathematica*, 1687) was going to offer a fuller and more lasting satisfaction to both the types of minds defined above. Newton as a scientist—prudent and modest—seems to have been at first a mathematician preoccupied with giving not an exhaustive explanation of the universe but a simple and elegant equation. He was also a religious man and wished to show the necessity of a permanent divine activity in the construction and working of the world-machine. He did not seem to have foreseen the many consequences of his theory that were often in conflict with one another.

To the classical type of imagination Newton offered certainty and balance; real space and real motion in relation to really immutable points; independent systems, each being supported by a practically fixed luminous body (a sun), around which dark bodies revolve at wisely measured distances, all arranged by an infallible Governor who is ready to repair any alteration. Thus, he offered harmony in motion, not so different from the Great Platonic Dance. But above all, his system is charming for the wonderful simplicity of its resources: once the Universe is set in motion by the initial push which inertia perpetuates, a single force suffices thereafter, namely, "universal attraction." From the Atomists and from Descartes, Newton inherited a unified idea of matter to which a universal law could be applied; now the latter did not end up with complications and disorder, as Cartesian mechanics did, but resulted in a more satisfying harmony. The limitless character of this universe no longer contradicts classical taste, henceforth adapted to the Infinite for various reasons. Philosophical reflection from Bruno to Henry More made acceptable, especially to the British, the idea that an infinite God could find his perfect image in an infinite creation. On their side the Cartesians believed that the simplicity and rigor of laws could suffice to assure the unity of a boundless universe. The natural bent of their minds was to emphasize among Newton's classical disciples the reassuring stability of this system as well as its unifying character. In the eighteenth century theories abounded in attempts to reduce the two laws of motion to a single one, and Louis de Tressan (1783) already utilized for this purpose an electric fluid as a universal agent.

Now the romantic mind found in the Newtonian world a still more complete satisfaction. The imagination in search of liberty and free flight found in Newton's space a propitious and exalting medium. Among the independent systems, all related to ours and yet different from ours, in which we can imagine an infinite variety of living forms, suited to delight the human visitor, large spaces open up which evoke not a dark and dry abyss, but a peaceful ocean welcoming the navigator. The Void assured the elasticity of a very tenuous ether and the smoothness of celestial motion; it is bathed by an omnipresent Light, and especially by the "very subtle Spirit" which Newton inherited from Henry More and which, from the depth of Newton's thought, assured the transmission of this unexplained force of Attraction. The contemporaries and successors of Newton went much farther and imagined worlds related to one another by mysterious life-messengers: imperishable seeds. The idea came from a fanciful cosmologist who had been speaking for Descartes, namely, B. de Maillet (*Telliamed*, 1748); but Newton's system contributed to the success of this fascinating dream, which was to be revived in the twentieth century by the Swedish astronomer Svante Arrhenius (*The Evolution of Worlds*, 1907). Thus Newton's system stirred the bold imagination of those who had inherited that proud confidence in the worth of man which inspired the Renaissance and burst out afresh in the eighteenth century. Newton is responsible for the cosmic voyages of the mind which have multiplied in poetry and fiction.

Furthermore, Newton brought about the triumph of a new pathos of dynamism. Universal gravitation for the first time gave a universal value to the idea of mass: the ancient and medieval celestial bodies were weightless. Now, the Creator became the athlete who shapes and hurls these cannonballs. His poetic emblem is no longer Milton's compass but Edward Young's scale-balance (*Night Thoughts*, 1742–44). If the classical mind tends to reduce to unity the agent of universal motion, the romantic mind tends to polarize the world and insists on seeing a conflict between the two forces, repulsion and attraction. In contrast to Newton, the romantic mind tends to make of both repulsion and attraction forces which, though working in exactly opposite directions, have the same nature; just as inexplicable on the physical plane as they appear similar to psychical forces—Love and Hate—a view which Empedocles had already declared.

According to H. Metzger, whom we follow here, the paradoxical force of attraction, which mysteriously acts at a distance, owed its career precisely to this unconscious or conscious assimilation by the imagination. The idea that a thing is attracted by what it resembles is also part of the primitive mentality; the "active power of desire" experienced within us directly is easily transferred to the external world. By reversing this transfer the romantic imagination went on to see in human love a particular case of the universal law of Attraction. This confusion already inspired the system of R. G. Boscovich (*Theoria philosophia naturalis*, 1758) and prevailed as late as the works of the astronomer Camille Flammarion.

The equilibrium of the two forces, an equilibrium so dear to classical minds, was capable of being shaken by the baroque imagination in love with conflict and in a close conspiracy with cataclysmic catastrophes. Attraction and repulsion could take turns in triumphing, the first reducing the world to a fabulously dense molecule, the second expanding it and scattering it anew, all this in accordance with a rhythm of alternating expansion and contraction: a dynamic and spatial variant of the ancient "Eternal Return," an idea which has had an influential career since the middle of the eighteenth century, enjoying favor that has lasted down to our own times, thanks to the theory of the expanding universe.

5. With Newton's system assuring the classical unity of explanation, there were also minds for whom the spatial unity of the architecture of the universe remained such a desideratum that they went ahead and worked at reconstructing the centralized universe of the ancients.

The desire among these minds for a regular arrangement of the stars on the celestial vault was at the base of their reconstruction. If from the earth the skies appear so irregular (a fact which Descartes found shocking), it was because our vortex could not be the center of the world; but there *should* exist a center from which the celestial vault would appear in a perfect harmony. The first astronomical observations on the displacement of the fixed stars (by E. Halley in 1718) favored the idea of the rotation of the whole of our galaxy (perhaps around Sirius, which would be its great sun) and of the entire universe around a central star. Thus appeared the system of Thomas Wright (*An Original Theory of the Universe*, 1750), which despite its mediocre mathematical value impressed important thinkers like Kant. In Wright's system there reappeared the old cult of the Circle and Sphere and the vast rotation of the whole starry vault, which had been at a standstill since Copernicus. But the original creation of this visionary cosmology was the fabulous "central body," the only stationary body, balancing by itself the Universe; the "central body" was not a sun of fire, but a habitable globe around which the stars appeared juxtaposed, forming a continuous vault of fire. It was the "First Mover," seat of the forces which move the universe, God's throne, and the "Abode of Recompense."

The central body and the great vortex appeared again among serious astronomers at the end of the eighteenth century; and among imaginative cosmologists like J. A. Lambert (*Kosmologische Briefe*, 1761) and J. E. Bode (*Anleitung zur Kenntniss des gestirnten Himmels*, 1768), whose influence on the *Sturm und Drang* dreamers was great.

Nevertheless these minds shared the then dominant yearning for infinite diversity. Wright established it in both space and time: he envisaged an unlimited plenum of creations, each with its central body, and conceived the blessedness of the elect to consist in the contemplation of the wonderful variety of the world. Bode insisted not only on the multiplicity of forms but also on their perpetually changing variety in which an inexhaustible creative power was displayed.

6. Henceforth, the cosmos definitively entered the historical scene. Newton's system was the last to have placed the "Harmony of the World" outside of time, installed and maintained by God, and transfigured by him on the "Last Day." Now, among Newton's disciples there was a slipping away; for the majority of minds curious about astronomy the fate of the universe was being progressively consummated in time.

As we have already indicated, starting from the middle of the eighteenth century there occurred a return of the imagination in favor of a cyclical conception of that destiny (such as Vico had just installed in human history). The "Eternal Return" may be a way of saving Parmenidean changelessness, but such was not the case with the men of that century, for it was the life cycle that mattered to them; we shall come back to this matter. Euler's calculations (*Mémoire*, 1746) on the progressive recession of the orbits of the planets provided an astronomical excuse for reviving an obscure desire. The idea spread that the planets of each system would return to the sun, and the latter to the "Sun of Suns," which periodically would absorb them, and then would disperse new worlds into space. Thus Unity alternated with Diversity. This obsession was exceptionally strong in the troubled time of the turn of the eighteenth into the nineteenth century, and inspired such visionaries as Delisle de Sales, Restif de la Bretonne, and Fabre d'Olivet; it was also to give birth to its masterpiece, the *Eureka* (1848) of Edgar Allan Poe. In this work, the cyclical idea retained only a minimal relation to obscure pulsations, and assumed a maximum of aesthetic satisfaction. Poe's idea of the cosmos as a poem inspired him with a pure intellectual joy resembling Kant's. What constituted Poe's delight was the law of Reciprocal Adaptation in virtue of which cause and effect flow into each other and become indiscernible. The Circle of Perfection was reestablished on an intellectual plane. "Beauty is truth, truth beauty," and that is all there is to know. Diversity was integrated with Unity in the form of the greatest possible totality of relationships in continuous growth until they are resolved. Matter was integrated with energy and the latter with pure Spirit. Finally the yearning to return to the Source was sublimated here into a mystical unity.

7. However, the cosmogony of *Eureka* was late and isolated—intellectually Poe was an offspring of the eighteenth century—at a time (1848) when the triumphant world view was not only Heraclitean but romantic, in the strict sense of the word, rather than baroque. The Great Vortex, without being abandoned (pure astronomers are still inclined to accept it, at least in the form of a complete rotation of our whole galaxy) enjoys less favor than the flight to infinity. The circle, and even the ellipse, yielded to the straight line or to curves (parabola, hyperbola) which are fascinating because they are open-ended. Scientific excuses were offered by Herschel and then by Laplace (*Exposition du système du monde*, 1796). "Several observations,"

519

Laplace says, "are represented well enough by supposing the solar system being carried towards the constellation of Hercules." It was only a mere hypothesis but the romantic imagination took hold of it. And for the intellectual delight of completely embracing the whole cosmos, the romantic substituted the joy of feeling himself projected outward, beyond all anticipation, the joy of resigning and losing one's self, relishing the mysterious and a certain intellectual vertigo with the savor of the "maybe." Carried away towards what? Towards regions of light, dense with stars, or towards some frightful collision? The romantic mind succumbed to the pathos of the "Voyage Out With No Return." This propensity for the "voyage out," associated with the desire for freedom, had created the prestige of comets. (We refer to the comet of the astronomical era, when the comet was recognized as a heavenly body and not as a supernatural apparition.) The comets' vast orbits, their unpredicted appearance, and the belief, due to Descartes, that they can escape from their own vortex and pass from one system to another—all that had made comets the model vagabonds; but now the whole solar system was in flight. Works, solidly documented for their time in astronomical matters, yielded to this intoxication and maintained it. For example, Alexander von Humboldt's *Kosmos* (1845) offered the reader an impressive speeded-up film of a universe in flight: "Countless stars are carried away, like whirlwinds of dust, in opposite directions." Jean Reynaud's *Earth and Sky* (*Terre et ciel*, 1854) also insisted on the exalted idea that navigation by the stars never followed the same route twice.

However, among the romantics (with a few exceptions like Byron and Leopardi) optimism carried the day; fear itself can be, after all, no more than a pleasurable intoxication. Faith in a Supreme Being was not given up. Only the "harmony of the world" was not divorced from time; it was in the process of becoming. Minds, preoccupied with socialism, like the Saint-Simonian socialism of J. Reynaud, or with an esoteric idea, like that of Flammarion (to name only truly informed astronomical writers), conceived the universe as "a great fraternal society" (Reynaud) or as a place reserved for souls allowed to rise from one world to a higher world in an indefinite progress.

Quite different was the reaction to the universe in flight by the pessimistic type of minds that formed the majority of sky-watchers at the end of the nineteenth century. What occurred now was a very intense negation of the "harmony of the world." The source of this current was *not* astronomical; the slow and steady progress of science did not justify it, but on the contrary, it offered grounds for creating enthusiasm. The discovery of Neptune in 1877, the study of Mars'

"canals" revived speculation on the plurality of inhabited worlds, and the flood of Martian fiction began to mount.

The influence of Schopenhauer and Hindu philosophy, accompanying perhaps an era of social stagnation and boredom, and perhaps also, the mysterious play of the psychological pendulum, imposed on cosmologists and poets the vision of an empty, dark, and icy space in which the imaginary voyage can only be a nauseating dizzy fall into the infinite. The hospitable space of Newton gave way to an uninhabitable space. And in this Sea of Darkness all that the earthly ship could expect thereafter without a pilot was shipwreck.

III

1. We must devote particular attention to the hypotheses about the birth and death of worlds; they were bound to have privileged connections with the imagination through the overtones they awaken in the darkest regions of human sensibility.

There is hardly any question here of anything suggestive of the Parmenideans. We are about to talk of those who are friends of Change when it assumes the form which is closest to our inner being: the life cycle. The lovers of change conceived the evolution of the world as a biological process, a favorite model of explanation especially from the start of the eighteenth century.

In particular two modes of the genesis of worlds excite the imagination, and one of them is especially explosive and violent. Out of a primordial star, father of worlds, are born secondary heavenly bodies; the planets escape from their suns, and these suns escape from the "Sun of Suns": by means of centrifugal force (Emmanuel Swedenborg, *Principia rerum naturalium*, 1734) or by means of a collision with a comet (G. L. L. de Buffon, *Théorie de la terre*, 1745). For the scientist, it seems, a rational explanation is in order, but reverie takes hold of it and the dreamer sees a seminal emission or childbirth instead. This fantasy slips easily into the dream of the Great Pulsation. The Sun-father becomes the God Saturn who devours his children; then, after a period of digestion, which is also a gestation, he procreates them again.

Opposed to this violent parturition there is a type of slow, mysterious genesis whose prestige is bound to be much greater than the violent type, since the Mother nostalgia is powerful among most men. Only this nostalgia can explain the capture of the imagination by the idea of "Prime Matter," which revives the old dream of primordial waters. In rationalistic centuries while scientific astronomy makes progress, we shall see the triumph of cosmogonies which owe not their development but their success among the profane or semi-profane to strong unconscious motivations.

The first and one of the most grandiose unitary systems of the formation and evolution of the world was Kant's *Theorie des Himmels* (1755), conceived six years earlier when he was twenty-five. Like many a great mind, Kant reconciled within himself two contrary tendencies. From the Parmenidean he sought a holistic structure: "a single system . . . a single general law in an eternal and perfect order." He inherited from his time a corpuscular Matter scattered to infinity in an infinite space. He reestablished an effective center, but it was not a geometric one, which would be absurd for an infinite universe. The first condensed nucleus was to become the Central Body of the Universe. And if it was not God's throne, as Wright would have it, at least this Sun of Suns had a most extraordinary density and power of attraction.

Nevertheless, the Heraclitean tendency is dominant in the young cosmologist. The order of the universe is always in the process of being worked out. As in Laplace's hypothesis of the origin of the solar system, rings of gaseous vapors start turning around the primitive star, break off, condense, and thus form systems of concentric zones farther and farther away from the center. As the organized universe wins over chaos, the earliest born worlds grow old and disintegrate through the wear of motion. And so there reappears an internal zone of unorganized matter, though this chaos cannot remain at rest more than an instant; active forces start to work on it again, and while the cosmic bubble expands to infinity, a new bubble swells at its center. Whence the dynamic Universe has an equilibrium guaranteed by a central mass, but it is perpetually broken and reestablished like the march or progress of man. The Scale of Perfection is not a fixed one either, but is constantly adding new gradations. In fact, the further one goes away from the center, the more does the finer attenuated matter show itself gently yielding to the soul embodied in it, and the distant planets are the most perfect abode of the most perfect creations. However, that absolute Beauty which resides in the realization of all possible worlds is never completely attained.

No matter how intellectual the young philosopher Kant may be, he is still under the shadow of the prestige of the idea of genesis. When he approaches this chapter, he speaks of the "ravishing charm of the subject." He takes some delight in evoking a primordial matter buried "in a silent night," but possessing "in its essence" the forces which are the sources of motion and life. Sleep is only apparent in this maternal obscurity, in the depths of which Kant saw seeds of worlds germinating: "It is not a minor pleasure to let the imagination wander to the limits of the creation achieved in the realm of chaos." More than that is the way the death of worlds is seen as a phase of that eternal process, visible also in flowers and insects, a process which the philosopher has to accept, not with resignation but with a certain delight.

2. Kant's hypothesis, like many syntheses of geniuses, remained ignored in his time. But at the beginning of the nineteenth century, another hypothesis emerged which was to enjoy a resounding success through the associations it awakened in the imagination, namely, the idea of a Primordial Nebula.

The idea did not come out of Kant's system, but from the observations of J. F. W. Herschel on nebulae. These remote cosmic clouds exercised a strange attraction as soon as they were discovered. Herschel had discerned in these accumulated gases that the nebular matter condensed more or less around more luminous nuclei; he had thought he recognized in them embryonic stars in various stages of development (*Memoir*, 1811). Laplace took up the idea, and brought it closer to home by applying it to the formation of the solar system (*Système du monde*, 1824). For Laplace, a particularly objective scientist, astronomy was "the solution of a large problem in mechanics." Concerned solely with explaining the direction of planetary motion, he offered his account "with all the reservations that should be induced by everything which is not a result of observation and reasoning." And he said this in a terse and coldly neutral tone. Now we know that this theory met with an enormous success, a success whose causes are far from being purely intellectual (even among true astronomers).

Thanks to Herschel, and then to Laplace, an exalted idea, taken up again by many cosmologists (e.g., H. Faye, and by J. H. Jeans, *The Nebular Hypothesis*, 1923), was to fascinate the imagination: the genesis of the universe is in continual process under our very eyes. And philosopher-poets like Lamennais multiplied such metaphors: for example, the worlds "appear to us at first like the small egg in which the liquid of life thickens gradually" (*Esquisse d'une philosophie*, IV [1846]).

The gropings of scientific explanations take turns in thwarting or favoring the nebular reverie. Telescopes of increasingly greater power reveal in the nebulae no longer fragments of primordial chaos waiting to give birth to new worlds, but simple masses of stars, a far less exciting idea. Herschel was familiar with this disappointment, but the strongest disappointment was caused by the giant telescope of Lord Rosse (1845). The imagination, however, takes refuge in its origins; if prime matter no longer exists 'as the mother of worlds, at least it has existed. The joy of seeing creation in the process makes room for the nostalgia of the vanished Mother, and especially of *our* nebula, the Mother of our solar family (in the poetry of J. Laforgue). The resurrection, by means of spectrum analysis, of the gaseous nebula (1864) released, for example, in Flammarion's *Astronomie populaire* (1864; *Popular Astronomy*, 1879), a delight whose sources are suspicious. Henceforth, said the astronomer, we can see in these "lights which palpitate on the frontiers of creation" the "genesis which shows us the birth of other Universes." It was the same emotion of young Kant concerning the fringes of Chaos.

The discovery of spiral nebulae (1845) threw the dream again on to new paths. The observer thought himself the eyewitness of the great tournament thanks to which systems have been formed. The arms of the spiral can only be imagined as moving, as either curling up or unrolling. Whether it is a condensation or dispersion, it is still a matter of genesis. The whirlwind motion (very different from circular rotation, eternally the same) is essentially creative. Dispersion triumphs in the hypotheses of S. Arrhenius (*Evolution of Worlds*, 1907) and of J. H. Jeans (*The Universe Around Us*, 1929) which have so powerfully affected the modern imagination.

3. The death of universes appeals to the imagination no less than their birth; but it does so in two very different ways. It can exert a horrifying fascination or can be joyfully accepted as a stage of the cycle of life and condition of rebirth.

There is a problem here in which hidden individual or social preferences play an important role; for from the day when we are to be faced with the death of universes as a physical phenomenon, several ends are considered possible: death by cold, after the extinction of the sun; by slow disintegration; by the return of the planets to the Father Star in a final flare-up; by collision with an intruder, e.g., an extinct star. These kinds of death—for the earth, for the solar family, and for the entire universe—may be reduced to two types, which approximate the two old myths of the flood and the burning: a slow death at night, a sudden death by fire.

Now there are eras in which concern for the end of the world is absent, others in which eschatology becomes obsessive. And the prevailing choice is not made for reasons that are essentially scientific, even among scientists. Apparently before and during periods of crisis, the imagination finds some satisfaction in imagining a cosmic cataclysm, followed or not by a renovated world; whereas in periods of disappointment and political stagnation, the nightmare of a slow death predominates. Thus, before and during the French Revolution and the Empire, the expectation of a catastrophe dominated the mind; on the other hand, after

1815, and then again in the 1880's, the obsession of universal darkness weighed on the imagination. Of course, there are exceptions and distinctions that should be made.

The appeal of a slow death during the night may manifest itself in two very distinct ways, for there are two nights: one, the gentle enveloping night, represents to the unconscious the Mother rocking her child; worlds allowed to fall asleep in her arms return to primordial matter or to the nebulous in order to be born again rejuvenated. But there is another night, which is a Void at absolute zero, and is associated in the unconscious with a devouring mother, who is far from preparing for any rebirth. Now there are types of men who not only aspire to an annihilating void but desire to extend it to all, to "being" itself; and this suicidal desire extends to the cosmic plane. This disease of the imagination, encouraged by the vogue of Schopenhauer, prevailed all over Europe during the 1880's and 1890's. We can also see a return of the Parmenidean imagination in the haunting fear, then current, of petrifaction in various forms: the complacent evocation of a dried-up earth reduced to a skeleton of rock, caught in a shroud of ice or salt. The vision that Galileo scoffed at, an earth turned to a desert of sand or block of jasper, became once again, through disgust with life, the nostalgia of a decadent generation.

Among cosmologists the physics of that period justified an increasing and total torpor of the universe worn out by its motion and by the degradation of its energy. Hervé Faye (*Théories cosmogoniques*, 1884), for instance, offers an impressive table of these "dark and icy globes circulating in the gloom of eternal night." Similarly with Flammarion (*La fin du monde*, 1894) and with countless works of fiction and poetry, we find the same images reproduced.

4. The death of worlds by the ordeal of fire exerts a strange fascination on other minds. The appeal of flames has retained the attention of psychoanalysts, in particular, of G. Bachelard (*Psychanalyse du feu*, 1938). Fire for the unconscious mind has two opposing functions, one destructive and the other regenerative. On the cosmic plane, the destroyer Fire, the Fire of Anger, devours and volatilizes worlds. But beneficial and fecund Fire, like the burning woodpile of the Phoenix, restores new life to the world transfigured.

This great flame, which is an integral part of biblical prophecies of the Doomsday, as also of the pagan myth of the "Eternal Return," is one that cosmologists find excuses for integrating into the evolution of their universe, not so much through their fidelity to tradition as through a deep attraction to it. In England, Thomas

Burnet (*Telluris theoria sacra*, 1681), William Whiston (*New Theory of the Earth*, 1696), and J. Ray (*Three Physico-theological Discourses*, 1713) fell back on the Holy Book. The French enlighteners, like Delisle de Sales or Restif de la Bretonne, who were little concerned with the Bible, opted for the flames and the eternal return because these satisfied their insatiable appetite for life and enjoyment. But right in the middle of the nineteenth century, a genuine astronomer, J. P. Nichol, believing he saw the nebulae rolling up and turning into globes, secretly hoped that the universe was marching "up to that mysterious terminating glory" (*Architecture of the Heavens*, 1838). And this was the message which aroused in the fantasy of Poe the final flames of his *Eureka*.

In order to spark the conflagration, as an unconscious desire urges, cosmologists at the end of the century resorted to the shock of the collision of two worlds. It was a matter of a more fortuitous and more partial version of the eternal return, lacking the aesthetic rigor of Poe's system, but having a more immediate physical verisimilitude. The comet has always been given the role of torch-bearer; meeting it is a fearful thing, like meeting love, but a new life can be expected of it. The comet stands in line among the hypotheses of Flammarion concerning the end of the world, and in 1910, materialized by Halley's comet, it was to let loose a flood of fears and hopes. At the end of the nineteenth century, the comet found rivals in the extinct stars with which Faye, Flammarion, and their followers peopled space, and which revived the old myth of the Dark Sun.

Universal death by the degradation of energy and total stabilization at absolute zero in absolute night was a tolerable vision only for the decadent family of minds of the catastrophists obsessed with the idea of the impending death of the universe. Others refused to accept it. This deathly equilibrium, before being definitely established, was to be broken constantly by some shock, transforming into heat the energy of motion; such was the "impact theory" of James Croll (*Stellar Evolution*, 1889). So it was at the beginning: the primordial spark jumped between two cold and black masses. So will it eternally be. This fascinating vision, resembling the alchemists' dreams, the marriage of two dead stars giving birth to a glorious child, is the view adopted by Flammarion (*Astronomie populaire, La fin du monde*). It was also the vision of a cosmologist who enjoyed great prestige in the first third of the twentieth century: Svante Arrhenius (*L'Évolution des mondes*, 1907). He insisted on the fabulous reserve of energy—therefore, of life and fecundity—which can remain in an extinct star until a collision

awakens it; and this impact gives birth either to a new star (*nova*) or to a spiral nebula; a striking sketch shows the two powerful jets of fire shooting out and whirling about. This impact theory was then popularized by H. Poincaré (*Hypothèses cosmogoniques*, 1911), by Abbé Moreux, and by M. Maeterlinck (*La grande féerie*, 1929).

Now, starting in 1927, the theory of the expanding universe took shape and satisfied once again the need for a unitary pulsation of the great Totality of the universe. Minds repugnant to the idea of Infinity took refuge in the curvature of space. To those who fear cold and darkness, the nuclear furnace of the sun has appeared inexhaustible; the *quasars* enable one to dream of fabulous stores of energy. Articles popularizing science suggest to us every day that light, the cosmic voyager par excellence, traveling for billions of years might end up by bringing back news of the Creation. Astronomy still appeals to all types of imagination, to lovers of the immutable as well as to lovers of change, provided that they can detach themselves from the individual destiny of man and lose themselves in that which surpasses them and all things.

BIBLIOGRAPHY

Gaston Bachelard, *La formation de l'esprit scientifique* (Paris, 1938); idem, *La psychanalyse du feu* (Paris, 1938); idem, *L'air et les songes* (Paris, 1943); idem, *La poétique de l'espace* (Paris, 1957). E. A. Burtt, *The Metaphysical Foundations of Modern Physical Science* (London, 1924; 1932). Pierre Duhem, *Le système du monde: Histoire des doctrines cosmologiques de Platon à Copernic*, 10 vols. (Paris, 1913–59). C. M. Edsman, *Ignis divinus* (Paris, 1949). Mircea Éliade, "Prestiges du mythe cosmogonique," *Diogenes* (1958). C. G. Jung, *Symbole der Wandlung* (Berlin, 1950). Arthur Koestler, *The Sleepwalkers* (London, 1959). A. Koyré, *La gravitation universelle de Képler à Newton* (Paris, 1951); idem, *From the Closed World to the Infinite Universe* (Baltimore, 1957). Arthur O. Lovejoy, *The Great Chain of Being: A Study of the History of an Idea* (Cambridge, Mass., 1933; New York, 1960). R. Lenoble, *Mersenne ou la naissance du mécanisme* (Paris, 1943); idem, "Origines de la pensée scientifique moderne," *Histoire de la science* (Paris, 1957). Hélène Metzger, *Attraction universelle et religion naturelle* (Paris, 1938). Marjorie H. Nicolson, *The Breaking of the Circle* (New York, 1949); idem, *Science and Imagination* (New York, 1956). G. Poulet, *Les métamorphoses du cercle* (Paris, 1961). Hélène Tuzet, *Le cosmos et l'imagination* (Paris, 1965). A. N. Whitehead, *Science and the Modern World* (Cambridge, 1926).

HÉLÈNE L. TUZET

[See also Chain of Being; Continuity; **Cosmic Voyages;** Cosmology; Creation; Cycles; Evolutionism; Hierarchy; **Infinity;** Macrocosm; **Metaphysical . . .;** Romanticism.]

COSMIC VOYAGES

I

THE DESIRE for the wings of a dove seems to have been perennial among human beings. At the dawn of recorded Chinese history we are told of Emperor Shun who was said to have made a successful flight and a descent in a parachute. In the Bible we hear of Elijah carried to heaven by good angels in a fiery chariot and of Christ's being transported by the devil to the top of a mountain and to the pinnacle of a temple. Solomon is said to have given the Queen of Sheba a vessel by means of which she could traverse the air. Greek legend told of flying gods like Hermes and flying mortals like Daedalus and Icarus. In Platonic myths we hear of the rise and fall of human souls through the heavenly spheres and of the winged chariots in the *Phaedrus*. In the myth of *Er* we are sometimes on the earth, sometimes above it, looking down. Both classical and later literatures use the device of dream or ecstasy in which the soul leaves the body to travel through space. Cicero's *Somnium Scipionis* set the pattern for much later dream literature: Scipio in his dream gains a conception of the universe and of the comparative insignificance of earth. Plutarch's *De facie in orbe lunare* is a cosmic voyage in its implications, concerned with the moon's size, shape, distance, light, and nature. In medieval literature such themes were picked up and others added as man in trance sought other worlds and Dante descended into Hell, then made his journey to Paradise.

In England the prehistory of aviation begins with a monarch, as in China, this one better known to us for his son than for himself. Bladud, legendary tenth king of Britain, was said to have made a flight on feathered wings, which resulted in his death and the accession of his son, King Lear. Into his death was read a lesson on overweening ambition expressed by one of many poets who wrote of him:

> As from a Towre he sought to scale the Sky,
> He brake his necke, because he soar'd too high.

During the Renaissance that myriad-minded man, Leonardo da Vinci, discovered the principle of the glider and invented a parachute, in addition to his many important studies of birds' wings and the principles underlying their flight. But it remained for the seventeenth century to make basic discoveries that presaged modern aviation and to develop the cosmic voyage into the important type of literature it remained for many years.

There were two main causes for the emergence of the cosmic voyage as a form of art, one literary, one scientific. The first English translation of Lucian's moon-voyages in 1634 was in part responsible for the popularity of the theme. In the *True History* men reached the moon not by design but by chance. Adventuring into unknown territory beyond the Pillars of Hercules, mariners found their ship caught up by a whirlwind. After eight days they reached the moon. Lucian's description of the moon-world, and his voyage among the stars to "cloud-cuckoo land" were the merest fantasy with no attempt at even semi-scientific verisimilitude. The voyage of Lucian's other moon-voyager, Icaromenippus, has more similarities with the cosmic voyage as it developed. Menippus reached the moon by design, not chance. He fastened to his body two wings, one of a vulture, the other of an eagle, and after a period of practice took off from the summit of Olympus. His first stop was at the moon, from which he looked back upon an earth, which—according to the Ptolemaic astronomy—remained stationary below him. But not content merely with a moon-voyage, he went on through the stars to heaven, which he reached in a few days. He was returned to earth by Hermes, and his wings stripped away to prevent further audacity. But, while the Lucianic voyages helped establish the literary pattern, the great stimulation of the cosmic voyage to imagination was a major scientific discovery.

In March, 1610, appeared the *Sidereus Nuncius* ("the starry messenger," or message) of Galileo Galilei, Professor of Mathematics at the University of Padua. In this little pamphlet, Galileo set down excitedly the chief discoveries he had made by his fifth telescope, the first one developed to a power sufficient for celestial observation. For centuries it had been taken for granted by Greek, Roman, and medieval men that all the stars were known and numbered and that they were arranged in the familiar constellations, by a knowledge of which men were able to travel by land or sea. Through his "optick tube"—it was not called "telescope" for some time—Galileo had observed "stars innumerable," and had solved the mystery of the Milky Way, which proved to be the radiance of myriads of stars never seen by the naked eye. What seemed to Galileo his major discovery was one that began with an incorrect surmise: he thought at first (1609) that he had discovered four new planets but not much later (Jan. 7, 1610) he found them to be satellites of Jupiter. This discussion will be limited, however, to his observations on the moon, which proved very different from the smooth lustrous body shining by its own light which man observes at night. "The Moon," Galileo reported, "certainly does not possess a smooth and polished surface, but one rough and uneven, and just like the face of the Earth itself, is everywhere full of vast protuberances, deep chasms, and sinuosities." This was not entirely new, since Plutarch and other classical philosophers had presupposed such a possibility, but their theories were based at most on logic. Galileo had seen the sinuosities of the moon with his own eyes through his tube. So too he could prove, not merely conjecture, that the moon has no light of its own but shines by reflected light. Most of all, Galileo had discovered moon-spots, as later he discovered sunspots. To some extent, the spots implied change or decay from perfection, which up to the time of Galileo had been limited to the sublunary world. The "great or ancient spots" on the moon man had always known, drawing them into various patterns of "the man in the moon." But Galileo had discovered "other spots smaller in size, but so thickly scattered that they sprinkle the whole surface of the moon." From his observation Galileo concluded that the surface of the moon, like that of earth, is varied by mountains and valleys, and, indeed, for a time he thought that some spots might indicate the presence of lunar seas and lakes. Galileo later denied the existence of water on the moon, though other astronomers continued for some years to presuppose its existence, making it possible for writers of moon-voyages to imagine moon-worlds with atmosphere in which their travellers could breathe as on earth.

The new moon-maps that began to appear during the seventeenth century were engrossing to the imagination. For a time England used one nomenclature, the Continent another, both imaginative and poetic. They agreed in giving names to the lunar mountains. There might indeed be, as Fontenelle suggested in his *Plurality of Worlds* (*Entretiens sur la pluralité des mondes*, 1686) "a promontory of dreams, a sea of tears, or a sea of nectar." Others suggested that there might be a desert uninhabitable because of heat or an ocean unknown to sons of Adam. So human imagination played with the idea of a new world in the moon, as one hardy mariner after another set off on voyages of discovery.

Among the themes that entered imagination in the seventeenth century was the possibility that man might colonize the moon. The original suggestion was German, made by no less a person than Johann Kepler, according to John Wilkins' *Discourse concerning a New World* (1638). England, with true British imperialism, inevitably adopted the idea, as Wilkins shows. Indeed, one of the reasons for the advance in aeronautics during the seventeenth century was the belief that, once the principle of space-flight was discovered, the first nation to raise its flag on the moon—and later on the planets— would possess new colonies. As time went on, the moon was to be claimed by Spanish, Italian, and Dutch romancers, as well as by German and British. In the various travels that make up *Voyages to the Moon*, this author looked eagerly at illustrations to see what flag floated over the new territory. Let us turn now to some of the various imaginary journeys.

II

It seems ironic that one of the last voyages to employ the supernatural as a device for journeying to the moon should have been the work of a great scientist. Johann Kepler's *Somnium* was published posthumously in 1634, though it had been written much earlier. Kepler had hesitated to publish it during his lifetime since it contained veiled references to his mother who had been condemned as a witch and would have been executed had it not been for the heroic efforts of her son. As the title indicates, the work was in the form of a dream. The author says that while he had been reading Bohemian legends, he fell into deep sleep, and dreamed that he was reading a book on magic. The story concerns a young man named Duracotus, whose mother was a "wise woman," who supported herself and her son by selling mariners little bags of herbs containing charms. Upon one occasion when her young son pried too curiously into the bags, Fioxhilda, a woman of ungovernable temper, gave the boy to a sea-captain in place of one of the bags. Duracotus—a disguise for Kepler himself—made a voyage to Denmark with the captain. He was set ashore to deliver letters to the astronomer Tycho Brahe, with whom Kepler actually spent several years at the observatory, Uraniborg, learning the principles of astronomy. After five years Duracotus returned home to find that his mother had long repented her rashness. He discovered that she knew as much astronomy as he did, since she was in league with the "daemons of Levania," spirits of the moon, whom she could call and with whom an occasional mortal travelled to the moon.

From the daemon who appeared at his mother's summons, Duracotus learned that mortals who travelled to the moon were given a "dozing draught," so that they remembered few details of the journey. Although this still sounds like magic, it was not. Kepler was pondering the effect of gravity upon a human body as it left the "attractive power" of the earth, considering too the probable effects of rarefied air upon human physique. He considered "weightlessness," since once the daemons had lifted their passenger above the "attractive power," they needed no extra force but carried the passenger without effort.

Fantasy and realism are mingled in the first part of the *Somnium*, but when Duracotus reaches the moon, fantasy falls away and we find ourselves on the moon Galileo had seen through his tube. Seasons, length of days and nights, climates are different from anything known on earth. The moon-world is divided into two zones, "Subvolva" and "Privolva." In Privolva, "night is 15 or 16 days long, and dreadful with uninterrupted shadow." No sun or moon shines there. All is intensely cold. In Subvolva the situation is less drastic, thanks to "Volva," the moon, yet the cold is more extreme, the heat more intense than anything experienced by man in this world. The terrain is much like that of earth, but the mountains tower to heights higher than Everest, the declivities are more profound than any terrestrial Grand Canyon.

In one detail Kepler departed from Galileo, since he continued to posit atmosphere on the moon, and believed that certain forms of life were possible. There is nothing corresponding to human life in Subvolva, but there are plants and animals. Some appear at dawn, only to die at night. Others seem to bask in the hot sun, then disappear into the caverns as evening comes. The animals are of serpentine nature, like great lizards or antediluvian monsters. The *Somnium* is a dream with nightmare touches, the scale of everything on exaggerated size, the lunar terrain forbidding and the prehistoric creatures monstrous.

The influence of the *Somnium* continued well down through the nineteenth century. There are reminiscences of its moon-world in Jules Verne's *From the Earth to the Moon* (1865), although Verne's is a dead world; if ever life existed there, it was in the remote past, and is now extinct. The last specific reminiscences to be found are in H. G. Wells, *The First Men in the Moon* (1900). Wells's lunar landscape reflects Kepler's, particularly in its mingling of beauty and terror. Wells posits the existence of vegetation growing to incredible heights in a single lunar day. When Bedford and Cavor land, they think the moon lifeless, but as they watch at dawn, what had seemed to be dry sticks and pebbles prove to be seeds, showing lines of yellowish green. The arid land becomes a combination of desert and jungle, with plants and flowers growing in lush profusion. When the lunar explorers are seized and thrown into subterranean caverns, Cavor's mind goes back to his reading. "Yes," he said, "Kepler with his *subvolvani* was right after all."

The idea of a supernatural voyage continued for some time, particularly among Roman Catholic writers such as Athanasius Kircher (1601–80) an important Jesuit traveller, Egyptologist, and scientist, whose *Itinerarum exstaticum* is in the tradition. The hero Theodidactus set off with an angel guide upon a cosmic tour as part of his education, an idea which Voltaire perhaps picked up in his *Micromégas*. But the only supernatural voyage that can vie with Kepler's in literary merit is Milton's in *Paradise Lost*, in which there are Keplerian reminiscences. When a group of fallen angels set out to chart the new world into which they

have fallen (II. 570–628), they find "fierce extremes, extremes by change more fierce," heat and cold, towering mountains and caverns vaster than any known on earth, "a frozen continent . . . beat with perpetual storms . . . a gulf profound as that Serbonian bog." Here the "parching air Burns frore, and cold performs the effect of fire":

> Through many a dark and dreary vale
> They passed, and many a region dolorous,
> O'er many a frozen, many a fiery Alp,
> Rocks, caves, lakes, fens, bogs, dens, and
>   shades of death . . .
> Where all life dies, death lives, and Nature
>   breeds,
> Perverse, all monstrous, all prodigious things.

In the meantime Satan, travelling in a different direction, has met Sin and Death, and arrives at the gates of Hell (II. 629–1055; III. 540–742). When Sin opens the doors, even the intrepid Satan is momentarily appalled, but after his first amazement

> his sail-broad vans
> He spreads for flight, and, in the surging smoke
> Uplifted spurns the ground; thence many a league,
> As in a cloudy chair ascending rides
> Audacious.

Satan was surprised to find that the intervening air was "neither sea, nor good dry land," requiring him to make use of every part of his body for navigation:

> O'er bog or steep, through strait, rough,
>   dense, or rare,
> With head, hands, wings, or feet pursues
>   his way,
> And swims or sinks, or wades, or creeps,
>   or flies.

Satan's is a cosmic rather than a moon-voyage. Unlike many mariners he did not pause at the moon. He takes

> His flight precipitant, and winds with ease
> Through the pure marble air his oblique way
> Amongst innumerable stars, that shone
> Stars distant, but nigh-hand seemed other worlds.

He proceeds to the sun, where an astronomer observing him would have taken him for another of Galileo's sunspots. The world of the sun Satan found "beyond expression bright." Within the light he saw "a glorious angel stand," the archangel Uriel. From him Satan learns about the new world which God has created for man, to take the place of the fallen angels. The unsuspecting Uriel gives him directions, and Satan completes his cosmic journey by landing in

> This little world, in bigness like a star
> Of smallest magnitude, close by the moon.

III

The idea of human flight by means of birds is probably as old as the supernatural voyage. Far earlier than Britain's King Bladud, the tale is found in Babylonian literature, in the *Zend Avesta* (ca. 650 B.C.), traditionally ascribed to Zoroaster, and in other Persian literature. In Greek literature Zeus performed the abduction of Ganymede by transforming himself into an eagle. The winged horse, Pegasus, who carried Bellerophon when he aspired to heaven, is a variant. Some forms of the tale entered Europe through "Alexander legends," ascribing every kind of feat to Alexander the Great. There is a passing memory of the legend of Ganymede in Dante's *Purgatorio* and a more extended one in Chaucer's *House of Fame*. During the Renaissance these combined with travellers' tales, particularly of Marco Polo, of gigantic rocs capable of scooping up a horse and rider or an elephant. If these birds could be trained, they might transport a man to the heavens. Even in modern times, after ascents of the balloon in 1783–84, attempts were made to harness to the lighter-than-air machine eagles to direct the steering.

The theme of the possibility of a flight to the moon by harnessing birds was picked up by Francis Godwin in a romance published (posthumously) in 1638, *The Man in the Moone: or A Discourse of a Voyage thither by Domingo Gonsales,* which had a greater vogue than Kepler's *Somnium,* since between 1638 and 1768, at least twenty-five editions were published in four European languages. The first English edition seems to have been so small that the British Museum copy is unique. Because of the hero's name the tale was often thought to be Spanish. Jules Verne and Edgar Allan Poe, both of whom borrowed from it, thought the romance French. How early it was written we cannot tell: Antony à Wood thought it was in Godwin's student days at Christ Church, 1578–84, but if so it was materially revised after Galileo's description of the moon in 1610. With the *Somnium,* which had appeared four years earlier, *The Man in the Moone* established the literary genre of the moon-voyage in France and England.

This romance of a castaway voyager foreshadowed *Robinson Crusoe* and *Gulliver's Travels,* both of which drew from it. The hero, Domingo Gonsales, a Spaniard of noble parentage, had had many adventures before we meet him in the Isle of St. Hellens, where he had been put ashore with a Negro servant, Diego, a "man Friday." In the island they remained for a year, encountering no difficulty in nourishing themselves by semi-tropical fruit, vegetables grown in the rich soil, fish, and birds. Among the last, the most interesting to Domingo were "gansas" or wild swans, which

Gonsales trained to come at his signal, then to carry provisions from one end of the island to the other. Secretly hoping it would be possible to train them to carry a man, Domingo made a harness for six or seven birds, by which they carried a lamb, "whose happinesse I much envied, that he should be the first living creature" to fly. "Surprized with a great longing to cause myselfe to be carried in the like sort," harnessing still more gansas, and providing himself with a little swinging perch, he took off from the top of a rock on one side of a river, and flew to another rock on the opposite side, where his pride knew no bounds: "I hold it farre more honour to have been the first flying man, than to bee another Neptune that first adventured to sayle upon the Sea." Three months later, when he was rescued, Gonsales took with him his birds and his "Engine," and when the ship was set upon by the British, he was saved by flying his machine to land. From his landing-place Domingo set out upon an adventure he had never expected. He had, of course, no way of knowing that this was the season for hibernation among gansas, and certainly could never have guessed that they hibernate in the moon. He thought his birds were making off for the peak of Teneriffe, but higher and higher they went until Gonsales realized that they were ascending to the moon.

With Kepler, but even more clearly with Godwin, there was established what became a literary convention in moon-voyages, the description of "weightlessness." The gansas had been laboring against Domingo's weight, but "At length, O incredible thing, they forbare moving any thing at all! and yet remained unmoveable, . . . the Lines slacked; neither I, nor the Engine moved at all, but abode still, as having no manner of weight." Weariness, hunger, and thirst proved all to have been effects of gravity upon the human body. Domingo was not sure in which direction his gansas flew, "whether it were upwards, downwards, or sidelong, all was one." Looking down at the earth he had left, Domingo assured himself of the truth of the Copernican hypothesis, that it turned upon its axis: "I will not go so farre as Copernicus that maketh the Sunne the Center of the Earth, and unmoveable. . . . Only this I say, allow the Earth his motion (which these eyes of mine can testifie to be his due) and these absurdities are quite taken away." Domingo's voyage to the moon took "Eleven or Twelve daies." He estimated it as 50,000 miles, a distance only one-quarter of that computed by the best mathematicians of the day who used a figure much closer to our own. Godwin was probably following Kepler but was not aware that Kepler spoke in German terms, not in miles as the British computed them.

Godwin paid some attention to the attractive power of the moon but not as much as to that of the earth when he left it. On the twelfth day the gansas set Domingo down on a high lunar hill. Godwin's moon-world is by no means scientific as was Kepler's. It is largely fantasy. He does posit the idea that lunar objects are on a vaster scale than terrestrial, "10, 20, I thinke I may say 30 times more than ours." There are anticipations here of Swift's Brobdingnag, and indeed of the land of the Houyhnhnms, since Domingo found himself regarded by the lunarians just as Gulliver was considered a Yahoo. But in spite of its charm and occasional moments of scientific imagination, Godwin's moon-world remains largely fantasy. Gonsales spent a year on the moon, and then, his gansas beginning to droop for lack of their annual terrestrial visitation, he returned to earth, landing in China where he was to continue his adventures.

The literary influence of Godwin's tale was great. Wilkins and Fontenelle introduced it to some readers. Cyrano de Bergerac, Defoe, and Swift borrowed from it. Samuel Butler and William Congreve wrote passing satire upon it. A minor poet, Samuel Wesley, produced a variant upon it in his "Pindaric Poem on Three Skipps of a Louse." Thomas D'Urfey made it into a comic opera in his *Wonders of the Sun*, and there were many reminiscences in Elkanah Settle's *The World in the Moon* and in Aphra Behn's *Emperor of the Moon*. The tale continued to be read and referred to well into the nineteenth century by Jules Verne, Edgar Allan Poe, and others.

The influence of Kepler and Godwin merged with that of another to establish the conventions of the moon-voyage as it remained for a hundred years. In the same year as Godwin's voyage appeared the first edition of John Wilkins' *A Discourse Concerning A New World* (1638). Wilkins was no mere romancer, but a member of the Philosophical Society of Oxford, and one of the founders of the Royal Society. His *Discourse* is one of the important works in seventeenth-century popular science, its science accurate, the general style so readable that its technicalities can be readily understood by a layman. For his first edition Wilkins had used the *Somnium;* in the second he used also Godwin's romance that had appeared in the same year as his own. Kepler, Godwin, Wilkins—these were the three pioneers in the cosmic voyage.

In careful detail Wilkins discussed various problems that Kepler and Godwin had raised, paying particular attention to the distance of the moon from earth, which he estimated at 179,712 miles; the nature and extent of gravity; the nature of air and intervening space; and "weightlessness." In many ways he advanced science, though in some ways he retarded it for writers of cosmic voyages, since some eighteenth-century authors were so impressed by the *Discourse* that they failed to realize that Wilkins had written in a pre-Newtonian era, and that Newton in the *Principia* had sometimes disproved and sometimes advanced principles of astronomy and physics which Wilkins had accepted without question.

Most charming among the many engrossing passages in the *Discourse* are those on diet and sleep. How is the traveller to rest and refresh himself on his long journey? "I believe he shall scarce find any lodging by the way," Wilkins wrote, slily picking up a passage from Ben Jonson's *News from the New World* (1621): "No inns to entertain passengers, nor any castles in the air (unless they be enchanted ones) to receive poor pilgrims or errant knights." As scientist Wilkins replied to his own questions by a passage in which he discussed "weightlessness." When the body is beyond the effect of gravity, it will feel neither hunger nor weariness. But his far-ranging imagination played also with old legends of the effect of the music of the spheres, of the "aethereal air" that nourishes plants growing without soil, of men who are said to have lived on the smell of a rose, of papists like Ignatius who fasted indefinitely. It was this Wilkins who replied to Margaret Cavendish, Duchess of Newcastle—herself a fancifier—when she inquired of his cosmic voyagers: "But where, Sir, shall they be lodged, since you confess there are no inns on the way?" Dr. Wilkins is said to have replied: "Surely, Madam, you who have written so many romances will not refuse my mariners rest and refreshment—in one of your castles in the air."

Only one full-length moon-voyage by the use of birds remains from the eighteenth century, *A Voyage to Cacklogallinia* (1727), by a pseudonymous Captain Samuel Brunt, who has never been identified. It has been attributed to both Defoe and Swift, neither of which attributions is valid. It is an obvious imitation of *Gulliver's Travels,* though it differs in one important way, since this is basically an economic satire, provoked by the inflation and crash of the South Sea Bubble. As Gulliver found a land peopled by horses, Brunt found one inhabited by birds. It was also a land peopled by "projectors" who were proposing to the government every conceivable scheme for investment. Project after project, tax after tax were suggested, one more fantastic than another. Brunt proposed one that caught both popular and governmental fancy: that an expedition be sent to the moon to extract gold from the mountains in the moon and bring it back to Cacklogallinia. The journey to the moon was no problem to birds who were natural fliers. For Brunt, who was to head the convoy, they designed a palanquin, powered by lower-class birds. Upon the announcement of the project, wild speculation broke out in Cacklogallinia. Men mortgaged their houses, women offered their children for adoption in order to invest in shares. On his journey, Brunt sent back bird-messengers daily to His Majesty with reports of progress. Good reports precipitated an orgy of speculation; the lack of a report sent the market to a new low.

A certain amount of science enters the *Voyage to Cacklogallinia*, though it looks back to Wilkins rather than to Newton. There is talk of the thinness of the air on the top of a mountain from which the caravan set out and the use of "humected sponges"—reminiscent of Kepler—which Brunt used for himself as the palanquin took off through the orb of gravity. Brunt pays some attention to "weightlessness" which he experiences once he passes the orb of gravity of the earth. In less than an hour the bird-leader comes to the palanquin to inform Brunt that he may now get out, since for a quarter-hour the bird-pilots have not felt his weight. Dismounting, Brunt found himself in a new world in which weight did not exist, where he could "with as much Ease lift a Palanquin of Provisions . . . as I could on our Globe raise a Feather."

The world on Brunt's moon is more like a comic opera than like Kepler's science, and will not be discussed here. The lunarians proved idealists with no material desires. They are an Englishman's reply to an England that had gone mad over gambling, forgetting eternal values. The lunarians did not want an Englishman in the moon, and Captain Brunt returned to earth, carefully steering his way to arrive in Jamaica rather than in England, and sending back his pilot to face in Cacklogallinia the bursting of the South Sea Bubble.

IV

The supernatural voyage and flight by harnessing birds remained literary conventions. During the seventeenth and eighteenth centuries, men devoted their efforts to the possibility of inventing artificial wings or a flying-machine for man. There is a tale—accepted by some historians, denied by others—that in the sixteenth century Giovanni Battista Danti attempted to fly over the lake of Trasimeno by the use of artificial wings, one of which failed him so that he fell on a roof and was seriously injured. The influence of Leonardo's careful study of birds' wings and their principle of flight lay behind many of the early attempts at artificial wings. Wings of potential fliers expanded until those of early ones came to seem absurd: e.g., Daedalus and Icarus or King Bladud attempting to soar on tiny wings attached only to the shoulders. Wings expanded and imagination expanded with them. Wilkins in various editions of his works pointed out the fallacy of thinking of wings as attached only to the arms, by means of which men could fly no further than domestic fowl. He advocated that, to the efforts of arms, be added "the labours of the feet," so that a man might swim through the air as now through water. The Ancients and the Moderns disputed learnedly about the possibility of human flight. Joseph Glanvill wrote in his *Vanity of Dogmatizing* (1661): "It may be some Ages hence, a voyage to the Southern unknown Tracts, yea possibly to the Moon, will not be more strange than one to America. To them that come after us, it may be as ordinary to buy a pair of wings to fly into remotest Regions, as now a pair of Boots to ride a Journey."

Whatever the facts about Danti's flight, there is no question that in 1679 a French smith named Besnier achieved a flight across a river by means of four folding wings transversely fastened to both arms and legs. Attested by the *Journal des Sçavans*, the contrivance was also described in the *Philosophical Transactions of the Royal Society*, before whose members Robert Hooke and Christopher Wren reported their own findings in experiments about flying.

So engrossing had the theme of human flight become that eighteenth-century literature is full of it. Addison and Steele had their fun with it in the *Guardian* for July 20, 1713: "The philosophers of King Charles' reign were busy in finding out the art of flying. . . . The humour so prevailed among the virtuosos of this reign, that they were actually making parties to go up to the moon together." In the same number was a pseudonymous letter from "Daedalus," who asserted that he had made considerable progress in the art of flying. "I flutter about my room two or three hours in a morning, and when my wings are on, can go above an hundred yards at a hop, step, and jump." On the next holiday he intends to sit astride the dragon on Bow steeple, from whence he will fly over Fleet Street to the maypole in the Strand. He plans to take out a patent for making wings so that none can make them but himself. He looks forward to a glorious future for England in a new era of air-travel, far superior to an age of coaches or packet-boats. But the editor, "Mr. Ironside," was outraged and declared that he would use every effort to discourage flying in his time. Consider what would happen to morals: "You should have a couple of lovers make a midnight assignation upon the top of the monument, and see the cupola of St. Paul's covered with both sexes like the outside of a pigeon-house." "Mr. Ironside" seems to have taken his point of departure from a Latin poem *In artem volandi* written by Francis Harding in 1692, in which the poet shook his head over the enthusiasm for human flight. What will happen in this insane new world? Will laborers fly to and from their work on artificial wings? Let the husband beware and strengthen the bolts on

529

his doors and windows, lest a new type of adulterer enter his wife's chamber on wings.

Among the many vanities of human wishes, Samuel Johnson satirized man's desire for wings in his "Dissertation on the Art of Flying," the sixth chapter of *Rasselas* (1759). On a visit Rasselas found a mechanically-minded man busily engaged in making artificial wings on the model of a bat's. With them he planned to fly, possibly even into space. To him the advantages of human flight would far offset its dangers. An ironic belief it proved to be since, when the wings were made, the mechanic took off—as usual from a hill. "He waved his pinions awhile to gather air, then leaped from his stand, and in an instant dropped into the lake. His wings, which were of no use in the air, sustained him in the water, and the prince drew him to land, half dead with terror and vexation."

But although artificial wings produced much satire and some attractive romances, they were not to take human beings on cosmic voyages. For that man needed what John Wilkins called a "flying-chariot." "I do seriously and upon good ground" he wrote in his *Discovery of a New World*, "affirm it possible to make a flying-chariot; in which a man may sit, and give such motion unto it, as shall convey him through the air. And this perhaps might be made large enough to carry divers men at the same time, together with food for their *viaticum*, and commodities for traffic."

Such a simple device as the kite—still a novelty in England in the early seventeenth century—played some part in the history of aviation, as did the elaborate fireworks of the period. But it is better not to pause over them but to turn to the brilliant satires on aviation of Cyrano de Bergerac, two of which involve flying-chariots. Cyrano was a satirist but his satire on this particular theme was as good as it was because—friend of Pierre Gassendi and Jacques Rohault—he was well versed in contemporary science. His *Histoire comique des estats et empires de la lune* (1656) included his first two attempts to reach the moon. The first is quite different from anything we have seen in the pseudo-scientific literature of the seventeenth and eighteenth centuries. The sun, said Cyrano, sucks up dew. If he fastened about himself vials of dew, would he not be sucked up? In contemporary illustrations we see him with his dew-vials, "a great many Glasses full of Dew, tied fast about me; upon which the Sun so violently darted his Rays, that the Heat, which attracted them, as it does the thickest Clouds, carried me up so high, that at length I found myself above the middle Region of the Air." So strong was the power of attraction and so rapidly did he rise that Cyrano began to break some vials in an effort to adjust gravity and attraction. In the space of a few hours he made a landing in a world

in which he found that the natives spoke French. The earth had turned on its axis and Cyrano was in French Canada.

Not caring for either the accent or the manners of the French Canadians, Cyrano occupied himself by building a flying-ship for the lunar voyage he still intended to make. He has told us little about the vessel except that it had wings and some form of spring. His first attempt was a failure. "I placed myself within and from the Top of a Rock, threw myself in the Air. But because I had not taken my measures aright, I fell with a sosh into the Valley below. Bruised as I was, however, I returned to my Chamber, and with Beef-Marrow I anointed my Body, so I was all over mortified from Head to Foot." Returning to his flying-chariot, Cyrano discovered a group of soldiers fastening to it bunches of firecrackers. His invention in peril, Cyrano plucked the match a soldier was lighting out of his hand "and in great Rage threw myself into my Machine . . . but I came too late, for hardly were both my Feet within, then whip, away went I up in a Cloud." Unwittingly Cyrano became the first imaginary voyager to reach the moon by rocket. It seems strange that, familiar as our seventeenth-century ancestors were with gunpowder and firecrackers, no other writer employed such form of propulsion before the eighteenth century, and then only two of them, neither well known in our time. On flew Cyrano, his machine rising higher and higher, until "all the combustible Matter being spent," speed slackened and the chariot fell beneath him, descending to earth. Cyrano himself continued to mount. He had an explanation: his body was covered with the marrow he had daubed on his bruises; "I knew that the Moon being then in the Wain, and that it being usual for her in that Quarter, to suck up the Marrow of Animals; she drank up that wherewith I was anointed." Three-quarters of the way to the moon, Cyrano found himself making a somersault dive, a device in which various later writers followed him. Peering between his legs, he looked back on earth which "appeared to me like a large Holland-Cheese gilded." On he went until he felt the attractive power of the moon's gravity, which caused him to make a crash landing in a tree. He recovered consciousness to find himself in a new Garden of Eden, "my face plaistered with an Apple."

Cyrano's moon-world was no such telescopic one as Kepler's. There are reminiscences of Godwin so that it is no surprise to meet Domingo Gonsales, who became Cyrano's lunar guide. In other ways Cyrano's lunar adventures are very different from Domingo's, with reminiscences of literature from Lucian to Rabelais and many fantastic adventures. The most amusing section is that in which the "philosophers" attempt to discover by logic and science whether Cyrano is or is not a human being, leading to Cyrano's trial for heresy, because he, who on earth had attempted to prove to his friends that the moon is inhabited, now tries to persuade the lunarians that their moon is our world and inhabited.

Curiously enough, although the lunarians are scientifically in advance of terrestrial beings and know much about the possibilities of flight, they do not send Cyrano home in a flying chariot. Momentarily we return to the theme of the supernatural voyage, when an attendant spirit rose like a whirlwind, and holding Cyrano in his arms, descended with him to earth in a day and a half. As on his arrival in the moon, so on his return to earth Cyrano suffered a brief period of unconsciousness, so that he had no clear memory of his arrival or the departure of his guide. But his memories of the moon-world remained vivid and he spent so much of his time trying to prove to his terrestrial friends that there were men in the moon that he was imprisoned for heresy.

There had been talk among the lunarians of their inventing a flying-machine that would carry three or four of them. Perhaps it was from them that Cyrano picked up details for the elaborate flying-chariot in which he made his voyage to the sun. This machine operated in part upon the principle of a burning glass:

It was a large, very light Box, that shut tight and close: of about six Foot high, and three Foot Square. This Box had a hole in it below; and over the Cover, which had likewise a hole in it, I placed a Vessel of Christal, bored through in the same manner, made in a Globular Figure, but very large, the Orifice whereof joyn'd exactly to and was enchaced, in the hole I had made in the head.

The Vessel was purposely made with many Angles, and in form of an Icosaedron, to the end that every Facet being convex and concave, my Boul might produce the effect of a Burning-Glass . . . It shut so close, that a grain of Air could not enter it, except by the two openings; and I had placed a little very light Board within for my self to sit upon.

As Cyrano rose from the tower of his prison, he further explained the machine:

When the Sun breaking out from under the Clouds, began to shine upon my Machine, that transparent Icosaedron, which through its Facets received the Treasures of the Sun, diffused by it's Orifice the light of them into my Cell . . . I foresaw very well, that the Vacuity that would happen in the Icosaedron, by reason of the Sun-beams, united by the concave Glasses, would, to fill up the space, attract a great abundance of Air, whereby my Box would be carried up; and that proportionable as I mounted, the rushing wind that should force it through the Hole, could not rise to the roof, but that furiously penetrating the Machine, it must needs force it upon high.

Cyrano had designed a sail for his ship but found it useless because of the force of wind he encountered as he ascended into the air. He had intended the machine for his escape from prison, planning, at least temporarily, to land elsewhere in France. But his vessel rose rapidly to the "Middle Region" of the air, then continued on a journey that was to take Cyrano to the sun. Again, he did not experience hunger or thirst. This, he suggested, might have been due to the lack of gravity, but also to the bottle of spirits he always carried, which seems to have been a perennial fountain of youth since it lasted him all the way. In four months he had approached only the outermost of "those little Earths that wheel about the Sun." It was nearly two years before he reached the sun. So human imagination was expanding with the expansion of space. He experienced neither weariness nor tedium as he studied the "new astronomy" at first hand. This time he bypassed the moon, his mind set upon the planets, other worlds, often with little worlds of satellites around them. "And therefore Mercury, Venus, the Earth, Mars, Jupiter, and Saturn, have been constrained to whirligig it, and move both at once around the Sun." As on his voyage to the moon, he ultimately lost his flying-chariot, which fell to earth, to be used by another mariner. According to his own cryptic statement, he continued his journey by "an ardour of Will." At the end of twenty-two months he arrived at the sun, so luminous that it looked "like flakes of burning snow." There we may leave this most amusing of cosmic voyagers, as he, like Milton's Satan, perhaps became another sunspot to be observed by a terrestrial astronomer.

In that extraordinary age of the seventeenth century, truth often proved as strange as fiction. Kepler, Godwin, Cyrano, and other mariners stimulated imagination with their tales of moon-flight, and Wilkins appealed to both literary and scientific imagination. But the most important stimulus to the history of aeronautics in the century occurred in 1670 when Francesco Lana, an Italian scientist, published his *Prodromo*, with a description and design of an airship. Although the vessel never flew, it marked a milestone in the history of aviation. Its principle is so simple that even a layman can readily understand it. It consisted of "a wooden car . . . fashioned like a boat," a canoe-shaped vessel. It had a sail and oars. Lana was aware of all the scientific work that had been done on the nature of air, which had been shown to be much like water. "It has weight owing to the vapours and halations which ascend from the earth and seas to a height of many miles and surround the whole of our terraqueous globe." As a boat is rowed against the resistance of water, Lana's boat was to be rowed against the resistance of air. The novelty of the airship lay

531

not in the sail and oars but in four evacuated globes attached to the boat by four ropes of equal length. The principle of the vacuum is familiar to laymen. By Lana's time philosophers no longer feared the *horror vacui*, the idea accepted for centuries that Nature abhors a vacuum. The Torricellian barometer of 1643, Otto van Guericke's air-pump of 1650, and the work of Francesco de Mendoza, Gaspar Schott, and Robert Boyle on specific gravity had put an end to the long "horror." Lana acknowledged his debt to all of these.

It soon became clear to the continental and British scientists who discussed the invention that, while a toy-model might fly, if the evacuated globes of glass, cooper, or any other thin metal Lana presupposed were increased to a size necessary to carry a man or men, they would be crushed under atmospheric pressure. Before man could hope to fly in an airship of this kind still more scientific work must be done on the nature of air. Robert Boyle, England's most important worker in the field, was close to making the discovery made later by Henry Cavendish (1731–1810), when he noted the effect of heat in causing the expansion of air. "It was experiments such as this," says J. E. Hodgson in his history of aeronautics, "that led to the assertion, met with after the invention of the balloon, that Boyle's investigation on the weight of the air gave birth to the new discoveries of Montgolfier." Mr. Hodgson suggests, too, how close John Clayton was to a solution of the problem when in 1739 he experimented with "spirit of coal," filling thick bladders with gas. But the discovery of hydrogen remained for Cavendish in 1766. The ascent of the first balloon of the Brothers Joseph and Étienne Montgolfier in 1783 resulted in disaster, but later that year a safe ascent was made near the Palace of Versailles. The balloon carried as passengers a cock, a hen, and a descendant of the "happy lamb" of Domingo Gonsales.

From the history of aviation, let us return momentarily to Francesco Lana and his little canoe. Scientifically Lana was an optimist who believed that he had solved the problem of human flight. But as a son of the Church, he did not believe that man would ever fly. "Other difficulties I do not see that could prevail against this invention, *save one only, which to me seems the greatest of them all, and that is that God would never surely allow such a machine to be successful.*"

The "benefit and use of man"—so Francis Bacon, one of the founders of science, optimistically anticipated its future. Francesco Lana was a scientist, but it was he who most clearly pointed out the dangers of aviation—then in its seminal stage—in his *Prodromo:*

Where is the man who can fail to see that no city would be proof against surprise, as the ship could at any time be steered over its squares, or even over the courtyards of dwelling-houses, and brought to earth for the landing of its crew? And in the case of ships that sail the seas, by allowing the aerial ship to descend from the high air to the level of their sails, their cordage would be cut, or even without descending so low iron weights could be hurled to wreck the ships and kill their crews, or they could be set on fire by fireballs and bombs; not ships alone, but houses, fortresses, and cities could be thus destroyed.

So the seventeenth-century inventor anticipated the possible destruction of civilization through the invention of flying-machines.

The literary influence of Lana's *Prodromo* was continental rather than English. With the addition of two more evacuated balls, mariners made a cosmic voyage to the moon and all the planets on the appearance in 1744 of Eberhard Kindermann's *Die Geschwinde Reise auf dem Lufft-schiff nach der obern Welt* ("Fast trip on an airship to the heavens"). In 1768 Lana's little ship was used by his countryman, Bernard Zamagna, in a Latin epic poem, *Navis aeria*, which described the first air-flight around the world. A variant of the canoe was proposed in Portugal by Bartholomeu Lourenco de Gusmão, the "Passarola." Motivated in large part by two amber balls operated by magnetism, a small model is said to have flown in a royal hall on August 8, 1709. Lana's and Gusmão's ships were combined in a long poem, *Gli Occhi di Gesú* ("The Eyes of Jesus" [1707]), in which Pier Jacopo Martello described a voyage to the Earthly Paradise under the guidance of the prophet Elijah. When we have a close view, as the airship draws near the world in the moon, we discover that the crew consists of one hundred apes, some dressed in blue, some in yellow, harnessed to each other and the boat by collars of thin metal.

Flying-machines in the imaginary voyage in England grew larger and larger until they were capable of carrying groups of men, in one case a whole race of people. Two such voyages were written by well-known men of letters, Daniel Defoe and Jonathan Swift. Defoe played with the theme of flight several times in 1705. His full-length use was in the *Consolidator*, in which Chinese men and lunarians plied between the earth and the moon. The work is strongly marked by the *chinoiserie* which was becoming important in English art, landscape gardening, and interior decoration. Defoe seems to shrug his shoulders at such tyros as Wilkins, Godwin, and other "moderns." He went back to the idea of China's excelling in aviation early in recorded history. In the libraries in China, he declares, there was a record of a man born in the moon, who had made a journey to earth to instruct the Chinese in the lore of lunar regions. Defoe's chief attention was upon an elaborate flying-machine, "a Consolidator":

. . . a certain Engine, in the shape of a Chariot, on the backs of two vast Bodies with extended Wings, which spread about fifty yards in breadth, composed of Feathers so nicely put together, that no air could pass; and as the Bodies were made of lunar Earth, which would bear the Fire, the Cavities were filled with an ambient Flame, which fed on a certain Spirit, deposited in proper quantity to last out the Voyage; and this Fire so ordered as to move about such springs and wheels as kept the wings in most exact and regular Motion, always ascendant.

Defoe's source for his happy anticipation of the gasoline age, in his "ambient Flame" which was fed by a fluid deposited in sufficient quantity to last a journey, is unknown. Actually he himself was less interested in that than in the "513 Feathers" of which his vessel was composed and which he describes in more detail, five hundred and twelve of them matched in length and breadth, one a "presiding or superintendent Feather, to guide, regulate, and pilot the whole Body . . . the rudder of the whole Machine," which probably symbolized the Prime Minister, Lords, and Commons who flew the ship of state.

In the room of this great flying Chariot, which plied between China and the moon, Defoe placed a European who remembered little of his journey, since Defoe went back to the use of anaesthesia suggested by Kepler, a "dozing Draught" administered to the traveller. He found the lunar world far in advance of ours, particularly in the invention of various kinds of glasses, including telescopes more powerful than our modern ones at Mount Wilson or Palomar. Through these the lunarians could clearly see the towers and cities of China. Defoe's lunar voyager summarizes his conversation with a man in the moon by saying: "He was *the Man in the Moon* to me, and I was *the Man in the Moon* to him; he wrote down what I said, and made a Book of it, and call'd it, *News from the World in the Moon*."

In his third adventure, *The Voyage to Laputa*, Gulliver looked up to see "a vast opaque body between me and the sun," moving forward toward the island. Through his pocket-perspective the captain was able to see numbers of people, though only later did he know what they were doing. When the body descended, Gulliver went aboard to find this a little world, inhabited by a whole race of men. Here is one of the most brilliant variations upon the theme of the cosmic voyage. For many years Mahomet had gone to the mountain; now the moon-world descends to Mahomet. When Gulliver had opportunity to study the little world more carefully he found it "exactly circular, its diameter 7837 yards or about four miles and a half," its bottom a plate of adamant "shooting up to the height of about two hundred yards. . . . Above

it lie the several minerals in their usual order." Adamant was considered in Swift's time the most magnetic of minerals, but it alone was not responsible for the path taken by the Flying Island. In the Astronomer's Cave in the heart of the island Gulliver was shown "a loadstone of prodigious size," by means of which the island is made to rise and fall and move from one place to another. One of its sides has attractive, the other repulsive power.

It has been shown (Mohler and Nicolson, 1937) that Swift's loadstone was a magnification of William Gilbert's famous dipping needle. As in the voyages to Lilliput and Brobdingnag, Swift readily changed feet to inches and inches to feet to keep his proportions exact. Swift had visited the Royal Society where he would have seen the Gilbertian terrella described in the catalogue as "an orbicular loadstone, about four inches and $\frac{1}{2}$ in Diameter." From it he created his "little world" of the Flying Island, "four and one half *miles* in diameter." If in Swift's "its diameter 7837 yards," we substitute "miles" for "yards" we find the approximate diameter of our own earth. It is not mere coincidence that the measurements agree so closely with those given by Isaac Newton and G. D. Cassini. The slight variation of nine miles between Swift's figure and Newton's may easily be explained: Swift slyly split the difference between Newton's average and least diameters of the world, which happens to work out at exactly 7837 miles.

The Flying Island of Laputa did not fly free or wild: it was governed by the mainland of Balnibarbi below, as is shown by the map which charts its course. William Gilbert (1540–1603) had pointed out that islands are more magnetic than seas. So the little world rose or fell, governed by the magnetic attraction of Balnibarbi. The great world and the lesser obeyed natural law. Each was dependent on the other. By physical laws man knows but cannot control, microcosm and macrocosm are combined: the terrella is "prodigious" as a magnet, yet it is a small power to govern the Flying Island. The island in turn is a macrocosm when compared to the loadstone, but it is a microcosm in comparison with Balnibarbi, which it governs in the sense that it had the power to shut out light and rain from the country below. In this voyage, unlike the others of *Gulliver's Travels* the author has considered less relationships between men than relationships in the Newtonian universe: planets, stars, or feathers observe the universal laws of motion and attraction. Swift's Flying Island is unique in the history of pseudoscience, since it carried a whole nation of men, and unique in its plausibility of motivation by the principle of terrestrial magnetism.

Swift was in part satirizing the engrossment of his

contemporaries in the idea of a world in the moon. Voltaire's *Micromégas* (1752) is the most satirical of all cosmic voyages. As the moon-world came to Gulliver in the *Voyage to Laputa*, so an inhabitant of Sirius came to earth in *Micromégas*. The circumference of Sirius, we learn, is 21,600,000 times that of earth; the hero of the tale is 120,000 royal feet in height. Micromégas had been well educated. He was an expert in telescopic and microscopic observations, on the basis of which he had written a book which was suspected of being heretical, since it suggested the existence of inhabitants in other worlds than his. For this he was exiled from Sirius for eight hundred years, a short period in his long life. He decided to spend the time in making a tour of the universe to discover at firsthand how much of his hypothesis of life in other worlds would prove true.

Micromégas needed neither wings nor a flying chariot. Over the Milky Way he merely stepped from one star to another. He was disappointed in the planet Saturn which seemed little more than an anthill to him. He remained there, however, for some time, having struck up an acquaintance with the Secretary of the Grand Academy. As the result of a protracted argument on the question of life in other planets, the Sirian and Saturnian undertook a cosmic journey. They leaped upon the ring of Saturn, then from one of its moons to another. A comet passed, by means of which they arrived at the satellites of Jupiter from which they could readily jump to the planet itself. On they went to Mars, which they found so insignificant that after a glance or two they passed by.

Why they bothered to stop at Earth—a most inferior planet—is not entirely clear, but stop they did, and gave themselves exercise circumambulating the globe which for a time they believed not only insignificant but unpopulated, since the Sirian and the Saturnian could not see the insignificant earth-dwellers. Except for an accident they would not have known of our existence. Micromégas happened to break his diamond necklace and amused himself by using one diamond as a microscope. On the ocean—a mere puddle to the travellers—they saw what seemed an aquatic animal, which proved to be a ship filled with scientists who were returning from an exploration of one of the poles. Reluctantly the travellers were forced to conclude that the tiny creatures had sense and also reason, when one of them computed the measurements of the Sirian by the method used on earth for computing the height of lunar mountains. They further astounded the visitors by informing them of the existence in their world of animalcules as invisible to them as they had been to their temporary guests.

Voltaire laughed, but even his laughter could not destroy the cosmic voyage, which continued on its way in the nineteenth century in the hands of Jules Verne, Edgar Allan Poe, and others. One of the most brilliant variations upon it was by the Danish dramatist and historian Ludwig Holberg (1684–1754) who wrote—originally in Latin—a world-classic. There are at least fifty-nine editions in eleven languages of the adventures of Nils Klim in *Iter subterraneum novam* (1741; published in English as *Niels Klim's Subterranean Journey,* 1742), his voyage to the center of the earth. As cosmic mariners had taken off from earth to discover a new world in the moon, Nils, in his enthusiasm to explore a Danish mountain, fell into its crater to find a new world in the center of the earth. Down the crater he fell until the attraction of the world drew him into its orbit, and Nils became for a time a satellite. He occupied himself with a round biscuit he took from his pocket but finding it nauseous—like other cosmic mariners he experienced neither hunger nor thirst—he threw it away to find that, as he described a circle around the earth, the biscuit described a circle around him. Around they went, Nils and biscuit, to learn later that astronomers in the world in the center of the earth had plotted the period of a new satellite, or—some said, since Nils' mountain-rope had fallen with him—a comet with a tail. Although we have English translations of the *Iter subterraneum novam*, we have none worthy of the Latin or Danish original. But we do have the finest imitation—*Alice in Wonderland*.

During the twentieth century the moon-voyage turned from the "imaginary voyage" to settle into a pattern of "science fiction." The literary career of H. G. Wells suggests something of a change that was occurring. His twentieth-century novels were to deal largely with social reform; during the last decade of the nineteenth, he wrote such pseudo-scientific works as *The Time Machine* (1895), *The Invisible Man* (1897), *The War of the Worlds* (1898). In 1938 Orson Welles startled and terrified large segments of the United States by a radio version of that last-named work of H. G. Wells, and was widely believed to be reporting an invasion from Mars. It is doubtful that any radio or television version of such a pseudo-scientific work could today startle many Americans, who seem to have drawn in scientific fiction with their mothers' milk. But even the most blasé readers and auditors remained close to their radios and televisions during the period which came to its climax on July 21, 1969, when the first two human beings landed on the moon.

BIBLIOGRAPHY

Samuel Brunt, (pseud.) *A Voyage to Cacklogallinia: With a Description of the Religion, Policy, Customs and Manners of that Country* (London, 1727). Cyrano de Bergerac, *His-*

toire comique des Estats et Empires de la lune (Paris, 1656; seven other editions 1659–87). Quotations in this article are largely from *The Comical History of the States and Empires of the Worlds of the Moon and Sun . . . newly Englished by A. Lovell* (London, 1687). Daniel Defoe, *The Consolidator: or Memoirs and Sundry Transactions from the World in the Moon* (London, 1705). Bernard de Fontenelle, *Entretiens sur la pluralité des mondes* (Paris, 1686). Galileo Galilei, *Sidereus Nuncius* (Venetiis, 1610). Quotations in the text are from *The Sidereal Messenger of Galileo Galilei*, ed. E. S. Carlos (London, 1880). Francis Godwin, *The Man in the Moone: or a Discourse of a Voyage thither. By Domingo Gonsales, The Speedy Messenger* (London, 1638). Francis Harding, "In artem volandi," *Musarum anglicanarum analecta*, (Oxford, 1692), I, 77–81. Ludwig Holberg, *Nicolai Klimii iter subterraneum novam telluris theoriam* (Hafniae and Lipsiae, 1741). Quotations are from *A Journey to the World Underground. By Nicholaus Klimnius* (London, 1742). Samuel Johnson, *The Prince of Abissinia. A Tale in Two Volumes* (London, 1759), the first edition of *Rasselas*. See also J. E. Hodgson, *Doctor Johnson on Ballooning and Flight* (London, 1925). Johann Kepler, *Joh. Keppleri mathematici olim imperatorii somnium seu opus posthumus de astronomia lunari* (Francofurti, 1634). Also in *Joannis Kepleri astronomi opera omnia*, Vol. VIII (Francofurti, 1858–71). Eberhard Christian Kindermann, *Die Geschwinde Reise auf dem Lufft-Schiff nach der obern Welt* (1744). Athanasius Kircher, *Itinerarium exstaticum quo mundi opificium, id est, coelestis expansi* (Romae, 1656). Francesco Lana, *Prodromo overo saggio di alcune inventioni nuove premesso all' Arte Maestra* (Brescia, 1670). There is a modern translation in *Aeronautical Classics*, No. 4 (London, 1910). John Milton, *Paradise Lost* (1667, 1674), *The Poems of John Milton*, ed. J. H. Hanford (New York, 1953). Jonathan Swift, *Travels into Several Remote Nations of the World. In Four Parts. By Lemuel Gulliver* (London, 1726). François Marie Arouet de Voltaire, *Le Micromégas de M. De Voltaire* (London, 1752). Quotations are from the English translation in *The Works of Voltaire, with notes by Tobias Smollett*, Vol. III. (London, 1901). John Wilkins, *A Discourse Concerning a New World and Another Planet* (London, 1638). The work is often called *The Discovery of a New World*, the title of the first book. Bernard Zamagna, *Navis aeria et elegiarum monobiblos* (Roma, 1768); republished with an English translation by Mary B. McElwain, *Smith College Classical Studies*, No. 12 (Northampton, 1939).

Secondary Bibliography. J. E. Hodgson, *The History of Aeronautics in Great Britain from the Earliest Times to the Latter Half of the Nineteenth Century* (London, 1924). Aldous Huxley, *Literature and Science* (London, 1963). Francis Johnson, *Astronomical Thought in Renaissance England* (Baltimore, 1937). Alexandre Koyré, *From the Closed World to the Infinite Universe* (New York, 1958). T. S. Kuhn, *The Copernican Revolution* (Cambridge, 1957). Marjorie Nicolson, *Voyages to the Moon* (New York, 1948; reprint, 1960); idem, *Science and Imagination* (Ithaca, 1956); idem, *The Breaking of the Circle* (New York, 1960); idem, with Nora M. Mohler, "Swift's 'Flying Island' in the 'Voyage to Laputa,'" *Annals of Science*, **2** (October, 1937), 405–30.

H. H. Rhys, ed., *Seventeenth Century Science and the Arts* (Princeton, 1961). Alfred North Whitehead, *Science and the Modern World* (New York, 1926; Cambridge, 1938; many reprints).

MARJORIE HOPE NICOLSON

[See also **Cosmic Images; Cosmology;** Macrocosm and Microcosm; **Myth;** Newton . . .; Optics.]

COSMOLOGY FROM ANTIQUITY TO 1850

COSMOLOGY as the endeavor to understand the motions of the heavenly bodies may well have begun with our earliest ancestors. In their unceasing efforts to feed on other animals, and to avoid being themselves devoured in turn, they found it advantageous to familiarize themselves with the habits of their prey and predators. It was important to know whether these beasts prowled by day and slept at night, or the reverse. Such knowledge could spell the difference between life and death for man the hunter and hunted. For this as well as other reasons he was sternly driven to note carefully the alternating cycle of day and night, thereby acquiring his first rudimentary concept of the cosmos in action.

The light that came down to him at night fluctuated far more conspicuously than daylight. As a cosmic body, the moon shone bright and full on certain nights, whereas on others it disappeared altogether. Between these extremes it displayed a recurring sequence of changing visible shapes, expanding steadily from the thin sliver of its crescent to the full roundness of its circular disk, and then shrinking in the opposite order until it vanished again from view. This striking series of lunar phases, constituting the synodic month, offered man another basic cosmological idea. It also provided him with a second unit of time as the measurement of cosmic motion. For longer periods the month was more useful than the day, which was reckoned as the interval between successive risings, culminations, or settings of the sun, moon, or stars.

The dark portion of such a day was discovered to vary in length. The months during which the nights lasted longer manifestly coincided with a distinguishable aspect in the life cycle of edible plants and animals. Comprehension of the revolving seasons, with their alternating warmth and cold, rainfall and drought, storms and fair weather, further aided mankind to survive and multiply by enlarging the food supply derived from agriculture, fishing, and hunting. The accompanying variations in the observed motions of the sun, mounting higher or lower at noon, shining a longer or shorter time on any given day, rising and setting at shifting points on the horizon, provided the basis for the year as man's third chronological tool in carving out for himself a more secure place in the cosmos. The calendar in any of its divergent forms was an invaluable achievement of early cosmological thought.

After being invisible for a considerable number of nights, a bright star would reappear briefly at dawn and then fade out of sight in the more brilliant light of the sun. But every morning following this heliacal rising, the star emerged from the eastern horizon earlier and earlier. The heliacal rising of Sirius, the most conspicuous star in Egypt, coincided with the start of the Nile's annual flood, on which the livelihood of that mainly agricultural country depended. Ten days after Sirius' heliacal rising, another notable star repeated its performance. Three such individual stars, or readily recognizable clusters of stars, were grouped together to form a month, and three sets of four months each constituted a fairly close approximation to a solar year. But the principal purpose of these thirty-six decans, or ten-day groups of stars, was to tell the time by night. Such a diagonally arranged star clock was employed in Egypt by 2500 B.C. For daylight a shadow clock was used a millennium later. The end of the shadow cast by an upright cross-piece on a horizontal beam reached a series of parallel marks indicating the principal divisions of the day.

The sun, like the other cosmic bodies and forces of nature, was manifestly much stronger than man's limited physique. Accordingly his unlimited mind imagined various divinities, which he proceeded to identify with the natural powers. Thus the ancient Egyptians sometimes conceived the sky to be the goddess Nut, whose enormously elongated body overarched the earth, the tips of her fingers touching the horizon at one side while her toes rested on the other side. Additional support was provided in the middle of her torso by the upstretched arms of her father Shu, the god of the air, who stood erect with both his feet firmly planted on the solid earth. As the sun or god Re set, he was swallowed by Nut's mouth in the west. During the night he was hidden while passing through Nut's body, from whose feet he reemerged the following morning in the east. Alternatively, he traveled in his night barge through the dark underworld (Dwat), which extended beneath the earth. The next morning, on terminating his subterranean sojourn, he transferred to his day boat.

Re's night barge could traverse Dwat because a great river ran through the netherworld. In Egyptian cosmo-

logical thought, the whole universe originated from water. In a valley inundated each year by the Nile's flood, the dry land, which emerged when the waters subsided, naturally suggested itself as a model for the imaginary creation of the cosmos. In the beginning there was nothing but the unlit abyss (Nun). From this primeval slime arose a hill, on which the god Atum created himself first, and then by masturbation generated a pair of divinities. From their sexual union the rest of creation proceeded stage by stage. Rival versions of this account were developed in religious centers which claimed primacy for the local divinity. No single hierarchical organization was strong enough to suppress competing dogmas. Later recensions tended to subsume their predecessors by absorbing the essential content and reducing it to a secondary level. As a result of these conflicting sacerdotal ambitions, Egypt developed divergent and mutually inconsistent cosmogonical schemes rather than a single unified view.

In Mesopotamia the Tigris and Euphrates rivers continually poured their fresh water into the salty brine of the Persian Gulf. Accordingly, for the local population the cosmos commenced with a mingling of salt water and sweet. These two forms of prime matter were personified as male and female divinities, from whose union sprang the rest of creation.

Similarly, in the Hebrew Bible the primordial substance was water, from which the dry land earth appeared. However, before the sun was created as the greater light to rule the day, and the moon as the lesser light to rule the night, the light of day was divided from the darkness of night. This unexplained pre-solar light, contrasted with utter darkness, recalls the dualistic Iranian conception of brilliant light and endless darkness as the twin primeval forces locked in ceaseless combat for control of the cosmos.

An alternative, and presumably earlier, cosmogony in the Hebrew Scriptures is affected by a physiographical environment vastly different from irrigational agriculture, with its abundant and sometimes excessive supply of water. Here the primordial substance is dry earth without vegetation, since there had not yet been any rain. The cosmic features mentioned in this creation story do not include the sea, nor are fish listed among the species brought to life.

The Hebrews rejected astronomical observations, systematically performed by "measurers of the heavens and stargazers who prognosticate each month what shall be." The exiled prophet's scornful condemnation of predictions based on recorded first visibilities of the lunar crescent was aimed at his Babylonian conquerors. They had long watched the western sky after sunset to note precisely when the moon emerged from complete obscuration during its conjunction with the sun, the phase in which it rose and set nearly simultaneously with the sun. When the new lunar crescent was seen thereafter for the first time, the month was officially declared to have begun. The number of whole days between any two such successive occurrences was either twenty-nine or thirty. To know in advance which of these two lengths of the lunation was applicable to any particular synodic month was the chief purpose of the Babylonian observers. In their unremitting efforts to solve this baffling problem they found it necessary to "measure the heavens," that is, to determine the angular distance between two cosmic bodies. By contrast, no such measurement of angular separation is found in indigenous Egyptian documents. Instead, there the observer is depicted facing an immobile, seated collaborator (or a life-size model of him) and identifying the stars near their culmination with reference to his right elbow, left eye, or other bodily feature.

In Mesopotamia the stars were used as reference points to locate the moon when, having passed beyond its crescent phase each month, it set later and later than the sun. Three stars, or striking configurations of stars, were assigned to each month. For the needs of urban life, such as the computation of interest on business loans, a uniform length of thirty days was conventionally adopted for the civil month, and twelve such months for the year. But such a curtailed year, however convenient for city-dwellers, was unsuitable for farmers. When the harvest month arrived before the grain was ripe for cutting, a thirteenth month had to be intercalated. If no such intercalation had occurred, the purely lunar calendar would soon have been out of phase with the seasons, as indeed it is today in Islamic countries, since twelve lunations fall many days short of a year. On the other hand, thirteen lunations would be excessive.

After centuries of spasmodic intercalations, the Babylonians recognized a near equation. Nineteen solar years were almost exactly equal to 235 lunar months. In this nineteen-year lunisolar cycle, twelve years received twelve months each for a subtotal of 144. The remaining seven years were each assigned thirteen months, bringing the full total to 235 (91 + 144). By 380 B.C. a definite pattern evolved in which the first, fourth, seventh, ninth, twelfth, fifteenth, and eighteenth years were made a month longer than the other twelve, with the intercalation being inserted after the twelfth month six times and once after the sixth month (of the eighteenth year).

Many stars, after traveling along arcs in the sky, dropped out of sight below the horizon in the west. By contrast with this disappearance, some northern stars remained visible above the horizon even at the lowest point on their nightly curves. These were complete circles, centered at various distances around an unseen point. This was conceived to be a pivot which turned, or around which turned, an invisible heavenly canopy bejewelled with the multitudinous sparkling stars. The distance between any two of them remained unchanged night after night, thereby reinforcing the impression that they were all attached to the imperceptible celestial awning.

Each star always rose at exactly the same point on the eastern horizon. But its time of rising was somewhat earlier on successive nights. Gaining a little on the sun every day, the star overtook it in the course of a year. This steady advance of the stars with respect to the sun, those east of it constantly approaching closer to it, and those west of it steadily withdrawing farther from it, could be interpreted otherwise. The stars could be regarded as fixed, and not as slipping westward away from the sun. Instead, the sun was deemed to be moving eastward slowly among the fixed stars in a journey that lasted a whole year, while every day of that year the sun traveled rapidly westward across the sky.

The speed of the sun in its annual eastward trek was discovered to change in a periodic manner. It was therefore indispensable to grapple with this period, since the moon's daily withdrawal from the sun was the basis of the Babylonian lunar calendar. Instead of assuming that the solar velocity varied continuously throughout the year, some Mesopotamian astronomers preferred to keep the speed steady at one level for about six months, drop it down to a lower constant level for the rest of the year, and then jump it back up again to the higher initial level, where it started to repeat the previous pattern. This discontinuous treatment of the varying speed, so that it steps up or down from one straight row of numbers to another, produces what is termed a "step function." Alternatively, the sun's eastward velocity was deemed to decrease continuously from its maximum to its minimum, and there alter its direction abruptly, climbing at the same rate of change back again to the maximum, where it began the second period of this so-called "linear zigzag function." Both step functions and zigzag functions were in use at the same time, the former more widely because somewhat easier to handle.

These two types of numerical tables made it possible to predict not only the beginning of the month but also the lunar eclipse at mid-month. It was noticed that the moon suffered eclipse, either total or partial, only when it rose near sunset or set near sunrise. This lunar phase of opposition to the sun, however, did not always coincide with an eclipse. This striking phenomenon occurred only when the moon was near the track followed by the sun in its annual eastward circuit

537

through the constellations. This solar path was later named the "ecliptic," because the moon was eclipsed only when its opposition to the sun took place in the vicinity of the sun's line of march. More often than not the moon at opposition was not eclipsed, because it was too far above or below the ecliptic; in other words, its northern or southern latitude was too great to permit the effect to occur. However, when the moon approached one of its nodes, where its path crossed the sun's, it underwent an eclipse, which would be followed by another in either five or six months. Continuous records of lunar oppositions with or without eclipses revealed a pattern that repeated itself after approximately eighteen years.

No such cycle was discovered for solar eclipses, which occur toward the end of the month, when the sun and moon are in conjunction. While a total or nearly total solar eclipse is a spectacular event, a minor partial eclipse of the sun might easily be overlooked in the daylight, and in any given case might not be visible to observers in Mesopotamia.

At an early date they distinguished the planet Venus, which on account of its extraordinary brilliance was grouped with the sun and moon to constitute a trinity of celestial divinities. From the day the observers first saw Venus rise in the east earlier than the sun, they watched it as a morning star for more than eight months, until it disappeared from the sky for three months. Then it reappeared in the west, setting later than the sun as an evening star. These recurring appearances and disappearances of Venus were faithfully recorded. In due course the observers recognized the remaining "stray sheep," as the planets visible to the naked eye were called.

One of them, Mercury, behaved like Venus, which disappeared twice during each cycle. By contrast, three other "stray sheep" became invisible only once in each cycle. The performance of these three (Saturn, Jupiter, and Mars) was remarkable also in another respect. They traveled eastward at a varying speed, stopped at their first stationary point, reversed their direction for a short while, halted at their second stationary point, and then resumed their normal eastward or direct motion. These critical junctures—where the planet stood still, first appeared, and disappeared—attracted the attention of the Babylonians. They compiled lists of the dates on which these transitions occurred. Dividing the planet's varying velocity into several discontinuous levels, they treated it either as a periodic step function or as a linear zigzag function. These functions were often modified in a variety of ways as different observers adopted divergent methods of approximating the planet's mean motion. These arithmetical planetary tables in general resemble those used for the moon. The lunar tables, however, are far more complicated, containing as they do supplementary column after column of the corrections needed to obtain increasingly accurate predictions of the highly erratic motion of the moon.

Like the other cosmic bodies, the moon was deemed to be a divinity. Each followed its own course in the sky, and in so doing gave signs to mankind. In the remote past the gods had on occasion spoken directly to this or that man. Now they wrote their will in the heavens. For those who professed to be skilled in the art of reading these celestial omens, there was foreknowledge of the near future: impending floods and storms, size of the crops, state of the public health, outbreaks of civil disorder, length of the ruler's life, intentions of foreign powers, duration of peace, and outcome of wars. Such political astrology was especially prominent in Assyria, whence it spread westward through the Hittite realm. On the other hand, those who revered the cosmic bodies were fiercely condemned by the monotheistic Hebrew prophet: their bones shall be spread "before the sun and the moon and all the host of heaven . . . whom they have worshipped"; their bones "shall not be gathered, nor be buried, they shall be for dung upon the face of the earth" (Jeremiah 8:2).

That oblique portion of the host of heaven within which the sun, moon, and planets travel was divided by the Babylonians into configurations resembling to a greater or lesser extent some terrestrial beast, real or fanciful, plant, human, or artifact. These imaginative constellations were later borrowed by the Greeks, who modified them somewhat and called them in their own language *zodiacal*, because their word for a little figure was *zodion*. The number of these Babylonian zodiacal constellations was gradually reduced to twelve. Each constellation was then assigned to one of the twelve months during which the sun completes its yearly course along the ecliptic or "line through the middle of the zodiac." To each such twelfth of the zodiac, or zodiacal sign, 30° of longitude were allotted. The dividing line between any two neighboring signs was drawn so that the constellation from which the sign took its name would fit as well as possible within the corresponding sign.

A planet could now be located as being at a given time at a definite degree within a specified zodiacal sign. This method of pinpointing the position of a cosmic body was more precise than the previous procedure of placing it in relation to a constellation, whose boundaries in the nature of things were bound to be much more difficult to define.

From the planetary tables it was now possible to say where each planet was at any given moment, even if it happened to be in the invisible portion of its orbit.

With the positions of all the planetary divinities known at the instant of any individual's conception or birth, it was believed possible to make a long-range prediction of his fate. Two of these deities, Venus and Jupiter, were regarded as benevolent; two others, Mars and Saturn, as malevolent; and Mercury as ambivalent. Their effect on the individual was strengthened or weakened by their presence in a particular zodiacal sign and by their aspects, or mutual angular distances within the zodiac. This kind of horoscopic or genethliacal astrology, based on the locations of the planets at a supposedly critical juncture and on their imagined potencies, could profess to read far into the future, where the planetary tables covered extensive periods of time. Moreover, the new predictive service was at the disposal of any person wealthy enough to afford the fee, and was no longer confined to royalty and other potentates.

The nations who worshipped the moon as a deity might predict its eclipses correctly, but could offer no physical explanation of them. Nor could the Hebrews who, although they deprived it of its divine status, regarded it as a self-luminous body, somewhat less brilliant than the sun. Their god announced that he would "show wonders in the heavens. . . . The sun shall be turned into darkness, and the moon into blood" (Joel 2:30–31). The copper color of the lunar eclipse was a product of the divine will, not a natural effect. So also among the Hindus, the moon was eclipsed because it was swallowed by a demon; the lunar nodes, the two points on its orbit where the moon crosses from north latitude to south and from south to north, were long called the dragon's head and the dragon's tail.

Anaxagoras, however, who was denounced for impiety and imprisoned in Athens, discovered that the moon's light is not its own, but comes from the sun. Hence the eclipses of the moon are caused by its falling within the shadow of the earth, which comes between the sun and the moon at that time.

Anaxagoras also recognized that the sun is eclipsed at new moon, when its dark and opaque bulk is interposed between the earth and the sun. By contrast, in pre-Hellenic cosmology, which made no effort to ascertain the earth's distance from the sun and moon, these bodies, or rather divinities, were regarded as equally remote. In like manner no attempt had been made to estimate their size. Anaxagoras, on the other hand, insisted that the sun was a red-hot rock bigger than the Peloponnesus. Did he suppose that the large meteorite which landed during his lifetime fell down from the sun? In any case he surmised that the moon is earthy, having mountains, plains, and ravines.

The shape of the earth had puzzled earlier Greek cosmologists. Thus, to account for its stability, Xeno-

phanes had supposed that it extended infinitely downward. But its roundness was proved visually by the convex shape of the shadow it always casts on the moon during a lunar eclipse. By the same token, the shadow thrown by the moon on the sun in a partial solar eclipse demonstrated ocularly the sphericity of the moon. This conclusion was confirmed by the lunar phases, with the half-moon regularly intervening between concave and convex illuminated segments. Since the moon was spherical, so were all the other cosmic bodies, and indeed the universe itself was one big ball. To the under surface of its exterior shell the stars were attached like bright studs, whereas the planets were free to roam.

As the planets revolved at various distances from the center at different speeds, they emitted diverse tones which blended into a celestial harmony, unnoticed because we mortals have all heard it from birth. This was only one indication to the mystically inclined Pythagorean brotherhood that the cosmos was constructed on mathematical lines. Philolaus, one of the brethren, held the earth to be a planet, revolving like the others around a central fire, the Hearth of the Cosmos. Ecphantus, another brother, maintained that the earth rotates about its own center from west to east. "Motion like an auger whirling around the same place" was attributed by Plato and the Pythagoreans to the fixed stars. Convinced that the planets could have no reason to speed up, slow down, stop, and retrace their steps in loops, the brotherhood asked how the phenomena seen in the sky could be explained on the assumption that the cosmic motions were all perfectly circular and absolutely uniform.

Although the same question was propounded by Plato, he insisted that "we shall dispense with the bodies in the heavens if we propose to obtain a real understanding of astronomy" (*Republic* VII, 530C). No perceptible object could furnish true knowledge, which comes only from pure reason, not from lowly sight. Like diagrams in geometry, the visible cosmic bodies merely furnished illustrations to facilitate a putatively "higher" study. Plato nevertheless proceeded to concoct a creation story, complete with an uncreated creator god and a divine cosmos animated by a universal soul. With regard to the three outer planets, he said that men "neither give them names nor investigate the measurement of them one against another by numerical calculation" (*Timaeus* 39C). With all its obscurity and obscurantism, Plato's *Timaeus* exerted a pervasive and pernicious influence on subsequent cosmological thought. It undertook to combat the speculations advanced by the founders of the atomic theory. According to them, space is infinite and contains innumerable atoms in ceaseless motion. From their collisions unnumbered worlds arise, some expanding, others

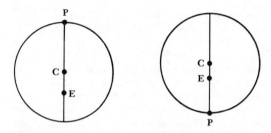

FIGURE 1. Eccentric orbit. P = moving planet, C = center of planet's orbit, E = Earth. In the left-hand diagram, P is at its apogee; in the right-hand diagram, P is at its perigee. From *Three Copernican Treatises*, Dover, 1959. COPYRIGHT BY EDWARD ROSEN.

collapsing, and still others devoid of moisture. Metrodorus, a pupil of the atomist Democritus, maintained that "a single plant growing in a broad field is just as absurd as one cosmos in infinite space" (Guthrie, II, 405; trans. E.R.).

The only cosmos we know was viewed by Eudoxus as a nest of twenty-seven homocentric spheres. To the sun, moon, and five known planets he assigned a combination of perfect spheres, each rotating with a constant angular velocity. The cosmic body was attached to the equator of its innermost sphere. As this carrying sphere rotated forward, its axis was borne backward by a second sphere to whose surface its poles were fixed, the axes of both spheres being inclined to each other. By adding a third similar sphere for the sun and moon, and two more for each of the planets, Eudoxus succeeded in representing the observed motions with qualitative fidelity, although not with quantitative precision, especially in the case of Mars.

The seven separate mathematical models of Eudoxus were later converted into a single physical mechanism by Aristotle. However, whether merely an abstract geometrical blueprint or a solid contrivance, no arrangement of concentric spheres could alter the distance of any planet from the eyes of the observer on the earth at the middle of the whole system. But Mars and Venus in particular, and the other planets too, vary considerably in brightness, and therefore in their distance from the earth. Moreover, the moon's distance from the earth also changes, as is shown by central solar eclipses, in some of which the sun's disk is entirely obscured, whereas in the annular eclipses a bright ring surrounds the moon's shadow.

These two fatal defects in the theory of homocentrics were overcome by removing the earth from the center of the cosmic body's uniform circular motion in its orbit. The displacement of the earth from the orbital center made the distance from the revolving cosmic body to the terrestrial observer a variable quantity. At its perigee, or closest approach to the earth, the body

was seen to move more rapidly than at its apogee, or greatest distance from the earth (Figure 1).

Such an "eccentric" pattern fits the sun's annual journey. This solar orbit is divided into four equal quadrants by the solstices and equinoxes, which mark the four seasons of the year. But the sun traverses these equal arcs in unequal times. Of the four seasons, the spring, extending from the vernal equinox to the summer solstice, lasts the longest. Because the sun travels most slowly then, it crosses its apogee. By the same token it passes through its perigee in the autumn, the shortest of the four seasons.

This simple eccentric scheme had to be modified in the case of Mars. When this planet culminates at midnight it is at its brightest, and therefore closest to the earth. At that same time it is in opposition to the sun. Mars' opposition, however, does not always occur at the same point of the zodiac. On the contrary, the opposition may take place anywhere along Mars' orbit. To permit the opposition to shift in this way, Mars' eccentric was provided with a moving, instead of a fixed, center. This center, always aligned with the sun, revolved around the earth in the course of a year. A similar moving eccentric suited the other two planets, Jupiter and Saturn, which are found at any angular distance, or elongation, from the sun (Figure 2).

In the case of Venus and Mercury, however, the circle described by the eccentric's center would have to exceed the eccentric itself in size. This arrangement would be tantamount to each of these planets riding on a small epicycle whose center traversed a large deferent. This moving center could be identified with

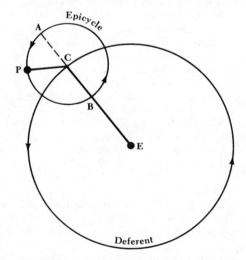

FIGURE 2. Epicycle and deferent, from Angus Armitage, *Sun, Stand Thou Still.* COPYRIGHT 1947 BY HENRY SCHUMAN, INC. BY PERMISSION OF ABELARD-SCHUMAN LIMITED.

the sun, since Venus and Mercury are never seen very far away from that luminary, their greatest elongations from it being quite moderate. Moreover, they are sometimes east of it, and at other times west of it. This alternate crisscrossing and perpetual proximity suggested the inference that Venus and Mercury revolved around the sun like satellites, while at the same time the sun executed its annual orbit around the earth.

The epicycles of Venus and Mercury had a material body, the sun, for their moving center. If this became an immaterial point, revolving around an earth-centered deferent, the planet-bearing epicycle produced the same visual effect for a terrestrial observer as an eccentric with a fixed center. The radii of the eccentric and deferent were equal and parallel to each other, while the eccentricity was equal to the radius of the epicycle. The kinematic equivalence of these two simple schemes was demonstrated by Apollonius. The introduction of eccentrics and epicycles in place of geocentric spheres gave mathematical cosmology a new freedom to choose any center of rotation outside the earth and at any suitable distance from it. In every case the accepted procedure was to adopt the fewest and simplest hypotheses that would produce results conforming as closely as possible to the observed phenomena, or "save the phenomena," as the Greeks liked to say.

A startling phenomenon, either a nova or a comet, impelled Hipparchus to compile for posterity the first catalogue of fixed stars, "indicating the position and magnitude of each, so that from this catalogue it could be readily determined not only whether stars perish and are born but also whether some of them actually shift and move" (Pliny the Elder, *Natural History*, II, 24, 95; trans. E.R.). While comparing previous observations of eclipses with his own, Hipparchus noticed that a certain star's longitudinal distance from the nearby equinoctial point had decreased somewhat between the two observations. He interpreted this decrease as a slow westward displacement or precession of the equinoxes, carrying the equator with them. Afterwards the alternative explanation prevailed, that the celestial sphere rotated eastward about the poles of the ecliptic.

Hipparchus refrained from attempting to construct theoretical schemes for the five planets because he did not have at his disposal an adequate supply of accurate observations. In remedying this deficiency he learned that the planetary retrograde arcs vary. Building on the foundations prepared by his highly admired predecessor, Ptolemy was able to complete the edifice of ancient cosmology.

In the Ptolemaic system the finite spherical cosmos was bounded by the fixed stars, more than a thousand

of which were catalogued in forty-eight constellations (twelve zodiacal, twenty-one northern, and fifteen southern). Each star was attached to the universe's outermost sphere, which completed a daily rotation from east to west around the poles of the celestial equator. This diurnal rotation affected also the sun, moon, and five planets. Since a planet's apse-lines, drawn through its apogee and perigee, did not change their position in the starry sphere, the planets shared in that outermost sphere's slow eastward rotation around the poles of the ecliptic in 36,000 years. It was this rotation which produced the phenomenon still called the "precession of the equinoxes."

Below the sphere of the stars three planets—Saturn, Jupiter, and Mars in that descending order—participated in the daily cosmic rotation westward. But just as passengers may stroll slowly eastward on the deck of a ship traveling swiftly westward, each of these three planets at its own speed completed its orbital revolution in the zodiac. This prevailingly eastward march slowed down and halted at a first stationary point, reversed its direction for a time, and after a second stationary point resumed its direct motion. To account for these irregular loops Ptolemy had the planet revolve on an epicycle whose center was in turn carried around by an eccentric deferent. At a distance from this deferent's center along the apse-line connecting the apogee and perigee lay the earth. On the apse-line at a distance from the deferent's center equal and opposite to the earth's, Ptolemy placed an equant.

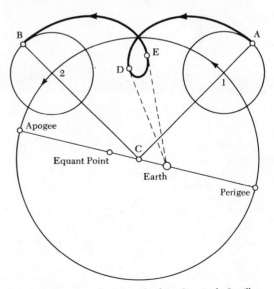

FIGURE 3. Function of an epicycle, from Giorgio de Santillana, *The Crime of Galileo.* COPYRIGHT 1955 BY THE UNIVERSITY OF CHICAGO. ALL RIGHTS RESERVED.

As measured from this equalizing point, and not from the deferent's center, the mean angular velocity of the epicycle's center was uniform (Figure 3).

These three outer planets could be observed at any elongation from the sun, which revolved around the earth in a year, either on a simple eccentric or an epicycle carried by a concentric deferent. In so doing the sun separated the three outer planets from Venus and Mercury, which never depart very far from it. Because Mercury's motion is so irregular, Ptolemy had to rotate the deferent's center on a circlet.

Below Venus and Mercury (the inner planets) the moon revolved around the earth. Its motion on an epicycle carried by a concentric deferent agreed fairly well with the observations when the moon was in syzygy, where an eclipse could occur because the moon was either in opposition to the sun or in conjunction with it. In quadrature, however, where the half-moon formed a right angle at the earth with the sun, the distance moon-earth had to be reduced to conform with this "evection," as it was called later. Ptolemy accomplished this result by making this distance depend on a line connecting the epicycle's center with a point moving around a circlet centered on the earth (Figure 4).

In the middle of this Ptolemaic cosmos the spherical earth, or rather terraqueous sphere, rested immovable. The interval extending outward from the surface of this sphere to the lunar perigee was filled with air and

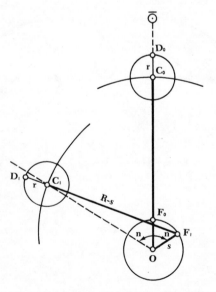

FIGURE 4. Ptolemy's lunar theory, from Otto Neugebauer, *The Exact Sciences in Antiquity.* DOVER PUBLICATIONS, INC., NEW YORK, 1957. REPRINTED THROUGH PERMISSION OF THE PUBLISHER.

elemental fire, in that order. The lunar apogee coincided with the perigee of Mercury, whose apogee was contiguous with Venus' perigee. This tight fit of apogee with the next perigee continued all the way out to the fixed stars on the principle that "in Nature a vacuum, or any meaningless and useless thing, is inconceivable" (Ptolemy, *Planetary Hypotheses*).

When viewed abstractly or theoretically, these neatly designed concentrics, eccentrics, deferents, and epicycles were merely indispensable mathematical aids in computing and predicting the positions of the cosmic bodies. Alternatively, these constructs were regarded as physical or material entities. Thus, "like a pearl on a ring" the spherical body of the planet was affixed to the equator of its epicycle, which was a solid ball running in a groove. This channel's lower surface was formed by the outside or convexity of the planet's deferent, which was now conceived as a spherical shell or hollow sphere. The groove's upper surface in like manner consisted of the interior or concavity of the next higher planet's deferent. From the stationary earth to the slowly rotating starry sphere, the celestial bodies, mounted on their epicycles, each confined within its own groove, performed their stately and intricate ballet. This absolutely full Ptolemaic universe devoid of empty space, or its mathematically equivalent blueprint, dominated cosmological thought for fourteen centuries (Figure 5).

Arab observers found that in their time the precession of the equinoxes moved faster than 1° in 100 years, the slightly mistaken figure announced by Ptolemy. Instead of discarding his value as too slow and accepting their own more rapid rate of 1° in 66 years as constant, some of them revived an ancient notion that the precessional speed swung back and forth between a maximum and a minimum. With this imaginary periodic oscillation or trepidation, they connected another supposed cyclic variation. This affected the angle at which the plane of the celestial equator is intersected by the plane of the ecliptic. This obliquity of the ecliptic had been somewhat overstated by Ptolemy at 23°51′20″. Putting the maximum at a rounded figure in this vicinity, the Arabs conceived the obliquity as oscillating slowly through an arc of about two-fifths of a degree.

Whereas the Koran was satisfied with only seven heavens (presumably one each for the moon, sun, and five planets), these Muslim cosmologists added Ptolemy's eighth sphere of the fixed stars. To account for the precession of the equinoxes, they introduced a ninth sphere, and then a tenth for the trepidation of the precession. For the related fictive cyclic variation in the obliquity of the ecliptic an eleventh sphere was adopted by some Muslims and their Christian followers.

FIGURE 5. Reconstruction of a fifteenth-century cosmological scheme utilizing solid spheres, from Giorgio de Santillana, *The Crime of Galileo.* COPYRIGHT 1955 BY THE UNIVERSITY OF CHICAGO. ALL RIGHTS RESERVED.

Early Christian writers had denied that the earth is round, since in that case on the opposite side of the globe there would be people with their feet upwards and heads downwards. In the Hebrew Bible, which they misappropriated to themselves under the extraneous designation "Old Testament," they professed to find sacred warrant for their contention that the earth is the floor of the cosmos. On this flat surface their imagination erected in the north a high conical mountain, whose summit created darkness by blocking out the light of the sun which passed from west to east during the night. In comparison with the earth, therefore, the sun was a small object. Its heat, like that of all the other celestial bodies, would be extinguished, at the dissolution of the cosmos, by the waters providentially stored for that purpose above the firmament.

While it still continued to function prior to that cataclysmic event, each cosmic body was propelled in its course by a tireless angel. This Christian angel replaced the pagan soul which Plato and the Neo-Platonists had assigned to each cosmic body as its driving force. On the other hand, Aristotle's First Mover, being incorporeal, could not itself move, but operated like a beloved object after which the First Movable, or sphere of the stars, strove and thereby communicated motion to the remaining cosmic bodies. They did not receive any impulse from without, according to Ptolemy. On the contrary, each of them had within itself its own vital energy propelling it forward. Every planet was the source of its own mo-

tion, like a living bird. Taken as a whole, the cosmic bodies flew through space like a flock of birds, each at its own pace and on its own course. In late antiquity Johannes Philoponus, a Christian commentator on Aristotle, early in the sixth century dismissed the angels who had formerly tugged and strained at the cosmic bodies. Instead, he had God implant within them at the time of creation an impetus which kept them going round and round.

The Christian version of the creation story insisted that with His unlimited might their God made the entire universe out of nothing at all. This denial of the existence of matter prior to creation reinterpreted the Hebrew Bible's primordial material abyss, and controverted the ancient atomists' teaching that "nothing is ever produced by divine action out of nothing." Nor, in the Nature of the atomists, is anything reduced to nothing. Instead, it is dissolved into its component indivisible atoms which, being indestructible, are everlasting. Then time itself has no end, although the several worlds created by Nature may come into being and pass away. For space is boundless. If it were confined within the stars, where would a javelin go when hurled outward from those "flaming ramparts of the cosmos"?

This was not the kind of question with which Aristarchus had grappled in the third century B.C., when he enormously enlarged the size of the cosmos without declaring it to be infinite. He ascribed to the earth a daily rotation about its own axis, so that the stars remained motionless. He also assigned to the earth an annual revolution around the sun, which he held stationary at the center of the earth's orbit. For he had computed the sun to be some 300 times larger than the earth in volume, and how could so big a mass revolve around the smaller earth? Did not the moon, whose bulk he calculated as about one-thirtieth of the earth's, revolve around the bigger body?

After lying dormant beneath the ruling geostatic cosmologies, the Aristarchan geokinetic thinking was revived early in the sixteenth century of our era by Nicholas Copernicus. Whereas Aristarchus had provided only the bare bones of the heliostatic system, Copernicus fleshed it out.

He was unaware that the followers of the fifth-century Hindu astronomer Aryabhata "maintain that the earth moves and heaven rests. People have tried to refute them by saying that, if such were the case, stones and trees would fall from the earth." But Brahmagupta, Aryabhata's seventh-century successor, disagreed, "apparently because he thought that all heavy things are attracted towards the center of the earth" (Sachau, ed. and trans., I, 372).

Copernicus was equally unaware that in 1377   543

Nicholas Oresme, while explaining his translation of Aristotle's *Heavens*—the earliest rendering in a modern language—considered many arguments for and against the daily rotation of the earth. Recognizing that it benefits from the sun's heat, Oresme reasoned that in familiar things what "is roasted at a fire receives the heat of the fire around itself because it is turned and not because the fire is turned around it" (*Le Livre du ciel et du monde*, eds. A. D. Menut and A. J. Denomy, Madison [1968], p. 533). Nevertheless Oresme, bishop of Lisieux, decided in favor of a static earth, on the basis of biblical passages.

At the same time in the Islamic world Ibn al-Shatir of Damascus rejected Ptolemy's equant as a violation of the principle that a cosmic body's orbit must be compounded from absolutely uniform circular motions. This Muslim timekeeper at the mosque in Damascus also introduced a second epicycle into Ptolemy's lunar theory in order to eliminate its grossly excessive variation in the length of the moon's apparent diameter. In these two respects Copernicus' theories resembled Ibn al Shatir's. But, unlike his Damascene predecessor, Copernicus did not use a second epicycle for the sun; he retained eccentric orbits; and his numerical results also differed, being based in part on his own observations. He knew neither Arabic nor French, and the relevant writings of Ibn al-Shatir and Oresme had not been translated into Latin. Copernicus evidently shared earlier uneasiness with aspects of the Ptolemaic cosmology. But entirely independently he went back to Aristarchus' heliostatic cosmos.

One objection thereto was that any motion of the earth must disrupt it. But, as regards its daily rotation, the only available alternative required the vastly greater heavens to whirl round with immensely swifter speed each day. Would not, Copernicus asked, a more devastating destruction necessarily be entailed thereby?

Then the daily rising and setting of the sun must be recognized as a mere appearance, due to the real axial rotation of the earth. In like manner, the cycle of the seasons is caused by the earth's annual tilted orbit. As it carries the observer around, the optical effect of his motion must be disengaged from the real revolutions of the planets. These bodies do not actually speed up, slow down, stop, and reverse their course. They seem to do so only because they are observed from that ceaselessly moving observatory which is our earth. In truth the planets always proceed in the same direction at a constant speed. So does the earth, which now took its rightful place in the cosmic order, a planet like the others.

Copernicus' rearrangement of the cosmic bodies for the first time clarified certain previously unexplained coincidences in the Ptolemaic system. The outer planets therein always appeared brightest in opposition; the radius of the epicycle remained at all times parallel to the line drawn from the terrestrial observer to the sun; and the arc of retrogression in the apparent loop diminished from Mars outward to Saturn. All these phenomena were now seen to be necessary consequences of the earth's orbital revolution.

In like manner the Ptolemaic system kept Venus and Mercury within their greatest elongations from the sun by requiring the line from the earth to the epicycle's center to be prolonged through the sun. But these two bodies became true inner planets in Copernicus' cosmos, and as seen from the earth they could not exceed their limited maximum elongations from the sun. Moreover, by evaluating the distance from Venus to the sun in terms of terrestrial radii, Copernicus finally found the way to determine the absolute dimensions of the planetary system. And he correctly reinterpreted the precession of the equinoxes as due to a continuous shift in the direction of the earth's axis of rotation, instead of to a slow eastward rotation of the sphere of the stars around the poles of the ecliptic.

In Copernicus' cosmos the earth revolved around the sun in a huge orbit requiring a whole year to be traversed. Then the direction of any star, as observed at an interval of six months from two diametrically opposite points on the earth's orbit, should exhibit the displacement known as the "annual stellar parallax." To account for the nonobservation of this phenomenon, Copernicus asserted that the enormous remoteness of the stars made the diameter of the earth's orbit a negligible quantity. In other words, Copernicus' universe became immensely great. But he stopped short of proclaiming it to be infinite, confining himself to the description "similar to the infinite." Unlike the Buddhists who declared that "the cosmos is neither finite nor infinite," Copernicus "left to the philosophers of nature the question whether the universe is finite or infinite."

One philosopher of nature who spoke his mind was Thomas Digges. In 1576 he declared that the sphere of the fixed stars reached "up in spherical altitude without end." Therefore, although the stars still stayed within the same sphere, their height varied. Thus Digges agreed with the ancient Greek expositor Geminus, who "would not assume that all the stars lie on a single surface, but rather that some are higher and others lower, the difference in their height being imperceptible because our sight attains [in all directions only] to an equal distance" (Cohen and Drabkin, p. 118; trans. E. R.). Just as the Roman poet Manilius had attributed the dimmer brilliance of some stars to their greater height, so Digges' stars looked smaller the more remote they were, and "the greatest part rest by reason of their wonderful distance invisible to us." Nevertheless the sun and its satellites remained in the middle of Digges' heliocentric cosmos.

On the other hand, the nonfinite universe preached by the mystical theologian Nicholas of Cusa had its circumference nowhere and its center everywhere. Then the earth could no longer be in the middle of the cosmos, and it therefore ceased to be the dregs of the universe. Instead, it became for Cusa a "noble star," whose motion was circular albeit not perfectly so.

Cusa's loosening of the rigid bounds of the traditional cosmos made a profound impression on an ill-fated genius who was publicly burned at the stake by the Roman Catholic church in 1600. But Giordano Bruno went far beyond his master Cusa in recognizing our sun as one of the countless stars in an infinite universe.

In Aristotle's finite universe everything had its natural place. Whether at rest therein or violently displaced therefrom, a body capable of motion was in a place bounded by the inner surface of a stationary nontransportable containing vessel. This Aristotelian concept of place was rejected by Bernardino Telesio, "the first of the modern men," as he was called by Francis Bacon. Telesio maintained that all bodies are contained in a single vast emptiness, for which he introduced the term "space."

This universal emptiness was made infinite by Telesio's contemporary, Francesco Patrizi. His infinite mathematical space, which he paradoxically described as an "incorporeal body," surrounds an inner physical space, containing the cosmic bodies. Thus Aristotle's hierarchically ordered set of finite places gave way to Patrizi's infinite emptiness, which in due course won acceptance as the concept of absolute space.

The new star of 1572 convinced Tycho Brahe that, contrary to the long accepted belief in the immutability of the perfect heavens, changes can occur there. However, he declined to speculate how the nova came into existence, although he concluded that it must have decreased in size.

The great comet of 1577 challenged the traditional sublunar location of these spectacular bodies. Aristotle had said that they were ignited below the moon as dry exhalations rose up from the earth. But a generation after Peter Apian remarked that a comet's tail always pointed away from the sun, the comet of 1577 showed no perceptible daily parallax. Therefore it had to be traveling far beyond the moon. In antiquity Seneca had said: "We see the comets mingling with the stars and passing through the higher regions."

Then the comet's head and tail must collide with the crystalline spheres carrying the planets. But, Tycho pointed out, no such collisions between comet and crystal occurred. The absence of these dreaded catastrophes demonstrated the entirely imaginary nature of the spherical machinery which had so long crowded the heavens before his time. Thereafter the cosmic bodies moved on their own through the upper regions.

Copernicus' reasoning that five planets revolved around the sun was accepted by Tycho. But he refused to believe that the heavy, sluggish earth was capable of motion, which, moreover, conflicted with the Bible as he interpreted it. In his own cosmology, therefore, he kept the earth motionless at the center of the universe. Around it revolved the sun, which in turn served as the center for the planets revolving around it. This Tychonian compromise appealed to those who, while feeling the force of Copernicus' argumentation, still clung to the remnants of their obsolete metaphysical prejudices and dogmatic bibliolatry.

No such hindrances prevented the intellectual development of Brahe's most famous assistant, Johannes Kepler. Inheriting the invaluable treasure of Tycho's accumulated observations, Kepler tried to fit them to the orbit of Mars while confining himself to the traditionally sanctioned cosmological devices. Unable to find a satisfactory agreement between Tycho's observations and any conceivable combination of uniform circular motions, Kepler finally discarded the bimillennial prejudice against all curved tracks save the circular. An ellipse, departing only slightly from a perfect circle, turned out to be the true (predictably correct) path of the planet. Its motion along the ellipse could be kept uniform by measuring, not the linear velocity, but the areas swept out in equal intervals of time by the straight line connecting the moving planet with the sun, located at one of the two foci of the elliptical orbit. The square of the time required by any planet to traverse its ellipse showed the same proportion in all cases to the cube of the planet's mean distance from the sun.

These three principles of planetary motion constituted Kepler's imperishable contribution to cosmology. They confirmed the essential truth of the Copernican system, while revising it drastically. Gone forever were the pre-Keplerian eccentrics, deferents, and epicycles in their complicated combinations.

Gone too was the conception that a cosmic body could revolve around a mathematical point not occupied by a physical body. For example, in Copernicus' cosmos the sun had been near, not at, the universe's center, which was also the center of the orbit of the earth. Hence this particular planet still retained a privileged status in Copernicus' nominally heliocentric system, wherein the physical sun was separated by a significant distance from the center of the universe. Kepler, however, elicited an implication from the Copernican cosmos which its architect himself had failed to draw. Since Copernicus' earth was a planet, then the other planets must be physical bodies like the earth. But when a physical body traverses an elliptical orbit, it must have the physical body of the sun present in one focus of its ellipse. The sun thereby acquired its rightful special status in the heliocentric system.

Since the planets had now become material bodies like the earth, some physical cause had to be invoked to explain their motion. Kepler could no longer accept Ptolemy's pronouncement that "the power and activity of an aster in its proper place and around its own center consist of self-coherent revolution." For Copernicus, revolution around a center was the motion natural to a sphere, although in his cosmos two spheres, the sun and the stars', were motionless. Before Kepler liberated himself from the grip of traditional notions, he had believed that the planets were driven around by "moving souls." But in the second edition of his youthful work he wrote:

If you substitute the word "force" for the word "soul," you have the very principle on which celestial physics is based in my *Commentaries on Mars*. . . . For previously I used to believe that the cause responsible for the motion of the planets was unquestionably a soul. But when I considered that this moving cause diminishes with distance, and that the sun's light is also attenuated with the distance from the sun, I concluded that this force is something corporeal (*Gesammelte Werke*, 8, 113; trans. E. R. See also, *Mysterium cosmographicum* [2nd ed. 1621], Note 3, Ch. 20).

Copernicus had correctly maintained that the cosmos must have more than one gravitational center, with each planet serving as the collecting core for its own detached heavy bodies. Accepting this plurality, Kepler reversed the traditional conception of the fall of a heavy object. No longer did the freely falling body seek its natural place as close as possible to its gravitational center. Instead, the gravitational center attracted to itself its separate parts. But Kepler's earth and moon were kindred bodies. Therefore they exerted a mutual attraction on each other. In exercising its gravitational pull on the earth, the moon helped to produce the ebb and flow of the oceanic tides on the earth's surface. So did the sun. And while imagining a flight to the moon, Kepler attributed to his fictional space vehicle the property of spontaneously persevering in the motion initially imparted to it, an incomplete expression of the principle of inertia, a term which he added to the vocabulary of the exact sciences. Moreover, he asserted that the light radiating spherically from a point source diminished in intensity with the square of the distance from the source. Then in 1644 G. P. Roberval insisted that "all the parts [of the matter in the universe] tend toward one another with unceasing pressure and mutually attract one another."

Meanwhile in a magnificent series of discoveries made with the recently invented telescope, Galileo Galilei helped to establish some characteristic features of the emerging cosmology. He revealed that the moon abounds in lofty mountains and depressed hollows. Then its surface is no more perfectly spherical than is our lowly earth's. Even more irregular was Saturn with its protruding ears, as that planet's rings looked for a time in Galileo's primitive instrument. Sunspots impaired the perfection of that luminary, and their rotation proved that the sun whirls around its own axis, like Copernicus' earth. Our planet reflects sunlight on the moon (as Kepler's teacher had publicly announced in 1596). Venus displayed phases resembling the moon's and due to the same causes. By detecting the four principal satellites of Jupiter, Galileo established that the earth was neither the only planet accompanied by a satellite nor the only center of a cosmic motion. He observed numerous stars invisible to the naked eye, and located them at various altitudes between two spherical surfaces, the more distant being regarded as concave, and the closer as convex. In the telescope the stars were not magnified, but remained vividly sparkling points. On the other hand, the planets showed enlarged pale disks. By thus proving the self-luminosity of the stars as contrasted with the darkness of the planets, Galileo settled the age-old controversy once discussed by al-Biruni:

Opinions of intelligent people differ . . . as to whether the planets are self-luminous like the sun, or merely illuminated by the rays of the sun falling on them. Many assert that light is exclusively the property of the sun, that all the stars [and planets] are destitute of it. . . . But others believe that all the planets are luminous by nature with the exception of the moon (*The Book of Instruction* . . . , p. 67, ¶156).

Disturbed by the Inquisition's condemnation of Galileo as a heretic and by his being sentenced to life imprisonment, René Descartes concealed his adherence to a cosmology very similar to the Copernican. In his own cosmos the earth was declared to be at rest, but only with respect to the celestial matter surrounding it. While this fluid vortex rotated around the sun, it pushed the earth along with it, as flowing water affects an unpropelled boat or a moving vessel transports a sleeping passenger. Similar whirlpools carried the other planets around the sun, while smaller eddies bore the satellites around the earth and Jupiter. Thus in Descartes' cosmos, as in Aristotle's, all action was by direct contact, and there could be no action at a distance. Nor could there be a void or empty space, the entire universe being filled with imperceptibly subtle matter.

Like Descartes, G. A. Borelli avoided assigning any motion to the earth by professedly confining his cosmological discussion to Jupiter's satellites. But, following Kepler, he ascribed to the rotating sun a physical force that drove the planets along. To explain why they do not fly off into space, as would a stone being whirled round in a sling, he attributed to the planets a "natural instinct" to approach the sun as the center of their motion. The equilibrium between these two centrifugal and centripetal motions kept the planets in their orbits, and their satellites circulating around them.

Whereas in 1666 Borelli attributed to the planets a natural tendency to approach the sun, that body attracted the planets and was in turn attracted by them, according to Robert Hooke's reflections early in 1665:

I suppose the gravitating power of the Sun in the center of this part of the Heaven in which we are, hath an attractive power upon all the bodies of the Planets, and of the Earth that move about it, and that each of those again have a respect answerable, whereby they may be said to attract the Sun in the same manner as the Load-stone hath to Iron, and the Iron hath to the Load-stone (R. T. Gunther, *Early Science in Oxford*, Oxford, VIII [1931], 228).

Then on 23 May 1666 Hooke advanced beyond mutual gravitational attraction between sun and planets by combining that cause of motion with the principle of inertia:

I have often wondered, why the planets should move about the sun according to Copernicus's supposition, being not included in any solid orbs (which the ancients possibly for this reason might embrace) nor tied to it, as their centre, by any visible strings; and neither depart from it beyond such a degree, nor yet move in a straight line, as all bodies, that have but one single impulse, ought to do: For a solid body, moved in a fluid, towards any part . . . must preserve [persevere] in its motion in a right line, and neither deflect this way nor that way from it. But all the celestial bodies, being regular solid bodies, and moved in a fluid, and yet moved in circular or elliptical lines, and not straight, must have some other cause, besides the first impressed impulse, that must bend their motion into that curve. And for the performance of this effect I cannot imagine any other likely cause besides these two: The first may be from an unequal density of the medium, through which the planetary body is to be moved. . . . But the second cause of inflecting a direct motion into a curve may be from an attractive property of the body placed in the centre; whereby it continually endeavours to attract or draw it to itself. For if such a principle be supposed, all the phenomena of the planets seem possible to be explained by the common principle of mechanic motions; and possibly the prosecuting this speculation may give us a true hypothesis of their motion, and from some few observations, their motions may be so far brought to a certainty, that we may be able to calculate them to the greatest exactness and certainty, that can be desired (idem, VI, 265–66).

Hooke's mathematical ability was not great enough to perform the requisite calculation, but he did proceed to demonstrate to the Royal Society of London a pendulum whose bob executed a continuous closed curve in a conical sweep, instead of simply oscillating to and fro in a vertical plane like the bob of a conventional pendulum. By imparting to the bob of his conical pendulum the right impulse in the right direction, Hooke produced a laboratory replica of planetary motion (Figure 6).

The previous assumption that "only a spherical shape" befitted a cosmic body was shattered when Christiaan Huygens announced anagrammatically in 1656 that with his eyes he had clearly seen Saturn "surrounded by a thin flat ring not touching it anywhere" (*Oeuvres . . .*, XV, 177, 299). Because the ring is tilted at a considerable constant angle to the plane in which Saturn revolves around the sun, it presented quite different appearances to observers from Galileo's time on. Their bafflement was finally cleared up by Huygens' discovery of the exterior formation, which is without any parallel.

Just as the planet Saturn departs from perfect sphericity, so does the planet earth. It is flattened at its two poles, thereby approximating the solid generated by an ellipse rotating about its minor axis. Then the gravitational pull felt at the earth's equator should be

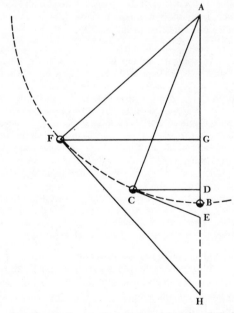

FIGURE 6: Hooke's drawing of a conical pendulum, from R. T. Gunther, *Early Science in Oxford*, Oxford, 1930. COURTESY OF A. E. GUNTHER, F. G. S.

weaker than at the less distant poles, and Huygens' pendulum clock should beat time more slowly at lower latitudes than at higher latitudes on this oblate spheroid which is our earth.

All the above mentioned partial successes achieved by Copernicus, Brahe, Digges, Bruno, Galileo, Kepler, Roberval, Borelli, Hooke, and Huygens were incorporated in the grand synthesis accomplished by Isaac Newton, who admitted that he "stood on the shoulders of giants." His cosmos consisted of discontinuous matter moving in continuous space and time.

Newton's matter was composed of

solid, massy, hard, impenetrable, movable particles; . . . these primitive particles being solids are incomparably harder than any porous bodies compounded of them, even so very hard as never to wear or break in pieces. . . . The changes of corporeal things are to be placed only in the various separations and new associations and motions of these permanent particles; compound bodies being apt to break, not in the midst of solid particles, but where those particles are laid together and only touch in a few points (*Opticks*, Book III, Query 31).

Newton's motion comprised the force of inertia or inactivity, "a passive principle by which bodies persist in their motion or rest, receive motion in proportion to the force impressing it, and resist as much as they are resisted" (loc. cit.). By contrast with the passive principle of inertia, there were also "active principles, such as is the cause of gravity, by which planets and comets keep their motions in their orbs, and bodies acquire great motion in falling" (loc. cit.).

Every body continues in its state . . . of uniform motion in a right [straight] line unless it is compelled to change that state by forces impressed upon it. . . . A stone, whirled about in a sling, endeavors to recede from the hand that turns it; and by that endeavor distends the sling. . . . That force which opposes itself to this endeavor, and by which the sling continually draws back the stone toward the hand and retains it in its orbit, because it is directed to the hand as the center of the orbit, I call the centripetal force. And the same thing is to be understood of all bodies revolved in any orbits. They all endeavor to recede from the centers of their orbits; and were it not for the opposition of a contrary force which restrains them to and detains them in their orbits . . . would fly off in right lines, with a uniform motion (*Mathematical Principles of Natural Philosophy*. Axioms or Laws of Motion, Law I; Definition V).

In particular, there was a centripetal ". . . force, whatever it is, by which the planets are continually drawn aside from the rectilinear motions, which otherwise they would pursue, and made to revolve in curvilinear orbits" (Definition V).

The force which retains the celestial bodies in their orbits has been hitherto called centripetal force; but it being now made plain that it can be no other than a gravitating force, we shall hereafter call it gravity. For the cause of that centripetal force which retains the moon in its orbit will extend itself to all the planets (idem, Book III, Proposition 5, Theorem 5, Scholium).

In the General Scholium inserted at the end of the second edition of his *Mathematical Principles of Natural Philosophy*, Newton said:

Hitherto we have explained the phenomena of the heavens and of our sea by the power of gravity, but have not yet assigned the cause of this power. . . . Hitherto I have not been able to discover the cause of those properties of gravity from phenomena, and I feign no hypotheses; for whatever is not deduced from the phenomena is to be called a hypothesis, and hypotheses, whether metaphysical or physical, whether of occult qualities or mechanical, have no place in experimental philosophy. . . . To us it is enough that gravity does really exist and act according to the laws which we have explained, and abundantly serves to account for all the motions of the celestial bodies and of our sea.

To one of his supporters Newton had previously written: "You sometimes speak of gravity as essential and inherent to matter. Pray do not ascribe that notion to me, for the cause of gravity is what I do not pretend to know" (*Correspondence* . . . , III, 240). About a month later Newton expressed himself even more emphatically to the same correspondent:

That gravity should be innate, inherent, and essential to matter, so that one body may act upon another at a distance through a vacuum, without the mediation of anything else, by and through which their action or force may be conveyed from one to another, is to me so great an absurdity that I believe no man who has in philosophical matters any competent faculty of thinking can ever fall into it. Gravity must be caused by an agent acting constantly according to certain laws, but whether this agent be material or immaterial is a question I have left to the consideration of my readers (op. cit., III, 254).

In Newton's cosmos there was no vacuum or void, because, as he told Robert Boyle, "I suppose that there is diffused through all places an aethereal substance capable of contraction and dilatation, strongly elastic, and in a word much like air in all respects, but far more subtle."

Newton's subtle aether was universally diffused through his absolute space, which, "in its own nature, without relation to anything external, remains always similar and immovable" (*Mathematical Principles* . . . , Definitions, Scholium II).

No other places are immovable but those that, from infinity to infinity, do all retain the same given position one to another, and upon this account must ever remain unmoved and do thereby constitute immovable space.

Yet he acknowledged that "it may be that there is no body really at rest to which the places and motions of others may be referred" (idem, IV).

In like manner Newton's "absolute, true, and mathematical time, of itself and from its own nature, flows equably without relation to anything external, and by another name is called 'duration.'" Yet "it may be that there is no such thing as an equable motion whereby time may be accurately measured. All motions may be accelerated and retarded, but the flowing of absolute time is not liable to any change" (idem, I).

In writing about the comet of 1652–53, Giovanni Domenico Cassini ascribed to those bodies a curved closed orbit, so that they would return periodically. That the orbit was nearly parabolic was suggested by Borelli. On 4 May 1665, Borelli wrote from Pisa to a private correspondent, requesting him to treat as confidential "until further attention and events throw light on the truth," the idea that

the real movement of the present comet [of 1664–65] can on no account be along a straight line, but along a curve so similar to a parabola as to be astonishing, and this is shown not only by computation but also by a mechanical contrivance, which I shall demonstrate to you when I arrive in Florence (*Lettere* . . . , I, 130–31; trans. E. R.).

Then in 1668 parabolic movement was publicly ascribed to comets by Hewelke (Hevelius). When the great comet of 1680 made a very close approach to the sun, Hewelke's follower, Georg Samuel Dörffel, in 1681 computed a parabolic orbit, with the sun in one focus. Thereafter Newton showed that the cometary path was really an ellipse, the visible portion of which might be indistinguishable from a parabola. Edmond Halley, without whom Newton's *Mathematical Principles of Natural Philosophy* might never have been published, then computed the orbits of twenty-four comets. By scrutinizing earlier descriptions of them, when they were still regarded as nonrepeating phenomena, he identified periodic returns of the same body. For instance, the comet observed by Apian in 1531 was identical with that described by Kepler in 1607 and studied by Halley himself in 1682. Thus a new regular member was added to the family of celestial bodies. Instead of being an unanticipated interloper, the comet was now an orderly constituent of the cosmos.

Halley discovered that the latitude of three conspicuous stars had altered perceptibly since antiquity. Consequently he suggested that the stars, whose angular distances from one another had seemed unchanged throughout the ages, wherefore they had traditionally been called the "fixed stars," had their own particular or proper motions. These were imperceptible or unobserved in the more remote stars, but visible in those that were largest and nearest to the earth, as Giordano Bruno had surmised.

Halley's discovery of stellar proper motion had a profound effect on an acute astronomical observer, Thomas Wright of Durham, who in 1750 turned cosmological thought in a new direction. Because the stars of the first three magnitudes are distributed irregularly throughout the heavens, Wright contended that the sun, and the solar system, cannot be located at the center of the universe. Instead, the sun, its planets, their satellites, and the comets are situated in the Milky Way. This vast ring, as Democritus had taught, contains an immense number of closely packed stars. These lie between two parallel planes. If we direct our gaze between these planes, we see the cumulative effect of the light emanating from the stars in the Milky Way. On the other hand, the rest of the heavens outside the Milky Way shows us only scattered constellations. The Milky Way, however, is only one such aggregation, other similar formations being visible elsewhere in the heavens. All the stars, including our sun, move round some still unknown common center. Wright likened their movement to that of the innumerable tiny bodies whirling around Saturn and appearing to us as that planet's compound ring.

An extensive summary of Wright's novel ideas was promptly dispatched by an alert German correspondent in London to a Hamburg journal. This report caught the eye of a young man then unsuccessfully pursuing the career of a private tutor. Immanuel Kant, however, went far beyond Wright, who was theologically oriented. Taking the precaution of publishing his *Allgemeine Naturgeschichte* (1755), subtitled (in translation) *Essay on the . . . Mechanical Origin of the Whole Universe*, anonymously, Kant undertook to set forth a natural history of the heavens, or evolution of the cosmos. He argued, for example, that the moon is more recent than the earth. In its original state the moon was fluid. The gravitational attraction exerted on this lunar fluid by the earth in due course slowed the moon's axial rotation down to the time required by the moon to revolve once around the earth. Reciprocally, the earth's day is gradually lengthening, and in the remote future will coincide with the month. When that condition occurs, only one side of the earth will always be presented to the moon, and the two bodies will journey through space face to face, so to speak.

Like the ancient atomists, Kant started his cosmic history with an initial stage in which primitive vaporous matter was universally dispersed. Through the operation of Newtonian attraction, heavier particles attracted lighter, which were deflected from their rectilinear path by mutual repulsion. The resulting whirling in a disk produced the cosmic bodies, which still continue to revolve in the same orbit, direction, and plane. This formation of an orderly system occurred not only around that center of attraction which is our sun but also around an infinite number of similar suns infinitely distant. Yet they all constitute a single system related to a single center. This process has already gone on for millions of centuries, and will continue to do so for myriads of millions of centuries.

The distribution of Kant's cosmogony was delayed by its publisher's bankruptcy. In any case a rival view was propounded by the celebrated French astronomer Pierre Simon de Laplace about half a century later. Unlike Kant, whose critics objected that his combination of attraction with repulsion could never produce a rotational motion, Laplace started his cosmos with a "protosun" already undergoing a slow axial eastward rotation. This immense vaporous mass was initially fiercely hot. Slowly it cooled, contracted, and speeded up. At its outer edge, when centrifugal force matched the attraction to the center, a ring around the equator became detached. This was only the first such product in a series of such crises. A ring might condense into a separate planet, which then proceeded to spin off satellites of its own. Or a ring might disintegrate into a group of small planets, such as was discovered between Mars and Jupiter at the turn of the century. Or a ring might persist in the form discovered by Huygens in Saturn. Laplace published his nebular hypothesis in four successively developed versions extending over a period of twenty-eight years (1796–1824).

While Laplace's attention was directed principally to the bodies composing the solar system, the stars were the chief subject of William Herschel's scrutiny. By discovering Uranus far beyond Saturn and thereby making in 1781 the first addition to the family of planets in historic times, Herschel was enabled to forsake music as his means of livelihood and devote his undivided talents to the advancement of science, previously his passionate hobby.

Herschel discovered the period of Saturn's axial rotation with only a minute error. He did the same for Mars, whose white polar caps he showed were subject to seasonal fluctuations:

If . . . we find that the globe we inhabit has its polar regions frozen and covered with mountains of ice and snow, that only partly melt when alternately exposed to the sun, I may well be permitted to surmise that the same causes may probably have the same effect on the globe of Mars; that the bright polar spots are owing to the vivid reflection of light from frozen regions; and that the reduction of those spots is to be ascribed to their being exposed to the sun

(*Philosophical Transactions of the Royal Society of London*, **74** [1784], 260).

While investigating the properties of sunlight, which Newton had demonstrated to be composed of differently refracted rays related to the colors of the spectrum, Herschel found that the various colors are linked with different heating effects. These increased toward the red end of the spectrum, but did not stop there. "The full red falls still short of the maximum of heat; which perhaps lies even a little beyond visible refraction. In this case radiant heat will at least partly, if not chiefly, consist . . . of invisible light" (op. cit. [1800], p. 272). Herschel's discovery in 1800 of the infrared radiation beyond one end of the spectrum was promptly followed by the finding of chemical reactions beyond the violet end of the spectrum in 1801. Thus the spectrum was revealed to be only the visible portion of a more extensive radiation possessing continuous properties.

In his *Dialogue* of 1632 Galileo had proposed a method of proving the Copernican thesis that the earth revolves around the sun. This orbital motion should produce the optical effect of a larger annual parallax in a nearby star than in a distant star situated nearly along the same line of sight. In pursuit of this so-called differential parallax Herschel undertook to discover and catalogue such pairs of stars. It had recently been pointed out that double stars, being too numerous to be the result of a random scattering throughout the heavens, must in at least some cases form a physically connected pair. Herschel reasoned that "as the mutual gravitation of bodies towards each other is quite sufficient to account for the union of two stars, we are authorised to ascribe such combinations to that principle" (op. cit. [1802], p. 485). The effect of Newtonian gravitational attraction in uniting such binary stars exemplified the essential unity of the cosmos.

A binary may consist of two components differing in brightness. As the fainter star passes in front of its brighter partner, the latter's light diminishes. The first such periodically variable star was detected in 1596 by Kepler's correspondent, David Fabricius, a minister who was murdered by an enraged parishioner. Fabricius' Mira Ceti varies in a long period averaging 330 days from its brightest as a star of the second magnitude down to its minimum of ninth magnitude, invisible to the naked eye. On the other hand, such a short-period variable as Algol was known to complete its cycle in about 69 hours. Herschel found a variable having a period of about two months, lying in the interval between a few days and a year, and bringing the variables into a single class of stars, with which he associated our sun.

Herschel was convinced "that there is not, in strictness of speaking, one *fixed* star in the heavens," and that our sun too must have its own proper motion (Armitage, p. 94). As a German contemporary had pointed out, when we take a walk through the woods, the trees in front of us seem to move farther apart as we approach them, while those behind us appear to close up. By analogy, if the solar system of which our earth is a part is moving toward some point in the heavens, which Herschel called the "apex of the solar motion," then the stars in that direction should seem to open out, whereas those in the opposite direction should appear to come closer together. By analyzing the then known proper motions Herschel located the apex somewhere near Lambda in the constellation Hercules, a conclusion regarded by astronomers today as reasonably close to the truth (Figure 7).

Herschel placed the sun in

the Milky Way, which undoubtedly is nothing but a stratum of fixed stars. . . . This . . . immense starry bed is not of equal breadth or lustre in every part, nor runs on in one straight direction, but is curved and even divided into two streams along a very considerable portion of it. . . . Suppose a number of stars arranged between two parallel planes, indefinitely extended every way, but at a given considerable distance from each other; and, calling this a sidereal stratum, an eye placed somewhere within it will see all the stars in the direction of the planes of the stratum

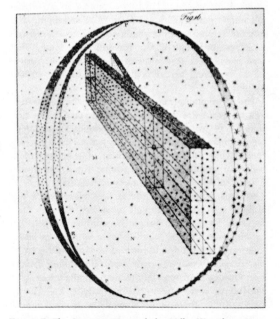

FIGURE 7. The Starry stratum and the Milky Way, from Angus Armitage, *William Herschel*, London, 1962. COURTESY OF THE ROYAL SOCIETY, LONDON.

projected into a great circle, which will appear lucid on account of the accumulation of the stars; while the rest of the heavens, at the sides, will only seem to be scattered over with constellations, more or less crowded, according to the distance of the planes or number of stars contained in the thickness or sides of the stratum (*Philosophical Transactions . . .* , **74** [1784], 442–43).

In the hope of determining the sun's place within the Milky Way Herschel introduced a statistical method in stellar astronomy. Dividing the sky into hundreds of regions, he directed his telescope to each region in turn, and counted the stars visible therein. As he thus "gaged the heavens," he could see many more stars in some directions than in others. The more tightly packed they were, the farther out they extended into space. Herschel surmised that our sun is situated "very probably not far from the place" of division of the Milky Way, that "very extensive, branching, compound Congeries of many millions of stars" constituting a "detached Nebula" or island universe, bounded on all sides by empty space (op. cit., **75** [1785], 244, 254). "It may not be amiss to point out some other very remarkable Nebulae which cannot well be less, but are probably much larger than our own system," from which they are separated by vast distances, no less vast than those by which they are separated from one another (idem, 258).

In many star clusters Herschel noted "a number of lucid spots, of equal lustre, scattered over a circular space, in such a manner as to appear gradually more compressed towards the middle" (op. cit., **79** [1789], 214). Those clusters showing the greatest density "must have been the longest exposed to the action of" centripetal force. Utilizing the implications of Olaus Römer's demonstration that the transmission of light is not instantaneous but requires a finite time, Herschel maintained that

a telescope with a power of penetrating into space . . . has also . . . a power of penetrating into time past. . . . When we see an object of the calculated distance at which one of these very remote nebulae may still be perceived, the rays of light which convey its image to the eye, must have been . . . almost two millions of years on their way; and . . . consequently, so many years ago, this object must already have had an existence in the sidereal heavens, in order to send out those rays by which we now perceive it (op. cit. [1802], pp. 498–99).

Herschel became convinced that not every nebulosity could be resolved by increased telescopic power into an aggregation of stars. In the middle of some nebulae he saw a somewhat greater brightness, which could serve as "a seat of attraction" for the formation of stars.

Since we are already acquainted with the centripetal force of attraction which gives a globular figure to planets, keeps them from flying out of their orbits in tangents, and makes one star revolve around another, why should we not look up to the universal gravitation of matter as the cause of every condensation, accumulation, compression, and concentration of the nebulous matter? (op. cit. [1811], p. 284).

For "what might be called the growth of stars" "millions of years perhaps are but moments." "We have an eternity of past duration to recur to."

For cosmologists the nineteenth century opened most auspiciously with the discovery of an asteroid on the very first evening of the new century. The successive distances of the planets from the sun had showed a disproportionately wide gap between Mars and Jupiter. In that gap the relatively tiny asteroids (as this class of cosmic bodies was constituted and christened by Herschel) have been found in great numbers. Since their brightness fluctuates considerably, their shape may be irregular rather than round. Writing to Herschel on 17 June 1802, Wilhelm Olbers, the discoverer of the second asteroid, suggested that the two known asteroids might be "just a pair of fragments, of portions of a once greater planet which at one time occupied its proper place between Mars and Jupiter, and was in size more analogous to the other planets, and perhaps millions of years ago, had, either through the impact of a comet, or from an internal explosion, burst into pieces" (Lubbock, p. 273).

An alternative origin of the asteroids was proposed about a century later by two American scientists. Convinced that the technical defects in the nebular hypothesis could not be overcome, they imagined that in the remote past while our sun still had no planets, it was approached by another star closely enough to raise huge tides upon it. Where the matter ejected by the sun was dominated by a nucleus, a planet was formed. But the asteroids or planetoids occupy a region in which no dominating nucleus existed to assemble them as a single planet.

Herschel's discovery of the planet Uranus led to a search for earlier determinations of its position, which had often been noted under the mistaken impression that it was a star. When these prior observations were compared with those made after Herschel's discovery, it was found that the two sets of data could not be combined into a unified theory of the motions of Uranus. Moreover, the computed tables of the planet's places increasingly diverged from fresh observations. Hence the suspicion grew that Herschel's planet was subject to perturbations caused by an unknown cosmic body. Could the position of this trans-Uranian planet at a given time be mathematically deduced from its disturbing effect on Uranus? A young French mathe-matician, U. J. J. Leverrier, wrote to Johann Gottfried Galle, an assistant at the Berlin Observatory, the two countries not being at war:

I would like to find a persistent observer who would be willing to devote some time to an examination of a part of the sky in which there may be a planet to discover. I have been led to this conclusion by the theory of Uranus. . . . I demonstrate that it is impossible to satisfy the observations of Uranus without introducing the action of a new planet, thus far unknown; and remarkably, there is only one single position in the ecliptic where this perturbing planet can be located. . . . The mass of the planet allows us to conclude that its apparent diameter is more than 3″ [three seconds] of arc (Grosser, pp. 115–16).

Leverrier's communication reached Galle on 23 September 1846. Two days later Galle replied: "The planet whose position you have pointed out *actually exists*. The same day that I received your letter, I found a star of the eighth magnitude. . . . The observations made the following day determined that this was the sought-for planet"—Neptune. Further examples of international cooperation in the peaceful investigation of our cosmos were provided by corrections of Leverrier's computations by John Couch Adams in England and Benjamin Peirce at Harvard.

Later unexplained perturbations of Uranus as well as irregularities in the motion of Neptune led to a search in the twentieth century for a trans-Neptunian planet. Pluto was found in 1930 by an American farmer and amateur astronomer, Clyde W. Tombaugh, who detected in photographic plates exposed two days apart a shift in an image of the fifteenth magnitude. This most recently discovered satellite of our sun turned out to be much less of a giant than its four closest neighbors.

The art of photography, invented in the nineteenth century, proved to be of inestimable value to the cosmologist. It provided him with a precise, impersonal, and permanent record of the object or field he was investigating. It could make faint objects or details visible by prolonging the exposure, since the action of light on the sensitive plate is cumulative.

At least equally valuable is spectroscopy. When sunlight was passed through a narrow slit and then dispersed by a prism, Joseph Fraunhofer noticed that the continuous bright band of color in the solar spectrum ranging from red at one end to violet at the other was crossed by many narrow dark lines. These Fraunhofer lines, as they were later called, signified that some constituents were missing from sunlight. Laboratory investigations subsequently showed that every chemical substance, when heated to incandescence, gives off its own characteristic line spectrum. When light from a hotter source passes through a cooler gas, the latter absorbs and does not transmit those components of the source's light that correspond to the bright lines in the spectrum of the gas. Bright lines in the spectra of some common chemical elements were shown by Gustav Kirchhoff to coincide with dark lines in the solar spectrum. He therefore concluded that these elements were present in the atmosphere of the sun. Then that body consists of an intensely hot core surrounded by layers of somewhat cooler gases containing in incandescent form chemical elements found on the earth. The spectra of the other stars likewise reveal the presence in them of known terrestrial chemical elements. In one case, helium was first detected spectroscopically in the sun before its existence on the earth was discovered, and its lightness and noninflammability utilized in balloons. Spectroscopy has proved that the cosmos is built up of the same elements throughout its enormous extent.

When a chemical element is heated to incandescence in the laboratory, its line spectrum coincides with that derived from its counterpart in a distant star. A displacement of the corresponding lines may indicate that the two sources are not at rest with respect to each other. If they are in relative motion, a displacement toward the violet end of the spectrum indicates a lessening of the distance between them. On the other hand, a displacement toward the red end of the spectrum signifies an increase of the distance between them. This principle was formulated by Christian Doppler in 1842. Since then the spectra of remote nebulae have exhibited a shift toward the red. Regarded as a "Doppler effect," this red shift indicates that these nebulae are receding into space at speeds proportional to their distances from us, with important implications for the history of the cosmos.

Whereas it had always been assumed that the atom as the ultimate constituent of matter was indivisible, in 1896 Henri Becquerel discovered that uranium and its compounds in their natural state spontaneously gave off an invisible radiation capable of affecting a photographic plate. When similar radioactivity was found in other heavy chemical elements, their atoms were regarded as breaking down into lighter atoms, while the process of disintegration was marked by the emission of charged particles. The rate at which this transformation proceeds can be computed and used to form an estimate of the age of the earth.

Such release of energy stored up within the atom was soon accomplished artificially by man-made devices. An atomic nucleus bombarded by particles penetrating it at extremely high velocities was transformed into a different atomic nucleus. At the enormous temperatures prevailing in the interior of the sun thermonuclear reactions could convert hydrogen into helium

with an accompanying output of energy approximating the present radiation of the sun. The other stars may be considered to be similar atomic furnaces at various stages of development.

On the basis of the different kinds of spectra which they exhibit the stars have been grouped into a number of classes capable of being arranged in a single sequence. These various types have been viewed as successive chronological stages in the evolution of the stars, some of which are giants while others are dwarfs. Variable stars of a certain variety have been regarded as gaseous spheres alternately expanding and contracting rhythmically in response to balanced opposing forces of gravitational attraction and internal pressure. When the latter crosses a critical threshold, the resulting explosion produces a nova. After it subsides, in its defunct state the former nova resembles the so-called planetary nebula.

Ingenious measurements of the velocity of light on the surface of the earth showed that this velocity was unaffected by the direction. Whether the beam of light traveled in the direction of the earth's orbital motion or in the opposite direction, the speed remained the same. This experimental result was combined by Albert Einstein with his own theoretical analysis to yield the postulate that the velocity of light is a constant of nature. Accordingly he dismissed as superfluous the supposed existence of a luminiferous aether, widely accepted throughout the nineteenth century. He likewise denied the reality of absolute space and absolute time, insisting that all motion is relative, with no system of coordinates possessing any privileged status. Thus the fundamental underpinning of the Newtonian synthesis was removed to make way for the sweeping rival speculative cosmologies of the twentieth century.

BIBLIOGRAPHY

Al-Biruni, *The Book of Instruction in the Elements of the Art of Astrology,* trans. R. Ramsay Wright (London, 1934). A. Armitage, *A Century of Astronomy* (London, 1950); idem, *William Herschel* (New York, 1962). For G. A. Borelli, see *Lettere inedite di uomini illustri,* ed. Angelo Fabroni, 2 vols. (Florence, 1773–75). S. G. F. Brandon, *Creation Legends of the Ancient Near East* (Mystic, Conn., 1963). David R. Dicks, *Early Greek Astronomy to Aristotle* (London, 1970). For Geminus, see M. R. Cohen and I. E. Drabkin, *A Source Book in Greek Science* (Cambridge, Mass., 1966). Morton Grosser, *The Discovery of Neptune* (Cambridge, Mass., 1962), pp. 115–16, translating from the French text in *Monthly Notices of the Royal Astronomical Society,* **71** (1910–11), 278–79. W. K. C. Guthrie, *A History of Greek Philosophy,* 3 vols. (New York, 1962, 1965, 1969). T. L. Heath, *Aristarchus of Samos* (Oxford, 1959). M. A. Hoskin, *William Herschel and the Construction of the Heavens* (Chicago, 1968). Christiaan Huygens, *Oeuvres complètes . . .*

(The Hague, 1888–1950). Johannes Kepler, *Gesammelte Werke* (Munich, 1937—); see also idem, *Mysterium cosmographicum* (1596; 2nd ed., 1621), Note 3, Ch. 20. A. Koyré, *From the Closed World to the Infinite Universe* (Baltimore, 1968); idem, *La révolution astronomique* (Paris, 1961); idem, *Newtonian Studies* (Chicago, 1968). B. and J. Lovell, *Discovering the Universe* (New York, 1963). Constance A. Lubbock, *The Herschel Chronicle* (Cambridge, 1933). H. Messel and S. T. Butler, *The Universe and its Origin* (New York, 1964). M. K. Munitz, ed., *Theories of the Universe* (New York, 1965). O. Neugebauer, *Astronomical Cuneiform Texts* (Princeton, 1955); idem, *The Exact Sciences in Antiquity*, 2nd ed. (New York, 1969); idem and R. A. Parker, *Egyptian Astronomical Texts* (Providence, 1960–68). Isaac Newton, *The Correspondence of Isaac Newton*, 4 vols. (Cambridge, 1959–67). Nicholas Oresme, *Le Livre du ciel et du monde*, eds. Menut and Denomy (Madison, 1968). A. Pannekoek, *A History of Astronomy* (New York, 1961). Ptolemy, *Planetary Hypotheses*, Book I, in *Transactions of the American Philosophical Society*, new series, **57** (1967), Part 4, p. 8. A. Romer, ed., *The Discovery of Radioactivity and Transmutation* (New York, 1964). E. Rosen, ed., *Three Copernican Treatises*, 3rd ed. (New York, 1971); idem, ed., *Kepler's Conversation with Galileo's Sidereal Messenger* (New York, 1965); idem, ed., *Kepler's Somnium* (Madison, 1967). Edward Sachau, *Alberuni's India*, 2 vols. (Lahore, 1962). H. Shapley, ed., *Source Book in Astronomy, 1900–1950* (Cambridge, Mass., 1960). E. T. Whittaker, *A History of the Theories of Aether and Electricity*, 2 vols. (New York, 1910; 1960). Wanda Wolska, *La topographie chrétienne de Cosmas Indicopleustès* (Paris, 1962).

Translations identified as E. R. are by the author of this article.

EDWARD ROSEN

[See also Astrology; **Atomism; Cosmic Fall;** Cosmic Images; **Cosmic Voyages;** Islamic Conception; **Pythagorean Harmony; Relativity;** Space; Time and Measurement.]

COSMOLOGY SINCE 1850

I. INTRODUCTION

THE LAST FORTY YEARS of the nineteenth century were among the most remarkable in the history of science, for this was a period of amazing scientific achievements and contradictions; on the one hand classical physics and astronomy were enjoying some of their greatest successes during this period, but at the same time observational and experimental data, which were ultimately to overthrow the classical laws of physics, were slowly being collected. Until the year 1860 physics and astronomy were dominated by Newton's concepts of space and time and by his laws of mechanics and gravitation; these seemed sufficient to explain observa-

tions ranging all the way from the motion of the planets to the behavior of the tides on the earth. The great eighteenth- and nineteenth-century mathematicians such as Euler, Laplace, Lagrange, Hamilton, and Gauss had cast the Newtonian laws into beautiful and magnificent mathematical forms which had their greatest applications to celestial mechanics. Astronomers happily used these techniques to show how excellent was the agreement between observation and theory. The two domains of physics that still lay outside the Newtonian laws—electromagnetism and optics—were also soon to be incorporated into a satisfying theoretical structure. In the year 1865, James Clerk Maxwell published his famous papers on his electromagnetic theory of light, which gave a precise and beautiful mathematical formulation of Faraday's experimental discoveries, unified electricity, magnetism, and optics, and opened up the whole field of electromagnetic technology.

Thus, at the end of the first decade of the last forty years of the nineteenth century, everything seemed to fall neatly into place in the world of science. To the scientists of that period, the universe appeared to be a well ordered arrangement of celestial bodies moving about in an infinite expanse of absolute space, and with all the events in the universe occurring in a unique and absolute sequence in time. There was no question at that time as to the correctness of this Newtonian universe based on the concepts of absolute space and time; only the observational and experimental details were lacking to make the picture complete, and everyone was confident that, with improved technology, these details would be obtained in time.

This absolute concept of the universe and of the laws of nature was very satisfying to the late nineteenth-century man, who saw in the orderly and absolute scheme of things the demonstration of the Divine Omnipotence which he worshipped and which gave him the reason for his existence; moreover, the infinitude of space and time required by the Newtonian universe was also required by the concept of an infinitely powerful deity, as described by Alexander Pope:

> He sees with equal eye as God of all
> A hero perish or a sparrow fall;
> Atoms or systems into ruin hurl'd;
> And now a bubble burst, and now a world.
> (*An Essay on Man* III. 87–90)

II. DISCREPANCIES IN THE NEWTONIAN UNIVERSE

But even while this neat, orderly scheme of the universe was being eagerly incorporated into Victorian philosophical and social concepts, its very basis was being undermined by experimental and observational data, and by logical analysis in four different realms of physics and astronomy: in the realm of optics, the experiments of Michelson and Morley on the speed of light were to destroy the Newtonian concepts of absolute space and time and to replace them by the Einsteinian space-time concept (the special theory of relativity); in the realm of radiation, the discoveries of the properties of the radiation emitted by hot bodies were to upset the Maxwell wave-theory of light and to introduce the quantum theory (the photon) with its wave-particle dualism; in the realm of observational astronomy, the discrepancy between the deductions from Newtonian gravitational theory and the observed motion of Mercury (the advance of its perihelion) indicated the need for a new gravitational theory which Einstein produced in 1914 (the general theory of relativity); finally, in the realm of cosmology, various theoretical analyses showed that the nineteenth-century models of the universe, constructed with Newtonian gravitational theory and space-time concepts, were in serious contradiction with stellar observations.

Although the investigation of each of these departures from classical physics is of extreme importance and each one has an important bearing on the most recent cosmological theories, we limit ourselves here to the cosmological realm and, where necessary in our discussion, use the results of modern physics without concern about how they were obtained. However, before we discuss the difficulties inherent in Newtonian cosmology, we must consider one other important nineteenth-century discovery which, at the time, seemed to have no bearing on the structure of the universe but which ultimately played a most important role in the development of cosmology. This was the discovery of the non-Euclidean geometries by Gauss, Bolyai, Lobachevsky, Riemann, and Klein. At the time that these non-Euclidean geometries were discovered, and for many years following, scientists in general considered them to be no more than mathematical curiosities, with no relevance to the structure of the universe or to the nature of actual space. Most mathematicians and scientists simply took it for granted that the geometry of physical space is Euclidean and that the laws of physics must conform to Euclidean geometry.

This attitude, however, was not universal and Gauss himself, the spiritual father of non-Euclidean geometry, proposed a possible (but in practice, unrealizable) test of the flatness of space by measuring the interior angles of a large spatial triangle constructed in the neighborhood of the earth. Also, the mathematician W. K. Clifford, in *The Common Sense of the Exact Sciences* (1870; reprint, New York, 1946), speculated that the geometry of actual space might not be Euclidean. He proposed the following ideas: (1) that small portions of space are, in fact, of a nature analogous to little hills on a surface which is, on the average, flat—namely, that the ordinary laws of geometry are not valid in them; (2) that this property of being curved or distorted is continually being passed on from one portion of space to another after the manner of a wave; (3) that this variation of the curvature of space is what really happens in that phenomenon which we call motion of matter, whether ponderable or ethereal; (4) that in the physical world nothing else takes place but this variation, subject (possibly) to the laws of continuity.

Clifford summarized his opinion as follows:

The hypothesis that space is not homaloidal and, again, that its geometrical character may change with time may or may not be destined to play a great part in the physics of the future; yet we cannot refuse to consider them as possible explanations of physical phenomena because they may be opposed to the popular dogmatic belief in the universality of certain geometrical axioms—belief which has arisen from centuries of indiscriminating worship of the genius of Euclid.

These were, indeed, prophetic words, for, as we shall see, in the hands of Einstein the non-Euclidean geometries became the very foundation of modern cosmological theory. But let us first examine the flaws and difficulties inherent in the Newtonian cosmology of the nineteenth century.

III. CONTRADICTIONS IN THE NEWTONIAN COSMOLOGY

We first consider what is now called the Olbers paradox, a remarkable conclusion about the appearance of the night sky deduced by Heinrich Olbers in 1826. Olbers was greatly puzzled by the fact that the night sky (when no moon is present) appears as dark as it does instead of as bright as the sun, which, he reasoned, is how it should appear if the basic Newtonian concepts of space and time were correct. In deducing this paradox, Olbers assumed the universe to be infinite in extent, with the average density and the average luminosity of the stars to be the same everywhere and at all times. He assumed, further, that space is Euclidean and that there are no large systematic movements of the stars. With these assumptions we can see, as Olbers did, that each point of the night sky should appear as bright as each point of the surface of the sun (or any other average star). The reason for this is that if the stars were distributed as assumed, a line directed from our eye to any point in space would ultimately hit a star so that the whole sky should appear to be covered with stars.

Until quite recently this apparent paradox was taken as a very strong argument against an infinite Newtonian universe (or at least against Olbers' assumptions) but E. R. Harrison (1965) has shown that Olbers' conclusions are contrary to the principle of conservation of energy. To understand this, we first note that a star (like the sun) can radiate energy at its present rate for only a finite time because only a finite amount of nuclear fuel is available for this release of energy. Now if we assume that stars (or galaxies) are distributed everywhere the way we observe them to be in our part of the universe, it would take about 10^{23} years before the radiation from these stars would fill the universe to give the effect deduced by Olbers. But all stars would have used up their nuclear fuel long before this time and their luminosities would have changed drastically. Thus Olbers' assumption that the luminosities of the stars do not change during their lifetimes is not tenable. Harrison has shown that the radiation emitted by stars in a period of about 10^{10} years (which, on the basis of modern theories we may take as a reasonable estimate of the age of the universe) should give just about the kind of night sky we observe.

Although Harrison's analysis of the Olbers paradox removes this flaw in a static infinite Newtonian universe, another difficulty, first pointed out by Seeliger in 1895 and also by C. G. Neumann, still remains. In a static Newtonian universe (one which is not expanding), with stars (or galaxies) extending uniformly out to infinity, the gravitational force at each point must be infinitely large, which is contrary to what we actually observe. This difficulty with a Newtonian universe can be expressed somewhat differently by considering the behavior of the elements of matter in it. These elements could not remain fixed but would move towards each other so that the universe could not be static. In fact, a Newtonian universe can remain static only if the density of matter in it is everywhere zero. To overcome this difficulty Neumann (1895) and Seeliger (1895) altered Newton's law of gravity by the addition of a repulsive term which is very small for small distances but becomes very large at large distances from the observer. In this way a static, but modified, Newtonian universe can be constructed.

We may also exclude a Newtonian universe of infinite extent in space but containing only a finite amount of matter. The principal difficulty with such a universe is that, in time, matter would become infinitely dispersed or it would all coalesce into a single globule—contrary to observation.

IV. COSMOLOGY AND THE THEORY OF RELATIVITY

When it became apparent at the end of the nineteenth century that pure Newtonian theory (that is,

without the addition of a repulsive term to Newton's law of force) could not lead to a static model of the universe, most scientists lost interest in the cosmological problem and very little work was done in this field until the whole subject was dramatically reopened by Einstein in 1917, when he published his famous paper on relativistic cosmology. New life was suddenly given to cosmology by the appearance of this paper, since it now appeared that the flaws in Newtonian cosmology would be eliminated with the introduction of the Einsteinian space-time concept. As we shall presently see, this is indeed true, but difficulties still arise because a number of different model universes can be obtained from general relativity theory, and we are then left with the problem of deciding which of these is the correct model. This is a somewhat unsatisfactory situation since one of the purposes of a theory is to restrict the theoretical models that can be deduced from it to just those that we actually observe in nature; but in spite of this drawback, we must turn to the general theory of relativity for an understanding of cosmology, since it is the best theory of space and time that we now have and Newtonian theory has certainly been disproved. However, before we can discuss relativistic cosmology meaningfully, we must understand the basic concepts of the theory of relativity itself.

This theory was developed in two stages: the first (1905) is called the special or restricted theory of relativity and the second (1915) is called the general theory. The basic feature of the special theory is that all observers moving with uniform speed in straight lines relative to the distant background stars (such observers are said to be moving in inertial frames of reference) are equivalent in the eyes of nature, in the sense that the laws of nature are the same for all of them. Put differently, the special theory states that an observer in an inertial frame cannot determine his state of motion by any kind of experiment (or observation) performed entirely in his frame of reference (that is, without referring to the background stars). Before the time of Einstein, this formulation of the special theory was accepted by physicists only insofar as it applied to the laws of Newtonian mechanics. They believed that an observer in an inertial frame could not detect his uniform motion by means of any mechanical experiment, but they assumed that the principle did not apply to optical phenomena and that an inertial observer *could* detect his motion through the ether (whose existence had been postulated to account for the propagation of light) by observing the way light moves (that is, by measuring the speed of light) in various directions in his frame of reference. Physicists believed this to be so because the Newtonian concepts of absolute space and absolute time lead precisely to this very conclusion.

One can deduce from these concepts that the speed of light is not the same in all directions, as measured by a moving observer—the measured value of the speed of light should be a maximum for a beam of light moving against the motion of the observer and a minimum for a beam moving in the same direction as the observer. This deduction, however, is contrary to the experimental evidence. In 1887 Michelson and Morley demonstrated experimentally that the speed of light is the same in all directions for all inertial observers. Thus the constancy of the speed of light for all such observers must be accepted as a law of nature. This means, as emphasized by Einstein, that the special theory of relativity must apply to optical phenomena just as it does to mechanical phenomena, so that an observer in an inertial frame cannot deduce his state of motion from optical phenomena. Since this is contrary to the deductions from the Newtonian concepts of absolute space and absolute time, Einstein rejected these absolute Newtonian notions and replaced them by relative time and relative space.

To illustrate the essential difference between the two concepts (absolute and relative) we may consider two events separated in space by a certain distance d and in time by the interval t *as measured by some particular observer in an inertial frame.* Now, according to the absolute concepts of Newton, *all other* inertial observers recording these two events would find the same distance d between them and the same interval t. This is what Einstein denies, for, as we have noted, this contradicts the observed fact that the speed of light is the same in all directions for all observers. This means that the distance d and the time interval t are different for observers moving with different speeds, so that space and time separately vary as we pass from one inertial frame to another. The special theory of relativity replaces the separate absolute Newtonian concepts of space and time with a single absolute space-time concept for any two events, which is constructed as follows by any observer: Let this observer measure the distance between these two events and square this number to obtain d^2. Next, let him measure the time interval between the two events and square this to obtain t^2. He now constructs the numerical quantity $d^2\text{-}c^2t^2$, where c is the speed of light. *This quantity, which is called the square of the space-time interval between the two events, is the same for all observers moving in different inertial frames of reference.*

We see from this that the absolute three-dimensional Newtonian spatial universe, with its events unfolding in a unique (absolute) temporal sequence, is replaced by a four-dimensional space-time universe in which the spatial separation and the time interval between any two events vary from observer to observer, but in which all observers measure the same space-time interval. We may state this somewhat differently by saying that the universe of the special theory of relativity is a four-dimensional space-time universe *governed by Euclidean geometry.* The last part of this statement is important since it is equivalent to saying that the square of the space-time interval in a universe governed by special relativity is exactly $d^2\text{-}c^2t^2$. In such a universe, free bodies (bodies that are not pulled or pushed by ropes, or rods, or by some other force) move in straight lines in space-time.

We must now see how this theory, which is restricted to observers in inertial frames of reference, is to be extended when we introduce gravitational fields and observers undergoing any arbitrary kind of motion (rotation, linear acceleration, etc.). That the theory as it stands (that is, the special theory of relativity) is not equipped to treat observers in accelerated frames of reference or to deal with gravitational fields can be seen easily enough if we keep in mind that the special theory is based on the premiss that all inertial observers are equal in the eyes of nature and that there is no observation, mechanical or optical, that an inertial observer can make to indicate how he is moving.

Now it appears at first sight that such a statement cannot be made about observers in accelerated frames of reference since the acceleration causes objects to depart from straight line motion. If one is in a train which is moving at constant speed in a straight line, objects in the train behave just as they would if the train were standing still; thus one can as easily pour coffee into a cup when the train is moving with constant speed as when it is at rest. But any departure from constant motion (that is, any kind of acceleration) can at once be detected, because such things as pouring liquids from one vessel into another become extremely difficult. We should therefore be able to detect that we are in an accelerated frame by observing just such phenomena. It thus appears that inertial frames of reference and accelerated frames are not equivalent. This, then, at first blush, would seem to eliminate the possibility of generalizing the theory of relativity. But we shall presently see just how Einstein overcame this difficulty.

That the law of gravity, as stated by Newton, is not in conformity with the special theory of relativity, is evident from the fact that, according to this theory, clocks, measuring rods, and masses change when viewed from different inertial frames of reference. But, according to Newton's law of gravity, the gravitational force between two bodies is expressed in terms of the masses of the bodies and the distance between them at a definite instant of time. Hence this force can have no absolute meaning—in fact, there is no meaningful way for an inertial observer to calculate this force since he has no way of knowing which values to use for the masses of the two bodies and the distance between them. This breakdown of the Newtonian law of gravity, and the impossibility of incorporating accelerated frames of reference in the framework of special relativity, convinced Einstein that a generalization of the theory of relativity was not only necessary, but possible. For if it were not possible to generalize the theory, a whole range of observers and of physical phenomena related to gravity would not be expressible in terms of a space-time formulation.

To see how Einstein set about generalizing his theory, we may first note that two apparently unrelated classes of phenomena—those arising from accelerations and those arising from gravitational fields—are excluded from the special theory. Einstein therefore proceeded on the assumption that these two groups of phenomena must be treated together and that a generalization of the theory of relativity must stem from some basic relationship between gravitational fields and accelerated frames of reference. This basic relationship is contained in Einstein's famous principle of equivalence, a principle which permits one to state that all frames of reference (in a small enough region of space) are equivalent and that in such a region there is no way for an observer to tell whether he is in an inertial frame of reference, in an accelerated frame, or in a gravitational field. Another way of putting this is that the principle of equivalence permits one to use any kind of coordinate system (frame of reference) to express the laws of physics. This means, further, that no law of physics can contain any reference to any special coordinate system, for if a law did contain such a reference, this in itself could be used by an observer to determine the nature of his frame of reference. Thus all laws must have the same form in all coordinate systems.

To understand how the principle of equivalence leads to the general theory, we must first see just what the basis of this principle is and what it states. The principle itself stems from Galileo's observation that all bodies allowed to fall freely (that is, in a vacuum with nothing impeding them) fall with the same speed. This can be stated somewhat differently if we consider the mass of a body (the amount of matter the body contains). This quantity appears in two places in the laws of Newtonian physics. On the one hand, it is the quantity that determines the inertia of a body (that is, the resistance a body offers to a force that tries to move it). For this reason, the quantity is referred to as the *inertial mass* of the body. But the concept of mass also appears in Newton's formula that expresses the gravitational force that one body exerts on another; this mass is then referred to as the *gravitational mass* of the body. The fact that all bodies fall with the same

speed in a gravitational field means that the inertial mass and the gravitational mass of a body must be equal.

This remarkable fact had been considered as no more than a numerical coincidence before Einstein developed his general theory of relativity. Einstein started out on the assumption that the equality of the inertial and gravitational masses of a body is not a coincidence but, instead, must have a deep significance. To see what this significance is, consider the way bodies behave in an accelerated frame of reference somewhere in empty space (far away from any masses) and the way they behave in a gravitational field (for example, on the surface of the earth). Owing to their inertial masses, all the bodies in the accelerated system behave as though they were being pulled opposite to the direction of the acceleration and they all respond in exactly the same way (that is, they all "fall" with the same speed). To Einstein, this meant that there is no way to differentiate between an accelerated frame of reference and a frame that is at rest (or moving with constant speed) in a gravitational field. This is called the principle of equivalence. Another way of stating it is to say that the apparent force that a body experiences when it is in an accelerated frame of reference is identical with the force this body would experience in an appropriate gravitational field; thus inertial and gravitational forces are indistinguishable.

Since the principle of equivalence makes it impossible to assign any special quality or physical significance to inertial frames of reference, the special theory (which is based on the assumption that inertial frames are *special* in the sense that only in such frames do the laws of physics have their correct and simplest form) must be discarded for a more general theory which puts all frames of reference and all coordinate systems on the same footing. In such a theory, the laws of physics must have the same form in all coordinate systems. With this in mind, we can now see how Einstein constructed his general theory of relativity. We begin by noting that the special theory replaces the concepts of absolute distance d and absolute time t between events by a single absolute space-time interval whose square is $d^2-c^2t^2$. Consider now a freely moving particle as viewed by an observer in an inertial frame of reference in a region of space where no gravitational fields are present. If this particle moves a distance d in a time t, the quantity $d^2-c^2t^2$ must be the same for all observers in inertial frames. This simply means that the natural space-time path of a free particle for inertial frames of reference is a straight line and that the space-time geometry of the special theory of relativity is Euclidean. We may take this formulation then as the law of motion (and hence a law of nature) of a free particle.

Now if we are to carry out our program of extending the principle of relativity to cover observers in gravitational fields and in accelerated frames of reference, we must say that this same law of motion (straight line motion) applies to a body moving freely in a gravitational field or in an accelerated frame of reference. But we know that the space-time path of a free particle in a gravitational field (or in a rotating system) appears to be anything but straight. How, then, are we to reconcile this apparent contradiction? We must redefine the concept of a straight line! We are ordinarily accustomed to think of a straight line in the Euclidean sense of straightness, because the geometry of our world is very nearly Euclidean and we have been brought up on Euclidean geometry. In a sense, we suffer from the same kind of geometrical bias concerning space-time as does the man who thinks the earth is flat because he cannot detect its sphericity in his small patch of ground.

To overcome this parochial attitude, we note that we can replace the "straightness" concept by the concept of the shortest distance between two points. We can now state the law of motion of a free particle as follows:

A free particle moving between two space-time points always moves in such a way that its space-time path between these two points is shorter than any other space-time path that can be drawn between the two points.

This statement of the law of motion makes no reference to the way the space-time path of the particle looks, but refers only to an absolute property of the path which has the same meaning for all observers. If no gravitational fields or accelerated observers are present, the shortest space-time path is $d^2-c^2t^2$ and the geometry is Euclidean. But if gravitational fields are present, the shortest space-time path of the particle (that is, its geodesic) is not given by $d^2-c^2t^2$, but by a different combination of d and t because the space-time geometry is non-Euclidean. The essence of Einstein's general theory is, then, that a gravitational field distorts space-time (it introduces a curvature into space-time) and the behavior of a free particle (that is, the departure from Euclidean straight-line motion) is not due to a "gravitational force" acting on the particle, but rather to the natural inclination of the free particle to move along a geodesic. In a sense, this is similar to what happens whan a ball is allowed to roll freely on a perfectly smooth piece of ground. The ball appears to us to move in a "straight line," but we know that this cannot be so because it is following the contour of the earth, which is spherical. Actually the ball is moving along the shortest path on the smooth surface, which is the arc of a great circle.

From this discussion we see that in the general theory of relativity, the space-time path of a freely moving particle is not $d^2-c^2t^2$, but some variation of this, which depends on the kind of gravitational fields that are present, and on the acceleration of our coordinate system. We can therefore go from the special theory to the general theory of relativity by replacing the space-time interval ($d^2-c^2t^2$) by the quantity $gd^2-qc^2t^2$, where g and q are quantities that vary from point to point. The value of the quantities g and q at any point for a given observer will depend on the intensity of the gravitational field at that point and on the acceleration of the frame of reference of the observer. Just as the special theory of relativity is based on the statement that the quantity $d^2-c^2t^2$ is the same for all observers in inertial frames of reference, the general theory of relativity is based on the statement that the quantity $gd^2-qc^2t^2$ must be the same for all observers, regardless of their frames of reference.

Now the use of the latter expression as the absolute space-time interval instead of the former means that we pass from Euclidean to non-Euclidean geometry in going from the special to the general theory, and the quantities g and q (they are also referred to as the Einstein gravitational potentials) determine by how much the geometry at any point of space-time departs from Euclidean geometry—in other words, these quantities determine the curvature of space time at each point. If, then, we know how to find g and q, we can determine the nature of the geometry in any region of space-time and hence the path of a free particle in that region. The curvature of space-time thus becomes equivalent to the intensity of the gravitational field, so that the gravitational problem is reduced to a problem in non-Euclidean geometry. The next step, then, in this development was to set down the law that determines the quantities g and q, and this Einstein did in his famous field equations—a set of ten partial differential equations that show just how the quantities g and q (there are actually ten such quantities, but in the gravitational field arising from a body like the sun, only two of these ten quantities are different from zero) depend on the distribution of matter. These gravitational field equations are the basis of all modern cosmological theories which we shall now discuss.

V. THE EINSTEIN STATIC UNIVERSE

The first great step in the development of modern cosmology was taken by Einstein in his famous 1917 paper, in which he set out to derive the physical properties of the universe by applying his field equations to the kind of distribution of matter that one might reasonably expect to find in the universe as a whole. Here Einstein had to introduce some simplifying assumptions, since we have detailed knowledge

559

about the distribution of matter only in a relatively small region of space (within a few thousand light years of our own solar system) and we find that the matter here is concentrated in lumps (the stars) with some dust and gas between the lumps. Einstein therefore introduced the *cosmological principle*, which states that, except for local irregularities, the universe has the same aspect (the same density of matter) as seen from any point. This means that what we see in our region of the universe is pictured as being repeated everywhere, like a wall-paper or linoleum pattern.

Einstein next replaced the lumpiness of the distribution of matter (as indicated in the existence of stars and galaxies) by a smooth, uniform distribution which we may obtain by picturing all the matter in the stars as smeared out to fill space with a fog of uniform density (actually a proton gas with a few protons per cubic foot of space). Einstein made one other assumption—that the universe is static; that is, that the density of matter does not change with time and that there are no large scale motions in the universe. At the time that Einstein did this work, this assumption appeared to be eminently justified because the recession of the distant galaxies had not yet been discovered and the stars in our own neighborhood of space were known to be moving with fairly small random velocities. With these assumptions, Einstein still had to make one important extrapolation—he had to extend his field equations to make them applicable to the entire universe and not just to a small region of empty space around the sun.

It is useful here (as a guide in our discussion) to write down Einstein's field equations in the form in which Einstein first used them in his study of cosmology:

$$R_{ij} - \tfrac{1}{2} R g_{ij} = -\frac{8\pi G}{c^4} T_{ij}. \tag{1}$$

This equation really represents ten distinct equations since the quantities R_{ij}, g_{ij}, and T_{ij} are components of three different tensors, and there are just ten such distinct components in each of these tensors. The tensor components R_{ij}, which are constructed in a well-defined way from the potentials g_{ij} (which are also called the components of the metric tensor) determine the nature of the space-time geometry. The quantity R gives the curvature of space-time at any specific point, and the tensor T_{ij} is the matter-energy-momentum-pressure tensor. G is the universal gravitational constant and c is the speed of light. This set of ten equations thus tells us how the matter and energy that are present determine the metric tensor g_{ij} at each point of space-time and therefore the geometry at each such point. To determine the potentials g_{ij} and hence

the geometry of space time, one must thus solve the ten field equations for the known or assumed distribution of matter and energy as given by the tensor T_{ij}.

In the case of planetary motion, one simply places $T_{ij} = 0$; this leads to Einstein's law of gravity for empty space

$$R_{ij} = 0,$$

which reduces to Newton's law for weak gravitational fields. But for the cosmological problem, Einstein placed T_{ij} equal to a constant value (the average density of matter at each point) and then sought to solve the field equations (1) under these conditions. In other words, he attempted to obtain the potentials g_{ij} from equations (1) under the assumption that there is a constant (but very small) density of matter throughout the universe. His idea was that this small density would introduce a constant curvature of space-time at each point so that the universe would be curved as a whole. This initial attempt to obtain a static model of the universe was unsuccessful, however, because the equations (1) lead to a unique set of potentials g_{ij} only if one knows the values of these quantities at infinity. Now the natural procedure in this kind of analysis is to assume that all the values of g_{ij} are zero at infinity, but this cannot be done if one keeps the equations (1) and also retains the assumption that the density in the universe is everywhere the same. In fact, the values of g_{ij} become infinite at infinity under these conditions, so that the equation (1) can give no static model of the universe.

This very disturbing development forced Einstein to alter his field equations (which he did very reluctantly) by introducing an additional term on the left-hand side. Fortunately, the field equations (1) are such that this can be done, for it is clear that the character of these equations is not changed when one adds to the left hand side a second order tensor which obeys the same conservation principle (it must represent a quantity that can neither be destroyed nor created) as the other two terms together. Now it can be shown (as Einstein knew) that the only physical term that has this important property is λg_{ij}, where λ is a universal constant. Hence Einstein enlarged his field equations by the addition of just this term and replaced (1) by the following most general set of field equations:

$$R_{ij} - \tfrac{1}{2} R g_{ij} + \lambda g_{ij} = (8\pi/c^4) G T_{ij}. \tag{2}$$

These are now the basic equations of cosmology.

Before discussing the various cosmological models that can be deduced from these equations, we should say a few more words about the famous constant λ which has become known in scientific literature as the "cosmological constant." It is clear from the way this constant was introduced that it has an exceedingly small numerical value as compared to the terms in (2) that give rise to the ordinary gravitational forces. For if this were not so, the term λg_{ij} would destroy the agreement between the observed motions of the planets (that is, the motion of Mercury) and those predicted by (2). It turns out, in fact, as we shall see, that the square root of λ (for the static closed universe that Einstein first obtained) is the reciprocal of the radius of the universe. Finally, we note that the term λg_{ij} in (2) behaves like a repulsion—in empty space it has the opposite sign of the gravitational term and hence opposes gravitational attraction. A curious thing about it, however, is that the repulsion of an object increases with its distance from *any* observer and is the same for all objects (regardless of mass) at that distance.

With the inclusion of the cosmical term λg_{ij} in his field equations, Einstein was able to derive a static, finite model of the universe. In a sense, we can understand this result in the following way: the small amount of matter in each unit volume of space introduces the same curvature everywhere, so that space bends uniformly, ultimately curving back upon itself to form a closed spherical universe. If there were no cosmical repulsion term, the gravitational force of all the matter would cause this bubble with a three dimensional surface to collapse. But the cosmical term prevents this; in fact, the cosmical repulsion and the gravitational contraction just balance each other to give a static unchanging universe. An interesting property of this universe is that it is completely filled; that is, it is as tightly filled with matter as it can be without changing. For if we were to add a bit of matter to it, the gravitational attraction would outweigh the cosmic repulsion and the universe would shrink to a smaller size, which would be just right for the new amount of matter (again completely filled). If we remove a bit of matter, the universe would expand to a slightly larger size, but it would again be completely filled.

Now it may seem that such a completely filled universe must be jam-packed with matter like a solid, or like the nucleus of an atom, but this is not so. In fact, the density of matter in such a universe depends on its radius (that is, its size) and its total mass. Einstein found the radius of such a static universe to be about 30 billion light years, with a total mass of about 2×10^{55} grams. This would lead to a density of about 10^{-29} gm/cm^3, or about one proton per hundred thousand cubic centimeters of space. We see that this is a quite empty universe, even though it is as full as it can be! Before we see why the static Einstein universe had to be abandoned, we must try to explain more precisely the meaning of spherical space. When we speak of the

universe as we have up to now, we mean the four-dimensional space-time universe, but the curvature we have been referring to is the curvature of the actual three-dimensional physical space of our existence. To understand this, we may picture the physical space of the universe as the surface of a rubber balloon and all the matter (that is, the galaxies) is to be distributed over this surface in the form of little specks. Note that the physical three-dimensional space of the universe is the surface of the balloon, not the whole balloon itself. Of course, the surface of a real balloon is two-dimensional, so that we have lost one dimension in this picture, but that does not affect the picture seriously. The spatial distances of, or separations among galaxies are now to be measured along the surface of the balloon (just as the distance between New York and Chicago is measured along the surface of the earth).

With this picture, we thus establish an analogy between the three-dimensional space of our universe and the two-dimensional surface of a sphere like the earth. The analogy can be made complete by supposing that the inhabitants of the earth are capable of only a two-dimensional perception (along the surface of the earth) so that they know nothing about up or down and hence cannot perceive that the earth's surface is curved in a space of higher dimensions (the three dimensions of actual space). Even though we, as actual three-dimensional creatures, can assign a radius of curvature to the surface of the earth (the distance of the surface of the earth from its center) the two-dimensional inhabitants of the earth would find such a concept difficult to perceive or accept.

To carry this over to the three-dimensional space of the universe, we must picture the curvature of this three-dimensional space as occurring in a space of higher dimensions. The radius of the universe is thus a distance (actually a number) associated with a direction at right angles to the three-dimensional curved surface of the universe, and hence into a fourth dimension. In this type of universe, every point is similar to every other point and no point of this curved surface can be taken as the center of space; in fact, there is no center, just as there is no center on the surface of the earth. The center of the universe, if we can speak of it at all, is in the fourth dimension.

VI. THE DE SITTER EMPTY EXPANDING UNIVERSE

When Einstein first obtained his static universe theory, it seemed to be just what was wanted, for it agreed with the astronomical observations as they were known in 1917. The measured velocities of the stars were small, and the large scale speed of recession of the distant galaxies had not yet been detected. It thus appeared that the universe was indeed static. More-over, it appeared to Einstein at the time that the solution of the field equations he had obtained with the introduction of the cosmical constant λ was a logical necessity which intimately linked up space and matter, so that one could not exist without the other. He was led to this opinion because he thought that the field equations (2) with a positive value of λ have no solution for $T_{ij} = 0$ (that is, in the absence of matter). But, as de Sitter (1917) later showed, this conclusion was wrong. He found a solution for empty space; that is, for $T_{ij} = 0$ everywhere. Now such a universe is an expanding one in the sense that if a test particle (a particle of negligible mass) is placed at any point in the universe, it recedes from the observer with ever increasing speed. In other words, the speed of recession increases with distance from the observer. In fact, if the de Sitter universe had test particles distributed throughout, they would all recede from each other. The reason for this is found in the cosmical term λg_{ij} in the field equations. If we place $T_{ij} = 0$ in the field equations (2) they reduce to

$$R_{ij} = \lambda g_{ij}, \text{ or } R_{ij} - \lambda g_{ij} = 0,$$

and since the term R_{ij} represents the ordinary Newtonian gravitation of attraction, the term $-\lambda g_{ij}$ represents repulsion, owing to the minus sign.

The de Sitter universe aroused interest initially because it showed that the cosmological field equations (2) do not have a unique solution, and that more than one model of a universe based on these equations can be constructed. Beyond this, however, the de Sitter model of the universe was not taken seriously, since it seemed to contradict the observations in two respects: it is an empty universe, whereas the actual universe contains matter; it is an expanding universe, whereas the observations seemed to indicate that the actual universe was static. But then, in the early 1920's, the recession of the distant nebulae was discovered by Hubble, Slipher, Shapley, and others. The work of these investigators on the Doppler displacement (towards the red) of the spectral lines of the extragalactic nebulae (or galaxies) indicates that the universe is, indeed, expanding. Moreover, the rate of recession of the galaxies increases with distance (the famous Hubble law, 1927) in line with what one would expect from the de Sitter universe. These discoveries demonstrated the inadequacies of the Einstein universe and brought the de Sitter model into prominence.

Another difficulty associated with the Einstein static universe is that it is not a stable model but must undergo either expansion or contraction if there is the slightest departure from the precise balance between the gravitational attraction and the cosmic repulsion.

Thus, if by some process or other some of the mass were to be changed into energy, or if condensations were to occur, the universe would have to begin to expand or collapse. This point, taken together with de Sitter's work and the observed recession of the distant galaxies, led cosmologists to the idea that the actual model of the universe might be an expanding one, that is, intermediate between the empty de Sitter model and the Einstein static model. One must therefore look for solutions of the field equations which give models that are expanding, but not empty. Such models were first obtained by the Russian mathematician Friedmann in 1922 when he dropped Einstein's assumption that the density of matter in the universe must remain constant. By dropping this assumption, Friedmann was able to obtain nonstatic solutions of the field equations which are the basis of most cosmological models. This same problem was independently investigated later by Weyl (1923), Lemaître (1931), Eddington (1933), Robertson (1935), and Walker (1936). Since the treatment of this problem as given by Robertson, and, independently, by Walker, is the most general one, we shall use their analysis as a guide in our discussion of the current models of the expanding universe.

VII. THE NONSTATIC MODELS OF A NONEMPTY UNIVERSE

In the previous section we saw that an expanding model of the universe can be obtained without altering Einstein's original assumptions if we remove all the matter from the universe and, at the same time, introduce into the field equations a cosmical repulsion term. Friedmann escaped this unrealistic situation by removing Einstein's assumption that there are no large scale motions in the universe. He assumed immediately that the average distance between bodies in the universe does not remain constant but changes steadily with time. This means that the right hand side of the field equations (2) does not remain constant, so that the density of matter in the universe changes with time. Owing to this variation of density it is not necessary to keep the cosmical term λg_{ij} in the left hand side of (2) to obtain nonstatic solutions; in fact, Friedmann discarded this term in his work and obtained two nonstatic models of the universe—one which represents a universe that expands forever, and the other a pulsating universe. In the investigations that followed the work of Friedmann, the general field equations (2) with λg_{ij} present, and with the right hand side changing with time, were used. This introduces a whole range of expanding and pulsating models whose properties depend on whether λ is negative, positive, or zero, and on the value of still another constant (the curvature constant) which also enters into the final solution of the field equations and which we shall presently discuss.

To see how these two constants determine the various models of the universe, we first consider briefly the manner in which Robertson and Walker represented the solution of the field equations for a nonstatic universe. We first recall, according to what we said in Section IV, that the square of the space-time interval between two events for an unaccelerated observer in empty space is d^2-c^2t^2, and we have Euclidean space. The presence of matter alters this by distorting space and changing the geometry from Euclidean to non-Euclidean. Suppose now that the two events we are talking about are close together (so that d and t are small) and that they are both at about the same distance r from us. We then find (following Robertson and Walker) that the space-time interval between these events for an expanding universe with matter in it can always be written as

$$\frac{R^2d^2}{\left(1+\dfrac{kr^2}{4}\right)^2}-c^2t^2,$$

where R is a quantity that changes with time and k is the curvature constant referred to above; it can have one of the three values: -1, 0, $+1$. If $k = -1$, the curvature of the universe is negative (like a saddle surface) and the geometry is hyperbolic. The universe is then open and infinite. If $k = 0$, the curvature is zero and space is flat (Euclidean); the universe is open and infinite. If $k = +1$, the curvature is positive and the universe is finite and closed. The quantity R is the scale factor of the universe; it measures the expansion (or contraction) and is often referred to as the radius of the universe. However, it is not in itself a physical distance that can be observed or measured directly, but rather the quantity that shows how the distances between objects in the real universe change; if, in a given time, $R(t)$ doubles, all distances and dimensions in the universe double.

To obtain a model of the universe, one must find the law that tells us how R varies with time, and this is done by using the field equations (2) in conjunction with the above expression for the space-time interval. When we do this, we obtain the equations that tell us exactly how R changes with time, but we find that these equations also contain the cosmic constant λ and the curvature constant k so that many different models of the universe are possible, depending on the choice of these constants. Before Friedmann and those following him did their work, it was thought that λ necessarily had to be positive, but the equations for R show that we can obtain models of the universe for which λ can be negative, zero, or positive. If we combine these three possibilities for λ with the three possible

values $(-1, 0, +1)$ for k, we obtain a large variety of model universes, and there is no way for us, at the present time, to say with certainty which of these models give the correct description of the universe.

Owing to this uncertainty we shall give a brief discussion of these models as a group and then see which of these is most favored by the observational evidence. We designate a model universe as either expanding or oscillating (pulsating) depending on whether R in-

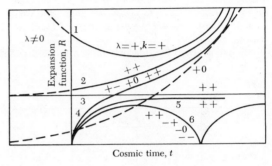

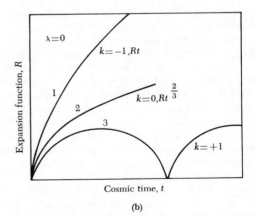

FIGURE 1(a). Expanding models of the universe with $\lambda \neq 0$ and $\rho \neq 0$. The labels refer to the signs of λ, k. The first sign on each curve refers to λ and the second to k.

1. Expanding II
2. Lemaître-Eddington—expanding II
3. Einstein static universe
4. Expanding I—"big bang" Gamow universe
5. Expanding I—"big bang," approaches the Einstein universe asymptotically
6. Pulsating "big bang" universe

FIGURE 1(b). Expanding models of the universe with $\lambda = 0$ and with $\rho \neq 0$. These are all "big bang" models.

1, 2. "Big bang" expanding I
3. "Big bang" pulsating universe

563

creases forever or increases to a certain maximum value and then decreases. In the expanding models, two cases are possible, depending on the choice of λ and k. In the first case (expanding I), R increases from a zero value, at a certain initial time, to an infinitely large value, after an infinite time. In the second case (expanding II), R increases from some finite value, at a certain initial time, to an infinite value, after an infinite time. In all the oscillating models, R expands from zero to a maximum value and then decreases to zero again. This fluctuation is then repeated over and over again. In Figure 1 graphs are shown giving the variation of R with time for the expanding and oscillating cases.

We summarize the various model universes in Table I.

TABLE I

λ	k (or curvature)		
	-1	0	$+1$
negative	oscillating	oscillating	oscillating
zero	expanding I	expanding I	oscillating
positive	expanding I	expanding I	oscillating
			expanding I
			expanding II

VIII. MODEL UNIVERSES WITH THE COSMICAL CONSTANT EQUAL TO ZERO

We have seen that the Einstein field equations lead to both expanding and oscillating models of the universe, but these field equations do not permit us to determine which one of the eleven models listed in Table I corresponds to the actual universe. The reason for this is that three unknowns, viz., the cosmical constant λ, the sign of the curvature k, and the scale of the universe (the units in which R and the time are to be expressed) appear in the final solutions, whereas direct observations of the galaxies can give us only the rate of expansion of the universe (Hubble's law) and its average density. Another possible observation is the deceleration of the expansion of the universe, and some work has been done on that possibility which we shall discuss later. If the deceleration could be measured accurately, we could decide among the various models, but until we have reliable observational evidence on this point, we must proceed by making some assumption about either λ or k.

For the time being, we proceed as Einstein did after Friedmann's work and place $\lambda = 0$. Einstein was very unhappy about the introduction of λ in the first place

since he considered it to be an ad hoc modification of the theory which spoiled "its logical simplicity"; he therefore felt that the models with $\lambda = 0$ were the ones to be favored. From Table I we see that $\lambda = 0$ leads to two expanding models of type I for $k = -1$ and $k = 0$, and to a single oscillating model for $k > 0$. To decide between the expanding and oscillating models, we must have the equation that tells us just how k depends on the density of the universe and its rate of expansion when $\lambda = 0$. This relationship, which is obtained from the solution of the field equations, is the following:

$$k = \frac{R^2}{c^2}\left(\frac{8}{3}\pi G\rho - H^2\right), \qquad (3)$$

where G is the gravitational constant, c is the speed of light, ρ is the average density of the universe, and H is Hubble's constant—that is, the rate of expansion of the universe.

The important quantity in equation (3) is that contained in the parenthesis on the right hand side; for it determines whether k is negative, zero, or positive, and hence whether the universe is expanding or oscillating. If we express distance in centimeters, mass in grams, and time in seconds, the quantity $(8/3)\pi G$ equals 5.58×10^{-7} and the parenthesis in (3) becomes $(5.58 \times 10^{-7}\rho - H^2)$. If we knew ρ and H accurately, we could see at once from this expression whether our universe (with $\lambda = 0$) is expanding or oscillating, but neither ρ nor H is well known. Hubble was the first to measure H by analyzing the recession of the galaxies and placed it equal to 550 km per sec per million parsecs; but we now know that this is too large. According to A. Sandage (1961), observations on the recession of the galaxies indicate that H is about 100 km per sec per million parsecs. If we use this value, H^2 becomes (in cm-gm-sec units) 9×10^{-36} and the quantity in the critical parenthesis becomes $(5.58 \times 10^{-7}\rho - 9 \times 10^{-36})$ or $5.58 \times 10^{-7}(\rho - 1.61 \times 10^{-29})$.

This is a most remarkable result, for it tells us that the model of the universe (for a given value of the recession) is determined by the density of matter in the universe. In our particular case (the cosmical constant zero) the density ρ must be larger than 1.61×10^{-29} gms per cc (one proton per 100,000 cubic cm. of space) for the universe to be an oscillating one. If the density just equals this value, the universe is expanding and Euclidean (no curvature), and if the density is less than this value, the universe is expanding but it has negative curvature. It is precisely here that we run into difficulty in drawing a definite conclusion because the density ρ is not accurately known.

In terms of our present data, the density appears to be about 7×10^{-31}, which would make $k = -1$, and the universe an expanding hyperbolic one (negative curvature). But there may be great quantities of undetected matter that can increase ρ considerably. One must therefore try to get other observational evidence which can permit us to decide between expanding and oscillating models. This can be done if one determines (from observational evidence) whether the Hubble constant H is changing with time, and, if so, how rapidly. If the value of H, as determined from the recession of nearby galaxies, is sufficiently smaller than the value as determined from the recession data of the distant galaxies, we must conclude that H was considerably larger when the universe was younger (the distant galaxies show us a younger universe) than it is now. This would mean that the rate of expansion had decreased and that ultimately the universe must stop expanding and begin to collapse. This means that the universe is oscillating. This sort of analysis has been carried out jointly by Humason, Mayall, and Sandage (1956) and the evidence favors an oscillating universe. This means either that the value of the density ρ has been greatly underestimated or that the correct model of the universe is one in which λ is different from zero. Of course, it may be that H is even smaller than 100 km per sec per M pc, but it cannot be much smaller than this value, and reducing H by a small amount does not help.

Before leaving these Friedmann models with $\lambda = 0$, we briefly consider the principal properties of the models associated with the three different values of k. For $k = 0$ there is no curvature and space is infinite. The age of the universe (as measured from some initial moment $t = 0$ when the expansion began) is then equal to $2/3(1/H)$, and we obtain about 8×10^9 years, which appears to be too small to account for the evolution of the stars and galaxies. For this kind of universe, the expansion parameter R increases as the 2/3 power of the time.

For $k = -1$, space is negatively curved and infinite; the expansion is continuous and endless, so that the universe finally becomes completely empty and Euclidean. At some initial moment, $t = 0$, the universe was in an infinitely condensed state and then began to expand. According to this model, the age of the universe is $1/H$ or 1.2×10^{10} years, which gives ample time for stellar evolution.

For $k = +1$, we obtain the oscillating universe which began from an infinitely condensed state at $t = 0$. This is a positively curved, closed universe, whose radius R will reach a maximum value and then decrease down to zero again. A similar expansion will then begin again and this will be repeated ad infinitum. The age of this model of the universe is smaller than that of the other two.

IX. MODELS OF THE UNIVERSE WITH THE COSMICAL CONSTANT DIFFERENT FROM ZERO

We saw in the last section that placing $\lambda = 0$ severely restricts the number of models, and that these models represent ages that are somewhat too small for stellar evolutionary comfort. For this reason, a group of investigators, particularly Lemaître, Eddington, Robertson, Tolman, and McVittie, in the early days (all independently of each other and without knowledge of Friedmann's work) and Gamow (1946) later, constructed various models with λ different from zero. There are many more such models than one can obtain with $\lambda = 0$, and among them are both the expanding and oscillating types, as we have already noted. The most popular of these models during the earlier period of this work is the one first proposed by Lemaître in 1927 and strongly supported by Eddington. This is the expanding II model listed in Table I, for which both λ and k are positive. In this model the universe is always closed and finite and began its expansion from some finite nonzero value of R. But the moment of the beginning of the expansion was not the moment of zero time (that is, the moment of the origin of the universe) because in this model the universe could have remained in a nonexpanding, static state for as long as one might desire—in fact, for an infinite time in the past.

Since this model starts expanding from a static model, both Lemaître and Eddington assumed this initial static model to be the original Einstein static model. In this model the value of λ and the radius R are chosen (in relationship to the mass M of the universe) in such a way as to give a closed spherical universe in which the cosmical repulsion is just balanced by the gravitational attraction. However, this Einstein universe is unstable, as we have already noted, so that any initial expansion reduces the density and causes this model to expand still more, with further reduction in density, and so on. The expansion thus proceeds faster and faster until the universe is infinitely expanded and the density is everywhere zero. On the other hand, a slight compression could have caused the Einstein model to have contracted indefinitely, finally ending up as an infinitely condensed point of matter.

If, then, we accept this Lemaître-Eddington picture, the universe was in a static Einstein state for an infinite time in the past and then at some finite time in the past, for some unknown reason, began to expand, attaining its present rate of expansion after a few billion years. Although Eddington never abandoned this concept and fought for it vigorously to the end of his life, Lemaître revised his thinking in 1931 and replaced this type II expanding model by a type I expanding model.

As we can see from Table I, three possible models of the universe can be constructed with λ positive and $k = 1$: an oscillating type, an expanding I type, and an expanding II type. If we reject the last of these (which corresponds to the original Lemaître-Eddington model, which we have just discussed) we still have the oscillating and the expanding I models.

The reason Lemaître replaced the expanding II model by the expanding I model is that he had no reasonable explanation for the start of the initial expansion of the actual universe from an Einstein static state. Although his own theoretical investigations and those of McCrea and McVittie (1931) strongly suggested that any local condensation of the matter in the Einstein static universe (for example, the formation of a single galaxy or star) would cause it to start expanding, these investigations left unanswered the question as to why other galaxies were formed. If expansion began after the formation of a single galaxy, the density of the universe would immediately begin to decrease and other condensations into galaxies would be precluded. This would mean, of course, that the cosmological principle defined in Section V would be untenable, since the distribution of matter in the neighborhood of this initial condensation would be different from that elsewhere in the universe. Moreover, it is difficult to see how the heavy elements such as iron, lead, and uranium could have originated in an Einstein static-state universe, since we know from nuclear theory that the formation of such elements from hydrogen in great abundance requires extremely high temperatures and pressures. This means that the entire universe, or at least parts of it, must have passed through a high temperature-high pressure phase. Thus the very existence of the stars and heavy elements argues against the Einstein static state as the initial phase of our present universe.

Owing to these difficulties, inherent in the assumption that our present universe evolved from an Einstein static universe of finite radius, Lemaître introduced the assumption that we live in an expanding universe of type I, which began its expansion from a highly condensed state. He referred to this initial condensation as the primordial atom or nucleus and assumed that a vast, radioactive explosion occurred in this atom and that what we now see in the recession of the galaxies all about is the result of this explosion. In this picture, the expanding universe is always finite in size, but closed like a sphere. The initial condensed state (that is, the Lemaître primordial atom) may be pictured as having been present for an infinite time in the past or we may suppose that the universe began its life in the Einstein static state and then collapsed violently into a primordial atom from which it began to expand.

According to Lemaître, this expansion carried the universe back to its initial Einstein state, but it did not stop there. Its velocity of expansion carried it beyond this static phase, and after that its expansion proceeded with ever increasing speed.

Whether we are discussing an Einstein-Friedmann expanding model, with λ = 0; or an oscillating model, with λ = 0; or a Lemaître model, with λ > 0 and $k = +1$ (expanding II or oscillating), we are dealing with a group of models that are referred to as the "big bang" models of the universe, since all of them picture the universe as having originated explosively from a point. The term "big bang" was first introduced by Gamow (1948) who, together with Alpher and Herman (1950), sought to account for the origin of the heavy elements by supposing that they were formed from the original protons and neutrons in the very early and very hot stage of the explosion. According to this picture of the origin of the universe, neutrons were the principal components of the original material ejected from the primordial atom or point source. Some of these neutrons quickly decayed into protons and electrons, and these protons then captured other neutrons to build up the heavy elements. This whole buildup of heavy elements must have occurred during the first thirty minutes after the initial explosion, for the temperature of this primordial material dropped very rapidly after that and everything then remained frozen.

Gamow's theory was very appealing at first since no other theory of the elements was available then; the theory of stellar structure and evolution had not yet reached a point of development where it could be shown that heavy elements can be and are built up inside stars, as they evolve from structures like the sun into red giants like Antares and Betelgeuse, with their internal temperatures rising to billions of degrees. Gamow's theory of the buildup of the heavy elements during the first thirty minutes of the life of the universe had to be discarded, however, since there are no stable nuclei of atomic masses 5 and 8, so that neutron capture alone could not have bridged the nuclear gap between the light and heavy nuclei. Even if some heavy nuclei were formed by neutron capture in this early fireball stage of the universe (and all nuclei capture neutrons very readily) a half hour would hardly have been long enough for the heavy elements to have been formed in their present abundances. Since we now know that the heavy elements can all be baked in the stellar furnaces at various stages of evolution, this phase of the Gamow "big bang" theory is not essential and one can discard it without invalidating the overall concept.

If we then accept this Lemaître-Gamow hot "big

bang" hypothesis, the universe must have passed through a very high temperature phase (about 10^{10} to 10^{11} degrees K) soon after the initial explosion, and some observable evidence of this may still be around. That this should be so was first pointed out by Gamow himself, who argued that there must have been a considerable amount of very hot black body radiation present in this initial phase of the universe and most of it must still be around, but in a very much red-shifted form. He estimated that its temperatures would now be 6°K. Without knowing about Gamow's suggestion, Dicke proposed the same idea in 1964 (he called it the "primordial fireball radiation") and later, in collaboration with Peebles, Roll, and Wilkinson (1965), demonstrated that the initial hot black body radiation (at a temperature of 10^{10} degrees K) must now be black body radiation (at a temperature of 3.5°K). The general idea behind this deduction is the following: if the universe was initially filled with very hot black body radiation (that is, of very short wavelength), this radiation would remain black body radiation during the expansion of the universe, but it would become redder and redder owing to the Doppler shift imparted to it by the expansion. This is similar to radiation that is reflected back and forth from the walls of an expanding container. This 3.5°K black body radiation was detected by Penzias and Wilson in 1965 and has since been verified by other observers. It is present in the form of isotropic, unpolarized microwave background radiation in the wavelength range from 1/10 to 10 cm.

One other residual feature of the "big bang" should still be visible, or at least amenable to verification—the present helium abundance. During the initial fireball period when the temperature was considerably larger than 10^{10} degrees K, the thermal electrons and neutrinos that were present would have resulted in very nearly equal abundances of neutrons and protons. When the temperature of the fireball dropped to 10^{10} degrees K these neutrons and protons would have combined to form deuterium, which, in turn, would have been transformed into He^4, and no heavier elements would have been formed. Two questions then arise. (1) Is the helium that we now observe all about us, in our own galaxy and in others, still this primordial helium? (2) If so, what can this tell us about the models of our universe?

The evidence relating to the first question is somewhat ambiguous because we know that helium burning occurs during the giant stage of a star's evolution, so that some of the original helium must certainly have been transformed into heavy elements in stellar interiors, and thus disappeared. But we may assume that the helium that is found in stellar atmospheres is primordial and the evidence here is that although there

is an overall helium abundance of about 25%, some stars have been observed with very weak helium lines. In spite of these, however, the overall evidence favors the 25% abundance, which is in agreement with the "big bang" hypothesis.

Taking all of the observed data into account (the 3°K black body radiation and the helium abundance) the preponderance of the evidence favors the "big bang" theory and points to an age of at least 10^{10}, i.e., ten billion years for our universe. The observed helium abundance (if we accept 25% as the primeval abundance) also indicates that the density of matter in the universe must be at least 4×10^{-31} grams per cc. But if the density of matter in the universe is no larger than this, we run into difficulty with the observations on the rate at which the expansion of the universe is decelerating. We have already noted that Humason, Mayall, and Sandage have given a value for this deceleration which indicates that the universe must ultimately stop expanding and begin to collapse. This means that the correct model of the universe is an oscillating one, rather than expanding, but, as we have seen, this requires the density of matter to be about 10^{-29} gms/cc, as compared to the observed density of 7×10^{-31}

In spite of this, the evidence for an oscillating universe has been greatly strengthened recently by the analysis of the distribution of quasars and of quasi-stellar radio sources in general. Since these objects (according to their red shifts) are at enormous distances from us, they give us the rate of expansion of the universe in its earliest stages. By comparing this with the present rate of expansion, we obtain a very reliable value for the deceleration, which shows the universe to be oscillating. To account for the discrepancy between the observed and required density of matter for such a model of the universe, we must suppose that there are large quantities of dark matter in intergalactic space—in the form of hydrogen clouds, black dwarf stars, and streams of neutrinos. But until we have direct evidence of this, we cannot be sure about the validity of the oscillating model.

X. THE STEADY-STATE THEORY AND OTHER COSMOLOGIES

We shall conclude our discussion of modern cosmologies with brief descriptions of theories that are related to, but do not spring directly from, Einstein's field equations, whether or not we place $\lambda = 0$. Of these, the most popular, and one which, has been strongly supported by outstanding cosmologists and physicists, is the steady state or continuous creation theory of Bondi and Gold (1948) and Hoyle (1948). On the basis of what they call the *perfect cosmological principle*, which is an extension of Einstein's cosmological principle, they assert that not only must the universe present the same appearance to all observers, regardless of where they are, but it must appear the same at all times—it must present an unchanging aspect on a large scale. The immediate consequence of this theory is that mass and energy cannot be conserved in such a universe. Since the universe is expanding, new matter must be created spontaneously and continuously everywhere so as to prevent the density from decreasing.

It can be shown from this theory that matter would have to be created at a rate equal to three times the product of the Hubble constant and the present density of the universe, in order to keep things as they are. One nucleon must be created per thousand cubic centimeters, per 500 billion years to maintain the status quo. Hoyle arrived at the same result by altering Einstein's field equations.

Although the steady-state theory was very popular because it eliminated entirely the question of the origin of the universe, it was rejected by most cosmologists because of its continuous creation and the consequent denial of the conservation of mass energy. But the strongest argument against the steady state theory is the existence of the $3°K$ radiation, which shows clearly that our universe has evolved from a highly condensed state. In addition, the observed distribution of quasars, radio sources, and other distant celestial bodies shows that the density of matter in the universe was much higher a few billion years ago than it is now. The observational evidence seems weighted against the steady-state theory.

Other general principles have been invoked to derive cosmological theories. Perhaps the most ambitious of these theories is that of Eddington (1946), who attempted, in his later years, to deduce the basic constants of nature by combining quantum theory and general relativity. Starting from the idea that the reciprocal of the square root of the cosmical constant represents a natural unit of length in the universe, and that the number of particles in the universe must determine its curvature, he derived numerical values for such constants as the ratio of the mass of the proton to that of the electron, Planck's constant of action, etc. But very few physicists have accepted Eddington's numerology since his analysis is often obscure, difficult to follow, and rather artificial. In any case, the existence of nuclear forces and new particles which Eddington was unaware of when he did his work, and which therefore are not accounted for in his theory, destroys the universality which he claims for his theory.

During the period that Eddington was developing his quantum cosmology, three other cosmological systems were introduced: the kinematic cosmology of Milne (1935) and the cosmologies of Dirac (1937) and Jordan (1947). Although these theories are extremely interesting and beautifully constructed, we can only discuss them briefly here. Of all the cosmological theories that we shall have discussed in this essay, Milne's is the most deductive, for instead of starting with the laws of nature as we know them locally, and then constructing a model of the universe based upon these laws, he introduces only the cosmological principle and attempts to deduce, by pure reasoning, not only a unique model of the universe, but also the laws of nature themselves. To do this, Milne had to assume the existence of a class of ideal observers attached to each particle of an ideal homogeneous universal substratum, which is expanding according to Hubble's law.

To carry out his analysis consistently, Milne had to introduce two different times; a kinematic time which applies to the ideal observer and which also governs electromagnetic and atomic phenomena, and according to which the universe is expanding; and a dynamic time, so that a good deal of arbitrariness is inherent in this theory, particularly at the boundary region where we pass from one kind of time to another. But the major objection to this theory arises from its basic assumption that an absolute substratum exists in the universe, and that a privileged class of observers is associated with this substratum.

Although a cosmological principle of one sort or another is at the basis of the cosmologies which we have discussed here, other types of principles have also been used. The most notable of these is that proposed by Dirac in 1937 (and later in a slightly different form by Jordan), according to which certain basic numbers associated with matter and the universe are not constant, as had been assumed in all previous cosmologies, but vary with time. The numbers Dirac had in mind are certain dimensionless quantities which are obtained by taking the ratio of atomic quantities to cosmological quantities of the same kind. Dirac expressed this principle as follows: "All very large dimensionless numbers which can be constructed from the important constants of cosmology and atomic theory are simple powers of the epoch."

One consequence of this principle is that the universal gravitational constant would have to decrease with time. But one can show, as E. Teller did (1948), that this would lead to a sun that was much too hot during the Cambrian period; the temperature of the earth would then have been so high that its oceans would have been boiling. Owing to this discrepancy, Dirac's theory has generally been discarded, although, more recently, C. Brans and R. H. Dicke have introduced a variation of it, starting from a different point of view.

SUMMARY

At this point in our narrative, the reader may well feel that modern cosmology is a welter of conflicting theories, all of which contain some elements of truth, but none of which gives a complete picture of the actual universe. This, however, would be a wrong conclusion to draw from the present state of affairs. It is true that a few years ago this would have been a fair assessment, since the observational evidence then was far too meager to permit us to choose from among the various cosmologies that stem from the basic field equations. But even then, the common heritage of all of these theories (the general theory of relativity) indicated that the basic differences among them are more apparent than real.

The situation in the early 1970's was quite different, for a threshold had been reached for a cosmological breakthrough; as we have seen, enough observational evidence was available to show us that our universe originated explosively, about ten to twenty billion years ago, from a highly condensed state. Even though we still could not decide unequivocally between an expanding and an oscillating universe on the basis of the observational evidence, the major problem of the origin of the universe had been solved and we had a self-consistent picture. It accounted not only for the recession and distribution of the distant galaxies but also for many diverse phenomena, ranging from the background radiation all around us in space (the 3° K. isotropic radiation which we have already discussed) to the formation of the stars and the heavy elements.

The most remarkable thing about the state of matter, whether in the form of stars or interstellar dust and gas all around us, is that it points to some momentous event that must have occurred some billions of years ago and which led to the pronounced differentiation that we see now. Starting from the "big bang," to which all these observations point, we can now arrange the succession of events that led to the present state of the universe into a well-ordered, meaningful, and understandable sequence. After the original explosion, when the temperature was still very high, about 30% of the primordial neutrons and protons were fused into He^4, but the expanding gas cooled off much too rapidly for elements above He^4 to be built up in any appreciable quantities, and these had to wait for the stellar ovens that were to be formed when the rapidly expanding gas of hydrogen and helium was fragmented into stars by turbulence and the gravitational forces.

The fragmentation of the original hydrogen-helium gaseous mixture into galaxies and stars occurred when the exploding universe had cooled off to very nearly its present value—about two hundred million years after the initial explosion. The density of matter and radiation was then favorable for gravitational contraction to take over in local regions and to compress the gas into huge clouds. This, however, could occur only after another process had come into operation—the natural and unavoidable fragmentation of the expanding gas into local eddies. One can show that a stream of gas becomes unstable against such a fragmentation when the length of the stream exceeds a certain number whose value can be derived from hydrodynamical theory. In an expanding universe this is bound to happen after the expansion has progressed beyond a given point. The average size of the turbulent eddies that are formed during this kind of fragmentation is determined by the speed and density of the expanding gas.

The details of this fragmentation process were worked out many years ago by J. H. Jeans. According to his calculation, we know that the expanding gas must have broken up into fragments having an average size equal to that of a typical galaxy. These galaxies in turn also suffered fragmentation (on a smaller scale) by the same process and the oldest stars were thus formed. These oldest stars (about 8 billion years old) were formed at the center of the galaxies; and that is where we find them now, although they also constitute the globular clusters that surround the core of a galaxy.

Since the very oldest stars were formed almost exclusively from the primordial hydrogen and helium, at least some of the heavy elements that we now observe all about us in the universe must have been synthesized in the interiors of these stars as they evolved. This, indeed, is the case, for we now know, from the theory of stellar interiors, that thermonuclear processes occur near the center of a star, resulting in the transmutation of the light to the heavy elements. When the oldest stars were first formed, they contracted very rapidly until their central temperatures reached about 10 million degrees, at which point thermonuclear energy was released with the transformation of hydrogen to helium; this process kept the stars in equilibrium and supplied them with their energy for the first few billion years of their lives—in fact, until about 12% of their hydrogen had been transformed into helium.

The core of each star, consisting entirely of helium, then began to contract quite rapidly under its own weight, and the central temperature rose (in a few hundred million years) to about 100,000,000 degrees. At this high temperature, the helium nuclei in the core were transformed to carbon—the first step in the buildup of the heavy elements. This led to the formation of a carbon core which contracted still further, resulting in still higher core temperatures. In fact, the temperature in the core continued to increase until the billion degree mark was reached, and the heavy elements, right up to iron, had been synthesized. But at that point a drastic change occurred in the evolution of the star, for very little of its nuclear fuel was left to supply the energy required to support its own weight. The star, which by this time had evolved into a very large and luminous object, collapsed violently and became a supernova, ejecting great quantities of material from its outer regions.

Following the supernova explosion, the hot residual core (consisting of such nuclei as iron, calcium, magnesium, and free electrons) continued to contract, finally becoming a white dwarf of enormous density. It remains in this stage when the outward pressure of the free electrons just balances the gravitational contraction. But this is not so in all cases, and the star must continue to contract beyond the white dwarf stage if it is massive enough—ultimately becoming a very hot neutron star, about ten miles in diameter. Although such stars have not yet been observed directly, astronomers believe that they constitute some of the X-ray sources now being observed and are the recently discovered "pulsars." But even neutron stars are not the final stage of stellar evolution, for the theory of relativity tells us that such stars must continue to contract until they disappear from sight.

But what of the material that was ejected from each star that became a supernova? This was swirled into the outer regions of the galaxy, where it became the gas and dust that formed the spiral arms that we now see. From this gas and dust—consisting not only of the primordial hydrogen and helium, but also of such heavy elements as carbon, oxygen, sodium, calcium, and iron—the second generation, and hence younger stars such as our sun, were formed. But something else happened at the same time—planets were also formed. It can be shown, as has been done by C. F. von Weizsäcker, G. F. Kuiper, H. Urey, H. Alfvén, and others, that the turbulences that must occur when a star like the sun is formed by gravitational contraction, from dust and gas, must lead to the formation of planets at fairly definite distances from the star. This is in agreement with the arrangement of the planets in our solar system.

We thus see that the cosmological theories that stem from Einstein's gravitational field equations agree with the overall architectural and dynamical features of the universe as we now observe them. At the same time, these theories show us how the present state of the universe has evolved from a highly condensed initial state, and tell us what to expect in the future evolution of the universe. Although many of the details are still missing from this forecast, the dominant features are clearly indicated, and we have every reason to believe that we shall soon be able to answer most of the ques-

tions about the universe that seemed so unanswerable just a few years ago, for never before in the history of science have so many capable scientists been working on this exciting problem.

BIBLIOGRAPHY

R. Alpher and R. Herman, *Reviews of Modern Physics*, **22** (1950), 153. H. Bondi and T. Gold, *Monthly Notices, Royal Astronomical Society*, **108** (1948), 252. R. H. Dicke, P. J. E. Peebles, P. G. Roll, and D. T. Wilkinson, *The Astrophysical Journal*, **142** (1965), 414. P. A. M. Dirac, *Proceedings of the Royal Astronomical Society, A*, **165** (1938), 199. A. S. Eddington, *The Expanding Universe* (Cambridge, 1933); idem, *Fundamental Theory* (Cambridge, 1946). A. Einstein, *Sitzungsberichte der Preussische Akademische Gesellschaft*, **142** (1917). A. Friedmann, *Zeitschrift für Physik*, **10** (1922), 377. G. Gamow, *Physical Review*, **70** (1946), 572; **74** (1948), 505. E. R. Harrison, *Monthly Notices, Royal Astronomical Society*, **131** (1965), 1. F. Hoyle, *Monthly Notices, Royal Astronomical Society*, **108** (1948), 372. M. L. Humason, N. U. Mayall, and A. Sandage, *The Astronomical Journal*, **61** (1956), 97. J. Jeans, *Astronomy and Cosmology* (Cambridge, 1928, reprint 1961). P. Jordan, *Die Herkunft der Sterne* (Stuttgart, 1947). G. Lemaître, *Monthly Notices, Royal Astronomical Society*, **91** (1931), 490. W. H. McCrea and G. C. McVittie, *Monthly Notices, Royal Astronomical Society*, **92** (1931), 7. A. A. Michelson and E. M. Morley, *Philosophical Magazine*, **190** (1887), 449. E. A. Milne, *Relativity, Gravitation, and World Structure* (Oxford, 1935). C. G. Neumann, *Über das Newtonische Prinzip der Fernwirkung* (Leipzig, 1895). A. A. Penzias and R. W. Wilson, *The Astrophysical Journal*, **142** (1965), 419. H. P. Robertson, *The Astrophysical Journal*, **82** (1935), 284; **83** (1936), 187, 257. A. Sandage, *The Astrophysical Journal*, **133** (1961), 335. H. Seeliger, *Astronomische Nachrichtungen*, **137** (1895), 129. W. de Sitter, *Monthly Notices, Royal Astronomical Society*, **78** (1917), 3. R. C. Tolman, *Relativity, Thermodynamics, and Cosmology* (Oxford, 1932). A. G. Walker, *Proceedings of the London Mathematical Society* (2), **42** (1936), 90. H. Weyl, *Physikalische Zeitschrift*, **24** (1923), 230.

GENERAL BIBLIOGRAPHY

H. Bondi, *Cosmology* (Cambridge, 1961); *Rival Theories of Cosmology* (Oxford, 1960). P. Couderc, *The Expansion of the Universe* (London, 1952). G. Gamow, *The Creation of the Universe* (New York, 1952). E. Hubble, *Realm of the Nebulae* (Oxford, 1961). G. C. McVittie, *Fact and Theory in Cosmology* (New York, 1961). M. K. Munitz, ed., *Theories of the Universe* (New York, 1957). D. Sciama, *The Unity of the Universe* (Garden City, N.Y., 1961). J. Singh, *Great Ideas and Theories of Modern Cosmology* (London, 1961). W. de Sitter, *Kosmos* (Cambridge, Mass., 1932). E. Teller, *Physical Review*, **73** (1948), 801.

LLOYD MOTZ

[See also Cosmic Images; Cosmic Voyages; **Cosmology from Antiquity to 1850;** Infinity; **Relativity;** Space; Time.]

CREATION IN RELIGION

CREATION, in religion, refers to a special way of relating physical things, plants, animals, and persons to God. All believers in God hold that whatever exists depends upon the nature of God, and that the worship of God is essential to supreme well-being. However, believers who use the word "creation" wish to defend both the supremacy of God, and the autonomy of persons.

The words in the Declaration of Independence (1776): ". . . that all men are created equal, that they are endowed by their Creator with certain unalienable Rights," involve the conviction that men, free before God, are responsible ultimately to Him. Believers in "creation" do not themselves agree about what exactly it means, although they intend the term to express their conviction that God is never identical with his creation, and with persons in particular. The most explicit expression of this view takes the form of *creatio ex nihilo* ("creation out of nothing," hereafter referred to as *creatio*) and this intention differentiates theists from religious monists or pantheists. Thus theists emphasize that God both transcends, and is immanent in, His creation. Their view is best understood in the context of other religious, moral, and intellectual concerns to be considered below.

I. THE RATIONALE OF CREATIO EX NIHILO

1. To the ancient Indian and Greek thinker the notion of *creatio* is unthinkable. Yet what captured the imagination of the dominant theistic strand in Jewish, Muslim, and Christian thought was expressed in the first two chapters of Genesis. "In the beginning God created the heavens and the earth. And the earth was waste and void; and darkness was upon the face of the deep: and the spirit of God moved upon the face of the waters. And God said, Let there be light: and there was light. And God saw the light, that it was good" (Genesis 1:1–4). The picture that unfolds in this first chapter is that of a Creator-God responsible for every created being.

What is further distinctive in this vision is the passage: "And God created man in his own image, in the image of God created he him; male and female created he them. . . . And God saw everything that he had made, and, behold, it was very good" (Genesis 1:27, 31. See also Genesis 2; Jeremiah 27:5, 31:35; and Isaiah 40:12–31). The phrase *creatio ex nihilo* is not a biblical phrase (though it does occur in Maccabees II:vii, 28).

The dominant if not exclusive image in the biblical account stands clear. God and the world are not identical; nor are the world and man "modes" of God's being. Furthermore, in creating man in his own image,

God makes man free in a world ultimately governed by God's purpose. When man freely chooses to abide by God's purpose for him, he will realize the best in himself and in Nature.

Thus in postulating *creatio*, Judeo-Christian-Muslim theism protects both God's unlimited freedom to create and man's limited freedom to be creative (or destructive). This postulate is also directed against the view that the human soul has existed in some form before its present existence. This view also leaves the door open to annihilation for, since man comes "from nothing," he may return to "nothing." Most theists, however, hold that God will grant personal immortality.

Furthermore, early Christian apologists, like Saint Augustine (*De civitate Dei* XI:24; XIV II) used *creatio* in order to stress that creation is God's own "free act," born of his goodness. They hold that the "stuff of his own being" is never involved in creating either the world or man. Or the stress, as in Philo, is on the fact that no inner "fate" governed God's creating this world. God could have created a different one, and he can override the laws of this present world if he sees fit.

2. In the *Timaeus* Plato seeks an account of the generation of the space-time world that is "inferior to none in likelihood" (*Timaeus* 29d). A good but not omnipotent Demiurge desired that all should be "so far as possible, like unto himself" (29d). He was limited by the fact that he must deal with two other kinds of being: the Receptacle and the Forms. The Receptacle is the "mother" of all becoming, a kind of "moulding-stuff" of everything "invisible and unshaped, all receptive." It could never be a cosmos unless "in some most baffling way" (51b), it could partake of Forms or Ideas. Plato's Demiurge, keeping his gaze fixed on "these co-eternal Forms" (29a), "persuades" the inchoate Receptacle to take on as much form as possible (48a). The world thus generated is "planned" as "a movable image" (37d) of the perfect Forms.

In postulating three co-eternal Beings, Plato departs from his contention in the *Republic* that the Good is the source of everything's being and being known. The imperfect world is there likened to the manifold radiations of the Sun (the Good). The theory in the *Timaeus*, of a Demiurge persuading a somewhat recalcitrant Receptacle to take on form, seems better able to explain imperfections in the world.

But a good Demiurge offends the religious consciousness of most theists. God, to be God, must be perfect, limited by nothing but his own will and reason. At the same time, Plato's view, even as a "likely" account, faces theoretical difficulties. For if God, the Forms, and the Receptacle are co-eternally independent of each other, why can God know the Forms? Or why should the Receptacle be such that it could be persuaded to take on the Forms?

To avoid such religious and theoretical difficulties the traditional theist substitutes *creatio ex nihilo*. He concedes that *creatio* too is baffling, that the *how* of creation is unknowable. But three co-eternal Beings, interacting and yielding a cosmos like ours, compounds mystery. Mysterious as the how of *creatio* may be, it offends no theoretical norm, and protects the absoluteness and perfection of God.

3. The words *creatio ex nihilo* are intended, then, to deny the existence of any other Being co-eternal with God, or any world identical with God.

For example, the theist cannot with Spinoza say *Deus sive natura* ("God or Nature"). Spinoza held that a God who created the world must have been imperfect before its creation. If God is perfect the world must follow from his nature "as the nature of a triangle that its two angles should be equal to two right angles" (*Ethics*, I, Prop. 17 Scholium).

In similar vein, the emanationist argues that the mystery of *ex nihilo* can be avoided by thinking of the world as "radiating" the unchanged One in different degrees. For Plotinus, influenced by Plato's image of the Sun, the world is the *efflux* of the ineffable, transcendent, "creative" One. Such emanation should not be confused with the "creative" or "emergent" evolution in which real novelty is produced "in time." For the emanationist the temporal order of "descent" is not real; the One and the many stages of "evolution" are in fact one. Hence, emanation hardly escapes monism in its attempt to avoid the *ex nihilo* that defies imagination and intellect.

The monist and emanationist usually urge that the One cannot be described in terms that reflect, as human thinking must, only a part of the world. The One is super-personal. The human at best is part of the world and can provide no adequate analogy to the nature of the One. Hence Spinoza declared that to conceive of the one Substance as a person is like comparing the constellation The Dog to a barking dog. Similarly, the most noble ideal of human goodness, or will, or reason, cannot serve to characterize the One.

The theist agrees with the monist and emanationist that God cannot be One among equals, or co-eternal with any other being or beings. But he counters that mystery is not decreased by considering an imperfect world, manifesting the One, ultimately good. Nor does he see how human freedom is consistent with emanationism or monism. *Creatio* allows him to think of the Unity as the ultimate Agent who in creating is self-guided by his ideals of goodness and of reason. God is not even, as Aristotle seems to have held, the Thinker whose perfection is the unifying lure of all finite beings.

God is the Creator who thinks and acts in accordance with goals intrinsic to his being. In creating the order of Nature which supports human effort without annihilating man's freedom, God expresses his loving purpose—a mutually respecting and responsible community of persons. Hence, this world, as Leibniz put it, is the best possible world once it is seen as the arena for the development of persons who cannot escape the responsibility for their own actions.

In the theistic view, the natural world may be conceived as the order of interacting nonmental entities (in Thomistic realism) or as part of the mental nature of God (as in Berkeley), or as a world of psychic unities of different grades (as in Leibniz' panpsychism).

The conception of man's interaction with Nature and with God varies in each of these theistic views. But the religious and moral relation of men to each other and to God is not significantly affected by viewing the natural world as mental or nonmental. Yet man's confidence that the natural world expresses God's reason and goodness, supports the scientific conviction that man's disciplined observation and reflection is not alien to the order of Nature.

In sum, then, the classical theistic model of the universe is of a self-existent God who, in accordance with his rational and loving nature, relates himself constantly to a world contingent on his creative activity. His general providence for free persons is expressed in the natural structure of things and persons. His individual providence depends on the fellowship each person freely seeks with God in prayer, worship, and action. Even when theists, like Calvinists, denied human freedom, the ethical effect seemed to be strenuous effort by individuals who used their worldly accomplishment as an index to their divinely ordained destiny.

This emphasis on responsible fellowship, as the ideal of worship and of human community, influences the theist's interpretation of the religious and mystical experience. Many mystics hold that in their experience of God the finite self is literally lost in God or the One, and they argue that this "union" favors monism. The theist objects: religious "union" is also frequently experienced, and interpreted, as interaction with, and not absorption in, God. In any case, the experience of love and worship is meaningless if the lover and the beloved are in fact one. Furthermore, to say that man is, and is not, identical with God is more mysterious than *creatio* and self-contradictory. How can the perfect God "somehow" include all the imperfection in man and in the world? Must not responsibility for all human error and for evils in Nature be God's? Indeed, if whatever happens in Nature and in man is ultimately good, there is neither final distinction between good and evil nor any standard for human progress.

4. Such reasoning in support of the doctrine of *creatio* helps to clarify what it is intended to mean: God creates what was not in existence and could not exist unless God created. Nothing less than a radically new model of coming-to-be and passing-away is advocated. A finite being is a no-*being,* a *no*-being, until it is created; it cannot come into existence or continue to exist on its own initiative.

This model, the creationist argues, is mysterious only in the sense that any ultimate state or quality of being is mysterious. Given this model of ultimate Being and coming-to-be, problems such as those indicated above can reasonably be resolved. *Creatio* itself cannot be understood by reference to any event within the world. The theist often refers to the creative activity of an artist as providing only a faint analogy, because the artist perforce uses materials not of his own making.

Indeed, the creationist is at pains to suggest that unfortunate picture-thinking leads to misunderstanding of *creatio.* Picture-thinking leads to the question: How can any being, however powerful, make something out of nothing, or, to put it crudely, how can he make something out of little bits of nothing? As Anselm said, *ex nihilo* does not mean *de nihilo ipso* (*Monologium,* VI–VII).

Incomplete understanding underlies the objection that "from nothing, nothing comes." Lucretius, for example, argues (I, 154), "if things came from nothing, any kind might be born of anything, nothing would require seed" (Oates, 1957). The creationist grants this. But creation, he argues, is the activity of the self-existent God, not of nothing. This God creates what was not existent. Hence, no beings come "*from* nothing"; the Creator-God creates, and this means that what was not, is now because of his act.

This model of *creatio* is intended to replace all others. But theists have nevertheless moved toward deism, emanationism, and pantheism as they dealt with such questions as: Having created, is God then indifferent to his creation? Does God need the world? Are the world and God thinkable without each other? How can the unchanging God remain unchanging if he is immanent in his changing world? The thought of several great thinkers makes such theoretical tensions within theism clearer.

II. PERSISTENT CREATIONIST ISSUES

1. Saint Augustine's God is self-identical, immutable, not in any way changed by the created world. The Ideas are God's ideas; they constitute eternal perfection imperfectly mirrored in all individuals and species. God did not have to create. He did so, in order that creatures might share in his goodness.

The material world, therefore, is not intrinsically bad. God endowed it with seminal principles (*rationes seminales*) which can be brought to fruition under appropriate conditions by created agents. The creating of the seminal principles is always the work of God. A mother and father, for example, do not create the child, but their "creative" action brings the form of the child as created by God into fruition.

In this view, God allows persons to make a difference in the actual history of the world. Yet, at every point, Augustine protects the insuperable glory, goodness, and creativity of God against any alternative that might even seem to limit his power. Thus, the doctrine of seminal principles enables Augustine to deny that anything kept God from creating the world and all it could become "from the beginning." Nor is God limited by time since he created time with the world.

Yet tension exists in this view. Augustine attributes free will to man. Man is responsible for whatever changes for good or evil depend upon his use of freedom. The goodness in the world and in man are not, therefore, a reflection of God only. But if God does create human freedom, must it not be possible for persons to contravene God's purpose? Augustine, intent on preserving God's sovereignty, holds that the outcome of human existence is predestined. He even adds that men cannot believe in God except as God in his grace moves them to do so, with no regard for their present and future merit. Thus Augustine's emphasis on both freedom and predestination, on both the immutability of God and his immanence in the changing world, raises difficulties which such theism must confront.

2. All the more fascinating, then, is Scotus Erigena's attempt to clarify both the Unity of God and the interrelated orders of existence (ca. ninth century). God is the Being who creates but is not created. To Him no categories of existence, even self-comprehension, apply. He is Nothing, that is, nothing like anything else. From this Nothing comes all else. Nevertheless, the essence of this intrinsically invisible God is manifest in creation. God without any world would be only a possible Creator, hence this world is not accidental to God's being. Just as the sun must shine, so the creative eternal Goodness must create; there can be no chasm between God's will, his thought, and his being. Yet God and the world are not one.

The stress is clear: creation must not be a divine fiat that is arbitrary, or unrelated to God's essential nature. Hence God is not one being alongside of other beings. As James Ward suggests (1935), words like "super-essential, super-rational, super-personal, nay, super-absolute unity" are intended to express the fullness of "inexhaustible positivity" (p. 35). God does not know himself (if to know is to know *what* some other is). Erigena's problem is to link his full Nothing with **573** the realms of immaterial and material beings and their composites. The Logos, created and creating, is the first manifestation of the Nothing of God. The Logos lures the created and uncreated realms "below" it, thus unifying the manyness of being with the One.

The traditional creationist will insist that such attempts do nothing ultimately to bridge "the ugly broad ditch" between the One and the many. Nor is the distance between the Unity of God and the manyness of the world decreased by introducing many grades of being that are lured by the immaterial Logos (or "Ideas") without which they would be nonexistent. Such juxtaposing of emanationism with creationism is not in fact helpful. For if it helps to argue that man's knowledge of Nature is possible because his mind "participates" in the mediating primal Ideas, it does not help us understand the existence of human freedom and natural evil. For the many, including man, still exist in the Absolute, Self-Determining, God. Nothing that appears to be evil, including man's misuse of his freedom, has reality apart from God. Thus, a high price is to be paid for unifying all Being and Goodness, for holding that evil is ultimate Harmony misunderstood.

3. In Thomas Aquinas the temptation to emanationism is overcome, and creationism is more clear-cut. Aquinas' God is changeless, transcendent in being and in self-knowledge. He is, nevertheless, immanent in the world without its changing Him in any respect. Nothing but God's own being and free decision determine the "moment" of creation or the duration and quantity of the created world. For Aquinas the question whether God can be God without the world is not answerable with logical necessity.

Aquinas concentrates on understanding how the one eternally perfect God can maintain his Unity and Perfection in creating both the many individuals and their forms of being. The controlling analogy here is that of an artist whose quality is expressed not in one work alone but in a variety that express his quality, and together display the many aspects of his perfection.

Aquinas' God, accordingly, creates individuals within species, but the individuals are concrete, graded ways that bring out the richness possible in each species. For example, eyes are eyes; they perform their limited function in all beings. But they, with other limited parts of the body, go to make up the harmony of the body. Similarly no species can express the perfection of God, for each species is limited. But the hierarchy of limited species, each with its imperfect but definite members are—all taken together—concrete manifestations of the perfection of God. God, in freely creating, perforce creates finite forms of his perfection; but their rich variety and hierarchical gradations together express the perfection of his handiwork.

There is a certain power in this argument once it is seen that the Creator and the created cannot be of the same quality in every respect. In Gilson's words: "No creature receives the whole fulness of divine goodness because perfections come from God to creatures by a kind of descent" (p. 155). But must the Perfection, expressed in limited creatures, also include their imperfections? Must the eyes be imperfect eyes? Granting that evil has no independent power but is the absence of good as defined for a given kind of creature, does the actual distribution of natural good and evil add up to perfection?

But Aquinas' main metaphysical model is clear. A self-sufficient God expresses his perfection in creating. The creative activity changes the Creator no more, presumably, than the knowing process changes what is known. God is not a member of any genus but he is the principle and cause of every genus. Were He incapable of creating in accordance with his will and reason, he would not be perfect. Only this kind of being, never Himself nonbeing, can create *ex nihilo*. Yet to create is to create some limited order of being as distinct from every other. This entails at best the creation of mutually supporting beings and of mutually supporting parts within them. These beings come into being and go out of being, within the limits of the divine plan. Their ultimate nature is not theirs to constitute or reconstitute; they affect and are affected in accordance with their particular created constitutions. Persons, however, have limited freedom, which can be strengthened by God's grace, which is respected by God even when it is abused.

4. This Thomistic theism has an outstanding counterpart in F. R. Tennant's *Philosophical Theology* (1930). Tennant argues that there is no denying the finite self, but that as regards all other philosophical questions, probability is the guide of life. He concludes that a cosmic Person is the most reasonable hypothesis for interpreting man's cognitive, aesthetic, moral, and religious experience as a whole.

Tennant struggles with the problem of the divine immanence in Nature. God, in creating, delegated spontaneous activity to unities ("substance-causes") in the subhuman world. A gradation, as biological evolution shows, eventuates in human self-consciousness, desire, reason, and free will. The facts of moral and natural evil are most intelligible if we hypothesize both the delegating of limited spontaneity to subhuman orders and the "planting out" and "positing" of persons. With such metaphorical expressions, Tennant stresses the fact that things and persons are no part of God.

More specifically, God is the Creator of the primary collocations of the world. He is transcendent insofar as the constitutive elements in Nature exhibit some spontaneity and persons enjoy limited moral freedom. Is God, then, a deistic spectator of the created world? Is he immanent as a painter is immanent in his paintings? Or does God, as in the Augustinian and Cartesian view, create from moment to moment and thus provide continuity in his creation?

Tennant answers each of these questions negatively. The Augustinian view does not take seriously enough the "planting out" of beings-for-themselves. Tennant thinks that evils in Nature, like cyclones and cancer, may be seen as an inherent, but not predetermined consequence of the delegated spontaneity at the subhuman level. Such evils and disorder, however, must be seen within the context of prevailing order and the possibilities for goodness in things. At the same time, Tennant urges, "through God's immanence all things *consist*" (II, 212). Purpose-foiling tendencies in the subhuman realm are not allowed to disrupt the purpose-realizing cosmos because of God's appropriate directive and creative activity in keeping "the world with all its differentiated detail and its ever emergent products" one whole (II, 216). Tennant reasons, accordingly, that "divine action upon the world-elements," be it occasional or continuous, is coherent with the intricate adaptations required for our understanding of cosmic evolution, including man (II, 215). The *how* of this direction, like the original act of creation, is not open to human analogy; but it contradicts nothing we know. Tennant leaves it as an empirical question whether interference with such law as we know in Nature has actually taken place when God acts to preserve the dependable unity of Nature. In any case, Tennant's God is no spectator; he is no artist; he is no continual creator (Augustine). God delegates autonomy, but does not remain helpless as he directs and creates in order to maintain and enrich the created realm.

Tennant distinguishes between God's action upon subhuman beings and his action on persons capable of reasonable, moral, and religious response. He rejects any theory of God's action upon man that suggests indwelling possession; no quasi-physical, impersonal coercion by God—even if it be called God's grace—is acceptable in a universe intended to support man's moral development.

Tennant also differs from other theists in holding that it is unempirical, and therefore unreasonable, to speak of God as creating the best possible world from an infinite number of contemplated possibilities. "God without a world is a superfluous abstraction, and a God who might have 'chosen' a different seminal world from this, or different 'primary collocations' would be a different God" (II, 183). Since this world is the only world we know, for us to talk of God's entertaining other eternal ideas is to talk as if we had some other evidence for thinking about God's nature other than this world with man in it. For Tennant, God has "no empty capacity which somehow hits upon definite modes of activity" (II, 184). "The world is what it is because God is what he is" (II, 184). It is this particular evolutionary world, not a "static perfection," which calls for a World-Ground.

In Tennant, the relation of the unchanging eternal God of classical theism to the temporal world is stated very cautiously. On the one hand, he does not wish to restrict God to the conceptual time of scientific description; on the other, he wishes to keep God functionally related to the created changing world. So he finally says, somewhat enigmatically, "We have no right to regard God as not supra-temporal. I admit that He cannot be regarded as supra-temporal" (P. A. Bertocci, *The Empirical Argument*, p. 255).

5. Theists who have less faith in such reasonable theorizing, and who hold to creation as an article of nonrational faith, tend to reinterpret *creatio* by emphasizing man's commitment to his own freedom. They are suspicious of any doctrine of transcendence that makes God one being alongside of others, or that conceives man as a thing and not creative in God's image. Hence they see *creatio* not as in any way separating man, world, and God, but as symbolizing both man's freedom and his dependence on unconditioned Being. John MacQuarrie's *Principles of Christian Theology* (1966) gives expression to this existential-ontological view.

MacQuarrie's conclusion is that the term "letting be" best expresses the meaning of creativity. The speculative questions about whether time had a beginning give way to the existential meaning of time. A creative, loving Being "lets be . . . only at the risk to itself, only by giving itself and going out into openness" (p. 200).

In this view man can understand himself as that being among dependent beings who, most open to fulfillment, is also most responsible for his development as part of the risk of being itself. What this view emphasizes is expressed in MacQuarrie's belief that *creatio* overstresses the difference between God and his creation, thus tending to make creation an arbitrary act. Hence MacQuarrie moves toward the image of emanation which "stresses affinity" and suggests "that God does really put himself into the creation so that the risk of creation really matters to him" (p. 202).

Clearly MacQuarrie uses emanation to avoid what could be arbitrary chasms between beings and Being. Like Paul Tillich he stresses the participation of conditioned beings in the unconditioned Being. At the same time, he has God "going out of himself" and "risking" the creation of the evolutionary order of subhuman and human beings who uniquely share in being and nonbeing. The stress remains on man's continuity with the subhuman world, and on the "leap" that differentiates man as rational, as responsible for his own development, and as capable of participation in Nature and in cooperative intimacy with God.

The contrast between Tennant and MacQuarrie is significant. Both stress human autonomy in particular, but Tennant would be suspicious of images like "participation" as inconsistent with creation, despite MacQuarrie's insistence that participation must never mean "absorption." MacQuarrie does say that creation means "the coming out or emergence of particular things" (p. 214). With what Tennant would approve MacQuarrie continues: "The more multiple the created beings, the richer is the unity, or at least the potential unity [of God], and all this richness would be shattered and destroyed by the collapse of everything into the stillness of an inert monolithic Being" (p. 214). There may seem to be only a verbal difference between Tennant's speaking of "planting out" and "positing" or "delegating" autonomy, and MacQuarrie's "creation where being confers itself, gives itself to the beings who have been called out of nothing" (p. 214). But MacQuarrie's concern for inner kinship inspires other images which for Tennant weaken both transcendence and mutual responsibility. Still both Tennant and MacQuarrie are not far apart when MacQuarrie says: "time is in Being rather than Being in time," and "Being must remain at once stable and dynamic" (p. 320).

6. It is clear that classical, absolutistic theism has produced uneasiness even in its more refined attempts to reconcile the transcendent, unchanging God with the God immanent in a changing world and presumably affected by the moral growth and sin of persons. When struggling with this problem classical theism has veered toward monism and emanationism: God's nature can be expressed in, but not affected by, change and suffering in all its finite centers.

Indeed, the classical God who creates *ex nihilo* suggests an omnipotent, sovereign King, the benefactor of his obedient creatures. But this image does not cohere with the image of God as cosmic Lover sensitive to all sentient creatures, and to overcoming sin and suffering in man. For some thinkers, such as S. Alexander, H. Bergson, C. Hartshorne, A. N. Whitehead and H. N. Wieman, this seems to mean the bankruptcy of the doctrine of *creatio ex nihilo*. They therefore supplant *creatio* with an ultimate creativity, congenial with the emergence of novelty in biological evolution and moral worth in man. The dominant model now is creative emergence within a temporalistic, teleological reality guided and directed in different degrees

by a God whose very being is involved with that of the world.

But all such views, despite their protestations to the contrary, are faced with the problem of protecting the nature of the individuality of both God and man. Their stress on human autonomy and independence of the world tends to be lost in a polarity between God and his creation. Such is the critique that underlies temporalistic personalism. E. S. Brightman, in particular, resists any blurring of *creatio,* individuality, and freedom, even as he takes both time and the problem of nondisciplinary suffering seriously (1958). The suggestion is that the working out of the purpose of the Creator-God is affected by changes in the world and by the free choices of persons. This suggestion may be expressed in four theses that at once summarize and develop the basic themes in this essay.

First, God in his metaphysical structure is a Person, aware of his own being and purposes. In creating, God brings into being what could not be apart from his willing it into being. Created beings are "posited" with their own quality and degree of activity-passivity (or, at the subhuman level, they may be identical with God).

Second, in creating free persons especially, God is both limiting his own power and the particular way in which he will affect them. Persons, with limited freedom, operating within the collocated structures that make the world a cosmos, cannot change these structures; but they can select among possible alternatives allowed by these structures. In so doing they influence the quality of their own experience and God's. The contrast with this classical theism is expressed in the next three contentions.

Third, God is not the stern cosmic Potentate, impassive to the suffering and enjoyments of men; nor is he the beneficent Overseer. He is indeed the Creator who in creating expresses his own being. The created world is indeed one in which co-creators arrive, survive, and are basically responsible for the quality of the responsive-responsible community involving God and man. God indeed continues to create without infringing the dependable order of being and in cooperation with human choice. And God can never become less than real, being a self-caused Person. But his creative acts in the evolution of world history, including man, make him a participant in, but not victim of, all that occurs. He responds creatively and mercifully to what is effected in the realm of delegated agency at all levels. This cosmic Creator is the redeeming Lover who is concerned that nothing valuable be lost as shared creation continues.

Fourth, God does not create the world and time together, for the Creator himself is temporal insofar as he creates and responds to his co-creators. The historic process is integral to the very being of the Creator, who, in creating any specific beings, expresses the nature of His own being in that specific way. Thus, the model of an unchanging Creator is supplanted by the model of a unified Creator who is self-continuous in creating and knows the agony and ectasy of all creativity and destruction.

Fifth, in this perspective, the notion that there is no model for *creatio ex nihilo* in the finite world is challenged. Man is indeed usually an artificer in a material given to him and in him. But the counter-suggestion is that man does create *ex nihilo* when, given his created nature, he does bring into being what was not. This is so when he creates in the realms of knowledge, ethics, art, and religion. Obviously this creation is within limits, but what comes to be would not be to the extent, and in the way that, a person wills it. There is an experiential person-model for *creatio ex nihilo*.

Accordingly, temporalistic personalists reject deism, emanation, monism, and a dialectical polarity. They seek to harmonize transcendence and immanence in a cosmological model of a Unified Person, who creates without being transformed, who maintains his unity and continuity as he creates and undergoes the consequences, good and bad, of his creations. This creationist model must be seen teleologically. A loving Person purposes a cosmic community of mutually responsible co-creators—the present and continuing goal of all creative activity. This view of God underlies the ethics and social philosophy not of authoritarian fascism or communism, but of communitarian personalism.

BIBLIOGRAPHY

Peter A. Bertocci, *The Empirical Argument for God in Late British Thought* (Cambridge, Mass., 1938); idem, "Toward a Metaphysics of Creation," *Review of Metaphysics,* **17** (1964), 493–510. Henry Bett, *Johannes Scotus Erigena* (New York, 1964). Edgar S. Brightman, *Person and Reality* (New York, 1958). Étienne Gilson, *The Christian Philosophy of Thomas Aquinas* (New York, 1956). Charles Hartshorne, *The Divine Relativity* (New Haven, 1948). Lucretius, *On the Nature of Things,* I, 154, in *The Stoic and Epicurean Philosophers,* ed. Whitney J. Oates (New York, 1940). John Mac-Quarrie, *Principles of Christian Theology* (New York, 1966). Robert C. Neville, *God and Creator* (Chicago, 1968). Frederick R. Tennant, *Philosophical Theology,* 2 vols. (Cambridge, 1930). James Ward, *Realms of Ends* (London, 1935). Harry A. Wolfson, *Religious Philosophy* . . . (Cambridge, Mass., 1961).

PETER A. BERTOCCI

[See also **Creativity in Art;** Death and Immortality; Deism; Evil; Existentialism; **Free Will in Theology; God;** Hierarchy; Nature; Right and Good; Time.]

CREATIVITY IN ART

PERHAPS the most significant interpretation of the conception of "creativity in art" which has appeared in the history of ideas, and certainly the one most fruitful for the aesthetician, is that couched in terms of freedom. Philologists have attributed the more extensive meanings of "make" and "grow" to the hypothetical root of "create," the Indo-European °*kerdh-* or the Sanskrit °*ker-* or °*kre-*. (See J. Pokorny, 1, 577; Walde-Hofmann, III, 288, Ernout and Meillet, III, 208, 260; and S. M. Kuhn, II, 713ff.) The proliferation of meanings of the word "create" in less hypothetical contexts has been extraordinary: "causing to grow," "ability to produce," "ability to make," "ability to call into existence, to construct, to give rise to, to constitute, to represent, to invest, to occasion, to form out of nothing." (See, for example, H. C. Wyld, *The Universal English Dictionary.*) A philosopher of art, in contrast to the philologist and to the maker of dictionaries, discovers that the identification of "creativity" with freedom is not hypothetical and that it is with widely received interpretations of freedom that he must deal. He finds, moreover, that the conception of freedom underlying speculation on art in all its phases—the artist's creativity, the autonomous judgment of works of fine art, and the productive imagination at work in the experience of profoundly moving works of art—is the theme of God's power and freedom to make or to originate the universe. This primarily theological and cosmological conception of creativity has influenced both philosophy of art and aesthetics principally through what has been called "the great analogy" between the artist and God (Nahm, *The Artist as Creator* and "The Theological Background of the Theory of the Artist as Creator").

Two dominant conceptions of deity have persisted within this analogy. These have provided conditions for two basic conceptions of the artist and for two main lines of speculation in the history of ideas concerning "creativity in art." The analogue to God the Creator is the inspired genius who, it has been maintained, is capable of producing works of art which cannot be explained solely in terms of artifacts. In classical speculation on art, the inspired genius was said to be *entheos*, "filled with god," and because he utters divine words, able to give "birth to beauty." In modern times, the genius is ordinarily regarded as a man endowed with a marked productive or creative imagination.

The analogue to God the Maker is the artist as imitator and technician, one who proceeds by "right reason," the ground for *technē* (τεχνη). Each conception of deity and of artist is presupposed by a contrasting conception of freedom. The creative god and the creative artist are free to originate; the artisan deity and maker are free to discover what is already there, to select, and to construct. These differing conceptions of deity and artist have influenced the entire aesthetic universe of discourse, with results happily suggested by Friedrich Schiller. In *The Aesthetic Education of Man* (Letter I), the poet writes of art that it is "a daughter of freedom" and adds that "through beauty . . . we arrive at freedom." It is with the principal implications of "creativity in art" as human freedom in terms of choice and origination, of *technē* and fine art which signifies more than *technē* that we shall be concerned here. Owing to the scope of a problem which touches the philosophy of art and aesthetics at almost every point, we shall limit this discussion principally to classical speculation on the subject, indicating in the conclusion by reference to various "heralds of creativity" some of the directions taken by writers on "creativity in art" in modern times.

In spite of the fact that for Greek philosophers art as making or *technē* is principally examined in terms of mimesis or imitation—and, indeed, it is for Plato's cosmic architect as he constructs the world (*Timaeus* 28A–B)—the basic outline for the speculative tradition concerning artistic creativity in the West is firmly drawn by them. For Aristotle, mimesis in the strictest sense is no longer adequate for the expression of his theory of the artist and the work of art (*Politics* 1340a 13ff.). Even the conception of productive or creative imagination, perhaps the most significant modern contribution to the subject, is foreshadowed by Philostratus. The notion of genius is clearly formulated in Platonic philosophy. A belief that the poet is free from the requirements of technique is firmly rooted in Greek speculation. The ground for creative freedom is present at the end of the classical period in the writings of Philo and Saint Augustine.

More specifically, we discover in ancient speculation that the theory of art as *technē* or intelligible making was developed within the context of Greek philosophy by thinkers who maintained both that the process of constructing a work of art is demonstrable and that criticism of the product of the process is adequate. This conception of art was argued at the same time that some of these philosophers sought to "explain" various aspects of the phenomena—principally those of creative productive activity—in terms of nonrational inspiration. For the most part, Greek theory tended to explain the experience of works of art in terms of responses to stimuli, without even hinting that the perceiver entered into the relation with the work of art in a productive and creative, rather than in a reproductive and re-creative way. As we shall observe, however, it clearly becomes increasingly difficult for speculative minds to entertain dogmatically either the theory that the work of art is a mere stimulus to imitation or that its experience is to be explained in terms of a catharsis of feelings.

Plato and Aristotle, the two principal speculative philosophers in classical Greece who systematically examined "creativity in art" in terms of freedom, both take art to be a basic and significant human activity, and they do so for a variety of reasons which are not directly relevant here. Their views diverge sharply as regards the nature and value of mimetic art. This is in part owing to the fact that for Plato the Idea of Beauty transcends the work of art, whereas for Aristotle the universal is in the thing. Still, as we shall argue, the transcendence for Plato is not for its own sake but for the establishment of a ground for a theory of technique intended to produce "absolutely and eternally beautiful" mathematical objects, whereas Aristotle is evidently confident that his assumption—art is "the rational state of capacity to make"—is adequate to the task of accounting for poetry, sculpture, music, and similar productions. It is *technē* which is significant in both philosophies, insofar as they treat "creativity in art," and the divergences are the clearer if we attend first to the different sources upon which Plato and Aristotle drew.

Plato is indebted to Pythagorean number-theory, to the Heraclitean conception of eternal process, to the Sophist doctrine of subjectivity, and to the opinions of Socrates concerning tragic and comic poets. He owed an important debt to earlier Greek cosmological theories, as we shall observe in an illustration drawn from the fragments of Empedocles' philosophy. Aristotle's indebtedness to Plato in speculation upon philosophy of art is enormous, as is evident whether we concentrate attention upon the agreements or the disagreements in theory of these two superb speculative minds. Still, Aristotle draws primarily upon nonmathematical sources, although he clearly values Pythagorean speculation on art (*Metaphysics* Book XIII). He abandons Plato's search for absolutely beautiful forms and places art in the area of the variable and contingent (*Nicomachean Ethics* VI. 4). The scientific tradition upon which Aristotle draws is largely that of the biologists and members of the medical schools, more particularly the cult of Asclepius at Epidaurus. The influence of this tradition is evident in his conception of the beautiful object (*Poetics* 1450b 34; *Metaphysics* XIII). It also conditions his interpretation of the experience of tragedy (*Poetics* 1449b 26, 1453b 1) and some kinds of music (*Politics* 1342a 6).

We may best begin a brief examination of Platonic and Aristotelian theories of artistic creativity by turning to an anticipation of the "great analogy" between the artist and God in Plato's cosmology and philosophy of art. For Plato, the cosmos is made by a *Demiurgos*, a world-artisan, who uses solid geometrical bodies for

FIGURE 1. *God, Cosmic Maker or Architect.* These miniatures are intended to illustrate Book XI, Chapter XIX of Saint Augustine's *The City of God.* Augustine's God is a creative deity but the miniaturist has illustrated the text as though the God he portrays is closely akin to Plato's Demiurgos. The Augustinean text tells us that ". . . God made two great lights. . . . He made both them and the stars: and God set them in the firmament of heaven. . . ." The process of "making" them in the miniatures requires that God use a drawing compass (compare Figure 4). From *Les Manuscrits et peintures de la cité de Dieu de St Augustin*, Vol. II by le Conte A. de Laborde. 1909

the task (Figure 1). The Demiurge models the universe after the Ideas and creates neither the pattern nor the "material" from which the cosmos is constructed. Empedocles had used a similar illustration: Love and Strife, the forces of nature which direct the cyclical processes in the cosmos, are compared to painters, men "well taught by wisdom in their art" ($\tau\acute{\epsilon}\chi\nu\eta s$) (Nahm [1964], p. 112, frag. 121).

It is to Pythagoras and the Pythagoreans, rather than to Empedocles, that we turn for one of the principal sources of Plato's conception of "creativity in art." The experience of beautiful forms induces pleasure unmixed with pain as a depleted body undergoes repletion and so returns to a state of harmony (*Philebus* 31B, 42D). The conception of harmony is central to the Pythagorean account of what the artist may do to introduce

intelligibility by definition into music. As regards "creativity in art," two specific contributions in Pythagorean philosophy are to be noted. In the first place, Pythagoras measured the length of vibrating taut cords and discovered that the concordant intervals of the scale can be expressed in terms of the ratio $6:8::9:12$. Secondly, in a brilliant act of imagination, the conception of this "harmony" was extended to the cosmos, and the image of a universe in which the planets and stars move in a circle and produce harmonious sounds (Aristotle, *Physics* 290b 15) has served since to light the imaginations of innumerable creative artists. Among these are Hindemith, Holst, Blake, and Yeats, and the notable instance among scientists, Johannes Kepler (Spitzer, pp. 14–17ff.).

A no less important but somewhat disregarded aspect

of Pythagorean philosophy, which is an integral part of a most significant tradition in the history of art, radically affected Plato's mature conception of "creativity in art." Like Pythagoras' reduction of "woodland notes wild" to mathematical ratio, the writers within this tradition have tried to make of painting and sculpture arts wholly intelligible in mathematical terms. The core of the tradition is the "canon of proportions," which has its antecedents in Egyptian theory of sculpture and its descendants in the formulations for art by artists such as Dürer, Leonardo, and Le Corbusier. (See W. M. Conway, pp. 165, 179; Leonardo da Vinci, *Trattato* . . . , Secs. 309, 313, 342, 366; C. E. Jeanneret-Grist [Le Corbusier], *Modulor 2*.) Plato argues in *Timaeus* 44D that God copied the figure of the universe, which was round and produced a spherical body, our head, "the most divine and sovereign" body. But, as we shall see he also advocated the retention of the Egyptian practice of using fixed and unchangeable patterns in their art. (See M. C. Nahm, *Aesthetic Experience* . . . , Chs. III and IV.) In this he was defending the Polycleitean canon of proportions in which it is stated that "Beauty . . . arises . . . in the commensurability of the parts, such as that of the finger to the finger . . . and . . . of everything to everything else. . . ." (See Galen, *De Placitis Hippocratis et Platonis*, ed. Müller, p. 45; P. Schuhl, *Platon et l'art* . . . , pp. 6ff.; E. Panofsky, "The History of the Theory of Proportions . . . ," in *The Meaning of Art*, pp. 55–108.) But he was defending the Egyptian tradition and the Polycleitean Canon in the face of the actual practice of artists who had acquired a sound knowledge of perspective. (For Egyptian practices, see C. R. Williams, *The Decoration of the Tomb of Per-nēb*, pp. 7ff., and E. MacKay, "Proportion Squares. . . .")

It is therefore not only to understand more completely Plato's theory of art but also to learn something concerning the actual processes believed to be adequate for "creativity in art" that we turn to a fragment of Pythagorean speculation. It is attributed to Eurytos, a student of the renowned Philolaus. Aristotle is the principal source of our information (*Metaphysics* 1092b 10; cf. Theophrastus, *Metaphysics* 11, 6a 19), and the obscurity of the reference suggests his own puzzlement as regards Eurytos' meaning. Aristotle says that Eurytos "determined which number belongs to which thing—for example, this number to man, and this to horse—by using pebbles to imitate the shape of natural objects, as those do who arrange numbers in the form of geometrical figures, the triangle and the square." Aristotle remarks that it has not been determined whether the Pythagoreans use numbers as the causes of substances and of Being as though the numbers are boundaries, "*e.g.* as points are the boundaries of spatial magni-

tudes" or because "harmony is a ratio of numbers, and so too is man and everything else. . . ."

Some of Aristotle's difficulty would appear to arise because his is a critical examination of the Pythagorean metaphysic of visible numbers (*Metaphysics* Book XIII), an important issue but not the immediately relevant one. The context of Eurytos' speculation is not the making of a living man or of a substance in Aristotle's interpretation of this passage. What the Pythagorean meant Aristotle does in fact suggest in the phrase "to imitate the shape of natural objects." The passage is meaningfully interpreted in terms of the relation of mathematics to art and it is of interest that in an earlier passage in *Metaphysics* (1078b 11ff.) Aristotle himself sets us on the right track. The main species of beauty, he writes, are orderly arrangement, proportion, and definiteness and he adds that as orderly arrangement and definiteness are causes of many things the mathematical sciences must to some extent treat of "the cause in the sense of the Beautiful." Eurytos, in relating mathematics to art, proceeds by "limiting" man by the number of pebbles required to define him. As the Pythagoreans defined numbers as "triangular," "oblong," and "square" in terms of the shape of the space enclosed by pebbles as "terms," so Eurytos is limiting or defining man by the number of pebbles needed to define him in contrast to a plant. Burnet quotes Alexander of Aphrodisias to the effect that 250 is the number which defines man, 360 the number which defines plant (Burnet, pp. 52ff., 90). Within the context of the theory of art, the point, as Alexander observes, is that he proceeded ". . . to fix some of the counters in the *outline* . . . of the man he had imaged by the number of counters equal in number to the units which he said defined the man." (He uses σκιαγραφία, i.e., "drawing.")

The Pythagorean theorist took the delineation or form to define the essence of man. Thus, his theory is integral to the ateleological theory of art as a mathematical form. Its source for the Greeks was Egypt and one of the principal speculative heirs was Plato. What Eurytos asserted concerning *outline* or delineation has an antecedent in Pliny's writing on the history of art. Pliny tells us (Pliny, Ch. XXXV) that either Philokles of Egypt or Cleanthes of Corinth invented painting, and proceeds to speculate on the possibility that the art originated "with the outlining of a man's shadow" (*omnes umbra hominis lineis circumducta*). We also learn (ibid., XXXV. 151) that Boutades, a potter of Sikyon, discovered with the help of his daughter how to model portraits in clay. It is of less consequence to determine whether or not this is sound history than to notice how persistently in the history of ideas on "creativity in art" the "outline," "form," or "delineation" has been taken to be the essential and permanent factor to be sought in the production of works of art. It is clear that a complex of reasons dictates this line of speculation. Boutades' daughter clearly wanted a permanent reminder of her loved one. Eurytos presumably searched for precision and accuracy. Plato, in *Philebus*, likewise wants accuracy and it is on this ground that he prefers building as an art to music (*Philebus* 56A ff.). What artists believed they could get by mathematical methods is suggested in the tale told of two brothers, Theodoros and Telekles. Each, one in Ephesus, the other in Samos, made one half a figure. When the two halves were brought together, so the story runs, they fitted perfectly into a single statue (*Diodorus Siculus*, I. 98).

There is no evidence that Eurytos believed that what the pebbles could define was beautiful; there is every evidence that Polycleitus' Canon is intended to enable the artist to produce beauty. Finally, there is no doubt that Plato believed that mathematical measure was the instrument most useful for the achievement of beauty, providing a technique for the attainment of perfected forms.

In line with the strong influence of Pythagorean philosophy which affected his speculation and in view of his own defence of the *Doryphorus*, Plato upheld what he believed to be the Egyptian practice of fixing and exhibiting patterns in their temples which "no painter or artist is allowed to innovate upon . . . or to leave the traditional forms and invent new ones." "To this day," he added, "no alteration is allowed in these arts, or in music at all. . . ." And, as a final fillip, he writes, "their ancient paintings and sculptures are not a whit better or worse than the work of today, but are made with just the same skill" (*Laws* 656D–E; cf. 799A).

Plato is not content, however, merely to defend what he interprets to be an Egyptian theory of painting and sculpture. He directs an argument against contemporary innovations in these arts and in doing so provides at once grounds from which attacks have been launched against his entire philosophy, points of departure for theories of Greek culture, and bases for detailed studies of the development of Greek art. These arguments, all pertinent to Greek and, more particularly, Platonic interpretations of "creativity in art" center on the interpretation of Plato's dialogue, *Sophist* 234–36. In this dialogue, Plato divides imitative art into the art of making "likenesses" and that of "fantastic art or the art of making appearances." This theory is applied to massive sculpture and mimetic painting. Plato asserts that the maker of "fantastic art" is, in the nature of the case, forced to deceive: if the true proportions of the upper part of a statue were given,

they "would appear to be out of proportion with the lower, which is nearer." It is strange to learn that sculptors or painters who employ perspective "give up the truth of their images (*eidōla; εἴδωλα*) and make only the proportions which appear to be beautiful, disregarding the real ones."

Two points should be noted. Plato is in search of a beauty which is not relative to context or person (*Hippias Major* 291D). The practicing artists of Greece, on the other hand—although they had turned to Egypt for the canon of proportions and had borrowed from that country the results of "the technically difficult achievement of extracting life-size solid images of men and animals out of quarried blocks of stone," a technique evolved "two thousand years before the classical era . . ." (Carpenter, pp. 164ff.)—unlike the Egyptians, had been bound neither by ritual nor the power of magic. To put the matter simply, they were not forced to follow a formula and so were able to attend to the essential problems of sculpture and painting, more particularly in the achievement of perspective and dynamic power.

Two stories illustrate the issue of *Sophist* 234ff. In the first, it is said that Phidias entered a contest to make a statue of Athena (Overbeck, No. 772). Two statues were to be made. Both were to be set on high columns. Alkamenes made one, Phidias the other. Phidias made his Athena as would one who knew optics and geometry and "knowing that things that are high will appear very small." His Athena was made with her mouth open, nostrils distended, and the rest in proportion to the height of the columns. As a result, the sculptor was in danger of being stoned by the outraged populace. But when both statues were raised on their columns, Phidias was seen to have produced a statue admirable for the excellence of its sculptural technique, whereas Alkamenes, whose statue had earlier been admired, was subjected to ridicule.

The second story concerns Socrates' visit to the sculptor Cleiton—probably Polycleitus—and indicates also how little likely it is for a sculptor to be bound by categorical formulae. Socrates asks the artist (Xenophon, *Memorabilia* III. 10. 6) how he produces the illusion of life in his statues and then proceeds to answer his own question. The sculptor, he says, faithfully represents the form of living things "by accurately representing the different parts of the body as they are affected by the pose . . . the limbs compressed or outstretched, the muscles taut and loose." The implication is that close observation of the variety of poses possible for the sitter is the basic requirement, rather than adherence to a strict canon of proportions. A work of sculpture is produced by its maker taking into account time, place, and pose. What is also needed, we

581

learn, is a capacity to represent in his figures "the activities of the soul." This is the proper method of procedure.

The story of the contest in which Phidias participated and the account of Socrates' visit to Cleiton suggest how alien to sculptural practice were Plato's desires, as expressed in his *Sophist*. Plato's reasons for what he wrote are basically philosophical. Still, it is illuminating to glance briefly at several of the alternative possibilities which have been put forward to explain his attitude. We have mentioned Plato's adherence to the canon of proportions, which is coupled with his distaste for the innovations by Lysippos and Euphranor, who distorted hair and neck of sculptured figures (Schuhl, pp. 6ff.). Mary Swindler has argued (p. 336) that Plato was one of the first writers "to criticize 'humbug' in painting" and that his belief that painting must be an exact copy of the original led him to attack Agatharchos and Apollodorus, "who had failed to follow in the old, plastic fashion" and had abandoned the older way of Polygnotus and Apelles for chiaroscuro and perspective. A not unrelated point of view is expressed by the philosopher-historian, R. G. Collingwood, who argues that Plato was inveighing against the decadent "amusement-art" which had emerged with the disappearance of the great artistic tradition (pp. 97ff.). A radically different interpretation is put forward by Arnold Hauser, who asserts (I, 99) that in the passage in the *Sophist* Plato offers an instance—consonant with the entire theory of Ideas—of a constant effort to champion the "cultural ideals of the nobility" (ibid., p. 110). Of the theory of Ideas, the sociologist writes that it is "the classical philosophic expression of conservatism, the pattern for all subsequent reactionary idealism" (ibid., pp. 110–11), a view seconded by an anthropologist, V. Gordon Childe (pp. 208ff.), who believes that the origin of the theory is to be found in the influence upon the individual of a serf or slave society.

The most that can be granted the sociologist and the anthropologist is that Athenian society was a conditioning factor in the development of Plato's thought. Nevertheless, the attention that has been paid to Plato's regard for the canon of proportions and Egyptian art is more relevant. Of more importance is Swindler's suggestion that Plato was attacking "humbug," a suggestion which verges on the basic problem of *Sophist* 234 as this affects an interpretation of Plato's notion of "creativity in art," a notion which turns on the distinction between the original inventor ($\phi \nu \tau o \hat{\nu} \rho \gamma o s$) and the artisan ($\delta \eta \mu \iota o \nu \rho \gamma o s$). These authors, however, all but ignore the philosophical problems of art presented to Plato by Heraclitus, the Sophists, and Socrates. It is not a reactionary society or an "archaiz-

ing" theory of art which must be understood, so much as Plato's effort to establish a theory of ideas or universals as an objective ground for truth and existence. What Plato implies concerning perspective and imitation is most fully understood in the light of his objections to Heraclitus' philosophy of constant change, in which the emphasis rests on the relations of contraries and on the consequences of the Sophists' doctrine that man is the measure of all things. Heraclitus' discovery of subjectivity finds its most vivid expression in the remark, "In the same rivers we step and we do not step. We are and we are not" (Nahm [1964], p. 73, frag. 81).

Its implications for the philosophy of art are best expressed (ibid., p. 74, frag. 99) in the judgment that "The fairest ape is ugly compared with anything of another kind and the fairest pot is ugly compared with any maiden." Few statements in the history of the philosophy of art express more cogently the implications of this Heraclitean remark for the doctrine, *de gustibus non est disputandum*, than those of the anonymous Sophist who wrote *The Argument on Both Sides*, just as few have ever asserted so baldly the opinion that the judgment of the fair and the ugly is not only subjective but unconditionally free as well: "Some say that the fair is one thing and the ugly another," writes the Sophist (Diels, II. 407ff.), "as the name differs. . . . If anyone bade all men to bring together into a single place the things that each thought were ugly, and then bade them take from this gathering the things each considered fair, nothing would have been left, and all would have taken every last thing. . . ."

The completely unconditioned creativity and freedom of judgment which the Sophists attributed to each subject are converted in Plato's philosophy of art into the complete and unconditioned freedom of the imitative artist to make everything. Plato believes that there is a class of "extraordinarily ingenious persons," practitioners of "shallow versatility" who not only can construct all manufactured articles but are able also to produce "everything that grows out of the ground . . . all living things, himself among others; and, in addition to this, heaven and earth and the gods and all heavenly bodies, and all beings of the nether world" (*Republic* 596C). In his interpretation of the imitative arts, Plato goes beyond Heraclitus and the Sophists. In the world of becoming, things "play double"; in the world of art, the mimetic artist produces a copy of a copy, an object twice removed from reality (ibid., 596–97). The imitative artist knows neither truth nor falsity (*Laws* 719B–C). What he practices is not in fact an art: his technique is likened to a mirroring of the world and since he copies what the artisan makes, his art has its essence in another.

It is evident that Plato believes that such creative freedom as the Sophist had evidently judged to be possible for the subject is for the imitative artist the worst form of bondage. Such a life is one spent in search of "images of beauty," a beauty "clogged with the pollutions of mortality, and all the colors and vanities of human life" (*Symposium* 211E–212A). For Plato, sound art and genuine classification are attainable but the imitative artist cannot achieve them. However, neither mimetic art nor craft is the sole product of *technē* which is possible. Plato's search is for that art which is master of its own subject matter and has its own technique. Almost by definition, the search cannot reach its goal by means of mimetic art, for this has its subject matter in the product of another art. Plato seeks the answer to the question by way of the Idea of beauty. In doing so he informs us concerning human creativity, insofar as creativity is to be achieved in terms of intelligibility.

It was remarked earlier that Plato's speculation on beauty transcends art, whereas Aristotle's does not do so. It should be noted, however, that the arduous ascent to the Idea of beauty in Plato's philosophy presupposes experience of works of art and, more significantly, that the transcendence is directed to the reestablishment of the theory of *technē* on grounds of beauty. In order to achieve this, Plato introduces the nonrational theory of inspiration. The transcendent experience achieved in inspiration establishes the absolute and eternal beauty of mathematical forms. The point is significant for many reasons, not the least of which is this; for Plato, in examining "creativity in art," the transcendence is not for its own sake. It tends to become so, and in Greek thought the tendency is the more notable because the explanation of the poet in terms of nonrational experience pervades even the most rational metaphysical theories (See Delatte). An example is found in the fragments of Democritus' philosophy (Diels, II. 145–46, frags. 17 and 18). The Atomist, builder with Leucippus of the greatest mechanist philosophy of ancient times, believed that without madness there is no poetry and that what the poet produces by divine inspiration and enthusiasm is "most beautiful." Plato's master, the rationalist Socrates, said of poets that they sing, not by art, but "by power divine" and do not understand fully what they make (*Ion* 534). Plato himself draws the sharp distinction between the inspired man and the interpreter of his words (*Timaeus* 71E, 72), and in the *Laws* (719B–C) makes a radical statement concerning the poet and the judge of the poetry, expressing a view which has exerted considerable influence upon the theory of criticism. When the poet "sits on the tripod of his muse," he writes, "he is not in his right mind,—like a fountain, he allows

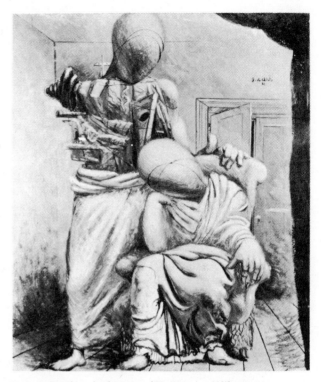

FIGURE 2. De Chirico's *The Poet and His Muse* (ca. 1925) portrays an essentially Platonic conception of "the shy, winged, and holy thing," the poet, who writes not by wisdom but "by a sort of genius and inspiration." When the poet "sits down on the tripod of his muse," writes Plato, he is "not in his right mind." PHILADELPHIA MUSEUM OF ART, THE LOUISE AND WALTER ARENSBERG COLLECTION

to flow out freely whatever comes in. . . . Neither can he tell whether there is more truth in one thing that he has said than in another . . ." (Figure 2).

The state of inspiration in Plato's philosophy is the end of an ascent to the world of Ideas, the suprasensible world of universals. "The true order of going . . . is to use the beauties of earth as steps along which" a man "mounts upwards . . . for the sake of that other beauty." He who searches for beauty proceeds from all fair forms to fair actions to fair notions until he arrives at absolute beauty and knows what its essence is (*Symposium* 211–12). Until beauty is reached, the procedure is rational, but the experience of beauty itself is nonrational, "a vision" and "a communion." What is revealed in this inspired state is "a single science which is the science of beauty everywhere" (Taylor, pp. 230–31).

Plato's Socrates had maintained that there is no invention in the poet until he is inspired and possessed (*Ion* 534C). Plato writes (*Phaedrus* 245) that only he who is inspired may enter the temple; the man who believes he will enter by the help of art, "he and his poetry will not be admitted." The importance of this for an understanding of Plato's theory of "creativity in art" is evident in his suggestion (*Symposium* 206ff.) that men who have experienced the "vision" of beauty are "creative souls." They achieve immortality. Their souls are pregnant with ideas. When inspired, they practice their creative arts, the processes by means of which passage from nonbeing to being is brought about. By implication the experience creates creativity.

Creativity here means freedom, most obviously freedom *from* the pollution of mortality. This freedom is, however, not the sole creative result of the "communion" with beauty. By its means, Plato relates the particular beauties of the ascent in *Symposium* to the "absolutely and eternally beautiful" mathematical forms of *Philebus*. It has been argued, on the contrary, that there is no relation between these two dialogues (see R. Hackforth, p. 99n.). The argument in *Symposium* shows that a man may proceed by an arduous ascent from the experience of objects which have their essence in another to the experience of the Idea of beauty which has its essence in itself and, unlike mimetic objects, has no external relations (*Symposium* 209–10; cf. *Timaeus* 52C, *Republic* 438D, *Parmenides* 133D).

This conception of the Idea of beauty leads Plato to employ inspiration as an epistemological theory different from that grounded on rational knowledge. In the latter, we know by means of external relations; subject and object are separate. In the inspired state, the self is related to the object by becoming one with it. From the point of view of "creativity in art," this way of knowing beauty is in sharp contrast to that by which the mimetic artist "knows," for what the latter "knows" has its essence in what is twice removed and therefore a double set of external relations is involved. In systematic terms, however, the identification of the self with the Idea is of vital importance.

As has already been suggested, this transcendence of the world of images is not only of value in itself but is valuable for the establishment of the grounds for a technique which will produce objects and events which are not mimetic, and are not relatively, but absolutely beautiful. The Idea of beauty provides the needed connotation in which mathematical objects are no longer merely spheres and straight lines but are beautiful. Plato tells us in *Phaedrus* (250E) that the beauty which shone bright in the world of forms is apprehended in this world below through sight, "the clearest of our senses" and that coming to earth we find beauty here, too, for it is "the privilege of beauty, that being the loveliest she is also the most palpable

to sight." The "vision" of absolute beauty is "communion" with the supreme value, beauty, and is the presupposition of the experience of the mathematical forms in *Philebus* as beautiful forms. Plato holds that they, like the Idea of beauty, are not relatively beautiful, nor are they imitative of men or animals (*Philebus* 51B–C).

As we turn to Aristotle, we come to a philosophy of art in which there is no transcendent beauty and one in which, for many, there is no theory of "creativity." It is certainly clear that creativity in the sense of origination, i.e., out of nothing, would violate a basic Aristotelian doctrine, repeated by Lucretius, *ex nihilo nihil fit*. For Aristotle there is no need for such transcendence as Plato describes for the experience of the Idea of beauty, because the universal is in the thing. One may accumulate considerable evidence, in fact, that there is no place in Aristotle's theory of art for "creativity": he (or his follower, Theophrastus) reduces "genius" to suffering by poets and philosophers from black bile (*Problems* XXXI). Works of art are to be explained in terms of man's "rational state of capacity to make"; art belongs to speculation concerning what is probable; the process of making a work of art involves the imposition of a form upon matter; this operation is physically possible because men have hands with retractable thumbs, the hand being an instrument for making instruments. Moreover, the *Poetics* and the *Rhetoric* give the impression that Aristotle proceeds on the assumption that works of art are intelligible and that criticism is an adequate correlative to art. Aristotle proceeds from the genus, imitation, to its differentiae. The work of art—the tragedy or music—is a stimulus for various responses, all explicable in natural terms.

Still, despite this evidence, the matter of "creativity in art" is not so simply disposed of. Two passages in Aristotle's writings merit attention. In the *Nicomachean Ethics* (VI. 1140a 11), we are told that "All art is concerned with the realm of coming into being, i.e., with contriving and considering how something which is capable both of being and non-being may come into existence." In the *Poetics* (IV. 1449a 11) we are told that "Tragedy advanced by slow degrees" from the dithyramb, "and each new element that showed itself was in turn developed. Having passed through many changes it found its natural form, and there stopped." In the latter passage, Aristotle is writing of tragedy as the actualization of the potentiality, the dithyramb, precisely as "potentially . . . a statue of Hermes is in the block of wood" (*Metaphysics* 1048a 25b 1). But clearly, while this is in agreement with the theory of potentiality and actuality, of form and matter, what Aristotle writes in both passages is not concerned merely with such natural processes as the development of the oak from the acorn. The freedom of the artist intervenes in the case of artistic making, and this fact suggests an interpretation of Aristotle's writings on art in terms of something other than an analysis in terms of *technē*. There are passages in the *Poetics* and in the *Rhetoric* which are not wholly explicable in terms other than "creativity" and "novelty." It is of interest in this regard that the texts led Sir Arthur Grant (*Aristotle's Ethics,* Book VI. 4.4) to translate *genesis* as "creation."

The issue is, however, not only a textual one. In part, it turns on the adequacy or inadequacy of Aristotle's theory of freedom to account for the facts he adduces. It is clear that Aristotle's artist is free—to discover, to select, and to make—and that the conception differs radically from the Platonic image of the mimetic artist as a mirror, reflecting everything and anything. For Aristotle, the origin of art is in the maker. He who errs willingly and voluntarily is to be preferred to the maker who errs involuntarily.

One might add other instances all of which underline the basic fact that the artist discovers the potentialities of the material and actualizes them in the work of art, and selects and makes an object or event separate from himself as the maker. Still it is more important to note that Aristotle raises issues which suggest not mere discovery or selection, but rather, that making produces what is new and that criticism is not adequate to explain certain results of technical processes.

It is evident, for example, that in its approach to the problem of ugliness as the artist copes with it, Aristotle's theory is an enormous advance over Plato's. (For Plato, see *Philebus* 48 A ff.) Both the *Poetics* and the *Rhetoric* imply that the power of the artist produces what is new, i.e., what is pleasant in the imitation from what is painful or unpleasant in the object imitated. "For," Aristotle writes, "it is not the object itself which here gives delight"; also, we may be pleased "even if the object imitated is not itself pleasant" (*Rhetoric* I. 1. 1371b 1; cf. *Poetics* 1446b 5). So far as the adequacy or inadequacy of *technē* to account for all aspects of works of art and so permit the critic to analyze these in wholly rational terms, we need cite here but two instances. Making may proceed "under the guidance of true reason" but this argument can account fully neither for the divergence of tragic excellence from technical skill nor for the production of metaphor. As for the first, we are told (*Poetics* XIII. 1453a 26) that Euripides is the most tragic of the poets, even if his execution, i.e., his technical skill, is inferior in every other respect. As for the second, "The greatest thing by far is to have command of metaphor," but metaphor alone cannot be imparted by another. It is

"the mark of genius, for to make good metaphors implies an eye for resemblances" (ibid., XX. 1459a 5). It is not implied that Euripides errs voluntarily, and it is argued that metaphor is not teachable and its making not demonstrable. "Creativity in art" does enter the Aristotelian theory in both instances, as well as in the argument concerning the artistic transformation of ugliness into what is aesthetically acceptable.

It is important to point out that whatever the implications may be concerning artistic creativity in Aristotle's own philosophy of art, these tend to disappear in the primarily critical and analytical interests of those who found in his philosophy the principal source for their own speculation. Jacques Maritain is the authority for the statement that the Schoolmen wrote no philosophies of art, and one may indicate the post-Aristotelian tendency to limit the scope of artistic creativity by following his interpretation of what Saint Thomas Aquinas argued in this field. We shall then turn to the tradition of artistic creativity which derives from Platonism and "the great analogy" of the artist to God.

Thomas defined the beautiful as *id quod visum placet* (*Summa theologica,* i.q.5, a.4 ad 1). "For beauty, three things are required, integrity or perfection, for whatsoever things are imperfect, by that very fact are ugly; and due proportion or consonance; and again effulgence; so bright colored objects are said to be beautiful" (ibid., i.q.39, a.8). Beauty is the "splendor of form shining on the proportioned parts of matter" (*Opus de pulchro et bono,* Thomas Aquinas or Albertus Magnus). God is beautiful and imparts beauty to all things (*De divinis Nominibus,* Ch. IV, lessons 5 and 6, Commentary of Thomas). The basis of the teaching, however, is that Art makes a work of art and, according to Maritain, the artist must content himself with good workmanship. In discussing abstract art, Maritain concludes that "to order contemporary art *to exist* as abstract art, discarding every condition determining its existence in the human subject" is to have it arrogate to itself the absolute self-sufficiency of God (*Art and Scholasticism,* p. 90).

In contrast, there *are* heirs to Greek rationalist theories of technique in which "creativity in art" is more than implicit, as one discovers in such a work as Leonardo da Vinci's *Trattato della pittura,* which has roots in classical medieval metaphysics and its elaboration in Renaissance theory and practice. But for the tradition of the genius, of artistic origination, of the ugly, and, finally for the effort to reconcile *technē* and inspiration in terms of the structure of the work of art in relation to imagination, we must turn to various interpretations of Platonism in conjunction with ideas derived from the theology of the Hebraic-Christian tradition.

One of the extraordinary contributions to the modern conception of "creativity in art" was made by the systematic philosopher, Plotinus (See Nesca Robb). It was, however, not a systematic philosopher but a great critic, Longinus (d. 273), who in *On the Sublime* influenced the eighteenth century as powerfully as did Plato in his *Ion* and *Symposium*, while another nonphilosopher, Philostratus (*Life of Apollonius*, VI, XIX) produced a brilliant and illuminating statement concerning imagination. Longinus abandons the theory that the work of art is simply a stimulus for a response and makes evident as well the fact that some aspect of creativity in the philosophy of art must be attributed to the man who experiences the product of art.

Briefly, Plotinus rethinks the conception of mimesis. Not only is the One, from which all emanates, creative (*Enneads* I.6.9), but the World Soul, a derivative principle, is free and autonomous (ibid., III.8.2). These explanatory principles are, however, the grounds for Plotinus' theory that the arts, which produce by imitation of natural objects, are not merely reproductive. The arts do go back to the Ideas but "much of their work is all their own." They are "holders of beauty and add where nature is lacking." In consequence, Phidias did not make Zeus from a model among things of sense but rather "by apprehending what form Zeus must take if he chose to become manifest to sight" (ibid., V.8.1).

Plotinus does retain, however, the notion of art as imitation. In contrast, his contemporary, Philostratus, asserts that it is not by imitation but by imagination that Phidias and Praxiteles work. According to Philostratus, there was no need for these men to mount to heaven and make a copy of the forms of the gods they reproduced in their art. It is imagination, "baffled by nothing," autonomous, and "marching undismayed to the goal it has itself laid down," to which Philostratus turns in order to explain what artists create. Similarly, Longinus in one of the great critical writings in the West, remarks that imagination, affected by the experience of great or sublime works, "oversteps the bounds of space." The man affected by sublimity, "the echo of a great soul," is made creative—he feels as though he himself had produced what stirs him.

To present a summary notion of the main line of systematic speculation concerning "creativity in art," it is of value to turn to the problem of ugliness. As we have observed, Aristotle's conception of the power of art includes the point that *technē* and mimesis may transform what is ugly into what is pleasing in art. What occurs to the conception of ugliness once it is involved in the complications of *theologia supernaturalis* and, more particularly, in "the great analogy" of the artist to God, is of value for an understanding

of the emergence of the theory of a genius and his originality in the seventeenth and eighteenth centuries.

Plotinus suggests (*Enneads* 3.2.4) that we should not complain that the colors in a painting are not everywhere beautiful. Contrast is necessary. This echoes the beginning of the Fourth Book of Plato's *Republic*. But Plotinus also argues that ugliness is nonexistent. Saint Augustine, similarly, maintains that ugliness is deficiency of the form of beauty (*Contra epistolam Manichaei . . . XX. XLIII, 49*). For Augustine, God is responsible neither for evil nor ugliness. His freedom to create is unconditioned. The contrast to Plato's conception of a cosmic artisan is radical. Plato's *Demiurgos* (see above) constructs the cosmos after the model of eternal Ideas which he does not create, and out of what Paul Shorey calls the "vaguely visioned preexistent chaos," which in later speculation is identified with matter (*Timaeus* 28B ff.). Augustine, in contrast, maintains that God creates the world out of nothing (Figure 3). He creates matter (*Confessions* XII, Ch. viii). The Ideas (*ratione*) exist ". . . in the very mind of the Creator" (*De diversis quaestionibus* LXXXIII).

The Platonic and the Hebraic-Christian conceptions of the making and creation of the world provide the ground for "the great analogy" of the artist to God. For the Platonists, God's freedom is conditioned by matter and Ideas. For the followers of Genesis, God's freedom is unconditioned. Moreover, in the demiurgic tradition man is a microcosm of the macrocosm and is a maker (Figure 4). In the Hebraic-Christian tradition, man is made in the Image of God (Genesis 1:27), and endowed with free will and the power to create. Harry Wolfson, discussing the contrasting views of Plato and Philo in an article, "Philo on Free Will" (pp. 138–40) makes the central point that both Plato and Philo believe that the laws of nature were implanted by God in the universe as an act of good will. For Plato, the laws once implanted could never be upset, whereas Philo believed that "God may change the order of natural events when it serves some good purpose." God is a miracle-worker for Philo and He endowed men with similar powers of freedom to upset the laws of nature.

If we return to Augustine's philosophy, we find that in it the artist's freedom is not equal to God's. Still, man is creative under the condition that the artist does not make the material with which he works (*Confessions* XI). It requires only that the analogy be drawn between the absolutely creative God and the wholly creative artist, and that this be conjoined with the ancient conception of the inspired genius in order for the full potentialities of productive imagination to be brought to bear on speculation concerning artistic freedom. The consequences for theories of criticism

FIGURE 3. *God the Creator*. Michelangelo's *God Creates the Sun and the Moon* (ca. 1510), in the ceiling of the Sistine Chapel, depicts a God whose creating is miraculous. In contrast to Figure 2, this is a portrayal of a *creating*—an exhibition of the power and freedom to originate without tools and without physical contact with what is created. ALINARI-ART REFERENCE BUREAU

FIGURE 4. In sharp contrast to de Chirico's poet, inspired by the Muse, is Blake's *Newton* (ca. 1795). The man portrayed by Blake is a maker or artisan, equipped with the drawing compass, one of the traditional tools which ensure accuracy and intelligibility in drawing a mathematical figure. He is Plato's microcosmic man. THE TATE GALLERY, LONDON

and taste become no less important for the conception of "creativity in art" than do those which concern the artist and the work of fine art.

What occurred to ancient speculation on "creativity in art," once it was conjoined to the theological doctrine of "the great analogy" and subsequently was established as autonomous in the philosophy of art and aesthetics, can only be sketched here. We need, however, merely quote from the writings of some of the many "heralds" of the modern conceptions of genius, of the critic, and of taste to suggest something of the modern temper. First, let us turn to George Puttenham's restatement in *The Arte of English Poesie* (p. 3) for poetry of Augustine's remarks concerning creativity in terms of man and God. Puttenham writes that the poet resembles God "who without any trauell to his diuene imagination, made all the world of nought, nor also by any paterne or mould as the Platonists with their Ideas do phantastically suppose." Second, Edward Young in *Conjectures on Original Composition* (p. 49), argues that the inspired genius is one who "differs from a good understanding as a magician from a good architect"; the former "raises his structure by means invisible," the latter "by the skilful use of common tools." Third, Joseph Addison in *The Spectator* (No. 421) holds that this "talent of imagination . . . has something in it like a creation . . . ," a view echoed by Coleridge's note that poetry is "a dim analogue to creation." Henry Home, in *Elements of Criticism* (p. 524), asserts that imagination is "a sort of creative power" which

587

can "fabricate ideas . . . of more surprising events, than in fact ever existed." Finally, as regards criticism, Daniel Webb reproduces Plato's image of the poet in *Laws* (719). Webb writes that ". . . the best critic, considered merely as such, is but a dependent, a sort of planet to his original; he does no more than receive and reflect that light of which the poet is a fountain . . ." (*Remarks . . .* , p. 63).

Addison and Home—as well as many others including Alexander Pope, William Duff, Alexander Gerard, Francis Hutcheson, and Shaftesbury—contributed to Kant's conception of aesthetics, but the reconciliation of the main elements which enter on the conception of "creativity in art" and which appear in the *Critique of Judgment* results from Kant's own systematization. Freedom is the core of creativity and taste in this most powerful of eighteenth-century works. The judgment of taste is the only free judgment and Kant contrasts it on this basis to judgments of morality and of pleasure. Taste is free. It is not, however, productive or creative. Productivity is the function of the genius who makes fine art. The genius employs imagination—no value is placed in Kant's aesthetic theory on imitation—and this productive faculty of cognition is "very powerful in creating another nature, as it were, out of the material that actual nature gives it" (Kant, Sec. 49). Kant calls the genius' originality "its first property." It is a natural talent; genius cannot be taught, nor can the genius teach another. Yet, in a brilliant interpretation of the function of the original genius, Kant argues that the work of fine or free art produced by a genius awakens another genius "to a feeling of his own originality" and "stirs him to exercise his art in freedom from the constraint of rules." Kant insists that productivity is not capricious. Genius cannot throw off the constraint of all rules. Imagination itself must be brought under the laws of the Understanding (the source of the categories, such as causality, relation, necessity, etc.).

Kant's interpretation of creativity encounters two primary obstacles. He follows David Hume in dismissing criticism and proceeds to argue the point on grounds that art is conceptual, mediated, and authoritative. The "taste" that is the core of Kant's aesthetic theory is immediate judgment and direct experience. The second obstacle is presented by the fact that some artistic representations "cannot be completely compassed and made intelligible by language." Clearly, fine art, the product of genius, is "ineffable" in some degree and, therefore, beyond intelligibility.

In part, one of the most radical results of Kantian speculation is the emergence over a century later of a theory of sheer creativity in art. This is the product of Benedetto Croce's speculation on language and art, most fully expressed in his *Aesthetic as Science of Expression* and elaborated in R. G. Collingwood's *The Principles of Art*. For Croce, criticism is nonaesthetic classification. It does not express the work of art, which is an image or intuition without external relations. Technique as the means of "externalizing" is likewise denied relevance to aesthetic: the work of art, the intuition, the image is completely expressed without such "externalization" as is involved in artistic "making." Moreover, the artist in creating, is inspired. He need have recourse neither to means nor ends. What the artist does is to express. The creativity of the artist is an act of complete imagination. Art is "free inspiration." What is imagined is an individual, neither to be compared nor contrasted to other individuals.

In Croce's theory of art as expression, the suggestion made by Kant that taste is free but not productive is denied. Genius and taste are identical in creativity (Croce, ibid., pp. 120ff., and J. E. Spingarn, p. 42). It is clearly on this issue that the theory of sheer creativity in Expressionism encounters a serious problem. If the man of taste may re-create the expression the genius creates, some externalized object of art must serve as the starting point for the experience which, for Croce, ends in the establishment for the man of taste of the same state of mind as that expressed by the artist.

Nietzsche offered the soundest beginning to a reconciliation of creativity in art and in criticism. "Valuing is creating . . ." (*Thus Spake Zarathustra* I. XI). There is criticism which is concerned solely with the accurate description of the facts of works of art—the symbols, media, forms, and the feelings they are presumably intended to evoke. But there is also criticism which is "creative," not only in the sense that some critics have produced works of criticism which are also works of fine art but have performed as well the highest function of criticism: to create and to apply the aesthetic values of the tragic, the comic, the sublime, the beautiful, and the ugly.

BIBLIOGRAPHY

Joseph Addison, *The Spectator* (London, 1867). Aristotle, *Aristotelis Opera*, ed. I. Bekker, 5 vols. (Berlin, 1831–70); idem, *The Works of Aristotle Translated into English*, ed. J. A. Smith and W. D. Ross, 12 vols. (Oxford, 1908–52). Saint Augustine, *Confessions*, trans. William Watts (New York, 1912); idem, *Opera Omnia*, ed. J. P. Migne, 12 vols. in 16 (Paris, 1841–77); *Patrologia Latina*, Vols. 32–46. E. de Bruyne, *Études d'estétique médiévale* (Bruges, 1946). John Burnet, *Greek Philosophy: Thales to Plato* (London, 1932), Part I. Rhys Carpenter, *Greek Sculpture* (Chicago, 1960). V. Gordon Childe, *What Happened in History* (New York, 1946). R. G. Collingwood, *The Principles of Art* (Oxford, 1938). B. Croce, *Aesthetic as Science of Expression*, trans. D. Ainslie (London, 1929); idem, *What is Living and What is Dead of the Philosophy of Hegel*, trans. D. Ainslie

(London, 1915). Armand Delatte, *Les Conceptions de l'ent-housiasme chez les philosophes pré-socratiques* (Paris, 1934). H. Diels and W. Kranz, *Die Fragmente der Vorsokratiker*, 2 vols. (Berlin, 1906–10). William Duff, *An Essay on Original Genius* (London, 1767). A. Dürer, *The Literary Remains of Albrecht Dürer*, trans. W. H. Conway (Cambridge, 1889). G. F. Else, *Aristotle's Poetics: The Argument* (Cambridge, Mass., 1957). A. Ernout and A. Meillet, *Dictionnaire étymologique de la langue latine* (Paris, 1932). Galen, *De Placitis Hippocratis et Platonis*, ed. I. Müller (Leipzig, 1874). Alexander Gerard, *An Essay on Genius* (London, 1774). Arthur Grant, *The Ethics of Aristotle* (London, 1885). R. Hackforth, *Plato's Examination of Pleasure* (Cambridge, 1945). J. Hambidge, *Dynamic Symmetry* (New Haven, 1920). Arnold Hauser, *The Social History of Art*, 4 vols. (New York, 1957). G. W. F. Hegel, *The Introduction to Hegel's Philosophy of Fine Art*, trans. B. Bosanquet (London, 1905); idem, *The Philosophy of Fine Art*, trans. F. P. B. Osmaston (London, 1920); idem, *Sämtliche Werke*, 26 vols. (Stuttgart, 1927–40). Henry Home (Lord Kames), *Elements of Criticism*, 5th ed. (Edinburgh, 1774). Francis Hutcheson, *An Inquiry into the Original of our Ideas of Beauty and Virtue*, 5th ed. (London, 1753). C. E. Jeanneret-Grist (Le Corbusier), *Modulor 2* (Boulogne, 1964). I. Kant, *Kant's Kritik of Judgement*, trans. J. H. Bernard (London, 1892). Leonardo da Vinci, *The Literary Works of Leonardo da Vinci*, ed. J. P. Richter, 2 vols. (London, 1883; 1939). Longinus, *On the Sublime*, trans. W. R. Roberts (Cambridge, 1899). E. MacKay, "Proportion Squares on Tomb Walls in the Theban Necropolis," *Journal of Egyptian Archaeology*, 4 (1917), 7ff. Jacques Maritain, *Art and Scholasticism*, trans. J. F. Scanlan (London and New York, 1930). Milton C. Nahm, *Selections from Early Greek Philosophy*, 4th ed. (New York, 1964); idem, *Aesthetic Experience and Its Presuppositions* (New York, 1946; 1968); idem, *The Artist as Creator* (Baltimore, 1956); idem, "The Theological Background of the Theory of the Artist as Creator," *Journal of the History of Ideas*, 8 (1947), 363–72. F. Nietzsche, *The Complete Works of Friedrich Nietzsche*, ed. Oscar Levy, 18 vols. (Edinburgh and London, 1909–1913; reprint New York, 1964). J. Overbeck, *Die antiken Schriftquellen . . . den Griechen* (Leipzig, 1868). E. Panofsky, *Meaning in the Visual Arts* (New York, 1955). Philostratus, *Life of Apollonius of Tyana* (London, 1912). Plato, *Opera Omnia*, ed. G. Stallbaum, 20 vols. (Gotha, 1857–85); idem, *The Dialogues of Plato*, trans. B. Jowett, 4 vols. (new impression, Oxford, 1952). Pliny the Elder, *The Elder Pliny's Chapters on the History of Art in the Historia Naturalis*, trans. K. Jex-Blake (London, 1896). Plotinus, *Ennéades*, ed. E. Bréhier, 7 vols. (Paris, 1924–38); idem, *Plotinus*, trans. Stephen Mackenna, 4 vols. (London, 1917–26). J. Pokorny, *Indogermanisches Etymologisches Wörterbuch* (Bern, 1948–). George Puttenham, *The Arte of English Poesie* (1589; Cambridge, 1936). Nesca A. Robb, *Neoplatonism of the Italian Renaissance* (London, 1935). F. Schiller, *On the Aesthetic Education of Man*, trans. R. Snell (New Haven, 1954). A. Schopenhauer, *The World as Will and Idea*, trans. R. B. Haldane and J. Kemp, 3 vols. (London, 1883–96). P.-M. Schuhl, *Platon et l'art de son temps* (Paris, 1933). Anthony, Earl of Shaftesbury, *Characteristics of Men,*

Manners, Opinions, Times . . . , ed. John M. Robertson (1711; London, 1900). Paul Shorey, *What Plato Said* (Chicago, 1933). J. E. Spingarn, *Creative Criticism* (New York, 1917). Leo Spitzer, *Classical and Christian Ideas of World Harmony* (Baltimore, 1963). Mary H. Swindler, *Ancient Painting* (New Haven, 1929). Saint Thomas Aquinas, *Opera Omnia*, 34 vols. (Paris, 1871–80). Alois Walde and J. B. Hofmann, *Lateinisches Etymologisches Wörterbuch* (Heidelberg, 1930–). Daniel Webb, *Remarks on the Beauties of Poetry* (London, 1762). C. R. Williams, *The Decoration of the Tomb of Per-nēb* (New York, 1932). H. A. Wolfson, "Philo on Free Will," *Harvard Theological Review*, 35, 2 (1942). H. C. Wyld, *The Universal Dictionary of the English Language* (London, n.d.). Xenophon, *Memorabilia of Socrates*, trans. E. C. Marchant (London, 1949). Edward Young, *Conjectures on Original Composition*, ed. M. W. Steinke (1759; New York, 1917).

MILTON C. NAHM

[See also Analogy; Art and Play; **Beauty; Creation in Religion; Expressionism;** Genius; God; Mimesis; Platonism; Pythagorean Harmony of the Universe.]

CRISIS IN HISTORY

DURING THE last fifty years the word "crisis" has achieved a popularity among writers and their audiences which stands in need of clarification. The proliferated use of the term can be attributed neither to vogue nor fad; it indicates, rather, an awareness of crisis as a salient feature of contemporary consciousness. However, the frequently indiscriminate use of the word has resulted in considerable confusion as to its exact meaning. Newspapers and magazines employ the expression to describe any change in human activities, whether impending or completed, thus permitting it to cover a multitude of topics from the production of moving pictures to political action. Historians have spoken of the *Crisis of the English Aristocracy*, or the *Crisis of the European Mind*, or the *Age of Crisis*, failing to give a precise meaning to the word, though we are occasionally warned that such terms should not glide inadvertently from the pen.

In view of the uncertainty pertaining to the word, we must without delay reach some understanding of the sense in which the expression is used. Even if there were a tacit consensus as to the significance of the word "crisis," such elucidation would seem necessary. The dictionary tells us that it is of Greek origin (κρίσις) and carries the meaning, to separate or to divide. Three different, though obviously related meanings are listed: "1. the turning point in the course of a disease, when it becomes clear whether the patient will recover or die, 2. a turning point in the course of anything; decisive or crucial time, stage or event, 3. a crucial situation; a situation whose outcome decides whether possible bad consequences will follow: as, an economic crisis" (Webster's *New World Dictionary*, 1966).

A precise history of the word does not exist. Of the three meanings given in Webster, the medical one was, we should judge, the oldest. It was used frequently in professional treatises and in literary descriptions to give an account of human illness. The wider purport of the word is of more recent usage and was rarely applied before the end of the eighteenth century. Thomas Paine wrote in 1776 about *The American Crisis*, saying, "These are the times that try men's souls."

Both his assertion and the date of his assertion are significant. The end of the ancien régime in the Western world was hastened by three great revolutions: the American, the French, and the Industrial Revolutions. Their impact on many observers was that of precipitous, even calamitous, change; in a word, crisis. Although premonitions of even greater transformations yet to come were voiced many times during the early nineteenth century, no general theory of crisis had been developed even by those thinkers most deeply concerned with the future of European civilization, such as Henri de Saint-Simon or Auguste Comte. It should be noted, however, that the term was introduced and acquired wider currency in the conceptual language of economic analysis.

Although earlier centuries had experienced frequent economic disturbances, it was only during the period following the great revolutions that economists undertook a preliminary analysis of what is today known as "the business cycle." It is in these descriptions and dissections of the business cycles that we first encounter a broader use of the term "crisis." Theorists did not at first distinguish between external influences, which might produce a disruption of the economic process, and internal causes produced by the dynamics of the business cycle proper. Gradually, however, it came to be recognized that the term "crisis" as used in economic theory should be applied in a restricted sense indicating the span of time required for the transformation of extraordinary phenomena from a pathological to a normal situation. Such a definition would imply that a crisis is only a transitory occurrence, and that after it has passed, the economy returns to a state of health. Indeed, this was the conviction of most economists of the nineteenth century, J. B. Say, for instance, or J. C. L. S. de Sismondi, Thomas Malthus, and J. S. Mill. The frequency of economic crises, occurring in 1815, 1825, 1836, and 1847, seemed to confirm this belief. Most economists were concerned with locating the cause or causes of economic crises, and they found them variously in overproduction, underconsumption, disequilibrium of production and consumption, oversaving, etc. Their findings might be summed up in the epigrammatic remark of Clement Juglar in *Les Crises commerciales et leur retour périodique en France, en Angleterre et aux États Unis* (Paris, 1862), that the only cause of depression was prosperity; in other words, crises were natural phases of the business cycle which ran its course in accordance with its own laws and dynamics.

The great exception to this interpretation was taken by Karl Marx, who saw in economic crises one of the characteristic features of the prevailing capitalistic system which he considered of enormous significance. Though Marx distinguished between general institutional conditions that allow for cyclical movement of the economy, and extempore conditions which actually spark the outbreak of crises, he accepted the notion of the periodical recurrence of crises as a matter of course. The idea was first expressed in the *Communist Manifesto* (1848): "In these crises a great part not only of the existing products, but also of the previously created productive forces, are periodically destroyed. Society suddenly finds itself put back into a state of momentary barbarism . . . industry and commerce seem to be destroyed. . . ." Furthermore, it was stated that crises tend to become more and more destructive in the course of capitalistic development, thus leading to the final breakdown of bourgeois society in a "super-crisis" from which the old society cannot recover and during which the working class will seize power through the dictatorship of the proletariat.

Marx restated his theory of crisis several times, especially in *Das Kapital* (1867–94), but he died before he could clarify some of the ambiguities of his doctrine. As Joseph Schumpeter has said in his *History of Economic Analysis* (p. 1131), it remains "the great unwritten chapter" of Marx's work. Consequently, his disciples disagree in their interpretations of this cardinal point in the Marxian theory. The crucial issue concerns the prognostication of the nature of the final crisis, whether it would be a violent overthrow of the existing order, or a gradual transformation. Lenin, in *Imperialism* (New York, 1939), assumed that a world war would bring on the end-crisis from which the world revolution would emerge with irrepressible force.

We need not delay over other details of the Marxian crisis theory which are still under debate. Its value lies not only in the explanation it offered for the cyclical movements of the capitalistic economy, but even more for allocating the latter in the framework of a universal historical process, making the final crisis the decisive step from man's pre-history to his history. Its limitations should likewise be transparent. It is heavily weighted toward the economic factors of history, thus precluding any objective evaluation of crises that stem from other sources. Finally, its eschatological determinism forces the crisis phenomenon into the pattern of a revolutionary development that allows of only one solution. Nevertheless, it seemed the most plausible explanation of the changes that took place in the world during the nineteenth century, and it was given added credence by the outbreak of the great depression of 1929. Since then, however, the resilience of the capitalistic economy in combination with the new Keynesian theories has greatly weakened the influence of Marx.

Several thinkers and statesmen of the nineteenth century felt, for different reasons, as did Marx, that the Western world was in a cataclysmic state, and they shared in his consciousness of crisis. Among them were Metternich, de Tocqueville, Kierkegaard, Nietzsche, and Henry Adams. Yet, strangely enough, none of these developed a theory of crisis. The Swiss historian, Jakob Burckhardt, would appear to be the only outstanding thinker who accepted the gambit. Burckhardt was as much concerned with the future of Europe ("Alt Europa," as he called it) as any one of the politicians, historians, and philosophers we have mentioned. However, he was a historian by profession, and thought it his duty to elucidate certain processes which had escaped the attention of other observers. He carried out this self-imposed obligation in a course of lectures at the University of Basel, first given in 1868. His notes were published posthumously under the title, *Reflections on World History* (*Weltgeschichtliche Betrachtungen*), and included a chapter on historical crises.

The earlier lectures dealt with the three great forces which make up the fabric of history: state, religion, and culture. But Burckhardt goes on to contend that these slow and lasting mutual influences and interactions are accompanied by certain phenomena which provoke an acceleration of the historical process. He called them historical crises. Bypassing the crises of primitive times, about which there is insufficient information, Burckhardt begins his review with migratory movements and invasions, such as the invasion of the Roman empire by the Germanic tribes, the rise of Islam, or the conquest of the Byzantine empire by the Ottoman Turks. Movements like these are important because they provoke a clash between old cultures and young ethnic forces. Invasions may bring on rejuvenation or barbarism, and, says Burckhardt, not every invasion rejuvenates; only those that carry a youthful race capable of assuming the culture of an older, already cultured race can do so. Clearly, as we might expect from the historian of the Italian Renaissance,

Burckhardt's criterion is culture. He goes on to say that there is a healthy barbarism just as there is a negative and destructive one. Thus in exhausted civilizations a crisis may bring out greatness, but it may be the euphoric vigor of the dying.

The next phenomenon Burckhardt considers as a contributing factor in the coming of crises is war. Inevitably his horizon here is the nineteenth century, a century that accepted war as necessary and even beneficial. Burckhardt admits to some of the standard arguments of his age, but his overall evaluation is skeptical and pessimistic. That wars may produce crises could not be denied, but, "Men are men, in peace as in war, and the wretchedness of earthly things lies equally upon them both."

In discussing wars as elements of crises, Burckhardt makes an important distinction between surface crises and genuine crises. For instance, he considered the wars of his own century as surface crises only. He even went so far as to describe the entire history of the Roman empire, from Augustus to Constantine, as untouched by genuine crises. Genuine crises are rare, he asserted; they should not be confused with civil or religious disputes which fill the air with deafening clamor and soon fade into oblivion. The test of the genuine crisis is that it leads to vital transformations, such as followed the invasion of the Roman empire by the Germanic tribes.

The distinction between surface and genuine crises is one of the significant contributions of Burckhardt's study, as is also his differentiation between genuine crises, abortive crises, and arrested crises. He asked the questions asked by every historian: Why do certain crises go unchecked?, Why do others fail to reach the turning point and fizzle out?, and finally, Are there some crises which could have been avoided, and if so, how could this have been accomplished? Burckhardt's originality lies not so much in the answers he offers (they were necessarily conditioned by the scholarship of his period), as in the queries he poses, for instance, his assertion that the Reformation could have been checked, and that the French Revolution might have been moderated. However that may be, what counts for our study of the problem of crisis is his observation of the dynamics of the true or genuine crisis. Genuine crises, he asserts, produce a sudden acceleration of the historical process in a terrifying manner. Developments which under "normal" circumstances might have extended over centuries, are completed in a matter of months or weeks.

At this point it might seem as though Burckhardt meant to identify crisis and revolution, but this would be an erroneous assumption. According to him, every revolution is a result of the interaction of one or several crises, though it does not follow that every crisis leads to or ends in revolution. Crisis is the general term, and it encompasses revolution. There can be little doubt, however, that many crises tend to unleash revolutionary upheavals. As Burckhardt sees it, one of the psychological motives for the eruption of crises is man's perennial and deep-rooted desire for change. Moreover, he seeks revenge for his sufferings, and since he "cannot reach the dead," his blame falls on the existing authorities. There are sufficient instances in the history of communism and fascism to support Burckhardt's observation. A blind coalition between all malcontents combines with a radiant vision of the future: the brilliant farce of hope.

One further comment of Burckhardt's deserves our attention. He maintains that the force and value of a crisis cannot be assessed at the initial stage; a crisis should not be appraised by its program but by the quantity of explosive material at hand. The test of a genuine crisis lies in its actual force under pressure. Once again, he introduces here a new concept to clarify his idea of the genuine crisis: "counterfeit crises" are easily paralyzed; only the real ones will prevail. In praise of crises, Burckhardt states that they are the result of real passions and that passion is the mother of great events.

Crises do not necessarily interfere with spiritual or cultural achievements. Whereas continuity and tradition may induce a favorable climate for culture, man may thereby be lured into a false security and his intellectual life become a matter of routine. Crises, argues Burckhardt, may be regarded as authentic signs of vitality. "All spiritual growth," he says, "takes place by leaps and bounds, both in the individual and in the community." Moreover, crises should be regarded as a proof of growth. Negatively speaking, they clear the ground of institutions that have long since withered away or of pseudo organizations which had no reason to exist except as obstacles to excellence. In proof of his point, Burckhardt says that *The City of God* would never have been written had it not been for the collapse of the Roman empire in Italy, and he adds that the *Divina Commedia* was composed while Dante was in exile. Crises teach men to distinguish between what is trivial and what is fundamental in human life, and he quotes Ernest Renan, who asserted that philosophy has never flourished more freely than it did during the great days of history. We may, however, be allowed to question whether the great days of history are perforce days of crisis. Crises may indeed fertilize human thought, but they may also annihilate it.

Viewed as a whole, what Burckhardt gives us is less an anatomy of crisis than a typology of crisis. As such

it has lasting value and may be used as a foundation for those crises which Burckhardt did not adequately analyze or which have been clarified by later events. Thus, the Reformation must be seen, regardless of Burckhardt's evaluation, as a chain reaction of crises. The personal crisis of Luther led to his confrontation with the authorities of the Old Church, and eventually his reforms engulfed the politics and the economy, first of Germany, and finally of nearly all Europe. Viewed from close range, a crisis often turns out to be composed of two or more interlocking crises in which the strongest element subdues the others or drives them underground, where they may live a subterranean existence and emerge again at a more propitious moment. Nor is it always an easy matter to determine the moment when a crisis has come to the end of its course. For instance, it would be fair to say that the Reformation had spent itself in Germany by 1648, whereas it was still vigorous in England and in the New World.

The Protestant Reformation did not overthrow the reign of the Papacy; it can be said, rather, that, since its triumph in the eleventh century, it has weathered all crises that threatened its existence, but that the marks left upon the institution are clearly visible.

It is worthy of note that Burckhardt in his treatment of historical crises never refers to the Renaissance, though he was without doubt the most outstanding historian of that period during the past century. Furthermore, his own treatment of the Renaissance seems to suggest that he did in truth see it as the end-crisis of the medieval world and as the nativity of modern man. We do not know what moved him to exclude the Renaissance from his analysis, but whatever the reason may be, he thereby came closer to the contemporary view of the Renaissance than might have been expected.

After a long debate about the origins, the character, and the impact of the Renaissance, most historians of today would agree that it should not be treated as a genuine crisis in the Burckhardtian sense. Certain historians have argued that the term "Renaissance" should be eliminated entirely (F. Heer); some emphasize the gradual transformation of the world from medieval times to the present (C. H. Haskins, J. Huizinga); still others point to the persistence of the Latin tradition which permeated literary expression throughout the Middle Ages, delivering itself to the future without benefit of crises (E. R. Curtius, 1954). These views support the belief that the Renaissance cannot be presented as a sudden break with the medieval perspective, but should rather be looked upon as a constant ground swell, reaching such proportions by 1500 that we are obliged to acknowledge a fundamental change in man's outlook upon himself and upon the world. Needless to say, violent upheavals occurred, and the struggle between the republican ideal prevailing in Florence and Venice, and the absolutism to which the rulers of Milan aspired created a favorable climate for the rise of the new humanism (H. Baron, 1955).

Nevertheless, these sporadic events do not permit us to classify the Renaissance under the heading of crisis. If we accept this stricture, we may be able to arrive at a more concise use of the word "crisis" than is commonly accepted: only a precipitous change over a short span of time affecting the very vitals of institutions, mores, modes of thought and feeling, power structures, and economic organizations, may rightly be termed a "crisis."

Economic and political crises are most easily detected, perhaps because they affect the lives of more people more directly and more brutally than intellectual or emotional changes. It does not follow, however, that they are always understood as such. More often than not, economic crises can only be properly understood in retrospect; take for instance the economic changes which took place after the Black Death in Europe, or the price revolution of the sixteenth century, which left observers completely bewildered. Political upheavals, on the other hand, seem less opaque and less difficult to group under the heading of crisis. But here, too, we should beware of hasty generalizations which stamp every change with the trademark of crisis. Political crises may be more readily recognizable because they have a greater degree of visibility; their protagonists attract the limelight in history and provoke a more complete documentation both of the actual events and of the motives behind them.

The most important political crises are to be found in the great revolutions; from them, as E. Rosenstock-Huessy (*Die europäischen . . .*, 1961) has said, the characteristics of the different European nations emerged. There was the Papal Revolution of the eleventh century, the English Revolution of the seventeenth century, the French Revolution, and the Russian Revolution. This writer would rank the revolt of the Netherlands and the American Revolution among the genuine historical crises which fulfill the criteria we have listed above. The revolution of 1848, however, must be rejected; it was, in the felicitous phrase of G. M. Trevelyan, "the turning point at which modern history failed to turn" (Trevelyan, 1946). It was an arrested crisis brought to fruition at a later date in those countries affected by it.

Many of the revolutions and pronunciamentos in Latin America and Africa are called revolutions,

whereas they are in reality only "counterfeit crises" which do not result in a vital transformation of the status quo, but merely a change of the guard with promises which remain unfulfilled after victory has been achieved.

The rise of the absolute monarchies in Europe, superseding feudalism without destroying it, furnished further examples of the genuine crisis. It is in the nature of crises to change complexion in accordance to the country in which they occur. Consequently the rise of absolutism presents a different picture in Spain, France, Germany, Denmark, Austria, and Russia. Yet in every instance the concentration of power in the hands of a dynasty supported by bureaucracy and military power seems essential. The crisis character of the situation lies in the political subjection of the nobility to the will of "The Prince" with the subsequent economic and social changes effected thereby. In many instances certain events marked the crisis, such as the *journée des dupes* ("the day of fools") by means of which Richelieu cemented his power in France. Such occurrences might be called sub-crises, since their full meaning can be grasped only within the framework of the greater genuine crisis.

Abortive political crises are frequent, though it is not always easy to distinguish them from arrested crises. The Russian revolution of 1905 might come under either heading. On the other hand, *La Fronde* is a classical example of the abortive crisis, as is also the Nat Turner rebellion of 1831. Another abortive crisis occurred in Prussia in 1819; it determined the policy of that country for half a century and prevented the liberalization of the state at a time when such a move could have had a decisive influence on the destiny of Germany.

Apprehension of the political crisis is not always followed by comprehension. There are some which resemble earthquakes; they are felt by everyone, but they defy explanation. The phenomenon of German national socialism is a case in point. In spite of the large body of literature on the subject, no convincing explanation of this greatest retrogression in the history of Western civilization has been provided thus far.

As we have said, wars must be counted among the most important causes of historical crises, and this is twice true. Wars may by themselves indicate a turning point in history, and we regard the great battles as engagements in which the survival of this or that power was at stake; we recall the Spanish Armada, or the battle of the White Mountain, or Trafalgar, the Battle of the Marne in 1914, or, more recently, Stalingrad. Yet wars spark crises in still another way. They release economic, social, and moral forces of unforeseen power and dimensions, which often make any return to the status quo impossible. Karl Marx called them the express trains of history. Not every war, however, is a genuine crisis; it may be a surface event or a counterfeit crisis.

Special attention should be given to the effect that technological changes produce on the course of history. Here too, one must beware of generic statements. Not all technological inventions have produced crises, and much depends on the cultural environment in which they occur. A comparison between Western and Chinese technology would be very enlightening in this respect. Yet, without question, technological discoveries or improvements must be counted among the prime agents of precipitous change. For instance, the invention of gunpowder, of the compass and the printing press, figure in every school book as instruments in the fracture of the medieval mold. During the last two centuries this process has continued with tremendous speed. The advances in communication, the new mass media, or the steady increase in firepower by the introduction of nuclear weaponry have become matters of almost daily acceptance. By themselves, these discoveries are rather symptoms of a long-lasting crisis than crises themselves, and in many instances we shall have to wait for their sequel. In other cases, the impact of technological artifacts on society becomes clear at the outset. The introduction of farm machinery deprived the southern American Negro of his job. This led to the migration of the Negro to the great industrial centers of the North, the Midwest, and the West, and the migration, in turn, contributed to the growth of the "ghettoes." Finally, the ghettoes provoked the urban crisis which began in the 1960's to shake the United States from one end to the other, causing in its very beginnings a profound transformation of the American society.

Medical discoveries are in the same category, and have had a far-reaching effect on the demographic structure of the world. Overpopulation is at least in part the result of medical advancements; on the other hand, it is not at all certain that medical remedies will be successful in checking the population explosion and the specter of a world famine which for some holds more frightening perspectives than a nuclear war. One is tempted to speak of a suspended crisis.

Since technology is basically applied science, our rapid survey must move into yet another field, namely the cultural sciences. As we have noted above, the permanent crisis in which we are forced to live has produced a crisis-awareness. This has opened our eyes to cultural changes and transitions which heretofore escaped notice. Huizinga, in one such attempt, described the forms of life, thought, and art in the four-

teenth and fifteenth centuries in *The Waning of the Middle Ages* (1948), and Paul Hazard's *La Crise de la conscience européenne* (1935) is even more in line with our reasoning.

In all probability, the First World War made the Europeans aware that all was not well with their civilization. A number of minds began to probe the depth of the sickness that had come over Europe; Rudolf Pannwitz's *Die Krisis der europäischen Kultur* (1921), was one of many efforts in this direction. It is impossible to say whether the general concern over the fate of the occident inspired Hazard's enterprise, though there are good reasons to think so. In the final chapter of his book, he speaks of the genius of Europe which is never content with itself, which at all times pursues contradictory aims, one of truth and one of happiness, whose labor is like the labor of Penelope, unravelling at night what she had woven during the day. Yet the immediate purpose of this remarkable work was a more limited one: Hazard wanted to establish the moment at which the European mind passed from its timid beginnings in the Renaissance to a determined revision of age-old prejudices and preconceived notions by applying the new standards of critical, rational thinking. Hazard proved that the "moment" spanned the years 1680 to 1715, that it provoked a violent clash of ideas, and that modern ideas emerged triumphant in the end, though some corners of Europe continued to harbor the old ones. Hazard demonstrated that over the thirty-five years to which his essay is limited there occurred a lasting and vital transformation of the European consciousness.

The word "crisis" seems to imply a break in continuity, but such breaks are often more apparent than real. The crisis of the late seventeenth century had been nourished by many subterranean waters until it finally broke ground and reached the light where historical decisions take place. Hazard is deeply conscious of this continuity, and presents the crisis with all its real and apparent contradictions.

The second cultural crisis—romanticism—of which we now must speak, would have been fortunate to find such a master analyst as Hazard; but although it caused an enormous amount of literature and discussion, no consensus emerged as to its origins, its essence, and its scope. The historian is obliged to grope through a labyrinthian profusion of scholarly effort to come to grips with the phenomenon.

Romanticism presents a crisis that in many ways parallels the one described by Hazard, but in other respects it gives evidence of fundamental differences. It too was European in scope, and was also accompanied by a deep-reaching change in perspective for almost all aspects of human life: poetry and philosophy, music and painting, political thought and social ideals. Yet any perusal of the literature devoted to its understanding shows the widest divergency. The movement was at first called the romantic school, later the romantic protest. It was alternately praised and vilified, its influence exaggerated or belittled. At the outset it seemed clear that its origins lay around 1790, and that its birth took place in Germany concurrently with the other great revolution across the Rhine. However, its beginnings have gradually been pushed back to 1750. Preludes have been discovered that are called preromanticism, and its origins have been traced back to such movements as German Pietism and the French and Spanish Quietism. To compound the difficulties, scholars have failed to realize that romanticism could not be comprehended simply by taking note of the ideals it proclaimed or the political parties it espoused. There was a conservative romanticism, just as there was a liberal and a democratic one, and one could even list a socialist one. But it is hopeless to arrive at any definition of romanticism by regarding the objects it emphasized or discovered, as for instance, the Middle Ages, or folk poetry, or the Catholic Church. Thus we come to the essential question: Was romanticism a matter of being or seeing or both, and in what order?

The distinction has been made of late between intrinsic romanticism and historical romanticism (Barzun), and this at least gives the basis for viewing the historical romanticism of the period between 1750 and 1850 as a change in mood and temper before it became a change in thought and ideas. Such shifts in mood had occurred in Europe in earlier times and had not always been recognized for what they were. In the case of the romantic movement an emotional subjectivism was brought to the fore, and it formed the core of the entire trend and constituted the criterion for the separation of the true romantic from the fellow traveller, of which there were many. It merits further study.

It is considerably more difficult to describe a third crisis in the cultural evolution of Europe. There is some reason to believe that it is still in process, and if this be true, the historian can do little more than note some of its aspects while its full impact is reserved for later writers. Keeping these reservations in mind, it may be said that around 1890 Europe entered into one of the most profound transformations of its entire history. There were those who interpreted the symptoms as indications of a final breakdown; such were the apocalyptic prophets Nikolai Danilewski (*Rossiia I Europa*, 1895) and Oswald Spengler (*Der Untergang des Abendlandes*, 1918). More restrained minds contented themselves with describing and analyzing the phenomena as they were revealed to a critical mind. H. S.

Hughes undertook such a study in his *Consciousness and Society* (1958), and the present writer offered a similar essay in *Prophets of Yesterday* (1961). There are differences of opinion as to the chronology of the crisis and about the comparative value of the contributions made by the various European nations, but these are minor matters. It is clear that the crisis was advanced by a "cluster of geniuses" somewhat like that which ushered in the crises of 1680 and 1790. To come upon a common denominator for the crisis is more difficult. Some observers have used the term, "the new irrationalism," and certainly this marks one, though not all, of the decisive changes that took place. The crisis of 1890 touches on the very vitals of the intellectual life of the West, its attitude toward science, the humanities, and religion, as well as toward poetry and the arts.

Future historians may well see the two World Wars with their social and economic concomitants as wave movements in the great transformation that is taking place at all corners of the earth. Few will doubt that the crisis which has engulfed our century is a genuine crisis in the Burckhardtian sense. One of its results appears to be the emergence of a consciousness which is learning or trying to learn a way of life that can accommodate the antitheses of crisis. We are beginning to wonder whether our destiny is to live under conditions of permanent crisis throughout any predictable future. The emergence of the New Physics, the experimental way in which modern art changes its methods and its goals every year, the questioning of historicism, all would seem to prove that old concepts are failing —i.e., that the idea of crisis is penetrating the most varied fields of human activities.

BIBLIOGRAPHY

The term "crisis" in its economic sense is discussed by H. Herkner in the article "Krisen," *Handwörterbuch der Staatswissenschaften*, 3rd ed. (Leipzig, 1910), VI, 253–76; and by J. Schumpeter, *History of Economic Analysis* (New York, 1955). Jakob Burckhardt's theory is presented in *Weltgeschichtliche Betrachtungen*, Vol. VII (Berlin and Leipzig, 1929); trans. J. Hastings Nichols as *Force and Freedom, Reflections on History* (Boston, 1964). See also: H. Baron, *The Crisis of the Early Italian Renaissance*, 2 vols. (Princeton, 1955); E. R. Curtius, *Europäische Literatur und Lateinisches Mittelalter*, 2nd ed. (Bern, 1954), trans. as *European Literature and the Latin Middle Ages* (Princeton, 1953); Paul Hazard, *La Crise de la conscience européene* (Paris, 1935), trans. as *The European Mind* (reprint New York); H. S. Hughes, *Consciousness and Society* (New York, 1958); J. Huizinga, *The Waning of the Middle Ages* (London, 1948; New York, 1954); Gerhard Masur, *Prophets of Yesterday* (New York, 1961); E. Rosenstock-Huessy, *Die europäischen Revolutionen und der Charakter der Nationen*, 3rd ed.

(Stuttgart, 1961); G. M. Trevelyan, *British History in the Nineteenth Century and After (1782–1919)* (London, 1946), p. 292.

GERHARD MASUR

[See also **Cycles;** Economic History; Historicism; **Marxism; Revolution;** Romanticism; War and Militarism.]

LITERARY CRITICISM

LITERARY CRITICISM may be defined as "discourse about literature," and in this wide sense, usual in English, it includes description, analysis, interpretation as well as the evaluation of specific works of literature and discussion of the principles, the theory, and the aesthetics of literature, or whatever we may call the discipline formerly discussed as poetics and rhetoric. Frequently, however, literary criticism is contrasted with a descriptive, interpretative, and historical account of literature and restricted to evaluative, "judicial" criticism. In other languages the more narrow conception is preferred, particularly in German where *Kritik* usually means only "the reviewing of literary novelties and the judging of literary and musical performances in the daily press" (*Reallexikon der deutschen Literaturgeschichte*, Bern [1959], 2, 63), though recently, probably under English and American influence, the wider use has again become common.

Criticism in English emerged early in the seventeenth century, apparently based on the analogy of such sixteenth-century terms as Platonism, Stoicism, skepticism, etc., devised to avoid the homonym which arose from the impossibility of distinguishing in English between "critic," the person, and "critique," the activity. Dryden, in the Preface to the *State of Innocence* (1677), said that by "criticism, as it was first instituted by Aristotle, was meant a standard of judging well," and in the same year in a letter (*Letters*, ed. C. E. Ward [1942]) he spoke of Thomas Rymer's *Tragedies of the Last Age* as "the best piece of criticism in the English language." Two years later, his play, *Troilus and Cressida*, was introduced by a preface on "The Grounds of Criticism in Tragedy." Pope's *Essay on Criticism* (1711) established the term for good, though for a time the term "critic," "critick," or "critique" was used in the eighteenth century where we would say "criticism."

Long forms, analogous to the English "criticism" are rare in other languages. *Criticismo* occurs in Spanish, in Baltasar Gracián's *El Heroe* (1637), and sporadically in eighteenth-century Italian, but disappeared as there was no problem of homonymy. In Germany, however,

Kritizismus was used by Schelling, Friedrich Schlegel, Jacobi, and Hegel for the philosophy of Kant. This nonliterary use penetrated then into French, Italian, and Spanish. In these languages *criticisme* or *criticismo* means today only Kantianism.

The term ultimately derives from the Greek *krínō*, "to judge," and *krités*, "a judge" or "juryman." *Kritikós*, as "judge of literature" was used as early as the fourth century B.C. Philitas, who came to Alexandria in 305 B.C. from the island Kos as the tutor of the future king Ptolemy II, was called "a poet and also a critic." Crates was at the head of a school of "critics" at Pergamon which seemed to have argued for a distinction from the school of "grammarians" headed by Aristarchos in Alexandria. The word "critic" is used in contradistinction from "grammarian" in the pseudo-Platonic *Axiochos* (366E). Galen, in the second century A.D. wrote a lost treatise on the question of whether one could be a *kritikós* and a *grammatikós* at the same time. But the distinction seems to have become blurred in antiquity. The term is rare in classical Latin: Hieron in the *Epistolae* speaks of Longinus as *criticus*. *Criticus* was a higher term than *grammaticus* but *criticus* was also concerned with the interpretation of texts and words. What today would be called literary criticism was, in antiquity, discussed by philosophers like Aristotle and by rhetoricians like Quintilian.

In the Middle Ages the word seems to occur only as a term in medicine: in the sense of "critical" illness. In the Renaissance the word was revived in its ancient meaning. Angelo Poliziano, in 1492 exalted the critic and grammarian against the schoolman. Grammarian, critic, philologist became almost interchangeable terms for the men engaged in the great revival of classical learning. With Erasmus "the art of criticism," (*ars critica*) was expanded to include the Bible. On the whole, however, among the humanists, the term "critic" and "criticism" was limited to the editing and correcting of ancient texts. For example, Karl Schoppe (1576–1649) defined the "only aim and task of critics" as "taking pains to improve the works of writers in either Greek or Latin." Joseph Justus, the younger Scaliger (1540–1605), made criticism even a subdivision of grammar, confined to distinguishing the spurious lines of ancient poets from the genuine, to correcting corrupt readings, in short to what today is called "textual criticism."

The elder Julius Caesar Scaliger (1484–1558) was the most influential propounder of a wider conception. In his posthumous *Poetics* (1561) the entire sixth book, entitled *criticus*, is devoted to a survey and comparison of the Greek and Roman Poets with the emphasis on weighing and ranking. The penetration of the term into the vernacular was, however, very slow. Modern books entitled "Literary Criticism in the Renaissance" obscure the fact that these questions were discussed in the sixteenth century only as rhetoric or poetics. In Italy the term *critica* seems to have occurred first as late as 1595 in the *Proginnasmi Poetici* of Benedetto Fioretti (published under the pseudonym Udeno Nisiely), while it was in France that the term caught on and spread rapidly early in the seventeenth century probably under the influence of Scaliger and his Dutch disciples, Heinsius and Vossius. Chapelain called Scaliger *le grand critique* in 1623. In 1687 La Bruyère could complain that the "critics and censurers" appear now in swarms and form factions which retard the progress of the arts (*Les Caractères*).

In France, in the seventeenth century, criticism emancipated itself from its subordination to grammar and rhetoric and absorbed or replaced "poetics," at least in part. This movement is connected with the growth and spread of the critical spirit in general, in the sense of increased skepticism, distrust of authority and rules, and later with the appeal to taste, sentiment, feeling, *je ne sais quoi*. The few writers who expressly reflected on the concept of criticism or the role of the critic, Father Bouhours in France and Alexander Pope in England, defended their ideal against pedants, censurers, and mere verbal quibblers, and described and exalted the true critic as a man of taste, a wit, a *bel esprit*. Pope, in particular, deplored the false divorce between wit and judgment and advocated a respect for antiquity and even of the rules while admitting "a grace beyond the reach of art" and praising the invention and imagination of Homer and Shakespeare.

During the eighteenth century, a term which had become confined to the verbal criticism of classical writers was slowly widened to include the whole problem of understanding and judging and even the theory of knowledge and knowing. Lord Kames, a Scottish judge, attempted in his *Elements of Criticism* (1762) to give criticism an elaborate groundwork in association psychology, and proudly claimed that he was founding a new science: "To reduce the science of criticism to any regular form, has never once been attempted." In practice, he defends neo-classical taste based on universal human nature which, he recognizes, is, however, upheld only by a small group of people who enjoy leisure, live in an enlightened age, and escape corruption. Dr. Johnson's ideal is also to "establish principles of judgment," but he does not rely on any psychology theoretically formulated and always finds "an appeal open from criticism to nature" (Preface to *Shakespeare*, 1765). He is both a classicist, who believes in "fundamental laws of criticism dictated by reason and antiquity" (*Rambler* No. 156), and an empiricist, who admits that many rules are temporal

and local, defensible only as custom or fashion. He is already touched by the new revolutionary force in the history of criticism: the historical spirit.

It was in Germany that the most radical consequences of the historical approach affected criticism. Johann Gottfried Herder was the first critic who completely broke with the ideal of the (fundamentally) Aristotelian tradition aiming at a rational theory of literature and permanent standards of judgment. He conceived of criticism as a process of empathy, of identification, of something intuitive and even subrational. He constantly rejected theories, systems, faultfinding. We find Herder quoting Leibniz with approval to the effect that "he likes most things he reads" (*Sämtliche Werke*, ed. B. Suphan, XVII, 338). The correct method "in order to understand and interpret a piece of literature is to put oneself in the spirit of the piece itself" (ibid., VI, 34). It is "the natural method, which leaves each flower in its place, and contemplates it there just as it is, according to time and kind, from the root to the crown. The most humble genius hates ranking and comparison. Lichen, moss, fern, and the richest scented flower: each blooms in its place in God's order" (ibid., XVIII, 138). Each work of art is seen as part and parcel of its milieu, fulfilling its function and thus needs no criticism. Literary study became a kind of botany.

Goethe, Herder's pupil, has the same gospel of tolerance. Criticism should be only criticism of beauties. He distinguishes between destructive and productive criticism. The first is easy as it is simply the application of a yardstick. Productive criticism is much harder. "It asks: What did the author set out to do? Was his plan reasonable and sensible, and how far did he succeed in carrying it out?" (Review of Manzoni's *Conte di Carmagnola*, *Werke*, Jubiläums-Ausgabe, 37, 180). Goethe hopes that such criticism may be of assistance to an author and admits that his own criticism describes largely the influence which books have had on himself. "At bottom this is the way all readers criticize" (ibid., 37, 280). Herder and Goethe with all their historical relativism and subjectivism have not yet broken their ties to the classical tradition: but by the nineteenth century their theories had led to complete critical relativism or to the subjective criticism, memorably phrased by Anatole France's definition of criticism as "the adventures of a soul among masterpieces."

Actually, about the same time, Immanuel Kant, in his *Critique of Judgment* (1790) had offered a solution to the central problem of criticism which recognized the subjectivity of aesthetic judgment but still allowed for its universality. Kant rejects any view of criticism by *a priori* principles, by laws or rules. Taste is subjective, yet aesthetic judgments differ from a taste, say, for olives or oysters by claiming universality. Aesthetic judgment, while subjective, appeals to a general judgment, to a common sense of mankind, to an ideal totality of judges. It is thus neither relative nor absolute, neither completely individual, which would mean anarchy and the end of criticism, nor absolute in the sense of an application of eternal norms. While Kant stresses the role of personal feeling he recognizes something like an aesthetic duty. We should respond to great art if we are to be fully human. It is a contemplative, problematical imperative—not a categorical imperative as in ethics. Kant's view of criticism rejects principles and doctrines. Criticism is always by examples, from the concrete. Criticism is historical, in the sense of being individual and thus different from generalizing science; it is comparative, in the sense of a confrontation with other men, and hence is introspection, self-criticism, an examination of one's feelings.

Kant had, however, little interest in concrete works of art. Still, the speculative movement inaugurated by him gave rise to a flowering of aesthetics in the philosophies of Schelling and Hegel and to the elaborate literary theories of Schiller, Wilhelm von Humboldt, and many others. The two brothers Schlegel (closely connected with Fichte and Schelling) formulated the most complex and coherent theory of criticism at that time. The younger, Friedrich (1772–1829), was the more original mind but August Wilhelm, the elder, (1767–1845) found the most influential formulas for the romantic-classical contrast, for the organic-mechanical dichotomy which through Coleridge became part of the history of English criticism. Friedrich Schlegel decisively rejected Herder's universal tolerance which would lead to an abdication of criticism. He knew that the critical view could not be superseded by the historical as books are not "original creatures." Criticism must "ascertain the value and non-value of poetic works of art" (*Prosaische Jugendschriften*, ed. Minor, 2, 11). It can be done by close attention to the text which must begin with an intuition of the whole. This whole is not only the individual work of art but the whole of art history. Every artist illuminates every other artist: together they form an order. The critic must "reconstruct, perceive, and characterize the subtle peculiarities of a whole" (*Lessings Geist*, 1, 40–41). This "characterization" is the business of criticism. But Schlegel also recognizes another function of criticism; polemics, incitory, anticipatory criticism, a criticism which would be not merely explanatory and conservative but productive, by guidance and instigation stimulating an emergent literature.

August Wilhelm, while in general agreement with his brother, emphasizes in his Berlin Lectures the role of history; "Even though a work of art ought to be enclosed within itself, we must consider it as belonging to a series" (Berlin Lectures, 3, 9). Criticism, in relation to theory and history, is the mediating middle link. The critic is subjective but can strive for objectivity by a knowledge of history, by reference to theory as "critical reflection is a constant experimentation to discover theoretical statements" (ibid., 1, 27). Disagreement does not necessarily result in general skepticism. "Different people may very well have their eyes on the same center, but since each of them starts from a different point of the circumference, they inscribe also different radii" (ibid., 1, 28). A "perspectivism" mediating between historicism and absolutism is thus envisaged.

This mediating function of criticism was exalted by Adam Müller (1779–1829) who arrived at a completely historistic point of view. In his Lectures of 1806 (*Vorlesungen über Wissenschaft und Literatur*) he conceives of the totality of literature as developing like an organism. Friedrich Schlegel is criticized for not seeing the complete continuity of literary tradition and for exalting one kind of art: romantic art. This reconciling, mediating criticism does not, however, imply a complete abdication of judgment; every work of art is to be judged by its place and weight in the whole of literature. Each work contributes to the whole and in so doing modifies the whole. Its goal is to achieve the reconciliation of judgment and history.

Compared to the attention given to the theory of criticism in Germany, England and France contributed little at that time. S. T. Coleridge, who was the one Englishman thoroughly familiar with German critical thought, said surprisingly little about his concept of criticism. Coleridge did formulate an ambitious program of aiming "at fixed canons of criticism, previously established and deduced from the nature of man," and, in retrospect, said of himself, referring to the 1790's, that "according to the faculty or source, from which the pleasure given by any poem or passage was derived, I estimated the merit of such a poem or passage" (*Biographia Literaria*, ed. Shawcross, I, 14, 44). The theory of criticism implied is a psychological one: a ranking of the faculties with the imagination higher than fancy, reason higher than the senses. But Coleridge never developed this as a theory of criticism.

Among the English critics of the time, William Hazlitt made a conscious attempt to formulate what would later be called "impressionistic criticism." "I say what I think: I think what I feel. I cannot help receiving certain impressions from things; and I have sufficient courage to declare (somewhat abruptly) what they are" (*Complete Works*, ed. Howe, V, 175). The task of criticism is the communication of feelings. He uses the new methods; elaborate evocative metaphors, per-

sonal reminiscences, a feeling of intimacy like an enthusiastic guide in a gallery or a host in a library.
Hazlitt faces a new middle-class audience; he wants
to win it over, to cajole it to the enjoyment of literature. The critic becomes neither a judge nor a theorist,
but a middleman between author and public.

Thomas Carlyle, in his early essays, adopted the idea
of sympathetic criticism drawing apparently on Herder
and the Schlegels. The critic's aim, he says, is "transposition into the author's point of vision"; he must
work his way into the poet's "manner of thought, till
he sees the world with his eyes, feels as he felt and
judges as he judged" (*Essays*, Centenary ed., I, 39). In
the act of enjoying a work of art "we partially and
for the time become the very Painter and the very
Singer" (ibid., III, 46). The older view survives, however, in Macaulay when he called the critic "a king
at arms versed in the laws of literary precedence, who
must marshall his author to the exact seat to which
he is entitled" (*Critical and Historical Essays*, Boston
[1900], VI, 50). Judging and ranking of authors was
Macaulay's passion.

Criticism in the United States echoes these views.
Edgar Allan Poe exalted the function of criticism and
hesitated whether to consider criticism a science or
an art. Criticism requires art in the sense that each
essay should be a work of art, but it is also a science
based on principles. R. W. Emerson like Carlyle knows
only a criticism of empathy and identification. He calls
the old saw that "every scripture is to be interpreted
by the same spirit which gave it forth," "the fundamental law of criticism" and he boldly asserts that "the
reader of Shakespeare is also a Shakespeare" (*Complete
Works*, Centenary ed., I, 35). Surprisingly, among
Americans Margaret Fuller reflected most concretely
on the nature and office of criticism. She distinguishes
three kinds of critics: "subjective" critics who indulge
in personal caprice, "apprehensive" critics who can
enter fully into a foreign existence, and finally "comprehensive" critics who also must enter into the nature
of another being but must, besides, judge the work by
its own law. The critic "must examine, compare, sift
and winnow." Saying that "I cannot pass on till I know
what I feel and why" (*Art, Literature and the Drama*,
Boston [1841], pp. 23–24) is not a bad expression of
a critic's conscience.

In France, prescriptive criticism survived longer
than elsewhere. In Julien-Louis Geoffroy (1743–1814)
it found a theorist who thought of it as serving the
government, "good taste, sound morals and the eternal
foundations of the social order" (*Journal des débats*.
Feb. 16, 1805). He would call in the police to punish
bad authors. Désiré Nisard attempted to establish criticism as an "exact science," by which he meant a setting

up of ideal norms—of the universal human spirit, of
the genius of France, and of the perfection of the
French language—which would allow him to judge
every work of French literature correctly. He expressly
condemned criticism of "each according to his taste"
and criticism which would reduce literature to a mirror
of history and social change (*Histoire de la littérature
française*, IV, 540). François-René de Chateaubriand, in
a famous essay on Dussault (1819) advised us "to abandon the petty and easy criticism of faults in favor of
the great and difficult criticism of beauties." With
Victor Hugo, particularly in his late book on *Shakespeare* (1864), the repudiation of judicial criticism is
complete. The complete negation of criticism as judgment is proclaimed complacently. "Genius is an entity
like nature and must, like her, be accepted purely and
simply. We must take or leave a mountain." Hugo
admires everything *comme une bête*.

Charles Augustin Sainte-Beuve, however, was the
French critic of the nineteenth century who most
consistently reflected on the concept of criticism. His
attitude shifted in the course of a long career from
an early, more subjective concept as personal expression to greater objectivity, detachment, and tolerance,
and at the same time from a rather uncritical, sympathetic acceptance of the role of "secretary of the public" (*Causeries du lundi*, I, 373) to an increasing emphasis on the role of judgment, to a definition of taste
and tradition. These two trends are often at cross-
purposes in Sainte-Beuve. His early romantic historicism goes with tolerance and relativism, but it is often
contradicted by his partisanship in the literary battles
of the time. He became, for a time, the "herald" of
Victor Hugo. The objectivity and the detachment of
Sainte-Beuve's later stage appeals rather to natural
science as the model. The late Sainte-Beuve aimed at
a theory of psychological types of men (see the essay
on Chateaubriand, 1862). Still, his return to classical
taste brought about a reassertion of the judicial function of criticism, a tone of authority and even of dogmatic certainty. "The true critic precedes the public,
directs and guides it" (*Chateaubriand et son groupe
littéraire* [1949], II, 95). The critic "maintains tradition
and preserves taste" (*Causeries*, XV, 356).

In the later nineteenth century, the divergence between concepts of criticism aiming at scientific objectivity and views that considered criticism an act of
personal appreciation became more accentuated. The
concept of criticism as judicial, as an upholder of the
tradition, receded into the background though in
England it found an influential spokesman in Matthew
Arnold. Arnold was an important apologist for criticism, for "disinterestedness," for a free circulation in
England of ideas from Europe. At times he believes

in a purely descriptive criticism, informative, liberating, preparatory to creation. But later Arnold stressed the judicial function of criticism, and defended the "real estimate" against the "historical" and "personal" estimate, both of which seemed to him fallacious. By personal estimate he meant an estimate in terms of "our personal affinities, likings and circumstances," which made it inevitably subjective while the historical estimate distorted values, overestimated works useful in a certain stage of the development of literature. The "real estimate" is the only critical one—it appeals to permanent standards, to "the best that has been thought and said in the world." (See "The Study of Poetry" in *Essays in Criticism*, 2nd Series [1888], pp. 6–7, 11.) Arnold's own criticism, appealing to impressionistic "touchstones" or to a historical concept of the "adequacy" of a literature to its time, may be riddled by contradictions but consistently upholds judgment as an ideal of criticism.

In Italy, the greatest critic and historian of the nineteenth century, Francesco De Sanctis, came to similar conclusions independently. He distinguishes three stages in the critical act: first an act of submission, a surrender to first impressions, then recreation and finally judgment. "Criticism cannot take the place of taste, and taste is the genius of the critic. Just as one says that poets are born, so also are critics born" (*Saggi critici*, ed. Russo, I, 307). The critic should "remake what the poet has done in his own manner and by other means" (ibid., II, 90), by translating into consciousness what is created in a work of art. Still, the proper critical act is deciding the intrinsic value of work and "not what it has in common with the times, or with its predecessors but what it has that is peculiar and untransferable" (*Saggio critico sul Petrarca* [1869], ed. Bonora, Bari [1954], p. 10). In Germany, Wilhelm Dilthey, who wrote a psychological poetics (*Die Einbildungskraft des Dichters, Bausteine für eine Poetik*, 1887) which aimed at scientific rigor, came late in his life to recognize the need for criticism. "Criticism," he argued, "is inevitably linked with the hermeneutic process. There is no understanding without a feeling of value, but only by comparison can the value be ascertained to be objective and universal" (*Gesammelte Schriften* V, 536).

Hippolyte Taine, with his theory of *la race, le milieu, le moment* ("race, environment, moment") was the outstanding figure who tried to model criticism on the pattern of deterministic science. Taine upholds the view that criticism is "analogous to botany, which studies the orange, the laurel, the pine, and the birch, with equal interest" (*Philosophie de l'art* [1865], p. 22). The historicism of this conception seems (as in Herder)

to lead to universal tolerance and hence to complete relativism. But actually Taine does not consider all works of art to be of equal value. He tries to overcome relativism by the criterion of representativeness. He asks whether a work represents a transient fashion, or a historical moment, or the spirit of a nation, or humanity in general, and ranks works according to such a scale. The work of art is always considered a sign or symbol of humanity, nation, or age. It is a mistake to consider Taine as a sociologist who thinks of works of art as social documents. They are rather in his scheme the essence or summary of history, in terms which are ultimately Hegelian.

Among Taine's followers Émile Hennequin tried in *La Critique scientifique* (1888) to give a different scientific basis to criticism than Taine. He criticized Taine's triad of *milieu-moment-race* and preferred a psychology of the author and the audience. The emphasis on the audience as a mental analogue of the work was particularly new though it remained only a suggestive proposal. Still, Hennequin offered a way out from the purely causal thinking into a "synthetic" literary criticism which would include an aesthetic, a psychology, and a sociology in a discipline he called "anthropology."

Ferdinand Brunetière, who followed Taine in his adherence to a scientific ideal (in his case, biological evolution), reflected more systematically on the theory of criticism. He believed that criticism must focus on the work of literature itself and must distinguish the study of literature from biography, psychology, sociology, and other disciplines. He defended the final aim of criticism as that of judging and even ranking, and distinguished this act of judgment from any purely personal preference, impression, or enjoyment. Brunetière saw clearly that the work of literature itself and not the soul of the author or the social background is the object of criticism. "If criticism," he argued, "forgets that a poem is a poem, when it claims to refrain from judgment, it is no longer criticism but history and psychology" (*Études critiques*, IX, 50). Taine's and Hennequin's attempt to make criticism scientific in the sense of abstaining from praise or blame is inevitably a failure. Brunetière also argued passionately against the impressionist creed which at that time was wittily stated by Anatole France when he declared the ideal of objective criticism an illusion. "The truth is that one never gets outside oneself. What would we not give to see for a minute, the sky and the earth with the faceted eye of a fly or to understand nature with the crude, simple brain of an orangutan? . . . The critic should say if he is candid: gentlemen, I am going to speak about myself in connection with Shakespeare,

Racine, Pascal, or Goethe" (*La Vie littéraire*, I, 5–6). Brunetière answers that we are neither flies nor orangutans but men, and that the whole of life consists in a going out of oneself. "Otherwise there would be no society, no language, no literature, no art" (*Essais sur la littérature contemporaine* [1892], pp. 7–9). He proves that even the most extreme impressionists make judgments all the time and that they themselves cannot obscure the fact that "there are differences in rank between Racine and Campistron, or that one cannot put Victor Hugo below Madame Debordes-Valmore, or Balzac below Charles Bernard" (ibid.). Brunetière sees in criticism "a common effort" (*Études critiques*, IV, 28) and finds a wide agreement about the classics. Mere enjoyment is not a criterion of value. We laugh more at a farce than at Molière's *Misanthrope*. Still "we can raise ourselves above our tastes" (*L'Évolution de la poésie lyrique* [1894], I, 25). Sympathy and judgment, sensibility and reason in this case are dangerously divorced.

An English writer equally preoccupied with the scientific ideal, John Addington Symonds, also saw, like Brunetière, that the evolutionary scheme with its fatalistic assumption of a necessary rise and decline raises the problem of criticism in its most acute form. The analogy with the life of a plant or animal must lead to universal tolerance, to an abdication of criticism. It is impossible to criticize youth for being young, or old age for being close to death. But he sees the need for overcoming such relativism. The critic cannot be confined by history. "He must divert his mind from what is transient and ephemeral, must fasten upon abiding relations, *'bleibende Verhältnisse'*" (*Renaissance in Italy: the Catholic Reaction* [1886], II, 396). There are three types of critics: the judge, the showman, and the natural historian of art and literature. The judge is the classical critic who judges by principles and the decisions of his predecessors. The showman is the romantic critic who exhibits his own sensibilities. The scientific analyst is the morphological historian who sees literature in terms of evolution. But even this scientific analyst does not satisfy Symonds, who demands that the true critic must combine all three types. "He cannot abnegate the right to judge" but ". . . it is his supreme duty to train his faculty of judgment and to temper his subjectivity by the study of things in their historical connections" (*Essays, Speculative and Suggestive* [1890], I, 98–99). Ultimately Symonds admits that criticism is not a science but can be exercised in a scientific spirit.

In many variations the importance of sympathy, even of identification, is stressed by many writers. Charles Baudelaire formulates this ideal well: "You must enter into the skin of the created being, become deeply imbued with the feelings which he expressed, and feel them so thoroughly, that it seems to you as if it were your own work" (*L'Art romantique*, ed. Conard, p. 198). But often Baudelaire thought of criticism as self-expression and self-criticism. It should "be partial, passionate, and political, that is to say, written from an exclusive point of view, but a point of view that opens up the widest horizon" (*Curiosités esthétiques*, ed. Conard, p. 87).

For Jules Lemaître criticism is nothing but "the art of enjoying books and of enriching and refining one's impression of them." The divorce between admiration and liking accepted by Brunetière is not only deplorable but false. "One calls good what one loves." The critic is not a judge but only a reader. He needs "sympathetic imagination" (*Les Contemporains*, III, 342; II, 85; I, 164). The same was said, in the United States, by Henry James who greatly admired Sainte-Beuve. As early as 1868 he wrote that "the critic is simply a reader like all the others—a reader who prints his impressions" (in *The Nation*, I, 330–31), and repeated that "Nothing will ever take the place of the good old fashion of 'liking' a work of art or not liking it" (*Partial Portraits* [1888], pp. 395–96). Criticism is "the only gate of appreciation" (*Future of the Novel*, p. 97). The true method of criticism is always that of sympathy, of identification with the work of art.

The English aesthetic movement presents arguments along the same lines. But Walter Pater is wrongly called a mere impressionist. He stresses the duty of the critic to grasp the individuality, the uniqueness of a work of art. He considers the question, does this book give one pleasure, as no more than a first step in criticism. The critic must go beyond it: penetrate "through the given literary or artistic product, into the mental and inner constitution of the producer, shaping his work" (*Guardian* [1901], p. 29). He must, moreover, know how to communicate this insight by finding what Pater calls the "formula," the "active principle" or the "motive" of a work. Oscar Wilde, among English writers, is the one who went furthest in advocating subjectivity. In the "Critic as Artist" (1893) he argues for criticism as a creative art. Criticism is a form of autobiography. The work of art is only a starting point for a new creation, which need not bear any obvious relation to the thing it criticizes. Objectivity is an absurd ideal, "Only an auctioneer can equally and impartially admire all schools of Art." Wilde sees the dialectics of subjectivity and objectivity; "It is only by intensifying his own personality that the critic can interpret the personality and work of others." Wilde's position thus fluctuates between an advocacy of criticism as empathy and historical imagination, as an exercise in cosmopolitanism, and a paradoxical plea for sheer wilfulness and caprice. His concept of criticism represents the other extreme at which nineteenth-century thinking had arrived.

The twentieth century brought a new sharpening of the conflicts between the main concepts of criticism: judicial, scientific, historical, impressionist, and "creative," and added some new motives and refinements. In England, an empiricist and antitheoretical point of view prevailed even in such a critic as T. S. Eliot. Eliot is suspicious of aesthetics and thinks of criticism for the most part as that of a poet "always trying to defend the kind of poetry he is writing" (*The Music of Poetry*, 1942). In distinguishing three types of criticism: the so-called "creative criticism," really "etiolated creation" for which Pater serves as a horrifying example, "historical" and moralistic criticism represented by Sainte-Beuve, and "criticism proper" or the criticism of the poet, Eliot forgets or ignores theory completely. The only exception Eliot allows is Aristotle, whose influence as a critic seems quite inexplicable in Eliot's scheme (*Chapbook*, No. 2, 1920). Criticism is left with little to do. Occasionally Eliot described the function of criticism as "the elucidation of works of art and the correction of taste" or even as "the common pursuit of true judgment" (*Selected Essays*, pp. 24–25). But he rejects both interpretative and judicial criticism in any case. "Interpretation" seems to him only a necessary evil productive of fictions, and judgment is expressly forbidden to the critic. "The critic must not coerce, and he must not make judgments of worse and better." The critic "must simply elucidate" (an activity which differs obscurely from interpretation); "the reader will form the correct judgment for himself" (ibid., p. 10). In practice, Eliot judges, however, on almost every page and conceives his own role as that of an upholder of the tradition or even as "the creator of values" (*Criterion*, 4 [1926], 751). Eliot's concept of criticism seems thus quite inadequate in the light of his practice.

Eliot's rival I. A. Richards belongs to the upholders of a scientific ideal. Criticism should become a new science, or at least "a cooperative technique of enquiry that may become entitled to be named a science" (*Coleridge on Imagination* [1934], p. xii). Richards hopes for an ultimate total victory of science: "We have," he said in 1952, "to seek a way by which Value must unrestrictedly come into the care of Science" (*Speculative Instruments*, p. 145). The science on which he leans is psychology and in his early books neurology. But in his *Practical Criticism* (1928) no scientific experimentation is used, no analysis in quantitative terms nor any controlled method of formulating the ques-

tionnaire. Richard's work is rather an attempt to analyze the sources of misreadings made by students when confronted with anonymous poetic texts. A theory of emotive language obscures Richards' successful manner of looking at texts and judging them sensitively.

Both Eliot and Richards deeply influenced F. R. Leavis. His concept of criticism is equally tentative and empirical but he is more deliberately moralistic and pedagogical. Criticism trains "intelligence and sensibility together, cultivating a sensitiveness and precision of response and a delicate integrity of intelligence." "Everything must start from and be associated with the training of sensibility" (*Education and the University*, pp. 34, 120). Criticism begins with the texture of texts in front of us. Hence literary history and scholarship are useless, though on occasion Leavis recognizes the necessity of a "critique of criticism." The central ethos of criticism is the preserving of the tradition, but tradition, in Leavis, is very different from Eliot's view of tradition. Leavis' view is nonreligious, Arnoldian, and appeals to the basic values of the old English organic society, though in recent decades this Arnoldian concept has been modified or subverted by Leavis' unbounded admiration for D. H. Lawrence and his worship of "Life." Life, with Leavis, is a vague and shifting term. Ultimately he has to appeal to intuitive certitude. "A judgment," he tells us, "is a real judgment, or it is nothing. It must, that is, be a sincere personal judgment; but it aspires to be more than personal" (*Scrutiny*, 18 [1951], 22).

English criticism has not extricated itself from these antinomies, though very diverse formulas can be found for alternatives. Herbert Read, in a piece on "The Nature of Criticism," advocates simply Jungian psychology as the solution. William Righter, in *Logic and Criticism* (1963), argues for the "irrelevance of precise intellectual machinery to the general criteria of critical success," while John Casey, in *The Language of Criticism* (1966), which is indebted to Wittgenstein's critique of language, comes rather to rejecting the whole English tradition of a theory of emotion and to stress the need of history. Historical criticism was also defended by Helen Gardner in her *The Business of Criticism* (1959) while George Watson in *The Literary Critics* (1962) distinguishes "legislative" (i.e., judicial) and "theoretical" criticism, and judges that "descriptive" criticism is "the only one which today possesses any life and vigour of its own." The history of criticism appears to Watson as "a record of chaos marked by a sudden revolution." "The great critics do not contribute: they interrupt." Against these excesses of empiricism in England one can quote, at least, one book, such as Harold Osborne's *Aesthetics and Criticism* (1955), which makes a reasoned defense of the dependence of criticism on aesthetics and expounds a theory of "organic configuration" which appeals to the main tradition of aesthetics. Criticism is, for Osborne, applied aesthetics. Also Graham Hough, in *An Essay on Criticism* (1966), sees criticism as rational discussion and as leading to judgments of value. The principles of literary criticism are not "just matters of taste." In principle, literary judgments are objective: some things are really better than others. The most recent theoretical discussion of the concept, F. E. Sparshott's *Concept of Criticism* (1967), while scholastically elaborate in its distinctions, comes to the conclusion that there is "no general theory of evaluative discourse," though criticism is, in his definition, a "discourse apt to ground evaluations" (p. 39).

In the United States, early in the twentieth century, criticism became largely social, and generalized to embrace a criticism of American society. H. L. Mencken showed, however, a surprising sympathy for the view of Joel E. Spingarn, the propounder of a somewhat diluted version of Croceanism. What appealed to Mencken in aestheticism was the rejection of the old didactic view of criticism: the critic as constable or "birchman." Mencken saw only another version of the old kind in the criticism of the New Humanists: of Paul Elmer More and Irving Babbitt who defended judicial criticism, a criticism with standards which were basically classical and ultimately moral. Norman Foerster argued most clearly for the view that an aesthetic judgment is equally an ethical judgment in *The Intent of the Critic* (1941).

With the advent of the New Criticism closer definitions of the nature of criticism were attempted. They all reflect the deep divisions even in the movement misleadingly called the "New Criticism," a name derived from a book (1941) by John Crowe Ransom which was actually extremely critical of T. S. Eliot, I. A. Richards, and Yvor Winters. Ransom has most consistently advocated the necessity of grounding criticism in theory and aesthetics. He has focussed on the central object of criticism: the work itself, the "criticism of the structural properties of poetry." His philosophic alignment with Croce and Bergson is obvious.

Ransom's followers and disciples differ from him widely; Allen Tate asked skeptically whether literary criticism is possible and came to the conclusion that criticism is "perpetually obsolescent and replaceable," a parasitic growth on creation. He hands over philosophical and stylistic criticism to other disciplines and asks for a criticism which would "expound the knowledge of life contained in a work"—surely something that has been done for centuries—and finally queries whether criticism is possible without a criterion of absolute truth. Criticism is paradoxically both "per-

petually necessary" and "perpetually impossible" (*The Forlorn Demon*, 1952).

No such anti-intellectualism pervades the critical writings of either Cleanth Brooks or William K. Wimsatt. Brooks has argued against critical relativism and for standards, and Wimsatt has defined the "domain of literary criticism" as "the verbal object and its analysis." Wimsatt sees the critical act largely as an act of explication out of which a judgment of value grows almost spontaneously. "The main critical problem is always how to push both understanding and value as far as possible in union, or how to make our understanding evaluative" (*The Verbal Icon*, p. 251). Brooks and Wimsatt's *Literary Criticism: A Short History* (1957) and Wimsatt's classifications of critics allow a combination of methods, a pluralism which belies the reputed charge of dogmatism or formalism often made against the New Critics.

Dogmatism can be ascribed rather to Yvor Winters, who has most strongly urged the need for ranking and has practiced it. "Unless criticism succeeds in providing a usable system of evaluation it is worth very little," he says, and he proceeds to supply such a system which, in practice, amounts to the application of a criterion of rational coherence and moral soundness.

Two twentieth-century critics, R. P. Blackmur and Kenneth Burke, have expanded the field of criticism far beyond the boundaries of literature. Burke has become a philosopher aiming at a system which combines psychoanalysis, Marxism, semantics, and "whatnot" with literary criticism. He tries to absorb literary criticism into a philosophy of motives which he calls "dramatism." The critic, for Burke, is a prophet who is to remake society and life. Blackmur, who diagnosed the pathologies of our culture, speculated more modestly also on the concept of criticism. Oddly enough he defines it at first as "the formal discourse of an amateur" but then argues that "any rational approach is valid to literature and may be properly called critical which fastens at any point upon the work itself" ("A Critic's Job of Work," 1935, in *Language as Gesture*, 1952). He recognizes that aesthetics is at least implicit in any criticism. Still it is no science because "science cannot explain the *feeling* or existence of a poem." In these pronouncements Blackmur is near the New Critics, but later he felt that they provide methods only for the early stages of criticism, viz., analysis and elucidation, but fail to compare and judge. He advocates a rational judgment but neither his practice nor his later theory lives up to this ideal. The critical act becomes with him the creative act, the product of the tension of the writer's lifetime, a self-definition which, in many later essays, seems hardly related to any literary text.

603

Other American New Critics upheld concepts of criticism which can be described as broadly social. F. C. Matthiessen pleaded in 1949 for the social "responsibilities of the critic," in *The Responsibilities of the Critic* (1952). Lionel Trilling is mainly concerned with the moral and political issues in modern literature. Harry Levin also conceives of literary criticism in broadly cultural terms, viewing literature "as an institution," but is relativistic and historistic in his orientation. The relativity of all critical judgments has been argued in many contexts; e.g., in George Boas' *Primer for Critics* (1937, new edition *Wingless Pegasus*, 1950), in Bernard Heyl's *New Bearings in Esthetics and Art Criticism* (1943), and in Wayne Shumaker's *Elements of Critical Theory* (1952). A pluralistic and instrumentalist view of criticism is also defended by Ronald S. Crane, the main spokesman of the so-called "Chicago Aristotelianism." Criticism is defined as "reasoned discourse, an organization of terms, propositions and arguments," which is subject to the critic's choice and hence necessarily relative. Still, in practice, the group has been committed to a rigid application of a doctrine of genres and ranking within the elements of a work of art, appealing to Aristotle as its ultimate source. In contrast to the New Critics, language and symbol are slighted in favor of plot and character. The Chicago Aristotelians consider criticism "a department of philosophy" and claim for their doctrines an immense certainty.

These pretensions have been questioned insistently in the twentieth century by poets such as Karl Shapiro, who shies away from anything that has to do with philosophy. He recommends "creative criticism, as a work of art about another work of art" (*In Defense of Ignorance*, 1960), while Randall Jarrell has pleaded for the strict subordination of criticism "to help us with works of art." "Principles and standards of excellence are either specifically harmful or generally useless; the critic has nothing to go by except his experience . . . and is the personification of empiricism" (*Poetry and the Age*, 1955). No theory, no history.

There is only room for theory in Northrop Frye's *Anatomy of Criticism* (1956). In a "Polemical Introduction" Frye excludes all value judgment from criticism, as criticism "should show a steady advance toward undiscriminating catholicity." The book tries to construe an all-inclusive scheme where literature is conceived as "existing in its own universe, no longer a commentary on life and reality, but containing life and reality in a system of verbal relationships." Criticism in Frye's sense clarifies this order and should succeed in "reforging the links between creation and knowledge, art and science, myth and concept." Criticism in Frye becomes not only a theory of literature

but a form of theology, an all-inclusive system, a world hypothesis. R. W. Lewis formulated this well when he said that "criticism, ceasing to be one of the several intellectual arts, is becoming the entire intellectual act itself," and the critic has become a "prophet announcing to the ungodly the communication of men with ultimate reality." This is meant as serious praise; it shows that this concept has broken completely loose from the traditional concern with literature. It has ceased to be *literary* criticism, and has become a version of philosophy.

In France, despite the great differences in the ideologies and concrete taste of the critics, the same variety of concepts of criticism was stated and restated. There is the rationalist tradition of the new classicists who upheld an ideal of judicial criticism, eloquently put, e.g., by Charles Maurras. Ramon Fernandez, who had his affinities with T. S. Eliot, formulated an ideal of a rather philosophic criticism, whose aim would be an "imaginative ontology," a definition of the problem of being. Fernandez believes that there is a "philosophic substructure" of a work, a body of ideas which the critic has to relate to the problems of general philosophy. But Fernandez knows well that critical consciousness is not the task of the author: it is reserved for the critic (*Messages*, 1926).

Generally, however, in the France of the early twentieth century irrationalistic tendencies were victorious: Bergson became the philosopher inspiring, e.g., the theory of criticism in Albert Thibaudet (1874–1936), who among the French reflected most fruitfully on the concept of criticism. Still, Thibaudet understands while pursuing an intuitive and metaphorical method of criticism that the critic translates what is conceived in poetic terms into intellectual terms, changes the concrete into the abstract, though he is also aware of the perils. He is afraid "to substitute for the profound clarity of an image the semi-obscurity or the shadow of an idea" of such a translation (*Valéry* [1924], p. 160). Besides translation, Thibaudet recognizes two other kinds of criticism: "pure" criticism which is theory of literature, thinking about genres and principles, and historical criticism. He sees also that "there is no criticism without a criticism of criticism" and has written sketches of the history of French criticism (*Physiologie de la critique*, 1930) in which he attacks the *certitudiens*, the dogmatists of the Right. He wanted mobility, flexibility, or what he called "literary pantheism." What in Thibaudet is phrased as a defense of tolerance, became in some contemporaries an emphasis on complete submission, on a lack of critical personality, on identification which, at times, sounds like mystical union. Jacques Rivière laments his "frightening plasticity" while Charles Du Bos made much of his "liquidity," of the central virtue of the critic as a "pure receptacle" of the life of another. Also Marcel Proust, in many scattered pronouncements, sees the critic as entering the mind of others and complains of Sainte-Beuve's detachment and irony as well as of his confusion of life and art. Imitation, the *pastiche*, is the proper form of criticism for Proust.

The second World War brought a reaction against all theories of pure art and pure criticism. Jean-Paul Sartre's watchword *"La littérature engagée,"* propounded in *Qu'est-ce que la littérature* (1947), implies a concept of committed criticism, criticism committed to a social and political cause. Sartre chides academic critics for "having chosen to have relations only with the defunct." Pure art and empty art are the same thing. But Sartre reserves a nook for pure poetry and in his actual criticism uses largely psychoanalytical methods to criticize Baudelaire as a man or to exalt Genet for the identity of man and work.

Surprisingly enough, the finest, most intellectual critic of the first half of the century, the poet Paul Valéry, held a theory of criticism which opens the way to a total divorce between the work of art and the reader or critic. Valéry believed that a work of art is so ambiguous that it has no proper meaning and that it is open to what he calls "creative misunderstanding." "There is no true sense of a text. The author has no authority." The critic is completely free to read into a work his own mind. The solution seems to be "creative criticism" which sounds like Oscar Wilde's defense of caprice or Anatole France's "adventures among masterpieces," but is in Valéry rather motivated by a deep conviction of the unbridgeable gulfs between author and work and work and reader.

This liberty of interpretation is then preached and practiced by the so-called "new critics" in France. The concerns may be very different: psychoanalytical, mythographical, structuralist, or what is called *la critique de conscience;* in all cases, the new French critics argue that the work of art is not something out there which has a proper meaning for the critic to discover and to formulate, but that the work itself is a mental construct realized only in collaboration with the subject. The conflict of concepts of criticism came out most clearly in the recent debate between Raymond Picard and Roland Barthes. Picard attacked Barthes' interpretation of Racine from a historicistic and philological point of view. Barthes, in replying (*Critique et vérité*, 1966), criticized cogently the limitations of conventional historical criticism, its ignoring of the changing "life" of a work through history, its obtuseness toward ambiguity and symbolism, but he goes far beyond this in asserting the right of criticism to "duplicate" a work of art. The term *écriture* is used to

assimilate the critic to the poet, the critic transforming the work of art into his image.

The other new critics seem to take the opposite position: Georges Poulet, for example, advocates participation or better "identification" with an author, the "integral transposition of a mental universe into the interior of another mind." This is an old idea known to the Schlegels or Croce, proclaimed as great novelty. The declaration, "The basis and substance of all criticism is the grasping of a consciousness by the consciousness of another" (*Les chemins actuels de la critique,* 1968), gives it a new twist: the "identification" is not with a text but with the "consciousness" of a writer which is not identical with his biographical *psyche* but is a construct accessible through the totality of his writings. His attitudes toward time or space (Poulet), or toward the life of the senses (J.-P. Richard) are to be reconstructed without regard to the individual works or their form. It follows even for a critic such as Jean Rousset who does pay attention to the form of individual works that the aim of criticism is "to participate in the existence of another spiritual being" by "an act of adhesion so total that it excludes, at least provisionally, all judgment" (*Forme et signification* [1962], p. xiv). The older concepts of criticism, judicial and aesthetic in the sense of an analysis and interpretation of a single work as an entity, are dismissed or minimized.

In Italy, Benedetto Croce had come to deceptively similar conclusions long before. One of Croce's earliest publications was a book *La Critica letteraria* (1894) which simply denied that the various operations and approaches which are called "literary criticism" make a unified and meaningful subject. But later Croce defended a view of criticism as identification. He went so far as to say that "if I penetrate the innermost sense of a canto of Dante, I become Dante" (*Problemi di estetica* [1909], p. 155). But at an even later stage of his thinking he considered imaginative re-creation only a presupposition of criticism and concluded that criticism is a translation from the realm of feeling into the realm of reason and thought. He found that critics should be reminded of the prohibition posted in some German concert halls in his youth: *Das Mitsingen ist verboten.* In practice Croce asked of criticism nothing else than that it "know the true sentiment of the poet in the representative form in which he has translated it" (Letter to R. W., June 5, 1952). But besides this task of characterization the critic must also judge. There is, however, no other criterion than the distinction between art and non-art, poetry and non-poetry, as in Croce there can be no intermediary between the individual and the universal. No classification of the arts, no genres, no styles or technical services matter, because "what is external is no longer a work of art."

After the death of Croce, different concepts of criticism have become more vocal: Marxism and stylistics. An adherent of Croce, Mario Fabini, advocates a broadening of criticism to include the study of style and genres (*Critica e poesia*, 1956), and a whole group of Italian scholars has returned to a concept of criticism as a study of the aesthetic surface, of language and style. In recent years French existentialism and structuralism have made their impact in Italy.

The peculiarity of the German situation is the sharp divorce between criticism as carried on in the daily press and the *Literaturwissenschaft* of the Academy which was traditionally philological but early in the twentieth century became largely speculative, philosophical (under the influence of *Geistesgeschichte*). Concepts of criticism were not widely examined, though the trends prevailing in the West are also reflected in German discussions. Alfred Kerr, for example, argued (in *Vorwort zum neueren Drama*, 1904) for the superiority of criticism over creation, for criticism as a kind of poetry, thus going even beyond Oscar Wilde. The scholars went the other way, arguing for criticism as a science, though Ernst Robert Curtius, for instance, sees criticism "as the form of literature whose subject is literature" (*Kritische Essays über europäische Literatur*, 1958). The creed of most German scholars was relativism and historicism: it is formulated by Erich Auerbach, for example, in a review of Wellek's *History of Modern Criticism* in *Gesammelte Aufsätze zur romanischen Philologie* (Bern, 1956).

Still, there were many critics interested in judging and ranking. Hugo von Hofmannsthal, who usually defends empathy and understanding, recognizes also the need for ranking, as does, in practice, the whole circle around Stefan George, who thinks of its master as prophet and judge laying down the law. Among more recent German critics Hans Egon Holthusen shows a concern for ethical judgments, commitments also in political matters, arguing that there is no such thing as "pure" literary criticism. He is one of the few Germans who have written on critical understanding (*Kritisches Verstehen*, 1961) and have thought about the concept of criticism while there is, of course, a proliferation of theories of poetry and much that could be called close reading or interpretation. Emil Staiger's preface to *Die Zeit als Einbildungskraft des Dichters* (1939) formulated the rejection of *Geistesgeschichte*, the new focus on the text.

Russian criticism has great interest because in Russia radically opposed conceptions were formulated most sharply. As late as 1825 Alexander Pushkin could complain that "we have no criticism . . . we have not a single commentary, not a single book of criticism." But this changed soon with the advent of Vissarion Belinsky (1811–48) who dominated Russian criticism for the rest of the century. Belinsky's concept of criticism is expounded in a "Speech on Criticism" (1842) in which he rejects arbitrary pronouncements of taste or judgment by rules and defines "criticizing as seeking and discovering the general laws of reason in particulars." Criticism is philosophical knowledge while art is immediate knowledge. In practice, criticism in nineteenth-century Russia was ideological and social. Apollon Grigoriev seems to be an exception. He advocated an "organic criticism" which is intuitive, immediate. The aim of the critic is to grasp the individuality and tone of an author or of an age, its particular atmosphere or "drift." Grigoriev rejected historical relativism but in practice was, like his radical rivals, mainly concerned with social types. Impressionistic and aesthetic concepts emerge only late in the nineteenth century. A symbolist poet like Alexander Blok, in an article on criticism (1907), complains rather of a lack of philosophy, of a "soil under one's feet." The Russian Formalists on the whole dismissed criticism in favor of a technical science of literature, while Soviet criticism constitutes a return to nineteenth-century demands for ideological clarity, for the "social mandate" of both writer and critic.

Today in Russia and generally behind the Curtain, the Marxist concept of criticism prevails. In its official version it is simply didacticism: criticism serves the inculcation of Communism and writers are judged according to whether they do so or not. This didacticism is combined with sociologism: a study of the society which assumes that the writer is completely determined by his class origins and reflects and should reflect the society he describes. In subtler versions of Marxism, mainly in the writings of the Hungarian György Lukács and his follower Lucien Goldmann in France, this simple version is rejected; rather, the critic's task is to analyze the structure of his society and that of former ages and to interpret and judge authors in their historical place, dividing them into reactionary and progressive without regard, however, to their overt intentions and allegiances. Goldmann draws a distinction between comprehension and explication. Explication is the insertion of a work into the context of a social structure. In the dialectical thinking of Lukács no contradiction is felt between asserting that the relative truth of Marxism is absolutely valid (*Beiträge zur Geschichte der Ästhetik*, Berlin [1954], p. 102) and that the party spirit demanded of the critic is not in contradiction to the other duties of an author: the objective reproduction of reality. In practice, the exact rules for criticism are laid down by solemn deliberations of the party congresses. Marxist criticism has returned to prescriptive criticism, to the imposition of specific themes, views, and even styles imposed by the immense power of the state, the party, and the literary organizations, which enforce the edicts in ways undreamt of even in the days of Richelieu.

Such a survey of the diverse concepts of criticism in history leads to the inevitable conclusion that "criticism" is an "essentially contested concept," that in the last two hundred years the possible positions were formulated and reformulated in different contexts, for different purposes, in different countries, but that the issues are reducible to a strictly limited number. The conflict between objective and subjective standards is basic and overlaps somewhat the debate between absolutism and relativism which may be historical. Subjectivism may be absolute in its claims. The methods of criticism also divide easily into intuitive and objective, while objective may mean an appeal to absolute standards of beauty or may appeal to the model of science with an implied indifference to criteria of quality. Intuitive (misnamed impressionistic) criticism can be judicial. Judicial criticism is usually absolutist, at least by implication. Scientific criticism can abdicate all judgment but may try to arrive at it by new criteria. All kinds of crossbreedings and compromises between these positions are possible and were actually formulated. While the dominance of judicial criticism, until the latter part of the eighteenth century, is incontestable, the development since about 1760 cannot be described in terms of a simple succession of concepts which can be clearly related to social, political, or even literary contexts. There appears to be a tug of war between the main trends—judicial, personal, scientific, historical—a tension which was still continuing unabated in the 1960's.

BIBLIOGRAPHY

There is no extensive history of the concept of criticism. See, however, "The Term and Concept of Literary Criticism" in René Wellek, *Concepts of Criticism* (New Haven, 1963); and most histories of criticism, e.g., George Saintsbury, *A History of Criticism and Literary Taste in Europe*, 3 vols. (Edinburgh and New York, 1900–04); J. W. Atkins, *Literary Criticism in Antiquity*, 2 vols. (London, 1934; reprint New York), and three sequels on English Criticism up to the end of the eighteenth century; René Wellek, *A History of Modern Criticism, 1750–1950*, 4 vols. (New Haven, 1955–65); up to 1900. Cleanth Brooks and William K. Wimsatt, *Literary Criticism; A Short History* (New York, 1957). There is no large history of French criticism. In German: G. Gudemann, "Kritikos," in Pauly-Wissowa-Kroll, *Real-Encyclopädie der Classischen Altertumswissenschaft* (Stuttgart, 1921), II, 1912–15; Bruno Markwardt, *Geschichte der deutschen Poetik*, 5 vols. (Berlin, 1937–67). In Russian: B. P. Gorodetsky, A. Lavretsky, and B. S. Meilash, eds.

Istoriya russkoi kritiki, 2 vols. (Moscow, 1958). In Italian: Luigi Russo, *La Critica letteraria contemporanea*, 3 vols. (Bari, 1946–47). G. Marzot, "La Critica letteraria dal De Sanctis ad oggi," in *Letteratura italiana: Le Correnti*, 2 (1956). On English criticism: George Watson, *The Literary Critics* (Harmondsworth, 1962). On American criticism: Norman Foerster, *American Criticism* (Boston, 1928); Bernard Smith, *Forces in American Criticism* (New York, 1939); Stanley Edgar Hyman *The Armed Vision* (New York, 1948); William Van O'Connor, *An Age of Criticism: 1900–1950* (Chicago, 1952); Floyd Stovall, ed., *The Development of American Literary Criticism* (Chapel Hill, 1955); Walter Sutton, *Modern American Criticism* (Englewood Cliffs, N.J., 1963).

RENÉ WELLEK

[See also Beauty; **Empathy;** Historicism; **Literature;** Style.]

CULTURAL DEVELOPMENT IN ANTIQUITY

IT IS A commonplace of modern thought that culture is always in a state of transformation; that the complex of arts, institutions, and ideas by which any society lives has been built up gradually through a long process of development that is still going on. This idea of culture entered modern thought as an inheritance, taken over more or less intact, from certain thinkers of classical antiquity; but the classical versions of it were, like culture itself, the products of an evolutionary process, one whose various stages can be traced in the writings of early Greek poets and philosophers.

Two attitudes dominate the earliest recorded Greek thought about the remote past of the human species. Neither is uniquely Greek, and neither can easily coexist with the notion of culture as evolving gradually from the simple to the complex. One attitude derives from retrospective admiration for the unparalleled achievements of an age of heroes; the other from longing for an earthly paradise of abundance and ease, a paradise which, like the biblical Garden of Eden, was imagined as having actually existed in the remote past of the human race. The former attitude is characteristic of Homeric epic, which presents its leaders as men of an earlier time, directly descended from the gods, and deriving all their arts and institutions from the gods. Individual feats of skill and strength, as well as the general level of power, wealth, and military organization in this heroic age are pictured as far surpassing anything which the poet or his hearers might have experienced themselves.

The age of heroes appears in Hesiod as well as

Homer, but alongside the earthly Paradise or Eden-motif and in the framework of a myth, probably Near Eastern in origin, in which a succession of races or epochs in human history is likened to a series of successively baser metals: gold, silver, bronze, and iron (*Works and Days*, 106–201). In this scheme of history the golden race becomes the inhabitants of the Greek Eden, the race of heroes is inserted somewhat oddly after the races of silver and bronze, and Hesiod's own contemporaries are the race of iron. Hesiod is far more interested in contrasting the iron present with the golden and heroic pasts than he is in developing in detail the idea of a step-by-step deterioration. The latter idea may, in fact, have been adopted by him chiefly as a means of working these two different notions of the past into a single historical narrative. When the Eden-motif appears alone in early Greek thought it is regularly in the context of another myth altogether, that which connects the harsh lot of contemporary man with the stern rule of Zeus and the ease of an earlier time with the mild rule of Zeus's father, Cronus. It was only when the myth of the Ages of Man was revived in Hellenistic and later times that it came to be used as a setting for the Eden-motif alone—a change which led, almost without exception, to the elimination of the age of heroes from the scheme altogether. But Hesiod's later imitators were true to their model in that they continued to emphasize the first and last phases of the cycle at the expense of the intervening two. The borrowed notion of a degenerating succession of epochs was never really assimilated either by Hesiod or his successors: the oriental cycle became and remained a Greek antithesis.

Both Homer and Hesiod are products of a transitional period between the relatively static era that followed the breakup of Mycenaean civilization in the twelfth century B.C., and the Greek renaissance of the seventh and sixth centuries. Homer looks back over the static centuries to the highly complex Mycenaean world and locates the deeds of his heroes there; Hesiod dislikes the signs of incipient change he sees around him and, by way of reaction, idealizes the fixed agricultural existence of a less remote past into the life of the Golden race. Change is still seen only as a disruptive process, and so this past is not a simpler or more primitive time but essentially Hesiod's own society minus the aspects of it he dislikes: sea-borne commerce, covetousness and litigation, and the hard labor in the fields which the gods have imposed on man as a punishment for his wickedness.

It was probably the pressure of external events which, more than anything else, led to the ultimate abandonment of such views of the past. Hesiod lived at the beginning of two centuries of continuous and radical change (ca. 700 B.C.). The period witnessed the opening of all the Mediterranean to Greek trade and colonization, the diffusion of the art of writing, the invention of coinage, the first written constitutions, extensive reorganization of political and social structures over much of Greece, and important developments in technology, mathematics, and the fine arts. It was natural for Greeks of this time to assume that the step-by-step transformation of all aspects of human life which could be observed in recent history had gone on throughout all of history and that the earliest human existence must have been, as a consequence, far simpler and poorer than any within memory.

The new view is already found in the writings of the sixth-century philosopher Xenophanes (frag. 18), but there is no evidence to suggest that it crystallized into a comprehensive reconstruction of the life of early man before the mid-fifth century. The first revisions of earlier notions seem to have been piecemeal in character: gods who had once been the divine patrons or supreme practitioners of a given art came to be regarded as the ones responsible for first acquainting mankind with its use, or the earliest men associated in mythological tradition with a given technology as its inventors. So Demeter becomes the bringer of agriculture, Prometheus the discoverer of fire, Daedalus the inventor of sculpture, and the Argonauts the world's first sailors. When a group of such "firsts" was assembled the result would not be an analysis of cultural development but a catalogue of inventions, and this is the form taken by the earliest connected piece of Greek cultural history that has survived: the Titan Prometheus' description of his services to mankind in Aeschylus' *Prometheus Bound* (ca. 460 B.C.). The gap which separates this account from the more genuinely scientific speculations of later thinkers is evident not only in its form, but also in the character of Prometheus himself. On one level, he is a personification of the intelligence of man the deviser (*promētheia* in Greek means "forethought"); but on another level he is an early fifth-century scientist or natural philosopher. The remote past is still seen very much in the image of the recent past, so that the inventions by which Prometheus is supposed to have raised man from his primitive savagery are largely in those fields—such as written communication, astronomy, medicine—where advances in the preceding century had been especially remarkable.

The first comprehensive attempt to envisage the character of human life in its pre-technological stages belongs to the generation following Aeschylus' if, as is now generally assumed, the doctrines ascribed to the Sophist Protagoras (fl. ca. 440 B.C.) in Plato's *Protagoras* are in fact his. Protagoras sees the development of technology in the context of the struggle which men, like all other animals, must wage for survival. Fire, housing, clothing, and agriculture are techniques devised to avoid death by starvation or exposure to the elements; the various social virtues (reverence, justice, piety) are a similar set of techniques (called by Protagoras "the civic technology") devised to secure the peaceful communal existence that is necessary if men are to cooperate effectively with one another in fighting for survival against other animals.

The civic technology is one in whose development all men participate, and Protagoras' whole theory can be regarded as a secularization and democratization as well as an extension of the approach which gave rise to the catalogues of inventors. The latter tended to concentrate on the outstanding achievements of individual inventors, often divine or semi-divine in character, and to neglect the more primitive and basic skills which could be felt as the property of the whole race. The transformation may be the work of Protagoras himself, who was the first man to take higher education out of the control of the family or professional guild and make it the subject of public lectures; but there is reason to believe that the evolutionary cosmology and biology of the Pre-Socratics were influential as well. Protagoras introduces his account of early man by a zoogony and regards the capacity for technology as a human trait which stands in lieu of the various natural advantages (claws, wings, bodily strength) which fit animals for survival. Man's ability to exploit his environment by various arts and crafts is similarly described as compensating for physical weakness in a fragment of a Pre-Socratic who was Protagoras' contemporary, namely, Anaxagoras (frag. 21b); and the latter's pupil Archelaus is credited with an account of the way in which "human beings were separated out from the other animals and then developed leaders and lawful usages and techniques . . ." (frag. A4). He must have covered much the same ground as Protagoras does in Plato's dialogue.

Protagoras, Anaxagoras, and Archelaus are probably symptomatic of the thoroughgoing character of the revision of earlier ideas which was going on in the middle of the fifth century, and it is a reasonable inference that by the end of the century few if any educated Greeks would have questioned the view that man's life had been radically transformed and enriched by his own technology. Later pictures of the Golden Age and reign of Cronus, whether Greek or Roman, are either consciously fanciful and metaphorical, or are modifications of the Hesiodic myth in that they describe the earliest men as living with no technology at all, or only its rudiments, and seek to show that they were better off as a consequence.

Once the fact of technological and material progress was generally accepted, the emphasis in discussions of cultural development tended to shift away from the simple assertion of the importance of technology and a catalogue of its achievements—even though the catalogue of inventors continued to be an established minor genre down to the end of antiquity and into the early Middle Ages. The capacity for technology is no longer, as it had been for Protagoras and his predecessors, simply a characteristic excellence of man. It is rather something whose existence calls for explanation within the context of a more general theory, often psychological in character, of the nature of man and the sources of man's actions. Here it is possible to distinguish two main lines of thought—a naturalistic and a teleological one.

The former antedates the latter, which arose partially in response to it. It recalls Protagoras in connecting the beginnings of technology and society with the struggle for survival, and in its view of social and ethical usages as a kind of "civic technology" acquired in the same way as the other arts and crafts. But the Protagorean notion of technology as a mechanism of survival that comes into being through a vaguely conceived process of "challenge and response" is replaced by something far more precise.

In some authors this more precise formulation involves a fairly simple historical determinism. Prodicus, a Sophist of the generation following that of Protagoras, held that society, religion, and most civilized usages followed inevitably as soon as man's natural quest for food led him to take up farming; and Thucydides in the opening chapters of his history of the Peloponnesian War seems to derive political and economic institutions exclusively from man's inevitable quest for security and power. Theories of geographical or climatic determinism also found their adherents; and the whole method was soon taken over by rhetoricians as a standard *topos*, by which any given art or activity could be praised as the principal cause of man's rise from savagery to civilization. Love between the sexes, oratory, poetry, sailing, even cooking are all exalted in this fashion.

Other thinkers within the naturalistic tradition seem to have posited a more complex process, one in which there is an interaction between a number of instincts or drives common to man and other animals—for food, shelter, physical comfort, sexual satisfaction, security from attack, proximity to members of one's own kind—and, on the other hand, certain physical and mental endowments—hands, upright stature, the capacity for articulate speech, the ability to calculate the future consequences of a decision—which are peculiar to man or possessed by him to a peculiar degree.

609

This ability to calculate functions passively rather than actively at the outset of human development, allows men to seize on the advantages of a situation that has already been presented to them (e.g., a chance fire, first terrifying, then fascinating and comforting momentarily with its warmth, eventually preserved as a continuing source of comfort and put to other uses) rather than to plan methodically for the future. With the passage of time men come to look for such situations and to seize upon their implications even when they are not immediately obvious, and so to expand constantly on the suggestions and models provided by nature and accident. Such advances always begin with one individual, but are quickly imitated by others, so that the rate of progress is much faster than if the talents of only one person were involved. Only when such activity, carried on over a long period of time, has produced a surplus of the necessities of life does pleasure as well as need become the goal toward which men work; hence the late origin of the fine arts as opposed to the useful arts.

Language and social mores arise in a similar manner: the first step in the transformation of the inarticulate cries men share with other animals occurs when a chance incident creates an association between a sound and a certain meaning and the utility of the resulting signal makes it a model for the creation of other meaningful utterances. (So, for example, a cry of terror in a moment of danger may save the utterer by attracting the attention of others who come to his aid, and then may be retained as a rallying cry).

A characteristically human society begins to evolve out of an animal-like herd when the vague patterns of cooperation and more or less amicable coexistence which characterize herd-existence are broken by acts of unprovoked aggression. Such departures from the expected pass unnoticed in other animal herds, but the human animal looks to the future and, foreseeing situations when he may be in the place of the injured party, registers indignation and disapproval in such a way as to inhibit future occurrences of the particular asocial or "unjust" act involved. Similar chance occurrences of desirable modes of behavior (e.g., exceptional bravery in combating the common enemies of the herd) are the occasion of approbation and rewards, and are thus encouraged. The result is a gradual and progressive standardization of behavior along the lines most conducive to the welfare of the whole herd, and the behavior patterns acquired in this way become second nature for each successive generation. The purely social system of rewards and punishments that is involved in this process is reinforced by government when the herd's leader (regularly, as in animal herds, its strongest member) for one reason or another decides to employ his own strength on the side of what the herd considers just; the advantages of having such a leader are perceived, and rule is henceforth based on consent rather than submission to superior force.

Such are some of the main ideas that enter into the composite picture of cultural development which can be pieced together from scattered accounts in a number of Greek and Latin texts, most of them dating from the late Hellenistic or early imperial period (the first book of Diodorus Siculus' universal history, the fifth book of Lucretius' exposition of Epicurean philosophy, the account of the origin and transformation of political constitutions found in the sixth book of Polybius, the description of the beginnings of architecture in the second book of Vitruvius). The passages in question are linked by general agreement as to the factors at work in the growth of culture (the continuing presence of certain basic human needs plus a continuously increasing ability on the part of man to calculate consistently for his future satisfaction) and, more strikingly, by the shared notion of cultural development as proceeding via a series of chance situations which provide opportunities or suggestions that man exploits for his own benefit. Whether all aspects of the general picture were ever present in a single account is uncertain, but the basic ideas or principles involved, and many of their specific applications, were probably first found in the writings of the late fifth-century atomist Democritus. Indeed, the whole theory, since it decomposes the seeming continuity of human life and culture into a series of discrete events each involving an abrupt transformation of a small portion of the life of a society, can be regarded as a kind of sociological atomism. It thus forms a natural counterpart to the atomistic analysis of change in the physical world as resulting from a series of sudden rearrangements of two or more of the tiny particles of which matter is composed.

This version of the process of cultural development, like the physical systems of Democritus and other Pre-Socratics, did not posit the existence of a final or formal cause, and as such was unlikely to appeal to thinkers trained in the Platonic and Aristotelian traditions. It is accordingly common to find in Aristotelian and post-Aristotelian philosophy an altogether different view of cultural development—one which sees it as a gradual unfolding of the capacities inherent in man's nature, a process which proceeds in orderly fashion toward its *telos*, which is the realization of human nature in all its fullness and perfection. The various human endowments to which the naturalistic theory called attention cease to be efficient causes in this scheme and become symptomatic of the operation of a final or formal cause. Man, as Aristotle says (correcting Anaxagoras), is not the most intelligent of animals because he has hands but has hands because he is the most intelligent (*De partibus animalium* 687a 7–10). Moreover, since all the virtues of civilized man must have been present in embryonic form in his primitive ancestors, there is a strong—though not universal—tendency to idealize the state of nature as incomplete but also uncorrupted.

Human development for the teleologists is analogous to the growth of an organism, or to the gradual perfection of an art, science, or other discipline through a series of discoveries which bring men progressively closer to the practice of the discipline in its ideal form. Perhaps as a consequence, teleological accounts of the growth of culture often seem to have included not simply a speculative reconstruction of prehistory but also historical research aimed at fixing the place, time, and author of each of the discoveries which went into the creation of a given art or science, somewhat in the manner of the earlier catalogues of inventors. The account of the growth of tragedy found in Aristotle's *Poetics* is the best-known surviving example of the method.

Technology, viewed as an organized system of skills, thus continued to receive a share of attention from the teleologists, but it is regularly relegated to an earlier stage in the process of cultural development, as being a product of that lower portion of man's capacities which is directed toward the satisfaction of material needs. Disinterested speculation on the constitution of the universe and the nature of Being constitute the final and culminating stages of man's cultural progress, with the fine arts occupying occasionally an intermediate stage.

This view of cultural development is implicit in a passage of the *Epinomis*, ascribed to Plato's pupil Philip of Opus, and seems to have appeared in Aristotle's early work (now lost) called *De philosophia*. It is best known, however, in the form given it by the Stoic Posidonius (ca. 135–51 B.C.). The latter held that man's earliest existence was under the guide of "philosophers," who showed man the various necessities of life, then led him to discover all the arts, and finally taught him the methods of philosophy proper—the implication being that technology is an early and imperfect version of a discipline which finds its fullest embodiment in pure theory.

The teleological view is not maintained with complete consistency by all of its proponents. Posidonius himself, in describing the growth of technology, posited a process of discovery which closely resembles that envisaged by Democritus and was probably influenced by Democritean doctrines; Aristotle's pupil Dicaearchus, though he argued for a progression from food-gathering to herding to agriculture in the life of early

man (evidently guided by the feeling that these are progressively more complex and advanced forms of activity and hence must follow in this order) seems not to have felt that the progression was in the direction of a better life for man; and another pupil of Aristotle, Theophrastus, in tracing the development of religious usages, assigned considerable importance to historical accident. But these are minor deviations which do not affect the basic character of the doctrines involved.

Insofar as such doctrines are not specifically teleological but simply a form of historical determinism, and insofar as they tend to minimize the importance of communities and social conditioning in the creation of man's civilized traits, they have parallels in Hellenistic thought outside the teleological schools. For most of the thought of this period, whether teleological or nonteleological, tended to eliminate the contingent in favor of the necessary in its theories of causation, and in the study of man to regard human nature as a universal, essentially the same regardless of the particular social context in which it might find itself. The points at which the Epicurean account of cultural origins found in the fifth book of Lucretius seems to depart from its Democritean model are indicative of both these characteristically Hellenistic tendencies. On more than one occasion Lucretius' account gives biological and environmental determinism a greater causal role as against the play of accident and human calculation, working in a particular social context, stressed by Democritus. Primitive language and primitive ethical notions are thus regarded as physiologically and geographically determined: men are impelled by their physical and psychic makeup and the climatic features of a given region to attach certain designations to certain objects, and, when brought together with other men for mutual protection, to recognize as immediately self-evident the advantages of certain modes of behavior, which are thus the basis of the moral codes operative in all societies.

Elements of the teleological view of the development of civilization appear as early as the late fifth century. Euripides and Xenophon, for example, refer to man's capacity for speech and his other physical advantages as the gifts of a benign providence to facilitate the development and exercise of his higher faculties. But the theory seems to have become fully formulated only in the Academy of Plato's later years (cf. the works of Philip of Opus and the young Aristotle mentioned above). Even in Plato's own works the idea of technology as preparation for philosophy never appears. Plato's concern in the three dialogues (*Republic, Politicus, Laws*) in which he deals most extensively with the question of cultural development is rather to separate the intellectual and technological elements in civilization and to emphasize the fact that it is only the former, not the latter, which can ensure man's happiness. He does this by contrasting the culture of his contemporaries with culture at an entirely different stage of technological and material development in such a way as to show that not technological superiority but the possession of philosophical wisdom is the criterion to be used in determining which culture is better for man.

In the *Republic* the contrasting culture is that of a "simple" state in which a rudimentary division of labor and exchange of services satisfies man's essential needs; in the *Laws* it is a primitive pastoral society (peopled by the survivors of one of the cataclysms which occur periodically through human history), which has retained from the period prior to the cataclysm certain rudimentary arts (weaving and pottery) and social institutions (the patriarchal family) but lost all the rest. Plato clearly suggests that the rudimentary technologies of this pastoral society and of the simple state in the *Republic* are more conducive to virtue and happiness than the more advanced technology of his own day. The only thing that makes life unsatisfactory in both these primitive states is the absence of philosophy. Philosophical wisdom is not among the virtues which Plato ascribes to the primitive shepherds in the *Laws* (679e), and the philosopher class only arises in the "luxurious" state which succeeds the simple one in the scheme of development posited in the *Republic*. In the *Politicus* Plato pictures the Hesiodic reign of Cronus as existing in a cycle of human existence prior to the present one. Cronus' subjects enjoy an easier and more abundant supply of material wants than technology in the present cycle can supply, but cannot be considered to have been truly happy if they lacked philosophy (272b–c).

The three passages in which Plato treats cultural development at some length do not present a coherent theory of it, but they were of fundamental importance for the development of later ideas. The teleological notion of the relation between technology and philosophy was probably an outgrowth of Plato's strict separation of the two, a kind of compromise designed to preserve the supremacy of the latter without totally rejecting the importance of the former. In the *Republic* and the *Laws* Plato envisaged the minimum of technological development that is requisite for human happiness, and attributed this level of technological development to the inhabitants of an early society. In so doing he created an intellectually acceptable modernization of the Hesiodic Eden myth that was to become the ultimate model for the state of nature as praised by primitivists throughout later antiquity. Fi-

nally, the system of world-cycles separated by cataclysms which appears in the *Politicus* and *Laws* was to provide the most common setting for the teleological theory of cultural development, providing as it did a series of appropriately finite chronological settings for the finite evolutionary processes posited by this theory.

The teleological conception of cultural history does not allow for further technological, social, or political development of any significance once the stage of philosophical inquiry has been reached. One would not expect, therefore, to find in writers who belong to or anticipate this tradition any counterpart to the modern idea of potentially unlimited progress, except insofar as it applies to the realm of philosophy. The idea is not in fact found in such writers when they are concerned with cultural development in general—though they may on occasion allow for the possibility in connection with a specific technology (see, most strikingly, *Politicus* 298b–99c). When the prospect of a radical transformation of man's way of life must be contemplated, writers working within this tradition can only describe it as a return to the Golden Age or a realization of it—as, for example, the Roman poets described the renovation of the Roman body politic attempted by Augustus.

The Democritean theory and its antecedents are, by contrast, not committed on principle to the rejection of unlimited future progress in any realm of human activity. The climate of the time in which such theories were formulated—middle and late fifth century—would have been favorable to such an idea, for the period saw the limitless aspirations of Periclean Athens and the first practical plans for reorganizing society along new lines, with provisions to ensure that the new societies should be themselves innovatory rather than static (see the suggestion of Pericles' friend, the city-planner Hippodamus of Miletus, reported in Aristotle, *Politics* 1268a 6–8). Democritus in several fragments seems to be proposing far-reaching reforms in the political and social structure of the city, and Plato may be drawing on earlier theories of cultural history when, in the *Laws* (683a), he suggests that the city itself is not the ultimate stage in political evolution but may be replaced by a larger unit—league, alliance, or confederacy. When the Democritean view of cultural development is transformed, as it is in several early Hellenistic texts, into monarchistic propaganda, the transformation is achieved by attributing man's early progress to beneficent kings and by suggesting that contemporary monarchs, like their primitive forerunners, can be expected to bring new levels of prosperity and technological achievement to their realms and to extend the blessings of civilization to ever larger portions of the habitable world. Even Democritus' conception of cultural development as a response to certain constant elements in human nature does not preclude the idea of infinite progression, since Democritus recognizes the existence of such a thing as second nature. Nature is not simply inborn but may be implanted through education and training (frag. 33).

Yet we cannot be sure how far such faith in progress went. Protagoras' contemporary, Sophocles, wrote the most enthusiastic proclamation of man's ability to control and transform the world that survives from antiquity (*Antigone* 332–75), yet he closed his encomium with a cautionary reference to the fact that such power can be a mixed blessing. And the Democritean fragments just mentioned must be compared with others, which stress the necessity of always limiting one's needs and being content with little. Greek distrust of power and affluence was perhaps too strong ever to allow the ancient apostles of progress to be as confident as some of their modern counterparts, and it is reasonable to assume that their voice became less and less confident as time went on. Political progress was so intimately bound up with technological progress in the minds of those who accepted the possibility of both processes continuing indefinitely, that the whole notion would have been difficult to maintain after the end of the fourth century B.C. By then Greece's control over her destiny had passed out of her own hands, and the most that the educated class could hope for politically was to maintain the social status quo against the threat of internal revolution. Teleological doctrines would have had an especial appeal for this age, for by their view of the position of philosophy in human history they taught that man was simply fulfilling his destiny in ultimately abandoning action for thought.

The coming of Roman domination in the second century B.C. only intensified this trend in Greek thought; and Roman historical thought, insofar as it did not simply reflect Greek ideas, was dominated by retrospective admiration for its own race of heroes: the plain-living, self-denying warriors and statesmen of the early Republic. It is hardly surprising, therefore, that the teleological theory of cultural development was, either in combination or in alternation with the primitivists' idealization of a simple and unproblematic state of nature, canonical throughout later antiquity.

BIBLIOGRAPHY

The principal texts are collected and translated in A. O. Lovejoy and G. Boas, *Primitivism and Related Ideas in Antiquity* (Baltimore, 1935). The best general survey of the whole subject is still W. von Uxkull-Gyllenband, *Griechische Kultur-Entstehungslehren* (Berlin, 1924). For more specialized discussions, see B. Gatz, *Weltalter, goldene Zeit und sinnverwandte Vorstellungen* (Hildesheim, 1967); A. Klein-

günther, "ΠΡΩΤΟΣ ΕΥΡΕΤΗΣ," *Philologus* Suppl. 26.1 (1933) and K. Thraede, "Erfinder," *Reallexikon für Antike und Christentum*, 5 (1962), 1191–1278 (inventor catalogues); T. Cole, *Democritus and the Sources of Greek Anthropology*, in *American Philological Association Monographs* XXV (1967); W. Theiler, *Geschichte der teleologischen Naturbetrachtung bis auf Aristoteles* (Zürich, 1925); and E. A. Havelock, *The Liberal Temper in Greek Politics* (New Haven, 1957), 25–124 (theories of cultural development in the larger context of early Greek anthropological and political thought). As is inevitable, since so many of the principal authors survive only in fragments, all these studies make extensive use of hypothetical reconstructions; and any two scholars' reconstructions will show important areas of disagreement. For views differing sharply from those here presented of the importance of Democritus in the shaping of the tradition and of the place of the idea of progress in ancient thought see W. Spoerri, *Späthellenistische Berichte über Welt, Kultur und Götter* (Basel, 1959) and L. Edelstein, *The Idea of Progress in Classical Antiquity* (Baltimore, 1967), reviewed critically by E. R. Dodds, *Journal of the History of Ideas*, **29** (1968), 453–57. For other relevant passages from ancient authors see the very full survey in K. Thraede, "Fortschritt," *Reallexikon für Antike und Christentum*, 8 (1969), 141–61.

THOMAS COLE

[See also Atomism; **Culture and Civilization;** Historiography, Ancient Greek; Platonism; **Pre-Platonic Conceptions;** Progress in Antiquity; **Technology; Work.**]

CULTURE AND CIVILIZATION IN MODERN TIMES

Semantic Origins. Both "culture" and "civilization" derive their original meaning from Latin: from *cultura* which referred to the cultivation of the soil, and from *civis* which referred to the status of citizenship. In Latin, however, both words also acquired secondary meanings. Cicero, for example, used *cultura* in a transferred sense when he identified *cultura animi* ("culture of the soul") with philosophy or learning generally. *Civis* denoted not only the fact of Roman citizenship, but also its superiority over the primitive condition of the foreigner or barbarian. In each case the acquired as well as the literal meaning has lingered on into modern times, although the words "culture" and "civilization" themselves did not gain currency in European thought until the second half of the eighteenth century.

The inherited meanings were, however, soon joined by others. Indeed, even before the last decade of the eighteenth century, the proliferation of meanings led the German philosopher Johann Gottfried von Herder

613

to remark of "culture" that "nothing was more indeterminate than this word" (*Works*, Suphan ed., XIII, 4). Its extended usage in the subsequent period has not enhanced its clarity. "Nothing in the world," a twentieth-century writer, A. Lawrence Lowell, complains, "is more elusive. . . . An attempt to encompass its meaning in words is like trying to seize the air in the hand, when one finds that it is everywhere except within one's grasp" ("Culture," in *At War With Academic Traditions in America*, Cambridge, Mass. [1934], p. 115). Nonetheless, such attempts have been made. A recent survey of the concept, by A. L. Kroeber and Clyde Kluckhohn (*Culture*, 1952), brought no less than 164 definitions to light. Distinctions between "culture" and "civilization" have also been rather abundant.

In some cases man's spiritual development has been identified with culture, in others with civilization; the same is true of man's control over nature and his external social relations. Frequently man's moral development and the improvement of his material conditions or refinements of social manners have been viewed as opposing, rather than reinforcing, tendencies. Then again culture has been treated as a particular component or stage of civilization, a sort of subculture within a "superculture"; at other times culture has been considered the more generic term while civilization has been confined to the culture of cities. A distinction commonly made is in terms of modes of development, according to which civilization (defined as "techniques") is a continuous and cumulative process, susceptible to generalizing methods and capable of universal diffusion, whereas culture (defined as "creativity"), occurring sporadically, is not susceptible to these methods and not transferable.

On the other hand, a contemporary writer, Raymond Williams, in his *Culture and Society* (1958, p. 16), regards the concepts as sufficiently synonymous to warrant the attribution of four jointly applicable meanings: (1) a general state or habit of mind, having close relations with the idea of human perfection; (2) a general state of intellectual development in a society as a whole; (3) the general body of the arts; and (4) a whole way of life, material, intellectual, and spiritual. The first three meanings have come to be associated with what are called "humanistic" conceptions of culture, whereas the fourth meaning is usually associated with "anthropological" approaches. Humanistic conceptions are held to be selective, separating certain segments of man's activities from others, and designating them as cultural; anthropological conceptions are held to be nonselective, by applying "culture" to the total fabric of man's life in a given society, to his entire social heritage and whatever he may add to it. While anthropologists eschew value judgments for fear of

succumbing to ethnocentrism, humanists maintain the possibility, and indeed desirability, of evaluating diverse forms of human activity and human goals in the light of universal values which, they insist, are objectively ascertainable. Although there is agreement on the need to distinguish the cultural from the biological in human and social life, the fulcrum of opinion as to what is crucial and problematic differs between these two conceptions.

SPECULATIONS ON CULTURE AND CIVILIZATION

The last two hundred years have witnessed a sharpened interest in what causes men to do, believe, create, or destroy, and under what circumstances and influences; what has helped to sustain or threaten the preservation of their ideas, norms, values, symbols, manners and customs, institutions and artifacts; what degree of balance or tension has attended contemporaneous social configurations, or their chronological transformation through time (the "synchronic" and "diachronic" mode of culture in anthropological terminology). This growing preoccupation has been the cause and the symptom of what is meant by the historical and cultural self-consciousness of modern times. The chief practitioners in this search have been a hybrid species of historians *cum* philosophers, though some, M. J. de Condorcet, Auguste Comte, or Karl Marx, for example, might have preferred being thought of as social scientists. Frequently these thinkers were also social critics, no less eager to bring about change in the future than they were to trace it in the past. But notwithstanding divergences in orientation or method, they all derived inspiration from, or reacted to the challenge of the advances made in the physical sciences. The idea that the emergence, perpetuation, and development of human events were phenomena susceptible to discoverable principles was never far from their minds, even when they emphatically insisted that these principles were *sui generis* and attainable by methods radically different from those of the physical sciences.

Giambattista Vico (1668–1744), was one who indeed boldly declared that the cultural world of man, since it was created by man, was more likely to yield its secrets to human inquiry than the world of nature which only God, the sole creator of that world, can know with certainty. Explicitly or implicitly, this basic premise of Vico's *New Science* (*Scienza nuova*, 1725) became the bedrock of subsequent speculations about the genesis, content, and development of culture.

Ideas on the Genesis of Culture. When in his *New Science* (1744 ed., §331; trans. Bergin and Fisch) Vico claimed that "the world of nations, or civil world, which, since men had made it, men could come to know," he did not mean that man, as an individual, everywhere, and at all times, consciously made the institutions, symbols, and norms that characterize civil cultures or civilizations. The first steps in the building of the "world of nations" were, on the contrary, taken by creatures, the consequences of whose acts were not intended by them (ibid., §133). Thus religion, for example, came about "when men's intentions were quite otherwise, it brought them in the first place to fear of the divinity, the cult of which is the first fundamental basis of commonwealths" (ibid., §629). Unintended consequences, then, are clearly conceived of as integral to the emergence and development of social cultures. Vico concedes, indeed stresses, that men have finite minds, that they frequently do not know the outcome of their actions, yet he also insists that their intentions, their "wills" rest on consciousness, or *conscienza* (ibid., §137). There is no suggestion that men follow the dictates of some transcendent being or, as in the Third Proposition of Kant's "Idea of a Universal History" (*Idee zu einer allgemeinen Geschichte in Weltburgerlicher Absicht*, 1784), that they toil "for the sake of those who come after them," even without intending it. Men merely obey their own spirit and, in so doing, may or may not advance the cause of posterity (*New Science*, §§340, 376).

On the assumption, then, that men, being participants in and not only observers of their form of life or culture, can understand the working of human wills or purposes in a way they can never hope to understand the working of nonhuman phenomena, Vico proceeded to trace the origin of human cultures. Emphasizing that these cultures had "separate origins among the several peoples, each in ignorance of the others" (ibid., §146), he also sought to discover "in what institutions all men have perpetually agreed and still agree. For these institutions will be able to give us the universal and eternal principles (such as every science must have) on which all nations were founded and still preserve themselves" (ibid., §332). These primary institutions, without which culture would be inconceivable, Vico identified with religion and rituals of birth, marriage, and burial, events common to all cultures (ibid., §§330–37).

In effect, therefore, Vico advanced two theories of the genesis of culture. On the one hand he rejected cultural diffusion as an explanation for the emergence of a given culture in favor of a multiple-independent-origin theory. On the other hand he stipulated a common-origin theory, by viewing diverse manifestations of culture as "modifications" of certain archetypes "common to all nations," a proof for which he saw in "proverbs or maxims of vulgar wisdom, in which

substantially the same meanings find as many diverse expressions as there are nations ancient and modern." To observe the diversity of cultural manifestations and to uncover the "common mental language" underlying them was the task of philology which, for Vico, provided the essential empirical foundation upon which philosophy could erect its theoretical edifice (ibid., §§161–62).

Closest to Vico's thought is that of Herder. Inquiring into the genesis of culture Herder asks what characterizes man as a creature of culture as distinct from his biological existence as a creature of nature. In his first major philosophical work *On the Origin of Language* (*Über den Ursprung der Sprache*, 1772), Herder had refuted the idea of man as essentially a "rational animal," of reason as some sort of entity or "faculty" that was simply superimposed on man's animal nature. Man, he maintained, was *fundamentally* different from the animal. His capacity for speech, therefore, was a function of the *totality* of his powers, the manifestation of the "entire economy of his perceptive, cognitive, and volitional nature" (*Werke*, V, 28). By virtue of this wholly different direction of his energies man is no longer "an infallible mechanism in the hands of Nature." Although not endowed at birth with conscious self-awareness, he has the propensity to attain it, and thus, unlike the animal, he can attain a state of development in which by "mirroring himself within himself" he becomes a reflective being (ibid., V, 28, 95). Owing to this capacity for self-awareness man is acutely conscious of his imperfections and hence "always in motion, restless, and dissatisfied." Unlike the bee "which is perfect when building her first cell," man's life is characterized by "continuous becoming" (ibid., V, 98).

In addition to the capacity for reflection, Herder, like Vico before him, stresses man's sense of freedom. While the animal is wholly a creature of nature, and confined to that sphere of activity for which it is equipped by its natural instincts, man, not thus determined, is also a creature of freedom. His perfectibility or corruptibility is closely bound up with this distinguishing feature. "Man alone," Herder writes in his *Ideas for a Philosophy of History* (*Ideen zur Philosophie der Geschichte der Menschheit*, 1784–91), "has made a goddess of *choice* in place of *necessity* . . . , he can explore possibilities and choose between alternatives. . . . Even when he most despicably abuses his freedom, man is still king. For he can still choose, even though he chooses the worst" (ibid., XIII, 110, 146–47). Man's sense of imperfection and his sense of freedom, then, are posited as the essential (psychological) prerequisites for the emergence and development of human culture.

Herder's theme of self-consciousness was taken over by Hegel who made it the very condition of a people's sense of history, while the notion of restlessness reappeared in a more socially oriented form in Kant's essay on universal history. Kant identified men's "mutual antagonism in society" as the origin of "all the culture and art that adorn humanity" (op. cit., Fourth and Fifth Propositions).

But were man's imaginative, cognitive, and social propensities primary determinants, inherently self-generated and autonomous, or were they rather reactions, induced by and contingent upon the particular physical environment in which he found himself? This was the question with which Montesquieu essentially sought to come to grips. In his *De l'esprit des lois* (1748), he inquired into the nature and source of a "general spirit" within a given society. Fully aware of the interrelations between natural or physical and social or institutional elements, he seems on occasion quite undecided which to regard as the ultimate determinant, as in his hesitancy over the primacy of climate versus political constitutions, or in his vacillation concerning religion, which he alternately described as a determining and determined factor (Book XXIV, Ch. 3). However, the prevailing tenor of his account of the rise of civilizations was in terms of geographical and climatic determinants, echoes of which are still discernible in Arnold Toynbee's formula of challenge-and-response in his *A Study of History* (1934–61). Thus, when enumerating such culture-determining agents as religion, laws, maxims of government, mores, and manners, he mentioned these *after* climate (ibid., Book XIX, Ch. 4).

This emphasis on geo-climatic determinants has prompted commentators like R. G. Collingwood, in *The Idea of History* (1946, p. 79), to suggest that Montesquieu "in fact conceived human life as a reflection of geographical and climatic conditions, not otherwise than the life of plants." What lends support to this criticism was Montesquieu's basic assumption that human nature itself was a constant.

Like many Enlightenment thinkers Voltaire did not challenge this assumption, but he did question Montesquieu's emphasis on geo-climatic factors as the prime determinants of cultural differences. Not the physical facts of a given environment, Voltaire argued in his *Essai sur les moeurs et l'esprit des nations* (1769), but man's ingenuity in mastering these, constituted the root of civilization. If human life were a matter merely of biology, civilization would indeed be the same wherever natural conditions were alike. But "the realm of custom is much vaster than that of nature; it extends over manners and morals, over all habits; it gives variety to the scene of the universe" (*Oeuvres*, Paris [1877–85], Vol. XIII, Ch. 197). Therefore, it is not nature, Voltaire concluded, but "culture [which] pro-

duces diverse fruits" (ibid.). The crowning achievement of these diverse cultural endeavors, and the means of their perpetuation, Voltaire saw in the rise of great cities. In this close identification of culture with the emergence of cities he was, however, at odds not only with Montesquieu but with many subsequent writers, who viewed urban growth as a threat to the continuance of culture, if not as an unmistakable symptom of its decline.

Ideas on the Content of Culture. Broadly speaking, there are two distinguishable approaches: (1) those which essentially constitute a critique of modern civilization, stressing its cultural fragmentation, and (2) those which conceive of culture as an integral whole. At times both positions have been held concurrently, the critique of disunity being in fact a plea for unity.

(1) Culture versus Civilization. When Diderot, Rousseau, Herder, the romantics, or, more recently, Spengler, pointed up the contrast between the natural, organic, creative, genuine, on the one hand, and the artificial, mechanical, stereotyped, and superficial, on the other, between the nobility, deep-rootedness, freedom, and equality of the savage, or the contentment of medieval man, and the corruption, alienation, servility, and exploitation of modern man, the chief impetus was invariably polemical. That the apotheosis of primitive or medieval man was or was not supportable by anthropology or history was scarcely relevant. What mattered was to unmask the pretensions of contemporary civilization, to puncture the pride and complacency that went with it. Underlying the polemics was a craving for spontaneity, sincerity, and warm sensibility rather than cold rationality, the concrete rather than the abstract, and a recognition of the incomparability and immeasurability of things. Though Vico's ideas were seminal in a number of these directions, they were rarely known at first, and there can be little doubt that Diderot's influence was the most pervasive, soon to be followed by that of Rousseau and Herder.

Diderot's critique of contemporary society, centering on the self-estrangement of modern man, finds its most pungent articulation in his novel *Rameau's Nephew (Le Neveu de Rameau)* written in the 1760's but not published during his lifetime. The abject Rameau extols vice, but in doing so, uncovers the inversion and perversion of prevailing values. Rousseau's *Discourse on the Arts and Sciences (Discours sur les arts et sciences,* 1750), written some fifteen years earlier, though with Diderot's encouragement, also pursues the theme of alienation. Rousseau does not claim that human nature was intrinsically better before the advance of the arts and sciences, only that social life and mores were in closer harmony with it. Modern civilization imposed its pattern on men, unlike the original cultures which grew out of men's needs. What is more, modern civilization imposed a wholly uniform pattern, casting every mind in the same mold. "Politeness requires this, decorum that; ceremony has its set forms, fashion its laws, and these we must always follow, never the promptings of our own nature" (*Oeuvres*, Deterville ed., I, 10).

In the *Discourse on the Origin of Inequality* (*Discours sur l'origine de l'inégalité*, 1754) Rousseau assails, as Vico had done before him, the natural law theorists for mistaking the artificial for the original, for making man a philosopher before he is a man, and for giving the name of natural law to a collection of norms they happen to find expedient, thus rationalizing existing practices and institutions, in particular that of private property. Such natural laws may be in conformity with modern civilization, but they have nothing in common with original customs and traditions. Private property may indeed have ushered in the era of civilization, but what has it done to the traditional way of life of earlier cultures? "It now became the interest of men to appear what they really were not. To *be* and to *seem* became two completely different things." Men lost their sense of identity; they became estranged from themselves and from each other. In place of the bonds of organic community relations there arose "rivalry and competition on the one hand and conflicting interests on the other" (*Oeuvres*, I, 286).

Herder's indictment of his age was no less severe. Few documents constitute so devastating an attack on contemporary civilization as his *Yet Another Philosophy of History* (*Auch eine Philosophie der Geschichte*, 1774). With the incisiveness of a surgeon's knife it lays bare the sores of the eighteenth-century world. The so-called enlightenment and civilization have affected only a few in a narrow strip of the globe, and even where light has been shed, ominous shadows are never far afield. Civilization has forced people into mines, into treadmills, and into cities which are fast becoming slag-heaps of human vitality and energy. So much in the arts, in industry, in war and civil life has been mechanized that the *human* machine has lost its zest to function. Man is alienated from himself: head and heart are rent apart. The culture of the age is a paper culture, its ideals mere abstractions, instruments of self-deception (*Werke*, V, 532–41).

Much of what these critics had to say on the ills of eighteenth-century civilization in Europe, on alienation, acquisitiveness, colonialism, and so on, reverberates in subsequent sociopolitical writings; but nowhere is the parallelism of mood and terminology quite so striking as in Oswald Spengler's *Decline of the West* (*Der Untergang des Abendlandes*, 1918–23). For Spengler civilization marks the disintegration, the last dying phase of a culture. In his characterization of civilization one encounters practically every one of the themes just traced. The basic source of cultural decline Spengler sees in the giant city, the "megalopolis," as he calls it. Its society is not a community but a "mass," leading a sort of nomadic, parasitic life, devoid of past or future. Rootless, restless, traditionless, it is constantly on the move, knowing neither whither nor why. In the end the city—and with it civilization—proves the negation of the negation, the seed of its own destruction (I, 31–34, 424; II, 310; trans. C. F. Atkinson, New York [1926–28]).

For writers such as Kant, Coleridge, and Matthew Arnold, culture represents essentially the moral condition of the individual, while civilization means the conventions of society. Invariably the former is also associated with "spiritual" values, the latter with "material" values. Remarking that Rousseau was not so far wrong when he preferred the state of the savages, Kant adds (in the Seventh Proposition of the "Idea of a Universal History") that though we are civilized, "even to excess in the way of all sorts of social forms of politeness and elegance . . . there is still much to be done before we can be regarded as moralized." External propriety merely constitutes civilization; only the idea of morality "belongs to real culture." This distinction, and to some extent the skepticism about the value of civilization, became quite common in nineteenth-century English writing, largely owing to the influence of Samuel Taylor Coleridge, an ardent disciple of Kant. "Civilization," Coleridge writes in *On the Constitution of Church and State* (1830, Ch. V):

. . . is itself but a mixed good, if not far more a corrupting influence, the hectic of disease, not the blossom of health, and a nation so distinguished more fitly to be called a varnished than a polished people, where civilization is not grounded in cultivation, in the harmonious development of those qualities and faculties that characterize our humanity.

Matthew Arnold, another leading advocate of culture in terms of moral self-perfection, interestingly anticipated in his *Culture and Anarchy* (1869) C. P. Snow's theme of the "two cultures." Culture is first and foremost moral improvement and not "merely or primarily [the perfection] of the scientific passion for pure knowledge" (Ch. 1). Toynbee, by contrast, generally understood by civilization the highest development of social cultures from their primitive origins (op. cit., I, 438).

None of these distinctions, however, has found resonance in the writings of modern cultural anthropologists, the first leading exponent of whom was E. B. Tylor. In his *Primitive Culture* (1871, p. 1) he defined 617 culture as "that complex whole which includes knowledge, belief, art, law, morals, custom, and any other capabilities and habits acquired by man as a member of society." This holistic conception was, however, not entirely novel; it had its intellectual antecedents from Vico to Herder and beyond.

(2) Culture as an Integral Whole. Vico's ideas prove highly original in this direction also. Both his multiple-independent-origin theory and his theory of cyclical development clearly indicate that he thought of cultures in terms of wholes or configurations. At each stage of its development a given culture represents a complex of interrelated and interdependent constituents, each of which shares with the others certain distinctive characteristics. "As from a trunk, there branch out from one limb logic, morals, economics, and politics," Vico wrote in the *New Science* (§367). Diderot, in *D'Alembert's Dream* (*Le Rêve de D'Alembert*, 1769), employed the image of a swarm of bees in order to give expression to this notion of organic unity, i.e., to the idea that a whole is qualitatively unique and different from a mere aggregate of individual parts. The conception of a whole as a *complex* whole characterizes also Voltaire's epoch-making contribution to the study of culture, the *Essai sur les moeurs*. Civilization, for Voltaire, is a totality forged by men in their social life and actions. Few thinkers before or after him penetrated more profoundly into the "spirit of the time," a concept he was the first to express; yet only rarely did he succeed in transcending the values of his own times. While he strongly emphasized the need for a harmonious balance of diverse human aspirations, his criterion for what constituted a proper balance was highly culture-bound, a fact which the young Herder was not slow in observing. Why, Herder asked in *Yet Another Philosophy,* should we take for granted that the beliefs of past ages were the same as ours, their standard of happiness identical to our own? "Has not each man, each nation, each period, the center of happiness within itself, just as every sphere has its center of gravity?" (*Werke*, V, 509).

Though Herder's thought owed much to Voltaire, it marks an important departure from Voltaire's cultural monism. Herder felt it would be more accurate to speak of specific cultures—in the plural—rather than of culture in general. There is no such thing, Herder further declared, as a people devoid of culture. To be sure, there are differences, but these are differences of degree, not of kind. To apply the standard of European culture as a standard for comparison, let alone as a universal yardstick of human values, is plainly meaningless. Each culture carries within itself its own immanent validity, and hence we have to think of the world as being composed of uniquely different socio-cultural entities, each with its own pattern of development, its own inner dynamic growth.

Although Herder was mainly concerned with eliciting sources of integration within a given culture, he recognized that there were subcultures that could exercise a divisive no less than a unifying influence. "A nation," he writes, "may have the most sublime virtues in some respects and blemishes in others . . . and reveal the most astonishing contradictions and incongruities" (ibid., V, 506). To speak, therefore, of a cultural whole is not necessarily a way of referring to a state of blissful harmony; it may just as conceivably refer to a field of tension. In contrast to those who identified culture with spiritual pursuits, and civilization with material progress, Herder rejected the dualism between "material" and "non-material" activity. Artifacts are as much part of culture as ideas, beliefs, and values. Culture comprises all of man's creative activities, both what he *does* and what he *thinks*. Of particular concern to Herder were culture determinants that help to produce a sense of collective identity, and these he identified chiefly with language, shared symbols and values, customs and norms of reciprocity. Physical environmental factors he considered of secondary importance, capable of "only influencing, favorably or unfavorably, but not of compelling a given course of development," as he put it in the *Ideas* (ibid., XIII, 273). It is interesting, both from the point of view of modern anthropology and also against the historical background of the "age of reason" to find that Herder saw in nonrational elements significant molding agents of social cultures. Neither myths nor prejudices are dismissed by him as irrelevant aberrations. Furthermore, unlike subsequent thinkers, Marxists in particular, Herder did not view ideas and beliefs as epiphenomenal, as mere superstructures. Certain myths or religious doctrines, he agreed, may indeed be intimately associated with economic and political institutions and practices; but this does not prove anything about their respective origins or significance, nor does it deny their essential autonomy. By the same token, whatever "functions" either of them may be said to perform within a given "system" proves nothing about their necessary or even sufficient conditions or interrelationships. Myths and religions may or may not serve the function of maintaining authoritarian (religious and/or political) structures, but this is not tantamount to saying that such structures would necessarily disappear with the disappearance of myths and religions (or vice versa), or that shamans, priests, or dictators invented certain beliefs, or invariably used them to deceive others without accepting them themselves. "By dismissing them as cheats," Herder observes in the *Ideas* (ibid., XIII, 307), "one is inclined to think that one has explained everything. They may well have been cheats in many or most places, but this should not induce us to forget that they were people too, and the dupes of myths older than themselves."

Herder's historical relativism and cultural pluralism affected, directly or indirectly, the thinking of J. G. Fichte, Friedrich Schlegel and Hegel, the historical law school of Savigny, the political romantics, J. S. Mill, and the writing of cultural history up to Spengler, T. S. Eliot, and Toynbee. Nor has Herder's anatomy of culture lost relevance for modern sociology and anthropology. In particular it demonstrates that situational-functional analysis, taken by itself, is inadequate as an explanatory tool if what we seek in terms of explanation is evaluation of content and/or determination of purpose, and that, therefore, functionalism can scarcely dispense with process analysis. Thus, far from being inconsistent, functional and historical approaches are indeed complementary or interdependent. Furthermore, Herder's heuristic principle of treating every manifestation of culture as essentially autonomous, though interrelated in the two-dimensional sense indicated, also implies that the applicable mode of causality is that of multiple causation. Both the idea of two-dimensional interaction and the idea of multiple causation have come to be recognized as potentially fruitful perspectives or conceptual aids in the study of social cultures.

Ideas on the Development of Culture. As a result of eighteenth-century progressivism and nineteenth-century evolutionism the very notion of "development" has become culture-impregnated. It has assumed the status of an absolute, a universal value, a symbol of modernity and, as such, a conscious goal or ideal in a growing number of social cultures. Ideas *on* the development of culture are, therefore, in a real sense, also ideas *of* the development of culture.

Apart from the assumption of continuous improvement (intimately associated with unilinear ideas on progress), three other assumptions commonly underlie the notion of cultural development. First, there is the belief that despite discontinuities there is a substantial degree of continuity between phases or stages of a given culture, although writers differ regarding the individual significance and the mutual linkage of such stages. Secondly, there is a widely shared consensus that striving towards ends is implicit in the notion of human or cultural development, even if it is frequently not clear whether a thinker is discussing teleology *in* history or the teleology *of* history, or both. Lastly, there is the assumption that culture constitutes not a "thing," but a relational continuum in and through time, so that culture is both a product of the past and a creator of the future.

It is evident from these assumptions, particularly the last, that the notion of cultural development raises the problem not only of change but also of persistence. Generally speaking, writers employing the organismic paradigm of growth—and these tend to coincide with the "holists"—have acknowledged the significance of persistence. Civilization, Edmund Burke, for example, insisted in his *Reflections on the Revolution in France* (1790), was chiefly a matter of past achievements over the ages (*Works*, London [1899], II, 351). The political romantics, likewise, preferred to cast their gaze backwards rather than forwards.

The prevalent orientation, however, was forward-looking or progressivist, even among those who traced cyclical or dialectic patterns in development. Vico, for example, envisaged the course of development in terms of recurrent cycles, with each cycle comprising three ages, of gods, heroes, and men, dominated by religion, myth, and philosophy, respectively, and reappearing, not in identical form, but in a "diversity of modes" as an upward-spiralling movement (*New Science*, §1096). Kant, Hegel, and Marx insisted in their different ways on dialectic rather than unilinear change, but at the same time saw each stage subservient to the next, inexorably leading to a predetermined end. Even Herder, the most outspoken opponent of the idea of linear progress, never concealed his faith in secular redemption as the terminal goal of the historical process. Curiously enough, the man who set the tone of the progressivist era, Voltaire, was no sanguine progressivist himself. It is true that the distant past was for him an age of darkness or semidarkness, yet he expressed no inordinate trust in the future as the harbinger of apocalyptic portents. Acutely conscious of the debits that accompanied the credits in the ledger of history, "later" did not self-evidently mean "better" for him. In comparing his own age with that of Louis XIV, for example, he left no doubt about his preference for the latter. It would seem, therefore, that it was Voltaire's contempt for the more remote past, in particular the Middle Ages, rather than his faith in continuous progress which cast him into the mold in which others came to see him.

But if the origin of the idea of uninterrupted cultural progress has somewhat erroneously been associated with Voltaire, its culmination is rightly identified with Condorcet's *Sketch for a Historical Picture of the Progress of the Human Mind* (*Esquisse d'un tableau historique des progrès de l'esprit humain*, 1794), which expressed unbounded optimism in man's progressively mounting capacity to understand and hence to control the "laws" of his own development. For Condorcet, no less than for Thomas Paine and Thomas Jefferson after him, the "march of civilization" was continuous.

619

Barbarism was bound to recede before the advance and diffusion of knowledge and the emergence of a new social and political ethic. Scientific procedures would liberate man from the excess baggage of the past While for Vico and Herder religion and myth were vital ingredients of culture, Condorcet dismissed them summarily as the work of cheats and scoundrels. And in contrast to their skepticism towards cultural diffusion, Condorcet displayed complete confidence in the transferability of cultures from more to less developed countries, maintaining indeed that the latter would, after importing the "know-how," actually overtake the former, whenever they were able to avoid their mistakes. For Condorcet cultural development consisted essentially in technological and scientific advance, and his *Sketch* surveyed the history of man's intellectual achievements, divided into ten stages of scientific and technologically based progress. Arriving at his own age he felt that "philosophy has nothing more to guess, no more hypothetical surmises to make; it is enough to assemble and order the facts and to show the useful truths that can be derived from their connection and from their totality" (Introduction, trans. June Barraclough).

Condorcet's faith in strict empiricism and scientific procedures profoundly inspired Auguste Comte's *Cours de philosophie positive* (1830–42). In it Comte sought to establish universal historical laws, the most fundamental of which stipulates three phases through which all human societies must pass, the theological, metaphysical, and positive. Of considerable interest is Comte's analysis of cultural development in terms of social statics and social dynamics, in that it emphasizes the two-dimensional nature of interaction to which Herder had drawn attention. Social statics seeks to study the interconnections and functions of cultural components within a cultural whole at a given time, while social dynamics focuses on the vertical interrelations and changes over time. Comte's demand that sociocultural development should be studied in a manner analogous to that applicable to causal uniformities in the realm of nature did not fall on deaf ears.

Two influential works that appeared in close succession, Henry Thomas Buckle's *History of Civilization in England* (1857) and Karl Marx's *A Contribution to the Critique of Political Economy* (1859) attempted to pay heed to Comte's insistence on inductive inquiry. Buckle sought to demonstrate that "the actions of men being determined solely by their antecedents, must have a character of uniformity, that is to say, must, under precisely the same circumstances, always issue in precisely the same results" (Buckle, Vol. I, Ch. 1). Like Comte, he was convinced of the superiority of European (and particularly English) culture and the

derivability of universal laws from its study. Marx also generally wrote as if he regarded historical tendencies to be akin to the operation of natural laws, having universal applicability and "working out," as he put it in the Preface of the first edition of *Das Kapital* (1867), "with iron necessity towards an inexorable destination," so that the laws of development operating in industrially advanced countries "simply present the other countries with a picture of their own future development." The most succinct statement of Marx's views on cultural development is in the Preface to *A Contribution to the Critique of Political Economy* (*Zur Kritik der politischen Oekonomie*), according to which "the sum total of the relations of production constitutes the economic structure of society—the real foundation, on which rise legal and political superstructures and to which correspond definite forms of social consciousness." In addition to his descriptive theory of sociocultural development Marx advanced a prescriptive doctrine intended to meet the problem of alienation, on which he had focused in his earliest writings and in particular in *The German Ideology* (*Die Deutsche Ideologie*, 1846, with Engels). The theme of alienation links Marx most intimately with the romantics, but whereas Marx sought the cure of man's alienation in the future, the romantics reverted to the past, finding that man had taken the wrong turn by seeking liberation from a traditional order of society.

Among attempts to reconcile traditionalism with progressivism, or persistence with change, Herder's treatment of *Bildung* and *Tradition* is undoubtedly the most original contribution which still has lost none of its relevance. Both these terms were used by him in their original dynamic sense of "becoming" or "building up" and of "passing on," respectively, and not in their better-known acquired sense. Thus *Bildung* is not equated with a particular *state* of development or confined in its connotation to intellectual or strictly individual pursuits. Instead it is viewed as an interactive social process in which men receive from and add to their distinctive cultural heritage. The modern concept of "socialization" comes, perhaps, closest to Herder's interpretation of *Bildung*.

It is also of interest that Herder conferred upon *Bildung* a distinctly dialectic meaning by identifying it with evaluation as well as assimilation (*Werke*, XIII, 343–48). Thus understood, it is not simply a replicative process but also a process of change. Indeed, Herder saw in *Bildung* the only alternative to sociocultural discontinuities attending the replacement of values through their destruction rather than their transformation. But he was aware that the merging of the old and the new involves in its operation both affirmative and negative properties, and that change is not tantamount to a smooth advance or progress. Every discovery in the arts and sciences, he wrote in the *Ideas*, knits a new pattern of society. New situations create new problems, and every increase in wants (even if they are satisfied) does not necessarily augment human happiness (ibid., XIII, 372–73).

Tradition, likewise, is not identified with a *stock* of accumulated beliefs, customs, and ways of doing things, but with an ongoing process of intergenerational transmission. *Bildung* and *Tradition* entail culture as both a product and an emergent force at any given time, insofar as *Bildung* leads to shared patterns or forms of life that have become "patterns" by virtue of a greater or lesser degree of institutionalization through *Tradition*. Although Herder opposed the idea of linear progress, he nonetheless refused to view stages of development in a dichotomous manner. Hence, in place of the idea of polarity he advanced the idea of *interplay*. Tradition and progress no longer embody two opposed tendencies, but a single continuum. Progress, or more precisely change, becomes a built-in characteristic of tradition, and development is seen, therefore, as at once part of a given culture continuum *and* the instrument for its transformation. It requires not only historical antecedents but also emerging goals pointing to the future. What is also worth noting is that, while Herder admitted conflict and tension as potentially inherent in the processes of *Bildung* and *Tradition*, he categorically denied the possibility of *complete* discontinuity within any given culture. In this he revealed considerable astuteness. For it is difficult to see how one can speak of "development" in terms of complete or total change without raising serious problems of identity. Finally, Herder's analysis of socialization as a nonreplicative process and his interpretation of tradition as a dialectic continuum clearly suggest that any attempt to explain change must entail a recognition of persistence or vice versa. A theory which cannot account for both is therefore unlikely to account for either.

BIBLIOGRAPHY

Translations of Kant, Herder, Voltaire, Rousseau, and Marx are by F. M. Barnard.

Philip Bagby, *Culture and History* (Berkeley and Los Angeles, 1959). F. M. Barnard, "Culture and Political Development," *American Political Science Review*, **63** (1969), 379–97. William R. Dennes, ed., *Civilization* (Berkeley and Los Angeles, 1959). T. S. Eliot, *Notes Towards a Definition of Culture* (London, 1948). L. Febvre, ed., *Civilisation: Le mot et l'idée* (Paris, 1930). Patrick Gardiner, ed., *Theories of History* (Glencoe, Ill., 1959). Johann Gottfried von Herder, *Sämtliche Werke*, ed. Bernard Suphan, 33 vols. (Berlin, 1877–1913). Gertrude Jaeger and Philip Selznick, "A Normative Theory of Culture," *American Sociological Review*, **29** (1964), 653–69. A. L. Kroeber and Clyde Kluckhohn, *Culture* (Cambridge, Mass., 1952), contains a detailed bibliography. Karl Mannheim, *Essays on the Sociology of Culture* (London, 1956). Bruce Mazlish, *The Riddle of History: The Great Speculators from Vico to Freud* (New York and London, 1966). Wolfgang Schmidt-Hidding, ed., *Kultur und Zivilisation* (Munich, 1967), includes extensive bibliographies. Giambattista Vico, *Scienza nuova* (1725), trans. H. Bergin and M. Fisch as *The New Science* (Ithaca, 1948; 1963). Alfred Weber, *Kulturgeschichte als Kultursoziologie* (Leiden, 1935). Karl J. Weintraub, *Visions of Culture* (Chicago and London, 1966). Raymond Williams, *Culture and Society: 1780–1950* (London, 1958).

FREDERICK M. BARNARD

[See also **Cultural Development; Environment and Culture;** Hegelian . . .; Marxism; Positivism in Europe to 1900; *Volksgeist; Zeitgeist.*]

CYCLES

THE CYCLICAL Theory of History is a doctrine that all events occur in cycles that are more or less alike. It has two main forms, one that posits cosmic cycles and one that posits cycles only in human affairs. Though the second of these concepts is logically independent of the first, it is sometimes found in company with it. One must also distinguish those thinkers, like Plato and Aristotle, who believed in periodic cataclysms and beginnings, from those, like the Stoics, who believed in the return of identical events. The doctrine in some of its forms is found in ancient India, in Babylonia, and in Greece.

I. COSMIC CYCLES

The notion of the rhythmical recurrence of cosmic events may well have developed out of the characteristics of the solar year, the periodicity of the lunar phases, the round of the seasons in regular order, the life cycle of the individual human being. That the idea of birth, maturation, senility, and death followed by rebirth interested the ancients is shown by the many myths and rites in which this series of events is figured. We no longer possess the documents which might have provided the evidence on which the concept was based, assuming that such documents ever existed, but there are certain hints from early intellectual history which suggest an answer. The observation of astronomical rhythms goes back to Babylonian times; the Pythagoreans as early as the sixth century B.C. had speculated on numerical repetitions such as are found in decimal fractions; in India various theories about ages, periods, recurrences were elaborated; and the early Greek philosophers in general were given to mentioning cyclical changes in the transmutations of the four elements: earth, water, air, and fire. In many of the thinkers who believed in cosmic cycles one also finds traces or definite assertions of the transmigration of souls.

1. *India.* In India the doctrine appears in the form of the four *yugas*, or ages, which make up the *mahâyuga* (Great Year), a period lasting for 4,320,000 solar years. Each of the *yugas* differs from its predecessor much as the Ages of Hesiod did, in that wickedness and general evil grow greater. The last *yuga* in the series is our own, and will come to an end with a great conflagration followed by a deluge. Between each two ages there is a twilight and a dawn lasting for one tenth of the duration of the preceding or following age. By the time the fourth age, the *Kaliyuga*, has come to an end, the world is made ready for the beginning of a new Great Year. But Indian imagination was such that the Great Years themselves were organized into groups of a thousand, called *kalpas*, a concept which was introduced at the time of the Emperor Asoka, in the third century B.C. It should be observed that the *yugas* varied in length: the first, the *Satyayuga*, corresponding to the Golden Age in Greek mythology, was the longest; the *Kaliyuga*, which began on 18 February 3102 B.C. will be the shortest. It is interesting that the four *yugas* have some of the characteristics of the human life-cycle in that the capacity for committing evils enters after childhood and increases until old age.

2. *Greece and Rome.* In Greece a distinction must be made between those philosophers who believed in cycles and those who believed that each cycle repeated the characteristics of its predecessor, or what was called by Friedrich Nietzsche the Eternal Recurrence. Among the latter was Empedocles (fifth century B.C.), but even he, as far as the evidence goes, did not say that every event was endlessly repeated. Yet Empedocles did assert that the general course of each cycle was repeated in its successor and he also seemed to believe in the transmigration of souls. The course of cosmic history ran from a period when the force of Love was in command, a time very like the Golden Age or the Age of Kronos. This was followed by the entrance of Strife upon the scene, to be followed in turn by the predominance of Strife, apparently the worst of times. But when Strife was uppermost it began to give way again to Love, and finally Love returned to take over the management of the universe. The rhythm was endless.

None of the Greek philosophers believed that the cosmos had a beginning in time; that idea entered the Western world with Judaism and Christianity. In contrast to the mythographers, the philosophers all believed the world to be everlasting, though the present condition of the world might come to an end. Even Plato in his *Timaeus*, which was later used as a creation myth, held that the matter out of which the world was made was everlasting, and for him the work of creation was the forming of this preexisting matter into a cosmos. If then the world was endless in its duration, there were either no changes in it at all, or the changes must have occurred in random or orderly fashion. The Greek philosophers, like their modern successors, were unwilling to accept a chaotic world and indeed some changes were so obvious that they could hardly escape the notice of a normal man. Among such were the familiar examples of birth and death, the apparent disappearance of matter when it is burned or dissolved in water, the freezing and melting of liquids and solids, sickness, growth, decay, the processes of digestion, and the chemical changes involved in metallurgy. It was one of the intellectual achievements of the early Greek philosophers to attribute all such changes to various phases of one or more of what were later to be called the "elements."

By the time of Heraclitus (early fifth century B.C.) three and possibly four of the elements were already distinguished: fire, air, and water. This might seem to be a great reduction in itself of complexity to simplicity, but Heraclitus went further. We find him saying in one of his fragments, "Fire lives the death of air, and air lives the death of fire; water lives the death of earth, earth that of water." There are justifiable grounds for doubts about the authenticity of the details in this series of changes, but that the author believed in a general pattern of elemental transmutations is clear. This pattern becomes even clearer in Aristotle and the changes occur in definitely described manners. Fire changes to air by losing its heat and earth changes to water by losing its dryness. But Aristotle does not say that at one time the cosmos was entirely composed of one of the four elements and then produced the others step by step, after which they all eventually returned to their primitive material unity. The changes occur as the sun moves along the ecliptic and to that extent there is a cosmic cycle in Aristotle's thinking. Each year brings about the same series of elemental changes but the whole never changes as a unit.

The Stoics are responsible for the clearest theory of cosmic cycles, though they attributed the source of the idea to Heraclitus. According to Stoicism there would occur at a given time a general conflagration, the *ekpyrosis*, after which the world would begin again as it was in the distant past. The cycle as a whole was called by Cicero the Great Year (*Annus Magnus*). Its length was variously calculated, now being 18,000 solar years, now 10,800. But that it was the year of all years is clear enough. What was desired was the length of time which it would take for the heavenly bodies to return to the position that they had held at a defined time, thought of as a beginning.

One of the founders of Stoicism, Cleanthes (early third Century B.C.), is said to have described the *ekpyrosis* as a process of death and growth. The fire burns up all things but is followed by a period of moisture in which the "seeds" of everything remain. These seeds begin to grow again at the proper time and eventually the cosmos is restored to what it was. The seeds in question were called the spermatic *logoi* or perhaps "principles," (for only a vague word can name them), which are material but probably as everlasting as fire itself. Mysterious as the doctrine is, the world turns out to be self-destructive and self-regenerative, like the phoenix which may indeed be a symbol of the process.

According to Cicero one of the later Stoics, Panaetius (second century B.C.), did not accept the doctrine of the *ekpyrosis*. But in spite of Cicero's well-known admiration for Panaetius, he himself did accept it. He describes it in his treatise *On the Nature of the Gods* (Book II, 46): "There will ultimately occur a conflagration of the whole world, because when the moisture has been used up neither can the earth be nourished nor will the air continue to flow, being unable to rise after it has drunk up all the water; thus nothing will remain but fire, by which, as a living being and a god, once again a new world may be created and the ordered universe restored as before." The process is based on sensory observation. Moisture, i.e., water, is dried up by fire; the air, which normally is found between the level of fire and that of water, is exhausted by the combustion, and thus fire alone is left. What happens to earth is not revealed. But by the time of Cicero Greek science was either the collection of data, such as are found in Pliny and Seneca, or it had turned to mathematics, astronomy, and geography. One finds little scientific clarity in the philosophers.

The other pagan witnesses to the Stoic belief in the *ekpyrosis* and the renewal of the world are Seneca, Diogenes Laërtius, and Plutarch. But they add little in the way of detail, and for the most part we are forced to rely on Christian writers who referred to the process in order to combat the ideas on which it was based or its supposed implications. It is they who tell us that the details of a given age will be repeated identically in later ages. Tatian (second century A.D.), for instance, in his *Adversus Graecos* says, "Zeno [the founder of Stoicism] has shown that after the *ekpyrosis* . . . men will be resurrected as they were. And I say that this must imply that Anytus and Meletus will again

bring their accusation [against Socrates] and Busiris slay the Strangers, and Hercules perform his labors." It is Tatian clearly who draws this inference, though Eudemus, a pupil of Aristotle, had attributed the same belief to "the Pythagoreans." In fact the accusation and trial of Socrates became a favorite example of what the eternal recurrence involved.

Yet Vergil in his *Fourth Eclogue* also plays on the theme and mentions specific events and individuals that will reappear in the new age which is to come. In our own time Shelley in the final chorus of his dramatic poem, *Hellas*, imitated Vergil, verbally in places; and a less important literary figure, George Moore, the Irish novelist, in his story "Resurgam," depicts the destruction of the world and its restoration in some detail.

3. *The Christian Fathers.* There were two basic reasons why the Christian apologists tried to refute the doctrine of cosmic cycles. First, it seemed to contradict the essential Christian dogma of free will, for if everything recurs in the same manner *ad indefinitum* and if the same identical persons commit the same deeds, then all choice is eliminated. This was the position of Origen. Since his statement in *De principiis* is clear, it may be well to quote it in full.

The disciples of Pythagoras, and of Plato, although they appear to hold the incorruptibility of the world, yet fall into similar errors. For as the planets, after certain definite cycles, assume the same relations to one another, all things on earth will, they assert, be like what they were at the time when the same state of planetary relations existed in the world. From this point of view it necessarily follows that when, after the lapse of a lengthened cycle, the planets come to occupy towards each other the same relations which they occupied in the time of Socrates, Socrates will again be born of the same parents, suffer the same treatment, being accused by Anytus and Meletus, and condemned by the Council of the Areopagus. . . . We who maintain that all things are administered by God in proportion to the relation of free will of each individual, and are ever being brought into better condition, so far as they admit of being so, and who know that the nature of our free will admits of the occurrence of contingent events . . . yet we, it appears, say nothing worthy of being tested and examined.

But, he goes on to say, we do believe in the resurrection of the body. In view of Origen's mistaken idea of Plato's views, it is probable that he did not understand what the Stoics said either, and we quote his words not as testimony to what any Platonist, Stoic, or Pythagorean actually said, but as testimony to current opinion among the Fathers.

One of the difficulties that the Church Fathers faced is the verse in Ecclesiastes which says that there is nothing new under the sun. Where Stoicism was held to imply the recurrence of individuals, this verse was interpreted as implying only the steady occurrence of the same kinds of things. Saint Augustine in his *City of God* (Book XII, Ch. 13) takes this up and replies that it does not imply the total recurrence of the past, but speaks simply of the course of generations, solar phenomena, floods—in short, of the coming into being and the passing away of kinds of things. It does not mean, he says, that the philosopher Plato, who in a certain century in Athens in a school called the Academy, formed of his pupils, must reappear in the future during an infinity of centuries in the same city, in the same school, before the same public, and teach the same lessons. For otherwise, and this is the second objection that the Christian apologists had to the doctrine of cosmic cycles, it would mean that Christ would have to be born again, crucified again, resurrected again. And this thought is repugnant to Saint Augustine. He knows that Christ died once for our sins and furthermore that His resurrection has freed mankind from death forever. The world will last for six thousand years and then be destroyed, but its destruction will not be followed by its resurgence.

The doctrine of cosmic cycles plus that of the eternal recurrence was dropped by Christian writers, though their continued exposition of it and arguments against it must imply that it had a certain popularity among the laity. It was revived again by Friedrich Nietzsche in the nineteenth century, but his arguments in support of the idea were different from those of the Stoics, as far as we have the latter. The idea seems to have come to him while resting after a walk from Sils-Maria to Silvaplana. He thought that since there is no end to time, and presumably only a finite number of possible events and things, everything now existing must recur. The obvious basis of this argument is that any calculable probability must happen in infinite time. Nietzsche took the reasoning seriously and contemplated writing a book (for which only notes remain) to be called *The Eternal Recurrence*. In *Thus Spake Zarathustra* (par. 270–71) we find the Superman saying:

The plexus of causes returneth in which I am intertwined,—it will again create me! I myself pertain to the causes of the eternal return.

I will come again with this sun, with this earth, with this eagle, with this serpent—*not* to a new life, or a better life, or a similar life: I come again eternally to this identical and selfsame life, in its greatest and its smallest, to teach again the eternal return of all things,—to speak again the word of the great noontide of earth and man, to announce again to man the Superman.

In the notes for *The Eternal Recurrence* he extends the reasoning to this end. The extent of universal energy, he says, is finite. Since all events are the result of changes based on the expenditure of energy, the number of kinds of things is finite. Since the duration of time is infinite, has already lasted for an infinite series of moments and will continue to exist for another infinite series of moments, all possibilities must have been already realized and the future will inevitably repeat the past. It is perhaps unnecessary to point out that at most this argument would imply the recurrence of kinds of things, something that every man has observed in his daily life. This is very different from the recurrence of identical individuals. But Nietzsche had been a professor of classical philology and, though he may have forgotten his Stoic forebears, he was repeating their conclusions if not their reasoning.

The importance of the argument for him was its supposed ethical implications. To accept to the full the eternal recurrence meant for him to live "beyond good and evil." Good and evil could be relevant within the context of a given cycle, but had no transcendent importance. Believers in Judaism and Christianity, however, had grown up in the belief that good and evil were standards laid down by God eternally, not for now and here. And since Nietzsche above all wanted to liberate his reader from what he called the slave-morality of the Judeo-Christian tradition, he perceived an escape in this idea of eternal recurrence.

II. CYCLES IN HUMAN AFFAIRS

1. Plato. That the cosmos itself goes through a series of changes is clearly stated by Plato in the *Statesman* (269D). During one period, he says, God accompanies the course of the world but "when the periods have run the measure of time allotted to it by him, he leaves it, and automatically it moves in the opposite direction, for it is a living creature endowed with thought by him who constituted it in the beginning." As in the *Timaeus*, God organized the world; He did not create it. Its history has two periods, one in which God is its guide and one in which it changes its course and moves under its own power. The reason for the reversal is its corporeal nature. Only the incorporeal has the power of remaining unchanged. Hence when the world is left to itself, it can only reverse its direction and this happens "through myriads of times." The change of direction entails a "very great destruction of all animals," and only a few humans are left alive. After this, history is just the reverse of what we are used to. The living grow younger and finally disappear and a new race is born of the earth. All this is related by Plato in the form of a myth, but it was a myth more or less harmonious with Greek folklore, and the birth of the postdiluvian race from stones. The occurrence of catastrophes in the past which annihilated almost all life was not an uncommon belief. One finds a similar story in Ovid's account of the Deluge in his *Metamorphoses* (Book I).

Plato's account of such catastrophes is given in *Timaeus* (22C) where he tells the story of Solon's meeting with an Egyptian priest who says: "There have been and will be many and diverse destructions of men. The greatest by fire and water, and the lesser by thousands of other means." When a flood occurs, only those who live on mountain tops are saved, but those who live in cities are borne into the sea by the rushing waters. Happily Egypt is preserved for it has no high mountains from which torrents can descend; its waters well up from below. But in other parts of the world the celestial waters pour down and drown all but the "illiterate and uncultured," who naturally have no memory of what has transpired in ancient times. That is why the Greeks speak of one flood, whereas there have been several. A similar account of cataclysms is given in *Critias* (111B) and in *The Laws* (677). The latter version also includes the story of man's progress after the Deluge. The main difference between this version and that given in the *Statesman* is that the race whose history begins the new period is not earth-born but descends from those few shepherds who lived on the hills.

The details of these stories are fanciful but it is likely that the principal fact of multiple cataclysms was taken seriously by Plato. For he had no conception of the "infinite perfectibility of mankind," such as was entertained by Condorcet and others in the eighteenth century. He knew that any change this side of Heaven must come to an end. But since there was no logically deducible end for human affairs, and since they could not continue unchanged forever, the best way to explain their cessation was by a conflagration, a deluge, or a plague. Such catastrophes could in turn be explained by a myth and that myth we have seen in our previous reference to the *Statesman*. Put in its barest terms, Plato's view is that all history is advance and retrogression. These occur in cycles. But only the most prominent features of them are repeated, not the details; and, if we are to believe Solon's Egyptian priest, the calamity varies in its severity, Egypt being specially favored. It is clear that none of this anticipates the notion of the Great Year.

2. Aristotle. The general idea of cyclical history is repeated by Aristotle, but only in passing, as if it was so generally accepted that it needed no support. He flatly says in the *Metaphysics* (1074b. 11) that the arts and sciences have been lost and regained many times; in the *Politics* (1264a. 1) that all ideas of any value have already been discovered and tried; and in *De caelo* (270b. 19) that the same doctrines have been discovered innumerable times. But he gives no account of how

and why men lost their acquired knowledge, no story of cataclysmic destruction of races or nations. Nor does he attempt to connect the periodic recurrence of ideas with any set of cosmic cycles. In the *Meteorologica* (352a. 32) he does mention Deucalion's Deluge, but limits its extent to the Greek world, though later (352b–353a) he speaks of geological changes as occurring at all times, but not in identical cycles. In the *Politics* (1269a. 3) he accepts the theory of cataclysms as possibly true and that of primitive men as either born of the earth or survivors from some catastrophe. In the Pseudo-Aristotelian *Problemata* (910a. 35) the Deluge is again mentioned. Aristotle apparently dealt with periodic catastrophes in his lost work *On Philosophy* (frag. 8) in which he also described the rebirth of civilization after the Deluge. But none of this is precise and we have no speculations about the length of cycles nor about the similarities of their details. Aristotle's works do, however, show how widely accepted was the idea of periodic cataclysms and the periodic rediscovery of the arts and sciences.

Aristotle is also responsible for the idea (which was to be developed by Polybius) of the degeneration of forms of government. There are, he says in his *Politics* (Book III, Ch. 7, 1279a. 23ff., and 1279b. 1ff.), three kinds of good government: the rule of one man, Monarchy; of a few, Aristocracy; and of many, Constitutional Democracy. Corresponding to these are three forms of bad government; tyranny, which is government in the interest of the ruler; oligarchy, in the interest of the rich; democracy, in the interest of the needy. But he is careful to point out that the number of people in the governing body is not so important as wealth. Government by the rich is an oligarchy even if the rich are numerous; government by the poor is a democracy even if the poor are few. So far nothing has been said about historical changes in governmental forms. But later (1286b. 7) he points out that the first governments were monarchical. They degenerated into oligarchies, then into tyrannies, and finally into democracies. But Aristotle does not say that monarchies will arise anew out of democracies. The process is not eternal, though one suspects that after a flood or conflagration the kind of government that will arise will again be monarchical.

3. Polybius. The Aristotelian formula was taken up by Polybius (ca. 204–122 B.C.). For him, as he says in his *History* (Book VI, 3), there are six kinds of government, as in Aristotle, but they occur in a definite series. By a natural growth monarchy comes first and turns into "kingship" by the aid of art and the correction of defects. Both are government by one man. Monarchy inevitably turns into tyranny against which aristocracy is organized. Aristocracy in turn degenerates into oli-

625

garchy. Revulsion against oligarchy produces democracy which in its turn becomes mob-rule. All this proceeds as by a natural law.

Governments, says Polybius, are instituted after the human race has been destroyed by floods and famines, "as tradition tells us has more than once happened and as we must believe will often happen again, all arts and crafts perishing at the same time." Then the survivors herd together because of their weakness. The strongest and most courageous rules over the others and thus monarchy arises. Primitive monarchy is the rule of force. But once order is established, notions of goodness, justice, evil, and injustice arise because of the conduct of ungrateful children "and others." There thus is formed an idea of duty and a benefactor wins gratitude and respect.

At that point the monarch is obeyed because of his administration of justice and then reason replaces force. The people trust in the descendants of their kings from the conviction that their qualities are inherited. But the heirs yield to their appetites, even wearing special clothes, and live so that their conduct gives rise to envy and offense, hatred and resentment. At this point tyranny takes over. The noblest members of the community, however, being unable to tolerate tyranny, conspire to overthrow the government, succeed, and establish an aristocracy. Unfortunately the children of the best may be bad. They give in to love of money, to lust, to pleasures of all sorts; and aristocracy becomes oligarchy. Oligarchy then becomes intolerable and turns into democracy; and, for the same reason that kings become tyrants, aristocrats, oligarchs, democrats become mob-leaders.

Thus Polybius anticipates Lord Acton's dictum that power corrupts. But to Polybius' way of thinking the cycle is established by natural law: it is the course appointed by nature in which constitutions, states, the arts change, disappear, and finally return to the point from which they started. Polybius is so convinced of this position that he says it may be used as a basis for prophecy. The only remedy is a mixed constitution. He found one, he thought, in Rome, where the Consuls were monarchs, the Senators aristocrats, the Many democrats. Nevertheless the course of history was one of constant decay.

4. The Italian Renaissance. Reflections upon the course of human events were reoriented during the Middle Ages when the moral behavior of states was of more importance than natural law. But early in the Renaissance the ideas of Polybius were revived. Before Polybius was translated from Greek to Latin and printed in 1473, we find in Giovanni Villani's *Chronicle of Florence* the cyclic pattern emphasized. Whether Villani (ca. 1275–1348) could have read Polybius in

Greek is doubtful since the Greek manuscripts came later to Italy. Villani's cycle depends on the supposed psychological fact that success engenders pride, pride sin, and sin brings on decline.

It was Machiavelli who carried on the tradition of Polybius. In his *Discourses* (Book I, Ch. ii) he argues that the mixed form of government is the best and that it was found in Rome. He bases his argument on the same points as those made by Polybius. Also Francesco Guicciardini in his *Ricordi* argues that the future repeats the past and that only the names of things change. But the history of this particular idea, which is one of the bases for the program of mixed constitutions belongs elsewhere We shall here merely point to its outcome in the Constitution of the United States.

III. TWENTIETH-CENTURY DEVELOPMENTS

Only two influential theories of cycles need be cited as representative of twentieth-century thinking on this problem, the theories of Oswald Spengler and those of Arnold Toynbee.

According to Spengler, and Toynbee as well, human history must be divided longitudinally into the biographies of civilizations, cultures, nations. These historical items are to be considered under the metaphor of a living organism which is born, matures, and dies. In Spengler's view, as given in his *Decline of the West* (German 1918; English 1926–28), people begin in a creative state of mind, which he calls "Faustian"—very similar to what Nietzsche had called in his *Birth of Tragedy* "Dionysian," where music and the dance, where the dramatic and the lyrical, are the dominant features of life. This period he calls that of a culture. But as a culture develops, it inevitably gives way to rationality, and the Apollonian attitude, where the geometric, the static, the formal predominate. When such features reach their height, there is no longer a culture, there is only a civilization. As a result the people's creative spirit dies. *The Decline of the West* is the story of how this has happened in the Occident. The same story has been repeated and presumably will be repeated again in the Orient. Thus the cycle of culture-civilization-death-culture goes on forever.

Toynbee is a bit less discouraging. For to his way of thinking there have been twenty-six nations or civilizations so far in world history. All have undergone the same stimuli, known as challenges. To these challenges they have responded in various ways and the ways are what we call their histories. So far none has succeeded in successfully meeting the challenges which have been put to them. But there is always the possibility that some civilization will succeed in doing so. The latter half of the twentieth century will see how successfully occidental civilization can meet the challenge which has confronted it. Just what this challenge is, is far from clear, unless it is the challenge that communism has put up to capitalism. But since capitalistic countries have absorbed certain socialistic devices and communistic countries have either retained or introduced capitalistic devices, there must be some other explanation that Toynbee has in mind. What recurs eternally in both Spengler and Toynbee is the general pattern of history, not the individual events. There have been and probably will continue to be international wars, for instance, but no given war will be repeated. The problem that such historians have to face is how to use their classifications, how much similarity they will demand of those events to which they give the same name. In one sense of the word, every time a person is born there is a repetition of a set of events. But what is born, beyond that which is named by the noun "person," is individual and different from every other member of his class. This problem is one that few historians have been willing to face, for it carries one off into the regions of metaphysics.

Related to the doctrine of historical cycles is that based on the metaphor of the swinging pendulum, according to which an historical movement will reach an extreme and then turn back until it reaches an opposite extreme. Thus radicalism and conservatism in politics, romanticism and classicism in art, ·skepticism and authoritarianism in religion, have all been said to occur in this manner. But the extremes have never been clearly defined except possibly by Hegel, whose historical theory is discussed elsewhere.

BIBLIOGRAPHY

For Empedocles and Heraclitus, see John Burnet, *Early Greek Philosophy*, 4th ed. (London, 1945); cf. A. O. Lovejoy and G. Boas, *Primitivism . . . in Antiquity* (Baltimore, 1935), pp. 79ff. For Pagan testimony to the Stoic doctrine of cycles and the *ekpyrosis*, Cicero, *Academics*, II. 37, 119; idem, *De natura deorum*, II. 46, 118, trans. H. Rackham (London and Cambridge, Mass., 1933), pp. 621 and 635 respectively; Seneca, *Consolatione ad Marciam*, XXVI. 5 to end; idem, *Consolatione ad Polybium*, I. 2, in *Moral Essays*, trans. John W. Basore (London and Cambridge, Mass., 1935), II. 95, 357; Plutarch, *The E at Delphi*, 388 F, in *Moralia*, trans. Frank Cole Babbitt (London and Cambridge, Mass., 1936), V. 221f.; Marcus Aurelius, *Meditations*, VII. 19; XI. 1. For the "reverse in cosmic history," see Plato, *Statesman*, 269D; for conflagrations and floods, *Timaeus*, 22B; for cataclysms, *Critias*, 110A, *Laws*, 677. For historical repetition in Aristotle, works as indicated in the text above; for political cycles, *Politics*, III, 7 (1279a. 23ff. and 1286b. 7). For the same in Polybius, see *History*, Book VI. 3 and 5. For political cycles in the Italian Renaissance, see Louis Green, "Historical Interpretation in Fourteenth-Century Florentine Chronicles," *Journal of the History of Ideas*, **28**, 2 (April–June, 1967), 161–78; Machiavelli, *Discourses*, Book I, Ch. ii; Guicciardini, *Maxims and Reflections of a Renaissance Statesman (Ricordi)*, trans. Mario Domandi (New York, 1965), pp. 60, 89. For comment on cycles in early Christian writers: Justin Martyr, *Apology*, I. 20, trans. Marcus Dods, George Heath, and B. P. Bratten (Edinburgh, 1872); Origen, *De principiis*, Book II. Chs. 3, 5 from *Patrologia Graeca*, Vol. XI, col. 192, trans. Frederick Crombie (Edinburgh, 1871) p. 84; idem, *Contra Celsum*, Book V. Ch. 20, from *Patrologia Graeca*, Vol. XI, cols. 1213, 1216, trans. Alexander Roberts and James Donaldson (Edinburgh, 1872). F. W. Nietzsche, *Complete Works*, ed. Oscar Levy, 18 vols. (London, 1909–13), 16, nos. 237–47; Karl Jaspers, *Nietzsche*, trans. Charles F. Wallraff and Frederick J. Schmitz (Tuscon, 1965), pp. 352ff.

GEORGE BOAS

[See also Analogy in Early Greek Thought; Christianity in History; Historiography; **Periodization in History; Primitivism;** Renaissance Literature and Historiography.]

CYNICISM

1. The Problem. The problem of the origins or sources of Cynicism has attracted the interest of scholars since Ferdinand Dümmler published his dissertation *Antisthenica* in 1882. Dümmler thought he had found a whole series of polemical allusions to Antisthenes in Plato's works. Dümmler's thesis was soon pushed to extremes by other scholars, who gave Antisthenes a central position in Greek philosophy. Antisthenes' role as the founder of a philosophical school was not called in question. Diogenes of Sinope was regarded as his immediate pupil in accordance with ancient tradition. Cynicism was regarded as an ethical and mainly practical philosophical movement with later additions of certain abstruse traits but still essentially a bearer of a Socratic tradition.

Contrary to this conception of the problem we find another radically different view. In this view Antisthenes was not an independent thinker or writer of any particular importance and had nothing at all to do with Cynicism. The linking together of Antisthenes and Diogenes is then explained as a Stoic attempt to derive the Stoa directly from Socrates. Cynicism is not a philosophy, it is an asocial, amoral, and anti-intellectual way of living. Without Diogenes there would be no Cynics. He is the creator of the true Cynic type with all its burlesque, asocial and anticultural features, described in an abundance of Cynic anecdotes. The picture of Diogenes as a type, conveyed by the anecdotes, is true in its main features, even though the details are invented.

The problem of Cynicism is essentially a problem concerning the sources. No original writings, with few exceptions, have survived. Our knowledge of Cynicism rests largely on quotations from late authors, on a rich profusion of anecdotes, and on late spurious letters. The interpretation of isolated sentences, torn from their context, and of résumés must therefore be conjectural and need to be viewed from the standpoint of the history of the ideas associated with the so-called Cynics. The widely differing positions taken up in this field of research are due to the conditions suggested here. The account of a few central themes in Cynicism that will be given here rests solely on doxographical material or such material as can be related to the doxographies.

2. Early Authors. First we present a short survey of persons and authors in the Cynic tradition during the fourth and third centuries B.C.

Antisthenes—dates unknown, but still living at an advanced age in Athens in 366—came from the Sophists as a disciple of Gorgias. According to the practice of the Sophists he gave instruction for a fee in the gymnasium of Cynosarges outside the city-wall of Athens, offering lessons intended for the education of young Athenians without full citizenship. Antisthenes himself was not a full citizen of Athens, his mother being a Thracian woman. The Cynosarges contained a famous shrine of Heracles; the name "Cynic," it is usually believed was derived from Cynosarges. Heracles as Cynic hero has his origin here. Antisthenes was a prolific writer. Diogenes Laërtius, in his *Lives of Eminent Philosophers,* gives us under Antisthenes' name one of the longest lists of books, 66 titles in all, divided into ten sections. His literary output belongs within the scope of the problems which were of interest to the Sophists. Of this immense literary output nothing remains except two declamations about Ajax and Odysseus, which betray the influence of Gorgias' rhetorical style but show manifest traces of Cynic "king-ideology" (which is discussed below). Besides the life in Diogenes Laërtius there are only a few scattered quotations, mostly in the writings of late authors.

Diogenes of Sinope probably came to Athens as a political exile in connection with the Persian satrap Datames' capture of the Athenian colony of Sinope on the south coast of the Black Sea in 370. He possibly taught in Athens after the decade of 360–50. Among his better known pupils were Onesicritus, Alexander's admiral, who took part in the expedition to India and wrote a novel on Alexander and descriptions of India; furthermore, Anaximenes of Lampsacus, who carried

on an extensive literary activity, was the instructor of Alexander and wrote a history of him. He is said to have lived ca. 380–20. The ancient testimonies are unanimous in placing Diogenes' death towards 320. There are no reasons for doubting the existence of personal contact between Antisthenes and Diogenes. Besides direct teaching, Diogenes also carried on a rather extensive literary activity. Diogenes Laërtius gives a list of writings attributed to him that comprises thirteen dialogues, seven tragedies, and letters; in a second, shorter list, with mostly other titles, Diogenes Laërtius enumerates thirteen works, besides letters. With the letters are probably those spurious letters that under the names of various philosophers were current in the first centuries B.C. and A.D. No tragedies are mentioned in this second list. That the teaching activity presupposes some kind of literary activity and literary reputation can hardly be doubted, but nothing remains.

Among Diogenes' personal pupils, besides the above-mentioned Onesicritus and Anaximenes, were a number of Cynic authors, among others Monimus of Syracuse, who wrote jocular poems with a serious intent; Philiscus of Aegina, who besides dialogues wrote tragedies intended for reading, in which Cynic paradoxes were paraded; also, Crates of Thebes, who likewise wrote jocular poems of which we get a fairly good idea from fragments that have been preserved. Metrocles of Maroneia, Crates' brother-in-law, originally a Peripatetic but later a pupil of Crates, played an important role, in the generation immediately after Diogenes, through his writings containing helpful words for everyday use intended to strengthen the philosophical attitude towards life. He had a decisive influence on the creation of the type of Cynic philosopher, and of the Diogenes legend.

In the generation after Metrocles we find a number of important writers. Diogenes Laërtius mentions as a pupil of Metrocles among others Menippus of Gadara, originally a slave at Sinope, who continued in the way which Monimus made vivid by putting forth philosophical maxims in a jocular form. His style, a mixture of prose and poetry, was imitated by Varro in the latter's *Saturae Menippeae,* of which about 600 fragments have been preserved. In addition, to this generation of authors belongs Bion the Borysthenite, also a freedman, and a pupil of Theophrastus and Xenocrates, but above all of Crates, the Cynic. Bion was already considered in antiquity to be the originator of the so-called diatribe style. Then we have Teles of Megara, diatribist after the manner of Bion (of whom a considerable number of extracts have been preserved by Stobaeus), and Cercidas of Megalopolis. Cercidas does not at all conform to the vulgar conception of a Cynic. He served his native city as general, diplomat, and lawgiver, but attained his greatest fame as Cynic philosopher and poet. He was strongly influenced by Diogenes as well as by Bion, whose diatribic style he developed.

In the latter half of the third century Menedemus from Asia Minor was active as a writer in a sternly moralizing, polemical style. Finally, mention must be made of the satirist Meleager of Gadara, poet and Cynic philosopher in the Menippean style, who lived at the end of the second century B.C.

3. Sophistic Background. From the point of view of the history of ideas Cynicism as a practical-philosophical movement begins with the Sophists. Most of its theoretical motivation and ideological substance is derived from the Sophists' nominalistic theory of knowledge and materialism, the radical opposition to society and its conventions through the assertion of natural law as against positive law, and a ruthless and unrestricted individualism. From the pedagogy of the Sophists came also the interest in practical ethical questions and educational problems. Antisthenes, who began as a Sophist and in spite of his attacks on his former teacher Gorgias always remained a Sophist, later on attached himself to Socrates, whom he admired highly and to whom he probably stood in a close relationship. He was with Socrates in the prison, when Socrates drank the hemlock. In Socrates Antisthenes met with what was later associated with the Cynic type in its serious form: poverty, voluntary asceticism, physical insensibility and hardiness, psychical firmness, and absolute personal integrity. Out of this encounter Cynicism was born. With Antisthenes' successor Diogenes the theoretical motivation receded to give place to a practical demonstration against established social behavior for the benefit of an individualism pushed *ad absurdum*.

4. Political Ideas. The Sophists, who almost without exception were of non-Athenian descent, wrote a number of critical and comparative descriptions of the constitutions of various states. The points of view varied considerably between conservative and radical ideas, and various attempts were made at justifying society's demands for subordination. Protagoras put this justification in a mythical form as innate feelings of right and wrong, thus giving society a foundation in irrational, religious conceptions. Law and nature are not contradictory notions; on the contrary, they are complementary to each other. The Sophist Antiphon, on the other hand, equated nature and truth in contrast to law, which means a violation of nature. As an example he cites the fictitious difference between social classes and between Greeks and barbarians, differences which have no foundation in nature.

In this political literary activity Antisthenes took part. According to Diogenes Laërtius he wrote a considerable number of political pamphlets under traditional titles. Our information about this literary output is scanty. Antisthenes criticized the tyrants for their excessive greed which led them to the greatest crimes. He also criticized Pericles and other politicians in special pamphlets, and appeared in public with his political criticism. More important are the conclusions that can be drawn about Antisthenes' political writings by viewing the fragments in relation to the Sophistic writings.

The Sophist Antiphon wrote a book about Concord. The word has on one side a political sense, concord between warring groups of society, but on the other side it had undergone a development in an individualistic direction and acquired the sense of harmony with oneself. Plato defines the wicked man as one who is not in harmony with himself, and he says that what is in opposition to itself, can hardly be a friend of anything else. The formula "to be in harmony with oneself" was familiar to Plato in his early writings. In the Stoa the concept of concord was defined as knowledge about common advantages. Only the wise possessed this knowledge. A number of fragments from Antisthenes' writings must be read in this connection: criticism of the existing society with its demand for political concord on the basis of the law, in contrast to this the concord that exists in accordance with nature above the law and in opposition to it, e.g., between brothers and above all between the wise. This concord is based on the philosopher's ability to hold converse with himself, to be in harmony with himself, which is possible only for the wise.

Antisthenes, like Antiphon, took up the cudgels against the traditional code of morality and its laws, and set up the antithesis: *nomos* versus *physis* ("custom" or "convention" versus "nature"). In a religious fragment he makes use of this antithesis to show that polytheism exists only according to law; according to nature there is only one god. In a political fragment this antithesis recurs: the wise man must not live in accordance with the established laws but with the law of virtue. There are other utterances that seem to show that Antisthenes used this and similar expressions in polemics against democracy.

The wise man's ethical superiority to other men leads to another antithesis with political consequences, the contrast between the good and the bad. The bad must be separated from the state just as the weeds are separated from the corn or the cowards from the battle. The good must unite, become friends and allies in the ethical battle. Their weapon is virtue and this weapon can never be lost. This virtue, which is itself a law in opposition to the laws of society, is teachable. Still

629

it demands no great learning but practical training. Family ties and difference of sex do not count here. Human fellowship can only be based on equal spiritual qualities, irrespective of all conventions. It can as a matter of fact exist only between the wise.

Politics and pedagogy were closely connected in the Sophistic. The aim of the Sophists was to create by instruction conditions for success in society. But the content and value of this Sophistic instruction were called in question. Antisthenes sought a solution of the problem of politics in opposition to Plato, whose theory of ideas he polemized against and rejected. We do not know how far the state in Cynic writings approximated Plato's ideal of the state, but there were some striking parallels: in both cases there was a question of an ethical aristocracy with justice and virtue as central concepts, a philosopher state with no possibility of realization in practical life. As to the Cynics this led to the idea of a simple and remote life in harmony with nature, which education should aim at.

5. Cynic Pedagogy. Diogenes Laërtius' account (VI 70f.) of Diogenes' maxims is a summary of early Cynic pedagogy. The theme is "the double training," the necessary training of body and soul, and the passage is one of the few sources of information about early Cynic ideology of Heracles. Both forms of training are equally necessary for him who wants to learn how to act rightly. More explicit information as to the methods of this pedagogy is given in Diog. L. VI 30f. Diogenes Laërtius quotes a certain Eubulus who wrote a book about how Diogenes was sold as a slave and became the teacher of Xeniades' two sons. These he trained in various sorts of athletics, not in an exaggerated way but only enough to keep them in good physical condition. The pupils also had to learn by heart passages from poets and historians, and the writings of Diogenes himself. Part of the education also consisted in learning a simple way of living as to food, drink, and clothes, and modest behavior. Thus Diogenes appears here as a representative of the traditional type of education, which reminds one of Xenophon's *Cyropaedia* and shows a certain affinity to Prodicus' allegory on Heracles. As a youth Heracles chose the virtuous woman Aretē instead of the woman of pleasure, Kakia, when he was confronted by both where paths crossed. The passages in Diog. L. VI 30 and 70 correspond to each other. Diogenes proclaimed a pedagogical doctrine which has left traces in early Cynic literature. The story of the sale of Diogenes into slavery has been treated by several Cynic writers in the next generation. The quotation from Eubulus (Diog. L. VI 30) represents a serious variant of the story. In this variant Diogenes appears outwardly as a slave but inwardly as free and a master. Whether and how far the version of the sale

into slavery given by Lucian, where Diogenes appears in a caricatured form, goes back to an early burlesque variant (Menippus?) is doubtful. The pedagogy of the Eubulus version is of an idyllic character which has its counterpart in a hedonistic theme in the doxography Diog. L. VI 71: the despising of pleasure is the greatest pleasure. In Lucian we meet a Cynic pedagogy of quite another character in line with the many Diogenes anecdotes representing traits of rigorous asceticism and abstruse shamelessness.

It is easy to relate the varying motifs in the Eubulus pedagogy to ideas generally known in the fourth century B.C.: the ruler-teacher motif, the slave-ruler motif, the idyllic training in hunting, archery, riding, and other forms of athletics as a complement to reading and learning by heart select passages from the works of poets and other writers. Even the framework itself, the sale of Diogenes into slavery, had its model in Euripides' play *Syleus*, where Heracles is sold as a slave. But while Eubulus' pedagogy with its archaic, Spartan education (*paideia*) was disappearing from the Cynic tradition, a burlesque variant was being created which left its most important traces in Lucian several centuries later. Instead of Eubulus' mild, hedonistically tinged asceticism we find a coarse and vulgar asceticism which was self-contained and was the form of Cynicism that Lucian criticized, and which furnished the material for countless popular anecdotes.

The idyllic existence which Eubulus' pedagogy describes has to a certain extent its counterpart in some fragments of an early Cynic poem (Crates' poem, *Pera*) which describes in allegorical form an ideal society.

Crates' social background was different from that of Antisthenes and Diogenes. He was a full citizen of Thebes but distributed his wealth, which was considerable, among his fellow citizens. Teles describes him as a sort of pre-Christian Saint Francis, who derived the highest ethical values from his voluntary poverty. Apuleius provides an interesting example of Heracles as an ethical model in his description of Crates. Here we find a picture of the Cynic saint, reconciler and adviser of men, punisher of all evil. In Crates we find the dream of the far-off state, which no evil men or evil conditions can reach. Pera—the type of wallet associated with the Cynics—stands as name and symbol of this state. Crates praises self-sufficing simplicity, isolation, and freedom. A simple way of life brings contentedness. The inhabitants of Pera are men who are not the slaves of pleasure, but who love freedom, the eternal queen.

In Crates' new kingdom there is no war. Men do not fight with each other for food since where frugality reigns there is enough for all. Crates embraces Cynic pacifism, which may well have been introduced by

Antisthenes. The poem is a mixture of fun and serious-ness. What Crates describes in the *Pera* is a never-never land. There is no question of a state in the usual sense: Pera is a dream, which the Christian Fathers compared with the heavenly Jerusalem. It is the Cynic ideal community, without the difficulties of sustaining itself, of war or wickedness, a society in which dwell such men as the Cynics endeavor to fashion by education.

The doxography Diog. L. VI 70ff. contains in section 72 an account of Diogenes' political views. It is possible that the passage is a summary of the content of Diogenes' book, *Politeia*, which described a philosopher state and contained principles that were later adopted by the Stoa. The elements of this account can in any case easily be related to the political debate of the fifth and fourth centuries: the wise are god's friends, hence everything belongs to them; noble birth and fame are valueless things; common possession of wives and children should take the place of marriage; the purpose of the state is to afford its citizens protection and help; this the state cannot do without law, conse-quently, law is necessary for the state. Then the ques-tion arises, which state is the right one. The Sophist Antiphon had shown in his book *Truth* that the histori-cal state was unable to provide the legal protection that men needed. The answer to the question about the right state is also given: the only right state is the world state. The expression "the right state" was a term accepted in the political writings of the fourth century. What is new in the Diogenes doxography is that it is applied to a "cosmos-state."

6. Scientific Views of the Cynics. The doxography contains in section 73 a passage of scientific, theoretical character. Cynicism may have derived its view of nature via the Sophists from Anaxagoras (who had considerable influence on Athenian philosophical views), from Diogenes of Apollonia, and from the Atomists. It is easy to find fragments which tie up with the main theme of this passage. The source quoted is Diogenes' tragedy *Thyestes*, with the reservation that the tragedies may not be genuine. Diogenes

. . . saw no impropriety either in stealing anything from a temple or eating the flesh of any animal; nor even anything impious in touching human flesh, this, he said, being clear from the custom of some foreign nations. Moreover, accord-ing to right reason, as he put it, all elements are contained in all things and pervade everything: since not only is meat a constituent of bread, but bread of vegetables; and all other bodies also, by means of certain invisible passages and particles, find their way and unite with all substances in the form of vapor.

It is quite possible to date this passage to the fourth century B.C. The idea that lies behind it is old; the scientific terms are early technical terms, and even if

the whole line of reasoning in this section is foreign to the traditional view of Diogenes, which ignores his intellectual side, we must still reckon with the possi-bility that Diogenes justified his radical views with plausible and appropriate scientific arguments. He was not, however, interested in physical or logical problems for their own sake.

This part of Diogenes' doxography is the only place in the whole Diogenes tradition where we have a reference to a really scientific theory as a justification of Diogenes' views. Elsewhere he adduces simple, eristic arguments to support a radical thesis or to explain an objectionable phenomenon. The passage contains no word about the desirability of the realiza-tion of the theory in actual society or in any ideal state.

7. Cynic Asceticism. Lucian's version of Cynicism represents the aspect of Cynicism that has become best known thanks to a profusion of anecdotes. The most varied anecdotes, some strictly rigorous and coarsely hedonistic, some serious and burlesque, and both sym-pathetic and hostile to civilization, have attached themselves to Diogenes of Sinope. Various scholars have maintained that the rigorous type of anecdotes is primary and genuinely Diogenic, whereas the hedonistic type of anecdotes was introduced in the Diogenes tradition by Crates and especially his disci-ples Bion and Menippus, as a more human reaction. A strict and rigorous movement also continued, which actually even attempted to outdo Diogenes himself. Diogenes appears as a misanthrope in the pessimistic 28th letter. Most words of rebuke occur in the Cynic texts of Roman imperial times. The creation of the legend began immediately after Diogenes' death and took place simultaneously along two lines—the strict and rigorous, and the hedonistic.

At a definite point we can see how a rigorous type of asceticism evidently influenced the Diogenes legend. Onesicritus, Alexander's admiral, tells, in Strabo, the story of his encounter with an Indian ascetic sect, the so-called Gymnosophists. Naked and motionless, in various positions on the rocks, they endured the heat of the equatorial sun until the evening. The motive for their harsh asceticism is conveyed in the following words:

Man trains the body for toil in order that his opinions may be strengthened, whereby he may put a stop to dissensions and be ready to give good advice to all, both in public and in private.

Onesicritus is comparing oriental asceticism with the form of asceticism he had come to know at home in Greece in the Cynicism of Diogenes. The comparison is to the disadvantage of Cynicism. In the Gymnosoph-ists he found ascetics of a far more radical type than he had previously encountered. In this respect he puts Pythagoras, Socrates, and Diogenes on the same plane: they failed because they put law before nature. This rigorous type of asceticism is reflected in the anecdotes about Diogenes rolling in the hot sand or embracing in winter statues covered with snow, and others.

Within the Cynic movement itself the increasing oriental influence on Greek religion, following the time of Alexander, created a necessity to maintain the school's saint Diogenes as a thoroughgoing, rigorous ascetic. Onesicritus' comparison between Indian and Greek ascetic philosophy was no isolated phenomenon. The story recurs as one of the sources in a papyrus from the second century B.C.

It remains an open question how much of the harsh, rigorous asceticism goes back as far as the historical Diogenes. It may be assumed that it does, to a certain extent. The history of ideas shows clearly that the eudaemonistic, Socratic asceticism, which is pedagogically motivated and has its background in the pedagogical debate of the fifth and fourth centuries, belongs to Cynic philosophy from its beginning.

8. Cynic Hero and King Ideology. The Heracles mythology contained a great many features that let themselves be easily applied to Cynic philosophy. The suffering Heracles appears as a benefactor in the drama. In Euripides' *Heracles* the theme *philanthropia* through suffering is clearly delineated. But the drama did not advance to the position of Antisthenes in regarding pain as something good. Antisthenes demonstrated that pain is a good thing by instancing the great Heracles and Cyrus, drawing the one example from the Greek world and the other from the barbarians. An important step towards the possibility of using Heracles for philosophical, ethical purposes had already been taken in the Ionian criticism of the myths. In the extensive Ionian literature about Heracles the Sophist Herodorus of Heraclea in Pontus was the creator of the allegories of the philosophic Heracles. In the Sophist Prodicus' allegory of the Choice of Heracles there appears a philanthropical as well as an ascetic theme, a hedonistic attraction towards a simpler, more natural way of life as a reaction against artificiality and excessive civilization. Antisthenes' view of pain as something good is fully consistent with Prodicus' description of Heracles. The myth of Heracles offered a multitude of possibilities for a philosophic sect which, because of its origin in circles without full political rights, was burdened by social and political discontent.

The fragments of Antisthenes' *Heracles* are not very extensive. The main points are: Heracles receives instruction in virtue from the wise centaur Chiron, pain is something good, the purpose of life is to live according to virtue, virtue can be taught and when once acquired cannot be lost.

As to Diogenes the doxography Diog. L. VI 70 offers an example of early Heracles ideology. Heracles is the prototype for the pedagogic ideas propagated here. The passage ends with a reference to Heracles:

. . . allowing [sc. Diogenes] convention no such authority as he allowed to natural right, and asserting that the manner of life he lived was the same as that of Heracles when he preferred liberty to everything.

The Heracles mythology had been dealt with at great length and in various aspects in the fifth century, but Heracles declined rapidly in popularity both in Cynic and in extra-Cynic literature. The vogue he enjoyed during the whole fifth century in epic, lyric, tragedy, and finally in the allegorical and rationalistic interpretation of myth did not continue into the fourth century. The only thing which survived apart from the sterile references scattered throughout literature is the allegory and the ethical propaganda in Cynic circles.

In Dio Chrysostomus in the first century A.D. we find relatively unequivocal themes of Cynic Heracles propaganda; there is an attempt to achieve a refined picture of Heracles along Cynic lines, in which the divine character of the hero is rationalized and his labors are given an allegorical interpretation. His virtues are individual-ethical, but the philanthropia theme is preserved and a firm front maintained against intellectualism and athleticism. This use of Heracles by Dio was due to Dio's becoming acquainted with a Cynic way of life and Cynic literature. Diogenes in Dio Chrysostomus Or. 8 compares himself with Heracles. The moral struggle against pleasure is designated by the term labor, and Heracles is held up as an example. We find in Dio Chrysostomus a picture of Heracles which has nothing in common with the athletic, sensual Heracles of satyrical drama and comedy. He is adapted to the Cynic ideal of behavior and appears in his new guise as a Cynic saint, a portrait for which Dio was indebted to earlier Cynic sources.

The most important feature in Dio's characterization of Heracles is the education, the double *paideia,* the "human" and the "divine"; the "divine" *paideia* represents the true Cynic pedagogics with Heracles as a model in opposition to Sophistic Rhetoric and vulgar Cynicism. Dio's views on this subject, maybe through early Stoic intermediaries, were influenced by classical Cynicism. In Dio we find the ideas and problems of the fourth century B.C. with its interest in the relationship between education and politics, its opposition to the Sophists' unsuccessful efforts in this field, and the individual-ethical form given to educational and political theories with the important central themes:

to govern oneself = to govern men; education = authority; philosopher = ruler. The Cynic educational theory is a pedagogy for rulers. From the point of view of the history of ideas it belongs together with Xenophon's *Cyropaedia* and the Aristippean polemic in Xenophon's *Memorabilia* II 1. A basic idea common to these texts is the part played by the paragon in their pedagogic theory: the ruler is a model and his position is based on his moral supremacy.

Antisthenes described Cyrus' development according to the scheme slave-king (*doulos-basileus*), and used the same theme in his portrayal of Odysseus. The theme recurs in the idealization of Diogenes, and its main point was to show the philosophical inner freedom which is founded on moral perfection and not on outward circumstances. The application of the theme to Diogenes has taken place among the authors of the generation after Diogenes. In Dio Chrysostomus we find this Cynic theme elaborated in detail, and there is no doubt that Dio reflects early Cynic basileus-ideology. In Dio's Cynic speeches there occur a number of catalogues of virtues and vices of a relatively fixed form. The man who does not possess the right qualities, i.e., a character firmly formed along individual-ethical lines, is not a basileus at all. Although Xerxes is by external standards the most powerful of kings and by his external power can perform the most unbelievable things, he is weaker than those who do not even possess an obol, if he does not possess the right, i.e., the Cynic character. The term "basileus" belongs properly only to the morally perfect ruler, a king with pronounced individual-ethical qualities, with simple, uncomplicated social functions illustrated by comparison to a herdsman, and by the father figure. He is an idyllic type who belongs historically to Xenophon's portrait of Cyrus.

But in his writings Dio presents a further portrait of the king, namely the basileus as a solitary, poor, and suffering figure. This portrait is modelled on Diogenes, but probably originated in the works of Antisthenes. The model for this type of basileus was Heracles with his solitariness, nakedness, poverty, homelessness, suffering. Yet with all this Heracles was the son of Zeus and worthy of kingship. In Dio we find that Diogenes plays the part of the suffering basileus: in his humiliation, exposed to men's abuse and ill-treatment he resembled a real king and ruler in his garment of a poor man. The philosopher in his simple tribon (the philosopher's cloak) must submit to suffering and ignominy. This "abuse" theme is an inseparable component of the Cynic type of behavior. The Cynic is reviled for his poverty, for consorting with bad men, for his humble origin, and for his appearance and demeanor. We have in Dio veritable catalogues of suffering and struggle. The philosopher must endure hunger, thirst, cold, ill-treatment, poverty, and ignominy, but he does so without complaining; on the contrary, he considers these burdens easy to carry. The eudaemonistic motivation of the moral struggle, the endurance, the absence of effort and strain in this struggle, in which, on the contrary, he engages with ease and joy, are all typical Cynic traits. The noble man, who is also perfect, is identical with the true king, the basileus disguised as a slave.

The best known example of the use of the *doulos-basileus* motif is the antithesis Diogenes-Alexander the Great. This antithesis belongs to the first half of the third century B.C. Dio Chrysostomus describes Alexander as an unfree and unhappy man full of erroneous ideas about the true values of life. Diogenes' aim is to teach Alexander what true kingship is. Diogenes not only gives instruction about the true king, but he views himself as the real king. Alexander is unfree or a slave, whereas Diogenes is the freest of men. In order to become a real king Alexander must exchange his royal splendor for the philosopher's ragged cloak and first learn to master himself before he can rule others. Still more, he must put on the slave's garment and serve those who are superior to himself. He must deliberately walk the road of suffering and service and submit to the philosopher's instruction and way of life, in order that in this way he may avoid false kingship.

The Cynic preaching contained, among other things, a conception of kingship of a unique character—the solitary, poor, and suffering basileus. The Cynic Heraclean allegory has played a decisive role in this connection. Even Antisthenes' works on Odysseus and Cyrus have been influenced by the same and similar motifs. After his death Diogenes is described in the role of the slave-king who is mocked and ridiculed, but at last raised above all surrounding adversities.

The other side of this Cynic conception of kingship is the purely ethical. We are concerned with a question, popular and much discussed in the fourth century B.C., the question of the true king's ethical qualifications and their indispensability as conditions for the position of basileus. Xenophon and Plato have both given evidence, each one in his own way, of the central role which this pedagogical motif has played in the Socratic circle. The Antisthenic-Diogenic theory of the double *paideia* must be looked upon as emanating from the same Socratic source. The stress falls on individual ethics, the "divine" *paideia*. "Human" *paideia*, although hazardous and misleading, is allowed to have some value, but only in relation to "divine" *paideia*. The pedagogical theories of Dio Chrysostomus, brought forth in argument against the Sophists, are directly influenced by the Socratic-Cynic pedagogy.

BIBLIOGRAPHY

F. D. Caizzi, *Antisthenis Fragmenta* (Milan, 1966). D. R. Dudley, *A History of Cynicism. From Diogenes to the 6th Century* A.D. (London, 1937). R. Höistad, *Cynic Hero and Cynic King: Studies in the Cynic Conception of Man* (Uppsala, 1948). A. O. Lovejoy and G. Boas, *Primitivism and Related Ideas in Antiquity. A Documentary History of Primitivism and Related Ideas* (Baltimore, 1935). K. Praechter, *Die Philosophie des Altertums* (Berlin, 1926), gives exhaustive lists of text editions and literature. F. Sayre, *Diogenes of Sinope. A Study of Greek Cynicism* (Baltimore, 1938); idem, *The Greek Cynics* (Baltimore, 1948). R. Vischer, *Das einfache Leben* (Göttingen, 1965). C. J. de Vogel, *Greek Philosophy: A Collection of Texts* (Leyden, 1950–59). K. von Fritz, *Quellenuntersuchungen zu Leben und Philosophie des Diogenes von Sinope, Philologus*, Supplementband 18:2 (Leipzig, 1926).

RAGNAR HÖISTAD

[See also Law, Natural; Nature; Platonism; Pre-Platonic Conceptions of Human Nature; Rationality; Stoicism.]

DEATH AND IMMORTALITY

DEATH

1. The Discovery of Death. It is a matter of debate whether animals have an awareness of mortality, but it is certain that man alone among all living creatures knows that he has to die. Yet even Homo sapiens acquired this knowledge relatively late in the long history of the species. It is reasonable to assume, as Voltaire did in his *Dictionnaire philosophique* (article, "Tout va bien"), that man has learned about death "through experience." More recently some philosophers, notably Max Scheler, asserted that man possesses an intuitive awareness of his mortality, and Paul Landsberg suggested that it is not through experience in the usual meaning of the term but by way of a particular "experience of death" that one realizes one's own finitude. There is undoubtedly some truth in this view but as numerous anthropological studies have shown, primitive man is totally unaware of the inevitability as well as the possible finality of death. For him it is neither a natural event nor a radical change: death occurs only as a result of violence or of a disease brought on by magic, and those who do die merely enter into another mode of living in which the need for food, drink, and clothing does not cease.

Therefore it is misleading to speak of the primitive's belief in immortality, because his view of death is rooted not in a denial of death but in the ignorance of its nature. And the term "immortality" would have to signify deathlessness as well as survival after death, whereby survival would be that of the whole man and not merely of a hypothetical incorporeal entity. It was only after it had become apparent that death was not a mere temporary lapse and that the change was irreversible and extreme that the notion could occur that what survives is something other than the whole man. Even then the "survivor" was not conceived of as something immaterial, but as a replica of the body, a "ghost" or "shadow," and only much later did it become the completely disembodied "soul."

The primitive's misconception of death is due primarily to his inability to draw the proper conclusions from his observations, but it is also strongly favored by the difficulty of visualizing the end of one's existence. This psychological peculiarity is not characteristic of the primitive alone. As Freud and Schopenhauer before him, have pointed out, "deep down" even contemporary man does not "really" believe in his own death. And Martin Heidegger shrewdly observed that the proposition, "all men are mortal" usually involves the tacit reservation "but not I."

Neither the time nor the historical sequence of the two elements in the discovery of death—its inevitability as well as its possible finality—can be determined with any degree of accuracy. On the one hand, the realization of the inevitability of death may conceivably have preceded the suspicion of its finality. On the other hand, the finality of death is in no way predicated on its inevitability. But if we judge by the testimony of the first written record of man's discovery of death, the Gilgamesh Epic (ca. 2500 B.C.), the realization of the inevitability of death as well as its possible finality would seem to have occurred simultaneously. If this is so, it is pointless to ask which of the two produced the greater shock. But again on the basis of the Gilgamesh legend, there can be no doubt about its severity. As a result we find in Gilgamesh most of the themes of the meditation on death as we know them today. But while King Gilgamesh strongly suspects that death may well be total extinction, the predominant view of death of his contemporaries, obviously still rooted in primitive ideas, was that the dead somehow continue to exist. But one cannot help but be impressed by the somber and frightening nature of the afterlife as it appears in the Babylonian and Greek mythologies. Typical is Achilles' complaint in the *Odyssey* that it is better to be a slave on earth than a king in the realm of phantoms. Such an image of a miserable existence as a mere "shadow" ought to throw considerable doubt on the usual interpretation of the belief in immortality as a mere "wish fulfillment," at least as far as the earliest manifestations of this belief are concerned. This kind of survival must have appeared, at least to some, as worse than complete extinction. For most people, however, the prospect of total annih..ation was as frightening and repulsive as that of a miserable afterlife. Seen against this background, the earliest philosophical speculations about the soul's ultimate blissful immortality must have appeared as welcome news.

We shall deal with these, and subsequent, doctrines of immortality in the second part of this article and consider the various attempts to come to terms with mortality without taking refuge in comforting visions of post-mortem existence.

2. Epicurus. These attempts were mainly concerned with gaining mastery over the fear of death. It is important, however, to realize that the first such attempts made by Democritus, and in particular by Epicurus, have been undertaken at a time when the predominant view of death was that of dismal survival in a bleak Underworld. Consequently Epicurus' liberating message consisted primarily in the denial of the reality of Hades. Later thinkers, however, had a different, and clearly a more difficult, task of trying to reconcile man with death meaning total extinction. According to Epicurus the fear of death is one of the two major afflictions of mankind, the other being the fear of the gods. Man fears death because he erroneously believes that he will experience pain and suffer after he has died. But, says Epicurus, death is deprivation of sensation. As to the soul it too does not survive death because, as Democritus has taught, like all things, it too consists of atoms (albeit particularly fine ones) which will disperse at death. Consequently "Death, the most terrifying of all ills, is nothing to us, since as long as we exist, death is not with us, and when death comes, then we do not exist" (Fragment XLVII, in Whitney J. Oates, *The Stoic and Epicurean Philosophers* [1940], p. 42).

This argument is frequently invoked even today in spite of the fact that it can be effective only against the fear of what comes after death—what may be done to the dead body, as well as what is supposed to happen to one's "shadow" in Hades. (The fear of mutilation and desecration of the corpse and the fear of being deprived of a proper burial were widespread in antiquity and sometimes appear to have been stronger than the fear of death itself.) But what is mostly feared today is precisely that which has been so lightly dismissed by Epicurus, namely, that one shall not exist anymore.

Another obvious shortcoming of the Epicurean argument is that it might alleviate the fear of death "at the thought of death," but not in its actual presence. The inadequacy of the argument in this respect, as well as with regard to the fear of annihilation, has

been noted even by some of Epicurus' contemporaries. In one of the Platonic apocrypha, the *Axiochus*, the dying ruler rejects it as "superficial twaddle which can impress only little boys." Perhaps this was the reason for which Lucretius, while exalting Epicurus as the great liberator from the "dread of Acheron," introduced the additional argument of a pessimistic evaluation of life: "And quitting life you quit thy living pain. . . . For all the dismal tales, that poets tell, are verified on earth and not in Hell" (*De rerum natura*, trans. John Dryden, Book III, 978–79).

3. Methods of Mastering the Fear of Death. The pessimistic evaluation of life can be considered as the oldest "remedy" against the fear of death. That "the best thing is not to be born, and the second best is to escape life as soon as possible" has been, since Theognis of Megara (sixth century B.C.), a recurrent theme of Greek poetry and drama. Pessimism is an important element also in Emperor Marcus Aurelius' approach to mastering the fear of death. But for most people the pessimistic stance carries no real conviction. Thus, another Roman Stoic, the slave Epictetus, relies more on self-discipline and the sense of decorum when it comes to death. His answer is that we have to take modestly the place assigned to us by God or Nature at the banquet of life and when the end approaches to leave it quietly and gracefully. This is also the view of Seneca. But he realized, however, that such an attitude is rather the result of the conquest of the fear of death than its condition. He was, therefore, more specific in suggesting as a remedy the constant thinking of death.

However, this second method of conquering the fear of death, even if it is done in the framework of hope of a future life, is scarcely realistic. And without that hope it is a "remedy" which may be worse than the affliction. The shortcomings of this method gradually became clear to Montaigne. In the chapter of his *Essays* significantly entitled "That to philosophize is to learn to die," he reports that being bothered by attacks of dread of dying, he at first tried to follow Seneca's advice. As time passed, he came to the conclusion that the only proper remedy against the fear of death is not "philosophy, which orders us to have death constantly before our eyes," but the attitude of the unsophisticated peasant whom "nature teaches not to think of death except when he actually dies. . . . If this be stupidity, let's all learn from it" (*Essays* [1595 ed.], Book III, Ch. 12). But how can not thinking of death be effective in the "presence" of death? What about the problem of "easy" dying? Here Montaigne is somewhat vague. He praises Nature which arranged things so that dying is in reality not too hard. And he says that "if we have known how to live properly and calmly, we will know how to die in the same manner."

However, Nature's cooperation is not necessarily realized in every case, although it was in Montaigne's: he did not have a chance to put the above statement to a test, having died suddenly of a stroke. His expectation of a peaceful death as an outgrowth of a "proper life" does not really convey Montaigne's radically new attitude toward life which determines his eventual attitude toward death. It is quite different from the Stoic position and even more so from that of Christianity; it is the expression of the Renaissance spirit with its appreciation of the exciting and wonderful world surrounding man of which he feels himself to be a part. Life is not seen any longer as something to be endured but something to be enjoyed and which can be shaped and changed for the better by man's own effort. In short, the *memento vivere* replaces the Christian *memento mori*. (It is plausible to assume that this radical reversal was, at least in part, an anticlimax to the pathologically heightened consciousness of mortality characteristic of the fourteenth and fifteenth centuries, which grew out of the disaster of the "Black Death.") What a "proper and calm" life was for Montaigne, a useful and productive life was for Leonardo da Vinci. "As a day well spent bestows pleasant sleep, so a life well used bestows pleasant death."

This has become the most often suggested secular answer to the problem of coming to terms with the fact of death. A variant of it, which puts even a greater emphasis on achievement, has been given expression by the German poet Hölderlin: "Should my verse grow perfect/ Most welcome then, O stillness of shades below . . . ("To the Fates"). It is obvious, however, that such a condition for overcoming the reluctance to die is well beyond the reach of the majority of mortals. Moreover, even the consciousness of having led a "full" life, and achieved great things may not be enough to make death welcome. What usually makes death acceptable is its coming as a well deserved surcease from a life of continuous hardship and particularly from the indignity and suffering of old age. However, it is hardly necessary to point out that the problem posed by premature death still remains in all its poignancy.

The weakness of the method of allaying fear of death by not thinking of it is that under certain circumstances it is easier said than done. Robert Burton realized it when he wrote in his *Anatomy of Melancholy* (1621) that "if our present weakness is such that death frightens us, we cannot moderate our passion in this behalf. We must divert them by all means, by doing something else, thinking of another subject. Study is above all the best means to divert one's thoughts" (Part a, sec. 3, mem. 5 [1907 ed.]). Spinoza too was well

aware of this. But, according to him, not any kind of study but only philosophical reflection which leads to what he calls "a higher kind of knowledge" can be truly effective. Therefore, his famous proposition LXVII (in the fourth part of *Ethics*), "A free man thinks of nothing less than death, and his wisdom is a meditation not of death but of life," is not advice to avoid thinking of death as a means of overcoming fear of it. To interpret this proposition as meaning that only fools waste their time on meditating about death is to misunderstand it completely. Spinoza's "free" man is the wise man, and the latter is defined as "one who lives under the guidance of reason and is not led by fear." But as Spinoza points out at the end of his *magnum opus*, the attainment of wisdom is one of the most difficult things in the world. Thus the above proposition is not an admonition not to think of death because no reasonable man does such a foolish thing, but a promise of a reward for the effort of becoming wise. It asserts that when one finally attains wisdom (that is, becomes "free") he will be able not to think of death, but of life. And it is obvious that only after having thought of death a great deal did Spinoza himself become able not to think of it any longer because he had learned not to fear it.

Although the method of allaying the fear of death by not thinking about it is a defective one, particularly since one usually thinks of it for some good reason (be it real danger of death to a loved one, or to oneself), the proffering of such advice is understandable if we consider man's uncanny ability to ignore his mortality. There is also the previously mentioned phenomenon that, in Freud's words, "in the unconscious no one really believes in one's own death." Were it not for these psychological defense mechanisms, who knows what havoc the knowledge of death would create in man's psyche.

Finally, a fourth method of mastering the fear of death is that of "minimizing" death. We have noted already that Epicurus' argument against the fear of death was, to a large extent, based on such an approach. But it was Socrates who must be considered as its initiator when, in Plato's *Apology*, he presses the analogy between death and sleep. "For fear of death is indeed the pretense of wisdom . . . being the pretense of knowing the unknown. . . . We may well hope that death is good, since it is either dreamless sleep or migration of the soul from this world to another . . ." (*Apology* 39D).

A telling criticism of the sleep analogy is Keats' complaint that "Mortality weighs on me like unwilling sleep" ("Endymion," 1818), and John Dryden's insistence that death is a very special kind of "sleep": "to sleep, and never wake again." These are valid reasons why the other alternative suggested by Socrates has been so popular. From the point of view of the conquest of the fear of death, the belief in immortality is nothing but another way of "minimizing" death.

While the method of not thinking of death could be effective only in instances of the fear of death "at the thought of it," that of thinking of it constantly (and thus becoming "familiar" with it) could probably be of help also in the "presence" of death. The two other methods, that of minimizing death, and that of minimizing the value of life may be helpful in both instances and unlike the first two are not mutually exclusive, but can and have been combined for greater efficacy. None of the four, however, is effective in the case of pathological fear of death. As the fifteenth-century Scottish poet, William Dunbar, stated in his "Lament for the Makaris" (stanza 10),

> . . . Art magicians, and astrologis,
> Rhetoris, logicians and theologis,
> Thame helpis no conclusions slee;—
> Timor mortis conturbat me
> ("Fear of death shatters me").

Before we consider what, if anything, contemporary psychology and psychotherapy have to contribute to this issue, we have to say a few words about death as the motive as well as the theme of philosophy.

4. Philosophers and Death. Schopenhauer maintained that death is the muse of philosophy and that "all religious and philosophical systems are principally directed toward comforting us concerning death, and are thus primarily antidotes to the terrifying certainty of death" (*The World as Will and Idea*, III, Ch. 16). This is an obvious oversimplification and overstatement. The origin of religion involves many other factors than just the dimension of human anxiety with regard to death, and this is true even more of philosophy where "wonder" (Plato) and intellectual curiosity were motives of equal if not greater importance.

Still almost from the very first, death was a major topic of philosophical reflection. Of the 126 known fragments of Heraclitus, no less than sixteen deal with death. And while it is a mistake to impute to Plato the proposition that philosophy is a meditation on death or to suspect him of an inordinate fear of it, there can be no doubt whatsoever that it held a prominent place in his thought. What Plato did say was that "the true philosopher is ever pursuing death and dying" (*Phaedo* 64A). This statement can be understood correctly only in the context of Plato's notion that the soul is a prisoner in the body, that the body is an obstacle to the acquisition of knowledge, that the philosopher is a seeker after truth, and that the attainment of true knowledge is possible only when the soul is liberated from the chains of the body, which is what death means to Plato. Thus, in the pursuit of true

knowledge, the philosopher strives in this life to approach the condition in which his soul will be after death. In philosophizing, he is, as it were, rehearsing death.

Death was also an important theme among the Stoics, Montaigne, Bruno, Descartes, Pascal, Spinoza, Leibniz, Kant, Hegel, Schopenhauer, Feuerbach, Nietzsche, and many others of lesser stature.

In any case, not until very recent times did philosophers—with the notable exception of "existentialists"—deliberately shun the problems arising from the fact of mortality. This is the more surprising since the prominent place which the topic of death occupies in contemporary literature (Malraux, Camus, Hemingway, Faulkner, Beckett, Ionesco to mention but the most outstanding examples) seems to reflect the profound uneasiness concerning man's ultimate fate.

One of the reasons for the reluctance of most contemporary philosophers to deal with death is their disenchantment with metaphysical speculation which seemed to yield nothing but contradictory opinions. Moreover, the "glamor" of science, due to its spectacular advances and the visibility of its practical applications, awakened the ambition to make philosophy an "exact" science in its own right. Both of these tendencies led to a considerable restriction of the scope of philosophy. "Professional" philosophers today are neither disposed nor expected (at least by their peers) to concern themselves with "ultimate questions." But if the so-called analytical philosophers, who predominate in the English-speaking countries, exclude death as a legitimate topic of philosophy because of a narrow view of the task of philosophy, some of those who still cling to a broader and more traditional view of the philosophical enterprise disregard death because individual man and his death appear to them to be of little importance.

Typical is the remark of the German philosopher Nicolai Hartmann that only "self-tormenting metaphysicians" waste their time on meditating on death and speculating about immortality. And most pragmatists are, in addition, haunted by the fear that concern with "otherworldly" things will interfere with the task of improving the conditions of existence here and now. It may be argued, however, that a better life includes also a satisfactory coming to terms with death. In any case, for better or for worse, a great many contemporary philosophers have abandoned the field almost entirely to psychologists and sociologists.

5. Contemporary Psychology and Death. Systematic studies of man's attitudes toward death and dying have begun only around the turn of this century. They have elicited information with regard to different age groups, sex, occupation, marital status, education, and physical as well as mental health and sickness. Most of the results are, however, conflicting, and no universally accepted theory of the genesis of the fear of death has emerged. But it has become amply clear that the term "fear of death" is a catch-all label which hides heretofore unsuspected complexities. Not only do the emotions described as death-fear range from simple reluctance or aversion to think of death to outright terror, but these emotions refer to a variety of "objects." There is fear of what comes after death (fear of the effects of death), and fear of the process of dying (fear of the pain and anguish of dying). As to the therapy of the (pathological) dread of death and dying, (that is, when no valid medical reasons to expect impending death exist), it appears that the two most effective approaches so far are that of psychoanalysis, which considers "anxiety" over death as but a special case of a general anxiety state which has become "fixated" on this particular subject, and hypnotic suggestion therapy, for which Russian psychiatrists claim outstanding successes. In the case of apprehension and fear in people actually dying, recent experiments with LSD have shown promising results. One should be careful, however, not to confuse the cure of the pathological fear of death or the chemically induced relief of the anxiety of the dying with a "solution" of all the problems which the fact of death continues to present to the inquiring mind.

This does not mean that there is, or must be, such a "global" solution. However, it is important to remember that until very recently it was generally assumed that the answer to the problems of death was known, universally accepted, and it is still considered valid by many. This answer was "immortality."

IMMORTALITY

Before discussing the main doctrinal formulations of the idea of immortality, a few preliminary remarks will be useful.

In order to be a satisfactory solution to the problems arising in connection with the fact of death, immortality must be first a "personal" immortality, and secondly it must be a "pleasant" one. Only pleasant and personal immortality provides what still appears to many as the only effective defense against the fear of death. But it is able to accomplish much more. It appeases the sorrow following the death of a loved one by opening up the possibility of a joyful reunion in the hereafter. It satisfies the sense of justice outraged by the premature deaths of people of great promise and talent, because only this kind of immortality offers the hope of fulfillment in another life. Finally, it offers an answer to the question of the ultimate meaning of life, particularly when death prompts the agonizing query, "What is the purpose of this strife and struggle

if, in the end, I shall disappear like a soap bubble?" (Tolstoy, *A Confession*, 1879).

It is important to realize, however, that the notion of a pleasant immortality for all and sundry runs counter to the sense of justice which otherwise plays such a prominent role in man's claim to immortality. While it was felt that it would be an "injustice" if man were condemned to total annihilation, it did not make sense that evil men should enjoy the same privileges in the hereafter as did the good ones. Thus we find in all doctrines of immortality some restrictions as to the enjoyment of a blissful afterlife, be it a permanent exclusion from it of those guilty of crimes, or a merely temporary one, allowing for rehabilitation, expiation, or purification. The main difficulty with personal immortality, however, is that once the naive position which took deathlessness and survival after death for granted was shattered, immortality had to be proved. All serious discussion of immortality became a search for arguments in its favor.

The three main variants of the idea of immortality are the doctrine of reincarnation, or transmigration of the soul, the Platonic theory of the immortality of the soul (which also admits the possibility of transmigration), and the Christian doctrine of resurrection of the body, which includes "Platonic" immortality. Historically they seem to have appeared in the Western world in that order. But we shall begin with the doctrine of the immortality of the soul as expounded by Plato, partly because his position was the best argued, and because it is around it that in subsequent times most serious discussions revolved.

I. IMMORTALITY OF THE SOUL

1. Plato. The two basic premises of Plato's doctrine of the immortality of the soul are a radical dualism which sees man as a composite of a material body and an incorporeal soul, and the assertion that the soul, and not the body, is the essential, the true man. The soul is not only totally independent of the body, but it is of divine origin and only an unwilling guest in the body. This is what makes Plato define death as a liberation of the soul from the bodily "prison." The probable source of this view is the Orphic "soma-sema," the body is the prison (of the soul). Whether it is this view of the soul which leads to the notion that the soul is the essential person or the other way around, is impossible to determine. In any case, when Crito asks Socrates how he wants to be buried, the latter expresses surprise that his listeners apparently still did not get the main point of his discussion, namely, that it is the Socrates who is now conversing with them, and not the corpse he will soon become, who is the real Socrates (*Phaedo* 115C–D).

Plato advances the following arguments for the immortality of the soul: (1) the argument from reminiscence. Man has certain ideal concepts as well as some knowledge of *a priori* (e.g., mathematical) truths which could not have been derived or been acquired through experience (*Phaedo* 72A–77A; *Meno* 81B–86B). Thus we must have acquired them before this life began, which indicates that the soul is prior to the body. But this would prove only the preexistence of the soul, not its immortality, although the latter is made more plausible if preexistence is true. The case for immortality is strengthened, however, when we consider that in order to apprehend the eternal "Ideas" or "Forms," the soul must itself be eternal for "nothing mortal knows what is immortal."

(2) Argument from the "fact" that the soul is the principle of life: the soul, whose essence is life (vitality) and thus the very opposite of death, cannot be conceived as dying any more than fire can be conceived as becoming cold. This argument (*Phaedo*, 100B–107A) is based on Plato's arbitrarily equating "soul" as the principle of life with soul as the bearer or originator of mental and emotional activity. Moreover, to hold that as the principle of life the soul is the "Idea" of life and, as such, deathless and eternal has no bearing on the immortality of the individual soul, since the "Idea" of a thing is, according to Plato himself, very different from its individual manifestation.

The same unwarranted equation of the two meanings of soul underlies the third argument, (3) the soul as self-moving, which states that since the soul moves itself and is the source of movement and life, it must be immortal because that which moves itself is incorruptible and ingenerable (*Phaedrus* 245C–246A).

(4) The soul as "simple." Plato argues that the soul must be immortal since it is "simple" and incorporeal. An incorporeal substance is "naturally" incorruptible, and "simple" means that it is uncompounded and therefore incapable of dissolution (in the sense of falling apart; Kant has later argued that even if it has no "extensive quality," it nevertheless possesses "intensive quality" and can therefore dwindle to nothingness "by a gradual loss of power").

Plato himself was well aware of the inadequacy of his arguments for the immortality of the soul (and this may be taken as a proof that he never doubted its truth). He admitted that the divine origin of the soul as well as the existence of eternal "Ideas" require further investigation (*Phaedo* 107B). His former pupil, Aristotle, rejected these basic assumptions on which Plato's doctrine of immortality of the soul rested. Aristotle held that the soul is one with the body as its "form" (which term is quite different from Platonic sense of "Form" or "Idea"). There is no necessity for the separate existence of Ideas, because "the shape of a bronze sphere exists at the same time as the bronze sphere exists," but it is not at all certain that "any form survives afterwards" and "the soul may be of this sort" (*Metaphysics* 1070a).

But while he was quite positive in his denial that the soul could survive in its entirety, Aristotle spoke of the possibility of survival of the intellectual part of it. Unfortunately, it is not at all clear what he meant by the term "pure intellect": on the one hand he described it as a capacity, but then there are passages where he speaks of it as if it were an incorporeal substance. Clearly, only the latter could be conceived as immortal. What Aristotle may have had in mind is that if not the whole soul, then at least man's active intellect is of divine origin (since he spoke of it as coming from the "outside") and as such can be said to be eternal. But this is not the immortality of the soul as Plato conceived it. Not only does Aristotle seem to be contemptuous of this doctrine (*Nicomachean Ethics* 1111b), but most of his commentators beginning with Alexander of Aphrodisias, and particularly Averroës, were of the opinion that "The Philosopher" did not believe in any kind of individual immortality.

2. Descartes. For almost two thousand years, few new arguments were propounded in favor of the doctrine of the immortality of the soul until Descartes turned his attention to the problem. In the meantime the reintroduction to the Western world of Greek philosophical works, in particular those of Aristotle, by Arabic scholars about the middle of the twelfth century, brought with it the first serious threat to the universally accepted belief in immortality, since these works, and the commentaries on them, contained shocking but well-reasoned arguments against immortality of the soul.

The reaction among Christian philosophers to this threat was exemplified by Siger of Brabant in the twelfth century, and set the pattern for the next six hundred years. This reaction consisted in the distinction between the truth of reason and the truth of faith. Although on rational grounds the immortality of the soul is, at best, doubtful, human reasoning must yield to the divinely revealed truth as set forth in the Holy Scriptures.

Descartes shared the view of the religious apologists about the morally disastrous effects of disbelief in the immortality of the soul. In Part V of the *Discourse on Method*, he wrote that "next to the error of those who deny God . . . there is none which is more effectual in leading feeble minds from the straight path of virtue than to imagine that . . . after this life we have nothing to fear or to hope for, any more than the flies or the ants" (Haldane and Ross, trans. throughout).

639

He asserted that "our soul is in its nature entirely independent of the body, and in consequence it is not liable to die with it. And then, inasmuch as we observe no other causes capable of destroying it, we are naturally inclined to judge that it is immortal." How did he justify the first assertion? Harvey's discovery of the circulation of the blood gave Descartes the idea that both animal and human bodies might be regarded as "machines." But, although, according to Descartes, there is no real difference between a machine and a living organism, man is much more than just a body. For he is able "to reply appropriately to everything . . . said in his presence" and "act from knowledge, whereas the animal can do so only from the disposition of its organs" (*Discourse*, Part V). What this means is simply that man alone "thinks." Thinking, however, was conceived by Descartes rather broadly to include "all that we are conscious as operating in us . . . willing, imagining, feeling" (*Principles of Philosophy*, I, IX). And "all that is in us and which we cannot in any way conceive as pertaining to the body must be attributed to our soul" (*Passions of the Soul*, I, IV).

Since the idea that something material may be endowed with thought is not contradictory and must have been known to Descartes (it was the view of the Greek atomists and presented with eloquence by Lucretius), what were his reasons for attributing thought to an immaterial soul apart from his commitment to religious dogma? The "proof" that there is a soul totally independent of the body appears as a by-product of his revolutionary approach to the problem of a criterion of certainty. In the *Discourse* (Part IV) he describes how he arrived at what he claimed to be rock-bottom certainty of the *cogito ergo sum*—"I am thinking, therefore I exist": ". . . I saw that I could conceive that I had no body, and that there was no world nor place where I might be; but yet that I could not for all that conceive that I was not." Thus he concluded that he was ". . . a substance the whole essence and nature of which is to think, and that for its existence there is no need of any place, nor does it depend on any material thing; so that this 'me,' that is to say, the soul by which I am what I am, is entirely distinct from the body . . . and even if the body were not, the soul would not cease to be what it is."

The strength of the above argument in favor of a soul entirely distinct from the body derives from the ease with which everyone can follow it, and from the familiarity with the experience described therein, because everyone at one time or another did have the impression of being a disembodied "spirit." The main objection to Descartes' conclusion is his unwarranted equating of "me" with the soul. It is a far cry from the reasoning that "while trying to think everything

false, it must needs be that I, who was thinking this was something" to the conclusion that this something was the incorporeal soul, that it was entirely distinct from the body, and thus will survive bodily death.

It is interesting that Descartes sometimes appears to have been more concerned with proving the existence of the soul than with the search for ultimate certainty. Having been advised by his friend, the mathematician Father Mersenne, that his *cogito, ergo sum* is not an original discovery since it can be found in Saint Augustine's *The City of God* (XI, 26), Descartes defends himself in a letter to Andreas Colvius (November 14, 1640) by pointing out the difference between them: "The use I make of it is in order to show that that 'I' which thinks is an immaterial substance which has nothing corporeal about it."

Descartes' difficulties in attempting to explain how such two radically different substances as the immaterial soul and the extended body could interact, since they obviously do interact, are well known. In themselves, they do not invalidate the notion of an incorporeal and immortal soul. But he must have felt in the end that to prove it may be as impossible as to solve the problem of the interaction between body and soul. It is significant that he changed the original subtitle of his *Meditations* from "In which the existence of God and the Immortality of the Soul are demonstrated" to "In which the Real Distinction between Mind and Body is demonstrated." But this does not mean that Descartes gave up his deep conviction that the soul was immortal.

The belief in immortality did not have to rely on rational proofs. As early as the ninth century, the Irish monk John Scotus Erigena held that personal immortality cannot be proved or disproved by reason. A much more forceful, detailed, and influential statement of the same position was made by Pietro Pomponazzi in his *De immortalitate animae* (1516). After having examined various arguments in favor of immortality and discussed several sets of objections to them, he concluded that the question should be regarded as a "neutral" one since man's natural reason was not strong enough either to demonstrate or to refute immortality of the soul. Pomponazzi added, however, that the question of the immortality of the soul had been answered affirmatively by God himself as reported in the Holy Scriptures. This is, in essence, a reiteration of the position advanced by Siger of Brabant. Pomponazzi's conclusion was interpreted by some of his contemporaries, and many modern historians have agreed with them, as implying that Pomponazzi himself did not believe in the immortality of the soul. Nevertheless, the imputation of hypocrisy in Pomponazzi has very little real evidence to support it.

In any case, in spite of the position that the truth of immortality of the soul should be based on faith and revelation, and asserted on this ground alone, philosophers continued to seek proofs of immortality. However, Descartes' fiasco made it clear to some that a radically new approach had to be tried, the more so because of new arguments against immortality.

The most cogent and influential were those advanced by David Hume. According to Hume, the doctrine of immortality is suspect since it is so obviously favored by human desire. Man would not cling so tenaciously to this belief if he did not fear death. But the very fact of this fear points rather in favor of the assumption that bodily death brings with it also the end of the conscious personality. Since "Nature does nothing in vain, she would never give us a horror against an impossible event." But what is the point of making us afraid of an unavoidable event? Hume answers that without the terror before death, mankind would not have survived. Moreover, why does Nature confine our knowledge to the present life if there is another? All the arguments from analogy to nature, Hume dismisses as being rather "strong for the mortality of the soul." Finally, "What reason is there to imagine that an immense alteration, such as made on the soul by the dissolution of the body, and all its organs of thought and sensation, can be effected without the dissolution of the soul?" ("Of the Immortality of the Soul," *Unpublished Essays* [1777], pp. 401–06).

The last argument was, in essence, the one advanced also by the French Encyclopedist d'Alembert and by the materialists, La Mettrie, Cabanis, and d'Holbach.

3. Kant. The most notable attempt to provide a new basis for ascertaining immortality of the soul, was Kant's "moral" argument. His starting point was that man is not only a rational but also a moral being, and that human reason has two functions, one "speculative" or theoretical ("pure reason"), and the other concerned with moral action ("practical reason"). In his *Critique of Pure Reason* (1781; revised 1787), Kant showed that God, freedom, and immortality are ideas which speculative reason can form but cannot prove. They are, however, "postulates" of "practical reason," that is, they "are not theoretical dogmas but presuppositions which necessarily have only practical import . . . they give objective reality to the ideas of practical reason in general." Thus the immortality of the soul must be true because morality demands it. In his *Critique of Practical Reason* (1789), Kant argued that the highest good (*summum bonum*) is the union of happiness and virtue. But while happiness can be attained in this life, perfect virtue ("holiness") cannot and requires, therefore, that the existence of man be prolonged to infinity. Thus there must be another, future life. Later on, Kant

modified this argument somewhat by stating that we are required by moral law to become morally perfect. But "no rational being is capable of holiness at any moment of his existence. Since, however, it is required as practically necessary, it can be found in a progress which continues into infinity. . . . This infinite progress, however, is possible only if we assume an infinitely lasting existence of the same rational being (which is called the immortality of the soul)" (*Critique of Practical Reason*, trans. L. W. Beck [1949], pp. 225–26).

Unfortunately, there is no absolute necessity that reality will yield to moral demands unless, of course, we assume that the world is ruled, as Kant asserts, "with great wisdom" and with a purpose which includes the moral perfection of man. This, too, however, can be "proved" only as a postulate of practical reason. No wonder, then, that Kant's moral argument for immortality of the soul failed to impress even his admirers.

4. Some Recent Philosophical Arguments. The influential French philosopher, Henri Bergson, the Englishman, John McTaggart, and the German, Max Scheler, were probably the most notable twentieth-century thinkers who opposed the predominant anti-immortalist trend of the nineteenth century, and argued in favor of immortality. All three embraced more or less the position that we cannot form a correct judgment on the issue of immortality because we do not know all the relevant facts about mental life. Bergson felt that to consider man as limited to his bodily frame is "a bad habit of limiting consciousness to a small body and ignoring the vast one." He argues that the only reason we can have for believing in the extinction of consciousness at death is that we see the body become disorganized. But this reason loses its force if it can be shown, as Bergson believed, that almost all of consciousness is independent of the body (*Time and Free Will* [1913], p. 73). But if the "mental life overflows the cerebral life, survival becomes so probable that the burden of proof comes to lie on him who denies it" (ibid.). Max Scheler took a similar position and declared that the burden of proof (*onus probandi*) falls on those who deny immortality.

McTaggart, however, was much more of an old-fashioned metaphysical idealist. He believed that "all that exists is spiritual," that reality is rational and external, and that time and change are only apparent. Death is not the end of the self, even though it deprives the spirit of an apparent finite body.

Basic to the views of all three philosophers is their conviction that the self—the unchanging, unifying core of man's personality—is not identical with the body and not wholly dependent on the brain, since it controls and drives the body in ways which are not native to

641

it. The body gives to the self merely a location and an opportunity to act. This is also the view of William Ernest Hocking, and of Gabriel Marcel who essentially repeats Socrates' assertion that "I am not my body." William James, however, held that even if the "soul" may be the function of the brain, this does not at all exclude the possibility that it continues after the brain dies. According to James, this continuity is, on the contrary, quite possible if we think of their relation as one of "functional dependence," that is, if the brain just fulfills a "permissive" or "transmissive" function.

In addition to the sometimes very subtle arguments for the immortality of the soul advanced by philosophers, there are several less sophisticated ones. Among them are the following.

A. Argument of "General Consent." This argument is simply that the universality of the belief in immortality is evidence of its truth. Others see such evidence in the universal desire for immortality. However, both arguments are fallacious, if for no other reason than the fact that such a belief is neither universally held nor is immortality universally desired. Moreover, no matter how intense and widespread such desire may be, there is no guarantee that the object of a desire must actually exist or be realized.

In addition, it must be pointed out that what is actually desired (although far from being a universal wish) is not the immortality of the soul but "deathlessness": most people would rather go on living indefinitely, and the belief in an immortal soul is merely a "compromise," a "second best" for those who are reluctant to face the prospect of total extinction but know that death is inevitable.

B. Argument that Cessation is "Inconceivable." The difficulty of imagining one's own demise has been used, among others, by Goethe as an argument for immortality: "It is quite impossible for a thinking being to imagine nonbeing, a cessation of thought and life. In this sense everyone carries the proof of his own immortality within himself" (Johann Peter Eckermann, *Conversations with Goethe*, 1852). He tries to compensate for the obvious weaknesses of this "proof" by taking refuge in the difficulties of proving immortality. "As soon as one endeavors to demonstrate dogmatically a personal continuation after death, one becomes lost in contradictions" (op. cit.). But Hume has disposed of this excuse by asking why, if man is indeed immortal, he does not have a clearer knowledge of it.

C. Mystical "Evidence." As a counterargument against the above, Jacques Maritain affirms that there is in man "a natural, instinctive knowledge of his immortality." The question is whether this "instinctive knowledge" is not the very same psychological phenomenon of disbelief in one's mortality that we have

referred to above. But Maritain may have in mind certain experiences which, for the lack of a better word, we can call "mystical," like those described in Goethe's *Wilhelm Meister:* "During some sleepless nights, especially, I had some feelings . . . as if my soul were thinking unaccompanied by the body. . . . The grave awakens no terror in me; I have eternal life." But this and similar experiences are strictly "private" insights and, as such, not very convincing. Sometimes they are not convincing even to those who have such "revelations," especially since they are counterbalanced by other experiences recently emphasized by some "existentialists." For example, Karl Jaspers speaks of the "awareness of fragility," and Heidegger speaks of the "experience of progressing toward death."

What is needed, then, in order to make immortality credible would be empirical, publicly verifiable evidence, without which the subjective feeling of one's indestructibility will have great difficulties in overcoming the formidable obstacle voiced by Omar Khayyam that ". . . of the myriads who/ Before us passed the door of Darkness/ Not one returns to us. . . ."

D. Spiritism and Psychical Research. It is precisely because it claims to offer empirical proof that the dead do survive, and can be communicated with, that "Spiritualism" (or "Spiritism") exercises a strong appeal to more people than is usually realized. "Spirits" and the doctrine of Spiritism were revived in the United States in 1844, in Hydesville, New York, where mysterious happenings occurring in the farmhouse of the Fox family were assumed by the members of the family to be due to the "spirits" of people, now dead, who had previously occupied the house. The "experiences" of the Fox sisters, who claimed to be able to communicate with these spirits, served as a basis for the book of a Frenchman, Léon Rivail (who assumed the spirit-inspired name of Allan Kardec), entitled *Le Livre des esprits*, which is considered the "bible of Spiritism."

There are two schools of Spiritism. The one prevalent in Anglo-Saxon countries believes in a single embodiment of the soul. The other, popular in Latin countries, follows Kardec who teaches multiple incarnation. Both posit the existence of an "astral" body which is conceived as an infinitely fine matter, or subtle fluid, which envelops the immaterial soul. It is said to be observable when a person dies and the soul reverts from the carnate to the disincarnate state. This "visibility" as well as the communication between the living and the dead (by means of the tapping of a three-legged table or the utterances of medium in trance) is the "proof" of immortality which the spiritists offer. And since immortality is thus for them a proven fact, they claim that they bring it down to earth as a purely naturalistic phenomenon and not something that involves supernatural intervention or magic. The idea of an astral body had been entertained by several early church fathers. Thus Tatian speaks of an ethereal body which envelops the soul, and Irenaeus maintains that the soul retains the imprint of the body like water which retains the shape of the receptacle in which it froze.

The obvious criticism of the spiritist doctrine of immortality is that although there may be mental and even physical paranormal phenomena, it is quite far-fetched to assume that they are caused by the spirits of the dead. Moreover, not only are the messages from "beyond the grave" uniformly trivial, not to say asinine, but all the mediums have been so far exposed as frauds, even by sympathetic investigators of the "occult" world. The more serious among the students of these strange phenomena assert only that they are the result of the hidden or neglected powers of the mind, that these point to the mind's independence of, and mastery over, the body, which renders the hypothesis of its survival after death not only plausible but even probable.

More recently, experimental studies of these unusual powers of the human psyche have been undertaken, of which those of J. B. Rhine of Duke University have received the most publicity. Without necessarily denying the existence of "extrasensory perception" (ESP), critics point out that it may be superfluous to assume a spiritual entity in order to explain parapsychological powers and that these are not more spectacular or uncanny than other psychological capacities which are taken for granted.

E. Conclusion. It has become clear from our brief survey of the arguments for immortality that they are perhaps sufficient to reinforce an already existing conviction, but not good enough for someone skeptical about the possibility of survival after death. Nor is the position that the burden of proof lies on those who deny immortality particularly persuasive.

William James noted that on this subject there are two kinds of people, "those whom we find indulging to their hearts' content in the prospects of immortality, and . . . those who experience the greatest difficulty in making such a notion seem real to themselves at all. These latter persons are tied to their senses . . . and feel a sort of intellectual loyalty to what they call hard facts" (*The Will to Believe* [1897], p. 40). But today, even among the first kind, we find rather a hope of immortality than a firm belief in it.

Several causes of the erosion of the immortalist's position have been suggested, among them the general decline of religious beliefs, the refutation of "proofs"

of immortality by materialist philosophers, and scientific data showing the dependence of mental phenomena on the brain. Another reason could well be that many may not really care about it. If this is so, it would signify a radical change in attitudes not only toward death but also toward life.

II. RESURRECTION

Bodily reconstitution combined with the immortality of the soul has been the universally accepted version of immortality in the Western world for almost two thousand years. Only recently (1968) Pope Paul VI reaffirmed this doctrine, thus categorically repudiating all attempts to interpret it symbolically.

The Christian view of the immortality of the soul differs significantly from the Platonic in that it is something which results from divine grace, whereas for the latter, immortality is a "natural" endowment of each and every soul. As Pope Paul formulated it, "We believe that the souls of all those who die in the grace of Christ, whether they must still be purified in Purgatory or whether from the moment they leave their bodies Jesus takes them to Paradise, are the people of God in the eternity beyond death which will be conquered on the day of resurrection when these souls will be reunited with their bodies" (*Time*, August 1968).

Most of those who accept this position as well as those who consider it unacceptable in such literal terms are unaware that the belief in the resurrection of the dead antedates Christianity. It is an integral part of the Zoroastrian eschatology and it is found among the Jews prior to Jesus' time. Although, according to Josephus Flavius, the sect of the Pharisees believed "that every soul is incorruptible, but that only the souls of the good pass over to other bodies," and thus appear to have believed in transmigration rather than resurrection, Saint Paul (Acts 23:6) attributes to them the latter belief.

Generally speaking, the idea of the resurrection of the body is not at all strange if we consider that, like the doctrine of the immortality of the soul, it was a reaction to the popularly held somber vision of postmortem existence in Sheol or Hades. Man is no more content with a sad conclusion to the drama of his existence than he is with this existence being an unmitigated calamity. Moreover, the awakening moral conscience demanded not only punishment but also rewards for one's actions in this life. And what better reward for a decent life could there be than restoration to life?

Significantly, however, what Saint Paul had been preaching seems to differ from the later, official Catholic doctrine. Not only did he speak of the resurrection of the *body* (*resurrectionem corporis*) and not of the flesh (*resurrectionem carnis*), but he insisted that the body will be resurrected in a new, changed form. Twice in I Corinthians he says, "We shall all be changed." In his view, God will recreate man not as the identical physical organism that he was before death but as a "spiritual body" (*soma pneumaticon*) endowed with the characteristics and the memory of the deceased.

Yet such a view of resurrection may have been troublesome. Skeptics doubted that Jesus had risen from the dead at all, and in order to convince them, it was imperative to be able to say that the disciples did recognize Him because He was physically exactly the same—"flesh and bones"—(*sarka kai ostea*, Luke 24:29). Obviously, such a positive identification would not have been possible in the case of a changed, "spiritual" body. In any case, the early church fathers did reshape the Paulinic view of resurrection to conform to these requirements.

This raises, however, the thorny question as to the condition in which the body will be resurrected, e.g., as it was at the time of death, or in its youthful splendor. Another perhaps even more serious problem was whether, on the day of the Last Judgment, the souls which were in Purgatory or Paradise awaiting that decisive hour would indeed rejoin the right bodies. The officially accepted answers to these and other problems are those of Thomas Aquinas.

Concerned as he was with proving the truth of resurrection, Aquinas was attracted to Aristotle's view that the person is the living human body. And faced with the necessity of asserting the immortality of the soul, he had, however, to show that it was a substance or, in his terminology, "something subsistent." Therefore, in his commentary to Aristotle's *De anima*, Aquinas tries to interpret Aristotle's remark that the intellect exists separately as meaning that "the principle of intellectual operation which we call the soul is both incorporeal and subsistent." Only in this way was a "synthesis" of the Aristotelian and the Platonic positions possible. And only if such synthesis could be accomplished and the unity of body and soul demonstrated can bodily resurrection, and not merely immortality of the soul, be asserted as man's true postmortem destiny. On the other hand, only if the soul is an incorporeal substance will it survive death and be available for the reunification with the resurrected physical body. That it will find the identical former body is, according to Aquinas, quite certain because the truth of resurrection is vouchsafed by the Holy Scriptures. He argues further that since man is created for happiness, and since it is unattainable here on earth, there must be an afterlife where this goal will be attained. But the whole man, body and soul, is destined for happiness. Thus only resurrection, and not mere

immortality of the soul, would fulfill this promise. And if the soul would not return to the very same body it left at death, it would not be true resurrection.

Modern man has considerable difficulty in accepting the doctrine of literal resurrection of the body. As Edwyn Bevin points out, "For many people today, the idea of a literal resurrection of the body has become impossible" (*The Hope of a World to Come* [1930], p. 53).

III. REINCARNATION

Various forms of this doctrine are transmigration, metempsychosis, palingenesis, and rebirth. It does not necessarily imply the eternity of the soul since Buddhism, which teaches reincarnation, denies it. The belief that the soul of a dead individual reenters immediately (or as in the Tibetan book of the dead, the *Bardo Tödol*, after 49 days) that of a newborn child eliminates the difficulty of visualizing a totally disembodied soul and the question of its destiny after it leaves the body. The doctrine of reincarnation seems to have originated in India, possibly in prehistoric times. Many primitives in various parts of the world believe that man possesses several souls, one of which reincarnates in a descendent of the deceased, a notion which may have been suggested by the sometimes striking resemblance between a child and his dead relative. It is interesting, however, that no traces of the belief in reincarnation can be found among the ancient Egyptians or the Assyro-Babylonians. There is also no hint of it in Homer, or Hesiod, and no mention of it in the Old Testament. Among the Jews we find it much later, and the sect of the Pharisees which adopted it had been obviously influenced by their Greek contemporaries. In Greece itself, the doctrine of reincarnation was first taught by Pythagoras in the sixth century B.C. and is usually assumed to be of orphic origin. Some scholars, however, claim that the doctrine was "invented" by Pherecydes of Syros and base their opinion on a passage in Cicero's *Tusculan Disputations*. Others point out that to trace it to Orphism of which little is known is to beg the question of an even earlier source.

It is tempting to seek it in the influence of Indian thought if it were not for the difficulty of finding concrete evidence for such a connection. Moreover, there is a basic difference between the Hindu version of the doctrine and that of Pythagoras. While the latter considers successive reincarnations as the opportunity for the purification and perfection of the soul, for the Hindus, Brahmanists and Buddhists alike, reincarnation represents merely a continuous repetition of the suffering and misery of earthly existence. It is tied in with the doctrine of cosmic eternal recurrence and the periodic disappearance and reappearance of humanity during which the soul transmigrates without end. And while, for the Hindu, salvation consists in an escape from the wheel of rebirths, in the Greek version the soul is ultimately united with God.

In the Western world, the doctrine of reincarnation has never achieved popularity. The Pythagorean brotherhoods were secret societies, and subsequently only sectarian and heretical movements like the Jewish Cabalists, the Christian Gnostics, and the Cathars embraced it. It fared somewhat better among philosophers. Aside from Pythagoras, one has to mention Empedocles and, in particular, Plato who gave a more or less systematic account of the doctrine of the transmigration of the soul in several of his dialogues (*Gorgias* 525C–526B; *Phaedrus* 248A–B; *Phaedo* 82A, 113E, 114A–B; *Republic* X, 614C–625A; *Theaetetus* 117A; *Timaeus* 91D, 92A–B). Plotinus incorporated this doctrine into his philosophical system. Soon thereafter it was completely displaced by the Christian doctrine of resurrection. It reappears again in the Renaissance among the Italian Platonists of the fifteenth century, in the Cambridge Neo-Platonists in the seventeenth century, and is sympathetically considered by Giordano Bruno, and later on by Leibniz. Even the skeptical Hume felt that if there were immortality, "metempsychosis is the only system of this kind that philosophy can hearken to" ("Of the Immortality of the Soul," op. cit.). In the twentieth century, McTaggart argued in its favor, and C. J. Ducasse considers it the most plausible hypothesis.

Apart from metaphysical considerations, what are the most important arguments for reincarnation? Here again we have to distinguish between the Hindu and Western proponents of this doctrine. In the West it is but one of several answers to the question of man's post-mortem destiny, and unless it is accepted uncritically, it adds the burden of proving multiple incarnations of the soul to the already sufficiently taxing task of proving its immortality. In Hindu thought, for which (with the exception of a few materialist philosophers) the immortality of the soul is axiomatic, its reincarnation is most often equally so. And if one should, nevertheless, want proofs, these are usually based on the soul's "obvious" immortality. Thus the leading contemporary philosopher (and ex-president) of India, S. Radhakrishnan, advances the following argument: since souls are eternal, and since their normal condition is to be associated with a body which is perishable, it is plausible to assume that in order for the soul to remain in its normal condition, it must inhabit an unending succession of bodies.

But the Western mind is not impressed and prefers empirical proofs. Among these, one of the favorite arguments is the undeniable fact that some children exhibit certain instinctive capacities, and a few are even geniuses at a very early age. This is supposed to prove that there must be reincarnation, since otherwise the possession of such extraordinary gifts remains totally uncomprehensible.

Another argument is the occurrence of the phenomenon known as *déjà vu*. But the most popular and supposedly clinching argument is that some people apparently remember their previous existences, sometimes without extraneous help, though usually under hypnosis.

The obvious counterarguments, as far as genius in children and the *déjà vu* phenomena are concerned, is that although they are difficult to explain, the recourse to such an extreme as the preexistence and reincarnation of the soul seems unjustified. And regarding people who claim to remember their previous lives, not only can the information elicited not be reliably verified, but such people are exceedingly few and far between.

It remains to mention the reply of the adherents of the reincarnation doctrine to the last counterargument. They contend that death is a traumatic experience of such a force that it seriously affects or obliterates memory. But this argument tacitly assumes the immortality of the soul, since only in such a case can one speak of the consequences of the traumatic experience of death. And while dying may well be traumatic for many, on all available evidence it appears to be the last experience of a person.

Substitute Immortalities. Some of those who bring forth arguments against immortality of the soul (or resurrection of the body) propose other kinds of "immortality," thus giving this term a broader and often misleading meaning. There is, first of all, what may be called the doctrine of impersonal immortality: the spirit, or mind of man, is not destroyed at death but returns to and merges with the universal or divine Soul, or mind. This is the possible meaning of Aristotle's hint about the eternity of the active intellect. The main representatives of this view are Averroës, Bruno, Spinoza, and the German and English romantic poets and philosophers of the late eighteenth and early nineteenth centuries. Of this kind of immortality, Madame de Staël remarked somewhat sarcastically that "if the individual inner qualities we possess return to the great Whole, this has a frightening similarity to death."

Another kind of "immortality" which is intended to console, as well as to justify death, is "biological" immortality of our germ plasm (genes). The prospect to live on in one's children has, however, lost much of its comforting power since the realization that mankind itself will some day disappear, and particularly now that the atomic and hydrogen bombs have made such an outcome not infinitely remote but a very real and even immediate possibility. It might not necessarily affect Santayana's "ideal" immortality which is reminiscent of Goethe's view that the "traces on one's earthly days cannot be erased in Aeons." Nor would it affect what is known as "cosmological" immortality, according to which our energy-matter does not cease to exist but is only transformed and dispersed. But to both of these "immortalities," Madame de Staël's criticism equally applies. Of course, many people would be satisfied with mere "social" or "historical" immortality—to have left traces of one's passage on earth in the form of an artistic achievement, scientific discovery, or other remarkable accomplishments. "How can he be dead, who lives immortal in the hearts of men?" asks Longfellow in speaking of Michelangelo. This was the meaning of immortality for the great men of Ancient Rome. In modern times, this kind of "immortality" was first suggested by M. J. de Condorcet in his *Outline of the Progress of the Human Mind*, and, with particular force, by Ludwig Feuerbach. The least ambitious immortality would be to live on for a short time in the memory of one's family and friends. Very probably this is the only kind of "immortality" that the overwhelming majority of people will ever have. But for many people, this is not a completely satisfactory thought.

BIBLIOGRAPHY

Death. Jacques Choron, *Death and Western Thought* (New York, 1963); idem, *Modern Man and Mortality* (New York, 1964), which contains an extensive bibliography of the most relevant philosophical and psychological works in English and foreign languages dealing with death. Herman Feifel, ed., *The Meaning of Death* (New York, 1959). Robert Fulton, ed., *Death and Identity* (New York, 1965). Arnold Toynbee, *Man's Concern with Death* (London, 1968).

Immortality of the Soul. W. R. Alger, *A Critical History of the Doctrine of a Future Life* (New York, 1871). Anthony Flew, ed., *Body, Mind and Death* (New York, 1964). James Hastings, ed., *Encyclopedia of Religion and Ethics*, 13 vols. (Edinburgh and New York, 1910), Vol. XI, article "The State of the Dead." Corliss Lamont, *The Illusion of Immortality* (New York, 1950). F. W. H. Myers, *Human Personality and its Survival of Bodily Death* (London and New York, 1903).

Resurrection. J. N. D. Kelly, *Early Christian Doctrines* (London, 1958). James MacLeman, *Resurrection Then and Now* (Philadelphia, 1967). K. Stendahl, ed., *Immortality and Resurrection* (New York, 1965), consists of four Ingersoll Lectures (1955, 1956, 1958, and 1959), by Oscar Cullmann, Harry A. Wolfson, Werner Jaeger, and Henry J. Cadbury.

Reincarnation. S. G. F. Brandon, "Man and His Destiny," *World Religions* (Manchester, 1962). C. J. Ducasse, *The Belief in a Life after Death* (New York, 1961). Ian Stevenson, *The Evidence for Survival from Claimed Memories of Former Incarnation* (New York, 1961).

JACQUES CHORON

[See also Antinomy; **Buddhism;** Existentialism; Faith; Idea; Platonism; Pythagorean. . . .]

DEISM

DEISM is the belief that by rational methods alone men can know all the true propositions of theology which it is possible, necessary, or desirable for men to know. Deists have generally subscribed to most of the following propositions, and have ranged widely from Christian rationalists or fideists to atheists:

1. One and only one God exists.
2. God has moral and intellectual virtues in perfection.
3. God's active powers are displayed in the world, created, sustained, and ordered by means of divinely sanctioned natural laws, both moral and physical.
4. The ordering of events constitutes a general providence.
5. There is no special providence; no miracles or other divine interventions violate the lawful natural order.
6. Men have been endowed with a rational nature which alone allows them to know truth and their duty when they think and choose in conformity with this nature.
7. The natural law requires the leading of a moral life, rendering to God, one's neighbor, and one's self what is due to each.
8. The purest form of worship and the chief religious obligation is to lead a moral life.
9. God had endowed men with immortal souls.
10. After death retributive justice is meted out to each man according to his acts. Those who fulfill the moral law and live according to nature are "saved" to enjoy rewards; others are punished.
11. All other religious beliefs or practices conflicting with these tenets are to be regarded critically, as at best indifferent political institutions and beliefs, or as errors to be condemned and eradicated if it should be prudent to do so.

Deism is thus the name given to a set of epistemological and metaphysical claims. It has sometimes been discussed in the light of what it positively affirms but more often with respect to what it denies. To discriminate positive or constructive deism as a view different from negative or critical deism, while it may be useful in emphasizing the characteristics of particular deists or their works, obscures the fact that deism is critical in its affirmations and constructive in its denials. Pyrrhic or academic skepticism, fideism, any view which relies upon nonrational intuitions or feelings to establish religious truth, or any claims to a nonrational revelation are implicitly rejected by deists. Also rejected is any philosophy which affirms the nonexistence of God or which claims that nothing can be known about any relations asserted to exist between God and men.

Deists have varied considerably in their views of what constitutes a rational methodology. Some have held their religious beliefs to be warranted by *a priori* arguments, while others claimed that their conclusions were based on wholly empirical evidence. A deistic view of the world is a static one which exacts from all men an identical religious response. Any thoroughgoing relativism is incompatible with deistic teleologies. Equally clear is the deistic presupposition of a uniform human nature. All reasoning men have and always will have the same religious views in any time or place. These views receive no support from tradition or authority, which, according to deists, are sources of pedantic error and corruption. History contains a history of religious error but not of religious evolution.

Deists claim that all or most of the true propositions of theology are and have been known with certainty whenever men have reasoned correctly about theology. Variations in religious belief, not the tenets of true belief, have to be explained and accounted for. Religious cults, the chief form taken by such variations, are the products of innocent or malicious human error. Among the innocent errors and mistakes giving rise to religious diversity are sickness, madness and delusion, fear, mistaken reasoning, and the transmission of false information. Malicious errors are propagated by priests, rulers, artists, and generally unscrupulous men who, having no regard for truth, impose false reasoning upon men whom they wish to control or in some manner use to their own advantage. Error once established is maintained by the force, authority, and cunning of men no different from the first deceivers.

Truth may be discovered only when men are free to reason. It can be maintained only where they have liberty to criticize errors, even those dogmatic errors maintained by authority. No society which wholly prohibits criticism, in the form of argument or ridicule, can be good, happy, or enduring. Free discussion is a necessity; any political practices or institutions which prevent this should be overthrown. Censorship and repression, if legitimate and feasible at all, should be extended only to the propagators of known falsehoods.

Abstractly considered, deism has an optimistic view of the human condition: there can be no radical evil in the well-ordered world created by a good God. Moreover it assumes that the true religion, if known, will be followed by men because they find it true and in their interest to follow it. Regarding the actual situation of men, deists could only be pessimistic, critical, and even politically subversive in their demands for reform.

Deism has flourished only among rationalists possessing, in relatively closed societies, the freedom and leisure to criticize popular and authorized religious beliefs. Its concern with reason, its reliance on classical sources, and its dislike of popular superstition contributed to make it rather aristocratic in outlook. Where it has not been so, notably in the United States, it has been a form of protest allied to republicanism. Lacking exponents of the first intellectual rank and exercising little hold on the emotions, it has never been a popular creed, not even in the Enlightenment. As is appropriate to a view with a negative philosophy of history, it has scarcely varied since its first appearance.

Elements of the deistic position are as ancient as critical religious thought itself. False gods and impostors appear in the Old Testament, as does a providential God who is both creator and preserver of the world. Saint Paul's statements concerning the law of the Gentiles (Romans 2:13–15) yield the base for a natural religion. Among the pre-Socratics there are sixth- and fifth-century B.C. fragments dealing with being, the One, and the *logos* which suggest attempts at the construction of a rational theology. The imposture theory of the origin of the gods and of popular, politically useful religious cults can be found in the fragment from the *Sisyphus* of Critias of Athens. Plato and Aristotle, in their differing ways, contributed both to rational theology and to the critical literature on the origin of the gods. Epicureans, Stoics, and Academics further elaborated and criticized rational theologies resembling deism, discussing the existence, attributes, and relation of gods to men. Cicero, who transmitted these speculations both to the Romans and to later thinkers, deserves the title, and perhaps was, the father of deism, the first deist, even though he never gives wholehearted assent to the deistic position.

All of the defining principles of deism appear in Cicero's works, notably in *De natura deorum* (Book III). Cicero, like later deists, distinguished between philosophical and popular religions, defending the latter by appeals to authority, reason, and utility. Writing in an age of political chaos and religious credulity in which cults were seen as political contrivances, Cicero outlined views appealing to later thinkers who found themselves in similar circumstances. Such views survived in the ancient schools, in the philosophical paganism of men such as Plutarch, Celsus, and the emperor Julian, even in works Christian apologists devoted to their refutation.

The Christianization of Europe put an end to deism until the Renaissance. Yet even in this long period ideas essential to a deistic outlook were kept alive in a variety of ways. Controversy over the limits of faith and reason usually ended with the assignment to reason of proofs for the existence of God and often allowed for the discussion of some of His attributes. Natural law remained an expression of divine general providence and specified moral obligations which, if fulfilled, entailed some merit if not saving grace. Christian and Muslim scholars speculated about the eternity of the world and the immortality of souls. In doing so they put their arguments more rigorously than the Stoics or Cicero had done. Schism, heresy, and anticlericalism were common to all of the western countries producing or keeping alive theories of imposture as well as giving convincing examples. The Middle Ages thus preserved ideas which, taken from their Christian contexts, might be reformulated in more rigorously monotheistic syntheses than they had received in classical or Christian works.

Deism revived with the new philosophy, science, and culture of the Renaissance but also owed something to the concomitant religious upheaval which offered freedom, opportunity, and incentive to the critical proclivities of religious thinkers. Moreover, concern rationally to ground revealed religion in natural religion, to find an irenic and fundamental basis for Christian unity, and to end sectarian controversies furthered the development of deism in the sixteenth and seventeenth centuries. Socinians and Baptists as well as Renaissance philosophers and scientists played a role in the reemergence of deistic views in Europe.

Perhaps the first reference to *deists* which employs that term is found in Pierre Viret's *Instruction Chrestienne* (1564), reliably reprinted in Bayle's *Dictionnaire* entry, *Viret*. To the Calvinist Viret, deism was a new species of heresy brought forth by Italian Renaissance naturalism in the turmoil of reform. Allowing the *déistes* a belief in God like the Turks and Jews (*comme les Turcs & les Juifs*), he went on to say that they thought the doctrine of the evangelists and apostles only "myths and dreams" (*la doctrine des Évangélistes & des Apostres* only *fables & resveries*). Deists tended to treat the creator in an Epicurean fashion. "There are some among them who have a belief in the immortality of the soul: others agree with the Epicureans, and likewise about the providence of God with respect to men: as He did not concern Himself with the conduct of human affairs, so these would be governed by

chance, prudence, or the folly of men accordingly as things happen" (trans. R. Emerson).

Viret thought these "atheists" greatly abused the liberty which the Reformation had given them to criticize idolatry and superstition. With horror he berated deists, much as Roger Ascham, writing the *Scholemaster* at the same time, did "Italianate Englishmen." Like Roger Ascham, he gave no names. As a representative thinker exemplifying these views we might pick Jean Bodin, the author of *Colloquium Heptaplomeres* (1588), a dialogue on religion which includes a diest among the discussants. One might also choose from the list of deists given by Robert Burton in the *Anatomy of Melancholy* ([1621], Part 3, Sec. 4, Member 2, Subsec. 1). Or, one could examine the natural religion in the *Utopia* (1516) of Sir Thomas More as a model of what sixteenth-century thinkers, inspired by discoveries in the New World, thought a religion of reason could be—a religion whose saving efficacy they denied.

Europe in the first half of the seventeenth century produced few deists. Numerous controversies over the nature and source of religious truth produced a body of literature used in the formation of deism in the second half of the century. Skepticism deriving from classical sources, the works of Michel de Montaigne and Protestant and Catholic fideists, was developed philosophically and applied to historical and religious works by *libertins* such as Cyrano de Bergerac and *érudits,* including Gabriel Naudé, La Mothe le Vayer, and Giovanni Diodati—respectively two nominal Catholic fideists and a somewhat indifferent Protestant. In the skeptical and fideistic literature can be found most of the arguments of critical deism. Other studies placed a premium upon reason and natural law which was to nourish the positive claims of deism. Jurists like Hugo Grotius appealed to reason and natural law as the bases of morality and law; religious thinkers such as the great Anglican apologist Richard Hooker sought in reason an irenic principle and recognized that reason constituted the common meeting ground of all religious polemicists. Christian humanists trained in Scholastic philosophy who sought to be reasonable men believed in a rational religion prior to, but compatible with, Christianity. Philosophers who refuted skepticism, René Descartes or Lord Herbert of Cherbury (often called the first English deist), to name but two, usually attempted to prove the existence of God and to work out a rational religion as part of their philosophic system. Thomas Hobbes did this in such a fashion that religion was reduced to a wholly natural phenomenon and one not very reasonable at that. As yet science played little role in the growth of deism which insofar as it emerged at all, did so in the context of debates in theology, philosophy, and history.

The deists of the early seventeenth century asked

only to be allowed to believe, in peace, the religion of wise men; like most wise men they did not imprudently preach it. We glimpse it as the rebellious protests of wits in the circle of Théophile de Viau, long thought to be the author of *Les Quatrains du Déiste* (ca. 1626), and we occasionally find it as an easy surrogate for conviction among wits and gentlemen who regarded it as quite compatible with the established religion. Among the scholars Thomas Campanella introduced it in his utopia, *The City of the Sun* (ca. 1602, published 1627), where it is joined to radical social and political views and to a philosophic outlook common in the Italian Renaissance. In France its most distinguished exponent was probably Isaac de la Peyrère, the author of *Du Rappel des Juifs* (1643) and *Praeadamitae* (1655). In England Lord Herbert of Cherbury's later works *De religione laici* and *Dialogue between a Tutor and His Pupil* (ca. 1641–45, published 1768), exemplify its critical side as his *De veritate* (1621) had stressed its constructive arguments.

The middle and late seventeenth century saw a change in the character of European deism. Continental deists continued to maintain their beliefs largely as they had in the past but modified them by supplying new scientific evidence of design in nature while supplementing the argument from universal consent by citations from travel literature. The skeptical tradition was nourished by Cartesianism. Libertine *érudits* found their natural successors in men like Simon Tyssot de Patot, Charles de Saint-Évremond, and Pierre Bayle, the first two of whom were deists while the latter shared and diffused their critical arguments. European deism continued to be both scholarly and aristocratic, apolitical even while condemning the vulgar religion. It existed in the protected homes of the wealthy, in the Bohemian world of journalism, among a few scholars, and in the places of exile and refuge such as Holland. In Rotterdam Peyrère's deism supplied Benedict Spinoza with a few critical analyses of the Old Testament; elsewhere Giovanni Marana's *L'Espion du Grand Seigneur* (*The Turkish Spy*, 1684) could defend a natural religion that was not Islam, and the Baron Lahontan's imaginary member of the Huron tribe, whom he named Adario, would show that even savages could reason better than Jesuits. The epistemic claims, the uniformities which deism asserted, and its rationalism, appealed to those who thought vulgar religion an imposture, sects equally wrong, and miracles unlikely to happen in a world composed of substances and modes behaving according to rules known with near mathematical exactitude.

In England a political and religious upheaval affected the course of development in several ways. The spectacle of sectarian strife, prophets in the countryside, and saints at Westminster deepened or produced a distrust of enthusiasm and religious emotion not to be overcome until the end of the eighteenth century. "Priestcraft," which until the 1640's had been primarily a sin of Catholics, now appeared as a universal clerical trait. Irenicism, based on appeals to natural theology and reason as essentials in religious debate, had marked Anglican apologetics since Archbishop Jewel's (1522–71) time. Richard Hooker was succeeded by men like William Chillingworth, John Hales of Eton, the Cambridge Platonists, and latitudinarians, who throughout the century in the interests of Christian unity appealed to reason and formulated a justification of Anglican practices which made Christianity itself supportable only as a reasonable revelation, moralistic rather than sacramental in character. Natural theology became, as it was not among Calvinists or Catholics, the apologetic mainstay. English rational theology, which became increasingly liberal as the century progressed, was the product of religious controversy, not a philosophic inquiry into epistemology. So much was this the case during the 1620's, '30's, and '40's that Lord Herbert's deistic works were not refuted until after the Restoration. Religion became an openly political issue in England and those who found republicanism congenial often tended to maintain religious views equally rationalistic. Levellers and near deists such as Henry Marten, William Walwyn, Major John Wildman, reputed deists like the first Lord Shaftesbury, James Harrington, and Henry Neville were republicans in political theory as English deists tended to be in the 1690's and throughout the eighteenth century. Political and religious protest joined not only in these men but in Puritans like Milton who moved progressively in the direction of a rational religion. Even Puritan mystics, Quakers or pantheistic Ranters, and those disturbed by the inner light often spoke in rationalistic terms, thus introducing into popular parlance a rational religion of sorts. "The light of reason," "the spirit of reason" were for the Digger, Gerrard Winstanly, synonyms for the divine in human consciousness: "When Mankind lives in the unity of the one Spirit of Righteousness, he lives in the light and the light lives in him, which is Christ in him, the light of the Father, or the restoring power." Such talk made a less heated rationalism in religion acceptable to many who on the Continent would have had no exposure to it. London judges worried over Peyrère's work on the pre-Adamites published in translation in 1655. Bulstrode Whitelock related in his *Memoirs* (March 22, 1651) "That one Boston . . . was cashiered for holding some dangerous opinions, as that god was reason, etc." Heresy was for a longer time more freely expressed than it had been hitherto in any Christian country save perhaps in Luther's Germany. From this confusion deism grew either as a rejection of sectarian extravagance or from revulsion against enthusiasm or in some cases as an outgrowth of the ideas held by Puritans and Anglicans themselves.

The Restoration of Charles II brought a reaction to Puritanism which made fashionable among rakes like Charles Sedley, George Etherege, the Duke of Buckingham "a general creed and no very long one" such as the Marquis of Halifax ascribed to Charles II. Halifax, "the Trimmer" in politics, was himself a Trimmer in religion. Thomas Shadwell and the young John Dryden shared the literary interests of the courtiers whose "atheism" they occasionally displayed on stage. Seldom really godless, it was much more a religion of reason and nature quite compatible with neo-classic tastes. Generally critical, as in Shadwell's *The Lancashire Witches* (1685), it could be more explicitly constructive. Dryden's *The Indian Emperour* (1665) has a Montezuma capable of the following statement of natural religion:

That which we worship, and which you believe,
From Nature's common hand we both receive:
All under various names, Adore and Love
One power Immense, which ever rules above.
Vice to abhor, and Virtue to pursue,
Is both believed and taught by us and you.
. . . this must be enough, or to Mankind
One equal way to Bliss is not design'd.
For though some more may know, and some know less,
Yet all must know enough for happiness (Act 5, Scene 2).

Dryden was later to attack such views in *Religio laici* (1682). In a more popular genre Richard Head's picaresque novel *The English Rogue* (1665) contains a portrait of an "atheist" whose deism is plainly apparent.

The publication of Dryden's *Religio laici* and the answer to it by Charles Blount in a pamphlet of the same name began in England a controversy over deism which was to last until after 1750. The initial years of this controversy, to which Blount was a major contributor, show that English deists had begun to appeal to the new science as well as to the classics and the philosophers. Science was widely held to reveal the will of God in a natural and rational way and it bolstered arguments from design with new evidence. The philosophy of Herbert, Hobbes, and Spinoza was searched for biblical criticism and their psychologies applied to the analysis of religion. The latter were plagiarized by the anonymous pamphleteers like the author of *Miracles No Violation of the Law of Nature* (1683) to show "that the power of God and the *power of Nature are one and the same, and that* all her laws are his eternal decrees" (p. 3). Due to the relative freedom of the press, deism could be openly advocated and was in a pamphlet by Charles Gildon entitled *A Summary Account of the Deist's Religion* (1686).

These developments in philosophy, science, and religion were given renewed impetus by the work of John Locke whose empirical methodology, reasonableness in religion, and conviction that the new physics revealed God's design in nature were widely shared. John Toland and Anthony Collins, whose writings appeared after Locke's great works of the 1690's and also after the lapsing of censorship laws in 1694, elaborated the implications of the new science and philosophical empiricism. For them clear and distinct ideas conforming to "their Objects, or the Things we think upon" are the "ground of all right Persuasion" (Toland, *Christianity Not Mysterious* [1696], p. 16). Reason, "That faculty of the Soul which discovers the Certainty of God's own Existence, so we cannot otherwise discern his *Revelations* but by their Conformity with our natural Notices of him, which in so many words, do agree with our common Notions," reason was to be the sole base of religion (ibid., p. 13). With ideas limited by experience and the mind's ability to reflect and compare ideas there could be no mysteries in religion. Toland wrote biblical criticism designed to rationalize the apparent mysteries found there. In *Nazarenus* (1718) and *Tetradymus* (1720) he used apocryphal and pseudo-epigraphic literature as well as Muslim sources to catalogue the errors and deviations from the true religion taught by Christ and reason. His biblical criticism went beyond that of Benedict Spinoza and Jean Le Clerc and fell short of Richard Simon's not in design but in erudition. Toland's history of religious error placed Christianity firmly in a secular context while his comparison of it with Celtic and Muslim sources stripped it of uniqueness. Without radically breaking with the Christian conceptions of history he introduced techniques which would make it imperative to do so. Collins and Toland both, like most English deists, were more interested in philosophical and critical problems than in the application of the discoveries of the new science to religion. Both argued forcefully against censorship but did not go as far in their demands for free expression as did Trenchard and Gordon.

Other English deists of this generation, e.g., Lord Shaftesbury, Matthew Tindal, Thomas Woolston, Thomas Chubb, John Trenchard, Conyers Middleton, Lord Bolingbroke, are of interest in several respects. They kept alive a controversy in religion, which, merging into polemics about the trinity and the nature of the church, kept England in heated debate for the better part of fifty years and provided open discussions of what had to be clandestine elsewhere in Europe. It was a discussion known on the Continent through translation, refutation, and even bibliographies such as those of Trinius, Alberti, and Thorschmid. Second, these writers show that empirical philosophy was not the only source of eighteenth-century deism, nor religion its only concern. Tindal and Chubb relied upon *a priori* reason to perceive the natural law and the eternal and immutable relations of things and less on the argument from design bolstered by science. Tindal's *Christianity as Old as the Creation* (1731) is probably the best summary of deism in its *a priori* form. Their work and that of Shaftesbury helped to divorce ethics from the religion of the churches. Third, Thomas Woolston and Conyers Middleton, the first a professed allegorist who scurrilously likened Christ to a gypsy, the second a clever historian and polemicist whose works on miracles cast doubt on the authenticity of any, forged arms which Voltaire and Gibbon were to employ against the "infamous" with greater effectiveness. Likewise John Trenchard and Thomas Gordon (d. 1750), editors of the *London Journal, Cato's Letters*, and *The Independent Whig*, extreme Whig opponents of Walpole, joined religious and political radicalism in amusing essays almost unique in the history of deism. Anthony Ashley Cooper, third Earl of Shaftesbury, made deism not only a good-natured religion, the mark of breeding, wit, good taste, and refinement but also gave its most optimistic formulation. Buoyed by Shaftesbury's moral-sense theory and aesthetics, tinged with a self-conscious rhetorical enthusiasm, it made a mark on the continent where Shaftesbury was translated by Diderot, and eagerly read and used by German writers, including Christlob Mylius, Johann Spalding, Gotthold Lessing, and Hermann Reimarus. In France there was less need of translation since many of the older *philosophes* had become deists. Bernard de Fontenelle, the Abbé de St. Pierre, Voltaire, and Montesquieu could be added to the list along with many authors of clandestinely circulated tracts.

Deism penetrated and influenced many aspects of life. Debated in the coffee houses and salons, it formed an essential ingredient of freemasonry and had the allegiance of *philosophes,* princes, soldiers, statesmen, abbés, and tradesmen. Its simple message of equality, optimism, and reason contributed to the ideas of progress and the complacency of the enlightened. Expressed in such works as Joseph Addison's rendition of Psalm 19, Alexander Pope's *Universal Prayer* (1738), James Thomson's *Seasons,* or the plays, essays, and stories of Voltaire, it became a cliché of poets and the readers of periodicals like *Le Journal Encyclopédique* (1756–93). Given a measure of endorsement by works as diverse as Samuel Clarke's *Demonstration of the Being and Attributes of God* (1704) or Maupertuis' *Essai de philosophie morale* (1750), it helped to liberalize Christianity and to accommodate it to the age of reason. It is central as a unifying conception in Lessing's plays and in the moral philosophy of Adam Smith. Even the political opportunism of Bolingbroke and Napoleon is partly explained by deistic views of vulgar religion and the credulity of the people. For republicans from Toland to Robespierre, Gordon to Thomas Paine, it justified and sanctioned republican government and served as a counterweight to theories of divine right. As a regulative principle its teleology structured the works of Abbé Pluche and other physicotheologians in the eighteenth century as well as scientists in royal societies and academies throughout Europe. In America Benjamin Franklin, Thomas Paine, and Thomas Jefferson among the great, and Ethan Allen and Elihu Palmer among the lesser, testified to the truth, political usefulness, and scientific accuracy of the deists' creed.

The eighteenth century saw not only the heyday of deism but the beginning of its demise. David Hume exposed its shoddiness: its teleology was unproven; its easy epistemology unsound; its rationalized universal human nature a myth exploded by the passions, diverse habits, and customs of essentially unreasonable creatures who never possessed a rational religion, just as they never lived in a state of nature. Bishops George Berkeley and Joseph Butler showed the deistic arguments to be fallacious or inconclusive, while a host of minor apologists in England attacked individuals, their scholarship and claims, with arguments now as dead as the deists' own. In France materialists put together not only a competing radicalism but evolved a theory of self-regulating nature which needed no creator and led to no divinely sanctioned moral duties. Denis Diderot's rationalism implied a vitalism which outmoded the stable mechanisms of the deistic cosmos. Rousseau's romantic appeal to conscience and the emotions as a source of religion and his concept of a normative general will undermined the deists' superficial religion and political rationalism. Gotthold Ephraim Lessing's conception of a progressive education of mankind, indeed the idea of progress as the immanent teleology of unfolding reason, was inimical to the deists' assumption of the fixity of things. The cultural pluralism of Edmund Burke and of J. G. Herder, insofar as it implied and prized uniqueness and variation, had no room for the uniformities upon whose existence deism was predicated. Even notions of utility called in question the deists' easy appeal to imposture and fraud.

Attempts to understand the minds of primitives, or in the case of Jean Astruc, Robert Lowth, and Herder, the genesis and form of inspired poetry, forced men to make less simple analyses of the origins and function of myth than deism had purveyed. Of equal importance was the fact that most Christians were willing to accept the validity of a natural religion as the basis upon which a revealed religion might be asserted. Fideism was dead. Imposters and fanatics no longer menaced states where standing armies moving over good roads had replaced the established religion as a means of control. Only in the United States, among republican revolutionaries and proletarians, was deism to have a further career. Tom Paine's style, thought, and appeal were vulgar; so were the readers of his books and those published by Elihu Palmer, Richard Carlisle, and the half-literate Chartists of the 1840's. As a secularizing force making for order and placing a premium upon reasonableness in all areas of life, deism ceased to live after 1800. This judgment, however, has been questioned by some scholars, notably E. C. Mossner, who point out that the heirs of deism are to be found among the liberal and freethinking religious critics of the nineteenth century and among those who defended toleration.

BIBLIOGRAPHY

Bibliographical Works. J. A. Trinius, *Freidenkers Lexicon* (Leipzig and Bernburg, 1759); many attributions are wrong but Trinius' work is useful as a guide not only to European deists but to the freethinking background from which they stemmed. U. G. Thorschmidt, *Versuch einer Vollständigen Engelländischen Freydenker-Bibliothek*, 3 vols. (Halle, 1765–66). N. R. Burr, *A Critical Bibliography of Religion in America* (Princeton, 1961), Parts I and II, pp. 184–237.

General Works Bearing on the History of Deism Containing Bibliographical Information. D. C. Allen, *Doubt's Boundless Sea* (Baltimore, 1964). H. Busson, *Les Sources et le développement du rationalisme dans la littérature française de la Renaissance*, rev. ed. (Paris, 1957). E. Cassirer, *Die Philosophie der Aufklärung* (Tübingen, 1932), trans. as *The Philosophy of the Enlightenment* (Princeton, 1951). J.-R. Charbonnel, *La Pensée italienne au XVIe siècle et le courant libertin* (Paris, 1919). P. Gay, *The Enlightenment: An Interpretation* (New York, 1966); contains a useful bibliographical essay. P. Hazard, *La Crise de la conscience européenne* (Paris, 1935), trans. as *The European Mind 1680–1715* (Cleveland, 1963); idem, *La Pensée européenne au XVIIIe siècle* (Paris, 1946), *European Thought in the Eighteenth Century* (New Haven, 1954). A. O. Lovejoy, "The Parallel of Deism and Classicism," *Modern Philology*, **29** (1932), 281–99, reprinted in idem, *Essays in the History of Ideas* (Baltimore, 1948). R. Pintard, *Le Libertinage érudit dans la première moitié du XVIIe siècle* (Paris, 1943). R. Popkin, *The History of Scepticism from Erasmus to Descartes*, Part I (Assen, 1960). T. S. Spink, *French Free Thought from Gassendi to Voltaire* (Bristol, 1960). L. Stephen, *History of English Thought in the Eighteenth Century*, 3rd ed. (London, 1902). R. N. Stromberg, *Religious Liberalism in Eighteenth Century England* (Oxford, 1954).

Studies of Deism and Deists. R. F. Birn, "Pierre Rousseau and the *philosophes* of Bouillon," *Studies on Voltaire and the Eighteenth Century*, **29** (1964), 170–79; a summary of the views of a typical deist, 1756–93. F. Brie, "Deismus und Atheismus in der Englishen Renaissance," *Anglia Zeitung*, **48** (1924), 54–98, 105–68. R. L. Colie, "Spinoza and the Early English Deists," *Journal of the History of Ideas*, **20** (1959), 23–46. G. Gawlick, "Cicero and the Enlightenment," *Studies on Voltaire and the Eighteenth Century*, **25** (1963), 657–79; idem, *Moralität und Offenbarungsglaube: Studien zum englischen Deismus* (Stuttgart, 1965). F. H. Heineman, "John Toland and the Age of Reason," *Archiv für Philosophie*, **4** (1950), 33–66. G. V. Lechler, *Geschichte des Englischen Deismus* (Tübingen, 1841). D. R. McKee, "Isaac de la Peyrère, A Precursor of Eighteenth Century Critical Deists," *PMLA*, **59** (1944), 456–85. H. M. Morais, *Deism in Eighteenth Century America* (New York, 1934). G. L. Mosse, "Puritan Radicalism and the Enlightenment," *Church History*, **29** (1960), 33–66. E. C. Mossner, "Deism," *Encyclopedia of Philosophy*, 8 vols. (New York and London, 1967), II, 326–36.

ROGER L. EMERSON

[See also **Agnosticism;** Enlightenment; **God;** Nature; **Religion.**]

DEMOCRACY

DEMOCRACY, a transliteration of the Greek δημοκρατία, is government by the people. The historians and philosophers of the Aegean world invented the term, situated it within a larger political vocabulary, again of their own invention, and provided a mode of political analysis that enjoyed authority well into modern times. Greek political institutions did not survive; Greek political theory did. As a consequence, attitudes about popular rule, characteristic of a slave-owning society, whose social organization permitted direct citizen-participation, received attention, even when the conditions that made Greek "democracy" possible had completely disappeared.

As late as the eighteenth century political classification schemes and value systems gleaned from classical Greek texts were current in the West. The Greek experience, transmitted through Rome, was still thought to be applicable. It mattered little that many who cited the Greek (or Latin) texts knew them badly; their citation was the significant fact. The texts, however ancient, carried authority. Just as Niccolò Machiavelli, seeking to reestablish the *virtù* of his native Florence, thought it entirely proper to recollect the glories of republican Rome, so the American constitution-framers showed themselves students of the classical world, anxious to discover classical texts that might be useful to their purposes.

The Greek achievement, then, was not a capacity for institution-building, but a genius for developing modes of analysis that survived even when filtered through Roman and Christian experience. There is, in Herodotus, a fairly primitive formulation of a debate embellished by Plato and Aristotle, that still produced an echo in the eighteenth century. Herodotus is led to inquire into the relative virtues (and vices) of three forms of political authority—monarchy, oligarchy, and democracy. The circumstances of the debate are not without interest: a decision has to be made concerning the establishment of a new government for Persia. The idea that governments are not immutable, that they are chosen, that their selection ought to depend in considerable measure on their prospective utility, and that reasonable men may differ about such matters, are all characteristic Greek attitudes. A civilization of city-states, with diverse political institutions, found the idea of debating the relative merits of one kind of rule rather than another entirely congenial.

The arguments in Herodotus are simple: democracy's advocate maintains that only "popular" government guarantees equality before the law; monarchy, by contrast, is said to encourage envy and pride; it is inherently unstable and leads almost invariably to violence (Book III, 80–82). Oligarchy's defender thinks such arguments specious; disparaging the rule of the many, he insists that the masses are feckless, ignorant, irresponsible, and violent; their capacity for capriciousness is certainly equal to that of any king. The multitude, having never been taught to know what is right, cannot be expected to pursue the right. Neither argument carries the day; instead the votes go to the spokesman for monarchy. He argues that democracy is a political system that encourages cliques; it stimulates rivalry among them and generally ends in tyrannical rule. The mob, peculiarly susceptible to the wiles of the demagogue is generally prepared to abdicate its authority. Oligarchy is held to be no more stable; it shows an equal tendency to degenerate into tyranny. The best guarantee of freedom, then, is to be found in monarchy, defined as the rule of an individual respectful of the laws.

The Greek preoccupation with order is apparent throughout; so, also, is the overwhelming and perpetual fear of tyranny. Governments are inherently unstable; one must search constantly for the least vulnerable form. The decision to vest authority—in an individual, a small group, the multitude—is recognized to be *the* significant political act. Stability and justice are the desired ends. Herodotus saw that equality before the law was the boon promised by democracy. If, however, that good might be obtained from monarchy, with the added advantage of stability, there was no doubting its superior claim.

The democratic theme figures only tangentially in Herodotus; with his successor, Thucydides, it is absolutely central to his purpose (Book II, 35–46). Pericles' funeral oration, often cited as the single most eloquent statement celebrating the virtues of Athenian democracy, is also the classic defense of democracy's claim to being the school of civic virtue. Athens, Pericles tells us, does not choose to copy the laws of its neighbors; it provides the pattern that others follow. Athens is well and justly administered; the many and not the few are favored; capacity is the sole criterion for office-holding. Personal relations are easy; lawlessness is uncommon; valor in the service of the city-state is habitual. Thucydides, in his dramatic rendering of the humbling of democratic Athens by Sparta, makes Periclean rule seem a "golden age" before ignominious defeats, produced by miscalculations in foreign and military policy, and before a deterioration in the Athenian populace causes the society to change. The citizens, tried by the rigors of war, are quite incapable of rising above their private ambition and private interest. No leader, after Pericles, is in a position to check the insolence and vanity of the citizenry. In the age of Pericles, Thucydides writes, "government was by the first citizen" (Book III, 37–40). Those who follow Pericles flatter the multitude, appeal to its baser instincts, and create conditions that encourage demagoguery. Athens is made to pay heavily for the blunders of its citizens.

In describing Cleon, a leader he abominates, Thucydides dwells on the violence of Cleon's words while never neglecting to emphasize the approval they inspire (Book III, 82–84). Cleon knows how to use the masses for his own purposes; contemptuous of gifted men, he ingratiates himself with those whom he aspires to rule. While passages in the history suggest a concern to assess individual blame for the final catastrophe that overtakes the city, this was clearly not Thucydides' chief interest. His larger purpose was to probe the vulnerability of the Athenian democracy, as it showed itself in time of war. In peace and prosperity, when individuals lead easy lives, and adversity is uncommon, tolerance comes naturally. In time of war, however, "imperious necessity" takes over; prudence, caution, and justice are the daily casualties of war. The war is catastrophic precisely because violence, excess, partisanship, greed, and a lust for power, are its inevitable results (Book II, 65). Civilized behavior is rare in time of war; debate enjoys little respect and becomes uncommon. Law itself finds itself impotent before the incessant calls for action; superiority of every kind becomes suspect.

The political reflections of Plato and Aristotle need to be read in the context of the history provided by Thucydides. Both philosophers reflect the widespread corruption and loss of confidence characteristic of their time. Plato, in commenting on the ignorance of democracy's political leaders, is appalled by the incompetence they show. He has no great admiration for the gifted amateur. Statesmanship is a disciplined calling: it depends on precise and full knowledge. All states are riven by a rivalry between those with property and those without; factionalism and partisanship are the inevitable consequences of the division between rich and poor. So long as extremes of wealth and poverty exist, Plato says, there can be no just society (*Republic*, Book VIII, 551f.). Democracy, by definition, must always be government by and for the many; the poor who lack property and birth will always control a democracy. Oligarchy, just as inevitably, must operate in the interest of the few who enjoy property and birth. Plato finds both democracy and oligarchy inherently unstable.

Plato, in the *Republic*, excludes the possibility that a just state can exist in which all citizens participate; he explicitly denies the Periclean ideal. In the *Statesman*, he gives a six-fold categorization of states. Three depend on fidelity to the law; three are essentially lawless. The rule of an individual produces monarchy or tyranny, depending on whether or not the individual at the head is law-abiding; when a few rule, the results are aristocracy or oligarchy; when the many rule, democracy exists, but again of two kinds, depending on whether or not the popular rule is law-abiding. Democracy, Plato accepts as the best of the lawless states, but the least desirable of the law-abiding. Aristotle's categorization of states is not very different from Plato's. What makes Plato's definitions important, however, is that he comes close to accepting in the *Laws*, the last of his works, that in the real world there ought in fact be a mixing of types (Book III, 691–94). If moderation is the quality hoped for, it comes only from combining the best in monarchy, aristocracy, and law-abiding democracy. In his *Republic*, Plato describes a quite different state, but clearly one that he does not expect to be realized in practice.

Aristotle, Plato's pupil, while interested in reflecting on the ideal state, showed a greater propensity to study actual conditions by analyzing the constitutions of a large number of existing states. Aristotle is particularly concerned to dwell on the class character of the political societies that he surveys. Farmers in an agricultural society with a democratic constitution may concern themselves very little with public affairs, preferring to leave such matters largely in the hands of wealthier men who have the leisure to attend to public business. This ought not to be taken to mean that citizens have given up their authority; they simply choose not to make use of it for as long as they think themselves well-governed. Aristotle clearly considered this kind of democracy better than one that saw large urban populations involving themselves in the daily management of their affairs; such democratic rule generally opened the way to demagogues and almost invariably ended in some form of tyranny. How to unite an intelligent administration with the power of the citizens was the problem that democracy had always to contend with; and Aristotle makes no effort to minimize its difficulty.

If democracy involves the whole body of citizens, oligarchy restricts the ruling function to some fraction of them; property qualifications, more or less stringent, are generally imposed in oligarchical states. Oligarchy, like democracy, easily runs to excess; when it does, effective government falls into the hands of a small band of wealthy men, factionalism becomes commonplace, and the results are scarcely different from what happens under the rule of a tyrant. So long as the property qualification is not too restrictive, there is a chance that oligarchy will not so mistreat the masses as to bring about disorder. When, however, it does become too closed, oligarchy may prove even more oppressive than democracy.

Aristotle hopes for a state that will combine the best features of democracy and oligarchy; this, he calls a *polity*, or constitutional government. Again, the significant feature of the constitution is its class base. If there are too many rich or too many poor, there is a danger to the stability of the state. The instruments of government ought to show themselves hospitable to various kinds of qualification; while there must be representation of wealth, birth, and ability, there must also be a sufficient regard for numbers. If oligarchy and democracy are inherently unstable, always tending towards tyranny, *polity* gives promise of that moderation which is the only sure guarantee of stability.

Aristotle thought in terms of class when so many before and after him did not. This, however, never led him to question slavery, an institution that dominated Greek society. The Greek city-state seemed unimaginable without slavery, and Aristotle never thought to abolish it. Only in extreme democracy, he wrote, would slaves be given "license." He had no doubts of how such a government would end. Aristotle knew that "most men find more pleasure in living without any discipline than they find in a life of temperance," but society could not be constructed on such a base (*Politics*, Book VI, Ch. 4). Always preoccupied with the state's survival, Aristotle feared for the stability of the political order that he knew. His principal concern was to delineate the conditions of political stability, to emphasize the relation between the constitution of the state and the character of its citizens.

The death of Aristotle in 322 B.C. came almost coincidentally with the demise of the Greek city-state. Its heir, republican Rome, was animated by new values, though its reliance on Greek thought remained considerable. The extent of the change may be suggested by the distance that separates Aristotle from Polybius. Polybius, born a century after Aristotle died, wrote his universal history to show "by what means, and thanks to what sort of constitution, the Romans subdued the world in less than fifty-three years." When Polybius describes constitutions, he uses the six categories employed by Plato and Aristotle, but his purpose is new; it is to explain Rome's success in unifying the world, which he attributes to her "mixed constitution," with the consuls representing the monarchical principle, the Senate the aristocratic, and the popular assemblies the democratic. In checking each other, these powers prevent disintegration and disorder. Polybius' history is a tribute to a constitution, but even more to a people, and to its imperial achievement. Greek political theory lives on in this history; Greek history, however, is effectively set aside. The stage is suddenly larger; what had seemed significant to Thucydides and Aristotle (the details of city-state existence) are scarcely alluded to. Polybius' purpose is to show why the Roman constitution worked, and why, even were the people to grow corrupted by flattery and idleness, showing a tendency to violence and arrogance, the constitution would survive. Its self-regulating mechanism is its genius: the three powers are interdependent; each checks and controls the other.

Cicero, influenced by Polybius, is again content to repeat the conventional Greek classification of states—monarchy, aristocracy, and democracy—and the conventional criticisms of each. If a preference is to be expressed, it is for monarchy, though the best state is not monarchical, but one that combines the virtues of all three. Cicero, following his Stoic masters, sees the equality of men neither in their possessions nor in their learning, but in their capacity to reason, to distinguish between right and wrong. The state is a *res publica*, an "affair of the people," which exists to give the people justice, and derives its authority from them. Cicero, like Polybius, created the myth of a Roman constitution that combined the love a king bears for his subjects (as incorporated in monarchy), the wisdom characteristic of aristocracy, and the freedom generally associated with democracy. Authority, in theory, proceeded from the people, but there was no indication of what remedies they might avail themselves of to thwart a ruler who in fact ignored them.

Republican Rome, in its self-praise, registered its defiance of those who thought only of the "corruption" of states and of their inevitable decline. Though it never represented itself as democratic, the Republic was proud of its popular instrumentalities, and took care to protect its fame as law-giver. Rome's capacity to survive and expand—to elicit service and enforce obedience—contributed to its later reputation. The Roman Empire never enjoyed an equivalent success. Contemporary judgments of its qualities were more modest; the old Republican *virtù* seemed to have given out. Epictetus, the Stoic philosopher, expresses a view markedly different from either Polybius or Cicero. He suggests that politics are not within the individual's power to change; the wise man will not be overly concerned with political activities. The citizen will, if asked to do so, consent to serve the state, but he will not push himself forward. This new "quietism," influenced also by the religious ferment of the first and second centuries, created a political climate distinctly different from the one that had previously existed. There were no new political institutions to celebrate, no new concepts of citizenship to proclaim.

With the barbarian invasions and the destruction of Roman political authority, local rule reasserted itself. In the feudal situation that developed, older concepts of citizenship became increasingly irrelevant. Democracy had no place in a society increasingly supportive of a value system that emphasized stability and custom; change was thought to be degenerate, political innovation was suspect. The world was a divine creation; man's obligation was neither to control it nor to make it over. Even the recovery of Aristotle's writings in the thirteenth century, important as they were for medieval scholarship generally, did not make the political concerns of the Aegean world altogether meaningful for men who were confronting problems different from those of the Greek city-state.

The genesis of Greek democracy has not been much studied; the genesis of modern democracy has been investigated in the most painstaking manner. In the nineteenth century, when the origins of modern democracy were closely inquired into, there was a tendency to give the most extensive intellectual and institutional genealogy for the "love of liberty and the capacity for self-government." William Lecky, the English historian, may be taken as a not unrepresentative Victorian scholar, searching for modern democracy's beginnings. His *History of the Rise and Influence of the Spirit of Rationalism in Europe* (1865) offers an almost classical nineteenth-century Liberal explanation of how democracy came into being. In a chapter entitled "The Secularisation of Politics," Lecky sees the increase of wealth and knowledge as predominant factors; roads, the printing press, universities, Protestantism—all are declared crucially important. So, also, Lecky insists, are changes in the art of war; in his words, "it is curious to trace from a very distant period the slow rise of the infantry accompanying the progress of democracy" (II, 213). The diffusion of Rationalism, as expressed in the "triumph of tolerance," and the growth of free trade are also contributing factors.

Another historian of the period might offer a slightly different and more sympathetic listing of factors. All such accounts would agree in emphasizing the importance of the French Revolution; some would think it necessary to dwell also on the American Revolution; a few would cite the English Civil War. While no one of these events had democracy as its goal, and while the term itself was little used in its modern form until after the French Revolution, ideas that carried with them the promise of a new politics circulated before 1789. Just as it would be inaccurate to say that puritanism *caused* capitalism, so it would be folly to claim that it *caused* democracy. Yet, puritanism was intimately involved in historical developments that were to have importance for the generation of a new democratic idea. So, also, were the theories of Hobbes and Locke, of Montesquieu and Rousseau, and of a great many others.

For a new democratic idea to develop, it was necessary that medieval attitudes be set aside, that man perceive himself in a new way and aspire to new political roles. Such perceptions began to be common in England and France after the Reformation; events in both countries were to have marked influence elsewhere. The anxiety that existed in Europe in the sixteenth and seventeenth centuries has been frequently remarked on. The disintegration of an earlier religious unity produced a marked disquietude; so, also, did rapid economic changes, with large social dislocations flowing from them. The seemingly interminable national and international wars conducted with a strikingly new armament—Machiavelli was one of the earliest to gauge their significance—contributed to feelings of insecurity and panic. In the circumstances, the theories of someone like Hobbes were compelling.

For Hobbes, the state was a human invention, created by man to satisfy a basic need, a release from the fear that existed when he could depend on no protection other than that provided by his own brute strength. Man made the state, created the authorities in it, and chose to obey them simply because he recognized the utility of doing so. Whatever rights existed derived from this decision to form a state and to vest authority in a sovereign. Hobbes effectively destroyed the medieval preference for corporate rights, hierarchy, and divine sanction. Man creates the state to avoid perpetual war; it is his reason that tells him to do so. When Hobbes, in 1628, published a translation of Thucydides, he described him as the most political of historians and the most hostile to democracy. In his

own *Leviathan* (1651), written many years later, he shows himself no less dubious about the virtues of democracy. In considering types of commonwealths, he recognizes only three—monarchy, aristocracy, and democracy. While others are named in the classical texts—oligarchy, tyranny, anarchy—Hobbes dismisses these as being essentially the same forms of government, disliked by the commentator. The question for Hobbes is simple: shall sovereignty rest with one, with a few, or with the multitude? On purely utilitarian grounds, he establishes the advantages of monarchy over democracy.

Contemporary with Hobbes, others saw the matter differently. The pamphlet literature for the years 1640–60, which compares not at all unfavorably with the outpouring of tracts in America after 1763, registers every kind of opinion. Some express a clear preference for democratic rule. The Levellers, who enjoyed a certain notoriety in the years 1646 to 1649, propounded no formal doctrine, but their leader, John Lilburne, argues for the sovereignty of the common people, who need to be made the masters of Parliament. Among the demands made by the Levellers and their supporters are: universal manhood suffrage, equal electoral districts, and biennial parliaments. Their doctrine seemed radical in the seventeenth century; when compared with other groups, the Diggers, for example, they emerge as the first of a long line of British radicals. Their purposes are overwhelmingly political; by comparison, the Diggers are early socialists. The rights of ownership, the Diggers recognize as God-given; they entitle every individual to share in the bounty of the land. Hostile to private property, they view it as the source of human suffering and vice. Democracy, for them, is not realizable without a social revolution.

The Levellers and Diggers were little known in their own time; they were minor sects. The same cannot be said of the larger body of Puritan "saints" who held no such radical economic and social views but who were the first modern revolutionaries. They developed and practiced a new kind of politics, scarcely democratic, but considerably more activist than any common in Europe (except in a few Italian cities). As has become increasingly obvious in the twentieth century, the English Civil War provided an early prototype of a new form of political revolution. As Michael Walzer has argued in his *Revolution of the Saints*, the Civil War in England had an international significance. It involved the execution of a king and the assertion by his adversaries of the legitimacy of their action and the propriety of their instituting new forms of governance to protect them in their rights. It emphasized the importance of participation: the traditional idea of accepting one's status as the subject of a monarch was shaken; while the modern idea of citizenship, with its emphasis on individual rights, was not fully articulated, there was a new "purpose" in politics, very different from what had been characteristic of medieval Europe. Finally, the events of the period were highly visible not only for those who remained in England but for those who emigrated abroad. The Puritans who came to the New World arrived with a suspicion of monarchy and a willingness to experiment with government.

If Hobbes and those who governed England in the 1640's and 1650's lived at a time when anarchy seemed a constant threat, giving them an incentive to search for forms of sovereignty that would not be easily set aside, that mood was no longer common after the Restoration. The greatest dangers appeared to have been traversed; it was possible to think of government in less catastrophic terms. English political thought, even before John Locke, showed a tendency to be more concerned with the rights of individuals and less preoccupied with the rights of the sovereign. Those who favored republican rule—Harrington, Milton, and Sidney were prominent—were to be influential in America years later; none was a democrat, but each was concerned with precisely the kinds of electoral and political safeguards that later democrats would value. The republicanism of the seventeenth century favored a "commonwealth" closely modeled on that of ancient Greece or republican Rome, with an "aristocracy of talent" governing in the name of the people.

John Locke emerges as *the* political philosopher of the later years of the seventeenth century. Like Hobbes, he is concerned with developing a rationale for political authority. His state of nature is not like that of Hobbes; it is not a time of terror and conflict; man, endowed with reason, enjoys a certain equality. Unhappily, however, there is no common authority to whom all men give obedience; each interprets the laws of nature as he wishes. The uncertainty that develops is contrary to the interests of the individual, and in order to escape the inconveniences of the state of nature, each joins with the others to form a society. It is man's reason that tells him to enter into this contract with his fellowmen; necessity does not drive him to it. By the social contract, the individual gives up his personal rights to interpret the laws of nature in return for a communal guarantee that his rights of life, liberty, and property will be maintained.

Once the political state is established, authority has to be fixed within it. In this, Locke follows the Aristotelian example in his categorization of states, but recognizes that the disposition of the legislative power is the all-important decision; the executive and judicial powers will be dependent on the legislative power.

Locke does not believe, as Hobbes had, that authority, once established, can never be broken; the community is always free to remake its constitution. While accepting that monarchy is the original form of government, he refuses to accept Hobbes' view that it is the best. As for oligarchy, it tends to favor the interests of a few, to the disadvantage of the many. Democracy offers the only adequate solution for a just rule. Locke argues that the legislative power ought to be one in which the delegates are controlled by popular election. Locke accepted the fact that monarchy would continue; his main concern was that the monarch should not have the supreme legislative power.

These ideas were important in the eighteenth century; they did not, however, create democratic government. In England they provided a defense for the Glorious Revolution and a rationale for the legislative supremacy that gradually developed under the Hanoverian kings. In France they provided an additional incentive for comparing the "free" institutions of Great Britain with the more despotic institutions of the Bourbon monarchy. Great Britain, for Voltaire and Montesquieu, and for many others as well, became the standard against which they compared their own society. This is most apparent in Montesquieu, particularly in his Book XI of the *Spirit of the Laws* (*De l'esprit des lois*, 1748), where he dwells on what he assumes to be the genius of the British Constitution—its separation of the executive, legislative, and judicial powers, and its balancing of these powers, one against the other. The inadequacies of the theory, and its irrelevance to historical facts, were not demonstrated until later in the century when Jeremy Bentham corrected William Blackstone, who had followed Montesquieu in this general description. Montesquieu's work, apart from its putative influence on the American revolutionaries, contributed to making the *philosophes* more aware of the British political achievement. Even in romanticizing that achievement, he, together with Voltaire, gave the French a sense of the gulf that separated England and France in the kinds of freedom that subjects enjoyed on either side of the Channel. Church and State in France were exposed to a kind of criticism that neither had previously known.

Still, neither Montesquieu nor Voltaire produced anything that could be appropriately described as a theory of democracy. This was the major contribution of Jean Jacques Rousseau; departing from Greek and Latin texts, showing himself independent of Aristotle and Polybius, but independent also of his Enlightenment contemporaries, he produced an original formulation of the problem of political obligation. While there are evidences of indebtedness to Locke in Rousseau's psychology and to Montesquieu in his sociology, his overall thesis is novel. With Rousseau, a new con-

657

cept of citizenship emerges; it is the awareness of interests in common that creates the bond between men. What are those interests? For Rousseau, they derive from a single determination—to prevent inequality among men. Though the term "general will" had been used before, it was Rousseau's use of the term that gave it a general currency.

The "general will" expressed the interest that men shared. Kings might pursue war and trade and seek to make it appear that they were acting in response to the will of the people; this was an elaborate fiction. The "general will" operates best in small states, where citizenship is felt, and where the identity of interests is real. Large states, ruled by monarchs, inevitably deteriorate into tyrannies. There is no "sovereignty of the people" possible in such societies. Without equality there can be no liberty. For Rousseau, neither kings nor representative parliaments can bring about justice; only the "general will" can enforce justice, since it is based on mutual respect and the absence of the type of subordination that is the essence of what passes for "civilization" in the modern world. The people, Rousseau believes, are capable of making and being faithful to such avowals of self-control and mutual respect; the rich and the intellectual can never be expected to abide by such an ethics. This, for Rousseau, is the essence of citizenship; it is the opposite of the subordination that "subjects" experience under a king or other form of imposed rule. Man, through the "general will," is inclined to do what duty tells him he ought to do.

Many have argued about the "modernity" of Rousseau's theory; some insist, however, on seeing him as the last of the ancients. Both interpretations are possible. In understanding the "passion for equality," Rousseau anticipates the nineteenth century, describing a phenomenon that will increasingly preoccupy both Socialists and Liberals. Rousseau, in linking equality and liberty, throws down a challenge to those who imagine that one is possible without the other, or even inimical to the other. In another sense, however, Rousseau is writing for a world still familiar with the ancient texts, and still respectful of classical insights. Rousseau, despite his efforts to disassociate himself from many of his fellow intellectuals, belongs to a European intellectual society for whom the events of Greece and Rome are immediate, and the categories developed by Plato and Aristotle are meaningful. His is a voice in a political dialogue that had been proceeding, with interruptions, for more than two millennia. That dialogue, however, even among intellectuals, was losing its force. It was not that the educated lacked the requisite Greek and Latin to consult the original texts (many had known the ancients imperfectly even before Rousseau), and many (in America and elsewhere)

quoted them without knowing them. What was new, after 1776, and even more after 1789, was not that men could not (or did not) consult the past, but that the more recent past became a more compelling subject of concern to them. Talk of democracy increased, but examples were no longer borrowed from Greece in the time of Pericles; the greatness of the American political experiment or the horrors of the Revolution in France, depending on the point of view taken, were the new subjects of major political discourse. The debate on democracy entered an entirely new phase; it was now linked to contemporary events and to theoretical reflections they had incited.

In the decade preceding the American Revolution, the British colonists in the New World produced a large and varied pamphlet literature to demonstrate the injustice of Parliament's claim to certain types of jurisdiction over them; they insisted that a new kind of social and political justice was possible in the New World. The colonists supported their arguments with citations from a political literature that originated in the English Civil War and continued on into the eighteenth century; it contained a radical critique of the prevailing political system. The warnings about political corruption, common in the age of Walpole, had dwelled on the dangers of autocracy. They were taken seriously and served the colonists' purposes in their own quarrel with the King and Parliament.

The Americans saw themselves as maintaining a tradition of opposition that had already shown its strength in the mother country. There was little explicit democratic sentiment in their philosophy; it was not overly concerned with either economic or social reform. Their hostility was to certain forms of government, based on corruption, that threatened traditional liberties. The power of a few—officeholders and members of Parliament—was endangering the freedom of the many. Despotic government, for the colonists at least, seemed a real possibility. There was a conspiracy abroad—its purpose was to destroy the English constitution and, with it, the liberties of free-born Englishmen. Parliamentary legislation after 1763 confirmed the colonists in their belief that a ministerial conspiracy existed to destroy their liberty, and that their mission ought to be to preserve it, to save it for all mankind. This was the special "duty" to which they felt themselves called. In the process, they developed a new idea of representation, one that was to have the greatest importance for democracy (though no one viewed the matter in this light at the time).

The colonists disputed Parliament's claim to authority over them. While members of Parliament might claim that the colonists were as much represented in Westminster as the "nine tenths of the people of

Britain" who did not vote, American pamphleteers criticized this notion of "virtual representation." In England, where representation was traditionally by "interests," the idea of personal (or individual) representation was unknown. The member of one seaport city could be held to represent the interests of all others. This, the Americans refused to admit. They saw no one in Parliament at Westminster who represented their "interests," who stood to lose or gain in the way they would through new taxation. The idea of "virtual representation" was condemned, and support grew for the principle that a man could be bound only by his own assent or by that of a representative for whom he had voted. This was a radical notion, whose democratic and republican implications were perceived, and refuted by many. Still, the idea of "virtual representation" was clearly on the defensive.

There were other changes also, no less subtle, with large implications for democracy, though scarcely recognized as having that import at the time. Increasingly, Americans came to define a constitution as a "set of fundamental rules" that even the legislature was forbidden to alter. These rules, they insisted, ought to be instituted by delegates elected by the people, and could be altered only by procedures that involved the people. This was a far cry from the notion that Parliament could by simple legislative enactment make or unmake any rule. For Blackstone, sovereignty rested in Parliament—King, Lords, and Commons. The American response was to question the notion, so popular in the seventeenth century, of the necessity of this undivided sovereignty. Sovereignty might be limited; an authority might have full power in one sphere and none in another (where a distinctly different authority might govern). The idea of federalism was nascent in the Americas of the early 1770's. Also, increasingly, there was talk of the fact that human rights existed above the law, and that the law's purpose ought to be to uphold these rights. The statement might have been made by Locke; the rhetoric suggested that something more was intended by it.

While all such criticisms of British constitutional practices showed hostility to the status quo, the colonists were reluctant to carry out the full implications of their theoretical positions. They used the term "republic" increasingly, as they did the term "democracy," but they felt embarrassed by both. Thomas Paine, in 1776, just a few months before the Revolution, published *Common Sense*; it was the first explicit defense of democracy. Paine saw America's cause as "the cause of all mankind," and, refusing to follow Montesquieu or Blackstone, saw the English constitution not as a finely balanced artifact with each authority checking the other, but a combination of two ancient tyrannies—monarchical and aristocratic—compounded with "new republican materials." The two powers, by being hereditary, were independent of the people, and "contribute nothing towards the freedom of the states." Paine saw monarchy as essentially oppressive, imposing a distinction between kings and subjects for which there could be no rational defense. The time had come for a "final separation" between the colonies and the mother country. Paine called for a "more equal" system of representation, one that would create unicameral assemblies in each of the colonies, and provide for a continental unicameral legislature as well. As for a King, there ought to be none; the *law* would be sovereign. The alternative to his proposal, Paine insisted, was a perpetuation of royal tyranny.

John Adams was only one of many who saw the democratic implications of Paine's scheme and who had reservations on that as well as on other accounts. Power could not be vested safely in a single national assembly elected democratically. Though one might do away with king and peers, Adams wrote in his *Thoughts on Government* (1776), other balancing authorities would have to be introduced. There were many who wondered what the final consequence of such emphasis on equality and the right of citizens to choose their governors would be. Would it not lead in time to a denigration of all authority and a constant defiance of existing institutions?

The Americans saw themselves as reinventing a form of government that had once existed but had fallen into decline. Their "republic" would not, however, end in the manner of Rome. The word republic, Paine explained, "means the *public good*, or the good of the whole, in contradistinction to the despotic form, which makes the good of the sovereign, or of one man, the only object of the government." When Americans set about establishing their new state governments, they showed little inclination to choose the "simple democracy" that Paine argued for. The greater number chose to establish bicameral legislatures; and only in Pennsylvania, where a radical spirit dominated, did the Constitution provide for a unicameral legislature, with annual elections and rotation of office. The Pennsylvania Constitution was subjected to immediate attack; first, by those who argued that only in a bicameral legislature would wealth and talent be duly represented; second, by those who insisted that the existence of two houses simply gave an additional guarantee against hasty and ill-considered action.

Important as this issue might be—it continued to arouse discussion at the time that the Federal Constitution was drafted and debated—another exercise of popular power was taking place that would have importance for democracy. It became increasingly common for the state constitutions to be drafted by conventions called explicitly for that purpose, and having no other responsibility. The convention that drew up the Constitution for Massachusetts was elected by universal male suffrage; other states showed an equal readiness to make the constitution-framing and constitution-amending procedure democratic. Ratification of the Massachusetts Constitution (1780) was by two-thirds vote, with all male residents of the state being eligible to vote. This did not mean, however, that all men would also vote for members of the legislature. In Massachusetts, as in many states, property qualifications were introduced. Still, the people had been consulted, as they were to be again at the time of the ratification of the Federal Constitution.

In the 1780's, alarms were sounded concerning the new republican system. Americans were said to be losing their traditional virtues—industry, frugality, and the like—and tending towards luxury and extravagance. In the absence of virtue, there would be no commonwealth. This threat led Jeremy Belknap to write in 1784 that "the people of this country are not destined to be long governed in a democratic form" (Wood, p. 425). Jefferson, however, refused to despair. To live in a European capital, he explained, was to be made aware of the worth of republican governance. Benjamin Rush expressed confidence that "our republican forms of government will in time beget republican opinions and manners. All will end well" (Wood, p. 426).

This opinion was not shared by John Adams. The experience after independence told him that though hereditary dignities might be abolished, the scramble for place and property would continue unabated. He believed that "a free people are the most addicted to luxury of any." The desire for luxury and distinction created new divisions, and there was no longer a hereditary monarch to serve as a scapegoat. Americans, he insisted, were no different from any other people; republican institutions make them no better than any other. The "rich, the well-born, and the able" were dangerous, but so also were the poor and the ignorant. Adams searched for an authority that would keep the peace between these contending elements; he thought he discovered such an authority in a strong executive. Adams continued to yearn for something like the balanced constitution that Montesquieu and Blackstone had admired (and, in part, invented). He thought in terms of monarchs, aristocracies, and popular representatives. Other Americans had gone far beyond this. They insisted that they had instituted a government and made its officials answerable to themselves. As John Taylor was to say in the nineteenth century, "all our governments are limited agencies"; the people remain

sovereign. It was the popular self-interest that had to be counted on, and not the people's virtue. This, alone, made a republic secure.

By the late 1780's Americans were referring to their governments as democracies, but democracies of a new kind, "Democratic Republics," or to put the matter another way, "representative democracies." Madison saw the novelty of the American experiment in "the delegation of the government to a small number of citizens elected by the rest." James Wilson said that the Federal Constitution was "purely democratical," since "all authority of every kind is derived by representation from the people and the democratic principle is carried into every part of the government."

The idea that authority existed outside the people and had to be limited by the people, so that government would not degenerate into tyranny, was felt to be old-fashioned. There were no longer evil kings or illegal acts of Parliament to rail against. Within government, in its several branches, the people were represented. The struggles would take place within government between authorities seeking to please constituencies who never lost sight of their self-interest. Madison, in defending the Constitution, said that his object was to establish a nontyrannical republic. To do this, it was necessary to avoid the accumulation of powers—legislative, executive, and judicial—in the hands of any one group; factions were always dangerous. Minority "factions" could be controlled by the operation of majority vote; majority "factions" would develop less easily if the electorate was large and disparate in its interests.

However much Europe might interest itself in the events of the American Revolution, honor its heroes— Ben Franklin and Thomas Jefferson—and construct its own mythology to explain what was happening across the Atlantic, the events of a distant continent, sparsely populated and little known, could not call forth the enthusiasms generated by the electrifying news that came out of Paris in the summer of 1789. The nation that had made "reason" the emblem of its modernity was seen to be dismantling the political institutions of an earlier age. This was an event of the greatest import to all who heard of it anywhere in the world. The fall of the Bastille, followed closely by the National Assembly's actions in destroying traditional feudal privilege, was overshadowed only by the issuance of the Declaration of the Rights of Man and the Citizen, adopted by the National Assembly on August 26, 1789.

Comparable statements had been issued years earlier in America, but neither the Virginia Declaration of Rights nor the Declaration of Independence itself could match the French statement in its appeal. That all sovereignty rested in the nation, that the aim of all political association was to preserve the natural rights of man, that no group and no individual might exercise authority that did not emanate from the nation, that all citizens had the right to participate personally, or through their representatives, in the making of law and in the voting of taxes, that every man was presumed innocent until judged guilty, that punishments had to be established by law, that freedom of speech and press was guaranteed, that no one could be disturbed for his opinions, even in matters of religion, provided that he did not trouble public order as established by law—to assert all these things was to bring into existence a new concept in Europe—that of the citizen, possessing rights that could not be trespassed on.

The sovereignty of the people was explicitly declared, and with it the principle that there would be one law for all, with public office open to citizens on the basis of their abilities. These ideas, in germ, circulated in Europe many years before the French Revolution, but there was a significant difference between the Abbé Sieyès, in a provincial assembly in 1787 urging the nobility to give up their privileges, and the National Assembly voting, in effect, to institute a democratic constitution. It was precisely the authorship of the declaration that gave it its dignity, its importance, and its legality.

Democracy, a term not much used in the eighteenth century, though a number of Swiss cantons and German cities thought themselves "democratic," now came into more general favor, though it was still not employed with the frequency that is sometimes imagined. Other terms—republican, Jacobin, patriot—were more common. What is important, however, is that whereas for Rousseau, Helvétius, and others it was taken for granted that "pure democracy" could exist only in small states, the question now raised was whether it was not also a viable system for large and complex kingdoms. The excitement that the revolutionary events generated, particularly in the intellectual classes, was well-nigh universal.

It was not until the end of 1790, when Edmund Burke's *Reflections on the Revolution in France* appeared, that someone of some intellectual prominence thought to condemn the events of the French Revolution. Burke's misgivings, expressed earlier in the year in Parliament, had not been generally noted. He had warned England that she would not be untouched by the "distemper" raging across the Channel. Were England to imitate the French example, he said, the result would be confiscation and plunder in the name of democracy and the replacement of religion by atheism. Even his threat to "abandon his best friends and join with his worst enemies" if he found them on the side of the revolutionaries caused no stir.

The same could not be said of the blast that he issued later in the year. The Revolution, Burke insisted, was a threat to all Europe and all mankind. It taught false principles; it questioned hereditary right and threatened inherited liberties; it justified the overthrow of governments on the flimsy charge of misconduct; it pretended that sovereignty lay with the people; it took power from the gifted and gave it to men who had no experience of government. Burke was unimpressed with the fact that Revolution gave citizens the right to elect representatives; small men were not made great by their having been popularly chosen. Burke fixed on a sermon preached by Richard Price and contemptuously dismissed him along with other "democratists" who spoke as he did.

Burke's attacks elicited a large number of responses; none was more devastating, perhaps, than that issued by Tom Paine, who, in *The Rights of Man* (1791–92), accused Burke of pitying the plumage but forgetting the dying bird. In *A Vindication of the Rights of Man* (1790) Mary Wollstonecraft wrote: "I pause to recollect myself; and smother the contempt I feel rising for your rhetorical flourishes and infantine sensibility." Others were more civil. All, however, contributed to an unparalleled international debate on the ends of government, the rights of the citizen, and the advantages of representative rule.

Throughout the 1790's, in England, but on the Continent more generally, groups argued about the sovereignty of the people and the implications of the concept. With the dethroning of Louis XVI and his execution, new attacks on the Church, and the imprisoning and beheading of the moderate Girondins, opinion grew increasingly divided. The term "Jacobin" or "democrat" became pejorative, at least in the mouths and writings of those who considered themselves part of the established order. When Europe's monarchs went to war with the "revolution," those who held "democratic" opinions were seriously threatened. Even in Britain, which so prided itself on its constitutional liberties, the life of the "radical" became exceedingly dangerous. The "treason trials" of 1794, following on the suspension of *habeas corpus*, testified to the hazards encountered by those suspected of holding "revolutionary" opinions.

Meanwhile, in France, a Jacobin idea of "the nation" developed. Increasingly, it was made synonomous with "the people." Popular sovereignty was also increasingly pitted against the "old order," with its royal, aristocratic, inegalitarian traditions. Robespierre, faithful to Rousseau, had great suspicion of parliamentary assemblies, which might easily become "representative despotisms." Only through direct popular control over assemblies—direct popular action in them—could representatives be kept honest. The constitution of 1793, with its universal suffrage, unicameral legislature, and collectivist Bill of Rights (very different from the American), expressed the political and social ambitions of the Jacobins. The constitution, overwhelmingly accepted in a national plebiscite, was, however, suspended until the end of the war. The Terror and the rule of Robespierre only raised new questions about popular rule, and while some imagined that Thermidor and the execution of Robespierre signalled the end of the Revolution, many saw that it only marked the end of an episode in the larger history.

A good argument can be made that "revolutionary democracy" reached its zenith in Europe in the eighteenth century not in 1794 but in 1798; it was then that democratic enthusiasm seemed most widespread. This was the time when republican ideas, as inspired by the French example, enjoyed currency with men of all classes who held "advanced" opinions. The basic rights to liberty, equality, security, and property were constantly reiterated; so, also, was the notion that sovereignty lay with the "citizenry as a whole," and that the right to vote ought to be extended generally to male citizens. The Revolution created its own mystique or mystery about the virtues of the people, in which ardent democrats believed. Those who espoused democratic ideas had a new sense of time, a new set of values, and a new kind of self-confidence. Democracy was a term scarcely used before the French Revolution; by the beginning of the nineteenth century it had its firm adherents and its equally ardent enemies.

The repression of democratic (or Jacobin) opinion was common during the last years of the eighteenth and the first years of the nineteenth centuries. During the long years of Napoleonic rule, in England there were the beginnings of a new democratic or "radical" school. The sources of the "philosophical radical" tradition are not easily given; it is generally accepted that Bentham's conversion to democracy began with his friendship with James Mill in 1808. Not until 1818, however, did Bentham draw up his *Resolutions on Parliamentary Reform*, which established his support of universal male suffrage and the secret ballot. The "philosophical radicals" were never numerous, but they were effective publicists and held views different from those of the "radicals" of the 1790's. They issued no call for violent revolution; they never suggested that government might one day be abolished. Instead, they propagated the idea that under a system of universal suffrage many opinions would be registered, that these would cancel each other out, and that what was common to the majority would in time become law.

Bentham believed that Blackstone was essentially mistaken in his ideas about the virtues of a constitution characterized by checks and balances; he refused to believe that bills of rights effectively restrained government. The only good government was derived from the people; the interest of the people needed to be the same as the interest of the government. Public opinion ought to weigh heavily; the education of the electorate was a prime responsibility, since it gave the greatest promise of opinion being informed. The middle class, in James Mill's opinion the wisest part of the community, ought to be enfranchised. They would give the lead to the lower classes, who could be expected to follow their example. Through each man pursuing his individual interest, the greatest good of the greatest number would result.

The philosophical radicals, believing in the middle class, argued for a form of government that would be responsive to educated opinion, that would, in short, be capable of rationalizing institutions and making them efficient. Crucial to their philosophy was the idea that the government must encourage each individual to pursue his own interest, and that there be no delusions about what government might do for man. This was to be a representative government, certainly, but if a certain level of competence was to be assured, there must be room in it for those who had special skills.

In his earliest writing, his anonymous *Fragment on Government,* published in 1776, Bentham wrote: "The age we live in is a busy age; in which knowledge is rapidly advancing towards perfection. In the natural world, in particular, everything teems with discovery and with improvement" (ed. Harrison, p. 28). Since nature had "placed mankind under the governance of two sovereign masters, *pain* and *pleasure*," it was essential that it not be placed under any other, but that it be free to determine its own destiny. Governors should not choose for the governed; this was to demean them. The right and proper end of government was the greatest happiness of the greatest number, "and this could not be legislated for." Men had to be prevented from doing harm to others, but governments ought not to seek to direct them in doing good for themselves. There were agencies in society other than the state which could be depended on to look after the social needs of men. A legislator inevitably imposed his will on others when he passed a law; he should do so only when he was persuaded that good would come out of his action. Men's needs were different; they ought to be permitted to seek their happiness in the way they thought most reasonable. There were some areas where governmental intervention was clearly called for, but these were fewer than was generally thought.

Modern democracy could be trusted. "I have not that horror of the people," Bentham wrote; "I do not see in them that savage monster which their detractors dream of" (Letwin, p. 152). Still, Bentham had no illusions about the people. He did not praise their virtues; it was simply that if all were permitted to pursue their interests, that would itself provide the check that was needed. The new society had no need of the mythological "natural rights" and "constitutional balances" that others favored; the principle of utility was a sufficient guarantee of good government.

Bentham's individualistic creed never lacked critics. What made his ideas important, however, was that they provided a rationale for a new kind of "liberalism," one that became the dominant political philosophy in Britain after the 1820's, influencing democratic theory in many countries for the rest of the century. In Bentham, as in his collaborators, there was an explicit preference for individual over collective action; and with it went an absolute confidence that there would be material progress and improvement in the condition of men's lives if men obeyed the new principles of political economy. Bentham and the philosophic radicals accepted the industrial revolution; they took for granted that they were living in a new age and that this required them to search for new knowledge. For the state to tamper with industry or trade was to say that government understood an individual's interest better than he himself did. This was unthinkable. The legislator was right to concern himself with the needs of the indigent, but he ought to take care to define that class closely and not make the mistake of believing that humanitarian impulses would be productive. Superstition, war, indolence—all the evils of the past were to be swept away through the pursuit by each of the possibilities inherent in an industrial society. Such an idea was anathema not only to men like Coleridge, Newman, and Carlyle, but also to many who might have been expected to be most sympathetic to such ideas.

John Stuart Mill, reared to be the heir of the Benthamite legacy, found himself increasingly alienated from what he thought to be its narrow, limited, and ungenerous perspectives. Influenced by the writings of Auguste Comte, he looked for a reform of government that would bring the "most virtuous and best-instructed" to the top in a position to give the lead to others. Increasingly, the theme of expert leadership insinuated itself into Mill's writings. After the passage of the Reform Act of 1832, Mill went out of his way to remind his readers that popular government meant not so much that the people govern as that they are in a position to choose their governors. The business of government had to be "by the few for the many." The science of politics was an exact one; not every elector could aspire to master it.

Mill's attitudes during this period were substantially influenced by the publication of Alexis de Tocqueville's *Democracy in America.* That two-volume study, published in 1835 and 1840, was the first large-scale empirical investigation of a modern democracy. It was also a prophetic work, seeking to indicate what Europe might itself soon be experiencing. Tocqueville, persuaded that the passion for equality would not be stilled, asked Europeans to reflect on whether liberty would in fact survive the move towards equality. While admiring certain attributes of America—its restless energy, industry, and traditions of self-governance—there was a good deal that Tocqueville found disquieting. If the democratic movement was indeed irresistible, if it originated in America principally because of the absence there of an hereditary aristocracy, would it end in the creation of a state with vastly increased authority, a new kind of tyranny, with the majority exercising its power over every minority?

The tyranny of public opinion, Tocqueville argued, could prove more burdensome than the tyranny of any monarch. New values would predominate in a democratic society; the desire for riches would take the place of the desire for glory; there would be few totally uninstructed men but few learned ones. The prejudices, passions, and interests of the multitude would always have great weight, and this would generally militate against the type of political careers possible in more "aristocratic" societies. Government would not attract great talent, precisely because the interest in equality would make any kind of superiority irksome. Men of wealth would be preoccupied with their own affairs and not with those of the state. Democracy does not guarantee efficient government; it does provide freedom for the pursuit of one's own interest, subject always to the tyranny that comes from the majority insisting that its values and ideas should be safeguarded. Democratic societies have a taste for easy success and present enjoyment; this is their strength and their weakness.

Equality, Tocqueville insisted, tends to isolate men, to cause them to concentrate on themselves only; it gives them an inordinate desire for material goods and comfort. For him, the liberal French aristocrat, the important question for the future was how to avoid the new kind of despotism that might be based on popular opinion, with the state's power being "absolute, minute, regular, provident, and mild." Tocqueville saw the new state power as rather like that of the parent, except that the parent prepared the child for manhood; the democratic state was interested in perpetuating childhood in man. It would provide for his necessities, facilitate his pleasures, and direct his industry. What remains, Tocqueville asked, "but to spare them all the care of thinking and all the trouble of living?" Tocqueville saw in religion, an independent

663

judiciary, voluntary organization, and the press certain restraining elements on state power. However, these guarantees were not sufficient to bring him to conclude his work with a verdict clearly favorable to democracy.

If a prevailing opinion existed in Europe in the 1850's and 1860's, it was certainly not that of Karl Marx, but probably of those who called themselves liberals. John Stuart Mill may be taken as a representative liberal. In his classic work, *On Liberty* (1859), he spoke out against the tyranny of public opinion; the common opinion ought not to be permitted to interfere with individual opinion. The individual is not accountable to society for actions that concern himself only; for those actions affecting others he may be judged. Mill's concern was always for the gifted individual whom the multitude might find objectionable. Persuaded that political responsibility was the greatest good that could come to a man, and that to be active and serve the public weal ought to be the objective of all in a position to do so, he saw that while not everyone could participate directly in public life, all could do so through representative institutions. This was Mill's ultimate reason for preferring representative government. Not all communities, however, were ready for it. The duty of a colonizing power was to prepare its dependencies for self-government. Britain clearly had such an obligation in India.

Towards the end of the century, liberalism moved increasingly in a collectivist direction and lost its earlier hostility to socialist experimentation. There was still some of the old-fashioned Benthamite individualism, but it was tempered by a willingness to support health and unemployment insurance, a widening of the franchise, a steady improvement in wages, and the granting of specific legal rights to trade unions. The working-class misery of the early industrial era seemed to be greatly attenuated. It was almost possible to believe that representative institutions had indeed resolved the political and social problems of industrial society. Many believed they had. Some, like Eduard Bernstein, felt compelled to "revise" Marxist doctrine, to take account of the new economic and political facts (not foreseen by Marx). Whether in the tradition of the "revisionists," or in its pure, unadulterated form, Marxism seemed to gain a new repute.

Marx, in accepting the industrial system—in refusing to posit an ideal society based on older agrarian models—in insisting that social inequities could be overcome through a rational organization of society, laid the basis for a doctrine that gained new adherents late in the century. On the Continent, though not in England or the United States, Marxist parties grew in prestige and power. France and Germany, whatever their mutual political antipathies, resembled each other

in spawning large Marxist parties. They were hostile to the anarchist and syndicalist spirit that remained prominent in certain segments of the working class. Eduard Bernstein, for all his acceptance of the benefits secured by the worker as the consequence of the new social legislation, had no doubt that Germany's political system was essentially undemocratic, and that a principal purpose of his political effort ought to be to achieve democracy. Socialism, he believed, could only come about through democracy; in his words, "democracy is a condition of socialism to a much greater degree than is usually assumed, i.e. it is not only the means but also the substance." Bernstein came very close to expressing what certain English social reformers had argued in the nineteenth century, and what Fabianism announced explicitly: socialism was a continuation and a fulfillment of industrialism *and* of democracy.

This was not a view that all working-class advocates would accept. The syndicalist spirit, going back to Proudhon and Blanqui, had deep appeal for many. Georges Sorel may be taken as typical of those who spoke glowingly of the possibilities of the "general strike" in the first decades of the twentieth century. Rejecting the democratic bias of Marxists like Bernstein, and detesting democracy generally as the creation of the bourgeoisie, Sorel feared what democracy was doing in weakening the revolutionary ardor of the working class. The *camaraderie* of workers ought not to be lost; the attack on the state had to continue; it could only lead, he insisted, to the collapse of the state. Sorel, a syndicalist at the time, passed through other ideological schools in time, but in every one he persisted in his diatribe against bourgeois democracy.

Others writing at the same time—Vilfredo Pareto, Robert Michels, Gaetano Mosca—inquired into the oligarchical tendencies of democracy. Where the nineteenth century prided itself on the suffrage—on the importance of extending the vote—these men expressed misgivings about the habits and tendencies of men selected by democratic ballot-box procedures. Could such men be entrusted with power? Would they not be self-serving or the servants of special interest groups? These questions had not been much asked in the nineteenth century.

So long as democracy was a political movement making its way, so long as there were classes to be enfranchised, constitutions to be written—so long, in short, as democracy was an uncommon thing—partisans of popular rule were disposed to be fairly uncritical of democracy. When, however, as in the early twentieth century, manhood suffrage was largely achieved, female suffrage was making progress, trade union rights were recognized, freedom of assembly, speech, press, and religion seemed assured, a new kind of questioning began. Perhaps elections were not as significant as nineteenth-century liberals imagined them to be. Perhaps political movements that insisted on instituting complex democratic mechanisms— "recall," "referendum," "proportional representation," and the like—dwelled on quite secondary matters. Mosca, Michels, Pareto—and others of their persuasion —argued that democracy was itself a fraud, a delusion by which men lived. Many, they said, could not bear to admit that self-government was impossible, that men lived under modern (bureaucratic) oligarchies and that there was no escape from that power. Government, for those who held such views, became a form of monopoly; the politician was the new monopolist, though he pretended to identify with the subjects over whom he exercised his authority. The ballot box, the glory of the nineteenth-century democrat, was made little of; so, also, were the political parties, with their pretensions to being checks on oligarchic power.

What the effects of such theories might have been had World War I not intervened, it is impossible to know. The war was important for democracy, not least because it catapulted into international prominence Woodrow Wilson and Nikolai Lenin, who, whatever their other gifts, knew the value of rhetoric. Each contributed to making new slogans for their age. Wilson, in bringing the United States into the war in April 1917, claimed that he was enrolling the country in a war to make the world safe for democracy. The fact that the Tsarist regime had been toppled some weeks earlier made it possible for Wilson to argue that the Entente powers were "democracies," while Germany remained victim of its authoritarian regime. He pledged a League of Nations—of peace-loving states— the institution of a permanent organization to which only democratic states would be admitted.

All this was predicated on the notion that self-government would be the prevailing political form of the future, and that the war was being waged to guarantee that possibility. Wilson thought that one of his purposes ought to be the encouraging of those elements in Germany that displayed "democratic" tendencies. They might prove useful in rendering assistance to the Allies in the democratic objective of overthrowing the Junker power. Such arguments were highly propagandistic; democracy became a word of common usage in a way that it had never been previously. An examination of the press, not only in the United States, but in other Allied states as well, shows a tendency to use the word democracy in ways that Wilson made respectable and possible.

Meanwhile, another new voice was heard, though not with anything like the same amplification. Lenin,

disgusted by the defection of Western Social Democrats from a pacifism they had long preached, persuaded that these men had abandoned their internationalist class-war ideology in favor of conventional patriotic nationalism, saw the war as advantageous only if it could be transformed from an "imperialist war" into an international "civil war," to hasten the inevitable revolution. Lenin's object was to bring into a common rebellion workers who were the subjects of modern capitalism and colonial peoples who were the subjects of capitalist imperialism. After March 1917, his only objective was to bring about revolution in Russia; this, he accomplished in November. His instrument was the Communist Party, for which he had labored since the early years of the century. A centralized party, of professional revolutionaries, it accomplished what social democracy had never been able to achieve in the West—absolute control, through party instrumentalities and a highly centralized bureaucracy, of the whole of a state's power. Lenin achieved this in the name of democracy; not the bourgeois democracy of parliaments, but the proletarian democracy of Soviets. Lenin, like his successor, Stalin, never doubted the legitimacy and superiority of the people's democracy established in the Soviet Union. Its institutions and values—so different from those of bourgeois democracy—were flaunted in a whole succession of written constitutions.

To the Communist disparagement of bourgeois democracy, democratic theorists have generally felt some obligation to give an answer. To the Fascist and Nazi critics of liberal democracy, increasingly vocal in the 1930's, there was less response; it was as if criticism from that quarter—with its simplistic racial and national myths, glorification of a "leader," and disparagement of representative institutions—scarcely merited a serious retort. In the 1930's, there was some disposition to argue; the defeat of Nazi Germany and Fascist Italy closed off the discussion.

The mood of the war years and of the immediate postwar period cannot be represented by any single work. Yet, that of Joseph Schumpeter, as expressed in *Capitalism, Socialism and Democracy*, merits attention. Schumpeter argued that the classical theory of democracy did not describe the political situation as we know it; there is no possibility of pretending, as the eighteenth century did, that "the democratic method is that institutional arrangement for arriving at political decisions which realizes the common good by making the people itself decide issues through the election of individuals who are to assemble in order to carry out its will" (p. 250). Schumpeter saw such description as an elaborate fiction; he preferred a new definition: "the democratic method is that institutional arrangement for arriving at political decisions in which individuals acquire the power to decide by means of a competitive struggle for the people's vote" (p. 269). This, Schumpeter said, implied nothing less than that "democracy is the rule of the politician." Modern democracy was the product of capitalism. If capitalism were to disappear and be replaced by socialism, he said, this would not necessarily mean that democracy's institutions would go. Parties, elections, parliaments—all these might prove convenient political instruments even for a socialist society. Central to the survival of democracy, for Schumpeter, was the agreement of the "vast majority of the people in all classes . . . to abide by the rules of the democratic game." This, in turn, "implies that they are substantially agreed on the fundamentals of their institutional structure" (p. 301).

Another critique of the classical theory of democracy, one that attracted great attention on its publication in 1956, was that of Robert Dahl. In his published lectures, *A Preface to Democratic Theory,* he showed an empirical grasp that had not been at all common in the prewar period. Contrasting his own theory of polyarchy, which focused primarily on the social prerequisites for a democratic order, with what he called Madisonian theory, which emphasized the constitutional prerequisites, Dahl insisted that a theory of social checks and balances was very different from one that dwelled on constitutional checks and balances. Dahl argued that "the bent given to American thought by the Constitutional Convention and the subsequent apotheosis of its product . . . hindered realistic and precise thinking about the requirements of democracy" (p. 83).

For Dahl, the possibility of majority rule on any specific policy was negligible. Where the prerequisites of polyarchy, as he outlined them, existed, then the election itself was "the critical technique for insuring that government leaders will be relatively responsive to non-leaders." Of the eight conditions he laid down for polyarchy, Dahl saw a small possibility of their being met. Elections were "a crucial device for controlling leaders," but "quite ineffective as indicators of majority preference." Specific policies tended to be the products of "minorities rule." Majority rule, in the sense that Madison had used the term, Dahl saw as largely a myth. In most societies minorities frustrate and tyrannize others, but this is a far cry from dictatorship.

Dahl concluded from all this that constitutional forms were not a principal device for protecting one group in society against another. What, then, were they useful for? He thought them significant mostly for determining "what particular groups are to be given advantages or handicaps in the political struggle." The

reason the American Constitution had survived, in Dahl's view, was not that Madison and his colleagues had constructed such delicate mechanisms for guaranteeing a political balance, but that the Constitution was frequently altered to fit a changing social balance of power. It was the American penchant for bargaining that made the whole political process work.

Debates that were once vivid about the relative advantages of presidential and parliamentary systems, about two-party versus multi-party constitutions, have lost some of their urgency in recent years. Increasingly, there is a tendency to distinguish between constitutional and autocratic regimes in a way that Eric Weil does in his *Philosophie politique* (1956); constitutional regimes involve a set of judicial institutions independent of political authority, and generally provide for a method whereby political leadership may be altered by the citizens' vote. In an autocratic state, the citizen has no legal recourse against administrative or political decision, and can neither legally challenge the decisions of government nor alter the political leadership. By this standard, democracy becomes the best form of government in a healthy society, since it has the best chance of bringing good men to major positions. In a community in decomposition, violent, passionate, and dominated by conflicts between rival interest groups, the reign of the mediocre and the wicked will generally be the rule; this will often lead to an autocratic government. This, Weil says, is the response of men who deem efficiency to be a paramount virtue, with all other values being secondary. In a healthy community, where rational discussion is possible, at least among those who participate in the direction and control of public affairs, democracy will bring the best men to power. Reasonable discussion must lie at the base of any stable democracy. Parliamentary institutions are no guarantee against tyranny; nor can universal suffrage be held to provide any defense. Even the law does not provide absolute assurance. Each is necessary to discussion, and each contributes to providing circumstances calculated to encourage the assertion of talent. The basis of democracy, then, is an administration capable of acting rationally, and capable of keeping the confidence of the electors. The electors cannot themselves decide; they cannot hope to master the complexities of fiscal or military reform. They must be prepared to accept the judgment of those who are qualified to know.

Today, when there is so much effort to appropriate the democratic label to governments that would not normally qualify as such, it becomes increasingly important to distinguish between the conditions for democracy and the criteria of democracy. Seymour Martin Lipset, in his *Political Man* (1960), has tried to do that, relating democracy to levels of economic development, but also to the effectiveness and legitimacy of particular governments. For Lipset, effectiveness has to do with actual performance, the extent to which the government satisfies powerful groups within the society, and is able to carry out its functions. Legitimacy, he defines as "the capacity of the system to engender and maintain the belief that the existing political institutions are the most appropriate ones for the society."

Increasingly, one returns to the ancient Aristotelian idea that there is a relation between a society's property distribution and its form of government. A large impoverished mass and a small elite will generally produce oligarchy or tyranny. Greater equalization of wealth favors democratic rule. As the relation between the educational level of a people and democracy is increasingly examined, the question of why certain developing societies achieve democratic forms while others do not becomes a matter of controversy. Industrialization is clearly possible in both democratic and nondemocratic societies. Material progress does not appear to depend on popular rule. What, then, are the incontestable advantages of democracy? The problem of Herodotus is as much the problem of the latter part of the twentieth century as it was of the Greek city-state where direct citizen participation was possible. There is a new sense today of the fragility of democratic institutions. Perhaps the preoccupations of Athens are not so foreign to the twentieth century as they were to the more self-confident nineteenth.

BIBLIOGRAPHY

Gabriel A. Almond and James S. Coleman, eds., *The Politics of the Developing Areas* (Princeton, 1960). Aristotle, *Politics*, trans. and ed. Ernest Barker (Oxford, 1946). Bernard Bailyn, *The Ideological Origins of the American Revolution* (Cambridge, Mass., 1967). Ernest Barker, *Reflections on Government* (Oxford, 1942). Jeremy Bentham, *A Fragment on Government*, ed. W. Harrison (Oxford, 1948). Isaiah Berlin, *Four Essays on Liberty* (London, 1969). Crane Brinton, *English Political Thought in the Nineteenth Century* (Cambridge, Mass., 1949). Maurice Cranston, *Freedom, A New Analysis* (London, 1953). Robert A. Dahl, *A Preface to Democratic Theory* (Chicago, 1956). William Y. Elliott, *The Pragmatic Revolt in Politics* (New York, 1928). Elie Halévy, *The Growth of Philosophical Radicalism* (London, 1949). Bertrand de Jouvenel, *On Power; Its Nature and the History of its Growth* (New York, 1949). Harold J. Laski, *A Grammar of Politics* (New Haven, 1925). Shirley Robin Letwin, *The Pursuit of Certainty* (Cambridge, 1965). A. D. Lindsay, *The Modern Democratic State* (London, 1943; New York, 1962). Seymour Martin Lipset, *Political Man: The Social Base of Politics* (New York, 1960). T. H. Marshall, *Citizenship and Social Class* (Cambridge, 1950). Richard McKeon and Stein Rokkan eds., *Democracy in a World of Tensions* (Chicago, 1951). Barrington Moore, *Social Origins of Dictatorship and Democracy* (Boston, 1966). Thomas Paine, *Complete Writings*, ed. Philip S. Foner, 2 vols. (New York, 1945). Robert R. Palmer, *The Age of the Democratic Revolutions*, Vols. 1 and 2 (Princeton, 1959; 1964). Plato, *Collected Dialogues*, ed. Edith Hamilton and Huntington Cairns (Princeton, 1963). George H. Sabine, *A History of Political Theory*, 3rd ed. (New York, 1961); contains a good bibliography of secondary works. Giovanni Sartori, *Democratic Theory* (Detroit, 1962). Joseph A. Schumpeter, *Capitalism, Socialism, and Democracy*, 3rd ed. (New York, 1950). Judith N. Shklar, *Men and Citizens: A Study of Rousseau's Social Theory* (Cambridge, 1969). E. P. Thompson, *The Making of the English Working Class* (New York, 1963). Alexis de Tocqueville, *Democracy in America*, ed. Phillips Bradley, 2 vols. (New York, 1960). Adam Ulam, *The Unfinished Revolution* (New York, 1960). Michael Walzer, *The Revolution of the Saints: A Study in the Origins of Radical Politics* (Cambridge, Mass., 1965). Eric Weil, *Philosophie politique* (Paris, 1956). Gordon S. Wood, *The Creation of the American Republic, 1776–1787* (Chapel Hill, 1969).

STEPHEN R. GRAUBARD

[See also Constitutionalism; **Equality;** General Will; Liberalism; Nation; Social Contract; **State.**]

DEMONOLOGY

DEMONOLOGY, the theory of beings intermediate between the divine and man, begins in European thought as a collection of religious and philosophical ideas. In general, classical and Hellenistic Greek thinkers ordered these ideas in relation to the philosophical concept of the One, while Jewish and Christian thinkers ordered them in relation to the religious concept of a unique Creator God. These two principles of order interact, Neo-Platonic speculation influencing angelology, as in the dependence of Pseudo-Dionysius' *On Celestial Hierarchy* (ca. 500) upon Proclus, and the reverse, as in the progressive degradation of the pagan "gods" to "demons."

Greek demonology includes the following religious ideas. There are incorporeal beings differing in rank but all requiring human respect to insure their favor. There is a being called a *daimon* who is either identical with *theos* or is the power or agency of *theos* (Homer). The souls of the dead who are distinguished—either for great goodness, as the men of the Golden Age (Hesiod, *Works and Days*), or for great evil—survive and have an influence upon the living. Some part of man's consciousness is akin to the divine, can be purified of sensual attachments and become a higher being called a *daimon* (Pythagorean). A *daimon* is a divine sign given to an individual (*Phaedrus*, 242B) or it is a guardian spirit that acts as a conscience.

The Pythagorean philosophical idea that there are spirits who are the necessary intermediaries between the gods and men, "because the divine will not mingle directly with the human," is expressed by Diotima in Plato's *Symposium* (203A) and is developed by successive Neo-Platonists. It is combined with the notion of the survival of the souls of the dead in the Xenocratic philosophical theory of *daimones* who are capable of good and evil, are suprahuman but limited, and who dwell near Hades and under the moon. Plato contributes the notion that the heavenly bodies are moved by divine souls, which develops into Aristotle's theory that the planets and stars are moved by "intelligences" (later called "separated substances" in medieval thought) which are perfect and incorporeal—a philosophical answer to the question of the origin of the movement of the heavenly bodies. The idea of a hierarchy of corporeal and incorporeal beings between earth and the outermost border of the world is a philosophical theory of the cosmos in the pseudo-Platonic *Epinomis* (ca. 347 B.C.?) and later works of the Neo-Platonic school.

In the Judaic religious tradition the concept of *mal'ak*, a "messenger" of the one God, entirely subject to his will, is found in the Old Testament, carried on in the New Testament, and developed as a theological idea in Christian thought. Also found in the Old Testament is the statement that certain "sons of God" (later interpreted as fallen angels) intermarried with women and gave birth to "giants" (Genesis 6:1–5). A *satan* ("adversary") or Satan is included in Jahweh's council of angels and functions as tempter of Job and David in the Old Testament (Zechariah 3:1; Job 1 and 2; I Chronicles 21:1). Alien national or nature gods are real though inferior spiritual powers in the Old Testament from 700–600 on.

In the Septuagint (200–100), the Greek *angelos* translates *mal'ak*, while *daimon* (or neuter *daimonion*) with the meaning "a spirit less than divine" translates the Hebrew for idols, alien gods, some hostile natural creatures, and natural evils, and *theos* is used for the one God. Hence, the hitherto morally ambivalent or neutral word *daimon* acquires an almost exclusively evil connotation in the monotheistic context. At nearly the same time the idea of the *angelos* develops in Hebrew Rabbinical commentary as a source for the explanation of the origin of evil. The "sons of God" in Genesis 6 are interpreted as angels who had descended of their own will and given birth through women to evil spirits in this world. Sammael, chief of these rebel angels had entered the serpent in Eden to

tempt man. Subsequently, the Jewish Pseud-Epigrapha and Apocalyptic literature elaborate on the angelic rebellion and descent to earth, the origin of evil spirits, the hierarchical ranking of the angels, their habitations, their physical and moral affliction of men, and their temporal and final punishment, as well as that of the evil spirits born of their union with women. The chief rebel angel is variously called Semjaza, Azazel, Mastema, Beliar, Satanail, Sammael, or Satan in this literature. The context of Jewish religious thought lies behind the frequent New Testament references to Satan, to the *diabolus* ("adversary"), and to *daimones* and *daimonia*. Also the idea of the evil spirits who issued from the union of angels and women and who remained on earth to plague mankind probably lies behind the New Testament concept of possession by disease-causing demons.

Greek and Judaic traditions mingle inextricably in the synthesizing comment of Philo Judaeus (20 B.C.–A.D. 50) on Genesis 6:1–5: "It is Moses' custom to give the name of angels to those whom other philosophers call demons (or spirits), souls that is which fly and hover in the air" (*De gigantibus*, Loeb trans.). In equating biblical *angelos* with *daimones* and in peopling the upper divisions of the universe with spirits, Philo anticipates the subsequent adaptation of Greek philosophical speculation to Christian exegesis, a most important result of which is *On Celestial Hierarchy*, which becomes in turn the basis for most medieval scholastic doctrine on angels. The blending of traditions persists throughout the Middle Ages and Renaissance; as late as 1621 Robert Burton writes: "*Substantiae separatae* and intelligences are the same which Christians call angels, and Platonists devils, for they name all the spirits *daemones*, be they good or bad angels" (*Anatomy of Melancholy*, Part I, Sec. ii, Mem. i, Subsec. 2).

Under Platonic influence Philo varies from the Hebrew view that the "gods" of the Gentiles are evil *daimones*, treating them as good subsidiary powers. He sees (*De somnium*) these intermediary spirits allegorically in the angels who ascend and descend the ladder in Jacob's dream (Genesis 28:11–13), a figure that parallels in Christian thought Plato's ladder of Love in the *Symposium* and becomes one of the most influential in Christian speculation and art.

Both Philo and Plutarch (*De defectu oraculorum*) anticipate the Christian Apologist Justin Martyr in explaining pagan myth, ritual, and oracles as the actions of *daimones*, but Justin's interpretation of them as deceits of the fallen angels and their offspring demons (*Dialogue with Trypho*, A.D. 155) is the background for Saint Augustine's treatment of the pagan gods in *The City of God*, Books 1–X.

The idea of a hierarchy of grades of being among the various spiritual beings—gods, daimons, heroes—correlative to their positions in the physical universe seems to originate with the Neo-Platonists. In the schematic order of spirits in *Epinomis* the greater the degree of participation in matter, the lower the status of the being. Between the stars (which are made of fire and are either gods or images of gods) and men are the daimons made of aether, air, and water. Like Plato's Eros in the *Symposium*—only in a physical sense—they fill the gap between gods and men and communicate in both directions. More abstractly, Xenocrates theorizes that daimonic souls exist between the divine and the human on the analogy of the isosceles triangle existing as a semi-perfect form between the equilateral triangle (perfect) and the scalene triangle (imperfect). The schematization of grades of being is even more abstract in Plotinus, where it takes the form of the doctrine of emanation of all grades of being from the One, who is beyond being. In Plotinus, there is a subdivision of species of intelligences within the Intelligence, which is the first of the degrees emanating from the One.

In Proclus' *Platonic Theology* (ca. A.D. 450) the hierarchical entities are correlated with the gods, goddesses, daimons, and heroes of Hellenistic religion. It can be said that in rationalizing thus their deities the Neo-Platonists developed a "theology," but their concept of *theos*, as a being less than the Good, the One, or some other philosophic principle, limited their "theology" to a "demonology"—a system dealing with beings less than the highest being or principle. In *Platonic Theology*, Proclus correlates his gods with the "intelligibles" organized hierarchically under the Plotinian "One." He has no reason to rank any of them on a level with the One, the first principle of reason, as Christian theology ranks its unique Creator God. In Christian thought the Creator is, philosophically speaking, the first principle, existing beyond nature but not beyond being; and there is created nature, which includes both angels and demons—all things except God.

The anonymous Christian thinker called Dionysius the Areopagite adapts Proclus' schema of incorporeal beings to the various angels of Judaic-Christian revelation. In his *Celestial Hierarchy* he places in the highest triad the Seraphim (OT), Cherubim (OT), and Thrones (NT); in the second, Dominations (NT), Virtues (NT), and Powers (NT); in the third, Principalities (NT), Archangels (NT), and Angels (OT, NT). The fusion of the philosophic idea of beings who are pure intellect with the religious idea of angelic messengers is complete when Dionysius says of the angels that "their life is only intellection." In Dionysius each rank contains in a simpler mode, and governs the functions of any rank inferior to it.

Saint Thomas Aquinas carries speculation on the angelic nature to its theological conclusion, using Aristotle's notion of the intelligences that move the spheres, Neo-Platonic ideas about pure spirits as degrees of being, and Scriptural accounts of angels and demons. Rejecting the early notion of their union with women, he affirms their incorporeality, and to the question of how to distinguish angels if they have no matter to provide a basis for distinction, numerical or otherwise, he replies that each is a species unto itself. More importantly, in order to distinguish them from God, Thomas discerns composition in them in that their immaterial form remains in potentiality in what concerns its actual existence, its own proper *esse*. Only in God is there no difference between his *esse* and his *essentia*, between the act-of-being and what God is. Thus Thomas places angels definitively within a God-created universe. Between God and creation there is "discontinuity in the way the act-of-being is possessed" although there is continuity of order of both knowing (becoming more and more simple reaching up to God) and of being (becoming more and more pure) (Gilson, 1957). Accepting the Judaic idea of the pre-Adamic fall, Thomas deals with the problem of the angels' sin as with the case of man's: the angels have liberty of choice. One fell through pride and envy in seeking to have final beatitude of his own power. Others, from all ranks (Saint Gregory) or from only the lower ranks (Saint John Damascene) followed the first; some are punished in hell and some in the cloudy atmosphere where they serve God by tempting men (*Summa theologica*, I, 63, passim).

The idea of beings intermediate between the divine and man changes definitively with the definition of God and his relation to nature in the Thomistic philosophy of being. In withdrawing from nature true "divinity," Thomas redefines the border between the "natural" and the "supernatural," not placing it between the corporeal and the incorporeal but between created nature and the Creator. Hence, created nature, having been made by a God who freely bestows existential reality though not the divine capacity for self-existence, becomes philosophically assured of the reality of its being and of its complete accessibility to human reason and experimental investigation.

In Renaissance Christian thought it is clear that the divine is not locatable in anything short of God, whose essence is unique, but the revived Neo-Platonism of Cornelius Agrippa, Marsilio Ficino, and Giordano Bruno brings with it the old gods and demons located in the stars, planets, and elements and the theurgy associated with them in the Hermetic tradition. Making use of the emanationist theory of the origin of being and the Pythagorean idea that man's soul is akin to the divine, they attempt to carry on the old idea of gods and demons in nature who are manipulatable by man.

In the seventeenth century demonology becomes for some a mistaken line of defense for Christianity based on the equation of the incorporeal with the supernatural. The power and reality of the devil were defended by polemicists such as Joseph Glanvill, *Sadducismus triumphatus* (1681) and Richard Baxter, *The Certainty of the World of Spirits* (1691) as if God's existence itself were involved. On the other hand, for rationalists such as Descartes the Thomistic distinction remains clear and demons themselves dwindle into sophisticated rhetorical figures, as for example in Meditation I of his *Discourse on Method*, where the first step in systematic doubt is to entertain the possibility that all perceptions are the delusive work of a malignant demon. Such rhetorical use is echoed in J. C. Maxwell's nineteenth-century figure of a demon who plays a logical role in his thought-experiment in statistical thermodynamics.

In the nineteenth century, Renaissance demonology together with its Neo-Platonic philosophical foundations survives in the use of the old nature gods and demons, with their Judaic-Christian accretions, as sources of feeling in romantic and symbolist literature. Concurrently, the history of demonology is used by some historians of religion for their theory that moral dualism may be inherent in all historic religions.

BIBLIOGRAPHY

Denys L'Aréopagite, *La hiérarchie céleste*, eds. R. Roques, G. Heil, M. de Gandillac (Paris, 1958). Marcel Detienne, *La notion de daïmôn dans le pythagorisme ancien* (Paris, 1963). E. R. Dodds, *The Greeks and the Irrational* (Berkeley, 1968). Gilbert François, *Le polythéisme et l'emploi au singulier des mots θεός, δαίμων dans la littérature grecque d'Homère à Platon* (Paris, 1957). Étienne Gilson, *Being and Some Philosophers*, 2nd ed. (Toronto, 1952); *The Christian Philosophy of St. Thomas Aquinas*, trans. L. K. Shook (London, 1957). Francis X. Gokey, *The Terminology for the Devil and Evil Spirits in the Apostolic Fathers* (Washington, D.C., 1961). Soren Jensen, *Dualism and Demonology* (Munksgaard, 1966). Edward Langton, *Essentials of Demonology* (London, 1949). Proclus, *The Elements of Theology*, rev. ed., trans. E. R. Dodds (Oxford, 1963). Erwin Rohde, *Psyche*, trans. W. B. Hillis (New York, 1925). Frances A. Yates, *Giordano Bruno and the Hermetic Tradition* (New York, 1969).

HELEN P. TRIMPI

[See also Evil; **Hierarchy; Music as a Demonic Art;** Neo-Platonism; Pythagorean. . . .]

DESIGN ARGUMENT

THE DESIGN argument in theology is often immediately identified with the "argument from design," i.e., the argument that from evidences of intelligent planning found in the world one may reasonably infer the existence of a purposeful Intelligence responsible for the world. Logically, however, the full design argument (or teleological argument) must be seen as more complex in structure, since the argument from design itself rests on the controversial premiss that there are significant similarities between objects in nature (or nature taken as a whole), on the one hand, and objects intelligently contrived by man for some purpose, on the other. Only after somehow supporting this preliminary analogical basis, which, if formalized, amounts to an "argument to (not from) design," can one properly even begin to move on "from" design to invoke the theoretical need for a deity as cosmic Designer. Historically both aspects have appeared in theological speculation, although more explicit attention has usually been paid to the move from apparently purposeful natural phenomena to a divine Purposer than to the logically prior question of the actual presence of purposeful design in nature.

I. ANCIENT ORIGINS OF THE ARGUMENT

The prehistory of the design argument is to be sought in the forms of thought characteristic of early man. Though these forms are difficult to reconstruct with any certainty, it does seem probable that mythopoeic consciousness was devoid of the sharp distinction between animate and inanimate that we suppose to be obvious. Since the natural world was simply addressed in personal or quasi-personal terms, there seems to have been no sense of analogy in attributing purposive behavior to the cosmos and its contents; purpose was immediately to be read off from natural events and things just as it was directly to be found in human society.

Thus far, of course, there is no question of argument. Argument arises in Greece with pre-Socratic speculation, and even then mythopoeic roots are not wholly severed to whatever extent the living, purposive character of nature is taken as a datum of experience rather than as an explicit consequence from evidence. It is not clear, in this context, exactly what was meant by Anaximander, a younger contemporary of Thales in Miletus, when he affirmed that the indefinite primal stuff (the ἄπειρον) of the universe "steers all." If this "steering" is to be understood as somehow conscious and purposeful, then in Anaximander we may have found at least the germ of the design argument as early as the first half of the sixth century B.C.; that is, Anaximander may have argued that only because the ἄπειρον "steers" all according to "justice" can one understand why the universe remains in orderly balance as it does. Aristotle, further, tells us that Anaximander credited this "steering" substance with being "divine" (*Physica* III 203b 7), though we must realize that such divinity would have had very little in common with the anthropomorphic divinities of popular religious thought or with any supernatural being. On the other hand, it is likewise possible that Anaximander conceived of the ἄπειρον as "steering" quite mechanically, or perhaps as manifesting only the immanent purposiveness common to the "life" of nature as a whole.

Another partial hint of the design argument is found in Heraclitus, at the very end of the sixth century or early in the fifth, B.C., whose emphasis on the fluxing character of all things led him to infer the need for a unifying formula of the flux, the Logos, which rules the struggle of opposites in the world of constant change and insures that long-term balance prevails. Once again it is not possible to be sure from extant sources whether Heraclitus conceived of the Logos as intelligent and purposeful, though subsequent significant Logos traditions in Stoicism and Christianity develop this theme, but at least the essential intellectual demand for some agent to account for observed order in a changing world was self-consciously sounded by Heraclitus himself.

Explicit appeal to "mind" (νοῦς) as the needed agent was first made by Anaxagoras, probably in Athens toward the middle of the fifth century, B.C., when he developed a theory of the universe in which some principle of ordered change was seen to be necessary over and above the infinite and confused swarm of qualitatively distinct but intrinsically inert items that he believed to make up the universe. Mind, being the one reality that can remain itself while ordering and controlling other natures very different from itself and from each other, is uniquely qualified to rule the mixed realm of nature. "For it is the finest of all things and purest, it has all knowledge about everything and the greatest power; and mind controls all things . . ." (Kirk and Raven, p. 373). Still this position falls short of a full design argument, however, if Socrates' complaint (*Phaedo* 98B) is justified, that Anaxagoras' appeal to "mind" as a cosmic orderer had no bearing on the deeper question "why" matters should stand as they do and not in some other way. It appears that "mind" was drawn in by Anaxagoras as an ordering dynamic principle only, and not as belonging to a moral agent expressing ends in view through the organization of the world order.

For an unequivocally clear statement of such an argument we must await the writings of Plato in the fourth century B.C., but a close approximation of what Socrates was hoping for can be found in one of Anaxagoras' somewhat younger contemporaries, Diogenes of Apollonia. Diogenes was an eclectic thinker, for the most part, combining the interests of the early Milesian philosophers in identifying a primal world-substance with the quest of Heraclitus and Anaxagoras for explanations of the ordered dynamics of change. Like Heraclitus, Diogenes was much impressed by the regularity of the world and the need to account for it; and like Anaxagoras he specified that this account could only be given in terms of "intelligence" (νόησις). Intelligence he identified with warm air, following Anaximenes (the Milesian successor of Anaximander), and he explained its method of working through the mechanism of rarefaction and condensation. Beyond all this, however, Diogenes made an explicit teleological claim—one that we shall find very prominently in Plato and later tradition—that intelligence disposes of all things "for the best" (κάλλιστα) (frag. 3, Simplicius *Phys.* 152, 13).

With this we find we are in possession of all the elements ingredient in the design argument: (1) the observation that there is order in nature or that nature as a whole is orderly, (2) the asseveration that natural order is not self-explanatory but requires an ordering agency of some kind, (3) the identification of this agency as explicitly aware and acting from intelligent design, and (4) the attribution to this Intelligence of benevolent moral purpose.

The first full articulation, in combination, of the various elements in the design argument was given by Plato. Here was no mere eclectic, however; the synthesis was distinctly his, and the argument he offered follows directly from central themes within his own philosophical position.

One such theme is rooted in Plato's view of soul as always the source of spontaneous motion. Our first experience of any genuine originative change springs from within ourselves. Changes observed in our bodies or in nature are always derivative, communicated from something else which is already in motion, that motion in turn borrowed from still something else, and so on—until a truly originative or spontaneous motion is finally introduced to ground the series. "Soul," therefore, comes to have a technical meaning for Plato as the "self-moving" or the "beginning of motion" wherever or whenever change genuinely originates: "He who affirms that self-motion is the very idea and essence of the soul will not be put to confusion" (*Phaedrus* 245D).

The changing universe, consequently, is not able to be understood on its own material terms alone. Its changes demand the postulation of something capable of initiating change, not merely of transmitting it.

How can a thing which is moved by another ever be the beginning of change? Impossible. But when the self-moved changes other, and that again other, and then thousands upon tens of thousands of bodies are set in motion, must not the beginning of all this motion be the change of the self-moving principle? (*Laws* X, 895).

The only known self-moving principle, however, is soul. Therefore it follows that soul must be invoked to account adequately for the changes that we observe.

In the above we have witnessed the birth of the famous "first cause" argument; and for Plato the design argument follows immediately upon it. Having established that the natural world is ultimately dependent upon soul, the question must be asked: "What kind of soul is it that rules the changing universe?" The answer, Plato says, depends on the kinds of changes we actually observe. If the soul ruling nature is "good"— and here Plato makes use of another of his prominent themes, urging the equation of goodness with rationality, harmony, intellectual coherence—the universe will exhibit lawful behavior. "But," Plato allows, "if the world moves wildly and irregularly, then the evil soul guides it" (*Laws* X, 897B). A survey of pertinent fact, however, particularly astronomical data, will convince any careful observer that nature changes with the utmost regularity and that, in consequence: "There would be impiety in asserting that any but the most perfect soul or souls carries round the heavens" (*Laws* X, 898C).

A more pictorially vivid version of this general position is found in Plato's *Timaeus* where the Demiurge is represented as a craftsman, fashioning the world of natural change by copying off eternal formal principles of reality into a matrix of flux. The myth adds little, however, to the design argument itself except in providing an answer to the ultimate question why the cosmic artisan should have done his work at all. Plato's suggestion is that the Demiurge acted from pure benevolence:

He was good; and in the good no jealousy in any matter can ever arise. So, being without jealousy, he desired that all things should come as near as possible to being like himself. . . . Desiring, then, that all things should be good and, so far as might be, nothing imperfect, the god took over all that is visible—not at rest, but in discordant and unordered motion—and brought it from disorder into order, since he judged that order was in every way the better (*Timaeus* 29E–30A).

Aristotle, although he shared Plato's keen sense of the order within nature and argued forcefully on other grounds for the existence of conscious deity at the apex of actuality, did not advance the design argument we have been following. Just as he objected to Plato's

alleged "separating of the Forms" from the substances of the world, so Aristotle argued against separating the source of order from the natural order itself. The universe contains goal-directed activity, even in areas of change where there is clearly no conscious deliberation, but Aristotle argued from this that in this case "purpose" must be understood as inherent and non-deliberative. "For natural things are exactly those which do move continuously, in virtue of a principle inherent in themselves, towards a determined goal . . ." (*Physics* 199b).

Thus, instead of making the inference from orderly processes in nature to an intelligent orderer above or beyond nature, Aristotle offers a thoroughly immanent view of natural teleology and offers an illustration: "The best illustration is the case of a man being his own physician, for Nature is like that—agent and patient at once" (*Physics* 199b). God, for Aristotle, necessarily exists as ultimate actuality, but he is too perfect even to know about the changing, self-correcting domain of nature, much less to have taken any part in designing it. Plato's greatest pupil abandoned both Demiurge and separate realm of Forms as theoretically redundant, and with them, as we see, the design argument for God.

II. THE MEDIEVAL "SYNTHESIS"

Despite significant support in the scientific writings of Galen (fl. A.D. 164) and in the philosophy of Boethius (480?–?524), there is little evidence of the design argument playing an important role in theological thought before the thirteenth century of our era. Biblical writers did not characteristically argue at all, though the wonders of nature are sometimes urged as illustrations of the might and grandeur of God (e.g., Psalms 8, 19). Likewise the Church Fathers spent their energies on other controversies than the existence of God; and even when the latter question did arise as a question at all, the defense of belief was typically based on what was taken as more worthy than the character of the natural world. It was in this era, for example, that Saint Anselm (1033–1109) created the famous ontological argument for God (*Proslogion*), purporting to depend on nothing beyond an understanding of what it means to be God in order to demonstrate his necessary existence.

With the rediscovery of Aristotle's philosophy, however, and with the attempt of Saint Thomas Aquinas to build an intellectually viable Christian theology on a fundamentally Aristotelian framework, the design argument reappears. This would be odd, since we have seen that Aristotle himself dispensed with this argument for God, if it were not for two pertinent considerations: first, Saint Thomas was by no means slavish in his use of Aristotle (as is sometimes falsely alleged), and, second, Plato's *Timaeus* had exerted great influence over the intervening centuries and had given philosophical reinforcement to the biblical vision of God as actively concerned with the created universe. Saint Thomas's design argument, therefore, stands out as a fundamentally non-Aristotelian correction of Aristotle in a corpus that is usually considered to be a synthesis of Christian faith with Aristotelianism.

The argument itself, the fifth of Saint Thomas's Five Ways (of which the first three are indeed Aristotelian), reads as follows:

We see that things which lack knowledge, such as natural bodies, act for an end, and this is evident from their acting always, or nearly always, in the same way, so as to obtain the best result. Hence it is plain that they achieve their end, not fortuitously, but designedly. Now whatever lacks knowledge cannot move towards an end, unless it be directed by some being endowed with knowledge and intelligence; as the arrow is directed by the archer. Therefore some intelligent being exists by whom all natural things are directed to their end; and this being we call God (*Summa Theologica*, Q. 2, Art. 3).

There are several interesting features of this argument. First, it is taken as obvious that there are end-directed activities within nature. This claim, on which the rest of the argument depends, is significantly different from Plato's appeal to the order of the visible universe, especially astronomical order which seems not to be directed at any identifiable goal. It may be that orderly change and end-directed change may be intimately related in some way. At the moment, however, it remains a disputable point and one which needs to be argued for.

Second, we see that Saint Thomas has adopted Aristotle's remarks about the presence of "purpose" in nature without accepting his conclusion that such observable regularities may be accounted for by appeal to an immanent teleology. This view, indeed, is not ever considered. In this dismissal by silence we find an implicit dualism between bodies and minds that Aristotle found objectionable in Plato. It is not self-evident, of course, which position is the stronger. Aristotle argued that such "separation" is in the end metaphysically redundant; Plato, on the other hand, could have replied that in this respect his great successor had not sufficiently advanced beyond the mythopoeic blurring of distinctions between the animate and the inanimate. Saint Thomas, in any event, we find to have applied to natural changes a very sharp distinction between the "ensouled" and the "unsouled," as shown by his choice of illustration of the archer and

the arrow. The model for nature is clearly technological as contrasted to Aristotle's mainly organismic examples of immanent teleology, such as the physician who treats himself.

Third, Saint Thomas concludes with the claim that his argument has shown that there must be "some intelligent being" who is responsible for the alleged design in the world. This, too, is a bolder claim that Plato permitted himself. Plato, as we saw, admitted the possibility of plural souls guiding the orderly phenomena of nature. Saint Thomas gives no argument here to show why his evidence points to only one intelligent being rather than several, and we shall see that this remains a persistent problem for the design argument taken by itself.

Fourth, and boldest of all, Saint Thomas equates the "intelligent being" of his argument with God. Perhaps this equation can be made good, but it must be recalled that insofar as Plato argued carefully in the *Laws* he claimed only to have shown the need for postulating "the most perfect soul or souls" to account for specific astronomical phenomena. Even in the mythological *Timaeus*, where a single perfect soul is depicted as ordering the whole cosmos, Plato does not go beyond presenting him as a Demiurge, limited by what he finds by way of formal possibilities and material medium for the always somewhat imperfect realization of these pure Ideas. Can the design argument support more than this? It all depends, assuredly, on what is supposed to be meant by "God" whether God's existence can be supported by this approach. Saint Thomas, at least, whose conception of God was shaped by both biblical and Aristotelian influences, seems unaware of the possibility that there may be a wide gap between what, on the most generous possible reading, he has shown, and the God of his theological concern.

III. MODERN DEVELOPMENTS OF THE ARGUMENT

It is significant that revival of interest in the design argument appeared in Europe along with the birth of natural science in its distinctly modern form. It is the most empirical of the arguments for God, requiring, as we have seen, observational premises about the kind of order we discover in nature. These are not the only premises, of course, that go into its structure, and we have already noted some of the distinctively philosophical disputes that may arise in connection with its use; but from this point forward we shall find that the design argument is intimately linked with the history of modern science.

Copernicus, who in many ways began this history, appealed to the wonderful harmony and divine reasonableness of the sun's placement at the center of the universe: "In the middle of all sits Sun enthroned. In this most beautiful temple could we place this luminary in any better position from which he can illuminate the whole at once?" (*De revolutionibus orbium caelestium* [1543], Book I, Part 10). Likewise Kepler, the great Neo-Platonist astronomer, advanced passionate arguments for the elegant and beautiful mathematical structure of the cosmic design.

Through the seventeenth century it continued to be the scientists, or those with deep scientific interests, who stated the design argument with most force. John Ray, author of *The Wisdom of God Manifested in the Works of Creation* (1691), was best known as a wide-ranging naturalist. Robert Boyle, the eminent physicist and chemist, was responsible for developing an early analogy between the universe and a clock, and the Boyle Lectures established by his will were influential in defense of Christianity among the intellectually advanced. Robert Hooke was also a brilliant scientist who, among other achievements, anticipated Newton's inverse square law and formulated the kinetic theory of gases, and lent his support to belief in God based on the order of nature. Even Ralph Cudworth, chief of the Cambridge Platonists, a philosopher who seems the one prominent exception to the list of scientists employing the design argument, also cast his argument for a divine intelligence into the scientific matrix of his day in *The True Intellectual System of the Universe* (1678).

The greatest scientist of the age, however, was Isaac Newton, whose publication of the *Principia* (1687) established the framework of the new science and drew the physical outlines of the great world-machine that was to dominate scientific imagination for centuries. Newton's own deployment of the design argument, therefore, is especially interesting. Newton summarized his view in the "General Scholium" added to Book Three, "The System of the World," of the *Principia* in 1713, and carefully revised it in 1726. There he argued that the beautiful arrangement of the heavenly bodies—especially the planets, the comets, and the moons of the planets—demands an intelligent agent to account for such formal perfection. The great law of gravitation, which he had first enunciated, could only deal with part of the facts:

The planets and comets will constantly pursue their revolutions in orbits given in kind and position, according to the laws above explained; but though these bodies may, indeed, continue in their orbits by the mere laws of gravity, yet they could by no means have at first derived the regular position of the orbits themselves from those laws (*Principia*, "General Scholium," 1713).

That "mere mechanical causes" could have given rise to such regular motions as the facts of science show is quite inconceivable, Newton insisted, and concluded, as Plato also had: "This most beautiful system of the sun, planets, and comets, could only proceed from the counsel and dominion of an intelligent and powerful Being" (ibid.).

But unlike Plato, whom we saw to have allowed the possible multiplicity of intelligent and powerful beings, Newton adds a new argument, now for the first time made scientifically possible by his having shown the existence of a single system of the world. "And if the fixed stars are the centres of other like systems, these, being formed by the like wise counsel, must be all subject to the dominion of One; especially since the light of the fixed stars is of the same nature with the light of the sun, and from every system light passes into all the other systems" (ibid.). Although we have previously seen this attribution of unity in the cosmic designer as mythically portrayed by Plato and as theologically affirmed by Saint Thomas, this is the first time we find the design argument itself extended to support such a monotheistic conclusion.

Newton went even further, however, and argued that such universal control over limitless space and endless duration as must be admitted for the One Being, given the Newtonian system of the world, requires that this Cosmic Intelligence also be recognized as Lord God. "He is eternal and infinite, omnipotent and omniscient; that is, his duration reaches from eternity to eternity; his presence from infinity to infinity; he governs all things, and knows all things that are or can be done" (ibid.).

For some time the prestige of the leaders of modern scientific thought supported the design argument they employed and believed. Even David Hume's brilliant attacks in the *Dialogues Concerning Natural Religion*, posthumously published in 1779, did not immediately dampen the enthusiasm of eighteenth- and early nineteenth-century exponents. The classical statement of the argument in its modern form, indeed, was not published until 1802 when William Paley brought out his celebrated *Natural Theology, or Evidences of the Existence and Attributes of the Deity collected from the Appearances of Nature*. In that work Paley argued explicitly for the presence of intelligently designed features in nature. The marks of design, he said, are what we observe in contrasting a watch with a stone. The stone, for all we can tell, might just have "happened"; but the watch is clearly put together out of parts that work together in an arrangement that is essential to their function, and the function of the whole has a discernible and beneficial use. Wherever we find such a constellation of characteristics, Paley said, we must admit that we are in the presence of "contrivance" and "design," and since in our experience the only known source of such contrivance is the intelligence of some designer, we are entitled—obliged—to infer an intelligent designer somewhere behind anything possessing the above mentioned marks of design. Given this general approach, Paley then multiplies instance after instance of natural phenomena that require the admission of intelligent design in their contrivance. Not astronomical phenomena alone, as had been the mainstay of design arguments from Plato to Newton, but biological mechanisms were Paley's stock in trade. The human eye, plants, anatomical and physiological features of men and beasts, instincts, birds, insects—all these and more went into Paley's massive argument, the constant theme of which was that all these data reveal elaborate structures made up of parts which work together with amazing ingenuity to perform useful functions for their possessors. Each taken separately, he contended, proved the need for an intelligent designer working behind the "appearances of nature"; taken together the case was crushingly conclusive.

Paley drew back, however, from the strongest of Newton's claims for the unity and infinity of the deity thus allegedly proved. With greater philosophic caution he admitted that attributes like "omnipotence," "omniscience," "infinity," and the like cannot be strictly derived from the design argument:

Nevertheless, if we be careful to imitate the documents of our religion by confining our explanations to what concerns ourselves, and do not affect more precision in our ideas than the subject allows of, the several terms which are employed to denote the attributes of the Deity may be made, even in natural religion, to bear a sense consistent with truth and reason and not surpassing our comprehension (*Natural Theology*, Ch. XXIV).

This more accurate way of dealing with such terms is to recognize their logical status as "*superlatives* expressing our conception of these attributes in the strongest and most elevated terms which language supplies" (ibid.). "Omnipotence," thus construed, can mean no more than "powerful beyond all comparison" since he must be allowed to be powerful enough to design and rule our observed universe. "Omniscience," likewise, literally means whatever enormous wisdom is required to account for the yet unmeasured intricacy of the world's intelligible structure. The uniqueness of this cosmic intelligence, too, is not demonstrable from the design argument: "Certain however it is," Paley acknowledged, "that the whole argument for the divine unity goes no further than to a unity of counsel" (*Natural Theology*, Ch. XXV). This is quite enough, how-

ever, Paley believed, since the limitations of natural theology can always be supplemented by revealed theology which, thanks to the design argument, has been shown to be wholly compatible with rigorous empirical thinking.

The pungent philosophical critique, however, of David Hume had raised serious questions about the claims on behalf of the design argument's empirical rigor. And Immanuel Kant had pressed equally severe objections against the assumption that traditional theology can find relevant support in the design argument. (For an earlier severe critique of the design argument, cf. Spinoza's *Ethics*, Part I, appendix.)

Hume was not the first to point out that the design argument is an argument from analogy. Samuel Butler had published his influential book, *The Analogy of Religion*, in 1736; and from then on it was generally acknowledged by users of the argument that their reasoning rested on the discovery of similarity between the world, or objects in the world, and products of human continuance. Hume, however, was the first to raise sustained and imaginative objections to the key analogy itself. In his *Dialogues Concerning Natural Religion* he attacked from several sides. Analogies are most trustworthy when the things compared are more or less comparable, he argued; but how comparable, really, are things in the world to the world as a whole? Comparing causes between things or events in the world may sometimes be justified, but logic stretches beyond its breaking point when one of the terms of the comparison is supposed to be beyond the world as somehow its cause. Again, how alike, really (asked Hume), are the forces now in existence with those which would have been in the world when it was being formed? We cannot say, and dare not suppose that our little analogies, drawn from the present state of things, can have fruitful application under such vastly different conditions. What a suspicious choice, in any case, to make human intelligence the model for the cosmic cause! The vice of pride may well be lurking here, especially when there are so many alternative analogies that might do equally well to account for the order observed in nature. Why not, Hume asked, take forces of generation or vegetation as explanatory of the world? Why not take the analogy, in other words, from what appears to be immanent ordering principles in nature, such as the spinning of a spider's web? The analogy to intelligence is not only farfetched, he challenged, but it is also far from uniquely serviceable—if any such explanation must be offered. But must it? Hume insisted not; any such explanation leads on to a never-ending regress of further questions (such as, "Who designed God's intelligence if all orderly things require a designer?"); any such analogy leads too far if it leads anywhere (e.g., can we deny that we experience intelligence only with embodied organisms? Must we therefore attribute hands, feet, sex to God?); and, finally, no causal argument for the whole universe seems logically possible in any event, since the universe, being unique, does not fall into the class of caused things—effects are only known to be such by repeated conjunction in experience with their causes—and therefore the world is improperly called an "effect."

Besides this volley of arguments against the logical underpinnings of the design argument, Hume pressed the darker side of the world's organization. If the well functioning nature is evidence for intelligence, benevolence, and power, he pointed out, then disease, disorder, and natural evil is counter-evidence for stupidity, malice, or impotence. Which shall it be? The design argument opens the door to natural evidence at a very high cost to one who would preserve belief in the perfection of God since the evidence, if taken seriously, can never lead to such a conclusion.

Kant, although more sympathetic to the design argument than Hume in some ways, develops the last point into a necessary principle. The argument, Kant said, "is the oldest, the clearest, and the most accordant with the common reason of mankind" (*The Critique of Pure Reason*, 2nd ed. [1787], B651); but it cannot possibly lead to a theologically significant conclusion about God. God is not, Kant insisted, merely a Demiurge; God is not only a Designer of nature's wonderful contrivances. God, to be theologically adequate, must be understood through a completely determinate concept as absolutely necessary, perfectly powerful, all knowing, utterly good, and all the rest. Between the essentially loose textured concept of an Author of the world which is appropriate to the empirical argument before us—the concept of a being who is (vaguely and at most) "very" powerful, "enormously" wise, "admirably" good, and the like—and the full determinate concept of God there is a radical logical gap. It is a gap that in the nature of the case, because empirical evidence is never complete, can never be closed by any amount of additional empirical evidence. The design argument, therefore, Kant concluded, can never succeed in helping theology in ways theology should welcome, though it may convince the speculative reasoner that:

If we are to specify a cause at all, we cannot here proceed more securely than by analogy with those purposive productions of which alone the cause and mode of action are fully known to us. Reason could never be justified in abandoning the causality which it knows for grounds of explanation which are obscure, of which it does not have any knowledge, and which are incapable of proof (ibid.).

IV. THE ARGUMENT SINCE DARWIN

Kant was generous to the design argument, as we see in the above quotation, on the ground that when he wrote these words there seemed to be no more theoretically adequate hypothesis on which to explain the amazing intricacy of the natural order than that of intelligent design. Hume's proliferation of alternatives was more ingenious than convincing if looked to for genuine help in understanding the facts such as those Paley had later piled so high. This situation, however, was radically changed by Charles Darwin's *Origin of Species* (1859); and the weight of scientific prestige, which had supported the argument since its championing by physicists of the seventeenth century, fell heavily against it because of the biologists of the nineteenth.

Darwin's primary contribution to the opponents of the design argument was to make available an intelligible and convincing alternative causal hypothesis—just such as Kant acknowledged he had failed to find—to take the place of intelligent contrivance. This alternative was the mechanism of natural selection, through which "adaptation to environment" took the place of "purposive design" as the concept by which Paley's evidences could be understood. Changes in biological species have occurred randomly over vast periods of time, Darwin argued, and the forms of life best equipped in the struggle for scarce resources have left their progeny to be admired by the natural theologians. Their intricate structures and admirable functioning need not be attributed to an intelligence behind nature, however, since the facts are as they must be if living forms are to survive at all.

It might be tempting to compare this position, on which nature is alleged to need no external intellect to bring about orderly and well adapted changes, with Aristotle's urging of immanent teleology against Plato's more dualistic view. To some extent the parallels hold: Plato, lover of mathematics, reminds us of Newton; and Aristotle, son of a physician and ardent collector of biological specimens, cannot fail to suggest an earlier Darwin. But the biology of Darwin is post-Newtonian, and it would be misleading to push the comparison too far. Precisely what is not present in the evolutionary process of natural selection is immanent purpose in the Aristotelian sense. Teleology, immanent as well as external, is dispensable, and totally non-telic processes of chance variations and physical interplay constitute all the parameters of the theory.

From its original home in biology, evolutionary thinking has spread to other fields as well. Theories of cosmic evolution have replaced Newton's appeal to intelligent design in the arrangement of the solar system and the galaxies. Historical geology, in a closely related development, has extended understanding of the present state of our terrestrial environment. In all this "evolution" has come to mean something more inclusive than Darwin's original theory, but in all its scientific applications evolutionary thinking has interposed itself between the "appearances of nature" and any easy appeal to the explanatory need for design.

Given this situation the design argument in its classical form has found few friends in recent times. There have been, however, post-Darwinian variations of the ancient argument intended to take account of the battering it has received from both philosophy and science since the mid-eighteenth century. The laws of the natural order itself, including the laws of evolution, may be taken as requiring some explanation in terms of a transcendent purpose. F. R. Tennant, for example, wrote:

The forcibleness of Nature's suggestion that she is the outcome of intelligent design lies not in particular cases of adaptedness in the world, nor even in the multiplicity of them. . . . The forcibleness of the world's appeal consists rather in the conspiration of innumerable causes to produce, by their united and reciprocal action, and to maintain a general order of nature (*Philosophical Theology*, Cambridge [1930], II, 79).

Others in the twentieth century, like Peter A. Bertocci, following Tennant, and Charles Hartshorne, following Alfred North Whitehead, have developed current variations of the argument; and Pierre Teilhard de Chardin worked out a form of design argument in his deeply evolutionary and widely influential posthumous work *The Phenomenon of Man* (1959). The ancient argument remains alive, therefore; and though it has lost much of its support in philosophical circles, its perennial appeal to religious persons and to others who approach the intelligible order of nature with a touch of wonder and awe will in all likelihood assure its continued survival as a live topic for meditation and debate.

BIBLIOGRAPHY

Careful examination of selected Greek texts is provided in G. S. Kirk and J. E. Raven, *The Presocratic Philosophers* (Cambridge, 1957), which also offers an excellent bibliography and useful indexes. Various translations of Plato, Aristotle, and Saint Thomas are readily available. A good translation of Nicholas Copernicus' *De revolutionibus orbium caelestium* (1543), Book I, is found in *Occasional Notes of the Royal Astronomical Society* (London, 1947), Vol. 2, No. 10, by J. F. Dobson and S. Brodetsky. David Hume's *Dialogues Concerning Natural Religion* (originally published 1779) may be found in a popular edition edited by Henry David Aiken (New York, 1948). Immanuel Kant's *Kritik der reinen Vernunft* (first ed. 1781) has been well translated by Max Müller (second ed. revised, 1927) as well as by Norman Kemp Smith, whose more interpretative translation (1929) reflects Kant's second edition of 1787. William Paley's *Natural Theology, or Evidences of the Existence and Attributes of the Deity collected from the Appearances of Nature* (London, 1802) is available in an abridged version edited, with a critical introduction, by Frederick Ferré (Indianapolis, 1963).

Modern works relevant to the support of the design argument include F. R. Tennant, *Philosophical Theology*, Vol. II: *The World, The Soul, and God* (Cambridge, 1930); Charles Hartshorne, *Man's Vision of God* (New York, 1941); P. Lecomte du Noüy, *Human Destiny* (New York, 1947); Peter A. Bertocci, *Introduction to the Philosophy of Religion* (New York, 1951), especially Chs. XXI–XV; and P. Teilhard de Chardin, *Le Phénomène humain* (Paris, 1955), translated by Bernard Wall as *The Phenomenon of Man* (New York, 1959).

Some recent works relevant to the attack on the argument include G. G. Simpson, *The Meaning of Evolution* (New Haven, 1949); C. J. Ducasse, *A Philosophical Scrutiny of Religion* (New York, 1953), Ch. XV; John Hospers, *An Introduction to Philosophical Analysis* (New York, 1953), Ch. V; and Michael Scriven, *Primary Philosophy* (New York, 1966), Ch. IV.

FREDERICK FERRÉ

[See also **Analogy**; Anthropomorphism; **Causation, Final Causes**; Evolutionism; **God**; Metaphor; Myth; Pre-Platonic Conceptions; Skepticism; Uniformitarianism.]